Manual of Woody Landscape Plants:

Their Identification, Ornamental Characteristics, Culture, Propagation and Uses

MICHAEL A. DIRR
Department of Horticulture
University of Illinois

ILLUSTRATIONS BY
MARGARET STEPHAN
and
ASTA SADAUSKAS

ISBN 0-87563-137-1

Published by
STIPES PUBLISHING COMPANY
10 - 12 Chester Street
Champaign, Illinois 61820

This book is
dedicated
to my very understanding and lovable wife,
Bonnie Lee Dirr
and my children,
Katherine Elizabeth Dirr
Matthew Albert Dirr

PREFACE

This book details the common and not so common woody ornamental deciduous trees, shrubs, ground covers, and vines as well as the narrowleaf and broadleaf evergreens which are adapted to Midwestern and Eastern climates. The book is designed as a teaching text for woody plant materials courses but should serve as a valuable reference to anyone interested in woody plants. As a teacher of woody plants I was often frustrated by the lack of a good text which included identification characters and the ornamental and cultural features. This text attempts to fill the gap and provide the student and interested plantsmen with concise, factual treatment of the subject matter.

Much of the information is based on my observations and subsequent inferences I have drawn concerning the relative merits of a particular plant. I plan to revise and enlarge the book in three years and would appreciate comments from interested individuals on how the book might be improved.

The line drawings were accomplished by Ms. Asta Sadauskas, one of my former students, from plant materials which I collected. An honest attempt was made to draw leaves which were most typical of the plant. The cover was designed by Ms. Sadauskas. Typing, proofreading and collating were accomplished by Ms. Suanne Layden, Ms. Kim Falkenstrom, Mrs. Barbara Armstrong, and Ms. Marcie Eberwine.

The greatest wealth of information was extracted from horticultural and botanical references most of which are listed in the bibliography. To L. H. Bailey, Alfred Rehder, Donald Wyman and the other great writers and teachers, I am indebted.

PREFACE TO THE SECOND EDITION

The initial version of this book was first published in August, 1975, and, at that time, I had planned to revise the book in approximately three years. Obviously my plans changed for the revision came about in little more than a year. The initial responses from teachers and students of plant materials were gratifying. The book received many kind comments from individuals I consider most knowledgeable in this area. Considerable constructive criticism was offered by readers and I have assimilated many of their comments and incorporated them into this edition.

Included in the second edition are hardiness zone maps, an extensive discussion, along with line drawings, of plant morphology as it relates to plant identification, a brief essay on the use of keys, over 150 additional plant descriptions, an index, and the finest line drawings of dormant buds and stems I have ever witnessed. One of my students, Ms. Margaret Stephan, asked if she could add line drawings of various vegetative features and I immediately collected *Aesculus hippocastanum,* Common Horsechestnut, and *Magnolia stellata,* Star Magnolia, and asked her to take them home and draw what she saw. The results are obvious from the drawings presented in this edition. Meg has the rare gift of being able to look at a plant, perceive the minutest detail, and transfer that perception to realism on paper.

The book will continue to be improved through the years by adding new drawings, up-to-date information on cultivars, propagation, diseases, insects, and the like. During my sabbatical leave, which will be spent at an arboretum, I will study plants more thoroughly through the seasons and, hopefully, accumulate additional worthwhile information for the book.

My students have been an inspiration in my desire to complete this second edition. University of Illinois students are inquisitive, challenging, innovative, intelligent, and these factors make teaching a real joy.

I would also like to thank our Department head, Dr. Charles J. Birkeland, who permitted me to undertake this work. Without his help, I doubt if the book could have been completed in as brief a time span as it was. Other individuals to whom I owe a debt of gratitude are Ms. Suanne Layden, Ms. Jo Ann Biedermann and Ms. Susan Burd who typed, collated, cut and pasted as if the book meant more to them than me. Thanks to Ms. Jenny Lyverse, Graduate Student, Purdue University, for allowing me to incorporate a horticultural glossary which she extracted from the literature.

Finally, my sincere appreciation and thanks to Professor Joseph C. McDaniel of our Department, one of the great plantsmen of modern times, who freely offered answers and supplied interesting anecdotes to my many questions.

INTRODUCTION TO THE USE OF THE MANUAL

Each plant type (taxon) is discussed in a defined sequence and usually accompanied by a line drawing and identification characteristics related to leaf, bud, and stem. Certain plants are discussed under the heading "Related Species". This approach was taken to avoid repetition and at the same time allow for a significantly greater number of plant discussions.

The plant's scientific, common, and family names are the first items treated under each description. After the family name has been listed for a particular genus it is usually omitted for the other species within the genus. The latin names are as accurate and current as is feasible. *The International Code of Botanical Nomenclature* (1966); and *International Code of Nomenclature of Cultivated Plants* (1969) were followed for scientific names while *Standardized Plant Names* was used, where feasible and logical, for common names. *Hortus III* (1976) was consulted and followed (where feasible) for a complete update on scientific names. If a scientific name was recently changed both the old and new names are listed.

Common names are a constant source of confusion and embarrassment. I have attempted, in most cases, to use the common name which is widely spoken. Certain plants might have 3 to 5 common names and they are usually included after the "accepted" common name. Common names should be written in lower case unless part of the name is proper and then the first letter of only the proper term is capitalized. For example, sugar maple would be written with lower case letters while Japanese maple would be written with the capital J. This is the accepted method for writing common names in scientific circles and should be familiar to the student. In this text and many others common names are written with capital first letters. This was done to set the name off from the rest of the sentence and make it more evident to the reader. Actually in modern horticultural writings the capitalized common name predominates.

The family name was included so that the reader could begin to see the common floral or fruit bonds which exist among genera which are dissimilar to each other in vegetative (leaf, bud, stem, habit) characters. For example, Kentucky Coffeetree does not appear similar or related to Redbud but the similarity of fruits should imply a familial relationship.

The use of SIZE delineations is a moot question and almost any description can be challenged due to the great variation which is to be found in a native population compared to a landscape population. I have attempted to estimate sizes which might be attained under "normal" landscape situations and, in many instances, have listed maximum heights so that the reader might get a feel for the differences. Plants can be maintained at various heights and widths by proper pruning. If a plant is listed as 25 feet in height and one only has space for a 20 foot specimen this is no reason to avoid using the tree. There are simply too many variables which affect the size of a tree or shrub. Plants which appear gnarled and dwarfed on high mountain tops where the soil is dry, rocky, and the exposure windy and cold, may grow to be gentle giants in the moist, fertile, well-drained soils of the valley below. Do not attempt to evaluate the size of a tree in one individual's yard with that in another's even though both may be of the same age. The conditions under which they are growing may be very different.

HARDINESS ratings are risky business since many factors other than low temperatures affect plant survival in a specific area. The hardiness zones mentioned in this book follow those compiled by the Arnold Arboretum. A picture of the map is presented on page 3.

The U. S. Department of Agriculture also publishes a hardiness map which is slightly different from the Arnold Arboretum map (See page 4). Each zone includes 10°F increments and is split into an *a* and *b* zone with the lower temperature occurring in the *a* zone. Since the maps do not coincide it is difficult to compare hardiness ratings but the following cross comparisons of USDA zones versus Arnold zones may serve as a guide.

USDA Hardiness Zones	Arnold Hardiness Zones
Zone 1 — below 50°F	Zone 1 — -50°F and below
Zone 2 — -50 to -40°F	Zone 2 — -50 to -35°F
Zone 3 — -40 to -30°F	Zone 3 — -35 to -20°F
Zone 4 — -30 to -20°F	Zone 4 — -20 to -10°F
Zone 5 — -20 to -10°F	Zone 5 — -10 to -5°F
Zone 6 — -10 to 0°F	Zone 6 — -5 to 5°F
Zone 7 — 0 to +10°F	Zone 7 — 5 to 10°F

Hardiness ratings are meant only as a guide and should not be looked upon as a limiting factor in plant use. Large bodies of water, well-drained soil, wind protection, and adequate moisture will help to increase hardiness. I have used *Ilex cornuta* 'Burfordii', a Zone 7 plant, in a protected part of my yard. Temperatures in the winter of 1975-76 dropped as low as -8°F yet the plant was not injured. Many plants such as forsythia are limitedly flower bud hardy but quite shoot hardy. Plants, such as *Abelia* x *grandiflora*, are best considered weakly shoot hardy and are often killed to the ground in Central Illinois but, as with a herbaceous perennial, develop new shoots and will make an attractive show during the growing season since it flowers on new wood.

One should never allow hardiness ratings to solely determine whether he/she will use a specific plant. Since plants have not been known to read what is written about them in terms of hardiness, they often surprise one and grow outside of their listed range of adaptability.

HABIT as used in this book should supply the reader with a mental picture of the ultimate form or outline of the plant and should prove useful to landscape architecture and design students.

RATE of growth refers to the vertical increase in growth unless specified differently. Rate, as is true for size, is influenced by numerous variables such as soil, drainage, water, fertility, light, exposure, ad infinitum. The designation *slow* means the plant grows 12" or less per year; *medium* refers to 13 to 24" of growth per year; and *fast* to 25" or greater.

TEXTURE refers to the appearance of the plant in foliage and without foliage. A plant that is fine in leaf may be extremely coarse without foliage. Best landscape effects are achieved when similar textures are blended. For example, a planting of catalpa next to a weeping willow is a definite contrast of textures.

The BARK COLOR and texture were included so that the reader could develop an appreciation for these ornamental characters. Too often they are overlooked and omitted as integral parts of the plant's aesthetic qualities. Considering that most deciduous trees and shrubs are devoid of foliage for six months in the northern states, it behooves us to use trees and shrubs with good bark character. To my way of thinking trees like *Acer griseum, Stewartia* sp., and *Ulmus parvifolia* are more beautiful without foliage.

LEAF COLOR refers to the shade of green in summer as well as the colors attained in fall. Again, nutritional and soil factors can partially influence the degree of greenness and to a lesser extent the quality of fall color for fall color is very strongly genetically controlled.

FLOWERS are discussed in terms of color, size, fragrance, period of effectiveness (based on my observations in Central Illinois), and the type of inflorescence. Some plants bear monoecious flowers (both sexes on same plant) while others are dioecious (sexes separate). This has profound implications if one is interested in fruit production. It does no good to buy 5 female American Hollies unless a male plant accompanies them. The male is necessary for pollination and subsequent fruit set.

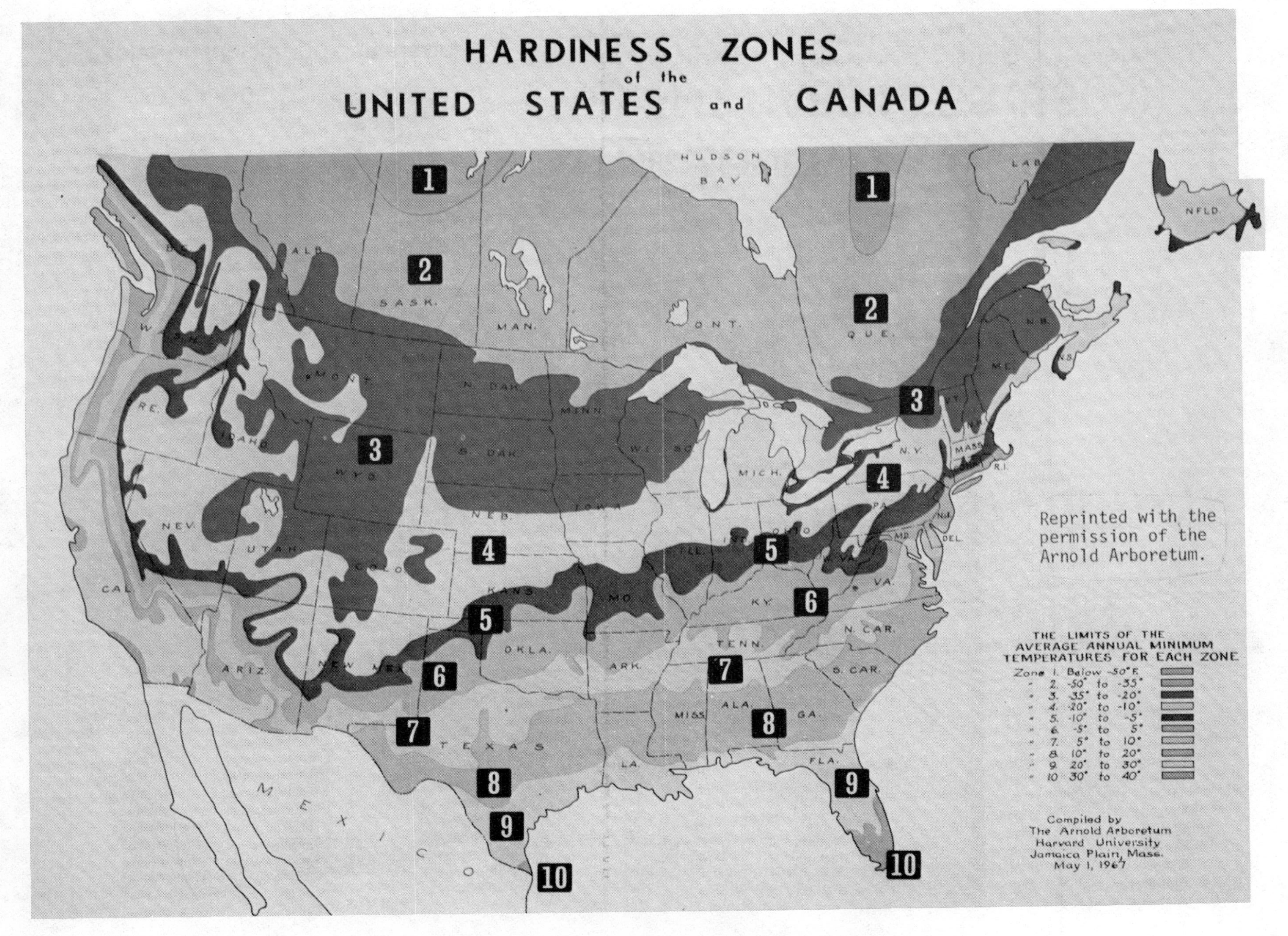

HARDINESS ZONES
of the
UNITED STATES and CANADA
HUDSON BAY
LAB.
NFLD.
ALB.
SASK.
MAN.
ONT.
QUE.
N.B.
N.S.
ME.
VT.
MASS.
CONN.
R.I.
N.Y.
PA.
N.J.
MD.
DEL.
W.VA.
VA.
N. CAR.
S. CAR.
GA.
FLA.
ALA.
MISS.
TENN.
KY.
OHIO
IND.
ILL.
MICH.
WIS.
MINN.
IOWA
MO.
ARK.
LA.
N. DAK.
S. DAK.
NEB.
KANS.
OKLA.
TEXAS
MONT.
WYO.
COLO.
NEW MEX.
IDAHO
UTAH
ARIZ.
NEV.
CAL.
ORE.
WASH.
MEXICO
1
2
3
4
5
6
7
8
9
10
Reprinted with the permission of the Arnold Arboretum.
THE LIMITS OF THE AVERAGE ANNUAL MINIMUM TEMPERATURES FOR EACH ZONE
Zone 1. Below -50° F.
2. -50° to -35°
3. -35° to -20°
4. -20° to -10°
5. -10° to -5°
6. -5° to 5°
7. 5° to 10°
8. 10° to 20°
9. 20° to 30°
10 30° to 40°
Compiled by The Arnold Arboretum Harvard University Jamaica Plain, Mass. May 1, 1967

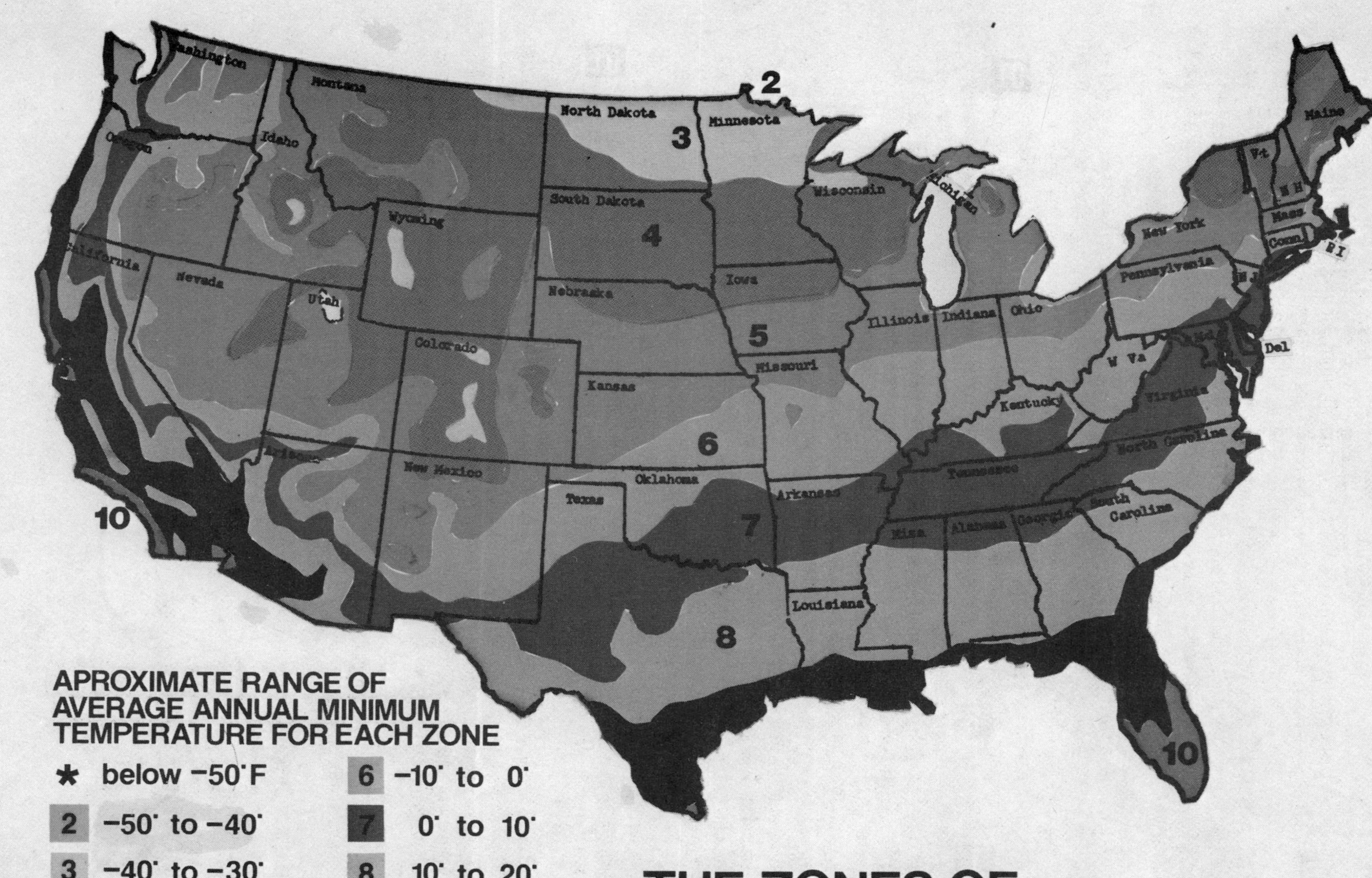

THE ZONES OF PLANT HARDINESS (USDA)

Reprinted with the permission of the National Arboretum and United States Department of Agriculture.

FRUIT discussion covers the type of fruit for each particular plant (i.e., whether it is a drupe, pome, berry); the size and color; period of effectiveness; persistence; and ornamental value.

The CULTURE section discusses the ease of transplanting, soil, light, pruning, pollution tolerance, and other factors which govern the successful growth of a particular plant type.

DISEASES AND INSECTS is a listing of problems encountered with various plant types. If a particular insect or disease is a significant problem it is usually discussed in some detail. Surprisingly most plants require limited maintenance. Ask yourself how often you have sprayed for insects or diseases on your ornamental plants.

LANDSCAPE VALUE is an arbitrary judgement on my part as to the best location or use for a particular plant in the landscape. Plants can be tailored to specific locations by pruning and other manipulations. The "pigeon holing" of plants is by far the worst crime one can commit. Certain plants are used for celebrated locations in the landscape and have become stereotyped. Blue Colorado Spruce or a White Birch are common occurrences in the front yard. Purpleleaf Plum is used on the corners of foundation plantings. Yews and many junipers are often reserved for foundation plantings. The effective use of a particular plant requires a thorough knowledge of all the factors discussed under that plant. It does no good to use a plant that has lovely flower and fruit qualities in wet soils if it is not adapted to this condition.

CULTIVARS are important components of the modern landscape and have been selected for growth habit, flower, fruit, pollution tolerance and myriad other factors. I have attempted to list the more common and recent introductions which are worthy of landscape consideration. Almost every juniper which is now sold is a cultivar which has been selected for good foliage and/or growth habit. The same could be said for many plants and you will note that many cultivar names are probably more familiar to you than the species.

PROPAGATION section lists the most effective methods of seed and vegetative reproduction. One of my research interests is in the area of propagation and much of the information in this section is based on actual experience.

RELATED SPECIES section discusses plant types which are similar to the species in many characters but differ in a few areas such as size, flower, or fruit color. Also included are those plants which are of negligible importance in the landscape but are worth considering if native to a particular area. Other plants discussed include plants which are limitedly known and available but seem to have excellent landscape potential.

ADDITIONAL NOTES is a potpourri of facts, trivia, or minutia related to the use of plant parts for food, fiber and man's enjoyment.

NATIVE HABITAT discusses the natural distribution or range of a particular plant type. The introduction or cultivation date is the earliest record of the plants.

PLANT MORPHOLOGY

In order to successfully identify woody plants it is necessary for an individual to have a keen awareness (working knowledge) of taxonomic terminology and concise mental pictures of leaf, bud, stem, flower and fruit morphology. The glossary in the back of the text capably defines the terminology. This section is devoted to line drawings of woody plant morphological characters which will aid in the identification of various plant types. Definitions and examples are also included.

LEAVES

Composition of a leaf

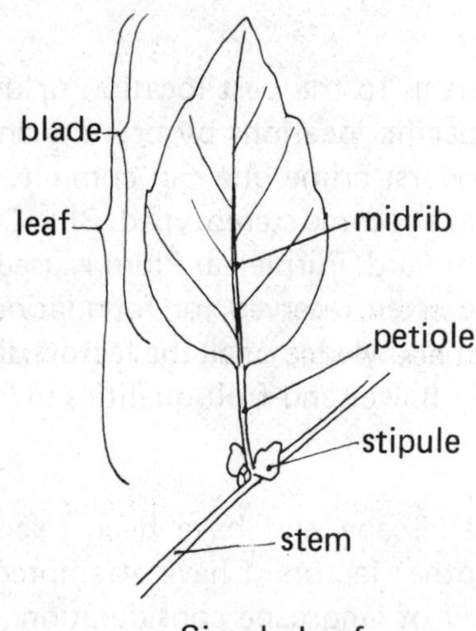

Simple Leaf

The position of the bud determines whether the leaf is simple or compound. In this case the bud is located in the axil of a single leaf and the stem, therefore, the leaf is classified as simple.

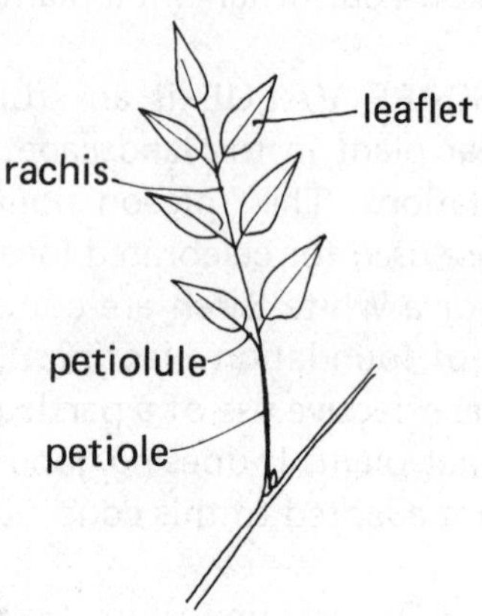

Pinnately Compound Leaf

In this case the bud is located in the axil of a structure with more than one leaf, therefore, the leaf is termed compound. Compound leaves are composed of anywhere from three (*Acer griseum*) to 400 to 1500 leaf-like structures in the case of *Albizia julibrissin*.

Other types of compound leaves.

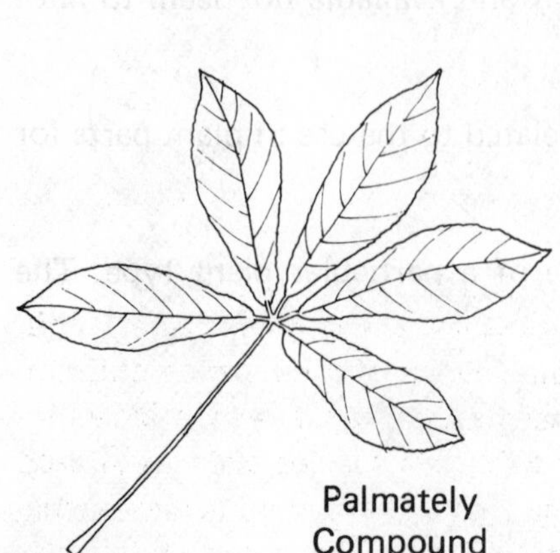

Palmately Compound

In this situation each leaflet is attached to a common point. Ex: *Aesculus, Acanthopanax, Parthenocissus quinquefolia*.

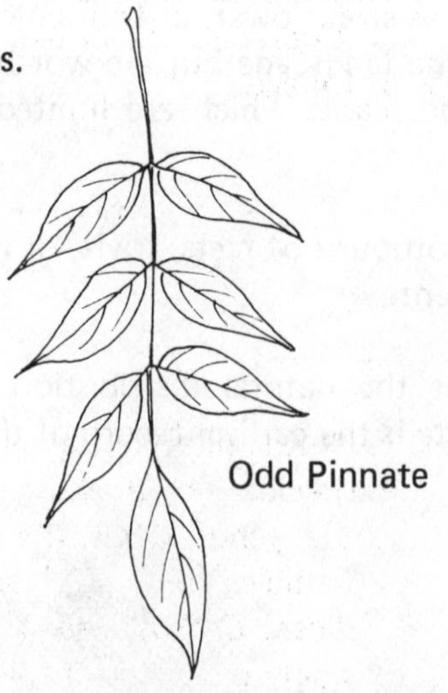

Odd Pinnate

A compound pinnate type of leaf with an odd number of leaflets. Ex: *Acer negundo* has 3 to 5 leaflets. *Fraxinus americana* has 5 to 9 leaflets.

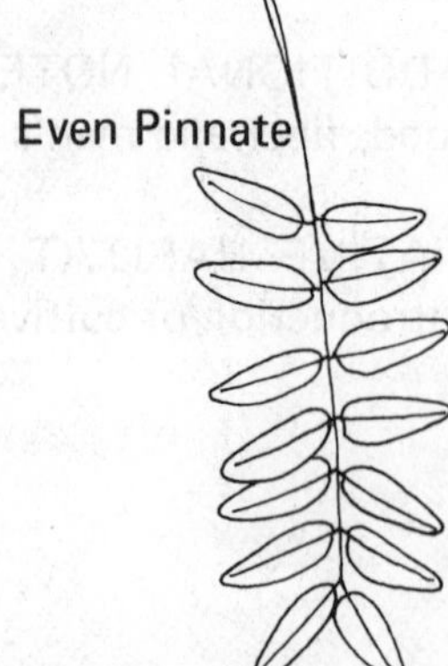

Even Pinnate

A compound pinnate type of leaf with an even number of leaflets. Ex: *Gleditsia, Caragana*.

Bipinnately compound

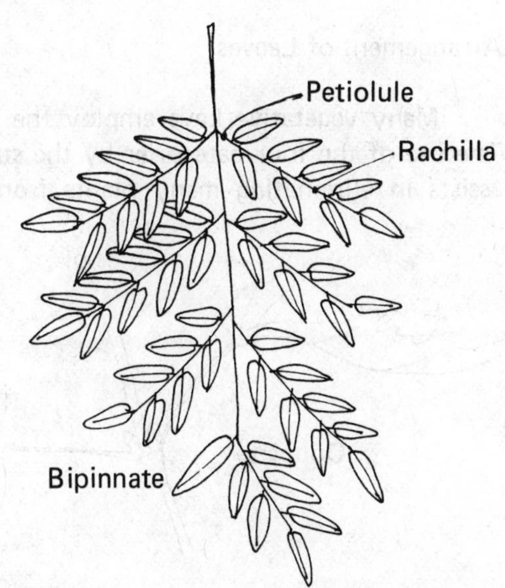

Bipinnately compound leaves are twice divided. What was considered the leaflet of the pinnately compound leaf is now another leaf-bearing axis to which additional leaflets are attached. The new leaf bearing axes are referred to as pinnae. Each pinnae has a certain number of leaflets. Ex: *Gymnocladus, Albizia, Gleditsia* (in certain instances).

Coniferous leaf types

Cone-bearing plants often display different leaf types than those associated with angiosperm plants. Not all conifers (or cone-bearers) have evergreen foliage (exceptions include *Taxodium, Metasequoia, Larix,* and *Pseudolarix*.)

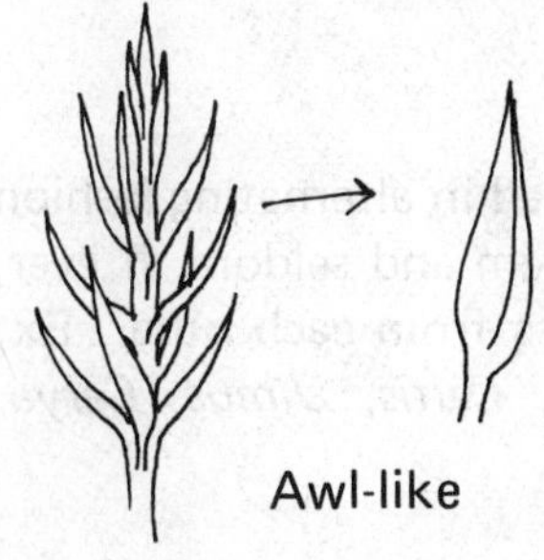
Awl-like

The needles (leaves) are shaped like an awl. They are usually very sharp to the touch. Many *Juniperus* (Junipers) exhibit awl-shaped foliage. This character is manifested in juvenile forms of juniper, however, there are many species and cultivars (*Juniperus communis, J. procumbens, J. chinesis* 'Pyramidalis' to name a few) which possess the awl-like or needle foliage in youth and old age.

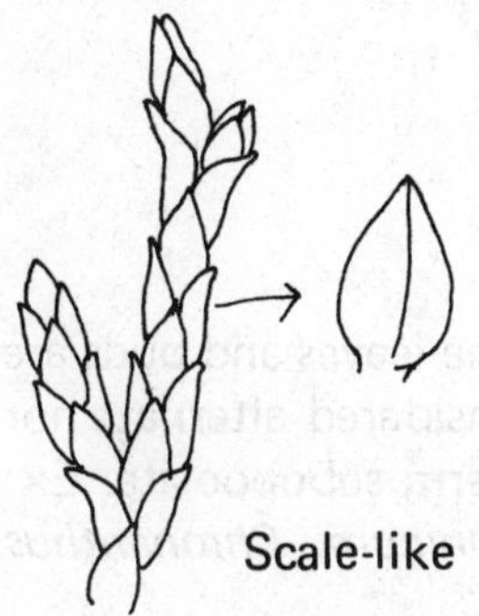
Scale-like

Scale-like foliage overlaps like the shingles on a roof or the scales on a fish. This type of foliage is relatively soft to the touch. *Thuja, Chamaecyparis, Cupressus, Libocedrus*, and many *Juniperus* species exhibit this type of foliage.

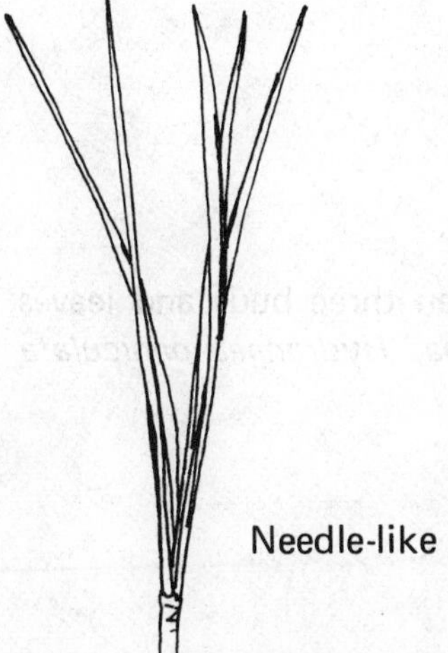
Needle-like

Needle-like foliage is typical of several evergreen genera and species. The drawing depicts the foliage of a 5-needled pine. In the genus *Pinus* the leaves (needles) are usually contained in fascicles of 2, 3, 2 and 3, or 5. Other species such as *Abies, Picea, Cedrus, Pseudotsuga*, and *Taxus* have the needles borne singly or in clusters along the stem. The needles may be relatively flat (2-sided) or angular (often quadrangular) in cross-section. See the respective genera for a detailed discussion of their leaf morphology.

Arrangement of Leaves

Many vegetative keys employ the arrangement of leaves and buds as a basis for separation. The use of the four categories by the student allows him/her to categorize plants into groups and assists in eliminating many plants from consideration in the process of positive identification.

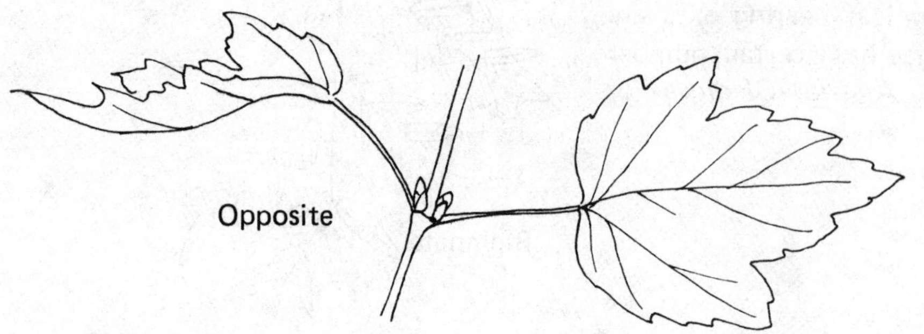

Leaves and buds directly across from each other on the stem. Ex: *Acer, Lonicera, Deutzia, Viburnum.*

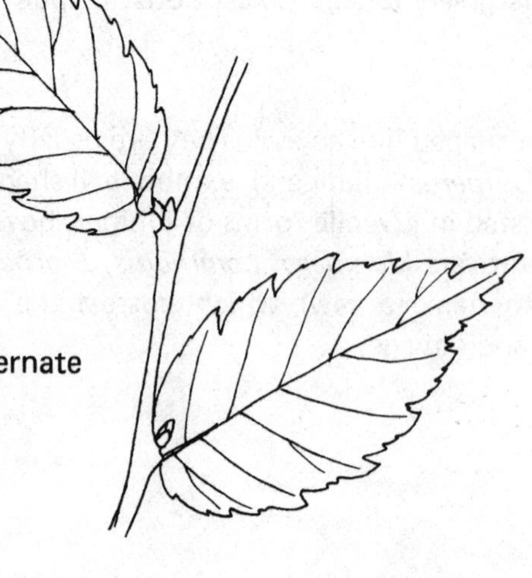

Leaves and buds are spaced in alternating fashion along the axis of the stem and seldom, if ever, are seated directly across from each other. Ex: *Betula, Fagus, Quercus, Celtis, Ulmus, Carya, Juglans*.

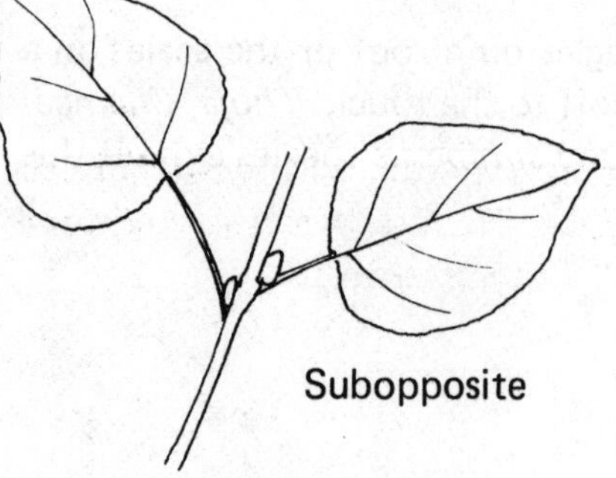

Subopposite refers to a condition where the leaves and buds are not spaced sufficiently far apart to be considered alternate nor are they perfectly opposite, hence, the term subopposite. Ex: *Rhamnus cathartica, Cercidiphyllum japonicum, Chionanthus virginicus*.

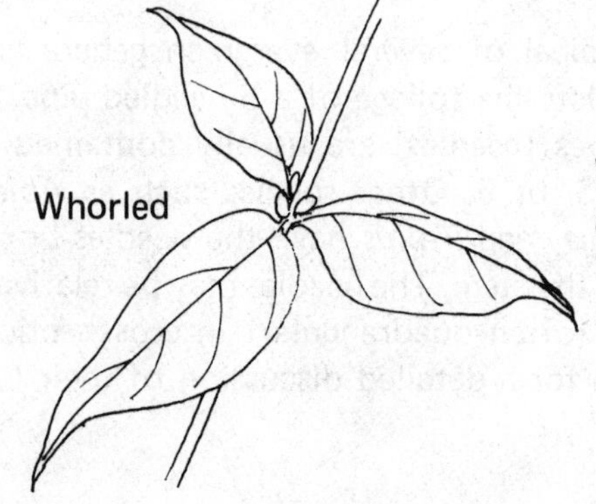

Whorled refers to a condition when three buds and leaves are present at a node. Ex: *Catalpa, Hydrangea paniculata* 'Grandiflora'.

Types of Venation

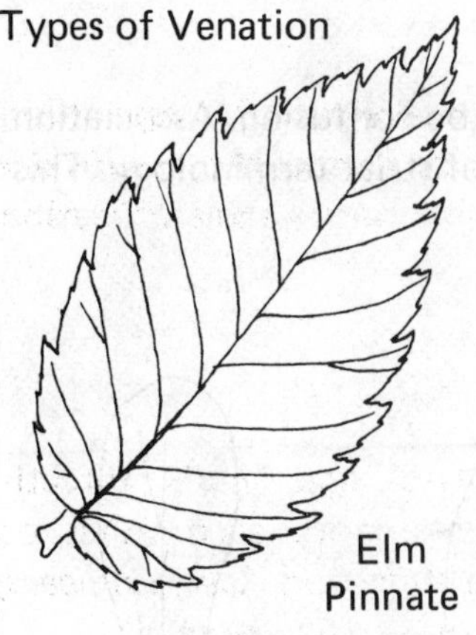
Elm
Pinnate

Pinnate. The leaf has a prominent central vein (often termed the midrib) which extends from the base, where the petiole attaches to the blade, to the apex of the leaf. If the interveinal areas were removed the overall effect would be that of a fishbone. Pinnate venation occurs in the leaves of many plant types. The elm (*Ulmus*) and oak (*Quercus*) are classic examples.

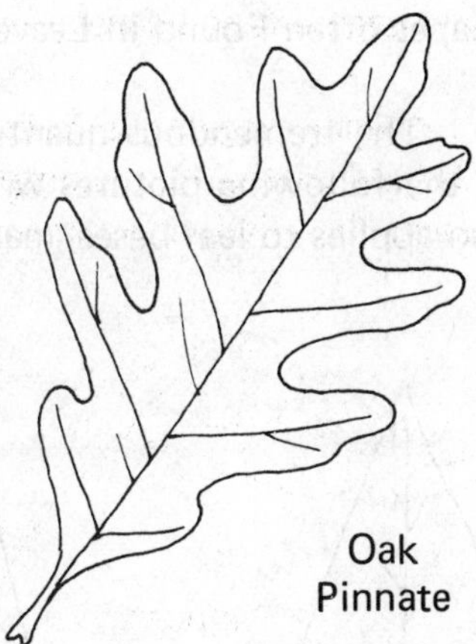
Oak
Pinnate

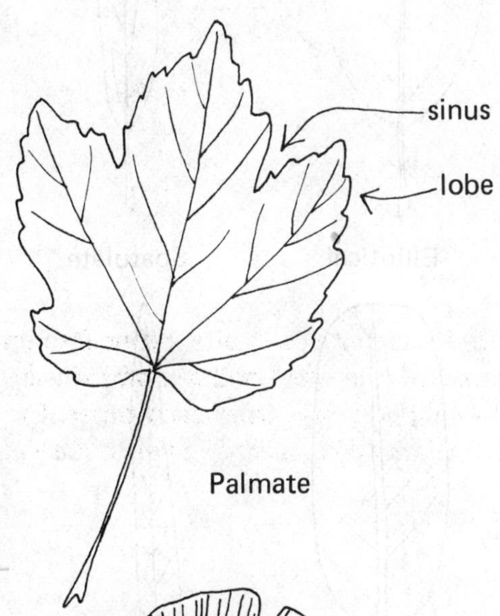

Palmate

Palmate. There are several main veins all of approximately equal size which extend from the base of the leaf to the apex of the lobe. Ex: *Acer, Platanus*.

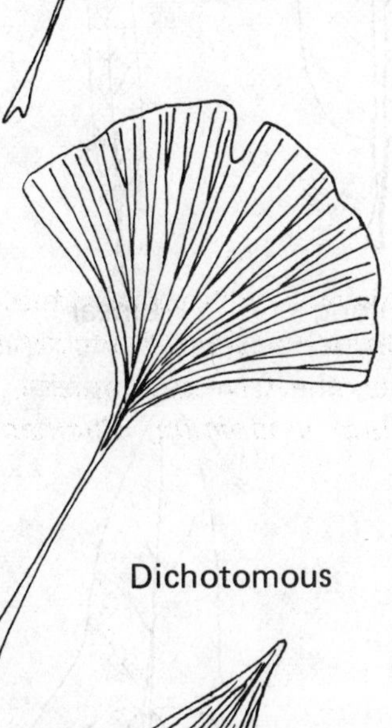
Dichotomous

Dichotomous. A very limited type of venation, the most familiar representative of which is *Ginkgo biloba*. The basal veins extend for a distance and then branch forming a "Y" type pattern.

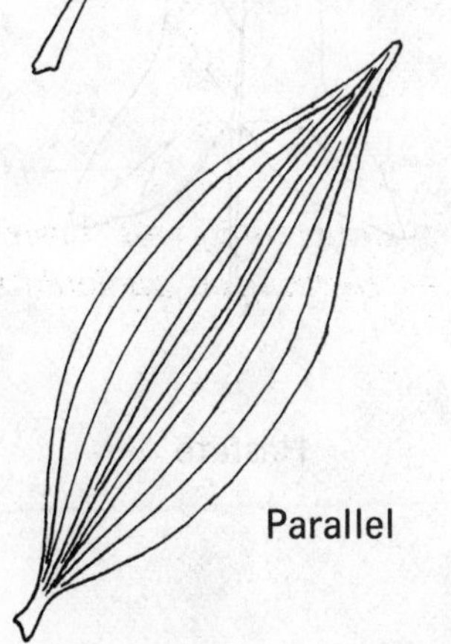
Parallel

Parallel. Typical of many monocotyledonous plants. The veins run essentially parallel to each other along the long axis of the leaf. Ex: *Zea* (corn).

Shapes often Found in Leaves

The tremendous quantity of terminology related to leaf shapes can be confusing. Association of the following pictures with the terms will help to alleviate the burden of strict terminology. This also applies to leaf bases, margins, and apices.

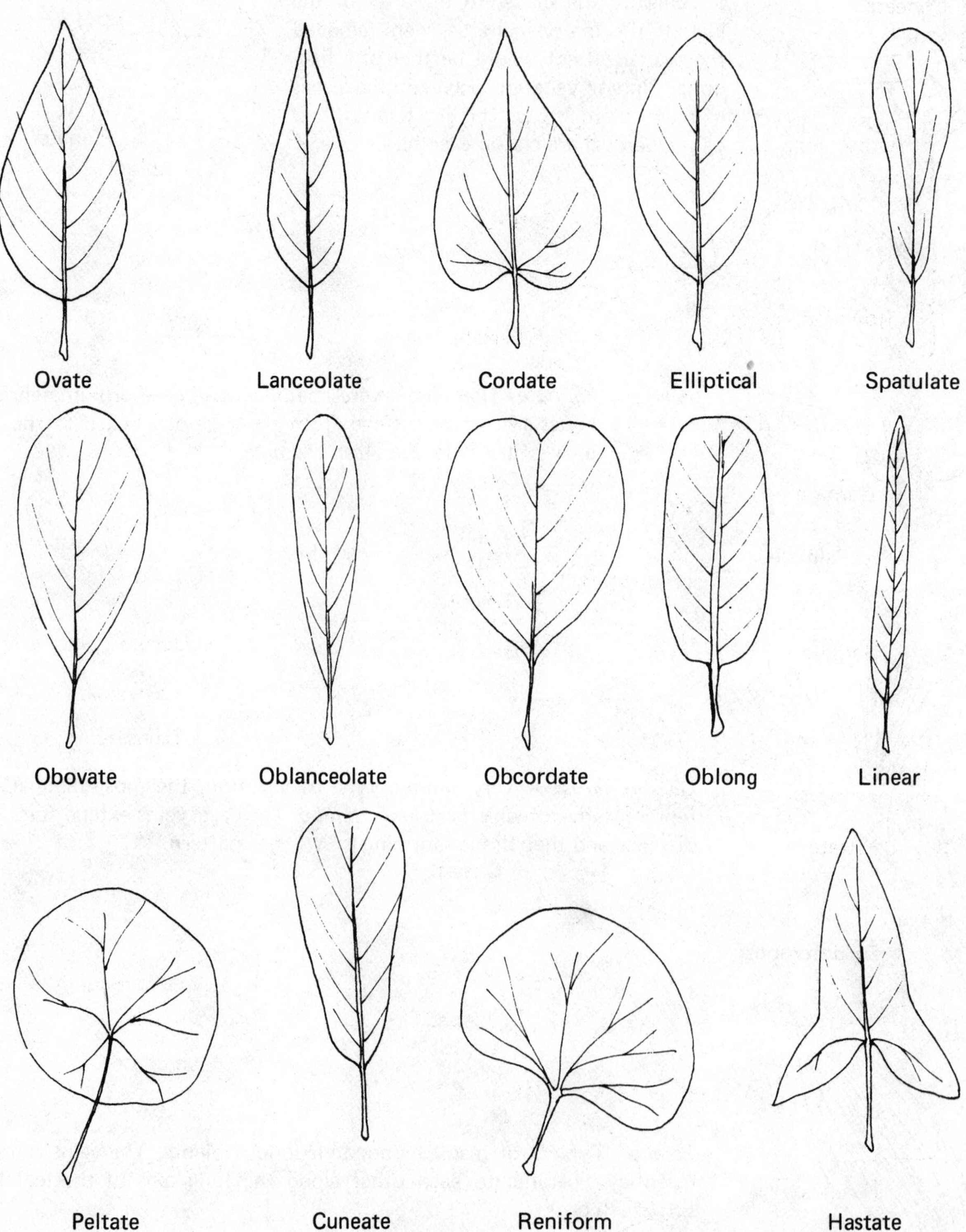

LEAF BASES, MARGINS, APICES

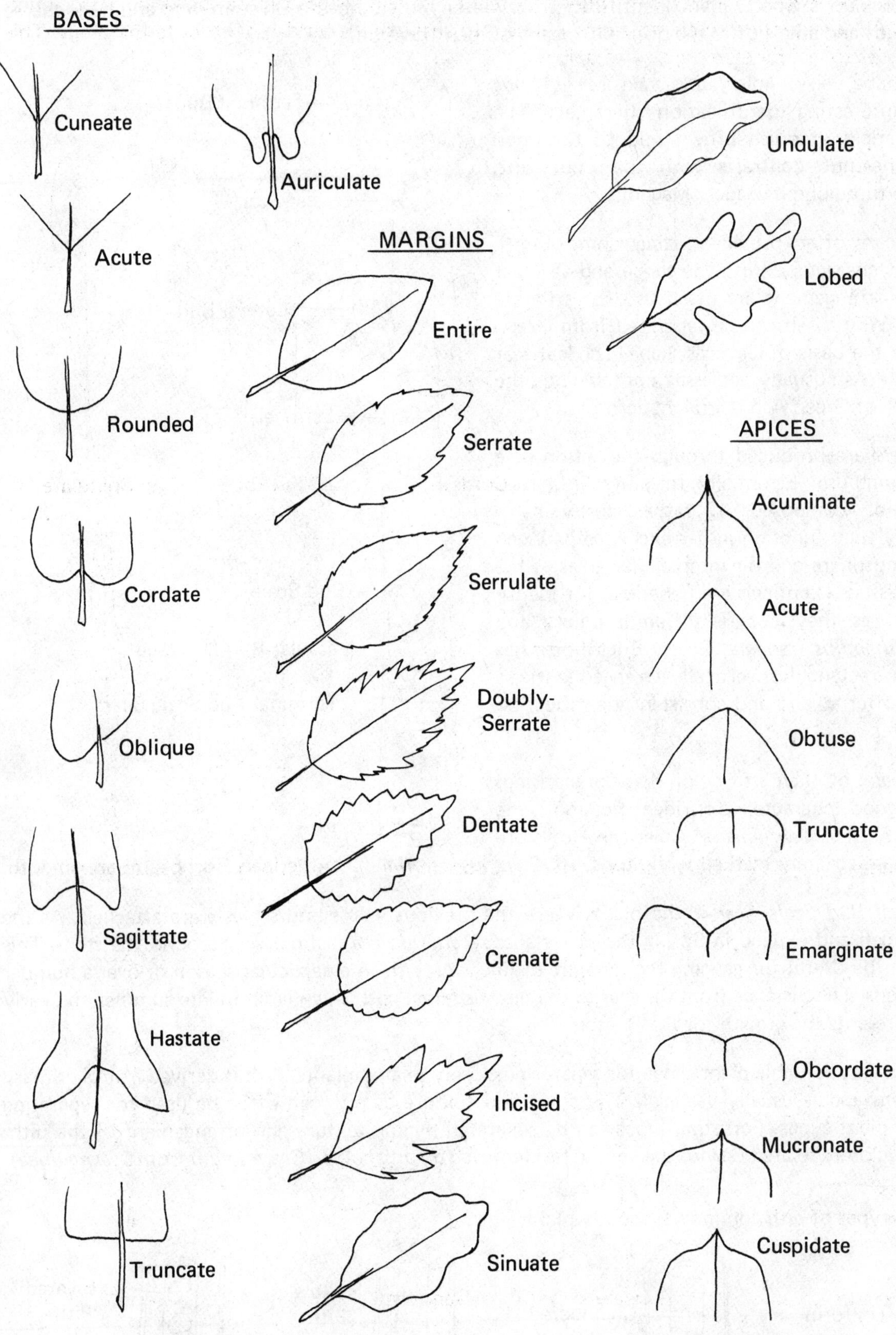
BASES
Cuneate
Auriculate
Acute
Rounded
Cordate
Oblique
Sagittate
Hastate
Truncate
MARGINS
Entire
Serrate
Serrulate
Doubly-
Serrate
Dentate
Crenate
Incised
Sinuate
Undulate
Lobed
APICES
Acuminate
Acute
Obtuse
Truncate
Emarginate
Obcordate
Mucronate
Cuspidate

STEM AND BUD MORPHOLOGY

Deciduous woody plant identification in winter must be based on stem, bud and bark characters. Buds and stems offer the principal means of identification.

The shape, size, color, and texture of *buds* offer interesting identification characters. The large, sticky, reddish brown bud of Common Horsechestnut contrasts with the pubescent, soft-textured bud of Saucer Magnolia.

Leaf scars often provide distinguishing identification characters. Both the shape and vascular bundle arrangement are often used to separate plants. White Ash can be separated from Green Ash on the basis of leaf scar shape. The leaf scar of White Ash usually possesses a notch while the leaf scar of Green Ash is straight across.

Lenticels are produced through the action of a cork cambium. Essentially they are lip-shaped structures composed of rather corky cells. Possibly they function in gas exchange between the atmosphere and the intercellular areas of the plant tissues. Lenticels are beneficial for identification as they possess different colors and sizes. *Rhamnus frangula*, Glossy Buckthorn, has whitish, rectangular, vertically arranged lenticels which offer a valid and consistent identification character.

Bud Scales by their size, color, shape or markings offer good characters for identification. The scales of *Ostrya virginiana*, American Hophornbeam, are striately marked while those of *Carpinus caroliniana*, American Hornbeam, are smooth.

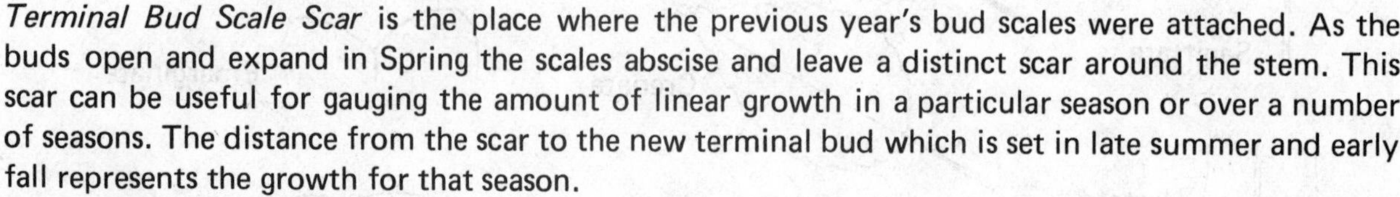

Terminal Bud Scale Scar is the place where the previous year's bud scales were attached. As the buds open and expand in Spring the scales abscise and leave a distinct scar around the stem. This scar can be useful for gauging the amount of linear growth in a particular season or over a number of seasons. The distance from the scar to the new terminal bud which is set in late summer and early fall represents the growth for that season.

Pith is a very valuable plant tissue for separating closely related plants. Pith is derived from a primary meristem and is usually vestigial. The color and texture of pith can often be used for separating similar plant types. Forsythia types can be separated by the texture and arrangement of the pith. Several closely related *Cornus* species can be identified by pith color. (*C. amomum* from *C. sanguinea*).

Several types of pith common to woody plants.

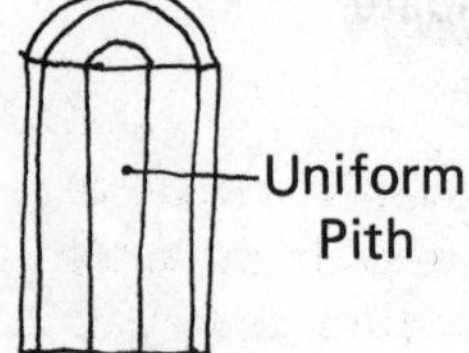

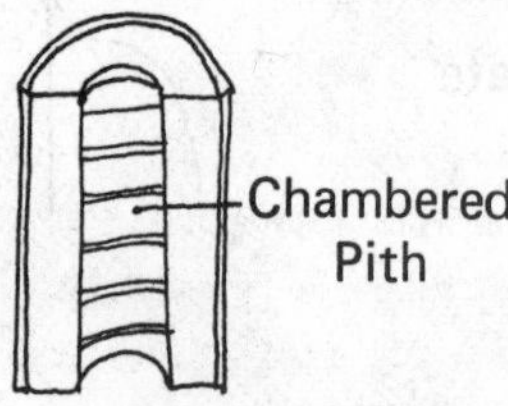

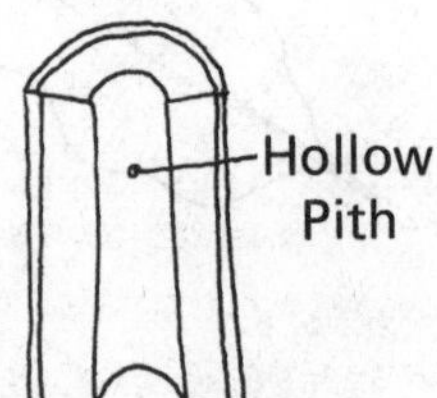

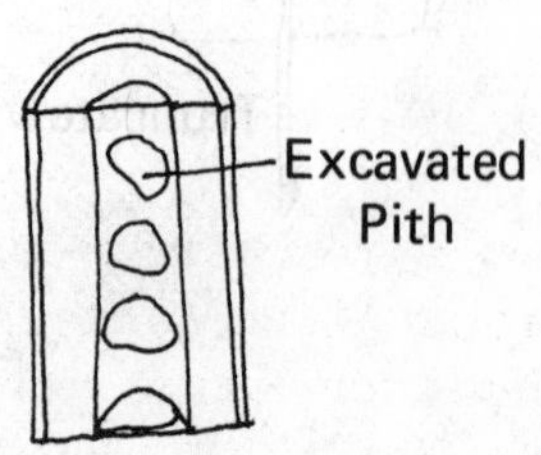

Bud types frequently found in woody plants.

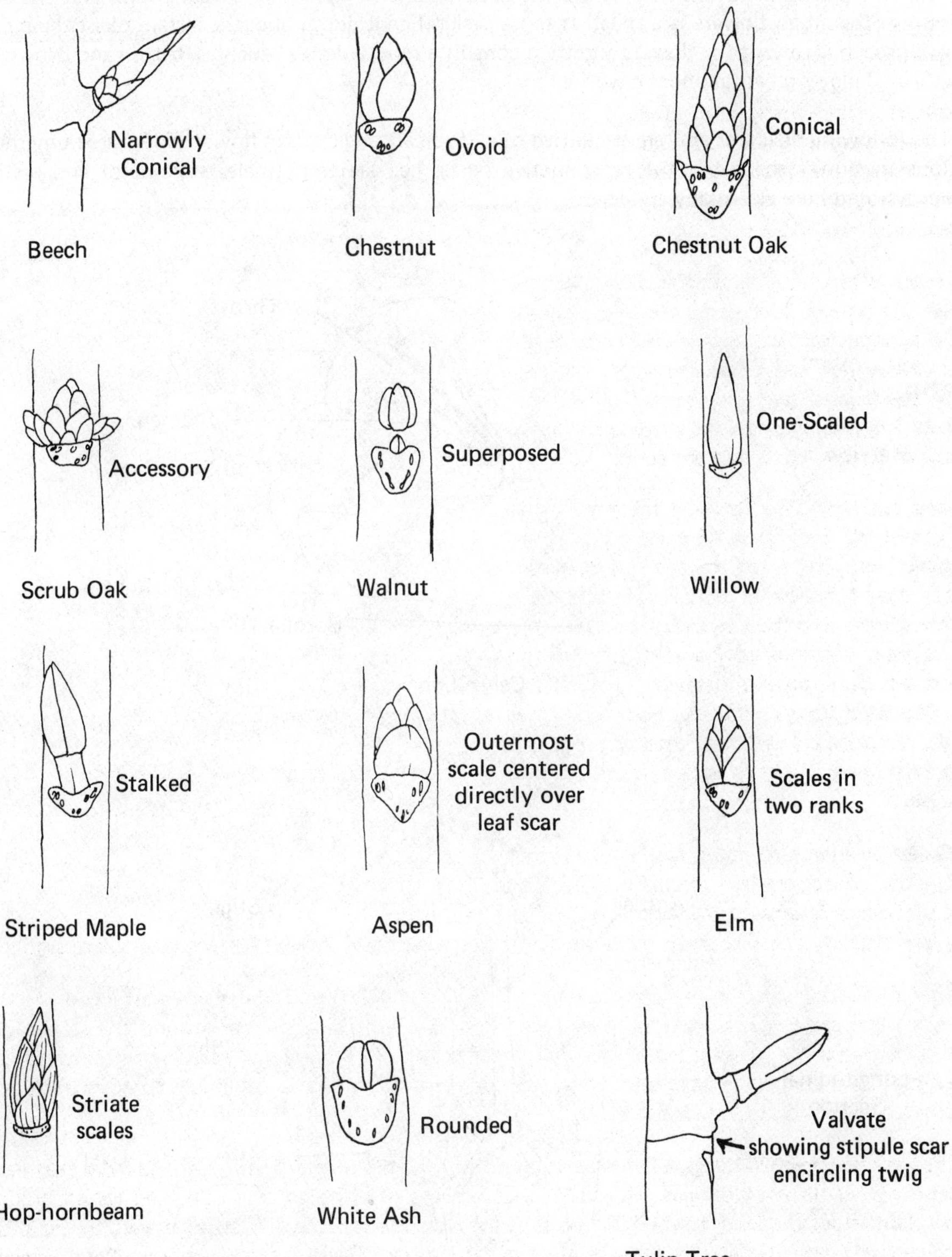

FLORAL MORPHOLOGY

Flowers are important components of most botanical keys and the positive identification of various plants is based on some aspect of floral morphology. This approach is acceptable but only allows for positive identification a short period of the year (on the average the flowering periods of most woody plants would average seven to fourteen days). The homeowner, nurseryman, student and interested plantsman often wish or are required to identify plants the year round and the use of features other than flowers is a must. If there is significant doubt about a certain plant the most logical approach is to wait for flowers and then consult a reputable text such as Britton and Brown's, Rehder's or Bailey's great taxonomic works.

The following diagrams are representative of a "typical" angiosperm flower. There are numerous variations in flower shape but the reproductive parts, i.e., stamens (male, staminate) and pistils (female, pistillate) are essentially similar.

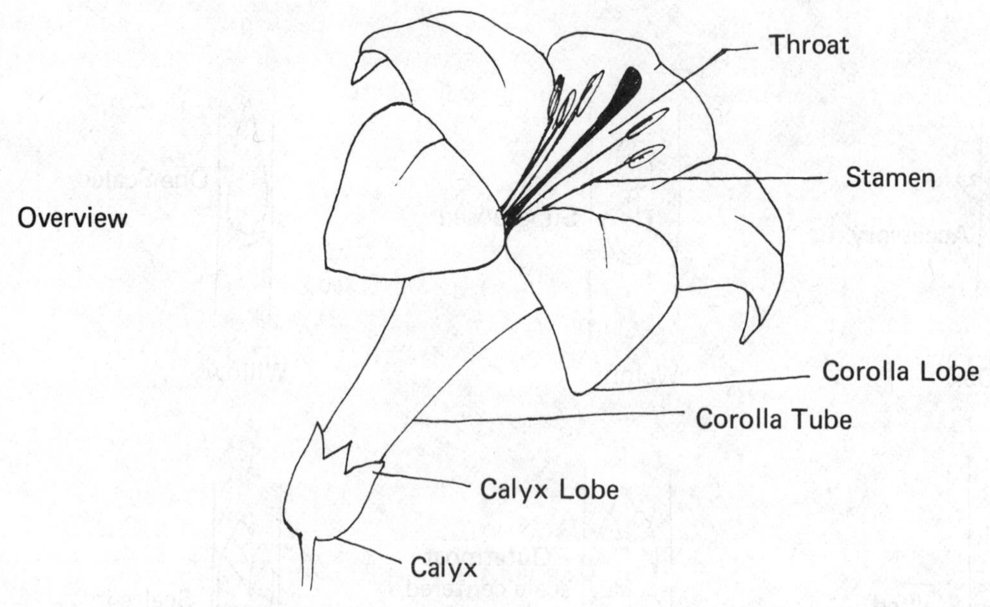

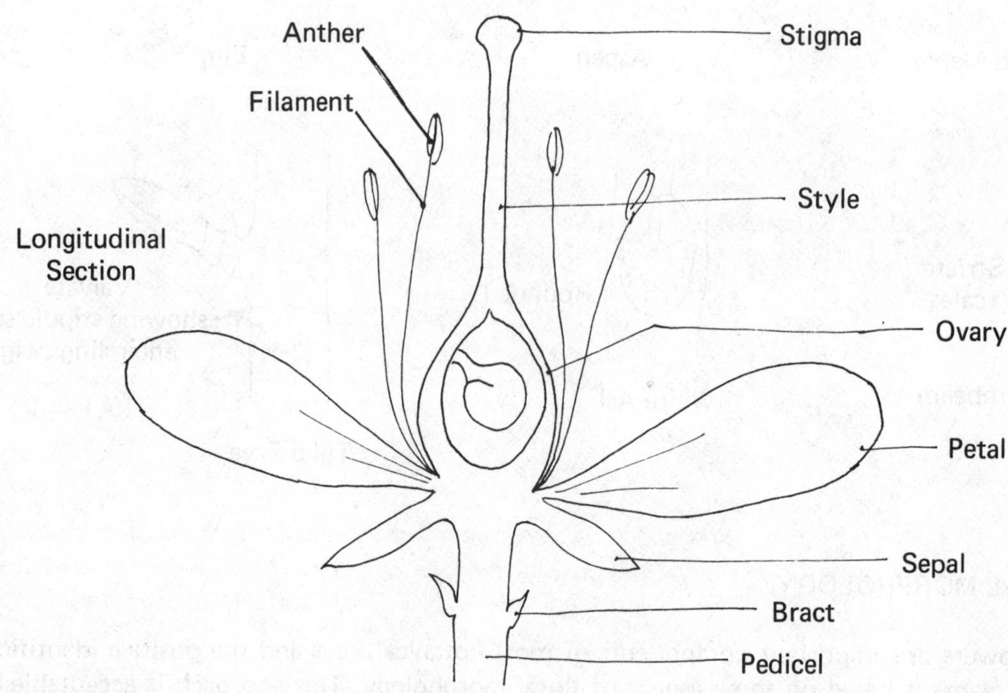

Flowers which have all the parts (sepals, petals, stamens, and a pistil or pistils) are termed *complete. Incomplete* flowers lack one or more whorls of floral parts such as the petals. *Imperfect* flowers lack either stamens or pistils. *Perfect* flowers have both stamens and pistils. *Monoecious* means that staminate and pistillate flowers are present on the same plant *(Betula, Carpinus, Ostrya, Carya, Quercus, Fagus). Dioecious* means the staminate and pistillate flowers are borne on different plants (Examples include *Gymnocladus dioicus, Ilex, Lindera,* and *Cercidiphyllum*). *Polygamo-monoecious* refers to a condition where perfect, pistillate and staminate flowers occur on the same tree. *Polygamo-dioecious* implies perfect and pistillate flowers on the same plant or perfect and staminate flowers. Several woody plants which show polygamous characters include *Gleditsia, Fraxinus, Chionanthus, Osmanthus,* and *Morus.*

Flowers are borne on structures which are referred to as inflorescences. An inflorescence is a collection of individual flowers arranged in some specific fashion. The following are some of the representative types found in both woody and herbaceous plants.

Spike. Individual flowers are sessile on the elongated axis (peduncle). The male flower of *Betula, Carpinus, Alnus, Populus, Quercus, Salix* and *Carya* are spikes with a special name termed catkin or ament (Indeterminate).

Spike

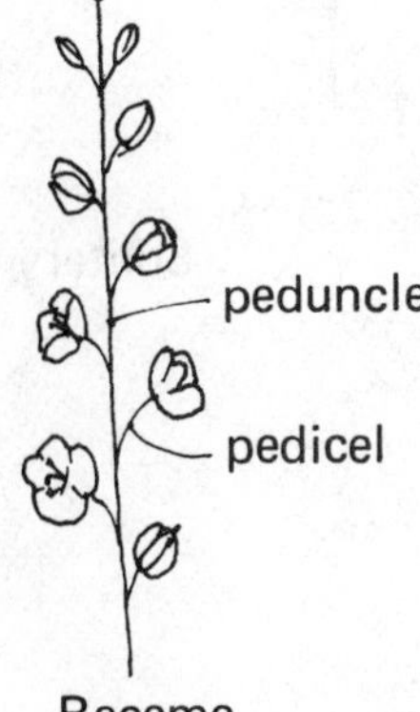

Raceme

Raceme. In the simplest terms it is a modification of a spike with the individual flowers stalked (on a pedicel). *Cladrastis, Laburnum, Wisteria* possess racemose flowers (Indeterminate).

Corymb. An indeterminate (can continue to elongate) inflorescence in which the individual flowers are detached at different points along the peduncle. The outer flowers open first. *Malus, Prunus,* and *Iberis* show corymb inflorescences.

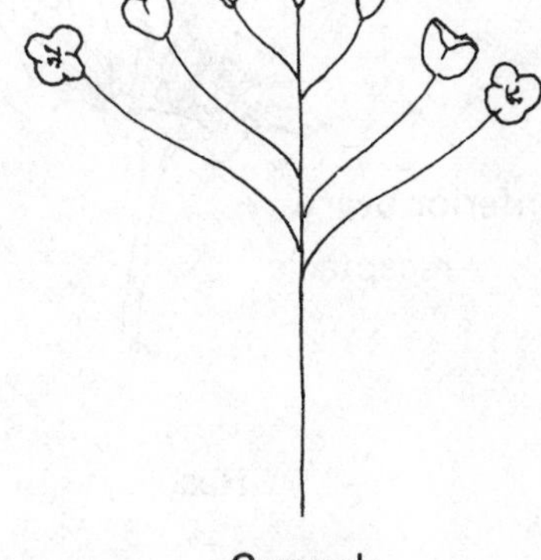
Corymb

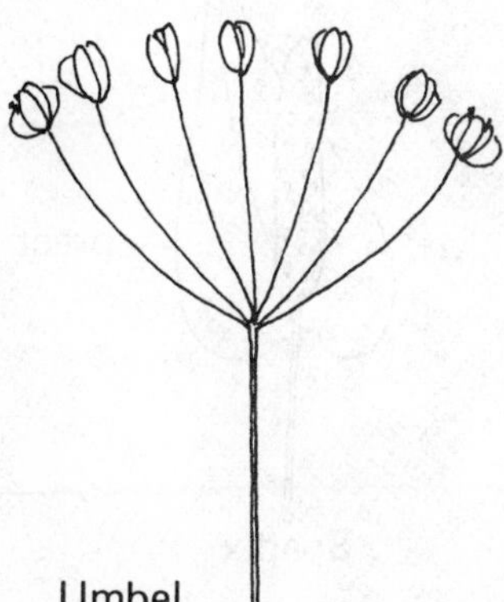
Umbel

Umbel. An indeterminate inflorescence in which the pedicels of the individual flowers radiate from about the same place at the top of the peduncle. Flowers open from outside in. *Hedera helix, Aralia, Daucus* (carrot) are examples.

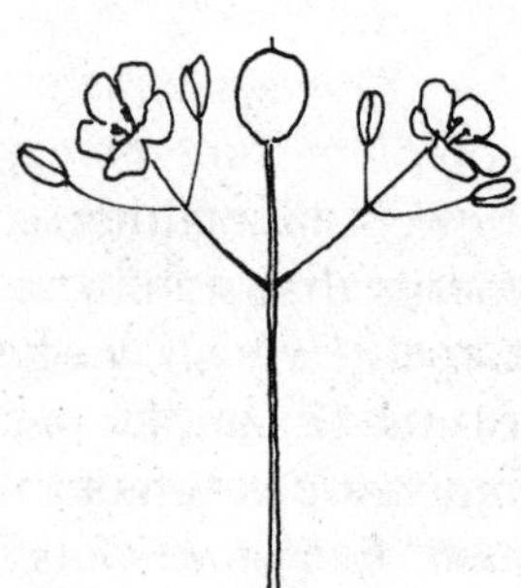

Cyme

Cyme. A determinate, flat or convex inflorescence, the central or inner flowers opening first. *Cornus, Viburnum, Geranium* are examples.

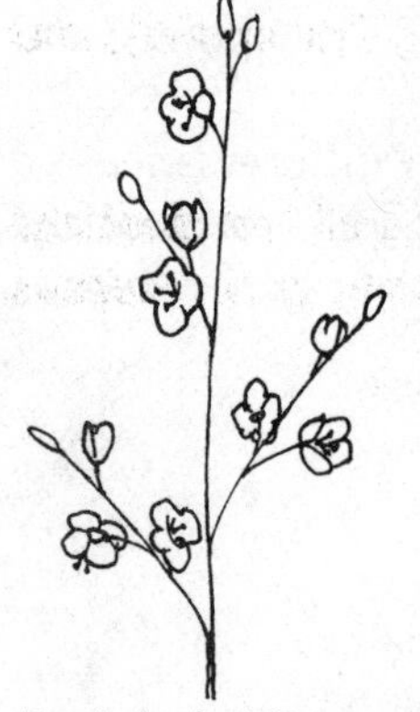

Panicle (of Racemes)

Panicle. An indeterminate inflorescence with repeated branching. Panicles can be made up of many racemes, spikes, corymbs, or umbels. Racemose-panicles are found in *Pieris, Koelreutaria;* spikose-panicles in corn; corymbose-panicles in *Pyracantha;* umbellose-panicles in *Aralia.*

Solitary

Solitary. Indicates a single flower with a pedicel attached to the stem. *Magnolia, Calycanthus, Kerria* and many other woody plant flowers fall into this category.

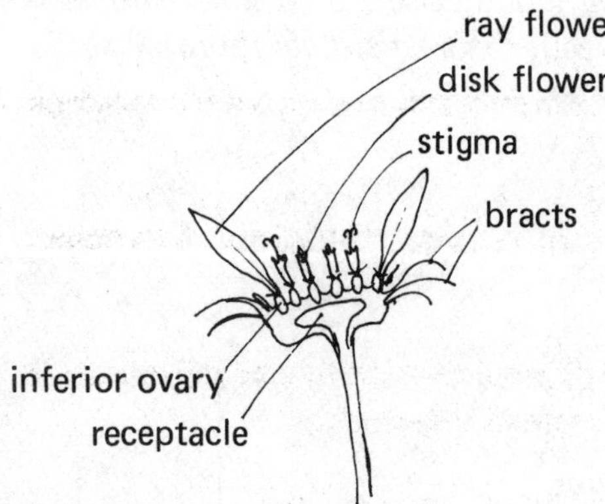

Head

Head. The typical inflorescence of the family Compositae. Made up of ray (sterile) and disk (fertile) flowers which are arranged on a flattened receptacle. *Chrysanthemum, Rudbeckia* are examples.

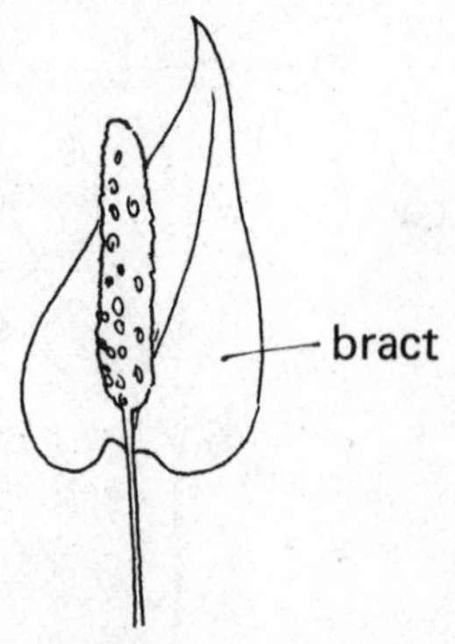

Spadix

A *spadix* is a specialized type of inflorescence typical of many tropical plants. The showy part is the bract or spathe while the spike-like structure which is partially surrounded by the spathe bears the fertile flowers. Examples include *Anthurium, Spathiphyllum, Caladium, Calla* and *Philodendron.*

FRUIT MORPHOLOGY

The longitudinal section of the "typical" flower offers a representative view of the ovary. The ovary is the forerunner of the fruit and is defined as an unripened fruit. The ovary is composed of carpel(s) which are highly modified leaf-like structures which inclose ovules (forerunner of seeds). An ovary may be composed of one carpel (simple fruit) or two or more carpels (compound fruit). Fruits are very important considerations in woody landscape plants for they offer good ornamental assets (color, texture) and positive identification features through late summer, into fall, and often persist until spring of the year following maturation. The fruits of *Ilex* (Holly) are often colorful for a long period of time while fruits of *Prunus* (Cherry), some *Malus* (Flowering Crabapples), and several *Crataegus* (Hawthorns) persist briefly after ripening (2 to 4 weeks).

The following classification scheme for fruits along with their definitions and line drawings should afford an idea of the diversity of fruit types which are manifested by woody or herbaceous plants.

I. SIMPLE FRUITS

A. Dry Fruits

1. *Indehiscent fruits* (not splitting open at maturity)

a. *Achene* — one-seeded fruit with seed attached at only one place to the pericarp. Pericarp is very close-fitting and does not split open, at least along regular established lines. Examples: Buckwheat, Sunflower, Calendula.

b. *Caryopsis* — similar to an achene but the pericarp is adherent to the seed, the two often being undistinguishable (seed coat is inseparable from the pericarp). Examples: Corn, Wheat.

c. *Samara* — usually one-seeded (not always) with a membranous wing which develops from the pericarp. Examples: Maple, Ash, Elm.

d. *Nut* — a bony, hard, one-seeded fruit. The pericarp is bony throughout. Examples: Oak, Chestnut and Filbert.

e. *Utricle* — similar to an achene but the ovary wall is relatively thin and inflated so it fits only loosely around the seed. Examples: Goosefoot, Pigweed.

f. *Nutlet* — diminutive of nut. Examples: Hornbeam, Birch, Hophornbeam.

2. *Dehiscent fruits* (splitting open when mature)

a. *Legume* (Pod) — composed of one carpel and opens along two sutures; characteristic of most members of the Leguminosae; contains several to many seeds. Examples: Redbud, Honey-locust, Coffeetree, Black Locust.

b. *Follicle* — composed of one carpel but splits open at maturity along one suture exposing several to many seeds. Examples: Larkspur, Columbine, Peony, Milkweed, Spirea, individual fruits of Magnolia.

c. *Capsule* — many-seeded fruits formed from more than one carpel. The carpels are united. *Loculicidal Capsule* opens along midrib; *Septicidal Capsule* divides through the partitions. Examples: Rhododendron, Mockorange, Deutzia, Forsythia, and Lilac.

d. *Silique* – composed of two carpels which separate at maturity, leaving a thin partition between. Example: Mustard family.

e. *Silicle* – a short, broad silique. Examples: Shephard's Purse, Peppergrass.

f. *Pyxis* – type of capsule which opens around a horizontal ring, the top of fruit falling away like a lid. Example: Purslane.

B. Fleshy Fruits

1. *Berry* – The entire pericarp (exo, endo, meso-carp) is fleshy. Examples: Tomato, Date, Banana, Blueberry, Cranberry, Honeysuckle.

   a. *Hesperedium* – a berry with a leathery rind. Examples: Orange, Lemon, Grapefruit.

   b. *Pepo* – a berry with a hard rind and fleshy inner matrix. Examples: Watermelon, Squash, Pumpkin.

2. *Drupe* – the pericarp is clearly differentiated into three layers; exocarp is the epidermis; middle layer, the mesocarp, is fleshy; and the inner layer, the endocarp, is stony. Examples: Cherry, Peach, Plum, Sassafras, Viburnum, Holly and numerous other woody ornamental plants.

3. *Pome* – the pericarp is surrounded by the floral tube (hypanthium) which becomes fleshy and tasty. Examples: Apple, Pear, Quince.

II. AGGREGATE FRUITS

Develop from a single flower which contains many pistils. Several to many fruitlets are massed on one receptacle. Examples: Raspberry–aggregate of drupes; Strawberry–aggregate of achenes; Tuliptree–aggregate of samaras; Magnolia–aggregate of follicles; Osageorange–aggregate of drupes.

III. MULTIPLE FRUITS

Consists of several flowers which are more or less united into one mass. Examples: Fig, Pineapple.

FRUIT TYPES

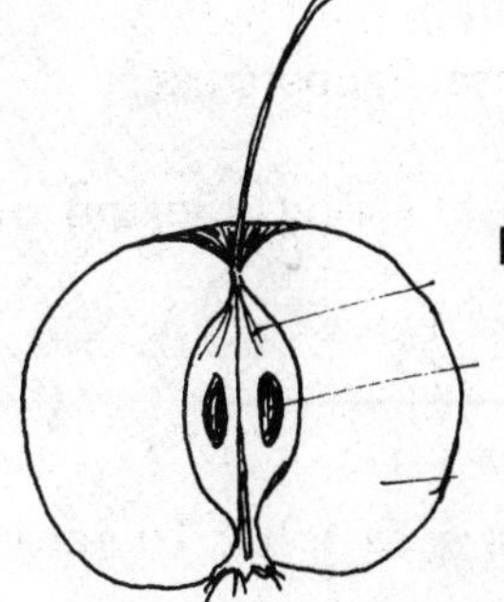

POME
(Malus, Pyrus, Chaenomeles)

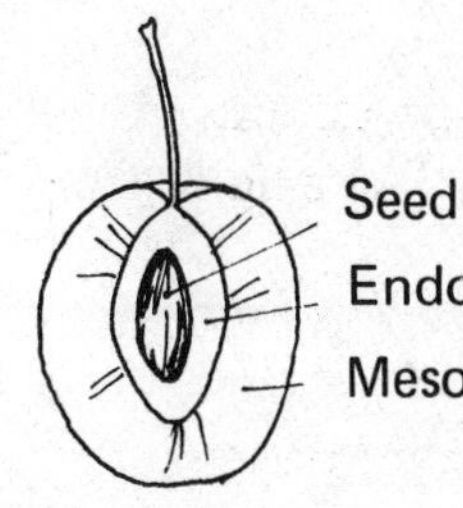

DRUPE
(Prunus, Viburnum, Celtis, Sassafras)

BERRY
(Asimina, Lonicera)

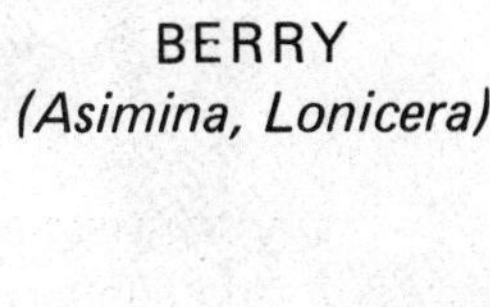

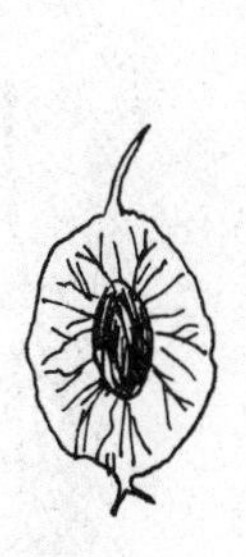

SAMARA
(Ulmus)

SCHIZOCARP
(Acer)

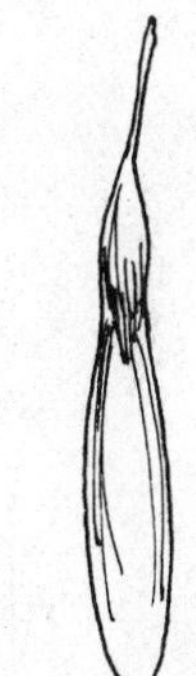

SAMARA
(Fraxinus)

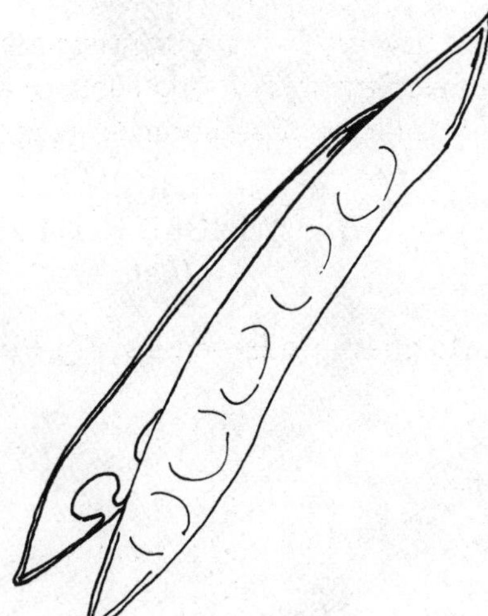

LEGUME (POD)
(Robinia, Cercis, Gleditsia)

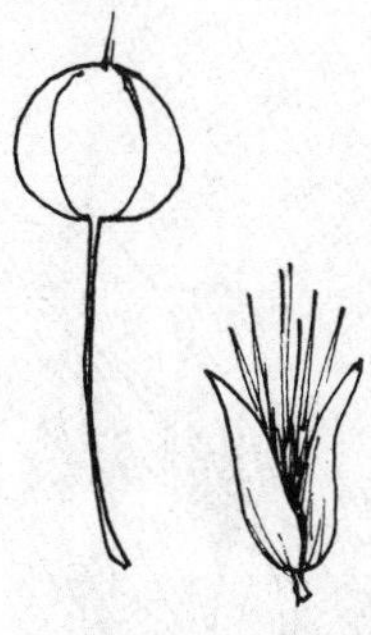

CAPSULES
(Kalmia, Forsythia, Rhododendron)

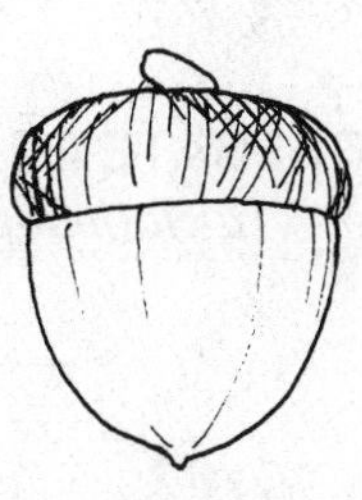

ACORN
(Quercus)

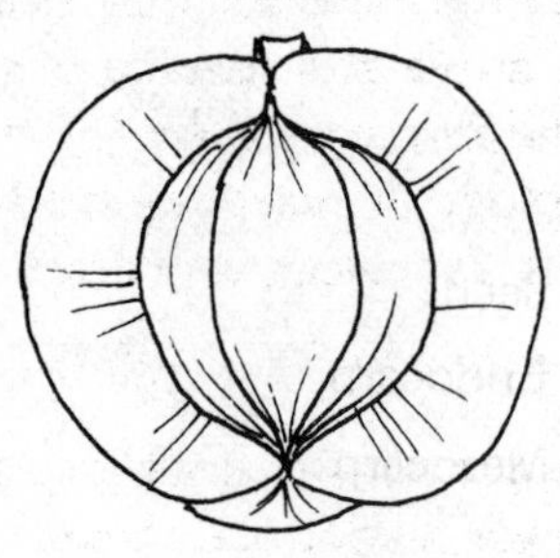

NUT WITH DEHISCENT HUSK
(Carya)

NUTLET
(Carpinus)

CONE
(Tsuga, Pinus, Abies)

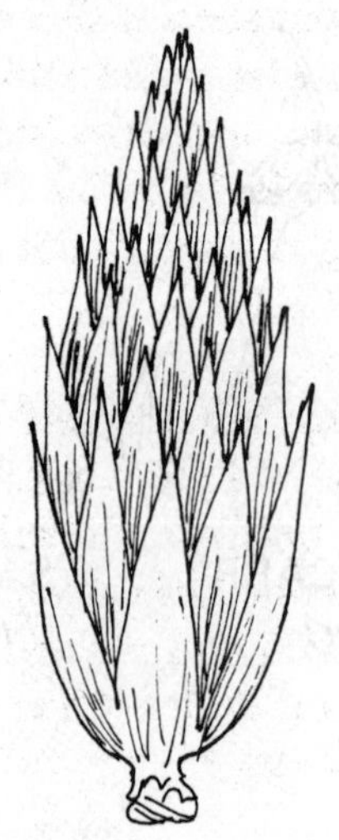

AGGREGATE OF SAMARAS
(Liriodendron)

MULTIPLE FRUIT OF SMALL DRUPES
(Morus)

STROBILE: WINGED NUTLET
(Betula)

AGGREGATE OF FOLLICLES
(Magnolia)

THE USE OF KEYS FOR IDENTIFYING WOODY PLANTS

A key is, in essence, an artificial contrivance which outlines specific morphological features in an organized manner that allows the identifier (user) to eventually arrive at a specific plant or at least reach a point where he/she can consult other references for further separatory information. The information in many keys is geared to flower and fruit morphology, however keys have been constructed from leaf, stem, bud, root, plant habit, anatomical traits and about any other feature be it macro- or micro-scopic.

A key is an aide to plant identification but far from the sole answer as many individuals would lead one to believe. Plants are variable entities! They may be in flower an average of only 7 to 14 days. The leaves of deciduous trees and shrubs, in the northern climes, are present, at most, 5 to 7 months. Bud and stem colors change drastically from fall through winter and into spring. A key that includes all season features is the utopian necessity but does not exist. Keys are often based on one or two morphological traits which suffice for a single time period. Gardening enthusiasts and those who work in horticultural related businesses must be able to identify plants throughout the seasons. I have seen more mixed up landscape plantings of birch, witchhazel, and honeysuckle simply because the buyer and seller could not distinguish between and among the various species. Our campus is a monument to this problem for we have pink and white flowering honeysuckles mixed unintentionally in hedges; Japanese and Mentor Barberries confused in the same planting; and Gray and European White Birch in total chaos. These examples are not isolated for I have seen foul-ups like this in many landscape situations. The moral is that plants must be learned by the characteristics which will permit separation in any season.

A key is a supplement and should not be used as the sole mode for teaching and/or learning plants. Innumerable times I have heard people say they can always "key" the plant out. Yet when I asked them to define several of the simple terms used in keys they were boggled. The successful use of a key demands a specific level of horticultural and botanical expertise. Considerable practice, patience, taxonomic vocabulary, and a more knowledgeable plant person (who can tell you if the answer is correct) are the necessary prerequisites. If one makes the wrong choice in the dichotomy of the key, he/she is hopelessly lost.

Too often keys attempt to simplify and reduce morphological characters to a paradigm. Maples are often construed as having the "typical" five-lobed leaves when; in fact, the genus *Acer* possesses species with trifoliate, compound pinnate, simple pinnate, and simple palmate leaves. The same is true for oaks where one gets the impression that White and Bur Oak leaves are characteristic of the genus. If one looks at enough oaks he/she quickly finds this more the exception than the rule.

A typical woody plant key might be constructed like the following.

Leaves Opposite or Whorled

1. Leaves compound.

    2. Leaflets pinnately arranged.

        3. Lateral buds hidden beneath petiole bases.

            4. Leaflets 3 to 7, coarsely toothed.
            Acer negundo — Boxelder

1. Leaves simple.

5. Margins of leaves lobed or toothed, not entire.

6. Leaves lobed.

7. Stipules absent.

8. Lateral buds hidden by the petiole bases; terminal bud absent.
Acer palmatum — Japanese Maple

8. Lateral buds visible; terminal bud usually present.

9. Terminal lobe of leaf much longer (2 or 3 times) than the lateral lobes; terminal bud present or absent.
Acer ginnala — Amur Maple

9. Terminal lobe of leaf not conspicuously longer than the lateral lobes; terminal bud present.

10. Leaves white beneath.

11. Buds green; leaves with depressed veins; axis of inflorescence long persistent, often for more than one season.
Acer pseudoplatanus — Planetree Maple

11. Buds reddish; . . . etc.

A key starts with a very general categorization and gradually works toward the smallest component. The above example is geared to four maple species and shows the pathway of least resistance for "keying out a plant". One would note that the maple leaves are opposite and would take that route rather than the "alternate" branch of the key. Are the leaves compound or simple? The user must take the choice and proceed to the next description. Eventually if he/she has made the correct choices the plant in question should be properly identified.

The following books offer valuable "keys" for distinguishing among plants. See bibliography for complete citation.

Apgar, Austin C. *Ornamental Shrubs of the United States.*
Trees of the Northern United States.

Bailey, L.H. *Manual of Cultivated Plants.*

Blackburn, Benjamin. *Trees and Shrubs in Eastern North America.*

Core, Earl L., and Nelle P. Ammons. *Woody Plants in Winter.*

Curtis, Ralph W., et al. *Vegetative Keys to Common Ornamental Woody Plants.*

Gray, Asa. *Gray's Manual of Botany* (Revised by M.C. Fernald).

Harlow, William M. *Fruit Key and Twig Key.*

Sargent, Charles S. *Manual of the Trees of North America.* Vol. I and II.

Trelease, William. *Winter Botany.*

Viertel, Arthur T. *Trees, Shrubs and Vines.*

PLANT NOMENCLATURE

Any discussion of plants should be prefaced by an explanation of how and why plants are named as well as a general understanding of the concepts of genus, species, variety and cultivar, all of which are used in this text. The following article (written by this author) was published in the *American Horticulturist* 54:32-34 and is reprinted here with only minor changes.

Recently I read a column by a noted garden authority (writer) who attempted to define the makeup of a plant's scientific name. His ideas and those of the taxonomic world were miles asunder. A name is a handle by which we get to know certain people, places and plants. We learn to recognize specific characters, for example, an individual's facial expressions, voice, or walk, which make him or her different from another. Plants are not unlike people in this respect for they possess characteristics which set them apart. Sugar maple, *Acer saccharum* Marsh., possesses opposite, simple, 5-lobed, medium to dark green leaves, sharp-pointed, imbricate, scaly, gray-brown to brown winter buds, upright-oval growth habit and brilliant yellow to burnt orange to red fall color. These features bring to this species an identity of its own which permit identification and separation from other types.

But what is this thing called a species? What do the latinized terms signify? How did the present system for naming plants evolve? Actually a historical sojourn would uncover several interesting facts concerning plant nomenclature. Before the Linnean system (binomial system) was accepted as a standard for naming plants, nomenclature was literally a disaster. Plants were named *Descriptively!* Latinized adjectives were added until sufficient verbiage was present to allow differentiation among plants. These latinized terms usually described morphological features of the plant. For example, the common carnation which is now *Dianthus caryophyllus* L. was, before 1753, "Dianthus floribus solitariis, squamis calycinis subovatis brevissimus, corollis crenatis." The Japanese maple, *Acer palmatum* Thunb., was "Acer orientalis, hederae folio" which, figuratively translated, means oriental ivy-leaved maple. Obviously, students of plant materials were at a distinct disadvantage in the embryonic stages of nomenclature. If this latinization approach seems cumbersome or confusing consider for a moment the *Common Name* syndrome. The common name of a specific plant in one part of the state, country or world often is not the same in another. *Carpinus caroliniana* Walt., American hornbeam, has been called the water beech, blue beech, ironwood and musclewood. *Nymphaea alba* L., the European white waterlily has 15 English common names, 44 French, 105 German, and 81 Dutch for a total of 245 common names. The term Mayflower means different things to different people. In the Middle West it refers to *Podophyllum* (mayapple), in New England to *Epigaea repens* (trailing arbutus), in England to *Caltha palustris* (marsh marigold), and in the West Indies to a member of the pea family.

The question which arises is how was this chaos made orderly? It is credited to Carl von Linne more commonly known by his pen name of Linnaeus. His book, *Species Plantarum* (1753), signaled the beginning of the binomial system of nomenclature. Essentially it means that plants acquire two latinized names, one representing the *genus* and the other termed the *specific epithet,* which in combination with the generic name constitute the *species* by means of which all plants or animals are known by all people in all countries who speak or write of them with precision. Take, for example, the European white waterlily. It is known to everyone as *Nymphaea alba,* however, it becomes a different entity when spoken of in common name terminology.

Those who work with and read about plants are continually exposed to the concepts of genus, species, variety, and cultivar. These terms appear in every nursery catalog, gardening article or publication concerning plants. However, what do they signify? Is there any practical significance to them and will understanding their meaning enhance one's appreciation for plants?

The genus is weakly defined as a more or less closely related and definable group of plants comprising one or more species. The genus is a category whose components (i.e. species) have more characters in common with each other than they do with components of other genera within the same family. Similarity of flowers and fruits is the most widely used feature although root, stems, buds, and leaves are used. There may be a single species comprising a genus such as in the case of *Ginkgo* where the species *Ginkgo biloba* L. is the only member. *Cercidiphyllum* possesses only one species, *Cercidiphyllum japonicum* Sieb. and Zucc. (katsura-tree), a beautiful tree of Japanese origin. At the other end of the spectrum the genus *Rosa* (rose) contains between 100 and 200 species. The generic name is written with a capital letter and underlined [*Quercus* (oak)]. The plural of genus is genera and not the often used genuses.

Possibly the most important unit of classification is the species, however, the term is more a concept than an absolute entity. Lawrence noted that botanists of every generation have attempted to define the term species for which there may be no single definition. L.H. Bailey defined a species as a kind of plant or animal distinct from other kinds in marked or essential features that has good characters of identification, and may be assumed to represent a continuing succession of individuals from generation to generation. He then went on to say that the term is incapable of exact definition for nature is not laid out in formal lines. Actually, the species term is a concept, the product of each individual's judgment. My concept of a species can be depicted by a bell-shaped curve. In any population of trees, shrubs or people there are those which fit under the common characteristic in the peak portion of the curve. These individuals adhere to the marked or essential identification features. Certain individuals do not fit the stereotype and appear to belong at the fringes of the bell curve. Intergrading between the normal types and the extremely divergent types are those of moderate adherence to the essential features but exhibiting some variance perhaps in degree of pubescence (hairiness) or some other salient feature. A casual stroll through the woods, meadow or any area where native stands of trees, shrubs, wild flowers and grasses co-exist will illucidate the great variation that exists within a species. All sugar maples within a given geographic area are not similar. They are members of the species, *Acer saccharum* Marsh., but exhibit discernible differences. A species name is composed of the following components and written as follows.

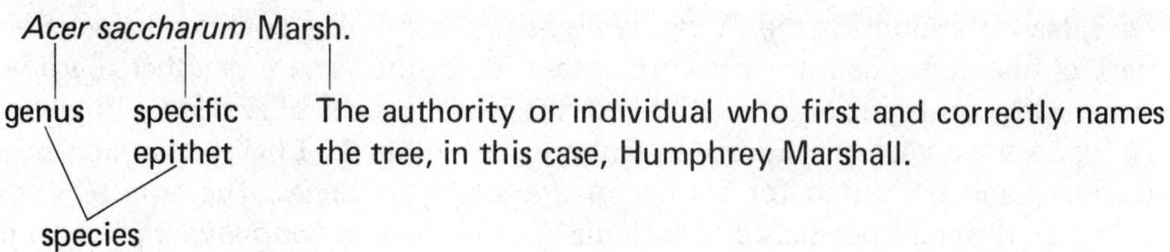

Note that the species name is always underlined and the specific epithet is lower case. The plural of species is species and the authority name does not have to be included in normal writing.

The term variety as used in the botanical sense constitutes a group or class of plants subordinate to a species (subspecies) and is usually applied to individuals displaying rather marked differences in nature. The crux is that these differences are inheritable and should show in succeeding generations. The difference between the thornless common honeylocust (*Gleditsia triacanthos* L. *inermis* Willd.), a true variety, and the species, common honeylocust (*Gleditsia triacanthos*), is the absence of thorns on the former. Seed collected from the variety will yield predominantly thornless seedlings, although a small percentage of the population will exhibit the thorny character. The redleaf Japanese barberry (*Berberis thunbergii* DC *atropurpurea* Chenault.), a true variety, yields 90 percent or greater redleaf progeny when grown from seed. Unfortunately, variety is often confused, and used interchangeably, with the term *cultivar* (a term coined by L.H. Bailey). The variety term is always written with the species, in lower case, and underlined or with the abbreviation var. placed before the variety term and the term underlined. The plural of variety is varieties. For example, the pink flowering variety of the white flowering dogwood (*Cornus florida* L.) may be written as follows.

Cornus florida rubra

or

Cornus florida var. *rubra*

A relatively new term and one which has important implications in horticultural circles is that of cultivar. A cultivar is an assemblage of cultivated plants which is clearly distinguished by any characters (morphological, physiological, cytological or chemical) and which when reproduced (sexually or asexually) retains its distinguishing characteristics. The difference between Norway maple (*Acer platanoides* L.) and the cultivar Crimson King (*Acer platanoides* 'Crimson King') is the purplish maroon foliage color of the cultivar. This cultivar cannot be reproduced from seed (hence does not fit the definition of variety) and must be reproduced vegetatively (grafting) to maintain the foliage characteristic. Essentially all other characters of identification between this species and the cultivar are similar. *Cedrus deodara* Loud. 'Kashmir', the Kashmir Deodar cedar, is similar to the species in leaf, stem, bud and other morphological characters except it is much hardier. Kashmir was the only plant of 200 set in nursery rows in Concordville, Pennsylvania which survived a rapid temperature drop to 25° F below zero. Obviously this difference is not apparent to the eye, as in the previous example, but the selection of this cultivar permits the use of this beautiful specimen much further north than could be accomplished with the species. This difference between the cultivar and species is of a cytological nature possibly related to protoplasmic resistance to low temperature stresses. Sexually reproduced cultivars include those plants (annuals such as petunias, marigolds, and asters) which are propagated from seed derived from the repetitive crossing of two or more parental breeding stocks maintained either as lines or clones. A line consists of a group of plants that are largely homozygous (similar in genetic makeup). *Clone* is a group of plants which originated from a single individual and, therefore, is genetically homogenous.

Cultivar names are written with single quotes and the first letter of each word comprising the term is capitalized or the insertion of cv. before the term and the deletion of the single quotes.

Example: *Acer platanoides* 'Crimson King'

or

Acer platanoides cv. Crimson King

It is possible to have a cultivar of a variety. *Cornus florida* var. *rubra* is the pink flowering form of the flowering dogwood. A cultivar of this variety is Cherokee Chief which possesses deeper red flowers. The term would read *Cornus florida* var. *rubra* 'Cherokee Chief'.

The basics of plant nomenclature are relatively simple to comprehend. A fuller, deeper appreciation of the great diversity which nature offers can be developed through an understanding of the previous discussion. A knowledge of the systematic naming of plants also has practical implications. Consider the great variation in the red maple, *Acer rubrum* L. The purchase of a seedling-grown tree does not guarantee red flowers in Spring nor brilliant red fall color, for trees may range from yellow to red in flower and fall color. The purchase of *Acer rubrum* 'October Glory', 'Autumn Flame' or 'Red Sunset' cultivars guarantees a tree with outstanding red to scarlet fall color for these trees were selected for their consistent ability to color.

A distillation of the preceding discussion should lead to the conclusion that an appreciation for plant nomenclature guarantees a deeper involvement with plants and their intricacies.

Abelia x *grandiflora* — Glossy Abelia

FAMILY: Caprifoliaceae

LEAVES: Opposite, simple, ovate, 3/5 to 1 2/5" long, acute, rounded or cuneate at base, dentate, lustrous dark green above, paler beneath and glabrous, except bearded near base of midrib.

BUDS: Small, ovoid, with about 2 pairs of rather loose scales.

STEM: Young-pubescent, reddish brown, fine textured appearance. Older stem-exfoilating and split to expose light inner bark. Leaf scars connected by a stipular line.

SIZE: 3 to 6' by 3 to 6' in northern areas.

HARDINESS: Zone 5.

HABIT: Spreading, dense, rounded, multistemmed shrub with slightly drooping branches.

RATE: Medium, tends to fill in quickly and form a dense mat.

TEXTURE: Medium-fine in leaf (summer) and in winter habit.

FOLIAGE COLOR: Dark glossy green in summer, bronze-purplish in late fall. Semi-evergreen in Central Illinois.

FLOWERS: White-flushed pink, each floret about 4/5" long, July through until frost, borne in prominent leafy panicles. Usually a profuse, prolific flowering plant.

CULTURE: Transplant balled and burlapped or from containers, prefers well-drained soil, full sun or 1/2 shade, often damaged in severe winters in Zone 5 and considerable pruning is necessary.

DISEASES AND INSECTS: Nothing especially serious.

LANDSCAPE VALUE: Excellent for textural effects, handsome in flower, often used as a bank cover, massing, facing plant. Combines well with broadleaf evergreens. Needs protection in Zone 5.

CULTIVARS: 'Sherwood'—Form not exceeding 3'.

PROPAGATION: Cuttings, anytime during the early summer with hormone treatment. I have rooted this plant with 100% success anytime foliage was present using 1000 ppm IBA.

RELATED SPECIES:

Abelia 'Edward Goucher' is a small, semi-evergreen shrub with lilac-pink flowers which are borne in great profusion similar to *A.* x *grandiflora*. Might be tender in the northern areas of Zone 5 but with proper siting and winter protection could be successfully grown. This cultivar is the result of a cross between *A.* x *grandiflora* x *A. schumannii* made at the Glen Dale Plant Introduction Station, Maryland. Flowers from July through September. Developed before 1911.

ADDITIONAL NOTES: About the hardiest and most free flowering of the abelias. Result of a cross between *A. chinensis* x *A. uniflora.*

Abeliophyllum distichum — Korean Abelialeaf or White Forsythia

FAMILY: Oleaceae

LEAVES: Opposite, simple, entire, 4/5 to 2" long, spreading in 2 ranks, ovate to elliptic-ovate, acuminate, broad-cuneate or rounded at base, appressed-pilose on both sides; petiole 1/12 to 1/5 " long.

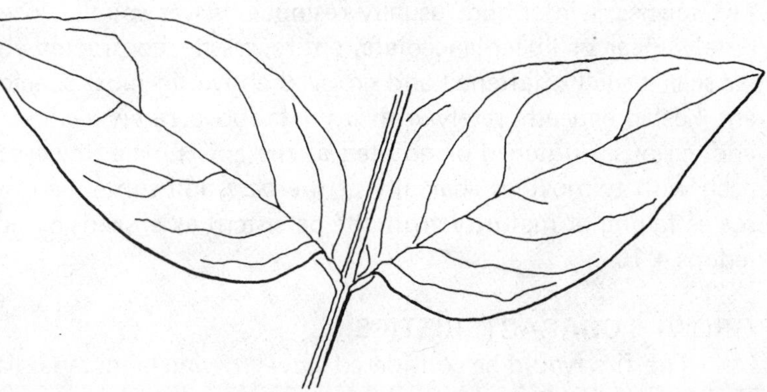

STEM: Squarish, brownish yellow, of rather weak constitution.

SIZE: 3 to 5' high by 3 to 4' wide.

HARDINESS: Zone 5, can grow in Zone 4.

HABIT: Multistemmed small shrub of rounded outline; developing arching branches.

RATE: Slow to medium.
TEXTURE: Medium in all seasons.
LEAF COLOR: Yellow-green to bright green in summer; no significant change in the fall.
FLOWERS: Perfect, white, or faintly tinged pink, 5/8" across, exceedingly fragrant, borne on previous year's wood just before forsythia, early April; axillary ½ to 1½" long racemes composed of 3 to 15 flowers.
FRUIT: Two celled compressed capsule which is winged all around, somewhat like the elm fruit.
CULTURE: Easily transplanted; adapted to many soils but the flower buds may be killed in severe winters; should be well protected; full sun or light shade; renew frequently by heavy pruning immediately after flowering.
DISEASES AND INSECTS: None serious.
LANDSCAPE VALUE: Provides early spring color to an otherwise dull landscape; since the flowers are borne along the leafless stems they make quite a show; makes a nice companion shrub for the forsythias.
PROPAGATION: Untreated hardwood cuttings taken in mid-March rooted 63 percent in sand-peat in the greenhouse in 10 weeks. In England it is propagated by cuttings of half-ripened wood, taken in July, and treated with IBA or IAA. Softwood cuttings are also effective propagules.
ADDITIONAL NOTES: I have seen one plant in Urbana which was barely surviving and, therefore, cannot adequately evaluate the plant. However, Dr. Roger's, in whose yard the plant struggles, indicated that it has never been happy since first arriving from the old Wayside Gardens. He has the plant well protected and sited but the harshness of the prairie is simply too much for it to endure. However, this species is performing quite well at the University of Minnesota Landscape Arboretum. They reported that it is a more reliable flowerer than forsythia in their climate. This seems to indicate that it should be considered a Zone 4 plant.
NATIVE HABITAT: Korea. Introduced 1924.

Abies — Fir

Pinaceae

Firs are limitedly used in midwestern landscapes but often appear in northeastern and northwestern United States. There are about forty species found in Europe, Northern Africa, temperate Asia and on the American continent from Canada to Guatemala. In youth they are mostly conical and extremely symmetrical in outline, and some types may grow over 200 feet.

MORPHOLOGICAL CHARACTERISTICS

Monoecious trees, evergreen, habit symmetrically pyramidal, or narrow-conical while young, or with age becoming large forest trees; trunk simple, rarely forked; bark usually smooth, thin on young trees, often thick and furrowed at the base on old trees; branchlets smooth, or grooved in a few species; winter-buds usually resinous; leaves spirally inserted, often spreading in 2 ranks (pectinate), linear or linear-lanceolate, entire, sessile, contracted above the base, leaving on falling a circular scar, usually flattened and grooved above, in most species with 2 white or pale stomatic bands and keeled beneath, rarely with stomata above, rarely 4-sided and with stomata on all 4 sides, rounded and variously notched or pointed at the apex; male flowers in cones composed of numerous scales, each with two ovules adaxially at the base and subtended by a narrow exserted or included bract; scales falling at maturity from the persistent axis; seeds ovoid or oblong; wing large and thick; cotyledons 4-10.

GROWTH CHARACTERISTICS

The firs would be considered slow-growing landscape plants especially when planted outside of their native habitats. It is safe to generalize that the majority of species are conical to pyramidal, almost spirelike, in outline. From this aspect they are somewhat difficult to work into the small, residential landscape. There are many cultivars among the various species including prostrate, compact, pendulous, contorted, fastigiate, yellow-foliaged, and blue-foliaged types. These cultivars fall in the novelty category and are difficult to find in the landscape trade, however, they do add different textures, colors and shapes not available from the fir species.

CULTURE

Firs require moist, well-drained, acid soil and high atmospheric moisture coupled with cooler temperatures. The hot, dry summers which occur in the midwest tend to limit their landscape usefulness. Firs are not suited for city plantings and do not tolerate air pollution. Transplanting is best accomplished in the spring using balled and burlapped specimens. Pruning should be kept to a minimum for when older branches are removed new growth seldom develops and, consequently, the trees become ragged and unkempt. They are most appropriately sited in full sun but light shade is also acceptable.

DISEASES AND INSECTS

Firs do not seem to be extensively troubled with disease and insect pests. At least this was true for firs which I have seen in landscape plantings. Needle and twig blight, leaf cast, rusts, cankers, shoestring root rot, wood decay, balsam twig aphid, bagworm, caterpillars, spruce spider mite, scale, balsam woolly aphid, spruce budworm and dwarf mistletoe (plant parasite) have been listed as problems.

PROPAGATION

Seed is the principal means of propagation. Dormancy of fir seed appears to be both physical and physiological in nature. There is considerable variation between seed lots in degree of dormancy. Part of this variability in dormancy is attributable to time of collection, methods of processing, seed cleaning, and storage. Seed is typically stratified under cool, moist conditions at 34° to 41°F for 14 to 28 days.

Cuttings have been rooted but the percentages were low and this approach is not practical on a commercial basis. The cultivars are usually grafted and some type of a side graft would be most appropriate.

LANDSCAPE USE

The only species which should be considered for the Midwest is *Abies concolor. Abies balsamea,* the short needled Christmas tree species, only does well in more northerly climates. Their stiff, rigid habit and specific cultural requirements place a restriction on extensive use. They are best employed in groupings, near large buildings, as specimens and screens.

SELECTED SPECIES

Based on observations I have made at various arboreta and in landscape plantings around the midwest and east the following firs would be my first choice.

Abies cilicica	Cilician Fir
Abies concolor	White Fir
Abies homolepsis	Nikko Fir
Abies procera	Noble Fir

Other firs which are worthwhile include:

Abies alba	Silver Fir
Abies balsamea	Balsam Fir
Abies cephalonica	Greek Fir
Abies fraseri	Fraser Fir
Abies holophylla	Manchurian Fir
Abies koreana	Korean Fir
Abies mariesi	Maries Fir
Abies nordmanniana	Nordman Fir
Abies veitchii	Veitch Fir

Abies balsamea — Balsam Fir

LEAVES: Variable, 5/8 to 1" long, 1/20 to 1/16" wide, horizontally arranged in 2 lateral sets with a V-shaped parting between, apex slightly notched, upper surface dark shining green with interrupted lines of stomata towards the tip, lower surface with 2 gray bands of stomata, typical balsam odor.

BUDS: Small, ovoid or globular, resinous and seemingly varnished, brownish.

STEM: Smooth, covered with fine, soft grayish hairs.

SIZE: 45 to 75' in height by 20 to 25' in spread.

HARDINESS: Zone 3.

HABIT: Stiff in habit, symmetrically pyramidal or narrow-conical when young before losing its pyramidal habit with age.

RATE: Slow.

TEXTURE: Medium.

BARK: Dull green, later with grayish areas, smooth except for numerous raised resin blisters; eventually breaking up into small reddish brown, irregular scaly plates; 1/2" thick.

LEAF COLOR: Lustrous dark green with white stomatic bands below.

FLOWERS: Yellow, male-catkin-like, developing from the underside of the leaf axil.

FRUIT: Cone, dark violet when young, 2 to 4" long, turning gray-brown and resinous at maturity. Soon after the ripening of the seeds the scales fall off leaving only the peduncle.

CULTURE: Shallow rooted, readily transplanted balled and burlapped; adaptable to cold-climates and there makes its best growth; prefers well-drained, acid, moist soils, however, in the wild it often forms pure stands in swamps but does best in association with spruce on ground which is better drained; it also grows on higher ground and is found in dwarfed, matted, pure stands, or entangled with Black Spruce, *Picea mariana*, near the windswept summits of mountains where great extremes in temperature occur. More shade tolerant than other firs but will not withstand polluted areas.

DISEASES AND INSECTS: Troubled by spruce budworm, woolly aphid and several canker diseases; see general *Abies* discussion.

LANDSCAPE VALUE: Used mainly as a specimen tree and popular as a Christmas tree. Does not hold its needles very long in a dry house and for this reason is not as desirable as the pines. In youth looks good but under the hot, dry conditions of the Midwest soon loses the older needles and becomes open and unkempt.

CULTIVARS: 18, none of which are grown commercially.

PROPAGATION: A brief stratification period of 15 to 30 days in moist medium at 34 to 41°F is recommended. There is variation among seed lots in degree of dormancy within firs and part of the variability can be attributed to time of collection and to methods of cone processing, seed cleaning, and seed storage.

ADDITIONAL NOTES: I have seen this species growing in the barren rock on top of Cadillac Mountain in Maine. The resin from this tree was used to mount thin specimens under slides but has now been supplanted by other materials.

NATIVE HABITAT: Native over a wide part of North America, especially in the higher altitudes from Labrador to Alberta to Pennsylvania. Cult. 1696.

Abies concolor — White (Concolor) Fir

LEAVES: Curving outwards and upwards or almost vertically arranged on the stems, 2 to 3" long and 1/12 to 1/10" wide, flattened, glaucous on both surfaces, apex short-pointed or rounded, upper surface slightly convex, not grooved, with faint lines or stomata, lower surface with 2 faint bands of stomata separated by a green band.

BUDS: Large, broadly conical, blunt, covered with resin which conceals the scales, light brown.

STEM: First year, glabrous or minutely downy, yellowish green; second year, grayish or silvery.

SIZE: 30 to 50′ in height by 15 to 30′ in spread in Illinois; can grow to 100′ or more.
HARDINESS: Zone 4.
HABIT: Conical and branched to the base. The branches on the upper half of the tree tend to point upward, the lower horizontal or deflected downward, creating a rather rigid, stiff appearance in the landscape.
RATE: Slow to medium, slow in Illinois; one authority reported that this species will grow 50 to 60′ in 30 to 60 years.
TEXTURE: Medium.
BARK: Smooth on young stems except for resin blisters; 4″ to 7″ thick on old trunks, ashy gray and divided by deep irregular furrows into thick, horny, flattened ridges.
LEAF COLOR: Bluish or grayish green with pale bluish bands beneath; new growth a light blue-green or bluish.
FLOWERS: Inconspicuous, monoecious; staminate red or red-violet.
FRUIT: Cones are stalked, cylindrical 3 to 6″ long, and pale green before maturity often with a purplish bloom.
CULTURE: The best fir for the Midwest. Transplant balled and burlapped. While withstanding heat, drouth and cold equally well, it prefers and makes best growth on deep, rich, moist, well-drained gravelly or sandy-loam soils; dislikes heavy clay. This species requires less moisture than other western firs and can exist on dry, thin layers of partially decomposed granite or nearly barren rocks. Although full sun is preferable, it will tolerate light shade; root system according to some authorities is shallow and wide spreading while others indicated there is a tap root. Seems to hold its needles better than any other fir. The 30 year-old specimen in my yard attests to this. A degree more tolerant of city conditions than other fir species.
DISEASES AND INSECTS: None serious, under the limited landscape use in the Midwest.
LANDSCAPE VALUE: Because of its growth habit and softer effect it could well replace the spruces in the landscape.
CULTIVARS: Only of botanical interest.
PROPAGATION: Seed shows variability in its chilling requirements. A period of 30 days in moist medium at 41°F is recommended. Cuttings taken in early December failed to root without treatment but rooted 50% after treatment with 100 ppm IBA/24 hour soak, followed by Phygon XL-talc, 1:1. In another study, cuttings taken in early December rooted 73% with the above treatment. but did not root at all without treatment. In another study, cuttings taken in late January rooted 76% in eight months without treatment, and 100% after treatment with Hormodin #3. In other work, cuttings rooted best when taken in March and treated with 100 ppm IBA for 24 hours.
NATIVE HABITAT: Western and Southwestern United States.

Abies fraseri — Fraser Fir

LEAVES: Crowded, directed forward, pectinate below, 1/2 to 7/8″ long, 1/24″ broad, entire or emarginate at apex, flat, grooved, shining dark green above, with stomates above near apex, with 2 broad bands of 8 to 12 stomatic bands beneath.
STEMS: Gray or pale yellowish brown, in the first winter reddish brown, very resinous.

SIZE: 30 to 40′ in height by 20 to 25′ spread.
HARDINESS: Zone 4.
HABIT: Pyramidal, with horizontal, stiff branches, opening up with age.
RATE: Slow.
TEXTURE: Medium.
LEAF COLOR: Shining dark green with stomata above near the apex and two broad bands of 8 to 12 stomatic lines beneath.
FLOWERS: Monoecious.

FRUIT: Cones ovoid or cylindrical, 1 1/2 to 2" long and 4" broad, purple when young becoming tan-brown.

CULTURE: Transplants well when root pruned, does well in dry situations compared to *Abies balsamea* but prefers a moist, well-drained loam and sun or partial shade.

PROPAGATION: Seed, again actual recommendations vary somewhat but a period of 15 to 30 days would probably be somewhat beneficial.

NATIVE HABITAT: Native to the mountains of West Virginia, North Carolina, and Tennessee at altitudes of 3000-6000 feet.

Abies procera — Noble Fir

LEAVES: Crowded above, the lower ranks spreading outward, those of the middle rank much shorter, appressed to the branchlet, curving upwards near the base, pectinate below and curved, 1 to 1 2/5" long, 1/16" wide, scarcely broadened, rounded or slightly notched at apex, grooved, bluish green, stomatiferous above, with narrow pale bands below.

SIZE: 180 to 270' in height in native stands, 50 to 100' under landscape conditions.

HARDINESS: Zone 5.

HABIT: Symmetrically pyramidal or narrow; conical in youth; mature trees develop a long, clear, columnar trunk, with an essentially domelike crown.

RATE: Slow to medium, will reach 75±' in 30 to 60 years; trees 100 to 120 years of age are commonly 90 to 120' in height.

TEXTURE: Medium.

BARK: Gray and smooth for many years, with prominent resin blisters; eventually dark gray, often tinged with purple and broken up into thin, nearly rectangular plates separated by deep fissures on old trunks; bark about 1 to 2" thick; this is thin in comparison to other trees and specimens are often ruined by fire.

LEAF COLOR: Bluish green, stomatiferous above with narrow pale bands below.

FLOWERS: Inconspicuous, monoecious.

FRUIT: A large, cylindrical cone, 6 to 10" long by approximately 3" broad, green before maturity, finally turning purplish brown.

CULTURE: Readily transplanted balled and burlapped if properly root pruned, prefers a moist, deep, cool, well-drained soil, sun or partial shade and dislikes high pH soils as well as windy conditions; good growth is also made on thin rocky soils if provided with an abundance of moisture.

DISEASES AND INSECTS: Damaged by the spruce budworm, woolly aphid and several canker diseases.

LANDSCAPE VALUE: Can be used as a specimen tree however best adapted in its native habitat.

CULTIVAR: 'Glauca' — Extremely glaucous foliage and a liberal cone bearer.

PROPAGATION: Stratified and non-stratified seeds gave good germination percentages.

NATIVE HABITAT: Native to the Cascade Mountains of Washington, Oregon and the Siskiyou Mountains of California. Western United States.

Abies veitchii — Veitch Fir

LEAVES: One half to (±)1" long and about 1/16" wide, flattened, gradually tapering to the base, apex truncate, notched; upper surface dark green, shining, grooved lower surface with 2 conspicuously white broad bands of stomata.

BUDS: Small, nearly globular, resinous, grayish brown.

STEM: Green, reddish brown to brown, more or less clothed with short pubescence.

SIZE: 50 to 75' high by 25 to 35' in spread.

HARDINESS: Zone 3.

HABIT: A broadly pyramidal tree with horizontal, spreading branches.
RATE: Slow to medium; one authority reported 25 to 50′ in height after 20 to 30 years.
TEXTURE: Medium.
LEAF COLOR: Lustrous dark green above with prominent, chalky-white bands below.
FLOWERS: Inconspicuous, monoecious, axillary.
FRUIT: Cones are sessile, cylindrical, 2 to 3″ long, 1 1/5″ broad and bluish purple when young, becoming brown.
CULTURE: Transplants well balled and burlapped if properly root pruned. Prefers moist, well-drained soils, sun or partial shade and dislikes high pH soils. Supposedly does all right in semi-urban conditions.
DISEASES AND INSECTS: As is the case with most firs it is troubled by the spruce budworm, woolly aphid and several canker diseases.
LANDSCAPE VALUE: Because of its extremely hardy nature and handsome foliage it should be considered more often for a specimen tree.
CULTIVARS: var. *nikkoensis* — Cones are smaller but eventually maturing to normal size.
PROPAGATION: There appears to be a significant increase in germination percentage with stratified versus non-stratified seeds. Stratify in a moist medium for 15 to 30 days at 41°F. Cuttings taken in late December rooted 60% with Hormodin #3; not at all without treatment. Rooting of winter cuttings has also been improved by IBA, 40 ppm for 24 hours.
NATIVE HABITAT: Central Japan at high altitudes.

Acanthopanax sieboldianus — Fiveleaf Aralia

FAMILY: Araliaceae
LEAVES: Alternate, partly fasicled on short spurs; leaflets 5 to 7, subsessile, obovate to oblong-obovate, 4/5 to 1 2/5″ long, acute, cuneate, crenate-serrate, glabrous; petiole-1 to 3″ long.
BUD: Solitary, sessile, conical-ovoid with about 3 exposed scales.
STEM: Light brown, warty, with 1 or 2 prickles beneath each narrow leaf-scar; pith-solid, white; leaf scars narrowly crescent-shaped or U-shaped, somewhat raised.

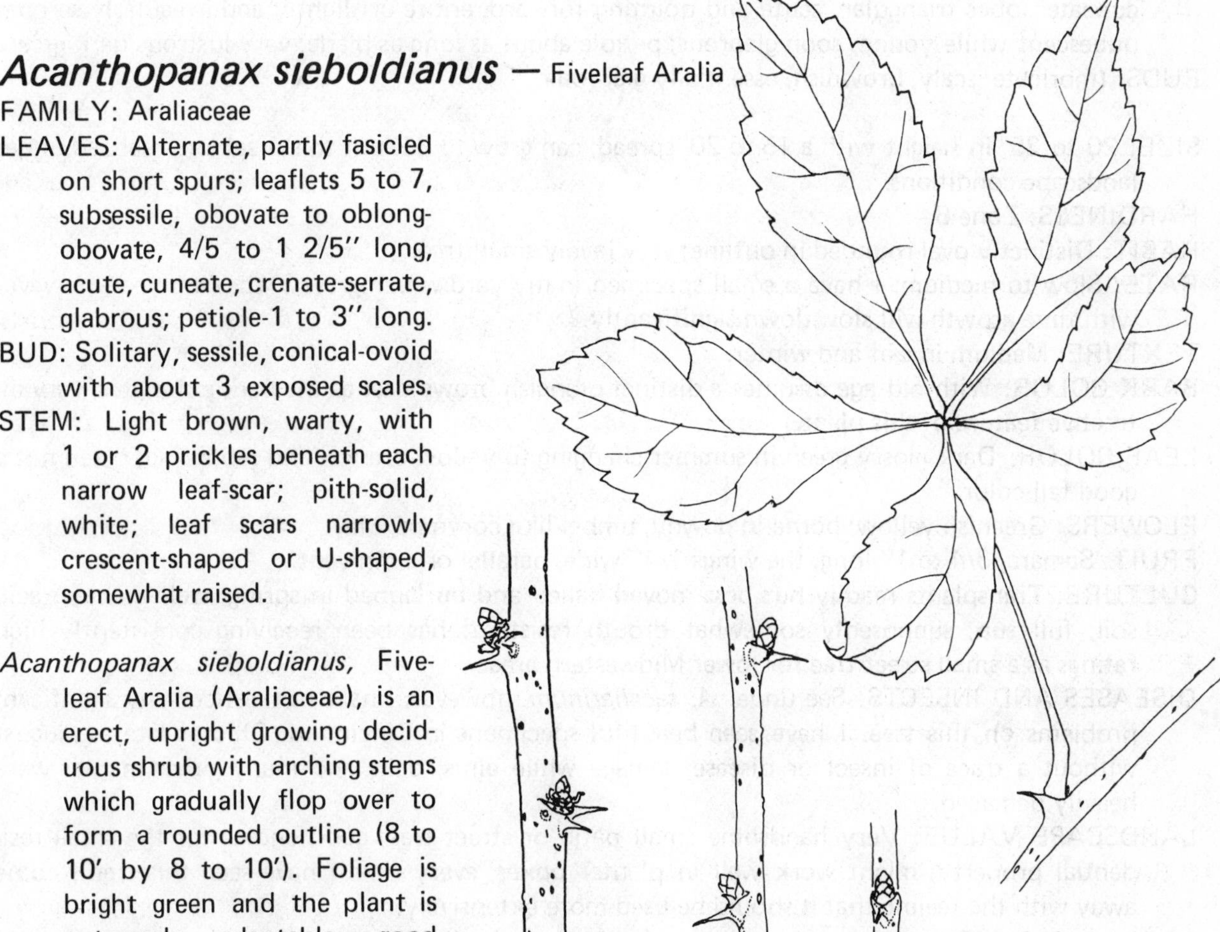

Acanthopanax sieboldianus, Five-leaf Aralia (Araliaceae), is an erect, upright growing deciduous shrub with arching stems which gradually flop over to form a rounded outline (8 to 10′ by 8 to 10′). Foliage is bright green and the plant is extremely adaptable; good plant for city conditions, will make a nice barrier plant; Cultivar:
'Variegatus' — Leaves which are edged white, listed as one of the daintiest of variegated shrubs. Roots readily from cuttings. China and Japan. 1859. Zone 4.

Acer buergerianum — Trident Maple

FAMILY: Aceraceae

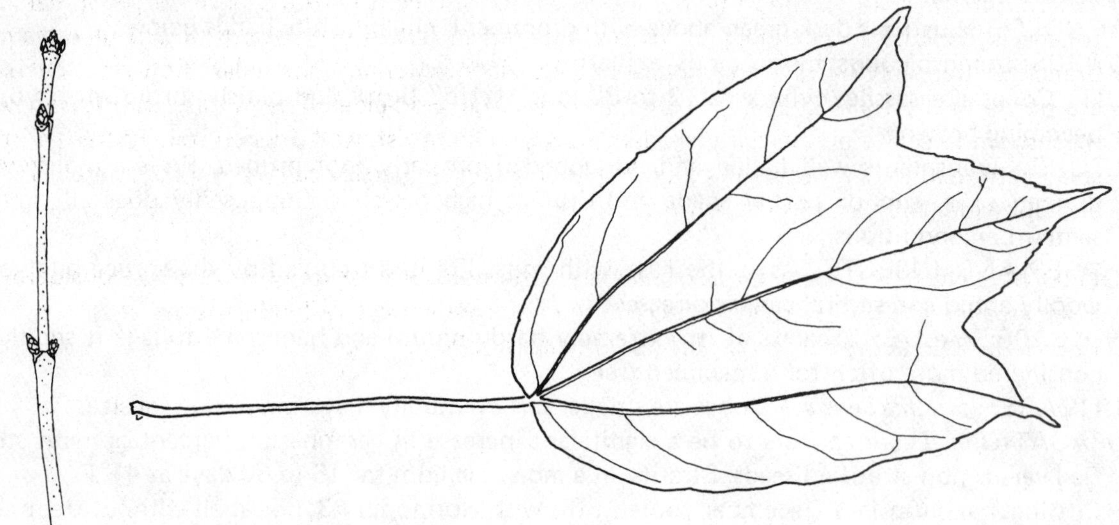

LEAVES: Opposite, simple, 3 lobed, 1 1/2 to 3 1/2" across, 3 nerved at base and rounded or broad-cuneate, lobes triangular, acute and pointing forward, entire or slightly and irregularly serrate; pubescent while young, soon glabrous; petiole about as long as blade; very lustrous dark green.

BUDS: Imbricate, scaly, brownish, essentially glabrous.

SIZE: 20 to 25' in height with a 15 to 20' spread; can grow to 35' but this is seldom realized under landscape conditions.

HARDINESS: Zone 6.

HABIT: Distinctly oval-rounded in outline; very lovely small tree.

RATE: Slow to medium; I have a small specimen in my yard which grew 3' the first year, however with time growth will slow down significantly.

TEXTURE: Medium in leaf and winter.

BARK COLOR: With old age assumes a distinct orangish brown cast as the bark exfoliates; very attractive feature of this plant.

LEAF COLOR: Dark glossy green in summer changing to yellow-orange, and red in fall; often not a good fall color.

FLOWERS: Greenish yellow; borne in downy, umbel-like corymbs; May.

FRUIT: Samara, 3/4 to 1" long, the wings 1/4" wide, parallel or connivent.

CULTURE: Transplants readily but best moved balled and burlapped in spring; well drained, acid soil; full sun; supposedly somewhat drouth resistant; has been receiving consistently high ratings as a small street tree for lower Midwestern areas.

DISEASES AND INSECTS: See under *A. saccharinum,* however, I have not noticed any significant problems on this tree. I have seen beautiful specimens in Cincinnati, Ohio as late as August without a trace of insect or disease damage while elms, oaks and many other maples were heavily damaged.

LANDSCAPE VALUE: Very handsome small patio or street tree; good choice for the small residential property; might work well in planter boxes; every time I have seen this tree I come away with the feeling that it should be used more extensively.

PROPAGATION: Probably requires a warm and then a cold stratification similar to *A. ginnala*, however, I have not found any absolute information.

RELATED SPECIES:

Acer carpinifolium, Hornbeam Maple, is a small (20 to 30'), vase-shaped, multi-stemmed, low branched tree of considerable merit. The foliage is similar in shape to hornbeam (*Carpinus*); dark green in summer changing to brownish yellow in fall. A very clean growing tree which might have possibilities in the residential landscape. Flowers are greenish, borne in short glabrous racemes in May. Native to Japan. Introduced 1881. Zone 5.

Acer cissifolium (has no common name) grows to 30′ in height with a slightly larger spread. The foliage is dark green changing to yellow and red in fall. A very beautiful and picturesquely branched tree. Its nearest ally appears to be *Acer negundo*, Box-elder, however the leaves are borne in 3′s rather than 5′s which are common to Box-elder. The overall habit is somewhat mushroom-like. Prefers partially shaded location and moist, well drained soil. There is a lovely specimen next to the observatory on the Ohio State University campus approximately 25′ tall and 35′ wide. Native to Japan. Introduced 1875. Zone 5.

ADDITIONAL NOTES: These three maples are little used but certainly worthy of consideration. Their smaller size, lovely foliage and growth habits are important landscape assets.

NATIVE HABITAT: Eastern China, Japan. Cultivated 1890.

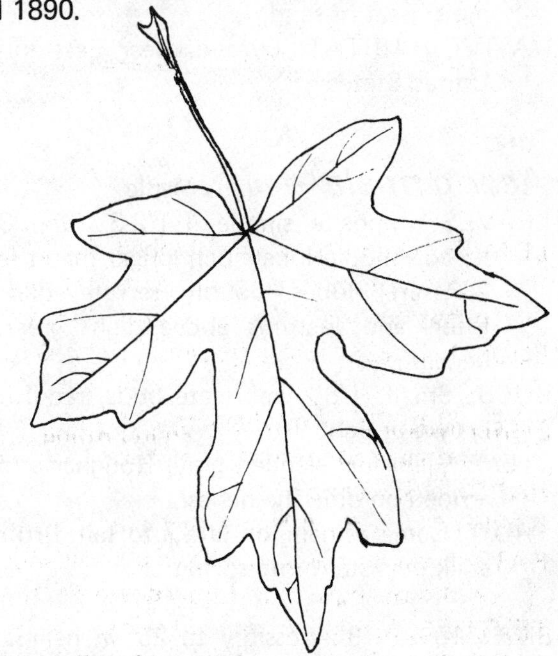

Acer campestre — Hedge Maple

FAMILY: Aceraceae

LEAVES: Opposite, simple, 2-4″ across, dark green above, pubescent beneath, 3-5 rounded, entire lobes. Thick in appearance. Petiole when detached from stem yields a milky white sap.

BUDS: Imbricate, similar to Sugar Maple but much smaller, brown-gray, woolly (Pubescent on scales).

STEMS: Pubescent or glabrous, light brown, fissured, often becoming slightly corky.

SIZE: 25 to 35′ in height, occasionally 70 to 75′; spread would be comparable to height especially specimens up to 30 to 35′.

HARDINESS: Zone 4.

HABIT: Rounded and dense, often branched to the ground making it extremely difficult to grow grass. Can be effectively limbed up and makes an excellent small tree.

RATE: Slow, 10 to 14′ over a 10 to 15 year period.

TEXTURE: Medium in leaf and winter.

FOLIAGE COLOR: Handsome dark green in summer changing to yellow-green or yellow in fall. Does not color consistently in Central Illinois as the leaves will drop green; intermediate in defoliation time.

FLOWERS: Greenish, May, in upright corymbs, ornamentally ineffective.

FRUITS: Samara, with horizontally spreading wings 1″ or more long, 1/2″ wide.

CULTURE: Readily transplanted, best in rich, well-drained soil, performs well in high pH soils although does admirably in acid soils (pH 5.5 and above); withstands severe pruning; full sun or light shade; air pollution tolerant.

DISEASES AND INSECTS: None serious compared to Silver, Norway and Sugar Maples.

LANDSCAPE VALUE: Excellent small lawn specimen, street tree in residential areas, good under utility lines because of low height, can be pruned into hedges and is often used for this in Europe. Answers the shears as well as a beech. I have never understood why this tree is not more popular.

CULTIVARS:

'Compactum' — A dwarf multi-stemmed shrub of very close, compact growth, 2 to 4' high and usually broader than high. Very effective and handsome dwarf shrub. I have attempted to root cuttings but with no success.

'Postelense' — Leaves golden yellow when young gradually changing to green.

'Schwerinii' — Leaves purple when first expanding, finally turning green.

PROPAGATION: Seed, 68-86°F. for 30 days followed by 36-40°F. for 90 to 180 days; stratify in moist peat or sand.

NATIVE HABITAT: Europe, Near East and North Africa. Introduced in colonial times into the United States.

Acer ginnala — Amur Maple

LEAVES: Opposite, simple, 1 1/2-3" long, 3 lobed, middle lobe much longer than the 2 lateral lobes, doubly serrate, dark green and lustrous above, light green beneath.

BUDS: Small, 1/8", imbricate buds, reddish brown or lighter.

STEM: Glabrous, slender, gray. Rougher and striped on older branches.

FRUIT: Samaras hang on late into fall. Fruit stalk persistent into spring.

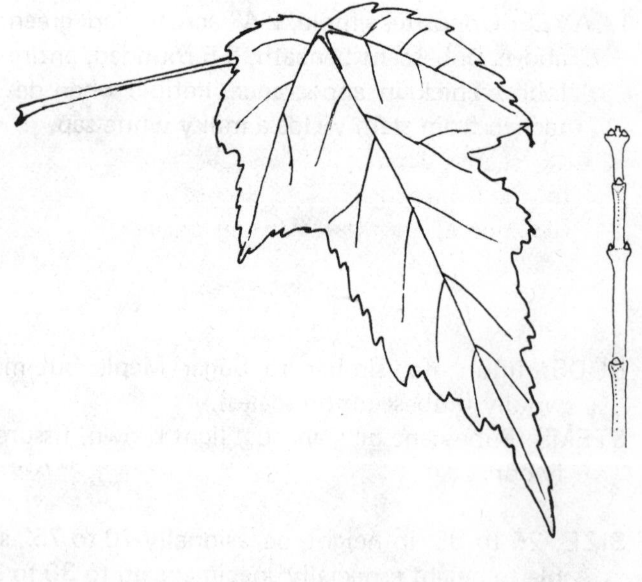

SIZE: 15 to 18', possibly to 25' in height, spread equal to or exceeding height especially multi-stemmed specimens.

HARDINESS: Zone 2.

HABIT: Multi-stemmed large shrub or small tree often of rounded outline. Shape is variable and can be successfully tailored to specific landscape requirements by pruning.

RATE: Over a period of 10 to 20 years the growth in height would average 12 to 20', however, in extreme youth can be induced into rapid growth by optimum fertilizer and moisture.

TEXTURE: Medium-fine in leaf; medium in winter.

BARK COLOR: Grayish brown on older branches.

LEAF COLOR: Handsome dark glossy green in summer changing to shades of yellow and red in fall. Does not fall color consistently. Best coloration is seen in full sun situations. Extreme variation in fall coloration and selections should be made for this trait; early defoliator.

FLOWERS: Yellowish white, fragrant as the leaves unfurl in late April to early May, borne in small (1 to 1 1/2" diameter) panicles. On of the few maples with fragrant flowers.

FRUIT: Samara, brown to red, variable in coloration but there are several good red fruiting types available; effective in September and October.

CULTURE: Very easy to transplant, quite adaptable to wide range of soils and pH ranges; performs best in moist, well-drained soil; withstands heavy pruning; can be successfully grown as a container plant; full sun or light shade.

DISEASES AND INSECTS: Relatively free of problems although can be affected by several of the pests listed under Silver Maple.

LANDSCAPE VALUE: Small specimen, patio tree, screen, massing, corners or blank walls of large buildings. Handsome small maple suited for the smaller landscape.

CULTIVARS:

'Compactum' — Superior to 'Durand Dwarf'; more dense and compact; exhibits good wine-red to red fall color.

'Durand Dwarf' — Dwarf, shrubby type; 5-year-old plant being 3' by 5' high; will probably grow twice this size, easily rooted from cuttings; originated before 1953 in Durand Eastman Park, Rochester, New York.

'Red Fruit' — A collective term for types whose fruit color a brilliant red. The Minnesota Landscape Arboretum has a clone whose fruits turn a good red. Based on observations in 1976 the tree fruits so heavily that vegetative growth is somewhat reduced.

var. *semenovii* — An interesting shrubby type (10 to 15') with smaller, more graceful, deeper cut lobes than the species; would make an effective screen or barrier plant; the leaves are a lustrous dark green in summer.

PROPAGATION: Seed, stratify at 68-86°F. for 30 to 60 days followed by 41°F. for 150+ days, or light scarification and then stratification for 90 days at 41°F. Cuttings, softwood, collected in June rooted 90 percent in peat: perlite under mist with 1000 ppm IBA treatment.

NATIVE HABITAT: Central and Northern China, Manchuria and Japan. Introduced 1860.

Acer griseum — Paperbark Maple

LEAVES: Opposite, trifoliate (pinnately compound), 3-6" long, acute, middle leaflet short stalked, coarsely toothed. Lateral leaflets almost sessile, not as toothed. Petioles pubescent.

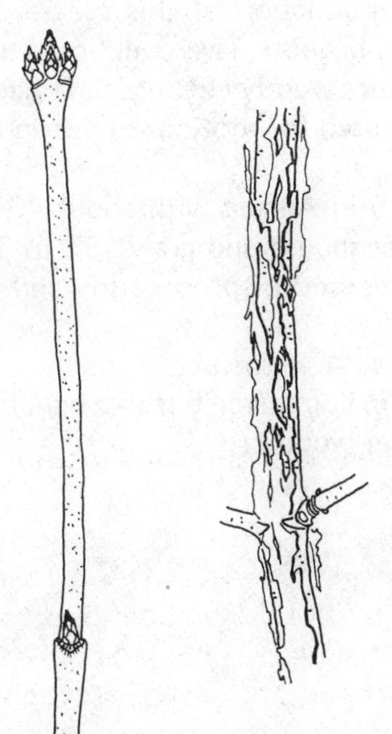

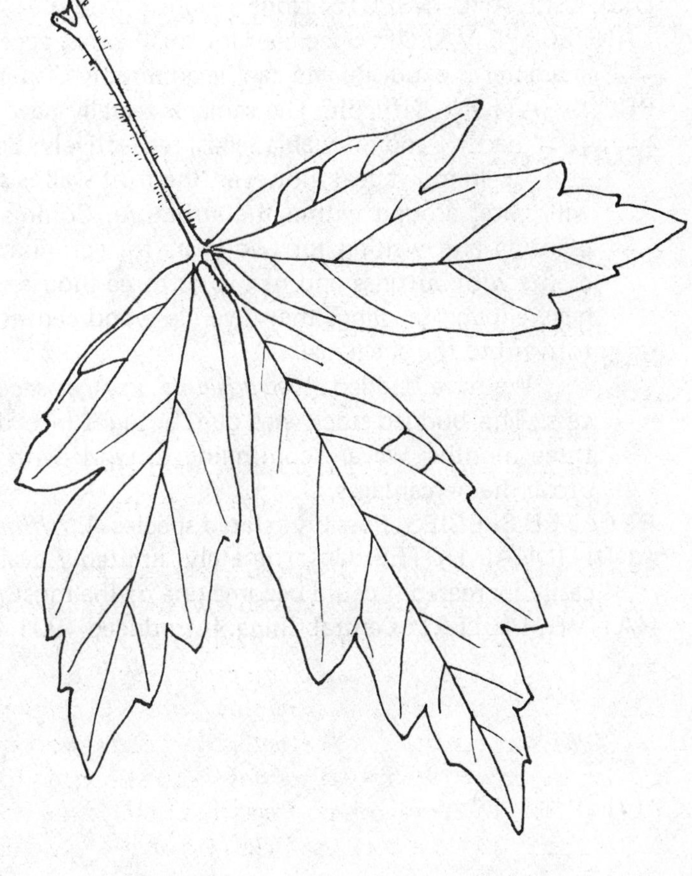

BUD: Imbricate, brown-black, small, 1/16-1/8" long, sharply pointed.

STEM: Fine branches, pubescent at first; finally glabrous. Excellent cinnamon-brown bark separating in thin papery flakes. Exfoliation starts on 2-3 year old stems.

SIZE: 20 to 30′ in height. Spread 1/2 or equal to height. Can reach 45 to 50′ but usually smaller under cultivation.

HARDINESS: Zone 5.

HABIT: Upright oval to oval-rounded; however, usually favoring the latter two descriptions. The splendid specimens on the University of Illinois campus are extremely variable but tend toward the oval-rounded habit. One specimen is of a distinct upright, oval character with strongly ascending branches and the most beautiful bark pattern I have had the privilege of viewing. If it were possible to asexually propagate Paperbark Maple then this specimen would be my first choice.

RATE: Slow, possibly 1′ per year over a 10-15 year period.

TEXTURE: Medium fine in leaf and winter habit.

STEM AND BARK COLOR: Young stems reddish brown; older wood (1/2″ or greater) a beautiful cinnamon or red-brown as the bark exfoliates to expose these colors. Second year wood usually starts to exfoliate, thus the exquisite bark character develops at a very young age. Verbal descriptions cannot do justice to this ornamental asset and only after one has been privileged to view the bark first hand can he or she fully appreciate the character.

LEAF COLOR: Flat dark green in summer changing to russet red, bronze, or red combinations. Very handsome in summer and fall foliage. Intermediate defoliator.

FLOWERS: Produced in limited quantities, borne in cymes.

FRUIT: Samara, not ornamentally important.

CULTURE: Transplant balled and burlapped or as a container-grown plant in spring; adaptable to varied soils; prefers well drained and moist but does well in the clay soils of the Midwest, full sun.

DISEASES AND INSECTS: None serious.

LANDSCAPE VALUE: Specimen for small areas, accent plant, focal plant in the shrub border, bark character is exquisite and can be admirably displayed anywhere in the landscape.

PROPAGATION: Difficult. The samaras usually have few viable seeds. Fruits collected in 1973 and 1974 had 1% and 8% viable seeds, respectively. Seeds will germinate after 90 days stratification at 41°F in moist peat; however, the fruit wall is so tough the root radical cannot penetrate and will spiral around within the structure. Commercial production of this species involves fall planting and waiting for two years for germination to begin. I have conducted many experiments with cuttings and of two or three thousand mature woody cuttings have had one root. I have enough seedlings that juvenile wood can now be used for rooting studies and am looking forward to the challenge.

We have budded *Acer griseum* on *Acer saccharum* in August with about 40 percent success. The budded-stock was dug, brought into the greenhouse and grew 18″ to 30″ the first three months. We are continuing to work with this method of propagation and hope to improve the percentages.

RELATED SPECIES: Possibly related species *A. triflorum* and *A. nikoense.*

ADDITIONAL NOTES: Unfortunately, limitedly available in commerce but if production could be easily increased it could become one of the most popular woody trees.

NATIVE HABITAT: Central China. Introduced 1901.

Acer miyabei — Miyabe Maple

LEAVES: Opposite, simple, 5-lobed, 4 to 6″ across, deeply cordate, lobes obtusely acuminate, obtusely lobulate or dentate, soft gray-green to moderately dark green and usually glossy above, pale green and pubescent beneath, pubescent above when young; petioles puberulous and exuding milky sap from the end when removed from the stem.

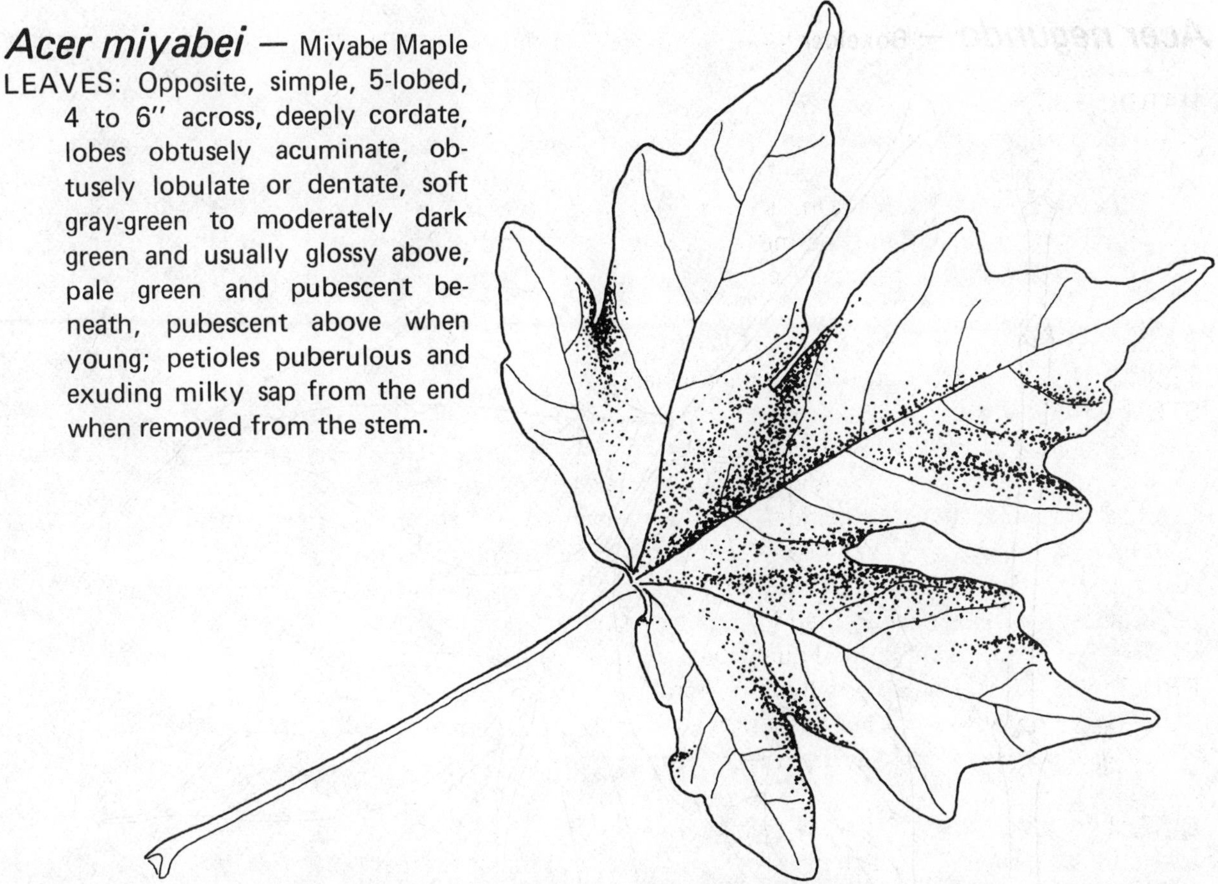

Acer miyabei, Miyabe Maple, is an upright-oval to rounded small tree growing 30 to 40′ either open or densely branched. The habit is quite lovely and may remind one of the outlines of *Acer campestre* or *Acer buergerianum*. The leaves stay green late into October and then turn rapidly to pale yellow and fall in early November. The flowers are greenish yellow, borne in slender-stalked, 10 to 15 flowered pyramidal corymbs in May. Culturally the species prefers moist, well-drained soils probably on the acid side. Several specimens are doing quite well in the Morton Arboretum where the soil could best be described as a clay loam. Propagation has been a problem as vegetative and seed attempts have met with limited success.

The Morton Arboretum has indicated that grafting onto volunteer seedlings has proven successful as well as onto seedlings of *Acer campestre*. The species is hardy to Zone 4 and I have seen a specimen doing quite well at the Minnesota Landscape Arboretum where winter temperatures may drop to -40°F. Would make a nice specimen tree for the small residential area.

The discovery of this rare tree took place quite by accident when Prof. C.S. Sargent of the Arnold Arboretum was waiting for a train at Iwanigawa, a railroad junction in Yezo, Japan. He had some time before the train arrived and, as any good plantsman, strolled out of the town to a small grove of trees. In this grove, occupying a piece of low ground on the borders of a small stream was *A. miyabei* covered with fruit. Japan. Introduced 1892.

Acer negundo — Boxelder

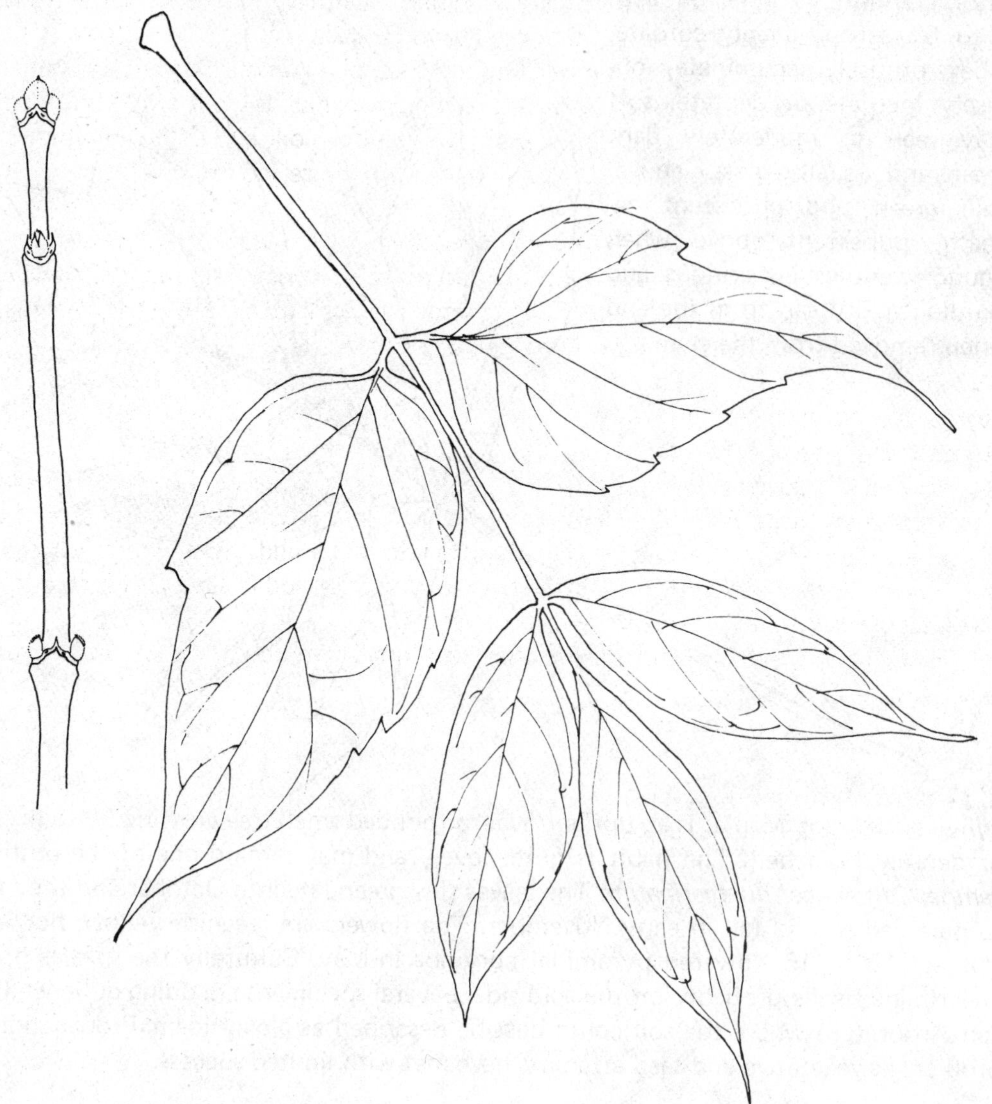

LEAVES: Opposite, pinnately compound, 3-5 leaflets (7-9), individual leaflet 2-4" long, coarsely serrate or terminal one-3 lobed. Bright green above, lighter green beneath and slightly pubescent.

BUD: Valvate in appearance. 1-3 scales visible, whitish, pubescent.

STEM: Reddish brown, more commonly green, polished, often with bloom which rubs off. Leaf scars completely encircle twig and meet at a sharp angle, has a malodor when crushed.

SIZE: 30 to 50′ in height, can reach 70′, but this is the exception; spread variable but usually equal to or greater than height.

HARDINESS: Zone 2.

HABIT: Usually rounded to broad rounded in outline, branches develop irregularly to support the uneven crown. Often a small "alley cat" tree with multistemmed character and ragged appearance.

RATE: Fast, extremely so when young, the wood is weak and will break up in ice and wind, can grow 15 to 20′ in a 4 to 6 year period.

TEXTURE: Owing to ragged habit, the tree is coarse in all seasons.

LEAF COLOR: Light green on the upper surface and grayish green below in summer, foliage turns yellow-green to yellow to brown in fall. Usually of no ornamental consequence; early defoliator.

FLOWERS: Dioecious, yellowish green, March to April, male flowers borne in corymbs; female in slender pendulous racemes and usually in great quantity. Not ornamentally effective but worth avoiding the female forms if the tree has to be used.

FRUIT: Samara, maturing in September or October, usually profusely borne, persisting into winter.

CULTURE: Easy to transplant, actually native to stream banks, lakes, borders of swamps but performs well out of its native habitat in poor, wet or dry soils and cold climates; pH adaptable; full sun. A necessary tree under difficult conditions where few other species will survive, usually a short-lived tree.

DISEASES AND INSECTS: Described under Silver Maple.

LANDSCAPE VALUE: Extensive use is limited due to lack of ornamental assets, however, has been used in Great Plains and Southwest. Falls in same category of *Ulmus pumila, Ailanthus altissima* and *Morus alba*. The cultivars have some landscape merit.

CULTIVARS:

'Auratum' — Leaves wholly yellow.

'Aureo-marginatum' — Margins of leaves etched in yellow.

'Variegatum' — Quite common form with white margined leaves. The small specimens I have seen were quite handsome but no doubt with age would assume some of the unworthy characteristics of the species. This is a female clone and the fruits are variegated like the leaves. Grew 15' high and 14' wide over a 10 year period in tests conducted in Oregon.

PROPAGATION: Seeds, 41°F. for 90 days in moist peat.

NATIVE HABITAT: New England and Ontario to Minnesota, Nebraska, Kansas, Texas and Florida. Cultivated 1688.

Acer nikoense — Nikko Maple

(now listed as *Acer maximowiczianum*)

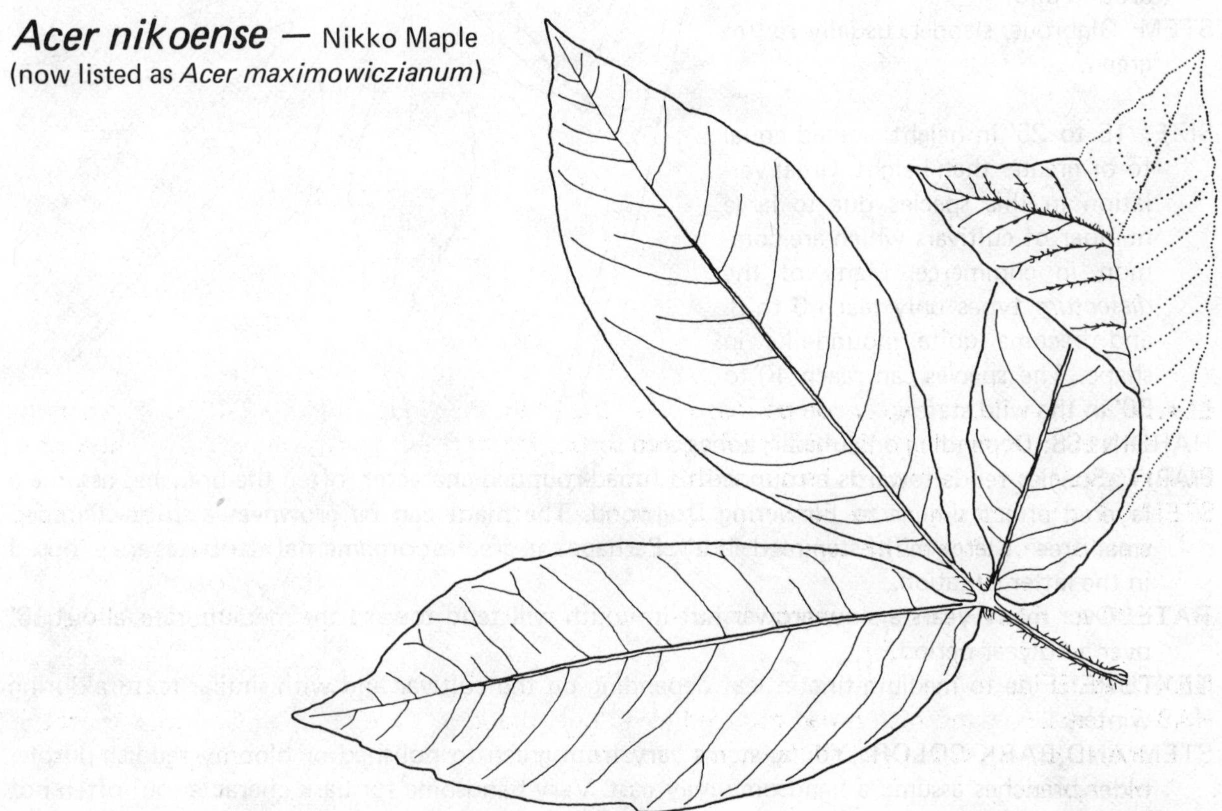

LEAVES: Opposite, trifoliate, leaflets ovate to elliptic-oblong, 2 to 5" long, middle-short stalked, lateral ones subsessile, acute, obtusely dentate or nearly entire, villous-pubescent beneath; petiole densely pilose, 4/5 to 1 3/5" long.

BUDS: Imbricate, long, pyramid-shaped, pubescent.

STEM: Slender, brownish, with pilose pubescence until the second year.

Acer nikoense, Nikko Maple, is a lovely, slow-growing, vase-shaped, round-headed, 20 to 30' high tree. Although very slow growing it is interesting throughout the seasons and would make a fine specimen for the small property. The leaves are bronzy when emerging, changing to medium green in summer and finally glorious and spectacular yellow, brilliant red and purple in fall. Flowers are yellow, 1/2" diameter, produced usually 3 together on drooping pedicels, 3/4" long, May. Fruit is a thick, densely pubescent samara; the upright wings curved inward or spreading at a right angle. This species seems to prefer a well-drained, loamy, moist, slightly acid soil. The bark is a handsome, smooth gray-brown. The largest tree I have seen was in the Arnold Arboretum and at the time I was so intrigued with it ten photographs were taken. Native to Japan, Central China now quite rare in its native haunts. Introduced 1881. Zone 5.

Acer palmatum — Japanese Maple

LEAVES: Opposite, simple, 2-5" long, deeply 5-7-9 lobed, being lance-oblong in shape, acuminate, doubly serrate. Color varies depending on cultivar.

BUD: Tend toward valvate character, small, green or red, hidden by base of petiole, frequently double terminal buds; margin of leaf scar much elevated forming flaring collar around bud.

STEM: Glabrous, slender, usually red to green.

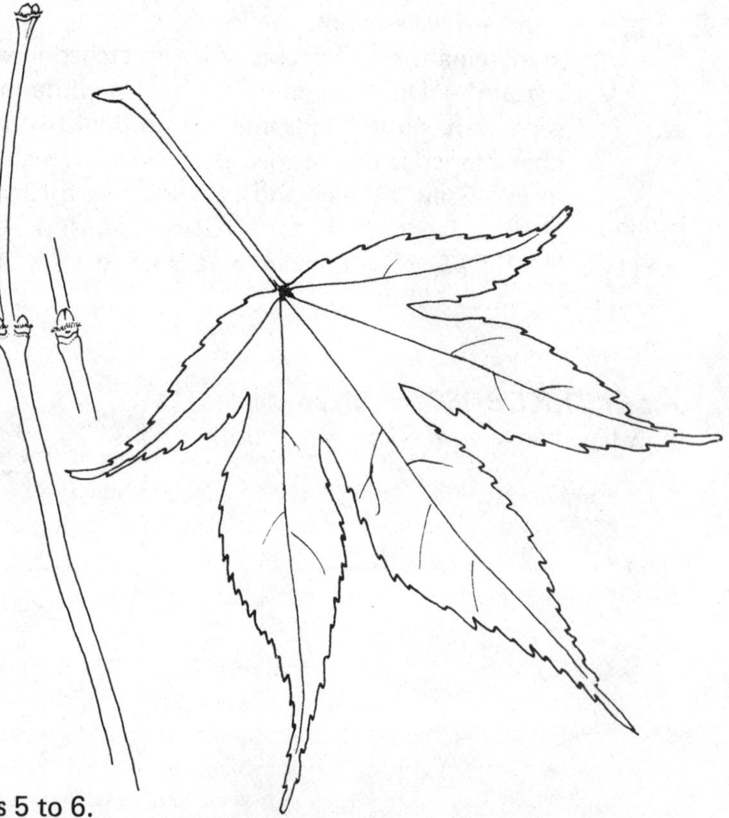

SIZE: 15 to 25' in height; spread equal to or greater than height. Great variation in this species due to large number of cultivars which are common in commerce. Many of the *dissectum* types only reach 6 to 8' and become quite mound-like in shape. The species can reach 40 to 50' in the wild state.

HARDINESS: Depending on cultivar, zones 5 to 6.

HABIT: Species tends towards a rounded to broad-rounded character, often the branches assume a layered effect similar to Flowering Dogwood. The plant can be grown as a single-stemmed small tree or large multi-stemmed shrub. Perhaps the greatest ornamental attributes are exposed in the latter situation.

RATE: Over many years a slow grower but in youth will tend toward the medium rate; about 10' over a 10 year period.

TEXTURE: Fine to medium-fine in leaf depending on the cultivar and with similar texture during winter.

STEM AND BARK COLOR: Young stems vary from green to polished or bloomy reddish purple; older branches assume a handsome gray cast. Very handsome for bark character but often not considered for this feature due to over-shadowing by excellent foliage.

LEAF COLOR: The species is green in summer, becoming bronzed or purplish in the fall. See cultivar descriptions for foliage colors ranging from yellow to green to blood red.

FLOWERS: Small, purple, May-June, borne in stalked umbels (possibly corymbs).

FRUITS: Samara, 1/2" long, wings 1/8" wide, ornamentally non-descript.

CULTURE: Transplant balled and burlapped or from a container; supposedly somewhat difficult to transplant but I have never had problems with small specimens; prefer good, well-drained, moist soil, preferably endowed with organic matter, pH range of 5.5 to 6.5 is probably optimum; should be sheltered from cold drying winds for the unfolding leaves of many of the delicate types are very sensitive to drying; may also be injured by late spring frosts; tolerant of shade and in some areas this is necessary to prevent scorching of the leaves; will survive in a moderately sunny location in the North but care should be taken in the selection and siting of the cultivar.

DISEASES AND INSECTS: Anthracnose, leaf scorch (physiological problem) in hot, dry weather; see under Silver Maple.

LANDSCAPE VALUE: Many uses: small lawn specimen, shrub border, accent plant, bonsai; lends an artistic and aristocratic touch to the landscape.

CULTIVARS: Numerous cultivars, the following are some of the better forms.

(Leaves usually with 5 main lobes)

'Asahi-juru' – Green leaves with "breaks" of white or pink.

'Atropurpureum' – One of the hardiest, leaves dark red throughout growing season, can be grown from seed but the seedlings vary in foliage color.

'Bloodgood' – Upright, strong growing, red-purple form.

'Burgandy Lace' – Fine foliage form with interesting reddish foliage displayed against green stems.

'Butterfly' – Small upright form, base color is deep green, with a blue cast. Edges are cream colored with a pink-tinge. In fall white edges become crimson.

'Corallinum' – Leaves light green, turning gold often with red edging, stems–coral-red in winter.

'Crispum' – Upright, vase shaped outline. Edges of small leaves roll inward; each leaf has a sharp, 5-pointed star shape. Green changing to rich gold.

'Hogryaku' – Pale green leaves with lobes recurved downward, give wavy pattern. Leaves turn rich orange in fall.

'Linearilobum' – Leaves divided into narrow lobes, slightly toothed. Foliage first appears red, turns green in summer.

'Nomura-nishiki' – Dark red leaves with brown and lighter colored variegations.

'Osakazuki' – Upright, somewhat spreading form with intense scarlet fall color.

'Oshio-beni' – Bright red leaves with long graceful branches.

'Roseo Marginatum' – Crinkled leaves with white and pink markings blended with green.

'Sagara-nishiki' – Mottled leaves of cream or pale yellow.

'Sanguineum' – Most hardy, leaves reddish above, green below, bark on young wood red.

'Scolopendrifolium' – Leaves cut to center, leaflets narrow, green.

'Sessilifolium' – Upright, leaves 3 to 5 divided, each lobe a separate "leaf", appearance quite different from any other form in cultivation.

'Sherwood Flame' – Red leaf form with strongly indented margins.

'Shishigashira' – Dwarf, slow growing, shrubby tree. Leaves are wrinkled, crinkled, almost puckered, beautiful green, often with reddish edge.

'Trompenburg' – Strong growing, red leaf form.

'Versicolor' – Leaves with white, pink and light green variegations.

'Yezo-nishiki' – Blood red leaves and bright red variegations.

(Leaves with 7 or more main lobes)

'Crimson King' – Red leaf form which holds color through the summer.

'Elegans' – Leaves 5" long, rose-margin when first open.

'Flavescens' – Yellowish foliage.

'Ornatum' – Beautiful wine-red foliage.

'Ozakazuki' – Large leaves, yellowish to light green, turning a brilliant red in the fall; one of the best for fall coloring.

'Purpureum' – Red purple foliage.

'Reticulatum' – Multicolored form, leaves with green veins, leaf spaces between veins are yellow, white and pale green.

'Rubrum' – Large leaves, deep red when young, turning green by summer.

PROPAGATION: Cuttings, softwood treated with 2% IBA, placed in peat under high humidity rooted 90 to 95%. This is not true for all *Acer palmatum* types for many must be grafted as they do not root or come true-to-type from seed. *Acer palmatum atropurpureum* is a botanical variety and produces purple-leaf seedlings which vary in intensity of coloration. Some nurserymen rogue out the off color plants and list the remaining plants as a specific cultivar (clone). It is wise to deal with reputable, knowledgeable plantsmen when purchasing Japanese Maples.

From my own experience, softwood cuttings collected in July, 1975, rooted 61 percent when wounded and treated with quick dip 10,000 ppm IBA/50% alcohol. Roots only developed from wounded areas along the cuttings. Rooting took place in about 2 months. Medium was peat: perlite.

RELATED SPECIES:

Acer japonicum, Fullmoon Maple, 20 to 30' in height with a comparable or larger spread (can reach 40 to 50' in the wild). Leaves are an extremely handsome soft green changing to rich crimson in fall; flowers purplish red produced in April before the leaves on long stalked corymbs; culture is similar to *Acer palmatum*; native to Japan; Zone 5. The following cultivars are probably more common than the species in gardens and include:

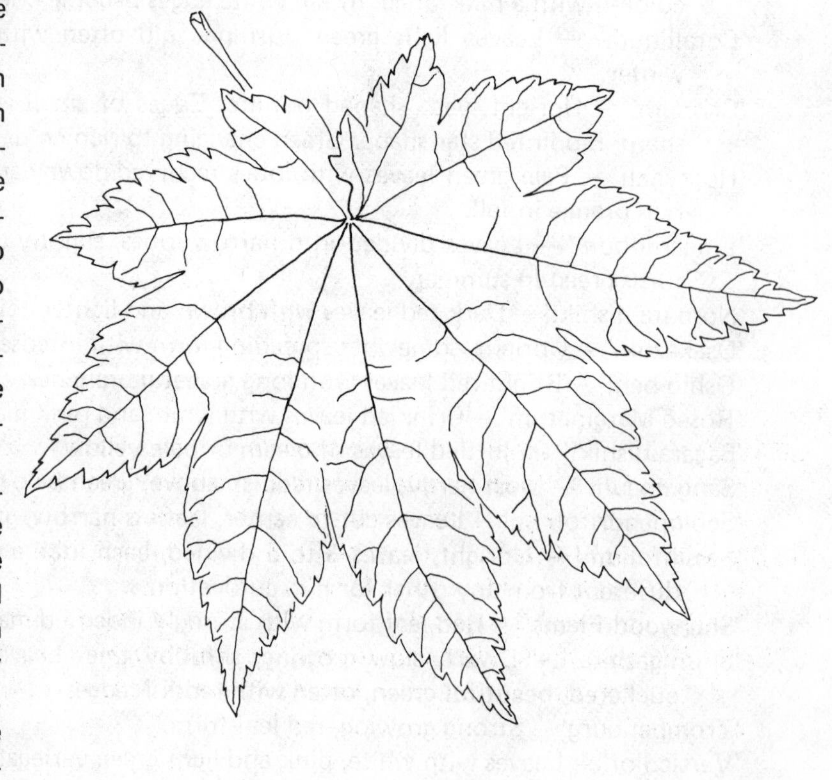

'Aconitifolium' – Lobes extend to 1/2 or 1/4" of the end of petiole, each lobe being again divided and sharply toothed; crimson fall color; rounded bushy habit to 8 to 10' in height.

'Aureum' – Leaves of a pale golden yellow and effective during the summer; reaching 10 to 20' in height with a comparable spread.

'Itayo' – Leaves larger than the species with good yellow fall color.

'Junshitoe' – Leaves smaller than the species, 2 to 3" across.

'Vitifolium' – Excellent type because of the rich purple, crimson, and orange fall colors, leaves are large up to 6" long and wide and of grape-like shape.

Acer pseudosieboldianum, Purplebloom Maple, native of Manchuria and Korea; develops excellent orange, scarlet and crimson fall colors.

Acer sieboldianum, Siebold Maple, differs from *Acer japonicum* in its yellow flowers and pubescence of young shoots; colors yellow in the fall; there is a handsome specimen at the Arnold Arboretum.

ADDITIONAL NOTES: The *Acer palmatum dissectum* types are especially handsome because of the delicate, lacy, deeply cut leaves and the small, mounded growth habit. A real gem in the green world providing they are properly cared for. Overall the Japanese Maples are high quality landscape plants valued for form, texture and color.

NATIVE HABITATS: Japan, China and Korea. Introduced 1820.

Acer pensylvanicum — Striped Maple, also called Moosewood

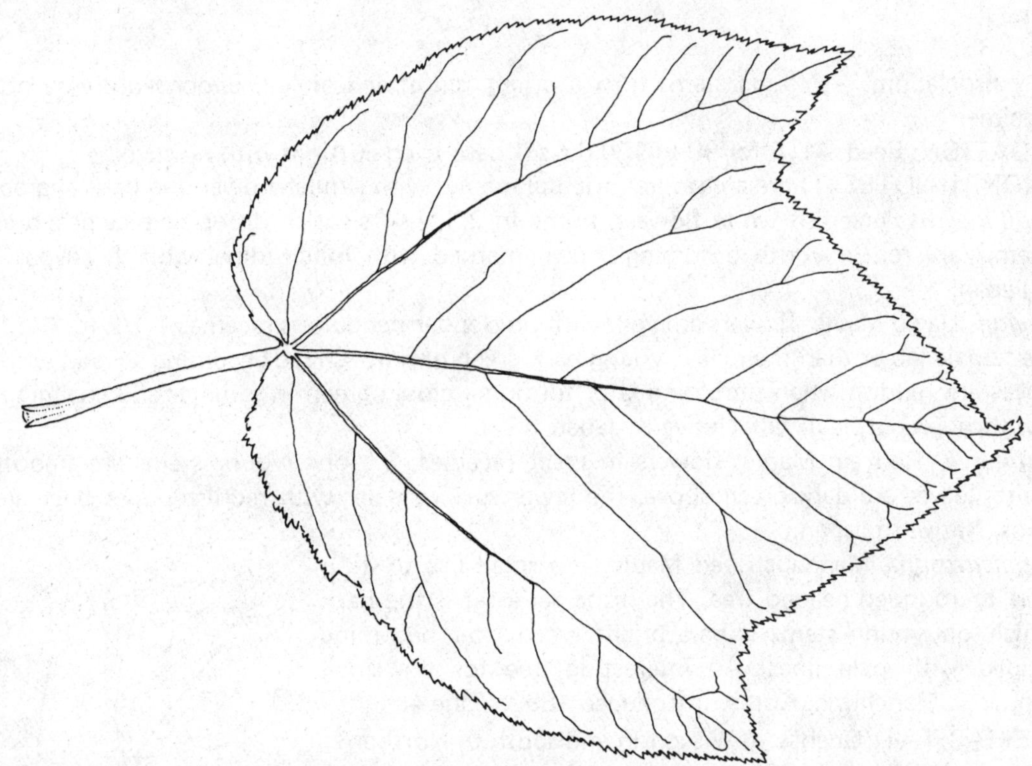

LEAVES: Opposite, simple, roundish-obovate, 3-lobed at apex, 5 to 7" long, subcordate, the lobes pointing forward, acuminate, serrulate, ferrugineous-pubescent beneath when young; petiole 4/5 to 2 4/5" long, rufous pubescent when young.

BUDS: Glabrous, 1/3 to 2/5" long, blunt, 2 scales, valvate; terminal-almost 1/2" long, much longer than the axillary buds, covered by 2 thick bright red spatulate boat shaped scales prominently keeled, inner scales green; stalked, about 1/25" long, red, glossy.

STEMS: Smooth, thick, changing to red; lenticels few; leaf scars "U" shaped, almost encircling twigs, older stems eventually becoming green striped with white; very handsome for this character.

SIZE: 15 to 20' in height but can grow to 30' or more in the wild, spread is less than or equal to height.

HARDINESS: Zone 3.

HABIT: Large shrub or small tree with a short trunk and ascending and arching branches that form a broad but very uneven, flat-topped to rounded crown.

RATE: Slow.

TEXTURE: Medium in leaf, medium to medium-coarse in winter.

STEM AND BARK COLOR: Young stems greenish brown or reddish, young branches (1" or greater) are green and conspicuously marked by long, vertical, greenish white stripes, hence, the name Striped Maple.

LEAF COLOR: Pinkish tinged when unfolding, bright green at maturity; apparently a great concentration of yellow pigments is present in the leaves; leaves change to yellow in autumn.

FLOWERS: Yellow, May, produced on pendulous, slender racemes, 4 to 6" long, each flower 1/3" diameter.

FRUIT: Samara, wings 3/4" long, not important ornamentally.

CULTURE: Does not proliferate under cultivation, prefers partially shaded woods; well-drained, cool, moist, slightly acidic soils. In native range exists as an understory plant which provides an index of its shade tolerance.

DISEASES AND INSECTS: See maple discussion.

LANDSCAPE VALUE: Very inadequate lawn specimen but for naturalizing purposes has possibilities.

CULTIVARS:

'Erythrocladum' – Young stems turn a bright red after leaf fall. Supposedly very attractive specimen.

PROPAGATION: Seed, 41°F for 90 to 120 days. I have tried cuttings with no success.

ADDITIONAL NOTES: There are several oriental maples with similar flower and bark characters.

Acer capillipes has greenish white flowers, borne in 2 1/4-4" slender, drooping racemes; branchlets (stems) are red in youth becoming brown marked with longitudinal whitish stripes. Native to Japan.

Acer davidii, David Maple, flowers are yellowish on slender pendulous racemes 1 1/2 to 2 1/2" long, the female larger than the males; young bark green or purplish red becoming striped with white; leaves are reddish when unfolding later turning a glossy green in summer and changing to yellow through purple in fall. Native to Japan.

Acer rufinerve, Redvein Maple, flowers in erect racemes, 3" long, young stems are smooth blue-white; leaves are dark green above, the lower surface paler with reddish pubescence along the veins. Native of Japan.

Acer tegmentosum, Manchustriped Maple, is a small (15 to 20'), oval to rounded headed tree. The principal asset is the bark which on young stems is pale bright green later becoming striped with pale lines. An interesting tree for the small property. Manchuria, Korea. Introduced 1892. Zone 4.

NATIVE HABITAT: Quebec to Wisconsin and south to Northern Georgia. Introduced 1755.

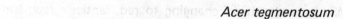

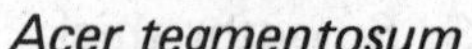

Acer tegmentosum

Acer platanoides — Norway Maple

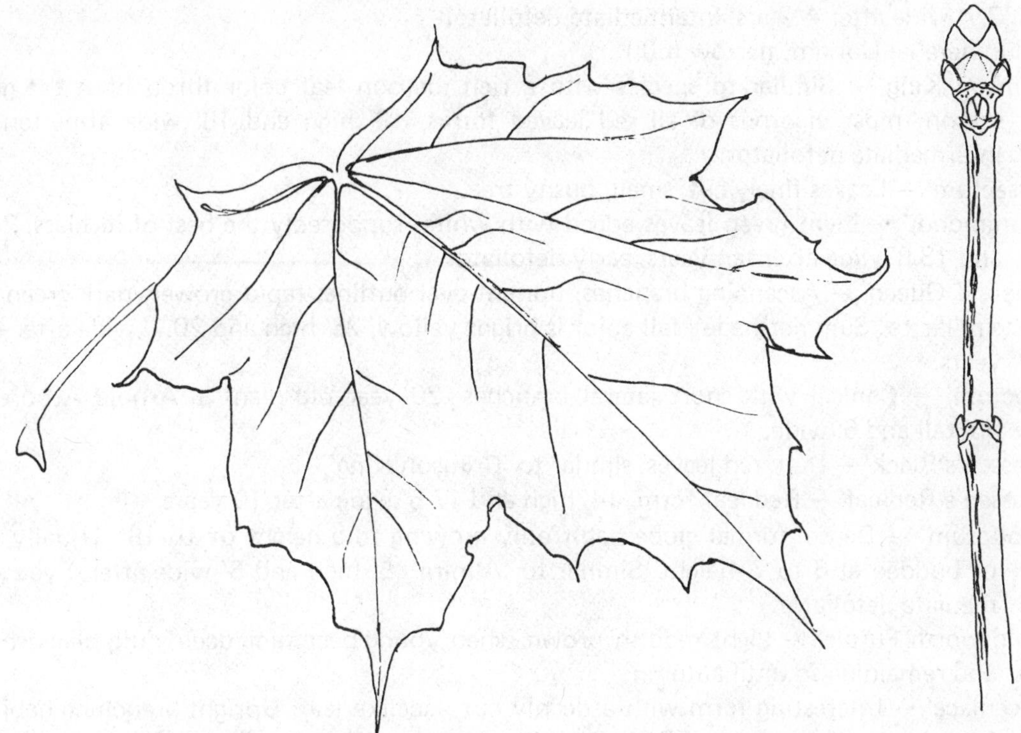

LEAVES: Opposite, simple, 4-7" across, 5-lobed, lobes sharp pointed, remotely dentate, dark green above, lustrous beneath often with hairs in axils of veins. Milky juice is visible when petiole is removed from stem.

BUD: Imbricate, terminal-large (1/4"), rounded, scales plump. Winter color—green to red to maroon.

STEM: Smooth, brownish, often somewhat olive-brown, leaf scars meeting forming a sharp angle.

SIZE: 40 to 50' in height occasionally over 90', usually spread is 2/3's or equal to height.

HARDINESS: Zone 3.

HABIT: Rounded, symmetrical crown, usually with very dense foliage and shallow root system which limit successful turf culture.

RATE: Medium, 10 to 12' in 5 to 8 years.

TEXTURE: Medium-coarse in summer and winter.

LEAF COLOR: Dark green in summer; sometimes changing to handsome yellow in fall. Colors during the fall of 1974 were golden yellow on many trees in the Champaign-Urbana area and rivaled *Betula lenta*, Sweet Birch, in intensity of coloration.

FLOWERS: Yellow or greenish yellow, each flower 1/3" diameter, April before the leaves, produced in erect, many flowered corymbs; quite effective in the early spring landscape; one of the most floriferous maples.

FRUIT: Samara, maturing in September-October.

CULTURE: Easy to transplant, well adapted to extremes in soils, will withstand sand, clay, acid to calcareous soils, seems to withstand hot, dry conditions better than Sugar Maple, tolerates polluted atmosphere. Especially those containing ozone and sulfur dioxide.

DISEASES AND INSECTS: *Verticillium* wilt, anthracnose, some leaf scorch.

LANDSCAPE VALUE: Over-used and probably over-rated tree. The species and several of the cultivars, especially 'Crimson King', are overplanted. Has been used as lawn, street and park tree. Should be given considerable room for it does cover large areas, often creates many problems along streets; the cultivars offer the greatest hope for the landscape.

CULTIVARS:

'Almira' — Small (20') globe shaped.

'Cleveland' — Upright oval in habit, dense dark green foliage, coarsely branched, 6.4' high and 2.7' wide after 4 years, intermediate defoliator.

'Columnare' — Upright, narrow (60').

'Crimson King' — Similar to species with a rich maroon leaf color throughout the growing season, most vigorous of all red leaved forms, 19' high and 16' wide after ten years, intermediate defoliator.

'Dissectum' — Leaves finely cut; small, bushy tree.

'Drummondi' — Light green leaves edged with white, supposedly the best of its class, 23' high and 13.9' wide after ten years, early defoliator.

'Emerald Queen' — Ascending branches, upright-oval outline, rapid grower, dark green leaves, similar to 'Summershade'; fall color is bright yellow; 26' high and 20.7' wide after twenty years.

'Erectum' — Conical with short lateral branches—20 year old plant in Arnold Arboretum is 30' tall and 6' wide.

'Faassen's Black' — Dark red leaves, similar to 'Crimson King'.

'Faassen's Redleaf' — Red leaf form, 14' high and 17.5' wide after 10 years.

'Globosum' — Dense, formal globe habit only growing to a height of 15-18'. Usually grafted or budded at 6 to 7' height. Similar to 'Almira', 5' high and 5' wide after 4 years, intermediate defoliator.

'Goldsworth Purple' — Light reddish brown when young becoming deep, dull, blackish purple and remaining so until autumn.

'Greenlace' — Interesting form with a deeply cut, lacelike leaf. Upright branching habit (50'), fast growing, 5.4' high and 8.3' wide after four years, intermediate defoliator.

'Jade Glen' — Similar to species, supposedly rapid growing and extremely sturdy.

'Laciniatum' — Smaller and more twiggy tree than the type, of more erect, narrow habit; leaves tapering and wedge-shaped at base, the lobes ending in long, often curved claw-like appendages.

'Lorbergi' — Leaves palmately divided to base of leaf but tips ascending from plane of leaf. A dense, rounded, very slow growing tree without a central leader.

'Olmsted' — Upright, similar to 'Columnare'.

'Royal Red' — Similar to 'Crimson King' but slower growing.

'Schwedleri' — Common older form with purplish red spring foliage changing to green in early summer, wider spreading than most selections, 17.5' high and 21' wide after 10 years, early defoliator.

'Summershade' — Rapid growing, heat resistant and upright-oval in habit, maintains a single leader. The foliage is more leathery than the other varieties, 12' high and 10.6' wide after 4 years, intermediate defoliator, ranked extremely high in the Shade Tree Evaluation Trials conducted at Wooster, Ohio.

'Superform' — Rapid growing with straight trunk and heavy dark green foliage (50'), 22.6' high and 21' wide after 10 years, intermediate defoliator.

PROPAGATION: Seed, 41°F for 90 to 120 days in moist peat or other media. The cultivars are budded on seedling understocks.

ADDITIONAL NOTES: A very popular maple and probably will continue to be in demand. Often the bark splits on the species and cultivars on the south or southwest side of the trunk where the sun warms the bark and then sudden low temperatures cause contraction and splitting occurs; often termed "frost cracks".

NATIVE HABITAT: Continental Europe, where it is widely spread in a wild state from Norway southwards, also has escaped from cultivation in United States.

Acer pseudoplatanus — Planetree Maple. Also called Sycamore Maple.

LEAVES: Opposite, simple, 3-6″ across, 5 lobed, veins impressed, dark green above, lighter greenish white beneath, sometimes pubescent on veins. Leaf margins tend to be regularly toothed; leaf is leathery.

BUD: Large, greenish, slightly pointed, only single buds above leaf scar. Buds similar to Norway, but remain green through winter.

STEM: Glabrous, gray-brown, dull, leaf scars do not meet as is the case in Norway Maple.

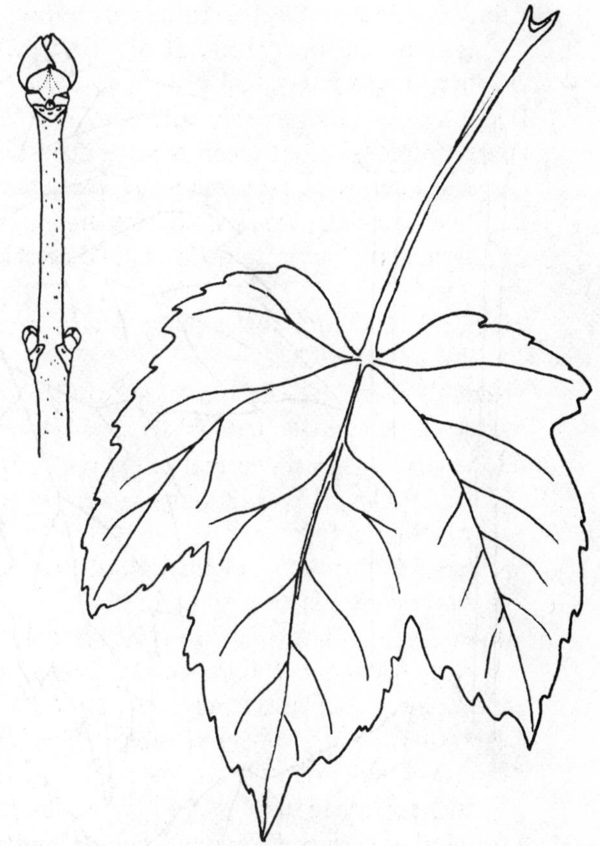

SIZE: 40 to 60′ in height under most landscape conditions but specimens of over 100′ are known, spread two-third's of, or equal to height.

HARDINESS: Zone 5.

GROWTH HABIT: Tree with upright, spreading branches forming an oval to rounded outline.

RATE: Medium, 10 to 12′ in 5 to 8 years.

TEXTURE: Medium in leaf and winter.

BARK COLOR: Reddish brown or grayish, flaking into small, rectangular scales.

LEAF COLOR: Dark green in summer; fall color a dingy brown or possibly with a tinge of yellow, intermediate defoliator.

FLOWERS: Yellowish green, May, borne in pendulous panicles, 2 to 4″ long.

FRUIT: Samara, maturing in September-October.

CULTURE: Transplant balled and burlapped in spring, very adaptable to soil types, preferably well-drained, tolerates high lime to acid conditions and exposed sites, supposedly will withstand the full force of salt-laden winds in exposed places near the sea. Often listed as a salt tolerant species and has been used extensively in Holland; full sun or light shade.

DISEASES AND INSECTS: Cankers, subject to considerable dead wood and requires ample maintenance for that reason.

LANDSCAPE VALUE: Probably too many better maples for this species to ever assume any popular status in American gardens. Where conditions warrant (exposed, saline environment) it might be used to good advantage.

CULTIVARS:

'Acubifolium' — Leaves blotched with yellow like the common *Acuba,* gold dust plant.

'Atropurpurem' — Leaves dark green above, rich purple beneath; may fall in the botanical variety category as apparently will come partially true from seed, 26′ high and 25′ wide after 10 years, favored with aphids, produces large quantities of fruits.

'Brilliantissimum' — Leaves of a beautiful pinkish color on unfolding, slow growing.

'Erythrocarpum' — Leaves smaller and glossier, fruit bright red.

'Leopoldii' — Leaves mottled with yellowish pink and purple.

'Worleii' — Leaves yellow to orange-yellow when young, petiole red.

PROPAGATION: Seed, 41°F for 90 plus days in moist peat. Cultivars are budded onto seedlings.

ADDITIONAL NOTES: Old world tree, cannot compete with American and Asiatic species for fall color.

NATIVE HABITAT: Europe, Western Asia. Cultivated for centuries.

Acer rubrum — Red Maple

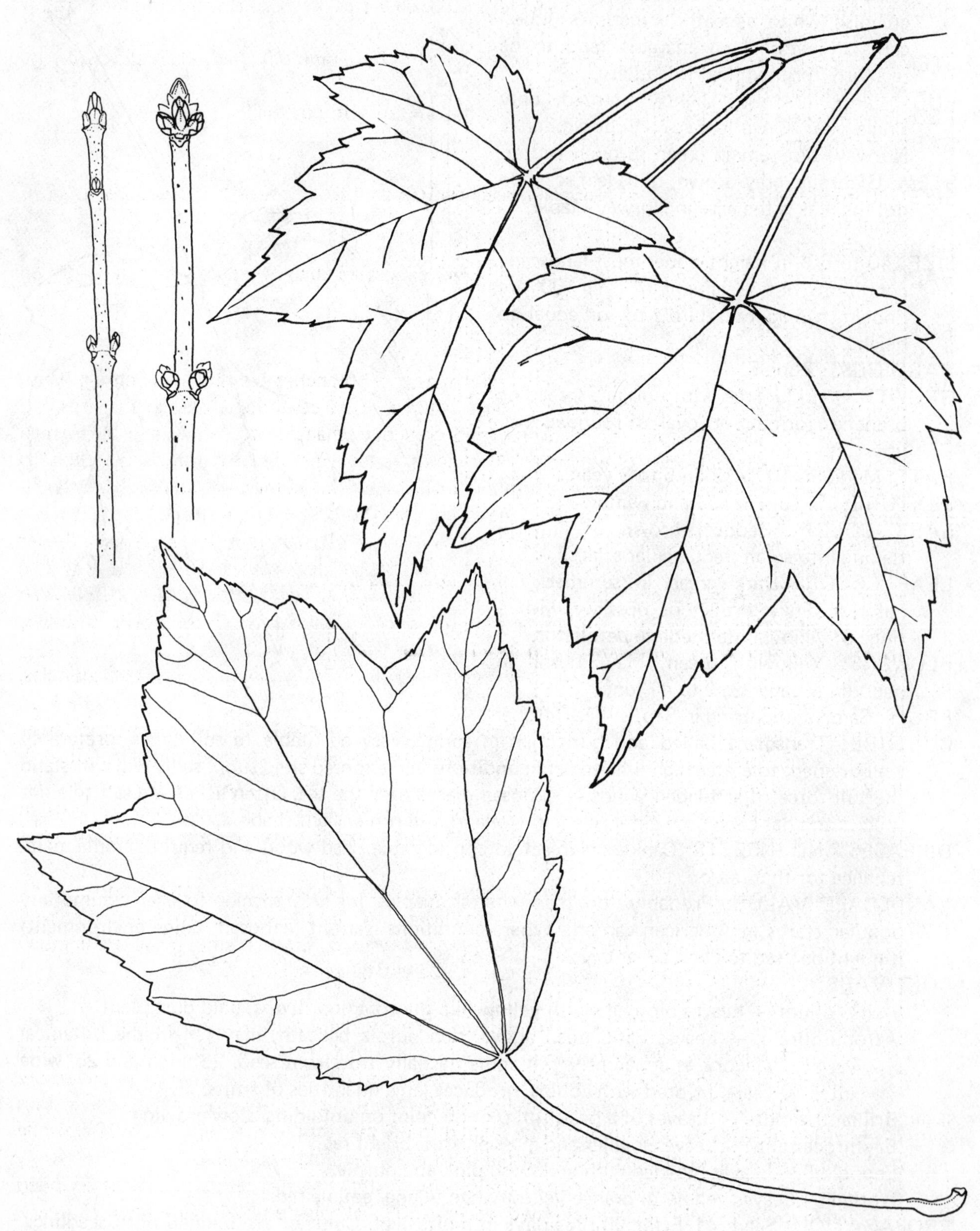

LEAVES: Opposite, simple, 2-4" long, 3 although often 5 lobed, triangular ovate lobes and sinuses are irregularly toothed. (note in Silver Maple the sinuses are entire). Medium to dark green above, grayish beneath with hairy veins, new growth often red and petioles often red.

BUD: Imbricate, red to green, blunt and several scaled, clustered, with rounded bud scales (Silver Maple scales are slightly pointed).

STEM: Glabrous, green, red, brown. When crushed does not have rank odor. Usually green becoming red as winter progresses.

FLOWER: Flowers are borne with petals. Silver Maple flowers without them.

BARK: Young-smooth, light gray; old-dark gray and rough.

SIZE: 40 to 60' in height, but occasionally reaches 100 to 120' in the wild; spread less than or equal to height.

HARDINESS: Zone 3.

HABIT: In youth often pyramidal or elliptical, developing ascending branches which result in an irregular, ovoid or rounded crown.

RATE: Medium to fast; 10 to 12' in 5 to 7 years.

TEXTURE: Medium-fine to medium in leaf; medium in winter.

BARK COLOR: Soft gray or gray-brown on intermediate sized branches eventually becoming flaky; dark grayish brown, separated into scaly ridges fastened at the center and loose at the ends.

LEAF COLOR: Emerging leaves are reddish tinged gradually changing to medium to dark green above with a distinct gray cast beneath. Fall color varies from greenish yellow to yellow to brilliant red. Red Maple does not always have brilliant red fall color and unscrupulous plantsmen who offer seedling trees and guarantee red fall color are frauding the public.

FLOWERS: Red, rarely yellowish; mid to late March, in dense clusters before the leaves, each flower on a reddish pedicel at first quite short but lengthening as the flower and fruit develop. The stigmas and styles as well as the small petals are the showy part of the flower. I have seen trees which are predominantly pistillate and others largely staminate. Both are showy, however, the male does not have the strong red colors compared to the female.

FRUIT: Samara, often but not always reddish maturing to brown; on slender drooping peduncles, 2 to 3" long; wings 3/4" long, 1/4" wide.

CULTURE: Transplants readily as a small specimen bare root, or balled and burlapped in larger sizes, move in spring, very tolerant of soils, however, prefers slightly acid, moist conditions; tolerant of ozone and intermediately tolerant of sulfur dioxide; occurs naturally in low, wet areas and is often one of the first trees to color in the fall; shows chlorosis in high pH soils, in the past this was thought to be due to iron deficiency, however, recent research has shown that manganese is the causal agent.

DISEASES AND INSECTS: Leaf hoppers have caused considerable damage in Central Illinois.

LANDSCAPE VALUE: Excellent specimen tree for lawn, park or street. Does not tolerate heavily polluted areas. Does not grow as fast as *Acer saccharinum,* Silver Maple, however, is much preferable because of cleaner foliage, stronger wood and better fall color.

CULTIVARS:

'Armstrong' — Fastigiate (30-50'), spire-like, beautiful light gray bark. Faster grower than Upright Sugar or Norway. Does not color well in Central Illinois, possibly a hybrid between *A. rubrum* x *A. saccharinum,* 15.4' high and 4.5' wide after 4 years, intermediate defoliator, often shows incompatibility problems and for no apparent reason older trees simply die; incompatibility could be related to the fact that 'Armstrong' is a hybrid, while the understock upon which it is grafted is usually a seedling Red Maple.

'Autumn Flame' — Leaves smaller than the species, brilliant scarlet fall color, dense rounded head. Colors earlier in the fall (two weeks) (60'), 21' high and 24' wide after 10 years, early defoliator.

'Bowhall' or 'Columnare' — Slow growing, narrow pyramidal shape, bright red fall color, 12.5' high and 3.6' wide after 4 years, received high rating in Shade Tree Evaluation Tests in Wooster, Ohio.

'Gerling' – Broadly pyramidal (35'), densely branched.

'October Glory' – Retains leaves late in fall, shiny foliage, brilliant orange to red color (50'), 11' high and 6.4' wide after 4 years, often holds leaves so late that severe early freezes reduce the intensity of fall coloration.

'Red Sunset' – Excellent red fall color for 1 to 2 weeks, leaves tend to droop slightly and are held late in fall, colors before 'October Glory', 13.6' high and 7.8' wide after 4 years, intermediate defoliator, highest rated shade tree in the Ohio Shade Tree Evaluation tests.

'Schlesinger' – Introduced for superior fall color (45-60'), 12.6' high and 6.9' wide after 4 years, intermediate defoliator, has fallen out of favor and no longer widely planted since the introduction of the smaller, better fall coloring types.

'Tilford' – Globe headed, uniform in shape, with vigorous habit.

PROPAGATION: Seeds, stratify at 41°F for 60 to 75 days or soak in cold running water for 5 days. Cuttings, collected in late June and treated with 200 ppm IBA for 6 hours rooted well.

ADDITIONAL NOTES: The cultivars should be used in preference to seedling stock if good red fall color is desired. The early spring flowers are attractive and forewarn that spring is just "around the corner".

NATIVE HABITAT: Newfoundland to Florida, west to Minnesota, Iowa, Oklahoma and Texas. Introduced 1860.

Acer saccharinum — Silver Maple

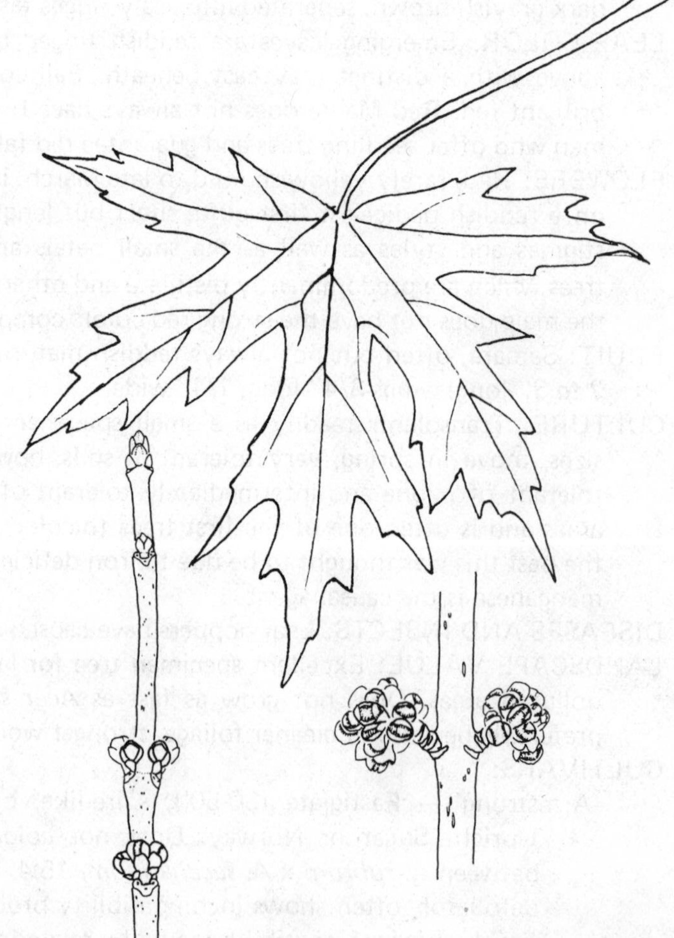

LEAVES: Opposite, simple, 3-6" across, 5 lobed, with entire deep sinus. End of lobes deeply and doubly serrate. Medium green above, silver white beneath.

BUD: Similar to red, except scales slightly pointed or acuminate. Flower buds spherical, accessory, margin of scales ciliate.

STEM: Similar to red except with rank odor when crushed. Lower branches frequently are slightly pendulous with upturned ends.

SIZE: 50 to 70' in height and can grow to 100 to 120'. Spread is usually about 2/3's the height.

HARDINESS: Zone 3.

HABIT: Upright with strong spreading branches forming an oval to rounded crown with pendulous branches which turn up at the ends.

RATE: Fast, 10 to 12' in 4 to 5 years from a small newly planted tree is not unreasonable. Unfortunately with fast growth comes a weak wooded tree. Often will break up in wind, ice, and snow storms.

TEXTURE: Medium in leaf, but coarse in winter. Actually the overall winter effect is difficult to digest.

BARK COLOR: On young branches (1" or more) color is an interesting gray or gray-brown and can be mistaken for the bark of *Acer rubrum.* However, the color is usually darker (or with a tinge of red) compared to that of *Acer rubrum.*

LEAF COLOR: Medium green above, gray or silver beneath in summer; fall color is usually a green-yellow-brown combination. A tinge of red is evident with certain trees during the fall but this is the exception rather than the rule.

FLOWER: Greenish yellow, sometimes reddish, without petals; opening before *Acer rubrum,* usually in early to mid-March in Central Illinois; borne in dense clusters similar to Red Maple.

FRUIT: Samara, not ornamentally important.

CULTURE: Of the easiest culture, transplants well bare root or balled and burlapped, tolerant of wide variety of soils but achieves maximum size in moist soils along stream banks and in deep, moist soiled woods; prefers slightly acid soil. Will cause sidewalks to buckle and drain tiles to clog because of vigorous, gross feeding root system. One of the best trees for poor soils where few other species will survive and for these areas should be considered.

DISEASES AND INSECTS: Anthracnose (in rainy seasons may be serious on Sugar, Silver Maples and Boxelder), leafy spot (purple eye), tar spot, bacterial leaf spot, leaf blister, powdery mildew, *Verticillium* wilt (Silver, Norway, Red and Sugar are most affected), bleeding canker, basal canker, *Nectria* canker, *Ganoderma* rot, sapstreak, trunk decay, forest tent caterpillar, green striped maple worm, maple leaf cutter, Japanese leafhopper, leaf hopper, leaf stalk borer, petiole borers, bladder-gall mite, ocellate leaf gall, Norway Maple aphid, boxelder bug, maple phenacoccus, cottony maple scale (Silver Maple is tremendously susceptible), other scales (terrapin, gloomy, and Japanese), flat-headed borers, Sugar Maple borer, pidgeon tremex, leopard moth borer, metallic borer, twig pruner, carpenter worm, whitefly and nematodes. Maples are obviously susceptible to a wide range of insect and disease problems. Several physiological problems include scorch where the margins of the leaves become necrotic and brown due to limited water supply. This often occurs on newly planted trees and in areas where there is limited growing area (planter boxes, narrow tree lawns, sidewalk plantings). Red and Silver Maple also show extensive manganese chlorosis in calcerous or high pH soils and should be grown in acid soils.

LANDSCAPE VALUE: The use of this tree should be tempered as it becomes a liability with age. Possibility for rugged conditions or where someone desires fast shade. There are far too many superior trees to warrant extensive use of this species.

CULTIVARS:

'Crispum' – Dense growing form with deeply lobed leaves and crinkled margins.

'Laciniatum' – A catch-all term for plants whose leaves are more deeply divided than the type; 'Beebee' and 'Wieri' are categorized here.

'Pyramidale' – A type of broadly columnar habit.

'Silver Queen' – Supposedly of better habit, fruitless, and leaves are bright green above with silvery lower surface.

'Wieri' – Branches pendulous, leaf-lobes narrow and sharply toothed.

PROPAGATION: Seed has no dormancy and germinates immediately after maturing. Seedlings grow in every idle piece of ground and gradually overtake an area. Cuttings have been taken in November and rooted with 84% efficiency.

ADDITIONAL NOTES: This species has been and will continue to be overplanted. It is one of the nurseryman's biggest moneymakers because of fast growth and ease of culture. Responds well to heavy fertilization and watering. I sometimes theorize that the red fall-colored Silver Maple may, in fact, be hybrids with *Acer rubrum.* They exist in a similar, geographic area and could readily hybridize.

NATIVE HABITAT: Quebec to Florida, to Minnesota, Nebraska, Kansas and Oklahoma. Introduced 1725.

Acer saccharum — Sugar Maple. Often called Rock Maple or Hard Maple.

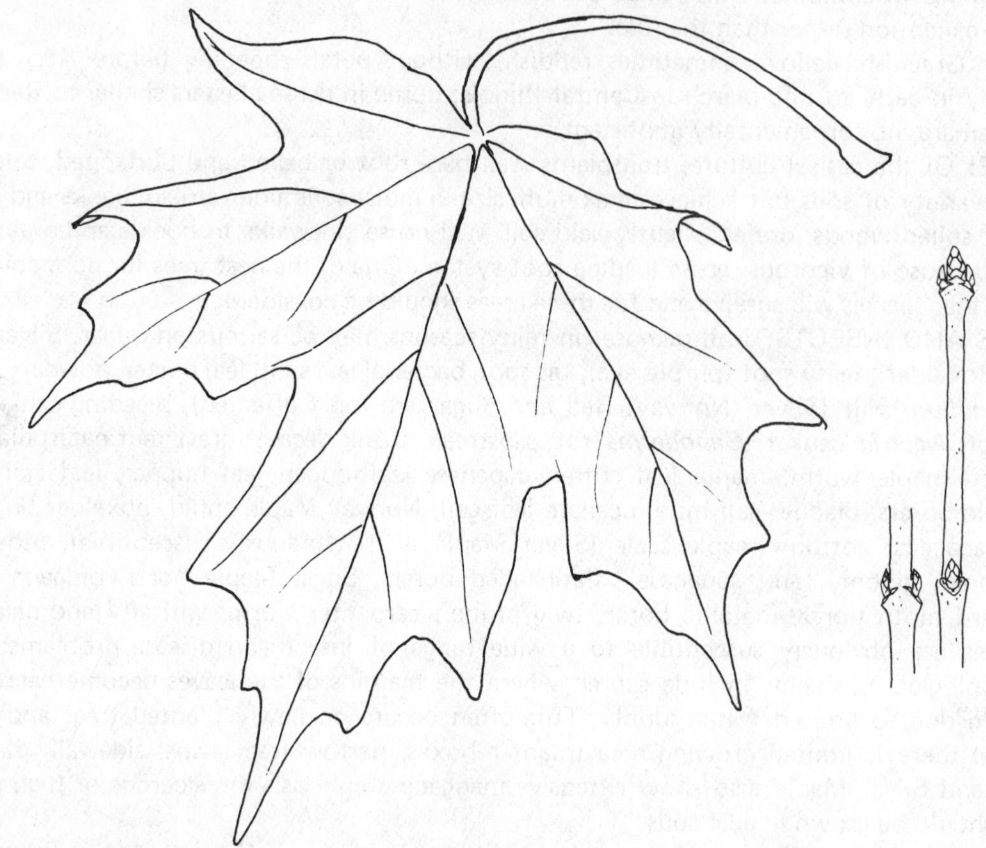

LEAVES: Opposite, simple, 3-6" across, 3-5 lobed, pointed, slightly coarsely toothed with narrow and deep sinuses. Lighter green than Black Maple and not as pubescent.

BUDS: Terminal-imbricate, long and sharp pointed, gray-brown, glabrous or hairy at apex. Axillary buds 1/2 as long as terminal. Hairs are found at upper edge of leaf scar and are brown in color.

STEM: Brown, often lustrous, lenticels are small and not as conspicuous as those of Black Maple.

SIZE: For the Midwestern states a landscape size of 60-75' could be attained; potential to 100-120' in height. The spread is variable but usually about 2/3's the height although some specimens show a rounded character.

HARDINESS: Zone 3.

HABIT: Upright-oval to rounded. Usually quite dense in foliage.

RATE: Slow, possibly medium in youth. The size of one recorded specimen was 23' in 28 years and 62' in 128 years. Obviously this indicates that Sugar Maple is of slow growth, however, has grown 23' high and 23' wide in ten years in Oregon tests.

TEXTURE: Medium in leaf and winter. I have seen delicately branched specimens of a distinct upright-oval character which appear fine in winter character.

LEAF COLOR: Usually a medium to dark green in summer (not as dark as Norway or Black Maple); changing to brilliant yellow, burnt orange and limited red tones in autumn. There is great variation in fall color among members of this species. The New England type seems to show more orange and red than the southern Indiana, Ohio and Illinois group which develops a beautiful golden yellow.

FLOWERS: Greenish yellow, each flower about 1/5-1/4" long; early April before the leaves; borne in pendulous corymbs. Attractive in a subtle way.

FRUIT: Samara, maturing in September.

CULTURE: Transplant balled and burlapped, prefers well-drained, moderately moist, fertile soil, pH—no preference although a slightly acid soil seems to result in greater growth, does not perform well in tight situations such as planter boxes, small tree lawns or other restricted growing areas. Probably not extremely air pollution tolerant; tolerates some shade and is often seen on the forest floor under a canopy of leaves gradually developing and assuming its place in the climax forest.

DISEASES AND INSECTS: Leaf scorch (a physiological disorder) can be a serious problem; *Verticillium* wilt; in the early sixties many New England Sugar Maples were declining or dieing and the cause was unknown. This "Maple Decline" was attributed to drought conditions which persisted in the fifties and affected the overall vigor of the trees and made them more susceptible to insect and disease attacks. Apparently, the problem has subsided for the noticeable decline has ceased.

LANDSCAPE VALUE: One of the best of the larger shade and lawn trees. Excellent for lawn, park, golf course, possibly as street tree where tree lawns are extensive. Definitely not for crowded and polluted conditions.

CULTIVARS:

var. *conicum* – Dense, conical habit.

'Columnare' – Compact and narrow upright 40′ by 12′.

('Newton Sentry')

'Monumentale' – Slender, ascending form, no central leader (50′). Very narrow in youth, gradually widening with maturity.

('Temples Upright')

'Globosum' – Dense, rounded form to 10′ in height.

'Sweet Shadow' – Interesting dark green leaves with deeply cut lobes. Light airy texture.

'Green Mountain' – Upright oval crown, dark green foliage, scarlet in the fall, a supposed hybrid of *A. saccharum* x *A. nigrum,* quite heat tolerant and performs better than species in dry, restricted growing areas, 7.2′ high and 5′ wide after 4 years, early defoliator. Does not fall color well in Midwest, according to Wandell's Nursery. Yellow is the predominant color.

PROPAGATION: Seed, stratify in moist peat at 36-41°F for 60 to 90 days. Cuttings collected in early June and treated with Hormodin #1 rooted 57%.

RELATED SPECIES:

Acer nigrum – Black Maple

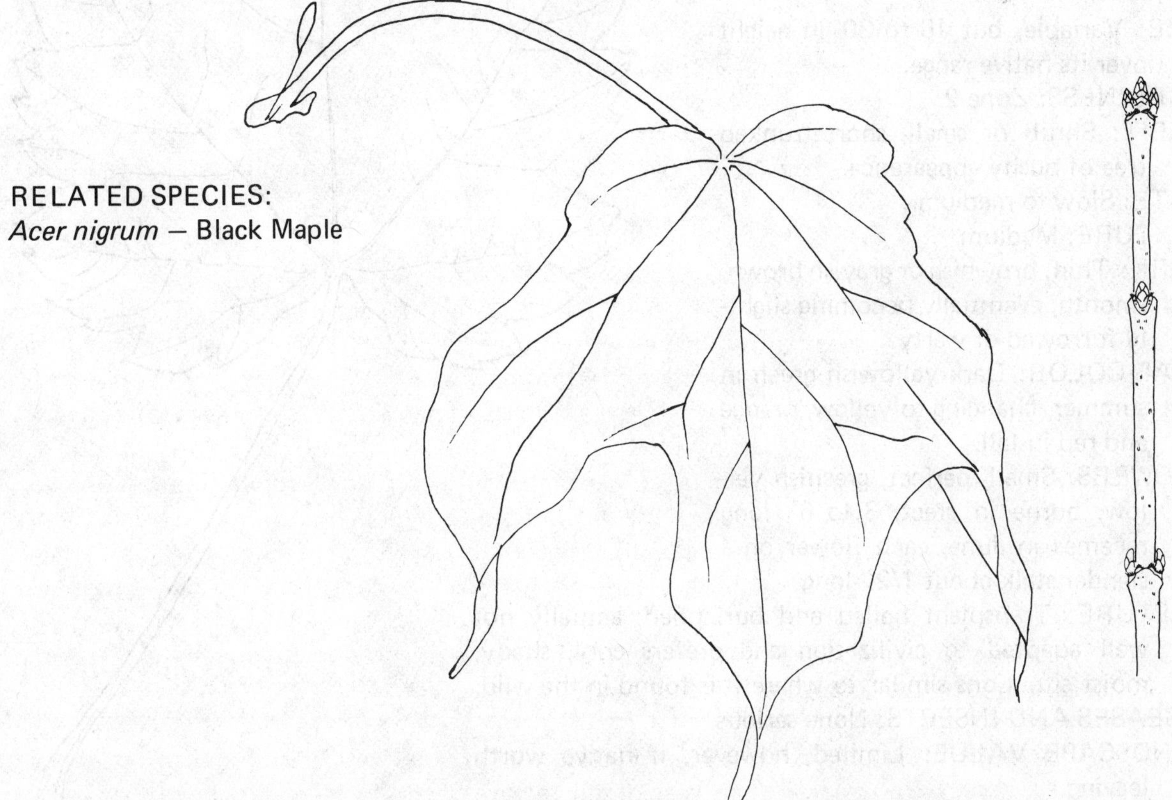

LEAVES: Opposite, simple, 3-6" wide, 3-5 lobed, deeply cordate with closed sinus, lobes acute, sides of blade drooping, dull dark green above, yellow green beneath, pubescent. Petioles pubescent, often enlarged at base. Stipules present.
BUD: Imbricate, pubescent, much more so than Sugar Maple, tend to be plumper than Sugar Maple buds and gray-dust-brown in color; 2 axillary buds at terminal, 1/2-3/4 as long as terminal.
STEM: Straw colored with prominent lenticels. Much more so than Sugar Maple.

ADDITIONAL NOTES: Outstanding native tree, unexcelled for fall color; sap is boiled down to make maple syrup; a trip to a sugar camp in February or March is a unique experience.
NATIVE HABITAT: Eastern Canada to Georgia, Alabama, Mississippi and Texas.

Acer spicatum — Mountain Maple, also called Moosewood, Whistle-wood, and Goosefoot Maple.

LEAVES: Opposite, simple, 3-lobed or sometimes slightly 5-lobed, 2 to 5" long, cordate, lobes ovate, acuminate, coarsely and irregularly serrate, dark yellowish green and smooth above, paler beneath and covered with a short grayish down.
BUDS: Usually less than 1/4" long, stalked, pointed, red but dull with minute, appressed, grayish hairs, 2 visible scales (valvate).
STEM: Young stems grayish pubescent, developing purplish red, or often greenish on one side, minutely pubescent with short, appressed, grayish hairs, particularly about the nodes and toward the apex. Leaf scars are narrowly crescent shaped.

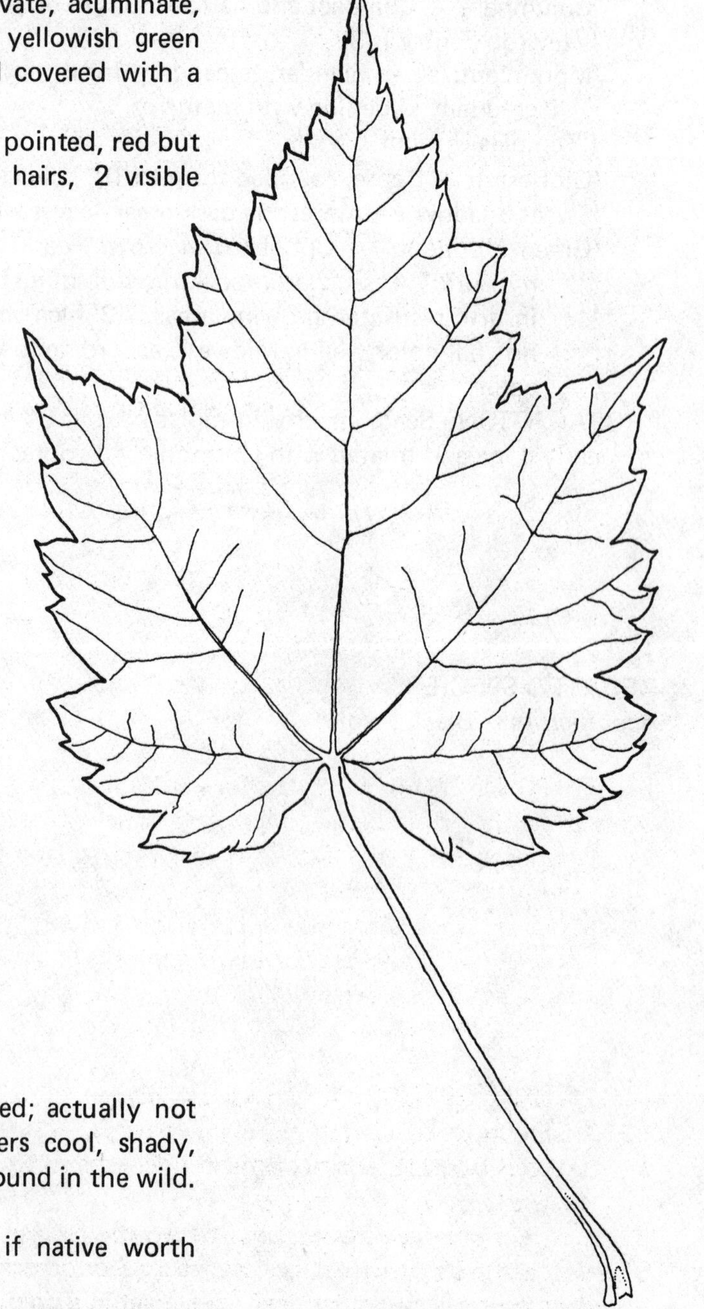

SIZE: Variable, but 10 to 30' in height over its native range.
HARDINESS: Zone 2.
HABIT: Shrub or small, short trunked tree of bushy appearance.
RATE: Slow to medium.
TEXTURE: Medium.
BARK: Thin, brownish or grayish brown, smooth, eventually becoming slightly furrowed or warty.
LEAF COLOR: Dark yellowish green in summer, changing to yellow, orange and red in fall.
FLOWERS: Small, perfect, greenish yellow, borne in erect, 3 to 6" long racemes in June, each flower on a slender stalk about 1/2" long.
CULTURE: Transplant balled and burlapped; actually not well adapted to civilization and prefers cool, shady, moist situations similar to where it is found in the wild.
DISEASES AND INSECTS: None serious.
LANDSCAPE VALUE: Limited, however, if native worth leaving.

PROPAGATION: Seed requires 90 to 120 days at 41°F.
NATIVE HABITAT: Labrador to Saskatchewan, south to Northern Georgia and Iowa. Introduced 1750.

Acer tataricum — Tatarian Maple

LEAVES: Opposite, simple, 2-4" long, usually unlobed, irregularly double serrate. Often pubescent when young on veins beneath.
BUDS: Imbricate, small, 1/8 to 1/4" long, brown-black, often hairy.
STEM: Slender, glabrous, brown, lenticelled.

SIZE: 15 to 20' in height with a comparable spread, can grow to 30' in height.
HARDINESS: Zone 4.
HABIT: A large multi-stemmed shrub of bushy habit or a small, rounded to wide spreading tree.
RATE: Slow to medium.
TEXTURE: Medium in foliage and in winter habit.
LEAF COLOR: Medium to dark green in summer; yellow, red, and reddish brown in fall.
FLOWERS: Greenish white; May; borne in 2 to 3" long panicles; not overwhelmingly ornamental but a definite asset in the landscape.
FRUIT: Samara, red—variable in intensity of color; August, effective 3 or more weeks before turning brown.
CULTURE: Transplant balled and burlapped, tolerant of adverse conditions including drought.
DISEASES AND INSECTS: None particularly serious.
LANDSCAPE VALUE: Handsome small specimen tree for the limited residential landscape, street tree use, perhaps planter boxes, groupings. Could be used more than is currently being practiced. Michigan State and Ohio State campuses have handsome specimens.
CULTIVARS:
'Rubrum' — Leaves color a blood red in the fall.
PROPAGATION: Seed, 41°F for 90 to 180 days.
ADDITIONAL NOTES: Nice small tree with landscape attributes similar to *Acer ginnala.*
NATIVE HABITAT: Southeast Europe, Western Asia. Introduced 1759.

Acer triflorum — Threeflower Maple

Acer triflorum, Threeflower Maple, is closely allied to *A. nikoense* but differs by virtue of the smaller leaflets, the fact that the wings of the fruit diverge at a much smaller angle, and the bark which is ash-brown, loose, and vertically fissured. The fall color is reported as brilliant crimson. The Minnesota Landscape Arboretum has a small tree and the most noticeable ornamental feature is the bark. The tree will grow 15 to 25' high. Manchuria, Korea. Introduced 1923. Zone 5, possibly 4.

Acer truncatum — Purpleblow Maple

LEAVES: Opposite, simple, deeply 5-lobed, 2 1/2 to 4" across, truncate at base, lobes acuminate, setosely pointed, entire or the middle lobe sometimes 3-lobed; very lustrous dark green summer foliage.
BUDS: Light brown, glabrate, about 4 exposed scales, end bud present.
STEM: Leaf-scars U-shaped, bundle traces 3 or occasionally 5 or 7 or 9; twigs slender, 1/8" diameter, leaf scars not glandular, leaf scars meet in a point.

SIZE: 20 to 25′ in height with a spread slightly less than or equal to height.
HARDINESS: Zone 5.
HABIT: Small, rounded-headed tree of neat outline with a regular branching pattern.
RATE: Slow.
TEXTURE: Medium in all seasons.
STEMS: Often tinged with purple when young; older branches assuming a gray-brown color.
LEAF COLOR: Reddish purple when emerging (very beautiful) gradually changing to dark glossy green in summer. Fall color, as observed at the National Arboretum, was an excellent combination of yellow-orange-red.
FLOWERS: Greenish yellow, 1/3 to 1/2″ diameter, each on a slender stalk 1/2″ long, borne in erect branching, 3″ diameter corymbs in May.
FRUIT: Samara.
CULTURE: Apparently a relatively hardy tree which thrives under conditions similar to those required for *Acer griseum.* I have seen several specimens and they appeared vigorous and healthy under Midwestern conditions.
DISEASES AND INSECTS: None particularly serious.
LANDSCAPE VALUE: A very lovely small maple with potential for street or residential areas.
PROPAGATION: Apparently similar to *Acer ginnala* in seed dormancy and requires stratification.
NATIVE HABITAT: Northern China. Introduced 1881.

Actinidia arguta — Bower Actinidia

FAMILY: Actinidiaceae
LEAVES: Alternate, simple, broad-ovate to elliptic, 3 to 5″ long, abruptly acuminate, rounded to subcordate at base, rarely cuneate, setosely and sharply serrate, green beneath and usually setose on midrib; petiole 1 2/5 to 3″ long, sometimes setose.
BUDS: Small, concealed in the thickened cortex above the leaf scar, the end bud lacking.
STEM: Brownish, heavily lenticelled (vertical); pith—brown, lamellate, leaf scars raised with single bundle trace (looks like an eyeball), glabrous.

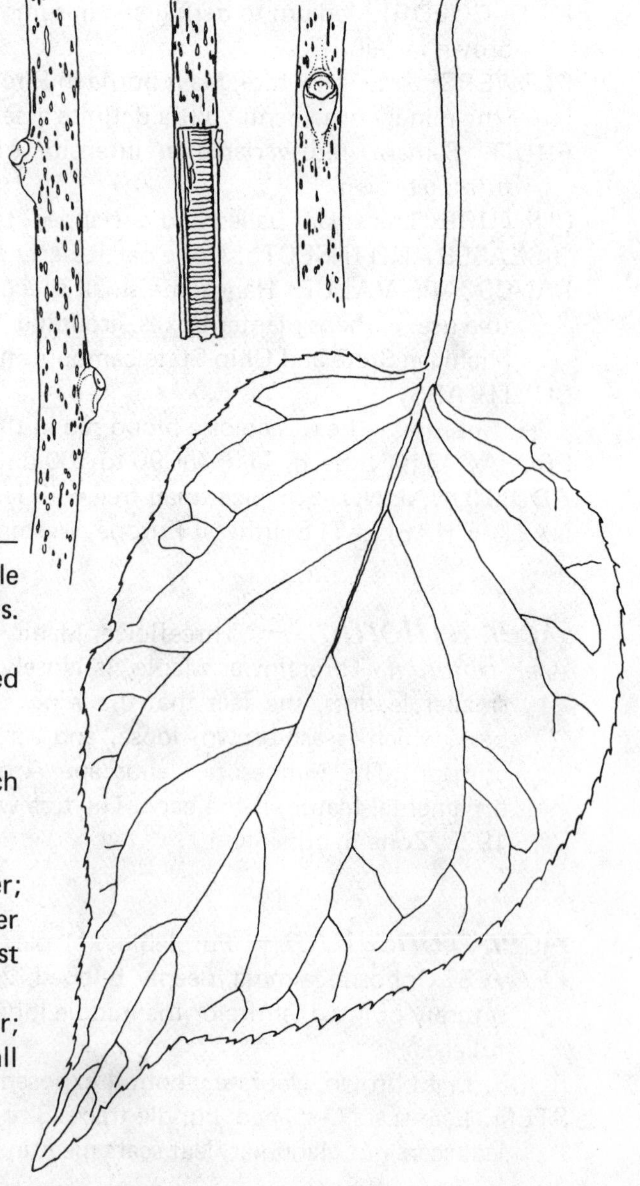

SIZE: 25 to 30′ in height but seems to be limited only by the structure to which it is attached.
HARDINESS: Zone 4.
HABIT: Vigorous, high climbing, twining vine which requires support.
RATE: Fast, can grow 20′ in 2 to 3 years time.
TEXTURE: Medium in leaf; medium-coarse in winter; actually the tangled, jumbled thicket of winter stems would be considered coarse by most observers.
LEAF COLOR: Lustrous dark green in summer; petioles often with slightly reddish tinge; fall coloration is yellowish green.

FLOWERS: Usually polygamo-dioecious, whitish or greenish white, 3 or more together, about 4/5" across, petals brownish at base; borne in June-July; seldom seen because of small size and the fact they are hidden by the foliage; slightly fragrant.

FRUIT: Berry, greenish yellow, ellipsoidal, about 1" long, edible; but not often seen in cultivation; effective September-October.

CULTURE: Like most rampant vines easy to transplant; this is probably the most vigorous of the *Actinidia* species; will tolerate any type soil but best sited in infertile soil to reduce rapid growth; full sun or partial shade; needs considerable pruning and this can be accomplished about anytime of year.

DISEASES AND INSECTS: None serious.

LANDSCAPE VALUE: Good vine for a quick cover but can rapidly overgrow its boundaries. The foliage is excellent and for problem areas where few other vines will grow *Actinidia arguta* could be used.

PROPAGATION: All species can be propagated by seed. Stratification for 3 months at 41°F in a moist medium is recommended, but *A. kolomikta* has shown a double dormancy and requires a warm plus cold stratification. Softwood and hardwood cuttings root readily.

RELATED SPECIES:

Actinidia kolomikta, Kolomikta Actinidia, is a deciduous twining vine growing 15 to 20' and more. The foliage is purplish when young, developing particularly on the male plant a white to pink blotch at the apex which may extend to the middle and beyond. The leaves are about 5" long and the variegated foliage is therefore quite showy. Supposedly this variegation is more colorful when the plant is grown on calcareous soils. The flowers are white, fragrant, 3/5" across, and the fruit is an edible, greenish yellow, 1" long berry. Native from Northeastern Asia to Japan and Central and Western China. Introduced about 1855. Zone 4.

Actinidia polygama, Silver-vine, is probably the weakest grower of the *Actinidia* group. It may grow 15' but is definitely not as vigorous as *A. arguta.* The 3 to 5" long leaves of staminate plants are marked with a silver-white to yellowish color. Cats apparently are attracted to this plant and will maul the foliage. The leaves of female plants are a duller green than *A. arguta.* The flowers are white, 3/5" across, fragrant, June-July; white; the fruit is an edible 1" long, greenish yellow berry of little ornamental significance. Native to Manchuria, Japan and Central China. Introduced 1861. Zone 4.

ADDITIONAL NOTES: An interesting group of vines but seldom used in modern landscaping. Their adaptability to difficult situations should make them more popular. The difference in foliage colors between male and female plants is a rarity among dioecious plants.

NATIVE HABITAT: Japan, Korea, Manchuria. Cultivated 1874.

Aesculus glabra — Ohio Buckeye, also called Fetid Buckeye.

FAMILY: Hippocastanaceae

LEAVES: Opposite, palmately compound, 5 leaflets, rarely 7, elliptic to obovate, 3 to 5" long, acuminate, cuneate, finely serrate, pubescent beneath, when young, nearly glabrous at maturity. Petioles present—approximately 1" long.

BUD: Imbricate, ovoid, sessile, terminal—2/3" long, brown, with prominently keeled scales, hairy on margins, lateral buds smaller.

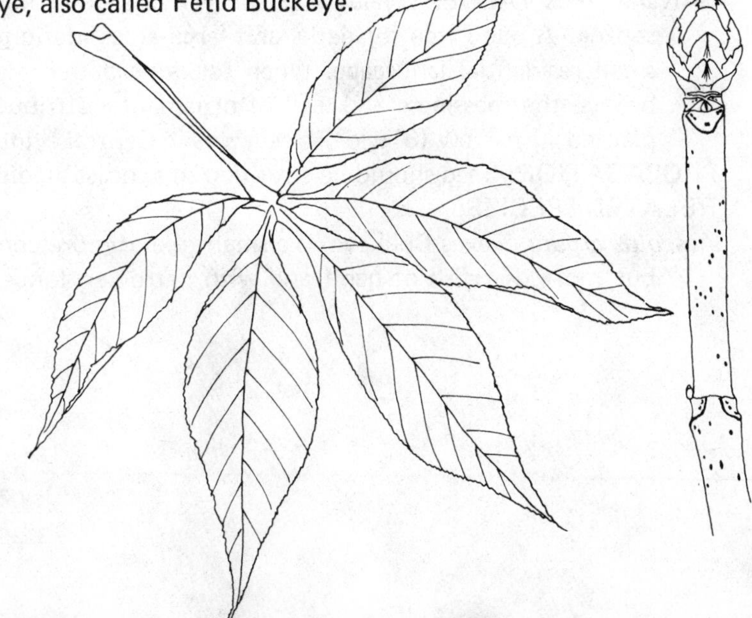

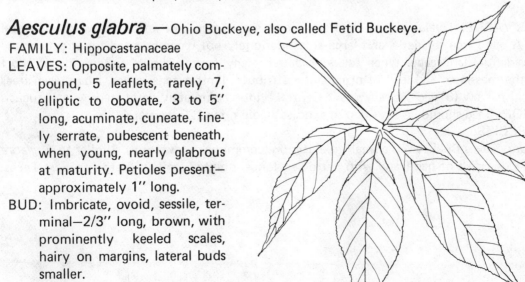

STEM: Stout, pubescent at first becoming glabrous and red-brown to ash-gray with disagreeable odor when bruised.

BARK: Ashy gray, thick, deeply fissured and plated.

SIZE: Usually in the range of 20 to 40′ in height with a similar spread although can grow to 80′. The largest specimen I have seen is located on the campus of Wabash College, Crawfordsville, Indiana. However, the tree is in poor condition.

HARDINESS: Zone 3.

HABIT: Rounded to broad-rounded in outline, usually low branched with the branches bending down toward the ground and then arching back up at the ends. Actually quite handsome in foliage, very dense and therefore difficult to grow grass under.

RATE: Medium, 7 to 10′ over a 6 to 8 year period.

TEXTURE: Medium-coarse in leaf; coarse in winter.

BARK: Ashy-gray, rather corky-warty, and on the older trunks is much furrowed and scaly.

LEAF COLOR: Bright green when unfolding (very handsome); one of the first trees to leaf out and also one of the first to defoliate in fall, changing to dark green in summer; fall color is often yellow but at times develops a brilliant orange-red to reddish brown.

FLOWERS: Perfect, greenish yellow, 1″ long, borne in early to mid May in 4 to 7″ long by 2 to 3″ wide terminal panicles. Not overwhelming but handsome when viewed close-up.

FRUIT: Capsule, light brown, dehiscent, 1 to 2″ long, with a prickly cover similar to Common Horsechestnut but not as pronounced, the seeds (buckeyes) are usually borne solitary. No childhood is complete without a pocketful of buckeyes! The seeds are poisonous but nonetheless often eaten by hungry squirrels.

CULTURE: Transplant balled and burlapped into moist, deep, well-drained, slightly acid soil; tends to develop leaf scorch and prematurely drop leaves in hot, droughty situations; found native in bottomlands along banks of rivers and creeks; full sun or partial shade; prune in early spring.

DISEASES AND INSECTS: Leaf blotch is very serious in Central Illinois on this species and *A. hippocastanum.* The leaves develop discolored spots which gradually change to brown. Powdery mildew is also a problem and some trees appear gray in color. Other problems include leaf spot, wood rot, anthracnose, canker, walnut scale, comstock mealybug, white-marked tussock moth, Japanese beetle, bagworm, flat-headed borer. If a problem occurs, and it is likely to be on the two species mentioned above, consult your extension agent for proper diagnosis and control measures. Another significant problem is leaf scorch which is physiological in nature. The margins of leaves become brown and curled. Trees located in tight planting areas are especially susceptible although it has been noted as occurring on selected trees even in moist years.

LANDSCAPE VALUE: I value this species as a good native tree best left in the wild or natural setting. A good tree for parks and large areas, definitely not recommended for streets or the small residential landscape. When selecting a tree many factors should be considered and I believe the messiness and lack of ornamental attributes limit extensive use. I have seen trees planted in narrow (3′ wide) tree lawns in Central Illinois completely defoliated by late August.

PROPAGATION: Seed should be stratified in a moist medium for 120 days at 41°F.

RELATED SPECIES:

Aesculus arguta, Texas Buckeye, is a small tree or more commonly a low shrub. Similar to *A. glabra* but more dwarfish of habit and with narrower, longer-pointed leaflets. Native to East Texas.

Aesculus octandra (A. flava), Yellow Buckeye, can reach 40 to 60′ in height with a spread of 2/3's the height; distinctly upright-oval in habit; similar in foliage to Ohio Buckeye but distinguished by absence of a fetid odor and the smooth, leathery, somewhat pear-shaped capsule. Very handsome buckeye, native from Pennsylvania to Georgia and Southern Illinois. Introduced 1764. Zone 3.

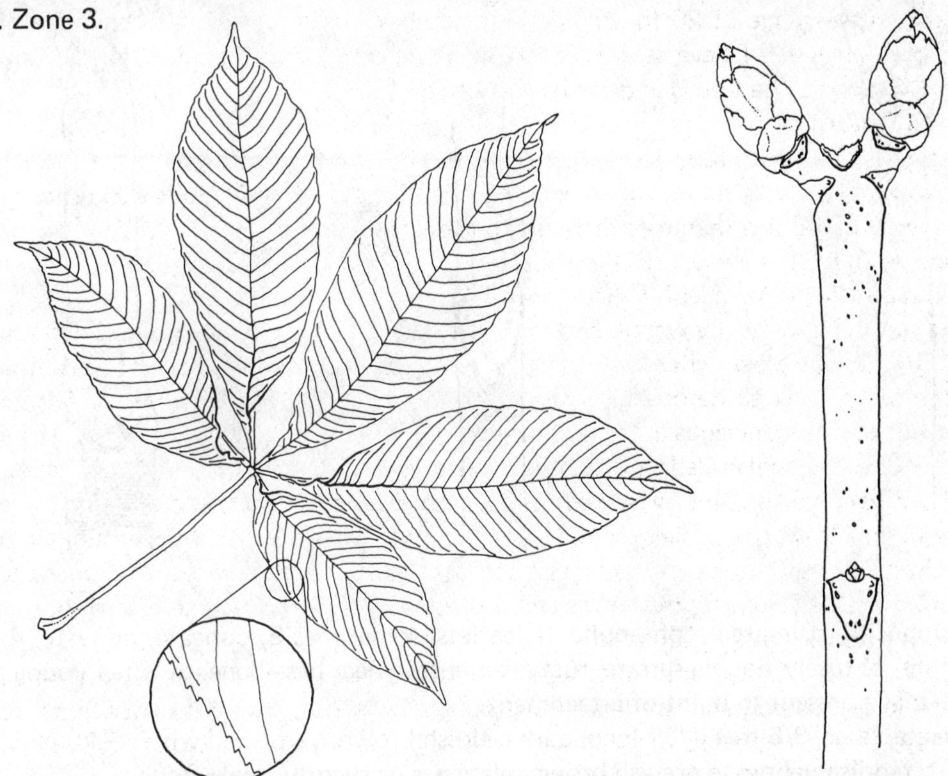

NATIVE HABITAT: Pennsylvania to Nebraska, Kansas and Alabama. Cultivated 1809.

Aesculus hippocastanum — Common Horsechestnut

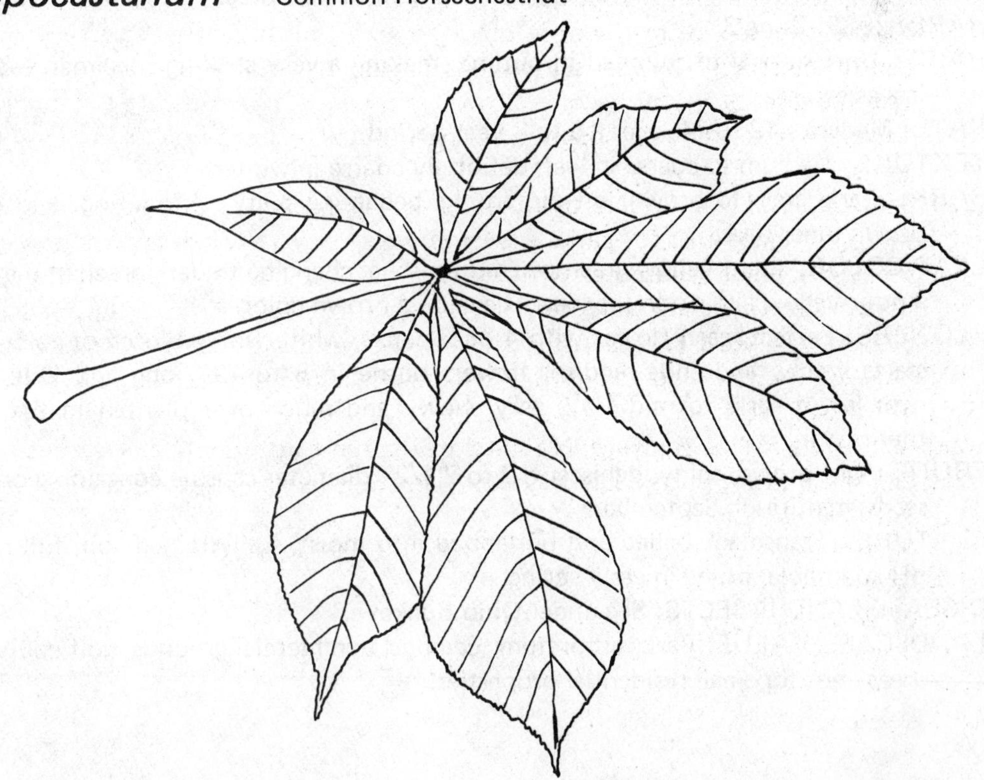

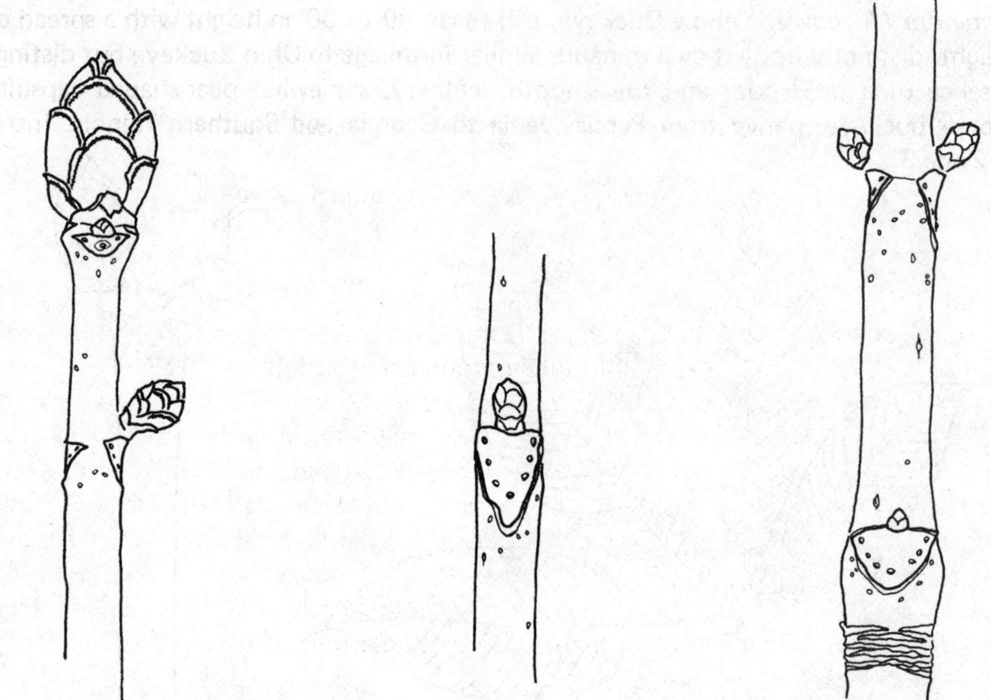

LEAVES: Opposite, palmately compound, 7 leaflets, sometimes 5, cuneate, obovate, 4-10" long, acuminate, obtusely double serrate, rusty tomentose near base beneath when young. Petiolules absent—blade present to point of attachment.

BUD: Imbricate, large, 3/5 to 1 1/5" long, dark reddish brown, varnished with sticky gum.

STEM: Stout, reddish yellow to grayish brown, glabrous or slightly finely-downy.

BARK: Dark gray to brown becoming shallowly fissured into irregular plate-like scales resembling bark of apple trees.

SIZE: 50 to 75' in height, will usually develop a 40 to 70' spread, can grow to 100' or larger.

HARDINESS: Zone 3.

HABIT: Upright-oval to rounded in outline, making a very striking specimen especially as the new leaves emerge.

RATE: Medium, 12 to 14' over a 6 to 8 year period.

TEXTURE: Medium to coarse in leaf; definitely coarse in winter.

BARK: Dark gray to brown, on old trunks becoming platy, exfoliating, and exposing orangish brown inner bark.

LEAF COLOR: Light yellow green when unfolding, changing to dark green at maturity; fall color is a poor yellow and often the leaves develop a brown color.

FLOWERS: Perfect, each flower with 4 or 5 petals, white with a blotch of color at the base which starts yellow and ends reddish, flowers borne in 5 to 12" long and 2 to 5" wide terminal panicles in early to mid May; very showy and much over planted in the Eastern states for that reason.

FRUIT: Light brown, spiny, dehiscent, 2 to 2 1/2" diameter capsule containing one, sometimes two seeds; matures in September.

CULTURE: Transplant balled and burlapped into moist, well-drained soil; full sun or light shade; pH adaptable; prune in early spring.

DISEASES AND INSECTS: See under Ohio Buckeye.

LANDSCAPE VALUE: Park, arboretum, campus, commercial grounds, golf courses and other large areas—not for small residential properties.

CULTIVARS:

'Baumanni' — Double white flowers, flowers last longer than the type, no fruits are produced, the best of the garden forms.

'Pyramidalis' — Sometimes referred to as 'Fastigiata', branches arise at 45° angle to the main stem.

There are other cultivars with yellow to white leaf variations as well as compact and weeping types.

PROPAGATION: Seed, 41°F for 120 days in moist medium.

RELATED SPECIES:

Aesculus x carnea, Red Horsechestnut, resulted from a cross between *A. pavia* x *A. hippocastanum.* Size is 30 to 40' in height with a similar spread, rounded in outline; extremely dark green leaves; flowers vary from flesh colored to deep red and are borne in 4 1/2 to 8" panicles in early to mid May; fruit is globose, slightly prickly, 1 1/2" diameter; originated as a chance seedling before 1818; the plant is an octoploid with 80 chromosomes and is considered a tetraploid species (according to Hui Lin Li). Plants grown from seed come relatively true-to-type with the flower colors showing different degrees of red. W.J. Bean in *Trees and Shrubs Hardy in the British Isles Vol. I.* tells a somewhat different story. He noted that the original *A. x carnea* must have been a diploid, with 40 chromosomes, as in the parents. At some stage in the history of the clone, spontaneous doubling of the chromosomes must have taken place, thus the 80 chromosome complement. Cultivars include:

'Briotii' — Larger flowers, bright scarlet color, panicle 10" long, dense and symmetrical.

'Pendula' — Type with weeping branches.

Aesculus x plantierensis, is the result of a backcross of *A. x carnea* x *A. hippocastanum.* Flowers are a soft pink or red with a yellow throat, panicles to 12" long. The tree does not set fruit and the fact that it is a triploid explains this sterility.

NATIVE HABITAT: Greece and Albania in the mountainous, uninhabited wilds. Introduced 1576.

Aesculus parviflora — Bottlebrush Buckeye

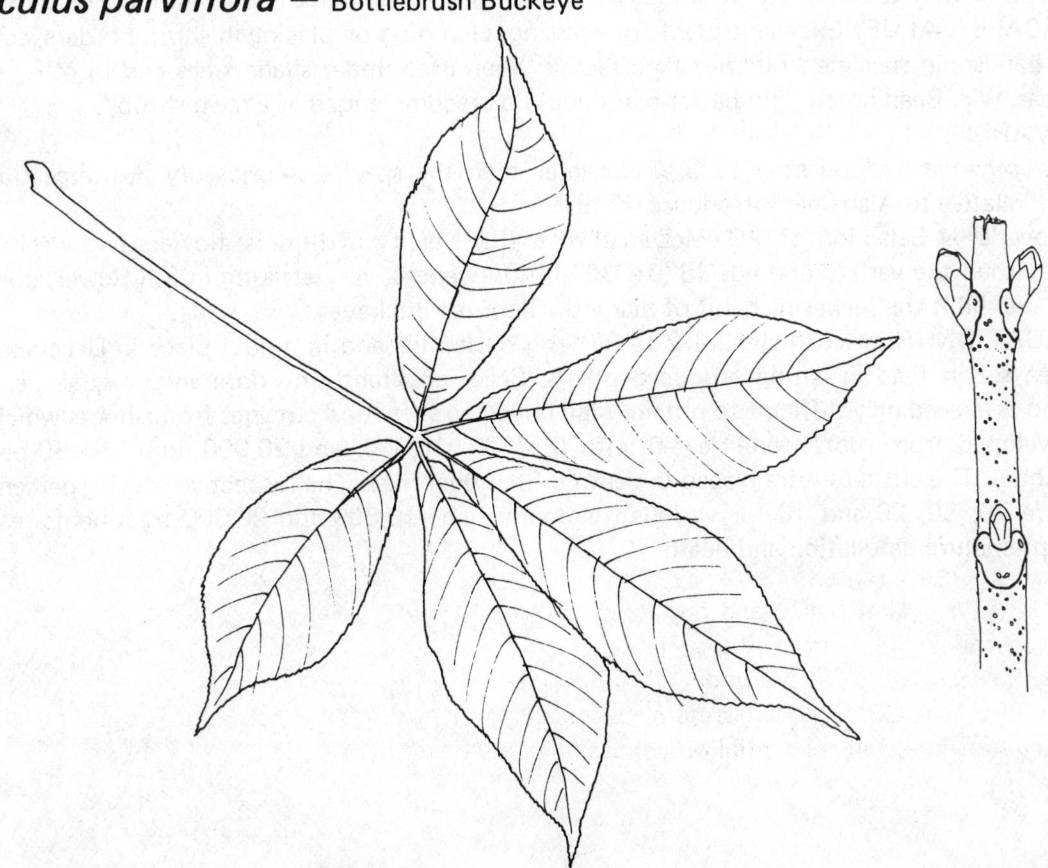

LEAVES: Opposite, palmately compound, 5-7 leaflets, nearly sessile, elliptic to oblong-obovate, 3 to 8" long, acuminate, crenate-serrulate, grayish, pubescent beneath.

BUD: Weakly imbricate, usually with 4 exposed scales, terminals—1/5" long, laterals minute, scales minutely pubescent and glaucous, gray-brown in color.

STEM: Stout, gray-brown, with raised light brown lenticels, leaf scar half encircling bud, vascular bundle traces forming a face-like image, usually 3 to 6 in number.

SIZE: 8 to 12' in height, spreading to 8 to 15'. I have seen a large specimen at the Arnold Arboretum about 15 to 18' tall.

HARDINESS: Zone 4.

HABIT: Wide-spreading, suckering, multi-stemmed shrub with many upright, slender branches. Often with an irregular, spreading almost stratified appearance, excellent form and texture in the branching structure.

RATE: Slow on old wood but shoots which develop from the base will grow 2 to 4' in a single season.

TEXTURE: Medium-coarse in summer and winter.

LEAF COLOR: Medium to dark green in summer, changing to yellow-green in fall. Foliage is little troubled by diseases which afflict *A. glabra* and *A. hippocastanum.*

FLOWER: Perfect, white with 4 petals, 1/2" long, stamens thread-like and pinkish white, standing out an inch from the petals, anthers red; produced in early July to late July in cylindrical 8 to 12" long panicles, 2 to 4" wide. Outstanding in flower; there are few summer flowering plants which can rival this species.

FRUIT: Dehiscent, 1 to 1 1/2" diameter capsule, light brown, rarely produced under Central Illinois conditions.

CULTURE: Transplant balled and burlapped or from a container in early spring into a moist, well-drained soil that has been adequately prepared with organic matter, prefers acid soil but is adaptable; full sun or partial shade, in fact, seems to proliferate in shade. Pruning is seldom necessary.

DISEASES AND INSECTS: None serious compared to Ohio Buckeye and Common Horsechestnut.

LANDSCAPE VALUE: Excellent plant for massing, clumping or placing in shrub borders; actually a handsome specimen plant; very effective when used under shade trees and in other shady areas. W.J. Bean noted, "no better plant could be recommended as a lawn shrub".

CULTIVARS:

var. *serotina* – Flowers 2 to 3 weeks later than the species, supposedly has large flowers. Native to Alabama. Introduced 1919.

'Roger's' – Selection of J.C. McDaniel of the University of Illinois; flowers two weeks later than the variety and has 18" to 30" inflorescences, very striking in full flower; does not exhibit the suckering habit of many Bottlebrush Buckeyes.

PROPAGATION: Root cuttings, 2 1/2 to 3" long buried in sand in a cool place in December and then set in field in spring produced plants. Seed—apparently no dormancy requirement but seed is exceedingly difficult to obtain. May collected softwood cuttings from shoots which had developed from roots were treated with 0, 1000, 10,000, and 20,000 ppm IBA/50 percent alcohol. The cuttings were placed in peat:perlite under mist. The respective rooting percentages were 70, 80, 20 and 10 for various treatments. The 10,000 and 20,000 treatments resulted in premature defoliation and death.

RELATED SPECIES:
Aesculus pavia – Red Buckeye

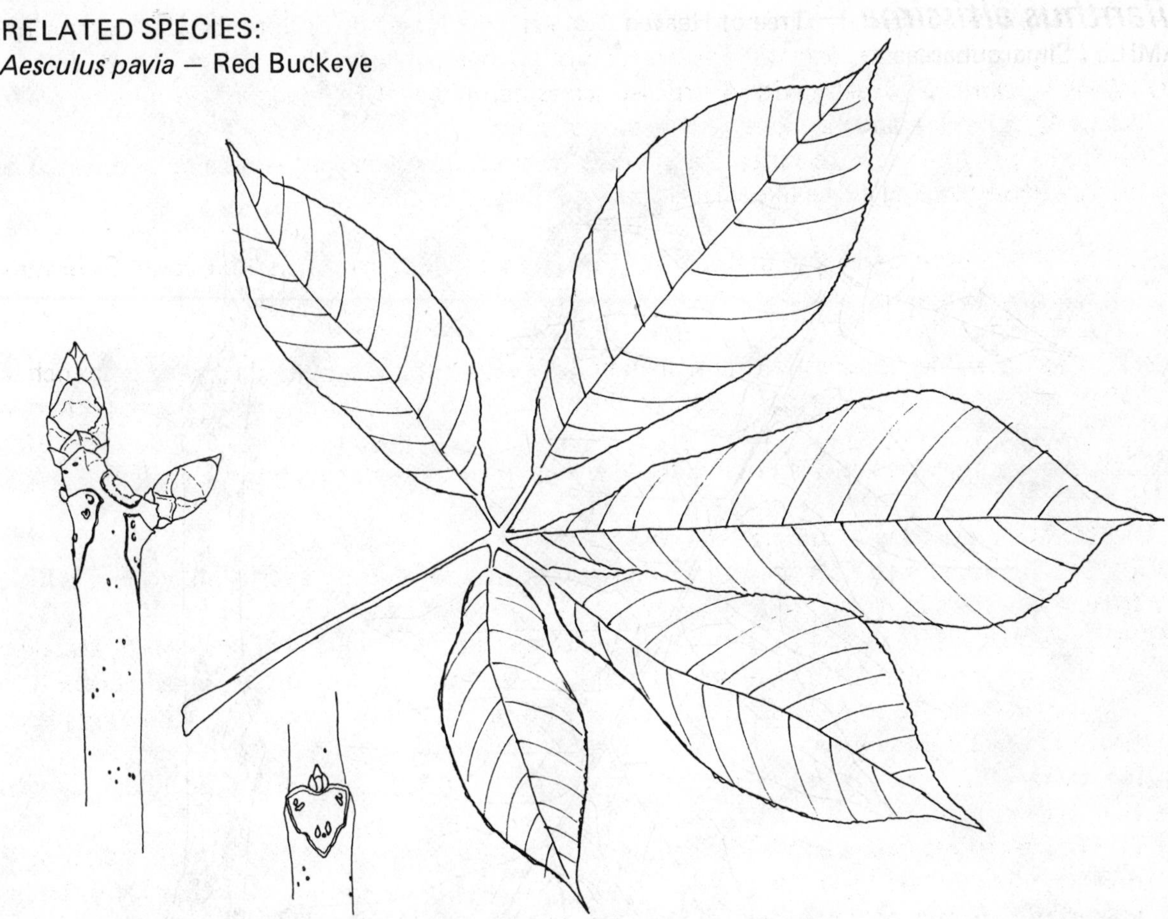

LEAVES: Opposite, palmately compound, 5 leaflets, short stalked, oblong-obovate or narrow elliptic, 3 to 6" long, acuminate, irregularly and often double serrate, glabrous or slightly pubescent beneath.

BUD: Imbricate, terminal—large, 1/3" long, brownish, glabrous, laterals—much smaller than terminal.

STEM: Stout, olive-brown in color with raised light brown lenticels, leaf scars triangular with "V" arrangement of leaf traces.

Aesculus pavia, Red Buckeye, is a small, clump forming, round-topped shrub or small tree reaching 10 to 20' in height under cultivation and spreading that much or more; can grow to 30 to 36' in the wild; each flower 1 1/2" long, mid to late May, very handsome small tree in flower; does not show significant blotch although mildew can be a problem. Cultivars include:

'Atrosanguinea' – Flowers dark red.

'Humilis' – Low, sometimes prostrate shrub, with red flowers in small panicles. Cultivated 1826.

Another species, *A. discolor,* is similar to *A. pavia* but differs in the whitish pubescence on the lower leaf surface, hence, the common name Woolly Buckeye; native from Georgia to Missouri and Texas. Introduced 1812. Zone 5. The Red Buckeye is native from Virginia to Florida and Louisiana. Introduced 1711.

ADDITIONAL NOTES: The small buckeyes are worthwhile additions to any garden and especially the small residential landscape where space is always at a premium. Their greater disease resistance coupled with outstanding floral traits places them at the top of the *Aesculus* group.

NATIVE HABITAT: South Carolina to Alabama and Florida. Introduced 1785.

Ailanthus altissima — Tree of Heaven

FAMILY: Simaroubaceae

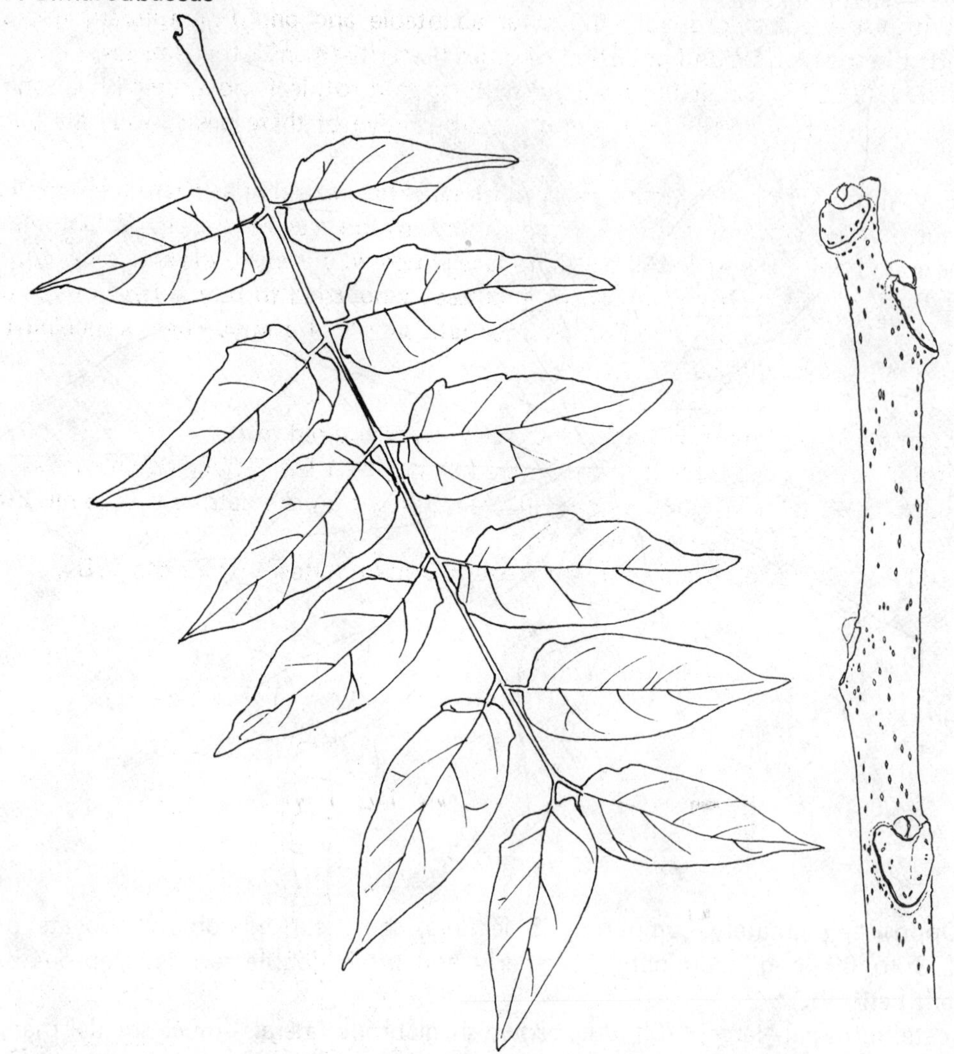

LEAVES: Alternate, pinnately compound, 18-24" long, leaflets—13 to 25, stalked, lance-ovate, 3 to 5" long, usually truncate at base, finely ciliate, with 2 to 4 coarse teeth near base, glabrous and glaucescent.

BUDS: Terminal-absent, lateral buds relatively small, 1/6" or less long, half spherical, reddish brown, downy. Scales—thick, the 2 opposite lateral scales generally alone showing.

STEM: Stout, yellowish to reddish brown covered with very short fine velvety down, or smooth, rather rank-smelling when crushed, older stems often shedding the down in the form of a thin skin and exposing very fine light longitudinal striations. Pith—wide, light brown.

SIZE: 40 to 60' in height with an extremely variable spread, but often 2/3's to equal the height.

HARDINESS: Zone 4.

HABIT: Upright, spreading, open and coarse with large clubby branches.

RATE: Fast, 3 to 5' and more in a single growing season.

TEXTURE: Coarse throughout the year.

BARK: Grayish, slightly roughened with fine light colored longitudinal streaks in striking contrast to the darker background.

LEAF COLOR: Dark green in summer; no fall color.

FLOWERS: Dioecious, although some trees with both sexes; yellow-green, borne in 8 to 16" long panicles in early to mid-June; male flowers of vile odor; females odorless.

FRUIT: Samara, yellow green to orange red, effective in late summer, finally changing to brown and persisting through the winter.

CULTURE: Without a doubt probably the most adaptable and pollution tolerant tree available; withstands the soot, grime and pollution of cities better than any other species.

DISEASES AND INSECTS: Verticillium wilt, shoestring root rot, leaf spots, twig blight and cankers have been reported. Verticillium is the most destructive of these pests; none are particularly serious.

LANDSCAPE VALUE: For most landscape conditions it has *no* value as there are too many trees of superior quality. However for impossible conditions this tree has a place. Selections could be made for good habit, strong wood, better foliage which would make the tree more satisfactory. I once talked with a highway landscape architect who tried to buy *Ailanthus* for use along polluted highways but could not find an adequate supply. I always knew a specialist growing *Ailanthus* could make money!

CULTIVARS:

'Erythrocarpa' – Pistillate type, with dark green leaves and red fruit.

'Pendulifolia' – Branches erect as in the type but the longer leaves hang downward.

PROPAGATION: Seed which I have worked with required no pre-treatment although 60 days in moist medium at 41°F is a recommendation.

NATIVE HABITAT: China, naturalized in the Eastern United States. Introduced 1784.

Akebia quinata — Fiveleaf Akebia

FAMILY: Lardizabalaceae

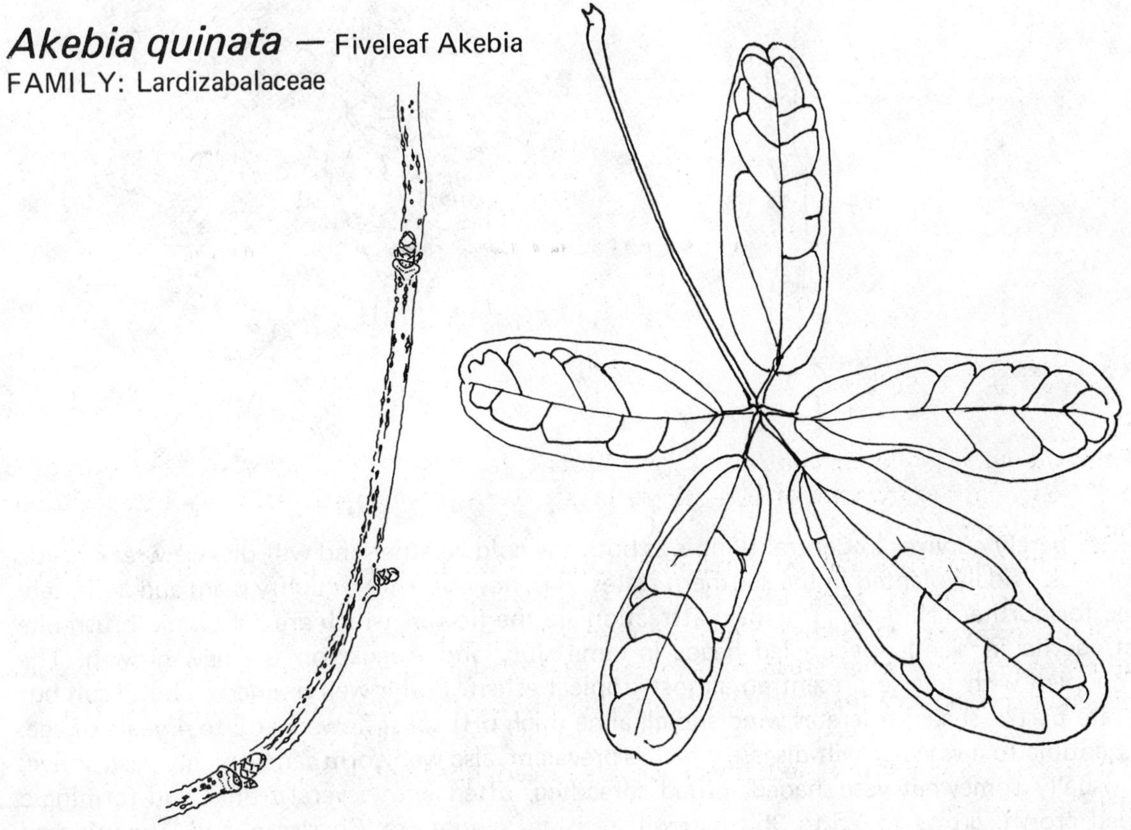

LEAVES: Alternate, palmately compound, 5 leaflets, obovate or elliptic to oblong-obovate, 1 1/5 to 2 2/5" long, emarginate, rounded or broad cuneate at base, glaucous beneath.

BUDS: Imbricate, glabrous, small, sessile, ovate, with 10 to 12 mucronate scales.

STEM: Slender, rounded, leaf scars—with 6 or more traces in a broken ellipse, half elliptic, much raised, green becoming brown, glabrous, heavily lenticelled.

Akebia quinata, Fiveleaf Akebia, is a twining evergreen or deciduous (depends on climate) vine which grows 20 to 40'. The foliage is bluish green in summer and quite attractive. The flowers are polygamo-monoecious, pistillate are chocolate-purple, staminate-rosy purple, both borne in the same pendent axillary raceme, the pistillate at the base and about 1" across, the staminate at the end of the raceme, about 1/5" across; May; flowers are fragrant, and uniquely attractive on close inspection. Fruit is a 2 1/4 to 4" sausage-like pod of purple-violet color, bloomy, ripening in September-October; apparently does not often develop under cultivation; need to hand pollinate; interesting vine and like most vines is extremely adaptable and requires little care. Central China to Japan and Korea. 1845. Zone 4.

Albizia julibrissin — Albizia, also called Silk-tree and Mimosa

FAMILY: Leguminosae

LEAVES: Alternate, bipinnately compound, to 20" long, with 10 to 25 pinnae, each with 40 to 60 leaflets, leaflets falcate, oblong, very oblique, 1/4 to 1/2" long, ciliate and sometimes pubescent on midribs below, often does not leaf out until late May or early June.

BUDS: Terminal absent, laterals with 2 or 3 scales, small, rounded, brownish.

STEM: Slender, greenish, heavily lenticelled, glabrous.

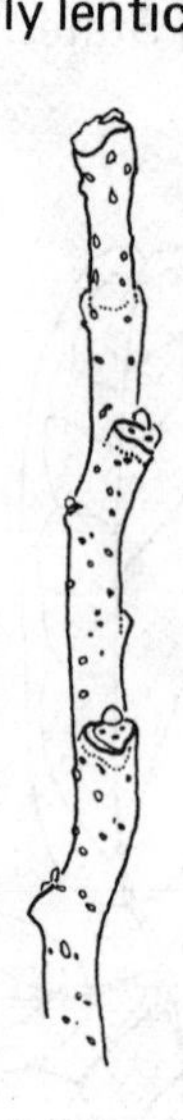

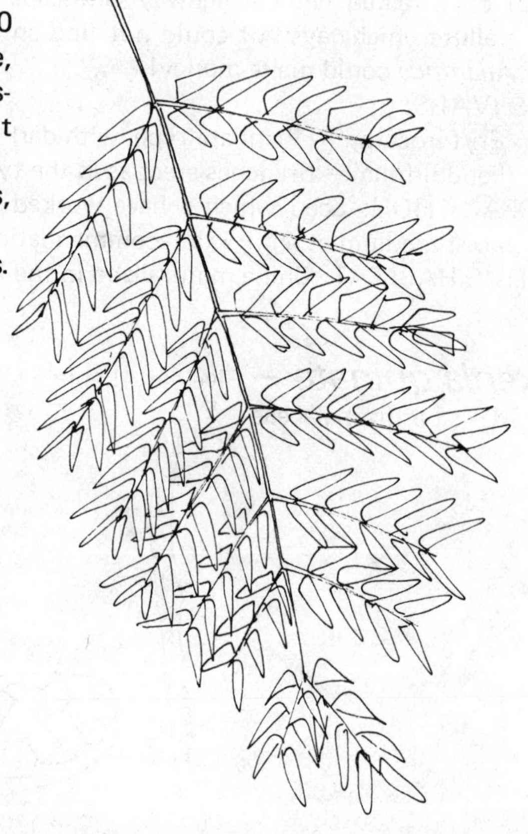

This species barely survives in Central Illinois as both the cold weather and wilt disease wreak havoc on this species. Widely planted in the southern states. It is, however, not a quality plant and definitely not suited for northern climates. The main attraction are the flowers which are light pink; brush-like in effect, borne in slender-peduncled heads in June, July and August on the new growth. The flowers coupled with foliage present an almost tropical effect. Prefer well drained soil; full sun but will tolerate partial shade; tolerates wind and alkaline (high pH) soils; flowers at 2 to 4 years of age. Very susceptible to a vascular wilt disease which is prevalent, also webworm can be highly destructive; habit is usually somewhat vase-shaped, broad spreading, often with several trunks and forming a flat-topped crown, grows to 25 to 35'; two wilt resistant clones are 'Charlotte' and 'Tryon'; seed dormancy due to hard seed coat and can be alleviated with acid scarification. Native from Iran to China. Introduced 1745.

Alnus glutinosa — Common Alder also called Black or European Alder

FAMILY: Betulaceae

LEAVES: Alternate, simple, 2-4" long, very gummy when young, rounded or emarginate at apex, coarsely and doubly serrate, dark green, glabrous above, axillary tufts beneath.

BUDS: Stalked, 1/4 to 1/2" long, reddish or reddish purple, valvate, very prominent.

STEM: Glabrous, green-brown, pith—small, three sided, continuous.

FRUIT: Nutlet, borne in persistent strobiles, on 1/2 - 1" peduncles, distinctly stalked. The long peduncle permits separation from *A. incana.*

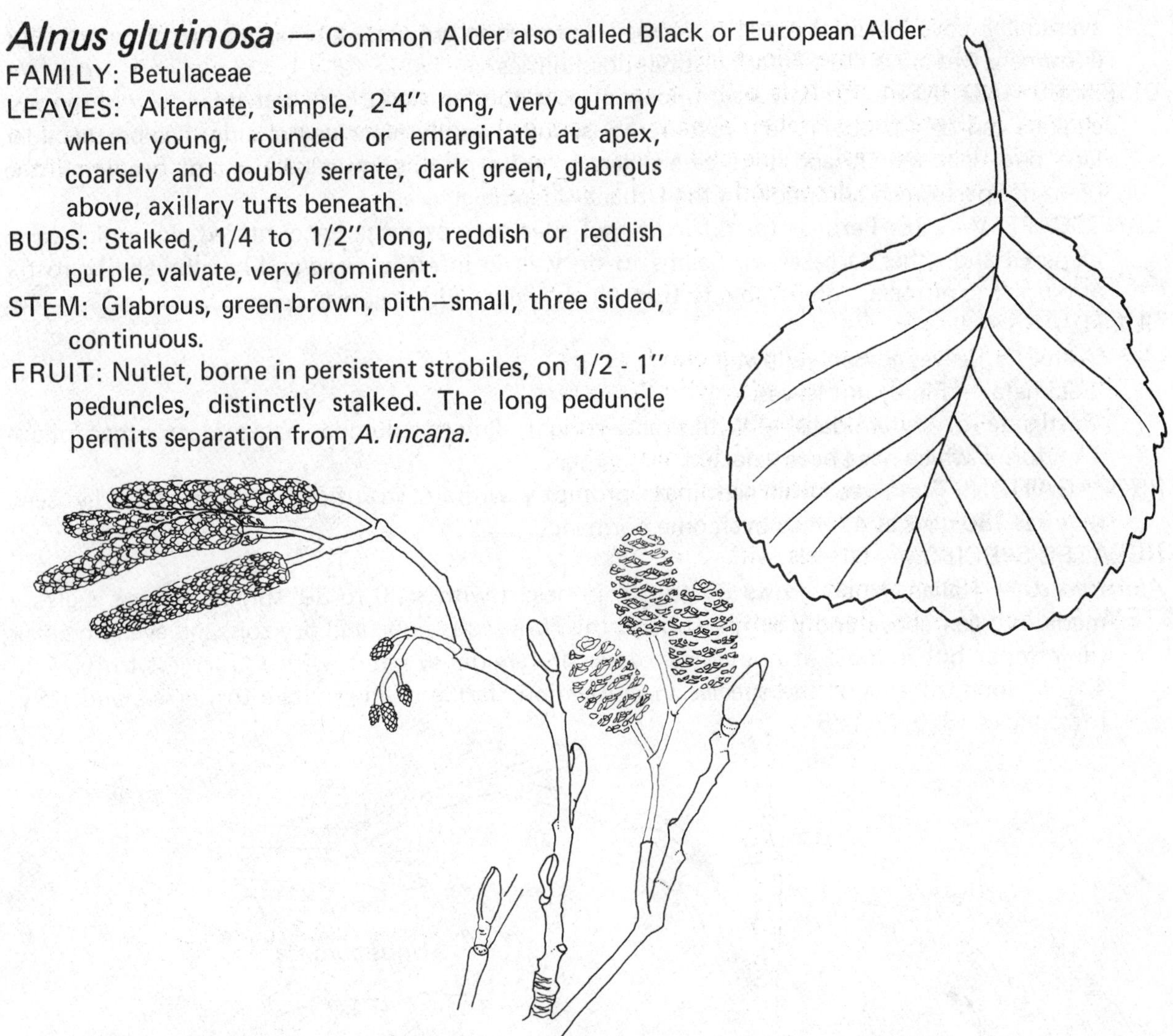

SIZE: 40 to 60' in height with a spread of 20 to 40', can grow to 90 to 100'.

HARDINESS: Zone 3.

HABIT: Often of weak pyramidal outline and at other times developing an ovoid or oblong head of irregular proportions. Small trees show a pyramidal habit. Often grown multistemmed and, in fact, has more ornamental appeal when cultured in this fashion.

RATE: Fast in youth, tends to slow down when abundant flowering and fruiting occur, although will average 24 to 30" per year over a 20 year period. The wood is not as weak and brittle as *Acer saccharinum,* Silver Maple.

TEXTURE: Medium in leaf and in winter.

BARK: Young bark is often a gray green or greenish brown and changes to soft gray-brown with age.

LEAF COLOR: Dark glossy green in summer; fall color does not occur as the leaves abscise green or brown. The foliage is extremely handsome and in the Central Illinois area little troubled by insects or diseases.

FLOWERS: Monoecious, reddish brown; male flowers in 2 to 4" long catkins; rather handsome but seldom noticed by most individuals. Female borne in a distinct egg-shaped strobile; early to mid March.

FRUIT: A small nutlet borne in a persistent woody strobile; maturing in October-November, strobile persisting through winter.

CULTURE: Transplants readily, prefer moist or wet soil but have grown well in the dry soils of Central Illinois; full sun or partial shade, seems to be tolerant of acid or slightly alkaline soils; prune in winter or early spring; if used along waterways will seed in along the banks and eventually cover large areas. I have seen the species growing submerged in the water. For extremely wet areas the tree has distinct possibilities.

DISEASES AND INSECTS: Powdery mildew attacks the female strobili but this is rarely serious, cankers can be a problem, leaf rust—rarely serious, woolly alder aphid, alder flea beetle, alder lace bug, leaf miner, and tent caterpillar. In spite of this impressive list of problems, the plant has performed admirably in the Urbana-Champaign area.

LANDSCAPE VALUE: Perhaps for difficult, wet sites such as those encountered along highways, in parks and other large areas. Seems to do well in infertile areas and has the ability to fix atmospheric nitrogen comparable to that which occurs with legumes.

CULTIVARS:

'Aurea' — Leaves golden yellow.

'Laciniata' — Finely cut leaves.

'Fastigiata' or 'Pyramidalis' — With erect, upright, almost columnar habit. Many other foliage forms which have been selected.

PROPAGATION: Fresh seed will germinate promptly without stratification, however, dried seed requires 180 days at 41°F to overcome dormancy.

RELATED SPECIES:

Alnus cordata, Italian Alder, grows 30 to 50' in height with a 20 to 30' spread; foliage is glossy medium green above and pale green beneath. Thrives on poor and dry soil, and even on chalk (limestone) but is most at home near water. Pyramidal in habit, with the largest fruits, 1 to 1 1/4" long, of any of the species in cultivation; fast growing; native to Corsica and Italy. Introduced 1820, Zone 5.

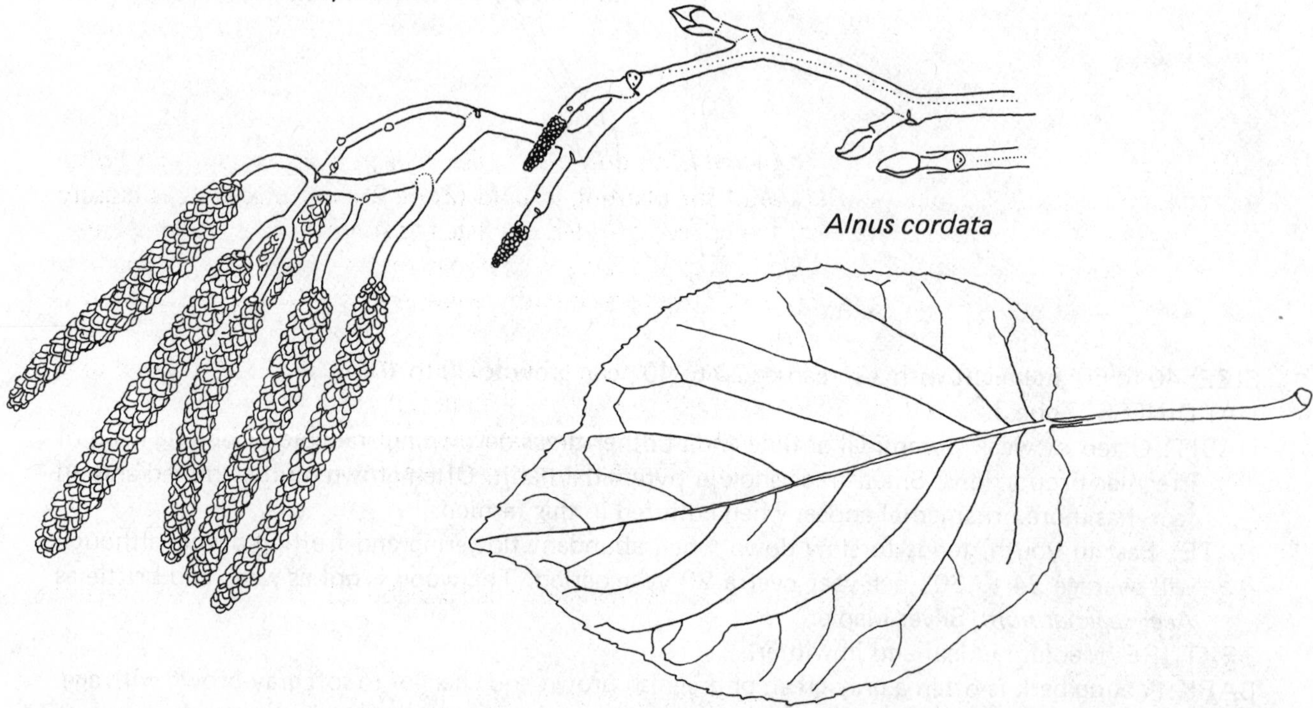

Alnus cordata

Alnus rugosa, Speckled Alder, is usually a coarse shrub or small tree to about 20 to 25' in height. Leaves are dull green with prominent straight veins, impressed above, projecting below. The name "speckled" comes from the appearance of the stems which are heavily lined with distinct horizontally borne lenticels. Native from Maine to Minnesota, south to Florida and Texas. Cultivated since 1769. Zone 4. At times called Smooth or Hazel Alder.

Alnus serrulata, closely allied species, differing chiefly in its leaves, which are usually broadest above the middle and have the margins set with fine nearly regular teeth. Confined to Eastern and North Central U.S. Lenticels fewer, shorter, darker.

Alnus incana — Gray Alder. Also called Speckled Alder.

LEAVES: Alternate, simple, 2 to 4" long, apex acute, double serrate and usually slightly lobulate, dull dark green above with impressed veins.

BUDS: Distinctly stalked, 1/4 to 1/2" long, reddish, more or less whitened with fine down, slightly sticky within.

STEM: Slender, finely downy or glabrous, grayish brown, hairy towards tips especially of fruiting twigs. Lenticels—scattered, whitish, conspicuous.

PITH: Dark green, 3-cornered.

FRUIT: Strobiles, sessile or short-stalked.

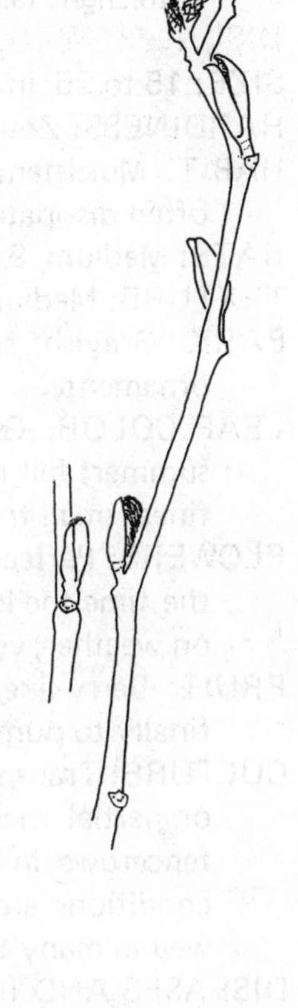

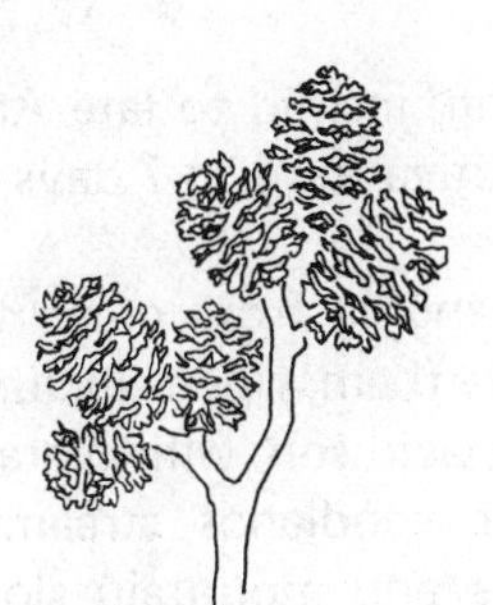

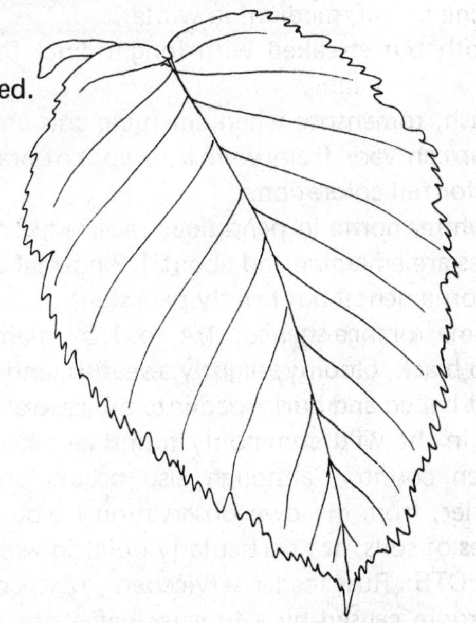

Alnus incana, a large tree 40 to 60' in height with dull dark green foliage. Next to *Alnus glutinosa* the commonest of the alders and is useful for planting in cold (Zone 2), wet places. It is closely allied to *Alnus rugosa* and, at one time, the Speckled Alder was listed as *Alnus incana* var. *americana.* There are several cultivars of *Alnus incana* which are more common in the landscape than the species:

'Aurea' — Leaves are yellow and young stems are reddish yellow and remain so throughout the winter, young catkins orangish.

'Laciniata' — The handsomest of the many cutleaved types with the blade divided into 6 or 8 pairs of lobes reaching 2/3's or more of the way to the midrib.

'Pendula' — A weeping form. Native to Europe and the Caucasus, long cultivated.

NATIVE HABITAT: Europe to Caucasia and Siberia, Northern Africa. Escaped from cultivation in North America. Long cultivated.

Amelanchier arborea — Downy Serviceberry also called Juneberry, Shadbush, Service-tree or Sarvis-tree

FAMILY: Rosaceae

LEAVES: Alternate, simple, generally obovate, less often ovate, elliptic or oblong, acute or acuminate, usually cordate at base, 1 to 3" long, sharply serrate nearly or quite at base, when young densely tomentose beneath, less so above, tomentum usually partly persistent, when unfolding grayish pubescent.

BUDS: Terminal-present, laterals of similar size, 1/3 to 1/2" long, imbricate, narrowly ovate to conical, sharp pointed, greenish yellow more or less tinged with reddish purple, glabrous or with white silky hairs at apex and edges of scales, mostly appressed.

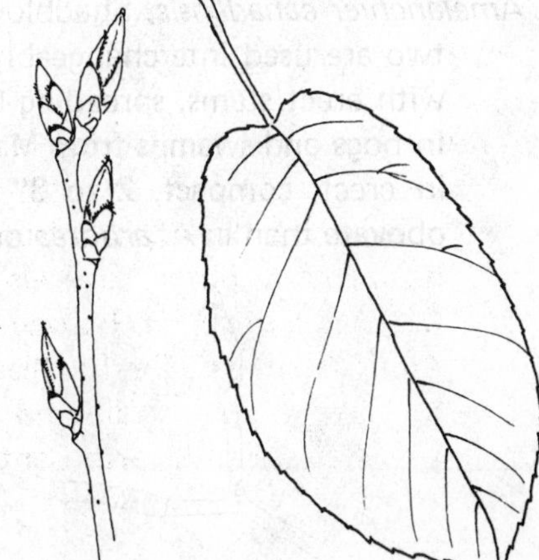

STEM: Slender, grayish, olive-green to red-brown often covered with a gray skin, generally smooth, with slight taste of bitter almonds. Pith—supposedly more or less 5-angled.

SIZE: 15 to 25′ in height with a variable spread; can grow to 40′ but this is rare under cultivation.

HARDINESS: Zone 4.

HABIT: Multistemmed large shrub or small tree with a rounded crown of many small branches; often dissipates in old age to a rounded form.

RATE: Medium, 9 to 10′ in 5 to 8 year period.

TEXTURE: Medium-fine in leaf; medium in winter.

BARK: Grayish; smooth but streaked with longitudinal fissures, often with a reddish cast, very ornamental.

LEAF COLOR: Grayish, tomentose when emerging and gradually changing to a medium green in summer; fall color can vary from yellow to apricot-orange to dull, deep dusty red; one of our finest small trees for fall coloration.

FLOWERS: Perfect, white, borne in pendulous racemes, 2 to 4″ long, in mid to late April, about the time the leaves are emerging and about 1/2 normal size; effective for 4 to 7 days depending on weather; very ornamental but briefly persistent.

FRUIT: Berry-like pome, orange-shaped, 1/4 to 1/3″ diameter, changing from green to red and finally to purplish black, bloomy, slightly sweetish, and birds love them; ripens in June.

CULTURE: Transplant balled and burlapped into moist, well drained, acid soil; will tolerate full sun or partial shade; in the wild commonly found along borders of woodlands, streambanks and fencerows in open country, although also occurs on hillsides and mountain slopes where conditions are drier; from my own observation I would expect the Amelanchiers to perform well in many types of soils; not particularly pollution tolerant; rarely require pruning.

DISEASES AND INSECTS: Rust (cedar serviceberry rust, comparable to cedar apple and hawthorn rusts), witches' broom caused by a fungus, leaf blight, fire blight, powdery mildews, fruit rot, leaf miner, borers, pear leaf blister mite, pear slug sawfly and willow scurfy scale.

LANDSCAPE VALUE: Very pleasing in a naturalistic planting and probably used to best advantage there; blends in well on the edges of woodlands near ponds and streambanks, blends into shrub borders especially with evergreen background; serviceberries are now used in all facets of landscaping but their most effective use is as described above.

PROPAGATION: Cold stratification for most species is recommended; 90 to 120 days at 41°F in moist medium would suffice. Not easily propagated by cuttings but reports indicate it is possible to get some (25%) rooting of softwood cuttings.

RELATED SPECIES:

Amelanchier asiatica, Asian Serviceberry, is a tree of very graceful form growing from 15 to 40′ high; flowers are white, fragrant, and borne about 2 to 3 weeks after *A. arborea* when the leaves are about full size; fruit is purple-black, about 1/3″ diameter. Native of China, Korea, and Japan. Zone 5. Winter buds are a very deep red and quite different in that respect from most of our native types.

Amelanchier canadensis, Shadblow Serviceberry, is often confused with *A. arborea* and, in fact, the two are used interchangeably in the nursery trade. *A. canadensis* as now understood is a shrub with erect stems, spreading by means of sucker growths from the base, 6 to 20′ tall, occurring in bogs and swamps from Maine to South Carolina along the coast; the white flowers are borne in erect, compact, 2 to 3″ long racemes and the petals are more distinctly and uniformly obovate than in *A. arborea* or *A. laevis* and somewhat shorter, 2/5″ long, fruit is black and juicy.

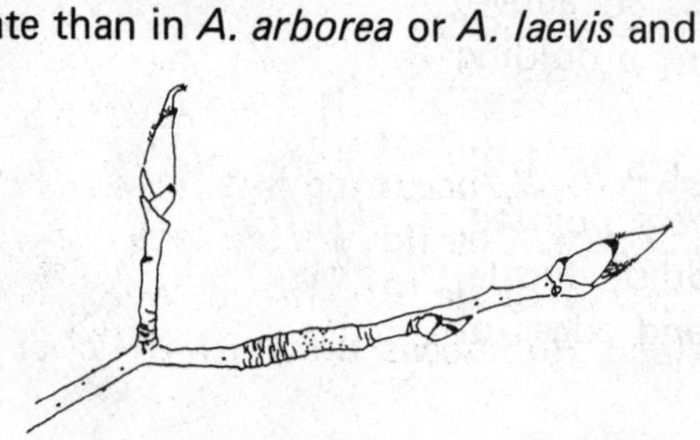

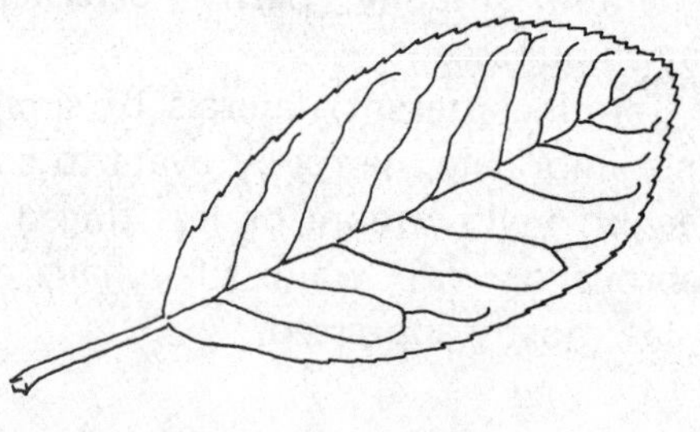

Amelanchier florida — Pacific Serviceberry

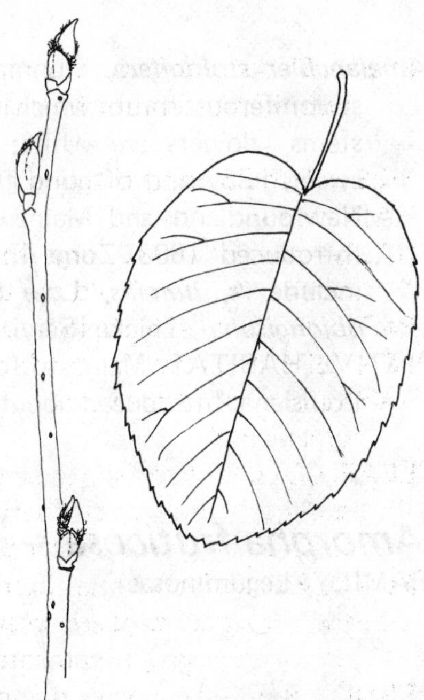

LEAVES: Alternate, simple, broad-oval to ovate, 3/4 to 1 1/2" long, truncate or subcordate at base, coarsely and sharply toothed above the middle, rarely below, quite glabrous or slightly floccose-tomentose at first.

BUDS: Ovoid to ellipsoidal, acute or acuminate, dark chestnut-brown, glabrous or puberulous, 1/4 to 3/4" long, scales of the inner ranks ovate, acute, brightly colored, coated with pale silky hairs.

STEM: Slender, pubescent when they first appear, bright red-brown and usually glabrous during their first season, darker second year, ultimately dark gray-brown.

BARK: Light brown, slightly tinged with red, smooth or slightly fissured.

FRUIT: Dark blue, 1/4 to 1/2" diameter, sweet and succulent.

Amelanchier florida, Pacific Serviceberry, is a shrub of erect stems to 10' or more high or a small tree; flowers are white, about 3/4 to 1 1/4" across, borne 5 to 15 together in erect racemes; fruit purplish black, juicy and edible although the birds do not seem to bother it like the fruit of other species. Southern Alaska to Idaho and Northern California. Introduced 1826. Zone 2. Another species which is closely allied to *A. florida* is *A. alnifolia,* Saskatoon Serviceberry. It differs in smaller flowers (to 4/5" across), rounder and thicker leaves, and dwarfer habit. Native from Sasketchewan to Colorado and Idaho. Introduced 1918. Zone 5.

Amelanchier laevis — Allegheny Serviceberry

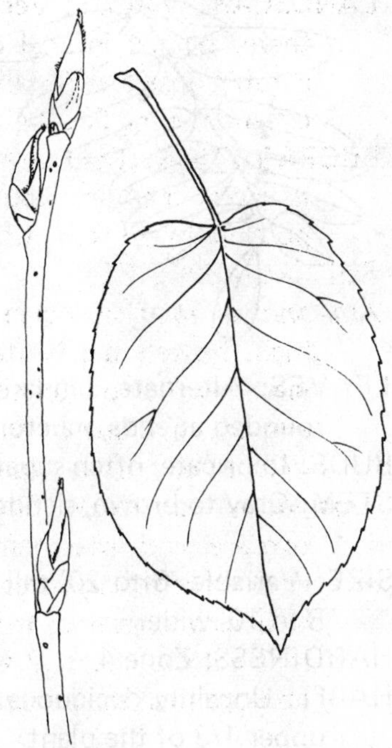

LEAVES: Alternate, simple, elliptic-ovate to ovate-oblong, 1 1/4 to 3" long, short acuminate, subcordate or rounded at base, quite glabrous and purplish when young.

BUDS: Imbricate, similar to *A. canadensis,* usually 1/2" long, green tinged with red, the inner scales lanceolate, bright red above the middle, ciliate with silky white hairs.

STEM: Slender, glabrous, reddish brown 1st year, dull grayish brown in their second season.

BARK: Supposedly reddish brown, divided by shallow fissures into narrow longitudinal ridges and covered by small persistent scales.

Amelanchier laevis, Allegheny Serviceberry, is closely allied to *A. arborea* but differs by reason of the bronzy purple color of the unfolding leaves and their lack of pubescence as well as the almost glabrous pedicels and peduncle of the inflorescence. The fruit is black and sweet. The fruits were preferred by the American Indians. Many birds and animals are also extremely fond of them. Native from Newfoundland to Georgia and Alabama, west to Michigan and Kansas. Cultivated 1870. Zone 4.

Amelanchier x *grandiflora,* Apple Serviceberry, is a naturally occurring hybrid between *A. arborea* x *A. laevis* with young leaves purplish and pubescent. The flowers are larger, on longer more slender racemes, tinged pink in bud. Two cultivars include 'Robin Hill' which is pink in bud and fades quite quickly after the flowers open, and 'Rubescens' on which the buds are purplish pink and tinged with pink when open.

Amelanchier stolonifera, Running Serviceberry, is a small 4 to 6′ stoloniferous shrub which forms small thickets of stiff, erect stems; flowers are white; fruit is purplish black, glaucous, sweet, juicy and of good flavor, ripening in July. Native from Newfoundland and Maine to Virginia in non-calcerous soils. Introduced 1883. Zone 4. Two related and confusing species include *A. humilis,* Low Serviceberry, and *A. obovalis (A. oblongifolia),* Thicket Serviceberry.

NATIVE HABITAT: Maine to Iowa, south to Northern Florida and Louisiana. Introduced about 1746.

Amorpha fruticosa — Indigobush Amorpha, also called Bastard Indigo

FAMILY: Leguminosae

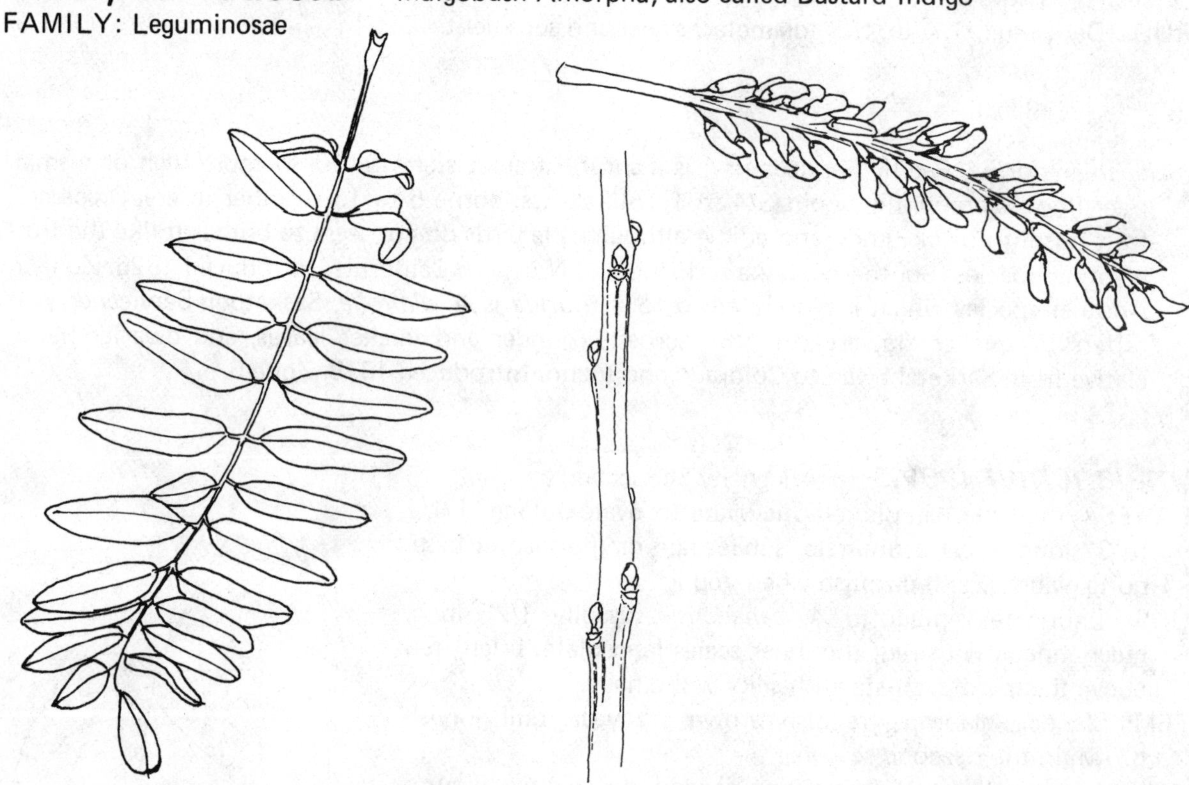

LEAVES: Alternate, pinnately compound, 11 to 25 leaflets, oval or elliptic, 3/5 to 1 3/5″ long, rounded at ends, mucronate, finely pubescent or glabrate.

BUDS: Imbricate, often superposed, essentially glabrous, appressed, brownish gray.

STEM: Gray to brown, slender, often looks dead.

SIZE: Variable, 6 to 20′ tall with a 5 to 15′ spread; a planting on our campus is about 12′ tall and 8 to 10′ wide.

HARDINESS: Zone 4.

HABIT: Ungainly deciduous shrub developing a leggy character with the bulk of the foliage on the upper 1/3 of the plant.

RATE: Medium in youth.

TEXTURE: Medium in foliage; coarse in winter.

LEAF COLOR: Light bright green in summer; slightly yellowish in fall.

FLOWERS: Perfect, purplish blue with orange anthers, each flower 1/3″ long; mid June, borne in 3 to 6″ long upright racemes; flowers are not extremely showy but the colors are unusual; flowers on new growth.

FRUIT: Small, 1/3" long, warty, kidney-shaped pod; persistent into winter and offers a good identification feature.

CULTURE: Transplants readily; does extremely well in poor, dry, sandy soils; pH adaptable; full sun; prune in late winter or early spring to keep the plant looking somewhat neat.

DISEASES AND INSECTS: Plants may be completely defoliated by the uredinal stage of the rust *Uropyxis amorphae.* Other problems include leaf spots, powdery mildew and twig canker. I have also observed a gall forming insect which causes a swelling of the spent inflorescences. Inside the gall is a small larva similar to those found in galls of oaks.

LANDSCAPE VALUE: Not a great deal of worth attached to this plant. Perhaps for poor soil areas where few plants will survive. Apparently can fix its own nitrogen and this may explain the adaptability. Spreads easily by seeds and can become a noxious weed.

PROPAGATION: Seed has an impermeable coat and dormant embryo. Light acid scarification for 5 to 8 minutes in sulfuric acid followed by cold stratification is recommended.

RELATED SPECIES:

Amorpha canescens — Leadplant Amorpha grows 2 to 4′ high and spreads 4 to 5′. The habit is broad, rounded and flat-topped. The foliage is an interesting gray-green in summer and can be used for foliage contrast. Flowers are similar to the above species. Should be used as a herbaceous perennial, accent plant, or useful in rock gardens. Can be propagated by cuttings; seed should be treated similar to *A. fruticosa.* Native from Michigan and Sasketchewan to Indiana, Texas and Northern Mexico. Introduced 1812. Zone 2.

NATIVE HABITAT: Connecticut to Minnesota, south to Louisiana and Florida. Introduced 1724.

Ampelopsis brevipedunculata — Porcelain Ampelopsis

FAMILY: Vitaceae

LEAVES: Alternate, simple, 2 1/2 to 5" long, broad-ovate, acuminate, cordate, 3-lobed, the lateral lobes broadly triangular-ovate, spreading, coarsely serrate, pilose beneath; hairy petioles as long as blade or shorter.

BUDS: Subglobose, solitary though collaterally branched in development, sessile, with 2 or 3 scales, brownish.

STEMS: Hairy when young; angled or nearly terete, brownish; pith-continuous, white.

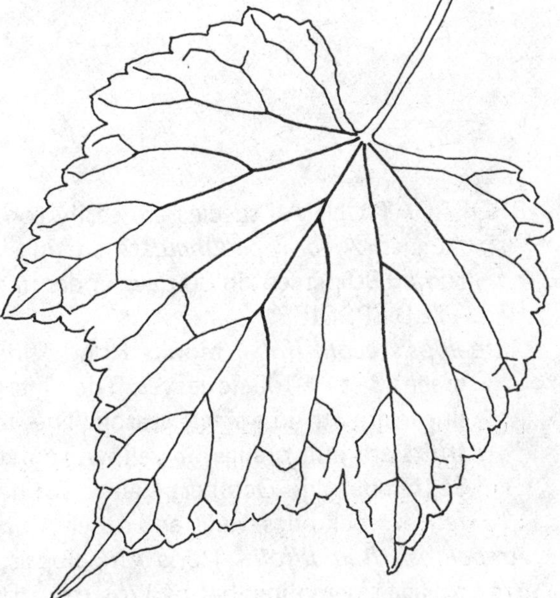

SIZE: 10 to 15 to 25′ and more.

HARDINESS: Zone 4.

HABIT: Vigorous, climbing vine clinging by tendrils, not as dense as some vines.

RATE: Fast, can grow 15 to 20′ in a single season; however, this is the exception.

TEXTURE: Medium in leaf and winter.

LEAF COLOR: Dark green in summer, not much different in fall.

FLOWERS: Perfect, greenish, unimportant; borne in long stalked cymes in July.

FRUIT: Berry, 1/4 to 1/3" diameter, pale lilac to yellow and finally to bright blue; often all colors are present in the same infructescence; effective in September and October.

CULTURE: Easily transplanted, adaptable to many soils except those that are permanently wet; best fruiting occurs in full sun; requires adequate support for climbing; plants should be sited where the root growth can be restricted, for, under this condition, fruiting is optimized.

DISEASES AND INSECTS: Some of the problems which are common to *Parthenocissus* could prove troublesome on *Ampelopsis* species.

LANDSCAPE VALUE: Another vine which is rarely visible in the landscape. The fruit is extremely handsome and is probably unrivaled by any other woody plant in vitality of color. Could be effectively integrated into a landscape by growing on a fence or over a rock pile. One authority calls the fruit an amethyst blue color.

CULTIVARS:

'Elegans' — A rather interesting type with slightly smaller leaves, variegated with white, greenish white and tinged pinkish when young.

var. *maximowiczii* — Leaves more deeply lobed, 3 to 5 lobes, interesting for textural difference compared to species.

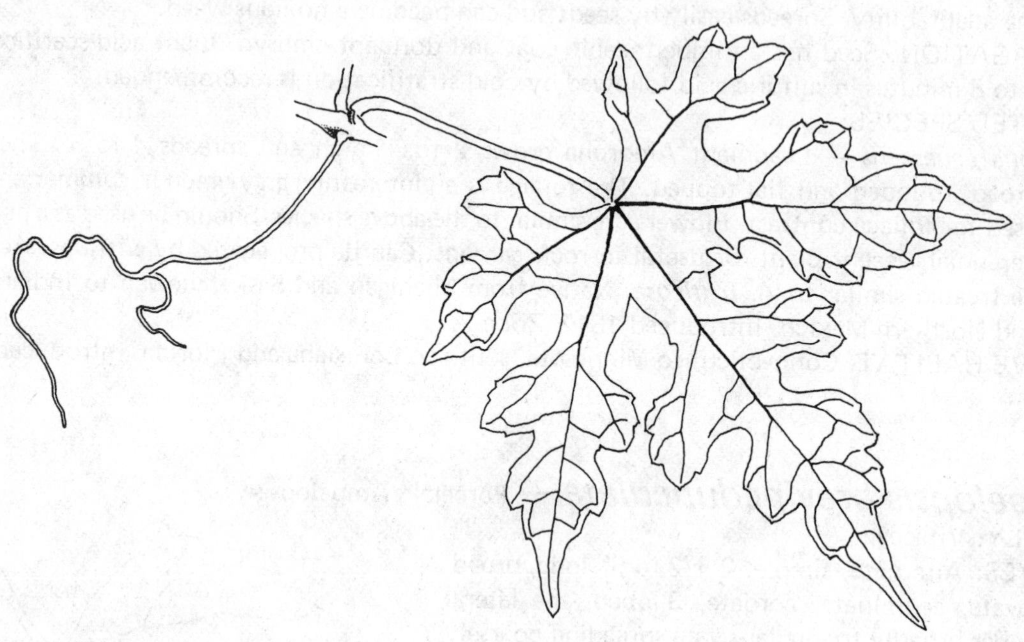

PROPAGATION: All species are easily rooted from leafy cuttings of firm growth taken in July and August. *A. brevipedunculata* cuttings taken in early summer, untreated, and planted in sand rooted 90 percent in 30 days under mist.

RELATED SPECIES:

Ampelopsis aconitifolia, Monks Hood Vine, is a slender luxuriant vine with delicate, deep glossy green, 3- to 5-foliate leaves. The vine grows 15 to 25′ and can develop as much as 12 to 15′ of linear growth in a single season. The flowers are perfect, greenish; August; borne in cymes. The fruits are dull orange or yellow, sometimes bluish before maturity, 1/4″ diameter, effective in September and October. Valued for delicate foliage; offers variation in texture; can be used on fences, rock piles, walls and other structures. Native to Northern China. Zone 4.

Ampelopsis humulifolia, Hops Ampelopsis, is a climbing, shrubby vine with lustrous bright green foliage resembling that of *Vitis* (true grape) in shape and texture. This species has been confused with *A. brevipedunculata,* but differs in the thicker, firmer leaves which are whitish beneath. The fruit is not borne profusely. The color ranges from pale yellow, changing partly or wholly to pale blue. Native to Northern China. Introduced 1868. Zone 5.

ADDITIONAL NOTES: I remember learning *A. brevipedunculata* in my plant materials courses at Ohio State in 1963 and did not see it again until the fall of 1975 when several students, who were involved in a fruit collecting project, brought in several clusters. Having not seen the plant for 12 years, I hesitated to immediately identify it, but the fruit color struck a mental note which I translated to *A. brevipedunculata.* The moral is that once one sees the fruit he/she never forgets with which plant to associate it.

NATIVE HABITAT: China, Korea, Japan and the Russian Far East. Cultivated 1870.

Andromeda polifolia, Bog-rosemary (Ericaceae), is an extremely intersting, slow growing (1 to 2′ high by 2 to 3′ wide) evergreen shrub with creeping rootstocks and upright limitedly branched stems. The foliage is stiff, leathery textured and deep dark green. The flowers are perfect, white tinged pink, 1/4″ long, urn-shaped; borne in May at the end of the shoots in umbels. The fruit is a capsule. The species requires a peaty or sandy soil which is constantly moist and cool; full sun or light shade; best to move it as a container-grown plant; in the wild it is most commonly found in peat or sphagnum bogs. A very lovely and interesting plant for edging or naturalized conditions but very exacting as to culture. Not very common in the trade but I have seen it offered in several garden centers as well as through mail order firms. Native to North and Central Europe, Northern Asia, North America south to New York and Idaho. Cultivated 1768. Zone 2.

Aralia spinosa — Devils-walkingstick or Hercules-club

FAMILY: Araliaceae

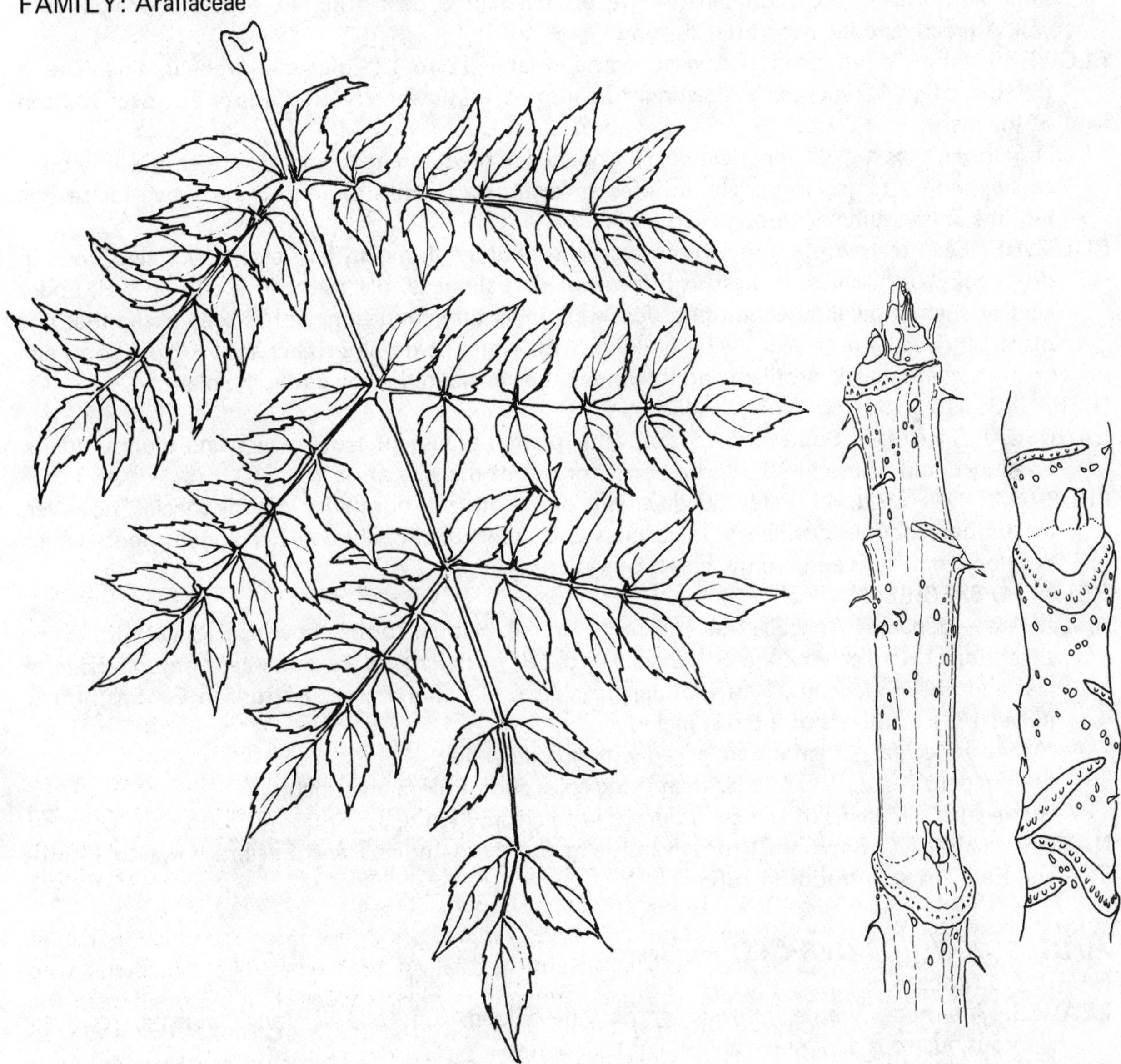

LEAVES: Alternate, bi-to-tri pinnately compound, 32 to 64" long, rachis with scattered prickles, leaflets 2 to 4" long, serrate.

BUDS: Ovoid-conical, solitary, with few scales.

STEM: Stout, gray-straw colored, glabrous, with prickles; pith large, pale, leaf scars fully half encircling stem, bundle traces, 15 in a single series.

SIZE: 10 to 20′ in height although can grow to 30 to 40′.

HARDINESS: Zone 4.

HABIT: Large, few-stemmed shrub or small tree with stout, coarse branches forming an obovate outline. Often renews itself by developing shoots from the base and forms a dense thicket of impenetrable branches. I have seen a large planting like this in Mt. Airy Arboretum, Cincinnati, Ohio, and the overall effect is quite handsome (soft-textured) in summer with the compound foliage; however, in winter the planting is extremely coarse.

RATE: Slow to medium on old wood, but fast from shoots which develop at the base of the plant.

TEXTURE: Medium, possibly medium-fine in leaf; appearing coarse in winter.

LEAF COLOR: Medium to dark green, sometimes lustrous, changing to purplish in fall according to some authorities. The specimens I have observed in Urbana, Illinois, turn a poor yellow or yellow-green, and fall soon after turning.

FLOWERS: Whitish, produced in August, borne in large 12 to 18" diameter umbellose panicles at the end of the branches. Interestingly handsome in flower creating a lacy veil over the top of the plant.

FRUIT: Drupe, black, 1/4" long; October; produced in great quantity and are either eaten by birds or fall soon after ripening. The inflorescence turns a pinkish red and is attractive for several months in late summer through early fall.

CULTURE: Easy to transplant, performs best in well-drained, moist, fertile soils, but also grows in dry, rocky or heavy soils; best in full sun or partial shade, pH tolerant as will do well under acid or slightly alkaline conditions, does well under city conditions, it has been noted that this plant "thrives with neglect". The freedom with which it develops new shoots from roots can create a maintenance problem and this should be considered when siting the plant.

DISEASES AND INSECTS: None serious.

LANDSCAPE VALUE: Somewhat of a novelty plant because of large leaves and clubby stems. Possibly could be used in the shrub border or out of the way areas.

PROPAGATION: Seed, 41°F for 60 days will overcome the dormancy of this species, however, others have double dormancy (seed coat and embryo). Possible to dig young shoots which develop from roots and use these as propagules.

RELATED SPECIES:

Aralia elata — Japanese Angelica-tree (Japanese Aralia). Similar to the above species with following exceptions: Hardier — Zone 3; Larger — to 50′ in height; more pubescent on underside of leaf and not as glaucous. Native of Japan, Korea, Manchuria and the Russian Far East. Introduced 1830. Cultivars of interest include:

'Aureo-variegata' — Leaflets are edged with golden-yellow.

'Pyramidalis' — Leaflets smaller than the species and of more erect habit.

'Variegata' — Margins of leaflets bordered with creamy white.

NATIVE HABITAT: Southern Pennsylvania and Southern Indiana and Eastern Iowa to Florida and East Texas. Introduced 1688.

Arctostaphylos uva-ursi — Bearberry

FAMILY: Ericaceae

LEAVES: Alternate, simple, obovate or obovate-oblong, 3/5 to 4/5" long, cuneate, revolute, glabrous, lustrous dark green above, lighter beneath.

BUDS: Solitary, sessile, ovoid, with about 3 exposed scales.

STEM: Minutely tomentulose-viscid, becoming glabrate; leaf scars small, crescent-shaped, bundle trace one; older branches covered with papery reddish to ashy exfoliating bark.

SIZE: 6 to 12" in height by 2 to 4' in width.
HARDINESS: Zone 2.
HABIT: Low growing, glossy leaved evergreen ground cover; forming broad, thick mats; single plant may cover an area 15' in diameter.
RATE: Slow.
TEXTURE: Fine.
LEAF COLOR: Glossy bright green to dark green in summer; bronze to reddish in fall. The foliage effect is unique and quite different from most ground covers.
FLOWERS: Perfect, white tinged pink, small (1/6" long) and bell shaped; late April to early May, borne in nodding racemes.
FRUIT: Fleshy drupe, lustrous bright red, 1/4 to 1/3" diameter, late July through August and persisting.
CULTURE: One of the more interesting species as far as cultural requirements. Difficult to transplant and container grown plants or large mats of plants should be used; although found in diverse soils and habitats it does best in poor, sandy, infertile soils; full sun or partial shade; pH 4.5 to 5.5 is preferable; exhibits good salt tolerance (I have seen the plant growing right next to beach grass on the beaches of Old Cape Cod; set plants 12 to 24" apart; pruning is seldom necessary; never fertilize.
DISEASES AND INSECTS: Nothing serious although black mildew, leaf galls and rust have been reported.
LANDSCAPE VALUE: Outstanding ground cover for that different effect; has been called "the prettiest, sturdiest, and most reliable ground cover." It is worth the effort of good bed preparation for this one plant alone.
PROPAGATION: Seeds have hard seedcoats and dormant embryos and scarification in H_2SO_4 for 3 to 6 hours followed by warm fluctuating temperatures and then cold stratification is recommended. Cuttings are somewhat difficult to root but one nurseryman takes 5 to 6" cuttings in winter, treats them with a fungicide and hormone, places them in sand with bottom heat out of sun, and roots form in 2 months.
NATIVE HABITAT: Circumboreal covering Europe, Asia, North America, south to Virginia, Northern Mexico and Northern California. Cultivated 1800.

Aronia arbutifolia — Red Chokeberry

FAMILY: Rosaceae

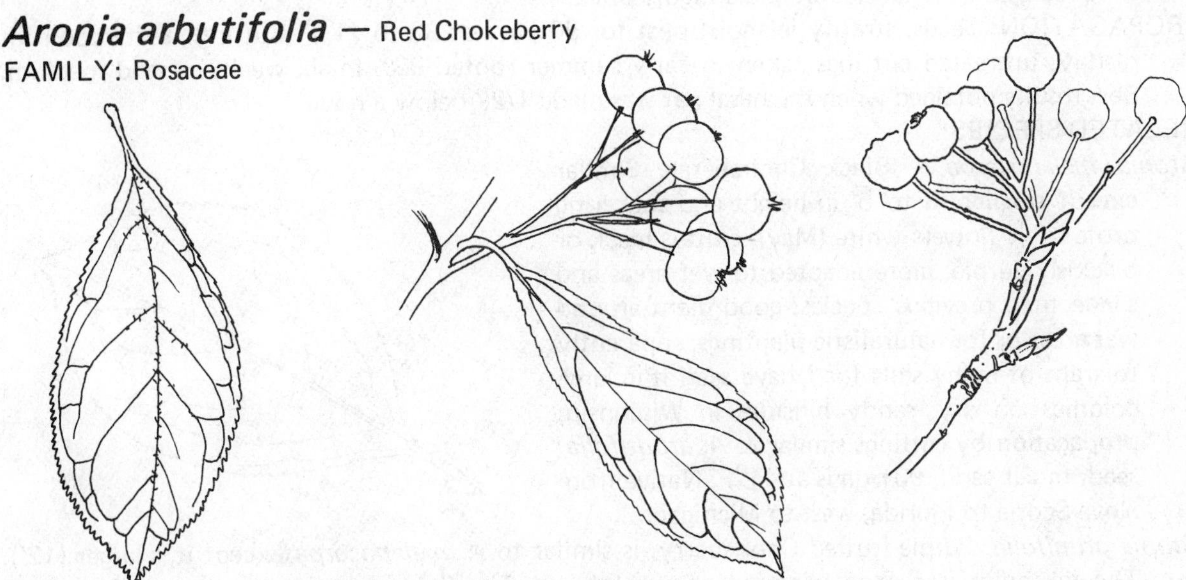

LEAVES: Alternate, simple, elliptic to oblong or obovate, acute or abruptly acuminate, glabrous above except the midrib, grayish tomentose beneath.
BUDS: Imbricate, 1/4 to 1/2" long, usually 5-scaled, green tinged red, often completely red, glabrous.

STEM: Slender, tomentose, brownish.
FRUIT: Pome, bright red, borne in tomentose corymbs, persistent into winter.

SIZE: 6 to 10′ in height by 3 to 5′ in spread.
HARDINESS: Zone 5.
HABIT: Distinctly upright, weakly spreading, multistemmed shrub, somewhat open and round topped. Shrub tends to become leggy with age as the majority of the foliage is present on the upper 1/2 or 1/3 of the plant. Breeding and selection for good habit, foliage and fruit could result in a superior landscape plant.
RATE: Slow, at least the case with the growth of plants I have recorded in Central Illinois.
TEXTURE: Medium in leaf; medium-coarse in winter although good fruit quality tends to minimize the ragged habit.
LEAF COLOR: Lustrous deep green above, grayish tomentose beneath in summer, changing to red, rich crimson or reddish purple in fall.
FLOWERS: White or slightly reddish, about 1/2″ diameter, mid May; borne in 9 to 20 flowered, 1 to 1 1/2″ diameter corymbs, not overwhelming.
FRUIT: Pome, 1/4″ diameter, bright red; September through November and later; fruits are firm and glossy into January in Central Illinois, borne in great abundance along the stems; called Chokeberry because of the astringent taste, even the birds do not like it.
CULTURE: Finely fibrous root system, transplants well, prefers good soil with adequate drainage but seems well adapted to many soil types, even poor soils; seems to tolerate both wet and dry soils; full sun or half shade, however, best fruit production occurs in full sun.
DISEASES AND INSECTS: Leaf spots, twig and fruit blight results in gray, powdery mold over affected plant parts, round-headed apple borer. None are serious.
LANDSCAPE VALUE: Border, massing, groups, very effective fruit character in the fall, the most useful way to compensate for the leggy character is to mass this species. Extremely effective when used in this manner. Almost a sea of red in fall and winter; might be a good choice for highway use because of adaptability and brilliant fruit display.
CULTIVARS:

'Brilliantissima' — Fruits supposedly more glossy and darker red.

'Erecta' — Form of narrow fastigiate habit; Wyman noted that after a few years of growth this form and the species are indistinguishable.

PROPAGATION: Seeds, stratify in moist peat for 90 days at 33 to 41°F. Cuttings, softwood root readily; untreated cuttings taken in early summer rooted 92% in six weeks in sand medium. Best results obtained when the basal cut was made 1/2″ below a node.
RELATED SPECIES:

Aronia melanocarpa — Black Chokeberry. Similar except smaller (3 to 5′ in height and suckering profusely); flowers white (May); fruit is black or blackish purple; more adapted to wet areas and shade than previous species; good plant around wet areas or for naturalistic plantings; apparently tolerant of many soils for I have seen it in large colonies on dry, sandy hillsides in Wisconsin; propagation by cuttings similar to *A. arbutifolia;* seed, moist sand, 90+ days at 41°F. Native from Nova Scotia to Florida, west to Michigan.

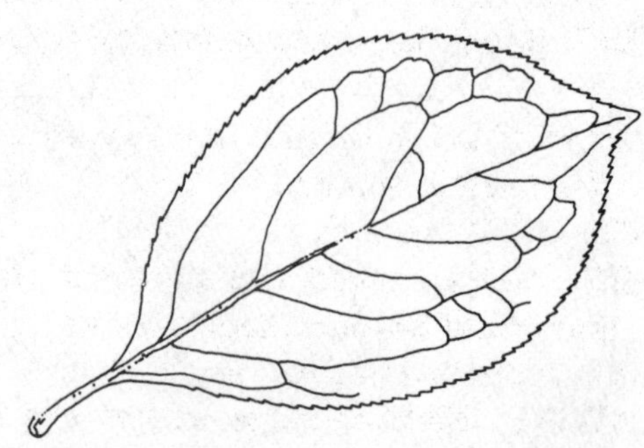

Aronia prunifolia, Purple-fruited Chokeberry, is similar to *A. melanocarpa* except it is larger (12′). The fall color is a good wine-red or purplish red. The flowers are white, about 1/2″ across, borne in terminal corymbs in late April through early May. The fruit is a lustrous, 2/5″ diameter, purplish black drupe which falls after the first frost. According to Rehder, this species is intermediate between *A. arbutifolia* and *A. melanocarpa,* but is not a hybrid. Current thinking has it that *A. prunifolia* is a hybrid species. Native from Nova Scotia to Florida, west to Indiana. Cultivated 1800. Zone 4.

NATIVE HABITAT: Massachusetts to Florida, west to Minnesota, Ohio, Arkansas and Texas. Introduced 1700.

Asimina triloba — Common Pawpaw

FAMILY: Annonaceae

LEAVES: Alternate, simple, entire, 6-12" long, obovate-oblong, apex short acuminate, base uniformly tapering, medium green. Usually glabrous at maturity.

BUDS: Terminal bud naked, larger than laterals, pubescent, red-brown, lateral buds naked, obliquely superposed, flower buds — pubescent, globose to rounded.

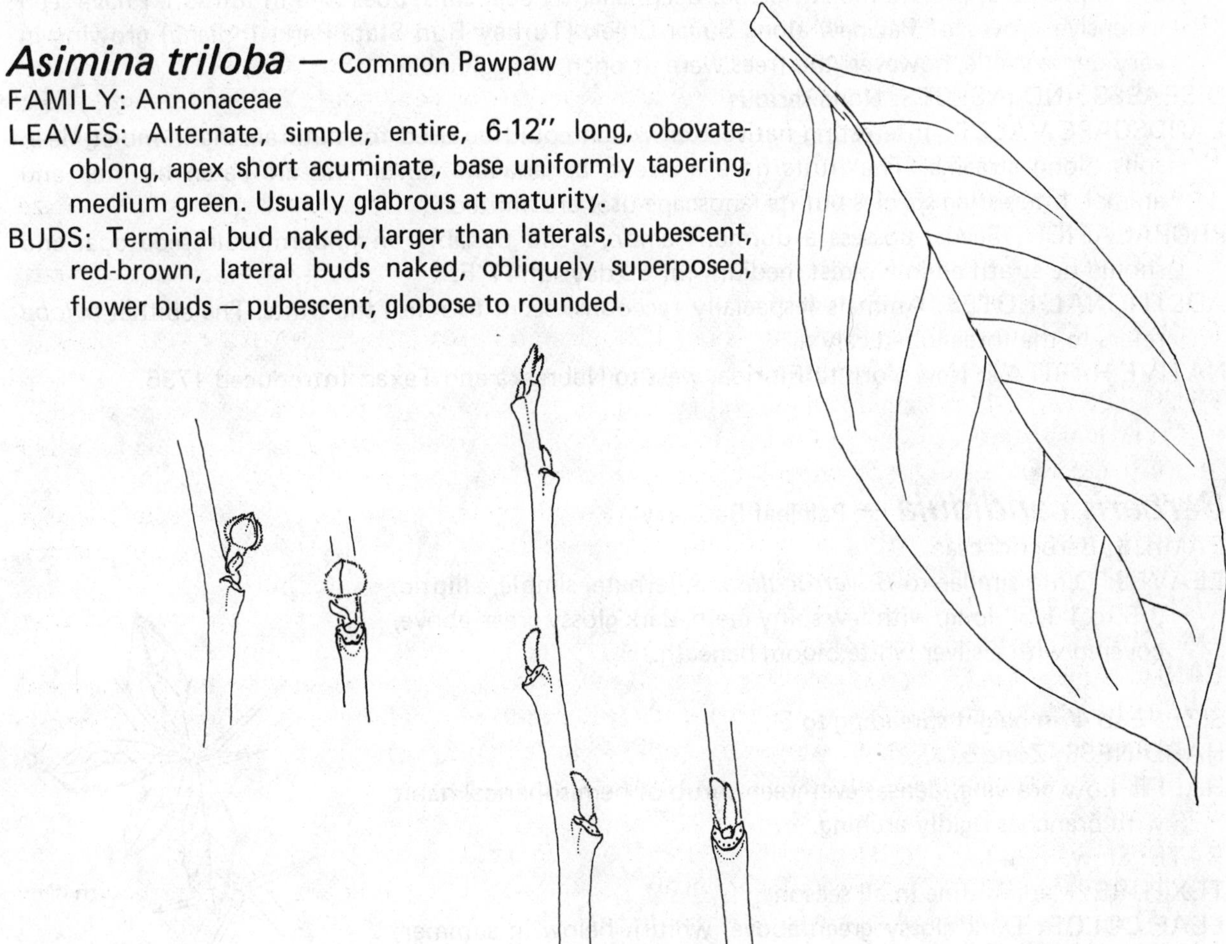

STEM: Essentially glabrous, brown, with fetid odor when broken, pith—continuous, white, with firmer greenish diaphragms at intervals in second year's growth.

FRUIT: Berry-like, green-yellow, turning dark, edible, banana-like taste.

SIZE: 15 to 20' in Central Illinois with spread equal to height; will grow 30 to 40' in height in more favorable locations.

HARDINESS: Zone 5.

HABIT: Multistemmed shrub or small tree with short trunk and spreading branches forming dense pyramidal or round-topped head.

RATE: Medium as a small tree.

TEXTURE: Medium-coarse in leaf and in winter habit. The summer foliage tends to droop and presents the tree with an overall sleepy (lazy) appearance. Easily recognizable by this feature.

BARK: Dark brown with grayish areas when young; becoming rough and slightly scaly with maturity.

LEAF COLOR: Medium green above, paler green beneath in summer changing to poor yellow or yellow-green in fall, early defoliator.

FLOWERS: Lurid purple, 1 to 2" across; early to mid May; borne singly. There are six petals, the outer three much larger than the inner three. Flowers before or as leaves are developing on thick, often recurved, downy, 1/2 to 3/4" long pedicels.

FRUIT: Edible, greenish yellow berry finally turning brownish black, 2 to 5" long, of many shapes—sometimes elongated, at other times rounded, has a taste similar to a banana; usually containing 2 to 3 large dark brown flattish seeds.

CULTURE: Somewhat difficult to transplant and should be moved as a small (3 to 6') balled and burlapped tree; prefers moist, fertile, deep, slightly acid soils; does well in full sun. I have seen extensive groves of Pawpaw along Sugar Creek (Turkey Run State Park, Indiana) growing in very dense shade, however, the trees were of open, straggly habit.

DISEASES AND INSECTS: None serious.

LANDSCAPE VALUE: Interesting native tree which could be used for naturalizing in moist, deep soils along streams. The fruits have a sweet, banana-like flavor and are eaten by man and animal. Interesting species but its landscape uses are limited.

PROPAGATION: Seeds, possess a dormant embryo and possibly an impermeable seed coat and should be stratified in a moist medium for 60 days at 41°F.

ADDITIONAL NOTES: Animals (especially raccoons) seem to relish the fruits. The epithet *triloba* refers to the three-lobed calyx.

NATIVE HABITAT: New York to Florida, west to Nebraska and Texas. Introduced 1736.

Berberis candidula — Paleleaf Barberry

FAMILY: Berberidaceae

LEAVES: Quite similar to *B. verruculosa.* Alternate, simple, elliptic, 3/5 to 1 1/5" long, with few spiny teeth, dark glossy green above, covered with a silver-white bloom beneath.

SIZE: 2 to 4' in height spreading to 5'.

HARDINESS: Zone 5.

HABIT: Low growing, dense, evergreen shrub of hemispherical habit with branches rigidly arching.

RATE: Slow.

TEXTURE: Medium-fine in all seasons.

LEAF COLOR: Dark glossy green above, whitish below in summer; leaves often turn wine-red in fall.

FLOWERS: Perfect, yellow, 5/8" diameter, borne singly in May-June. Very dainty and appealing.

FRUIT: True berry, purplish, bloomy, 1/2" long, August-September.

CULTURE: Transplants readily; prefers moist, well-drained, slightly acid soils; full sun or light shade; withstands pruning well; fertilize in spring.

DISEASES AND INSECTS: Nothing exceptionally serious.

LANDSCAPE VALUE: Very handsome and beautiful plant for rock gardens. I have grouped three together and they actually make a nice solid mat. Could possibly be used as a ground cover.

PROPAGATION: I have rooted cuttings using 1000 ppm IBA/50% alcohol, in peat:perlite, under mist with 90% or greater efficiency.

NATIVE HABITAT: Central China. Introduced 1894.

RELATED SPECIES:

Berberis x *chenaultii* — Chenault Barberry, a cross between *B. verruculosa* x *B. gagnepainii.* One of the best evergreen barberries for Northern United States because of vigorous growth and good condition of the foliage all winter; will grow to 3 to 4' high.

Berberis julianae — Wintergreen Barberry

LEAVES: Alternate, simple, narrow-elliptic to lanceolate or oblanceolate, 1 1/5 to 2 2/5" long, spiny-serrate, dark green above, much paler and indistinctly veined beneath, rigidly coriaceous.

STEM: Slightly angled, yellowish when young, light yellowish gray or yellowish brown the second year, spines rigid, 3-parted, 2/5 to 1 1/5" long; the inner bark and wood is yellow.

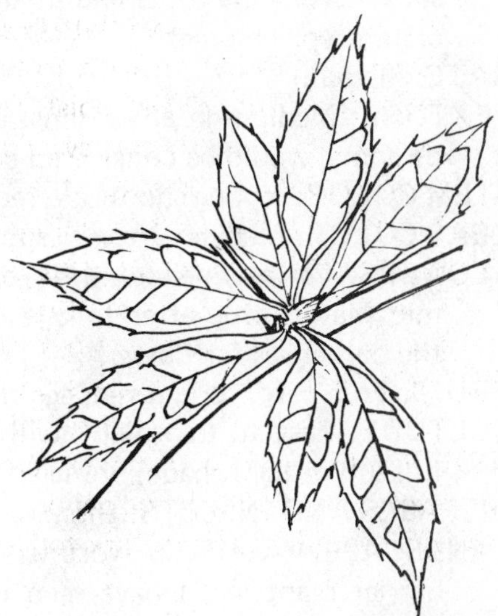

Grows to 6 to 10' in height with a comparable spread. The foliage is lustrous dark green in summer and often turns yellow to brown in winter. The flowers are yellow; the fruits bluish black, bloomy, 1/3" long; makes a good specimen, hedge, impenetrable barrier. Central China. Introduced 1900. Zone 5. Tends to be on the hardiness borderline in our area. Where it can be grown makes a nice specimen plant.

Berberis gladwynensis 'William Penn' caught my eye at Millcreek Valley Park, Youngstown, Ohio. The plant grows to about 4' in height and is rather wide spreading; the foliage is a beautiful lustrous green.

Berberis triacanthophora, Threespine Barberry, grows to 4 to 5'; shrub-like with spreading branches of graceful habit, evergreen foliage is bright green above, glaucous beneath; flowers are pale yellow or whitish tinged red; fruit is blue-black, slightly bloomy, 1/3" across. Native to Central China. Introduced 1907. Zone 5.

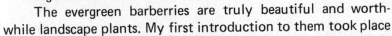

Berberis verruculosa, Warty Barberry, grows to 3 to 6' and forms a dense shrub; leaves are small and lustrous dark green above, whitish beneath and turn rich mahogany in winter, flowers are golden yellow, 5/8 to 3/4" diameter; fruit is violet-black, bloomy; closely related to *B. candidula.* Western China. Introduced 1904. Zone 5. Although listed as hardy in Zone 5 it was severely injured above the snowline during the winter of 1975-76 in Urbana and lowest recorded temperature was -8°F. *Berberis candidula* growing next to it was not affected.

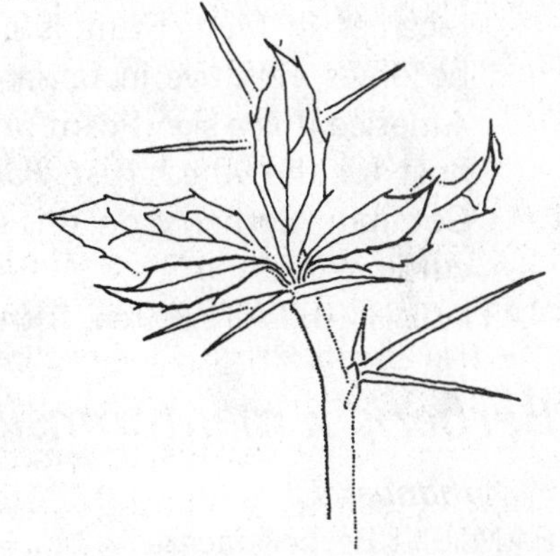

The evergreen barberries are truly beautiful and worthwhile landscape plants. My first introduction to them took place on a hot July day at the Arnold Arboretum. The barberries were crisp and cool looking and neat as a pin. It is unfortunate that they are not better known but the word barberry, to most people, only rings one bell and that is, alas, for *B. thunbergii.*

Berberis koreana — Korean Barberry

LEAVES: Alternate, simple, obovate or elliptic, 1 to 3" long, rounded at apex, cuneate at base, rather densely spinulose-serrulate, reticulate beneath, subchartaceous at maturity; medium green.

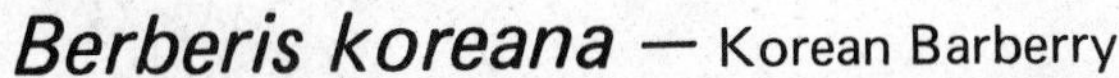

STEMS: Somewhat glabrous, red or orange or purple or brown; spines 3/5" long, grooved or dilated, usually simple.

SIZE: Small shrub growing 4 to 6' tall and slightly less in spread.

HARDINESS: Zone 4.

HABIT: Multistemmed oval to haystack shaped plant of rather dense constitution. However, it does sucker from the roots and at times becomes quite unruly in its growth habit. Will form large, clump-type colonies.

RATE: Medium.

TEXTURE: Medium in all seasons; this species has about the largest foliage of the barberries and, by some, would be considered coarse.

STEM COLOR: Young shoots are reddish and bloomy.

LEAF COLOR: Medium green in summer changing to deep red in the fall.

FLOWERS: Perfect, yellow, 1/4" diameter, borne in drooping, 3 to 4" long racemes in early to mid May. Borne after foliage has matured but still quite showy. Perhaps the handsomest of the barberries for flower.

FRUIT: True berry, bright red, egg-shaped, 1/4" long, effective through fall and into winter.

CULTURE: Easy to transplant; will tolerate about any soil except those that are permanently wet; full sun or light shade; prune anytime.

DISEASES AND INSECTS: Discussed under *B. thunbergii.* Usually very few problems.

LANDSCAPE VALUE: A worthwhile barberry for foliage, flower, and fruit. Makes an excellent barrier plant and I have seen it used in mass plantings with a degree of success. Presents an impenetrable barrier to unwanted neighbors.

PROPAGATION: Softwood cuttings of young growth collected in May or June and treated with 1000 ppm IBA rooted readily. Most barberry species have internal dormancy and require cold stratification to stimulate germination. A period of 60 to 90 days at 41°F is suitable.

RELATED SPECIES:

Berberis vulgaris, Common Barberry, grows 6 to 10' high producing a mass of stems; erect at the base, branching and spreading outwards at the top into a graceful, arching or pendulous form. The foliage is dull green, about 1 to 2" long. Flowers are yellow and borne on 2 to 3" pendulous racemes in May. Fruit is a bright red or purple, 1/3 to 1/2" long, egg-shaped berry which becomes effective in fall and persists. W.J. Bean is manifest in his praise of this shrub but in America it is a significant problem for it has escaped from cultivation and serves as the alternate host for the wheat rust, *Puccinia graminis.* In some states the laws require the destruction of Common Barberry on this account. Native to Europe, North Africa and temperate Asia. Long cultivated. Zone 3.

NATIVE HABITAT: Korea. Introduced 1905.

Berberis x *mentorensis* — Mentor Barberry. Result of cross between *B. julianae* and *B. thunbergii.*

FAMILY: Berberidaceae

LEAVES: Alternate, simple, elliptic-ovate, 4/5 to 2" long, subcoriaceous, sparingly spinulose toothed, pale beneath, very dark green. Tends to be semi-evergreen or hold leaves late in fall.

BUDS: Small and scaly, usually 6 pointed scales borne on spurs.

STEM: Glabrous, usually three spined, grooved, inner bark and wood yellow.

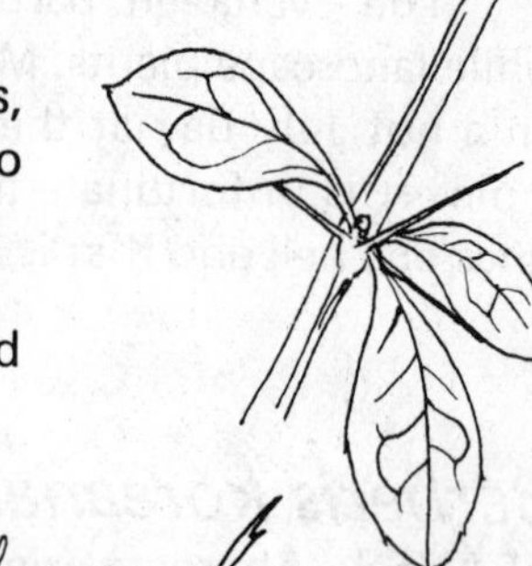

SIZE: 5' in height by 5' to 7' in spread.

HARDINESS: Zone 5.

HABIT: Upright, stiff, with many slender stems, becoming bushy with age, very regular in habit.

RATE: Medium to fast, good rapid growing hedge plant.

TEXTURE: Medium in foliage, medium-coarse in winter.

LEAF COLOR: Dark green, leathery in nature. Semi-evergreen, often developing yellow-orange-red late in fall.

FLOWERS AND FRUITS: Not important.

CULTURE: Easily transplanted, very adaptable, full sun to 1/2 shade situations, withstands cold (-20°F) and hot weather better than other barberries. A well drained soil is preferable.

DISEASES AND INSECTS: None serious, although *Verticillium* wilt has been reported, see under *B. thunbergii.*

LANDSCAPE VALUE: Excellent hedge plant because of uniform growth rate. Holds leaves into December in Central Illinois. Makes an excellent barrier plant because of thorny nature of stems. Can be used for massing, shrub border and foundation plant. Possibly the best of the barberries for hedging in the Midwest.

PROPAGATION: Cuttings, softwood, with hormone treatment (IBA) will yield 80 to 100%.

Berberis thunbergii — Japanese Barberry

LEAVES: Alternate, simple, very unequal, obovate to spatulate-oblong, 2/5 - 1 1/5" long, obtuse, rarely acute, narrowed at base into a petiole 1/12-2/5" long, quite entire, bright green above, glaucescent beneath.

BUDS: Small, ovoid, solitary, sessile, about 6 pointed scales borne on spurs.

STEM: Single spine (usually), does not always hold true.

SIZE: 3 to 6′ by 4 to 7′.

HARDINESS: Zone 4.

HABIT: Much branched, very dense, rounded shrub usually broader than tall.

RATE: Medium.

TEXTURE: Medium-fine to medium in leaf, medium-coarse in winter. Tends to attract leaves, papers, cans and bottles due to dense, multi-stemmed habit. I have personally looked upon this shrub as a winter garbage can because of this ability.

LEAF COLOR: Bright green in summer changing to orange and scarlet in the fall, usually quite variable in fall color.

FLOWERS: Perfect, yellow, mid to late April, solitary or 2 to 4 in umbellate clusters, actually not showy for individual flowers are small, 1/3 to 1/2" long, and are borne under the foliage.

FRUIT: Bright red, October and persisting into winter, an ellipsoidal berry, 1/3" long or greater.

CULTURE: Easily transplanted as a bare-root plant, extremely adaptable, withstands dry conditions, best in full sun.

DISEASES AND INSECTS: Bacterial leaf spot, anthracnose, root rots, rusts (Japanese Barberry is not susceptible), wilt, mosaic, barberry aphid, barberry webworm, scale, and northern root-knot nematode. Usually barberries are little troubled under ordinary landscape conditions.

LANDSCAPE VALUE: Hedge, barrier, groupings. The cultivars offer different foliage colors and forms and therefore other landscape possibilities.

CULTIVARS:

var. *atropurpurea* — Purplish leaves throughout season if grown in full sun; reddish green in shaded situations. Plants come about 90-95% purple leaf when grown from seeds.

'Aurea' — Bright yellow leaves throughout growing season especially if grown in full sun, somewhat gaudy, difficult to use in residential landscapes, a high contrast plant.

'Crimson Pygmy' — Dwarf form, red to purplish foliage if grown in full sun. Eight-year-old plants 2′ high and 3′ broad. Excellent low hedge, edging, or facer plant.

'Erecta' — Upright, compact form. Twenty-eight-year-old plant that was never clipped was 5′ tall and 10′ across, makes a handsome hedge.

'Globe' — Green-leaved globe shaped plant. Old specimen in Arnold Arboretum being 27" high and 48" across.

'Golden Ring' — Type with a distinct, uniform, golden margin to the leaf; inner portion reddish purple; when grown in shade the outer ring turns greenish.

'Minor' — Smaller leaves, fruits, flowers and habit than species. Dense, rounded and compact. Seventy-five-year-old plant is 3 1/2' tall and 5' wide. (Chance seedling from Arnold Arboretum).

'Rosy Glow' — Type with green-white leaves overcast with rose-red. Best in sunny spot to develop coloring. Hardy to Zone 4. New growth is exceptionally red.

'Sheridan's Red' — A vigorous selection from the *atropurpurea* group with large reddish purple leaves holding their color throughout the growing season.

'Silver Beauty' — A sprawly grower with variegated green and white foliage; not uniform in variegation patterns.

'Thornless' — Essentially thornless, globe-shaped, 1 1/2 times as wide as high at maturity.

'Variegata' — Leaves are variegated with spots or dots of white, light gray and yellow. Growth habit similar to species.

PROPAGATION: Easy to root from softwood cuttings. Seed should be stratified 15 to 40 days in moist sand:peat at 32° to 41°F.

NATIVE HABITAT: Southern Europe to Central China and Himalaya. Cultivated 1656.

Betula lenta — Sweet Birch, also called Black or Cherry Birch

FAMILY: Betulaceae

LEAVES: Alternate, simple, 2 1/2 to 5" long, oblong-ovate, doubly serrate.

BUDS: Imbricate, conical, sharp pointed, reddish brown, divergent, terminal-absent on long shoots, buds on short spurs—terminal.

STEM: Slender, light reddish brown, glabrous, shining, with strong wintergreen flavor when chewed or smelled, short spur-like lateral shoots abundant, bearing 2 leaves each season.

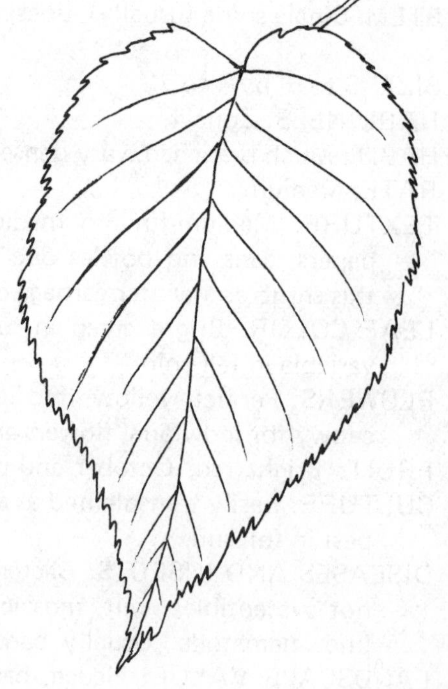

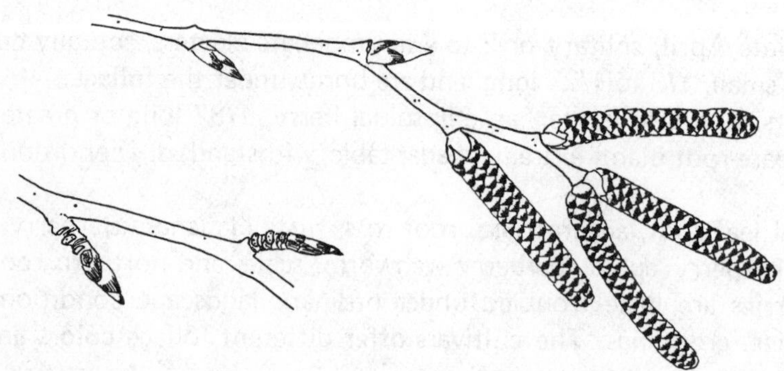

SIZE: Possibly 40 to 55' in height in a landscape situation with a spread of 35 to 45'. In the wild may reach 70 to 80' in height.

HARDINESS: Zone 3.

HABIT: Pyramidal and dense in youth forming an irregular, rounded, sometimes wide spreading crown at maturity.

RATE: Medium, 30 feet over a 20 year period.

TEXTURE: Medium in leaf and winter.

BARK COLOR: Reddish brown to almost black on young trees, with prominent horizontal lenticels; on mature trees brownish black and breaking up into large, thin, irregular, scaly plates.

LEAF COLOR: Deep dark green in summer changing to golden yellow. Exhibits the best fall color of the birches (among *B. nigra, B. papyrifera, B. pendula,* and *B. populifolia*) on the University of Illinois campus.

FLOWERS: Staminate catkins, 3/4" to 1" long; pistillate 1/2 to 3/4" long; the male flowers on birches are apparent on the tree during the winter as they are formed during summer and fall of the year prior to flowering. The pistillate flowers are enclosed in the bud and are usually borne upright while the male catkins are pendulous. In Central Illinois the birches flower in April before the leaves. They possess a hidden beauty which is lost to most people because they have never examined or considered the birches as flowering species.

FRUIT: Small nutlet, with no ornamental value; there are approximately 493,000 to 933,000 nutlets to the pound. This should afford some idea as to their size.

CULTURE: Reaches its best development in deep, rich, moist, slightly acid, well-drained soils, however, is often found on rocky, drier sites; has performed reasonably well on the heavy soils in Central Illinois.

DISEASES AND INSECTS: Birches are subject to many problems and the following list is applicable to this and the species which follow unless otherwise noted. Leaf spots, leaf blisters, leaf rust, canker (black, paper, sweet and yellow birches are particularly affected), dieback, woody-decay, and mildew are the most commonly noted pathogens. Insects include aphids, witch-hazel leaf gall aphid, birch skeletonizer, leaf miner (gray, paper, white are very susceptible), bronze birch borer and seed mite gall.

LANDSCAPE VALUE: Makes an excellent tree for parks, naturalized areas, does not have the white bark often synonymous with birches and for this reason is often shunned. Dr. Wyman mentions it is the best of the birches for fall color.

PROPAGATION: Seed, 40 to 70 days at 41°F, then germinate in sand at fluctuating temperatures of 90°F day and 59°F night. Light also seems to break the dormancy of birch seeds. (See *Seeds of Woody Plants in the United States*).

RELATED SPECIES:

Betula albo-sinensis, Chinese Paper Birch, is a little known and grown species with an exquisite bark character rivaled by few trees. E.H. Wilson in his *Aristocrats of the Trees* noted that "the bark is singularly lovely, being a rich orange-red or orange-brown and peels off in sheets, each no thicker than fine tissue paper, and each successive layer is clothed with a white glaucous bloom". Foliage is dark yellow-green in summer changing to yellow in fall. The habit is rounded and size in a landscape situation would range from 40 to 60' although it can grow 80 to 90'. The variety *septentrionalis* is similar but lacks the white glaucous bloom of the species. I have seen the species at Vineland Station, Ontario, Canada. The tree was about 25' tall and the bark had a distinct orangish cast but the exfoliating character was not evident. Native to Central and Western China. Introduced 1910. Zone 5.

NATIVE HABITAT: Maine to Alabama, west to Ohio. Introduced in 1759.

Betula alleghaniensis — Yellow Birch

LEAVES: Alternate, simple, ovate to oblong-ovate, 3 to 5" long, with pale hairs on the veins above and below, nearly glabrous at maturity, at the end of vigorous shoots often pubescent below, with 9 to 11 pairs of veins; petiole slender, 3/5 to 1" long.

BUDS: Imbricate, appressed at least along the lower part of the stem, often hairy.

STEM: Slender, dull-light yellowish brown; exhibiting the faint odor and taste of wintergreen.

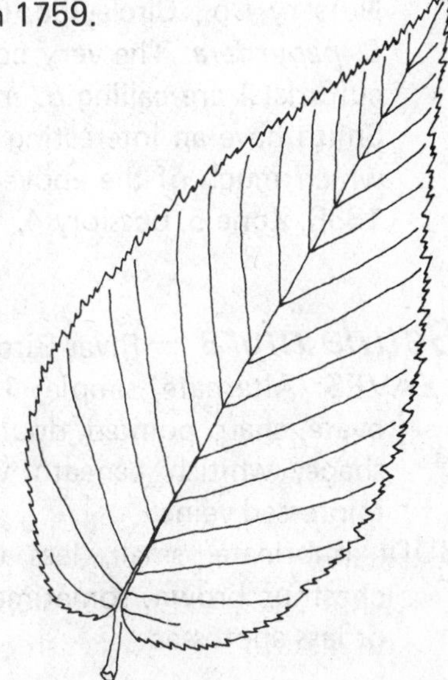

Betula alleghaniensis, Yellow Birch, is similar to *B. lenta* but grows to 60 to 75′ and occasionally 100′ in height; leaves are dull dark green above, pale yellow-green beneath in summer changing to yellow in fall; bark on young stems and branches is yellowish or bronze and produces thin papery shreds, gradually changing to reddish brown and breaking into large, ragged edged plates; prefers moist, cool soils and cool summer temperatures as it does not perform well in hot, dry climates; an important lumber tree as the wood is used extensively for cabinets, furniture, flooring and doors. Native to Newfoundland to Manitoba, south to high peaks of Georgia and Tennessee. Cultivated 1800.

Betula davurica, Dahurian Birch, is apparently used on the east coast to a small degree. The species grows 40 to 50′ in height and has rather wide spreading branches. The summer foliage is dark green changing to yellow in fall. The bark is not unlike that of *B. nigra,* River Birch, exfoliating in curly flakes of warm brown to reddish brown. Native of Manchuria, Northern China, and Korea. Introduced 1883. Zone 4 to 5.

Betula schmidtii, Schmidt Birch, is of interest because of its wood which according to Wilson is too heavy to float in water. I have seen the tree in the Arnold Arboretum and was much impressed by its neat rounded outline and clean foliage. The bark is gray-brown to black. Native to Japan, Korea and Manchuria. Introduced 1896. Zone 5.

ADDITIONAL NOTES: Wintergreen can be distilled from the stems and inner bark of *B. lenta* and *B. alleghaniensis.*

NATIVE HABITAT: Maine to Alabama, west to Ohio. Introduced 1759.

Betula maximowicziana — Monarch Birch

LEAVES: Alternate, simple, broad-ovate, acuminate, deeply cordate at base, 3 to 6″ long, double serrate, pubescent on young trees, nearly glabrous on old trees, with 10 to 12 pairs of veins, dark green, petiole 1 to 1 2/5″ long.

Betula maximowicziana, Monarch Birch, has attained heights of 100′ or more in its native habitat of Japan, however, experimental plantings in arboretums in the United States have indicated that it will generally be closer to 45 or 50′. The habit is roundish and of a mop-like nature. The foliage is dark green in summer changing to yellow in fall. The leaves and catkins are the largest of all known hardy birches. The young branches are reddish brown eventually becoming gray or whitish and the bark splits into long, broad thin sheets which cling to the tree in shaggy masses. I have seen trees labeled as *B. maximowicziana* at the Holden Arboretum, Mentor, Ohio and they were truly beautiful, however, the older bark was a uniform white, the leaves were small (about the size of *B. papyrifera*) and the leaf bases were not cordate as is supposedly typical for *B. m.* Significant advantages of this birch are the complete resistance to bronze birch borer and, unlike other birches, the tolerance to urban environments. According to Cole Nursery Co., Circleville, Ohio, this species grows about 33 percent faster than *B. pendula* or *B. papyrifera.* The very confusing aspect of the Monarch Birch is the fact that what we (horticulturists) are calling *B. m.* does not fit the taxonomic description. Drs. P.C. Kozel and R.C. Smith have an interesting article in *Horticulture.* 54(1):36, 1975, "The Monarch Birch", from which much of the above information was abstracted. Native to Northern Japan. Introduced 1888. Zone 5, possibly 4.

Betula nigra — River Birch also termed Red Birch

LEAVES: Alternate, simple, 1 to 3″ long, rhombic-ovate, sharp pointed, doubly serrate, base wedge shape, whitish beneath with 7 to 9 pairs of impressed veins.

BUD: Imbricate, small, less than 1/5″ long, light chestnut brown, sometimes pubescent, or more or less appressed.

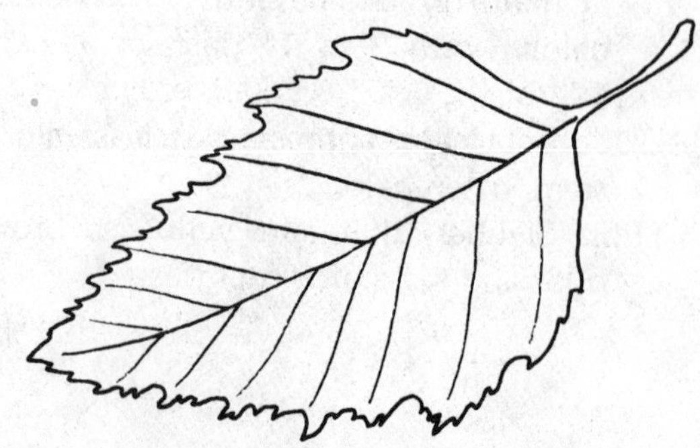

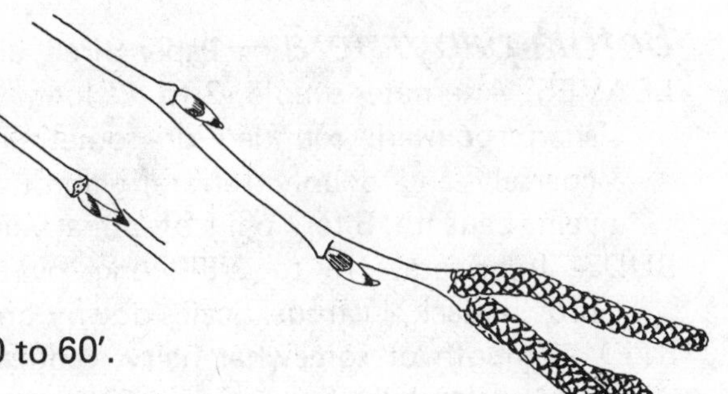

STEM: Pubescent at first, later essentially glabrous, reddish.

BARK: Young trunks and branches, thin, shining, light reddish brown to cinnamon brown, peeling freely. Older trunks, dark reddish brown, deeply furrowed, broken into irregular plate-like scales.

SIZE: 40 to 70′ and may reach 90′ in height; spread 40 to 60′.

HARDINESS: Zone 4.

HABIT: Pyramidal to oval-headed in youth, often rounded in outline at maturity. The trunk is usually divided into several large arching branches close to the ground. The tree is more handsome when grown as a multistemmed specimen.

RATE: Medium to fast, over a 20 year period can be expected to grow 30 to 40′.

BARK: On branches 2″ or greater diameter, exfoliating into papery plates and exposing the inner bark which is colored gray-brown to cinnamon-brown to reddish brown. Various authors list the color as salmon-pink but this is stretching the fact. There is tremendous variability in bark color among trees. Stands along the Illinois river exhibit extreme variability in bark color. All River Birch are seedling grown so differences in bark and other characteristics are the rule and not the exception. The biological world is composed of shades of gray and not black and white. There simply are no stereotypes in the species category. One cannot unequivocally say that all River Birch (or any other species) will have the same leaf, bark, or fall color. It is folly to think like this in relation to biological systems. Old bark of River Birch becomes brown and develops a ridged and furrowed character.

LEAF COLOR: Lustrous medium to dark green in summer changing to yellow in fall and soon dropping. The fall color on River Birch has not been effective.

FLOWERS: All birches are monoecious, staminate 2 to 3″ long; pistillate 1 to 1 1/2″ long, 1/2″ thick.

FRUIT: Small nutlet, approximately 287,000 to 548,000 seeds per pound.

CULTURE: Transplants well, best adapted to moist soils and is usually found in the wild along stream banks and in swampy bottomlands which are periodically flooded, will survive in drier soils although reaches its maximum development in moist, fertile areas, prefers an acid soil (6.5 or below) for chlorosis will develop in high pH situations.

DISEASES AND INSECTS: Listed under *B. lenta,* although leaf spots have resulted in partial or complete defoliation in 1973 and 1974. These seasons were extremely wet and in normal seasons this would not be a serious problem.

LANDSCAPE VALUE: Very handsome specimen tree for estates, parks, golf courses, campuses and other large areas. Particularly well suited to areas which are wet a portion of the year yet may be quite dry in the summer and fall. Very handsome for bark character and should receive wider landscape use as it becomes better known. The iron chlorosis on high pH soils has been extremely common in Champaign-Urbana. For this reason I would test the soil and make sure it read pH 6.5 or below before planting River Birch.

PROPAGATION: I have had good success with softwood cuttings treated with 1000 ppm IBA/50% alcohol and placed in peat:perlite under mist. Seed ripens in the spring and should be direct sowed.

ADDITIONAL NOTES: Most southernly distributed of the birches; possibly the best for hot, dry climates.

NATIVE HABITAT: Massachusetts to Florida west to Minnesota and Kansas, restricted to stream banks and other moist places.

Betula papyrifera — Paper Birch, also called Canoe or White Birch

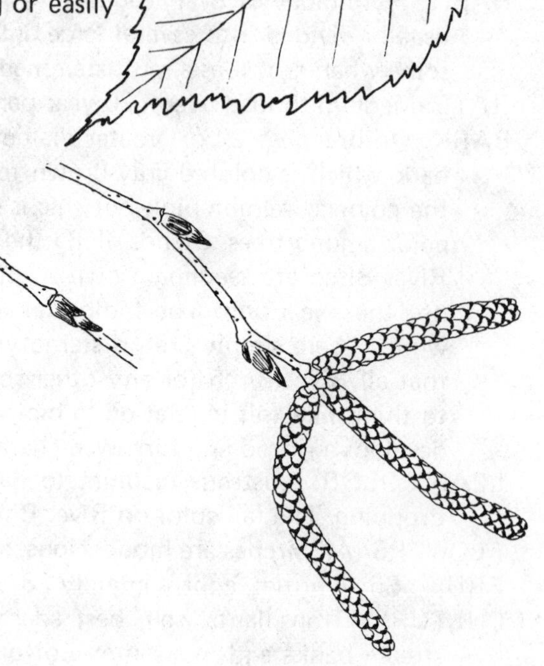

LEAVES: Alternate, simple, 2 to 4" long, ovate to narrow ovate, sharp pointed, rounded or sometimes wedge shape base, coarsely and doubly serrate, glabrous above, pubescent on veins beneath, 3 to 7 pairs of lateral veins.

BUDS: Imbricate, 1/5 to 2/5" long, ovate, pointed, divergent, brown-black, lustrous. Scales downy on margin.

STEM: Smooth or somewhat hairy, reddish brown, young stem-lightly glandular.

BARK: Trunk and older branches chalky-white, peeling or easily separated into thin paper-like layers.

SIZE: 50 to 70' in height with a spread equal to one-half to two-third's the height; Rehder noted it may reach 90 to 120' in height.

HARDINESS: Zone 2.

HABIT: Loosely pyramidal in youth developing an irregular, oval crown at maturity. Usually maintaining its branches close to the ground unless limbed up. Handsome as a single or multi-stemmed specimen.

RATE: Medium to fast, over a 10 to 20 year period averaging 1 1/2 to 2' of growth per year.

TEXTURE: Medium in leaf and in winter habit.

BARK: Thin, smooth, reddish brown on young branches, becoming creamy-white, perhaps the whitest of all birches; peels freely to expose a reddish orange inner bark which gradually turns black with age.

LEAF COLOR: Usually dull dark green in summer changing to yellow in fall. I rate this second to *Betula lenta* for excellence of fall color in Central Illinois. There is a particular specimen on campus which consistently colors a bright yellow each year.

FLOWERS: Staminate, 2 to 4" long, usually borne in 2's or 3's, pistillate 1 to 1 1/4" long, 1/4 to 1/3" thick.

FRUIT: Small nutlet.

CULTURE: Transplants readily as balled and burlapped specimen, best adapted to colder climates, adapted to a wide variety of soils, does best on well-drained, acid, moist, sandy or silty loams, full sun; not a particularly tough tree and should not be used in difficult, polluted areas.

LANDSCAPE VALUE: Handsome for bark and fall color attributes; good in parks, estates and large area plantings.

PROPAGATION: Cuttings, treated with 20 ppm IBA for 24 hours rooted 50 percent. Seed, 60 to 75 days of cold stratification, germinated under a daily light period of 8 hours resulted in percentages of 11 to 87 for various seed lots.

NATIVE HABITAT: Labrador to British Columbia and Washington south to Pennsylvania, Michigan, Nebraska and Montana. It is the most widely distributed of all American birches. Introduced 1750.

Betula pendula — European White Birch (formerly listed as *B. alba* and *B. verrucosa*)

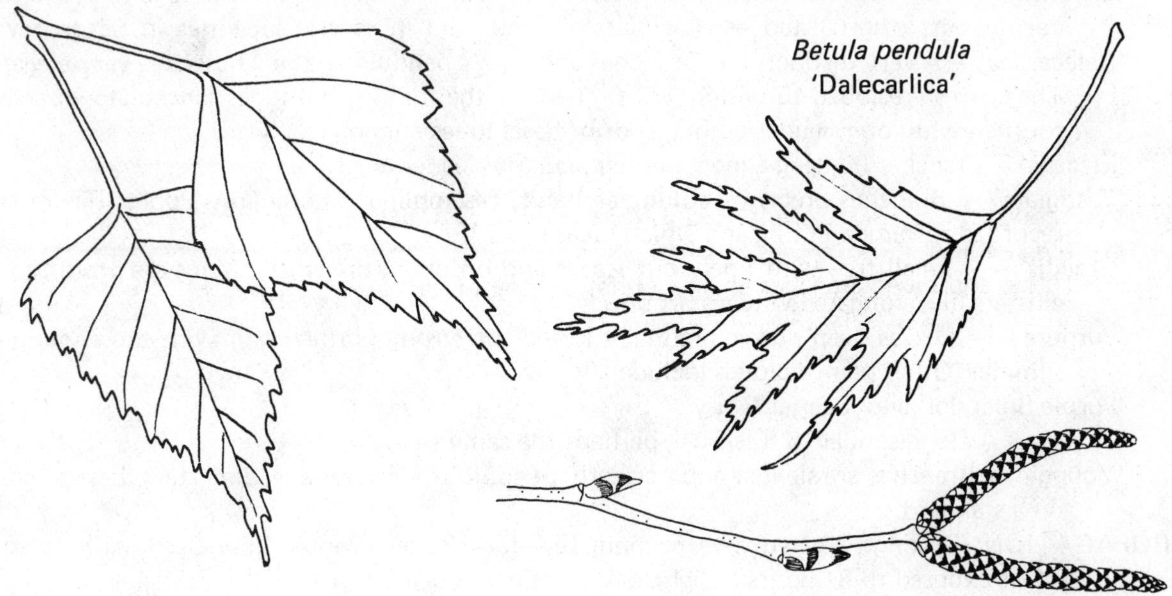

LEAVES: Alternate, simple, 1 1/4 to 3" long, apex-acuminate, base—cuneate or truncate, doubly serrate, glabrous.

BUD: Imbricate, curved, pointed, brownish black.

STEM: Glabrous, resinous-glandular, brown, smoother than paper or gray.

BARK: Whitish, does not peel (exfoliate) to degree of Paper Birch. With age trunk becomes black with relatively small amount of white bark showing.

SIZE: 40 to 50' in height with a spread one-half to two-third's the height, may reach 80 to 100' or more in the wild.

HARDINESS: Zone 2.

HABIT: Gracefully pyramidal in youth, developing an oval pyramidal to oval outline with time while maintaining the graceful pendulous branching habit; sometimes rounded in outline.

RATE: Medium to fast, growing 30 to 40' over a 20 year period.

TEXTURE: Medium-fine in leaf; medium in winter habit.

BARK: Brownish in youth (1 to 1 1/2" diameter) changing to white on larger branches and with time developing black fissured areas.

LEAF COLOR: Dark glossy green in summer changing to a poor yellow or yellow green in Central Illinois, seems to hold the green leaves later into fall than the other species.

FLOWERS: Staminate, approximately 2" long, usually in 2's, sometimes singly or in 3's; pistillate, 3/4 to 1 1/4" long, 1/3" wide, cylindrical.

FRUIT: Small nutlet, 730,000 to 860,000 winged seeds per pound.

CULTURE: Transplants readily, should be moved in spring, does best in moist, well-drained, sandy or loamy soil but will tolerate wet or dry soils, seems to be more pH tolerant than *B. nigra*, should be pruned in summer or fall as pruning in late winter or early spring causes the tree to "bleed" excessively.

DISEASES AND INSECTS: See under *B. lenta*. Leaf miner and bronze birch borer are serious pests; I do not recommend European White Birch for the Midwest because of the borer; it can be controlled but most people wait until considerable injury has occurred and then it is too late to save the tree. The top is infected first. If one has specimen trees a regular spray program is a worthwhile investment.

LANDSCAPE VALUE: Very popular tree gracing the front or back yard of one out of three homes in Champaign-Urbana, still widely sold by many nurserymen and, unfortunately, purchased by the uninitiated. Tree has been extensively used for lawns, parks, and cemeteries.

CULTIVARS:

var. *crispa* — Has been confused with 'Dalecarlica' but the leaves are more regularly and less deeply cut; often listed as 'Laciniata'; found wild in several localities in Scandinavia.

'Dalecarlica' — A very distinct tree, branches and leaves pendulous; the whole tree very elegant. The leaves are lobed to within 1/8 to 1/4" of the midrib, the lobes lanceolate, coarsely toothed with long slender points, ends of basal lobes curving backward.

'Elegans' — Branches hanging almost perpendicularly, leader erect.

'Fastigiata' — Branches erect, of columnar habit, resembling a Lombardy Poplar. There is a recorded specimen in England which measures 71'.

'Gracilis' — A small tree with finely cut leaves and drooping branches. Stems are produced in clusters like elongated witches brooms.

'Purpurea' — Leaves deep purple gradually losing the strong purple color with the coming of summer. Other named clones include:

'Purple Splendor' and 'Scarlet Glory'.

'Tristis' — A clone similar to 'Elegans', perhaps the same tree.

'Youngii' — Branches are slender and perfectly pendulous, without a leading stem; best to graft on a standard.

PROPAGATION: Cuttings, treated with 50 ppm IBA for 32 hours rooted 25%. Seed, with no cold period but exposed to 8+ hours of light/day germinated 30%.

RELATED SPECIES:

Betula platyphylla, Asian White Birch, is probably represented in cultivation by the varieties *japonica* and *szechuanica.* Dr. Ed Hasselkus, University of Wisconsin, mentioned that while other birches, especially *B. pendula,* were dying out in the U. of W. Landscape Arboretum this birch continued to thrive. The original planting of three still exists which would indicate bronze birch borer resistance. Variety *japonica* would be the preferred tree under landscape conditions for it is rather large (85'), with thin spreading branches and pure white bark on the trunk. Under landscape conditions the tree would grow 40 to 50'. The Wisconsin trees are 25 to 30' with a relaxed, pyramidal habit and have maintained a dominant central leader. The leaves are about 1 1/2 to 3" long, glossy dark green and shaped somewhat like those of *B. pendula* but differ by virtue of being broader with axillary tufts beneath, more numerous veins and usually single toothing. Bean noted that in England it thrives well in cultivation. Native of Japan and the Okhotsk peninsula. Cultivated since 1887. Zone 4. To date, I like what I have seen of the tree and based on observations of an old tree in the Arnold Arboretum the bark character (whiteness over time) may be better than *B. pendula.* The variety *szechuanica* is more open and wide spreading than the above but according to Bean a rather graceless tree, with a silvery-white bark. The leaves are thick, blue-green, and remain on the tree longer than other birches. Distinguished from var. *japonica* by the leaves which are dotted with glands beneath. Native to Western China. Introduced 1872. Zone 5.

ADDITIONAL NOTES: Other birches are more suitable for the Midwest and should be used in preference to this species. When purchasing a "white" birch make sure of the scientific name for any birch with white bark is a "white" birch.

NATIVE HABITAT: Europe (including Britain), especially high latitudes and parts of Northern Asia. Long cultivated.

Betula populifolia — Gray Birch, also called Old Field Birch, White Birch, Poverty Birch, and Poplar Birch

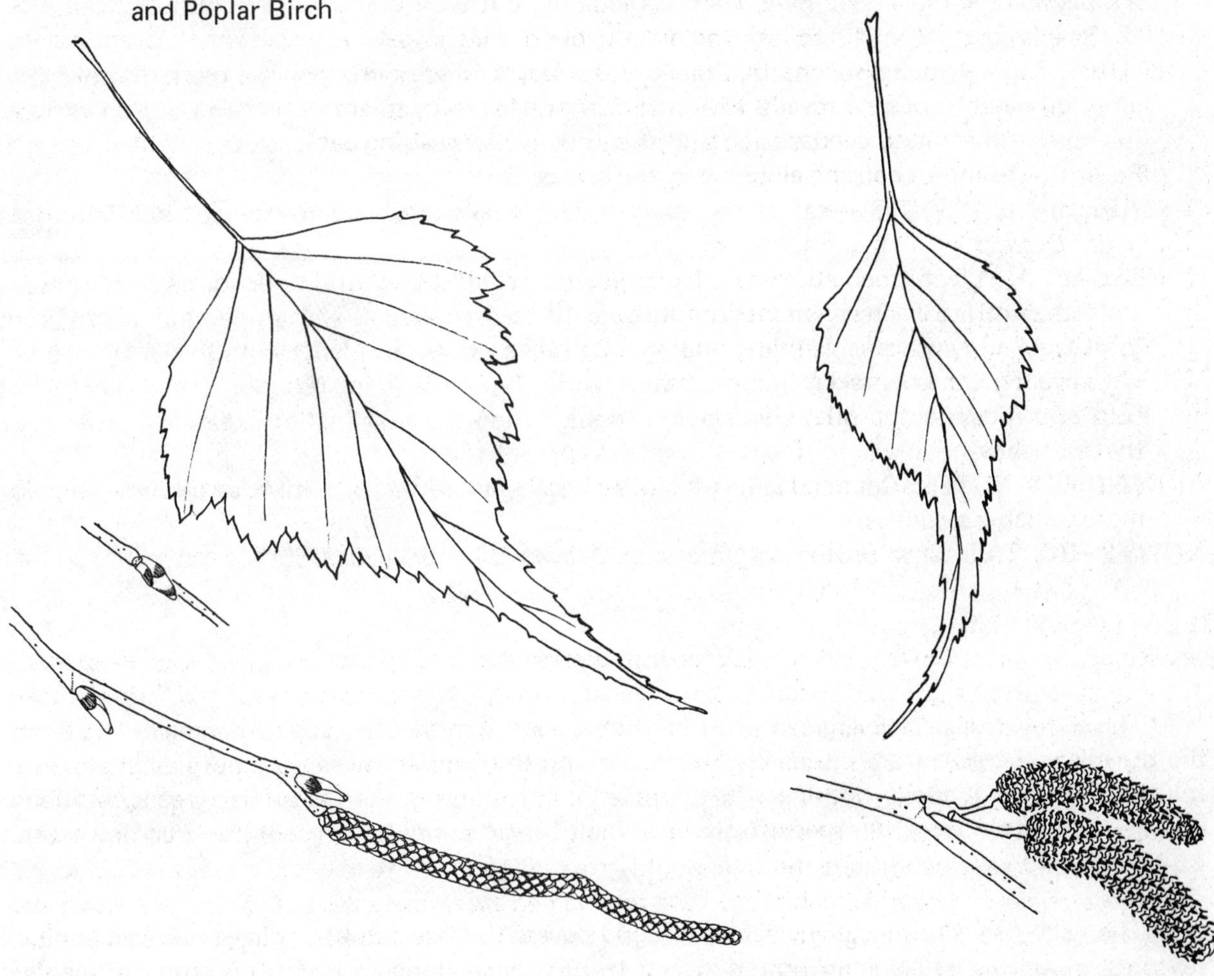

LEAVES: Alternate, simple, 2 to 3 1/2" long, triangular-ovate or deltoid, long acuminate, truncate at base, coarsely or doubly serrate, glutinous when young, lustrous dark green above.

BUD: Imbricate, 1/5" or less in length, brownish, smooth, somewhat resinous, ovate, pointed, divergent. Scales—finely downy on margin.

STEM: Slender, bright reddish brown or grayish, roughened by warty resinous exudations.

BARK: Dull chalky-white (older branches), close, not peeling, with distinct dark triangular patches below insertion of branches, inner bark reddish-orange-yellow.

MALE CATKIN: Borne singly at end of branches, 2 to 3 1/2" long.

SIZE: 20 to 40' in height with 30' a more reasonable size in the Midwest; spread is about 10 to 20'.

HARDINESS: Zone 3.

HABIT: Narrow, irregularly open, conical crown with slender branches ending in fine stems that are often pendulous. Usually a multiple stemmed tree in the wild but can be grown single-stemmed. Has a tendency to develop shoots from the roots and often forms thickets. One of the smallest of the birches and usually short-lived (15 to 25 years).

RATE: Medium to fast, averaging 2' per year over a 10 to 15 year period. Often forms pure stands in cut-over or burned forest lands in a very short time.

TEXTURE: Medium-fine in leaf; medium in winter habit.

BARK: Thin, smooth, reddish brown on young trunks becoming chalky white with prominent, triangular black patches below the bases of the branches. Does not peel readily.

LEAF COLOR: Dark glossy green in summer changing to yellow in fall. Does not color well in the Champaign-Urbana area.

FLOWERS: Staminate, 2 to 3 1/2" long, catkin borne singly at the end of the branches, rarely in 2's, pistillate 3/4 to 1 1/4" long, 1/4" diameter.

FRUIT: Small nutlet.

CULTURE: Transplant balled and burlapped in spring, relishes in the poorest of sterile soils, will grow on sandy, rocky, gravelly sites and also heavier soils, tolerates wet and dry conditions, full sun, intolerant of competition and this should be considered if it is used in the landscape. Probably the most widely used birch on the east coast.

DISEASES AND INSECTS: Leaf miner, cankers, but is quite resistant to bronze birch borer, see under *B. lenta.*

LANDSCAPE VALUE: Good for naturalizing, possibly could be used in poor soils along highways and other difficult sites. The ability to quickly seed an area as well as develop shoots from roots (suckering) is valuable in developing rough sites where few plants will survive.

PROPAGATION: Cuttings taken in July treated with 50 ppm IBA for 6 hours rooted 30%. Seed, cold stratification for 60 to 90 days or light during the germination treatment will break the dormancy.

ADDITIONAL NOTES: Commercially of limited value but serves in nature as a nurse plant for more valuable seedlings.

NATIVE HABITAT: Nova Scotia and Ontario to Delaware. Introduced 1780.

Broadleaf Evergreens

The term 'Broadleaf Evergreen' is in the literal sense a misnomer. The gardening public thinks the broadleaf evergreens are intimately associated with the Coniferales because both maintain green foliage all season. Actually nothing is further from the truth for the broadleaf evergreens, with only a few exceptions (*Podocarpus* species), are in actuality angiosperms and produce normal flowers and fruits.

The wide diversity of growth habits (ground covers to large shrubs), foliage types and unique textures as well as outstanding flowering and fruiting characteristics make this group of plants a valuable asset in any landscape planting.

The broadleaf coverage is fairly complete and includes many types not commonly found in this part of the country. However with artistic and scientific manipulation of the environment every type can be grown with a certain degree of success. The following cultural criteria, if followed, will result in successful broadleaf evergreen production.

CULTURE OF BROADLEAF EVERGREENS

1. Select plants which are reasonably hardy in your area.
2. Provide an open well drained soil with an ample supply of organic matter.
3. Maintain a cool, moist soil by providing partial shade and mulches.
4. Use mulches also to reduce cultivation which may damage the shallow, very fine silk-like roots of many broadleaf evergreens.
5. Transplant with a ball of soil or from container grown plants.
6. Do not plant these types under unfavorable environmental conditions such as *poorly drained* soils or where there is excessive exposure to *drying winds* or *winter sun.*
7. Provide acid soil conditions for acid soil types. These include most members of the Ericaceae which have unique cultural, nutritional and morphological characteristics. Flowers of sulfur and $FeSO_4$ can be used to acidify soils. One and one-half to 4 pounds per 100 square feet of soil surface will help. It is best to soil test for absolute pH values. A pH in the range of 4.5 to 5.5 is desirable. If your soil tests 8.0, use 8 1/4 lbs. of ferrous sulfate per 25 sq. ft. of soil; pH 7.5 use 7 3/4 lbs.; pH 7.0 use 6 lbs.; pH 6.5 use 4 3/4 lbs.; pH 6.0 use 3 1/2 lbs.; pH below 6.0, no correction is needed. Iron is actually the limiting element under high pH regimes as

the iron is rendered insoluble. The use of chelated iron (FeEDTA) as a foliage spray or soil additive will correct the problem often referred to as 'Lime Induced Chlorosis' or 'Iron Chlorosis'.

8. Water broadleaf evergreens in the fall. Do not let them dry excessively in winter. Applications of anti-desiccants may be helpful in some situations of sun and wind exposure. Cost and difficulty of application limit their use by average homeowners.

PROPAGATION:

Most broadleaf evergreens can be propagated by cuttings, however it is difficult to achieve 100% efficiency. Rhododendron, holly, ivy, barberry, boxwood, pachysandra, viburnum, euonymus, pachistima, bearberry, heather, leucothoe, pieris, laurel-cherry and pyracantha are relatively easy to root. There are types especially in the genus *Rhododendron* that are difficult to root. Rhododendrons are easy to grow from seed and often times an individual is sold hybrid stock rather than asexually propagated true-to-type material.

Broussonetia papyrifera — Paper Mulberry

FAMILY: Moraceae

LEAVES: Alternate, occasionally opposite, ovate, 3 1/2 to 8" long, acuminate, cordate at base, coarsely dentate, on young plants often deeply lobed, scabrous above, soft-pubescent beneath; petioles 1 1/4 to 4" long, sap milky; dull green.

BUDS: Moderate, conical, solitary, sessile, outer scale longitudinally striped.

STEM: Moderate, rounded, pith large and white with a thin green diaphragm at each node; leaf scars 2-ranked, large, rounded, elevated; bundle-traces about 5 aggregated in ellipse; stipule scars long and narrow; zig-zag, hispid when young.

SIZE: 40 to 50' in height with a comparable or greater spread.

HARDINESS: Zone 6.

HABIT: Tree with wide-spreading branches forming a broad, rounded crown; usually low branched.

RATE: Fast, 20 to 30' over a 6 to 8 year period.

TEXTURE: Medium-coarse in all seasons.

LEAF COLOR: Dull green and rough on the upper surface; lower-densely woolly until the leaves fall; no fall color of any consequence.

FLOWERS: Dioecious, male borne in cylindrical, often curly, woolly, 1 1/2 to 3" long and 1/4" wide, yellowish catkins; female flowers in ball-like 1/2" diameter head; May.

FRUIT: Red, 3/4" diameter, aggregate of drupes; September.

CULTURE: Apparently easy to grow. Thrives in any soil; does well in dirt and grime of cities; tolerates heat and drouth; highly alkaline soils; full sun.

DISEASES AND INSECTS: Canker, root rot, dieback, leaf spot, root knot nematode.

LANDSCAPE VALUE: Often planted for ornament; sometimes used as a street tree, casts heavy shade and will send up shoots from the roots. W.J. Bean mentions that this tree can make a nice street specimen.

CULTIVARS:

'Cucullata' — A male tree with curious leaves whose margins are curled upwards, so as to give the leaf the shape of a boat.

'Laciniata' — A dwarfish clone with the leaf reduced to a stalk and the three main veins, ends of which have a small, narrow, variously shaped blade.

PROPAGATION: Softwood cuttings collected in July and August of short shoots with a heel attached will root readily.

ADDITIONAL NOTES: Interesting tree which is closely allied to the mulberries *(Morus)* but is less woody. The common name is derived from the use of the bark for paper, and in the Polynesian islands for the fiber, which is made into a cloth. The lobed leaves occur primarily on young vigorous trees; the unlobed ones on flowering specimens.

NATIVE HABITAT: China, Japan. Cultivated 1750. Occasionally naturalized from New York to Florida and Missouri.

Buxus microphylla — Littleleaf Box or Boxwood

FAMILY: Buxaceae

LEAVES: Opposite, simple, obovate to lance-obovate, 1/3 to 1" long, rounded or emarginate, cuneate, entire, usually medium green often turning yellowish brown in winter.

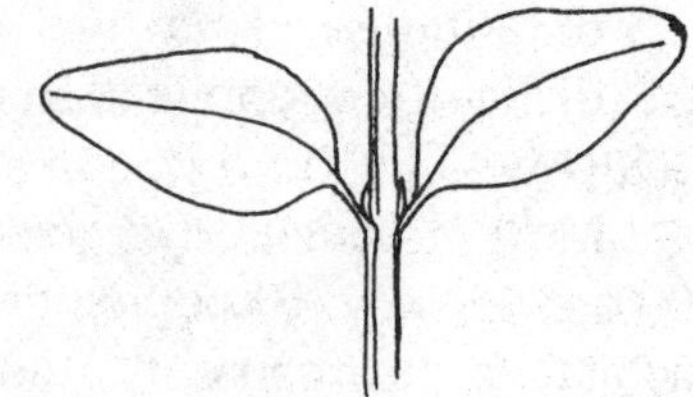

BUDS: Small, solitary, sessile, ovoid with 1 or 2 pairs of visible scarcely specialized scales.

STEMS: Slender, green, flat, grooved between each pair of leaves, stems appear sharply quadrangular.

SIZE: 3 to 4' in height by 3 to 4' in spread.

HARDINESS: Zone 6, although some cultivars are listed as Zone 5.

HABIT: Evergreen, much branched, compact, dense, rounded or broad rounded shrub.

RATE: Slow.

TEXTURE: Medium-fine in all seasons.

LEAF COLOR: Medium green in summer changing to repulsive yellow-green-brown in winter.

FLOWERS: Apetalous, in axillary or terminal clusters consisting of a terminal pistillate flower and several staminate flowers, early March; not showy but fragrant.

FRUIT: Capsule.

CULTURE: Transplant balled and burlapped or from a container into well-drained soil; responds well to mulching with peat or leaf mold for roots require cool moist conditions; full sun or light shade; protect from drying winds and severe low temperatures; often necessary to shade newly transplanted plants from summer sun; apparently boxwood roots should not be cultivated around since it is a surface rooter.

DISEASES AND INSECTS: Canker, blight, leaf spots, root rot, winter injury and sun scald (physiological injury), mealybugs, scales, boxwood psyllid, boxwood leaf miner, giant hornet, boxwood webworm, nematodes and boxwood mite. Most of these problems are more prevalent on *Buxus sempervirens.*

LANDSCAPE VALUE: Excellent as hedge plant, for foundations, edging situations, formal gardens.

CULTIVARS:

'Compacta' — Small, dense, slow growing form with excellent dark green foliage. 47-year-old plant is 1' by 4'.

'Green Pillow' — Similar to 'Compacta' except the leaves are twice as large.

var. *koreana* — (Zone 4) Extremely hardy geographical variety of the species. The foliage turns brown in the winter. Somewhat loose and open in habit and twice as wide as high at maturity.

'Tide Hill' — Cultivar of the above variety with green foliage all winter. 20-year-old plant is 15" by 5'.

'Wintergreen' — Cultivar of the Korean variety which retains its green foliage through the winter. Seems to do perfectly well in the Chicago area.

PROPAGATION: Cuttings root readily anytime of the year.

NATIVE HABITAT: Japan. Introduced 1860.

Buxus sempervirens — Common Box or Boxwood

LEAVES: Opposite, simple, elliptic or ovate to oblong, 2/5 to 1 1/5" long, obtuse or emarginate at apex, dark green above, light or yellowish green beneath, and usually lustrous on both sides.

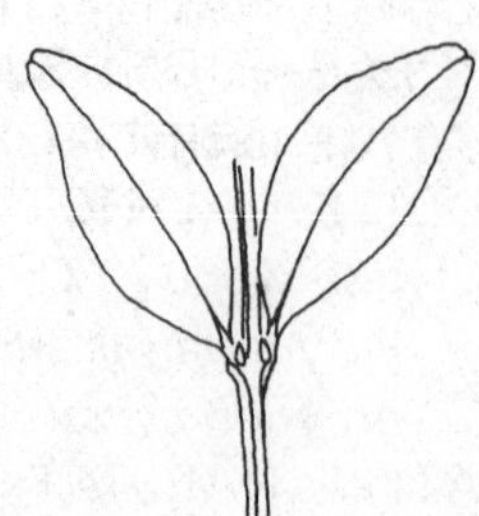

STEM: Somewhat angled but not like *Buxus microphylla.*

SIZE: 15 to 20' in height with an equal or greater spread; can grow to 30' but this size is rarely attained.

HARDINESS: Zone 5 to 6 depending on cultivar.

HABIT: Dense, multibranched shrub; of round or broad-rounded outline holding its foliage to the ground. Old, over-grown specimens in Spring Grove Cemetery, Cincinnati, Ohio, with 4 to 6″ diameter trunks were cut back to 1 to 2′ from the ground and have developed new shoots and are filling in nicely.

RATE: Slow, but faster than *B. microphylla.*

TEXTURE: Medium-fine in all seasons.

LEAF COLOR: Lustrous dark green above, light or yellowish green below in all seasons.

FLOWERS AND FRUITS: Ornamentally unimportant.

CULTURE: Similar to *B. microphylla* except does best in warm, moist climates that do not have extremes of summer heat or winter cold.

DISEASES AND INSECTS: See under *B. microphylla.*

LANDSCAPE VALUE: Excellent specimen and is used extensively on the East Coast; good for hedges, massing, topiary work, formal gardens; might be called the "aristocrat" of the hedging plants.

CULTIVARS:

'Angustifolia' — Treelike in habit with leaves 1 to 1 1/4″ long.

'Argenteo-variegata' — Leaves variegated with white.

'Aureo-variegata' — Leaves variegated with yellow.

'Bullata' — Low growing form with short blunt leaves that are decidedly green.

'Curly Locks' — Compact, upright growing form; the branches have a curling or twisting habit. 20-year-old plant is 2′ by 4′.

'Handsworthiensis' — Wide, strong growing, upright form with dark green foliage. Makes a good hedging plant.

'Inglis' — Hardy form, densely pyramidal in habit with a good dark green foliage all winter. Supposedly hardy to -20°F.

'Myrtifolia' — Low growing form, 4 to 5′ tall.

'Newport Blue' — Foliage is bluish green, habit is densely rounded. 14-year-old plant is 18″ by 3′.

'Northern Find' — Hardy form selected from a group of plants in Cooksville, Ontario, Canada, where it withstood temperatures of -30°F.

'Northland' — Hardy form from Central New York state. 14-year-old plant is 4′ by 5′ with dark green foliage all winter.

'Pendula' — Form with pendulous branchlets.

'Pullman' — Selected by W.A.P. Pullman, Chicago, Illinois, for incredible vigor and hardiness (-20°F), starts growth in mid May and is not injured by late freezes; a rounded, dense habit and will probably grow to about 6′ in height.

'Rosmarinifolia' — Low shrub with leaves 1/4 to 5/8″ long, about the smallest of any cultivar.

'Suffruticosa' — Dense, compact, slow growing form ideal for edging. Leaves quite fragrant and least susceptible to box leaf miner. 150-year-old plants are about 3′ high.

'Vardar Valley' — (Zone 4) Probably the best low growing form for Illinois. Basically, a flat-topped, dense form with good green foliage all winter. Found growing in the Vardar Valley of the Balkans in 1935.

'Welleri' — Dense, broad form, 13-year-old plant is 3′ by 5′ and green throughout the winter.

PROPAGATION: Cuttings root readily. I use 1000 ppm IBA/50% alcohol and achieve excellent results.

ADDITIONAL NOTES: Wood is of a hard, bony consistency; good for carving. The foliage has a distinctly malodorous fragrance.

NATIVE HABITAT: Southern Europe, Northern Africa, Western Asia.

Callicarpa japonica — Japanese Beautyberry

FAMILY: Verbenaceae

LEAVES: Opposite, simple, elliptic to ovate-lanceolate, 2 to 5″ long, long acuminate, cuneate, serrulate, glandular beneath.

BUDS: Small, superposed, often distinctly stalked or the uppermost developing the first season, round or fusiform oblong, naked, or the smaller appearing to have 2 nearly valvate scales.

STEM: Round, slender, gray-buff.

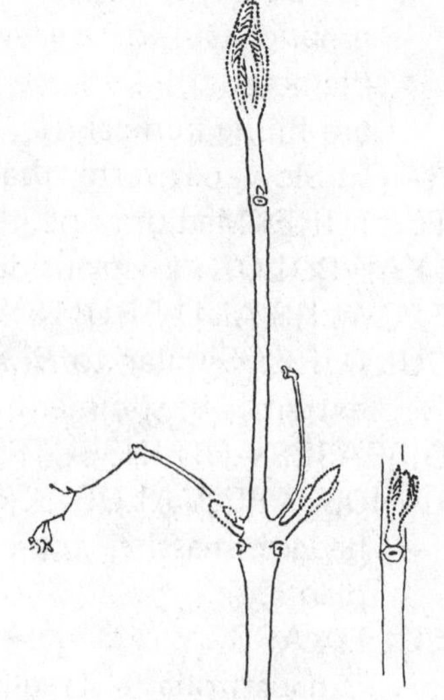

SIZE: 4 to 6′ in height by 4 to 6′ in spread.

HARDINESS: Zone 5.

HABIT: Bushy, rounded shrub with arching branches.

RATE: Fast.

TEXTURE: Medium in all seasons.

LEAF COLOR: Medium green in summer becoming yellowish in fall.

FLOWERS: Perfect, pink or white; July; many flowered cymes, 3/5 to 1 1/5″ across.

FRUIT: Berry-like drupes, 1/6″ across, violet to metallic-purple; effective in October for about 2 weeks after the leaves fall off.

CULTURE: Readily transplanted; well drained soil; full sun or light shade; prune to within 4 to 6″ of the ground every spring as the flowers are produced on new growth.

DISEASES AND INSECTS: Leaf spots, black mold, and various stem diseases. None of these are serious.

LANDSCAPE VALUE: Most effective when planted in groups in the shrub border. The fruit is very attractive and unusual in color among woody plants.

CULTIVARS:

'Leucocarpa' — White fruits.

PROPAGATION: Softwood cuttings root readily in sand under mist, in fact, all *Callicarpa* root readily from softwood cuttings.

RELATED SPECIES:

C. dichotoma, Purple Beautyberry, has deep lilac fruits set on purplish stems and leaves that turn purplish late in the fall. Possibly not as hardy as the above species, Zone 5.

NATIVE HABITAT: Japan. Introduced 1845.

Calluna vulgaris — Scotch Heather

FAMILY: Ericaceae

LEAVES: Opposite, scale-like, 4-ranked, sessile, keeled, oblong-ovate, 1/25 to 1/8″ long, sagittate at base, puberulous or nearly glabrous.

BUDS: Small, solitary, sessile, angularly globose, with about 3 scales.

STEM: Very slender, terete; pith-very small, roundish, continuous.

SIZE: 4 to 24″ in height; spread 2′ or more.

HARDINESS: Zone 4.

HABIT: Upright branching, small evergreen ground cover type shrub with densely leafy ascending branches forming thick mats.

RATE: Slow.

TEXTURE: Fine in all seasons.

LEAF COLOR: Medium green in summer; winter color varies from green to bronze.

FLOWERS: Perfect, rosy to purplish pink, urn-shaped; borne in 1″ to 10″ racemes in July-September. Exquisite, dainty, refined plants especially when in flower.

FRUIT: Capsule, not important.

CULTURE: Move as a container grown plant in spring; prefer acid (pH 6 or less), sand or organic, moist, perfectly drained soils; avoid sweeping winds as plants are very susceptible to drying; full sun or partial shade, however, plants do not flower as profusely in shade; prefer low fertility soils, otherwise become ratty looking; do not over fertilize, prune in early spring before new growth starts; do not cultivate soil around plants; mulch and water during dry periods.

DISEASES AND INSECTS: Japanese beetle, two-spotted mite and oyster shell scale.

LANDSCAPE VALUE: Good ground cover plant, edging, rock garden. Excellent flowers and foliage put this plant at the top of my groundcover list. Fastidious as to soil requirements and attention to cultural details is necessary.

CULTIVARS: There are so many cultivars that it would be impossible to do justice to them. Best to consult a reference text like Wyman's *Shrubs and Vines for American Gardens.*

PROPAGATION: Seed should be sown on peat moss. There is no dormancy and germination takes place in 2 to 3 weeks. I have raised many *Calluna* plants this way. Softwood cuttings treated with 1000 ppm IBA quick dip, rooted in 2 to 3 weeks in a peat:perlite medium under mist.

RELATED SPECIES: The genus *Erica* is similar to *Calluna* but not as hardy and popular in the midwest. Some of the important species include *Erica carnea,* Spring Heath; *Erica cinerea,* Twisted Heath; *Erica tetralix,* Crossleaf Heath; and *Erica vagans,* Cornish Heath. I have only seen a few heaths and they are quite similar in morphological features to *Calluna* differing only in time of flowering (Spring) and a greater abundance of species.

NATIVE HABITAT: Europe, Asia Minor; naturalized in Northeastern North America.

Calycanthus floridus — Common Sweetshrub, also called Carolina Allspice or Strawberry-Shrub.

FAMILY: Calycanthaceae

LEAVES: Opposite, simple, entire, ovate or elliptic to narrow-elliptic, 2 to 5" long, acute or acuminate, rarely obtuse, cuneate or rounded at base, grayish green and densely pubescent beneath.

BUDS: Superposed in a single bud-like aggregate, sessile, round or oblong, brown hairy, without evident scales, the end bud lacking.

STEM: Aromatic when bruised, stout, compressed at the nodes, pith—relatively large, somewhat 6-sided, white, continuous; leaf scars – U or horseshoe-shaped, raised, 3 bundle traces.

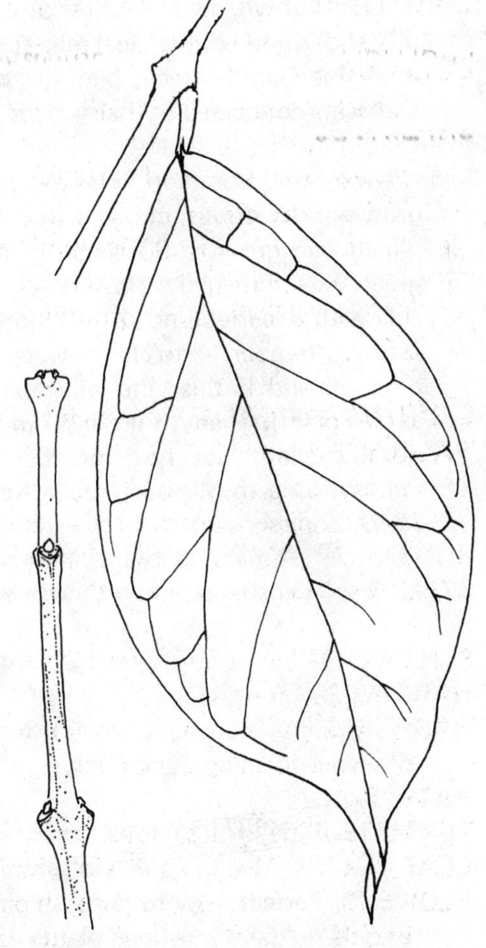

SIZE: 6 to 9' in height by 6 to 12' in spread.

HARDINESS: Zone 4.

HABIT: Dense, bushy, rounded or broad rounded shrub of regular outline.

RATE: Slow.

TEXTURE: Medium in leaf and in winter.

LEAF COLOR: Dark green in summer; yellowish in fall, but usually not effective.

FLOWERS: Perfect, dark reddish brown, 2" across, very fragrant, mid-May and flowering sporadically into June and July, borne singly.

FRUIT: Urn-shaped receptacle, somewhat capsule-like at maturity and enclosing many one seeded achenes; brown in color.

CULTURE: Easily transplanted, adaptable to many soils; preferably a deep, moist, loam; shade or sun, but does not grow as tall in sun as in shaded places; prune after flowering.

DISEASES AND INSECTS: Very resistant shrub.

LANDSCAPE VALUE: Worthwhile plant for every garden especially welcome in the shrub border or around an outdoor living area where the sweet strawberry scent can permeate the entire area.

PROPAGATION: Seeds are easy to germinate. I have collected them in December and sowed them immediately with good results. I do not know if there is an absolute stratification requirement. Cuttings collected in early July rooted 90% in sand in 60 days with Hormodin #2.

RELATED SPECIES:

Calycanthus fertilis, Pale Sweetshrub, is often confused with the above, however, the leaves are less pubescent and the flowers have little or no scent. Great quantities of fruit are set. Native over same territory as *C. floridus.*

ADDITIONAL NOTES: All parts and particularly the wood when dry exude a camphor-like fragrance; supposedly the bark was used as a substitute for cinnamon.

NATIVE HABITAT: Virginia to Florida. Introduced 1726.

Campsis radicans — Common Trumpetcreeper

FAMILY: Bignoniaceae

LEAVES: Opposite, pinnately compound, 9 to 11 leaflets, short-stalked, elliptic to ovate-oblong, 1 1/5 to 2 2/5" long, acuminate, cuneate, serrate.

BUDS: Small, mostly solitary, sessile, triangular, compressed, with 2 or 3 pairs of exposed scales.

STEM: Light brown, aerial rootlets develop between nodes, pith—solid, pale brown, leaf scar—crater like depression with one bundle trace, bud sits on top of leaf scar, leaf scars connected by hairy ridge.

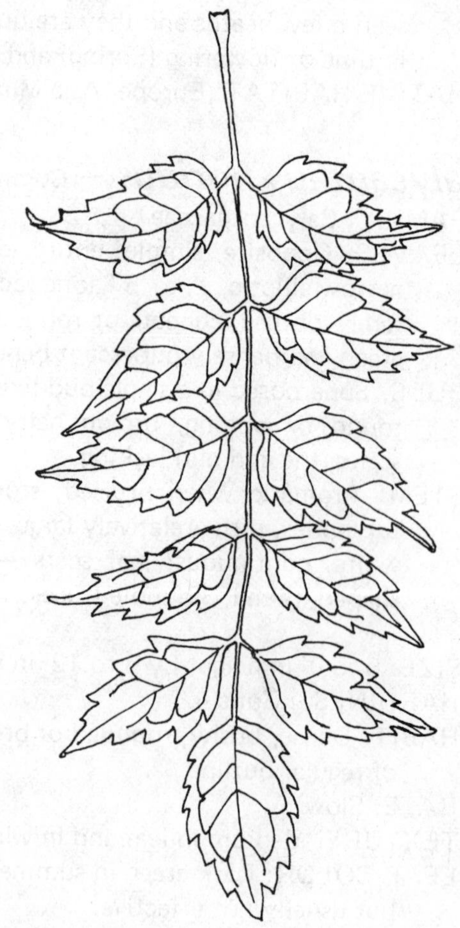

Campsis radicans, Common Trumpetcreeper, is a rampant growing, deciduous, clinging (rootlike holdfasts) vine which can grow to 30 to 50'. The foliage is bright green in summer; the flowers are orange on the outside with a scarlet limb, 2 to 4" long, July-August and into September, 4 to 12 flowers together; grows in any soil and if this vine will not grow there is little sense planting anything else in that area; tough, durable plant but not for the average landscape. Pennsylvania to Missouri, south to Florida and Texas. 1640. Zone 4.

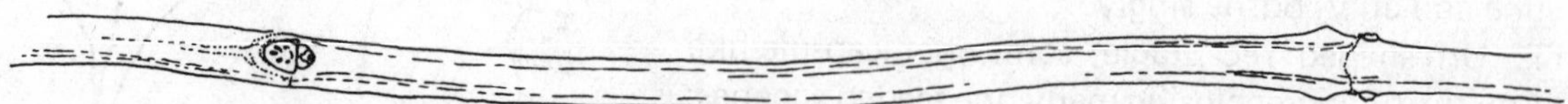

Caragana arborescens — Siberian Peashrub

FAMILY: Leguminosae

LEAVES: Alternate, pinnately compound, 8 to 12 leaflets, obovate to elliptic-oblong, 2/5 to 1" long, rounded at apex and acuminate, pubescent when young, later glabrescent, bright green.

BUDS: Weakly imbricate, light brown in color, bud scales—chaffy in nature.

STEM: Green in color, remaining so for several years, angled from the nodes, with pale, horizontal lenticels. Usually of scurfy appearance.

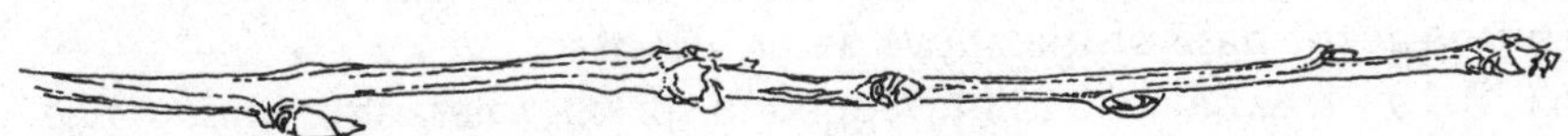

SIZE: 15 to 20' in height with a spread of 12 to 18'.

HARDINESS: Zone 2.

HABIT: Erect, oval shrub, often taller than broad with moderate, sparse branches; can also be grown as a tree.

RATE: Medium to fast.

TEXTURE: Medium in summer, coarse in winter.

LEAF COLOR: Light, bright green in summer; briefly yellow-green in fall.

FLOWERS: Perfect, bright yellow, 3/5 to 4/5" long, early to mid May on previous year's wood when the leaves are 2/3's to fully developed; borne singly or up to 4 in fascicles.

FRUIT: A pod, 1 2/5 to 2" long, yellow-green changing to brown.

CULTURE: Very easy to grow; extremely cold hardy and able to tolerate poor soils and drought as well as sweeping winds; an extremely adaptable but limitedly ornamental plant.

DISEASES AND INSECTS: Nothing too serious although leaf-hoppers have decimated the lone specimen on the University of Illinois campus.

LANDSCAPE VALUE: Good for hedge, screen, windbreak where growing conditions are difficult. I would not recommend it for wholesale use.

CULTIVARS:

'Nana' – Dwarf form with contorted branches.

'Pendula' – Weeping form, branches are not graceful but the effect is kind of interesting.

PROPAGATION: Seed should be stratified for 15 days at 41°F or longer. Cuttings taken in late July rooted 80% in sand without treatment.

NATIVE HABITAT: Siberia, Mongolia, Manchuria. 1752.

Carpinus betulus — European Hornbeam

FAMILY: Betulaceae

LEAVES: Alternate, simple, sharply and doubly serrate, 2 1/2 to 5" long, similar to *Carpinus caroliniana* except leaf of thicker texture, veins more impressed above.

BUD: Imbricate, angular-conical, usually appressed, brownish to reddish, curl around stem, scales with soft pubescence, 1/4 to 1/3" long.

STEM: Glabrous, olive-brown, prominently lenticelled.

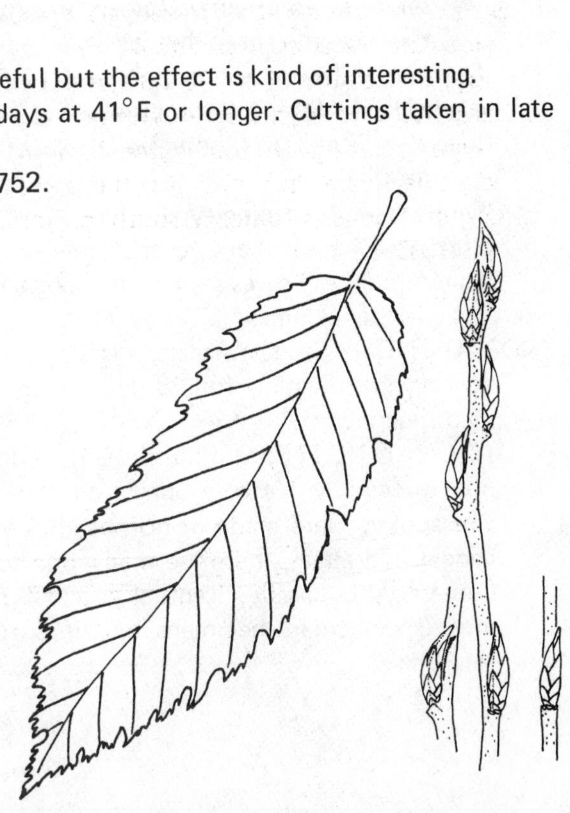

SIZE: 40 to 60' in height by 30 to 40' in spread; potentially can reach 70 to 80' in height.
HARDINESS: Zone 4.
HABIT: Pyramidal in youth, oval-rounded at maturity, appearing egg-shaped in outline.
RATE: Slow to medium, about 10' over a 10 year period, perhaps slightly faster.
TEXTURE: Medium-fine in leaf and winter habit; exquisitely tailored in winter with the slender branches dapperly arranged around the main leader.
BARK: Usually on old wood a handsome gray and the wood is beautifully fluted.
LEAF COLOR: Dark green in summer changing to yellow or yellowish green in fall. The summer foliage is usually very clean, i.e., no evidence of insect or disease damage.
FLOWERS: Monoecious, male not preformed as in *Betula*, not ornamentally important, the male catkins, 1 1/2" long; the female 1 1/2 to 3" long, furnished with large, conspicuous 3-lobed bracts, the middle lobe 1 to 1 1/2" long, often toothed, borne in April.
FRUIT: Nut, ribbed, 1/4" long, borne at the base of the above described bract.
CULTURE: Transplant as a small (8-10') tree balled and burlapped in spring; tolerant of wide range of soil conditions—light to heavy, acid to alkaline, but prefer well drained situations, performs best in full sun but will tolerate light shade, pruning is seldom required although this species withstands heavy pruning, partially tolerant of difficult conditions.
DISEASES AND INSECTS: None serious, in fact, unusually free of problems which lead to extensive maintenance.
LANDSCAPE VALUE: One of the very finest small landscape trees; excellent for screens, hedges, groupings, around large buildings, in malls, planter boxes; withstands pruning as well as or better than European Beech; a choice specimen with an air of aloofness unmatched in any plant. The many excellent cultivars are probably preferable to the species for landscape situations.
CULTIVARS:

'Asplenifolia' – Leaves deeply and regularly double-toothed.

'Columnaris' – A densely branched and foliaged, spire-like, slow growing tree usually maintaining a central leader. A very handsome plant, but little known and used.

'Fastigiata' – Somewhat of a misnomer as the tree develops an oval shape and reaches 30 to 40' in height with a spread of 10 to 15'. Larger specimens have been recorded but the size listed is representative for landscape conditions. Grew 25' high and 14' wide after 10 years in the Oregon Tests, very highly rated tree in the Ohio Shade Tree Evaluation Tests, serves as an effective screen in winter because of the dense, compact, close-knit nature of the ascending branches.

'Globosa' – Rounded and globose in habit without a central leader.

var. *horizontalis* – A flat topped variety supposedly similar to *Crataegus crusgalli* in outline.

'Incisa' – Similar to 'Asplenifolia' except with smaller and shorter leaves, coarsely and irregularly toothed.

'Pendula' – A weeping type.

'Purpurea' – Leaves are purplish.

'Quercifolia' – Leaves somewhat oak-shaped in outline; this cultivar has been mistakenly called 'Incisa' at times.

PROPAGATION: Seed, dormancy is apparently caused by conditions in the embryo and endosperm; stratification for 28 days at 68°F followed by 87 to 98 days at 41°F in sand:peat is recommended.
ADDITIONAL NOTES: Minimum seed bearing age is between 10 and 30 years; to date I have had poor success with seed propagation; the wood is extremely hard, heavy, and tough; cogs, axles, and spokes were made of hornbeam; used extensively in English and continental Europe for hedges and allees; there are many fine specimens of this species and the cultivars in Cave Hill Cemetery, Louisville, Kentucky, and Spring Grove Cemetery, Cincinnati, Ohio. Perhaps the most spectacular specimens of the species are located in Lexington Cemetery, Lexington, Kentucky.

Carpinus caroliniana — American Hornbeam, also called Blue Beech, Ironwood, Musclewood, and Water Beech.

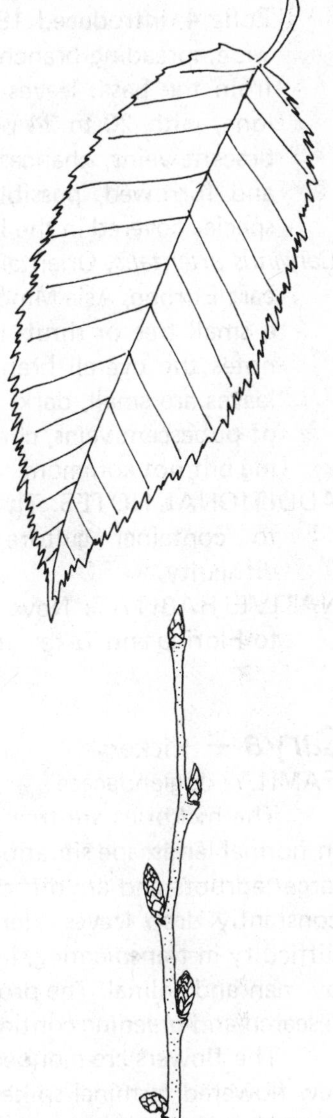

LEAVES: Alternate, simple, 2 1/2 to 5″ long, ovate-oblong, sharply and doubly serrate, glabrous, except pilose on veins beneath and with axillary tufts of hair, veins seldom forking at ends.

BUD: Imbricate, small, 12 4-ranked scales, 1/12-1/6″ long, narrowly ovate to oblong, pointed, reddish-brown-black, more or less hairy, especially buds containing staminate catkins, terminal bud absent. Scales—often downy on edges, frequently with woolly patch of down on tip.

STEM: Slender, dark red-brown, shining, smooth or often somewhat hairy, pith—pale, continuous.

BARK: Smooth, thin, dark bluish gray, close fitting, sinewy, fluted with smooth, rounded, longitudinal ridges. Wood-heavy and hard.

FRUIT: Small, ribbed, seed-like nutlet enclosed by a veiny, generally 3-lobed bract about 1″ long.

SIZE: 20 to 30′ in height, often smaller but with the potential to reach 40′.

HARDINESS: Zone 2.

HABIT: Small, multistemmed, bushy shrub or single-stemmed tree with a wide-spreading flat or round-topped (often irregular) crown. Somewhat unkempt in form.

RATE: Slow, averaging 8 to 10′ over a 10 year period.

TEXTURE: Medium in leaf; somewhat coarse in winter, possibly medium-coarse; coarseness is largely due to the disheveled winter appearance.

BARK COLOR: On older branches develops a slate gray, smooth, irregularly fluted appearance. The overall appearance is comparable to the flexed bicep and forearm muscles and, hence, the name Musclewood.

LEAF COLOR: Dark green in summer changing to yellow, orange and scarlet in the fall; fall coloration is poor in Central Illinois, the overall effect a yellow-red-brown on most trees.

FLOWERS: Monoecious, male, 1 to 1 1/2″ long; female, 2 to 3″ long; the bracts 3 lobed 1 to 1 1/2″ long, the middle lobe the widest (1″ diameter), toothed.

FRUIT: A nut(let).

CULTURE: Somewhat difficult to transplant and should be moved balled and burlapped or from a container in spring; performs best in deep, rich, moist, slightly acid soils although will grow in drier sites; does well in heavy shade and is often found as an understory plant in forests; probably if used in the landscape should be sited in partial shade; does not take pruning as well as *C. betulus* and is probably an inferior tree except for fall color.

DISEASES AND INSECTS: Leaf spots, cankers, twig blight, maple phenococcus scale, none of which are significantly serious.

LANDSCAPE VALUE: Best in naturalized situation; interesting native tree often seen in the woods and inappropriately called "beech" by the uninitiated.

CULTIVARS:

'Pyramidalis' — The tree is supposedly V-shaped with a rounded top. A tree in the Arnold Arboretum at 43 years of age was 40′ tall and 33′ in spread.

PROPAGATION: Seed, moist stratification at 68-86°F for 60 days followed by 41°F for 60 days.

RELATED SPECIES:

Carpinus japonica, Japanese Hornbeam, native to Japan, Zone 4, introduced 1879; 40 to 50′ in height with wide spreading branches but definitely fan shaped from the base; leaves are dark green, 2 to 4 1/2″ long, with 20 to 24 pairs of deeply impressed pubescent veins, changes to red in fall; bark is scaly and furrowed, possibly the coarsest of the four species covered in the book.

Carpinus orientalis, Oriental Hornbeam, native of Southeast Europe, Asia Minor, Zone 5. Introduced 1739; a small tree or shrub to 25′ in height, Dr. Wyman notes the overall branching structure is U-shaped; leaves are small, dark, glossy green, 12 to 15 pairs of pubescent veins, changing to red in fall. Interesting but not common.

ADDITIONAL NOTES: This species might be well suited to container culture because of transplanting difficulty.

NATIVE HABITAT: Nova Scotia to Minnesota, south to Florida and Texas. Introduced 1812.

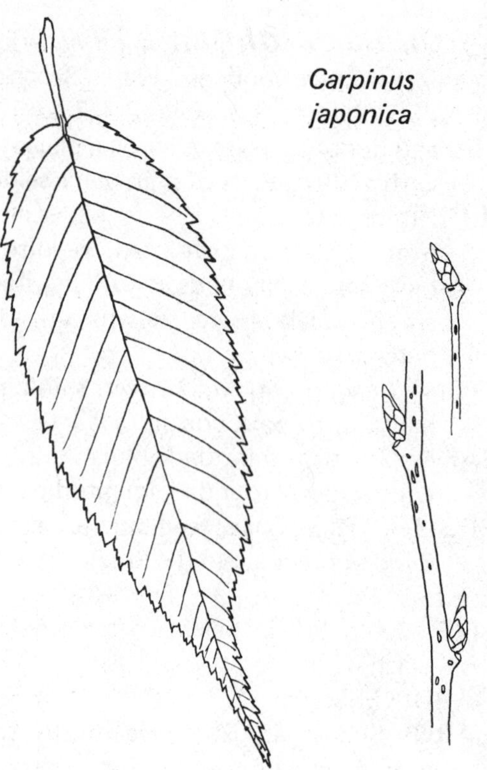
Carpinus japonica

Carya — Hickory

FAMILY: Juglandaceae

The hickories are treated as a group rather than individual entities because of their limited use in normal landscape situations. Although extremely beautiful and esthetic native trees, they develop large taproots and are difficult to transplant. Most are large trees reaching 60′ or more and seem to constantly drop leaves, stems, or fruits. Their size and limited ornamental assets, as well as the difficulty in transplanting, limit extensive landscape use. The nuts are edible and utilized extensively by man and animal. The production of pecan, *Carya illinoinensis,* is a large commercial business and research and breeding continues on this most important crop.

The flowers are monoecious with the male borne in drooping 3-branched catkins; the female in few flowered terminal spikes, developing with the leaves in late April into early May. The fruits are bony, hard-shelled nuts encased in a 4-valved "husk" (involucre?) often splitting away but in some species persisting. They usually ripen in October and soon drop from the trees. The seeds are either bitter or sweet. In the wild, seed dissemination is largely through squirrels who bury them in the forest floor as a food reserve. The hickories are typically American trees and the following are some of the more common.

ADDITIONAL NOTES: *Carya* exhibit embryo dormancy and should be stratified in a moist medium at 33° to 40°F for 30 to 150 days. Prior to the cold treatment nuts should be soaked in water at room temperature for 2 to 4 days with 1 or 2 water changes per day. Cultivars are budded or grafted on seedling understocks.

Carya cordiformis — Bitternut Hickory

LEAVES: Alternate, pinnately compound, 5-9 leaflets, 3 to 6″ long, ovate to lanceolate, acuminate, serrate, light green and pubescent below.

BUD: Valvate scales, strikingly sulfur yellow, terminal bud—1/5 - 3/5″ long, flattened, obliquely blunt pointed, scurfy-pubescent. Lateral buds—more or less 4-angled, much smaller than terminal.

STEM: Stout, buff, gray or reddish, smooth or slightly downy toward apex. Pith-brown.

Carya cordiformis — Bitternut Hickory can grow to 50 to 75′ in height and larger; usually a slender tree with rather irregular, cylindrical crown of stiff ascending branches, often widest at the top; supposedly the fastest growing of the hickories; seeds are bitter and squirrels tend to ignore them; native from Quebec to Minnesota, south to Florida and Louisiana. Introduced 1689. Zone 4.

Carya glabra — Pignut Hickory reaches 50 to 60′ in height with a spread of 25 to 35′ although can grow to 100′. It has a tapering trunk and a regular, rather open, oval head of slender, contorted branches; found along hillsides and ridges in well-drained to dry, fairly rich soils; seeds are bitter and astringent; native from Maine to Ontario, south to Florida, Alabama and Mississippi. Introduced 1750. Zone 4.

Carya illinoinensis — Pecan

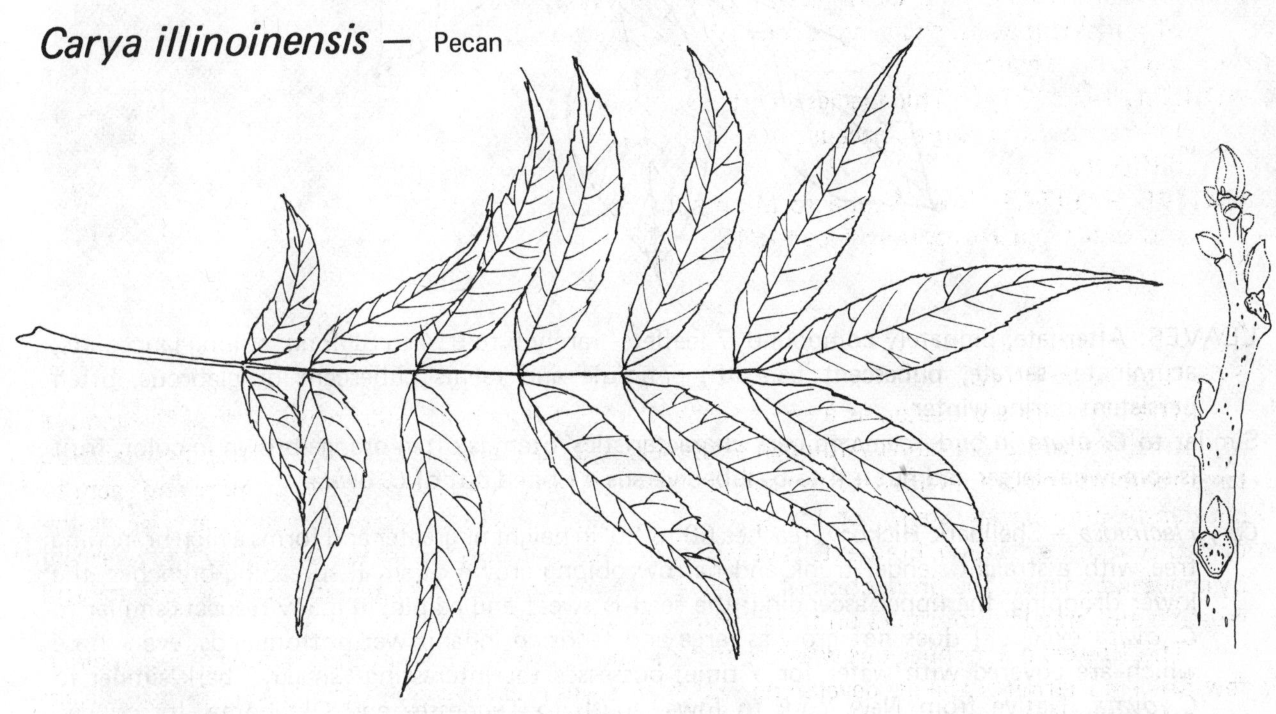

LEAVES: Alternate, pinnately compound, 11 to 17 leaflets, 4 to 7″ long, short-stalked, dark green, oblong-lanceolate, serrate or doubly serrate, glandular and tomentose when young, becoming glabrous; petiole-glabrous or pubescent.

BUD: Valvate, 1/5 - 2/5″ long, dark brown, pubescent, ovoid, apex pointed, looks like a small roasted almond.

STEM: Stout, olive-brown to brown, pubescent, leaf scar indented and partially surrounding bud.

Carya illinoinensis — Pecan will grow to 70 to 100′ in height with a spread of 40 to 75′ and can reach 150′; largest of the hickories, tall and straight with a uniform, symmetrical, broadly oval crown; extremely difficult to transplant as it develops a long taproot; on a 6′ tree the tap root may extend 4′ or more; prefers deep, moist, well-drained soil; the best hickory for fruits and many cultivars have been selected for outstanding fruiting characters. Native from Iowa to Indiana to Alabama, Texas and Mexico; follows the river basins very closely. Introduced 1760. Zone 5. Makes an interesting ornamental in Central Illinois but does not bear liberal quantities of fruit.

Carya laciniosa — Shellbark Hickory

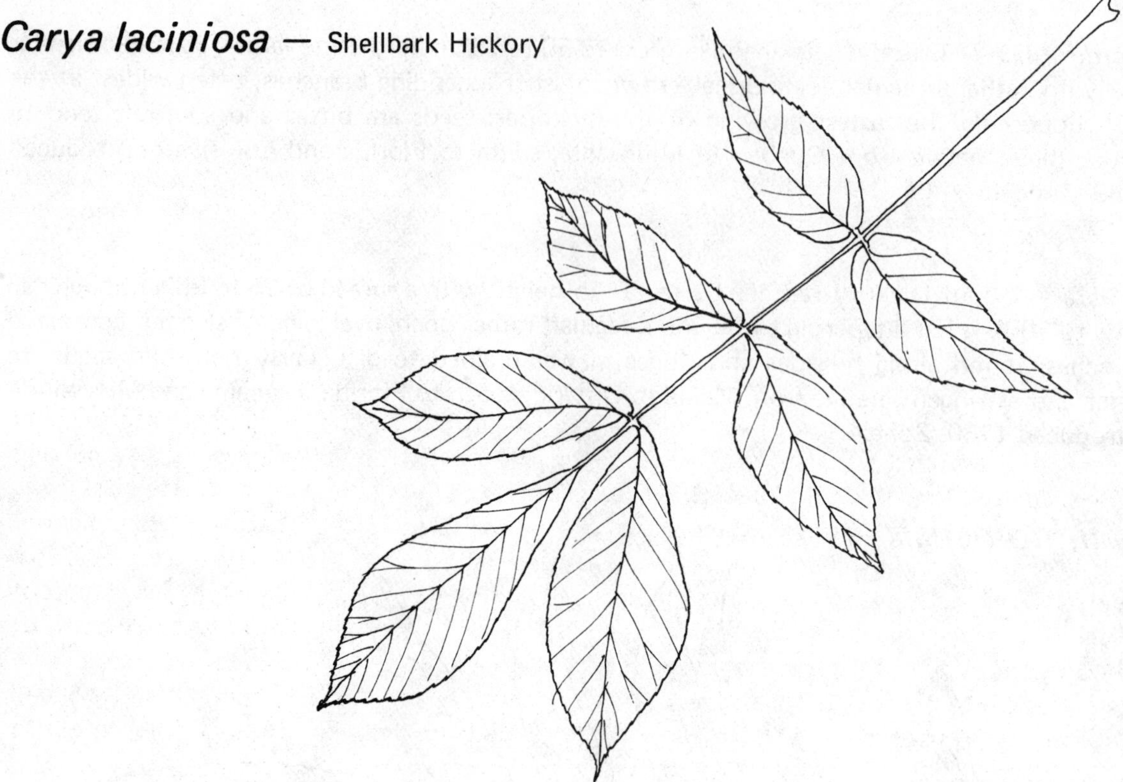

LEAVES: Alternate, pinnately compound, 7 leaflets—rarely 5 to 9, 4 to 8″ long, oblong-lanceolate, acuminate, serrate, pubescent beneath; petiolule and rachis pubescent or glabrous, often persistent during winter.

Similar to *C. ovata* in bud, stem and bark characteristics. Stem is often orange-brown in color, fruit is somewhat larger and nut is 4 to 6 ribbed versus 4 ribbed nut of *C. ovata.*

Carya laciniosa — Shellbark Hickory, reaches 60 to 80′ in height or greater and forms a high branching tree with a straight slender trunk and narrow oblong crown of small spreading branches, the lower drooping, the upper ascending; the seed is sweet and edible; in many respects similar to *C. ovata* except it does not grow as large and tends to inhabit wet bottomlands, even those which are covered with water for a time; possesses the interesting "shaggy" bark similar to *C. ovata.* Native from New York to Iowa, south to Tennessee and Oklahoma. Introduced 1800. Zone 5.

Carya ovata — Shagbark Hickory

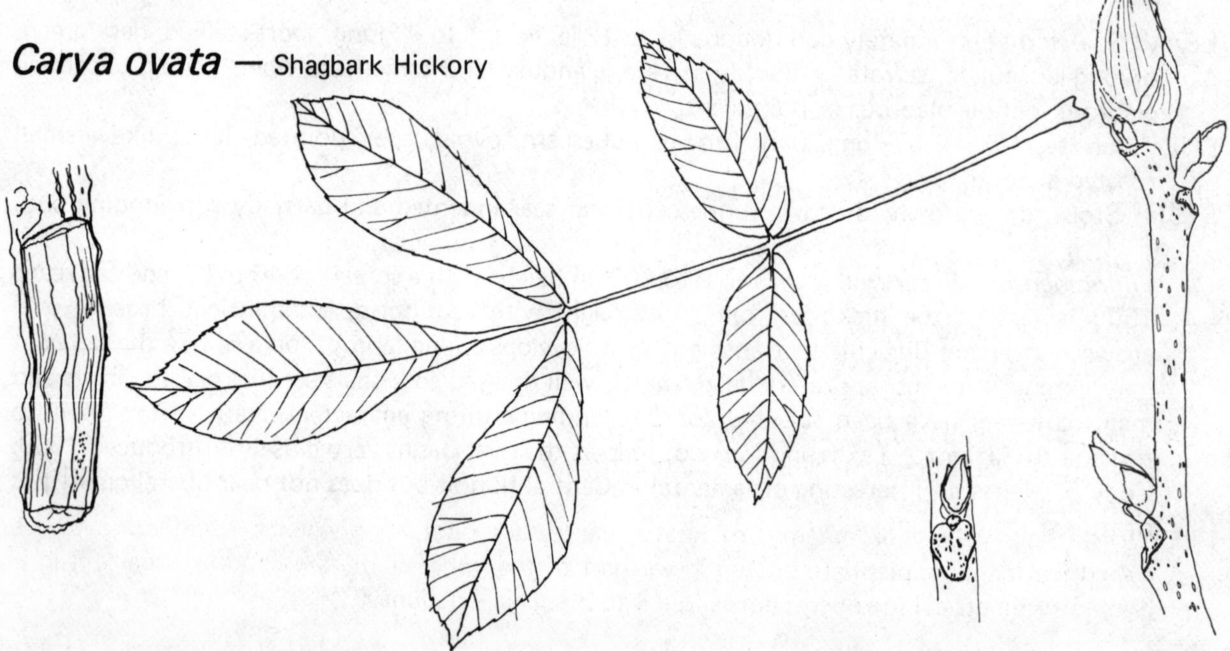

LEAVES: Alternate, pinnately compound, 5 leaflets rarely 7, 4 to 6" long, elliptic to oblong-lanceolate, acuminate, serrate and densely ciliate, pubescent and glandular below when young, finally glabrous.

BUD: Imbricate, terminal—2/5 to 4/5" long, broadly ovate, rather blunt-pointed, brown, with 2 to 4 visible, overlapping, pubescent, loose fitting scales.

STEM: Stout, somewhat downy or smooth and shining, reddish brown to light gray. Lenticels—numerous, pale, conspicuous, longitudinally elongated.

BARK: On old trunks shagging characteristically into long flat plates which are free at the base or both ends. Usually more pronounced than Shellbark.

Carya ovata, Shagbark Hickory, is a large tree reaching 60 to 80' in height but can grow to 100 to 120'; usually develops a straight, cylindrical trunk with an oblong crown of ascending and descending branches (similar to *C. laciniosa*); the foliage is a deep yellow green in summer and changes to rich yellow and golden brown tones in fall (this is also true for *C. laciniosa*); the seed is edible; what could taste better than hickory smoked hams and bacon; try some hickory chips in your next barbecue outing; prefers rich and well drained loams, but is adaptable to a wide range of soils; seedlings of this hickory develop a large and remarkably deep taproot which may penetrate downward 2 to 3' the first season with a corresponding top growth of only a few inches; this is typical of many hickories; the bark is gray to brown and breaks up in thin plates which are free at the end and attached at the middle; the overall effect is a "shaggy" character and, hence, the name Shagbark Hickory. Native from Quebec to Minnesota, south to Georgia and Texas. Cultivated 1629. Zone 4.

Two other species, *Carya tomentosa,* Mockernut Hickory, and *Carya ovalis,* Red Hickory, are native over much of eastern United States and may be encountered in the wild. They are of negligible importance for landscaping and further information can be obtained in appropriate forestry texts.

Castanea mollissima — Chinese Chestnut

FAMILY: Fagaceae

LEAVES: Alternate, simple, 3-6" long, elliptic-oblong to oblong-lanceolate, acuminate, rounded or truncate at base, coarsely serrate, whitish tomentose or green and soft-pubescent beneath.

BUD: Two to 3 scales, weakly overlapping, gray-brown, pubescent, 1/8" long or less.

STEM: Pubescent with long spreading hairs, olive-brown, prominent lenticels, pith-star-shaped; 4 to 5 sided, bark on second and third year stems is cherry-like in appearance.

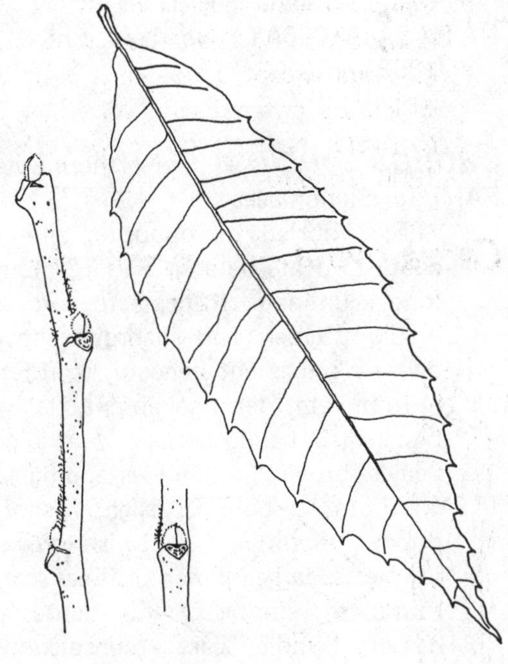

SIZE: 40 to 60' in height with an equal spread.

HARDINESS: Zone 4.

RATE: Slow to medium, 4 to 7' over a 3 to 4 year period.

TEXTURE: Medium throughout the seasons.

BARK: Gray-brown to brown and strongly ridged and furrowed.

LEAF COLOR: Reddish upon unfolding changing to a lustrous dark green in summer culminating with shades of yellow and bronze in fall.

FLOWERS: Pale yellow or creamy, of heavy, unpleasant odor, monoecious; staminate in erect cylindrical catkins, pistillate on the lower part of the upper staminate catkins, usually 3 in a prickly symmetrical involucre; borne in a 4 to 5" panicle in June.

FRUIT: Nut, 2 to 3 enclosed in a prickly involucre which splits at maturity into 2 to 4 valves, fruits are edible and relished by man and animals. Seed grown trees often produce fruit after 4 to 5 years.

CULTURE: Easily transplanted when young (5 to 6'); prefer acid (pH 5.5 to 6.5), well-drained, loamy soil; full sun; does well in hot, dry climates; responds well to fertilization.

DISEASES AND INSECTS: Blight (discussed under *C. dentata*), twig canker of asiatic chestnuts, weevils which damage the roots.

LANDSCAPE VALUE: Possibly for shade tree use; best as a replacement for the American Chestnut; valued for fruits.

PROPAGATION: Seed should be stratified under cool moist conditions for 60 to 90 days. Cuttings taken from young trees have been rooted.

RELATED SPECIES:

Castanea dentata — American Chestnut

LEAVES: Alternate, simple, oblong lance-shaped in outline, with cuneate base and long-pointed tips, 5-8" long.

STEMS AND BUDS: Glabrous, chestnut brown.

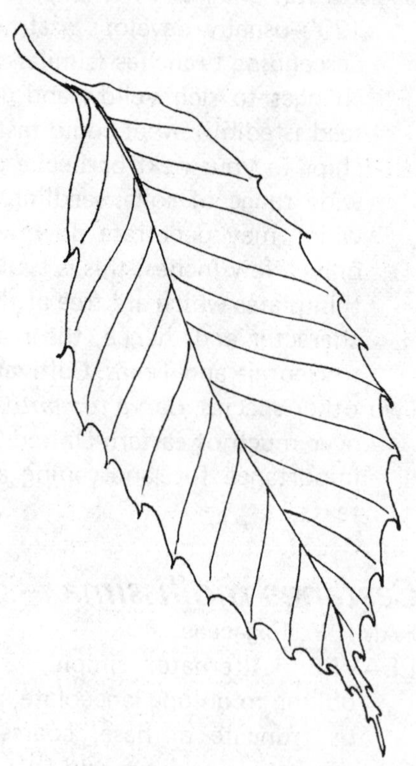

Castanea dentata, American Chestnut, was once native from Southern Maine to Michigan, south to Alabama and Mississippi. Cultivated 1800. This tree was once the queen of eastern American forest trees but now is reduced to a memory. About 1906 a blight, *Endothia parasitica,* was introduced along the east coast and spread like wildfire through the forests. All that remains are isolated stump and root sprouts which developed after the parent tree was killed. The tree reached heights of 100 feet and developed massive, wide-spreading branches, and a deep broad rounded crown. The flowers are similar to those of *C. mollissima* however the fruits are reported as being much sweeter and more flavorful than the asiatic species.

NATIVE HABITAT: Northern China, Korea. Introduced 1853 and 1903.

Catalpa speciosa — Northern Catalpa, also called Western Catalpa or Hardy Catalpa.

FAMILY: Bignoniaceae

LEAVES: Whorled or opposite, simple, ovate to ovate oblong, 6 to 12" long, long acuminate, truncate to cordate, medium green and glabrous above, densely pubescent beneath, scentless.

BUD: Imbricate, terminal-absent, lateral buds small, hemispherical, 1/12" high. Scales—brown, loosely overlapping.

STEM: Stout, smooth or slightly short-downy, reddish to yellowish brown. Lenticels - large, numerous. Leaf scars-round to elliptical with depressed center. Bundle scars - conspicuous, raised, forming a closed ring; pith is solid white.

FRUIT: Capsule, 8-20" long, 3/5" wide, wall thick, seeds fringed.

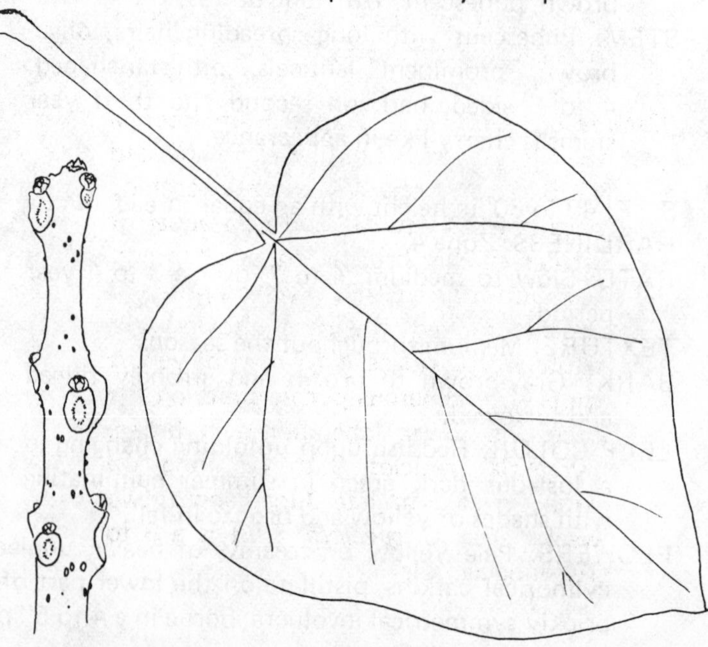

SIZE: 40 to 60′ in height with a spread of 20 to 40′ but sometimes reaching 100′ or more in the wild.

HARDINESS: Zone 4.

HABIT: Tree with a narrow, open, irregular, oval crown.

RATE: Medium to fast, 15′ over 7 to 8 year period.

BARK: Grayish brown on old trunks usually exhibiting a ridged and furrowed character although some trees exhibit a thick, scaly bark.

LEAF COLOR: Medium green although there is great variation in leaf colors, some leaves are a bright green in summer, fall color a poor yellow-green to brownish, often falling before turning.

FLOWERS: Perfect, corolla white, 2″ long and wide, the tube bell-shaped, the lobes spreading and frilled at the margin, the lower one with yellow spots and ridges as in *C. bignonioides,* but less freely spotted with purple, borne in early June, in large upright terminal panicles, 4-8″ long.

FRUIT: Capsule, green changing to brown, pendulous, 8 to 20″ long, about 1/2″ wide, persisting through winter.

CULTURE: Transplant balled and burlapped as a small tree, very tolerant of different soil conditions but prefers deep, moist, fertile soil; withstands wet or dry and alkaline conditions; sun or partial shade, seems to withstand extremely hot, dry environments.

DISEASES AND INSECTS: Leaf spots, powdery mildew, *Verticillium* wilt, twig blight, root rot, comstock mealybug, catalpa midge and catalpa sphinx.

LANDSCAPE VALUE: Limited value in the residential landscape because of coarseness, has a place in difficult areas but the use of this and the following species should be tempered.

PROPAGATION: Seeds germinate readily without pretreatment. Cuttings—root pieces taken in December can be used for most species.

RELATED SPECIES:

Catalpa bignonioides — Southern Catalpa, also called Common Catalpa and Indian Bear.

LEAVES: Whorled or opposite, simple, 4-8″ long, apex - abruptly acuminate, base truncate to subcordate, light green and nearly glabrous above, slightly pubescent beneath, especially on veins, of unpleasant odor when crushed. Similar to *C. speciosa* except of smaller size and rounded habit. Flowers 2 weeks later than *C. speciosa* and has a thinner walled fruit. End of seeds are tufted versus fringed of *C. speciosa.*

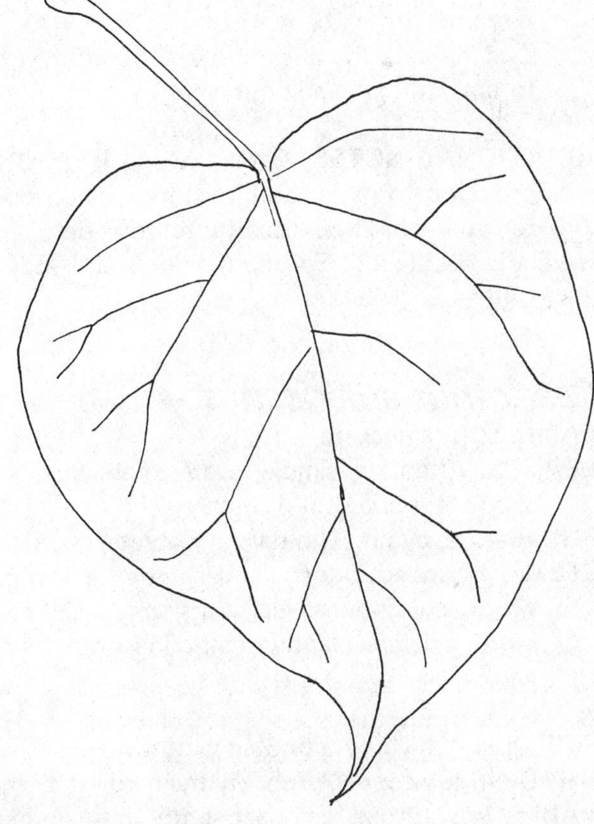

Catalpa bignonioides — Native from Georgia to Florida and Louisiana. Introduced 1726. Smaller than *C. speciosa* reaching heights of 30 to 40′ with an equal or greater spread; broadly rounded in outline with an irregular crown composed of short, crooked branches, flowers are white with 2 ridges and 2 rows of yellow spots and numerous purple spots on the tube and lower lobe, borne in broad, pyramidal panicles, 8 to 10″ long and wide, in mid to late June, about two weeks after *C. speciosa;* fruit is a 6 to 15″ long capsule.

Cultivars include:

'Aurea'— Rich golden yellow leaves which retain color throughout the summer.

'Nana' — A dwarf type reaching 3 to 6' in height, bushy, and rarely if ever flowers. Often grafted on the species about 5 or 6' high to form umbrella-like head.

Catalpa bungei, Manchurian Catalpa, is a small, bushy 20 to 30' tree; native to China; often confused with *C. bignonioides* 'Nana'.

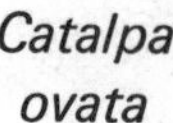

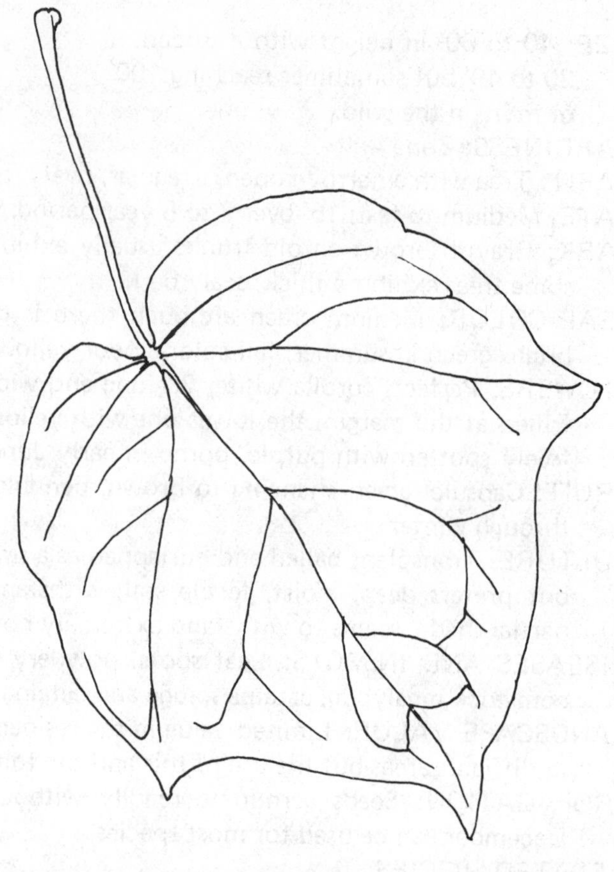

Catalpa ovata

Catalpa ovata, Chinese Catalpa, similar to other species except fruit is longer, 8-12", and thinner, less than 1/3". Leaves are glabrous, almost completely so. Seeds are smaller than *C. speciosa* and *C. bignonioides* and exhibit the fringed character of *C. speciosa. Catalpa ovata* is only mentioned here because of long, thin (1/3" diameter) fruits. I have raised many seedlings from seed donated by the Morris Arboretum, Philadelphia, Pennsylvania and am looking forward to evaluating them in our area.

ADDITIONAL NOTES: Catalpa wood is usually quite brittle and frequently small branches are broken off in wind and ice storms. The wood in contact with the ground is extremely resistant to rot and has been used for railroad ties.

NATIVE HABITAT: Southern Illinois and Indiana to Western Tennessee and Northern Arkansas. Cultivated 1754.

Ceanothus americanus — New Jersey Tea, also called Redroot

FAMILY: Rhamnaceae

LEAVES: Alternate, simple, ovate to obovate, 1 1/5 to 3 1/5" long, acute or acuminate, irregularly serrulate, pubescent or nearly glabrous beneath, petiole 1/5 to 3/10" long; dull green at maturity.

BUD: Sessile, ovoid, with several glabrate, stipular scales of which the lowest only are distinct.

STEMS: Rounded, rather slender, more or less puberulent, green or brownish; pith relatively large, white, continuous; leaf scars small, half-round, somewhat raised; 1 transverse bundle-trace, more or less evidently compound, sometimes distinctly 3; stipules small, persistent or leaving narrow scars.

SIZE: 3 to 4' high by 3 to 5' in width.

HARDINESS: Zone 4, probably the hardiest of the *Ceanothus*.

HABIT: Low, broad, compact shrub with rounded top and slender upright branches. The few that I have seen were quite low and dense.

RATE: Slow to medium.
TEXTURE: Medium in all seasons.
LEAF COLOR: Dull green in summer; perhaps yellow to tan in fall.
FLOWERS: Perfect, white, odorless, less than 1/8" diameter, borne in corymbose panicles at the ends of the stems in June and July; not particularly showy.
FRUIT: Similar to a capsule, dry, triangular, 1/5" wide, separating into 3 compartments at maturity, not showy.
CULTURE: Supposedly somewhat difficult to transplant; prefers light, well drained soil; tolerates dryness; full sun or shade.
DISEASES AND INSECTS: Leaf spots and powdery mildew are two minor problems.
LANDSCAPE VALUE: Essentially none except possibly for very poor soils. This species is a parent of many of the hybrids which are used extensively on the west coast.
PROPAGATION: Seed dormancy occurs in most *Ceanothus* species. Germination has been induced by a hot water soak, a period of cold stratification, or both. Seed should be stratified in a moist medium for periods of 30 to 90 days at 34° to 41°F. Cuttings, especially softwood, root readily when collected in summer. Treatment with IAA or IBA will hasten and improve rooting to a degree.
RELATED SPECIES:
Ceanothus ovatus, Inland Ceanothus, grows 2 to 3' high and is quite dense in foliage. This species is considered superior to *C. americanus* because of its growth habit and the dry capsules which turn bright red in July and August. The flowers are white and minimally showy. The summer foliage is a shiny green while fall coloration is of no consequence. Best reserved for out of the way areas and naturalizing. Native from New England to Nebraska, Colorado and Texas. Cultivated 1830. Zone 4.
NATIVE HABITAT: Canada to Manitoba, Nebraska, Texas and South Carolina. Introduced 1713.

Cedrela sinensis — Chinese Cedrela or Chinese Toon

FAMILY: Meliaceae
LEAVES: Alternate, pinnately compound, long-petioled, 10 to 20" long; leaflets 10 to 22, short-stalked, oblong to lance oblong, 3 to 6" long, acuminate, remotely and slightly serrate or nearly entire, pubescent beneath on veins or finally glabrous; young leaves smell like onions when crushed; reddish bronze in color on newly emerging leaves; eventually medium green.
BUDS: Solitary, sessile, short-ovoid, with about 4 short-pointed, exposed scales; terminal much larger.
STEMS: Coarse, terete, puberulent; pith large, homogeneous, roundish, white becoming colored; leaf scars alternate, cordately elliptical-shield-shaped, slightly raised, large; 5 bundle-traces; no stipular scars; could be mistaken for *Ailanthus* on first inspection.

SIZE: 30 to 40' tall under landscape conditions; can grow 60 to 70' in the wild.
HARDINESS: Zone 5 (6).
HABIT: I have seen this species at three places: National Arboretum, Washington, D.C.; Rowe Arboretum, Cincinnati, Ohio; and Cave Hill Cemetery, Louisville, Kentucky. The specimen at the National was upright-oval, single-stemmed and from a distance resembled *Carya ovata;* the specimens at the latter two places were strongly multistemmed and of erect habit.
RATE: Medium to fast.
TEXTURE: Medium-coarse in summer; coarse in winter.
BARK: Brown, peeling off in long strips; similar to that of *Carya ovata* in appearance.
LEAF COLOR: Reddish purple when unfolding; gradually changing to medium green in summer; fall color is of no consequence.
FLOWERS: Small, perfect, white, fragrant, campanulate, about 1/5" long, borne in pendulous 12" long panicles in June.
FRUIT: Woody capsule, about 1" long.

CULTURE: Apparently quite adaptable to different soils but performs best in calcareous soils.
DISEASES AND INSECTS: None serious.
LANDSCAPE VALUE: More of a novelty plant than anything else. Interesting, but will not take the place of Silver Maple.
PROPAGATION: Seed or root cuttings.
ADDITIONAL NOTES: Resembles *Ailanthus altissima* in morphological features except it does not bear the glandular teeth near the base of the leaflet and the leaves have an oniony smell. The young shoots are boiled and eaten as a vegetable by the Chinese. The tree was known to botanists since 1743, but was not introduced to Europe until 1862.
NATIVE HABITAT: Northern and Eastern China. Introduced 1862.

Cedrus atlantica — Atlas Cedar (Pinaceae)

IDENTIFICATION FEATURES: Closely related to *C. libani,* distinguished by the taller crown, less densely arranged branchlets, the bluish or dark green leaves which are mostly as thick as broad, the smaller cones (2 to 3″ long) and the smaller seeds (1/2″ long).
SIZE: 40 to 60′ high by 30 to 50′ wide but can grow to 120′ in height by 90 to 100′ spread.
HARDINESS: Zone 6.
HABIT: In youth and early maturity the form is stiff with an erect leader and the overall shape is pyramidal; in age it assumes a flat-topped habit with horizontally spreading branches; extremely picturesque and interesting tree; its beauty perhaps unmatched by any other conifer.
RATE: Slow (fast when young).
TEXTURE: Medium
LEAF COLOR: Bluish green, varying in color from light green to silvery blue.
FLOWERS: Monoecious, male cones very densely set, erect, finger-shaped, 2 to 3″ long, 1/2 to 5/8″ wide, shedding clouds of yellow pollen when mature (the above description applies to the other cedars). Female borne in stout, erect cones, purplish initially.
FRUIT: Cones rather short, long persistent, upright on upperside of branches, 3″ long and 2″ in diameter, requiring two years to mature.
CULTURE: Difficult to transplant and should be moved as a container plant. Prefers a well-drained, moist, deep loamy soil but will tolerate sandy, clay soils if there is no stagnant moisture. Sun or partial shade, needs shelter from strong, sweeping winds; preferably acid soil.
DISEASES AND INSECTS: Tip blight, root rots, black scale and Deodar weevil.
LANDSCAPE VALUE: A handsome specimen tree, especially the following cultivars.
CULTIVARS:

'Argentea' — Perhaps the best of the bluish needle forms, the whole tree is a beautiful pale silver-gray-blue color.

'Fastigiata' — Branches ascending; supposedly a very stately tree.

'Glauca' — Might well be listed as a true variety comparable to *Picea pungens glauca* as bluish forms can be selected from seedling populations; usually the foliage colors range from very blue to green in a given population.

'Glauca Pendula' — Weeping form with bluish foliage; the branches cascade like water over rocks; must be staked to develop a strong leader; truly a beautiful clone.

PROPAGATION: Seeds of *Cedrus* exhibit little or no dormancy, however, prechilling or cold stratification at 37° to 41°F for 14 days has been recommended.
ADDITIONAL NOTES: Closely related to *C. libani* from which it differs in the shoots always being downy and the cones do not taper above the middle so much. Bean noted that *C. atlantica* was thriving splendidly in various parts of the British Isles. At Kew Gardens, on dry, hot soil it grows more quickly and withstands London smoke better than *C. libani* or *C. deodara.*
NATIVE HABITAT: Algeria and Morocco on the Atlas Mountains. Introduced before 1840.

Cedrus deodara — Deodar Cedar

LEAVES: One to 1 1/2" long (occasionally 2"), 15 to 20 per whorl, dark green, glaucous or silvery, sharply pointed, on long shoots borne singly and spirally around the stem.

BUDS: Minute, ovoid, with brown scales which remain on the shoots after the appearance of young leaves.

STEM: Long stems bearing scattered leaves and short, spur-like stems with whorled leaves. Stems usually clothed with a grayish down; silvery, glaucous appearance.

SIZE: 40 to 70' after 30 to 40 years. Supposedly can grow to 150 to 200' high with a spread of 150'.

HARDINESS: Zone 7.

HABIT: Broadly pyramidal when young with gracefully pendulous branches; becoming wide spreading and flat-topped in old age.

RATE: Slow-medium, grows about 2' a year when young.

TEXTURE: Fine.

LEAF COLOR: Light blue or grayish green, sometimes silvery in color.

FLOWERS: Inconspicuous, monoecious and erect.

FRUIT: Cones solitary or two together on short branchlets, ovoid or oblong ovoid, 3 to 4" long by approximately 2" broad. Apex rounded, bluish, bloomy when young turning reddish brown at maturity.

CULTURE: Straight species is not hardy here, however, the 'Kingsville' and 'Kashmir' cultivars are. If root pruned, transplants easily, prefers a well-drained and somewhat dry, sunny location and protection from sweeping winds.

DISEASES AND INSECTS: None serious.

LANDSCAPE VALUE: Excellent specimen evergreen because of its extremely graceful and pendulous habit.

CULTIVARS:

'Kashmir' — Hardy form, silvery blue-green foliage, survived rapid temperature drop of 25°F below zero.

'Kingsville' — Similar to above, possibly hardier than 'Kashmir'.

PROPAGATION: Seed as previously described. Cuttings taken in October after growth hardened off rooted 80% under mist in peat:perlite when treated with 2000 ppm IBA.

NATIVE HABITAT: Himalaya from East Afghanistan to Garwhal. Introduced 1831.

Cedrus libani — Cedar of Lebanon

LEAVES: 30 to 40 per spur, 4/5 to 1 2/5" long, stiff, quadrilaterally compressed, broader than high, pointed at apex, dark or bright green.

STEM: Branchlets very numerous, densely arranged, spreading in a horizontal plane, short, glabrous or irregularly pubescent.

SIZE: 40 to 60' after 40 to 70 years but can grow to 75 to 120' in height by 80 to 100' spread.

HARDINESS: Zone 5.

HABIT: A stately tree with a thick, massive trunk and very wide-spreading branches, the lower ones sweeping the ground; pyramidal when young.

RATE: Slow.

TEXTURE: Medium.

BARK: Blackish gray, splitting or dividing.

LEAF COLOR: Dark or bright green.

FLOWERS: Inconspicuous, monoecious; yellow, erect catkins; pistillate purplish.

FRUIT: Cones stalked, solitary, upright, barrel shaped, 3 to 4" long by 1 3/5 to 2 2/5" across, impressed at the apex, sometimes resinous, requiring two years to mature, purple-brown in color.

CULTURE: Like other cedars difficult to transplant. A good, deep, well-drained loam. Open, sunny, spacious location. Intolerant of shade. Needs a pollution-free, dry atmosphere.

DISEASES AND INSECTS: None serious.

LANDSCAPE VALUE: A specimen tree of unrivalled distinction, uniting the grand with the picturesque. The dark green foliage, stiff habit, and rigidly upright cones, give this tree a popular interest.

CULTIVARS:

'Argentea' – Could be listed as a true variety; leaves of a very glaucous (silvery-blue) hue; supposedly is found wild in the Cilician stands.

var. *stenocoma* – Extremely hardy form and more stiff and rigid than the species.

PROPAGATION: Seed, see under *C. atlantica;* cuttings, taken in November rooted 30% in sand:peat without treatment.

ADDITIONAL NOTES: All the *Cedrus* are exquisite, lovely trees but *C. libani* has received the most notoriety, and justifiably so. There are disagreements as to the exact taxonomic status of the various cedars. Some botanists regard them all as geographical forms of one species. One botanist divided them into four subspecies. No matter how they are allied taxonomically they are similar aesthetically. The National Arboretum, Washington, D.C. has a notable collection of *Cedrus.*

NATIVE HABITAT: Asia Minor, best known from its historic stands in Lebanon, but attaining maximum size in the Cilician Taurus, Turkey; further west it occurs in scattered locales as far as the Aegean. Introduced in colonial times.

Celastrus scandens — American Bittersweet

FAMILY: Celastraceae

LEAVES: Alternate, simple, ovate to oblong-ovate, 2 to 4" long, acuminate, broad cuneate at base, serrulate, glabrous.

BUDS: Brownish, small, sessile, solitary, subglobose, with about 6 hard, mucronate scales, glabrous.

STEMS: Brown to tan, lenticels scarcely noticeable; pith—solid, white, one bundle trace.

SIZE: Often listed as 20' but seems to continue growing as long as there is something to climb upon.

HARDINESS: Zone 3.

HABIT: Vigorous, deciduous, twining vine which engulfs every fence in sight.

RATE: Fast; Wyman noted it can kill shrubs or small trees as it girdles the stems.

TEXTURE: Medium in leaf; medium-coarse in winter.

LEAF COLOR: Deep glossy green in summer; greenish yellow in fall.

FLOWERS: Polygamo-dioecious, primarily dioecious, greenish white, not showy; borne in 2 to 4" long terminal panicles, June.

FRUIT: Capsule, 1/3" across, yellow, with crimson seeds; ripens in October and is extensively collected and sold for dried flower arrangements.

CULTURE: Most nurserymen sell it as a small container plant. The problem occurs because the sexes are never labeled. In this respect, it is like holly for without the male, fruit set will be nonexistent. Quite easy to grow as it withstands about any soil condition including those that are dry; pH adaptable; full sun for best fruiting. Probably best to locate in a poor soil site as it will quickly overgrow its bounds when placed in good soil.

DISEASES AND INSECTS: Leaf spots, powdery mildews, crown gall, stem canker, *Euonymus* scale, aphids, and two-marked treehopper.

LANDSCAPE VALUE: Little, except in rough areas; could be allowed to scramble over rock piles, fences, old trees and the like. The fruit is handsome and is always welcome in arrangements.

PROPAGATION: Seeds have a dormant embryo and require after-ripening for germination. There is some evidence that the seed coat may have an inhibiting effect upon germination. Seeds or dried fruits should be stratified in moist sand or peat for 2 to 6 months at 41°F. Softwood cuttings root readily in sand without treatment, but rooting may be hastened or improved by treatment.

RELATED SPECIES:

Celastrus orbiculatus, Oriental Bittersweet, is similar to the American but the fruits are borne in smaller, axillary cymes. Japan, China. 1870. Zone 4.

NATIVE HABITAT: Canada to South Dakota and Northern Mexico. Introduced 1736.

Celtis occidentalis — Common Hackberry

FAMILY: Ulmaceae

LEAVES: Alternate, simple, ovate to oblong-ovate, 2 to 5" long, acute to acuminate, oblique and rounded or broad-cuneate at base, serrate except at base, bright green and usually smooth and lustrous above, paler below and glabrous or slightly hairy on veins; petioles 2/5 to 3/5" long.

BUD: Small, imbricate, 1/4" long or less, downy, chestnut brown, ovate, sharp pointed, flattened, appressed, terminal—absent.

STEM: Slender, somewhat zigzag, light olive-brown, prominently lenticeled, more or less shining, more or less downy; wood of stem light greenish yellow when moistened. Pith—white, finely chambered.

BARK: Trunk and older limbs with narrow corky projecting ridges which are sometimes reduced to wart-like projections.

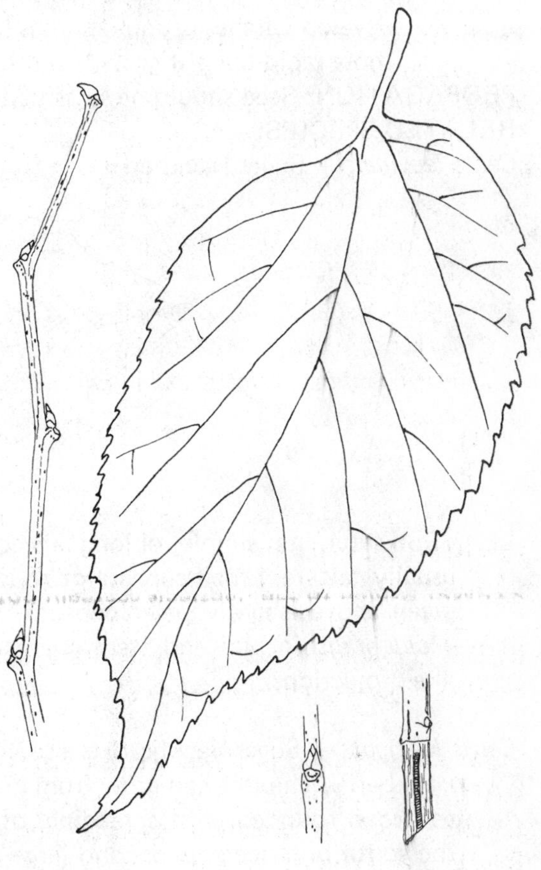

SIZE: 40 to 60' in height with a nearly equal spread; can grow to 100'.

HARDINESS: Zone 2.

HABIT: In youth weakly pyramidal; in old age the crown is a broad top of ascending arching branches, often with drooping branchlets; not unlike the American Elm in outline, however, by no means as esthetic.

RATE: Medium to fast, 20 to 30' over a 10 to 15 year period.

TEXTURE: Medium-coarse in leaf and in winter.

BARK: Grayish brown, with characteristic corky warts or ridges, later somewhat scaly.

LEAF COLOR: Dull light to medium green in summer; yellow or yellow-green fall color.

FLOWERS: Polygamo-monoecious, staminate ones in fascicles toward base; the perfect and pistillate flowers above; solitary in the axils of the leaves; early May.

FRUIT: Fleshy, orange-red to dark purple drupe, 1/2 to 3/4" long by 1/4 to 1/3" diameter, ripening in September and October, often persistent for several weeks; supposedly flavored like dates (I have never eaten any) and relished by birds and wildlife.

CULTURE: Easily transplanted bare root as a small tree or balled and burlapped in larger sizes; prefers rich, moist soils, but grows in dry, heavy or sandy, rocky soils; withstands acid or alkaline conditions; moderately wet or very dry areas; tolerates wind; full sun; withstands dirt and grime of cities.

DISEASES AND INSECTS: Leaf spots, witches' broom, powdery mildew, *Gonoderma* rot, hackberry nipple-gall, mourning-cloak butterfly and several scales are troublesome. Personally I find the witches' broom often caused by an *Eriophyes* mite and the powdery mildew fungus, *Sphaerotheca phytophylla,* particularly offensive for trees are often totally disfigured by broom like clusters of abnormal branch growth. Some trees show resistance and might be propagated vegetatively to avoid this problem. The nipple gall is another serious problem as the leaves are often disfigured by these bullet-like appendages.

LANDSCAPE VALUE: Good tree for plains and prairie states because it performs admirably under adverse conditions; good for park and large area use; has the innate ability to grow in dry soils and under windy conditions.

CULTIVARS:

'Prairie Pride' — Selected by Bill Wandell of Wandell's Nursery, Urbana, Illinois. The foliage is a good glossy green and as a small tree develops a nice uniform, compact crown; does not develop witches broom and has lighter than usual fruit crops. Young trees under cultivation show rapid upright growth and few spur branches.

PROPAGATION: Seed should be stratified for 60 to 90 days at 41°F in moist medium.

RELATED SPECIES:

Celtis laevigata — Sugar Hackberry

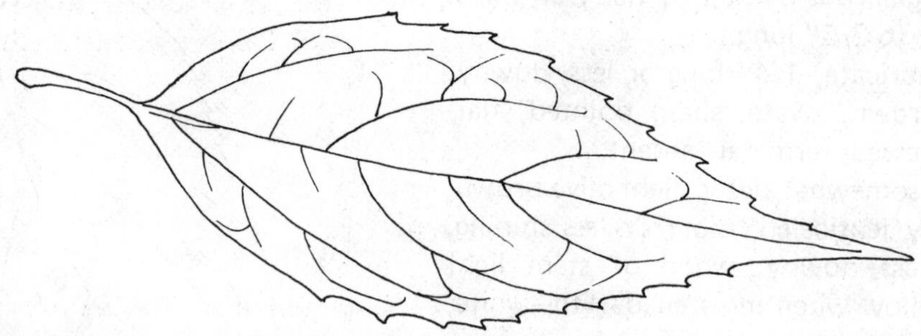

LEAVES: Alternate, simple, oblong-lanceolate, sometimes ovate, 2 to 4" long, long-acuminate and usually falcate, broad-cuneate or rounded at base, entire or sometimes with a few teeth, dark green above, slightly paler beneath, glabrous, thin; petioles 1/2 to 2/5" long. Similar to *C. occidentalis* in bud and stem characteristics. Bark is generally smooth and devoid of wart-like projections.

Celtis laevigata — Sugar Hackberry is also known as the Sugarberry, Southern Hackberry or Mississippi Hackberry. The tree can grow from 60 to 80' in height and similar spread. The habit is rounded to broad rounded with spreading, often pendulous branches. This tree is used extensively in the south on streets, parks and large areas; resistant to witches' broom; the fruit is orange-red to blue-black, very sweet and juicy, and relished by birds. The common name is derived from the sweet taste of the fruits. Native from Southern Indiana, Illinois to Texas and Florida. Cultivated 1811. Zone 5.

Cephalanthus occidentalis — Buttonbush

FAMILY: Rubiaceae

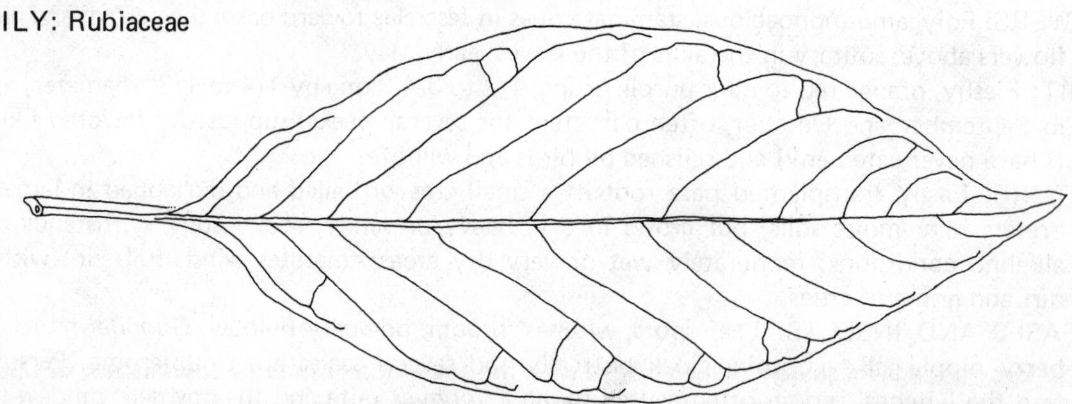

LEAVES: Opposite or whorled, simple, ovate to elliptic-lanceolate, 2 to 6" long, acuminate, lustrous bright green above, lighter and glabrous or somewhat pubescent beneath; petiole 1/5 to 4/5" long.

BUDS: Terminal-absent, laterals-solitary, sessile, conical, in depressed areas above the leaf scars, often superposed.

STEM: Slender, round, glabrous, young stems shining, olive-green; in winter often reddish.

Cephalanthus occidentalis, Buttonbush, is a rounded 3 to 6′ high, occasionally 10 to 15′ shrub (southern part of range), of rather loose, gangling proportions. The winter texture is quite coarse, however, the glossy summer foliage lends a medium texture. The flowers are creamy-white, crowded in globular heads, without the projecting styles, 1 to 1 1/5″ across, on peduncles 1 to 2 2/5″ long in August. The fruit is a nutlet and the compound structure is present throughout winter. Culturally, Buttonbush is best adapted to moist situations, and in cultivation is averse to dryness. Probably best reserved for wet areas in a naturalized situation. The glossy foliage is quite attractive and the late flower is interesting. Easily propagated by softwood and hardwood cuttings. Softwood cuttings taken in late July and early August rooted 100 percent in sand:peat in one month without treatment. Seeds will germinate promptly without pretreatment. Native from New Brunswick to Florida, west to Southern Minnesota, Nebraska, Oklahoma, Southern New Mexico, Arizona and Central California; also occurring in Cuba, Mexico and Eastern Asia.

Cercidiphyllum japonicum — Katsuratree

FAMILY: Cercidiphyllaceae

LEAVES: Opposite or subopposite, simple, 2 to 4″ long, suborbicular to broad ovate, obtusish, cordate at base, crenate-serrate, dark bluish green above, glaucescent beneath. Leaf resembles redbud, purplish when unfolding.

BUDS: Two scales, not overlapping, terminal bud lacking, reddish, 1/16 to 1/8″ long, appressed, glabrous, angular.

STEM: Slender, swollen at nodes, brownish, glabrous.

SIZE: 40 to 60′ in height and can reach 100′ in the wild; spread is variable as staminate trees tend to be upright while pistillate are more spreading. I have seen 40 to 50′ high trees with a 20 to 30′ spread and other trees of the same size with a spread equal to and in some cases greater than the height.

HARDINESS: Zone 4.

RATE: Medium to fast; once established about 14′ over a 5 to 7 year period and about 40′ over 20 years.

TEXTURE: Medium-fine in leaf; medium in winter habit.

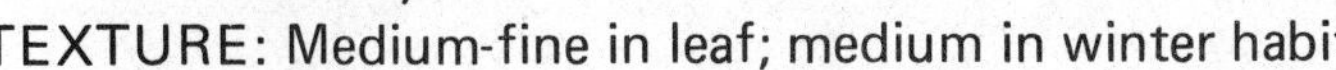

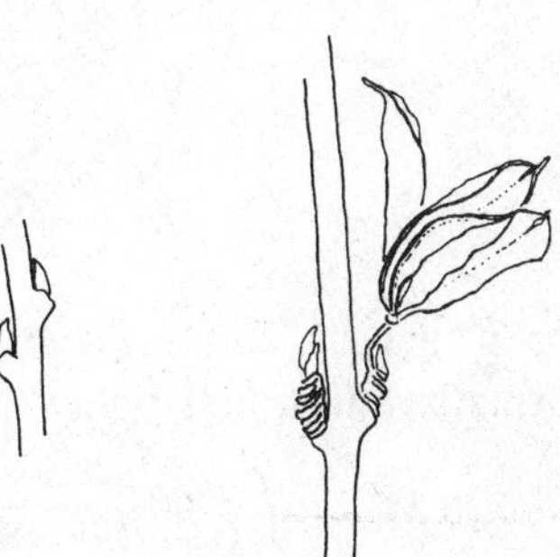

BARK: Brown, slightly shaggy on old trunks with the ends loose; limitedly reminiscent of Shagbark Hickory bark, very handsome and quite refined compared to Hickory.

LEAF COLOR: New leaves emerge a beautiful reddish purple and gradually change to bluish green in summer; fall color varies from yellow to scarlet with the emphasis on the yellow in Central

Illinois. Often a soft apricot-orange fall color develops. Leaf is shaped like a *Cercis* (Redbud) leaf, hence, the generic name *Cercidiphyllum.*

FLOWERS: Dioecious, male consists of a minute calyx and an indefinite number of stamens; pistillate of four green, fringed sepals, and four to six carpels, open from late March to early April.

FRUIT: Small, 1/2 to 3/4" long pods.

CULTURE: Somewhat difficult to transplant; move as a balled and burlapped or container grown-plant in early spring; soil should be rich, moist and well drained, pH adaptable although seems to fall color better on acid soils; full sun; an effort should be made to provide supplemental watering during hot, dry periods during the initial time of establishment.

DISEASES AND INSECTS: None serious.

LANDSCAPE VALUE: Possibly a street tree; excellent for residential properties, parks, golf courses, commercial areas; one of my favorite trees, overwhelming in overall attractiveness; choice specimens exist at Morton Arboretum, Arnold Arboretum, and Spring Grove Cemetery.

PROPAGATION: Seed requires no pretreatment and can be sown when mature. My students have collected seed from specimens on campus and grown numerous plants. We grew the seedlings in containers and produced beautiful 3 to 5' high plants in a single growing season.

ADDITIONAL NOTES: A landscape tree that will become more widely grown as it is introduced to the gardening public.

NATIVE HABITAT: China, Japan. Introduced 1865.

Cercis canadensis — Eastern Redbud

FAMILY: Leguminosae

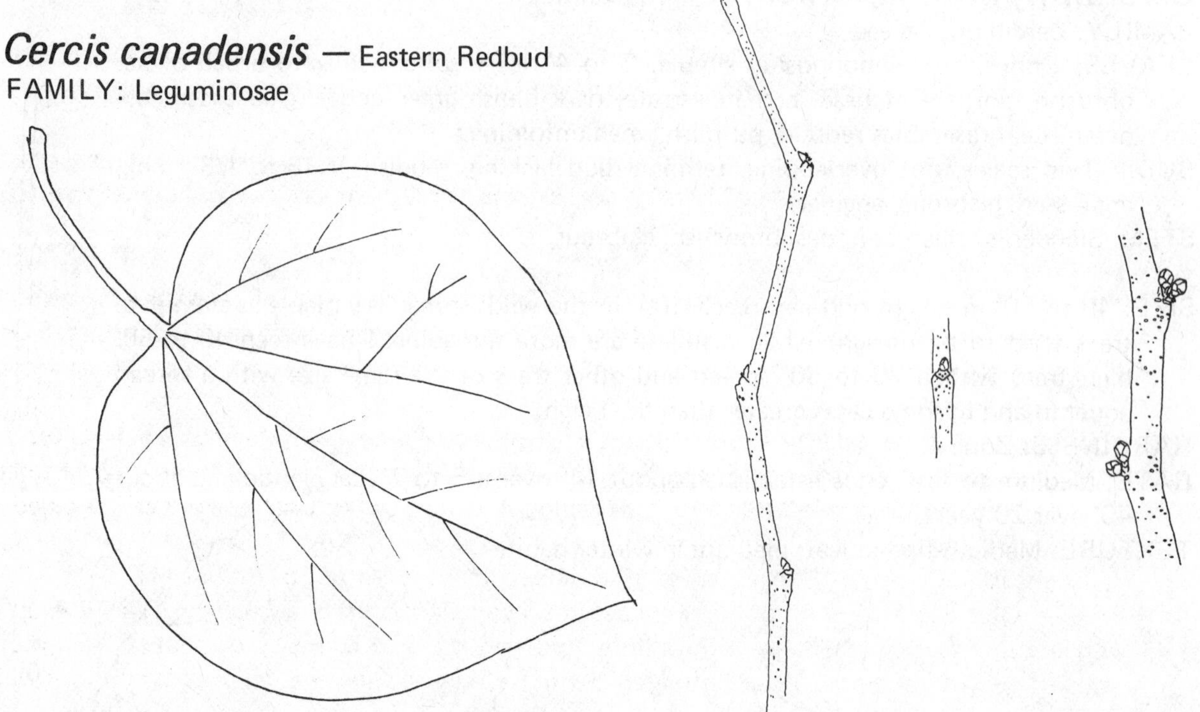

LEAVES: Alternate, simple, broad-ovate to suborbicular, 3 to 5" across, cordate at base, base with 5 to 9 prominent, radiating veins, petiole with conspicuous swelling just below blade, pubescent to glabrous beneath.

BUD: Terminal-absent, laterals—small, 1/8" or less long, blunt, dark purplish red, somewhat flattened and appressed, one or more superposed buds often present, the uppermost the largest, bud scales—overlap, somewhat hairy on edges, about 2 visible to a leaf bud, several to a flower bud.

STEM: Slender, glabrous, dark reddish brown, zigzag. Pith—especially of older growth generally with reddish longitudinal streaks.

SIZE: 20 to 30' in height by 25 to 35' in spread.

HARDINESS: Zone 4.

HABIT: Usually a small tree with the trunk divided close to the ground and forming a spreading, flat-topped to rounded crown; very handsome with its gracefully ascending branches; "a native tree with a touch of class".

RATE: Medium, 7 to 10' in 5 to 6 years.

TEXTURE: Medium-coarse in leaf; medium in winter.

BARK: Older bark black or brownish black usually with orangish inner bark peaking through; not often considered as a tree with interesting bark but it does possess ornamental value.

LEAF COLOR: New growth when emerging is a reddish purple and gradually changes to a dark, often somewhat lustrous green in summer; fall color is usually a poor yellow-green.

FLOWERS: Perfect, reddish purple in bud, opening to a rosy-pink with a purplish tinge, 2/5 to 1/2" long; open in mid to late April and are effective for 2 to 3 weeks; borne 4 to 8 together, fascicled or racemose; often flowers are produced on old trunks 4 to 8" in diameter; flowers at a young age, 4 to 6 years.

FRUIT: True pod (legume), brown, 2 to 3" long, October.

CULTURE: Transplant balled and burlapped as a young tree in spring or fall into moist, well drained, deep soils, however, does exceedingly well in many soil types except permanently wet ones; adaptable to acid or alkaline soils; full sun or light shade; keep vigorous by regular watering and fertilization. Trees rarely require pruning although I have found on my own trees that numerous small dead branches occur under the canopy of the tree. This could be due to excessive shade. I have rectified the problem by pruning out the dead wood and opening up the canopy to allow more light to filter through.

DISEASES AND INSECTS: Canker is the most destructive disease of redbud and can cause many stems to die, leaf spots and *Verticillium* wilt are other disease problems; tree hoppers, caterpillars, scales and in our area leafhoppers can also cause damage.

LANDSCAPE VALUE: Effective as a single specimen, in groupings, in the shrub border, especially nice in woodland and naturalized type situations; one of my many favorite eastern native plants.

CULTIVARS:

var. *alba* – White flowers.

'Forest Pansy' – A very handsome purple leaf type, the new foliage emerges a screaming, shimmering red-purple and changes to a more subdued color as the season progresses. One of my favorites for colored foliage and I do not rate too many purple leaf plants among my top 1000.

'Pinkbud' – A pure, bright true pink flower, discovered wild on an estate near Kansas City.

'Royal' – A selection made by Professor J.C. McDaniel of the University of Illinois, Department of Horticulture for outstanding and abundant white flowers. The parent tree is located in Bluffs, Illinois.

'Wither's Pink Charm' – Flowers soft pink without the purplish tint of the species.

PROPAGATION: Seeds have hard, impermeable seedcoats and internal dormancy. Scarification in concentrated sulfuric acid for 30 minutes followed by 5 to 8 weeks of cool (41°F), moist stratification is recommended. Untreated cuttings taken in June and July rooted 75 to 90% in sand at 72°F in about 4 weeks.

RELATED SPECIES:

Cercis chinensis, Chinese Redbud, is not particularly hardy in Central Illinois but will survive in the southern part of the state. Usually a small multistemmed shrub less than 10' in height. Flowers are rosy purple about one week later than *C. canadensis* and about 3/4" long. Native to Central China. Introduced before 1850. Zone 6. Very handsome and showy in flower.

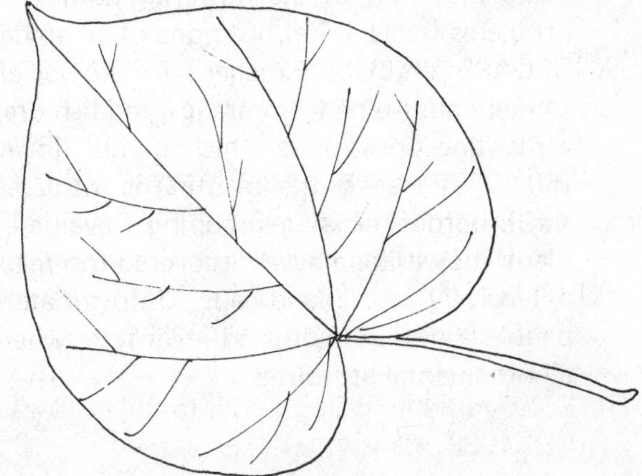

NATIVE HABITAT: New Jersey to Northern Florida, west to Missouri and Texas and Northern Mexico. Cultivated 1641.

Chaenomeles speciosa — Common Floweringquince

FAMILY: Rosaceae

LEAVES: Alternate, simple, ovate to oblong, acute, 1 to 3" long, sharply serrate, lustrous above, glabrous.

BUD: Similar to *C. japonica,* usually larger.

STEM: Slender, brownish, often slightly pubescent.

GROWTH HABIT: More upright in habit than *C. japonica.* 6 to 10' in height.

SIZE: 6 to 10' in height; spread 6 to 10' or greater; quite variable and may be smaller due to hybidization with *Chaenomeles japonica.*

HARDINESS: Zone 4.

HABIT: A shrub of rounded outline, broadspreading with tangled and dense twiggy mass of more or less spiny branches; some forms are more erect while others are quite rambling, variable in habit.

RATE: Medium.

TEXTURE: Medium in leaf; coarse in winter. Collects leaves, bottles and trash in the twiggy network; rates highly as a "garbage can" shrub. Over-rated plant, primarily because of flowers.

LEAF COLOR: Bronzy-red when unfolding gradually changing to dark, glossy green; fall color is nonexistent.

FLOWER: Scarlet to red in the type varying to pink and white; mid to late April before leaves, borne solitary or 2 to 4 per cluster on old wood, each flower 1 1/2 to 1 3/4" diameter, very showy, flower buds can be killed as happened in spring of 1974 when a late freeze eliminated the expanding flower buds.

FRUIT: Pome, 2 to 2 1/2" long and wide, yellowish green, fragrant, speckled with small dots (glands), ripening in October. Fruits are quite bitter when eaten raw but when cooked are used for preserves and jellies.

CULTURE: Transplant balled and burlapped, adaptable to a wide range of soil conditions, performs well in dry situations, full sun or partial shade with best flowering in sun, develops chlorosis on high pH soils, renewal pruning either by eliminating the older branches or simply cutting the whole plant to within 6" of the ground will result in more spectacular flower.

DISEASES AND INSECTS: Leaf spots have resulted in premature defoliation in 1973 and 1974 in Champaign-Urbana. There was abundant rainfall in the spring and early summer of those years and many of the flowering quinces were 50 to 75% defoliated in July. There are other problems (scale, mite) but none of an epidemic nature.

LANDSCAPE VALUE: Excellent for flower effect when fully realized. Range of flower colors is tremendous going from orange, reddish orange, scarlet, carmine, turkey red and white. There is a planting on campus which in full flower is beautiful, however, during the rest of the year (50 to 51 weeks) the planting is intolerable. Often used for hedge (makes a good barrier), shrub border, massing, grouping. I evaluate this species and its many cultivars as a single season plant (flower) and have discovered too many superior (multi-season) plants to justify using this extensively in the landscape. Unfortunately, it will continue to be widely sold because many people are only interested in flowers when, in essence, this feature is the most short-lived of all ornamental attributes.

CULTIVARS: Abundant; Wyman noted that the Arnold Arboretum was growing 150 forms. Most appropriate to check with the local nurseryman and note the colors he has available. White, pink and scarlet tend to be the most commonly available colors.

PROPAGATION: Cuttings, collected in August, dipped in 1000 ppm IBA solution rooted 100% in peat:perlite medium under mist.

ADDITIONAL NOTES: Often flowers sporadically late into spring and again in fall will show some color. This fall flowering syndrome has occurred in 1972, 1973, and 1974 in Champaign-Urbana. Interesting but not overwhelming as are the flowers which develop in April.

RELATED SPECIES:

Chaenomeles japonica – Japanese Floweringquince

LEAVES: Alternate, simple, broad-ovate to obovate, obtuse or acutish, 1 1/5 to 2" long, coarsely crenate-serrate, glabrous.

BUD: Imbricate, solitary, sessile, round-ovoid, with few exposed scales. Terminal-absent. Brown in color.

STEM: Slender, dark gray to brown, glabrous, sometimes spiny.

GROWTH HABIT: Low growing densely branched shrub to 3'.

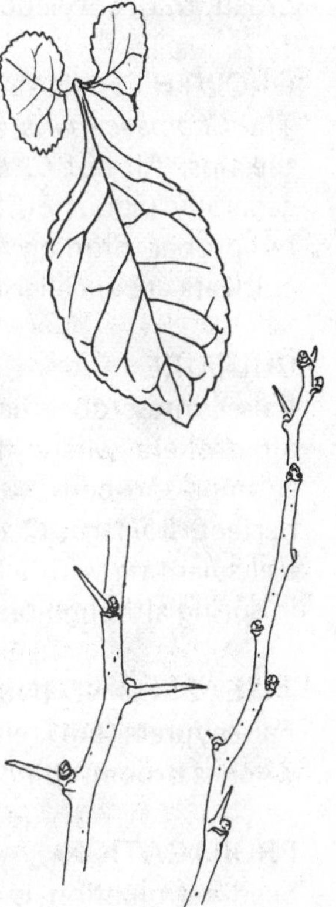

Chaenomeles japonica – Japanese Floweringquince. 3' in height or less and broad spreading, forming an interlacing network of thorny stems; "garbage can" shrub; flowers orange-red, scarlet or blood-red on year old wood; each flower about 1 1/2" across; early to mid April (before *C. speciosa* in Central Illinois); fruit is a greenish yellow, fragrant, 1 1/2" diameter pome, late September to October. A ratty shrub whose use should be tempered by astute judgment; not as ornamental as *C. speciosa;* native of Japan. *Chaenomeles* x *superba* represents a hybrid species between *C. japonica* x *C. speciosa.* Usually they are low spreading shrubs, 4 to 5' in height; most characters are intermediate between the parents; flower colors range from white, pink, crimson to shades of orange and orange-scarlet. Quite difficult to distinguish among various *C.* x *superba* forms and *C. speciosa* forms.

NATIVE HABITAT: China, cultivated in Japan. Introduced before 1800.

Chamaecyparis – Falsecypress

Cupressaceae

At one time I would have said that the falsecypress might as well be omitted from Midwestern landscapes but the more I travel the more convinced I become that many of the cultivars are suitable for the midwest. *Chamaecyparis* is generally considered the least important of the smaller evergreens used in Midwestern landscaping. They appear frequently on the east and west coast in cooler, more humid regions. All, except *C. thyoides* of eastern North America, are native of the lands bordering the Pacific Ocean, two in western North America and the other three in Formosa and Japan. With the exception of *C. formosensis* all the species are hardy. Cultivars of *C. obtusa* and *C. pisifera* are most common in the trade although *C. lawsoniana* has yielded many cultivars. The leaves of seedling and juvenile plants are very distinct from those of adult trees, being needle-like or awl-shaped, up to 1/3" long and spreading. Formerly plants with these features were placed in the genus *Retinospora,* but this genus is no longer recognized. It is interesting to note that some juvenile forms of more recent origin, having produced neither cones nor reversion shoots, still cannot be placed with certainty, either as to species or even to genus. It is easy to confuse *Thuja* with *Chamaecyparis,* however, the cones differ and the lateral leaves nearly cover the facial in the former, whereas in the latter, the facial leaves are more exposed.

MORPHOLOGICAL CHARACTERISTICS

Monoecious trees, pyramidal, leading shoots nodding; branchlets mostly frond-like, usually flattened; leaves opposite, scale-like (awl-shaped only in the juvenile state), ovate to rhombic, pointed or obtuse; flowers borne terminally on lateral branchlets; male flowers ovoid or oblong, yellow, rarely red, often conspicuous by their large number, stamens with 2-4 anther-cells; female flowers small, globular, less conspicuous; cones globose, short-stalked, solitary, ripening the first season (except *C. nootkatensis,* cones of which ripen in the second year); scales 6-8 (seldom 4, or 10-12), peltate, pointed or bossed in the middle; seeds (1)-2, rarely up to 5 per scale, slightly compressed; wings broad, thin, cotyledons 2.

GROWTH CHARACTERISTICS

The *Chamaecyparis* species are large pyramidal, almost columnar trees with pendulous branches at the tips. All but *C. thyoides* can regularly grow to over 100 feet in native stands, however, they are generally (about 50%) smaller under landscape conditions and can be maintained at suitable heights by proper pruning. The species are seldom in evidence in landscape plantings but many of the cultivars are excellent and offer diversity of form, color, and texture.

CULTURE

Falsecypress does best in full sun in rich, moist, well-drained soil. They thrive in a cool, moist atmosphere where they are protected from drying winds. *C. thyoides,* is found in fresh-water swamps and bogs, wet depressions and along stream banks and would obviously withstand less than perfect drainage. *C. obtusa* and *C. pisifera* types seem best adapted to the midwest. Fall or spring transplanting with a ball of soil or as a container-plant are satisfactory. Pruning is best accomplished in spring although branches can be removed about anytime.

DISEASES AND INSECTS

Falsecypress are relatively free of serious problems although blight *(Phomopsis juniperovora),* witches broom, spindle burl gall, root rot and other minor insect pests have been noted.

PROPAGATION

Seed germination is usually low, due in part to poor seed quality, and also to various factors of embryo dormancy. See specific recommendations under each species. Softwood or hardwood cuttings are the principal means of propagation although a few difficult to root types may be grafted.

LANDSCAPE USE

Falsecypresses can be used for about any landscape situation if the proper cultivar is chosen. They make good hedges, screens, foundations, and border plants. Some of the cultivars make strong accent or specimen plants and their use should be tempered so as not to detract from the total landscape. If not properly cared for the species will become ratty, open, and sorrowful looking. As a genus, this is relatively unimportant when compared to *Thuja, Juniperus,* and *Taxus;* for few plants are used in contemporary midwestern landscapes.

SELECTED CULTIVARS

The following cultivars are recommended for midwestern landscapes.

C. nootkatensis 'Pendula'
C. obtusa 'Gracilis'
C. obtusa 'Lycopodioides'
C. obtusa 'Nana Gracilis'
C. obtusa 'Pendula'
C. pisifera 'Filifera'
C. pisifera 'Filifera Aurea'
C. pisifera 'Plumosa' and types
C. pisifera 'Squarrosa' and types

Chamaecyparis lawsoniana — Lawson Falsecypress or Port Orford Cedar

LEAVES: Closely pressed, arranged in opposite pairs marked with white streaks on the undersurface; the lateral pair keel-shaped, 1/16 to 1/12″ long, slightly overlapping on the facial pair, which are rhomboidal and much smaller, about 1/20″ long, often glandular pitted, those on the main axis oblong, unequal; the lateral pair 1/4″, the facial pair 1/5″ long, with short or long spreading points.

STEM: Flattened, frond-like, arranged in a horizontal plane.

SIZE: Almost impossible to estimate landscape size but 40 to 60′ high under midwest conditions is reasonable; can grow 140 to 180′ high and greater in the wild.

HARDINESS: Zone 5.

HABIT: A tree with a massive, buttressed trunk and short ascending branches; drooping at the tips and ending in flat sprays.

RATE: Medium.

TEXTURE: Medium.

BARK: Silvery brown to reddish brown, fibrous, divided into thick, rounded ridges separated by deep irregular furrows; 6 to 10″ thick on old trees.

LEAF COLOR: Glaucous green to deep green.

FLOWERS: Monoecious, terminal; staminate ones crimson, pistillate steely-blue.

FRUIT: Cones numerous, globose, 1/3″ across, at first bluish green, afterwards reddish brown, bloomy; scales 8, with thin, pointed, reflexed bosses, each 2 to 4 seeds; seeds oblong, appressed, glossy brown, broadly winged.

CULTURE: Transplanted balled and burlapped if root pruned. Prefers a humid climate, well-drained, moist soil; full sun or partial shade, sheltered from winds and supposedly does not like chalky soils. See culture sheet.

DISEASES AND INSECTS: Until recently it was thought this tree to be insect and disease free, but there is a fungus, *Phytophthora lateralis,* which is devastating the species. It does its main damage by rotting the root system, which in turn kills the tree.

LANDSCAPE VALUE: A very handsome specimen with beautiful foliage and graceful habit for gardens and plantations where it can be grown; has numerous variations of form and color; in general not a plant for Midwestern conditions.

CULTIVARS: 200+ in arboretums, but hopelessly confused.

PROPAGATION: Germination of Falsecypress seed is characteristically low, due in part to poor seed quality, and also to various degrees of embryo dormancy. Sound, unstratified seeds of *C. lawsoniana* have germinated completely on moist paper in less than 28 days at diurnally alternating temperatures of 86°F for 8 hours and 68°F for 16 hours with light during the warm periods. However, in Britain, presowing stratification has yielded the most consistent results. Stratification for 60 to 90 days at 41°F is recommended. This species is easily propagated by cuttings taken in fall. Cuttings taken in October and placed untreated in sand:peat rooted 90% or more. Untreated cuttings taken in January rooted equally well but more slowly. IBA treatments will hasten rooting.

ADDITIONAL NOTES: This species performs best where there is an abundance of soil and atmospheric moisture although it is less exacting in this respect than Redwood, *Sequoia sempervirens,* and frequently occurs on rather high, dry, sandy ridges which are often 30 to 40 miles inland.

NATIVE HABITAT: Southwestern Oregon and isolated parts of Northwestern California.

Chamaecyparis obtusa — Hinoki Falsecypress

LEAVES: Closely pressed, of 2 sizes, the lateral pair much the larger, boat-shaped, 1/12″ long, blunt at the apex or with a minute point; the smaller pairs about 1/24″ long, triangular, with a thickened apex, all prominently lined beneath with white X-shaped markings produced by a coating of wax; dark green above.

STEM: Flattened, slightly drooping at the tips.

SIZE: 50 to 75′ in height with a 10 to 20′ spread.
HARDINESS: Zone 4.
HABIT: A tall, slender pyramid with spreading branches and drooping, frondlike branchlets.
RATE: Medium (25′ in 20 years).
TEXTURE: Medium.
BARK: Reddish brown, shed in long narrow strips.
LEAF COLOR: Shining dark green above, whitish markings beneath.
FLOWERS: Monoecious, terminal; staminate yellow, pistillate solitary.
FRUIT: Cones short-stalked, solitary, globose, 1/3 to 2/5″ across, orange-brown; scales 8, rarely 10, depressed on the back and with a small mucro; seed-2 to 5 on each scale, convex or nearly triangular on both margins, often with 2 glands; wings narrow, membranous.
CULTURE: Supposedly somewhat difficult to transplant but most of the cultivars are container-grown and move without great difficulty as is true with most *Chamaecyparis.* This species prefers a moist, well-drained soil and moderately humid atmosphere in a sunny, protected (from wind) area. According to an English reference the species and its cultivars thrive in moist, neutral soils and in those that have decided acid tendencies. From my own observations I would have to rank the cultivars of this species about the best suited for Midwestern conditions.
LANDSCAPE VALUE: Useful as a specimen, dwarf forms valuable for rock gardens and that different landscape touch.
CULTIVARS:

'Crippsii' — Foliage yellow when young turning dark green at maturity.

'Erecta' — Fastigiate, ascending branches.

'Filicoides' — A bush or small tree of open, irregular, often gaunt habit, branches long and straggly, clothed with dense pendulous clusters of fern-spray, green foliage.

'Gracilis' — Compact pyramid with pendulous branches, rarely exceeds 6′ in height.

'Nana' — Very slow growing type to about 3′ in height and slightly broader, a 90 year-old specimen is 20″ high and 25″ wide. Often confused with the following cultivar.

'Nana Gracilis' — Has thick dark green foliage; grows slowly to a height of about 4′ and has a spread of 3′ in about 8 years.

It is hopeless to list all the cultivars of this species or for that matter *C. lawsoniana* or *C. pisifera.* Many are so close in morphological features that as small plants it is impossible to distinguish among them. I have seen the fine dwarf conifer collection at the Arnold Arboretum and was thoroughly impressed by the many types of falsecypress. Mr. Al Fordham, the propagator at the Arnold, showed me some seedlings of Hinoki Falsecypress which had been grown from seed collected from a dwarf clone. The variation was endless and the possibilities for introducing more dwarf forms existed. I also saw a large seedling population which was grown from a yellow foliaged form of *C. pisifera.* Again, there were many different types for some had yellow foliage, some blue or bluish green, others had juvenile needles while some showed adult foliage. The point I am attempting to make is that production of new and different cultivars of falsecypress is about as simple as sowing seed.

PROPAGATION: Considerable variation in cutting rootability among different cultivars of this species; cuttings of the species and the cultivars 'Nana', 'Compacta', 'Lycopodioides', 'Filicoides', 'Gracilis' and 'Magnifica' were taken eleven times between late September and late January. The average percentage of rooting of untreated cuttings was 41%. Rooting of cuttings treated with 50 to 100 ppm IBA/18 to 24 hours soak, or Hormodin #3 was 96%. Cutting wood was collected from current seasons's growth although 2 and 3-year-old wood also rooted. Untreated cuttings rooted equally well when taken from September through January.
RELATED SPECIES:

Chamaecyparis nootkatensis, Nootka Falsecypress, Alaska-cedar, Yellow-cypress, is a medium-sized tree reaching 60 to 90′ in the wild but one-half of that under cultivation. The crown is conical and composed of numerous drooping branches with long, pendulous, flattened sprays. The leaves are a dark bluish green or grayish green, 1/8 to 1/4″ long, pointed, scale-like, with the tips often diverging, occasionally glandular on the back; turning brown during the second season but persistent until the third. The leaves do not possess white markings and are rank-smelling when bruised or rubbed. Branchlets are often quadrangular. This species does best where both soil and atmospheric moisture are abundant. Not seen in cultivation too extensively compared to *C. obtusa* and *C. pisifera* and their clones. Native from Coastal Alaska to Washington; the Cascades to Oregon. Zone 4.

NATIVE HABITAT: Japan and Formosa. Introduced 1861.

Chamaecyparis pisifera — Sawara or Japanese Falsecypress

LEAVES: Appressed, long pointed, ovate-lanceolate, with slightly spreading tips, obscurely glandular, dark green above, with whitish lines beneath. Branchlets flattened, 2-ranked and arranged in horizontal planes.

SIZE: 50 to 70′ in height by 10 to 20′ in width.

HARDINESS: Zone 3.

HABIT: A pyramidal tree with a loose open habit and numerous branchlets thickly covered with slender feathery branchlets.

RATE: Medium.

TEXTURE: Medium.

BARK: Rather smooth, reddish brown, peeling off in thin strips.

LEAF COLOR: Dark green above with whitish lines beneath.

FLOWERS: Monoecious, small, inconspicuous.

FRUIT: Cones crowded, short-stalked, globose, 1/4″ across, yellowish brown; scales 10 to 12, soft woody, upper side wrinkled, the middle depressed, with a small mucro at the depression; seeds 1 to 2, ovoid, bulbous on both sides, glandular; wing broad, membranous, notched above and below.

CULTURE: Moist, loamy, well-drained, humid climate; sunny, open conditions, prefers lime free soils.

LANDSCAPE VALUE: Handsome when small but loses its beauty with old age as the lower branches die. The chief advantage lies in the many cultivars which have a place in various parts of the landscape, especially in rock gardens or as accent plants.

CULTIVARS:

'Filifera' — Has drooping stringy branches and forms a dense mound, usually no higher than 6 to 8′ after 10 to 15 years. Very fine textured, a lovely and different accent plant.

'Filifera Aurea' — Similar to above with yellow foliage.

'Plumosa' — Foliage is very soft textured almost feathery in constitution. There are two in Urbana about 20′ tall and rather ratty looking due to our hot, dry summer weather.

'Plumosa Aurea' — Soft, feathery golden yellow foliage; retains color throughout the summer and ranks among the best in this respect.

'Squarrosa' — Foliage is almost needle-like, very feathery, definitely not flat and frond-like; of soft gray-green foliage.

'Squarrosa Cyano-viridis' — Foliage is similar to above but silvery-green in summer and grayish blue in winter.

PROPAGATION: Cuttings should be taken in October, November and December, treated with IBA, 1000 ppm and placed in sand:peat. There are other manipulations which can be performed to increase rootability but the above should work for most clones.

NATIVE HABITAT: Japan. Introduced 1861.

Chamaecyparis thyoides — Whitecedar Falsecypress or Atlantic Whitecedar

LEAVES: Bluish green to glaucous-green with white margins, 1/10 to 1/12″ long, lateral pairs boat-shaped with sharp-pointed, spreading tips, facial pairs closely pressed, ovate-triangular, short-pointed, flat or keeled; most of the leaves are marked on the back with a resinous gland; leaves turn brown the second year but persist for several years.

STEM: Branchlets slender, rather irregularly arranged (not flattened), spreading, not decurving, very thin.

SIZE: 75 to 90′ in height by 10 to 20′ spread.

HARDINESS: Zone 3.

HABIT: A slender column in youth, forming a narrow spirelike crown at maturity devoid of branches for 3/4's of its length.

RATE: Medium (25′ in 20 years).

TEXTURE: Medium.

BARK: Thin, on old trunks 3/4″ to 1″ thick, ashy gray to reddish brown.

LEAF COLOR: Dark bluish green turning brown the second year, but persistent for several years.

FLOWERS: Monoecious, small, terminal; staminate red or yellow and abundant; pistillate green, few.

FRUIT: Cones on small branchlets, globose, small, 1/4″ across, a bluish purple, bloomy; scales 4 to 5, rarely 6, acute often with a reflexed base; seeds 1 or 2 on each scale, oblong; wing narrow, as broad as the seed.

CULTURE: In the wild, characteristic of fresh-water swamps and bogs, wet depressions, or stream banks, and is rarely found except on such sites; extensive pure stands are the rule, occurring on shallow-peat covered soils underlain with sand. Under cultivation it is best to provide a moist, sandy soil; prefers full sun and can not compete with hardwood species.

DISEASES AND INSECTS: None serious.

LANDSCAPE VALUE: Useful on low lands and boggy sites where it is native.

PROPAGATION: Supposedly somewhat difficult to root from cuttings but cuttings taken in mid-November and treated with 125 ppm IBA/24 hour soak, rooted 96% in sand:peat in 6 months. Cuttings taken in mid-December and placed in sand:peat rooted 14% without treatment and 70% with Hormodin #3.

NATIVE HABITAT: Eastern United States in swamps, along the Atlantic coast from Maine to Florida.

Chionanthus virginicus — White Fringetree

FAMILY: Oleaceae

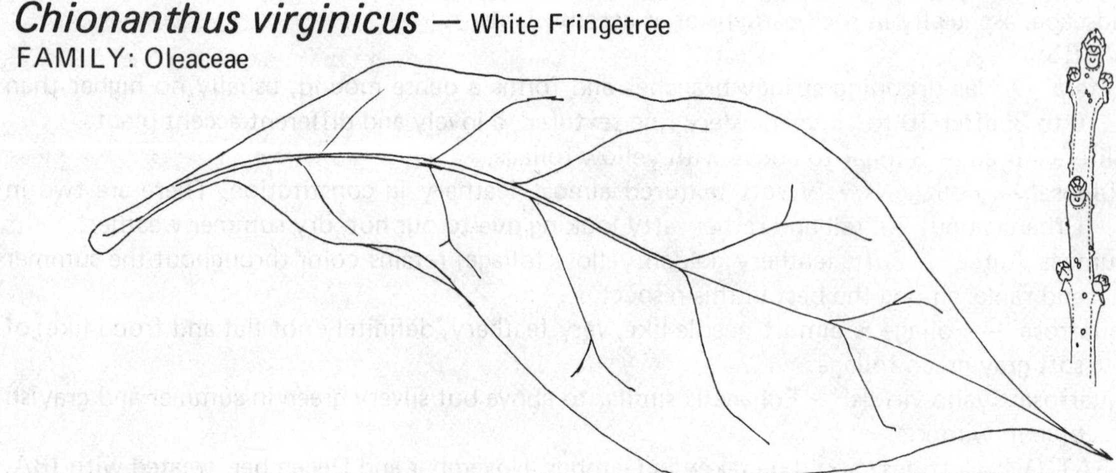

LEAVES: Opposite or subopposite, simple, narrow-elliptic to oblong or obovate-oblong, 3 to 8″ long, entire, acute or acuminate, cuneate, medium to dark green and often lustrous above, paler and pubescent at least on veins beneath, usually becoming glabrate.

BUD: Terminal-present, ovoid with keeled scales, acute, 1/8″ long, green to brown, 3 pairs of sharp-pointed keeled scales, angled appearance when looked upon from apical end.

STEM: Rather stout, green to buff to brown, glabrous or pubescent when young.

SIZE: In the wild may reach 25 to 30′ with an equal spread but under midwestern conditions is often a shrub or small tree 12 to 20′ with an equal spread.

HARDINESS: Zone 4.

HABIT: Large shrub or small tree with a spreading, rather open habit; often wider than high.

RATE: Slow, under ideal conditions possibly 8 to 10′ in 10 years but plants I have observed on our campus have averaged only about 4 to 6″/year over the last five years.

TEXTURE: Medium-coarse in leaf; fine in flower; medium-coarse in winter.

BARK: Gray and scaly on old trees.

LEAF COLOR: Medium to dark green, sometimes lustrous, in summer; fall coloring is poor in Central Illinois (yellow-green-brown combinations) but according to several east coast authorities can range from a bright to golden yellow.

FLOWER: Dioecious or polygamo-dioecious, white, fragrant, males more effective than females because of longer petals, borne in 6 to 8″ fine, fleecy, soft textured panicles in late May to early June just after leaves have matured. One of our more handsome native plants in flower.

FRUIT: Dark blue, bloomy, fleshy drupe, 1/2 to 3/5″ long, effective in September; interesting but often overlooked because the fruits are partially hidden by the foliage.

CULTURE: Transplant balled and burlapped in spring, supposedly difficult to move although several nurserymen I have talked with indicated they have had no problems; prefers deep, moist, fertile, acid (pH 6.0 to 6.5) soils; full sun; pruning is rarely required; in the wild is most commonly found along streambanks or the borders of swamps.

DISEASES AND INSECTS: None serious, occasionally scale, leaf spots, powdery mildew and canker.

LANDSCAPE VALUE: Very beautiful specimen shrub, excellent in groups, borders, near large buildings; outstanding in flower; supposedly will do well in cities as it is quite air pollutant tolerant.

PROPAGATION: Seed possesses a double dormancy and requires a warm period of 3 to 5 months, during which a root unit is made while the shoot remains dormant. Then cold temperature at 41°F for one or more months overcomes the shoot dormancy.

RELATED SPECIES:

Chionanthus retusus, Chinese Fringetree, is a large, multistemmed shrub in cultivation but can be grown as a small tree. Usually reaches 15 to 25′ in height but may grow 30 to 40′ in the wild. The outline is spreading, rounded. The leaves are leathery, smaller than those of *C. virginicus*, and lustrous. The flowers are snow-white, June-July, produced in erect, 2 to 3″ high and 2 to 4″ wide, cymose panicles, on terminating young shoots of the year. Fruit is an ellipsoidal, 1/2″ long, dark blue drupe which ripens in September through October. The flowers, fruits and foliage are highly ornamental but the fruit will only occur on female plants. Another asset is the handsome gray-brown bark which offers another season of interest. One traveler in China compared it in flower to a dome of soft, fleecy snow. China, Korea, Japan. Introduced 1845. Zone 6.

NATIVE HABITAT: Southern New Jersey to Florida and Texas. Introduced 1736.

Cladrastis lutea — American Yellowwood, Virgilia

FAMILY: Leguminosae

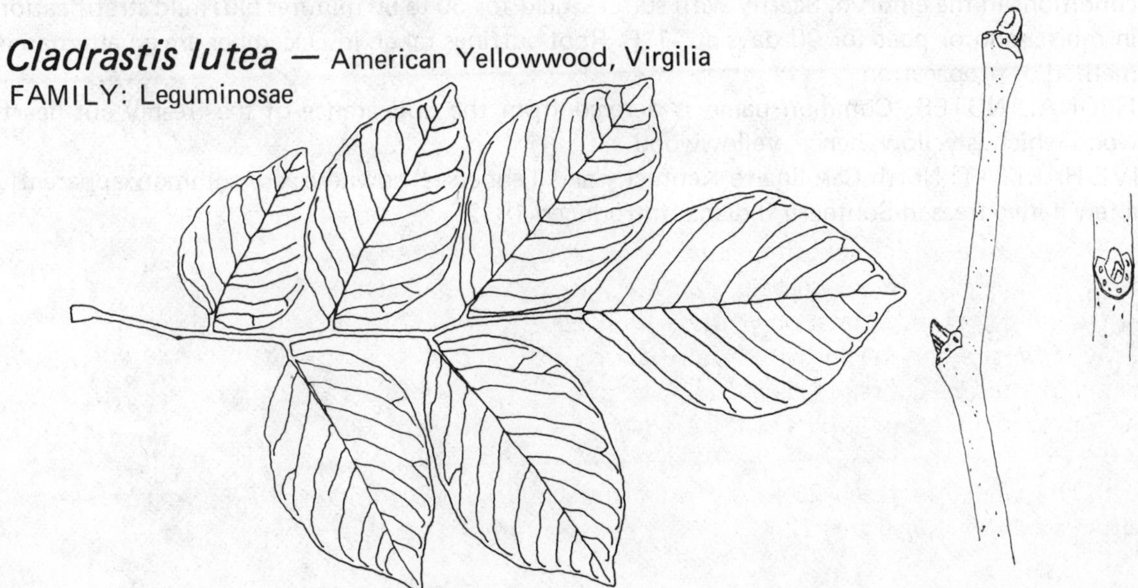

LEAVES: Alternate, odd-pinnately compound, 7 to 11 leaflets, elliptic to ovate, broad cuneate, glabrous, bright green, petiole enlarged at base, enclosing bud.

BUD: Terminal-absent, laterals-naked, superposed, the uppermost the largest and generally alone developing, flattened, closely packed together to form a pointed, bud-like, hairy "cone", generally less than 1/5" long, nearly surrounded by the leaf scar.

STEM: Slender, more or less zigzag, smooth bright reddish brown, often bloomy, odor and taste resembling that of a raw dried pea or bean.

BARK: Thin gray to light brown, resembling bark of beech, with slight protuberances of ridges and horizontal wrinkles.

SIZE: 30 to 50' in height with a spread of 40 to 55 feet.

HARDINESS: Zone 3.

HABIT: Usually a low branching tree with a broad, rounded crown of delicate branches.

RATE: Medium, 9 to 12' over a 8 to 10 year period.

TEXTURE: Medium in foliage and winter; very handsome in foliage because of the bright green color of the leaves.

BARK: On older branches and trunks very smooth, gray and beech-like in overall appearance and texture.

LEAF COLOR: Opening bright yellowish green gradually changing to bright green in summer; very prominent in a landscape when compared to the dark green of maples, oaks, or ashes; fall color is supposedly a bright yellow but in Central Illinois usually develops yellow-green.

FLOWERS: Perfect, white, fragrant, 1 to 1 1/4" long; borne in 8 to 14" long terminal panicles or racemes in late May to early June; tends to produce the greatest abundance of flowers in alternate years or every third year; flowers when 12 to 18' tall; bees really frequent the flower for nectar.

FRUIT: Pod, brown, October, 2 1/2 to 3" long.

CULTURE: Transplant balled and burlapped as a small tree into well drained soil; tolerates high pH soils as well as acid situations, native on limestone cliffs and ridges; full sun; prune only in summer as the tree bleeds profusely if pruned in winter or spring; often develops bad crotches which can split or crack in storms.

DISEASES AND INSECTS: Very few problems are associated with this tree; Verticillium wilt has been reported.

LANDSCAPE VALUE: Excellent tree for flowers and foliage; the medium size and spreading habit make it a choice shade tree for smaller properties; can be used as a single specimen or in groupings; there are beautiful specimens located on the University of Illinois campus and at Spring Grove Cemetery.

PROPAGATION: Seed dormancy is caused by an impermeable seed coat and to a lesser degree by conditions in the embryo. Scarify with sulfuric acid for 30 to 60 minutes plus mild stratification in moist sand or peat for 90 days at 41°F. Root cuttings taken in December are an alternative method of propagation.

ADDITIONAL NOTES: Common name is derived from the appearance of the freshly cut heartwood which is yellow, hence, yellowwood.

NATIVE HABITAT: North Carolina to Kentucky and Tennessee, nowhere very common; apparently a few native trees in Southern Indiana. Introduced 1812.

Clematis x *jackmanii* — Jackman Clematis

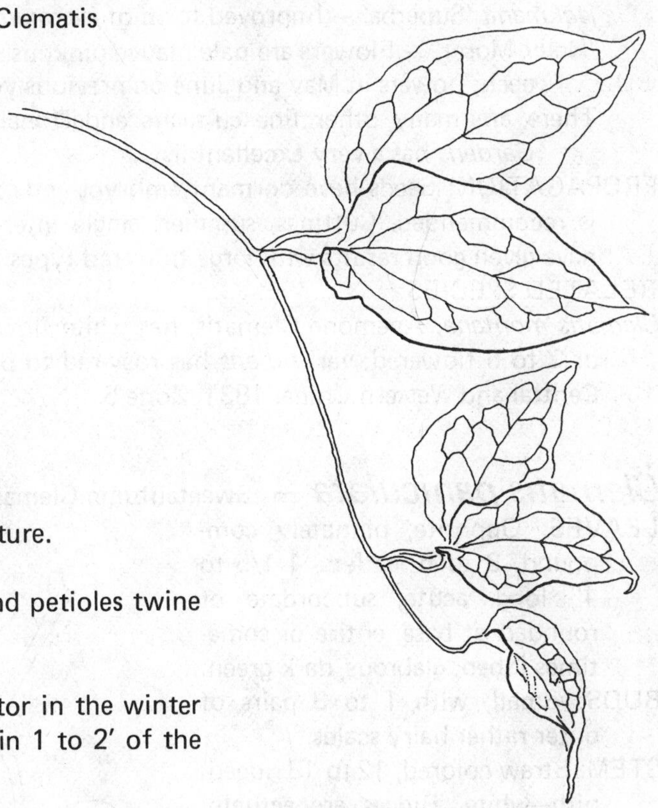

FAMILY: Ranunculaceae

LEAVES: Opposite, pinnate, the upper ones often simple; leaflets ovate, rather large, usually slightly pubescent beneath.

BUDS: Rather small, ovoid or flattened, sessile, solitary, with 1 to 3 pairs of exposed somewhat hairy scales.

STEM: Slender, light brown, ridged, with the 6 primary ridges prominent; pith-angular or star-shaped, white, continuous with thin firmer diaphragms at the nodes.

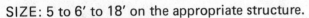

SIZE: 5 to 6' to 18' on the appropriate structure.

HARDINESS: Zone 4 to 5.

HABIT: A herbaceous vine whose stems and petioles twine around objects.

RATE: Fast, 5 to 10' in a single season.

TEXTURE: Medium in summer; not a factor in the winter landscape as it often dies back to within 1 to 2' of the ground.

LEAF COLOR: Bright green in summer.

FLOWERS: Perfect, violet-purple, 4 to 7" diameter, June through until frost; usually borne solitary or in 3-flowered cymes, sepals are the showy portion.

FRUIT: Achene, with 1 to 2" persistent style which is clothed with long silky hairs.

CULTURE: Attention to detail is important, the adage a warm top and cool bottom apply; transplant as a container plant in spring into light, loamy, moderately moist, well-drained soil (cool root environment); soil should be mulched; avoid extremely hot, sunny areas; place the plant so it receives some shade during the day; higher pH soils 6 to 7.5 are often recommended as being optimum but personally I do not think it makes much difference if the pH is 4.5; avoid extremely wet conditions.

DISEASES AND INSECTS: Leaf spot and stem rot can be a serious problem, black blister beetle, clematis borer, mites, whiteflies, scales and root-knot nematodes.

LANDSCAPE VALUE: Does not fit the absolute requirements of a woody plant but to omit these beautiful vines would be somewhat of an injustice to the reader. Excellent for trellises, fences, rock walls, any structure around which the stems and petioles twine is a good support; very beautiful in flower and many of the large flowered hybrids are worth experimenting with. Other cultivars: From my own observations I would recommend the following for Midwest culture:

'Comptesse de Bouchard' — Flowers are 5 to 6" diameter, satiny rose color, usually with 6 sepals, flowering from July to October on current season's wood.

'Crimson Star' — Handsome red-flowered type with 2 to 4" diameter flowers.

'Duchess of Edenburgh' — Excellent large flowering, double, pure white type with fragrant flowers appearing in May and June on previous year's wood.

'Ernest Markham' — Large red flowers, July to September on current season's growth.

'Henryi' — Creamy white, 6 to 8" diameter flowers with a center of dark stamens, June and July on current season's growth.

jackmanii 'Alba' — Large white flowers on current year's growth are at first double, produced from older wood, then single on current season's growth.

jackmanii 'Rubra' — Flowers are a deep red; sometimes flowers are double on old wood.

jackmanii 'Superba' – Improved form of *jackmanii* with dark purple, 5" diameter flowers.

'Nelly Moser' – Flowers are pale mauve-pink, usually with 8 sepals, with a deep pink bar down each; flowers in May and June on previous years' wood, sometimes again in summer.

There are many other fine cultivars and Donald Wyman's *Shrubs and Vines for American Gardens* has a very excellent list.

PROPAGATION: Seeds have dormant embryos and stratification for 60 to 90 days at 33° to 40° F. is recommended. Cuttings, summer, single inter-nodal cuttings with cuts between the nodes have given good results with large flowered types.

RELATED SPECIES:

Clematis montana, Anemone Clematis, has white flowers, 2 to 2½" across, May-June, borne singly or 2 to 5 flowered; var. *rubens* has rosy-red to pinkish 2 to 2½" diameter flowers. Himalayas, Central and Western China. 1831. Zone 5.

Clematis paniculata – Sweetautumn Clematis

LEAVES: Opposite, pinnately compound, 3 to 5 leaflets, 1 1/5 to 4" long, acute, subcordate or rounded at base, entire or sometimes lobed, glabrous, dark green.

BUDS: Small, with 1 to 3 pairs of outer rather hairy scales.

STEM: Straw colored, 12 to 18 ridged; pith–white. Ridges are actually vascular bundles.

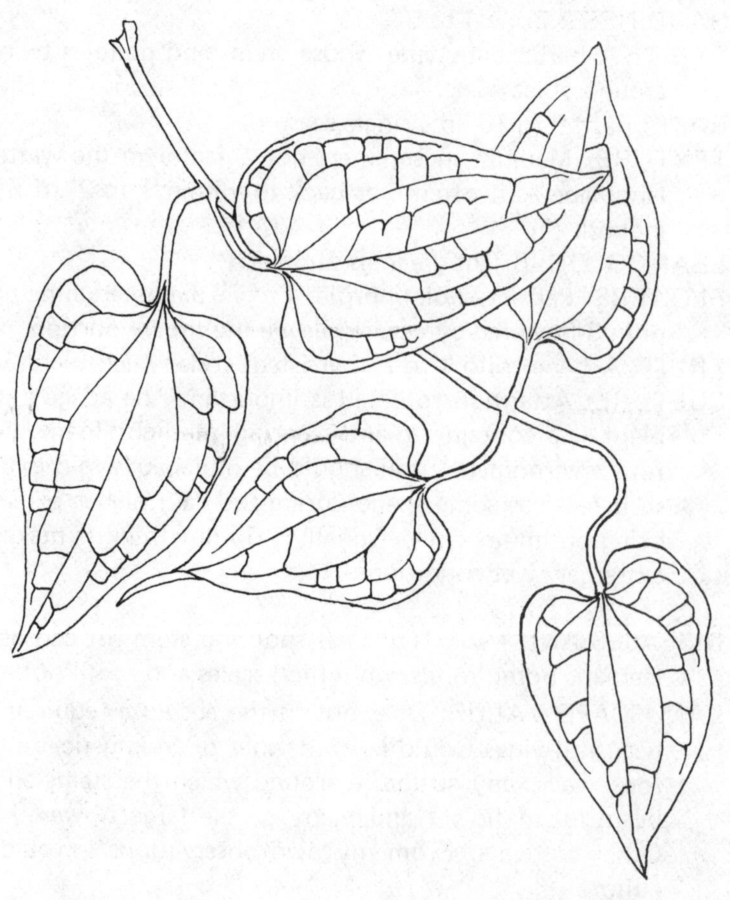

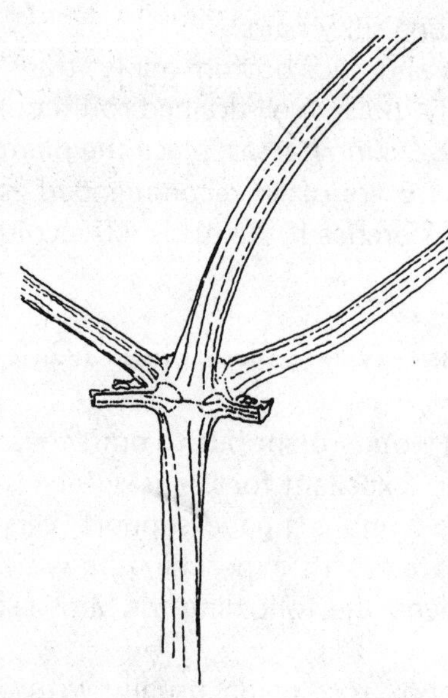

Clematis paniculata (correct name is now *C. dioscoreifolia robusta*), Sweetautumn Clematis, is a rampant, rampaging vine which engulfs every structure in sight. The flowers are white, 1 1/5" across, fragrant, 6 to 8 sepals, August into September and October, borne in many flowered axillary and terminal panicles; quite literally make the whole plant look like a new fallen snow; probably the easiest *Clematis* to grow as it seems to thrive with neglect. Japan. 1864. Zone 5.

Clematis tangutica, Golden Clematis, has bright yellow, 3 to 4" diameter flowers, June-July, solitary; listed as handsomest of yellow flowered *Clematis.* Mongolia to Northwestern China. 1890. Zone 5.

Clematis texensis, Scarlet Clematis, has carmine or bright scarlet flowers, urn-shaped, narrowed at the mouth, about 1" long and 3/4" wide; July through until frost; solitary and nodding. 'Duchess of Albany' is a pink flowered form. Texas. 1878. Zone 4.

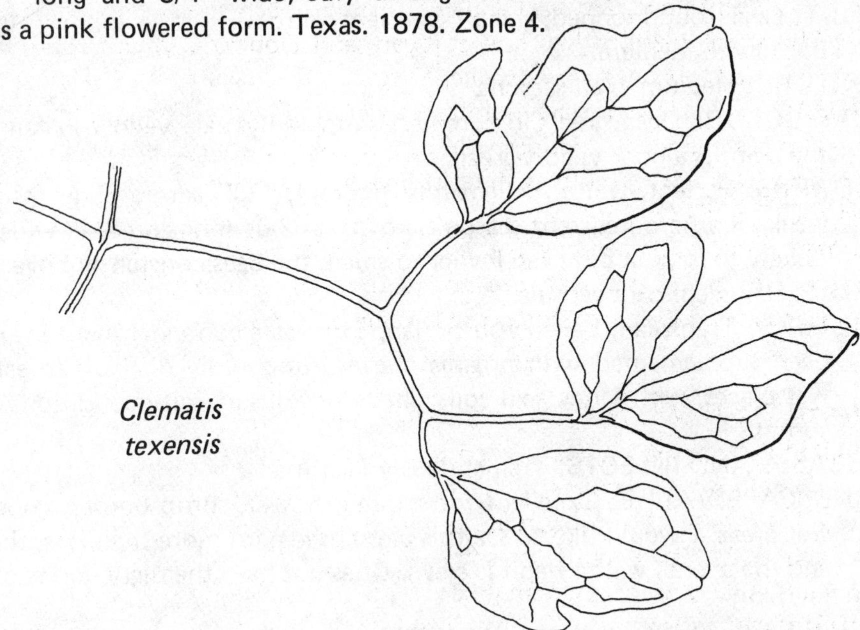

Clematis texensis

Clematis virginiana, Virginsbower, is a handsome vine growing 12 to 20' with bright green summer foliage. The flowers are whitish (supposedly this is a dioecious species with staminate flowers showy white; pistillate more dull); borne in 3 to 6" long axillary leafy panicles in July through September. Good vine for native situations; other types are more effective in flower. Native from Nova Scotia to Manitoba, south to Georgia and Kansas. Introduced 1720. Zone 4.

Clematis vitalba, Traveler's joy or Old Man's Beard, has white, 4/5" diameter, almond scented flowers in July through September which are borne in axillary and terminal 3 to 5" panicles. Common name comes from the fact the flowers are slightly fragrant and odor proves refreshing to the traveler on a hot summer's day. Europe, Northern Africa. 1820. Zone 4.

Clematis viticella, Italian Clematis, has purple, rosy-purple or violet, 1 to 2" diameter, 4-sepaled flowers which are borne in June through August singly or in 2's or 3's.
'Albiflora' — Has white flowers.
'Nana' — Dwarf type about 3'.
'Plena' — Double flowering form.
'Rubra' — Red-flowered form.
Southern Europe to Western Asia. 1597. Zone 4.

Clethra alnifolia—Summersweet Clethra

FAMILY: Clethraceae

LEAVES: Alternate, simple, obovate to obovate-oblong, 1 3/5 to 4" long, acute to short acuminate, cuneate, sharply serrate, glabrous or nearly so on both sides, with 7 to 10 pairs of veins.

BUDS: Small, loosely scaled, solitary, sessile, ovoid.

STEM: Brown, rounded or obscurely 3-sided, pith—light brown, continuous.

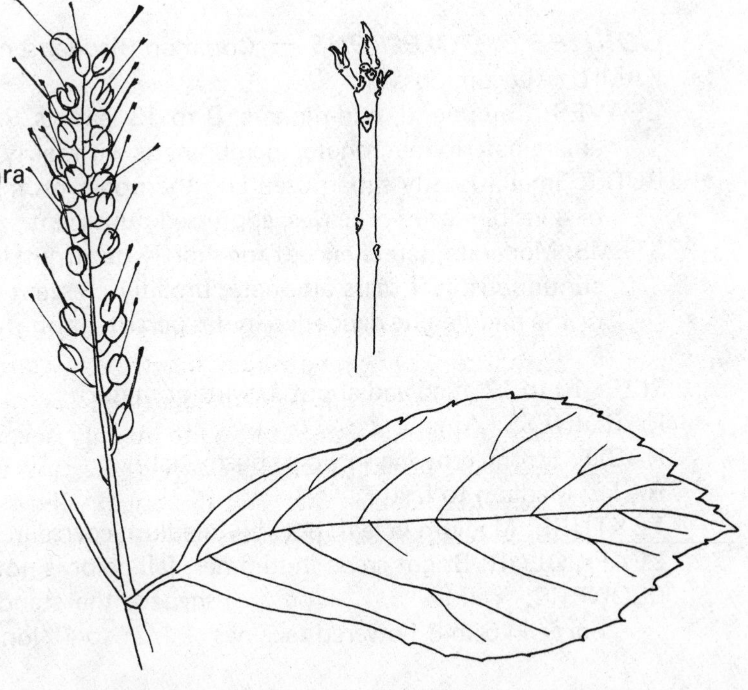

SIZE: 3 to 8′ high and 4 to 6′ wide.
HARDINESS: Zone 3.
HABIT: Oval, round-topped, erect, dense leafy shrub.
RATE: Slow to Medium.
TEXTURE: Medium in all seasons.
LEAF COLOR: Deep green in summer; supposedly pale yellow in fall but in Champaign-Urbana the color is a poor yellow-green.
FLOWERS: Perfect, white, delightfully fragrant, 1/3″ across, July into August, effective 4 to 6 weeks, borne on current season's growth in 2-6″ long and 3/4″ wide upright panicled racemes. Lovely to look at but even lovlier to smell; the bees constantly hover about.
FRUIT: Dry, dehiscent capsule.
CULTURE: Transplant balled and burlapped or as a container plant into moist, acid soil which has been supplemented with organic matter; supposedly difficult to establish; grows naturally in wet places, withstands acid soils, shade or full sun, salty conditions of seashore; prune in early spring.
DISEASES AND INSECTS: Tremendously pest free.
LANDSCAPE VALUE: Excellent for summer flower, shrub border, good plant for difficult shade, wet areas; I would like to see this plant used a lot more than it is; the foliage is very handsome and the overall winter habit is clean. Does not have the dirty habits of *Weigela* and *Lonicera*.
CULTIVARS:

'Paniculata' — Large terminal panicles and is superior to the type.
'Rosea' — Flowers buds pink; flowers at first pinkish.

PROPAGATION: Cuttings taken in summer root readily in sand and peat without treatment but treatments may hasten rooting.
RELATED SPECIES:
Clethra acuminata, Cinnamon Clethra, grows to 18′ and develops into a shrub or small tree. The foliage is dark green; flowers are white, fragrant, late July, borne in 3 to 8″ long, solitary, nodding racemes, the bark has a polished-cinnamon color. Virginia to West Virginia to Georgia and Alabama. 1806. Zone 5.
Clethra barbinervis, Japanese Clethra, grows to 6 to 10′ under cultivation but can reach 30′ in the wild. Similar to above. Japan. 1870. Zone 5.
ADDITIONAL NOTES: The late flowering is an asset to the summer garden, the preferred species is *C. alnifolia* for midwestern gardens.
NATIVE HABITAT: Maine to Florida. Introduced 1731.

Colutea arborescens — Common Bladder-senna

FAMILY: Leguminosae
LEAVES: Compound, odd-pinnate, 9 to 13 leaflets, 3/5 to 1 1/5″ long, elliptic to obovate, usually emarginate to mucronate, membranous with fairly distinct venation; stipules small.
BUDS: Small, usually superposed and the upper promptly developing into slender branches with 2 or 4 visible scales or leaves; appressed-pubescent.
STEMS: Moderate, terete except for shortly decurrent lines from the nodes; pith moderate, rounded, continuous; leaf scars alternate, broadly crescent-shaped, much elevated; bundle-traces 1 or 3 or the middle one divided; stipules persistent on the sides of the leaf cushion.

SIZE: 10 to 12′ high and about as wide at maturity.
HARDINESS: Zone 5.
HABIT: Strong growing shrub of bushy habit.
RATE: Medium to fast.
TEXTURE: Medium in leaf; possibly medium-coarse in winter.
LEAF COLOR: Bright green in summer; fall color is not effective.
FLOWERS: Yellow, 3/4″ long, pea-shaped, the standard with red markings; May through July; borne in 6 to 8-flowered racemes, 1 1/2″ to 4″ long; produced on current season's growth.

FRUIT: Inflated and bladder-like pod, 3" long and 1 to 1 1/2" wide; greenish to slightly reddish near the base; maturing July through September.

CULTURE: Easily grown in almost any soil except waterlogged; prefers full sun; prune back to old wood in winter.

DISEASES AND INSECTS: None serious.

LANDSCAPE VALUE: Most authorities consider this species too coarse and weedy for the home landscape. Because of its adaptability, it could be successfully used in poor soil areas where more ornamental shrubs would not grow. I have seen the species and the cultivar 'Bullata" in July at the Arnold Arboretum; at this time their foliage was in immaculate condition and they were the match of any other shrub for summer foliage effect.

CULTIVARS: 'Bullata' – A dwarf form of dense habit whose 5 to 7 leaflets are small, rounded and somewhat bullate. Probably about 1/3 to 1/2 the size of the species at maturity.

'Crispa' – A low growing form with leaves wavy on the margins.

PROPAGATION: Seeds have a hard seed coat and should be scarified in concentrated sulfuric acid. Half-ripened cuttings collected in early November (England) rooted 29 percent without treatment, failed to respond to NAA but rooted 73 percent after treatment with 100 ppm IBA/18 hr.

ADDITIONAL NOTES: Only *Koelreutaria* and *Staphylea* among hardy woody plants have similar fruits. The fruits explode when squeezed. W. J. Bean noted that "its accommodating nature had made it, perhaps, despised in gardens."

NATIVE HABITAT: Mediterranean region and Southeastern Europe. Introduced 1570.

Comptonia peregrina — Sweetfern

FAMILY: Myricaceae

LEAVES: Alternate, simple, linear-oblong, deeply pinnatifid with roundish-ovate, oblique, often mucronulate lobes, 2 to 4 1/2" long and 2/5 to 3/5" broad, pubescent, fragrant; looks somewhat like a fern frond hence, the name Sweetfern, pale green when emerging, eventually dark green often lustrous.

BUDS: Globular, minute, solitary, sessile, with 2 or about 4 exposed scales, hairy. Pistillate catkins crowded at the ends of the stems, 1/4" long, cylindrical, pale brown, hairy.

STEMS: Young stems green or yellowish or reddish brown and covered with resin dots; older stems yellowish brown with shining surface, somewhat hairy; oldest are reddish purple or coppery brown.

SIZE: 2 to 4' high and can spread 4 to 8'.

HARDINESS: Zone 2.

HABIT: Deciduous shrub with slender, often erect branches developing a broad, flat-topped to rounded outline as it spreads and colonizes.

RATE: Slow to medium.

TEXTURE: Medium-fine in leaf and no worse than medium in winter. The interesting fern-like foliage gives the plant a gentle, woodsie, graceful appearance.

LEAF COLOR: Dark green, almost lustrous, in summer; falls green or greenish brown in autumn.

FLOWERS: Monoecious (usually), staminate with 3 to 4, usually 4 stamens, borne in cylindric catkins; female-ovary surrounded with 8 persistent bracts at the base, borne in globose-ovoid catkins; April or early May; not showy; of yellow-green color.

FRUIT: Nutlet, 1/5" long, olive-brown, burr-like.

CULTURE: Not the easiest plant to move; people have suggested digging large pieces of sod and, hopefully, getting sufficient roots to effect establishment. Recent work has shown that Sweetfern can be container-grown and successfully transplanted from containers. See *Inter. Plant Prop. Soc.* 24:364-366, 1974. Sweetfern does best in peaty, sandy, sterile, acid soils. Some authorities indicated moist soils are beneficial, however, I have seen this plant in New England growing all over cuts and fills along highways. Sweetfern has the ability to fix its own nitrogen and this partially explains its adaptability to poor, infertile soils; full sun or partial shade.

DISEASES AND INSECTS: Nothing serious.

LANDSCAPE VALUE: Interesting plant with aromatic foliage and stems. Can be used for highways and other waste areas where the soil is sandy, infertile and somewhat dry. A nice novelty plant for the collector.

PROPAGATION: Is considered difficult to propagate, however, Bill Hamilton, from the University of Massachusetts has spent considerable time and effort and now has recommendations pretty well in hand. The following information is extracted from Mr. Hamilton's work (see reference under culture). Cuttings taken from mature wood rooted poorly. Cuttings taken from juvenile growth rooted readily when treated with Hormodin #2 and placed under mist. Best to collect juvenile stems 3" or less in length. The principal means of propagation was by root pieces which are dug in late winter or early spring before growth starts. The root pieces should be 4" long if 1/16" in diameter and 2" long if 3/8 to 1/2" in diameter. The medium should be a fine sand and Sphagnum peat. The cuttings should be placed horizontally at a 1/2" depth and will develop shoots and additional roots. As the new juvenile shoots developed they can be collected for cutting wood. Seed propagation has met with limited success but Dr. Torrey of the Harvard Forest in Petersham, Mass. obtained 80% germination using gibberillic acid.

ADDITIONAL NOTES: Similar to *Myrica* but differs in the monoecious flowers. Not used enough and the new findings in propagation may increase its usage.

NATIVE HABITAT: Nova Scotia to North Carolina, Indiana and Michigan. Introduced 1714.

Cornus alba — Tatarian Dogwood

FAMILY: Cornaceae

LEAVES: Opposite, simple, ovate to elliptic, 1 3/5 to 3" long, acute to acuminate, usually rounded at base, rugose, and often somewhat bullate above and medium green, glaucous beneath, with 5 to 6 pairs of veins; petiole 2/5 – 1" long.

BUD: Appressed, valvate, pubescent, deep red-brown-black in color.

STEM: Slender, appressed, hairy to glabrous, lenticels prominent, long oval, vertical, beautiful deep-red in winter. Pith—white.

FRUIT: Drupe, white or slightly bluish, stone higher than broad, acute at ends, flattened.

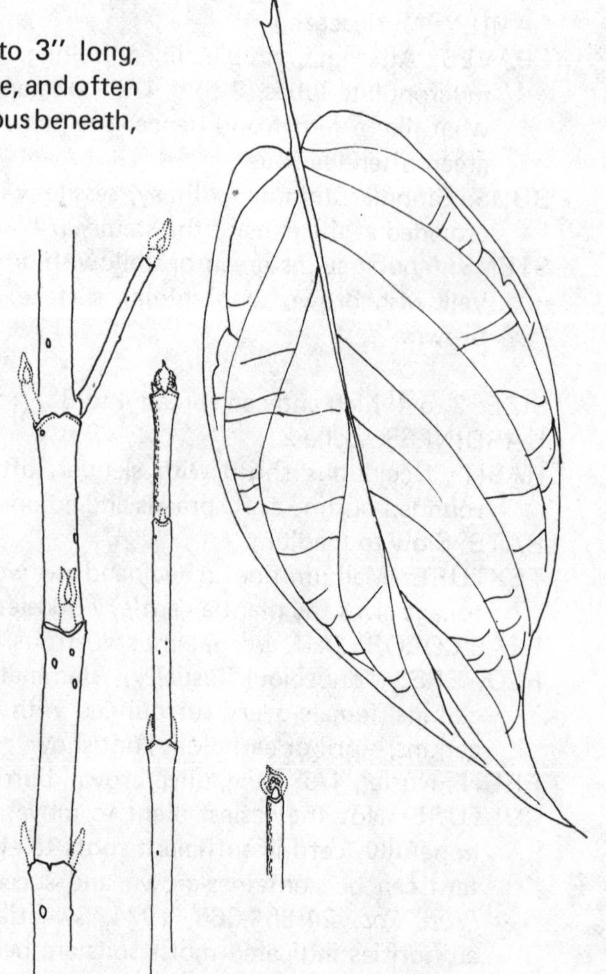

SIZE: 8 to 10′ in height, spread is variable ranging from 5 to 10′.

HARDINESS: Zone 2.

HABIT: Usually distinctly erect in youth, arching somewhat with age, the long branches sparsely branched creating an open, loose appearance. The lack of lateral bud development along the shoots is interesting. The branching (when it occurs) appears at the tops of the shoots.

RATE: Fast.

TEXTURE: Medium in leaf, somewhat coarse in winter although the rich red winter stems reduce the bold harshness of the erect ascending stems.

STEM COLOR: In winter the stems change to a blood-red color. The summer color is strongly greenish with a tinge of red. The color transformation can be correlated with the short, cool days of fall and the abscission of foliage which coincides quite well with the initiation of red coloration. The oldest canes should be removed as the young stems develop the most vivid reds.

LEAF COLOR: Soft yellow-green in early spring gradually changing to medium green. Fall color in our area is often a good reddish purple, however, some plants exhibit very limited coloration.

FLOWERS: Yellowish white, late May, after the leaves have matured, in 1 1/2 to 2″ diameter flat-topped cymes, effective 7 to 10 days. The flowers are not overwhelmingly effective; perfect.

FRUIT: Drupe, whitish or slightly blue tinted, about 3/8″ across, mid-June to early July, interesting but not long persistent. The stones (endocarp and seed) higher than wide, acute at ends, flattened. The fruit has ornamental appeal but is little recognized by most gardeners. In fact, a question to the most knowledgeable of gardeners concerning the fruit colors of the "red-stemmed" dogwoods (*C. alba, C. baileyi, C. stolonifera*) would probably yield an I do not know response.

CULTURE: Fibrous rooted, relatively easy to transplant, adapted to varied soil conditions but prefers well drained situation, sun or partial shade, quite vigorous and is apt to overgrow neighboring shrubs, prune 1/3 of old wood every year.

DISEASES AND INSECTS: Crown canker, flower and leaf blight, leaf spots, powdery mildews, twig blights, root rots, borers (at least seven kinds), dogwood club-gall, leaf miner, scales, and other lesser insects. The borers can be serious especially on stressed, weak growing trees.

LANDSCAPE VALUE: Difficult to use as a single specimen plant, best in shrub border, especially effective in large masses along roadsides, ponds and other large display areas. Definitely adds color to the winter landscape. Probably does not spread as rapidly as *C. stolonifera* and hence more desirable for the home landscape. The red-stemmed dogwoods are difficult to separate by winter characteristics especially as small plants and one is never absolute as to which species he is purchasing. Use with discretion for this species is a strong focal point in the landscape and may actually detract from the other plant materials.

CULTIVARS:

'Argenteo-marginata' — Leaves with an irregular creamy-white margin, the center a weak blue-
'Elegantissima' green; winter stems are red. This cultivar has often been listed simply
'Variegata' as *Cornus elegantissima* by many nurserymen. The second name is often accepted in this country but either one is probably acceptable.

'Gouchaltii' — The leaf margin is yellow and rose, the center of the leaf green and rose. Difficult to digest in any garden!

'Sibirica' — Coral-red stems, not as vigorous as the species, color is most intense on stems produced during the current growing season. Very handsome winter color but its use should be tempered.

'Spaethii' — Foliage strongly bordered with yellow, very effective. From my own observations I would find it difficult to integrate this shrub into the small home landscape.

PROPAGATION: Seed should be treated like *C. stolonifera*. Cuttings, any time of the year, softwood or hardwood, root easily. I have collected cutting wood in February, placed it in the mist bed and had 90% success.

NATIVE HABITAT: Siberia to Manchuria and Northern Korea. Introduced 1941.

Cornus alternifolia — Pagoda Dogwood

LEAVES: Alternate—but crowded near ends of twigs, appearing as if whorled, simple, slender stalked, usually crowded at end of branches, elliptic ovate, 2 to 5" long, acuminate, cuneate, nearly glabrous above, glaucescent beneath and appressed—pubescent, with 5 to 6 pairs of veins, petiole—4/5 to 2" long, medium to dark green.

BUD: Flower—1/4" long, purplish, essentially glabrous at base, pubescent toward tip. Valvate, terminally borne. Vegetative—minute, valvate, minutely hairy.

STEM: Slender, usually greenish to reddish or purplish, shiny, somewhat bloomy and glabrous. Pith—white.

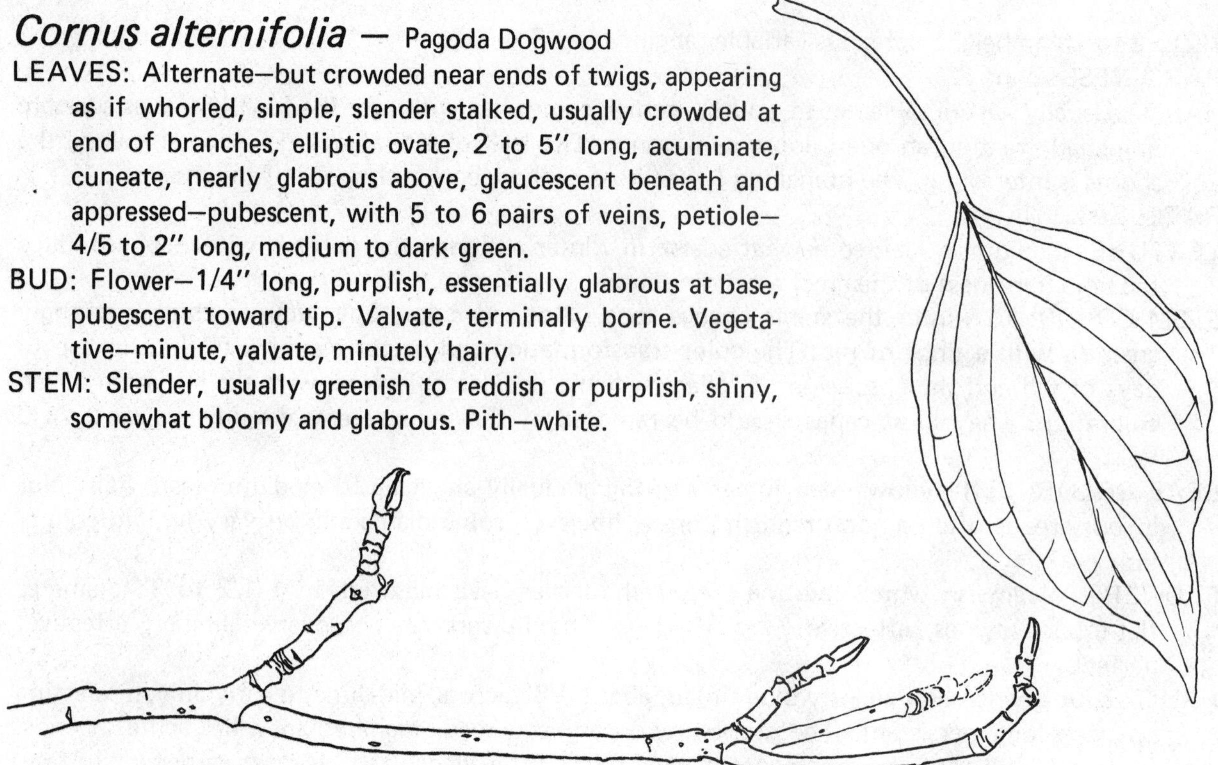

SIZE: 15 to 25' in height, possibly 1 1/2 times that in spread.

HARDINESS: Zone 3.

HABIT: Spreading, horizontal low-branched tree or large shrub with broadly horizontal branches forming horizontal tiers. Interesting branching habit.

RATE: Slow initially, medium when established.

TEXTURE: Medium in leaf and winter habit. Excellent textural effects because of the strong horizontal branches which are almost parallel with the ground. The sympodial or "Y" — type branching pattern creates an unusual mosaic along the stems.

STEM COLOR: Variable but first and second year stems are often lustrous brown to purple. Quite handsome on close inspection.

LEAF COLOR: Medium to dark green, fall color can develop reddish purple, however, I have yet to observe good color on this species.

FLOWERS: Yellowish white, sickeningly fragrant, effective 7 to 10 days in our area; late May to early June; borne in 1 1/2 to 2 1/2" diameter flat-topped upright cymes. The flowers are not eye catching but are sufficiently showy to be of ornamental value in the late spring landscape.

FRUIT: Drupe, bluish black, bloomy, 1/4 to 1/3" across; July-August, not long persisting, the fruit stalk turning a pinkish red; fruit changing from green to red to blue-black at maturity.

CULTURE: Fibrous, spreading root system, transplants best as young plant; requires moist, well drained soil; seems to do best in a partially shaded situation although I have observed plants in full sun which appeared quite prosperous.

DISEASES AND INSECTS: Leaf spot, twig blight or canker are problems, see under *C. alba*.

LANDSCAPE VALUE: Possibly for naturalizing, where horizontal characteristics needed, shrub border, where sharp vertical architectural lines are present. Interesting dogwood, little used for it has rough competition from *Cornus florida*.

CULTIVARS:

'Argentea' — Leaves variegated with white, tends toward shrubby habit.

PROPAGATION: Seed, 60 days at 68 to 86°F plus 60 days at 41°F in moist sand, peat or sand and peat. Cuttings, I have rooted cuttings collected in June but the percentage was low.

RELATED SPECIES:

Cornus controversa, Giant Dogwood, 60′; Zone 5; picturesque, wide spreading, horizontal branching; flowers are whitish in 3 to 7″ diameter flat-topped cymes, May, fruit is bluish black, August to September, has possibilities but seldom used; native to Japan, China.

NATIVE HABITAT: New Brunswick to Minnesota south to Georgia and Alabama. Introduced 1760.

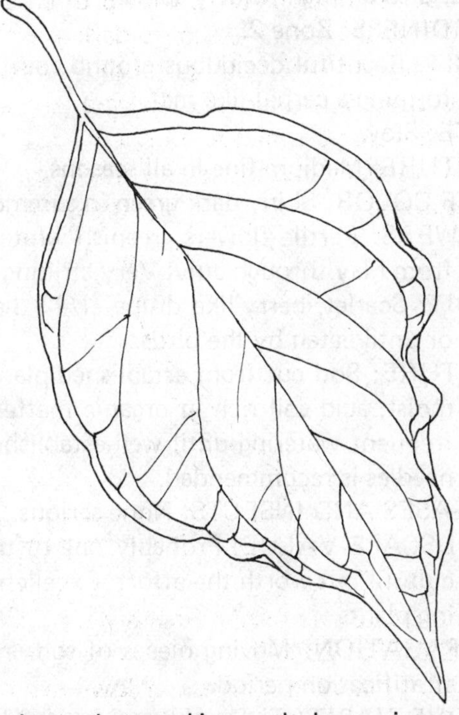

Cornus amomum — Silky Dogwood

LEAVES: Opposite, simple, elliptic-ovate or elliptic, 2 to 4″ long, short acuminate, usually rounded at base, medium to dark green and nearly glabrous above, glaucous beneath and with grayish white or brownish hairs on the veins, petiole—1/3 to 2/3″ long.

BUD: Flower—terminally borne, hairy, valvate, nearly sessile, relatively small. Vegetative—valvate, appressed, pubescent, small.

STEM: Slender, purplish, rarely greenish, appressed pubescence especially on younger branches, second year wood showing distinct fissuring pattern, pith-brown.

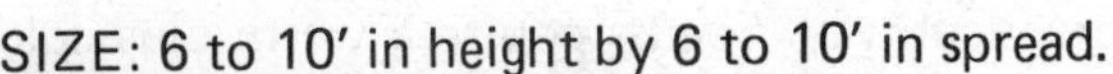

SIZE: 6 to 10′ in height by 6 to 10′ in spread.

HARDINESS: Zone 5.

HABIT: Rounded, multistemmed shrub usually twiggy and round-topped in youth, becoming open with age. The specimens on the University of Illinois campus attest to the growth habit. Actually several of the older plants are straggly, unkempt and without ornamental appeal.

RATE: Medium (possibly fast).

TEXTURE: Medium in foliage, coarse in winter.

STEM COLOR: Young branches reddish purple, sometimes greenish. Older wood is brownish purple and develops brown fissured areas.

LEAF COLOR: Medium to dark green in summer; fall color has been green to brown in our area although various authors mention reddish purple as a possibility.

FLOWERS: Yellowish white, not fragrant, mid-June, 7 to 10 days, borne in upright, 1 1/2 to 2 1/2″ diameter, flat-topped, slightly villous cymes.

FRUIT: Drupe, 1/4″ across, bluish often with white blotches, actually as I view it: a porcelain blue and of attractive quality. Unfortunately persisting only a brief time in August.

CULTURE: Native in low woods, along streams and borders of swamps over much of the eastern United States, fibrous rooted, easily transplanted, quite adaptable but prefers moist, partially shaded situations although it is performing well in our area in full sun and with less than optimum moisture.

DISEASES AND INSECTS: Scale may present a problem, see under *C. alba*.

LANDSCAPE VALUE: Possibly massing, shrub borders, naturalizing, in moist and wet soils where many shrubs do not grow well. Probably too coarse and with limited ornamental assets to ever become a common landscape shrub but, like all plants, in the proper setting it has a place.

PROPAGATION: Seed, 90 to 120 days at 41°F will break the dormancy. Cuttings, softwood, taken in July rooted well without hormonal treatment. Rooting can be enhanced with IBA treatment.

NATIVE HABITAT: Massachusetts to Georgia, west to New York and Tennessee. Introduced 1658.

Cornus canadensis — Bunchberry

LEAVES: Whorled at top of stem, oval to obovate, 1 to 3" long, acute, glabrous or slightly appressed-pubescent; glossy dark green.

SIZE: 3 to 9" high, widely spreading.
HARDINESS: Zone 2.
HABIT: Beautiful deciduous ground cover, in favorable areas forming a carpet-like mat.
RATE: Slow.
TEXTURE: Medium-fine in all seasons.
LEAF COLOR: Shiny dark green in summer changing to red and vinous-red in fall.
FLOWERS: Fertile flowers greenish white, not showy; bracts are borne in four's, white, appearing from May through July. Very striking in flower.
FRUIT: Scarlet, berry-like drupe, 1/4" diameter, ripening in August and later; persisting quite late or until eaten by the birds.
CULTURE: Sod cut from established plantings is probably the best mode of transplanting; requires moist, acid soil rich in organic matter; prefers a cool atmosphere; partial or full shade; needs frequent watering until well-established; mulching with acid material such as peat moss or pine needles is recommended.
DISEASES AND INSECTS: None serious.
LANDSCAPE VALUE: Probably one of our most beautiful native ground covers. Fastidious as to culture but worth the effort. Excellent under pines, broadleaf evergreens and other acid-requiring plants.
PROPAGATION: Moving pieces of sod is the most practical way. Seeds require a warm plus cold stratification period.
NATIVE HABITAT: Southern Greenland to Alaska, south to Maryland, west to South Dakota, New Mexico, and California. Found in high altitudes in cool, moist woods, and on hummocks in bogs.

Cornus florida — Flowering Dogwood

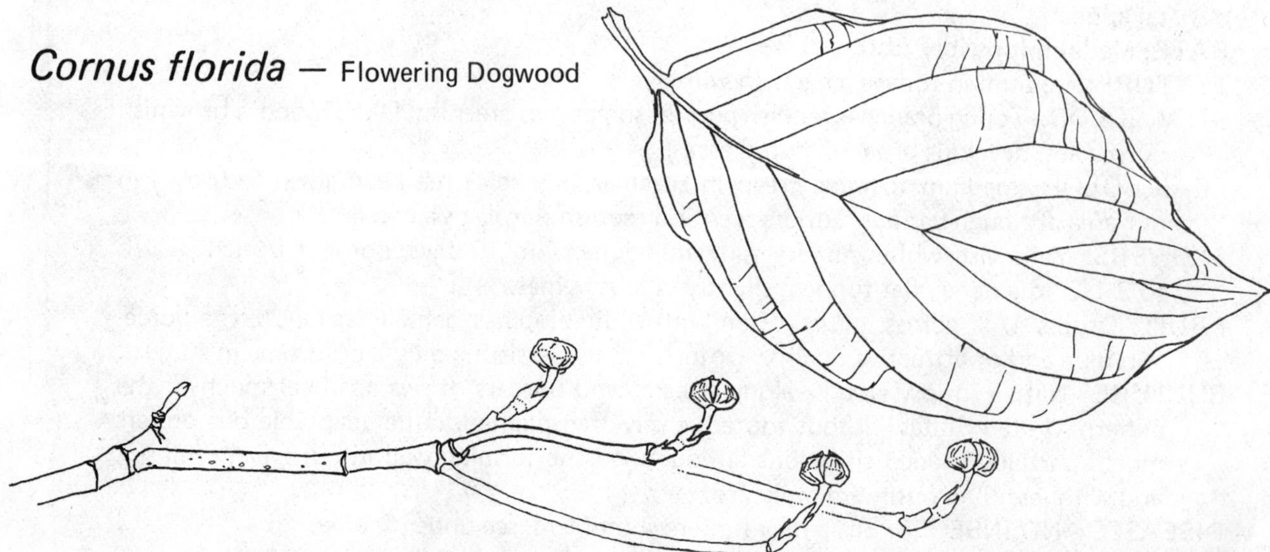

LEAVES: Opposite, simple, elliptic or ovate, 3 to 6" long, abruptly acuminate, broad cuneate to rounded at base, nearly glabrous above, glaucous beneath and usually only pubescent on the veins, with 6 to 7 pairs of veins; petiole 1/5 to 3/5" long.
BUD: Flower—usually at end of stem, globose, flower buds biscuit shape, flattened, valvate, covered by 2 large silky appressed pubescent scales. Vegetative—small, valvate, slender, almost hidden by raised leaf scar; leaf scars usually completely encircling stem.
STEM: Slender, green to purple, sometimes bloomy, pubescent when young, finally glabrous.

SIZE: Variable with location, in our area 20′ in height represents a magnificent specimen, however, the tree can reach 30 to 40′ in height with a spread equal to or considerably greater than the height.

HARDINESS: Zone 4. This represents a misnomer for seedling material from southern sources is not adequately hardy under Zone 4 conditions. Plants which are sold in Zone 4 and 5 regions should be grown from seed collected from trees indigenous to those areas. I have observed far too many Flowering Dogwoods in the Central Midwest with minimal flower production principally caused by lack of flower bud hardiness. If possible, always ask the nurserymen where the trees were grown and this, in turn, will save considerable disappointment when in 3 to 5 years time the trees may show limited flowering.

HABIT: Shrub (seldom) or small low-branched tree with spreading horizontal lines, sympodial, layered effect, usually with a flat-topped crown and often wider than high at maturity. Excellent plant for winter habit, very unique.

RATE: Slow upon transplanting, gradually assuming a medium rate.

TEXTURE: Medium in foliage; medium or finer in winter; the soft gray stems silhouetted against snowy or evergreen backgrounds are as handsome as the flowers.

STEM COLOR: Young stems are often purplish, gradually turning grayish. Older wood (3 to 4″ diameter) becomes scaly (grayish brown) and develops an "alligator" hide appearance.

LEAF COLOR: Usually a good dark green in summer, develops a handsome yellow-green when unfolding, fall color is a consistent reddish purple in the Midwest. One of the most consistent trees for excellent fall color. Tremendous variation from seedling grown material in all characters (habit, fall color, flower).

FLOWER: True flowers are greenish white or yellow and unimportant, showy parts of inflorescences are the 4 white bracts which are obovate or emarginate; they are about 2″ in diameter; borne in early to mid May, effective for 10 to 14 days depending on the weather, true flowers are borne in short stalked cymes (umbels?) and are subtended by the handsome bracts.

FRUIT: Drupe, glossy red, 2/5″ long, 3 to 4 in a "cluster", ripening in September to October and can persist until mid December. Birds seem to devour them or they often simply abscise soon after ripening.

CULTURE: Even as a small tree (3 to 4′) move balled and burlapped, provide an acid, well drained soil with sufficient organic matter; mulch to maintain a cool, moist soil; place in partial shade although full sun is acceptable. This particular species grows wild over the eastern United States and if you have ever witnessed a woodland dotted in flower, the reason for its popularity becomes evident. Trees planted in poorly drained soils and open areas where summer water is limited invariably decline and die.

DISEASES AND INSECTS: Very susceptible to borers especially trees under poor growing conditions.

LANDSCAPE VALUE: The aristocrat of native flowering trees, often overplanted but never becomes obnoxious as is the case with forsythia, deutzia and spirea. A plant with four-season character (excellent flower, summer and fall foliage, fruit, and winter habit). Excellent as specimen, near a patio, corners of houses and larger buildings, parks, groupings. Especially effective against a red brick background where the flowers are accentuated, as is the branching habit in winter. Dr. Wyman considers it the best ornamental of all the natives growing in Northern United States. Has the quality of flowering before the leaves and consequently vegetative competition is minimized.

CULTIVARS:

'Abundance' – Probably same as 'Cloud 9'.

'Apple Blossom' – Light pink flowers–shading to white in the center.

'Belmont Pink' – Flowers (bracts), blush pink.

'Cherokee Chief' - Flowers rich ruby-red and new growth reportedly reddish.

'Cherokee Princess' – Light pink flowers.

'Cloud Nine' – Slow growing with showy white flowers.

'Fastigiata' – Maintains upright habit only while young. After 20 years this form assumes habit of species.

'First Lady' — Variegated creamy-white and green foliage, a bit difficult to work into the common landscape, more vigorous than 'Welchii'.
'Fragrant Cloud' — White flowers, profuse, similar to 'Cloud 9'.
'Gigantea' — Large flowered form, flower bracts 6" from tip to tip.
'Hohman's Gold' — Variegated golden yellow and green foliage that turns deep red in fall.
'Magnifica' — Flower bracts about 4" from tip to tip.
'New Hampshire' — Hardy, flower producing clone from Atkinson, New Hampshire.
'Pendula' — Weeping form with stiffly pendulous branches and white flowers.
'Pluribracteata' — Form with 7 to 8 large flower bracts and many aborted smaller ones.
var. *pygmaea* — Dwarf, very diminutive, good foliage form. The few I have seen were beautiful.
'Rainbow' — Variegated deep yellow, green and pink foliage that turns carmine-red in fall. White bracts in spring.
'Royal Red' — New foliage opens blood-red; turns red in fall; flowers are deep red and very large.
var. *rubra* — Pink to red flowers, considerable variation in nature.
'Spring Song' — Deep rose-red flowers.
'Sweetwater Red' — Deep red flowers and reddish foliage.
'Welchii' — Leaves are a combination of green, creamy-white and pink. Stands out in a crowd; definite clashing of color.
'White Cloud' — Numerous creamy-white flowers especially when plant is very young.
'Xanthocarpa' — Yellow fruited form.
(var. *xanthocarpa*)

PROPAGATION: Seed, dormant embryo, 100 to 130 days at 41°F. Cuttings, softwood, collected immediately after the flowering period ended, rooted readily in three weeks. Softwood cuttings collected in June rooted 56 percent in sand under mist, when treated with 10,000ppm IBA, quick dip, after 8 weeks. This same clone rooted 93 percent in peat: perlite under mist in 10 weeks with the same hormonal treatment. Apparently, the acidity of the medium influenced the degree of rooting since other factors were constant.

NATIVE HABITAT: Massachusetts to Florida, west to Ontario, Texas and Mexico. Cultivated 1731.

Cornus kousa — Kousa Dogwood

LEAVES: Opposite, simple, elliptic-ovate, 2 to 4" long, acuminate, cuneate, dark green above, glaucous and appressed-pilose beneath and with large axillary fulvous tufts of hairs; petiole—1/6 to 1/4" long.

BUD: Flower—formed at end of stem, flattened and globose at base with 2 valvate silky appressed pubescent bud scales forming a sharp apex. Vegetative—valvate, appressed, brownish black, usually longer than those of *C. florida*.

STEM: Slender, glandular, light tan with tinges of purple and green, essentially glabrous.

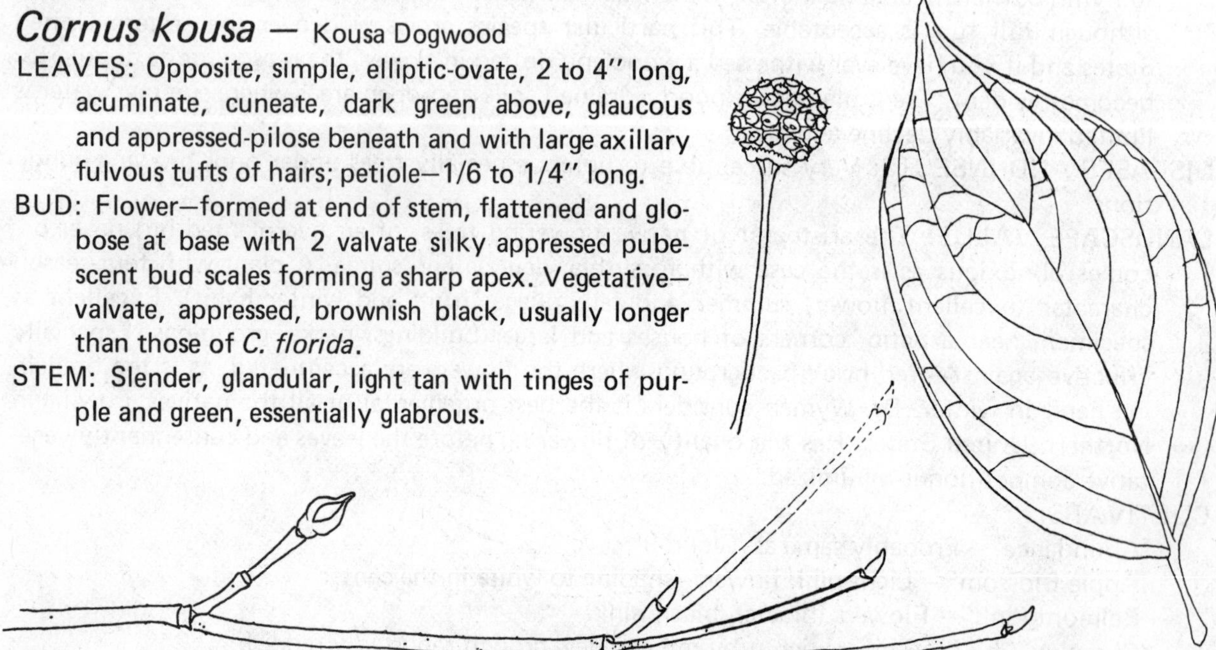

SIZE: About 20' in height with a spread of 15 to 20'.

HARDINESS: Zone 5, I feel an acid, well drained soil will improve the hardiness by a Zone (4).

HABIT: In youth, vase-shaped in habit, with age, forming a rounded appearance with distinct startified branching pattern. Very strong horizontal lines are evident in old age.

RATE: Slow, possibly medium in early stages of growth.

TEXTURE: Medium in leaf and winter character. Very handsome in the winter because of horizontal branching character.

STEM COLOR: Older wood often develops multicolored areas due to exfoliating nature of the bark.

LEAF COLOR: Dark green in summer foliage changing to reddish purple or scarlet in fall.

FLOWERS: The true flowers are small and inconspicuous and are produced on an upright 2" long peduncle in 5/8" diameter rounded umbel. The white bracts are the showy part of the inflorescence and are borne in early to mid June, approximately 2 to 3 weeks after those of *Cornus florida*. The 4 bracts are long, taper-pointed and about 2" across. The flowers, being stalked, are raised above the foliage creating a milky way effect along the horizontal branches.

FRUIT: Drupe, pinkish red to red, borne in 3/5 to 1" diameter globose structures (resemble a raspberry in appearance); late August through October, very effective.

CULTURE: Transplant balled and burlapped as young specimen, more difficult to grow in our area than *C. florida*; fastidious for acid, well drained soil, seems to perform best in sandy soil with good organic matter content; well worth the extra cultural efforts needed to successfully grow this plant. Requires a relatively sunny location.

DISEASES AND INSECTS: None serious, see under *C. florida*.

LANDSCAPE VALUE: Handsome small specimen tree or shrub, excellent near large buildings or blank walls, tends to break up harshness with horizontal structure, works well in shrub border or in a foundation planting at the corner of the house. The horizontal lines break up the vertical lines and make the home appear larger. Difficult to overuse this plant. The flowers appear in June when there is often a paucity of color.

CULTIVARS:

var. *chinensis* — According to Wyman and Bean there is not much difference between this form and the species, however, under cultivation the variety grows more freely and the flowers are larger than those of any form. Introduced from Japan.

'Milky Way' — Cultivar of var. *chinensis* with very floriferous habit. I have witnessed this specimen at Mill Creek Valley Park, Youngstown, Ohio, and was amazed at the flower and fruit production compared to the species. This was a very broad, bushy form suitable for the small landscape.

'Summer Star' — A form with bracts which hang on up to six weeks after the flowering period.

PROPAGATION: Cuttings, somewhat more difficult to root than *C. florida* but various investigators have been able to achieve 50% success from softwood cuttings treated with IBA.
From my own experience, softwood cuttings collected in June rooted 50 percent with 10,000 ppm IBA quick dip when placed in peat: perlite under mist after 12 weeks. All cuttings had callused and possibly would have rooted with increasing time.

NATIVE HABITAT: Japan, Korea, China. Introduced 1875.

Cornus mas — Corneliancherry Dogwood

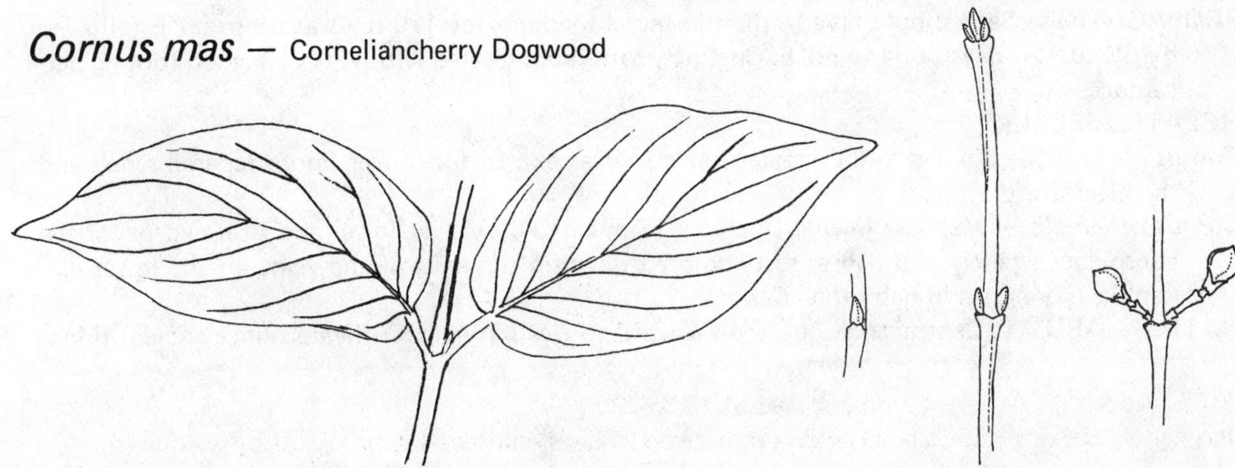

LEAVES: Alternate, simple, ovate to elliptic, 2 to 4" long, acute to acuminate, broad-cuneate at base, appressed-pilose and green on both sides, dark green above, with 3 to 5 pairs of veins; petiole 1/5 to 2/5" long.

BUD: Flower—borne in axillary position, appear stalked, valvate, globose, without sharp apex, greenish brown in color, appressed pubescence. Vegetative—valvate, more divergent than other dogwood vegetative buds, greenish with silky appressed pubescence.

STEM: Slender, angled on young stems, usually red above—green below, branches minutely appressed-pilose.

SIZE: 20 to 25' in height by 15 to 20' in width.

HARDINESS: Zone 4.

HABIT: Large, multistemmed shrub or small tree of rounded-oval outline, usually branching to the ground making successful grass culture impossible. It is possible to remove the lower branches and the result is a small tree of rounded habit. Excellent way to use this plant.

RATE: Medium.

TEXTURE: Medium in foliage and in winter habit.

LEAF COLOR: Dark green often somewhat glossy, attractive summer foliage; fall color can be purplish red, very poor fall color in our area; often the leaves fall off green.

FLOWERS: Yellowish, early to mid March, effective for three weeks, borne in short stalked umbels before the leaves from the axils of the previous season's wood; each umbel about 3/4" diameter, enclosed before opening in four downy boat-shaped bracts. Very effective in the early spring landscape for it receives little competition from other flowering shrubs. The buds have fully opened around March 10 to 20th in Champaign-Urbana.

FRUIT: Drupe, 5/8" long, bright cherry-red, July, often partially hidden by the foliage; the fruits are used for syrup and preserves. I have observed specimens with fruit more abundantly borne than that often found on sour cherry trees. Selections should be made for both flower and fruit production.

CULTURE: Transplants well when young, move balled and burlapped, adaptable as far as soil types and pH are concerned, but prefers rich, well drained soil, sun or partial shade. I would rate this the most durable of the larger dogwood types for midwestern conditions. Has performed admirably on the University of Illinois campus and other areas throughout the Midwest.

DISEASES AND INSECTS: None serious, actually a very pest-free plant.

LANDSCAPE VALUE: Shrub border, hedge, screen, foundation planting, around large buildings, optimum effect is achieved if the plant has a dark green or red background so the early yellow flowers are accentuated. This species is not used nearly enough in the modern landscape.

CULTIVARS:

'Alba' — White fruited form.

'Aureo-elegantissima' — Leaves with creamy white and red variegations.

var. *flava* — Yellow fruited.

'Variegata' — Leaves with margins bordered yellow or white.

PROPAGATION: Seed should be stratified in moist medium for 120 days at 68 to 86°F followed by 30 to 120 days at 34 to 56°F. Cuttings, softwood, treated with IBA gave good rooting percentages.

RELATED SPECIES:

Cornus chinensis — Similar to the previous two species except for longer, more tapered sepals and the black fruits.

Cornus officinalis — Japanese Cornel Dogwood. Similar to *C. mas* in flower and fruit except for the conspicuous patches of dense, rusty-colored down in the axils of the veins on the lower epidermis, more open in habit than *C. mas*.

NATIVE HABITAT: Central and Southern Europe and Western Asia. Cultivated since ancient times.

Cornus racemosa — Gray Dogwood

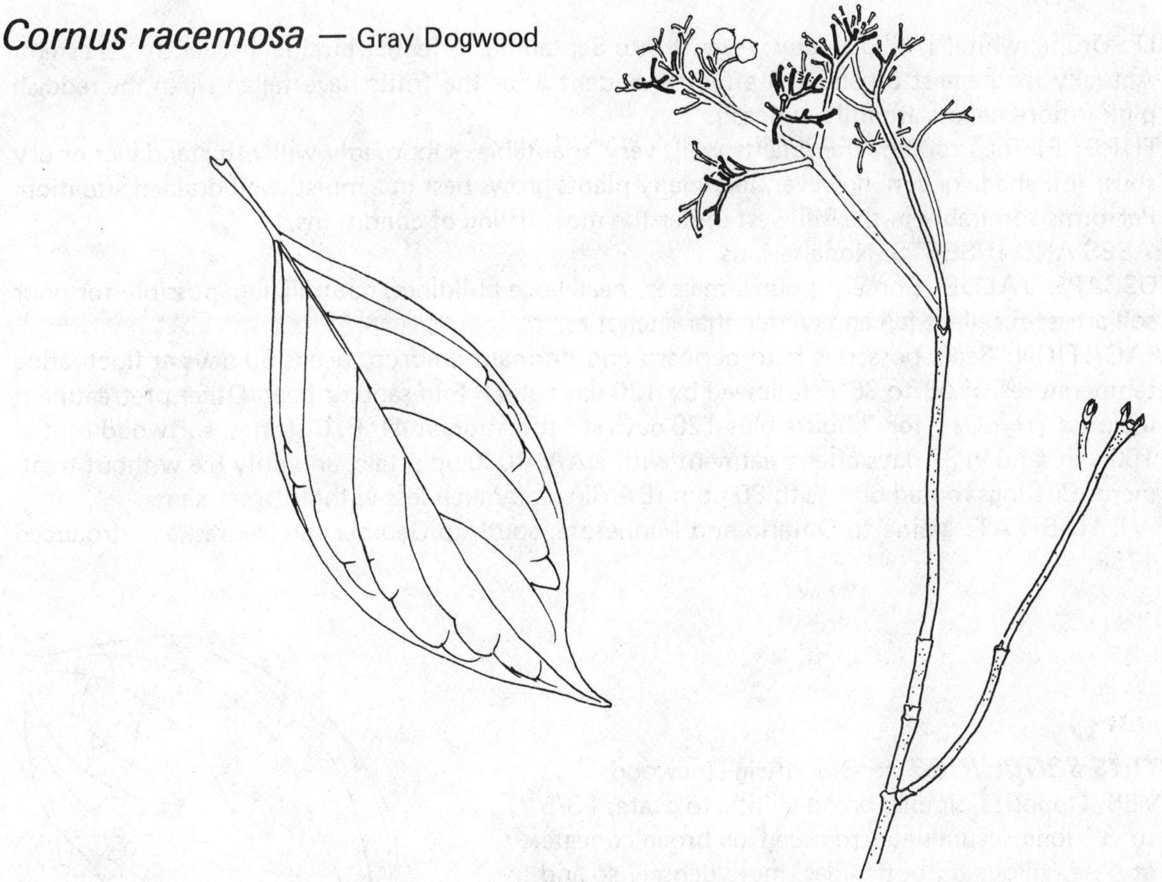

LEAVES: Opposite, simple, narrow-elliptic to ovate-lanceolate, 2 to 4" long, long acuminate, cuneate, appressed-pubescent or nearly smooth, glaucous beneath; petiole—1/2 to 3/5" long.

BUD: Flower—terminally borne, more plump than vegetative buds, slightly appressed hairy. Vegetative—valvate, very small in relation to flower buds, almost hidden by leaf scar.

STEM: Slender, young stems—somewhat angled, tan to reddish brown, essentially glabrous. Older stems—decidedly gray. Pith—small, white to brown, usually light brown.

FRUIT: Pedicels remain red into late fall and early winter.

SIZE: 10 to 15' in height by 10 to 15' in width. Actually it is difficult to define the spread of this shrub for it suckers profusely from the roots and forms a large colony of plants extending in all directions from the original plant. This should be considered when employing this plant in the home landscape for it often oversteps its boundaries.

HARDINESS: Zone 4.

HABIT: Strongly multistemmed, erect growing, suckering shrub with short spreading branches towards apex of stems.

RATE: Slow from old wood, however, shoots which develop from roots grow very fast (3 to 5' in a season).

TEXTURE: Medium-fine in leaf, medium in winter, probably more interesting and valuable in winter than in the foliage periods.

STEM COLOR: Three-year-old wood or greater is a distinct gray and quite attractive. The first and second year stems are a light reddish brown and form an interesting contrast. The inflorescences are reddish pink and are effective into December. The total winter character is valuable in the landscape.

LEAF COLOR: Dull gray-green in summer foliage, assuming purplish red tones in fall. Fall color is usually non-descript in our area.

FLOWER: Whitish, late May to early June, borne in 2" diameter cymose panicles which terminate almost every stem, effective for 7 to 10 days.

FRUIT: Drupe, white, 1/4" diameter; August into September; effective but inconsistently persistent. Actually its greatest ornamental effect is evident after the fruits have fallen when the reddish pink inflorescences are fully exposed.

CULTURE: Fibrous rooted, transplants well, very adaptable, supposedly will withstand wet or dry soils, full shade or sun, however, like many plants grows best in a moist, well-drained situation. Performs admirably in the Midwest under the most trying of conditions.

DISEASES AND INSECTS: None serious.

LANDSCAPE VALUE: Border, groups, masses, near large buildings, naturalizing, possibly for poor soil areas, excellent fall and winter characteristics.

PROPAGATION: Seed, possesses hard pericarp and dormant embryo, needs 60 days at fluctuating temperatures of 68 to 86°F followed by 120 days at 41°F in sand or peat. Other pretreatment includes [H_2SO_4] for 2 hours plus 120 days stratification at 41°F. Cuttings, softwood rooted 100% in sand in 37 days after treatment with NAA, 1000 ppm talc, and only 8% without treatment. Cuttings rooted 66% with 80 ppm IBA dip, and much less without treatment.

NATIVE HABITAT: Maine to Ontario and Minnesota, south to Georgia and Nebraska. Introduced 1758.

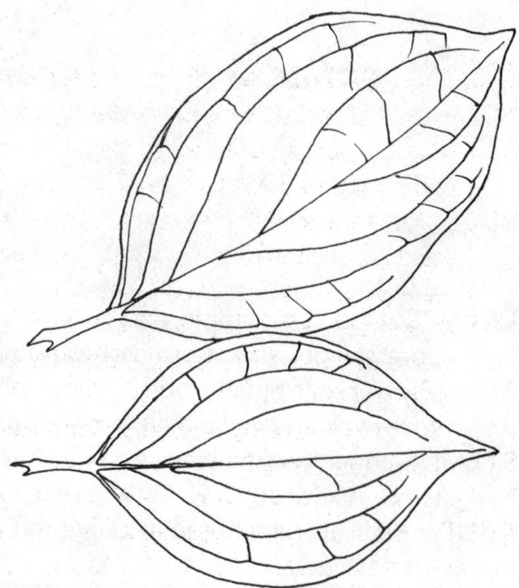

Cornus sanguinea — Bloodtwig Dogwood

LEAVES: Opposite, simple, broad-elliptic to ovate, 1 3/5 to 3" long, acuminate, rounded or broad-cuneate at base, villous on both sides, more densely so and lighter green beneath, with 3 to 5 pairs of veins; petiole—1/4 to 3/5" long.

BUD: Flower—terminally borne, pubescent with grayish silky hairs, fatter than vegetative buds which are valvate, appressed, coated with gray silky appressed pubescence.

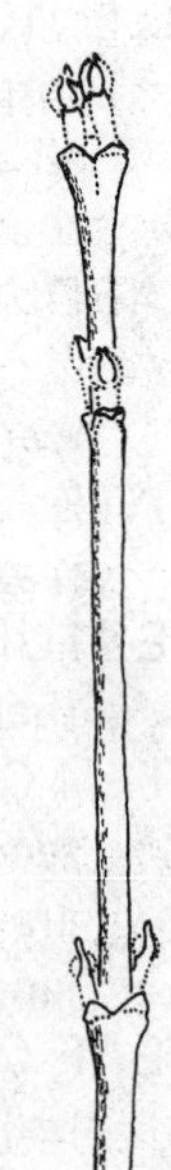

STEM: Slender, appressed hairy, usually purple or dark blood red often greenish on lower side. Pith-white. Older branches greenish gray in color.

SIZE: 6 to 15' in height, with spread ranging from 6 to 15'; very variable.

HARDINESS: Zone 4.

HABIT: A large, unkempt, sloppily dressed, spreading, round-topped, multi-stemmed shrub of a dense, twiggy nature suckering freely from the roots and forms a colony much like *C. racemosa*.

RATE: Slow to medium on old wood, fast on shoots which develop from roots.

TEXTURE: My opinion is somewhat biased, but I would rate it coarse in all seasons. Very difficult to blend into the landscape; a proverbial "sore thumb" plant.

STEM COLOR: I have never understood the name bloodtwig for the stems are usually more green than blood-red. Often the stem portion exposed to the sun is red and the rest is green. Bean noted that the name is derived from its fall color and not the young bark. There is considerable variation in habit and stem coloration.

LEAF COLOR: Dull, dark green in summer changing to blood-red autumnal color according to many authorities. This shrub has never shown good fall color on our campus, usually a sickly greenish purple.

FLOWERS: Dull white, of fetid odor, profusely produced in late May to early June in 1 1/2 to 2" diameter flat-topped pubescent cymes, effective 7 to 10 days, the total effect of the flowers is somewhat reduced by the abundant foliage.

FRUIT: Drupe, 1/4" across, purplish black, almost unnoticeable as they blend in with the dark green foliage.

CULTURE: Fibrous rooted, easily transplanted, very adaptable, supposedly tolerates lime better than other dogwoods, sun or partial shade, thrives in our area, needs frequent pruning to keep it clean (presentable).

DISEASES AND INSECTS: None serious.

LANDSCAPE VALUE: Possibly shrub border, massing, screening; definitely not for specimen use or the small residential landscape. Too large and clumsy, tends to look out of place with age.

CULTIVARS:

'Atrosanguinea' – Branches of deep red color.

'Variegata' – Leaves mottled with yellowish white.

PROPAGATION: Cuttings, taken in late June rooted 44% without treatment, and 68% in three weeks after treatment with 30 ppm IBA, 12 hours.

NATIVE HABITAT: Europe. Long cultivated.

Cornus stolonifera — Redosier Dogwood (Listed as *C. sericea* in *Hortus III*)

LEAVES: Opposite, simple, ovate to oblong-lanceolate, 2 to 5" long, acuminate, rounded at base, medium to dark green above, glaucous beneath, with about five pairs of veins, petiole–2/5 to 1" long.

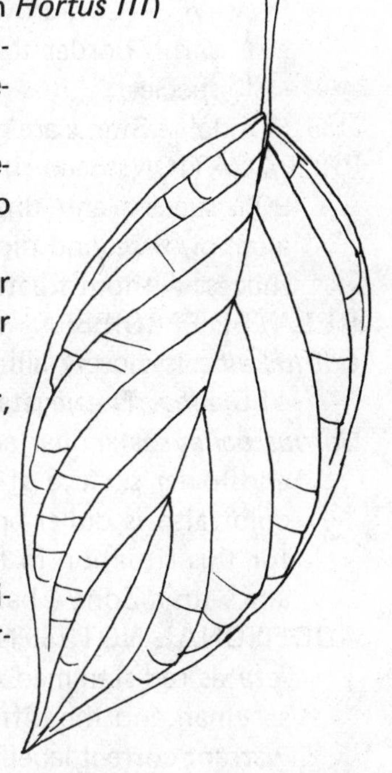

BUD: Flower–terminally borne, valvate, hairy, silky-appressed pubescence; Vegetative–valvate, appressed, elongated. Essentially no difference between this species and *C. alba*.

STEM: Slender, upright, dark blood red, appressed pubescence on younger stems, pith–white, large. Lenticels similar to *C. alba* except fewer per internode.

FRUIT: Drupe, white, globose; stone as broad as high or slightly broader, rounded at base.

SIZE: 7 to 9' in height spreading to 10' or more.

HARDINESS: Zone 2.

HABIT: Loose, broad-spreading, rounded, multistemmed shrub with horizontal branches at base. Freely stoloniferous as it spreads by underground stems.

RATE: Fast, seems to be quite vigorous.

TEXTURE: Medium in leaf and in winter.

STEM COLOR: Red, various authorities list the stem color as dark blood-red, dark purplish red, brilliant red. Very handsome and eye appealing in a winter setting especially with a sprinkling of snow to set off the stem color.

LEAF COLOR: Medium to dark green in summer; purplish to reddish in the fall. Fall color has been good in our area.

FLOWERS: Dull white, borne in 1 1/2 to 2 1/2" diameter flat-topped cymes in late May to early June, flowers are adequate but not overwhelming.

FRUIT: Drupe, 1/5" diameter, white, borne in September, briefly effective.

CULTURE: Fibrous rooted, easily moved bare root or balled and burlapped, extremely adaptable to wide range of soil and climatic conditions, does best in moist soil and is often observed in the wild in wet, swampy situations.

DISEASES AND INSECTS: There is a twig blight (canker) which can wreak havoc on this species and the cultivars. Scale can be a problem and, in Central Illinois, I have noticed a wealth of bagworms.

LANDSCAPE VALUE: Excellent for massing in large areas, along highways, parks, golf courses; interesting stem color makes it suitable for shrub border use in residential landscapes; can be an effective bank cover for it holds soil quite well.

CULTIVARS:

var. *coloradensis* 'Cheyenne' — Good selection for blood-red stem color; shows growth habit of the species but does not grow as tall.

'Flaviramea' — Form with yellow stems, often inflicted with canker, none-the-less widely sold and planted. Should be used with taste for a small planting goes a long way on any residential landscape.

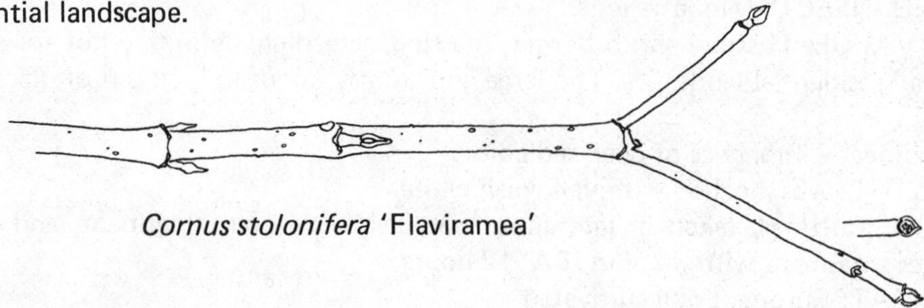

Cornus stolonifera 'Flaviramea'

'Isanti' — Compact form with bright red stem color, shorter internodes which make for a denser plant.

'Kelseyi' — Low-growing, neat, compact form of 24 to 30" in height. Nice facing plant in the shrub border to hide the "leggy" shrubs in the background; stems less colorful than the species.

'Nitida' — Stems are green.

PROPAGATION: Seed should be stratified for 60 to 90 days at 41°F. I have rooted cuttings with 90% success any time leaves were present by treating the cuttings with 1000 ppm IBA/50% alcohol, 5 second dip. Hardwood cuttings placed immediately in the field also give 90 to 100% success without treatment.

RELATED SPECIES:

Cornus alba is closely allied to *C. stolonifera* and some authors consider *C. stolonifera* a subspecies of *C. alba.* The vegetative differences are nonexistent.

Cornus baileyi is similar and much confused with *C. stolonifera* from which it differs in the shoots and lower surface of the leaves being distinctly woolly and in not being stoloniferous; the stem color also is duller and browner red; usually found native on sandy soils and is recommended for this situation in the landscape. Native to Ontario and Minnesota to Pennsylvania and Indiana with a Zone 4 hardiness designation.

ADDITIONAL NOTES: Nurserymen tend to sell all three species, *C. alba, C. baileyi,* and *C. stolonifera* as red-stemmed dogwoods. The homeowner is at the mercy of the garden operator or nurseryman and the differences in growth habit and stem color in old age are different enough to warrant correct labeling by the seller.

NATIVE HABITAT: Newfoundland to Manitoba, south to Virginia, Kentucky and Nebraska. Cultivated 1656.

Corylopsis glabrescens — Fragrant Winterhazel

FAMILY: Hamamelidaceae

LEAVES: Alternate, simple, ovate, acuminate, cordate to subcordate, 1 to 3" long, sinuate-dentate with bristle-like teeth, glaucescent beneath and sparingly silky on the veins or sometimes slightly pubescent when young, thin; petioles slender, 3/5 to 1 1/5" long; dark green.

BUDS: Rather large, sessile, solitary or finally short-stalked and collaterally branched, directly in the axil, fusiform or ovoid, with about 3 glabrous scales; terminal somewhat larger, brownish.

STEMS: Rounded, zig-zag, moderate or slender, mostly glabrescent; pith small, angular, continuous.

SIZE: 8 to 15′ in height with a similar spread.

HARDINESS: Zone 5, the hardiest of the *Corylopsis* and the best choice for northern gardens.

HABIT: A wide-spreading, dense, somewhat flat-topped, rounded, multi-stemmed shrub.

RATE: Slow to medium.

TEXTURE: Medium in leaf; possibly medium to medium-coarse in winter.

LEAF COLOR: Dark green above, glaucescent beneath in summer; fall color varies from yellow-green to clear gold.

FLOWERS: Perfect, pale yellow, fragrant, borne in 4/5 to 1 2/5″ long pendulous racemes; flowering in early to mid-April before the leaves develop.

FRUIT: Capsule, about 1/4″ across, not ornamental.

CULTURE: Transplant balled and burlapped into moist, acid, preferably well-drained soil which has been amended with peat moss or leaf mold; full sun or light shade; should be sheltered as they flower early and are susceptible to late spring frosts. This is especially true in the Midwest where invariably there is a warm period in March and the buds of many plants swell and often open only to succumb to the early April freeze. Pruning should be accomplished after the flowers pass.

DISEASES AND INSECTS: As is true with many members of the Hamamelidaceae this genus is free of significant problems.

LANDSCAPE VALUE: Good plant for early spring flower color and fragrance. Could be successfully integrated into the shrub border. Worthwhile considering if a protected area is available in the garden.

PROPAGATION: Softwood cuttings of new growth collected in May or early June will root; semi-hardwood cuttings taken in July or ground layering are alternative vegetative methods.

RELATED SPECIES: There are several other species that are not as hardy as the above but are more showy in flower. They include:

Corylopsis pauciflora, Buttercup Winterhazel, is a small (4 to 6′) shrub of spreading habit with fragrant primrose-yellow flowers, about 3/4″ diameter, produced 2, sometimes 3 on short inflorescences. I have seen this species at the National Arboretum, Washington, D.C. and was pleased with its restricted, dainty habit compared to the larger *C. glabrescens*. Native to Japan. Introduced 1862. Zone 6.

Corylopsis spicata, Spike Winterhazel, grows to 4 to 5′ high and wide with crooked, flexible branches. The flowers are yellow, fragrant, 6 to 12 developing on a pendulous raceme in March or April. This species is probably the most colorful of the three species discussed. Native to Japan. Introduced 1863. Zone 6.

ADDITIONAL NOTES: Somewhat similar to *Hamamelis* and *Parrotia*, its hardy allies, but differing in the flower morphology. The raceme on which the flowers are borne is really a short branch. At the base are a few thin, membranous, bract-like organs, which are not accompanied by flowers, but from the axils of which a leaf is developed after the flowers farther along the raceme have developed.

NATIVE HABITAT: Japan. Introduced 1905.

Corylus americana — American Filbert

FAMILY: Betulaceae

LEAVES: Alternate, simple, 2 1/2 to 6″ long, broad-ovate to broad elliptic, apex short-acuminate, sparingly pubescent above, soft pubescent beneath.

BUD: Imbricate, globose, gray-pubescent, small, 1/6″ long, greenish brown to purplish.

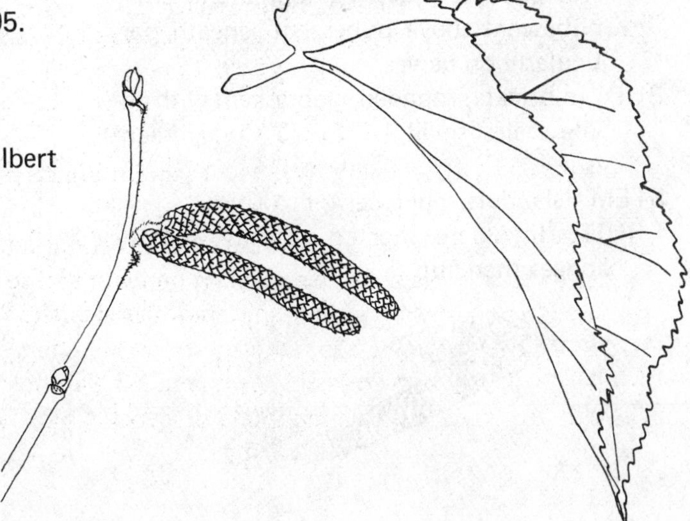

STEM: Young branches glandular-pubescent, brown, pith-continuous, 3-sided, pale or brown.

FRUIT: Involucre about twice as long as nut, usually tightly enclosing it, deeply and irregularly lobed.

SIZE: Listed as 8 to 10′ by many authorities but usually grows larger, possibly to 15′, spread is approximately 2/3's the height.

HARDINESS: Zone 4.

HABIT: Strongly multistemmed shrub forming a rounded top with a leggy or open base.

RATE: Medium to fast.

TEXTURE: Medium-coarse in summer and winter, this is also true for the types treated under the related species category.

LEAF COLOR: Dark green in summer, muddy yellow-green in fall, usually of negligible importance.

FLOWERS: Monoecious, male in catkins, 1 1/2 to 3″ long, brownish, quite showy in early spring, March. Female flowers inconspicuous, the stigma and style barely protruding out of the bud, color is a rich red.

FRUIT: Nut, 1/2″ long, set in an involucre nearly twice its length, involucre is downy and deeply touched.

CULTURE: Transplant balled and burlapped or as a container plant into well drained, loamy soil, pH adaptable, full sun or light shade, prune anytime, tends to sucker from the roots and must often be thinned out to maintain a respectable appearance.

DISEASES AND INSECTS: Blight, crown gall, black knot, leaf spots, Japanese leafhopper, caterpillars, scales. I have not noticed any extensive problems with our large *Corylus* collection on the University of Illinois campus although nurserymen have indicated that *Corylus avellana* 'Contorta' is affected by a blight which injures leaves and branches.

LANDSCAPE VALUE: The American Hazel is best reserved for naturalizing and other nonformal areas. The European Filbert and especially the cultivars might lend themselves to selected landscape situations.

PROPAGATION: Seed, similar to that described for *C. colurna*, softwood cuttings of *C. avellana* and *C. maxima purpurea* have been rooted but percentages were low.

RELATED SPECIES:

Corylus avellana — European Filbert

LEAVES: Alternate, simple, 2 to 4″ long, suborbicular to broad ovate, doubly serrate and often slightly lobulate, slightly pubescent above, pubescent beneath, particularly on nerves.

BUD: Imbricate, rounded, glabrescent with ciliate scales, small, 1/6 to 1/3″ long, greenish.

STEM: Glandular-pubescent, brownish.

FRUIT: Involucre shorter or only slightly longer than nut.

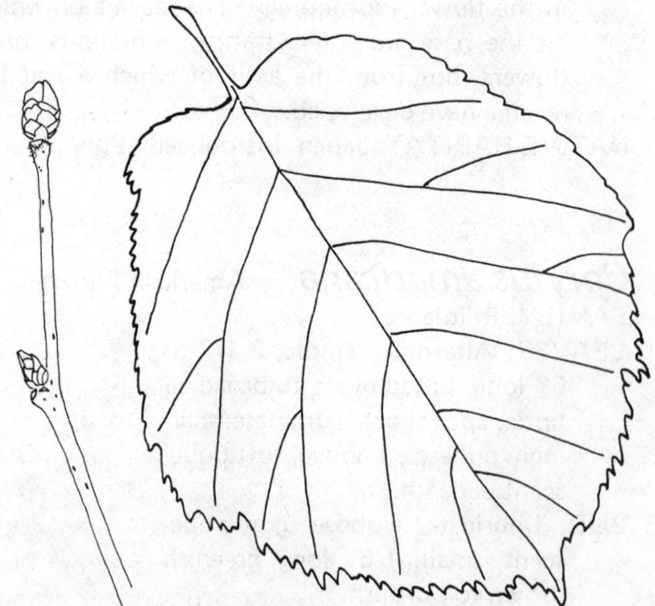

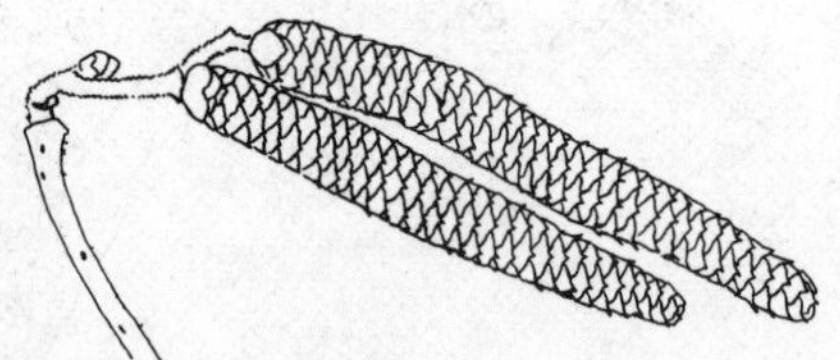

Corylus avellana, European Filbert, grows from 12 to 20′ in height; can be a small tree, but usually forms a dense thicket of erect stems and develops extensive shoots from the roots. Nut is 3/4″ long, set in an involucre about as long as the nut, the margins are cut into shallow, often toothed lobes; native to Europe, Western Asia, and Northern Africa; prized for its nuts in European Countries.

The cultivars include:

'Aurea' – A yellow leaf type.

'Contorta' – 8 to 10′, stems curled and twisted, quite an attraction when properly grown, often called Harry Lauder's Walkingstick.

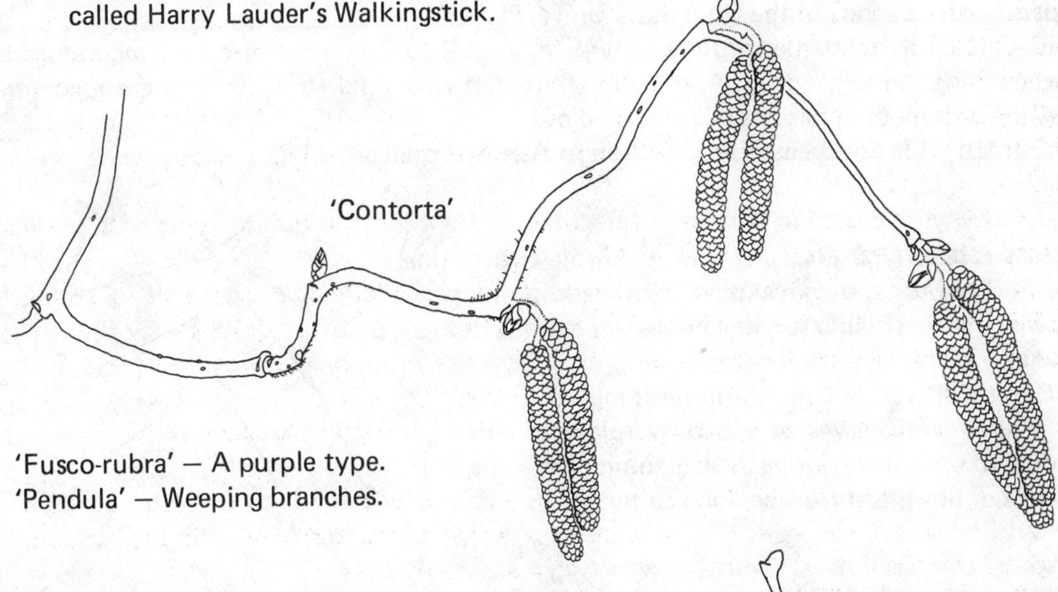

'Fusco-rubra' – A purple type.

'Pendula' – Weeping branches.

Corylus colurna — Turkish Filbert or Hazel

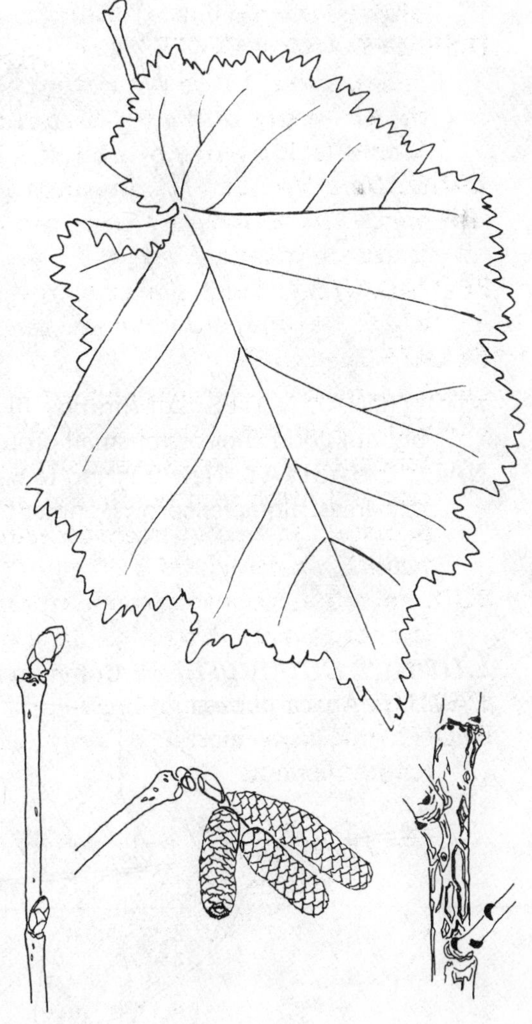

LEAVES: Alternate, simple, sometimes lobed, 3 to 5″ long, doubly serrate or crenate-serrate, broad ovate, nearly glabrous above, pubescent on veins beneath.

BUDS: Large–1/3″, softly pubescent, green-tinged brown.

STEM: Glandular-pubescent, gray-brown, coarse, with fissures up and down stem.

SIZE: 40 to 50′ in height with a spread of 1/3 to 2/3's the height, can grow to 70-80′.

HARDINESS: Zone 4.

HABIT: Broad pyramidal, very stately and handsome in form, usually with a short trunk and the bottom branches touching the ground.

RATE: Medium, 35 feet over a 20 year period.

TEXTURE: Medium in leaf and winter.

BARK: Pale brown, older bark develops a flaky character.

LEAF COLOR: Dark green in summer, potentially yellow to purple in autumn but seldom handsome in Central Illinois, drops yellow-green. The summer foliage is very handsome and seems to be free of insect and disease problems.

FLOWERS: Male, 2 to 3″ catkins, female, inconspicuous as only the two free styles protrude from the bud scale. Monoecious tree with flowers of little ornamental appeal.

FRUIT: Nut, 1/2 to 5/8" diameter, the involucre about 1 1/2 to 1" long, nuts are closely grouped 3 or more together.

CULTURE: Thrives in hot summers and cold winters, tolerant of adverse conditions, a well drained, loamy soil is preferable, pH adaptable, full sun, actually a very excellent tree but little known and grown, supposedly somewhat difficult to propagate.

DISEASES AND INSECTS: None serious.

LANDSCAPE VALUE: Excellent formal character, possibly for lawns, street tree use, also city conditions, where maples exhibit scorch this tree is still green and vigorous. A handsome specimen exists on the campus of the Ohio State University.

PROPAGATION: Most of the shrubby *Corylus* require 2 to 6 months of cold temperature before the germination will occur. Also warm alternated with cold stratifications are recommended but the best method has not been worked out.

NATIVE HABITAT: Southeast Europe, Western Asia. Introduced 1582.

Corylus maxima purpurea — Purple Giant Filbert

Similar to *Corylus avellana* except with dark purple leaves in spring fading to green in late summer. Buds and catkins retain purplish cast.

Purple Giant Filbert is a large shrub reaching 15 to 20' in height, with leaves of a dark purple gradually fading to dark green during the late summer months, Native of Southeast Europe, long cultivated.

ADDITIONAL NOTES: All shrubby filberts should be used with restraint in the landscape, probably not good choices for small properties, squirrels love the nuts.

NATIVE HABITAT: New England to Sasketchewan and south to Florida, often found in moist and dry areas, along fencerows, and at the edge of woodlands. Introduced 1798.

Cotinus coggygria — Common Smoketree or Smokebush

FAMILY: Anacardiaceae

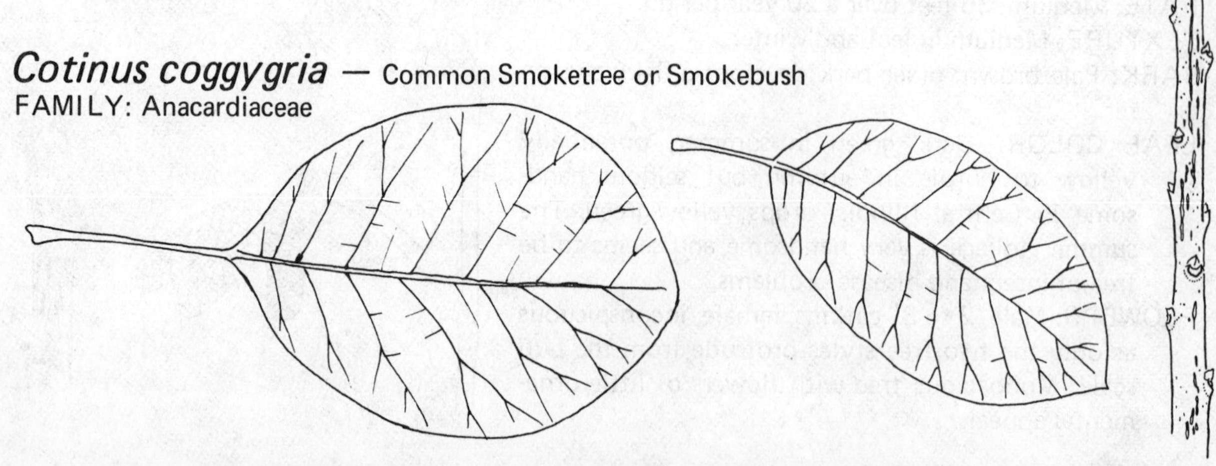

LEAVES: Alternate, simple, entire, oval to obovate, 1 1/4 to 3 1/4" long, rounded or slightly emarginate at apex, glabrous; petiole 2/5 to 1 3/5" long.
BUD: Small, solitary, sessile, with several imbricate dark red-brown scales, acute.
STEM: Stout, brown or purplish, with prominent lenticels, glabrate. Pith—orange-brown. When crushed emitting strong odor. Leaf scars not lobed.

SIZE: 10 to 15' in height by 10 to 15' spread.
HARDINESS: Zone 4, preferably 5.
HABIT: Upright, spreading, loose and open, often wider than high, multi-stemmed shrub. When pruned develops very long slender shoots creating a straggly, unkempt appearance.
RATE: Medium.
TEXTURE: Medium in leaf, coarse in winter.
LEAF COLOR: Medium blue-green in summer and yellow-red-purple in fall. Fall color is often poorly developed.
FLOWERS: Polygamous or dioecious, yellowish green changing to smoky-pink (variable), June-July, borne in large, loose terminal panicles, 6 to 8" long, showy parts of flower are the numerous sterile pedicels furnished with long spreading purplish or greenish hairs.
FRUIT: Drupe, small, dry, not showy.
CULTURE: Fibrous rooted, readily transplanted, adaptable to widely divergent soils and pH ranges, dry and rocky soils, prefers well drained loam and sunny exposure.
DISEASES AND INSECTS: None of serious magnitude; however, rusts, leafspot, leaf rollers and San Jose scale can attack this species.
LANDSCAPE VALUE: Good in shrub border, possibly in masses or groupings, not for single specimen use.
CULTIVARS: Several interesting purpleleaf and flower forms. Of special note is 'Velvet Cloak'.

'Daydream' — Floriferous form with fluffy and heavily produced inflorescences. Sterile hairs—brown initially—later turning pink.

'Flame' —
'Notcutt' —
'Purpureus' —
'Royal Purple' —
'Royal Red' —
'Rubrifolius' —
} Leaves and panicles are purplish, leaves tend to fade to a purple-green.

'Pendulus' — Weeping form.

'Velvet Cloak' — Handsome purpleleaf form maintaining good color through the summer months, developing excellent reddish purple fall color.

PROPAGATION: From my own experience softwood cuttings treated with 1000 ppm IBA gave 80 to 100% rooting.
RELATED SPECIES:
Cotinus obovatus — American Smoketree

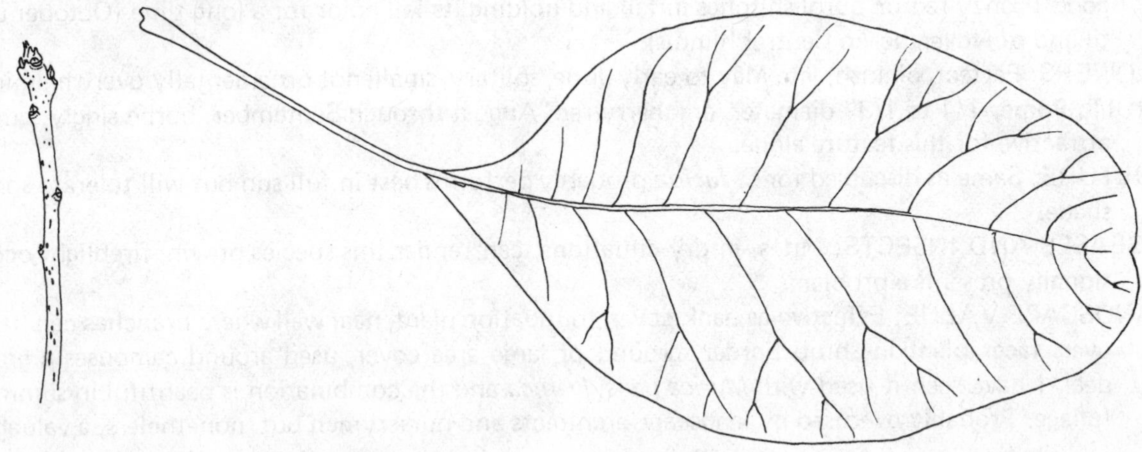

LEAVES: Alternate, simple, entire, obovate to elliptic-obovate, 2 1/4-5" long, rounded at apex, silky pubescent beneath when young, petiole - 3/5 to 1 2/5" long.

Similar to *C. coggygria* except leaf-scars lobed, stems orangish and usually an upright tree or shrub to 30 feet.

Cotinus obovatus, American Smoketree, is a large upright shrub or small tree growing to 30' high. The leaves turn a brilliant orange and scarlet in fall. The flowers are not as showy as *C. coggygria* and this species should only be grown for its fall effect. Native to Alabama to Eastern Tennessee and Western Texas. Introduced 1882. Zone 5.

NATIVE HABITAT: Southern Europe to Central China and Himalaya. Cultivated 1656.

Cotoneaster apiculata — Cranberry Cotoneaster

FAMILY: Rosaceae

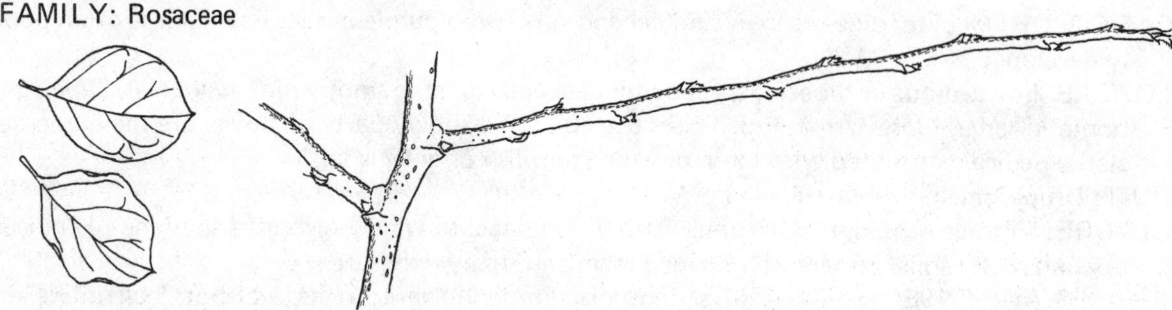

LEAVES: Alternate, simple, suborbicular to orbicular-ovate, apiculate, glabrous at maturity or only slightly ciliate, 3/5" long. Margin—wavy.

BUD: Similar to *C. lucida* except smaller.

STEM: Greenish red-brown with appressed pubescence. Older stems gray-brown and ragged in appearance. When bruised or broken, stems emit a distinct maraschino cherry odor. This smell is more distinct on the low growing types but all species I have sampled exhibit the odor.

SIZE: 3' in height by 3 to 6' in spread.

HARDINESS: Zone 4.

HABIT: Low, wide spreading shrub with stiff, cold branching pattern, young shoots growing herringbone fashion from the older ones. Tends to mound upon itself forming dense, inpenetrable tangles where leaves, bottles, and paper penetrate but rakes cannot enter. Somewhat of a "garbage can" shrub but useful because of good foliage and fruit.

RATE: Slow, growth can be accelerated in youth with optimum watering and fertilization, will cover an area fairly fast.

TEXTURE: Fine in leaf, but often coarse in winter because of its "pack-rat" ability to store many unwanted articles.

LEAF COLOR: Dark glossy green, extremely handsome for its summer foliage effect; changing to good bronzy-red or purplish tones in fall and holding its fall color for a long time (October until end of November in Central Illinois).

FLOWERS: Perfect, pinkish, late May to early June, solitary, small, not ornamentally overwhelming.

FRUIT: Pome, 1/4 to 1/3" diameter, cranberry-red, August through September, borne singly, quite attractive for this feature alone.

CULTURE: Same as discussed for *C. lucida* probably performs best in full sun but will tolerate some shade.

DISEASES AND INSECTS: Mites, in dry situations, can render this species brown; fireblight occasionally presents a problem.

LANDSCAPE VALUE: Effective as bank cover, foundation plant, near wall where branches can hang over, facer plant in shrub border, ground or large area cover, used around campuses a great deal. I have seen it used with *Myrica pensylvanica* and the combination is beautiful in summer foliage. Probably overused by landscape architects and nurserymen but, nonetheless, a valuable landscape plant which offers good foliage and fruit. Can present a maintenance problem for it is difficult to clean leaves and trash out of the interior of the plant.

PROPAGATION: Seeds, scarify in H_2SO_4 for 60 minutes followed by stratification in moist peat for 60+ days at 41°F. Cuttings, softwood taken in early summer, untreated, rooted 80% in sand in 84 days.

RELATED SPECIES:

Cotoneaster adpressa — Creeping Cotoneaster. A very dwarf, close growing, compact, rigidly branched, 1 to 1 1/2′ high shrub, spreading 4 to 6′ and rooting where branches touch the soil; leaves are dark glossy green; flowers are solitary or in pairs, white tipped rose; fruit—pome, 1/4″ diameter, bright red. Regarded by some authorities as a variety of *C. horizontalis.* According to Rehder hardy in Zone 4, but has not performed well in Central Illinois (Zones 5 and 6).

NATIVE HABITAT: Western China. Introduced 1910.

Cotoneaster horizontalis — Rockspray or Rock Cotoneaster

LEAVES: Alternate, simple, suborbicular to broad-elliptic, acute at ends and mucronate at the apex, 1/5 to 1/2″ long, dark lustrous green, glabrous above, sparingly strigose-pubescent beneath; petioles 1/12″ long, strigose-pubescent. Leaf blade lies flat and does not have the undulating character of *C. apiculata* with which it is often confused.

STEM: The interesting fishbone pattern in which the branches are borne provides a distinct identification feature (see drawing).

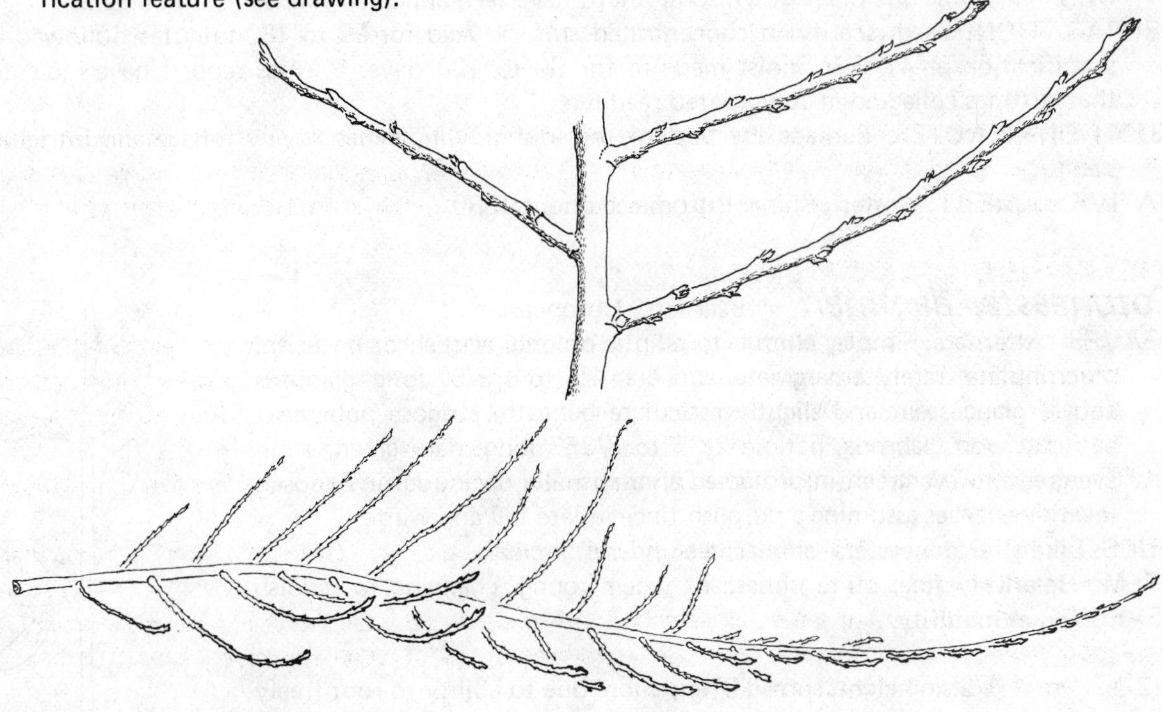

SIZE: 2′ to 3′ in height, spreading 5 to 8′.

HARDINESS: Zone 4, this might be somewhat open to question.

HABIT: Usually a low, flat, dense shrub with branches spreading horizontally. The branches almost form tiers and create a very unusual layered effect.

RATE: Slow to medium.

TEXTURE: Fine in leaf; possibly medium when defoliated although the branch detail does contribute to a rather fine winter character.

LEAF COLOR: Excellent dark glossy green in summer changing to reddish purple combinations in fall.

FLOWERS: Perfect, pink, rather small; borne in mid to late May and into early June; single or 2 together, subsessile. Flowers are very small but when present in great quantity make a nice show. The bees seem to like the flowers as I was almost stung collecting cuttings from a particularly handsome plant at the Holden Arboretum, Mentor, Ohio.

FRUIT: Small pome, bright red, 1/5" diameter; effective in late August through October.

CULTURE: Same as described for *C. lucida*. This species is deciduous or semi-evergreen to almost evergreen depending on location. In northern locations it would tend toward the former, in southern towards the latter. I have seen the plant in March at Bernheim Arboretum, Clermont, Ky., completely evergreen.

DISEASES AND INSECTS: Same as discussed under *C. lucida*.

LANDSCAPE VALUE: Nice ground cover plant; I have seen it used by gradually descending steps and it fit in very well; would work as bank cover, in masses or groupings.

CULTIVARS:

'Little Gem' – Dwarf, broad-mounded, dainty, slow-growing form. Would be excellent in the rockery; very handsome cultivar.

'Perpusilla' – A very prostrate form with leaves about 1/4" long; again a handsome clone.

'Robusta' – A clone I observed growing at the Morton Arboretum, considerably more upright and vigorous than the species.

'Tom Thumb' – Another dwarf form like 'Little Gem'. They look very much alike at least as I witnessed them in the Arnold Arboretum.

'Variegata' – Leaves are edged with white; not as vigorous as the species.

'Wilsonii' – The one plant of 'Wilsonii' that I have seen appeared similar to 'Robusta'.

PROPAGATION: Seed, scarify in concentrated sulfuric acid for 90 to 180 minutes, followed by stratification at 41°F in moist medium for 90 to 120 days. Various reports have indicated that cuttings collected in June rooted readily.

ADDITIONAL NOTES: Perhaps the best of the low growing types; lovely foliage and intriguing habit.

NATIVE HABITAT: Western China. Introduced about 1880.

Cotoneaster dammeri – Bearberry Cotoneaster

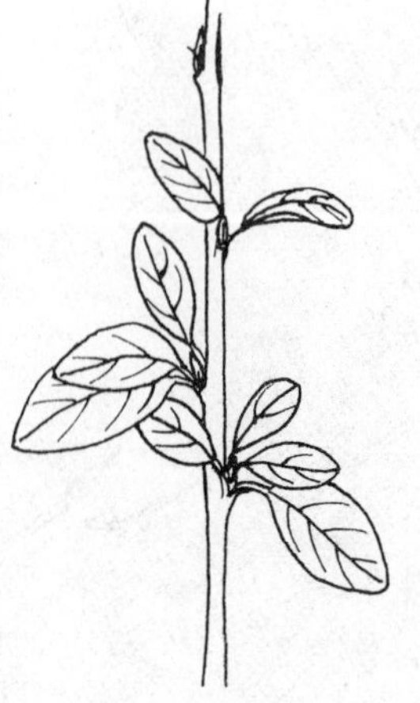

LEAVES: Alternate, simple, elliptic to elliptic-oblong, acutish or obtusish, mucronulate, rarely emarginate, cuneate, 4/5 to 1 3/5" long, glabrous above, glaucescent and slightly reticulate beneath, strigose pubescent at first, soon glabrous, petiole 2/25 to 3/25" long; dark green; semi-evergreen to evergreen in protected areas; usually deciduous in exposed locations; leaves assuming a purplish tinge in late fall and winter.

BUDS: Like all Cotoneasters—similar; see under *C. lucida*.

STEM: Relatively fine; quite pubescent when young, changing to reddish brown at maturity.

SIZE: 1' to 1 1/2' in height, spread 6' and more due to ability to root freely where branches contact soil.

HARDINESS: Zone 5.

HABIT: Very low, prostrate, evergreen to semievergreen shrub, with slender creeping stems keeping close to the ground. Will cover a large area in a short period of time.

RATE: Fast.

TEXTURE: Fine in all seasons.

LEAF COLOR: Lustrous dark green in summer and fall, assuming a wilted dull dark green in winter in Central Illinois.

FLOWERS: White, 1/3 to 1/2" diameter, solitary or in pairs, borne in late May, not abundant.

FRUIT: Pome, 1/4" wide, bright red, late summer, good for color, however, usually sparsely produced.

CULTURE: Transplants well, often container-grown as are most ground cover type cotoneasters, adaptable but prefers well drained soil, occurs wild on heaths (peaty areas) and rocky ground.

DISEASES AND INSECTS: Subject to usual problems. I have noticed great quantities of aphids on this plant.

LANDSCAPE VALUE: The species and cultivars are among the best everygreen ground covers. Excellent on banks, gentle slopes, masses, shrub border, low facing shrub, foundation and as a possible espaliered effect. The solid carpet of glossy green is difficult to duplicate with other ground covers.

CULTIVARS:

'Coral Beauty' ('Pink Beauty' 'Royal Beauty') — Excellent free fruiting form.

'Lowfast' — Supposedly extremely hardy with good dark glossy green foliage.

'Skogsholmen' — An extremely vigorous form with prostrate or serpentine branches. A two year old plant may be 3' across and can spread several feet each year. It is not a free fruiting form.

PROPAGATION: Cuttings, anytime during the growing season, treated with 1000 ppm IBA, quick dip, peat:perlite, mist, gave 100% rooting; perhaps the easiest *Cotoneaster* to root.

RELATED SPECIES:

Cotoneaster salicifolia — Willowleaf Cotoneaster. Actually a large evergreen shrub in the south, of spreading, arching habit. The variety *floccosa* remains semi-evergreen in the north, graceful shrub with arching branches and dark glossy green, narrow leaves often changing to purplish red. *C. s.* 'Repandens' is a low-growing form, semievergreen with excellent dark green foliage. Western China. Introduced 1908. Zone 6.

NATIVE HABITAT: Central China. Introduced 1900.

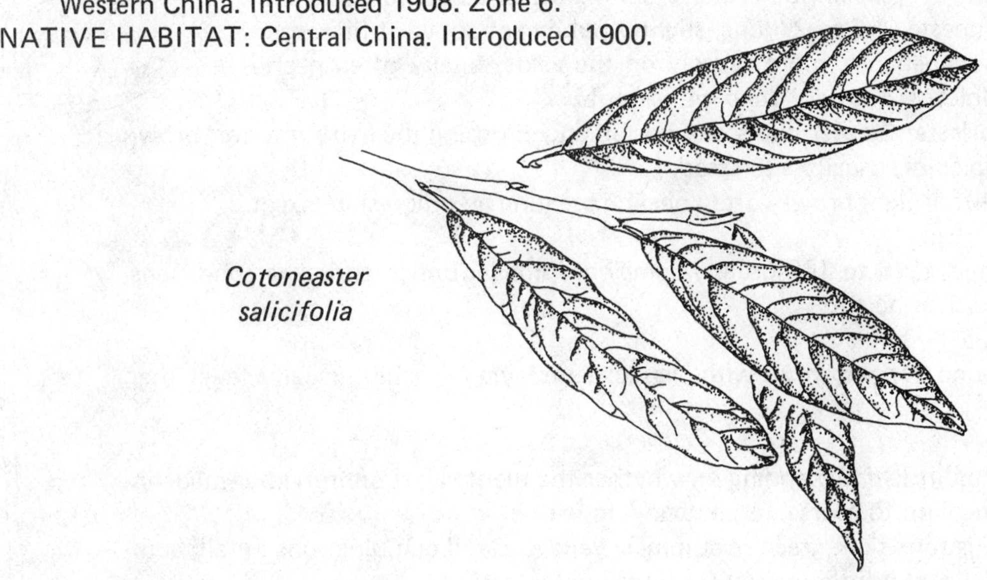

Cotoneaster salicifolia

Cotoneaster divaricata — Spreading Cotoneaster

LEAVES: Alternate, simple, elliptic or broad-elliptic, acute at ends or rounded at apex, 1/3 to 4/5" long, lustrous dark green above, lighter and slightly pubescent or glabrous beneath.

BUD: Similar to other cotoneasters.

STEM: Slender, purple, appressed pubescent, older stems becoming dark brown.

SIZE: 5 to 6' in height with a comparable or larger spread (6 to 8').

HARDINESS: Zone 5.

HABIT: Spreading, multistemmed shrub of rounded outline, outer branches are long, slender, and tend to droop creating a fine appearance.

RATE: Medium to fast.

TEXTURE: Fine in leaf; medium-fine in winter. Tremendous textural asset in the shrub border.

LEAF COLOR: Dark glossy green, unexcelled for summer leaf color; fall color has been outstanding in Central Illinois in 1973 and 1974 with the leaves changing to fluorescent yellow-red-purple combinations which persisted for 4 to 6 weeks. One of the last deciduous shrubs to defoliate in our area. One hedge on the campus was magnanimous in fall splendor.

FLOWERS: Rose, solitary or in threes, late May to early June, not spectacular.

FRUIT: Pome, 1/3" long and 1/4" wide, red to dark red, early September through November, one of the handsomest in fruit of the Chinese Cotoneasters.

CULTURE: Same as described for *C. lucida*.

DISEASES AND INSECTS: One of the most desirable, ornamental, and trouble-free of the cotoneasters although limitedly susceptible to the typical problems which beset cotoneasters.

LANDSCAPE VALUE: Multi-faceted shrub, can be successfully used in foundation plantings, hedges, groups, borders, masses; blends well with other plants; foliage is unrivaled in summer and fall, integrates well with broadleaf evergreens.

PROPAGATION: Seed, as described for *C. apiculata*. Cuttings, softwood collected in early June, dipped in 1000 ppm IBA solution, rooted 90% in three months in sand under mist (personal experience). Another worker reported 100% rooting in six weeks of untreated cuttings collected in early July.

NATIVE HABITAT: Central and Western China. Introduced 1907.

Cotoneaster lucida — Hedge Cotoneaster

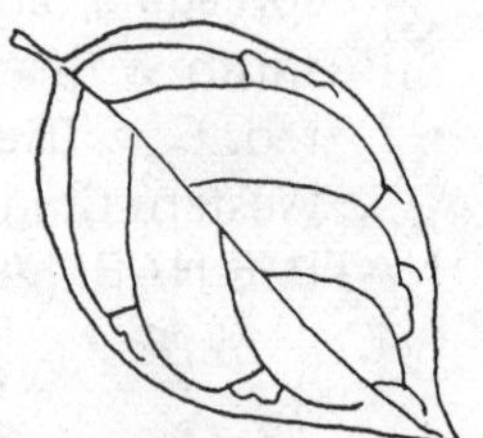

LEAVES: Alternate, simple, elliptic-ovate to oblong-ovate, acute, rarely acuminate, broad-cuneate, 4/5 to 2" long, slightly pubescent above at first, sparingly pubescent beneath, more densely on the veins, finally often nearly glabrous, petioles, 1/8 to 1/5" long, pubescent.

BUD: Weakly imbricate, 2 outer bud scales parted and exposing the hairy interior, brown to pale gray in color, usually appressed.

STEM: Slender, buff or light brown, often peeling creating an onion-skin effect.

SIZE: 10 to 15' high by 6 to 10'; usually somewhat smaller under landscape conditions, possibly 5 to 10' in height.

HARDINESS: Zone 4.

HABIT: Erect, round topped shrub with slender spreading branches, usually taller than broad.

RATE: Medium.

TEXTURE: Medium in leaf; depending on whether the plant is left unpruned or made into a hedge—medium to coarse, respectively, in winter.

LEAF COLOR: Lustrous dark green in summer; yellow to red combinations in fall; actually very effective but little praised for its fall coloration.

FLOWERS: Pinkish, rather small and ineffective; mid to late May; borne in 2 to 5-flowered cymes.

FRUIT: Berry-like pome, black, 2/5" diameter, September and persisting.

CULTURE: In general cotoneasters have sparse root systems and should be moved balled and burlapped or preferably as a container plant. They prefer well drained, loose, fertile soil with adequate moisture but do quite well in dry, poor soils; tolerant of wind; pH adaptable; somewhat tolerant of seaside conditions, prune almost anytime; once established they are very vigorous, strong growing landscape plants; full sun or light shade.

DISEASES AND INSECTS: Leaf spots, canker, fire blight, hawthorn lace bug, scales, spider mites, cotoneaster webworm, sinuate pear tree borer, and pear leaf blister mite.

LANDSCAPE VALUE: Primarily used as a hedge because of narrow, upright habit. Excellent for screens or groupings because of handsome foliage; tends to be overused as a hedge. Often plants are stereotyped as to landscape use and this plant has been relegated to the status of hedge plant.

PROPAGATION: Seed should be scarified in concentrated sulfuric acid for 5 to 20 minutes followed by cold stratification in moist peat at 40°F for 30 to 90 days. Cuttings rooted well when taken in early July.

RELATED SPECIES:

Cotoneaster acutifolia, Peking Cotoneaster, is confused with *C. lucida* in the trade. The principal difference is in the foliage which is dull green, not shining and more hairy. Native to Mongolia, Northern and Western China and the Eastern Himalaya. Zone 4. Introduced 1883. Bean considers this an inferior cotoneaster and possibly a poor form of *C. lucida*.

NATIVE HABITAT: Siberia and other parts of Northern Asia. Cultivated 1840.

Cotoneaster multiflora — Many-flowered Cotoneaster

LEAVES: Alternate, simple, broad-ovate to ovate, acute or obtuse, rounded or broad cuneate at base, 4/5 to 2" long, at first tomentose beneath, soon glabrous. Petioles, 1/8 to 2/5" long.

BUD: Similar to other cotoneasters.

STEM: Purple when young, to reddish green and finally gray. Slightly pubescent to glabrous.

SIZE: 8 to 12' and greater in height (17' specimens on campus) and 12 to 15' in spread.

HARDINESS: Zone 5.

HABIT: Upright, spreading, weeping or mounded at maturity with long arching branches forming a fountain much like Vanhoutte Spirea.

RATE: Medium; once well established develops very rapidly.

TEXTURE: Medium-fine in foliage; medium-coarse in winter; looks a bit naked in the winter landscape and is difficult to conceal due to large size.

LEAF COLOR: Soft gray-green when unfolding, changing to gray or blue-green in mature leaf; fall color not much different or with a hint of yellow. Summer foliage is different than most plants which adds unusual contrasting color to the normal green complement of most shrubs.

FLOWERS: White, each flower about 1/2" diameter, early to mid-May, abundantly produced in 3 to 12 or more flowered corymbs, unpleasantly scented. Very spectacular in flower as the flowers are borne upright along the stem on slender peduncles and effectively use the gray-green foliage as a background for accentuation of their beauty. Could be mistaken for *Spiraea* x *vanhouttei* but it is most definitely a superior plant.

FRUIT: Berry-like pome, 1/3" diameter, red, late August holding into early October, borne in great quantities, appears with the foliage and falls before leaf abscission, so the total ornamental effect is somewhat masked. Very beautiful in full fruit; I rate this the best flowering and fruiting shrub of the cotoneaster group.

CULTURE: Supposedly somewhat difficult to transplant, should be root pruned to develop good, fibrous root system, probably well adapted to container production at least in small sizes; strongly prefers well drained soil, sunny, airy location and no standing water.

DISEASES AND INSECTS: Comparing the cotoneasters on our campus, this species seems to be the most trouble-free and exhibits abundant growth every year. I have not observed the fireblight or mite problem which have occurred frequently on *C. apiculata*.

LANDSCAPE VALUE: Requires room to spread, shrub border, massing, parks, golf courses, almost any public area because of low maintenance aspect. There are several large (16 to 18') specimens on campus which are bountiful in flower and fruit. Unfortunately, I have not been able to successfully propagate them.

CULTIVARS:

var. *calocarpa* — Leaves long and narrower than the type; fruit larger and more numerous. W.J. Bean termed this variety "a singularly beautiful fruit bearing shrub".

PROPAGATION: Cuttings, collected in June by this author, treated with 1000 ppm IBA solution, placed in sand under mist yielded 1% rooted cuttings. According to an Illinois nurseryman, *C. multiflora* roots readily from June-collected softwood cuttings. Further experiments are planned, for several of the plants on campus are worthy of perpetuation. Seed should be treated as described under *C. lucida.*

RELATED SPECIES:

Cotoneaster racemiflora soongorica — Sungari Redbead Cotoneaster. Similar in form, but hardier (Zone 3) with bluer foliage and great abundance of pink (rose) fruits; in cultivation it has proven to be a graceful and exceptionally free fruiting shrub, thriving in dry, sandy soil; native of Central Asia, introduced by E.H. Wilson, the great plant explorer.

ADDITIONAL NOTES: These species are little known and used, but definitely should be brought to the gardener's eye. Asset in any garden while the liability shrubs (forsythia, deutzia, mock-orange) continue to be overplanted.

NATIVE HABITAT: Western China. Introduced 1900.

Crataegus crusgalli — Cockspur Hawthorn

FAMILY: Rosaceae

LEAVES: Alternate, simple, obovate to oblong-obovate, usually rounded at apex, cuneate, 4/5 to 3" long, sharply serrate above the entire base, quite glabrous, subcoriaceous, dark glossy green.

BUDS: Applies to the genus: solitary or collaterally branched in spine formation, sessile, round or oblong ovoid, with about 6 exposed fleshy and bright red to reddish brown scales.

STEM: Moderate or slender, terete, usually armed with slender, numerous 1 1/2 to 3" long thorns.

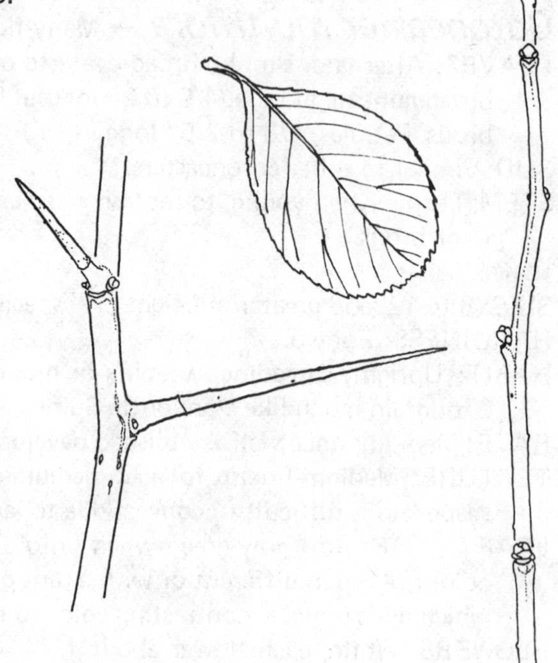

SIZE: 20 to 30' in height with a spread of 20 to 35'.

HARDINESS: Zone 4.

HABIT: Broad-rounded, low branched tree with wide spreading, horizontal thorny branches which are densely set and make it difficult to grow grass under.

RATE: Slow to medium, 10 to 14' over 6 to 10 years.

TEXTURE: Medium-fine in leaf; medium in winter.

LEAF COLOR: Lustrous dark green in summer; bronze-red to purplish red in fall.

FLOWERS: Perfect, 1/2 to 2/3" diameter, white, of disagreeable odor; mid to late May; effective for 7 to 10 days, borne in 2 to 3" diameter flat corymbs, flowers with 10 stamens, pink anthers, usually 2 styles.

FRUIT: Pome-like drupe, deep red, 3/8 to 1/2" diameter; ripening in late September, October and persisting into late fall.

CULTURE: Transplant balled and burlapped in early spring as a small tree; tolerant of many soils but they should be well drained; pH adaptable, however, on the University of Illinois campus I have noticed a few trees with chlorosis; full sun; tolerates soot and grime of cities; prune in winter or early spring.

DISEASES AND INSECTS: Fireblight, leaf blight, rusts (at least 9 species attack hawthorns), leaf spots, powdery mildews, scab, aphids, borers, western tent caterpillar, apple leaf blotch miner, lace bugs, apple and thorn skeletonizer, plant hopper, scales and two spotted mite. Hawthorns, though lovely ornamentals, are severely affected by pests. The cedar hawthorn rust has been extremely bad as has the leaf blotch miner especially on *C. crusgalli* in Central Illinois.

LANDSCAPE VALUE: Single specimen, groupings, screens, barrier plant, hedges; on campus this species has been effectively used around large buildings and helps to soften the strong vertical lines. Extensive use around residences must be tempered with the knowledge that the 2" thorns can seriously injury small children. In fact, I would not use this hawthorn in the landscape where small children are apt to play.

CULTIVARS:

var. *inermis* — Thornless type with the good features of the species. I have three in our plant evaluation plots and have found them to be vigorous and attractive trees.

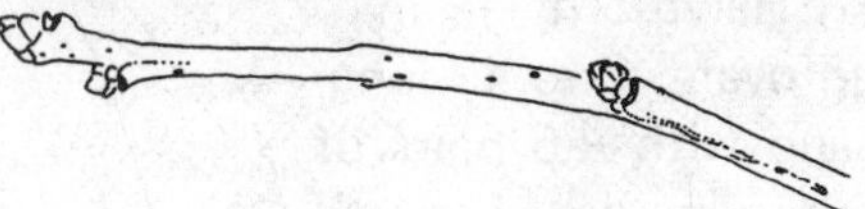

PROPAGATION: Seed should be immersed in H_2SO_4 acid for 2 to 3 hours (seed should be dry) then warm stratified at 70-77°F. for 120 days followed by 135 days at 41°F. Other species do not have the bony endocarp and require only the warm-cold treatment. Selected clones are budded on seedling understock.

RELATED SPECIES:

Crataegus punctata, Thicket Hawthorn grows 20 to 35' high and is usually wider than tall at maturity. The leaves are dull grayish green in summer. Flowers are white; fruit is dull red, 3/4" diameter, ripening in October and falling soon after.

'Aurea' — Yellow fruits and could be considered a variety as it has been found in the wild.

var. *inermis* ('Ohio Pioneer') — An essentially thornless type selected from a tree at the Secrest Arboretum, Wooster, Ohio with good vigor, growth, and fruiting characteristics.

Quebec to Ontario, Illinois and Georgia. Introduced 1716. Zone 4.

ADDITIONAL NOTE: Only a few birds like the fruits of *Crataegus* and, consequently, they remain effective for a long time.

NATIVE HABITAT: Quebec to North Carolina and Kansas. Introduced 1656.

Crataegus x *lavallei* — Lavalle Hawthorn

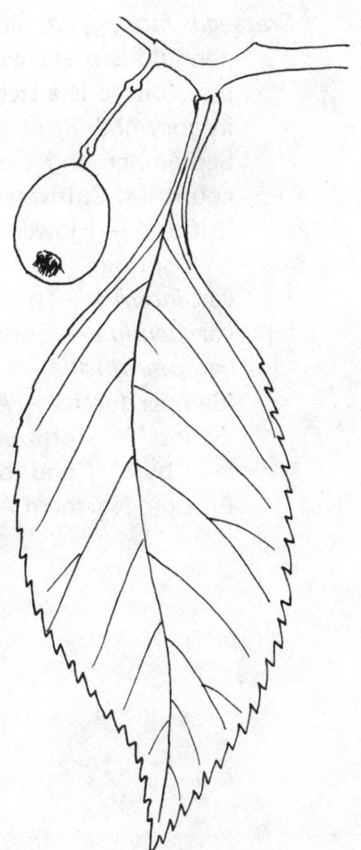

LEAVES: Alternate, simple, elliptic to oblong-obovate, acute, cuneate, 2 to 4" long, unequally serrate from below the middle, slightly pubescent above when young, finally glabrous and lustrous dark green, pubescent beneath.

STEMS: Greenish, glabrous, glaucous, usually without thorns.

Crataegus x *lavallei*, Lavalle Hawthorn, is a hybrid between *C. crusgalli* and possibly *C. pubescens.* It is a small, dense, oval-headed tree growing 15 to 30' tall. The foliage is a lustrous dark green in summer followed by bronzy or coppery-red colors in fall. Flowers are white, 3/4" diameter; late May; borne in 3" diameter, erect corymbs. Fruit is brick red to orange-red speckled with brown, 5/8 to 3/4" diameter pome-like drupe which ripens in November and persists into winter. I have seen many specimens and most exhibit a one-sided habit. They are not the most uniform growing trees.

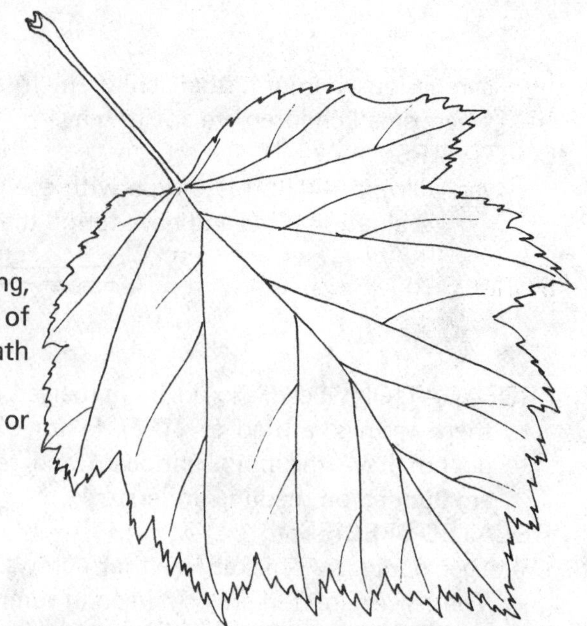

Crataegus mollis — Downy Hawthorn

LEAVES: Alternate, simple, broad ovate, 2 to 4" long, sharply and doubly serrate and with 4-5 pairs of short and acute lobes, densely pubescent beneath at first, later chiefly on the veins, medium green.

STEM: Moderate, thorns to 2" long, curved, stout or absent; older branches turn a grayish cast.

Crataegus mollis, Downy Hawthorn, is a rounded to wide-spreading tree with varying degrees of thorniness reaching 20 to 30' in height. The branches take on a gray cast and are quite different from most hawthorns. The young leaves are very downy when unfolding and gradually change to a flat medium green in summer and can turn bronze to bronze-red in fall. Flowers are white, 1" diameter, malodorous, early May (earliest hawthorn to flower in Central Illinois), borne in 3 to 4" diameter corymbs. Fruit is red, 1/2 to 1" diameter, ripening in late August and September and falling soon after. Good native tree but extremely variable; not for the modern landscape as there are too many superior species and cultivars. Southern Ontario to Virginia, west to South Dakota and Kansas. Cultivated 1683. Zone 4.

Crataegus monogyna, Singleseed Hawthorn, is a round headed, densely branched tree with slightly pendulous branches and moderate thorny character which grows to 20 to 30' high. The summer foliage is a rich, polished green; flowers are white, 5/8" diameter, mid to late May, borne in corymbs. Fruit is red, 3/8" diameter, one-seeded (hence the name Singleseed), effective in September and October. This species has been widely used as a hedge plant in European countries. Cultivars include:

'Biflora' — Flowering in mild seasons in midwinter, producing a second crop of flowers in the spring.

var. *inermis* — Thornless, excellent mushroom habit.

var. *pendula* — Form with pendulous branchlets.

var. *pteridifolia* — Leaves deeply-lobed and closely incised.

'Semperflorens' — A low shrubby form often flowering continuously until August.

'Stricta' — Form with upright branches and narrow habit. A specimen at the Arnold is 30' by 8'. Good for street tree and other areas where space is limited.

Europe, Northern Africa, Western Asia. Long cultivated. Zone 4.

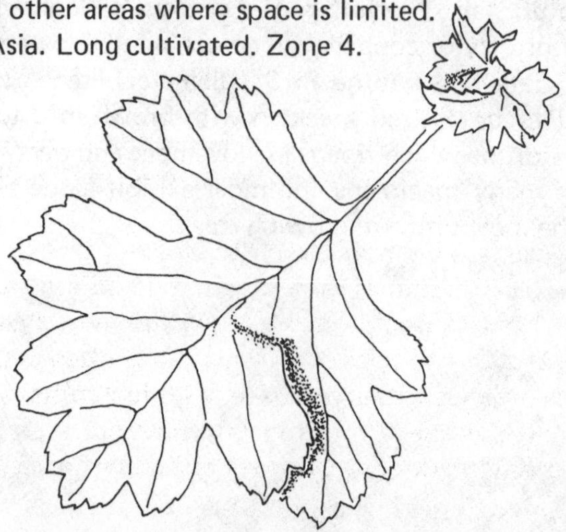

Crataegus nitida — Glossy Hawthorn

LEAVES: Alternate, simple, elliptic to oblong-obovate, acuminate, cuneate, 4/5 to 3″ long, coarsely serrate and often slightly lobed, dark green and lustrous above, paler below, glabrous.

STEM: Slender with thorns to 2″ long, straight or absent.

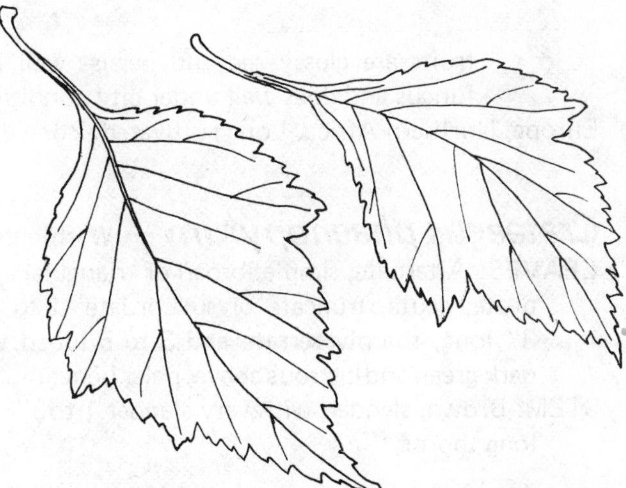

Crataegus nitida, Glossy Hawthorn, grows to 30′ and forms a dense, rounded outline. The foliage is lustrous dark green (extremely shiny) in summer and turns orangish to red in the fall. Flowers are white, small, mid to late May, borne in 1 to 2″ diameter corymbs. Fruit is dull red, 3/8″ diameter, ripening in October—November and persisting into spring. This species is supposedly similar to *C. viridis,* Green Hawthorn. Illinois to Missouri and Arkansas. Introduced 1883. Zone 4.

Crataegus oxyacantha — English Hawthorn (Listed as *C. laevigata* by *Hortus III*)

LEAVES: Alternate, simple, broad-ovate or obovate, cuneate, 3/5 to 2″ long, with 3 to 5 broad serrulate, obtuse or actuish lobes, glabrous.

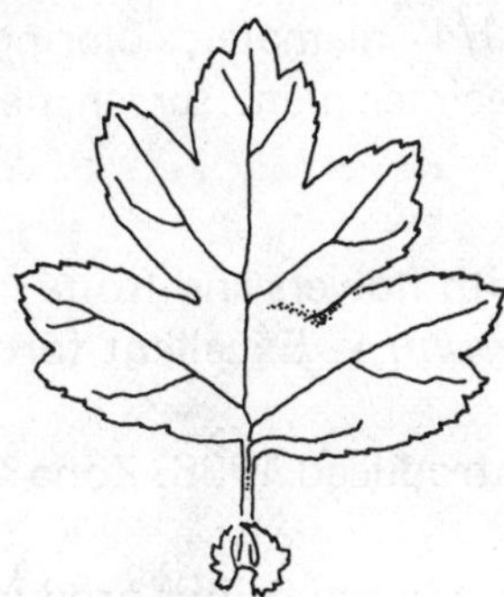

Crataegus oxyacantha, English Hawthorn, is a shrubby, low branching, round topped tree with a close, dense head of stiff zig-zag ascending branches reaching 15 to 20′ in height and 12 to 20′ in spread. The foliage is a deep dark green in summer. Flowers are white, 5/8″ diameter, mid May, borne in 5 to 12-flowered corymbs. Fruit is scarlet, 1/4 to 3/4″ long, ripening in September and October. The cultivars offer the greatest diversity in the landscape and include:

var. *aurea* — Fruit bright yellow.

'Autumn Glory' — Good growth habit, white flowers and giant red fruit; however, probably a Zone 6 plant.

'Crimson Cloud' — A selection by Princeton Nurseries with good red flowers and resistance to the leaf blight which is so troublesome to *C. o.* 'Paulii'.

var. *rosea* — Flowers light rose, single.

var. *rosea-plena* — Flowers light rose, double.

var. *rubra* — Best fruiting form, bright red, 3/8″ diameter, flowers single, white.

'Paulii' — Flowers double, scarlet, and the most showy of all the hawthorns, very susceptible to leaf spot and blight problems and is often defoliated.

var. *plena* — Flowers double, white, with few fruits.

'Superba' — Another Princeton introduction; a cross between 'Charles X' and 'Paulii', with large single bright red flowers and each flower has a white star-shaped area in the center;

fruits are glossy red and persist well into winter. It is highly resistant to the leaf spot fungus and does well under city conditions (apparently same as 'Crimson Cloud').

Europe, Northern Africa. Long cultivated. Zone 4.

Crataegus phaenopyrum — Washington Hawthorn

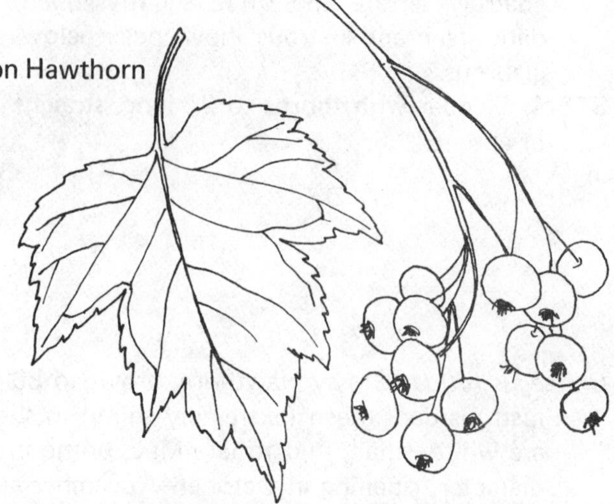

LEAVES: Alternate, simple, broad or triangular-ovate, acute, truncate or subcordate, 1 to 3" long, sharply serrate and 3 to 5 lobed, dark green and lustrous above, paler beneath.

STEM: Brown, slender, with very slender 1 to3" long thorns.

Crataegus phaenopyrum, Washington Hawthorn, grows to 25 to 30' high with a 20 to 25' spread. The overall effect is a broadly columnar, dense, thorny tree eventually somewhat rounded. The foliage is a reddish purple when unfolding gradually changing to lustrous dark green at maturity; fall color varies from orange to scarlet through purplish; flowers are white, 1/2" diameter, not badly scented compared to *C. mollis* and *C. crusgalli*; early June, effective for 7 to 10 days (the last hawthorn to flower in Central Illinois); borne in many flowered terminal and axillary corymbs. Fruit is bright, glossy red, 1/4" diameter, coloring in September and October and persisting all winter. Excellent single specimen plant, screen, near buildings, streets, borders, hedges. Cultivars include:

'Clark' — Heavy fruiting clone.

'Fastigiata' — Columnar type with flowers and fruits smaller than the species.

'Vaughn' (*crusgalli* x *phaenopyrum*) — Excellent for the abundance of glossy fruit it produces.

Virginia to Alabama and Missouri. Introduced 1738. Zone 4.

Crataegus succulenta, Fleshy Hawthorn, is a heavy fruiter producing bright red, 3/8 to 1/2" diameter pome-like drupes in September and October. I remember this tree from my woody plant materials courses at Ohio State and can still picture the heavy fruit crops as I walked past this tree on my way to the Botany building. The fall color is a good purple-red. Does not seem to be common and in many respects (foliage, flower, fruit) is similar to *C. crusgalli*. Charles S. Sargent considered it one of the 6 best hawthorns in America and that is quite a tribute considering the great number which are native. Quebec and Ontario to Massachusetts and Illinois. Cultivated 1830. Zone 3.

Crataegus 'Toba' is a cross between *succulenta* x *oxyacantha* 'Paulii'. The flowers are light to bright pink fading to deep rose, double, fragrant; mid to late May; corymbs. Fruit is bright red, 1/2" diameter, October and persisting most of the winter. Chief claim to fame is extreme hardiness (Zone 3) compared to *C. oxyacantha*.

Crataegus viridis, Green Hawthorn, is a rounded, sharply thorny, spreading, dense tree growing 20 to 35' high. The foliage is a lustrous medium green in summer and can change to purple and scarlet in the fall. Flowers are white, 3/4" diameter, mid May, borne in 2" diameter corymbs. The fruits are bright red, 1/6 to 1/4" diameter, coloring in September-October and persisting.

'Winter King' — Selection with lovely rounded habit, almost vase-shaped branching structure and distinct green, bloomy stems. The fruits are larger than the species and a good red. Could be hybrid as it does not match the characteristics of the species; less susceptible to rust than other thorns.

Maryland and Virginia to Illinois, Iowa, Texas and Florida. Cultivated 1827. Zone 4.

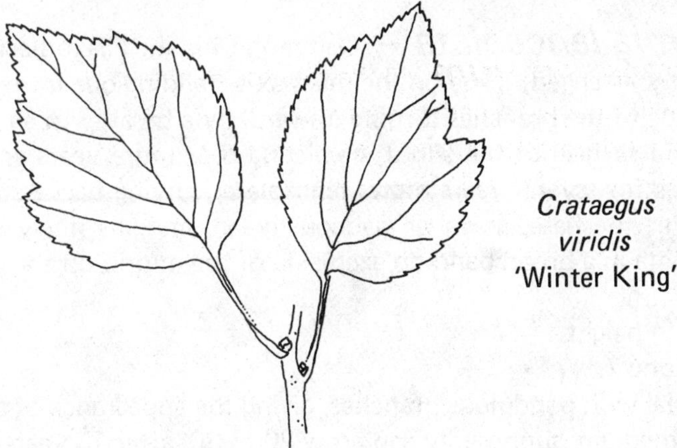

Crataegus viridis 'Winter King'

Cryptomeria japonica — Japanese Cryptomeria (Taxodiaceae)

LEAVES: Spirally arranged, persisting 4 to 5 years, awl-shaped, 1/4 to 1/2" long, the first leaves of the year shorter than the later ones, curving inwards, sometimes slightly twisted, point forwards, keeled on both surfaces, margins entire, apex tapering to a blunt point, base spreading and clasping the shoot, stomata on each surface.

STEM: Green, glabrous; the branchlets spreading or drooping, eventually deciduous.

SIZE: 50 to 60' high by 20 to 30' wide; can grow to over 100'.

HARDINESS: Zone 5-6, hardy to Boston, Massachusetts.

HABIT: A pyramidal or conical tree with a stout trunk and erect, wide-spreading branches with numerous branchlets.

RATE: Medium, can grow 50 to 60' after 30 to 40 years; the few that I have seen in the lower Midwest (Cincinnati) were slower growing than this.

TEXTURE: Medium.

BARK: Reddish brown peeling off in long shreds.

LEAF COLOR: Bright green to bluish green in summer; during the winter the needles take on a bronzy hue (brown if in windy locations), but become green again in spring.

FLOWERS: Monoecious, inconspicuous.

FRUIT: Cones are terminal, globular, 3/5 to 1" broad and dark brown.

CULTURE: Easy to grow, prefers a rich and deep, light, permeable, acid soil with abundant moisture; open, sunny location, sheltered from high winds.

DISEASES AND INSECTS: Leaf blight and leaf spot.

LANDSCAPE VALUE: An accommodating tree, graceful, stately and handsome; useful as a specimen or for avenues.

CULTIVARS:

'Compacta' — Compact, conical tree to 45', leaves short and bluish green.

'Elegans' — Juvenile form 9 to 15' tall, sickle shaped needles, green in summer, bright brownish red in winter.

PROPAGATION: Seed germination is usually quite poor. The seed should be soaked in cold water (32°F) for about 1/2 day, then put moist into plastic bags and stored at 34°F for 60 to 90 days before sowing. Bags should be left open for adequate aeration. Cuttings taken in summer and fall will root, although slowly. Effective treatments are 40 to 80 ppm IBA soak/24 hours.

ADDITIONAL NOTES: A lovely conifer where it can be grown. The National Arboretum has a wealth of *Cryptomeria* and in November, 1975, were planting a considerable number in the back of their administration building for a screening effect.

NATIVE HABITAT: China and Japan, and was originally discovered in the former country in 1701 by James Cunningham, and by Kaempfer in Japan in 1692. Introduced into America 1861.

Cunninghamia lanceolata — Common Chinafir (Taxodiaceae)

LEAVES: Spirally arranged, those on the main axis standing out from all around the stem, those on the underside of the branches turning upwards by a basal twist so that all appear to spring from the sides and surface of the shoot; persisting 5 or more years and remaining dry and dead on the branches for several years more; lanceolate, curving backwards, 1 to 2 3/4" long, 1/16 to 1/8" wide at the base, green or glaucous green, margins finely toothed, apex a long, slender point; stomata in a broad band on each side of the midrib on the under-surface.

SIZE: 30 to 75' in height.
HARDINESS: Zone 7.
HABIT: Pyramidal with pendulous branches, giving the appearance of an exotic-looking tree.
RATE: Slow to medium; supposedly can grow 20 to 30' after 15 years.
TEXTURE: Medium-fine.
BARK: Brown, scaling off in long irregular strips, exposing the reddish inner bark.
LEAF COLOR: Bright medium green or glaucous green becoming dark and bronzy by fall.
FLOWERS: Monoecious; male flowers in terminal clusters; female flowers terminal.
FRUIT: Cones usually several together, rarely solitary, globose, ovoid, 1 1/5 to 1 3/5" broad.
CULTURE: Prefers moist, acid, well-drained soils. Not very hardy, grows best in open spaces shaded by trees and protected from windswept sites.
DISEASES AND INSECTS: None serious.
LANDSCAPE VALUE: Only of value in the warmer parts of the country. Possibly used as a specimen or mass planting.
CULTIVARS:
'Glauca' — Leaves with a conspicuous glaucous bloom.
PROPAGATION: Propagated by seeds and cuttings.
ADDITIONAL NOTES: Highly prized tree in China and, next to bamboo, is the most useful for all around work. The wood is light, soft, fragrant, pale yellow or almost white, easily worked, durable, and used for housebuilding, indoor carpentry, masts, planking, box-making, and largely for coffins. The wood is very rot resistant in contact with the soil.

In the wild, under forest conditions, it develops a long, straight, mast-like trunk, 80 to 150' high, clear of branches for half its height. It has the ability when cut to produce sprouts from roots and revegetate an area.

NATIVE HABITAT: Central and Southern China. Introduced 1804.

Cytisus scoparius — Scotch Broom

FAMILY: Leguminosae

LEAVES: Alternate, 3-foliate, obovate or lanceolate, 1/3 to 3/5" long, sparingly appressed pubescent, the upper leaves reduced to 1 leaflet. Bright to medium green.

BUDS: Small, solitary, sessile, round-ovoid, with about 4 often indistinct scales.

STEM: Slender, finely granular, almost winged on the ridges; pith—small, roundish, continuous; bright-green in summer and winter.

SIZE: 5 to 6' when open grown and twice that when used in shrub borders and tight situations; spread is equal to or considerably greater than height.

HARDINESS: Zone 5.

HABIT: A broad, rounded-mounded deciduous shrub with very erect, slender, grass green stems and twigs.

TEXTURE: Medium-fine if kept in bounds during summer; similar texture in winter.

STEM COLOR: Distinctly winged stems of grass green color.

LEAF COLOR: Light to medium green in summer; fall color of no consequence.

FLOWERS: Perfect, glowing yellow, 1" long and 4/5" across, May-June and profusely borne along the stems on old wood either singly or in two's.

FRUIT: 1 2/5 to 2" pods, not ornamental.

CULTURE: Supposedly does not transplant well but I have had good success with container-grown material. Prefers sandy, infertile soils which are somewhat on the dry side; full sun; pH adaptable; prune after flowering.

DISEASES AND INSECTS: Leaf spot and blight can kill the plants. Small irregular spots first appear on the leaf blades, enlarge rapidly, and cause a blotch or blight.

LANDSCAPE VALUE: Very good plant for poor soils; has been used for stabilizing sandy right-of-ways along eastern highways. I have seen it used in Massachusetts along highways and it appeared to be an effective cover. Yields a fantastic splash of color when in flower.

CULTIVARS: Apparently there are over 60 clones offered for sale by American and European nurserymen.

PROPAGATION: Seeds should be soaked in hot water or H_2SO_4 to break seed coat dormancy. For germination, diurnally alternating temperatures of 68°F (night) and 86°F (day) for 28 days are recommended. Cuttings taken in August with a heel of older wood and placed in sand in cold frames will develop roots by the following spring.

NATIVE HABITAT: Central and Southern Europe.

Daphne cneorum — Rose Daphne

FAMILY: Thymelaeaceae

LEAVES: Alternate, simple, 2/5 to 4/5" long, crowded, oblanceolate, usually obtuse and mucronulate, cuneate, lustrous olive-green above, glaucescent beneath.

BUDS: Sessile, usually solitary but sometimes superimposed or collaterally branched, ovoid, with 4 to 6 exposed scales.

STEMS: Moderate, rounded or somewhat 4-sided; pith small, roundish, continuous; leaf-scars crescent-shaped, small, exceptionally elevated; 1 bundle-trace.

SIZE: 6" to 12" in height by 2' or more in spread.

HARDINESS: Zone 4

HABIT: A low spreading evergreen shrub with long, trailing and ascending branches forming low, loose masses.

RATE: Slow.

TEXTURE: Medium-fine in all seasons although often looks ragged in winter.

LEAF COLOR: Grayish green overall effect.

FLOWERS: Bright rosy-pink, 2/5" across, delightfully fragrant; April and May and often flowering again in late summer; borne in 6 to 8-flowered umbels; often reminds one of the flower of Candytuft.

FRUIT: Berry, yellowish brown.

CULTURE: Transplant as a container plant; does not move readily; should be done in early spring or early fall; there is considerable incongruity in soil recommendations but the following composite was gleaned from several sources; prefers well-drained, moist, near neutral (pH 6 to 7) soil; light shade, possibly full sun in coastal areas; snow-cover is beneficial; protect with pine boughs where winter sun and wind present a problem; mulch to maintain moist root zone; prune annually after the plants have become established, preferably after flowering and before mid-July; the plant resents disturbance and once located should be left there permanently.

DISEASES AND INSECTS: Leaf spots result in brown spots on both sides of the leaves, crown rot occurs more commonly on plants in shady areas; twig blight, canker, viruses, aphids, mealybug and scales present problems.

LANDSCAPE VALUE: Good small evergreen ground cover; works well in a rock garden or slightly shady spots; very fastidious as to culture and perhaps *Iberis sempervirens* is a decent substitute especially for Midwestern states.

CULTIVARS:

'Alba'– White flowering type.

'Ruby Glow' – Dark pink flowers.

'Silverleaf' or 'Variegata' – Leaf margins with a white band.

PROPAGATION: Cuttings taken in summer and fall yield the best results. December cuttings failed to root without treatment but rooted 56 percent after treatment with 100 ppm IAA for 16 hours. July cuttings rooted 74 percent without treatment, and 93 percent with Hormodin #1.

RELATED SPECIES:

D. x *burkwoodii,* Burkwood Daphne, is a cross between *D. caucasica* x *D. cneorum.* The flowers are creamy white to pinkish tinged, fragrant, and borne in dense, terminal, 2" diameter umbels in mid-May. Individual flowers are about 1/2" wide while the red berries are about 1/3" wide. This species is performing quite well at the Morton Arboretum in Lisle, Illinois. The species will grow 4 to 6" high. Zone 5. There are two clones, one termed 'Arthur Burkwood' the other 'Somerset' which have received considerable attention because of the old Wayside Gardens. Apparently, when the original cross was made only three seeds resulted but all germinated. Of the three plants, one died and the other two are the clones listed. Both forms make vigorous bushes to at least 3', but of the two, 'Somerset' is larger and can grow to 4' high and more in diameter. The foilage is semi-evergreen on both and, in this respect, intermediate between the parents. Wyman noted that a 20-year-old specimen was 4' high and 6' wide, very rounded and dense. This group is easily propagated by cuttings taken in summer and treated with IBA.

Daphne genkwa, Lilac Daphne, grows 3 to 4', is deciduous and composed of erect, slender, sparsely branched stems. Flowers are lilac-colored, produced during May at the nodes of naked wood of the previous year in 1/2" stalked clusters. Native to China. Introduced 1843. Zone 5. Easily propagated by cuttings taken when the new growth is very soft.

Daphne giraldii, Giraldi Daphne, is a deciduous 2 to 3′ shrub of bushy habit. The flowers are slightly fragrant, golden yellow, produced during May in umbels terminating the young shoots, 4 to 8 per inflorescence. The fruit is an egg-shaped, 1/4″ diameter, red berry which matures in July-August. It is quite hardy (Zone 3) but difficult to culture successfully. Native of Northwestern China. Introduced 1910.

Daphne mezereum, February Daphne, is a deciduous, erect branched shrub growing 3 to 5′ high and as wide, usually becoming leggy at the base. The flowers are lilac to rosy-purple, very fragrant, produced from the buds of the leafless stems in late March to early April; grouped in 2′s and 3′s; each flower 1/2″ across. The fruit is a red, 1/3″ diameter berry which matures in June. Several authorities have noted that the shrub will do well for years and then suddenly die. No one has a good explanation for the whims of *Daphne*, however, there is a lethal virus which affects *D. mezereum* and this could explain its sudden failings. The variety *alba* has dull white flowers and yellowish fruits; comes true to type from seed and is found in the wild. Selections called 'Paul's White' and 'Bowles' White' have pure white flowers. 'Autumnalis' flowers in the fall and the flowers are larger than the species and equally fragrant and colored. It does not usually bear fruit. *D. mezereum* and the clones can be propagated, although not very easily, by cuttings taken and planted in a mixture of peat moss, loam and sand. Native of Europe and Siberia; found wild, although limitedly so in England; occasionally naturalized in Northeastern states. Introduced in colonial times.

ADDITIONAL NOTES: A choice group of plants for the garden but unfortunately are so fastidious as to cultural requirements that they can rarely be successfully grown. I looked at my extensive slide collection and realized there are only 6 slides of *Daphne*. One can travel to private and public gardens without ever seeing a wealth of *Daphne*. English authorities speculated that most *Daphne* species do best in limestone soils, however, in the Arnold Arboretum several species are growing in a soil of pH 5 to 5.5 which has been amended by peat moss. I do not know the answer to *Daphne* culture and if anyone has the problem solved, please write and I will include it in future editions.

NATIVE HABITAT: Europe, from Spain to Southwest Russia. Introduced 1752.

Davidia involucrata — Dove-tree, sometimes called Handkerchief Tree

FAMILY: Nyssaceae

LEAVES: Alternate, simple, 3 1/5 to 5 1/2″ long, broad-ovate, acuminate, cordate, dentate-serrate with acuminate teeth; strongly veined, finally glabrous above, densely silky-pubescent beneath; petiole 1 2/5 to 2 3/4″ long.

BUDS: Solitary, sessile or the lateral developing into short spurs, rather large, with about half-a-dozen blunt, pale-margined scales.

STEMS: Moderately stout, terete, somewhat zig-zag; pith moderate, rounded, pale, continuous with firmer plates at short intervals; leaf scars moderate, half-elliptical or 3-lobed; little raised; 3 large bundle-traces.

SIZE: Under cultivation 20 to 40′ high and as wide; supposedly in the wild can roam from 40 to 65′ in height.

HARDINESS: Zone 6.

HABIT: Broad pyramidal tree, resembling a linden, especially in youth. The one tree of any size which I have seen was nestled in and under other plants at the National Arboretum. This specimen was rather flat-topped, spreading, with the younger branches slightly pendent. One quickly learns that the literature concerning a particular facet of a tree is often conflicting, i.e., what one writer sees in the shape of a tree another may discern a little differently.

TEXTURE: Medium in leaf; would also be medium in winter.

LEAF COLOR: Bright green in summer, leaves supposedly strong scented; fall color of no consequence.

FLOWERS: Andro-monoecious, crowded in a 3/4" diameter rounded head at the end of a 3" long pendulous peduncle; staminate flowers composed of numerous long stamens with white filaments and red anthers, forming a brush-like mass; pistillate reduced to an egg-shaped ovary, with a short 6-rayed style and a ring of abortive stamens at the top. The real beauty of the *Davidia* lies in two large bracts which subtend each flower. They are white or creamy white of unequal size, the lower being the larger (7" long by 4" wide); the upper bract being 3 to 4" long and 2" wide. They are effective for 10 to 14 days in May. Often the tree does not flower until about 10-years-of-age and even then some trees do not flower every year.

FRUIT: Solitary, ovoid, 1 1/2" long drupe, green with a purplish bloom; becoming russet-colored and speckled with red when ripe; contains a single, hard, ridged nut (endocarp) with 3 to 5 seeds; matures in fall.

CULTURE: Transplant balled and burlapped; prefers a well-drained, moist soil that has been amended with peat moss and the like; prefers light shade but will tolerate sun if the soil is kept moist; water during drought periods; prune in winter.

DISEASES AND INSECTS: None serious.

LANDSCAPE VALUE: Acclaimed by many gardening enthusiasts as the most handsome of flowering trees. That is quite an accolade when one thinks of all the beautiful flowering trees we have at our disposal. The obvious use is that of a specimen. Any tree so grand should not be hidden in the shrubbery. Wyman noted that, for all its good features, it has the bad habits of being slow to flower, does not consistently flower every year and, even though stem and vegetative bud hardy, may not set flower buds in colder climates.

CULTIVARS: Variety *vilmoriniana* differs from the species in that the underside of the leaves are yellowish green or somewhat glaucous, slightly downy on the veins at first but otherwise glabrous. The variety is more common in cultivation than the species and is hardy in Zone 5.

PROPAGATION: According to Bean it is easily propagated by cuttings or by seed. One research report stated that hardwood cuttings taken in mid-January rooted 20 percent without treatment and there was no response to IBA. Leaf-but cuttings taken in September treated with Hormodin #2, placed in sand, shaded, and frequently syringed, rooted 85 percent in five weeks.

NATIVE HABITAT: Native of China in West Szechwan and parts of West Hupeh. Introduced 1904.

Deutzia gracilis — Slender Deutzia

FAMILY: Saxifragaceae

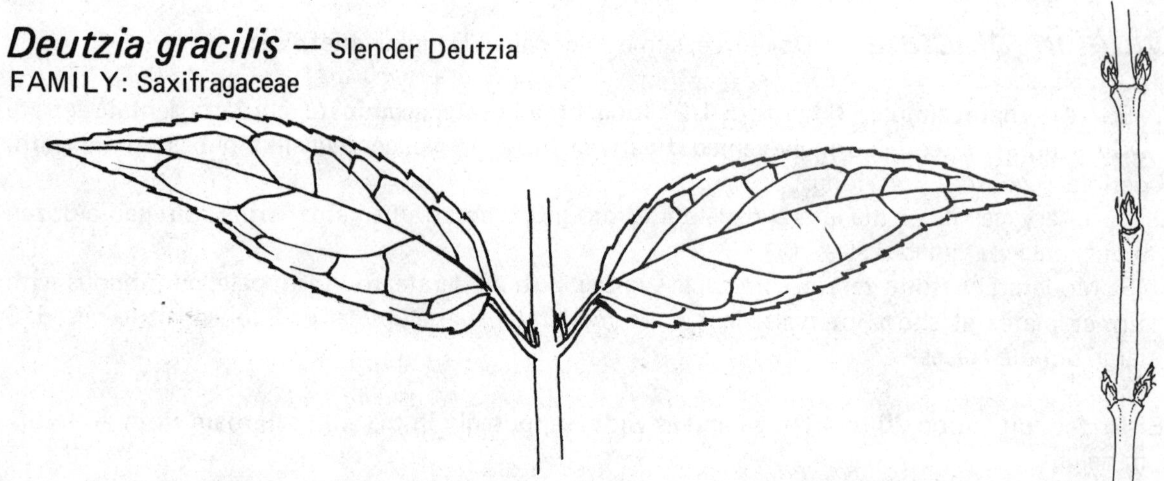

LEAVES: Opposite, simple, oblong-lanceolate, 1 1/5 to 2 2/5" long, rarely to 3 1/4" long, long acuminate, broad-cuneate or rounded at the base, unequally serrate, with scattered stellate hairs above, flat green, nearly glabrous beneath.

BUDS: Ovoid, nearly sessile, with several pairs of outer scales, glabrate, brownish. This bud description is applicable to the following species.

STEM: Yellowish-gray-brown in color; leaf scars—linear; pith-white, hollow after a time.

SIZE: 2 to 4' high by 3 to 4' in width; can grow to 6' high.

HARDINESS: Zone 4.
HABIT: A low, broad mound, graceful and free flowering, with slender ascending branches.
RATE: Slow to medium.
TEXTURE: Medium-fine in leaf; medium in winter.
LEAF COLOR: Flat green in summer, does not color effectively in fall.
FLOWERS: Perfect, pure white, 1/2 to 3/4" across; mid to late May; borne in erect racemes or panicles, 1 1/2 to 3" long. The plants are literally covered with flowers and are quite attractive at this time of year.
FRUIT: Capsule.
CULTURE: Transplant readily, best moved in spring; any good garden soil is acceptable; seems to be pH adaptable; full sun or very light shade; prune after flowering.
DISEASES AND INSECTS: Leafspots, aphids, and leaf miner; basically problem free plants.
LANDSCAPE VALUE: This is probably the best of the deutzias and makes a good hedge, mass, facer or shrub border plant. On our campus seems to be a much more prolific flowerer than *D.* x *lemoinei* and does not exhibit winter injury to the degree of Lemoine.
CULTIVARS: *D. gracilis* was used as a parent of several hybrid deutzias including *D.* x *rosea* with pink petals on the outside and paler within. The cultivar 'Carminea' is a selection from the *D.* x *rosea* group with pale rosy pink petals within, darker pink outside and in bud, about 3/4" across, in large panicles. It is a rather spreading plant, with arching branches, to about 3' high. W. J. Bean calls it one of the most delightful of dwarf deciduous shrubs.
PROPAGATION: All deutzias can be easily rooted from softwood cuttings collected any time in the growing season.
ADDITIONAL NOTES: Deutzias, although usually dependable for flower display, rarely overwhelm one at any time of the year. In northern areas they require annual pruning to remove the dead wood and to keep them looking acceptable. The summer foliage is a blasé green while fall color and fruits are not interesting. The crux of the matter is that if one has limited garden space he/she should look elsewhere for ornament; but in large landscapes, especially shrub borders, the excellent flower display provided by the deutzias is warranted.
NATIVE HABITAT: Japan. Introduced 1880.

Deutzia x *lemoinei* — Lemoine Deutzia

LEAVES: Opposite, simple, elliptic-lanceolate to lanceolate. 1 1/5 to 2 2/5" long, on shoots to 4" long, long acuminate, cuneate at base, sharply serrulate, green on both surfaces, with scattered 5 to 8 rayed hairs beneath.
STEM: Glabrous or nearly so, older with brown exfoliating bark; pith—white.

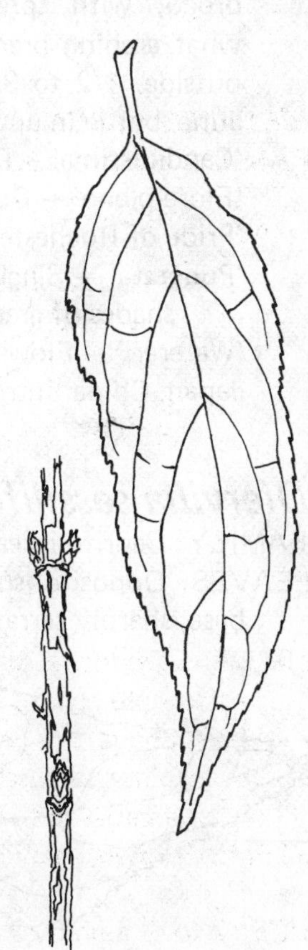

Deutzia x *lemoinei*, Lemoine Deutzia, grows 5 to 7' tall with a similar spread. It is a very twiggy, dense, round, erect branched shrub. The flowers are pure white, 5/8" across, after *D. gracilis* usually about late May; borne in 1 to 3" long erect pyramidal corymbs. Some authorities say this species is more beautiful and effective than *D. gracilis*.

'Avalanche' — bears white flowers in small clusters on arching branches, very dense and compact, about 4' high.

'Compacta' — Dwarf and compact in habit.

Zone 5 (4).

Deutzia x *magnifica*, Showy Deutzia, is the result of a cross between *D. scabra* x *D. vilmoriniae.* This hybrid species is often listed as growing 6' high but I have seen 8 to 10' specimens. The plant is strongly multistemmed, usually leggy at the base, and clothed with foliage over the upper one-half. The flowers are the best I have seen among the deutzias. They are white, double, borne in dense 1 1/2 to 2 2/5" long panicles in late May or early June and are extremely eye-catching. Originated before 1910. Zone 5. Several clones include:

'Eburnea' – Single white flowers in loose panicles.

'Latifolia' – Single white flowers up to 1 1/2" across.

'Longipetala' – White, long petaled flowers.

Deutzia scabra — Fuzzy Deutzia

LEAVES: Opposite, simple, ovate to oblong-lanceolate, 1 to 3" long, acute or obtusely acuminate, usually rounded at the base, crenate-denticulate, dull green, stellate-pubescent on both sides, beneath with 10 to 15 rayed hairs.

STEMS: Brown, rarely gray-brown, tardily exfoliating bark; stellate pubescent when young, pith–brown, excavated, finally hollow.

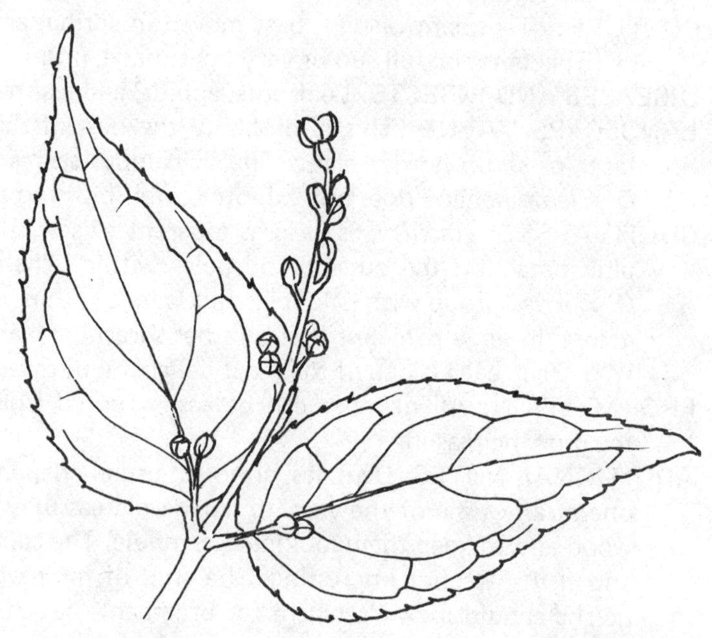

Deutzia scabra, Fuzzy Deutzia, grows 6 to 10' tall with a spread of 4 to 8'. It is an oval or obovate, round topped shrub, taller than broad, with spreading, somewhat arching branches and often straggly in appearance. Flowers pure white or tinged pink outside, 1/2 to 3/4" long and wide; flowers 10 to 14 days after *D. gracilis,* usually in early June, borne in upright, 3 to 6" cylindrical panicles. Cultivars include:

'Candidissima' – Double, pure white.

'Flore-pleno' – Double, white, tinged with rosy purple on outside of corolla.

'Pride of Rochester' – Similar to the above but the rosy tinge is paler.

'Punctata' – Single, pure white flowers, with leaves strikingly marbled with white and 2 or 3 shades of green.

'Watereri' – Flowers 1" across, single; petals rosy outside.

Japan, China. Introduced 1822. Zone 5.

Diervilla sessilifolia — Southern Bush-honeysuckle

FAMILY: Caprifoliaceae

LEAVES: Opposite, subsessile, ovate-lanceolate, 2 to 6" long, acuminate, cordate or rounded at base, sharply serrate.

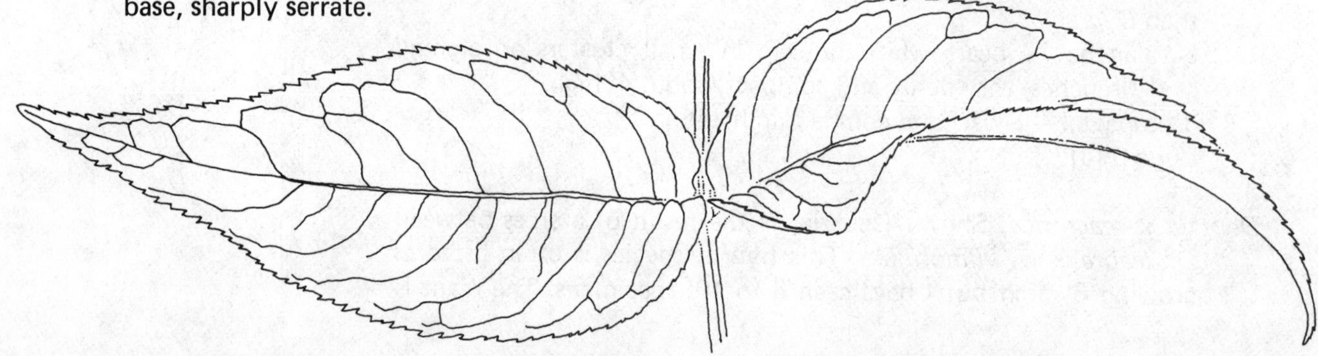

BUDS: Often superposed, sessile, oblong, appressed with about 5 pairs of exposed scales.

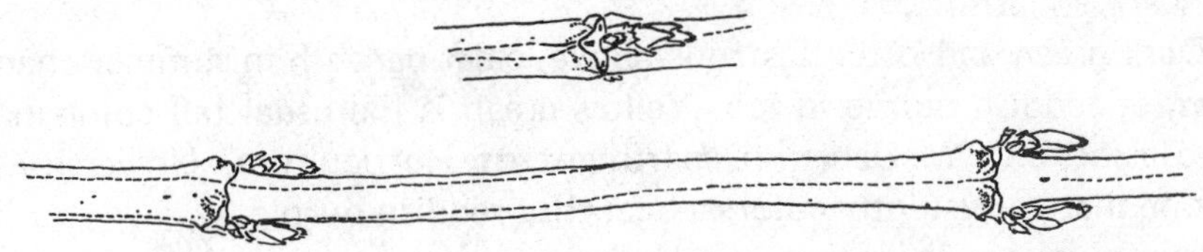

STEM: Rounded, brownish, with 4 crisp-puberulent ridges decurrent from the nodes; pith—moderate, pale, continuous.

Diervilla sessilifolia, Southern Bush-honeysuckle, is a low growing, stoloniferous, 3 to 5′ high and 3 to 5′ or greater spreading, deciduous shrub; the foliage is glossy dark green; the flowers are sulfur yellow, 1/2″ long, June-July into August, borne in 2 to 3″ diameter, 3 to 7-flowered cymes on current season's growth; very adaptable and should be pruned back in early spring; makes a good filler, possibly facer plant; roots readily from cuttings; Long Island to Georgia and Alabama. 1844. Zone 4.

Diospyros virginiana — Common Persimmon

FAMILY: Ebenaceae

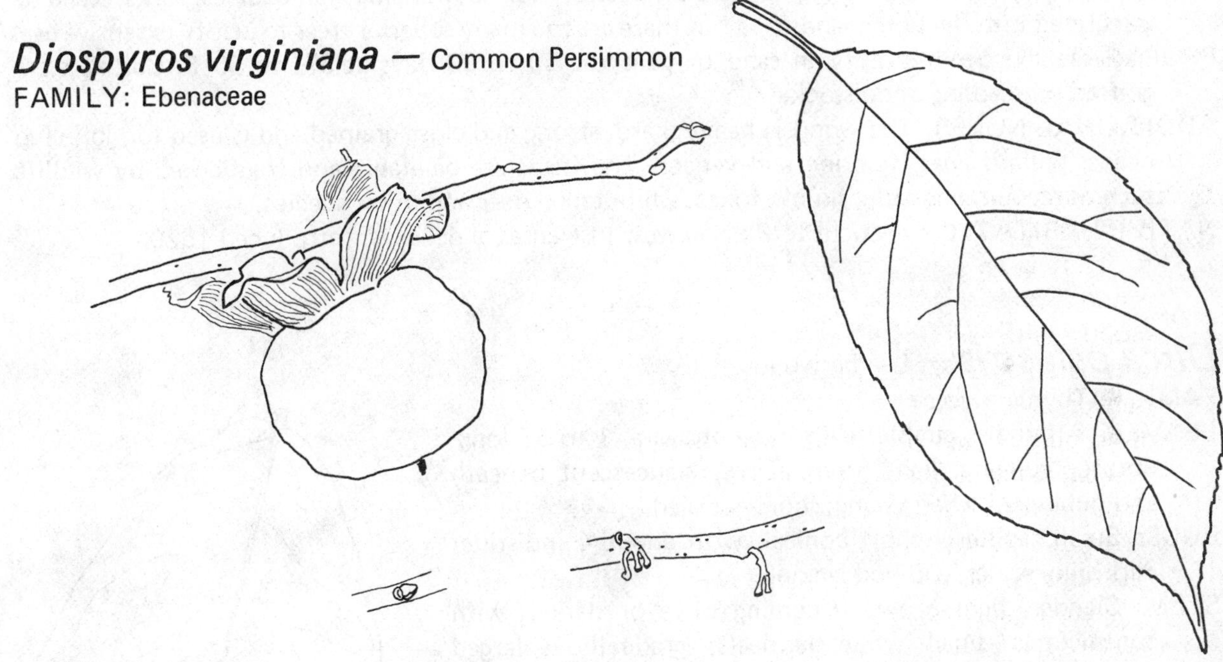

LEAVES: Alternate, simple, 2 1/4 to 5 1/2″ long, ovate to elliptic, rounded at base, lustrous dark green above, paler beneath, glabrous at maturity.

BUDS: Solitary, sessile, with 2 greatly overlapping scales, 1/8″ long, ovoid, acute, reddish black, glabrous, terminal bud lacking.

STEM: Slender, gray-red-brown, pubescent or glabrous.

FRUIT: Berry, globose, 1 to 1 1/2″ long, yellowish to pale orange, 1 to 8 seeded, edible, subtended by 4 persistent calyx lobes, persistent into winter.

BARK: Thick, hard, dark gray-black, in distinctive square, scaly blocks.

SIZE: 35 to 60′ in height with a spread of 20 to 35′; can grow to 90′ or larger but this rarely occurs.

HARDINESS: Zone 4.

HABIT: Tree with slender oval-rounded crown, often very symmetrical in outline.

RATE: Slow to medium; one authority reported 15′ over a 20 year period in England.

TEXTURE: Medium in leaf and winter.

BARK: On old trunks the bark is thick, dark gray or brownish to almost black and is prominently broken into scaly, squarish blocks.

LEAF COLOR: Dark green and often lustrous above, paler beneath in summer changing to yellow-green, yellow, or reddish purple in fall. Yellow-green is the usual fall color in Central Illinois although Professor J.C. McDaniel, Department of Horticulture, University of Illinois has selected a clone that consistently colors a beautiful reddish purple.

FLOWERS: Dioecious, although sometimes both sexes present on same tree; white or whitish; staminate usually in three's about 2/5" long, with 16 stamens; pistillate short-stalked, solitary, 3/5" long, borne in May; the peduncle of the male flower persistent and woody.

FRUIT: An edible berry, yellowish to pale orange, 1 to 1 1/2" across, subtended by 4 persistent calyx lobes; ripens after frost in late September through October, although cultivars are available which produce edible fruit without frost treatment.

CULTURE: Somewhat difficult to transplant and should be moved balled and burlapped as a small tree in early spring; prefers moist, well-drained, sandy soils but will do well on low fertility, dry soils; in Southern Illinois the tree grows on coal stripped lands and often forms thickets on dry, eroding slopes; pH adaptable; full sun; prune in winter; does well in cities.

DISEASES AND INSECTS: None serious if the tree is grown for ornamental purposes.

LANDSCAPE VALUE: Interesting native tree, possibly for naturalizing, golf courses, parks, could be integrated into the home landscape but there are too many superior trees to justify extensive use.

PROPAGATION: Seed, stratify in sand or peat for 60 to 90 days at 37° to 50°F. Cultivars are grafted on seedling understock.

ADDITIONAL NOTES: The wood is heavy, hard, strong and close grained and is used for golf club heads, billiard cues, flooring and veneer. The fruits are palatable and frequented by wildlife such as racoon, opossum, skunk, foxes, white-tailed deer and other species.

NATIVE HABITAT: Connecticut to Florida west to Kansas and Texas. Introduced 1629.

Dirca palustris — Leatherwood

FAMILY: Thymelaeaceae

LEAVES: Alternate, simple, elliptic to obovate, 1 to 3" long, obtuse, cuneate, light green above, glaucescent beneath and pubescent when young; short petioled.

BUDS: Small, solitary, short conical, with about 4 indistinct dark silky scales; end-bud lacking.

STEM: Slender, light brown becoming olive or darker, with conspicuous small white lenticels; gradually enlarged upwards through the season's growth. Called leatherwood because the bark is very leathery and it is quite difficult to remove a piece of broken stem.

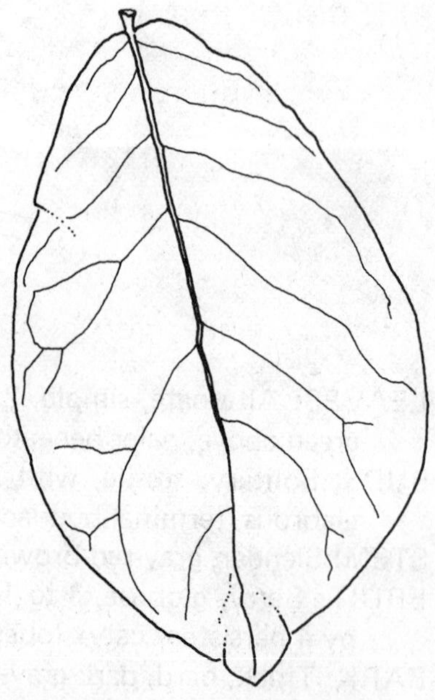

SIZE: Variable over its native range; 3 to 6' in height.

HARDINESS: Zone 4.

HABIT: Much branched, rather dense, oval to rounded shrub.

RATE: Slow to medium.

TEXTURE: Medium.

LEAF COLOR: Light green, by some authorities yellow-green; may turn clear yellow in fall.

FLOWERS: Perfect, pale yellow, 3 to 4 in an inflorescence; not overwhelming but interesting by virtue of their March flowering date.

FRUIT: Oval drupe, 1/3" long, pale green or reddish; containing one large, shining, brown seed; June-July; seldom seen as it is hidden among the leaves and falls soon after maturity.

CULTURE: Thrives in moist to wet, shady areas; prefers a deep soil supplied with organic matter; in Turkey Run State Park, Indiana, the plant appears to follow the water courses through the ravines and dominates in the alluvial soils.

DISEASES AND INSECTS: None serious.

LANDSCAPE VALUE: Interesting native shrub well-adapted to wet shady areas. If natural in an area it is worth leaving. The flowers are borne on leafless stems and are interesting.

PROPAGATION: Seed can be sown as soon as ripe. Layering offers a method of vegetative propagation.

ADDITIONAL NOTES: The Indians used the bark for bow strings and fish lines and in the manufacture of baskets.

NATIVE HABITAT: New Brunswick and Ontario to Florida and Missouri. Introduced 1750.

Elaeagnus angustifolia — Russian-olive

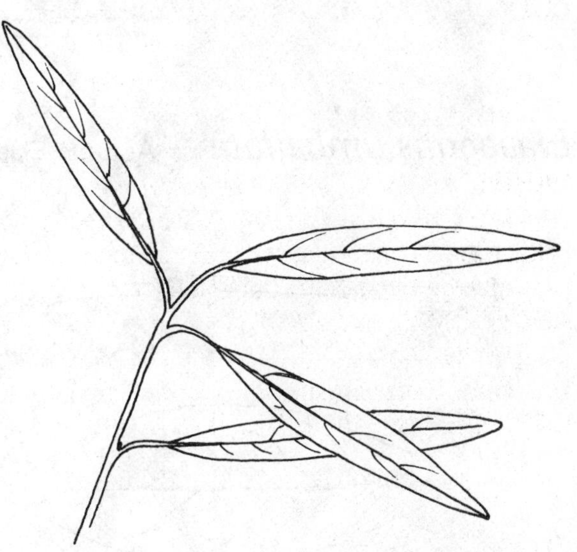

FAMILY: Elaeagnaceae

LEAVES: Alternate, simple, oblong-lanceolate to linear-lanceolate, 1 3/5 to 3″ long, acute to obtuse, usually broad-cuneate at base, petiole—1/5 to 1/3″ long.

BUDS: Small, solitary, gray-brown, sessile, round, conical or oblong, with about 4 exposed silvery scales.

STEM: Young branches silvery, sometimes thorny, covered with scales. Older branches assuming a glistening brown color, pith—brown.

SIZE: 12 to 15′ (20′) tall and as wide, occasionally will grow to 30 to 40′.

HARDINESS: Zone 2.

HABIT: Large shrub or small tree of round outline, often quite open and of light texture.

RATE: Medium to fast.

TEXTURE: Medium-fine in leaf; medium-coarse in winter.

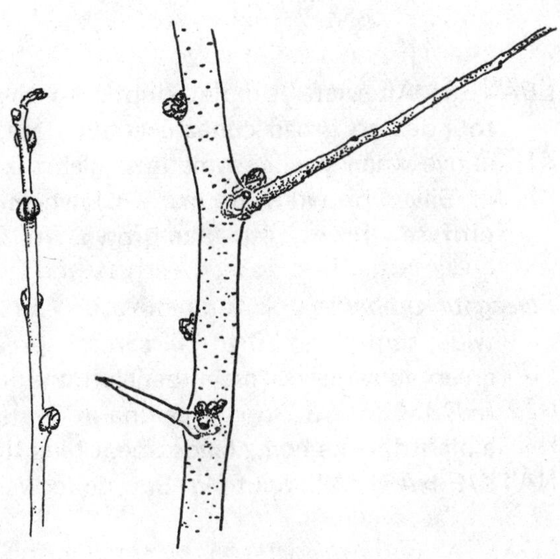

LEAF COLOR: Silver-green to gray-green in summer and one of our most effective plants for gray foliage.

FLOWERS: Perfect or polygamous, apetalous, silvery or whitish outside, yellow inside, 3/8″ long, fragrant; mid to late May; one to three together.

FRUIT: Drupe-like, 2/5″ long, yellow and coated with silvery scales, August through September, the flesh is sweet and mealy and in the Orient a sherbet is made from it.

CULTURE: Transplants readily, can be grown in any soil, but does best in light, sandy loams; withstands seacoast, highway conditions, drought and alkali soils; prefers sunny open exposure; can be pruned into a tight structure. The secret to keeping this plant looking good is to keep it vigorous.

DISEASES AND INSECTS: Leaf spots, cankers, rusts, *Verticillium* wilt, crown gall, oleaster-thistle aphid, and scales.

LANDSCAPE VALUE: For grayish foliage effect it is difficult to beat; can be used for hedges, highways, seacoasts, about anywhere salt is a problem; possibly an accent plant in the shrub border.

PROPAGATION: Seed should be stratified for 60 to 90 days at 34 to 50°F. Cuttings collected in mid-October rooted after treatment with 40 ppm IBA for two hours but the percentage was poor.

RELATED SPECIES:

Elaeagnus multiflora, Cherry Elaeagnus, is a wide spreading almost flat-topped shrub with rather stiff branches (grows 6 to 10′ high and as wide). Foliage is a silvery green (green above, silvery below); fruits are red, scaly, 3/5″ long, of pleasant acid flavor, June; birds seem to like the fruits; as adaptable or more so than *E. angustifolia.* China, Japan. 1862. Zone 4.

Elaeagnus umbellata — Autumn Elaeagnus

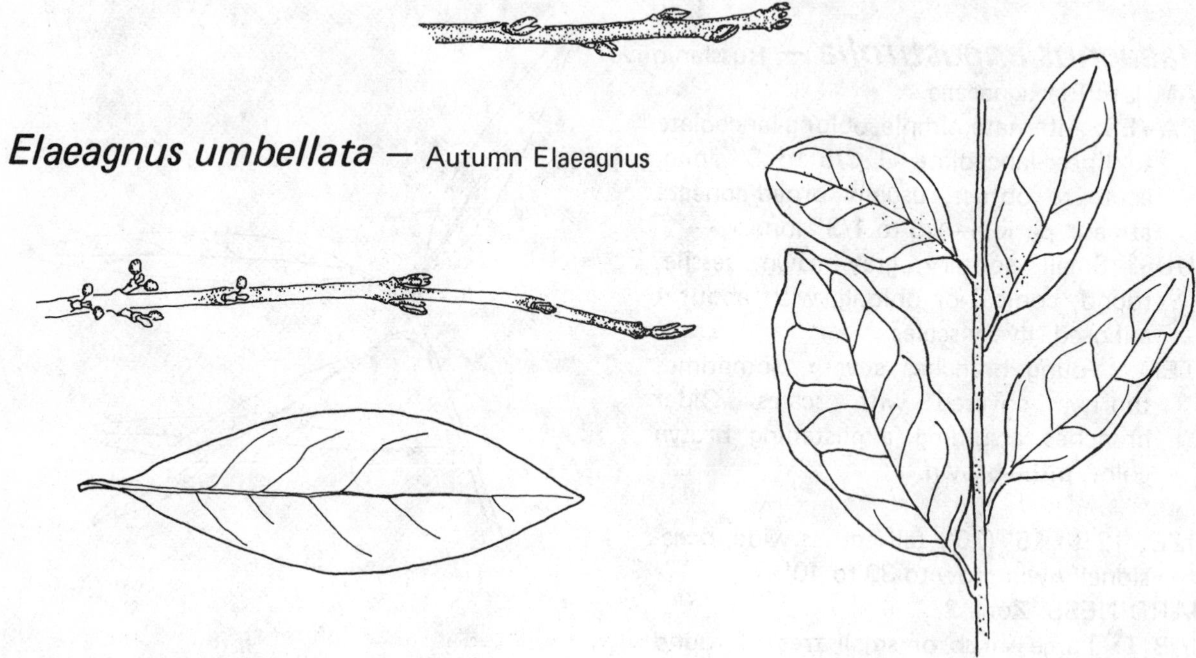

LEAVES: Alternate, simple, elliptic to ovate-oblong, 1 to 3″ long, obtuse to short-acuminate, rounded to broad cuneate at the base, often with crisped margin, usually with silvery scales above when young, sometimes glabrous, silvery beneath and usually mixed with brown scales.

STEM: Silver brown with many brownish scales which give a speckled appearance, spines are profusely borne, pith—rich brown.

Elaeagnus umbellata, Autumn-olive or Autumn Elaeagnus, is a large (12 to 18′ tall by 12 to 18′ wide, sometimes 20 to 30′ across) spreading, often spiny branched shrub. The foliage is bright green above, silver green beneath; the fruits are silvery mixed with brown scales finally turning red, 1/4 to 1/3″ long, ripening in September to October; sold for conservation purposes; not a plant for the home landscape. China, Korea, Japan. 1830. Zone 3.

NATIVE HABITAT: Southern Europe to Western and Central Asia, Altai and Himalayas.

Enkianthus campanulatus — Redvein Enkianthus

FAMILY: Ericaceae

LEAVES: Alternate, mostly crowded at the end of branches, elliptic to rhombic-elliptic, 1 1/5 to 3″ long, acute or acuminate, appressed-serrulate with aristate teeth, with scattered bristly hairs above and on the veins beneath.

BUDS: Minute, sunken and in the notch of the leaf scar, solitary, sessile, indistinctly scaly, the flower buds large.

STEM: Slender, 3-sided or rounded, often reddish.

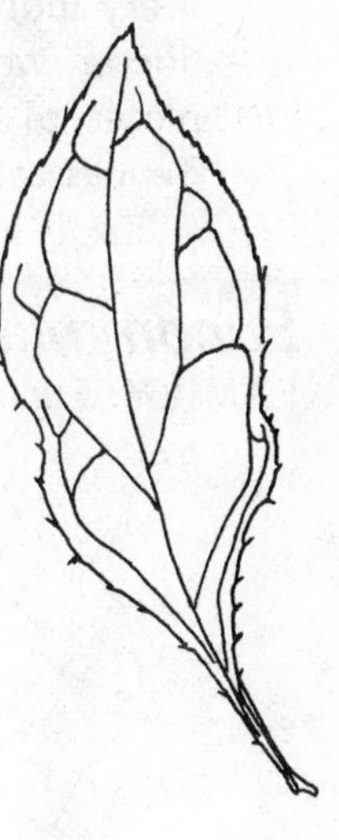

SIZE: 6 to 8′ in cold climates but can grow from 15 to 30′.

HARDINESS: Zone 4.

HABIT: Narrow, upright shrub or small tree with layered branches and tufted foliage.

RATE: Slow.

TEXTURE: Medium in all seasons.

LEAF COLOR: Bright to medium green in summer; brilliant orange and red in fall.

FLOWERS: Perfect, yellowish or light orange, veined with red, 1/3 to 1/2″ long; May, about the time the leaves are developing, from terminal bud of previous year's growth; very dainty and delicate.

FRUIT: Capsule.

CULTURE: Similar to rhododendrons, definitely acid soil requiring; full sun or partial shade.

DISEASES AND INSECTS: None serious.

LANDSCAPE VALUE: Excellent for flower and fall color, nice specimen, combines well with rhododendrons, nice around a patio.

CULTIVARS:

'Albiflorus' — White flowers with no veins.

var. *palibinii* — Red flowers.

PROPAGATION: Seed, see under *Calluna,* very easy to grow from seed, almost like beans. Cuttings collected in late May rooted 80% without treatment.

RELATED SPECIES:

Enkianthus deflexus, Bent Enkianthus, is a narrow, upright shrub with layered branches reaching 10 to 20′ in height. Foliage is dark green in summer; scarlet in fall; flowers are yellowish red with darker veins, 1/2″ diameter, May, borne in umbel-like racemes; flowers are larger and showier than Redvein, however, not as hardy. Himalayas, Western China. 1878. Zone 5 to 6.

Enkianthus perulatus, White Enkianthus, grows to 6′ high and about as wide. The foliage is bright green in summer; scarlet in fall; flowers are white, urn-shaped, 1/3″ long, early May before the leaves in 3 to 10-flowered nodding umbel-like racemes. This is a neater shrub than the other species but hard to find in the trade. Japan. 1870. Zone 5.

NATIVE HABITAT: Japan. 1870. Zone 4.

Epigaea repens — Trailing Arbutus

Epigaea repens, Trailing Arbutus (Ericaceae), is, like *Andromeda polifolia,* one of the untamed members of Ericaceae. It resists cultivation but is deserving of every attempt that die-hard plantsmen make. The habit is one of a flat (4 to 6″ high by 2′ spread) evergreen mat which forms dense cover; in favorable locations it will carpet large areas but, alas, intrusion and disturbance by man puts it to rot. The foliage is leathery, of a rather dark glossy green, slightly bronzed by rusty hairs. The flowers are perfect, white through pink, 5/8″ long by 1/2″ wide, exceedingly fragrant; April; 4 to 6 together in a dense terminal raceme. Fruit is a whitish, berry-like, 1/2″ diameter capsule. Extremely difficult to transplant and perpetuate; requires an acid, sandy or gravelly soil which has been mulched with decayed oak leaves or pine needles; best to move as a container-grown plant for the delicate roots are easily injured; shade or partial shade is advisable but freedom from man and his activities is even more necessary. This plant could be one where a mycorrhizal association plays a significant role in its survival. It could be that transplanted specimens do not develop the fungal relationship that is necessary for their survival. A very dainty, delicate evergreen ground cover that presents a challenge to every individual who considers him- or herself a true plant-person. There is a cultivar termed 'Plena' which is a double-flowered type. Usually propagated from cuttings although large pieces of "sod" may be utilized. Native from Massachusetts to Florida west to Ohio and Tennessee. Introduced 1736. Zone 2. The state flower of Massachusetts.

Eucommia ulmoides — Hardy Rubber Tree

FAMILY: Eucommiaceae

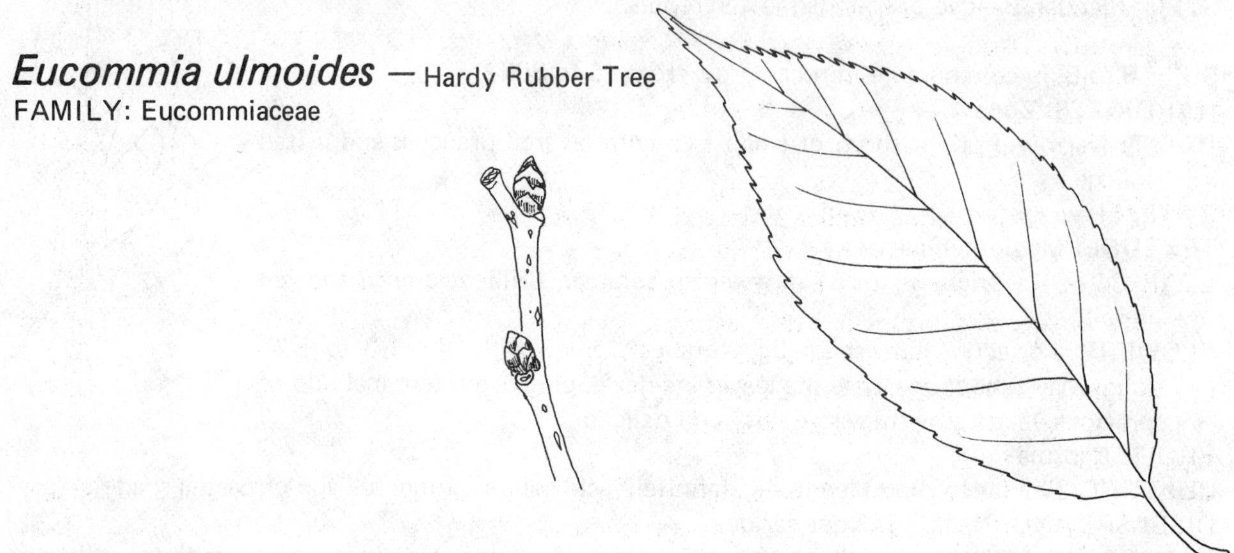

LEAVES: Alternate, simple, 3 to 6" long, elliptic or ovate to oblong-ovate, acuminate, broad-cuneate or rounded, serrate, glabrous above and slightly rugose at maturity. Leaf when torn exhibits rubbery substance.

BUDS: Imbricate, sessile, ovoid, 3/16" long, terminal lacking, ending in a leaf, chestnut brown.

STEM: Stout, bloomy, olive brown, pith — chambered. Bark when stripped exhibiting elastic (rubbery) strings.

SIZE: 40 to 60' in height with an equal or greater spread.

HARDINESS: Zone 4.

HABIT: Rounded to broad-spreading tree of dapper outline.

RATE: Medium, 30' over a 20 year period.

TEXTURE: Medium in all seasons.

LEAF COLOR: Lustrous dark green in summer (very handsome); fall color is non-existent as the leaves fall green or a poor yellowish green.

FLOWERS: Dioecious, inconspicuous and ornamentally unimportant.

FRUIT: Capsule-like with compressed wings, 1 1/2" long.

CULTURE: Transplants readily; very soil tolerant; resists drought; pH adaptable; full sun.

DISEASES AND INSECTS: None serious.

LANDSCAPE VALUE: Excellent shade tree for many areas; outstanding summer foliage that is completely free of pests; excellent for Midwest, at least the Central Illinois area; the largest male specimen east of the Mississippi is located on the University of Illinois campus and the largest female in Spring Grove Cemetery, Cincinnati, Ohio.

PROPAGATION: Cuttings made from the current year's growth and taken in mid-summer will root in sand in a few weeks.

ADDITIONAL NOTES: Only rubber producing tree for the central and northern parts of the country. Rubber content is about 3% on a dry weight basis, however, the extraction is difficult.

NATIVE HABITAT: Central China. Introduced 1896.

Euonymus alatus — Winged Euonymus

FAMILY: Celastraceae

LEAVES: Opposite to subopposite, simple, short-stalked, elliptic to obovate, 1 1/5 to 2" long, acute, finely and sharply serrate.

BUDS: Imbricate, green-brown-red, 6 to 8 pairs of bud scales, conical, ovoid, acute, glabrous, strongly divergent, actually breaking the continuous wing.

STEM: Green to brown with 2 to 4 armed corky wings (prominent).

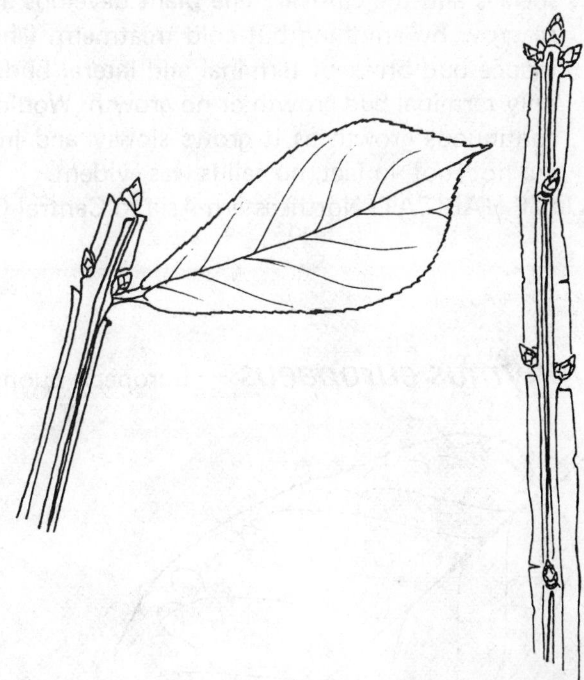

SIZE: 15 to 20′ in height, similar in spread. Here is a classic example of how the size descriptions given in the literature do not adequately estimate the actual landscape size. Usually listed as 9 to 10′, this shrub defies description and develops into a 15 to 20′ well-preserved specimen.

HARDINESS: Zone 3.

HABIT: Mounded to horizontal spreading flat-topped shrub, usually broader than high. Extremely effective and well-preserved in the winter landscape. Does not develop the "garbage can" look of many shrubs, always an aristocrat even under the most demanding of conditions.

RATE: Slow.

TEXTURE: Medium in leaf; medium in winter, the distinctive corky-winged branches are very effective in the winter landscape and their beauty is renewed with each new fallen snow.

LEAF COLOR: Flat medium to dark green, very clean looking foliage, fall color is usually a brilliant red. One of the most consistent fall coloring shrubs, seldom disappointing. Seems to color as well in the Midwest as it does in the eastern states.

FLOWERS: Ornamentally unimportant, perfect, yellow-green, May to early June.

FRUIT: Capsule, red, September through late fall, not particularly showy for fruits are borne under the foliage. Seed is actually the ornamental part of fruit as it possesses an orange-red seed coat (aril) which is exposed when the capsule dehisces. By the time the leaves have fallen many of the fruits have also abscised thus minimizing the ornamental quality.

CULTURE: Easily transplanted balled and burlapped, very adaptable plant tolerating widely divergent soils, seems to do well in heavy shade and still develop good fall color, not tolerant of water logged soils, best growth is achieved in well-drained soils; pH adaptable; withstands heavy pruning.

DISEASES AND INSECTS: None serious.

LANDSCAPE VALUE: Unlimited and, therefore, overused; excellent for hedging, in groups, as a specimen plant, borders, screening, massing; plants used near water are very effective in the fall where the brilliant red foliage color is reflected off the water; makes an excellent foundation plant because of horizontal lines, clean foliage, and interesting stem characters.

CULTIVARS:

Euonymus alatus 'Compactus' — Dwarf Winged Euonymus

Corky wings usually not as pronounced. Finer textured branches and more compact habit. Finer, slender branches, usually more densely borne, quite rounded in habit, ultimately growing to 10′, definitely not a small, diminutive form; makes an excellent hedge plant without pruning; perhaps growing to 15′.

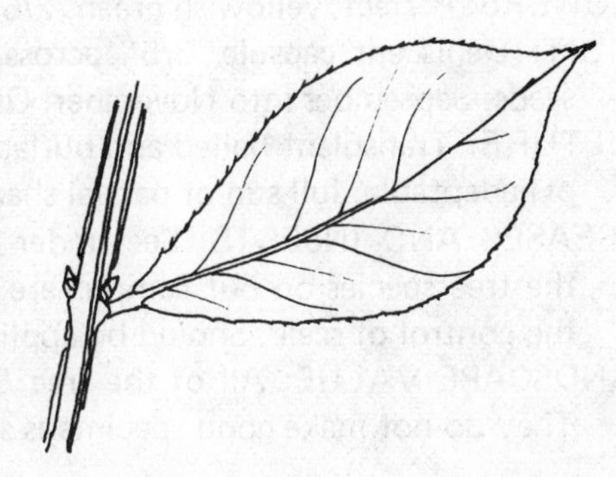

PROPAGATION: Cuttings, anytime in leaf, 1000 ppm IBA. I have had 100% success every time with this species and the cultivar. The plant develops a deep bud rest and cannot practically be induced to grow by anything but cold treatment. I have found 90 to 120 days at 40°F sufficient to induce bud break of terminal and lateral buds. Any time period less than this has resulted in only terminal bud growth or no growth. Would be a good plant to experiment with for inducing continuous growth as it grows slowly and in short flushes. Interestingly, hardwood cuttings did not root, in fact, no callus was evident.

NATIVE HABITAT: Northeastern Asia to Central China. Introduced about 1860.

Euonymus europaeus — European Euonymus

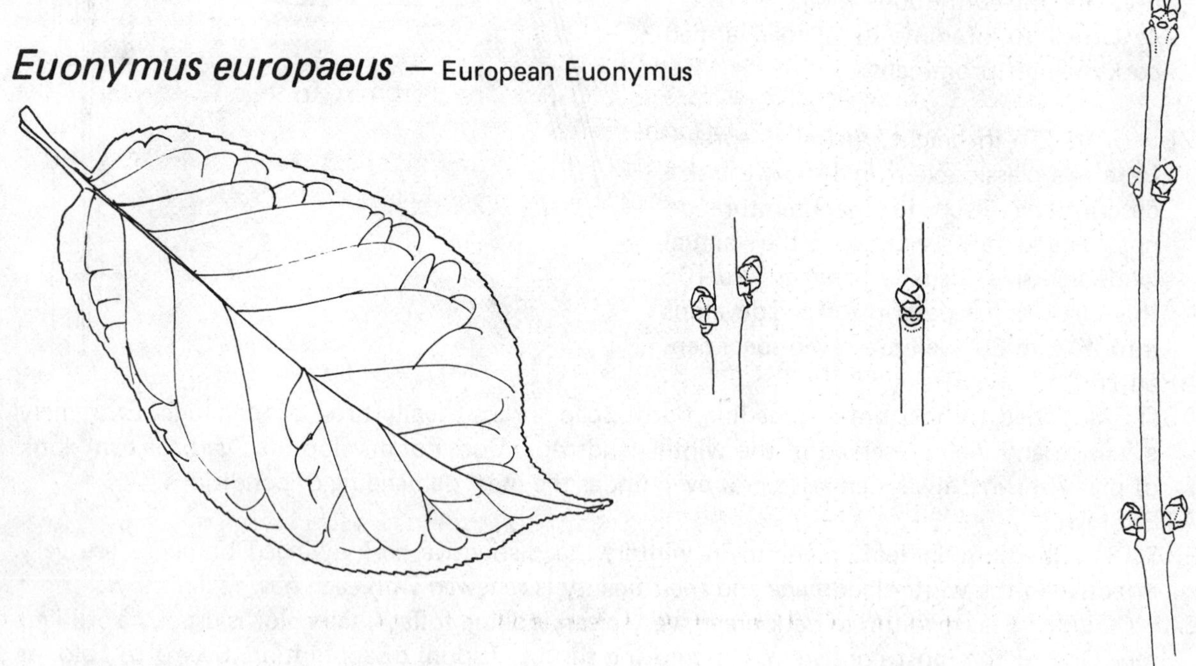

LEAVES: Opposite, simple, elliptic-ovate to lance-oblong, 1 1/5 to 3 1/5" long, acuminate, cuneate, crenate-serrate, petiole 1/4 to 1/2" long.

BUDS: Imbricate, plump, resembling Norway Maple bud, greenish often tinged with red.

STEM: Slender, green-red, glabrous the first year, usually becoming light gray-brown the second.

FRUIT: Capsule, 4-lobed, pink to red, seed white, aril orange.

SIZE: 12 to 30' high and 10 to 25' wide.

HARDINESS: Zone 3.

HABIT: Narrow upright when young, broadening with age, taller than broad at maturity, dense.

RATE: Medium to fast.

TEXTURE: Medium in leaf and winter.

LEAF COLOR: Dull dark green in summer; fall color varies from yellow-green to yellow to a good reddish purple.

FLOWERS: Perfect, yellowish green, 2/5" across; May; 3 to 5 flowered cyme. Not showy.

FRUIT: Dehiscent capsule, 3/5" across, of pink to red color, 4-lobed, opening to expose orange seeds; September into November. Quite attractive in fruit.

CULTURE: Transplant balled and burlapped; tolerant of most soils as long as they are well-drained; pH adaptable; full sun or partial shade; very tough and tolerant.

DISEASES AND INSECTS: See under *E. fortunei.* The most significant problem is scale and all the tree species on our campus are affected. Timing of spray application is very important in the control of scale. Should be applied when the young crawlers are moving about.

LANDSCAPE VALUE: All of the tree *Euonymus* can be used in groupings, screens and massings. They do not make good specimens simply because of lack of ornamental characters.

CULTIVARS:

'Albus' or var. *albus* — Fruits white. Does not produce the rich effect of the species but is very striking in contrast with it.

'Aldenhamensis' — Brilliant, large pink capsule borne on longer, more pendulous stalks than the species; more fruitful than the species.

var. *intermedius* — A heavy fruiter with bright red capsules; supposedly produces enormous crops of fruits.

'Pumilus' — Dwarf, upright form, about 3 to 4' high.

'Red Cascade' — A free-fruiting form. There is a cultivar called 'Red Caps' which, according to several individuals in the midwest, has proven the best of the tree *Euonymus.* Whether 'Red Caps' and 'Red Cascade' are synonyms for the same plant is not known by this author. Wyman noted that the color of the fruit may vary slightly, but when viewed from a distance there is little to choose among them, unless one is very particular about the exact shade of red or pink color in the fruits.

PROPAGATION: Seed should be stratified at 68 to 77°F for 60 to 90 days followed by 32 to 50°F for 60 to 120 days. Cuttings should be taken in June and July and treated with IBA.

RELATED SPECIES:

Euonymus atropurpureus — Eastern Wahoo

LEAVES: Opposite, simple, elliptic to ovate-elliptic, 1 3/5 to 5" long, acuminate, serrulate, pubescent beneath, petiole 2/5 to 4/5" long, dark green.

BUDS: Small, green tinged red, appressed with 5 to 6 scales.

STEM: Slender, greenish, glabrous, usually more or less (mostly less) 4-angled, often with slight corky lines.

FRUIT: Capsule deeply 4-lobed, crimson, seed brown with scarlet aril.

GROWTH HABIT: Large shrub or small tree with wide, flat-topped, irregular crown. 12 to 24' high.

NATIVE HABITAT: New York to Florida, west to Minnesota, Nebraska, Oklahoma and Texas. Introduced 1756. Zone 4.

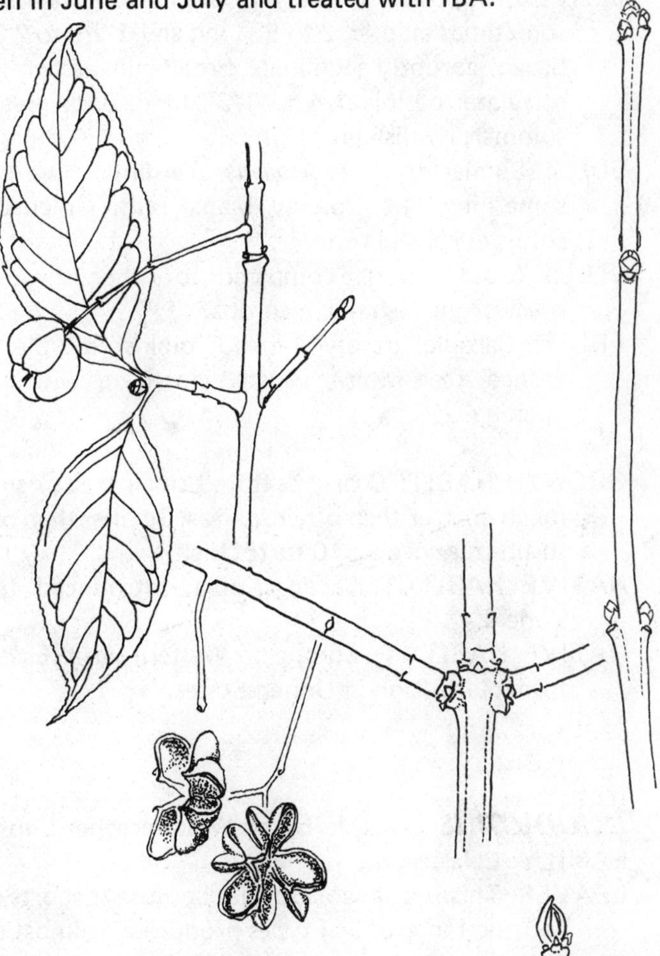

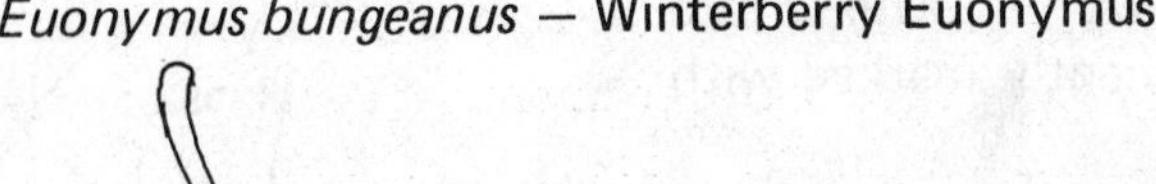

Euonymus bungeanus — Winterberry Euonymus

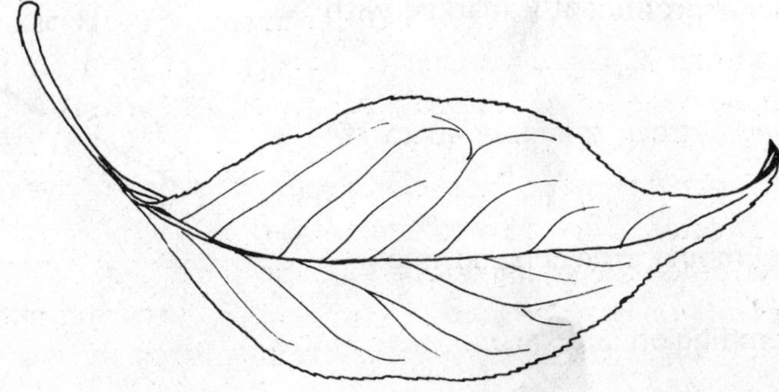

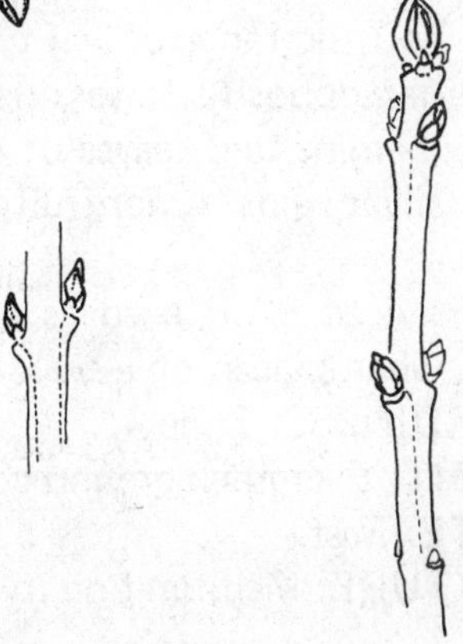

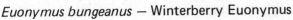

LEAVES: Opposite to subopposite, simple, elliptic-ovate to elliptic-lanceolate, 2 to 4" long, long acuminate, broad-cuneate at base, serrulate, petiole 1/3 to 1" long; light to medium green.
BUDS: Terminal (unique), outer bud scales upright creating a stockade-like appearance around meristem; lateral-imbricate, appressed, green-red-brown.
STEM: Slender, often weeping, greenish, glabrous, almost round, often with slight corky lines.
FRUIT: Capsule, deeply 4-lobed, yellowish to pinkish white, seeds white or pinkish with orange aril, usually open at apex.

GROWTH HABIT: Rounded small shrub or tree with pendulous branches to 18 to 24' in height.
NATIVE HABITAT: Northern China and Manchuria. Introduced 1883. Zone 4. Variety *semipersistens* has fruits which remain late in fall; *pendulus* has weeping branchlets.

Euonymus hamiltonianus sieboldianus — Yeddo Euonymus

(Euonymus yedoensis)
LEAVES: Opposite, simple, obovate to obovate-oblong, sometimes elliptic, 2 to 5" long and 1 2/5 to 2 2/5" broad, abruptly acuminate, broad-cuneate, crenate-serrulate; petiole 1/4 to 1/2" long, dark green in summer; reddish purple in fall.
BUDS: Similar to *E. europaeus.* Terminal bud looks something like Norway Maple bud. Greenish in color, purplish in winter.
STEM: Stout, coarse compared to other shrub-tree species, greenish red, glabrous.
FRUIT: Capsule, deeply 4-lobed, pinkish purple, aril orange, seed white, usually closed or with small opening.

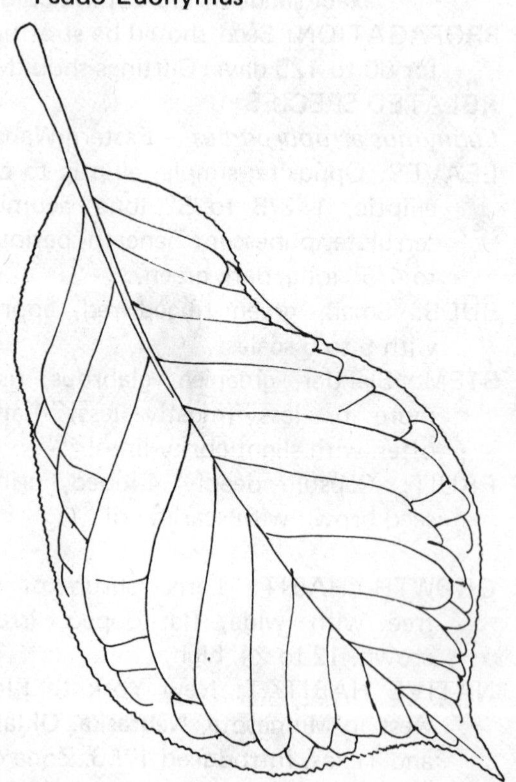

GROWTH HABIT: Coarse textured small tree or shrub, much coarser than other species. Smaller than other shrub-tree species, 10 to 15' high.
NATIVE HABITAT: Japan, Korea. Introduced 1865. Zone 4.
NATIVE HABITAT: Europe to Western Asia. Escaped from cultivation in United States.

Euonymus fortunei — Wintercreeper Euonymus

FAMILY: Celastraceae
LEAVES: This is a variable species because it sports (mutates) so readily and the range of leaf types produced is almost endless. The species has opposite leaves, usually 1" long or less, with crenate-serrate margins and leaves of dark green color prominently marked with silver veins. A nonfruiting form.

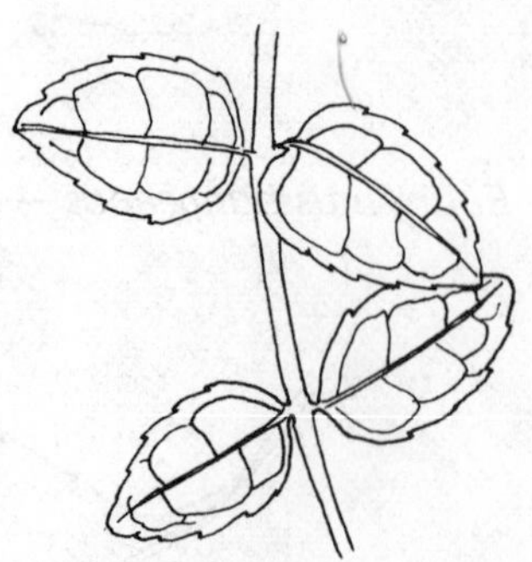

SIZE: 4 to 6" if used as a ground cover but can scramble 40 to 70' when placed on a structure.
HARDINESS: Zone 4.
HABIT: Evergreen ground cover or high climbing, true clinging vine.
RATE: Fast.
TEXTURE: Medium-fine to medium depending on cultivar.

LEAF COLOR: Depends on cultivar but the species as I interpret it has small leaves less than 1" long, the leaves are dark green almost bluish with silver-nerved veins. The morphology changes considerably from the juvenile to the adult forms.

FLOWERS: Only on adult types. Perfect, whitish, June-July, axillary cymes; not particularly showy.

FRUIT: Dehiscent capsule usually with a pinkish to scarlet color which opens to expose the seeds which have an orange-red aril (fleshy seed coat), October-November and often persisting.

CULTURE: Extremely easy to culture, transplants readily; tolerant of most soils except swampy, extremely wet conditions; tolerates full sun and heavy shade; pH adaptable.

DISEASES AND INSECTS: Anthracnose, crown gall (bacterial disease of considerable importance), leaf spots, powdery mildews, aphids, thrips, and scales (these have proved lethal on many plantings especially those containing 'Vegetus', 'Coloratus' and the tree species such as *E. europaeus, E. bungeanus* and *E. yedoensis*). Many of our campus plantings have been ruined.

LANDSCAPE VALUE: Multitudinous depending on cultivar; ground cover, vine, wall cover, low hedge, massing and groupings. Tremendous variation occurs as a result of vegetative mutations.

CULTIVARS:

'Azusa' — Ground cover type with prostrate branches, small dark green leaves with lighter colored veins. Underside of foliage turns intense maroon in winter.

'Berryhilli' — Upright form with leaves 1 1/2 to 2" long. 5-year-old plants are 2 1/2' tall, definitely upright, and the leaves are evergreen.

'Carrierei' — Semi-shrub form or climbing if supported, leaves glossy deep green about 2" long. Fruiting freely.

var. *coloratus* (often listed as cultivar 'Coloratus') — Vigorous ground cover form, foliage is a deep glossy green and turns plum-purple in the winter. There seem to be several clones in the nursery trade. Some clones do not develop the good plum-purple color on both leaf surfaces, while others show excellent color over the entire plant.

Leaves: Without the prominent venation, usually lustrous dark green, 1 to 2" long, changing to purple during the winter. This variety is variable for often the underside of the leaf is purple and the upper portion green. Usually nonfruiting.

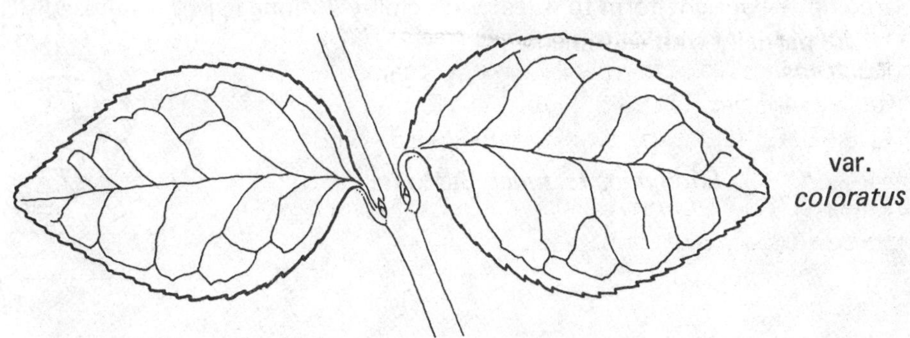

var. *coloratus*

'Emerald Beauty' — Grows to 6' and spread 8 to 10' and bears abundant pink capsules with orange seeds.

'Emerald Charm' — Similar to the following form, 5 to 7', spreads 18", makes a very fine hedge.

'Emerald Cushion' — Dwarf mounded form, dense branching habit, holds rich green foliage, 3'.

'Emerald Gaiety' — Small, erect form of dense branching habit, distinguished by the pronounced white margin on the deep green, rounded leaves, 4 to 5'.

'Emerald and Gold' — Low growing, tight branching habit, foliage dark glossy green with yellow margins, 4 to 5'.

'Emerald Leader' — Similar to 'Emerald Beauty' in fruitfulness but grows to 5' with a 30" spread.

'Emerald Pride' — Small, erect form with lustrous dark green foliage and a close branching habit, 4 to 5', spreading 42".

'Erecta' — Often a catchall term for upright woody forms of the species.

'Golden Prince' — Vigorous, mounded form with new foliage tipped a bright gold. Older leaves turn solid green.

'Gracilis' — Used to designate a group of variable and inconstant forms which possess variegated white or yellow or pink foliage.

'Green Lane' — A better green foliage form, and not as upright growing as 'Sarcoxie'.

'Kewensis' — Dainty prostrate form with leaves about 1/4" long.

'Minimus' — Low growing form with leaves 1/4 to 1/2" long.

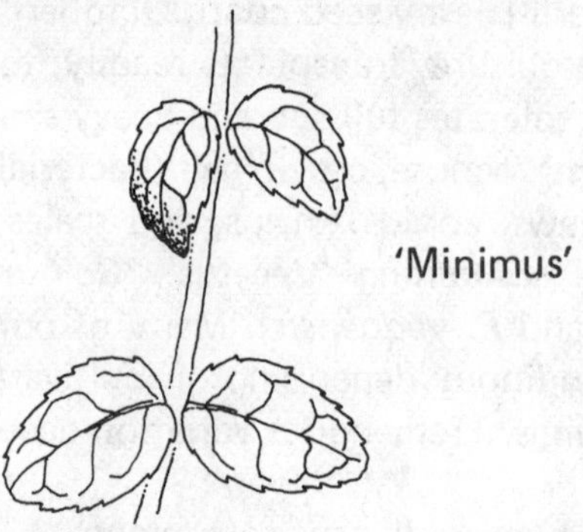

'Minimus'

var. *radicans* — Intermediate form trailing or climbing, fruiting, leaves ovate or broad-elliptic to elliptic, 1 1/2 - 2" long, acute or obtusish, distinctly serrate, of thicker texture, veins obsolete. This variety represents an intermediate stage between the species and the 'Vegetus' type. Trailing or climbing in habit forming woody stems and exhibiting sporadic flowering and fruiting. Leaves are about 2" long, shiny medium to dark green and wavy in appearance.

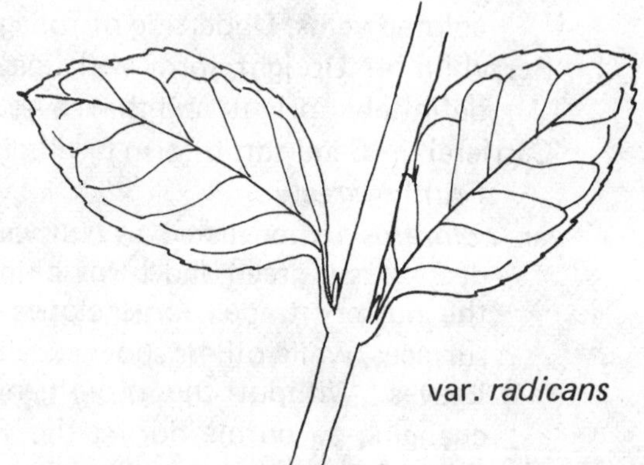

var. *radicans*

'Sarcoxie' — Upright form to 4 feet with glossy 1" long leaves; supposedly a non-fruiter, leaves are partially whitish veined.

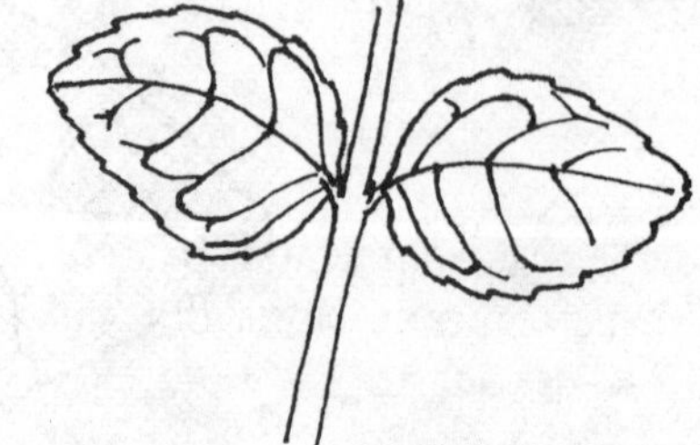

Euonymus fortunei 'Sarcoxie'

'Vegetus' — Somewhat similar to above; however, a fruiting form; the leaves are a light glossy green without the venation and of a more rounded, thicker nature. Actually the super-adult form. An upright shrub to 4 to 5' or a true clinging vine if trained. Leaves are broad-elliptic to nearly suborbicular, 1 to 2" long, acute or obtusish, crenate-serrate, dull green to medium-green; fruiting freely. The 'Sarcoxie' form is more upright and does not fruit.

'Vegetus'

PROPAGATION: Seeds have dormant embryos and moist stratification at cold temperatures is recommended. Softwood cuttings root easily.

RELATED SPECIES:

Euonymus kiautschovicus – Spreading Euonymus

LEAVES: Opposite, simple, broad-elliptic or obovate to oblong-obovate or elliptic-oblong, 2 to 3" long, acute or obtusish, cuneate, crenate - serrulate, subcoriaceous with obsolete veins beneath; petiole 1/6 to 1/3" long.

BUDS: Imbricate, conical, sharp pointed, greenish and often tinged with red in winter.

STEM: Slender, green, rounded, not developing a woody character until the second or third year.

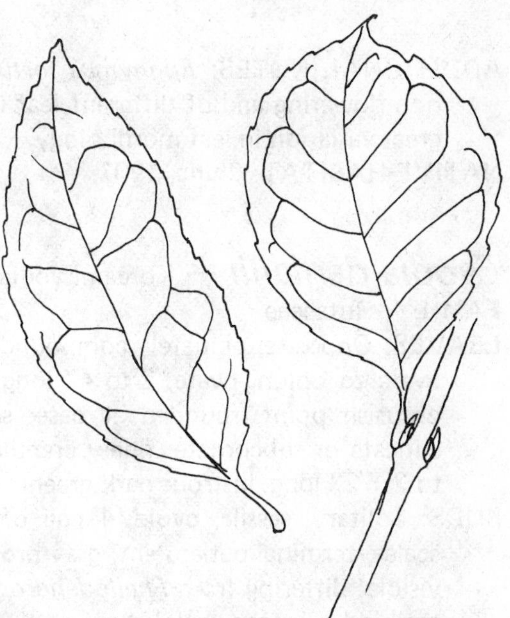

Euonymus kiautschovicus, Spreading Euonymus, is a semievergreen shrub of rounded habit reaching 8 to 10' in height; the foliage is a good dark green in summer but usually burns in winter and looks quite unkempt. Flowers are greenish white and borne in August; the flies hover about this shrub when in flower and it is not a good plant for patio areas and like; fruit capsule is pink, seed coat is orange-red, matures in November; decent plant for informal hedges, screens, and massing; the cultivars:

'Dupont' – Hybrid form with large leaves (2 1/2") and vigorous growth habit. 4-year-old plants are 4' tall, quite hardy.

'Manhattan' – Hybrid, excellent dark green glossy foliage form with leaves 2 1/2" long and 1 1/4" wide.

'Newport' – Similar to above forms.

'Sieboldiana' – New form, supposedly with good foliage and not as susceptible to scale as other types.

The cultivars are superior to the species. Native to Eastern and Central China. Introduced 1860. Zone 5.

Euonymus nanus turkestanicus

LEAVES: Alternate, whorled or occasionally opposite, simple, narrow-to-linear-oblong, 1 3/5 to 3" long, 1/5 to 2/5" broad, not revolute; bluish green.

Euonymus nanus turkestanicus, Dwarf Euonymus, is a small (3') shrub with erect slender branches and leaves which may be alternate, opposite, or subopposite. The foliage is of a bluish green consistency in summer and changes to brilliant red tones in fall. The flowers are about 1/6" across, brownish purple, and borne 1 to 3 on a slender stalk in May. The fruit is a 4-lobed, pink capsule; the seeds are brown and not wholly covered by the orange aril. The variety *turkestanicus* is the type in cultivation. The species is native from Caucasian Mountains to Western China. Introduced 1830. Zone 2. This plant has performed well in Central Illinois and the fall color has been brilliant. It is easily rooted from softwood cuttings treated with a quick-dip of 1000 ppm IBA. May become a popular plant with exposure.

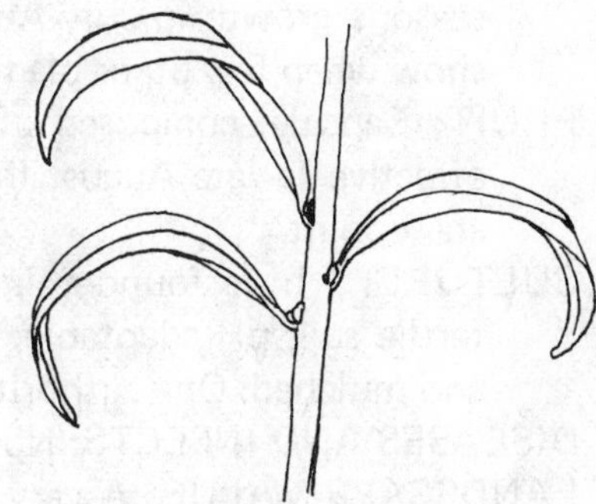

ADDITIONAL NOTES: *Euonymus fortunei* behaves similar to *Hedera helix.* The juvenile form is non-flowering and of different leaf morphology. The adult form flowers and fruits and shows great variation in leaf morphology.

NATIVE HABITAT: China, 1907.

Evodia daniellii — Korean Evodia

FAMILY: Rutaceae

LEAVES: Opposite, pinnately compound, leaflets 7 to 11, ovate to oblong-ovate, 2 to 4" long, acuminate with obtusish point, rounded at base, sometimes broad-cuneate or subcordate, finely crenulate, petiole 1 1/2 to 2 1/2" long; lustrous dark green.

BUDS: Solitary, sessile, ovoid, 1 pair of rather indistinct scales, terminal-puberulent, gray-brown; exposed and visible; differing from *Phellodendron* where the buds are hidden by the petiole base.

STEM: Round or somewhat 4-angled or wrinkled; pith—moderate, somewhat angular, firm, continuous; leaf scars broadly crescent-shaped, low; 3 bundle-traces.

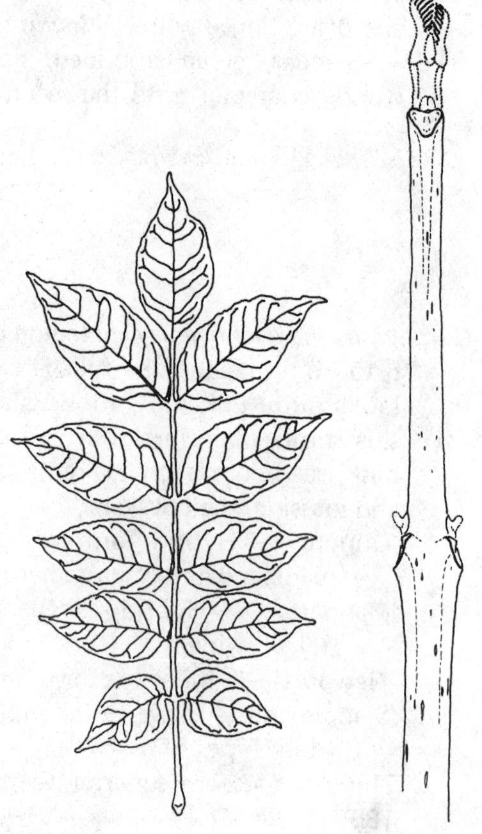

SIZE: Will probably grow 25 to 30' high under landscape conditions but can reach 50'. The spread is equal to or greater than the height.

HARDINESS: Zone 4; I have seen excellent specimens at the Morton Arboretum, Lisle, Illinois, which showed good vigor and abundant fruit.

RATE: Medium to fast, especially in youth. Seedlings which I grew in containers reached 5 to 6' in a single growing season.

TEXTURE: Medium in leaf and in winter.

BARK: Older stems and branches develop a smooth gray appearance which is interrupted at irregular intervals by raised lenticels.

LEAF COLOR: Dark lustrous green in summer. The foliage is quite free of pests and diseases and looks as good in August as it did when first maturing in May. Fall color is of no consequence as the leaves usually drop green or yellowish green.

FLOWERS: Often unisexual, small, white; borne in 4 to 6" broad, flattish corymbs on current seasons growth in July-August. The flowers are borne in great quantities and provide quite a show when few other plants are in flower.

FRUIT: Capsule, composed of 4 or 5 carpels which split from the top; red to black in color and effective in late August through November. The fruits are very effective from an ornamental standpoint.

CULTURE: I have found this species easy to transplant; seems to prefer a well drained, moist, fertile soil; pH adaptable; full sun; may be a bit tender when young and should be well sited and mulched. One authority noted that any soil is acceptable for culturing this plant.

DISEASES AND INSECTS: None of any consequence.

LANDSCAPE VALUE: A very interesting tree, but unfortunately little known and used. A lovely, small tree which can be used in the small landscape. Excellent summer foliage, flower, and fruit characters make this tree worthy of additional use. Wyman noted that the wood is comparatively weak and splits easily and the tree is short-lived (15 to 40 years).

PROPAGATION: Seeds which were sent from the Morris Arboretum, Philadelphia, were direct sowed and germinated almost 100 percent.

RELATED SPECIES:

Evodia hupehensis, Hupeh Evodia, is closely allied to *E. daniellii* and may be an ecotype. Supposedly it differs in larger-stalked leaflets and the longer beak of the fruit, but according to W.J. Bean the characters are not reliable. *E. hupehensis* can grow to 60′ and may be slightly less hardy than *E. daniellii.* Native to Central China. Introduced 1907. Zone 5.

ADDITIONAL NOTES: The Evodias are closely allied to *Phellodendron* but differ in the buds which are exposed in the leaf axils rather than covered by the base of the petiole as in *Phellodendron. Evodia* is often written *Euodia* and this was the original spelling as rendered by the Forsters who founded the genus in 1776.

NATIVE HABITAT: Northern China, Korea; introduced by E.H. Wilson in 1905.

Exochorda racemosa — Common Pearlbush

FAMILY: Rosaceae

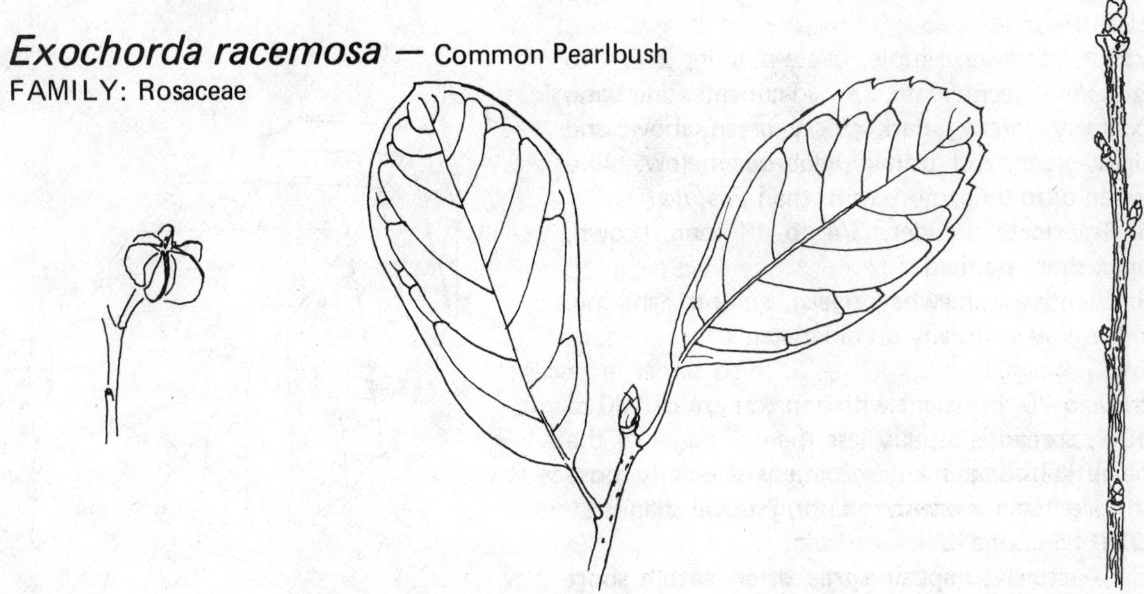

LEAVES: Alternate, simple, elliptic to elliptic-oblong or oblong-obovate, acute and mucronate, cuneate, 1 to 2 1/2″ long, entire or on vigorous shoots serrate above the middle, whitish beneath.

BUDS: Moderate, solitary, sessile, ovoid, with about 10 more or less pointed and fringed scales.

STEM: Round, slender, brown, glabrous, roughened by lenticels and longitudinal fissures; pith—small, continuous, pale.

SIZE: 9 to 15′ by 10 to 15′.

HARDINESS: Zone 4.

HABIT: An upright, slender branched, loose, irregular shrub becoming floppy, often unkempt with age; often somewhat fountain-like in outline.

RATE: Medium.

TEXTURE: Medium in leaf, coarse in winter.

LEAF COLOR: Medium green in summer; no fall color of any consequence.

FLOWERS: Perfect, white, 1 1/2″ across, odorless; mid-May (7 to 14 days); borne in 6 to 10 flowered, 3 to 5″ long racemes at ends of short lateral stems from branches of previous year.

FRUIT: Broad turbinate, 5-valved capsule ripening in October and persisting.

CULTURE: Transplant balled and burlapped or as a container plant in early spring; prefers well-drained, acid, loamy soil; full sun or partial shade; prune after flowering.

DISEASES AND INSECTS: None serious.

LANDSCAPE VALUE: Good for flower effect, probably should be reserved for the shrub border.

PROPAGATION: Softwood cuttings in June, treated with IBA, and placed in sand under mist will root.

RELATED SPECIES:

Exochorda giraldii, Redbud Pearlbush, is closely allied and very similar to the above but less available.

The variety *wilsonii* has flowers 2″ across, and is of more upright and floriferous habit. Northwestern China. Introduced 1897. Zone 5.

Exochorda x *macrantha* is a hybrid between *E. racemosa* and *E. korolkowii* and supposedly a shrub of great beauty producing a raceme of flowers from every bud of the previous year's growth. There is one large mailorder nursery firm which offers a cultivar called 'The Bride' and claims it grows only 3 to 4′ tall and is quite bushy. This could be, but since both parents grow 12 to 15′ in height I would have to view this cultivar first hand to remove my suspicions.

NATIVE HABITAT: Eastern China. Introduced 1849.

Fagus grandifolia — American Beech

FAMILY: Fagaceae

LEAVES: Alternate, simple, ovate-oblong, 2 1/4 to 5″ long, acuminate, broad-cuneate at base, coarsely serrate, dark glossy green above and light green and usually glabrous below, silky when unfolding; more veins than *F. sylvatica.*

BUDS: Imbricate, slender, 3/4 to 1″ long, brown, apex sharp-pointed.

STEM: Slender, somewhat zigzag, smooth, shining, silver-gray especially on older stems.

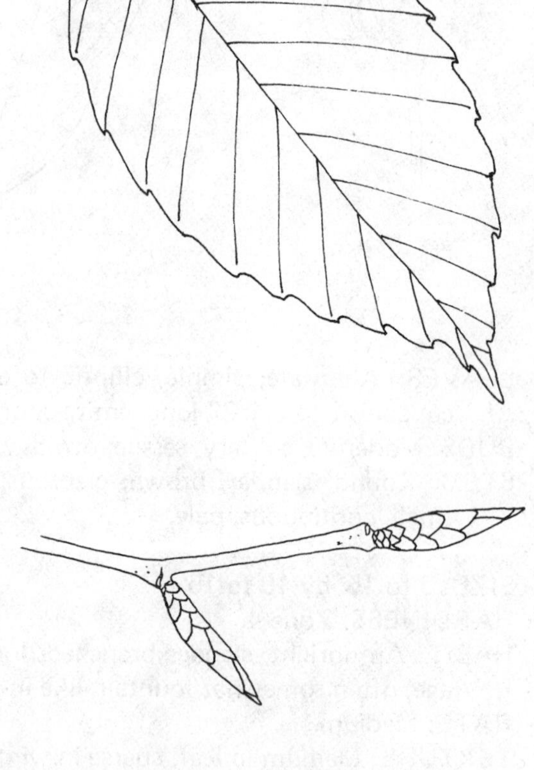

SIZE: 50 to 70′ in height with a maximum of 100 to 120′; spread is usually less than or equal to the height, although many specimens especially those in forest stands assume an upright-oval shape.

HARDINESS: Zone 3.

HABIT: A sturdy, imposing tree often with a short trunk and wide spreading crown, a picture of character in a native situation.

RATE: Slow, possibly medium in youth, averaging 9 to 12′ over a 10 year period.

TEXTURE: Medium throughout the season.

BARK: Thin, smooth, light bluish gray almost silvery on young stems; similar on mature trees but darker.

LEAF COLOR: Silvery when opening, gradually changing to dark green in summer; fall color is a beautiful golden bronze and the leaves (especially on the lower portion of the tree) often persist into winter.

FLOWERS: Monoecious; male and female separate on the same tree; male in globose heads; pistillate in 2- to 4-flowered spikes, however, sometimes at base of staminate inflorescence. Usually flowers in late April to early May in Urbana.

FRUIT: Nut, solitary or 2 to 3, partly or wholly enclosed by a prickly involucre.

CULTURE: Transplant balled and burlapped in spring; moist, well-drained, acid (pH 5.0 to 6.5) soil is preferable; will not withstand wet or compacted soils; soils with oxygen concentrations of less than 10 to 15% are not suitable; root system is shallow and it is difficult to grow grass under this tree; does best in full sun although withstands partial shade; prune in summer or early fall.

DISEASES AND INSECTS: The following problems have been reported but are not particularly serious: leaf spots, powdery mildew, bleeding canker, leaf mottle, beech bark disease, cankers, aphids, brown wood borer, beech scale, two-lined chestnut borer and caterpillars.

LANDSCAPE VALUE: Beautiful native tree; restricted to large area use; beautiful in parks, golf courses, and other large areas; a beech forest is worth viewing especially in early spring and again in fall.

PROPAGATION: Seed, 41°F for 90 days in moist sand.

ADDITIONAL NOTES: F.B. Robinson has termed the beech "The Beau Brummel of trees but clannish and fastidious as to soil and atmosphere, magnificent specimen casting a dense shade which does not permit undergrowth." J.U. Crockett noted, "If the word noble had to be applied to only one kind of tree, the honor would probably go to the beech." The nuts were once fed to swine and were a favorite food of the extinct passenger pigeon, squirrels, blue jays, titmice, grosbeaks, nuthatches and woodpecker. The American Beech is a variable species and there are at least three different races. The northern type is "gray beech" found from Nova Scotia to the Great Lakes, and on the higher mountains of North Carolina and Tennessee, mainly on neutral to alkaline soils. "White Beech" is found on the southern coastal plain and northward on poorly drained acid sites. Between these two forms, mainly on well-drained acid sites and mixing with them is "Red Beech."

NATIVE HABITAT: New Brunswick to Ontario, South to Florida and Texas. Introduced 1800.

Fagus sylvatica — European Beech

LEAVES: Alternate, simple, 2 to 4" long, ovate or elliptic, acute, broad-cuneate or rounded at base, undulate, lustrous dark green above, light green beneath, glabrous at maturity, silky and ciliate when young.

BUDS: Similar to *F. grandifolia.*

STEM: Similar, except olive-brown in color.

GROWTH HABIT: Tends to branch to ground, dense, upright, oval character when young.

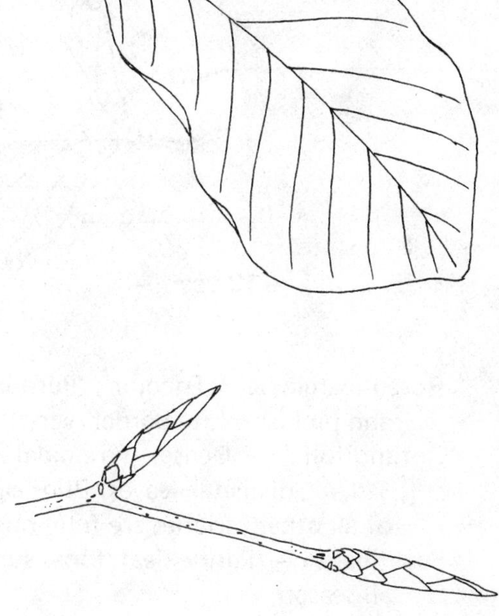

SIZE: 50 to 60' in height with a spread of 35 to 45'; can reach 100' in height.

HARDINESS: Zone 4.

HABIT: Densely pyramidal to oval or rounded, branching to the ground. Very formal (stately) in outline.

RATE: Slow to medium, 9 to 12' over a 10 year period; an English reference noted 35' in 20 years.

TEXTURE: Actually fine when first leafing out, otherwise of medium texture in full foliage and winter.

BARK: Smooth, gray, usually darker than the American Beech; developing an elephant hide appearance on old trunks. A beauty unmatched by the bark of other trees.

LEAF COLOR: When unfolding a tender shimmering green unmatched by any other tree gradually changing to lustrous dark green in summer followed by rich russet and golden bronze colors in fall. The leaves are slow to emerge and do not fully develop until mid-May in Central Illinois. There is one specimen on campus that develops its leaves a full 2 to 3 weeks ahead of the others.

FLOWERS AND FRUITS: Essentially as described for American Beech.

CULTURE: More tolerant of soils than American Beech but otherwise requirements are comparable.

DISEASES AND INSECTS: See under *Fagus grandifolia.*

LANDSCAPE VALUE: There is no finer specimen tree; so beautiful that it overwhelms one at first glance, excellent for public areas, also makes an excellent hedge for it withstands heavy pruning.

The cultivars are especially beautiful and at least one will blend into every landscape. My favorites are 'Asplenifolia', 'Fastigiata', 'Pendula', and 'Riversii'.

CULTIVARS: There are a great number of cultivars which have developed in the wild and under cultivation. The following list represents the best.

'Asplenifolia' — Fern-like feathery foliage texture, very delicate and refined, a jewel in the gardening crown.

'Atropunicea' — Purple leaf form showing considerable variation because it is often grown from seed.

'Cuprea' — The younger foliage has a lighter reddish bronze color than that of 'Atropunicea', gradually fading to dark green.

'Dawyckii' — Fastigiate in habit, good narrow beech.

'Fastigiata' — Narrow columnar form, good plant for "tight" areas.

'Laciniata' — Cutleaf Beech, differs from 'Asplenifolia' in having wider, more regularly shaped leaves.

'Pendula' — Weeping form, interesting in all seasons because of branching habit.

'Purpureo-pendula' — Pendulous branches and purple leaves.

'Quercifolia' — Oaklike foliage.

'Riversii' — Young foliage is reddish but turns a deep purplish later and holds the color through the summer. The best of the purple forms.

'Rohanii' — Purple leaves very similar in shape to those of 'Quercifolia', leaves are not deeply cut or incised.

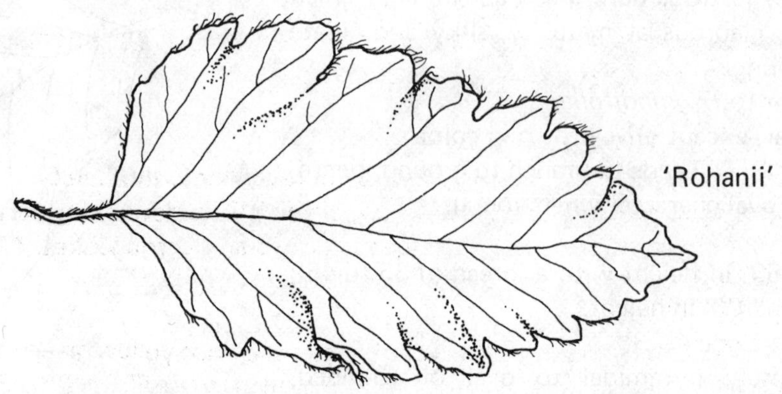
'Rohanii'

'Roseo-marginata' ('Tricolor', 'Purpurea Tricolor') — Purple leaves with an irregular light pink and pinkish white border, very handsome.

'Rotundifolia' — Dense, pyramidal tree with rounded 1/2 to 1 1/4" diameter leaves. Buds open two weeks after those of all other varieties are fully open.

'Spaethiana' — Purple leaf form supposedly holding its color all season.

'Tortuosa' — Wide-spreading, flat-topped variety with a picturesque growth habit. Extremely slow growth rate.

'Zlatia' — Yellow foliage at tips of branches changing to normal lustrous dark green when mature.

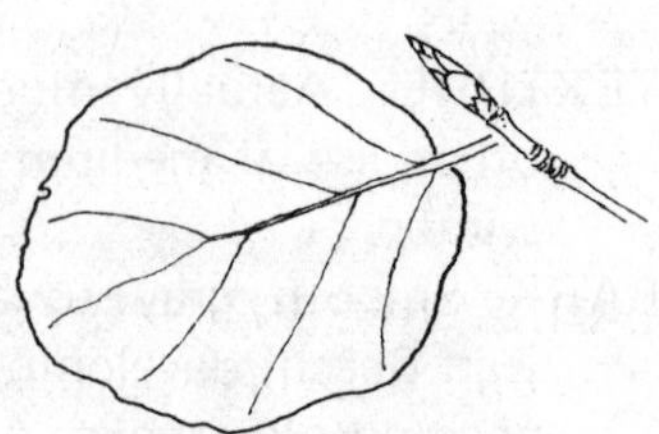
'Rotundifolia'

PROPAGATION: Seed, stratify in moist sand:peat for 150 days at 41°F. I have attempted, on several occasions, to root soft and hardwood cuttings of various trees on campus but to no avail.

ADDITIONAL NOTES: The bark is often disfigured by fledgling poets, lovers and other irresponsibles.

NATIVE HABITAT: Europe. Long cultivated.

Forsythia x *intermedia* — Border Forsythia

FAMILY: Oleaceae

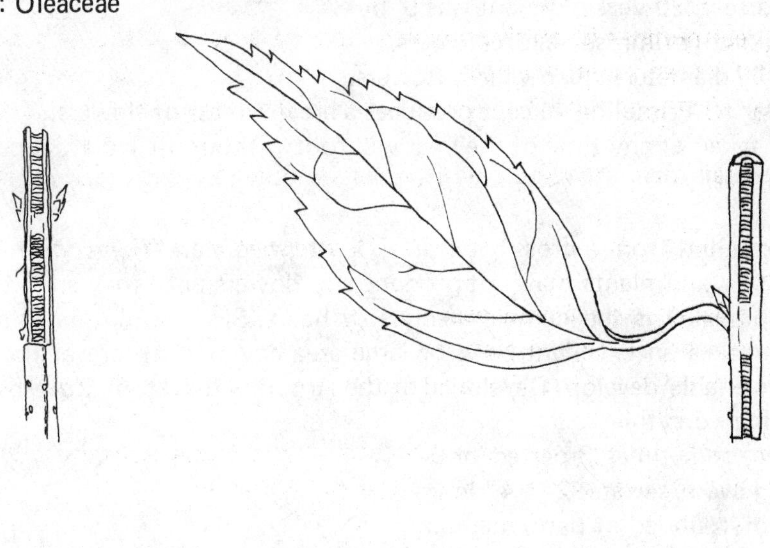

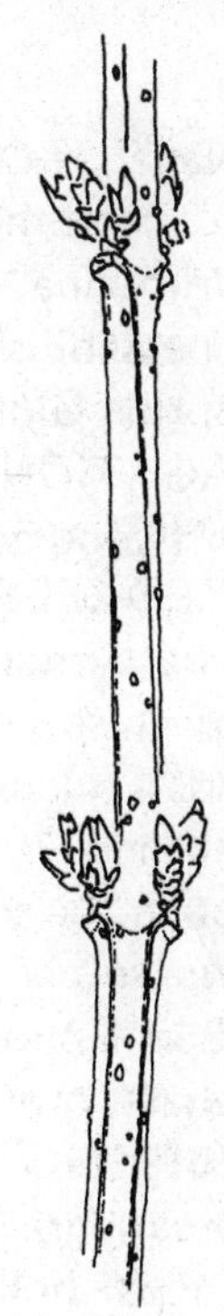

LEAVES: Opposite, simple, toothed, ovate-oblong to oblong lanceolate, 3 to 5" long, medium green above.

STEM: Often somewhat squarish or 4-sided; pith—chambered in the internodes, solid at the nodes; stems yellowish brown and strongly lenticellate.

SIZE: 8 to 10' high by 10 to 12' wide.

HARDINESS: Zone 4, however, flower buds are limitedly hardy in Zone 5.

HABIT: Upright, rank growing deciduous shrub, differentially developing upright and arching canes which give it the appearance the roots were stuck in an electric socket. Always needs grooming. One of the most over-rated and over-used shrubs!

TEXTURE: Medium in leaf; wild in winter.

LEAF COLOR: Medium-green in summer; green or a ridiculous yellow green in fall.

FLOWERS: Perfect, pale to deep yellow, scentless, usually April for 2 to 3 weeks; borne 1 to 6 together or often in 2's and 3's on old wood.

FRUIT: Capsule, brown, not ornamental.

CULTURE: Fibrous, transplants readily bare root or balled and burlapped; prefers a good, loose soil but will do well in about any soil; full sun to maximize flower; pH adaptable; withstands city conditions; prune after flowering either by cutting plant to ground or removing the oldest stems.

DISEASES AND INSECTS: Crown gall, leaf spots, dieback, four-lined plant bug, Japanese weevil, northern root-knot nematode and spider mites. None of which are extremely troublesome.

LANDSCAPE VALUE: Chief value is in the early spring flower; forsythias do not belong in foundation plantings but are often used there; shrub border, massing, groupings, bank plantings are the most appropriate places. The early spring color is a strong selling point and when forsythia is in flower it is one of the hottest selling items at a garden center. Often injured by late freezes and flower quality is reduced.

CULTIVARS:

'Beatrix Farrand' — Flowers vivid yellow and about 2" in diameter. Excellent for early yellow color; reasonably flower bud hardy.

'Densiflora' — Pale yellow flowers, more upright than most cultivars.

'Karl Sax' — More flower bud hardy in the Middle West than 'Beatrix Farrand', otherwise similar.

'Lynwood' or 'Lynwood Gold' — Sport of 'Spectabilis', flowers are more fully opened and better distributed along the stems than those of 'Spectabilis'. Upright in habit.

'Nana' — Collective term for dwarf forms. May take 7 years from a cutting before it flowers and then only sparsely. 20-year-old plant was 5' by 8'.

'Primulina' — Light-colored, primrose-yellow flowers.

'Spectabilis' — Large (2" diameter), deep yellow flowers.

'Spring Glory' — Similar to 'Primulina' except produces a greater mass of flowers.

PROPAGATION: Cuttings taken at any time of the year will root without difficulty. June and July softwood cuttings root easily.

RELATED SPECIES:

Forsythia 'Arnold Dwarf' resulted from a cross between *F.* x *intermedia* and *F. japonica.* It flowers (greenish yellow) sparsely and plants may not produce any flowers until they are 5 to 6-years-old. Principal landscape value is the comparatively low habit. Six-year-old plants may be 3' tall and 7' across. It makes an excellent bank or large area cover for wherever the branches touch the soil, roots invariably develop. Developed at the Arnold Arboretum. Zone 5.

Forsythia suspensa — Weeping Forsythia

LEAVES: Opposite, simple, sometimes 3-parted or 3-foliate, ovate to oblong-ovate, serrate, 2 to 4" long, acute, broad-cuneate or rounded at base, medium to dark green.

STEM: Pith—hollow in internodes and solid at the nodes, yellowish brown stem color; also stem appears more rounded than *F.* x *intermedia.*

Forsythia suspensa, Weeping Forsythia, grows 8 to 10' tall and 10 to 15' wide. The habit is upright, arching, almost fountain-like with slender, long, trailing, pendulous branches. The flowers are golden yellow, 1 to 1 1/4" across, April, usually 1 to 3 together. This species does not flower as heavily as *F.* x *intermedia.*

Cultivars and varieties include:

var. *fortunei* — Vigorous upright habit with arching or spreading branches (7 to 8').

'Pallida' — Light-yellow flowers.

var. *sieboldii* — Form with very slender pendulous branches, often trailing on the ground and rooting at the tips. Nice plant for banks, waterways where trailing branches can sweep the ground. China. Zone 5.

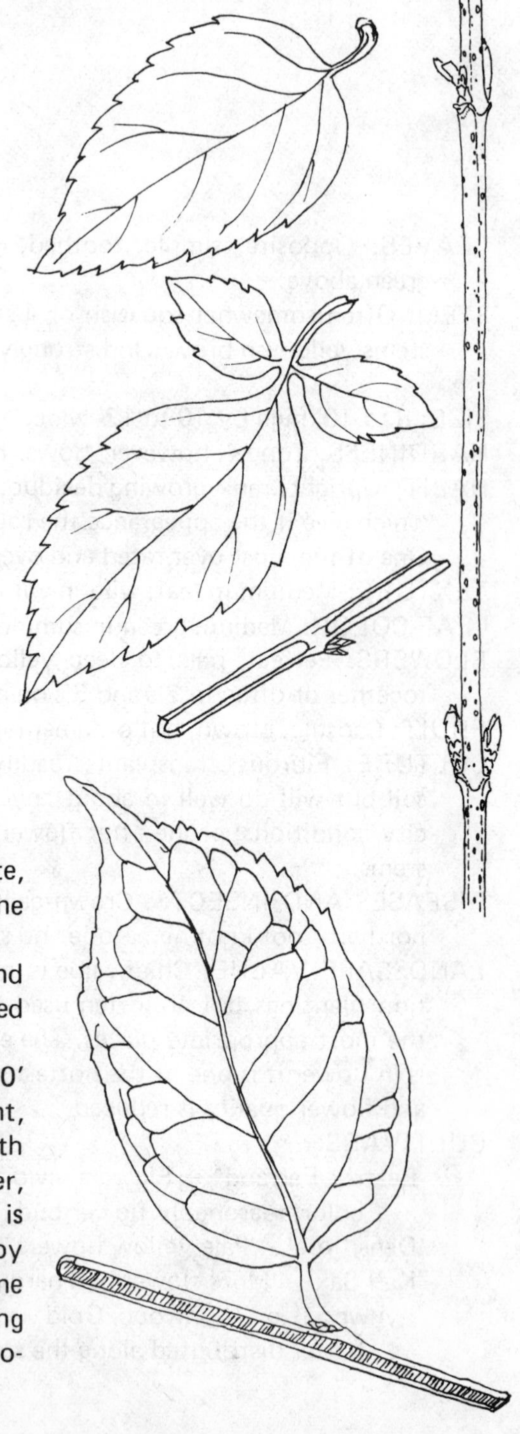

Forsythia viridissima — Greenstem Forsythia

LEAVES: Opposite, simple, elliptic-oblong to lanceolate, rarely obovate-oblong, broadest about or above the middle, sometimes nearly entire, dark green.

STEM: Often greenish, pith chambered through nodes and internodes on young branches, or finally all excavated on old wood.

Forsythia viridissima, Greenstem Forsythia, grows 6 to 10' high with a similar spread. The habit is stiff and upright, more or less flat-topped. Flowers are bright yellow with a slight greenish tinge, 1" long, April, 1 to 3 together, not particularly effective. The cultivar 'Bronxensis' is a very dwarf form as 10-year-old plants are 1' high by 2' wide; supposedly flowers well; I have heard this clone was difficult to root but have had no difficulty using softwood cuttings and 1000 ppm IBA. China. Introduced 1844. Zone 5.

Fothergilla gardenii — Dwarf Fothergilla

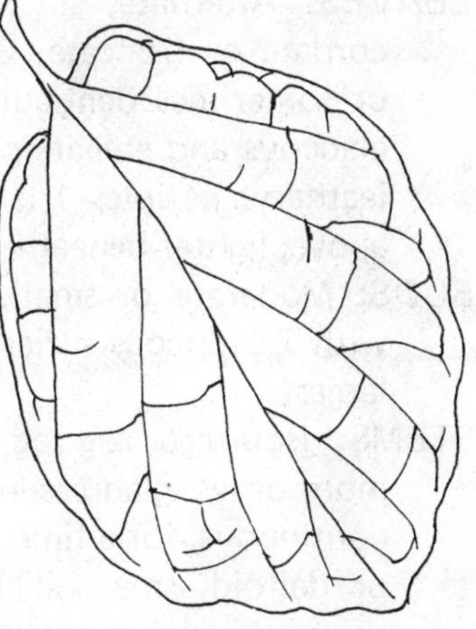

FAMILY: Hamamelidaceae

LEAVES: Alternate, simple, obovate to oblong, rounded or broad cuneate, 4/5 to 2" long, dentate above the middle, pale or glaucous and tomentose beneath; petioles 1/5 to 2/5" long. Leaves resemble those of *Hamamelis vernalis*.

BUD: Stalked, oblique, obovate or oblong, with 2 caducous scales, often collaterally branched, the end bud largest.

STEM: Rounded, zig-zag, slender, dingy stellate-tomentose; pith—small, somewhat angular, continuous, for a time greenish.

SIZE: 2 to 3' in height; similar or greater in spread.

HARDINESS: Zone 5.

HABIT: Small shrub with slender, crooked, often spreading branches, weakly rounded in outline.

RATE: Slow.

TEXTURE: Medium-coarse in foliage, medium in winter.

LEAF COLOR: Dark green summer foliage, quite attractive, somewhat leathery in texture. Fall color is a brilliant yellow to orange to scarlet, often a combination of colors in same leaf. Colors extremely well in our area.

FLOWER: White, fragrant, actually apetalous; showy parts are the stamens (white filament; yellow anthers), borne in terminal 1 to 2" long by 1" diameter spikes, late April to early May, flowers appear before leaves, actually look like small bottle-brushes.

FRUIT: Capsule, not showy.

CULTURE: Move balled and burlapped, requires acid, peaty, sandy loam, does well in partial shade, flowers and colors best in full sun, requires good drainage.

DISEASES AND INSECTS: Trouble free, making it worthy of wider landscape use.

LANDSCAPE VALUE: Foundation plantings, borders, masses, excellent for interesting flowers, good summer foliage and outstanding fall color.

PROPAGATION: Cuttings, wood taken from suckers or root cuttings yielded good results, best with bottom heat. *F. monticola* — untreated cuttings taken when shrubs were in flower rooted 67% in sandy soil in 60 days. *F. major* — June cuttings set in sand:peat rooted 67% without treatment, and 100% in 42 days after treatment with 200 ppm IAA/24 hours. The best information comes from Mr. Alfred Fordham, Propagator, at the Arnold Arboretum [See *Arnoldia* 31:256-259 (1971)]. Seeds are somewhat difficult to germinate for they exhibit a double dormancy and pretreatment must be accomplished in two stages. Seeds require warm, fluctuating temperatures followed by a period of cold.

Fothergilla major seeds have required exceptionally warm periods with 12 months being optimum. After warm treatment they should be placed at 40°F for 3 months. *Fothergilla gardenii* has germinated well after 6 months of warm pretreatment followed by 3 months at 40°F.

Often after rooted cuttings are transplanted they enter a dormancy from which they never recover. The problem can be avoided if the cuttings, when rooted, are left in the flats and hardened off. The flats of dormant cuttings are transferred to cold storage, which is maintained at 34°F. In February or March the flats are returned to a warm greenhouse and when growth appears the cuttings are potted.

ADDITIONAL NOTES: Anyone interested in furthering their *Fothergilla* education should consult Dr. Richard Weaver's excellent article in *Arnoldia* 31:89-97 (1971).

NATIVE HABITAT: Virginia to Georgia. Introduced 1765. All species are localized in Southeastern United States.

Fothergilla major — Large Fothergilla

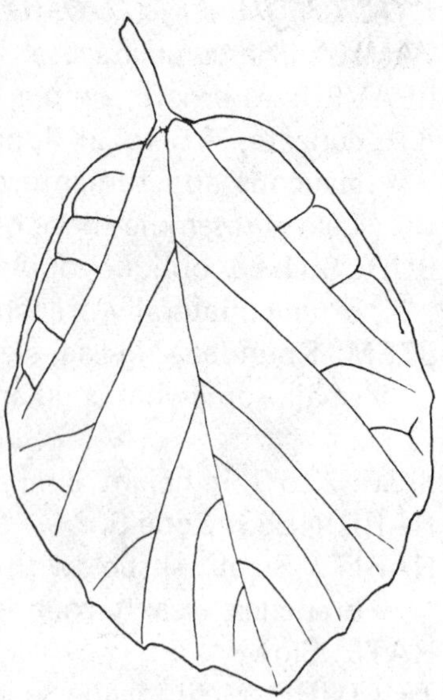

LEAVES: Alternate, simple, suborbicular to oval or obovate, cordate or truncate, 2 to 4" long, coarsely crenate-dentate or sometimes denticulate above the middle, glabrous above, glaucous and stellate-pubescent beneath at least on the veins, leathery; petioles 1/5 to 2/5" long, tomentose. Dark green above, lighter beneath.

BUDS: Moderate or small, stalked, oblique, obovate or oblong, with 2-caducous scales, often collaterally branched; terminal largest.

STEMS: Rounded, zig-zag, slender, dingy stellate-tomentose or more or less glabrescent; pith rather small, somewhat angular, continuous, for a time greenish; leaf-scars 2 ranked, half-round or deltoid, small, slightly raised; stipule-scars unequal, one short the other elongated; 3 bundle-traces, more or less compound or confluent.

SIZE: 6 to 10' in height; slightly less in spread. A very neat shrub.

HARDINESS: Zone 5.

HABIT: A rounded, multistemmed shrub with mostly erect stems; very dense due to the leaves which are closely borne along the stems.

RATE: Slow.

TEXTURE: Medium in leaf and in winter.

LEAF COLOR: Dark green in summer; fall color ranges from yellow to orange and scarlet often with all colors present in the same leaf. One of our more handsome native fall coloring shrubs.

FLOWERS: Whitish, apetalous, the showy portion of the flower being the stamens; borne in 1 to 2" bottlebrush-like spikes in late April to early May. The flowers are fragrant and remind one of the smell of honey.

FRUIT: Capsule, 1/2" long, splitting at the top, usually containing two seeds.

CULTURE: The need for acid soil conditions is of paramount importance. Most authorities indicated that *Fothergilla* species are not suitable for limey soils.

DISEASES AND INSECTS: See under *F. gardenii*.

LANDSCAPE VALUE: Excellent shrub for the residential landscape. Adds considerable color from late April to October by virtue of flower and fall color. The summer foliage is a dark, leathery green and is not affected by diseases or insects. Probably best used in the shrub border but could be employed in groupings, masses and foundation plantings.

PROPAGATION: See under *F. gardenii*.

ADDITIONAL NOTES: This species and *F. monticola,* Alabama Fothergilla, are quite similar and now are treated as one species *F. major.* In the past, plants with more glabrous vegetative parts were listed as *F. monticola.* Also *F. monticola* was supposedly smaller in size (6') but these differences are not absolute. The current thinking is the lumping of the two species into the *F. major* category.

NATIVE HABITAT: Indigenous to the Allegheny Mountains from Virginia to South Carolina. Introduced late 1800's.

Franklinia alatamaha — Franklinia, Franklin Tree

FAMILY: Theaceae

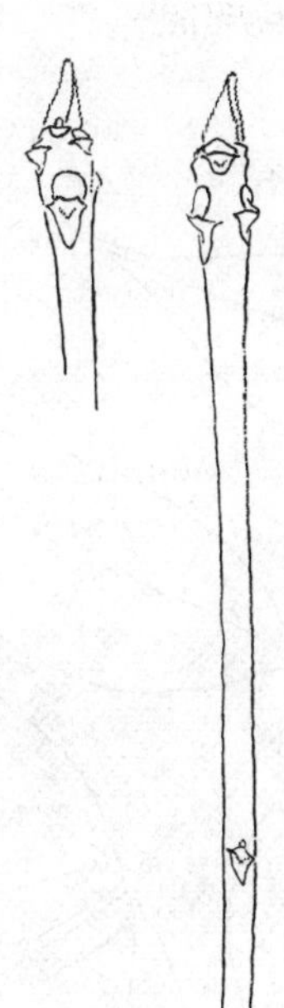

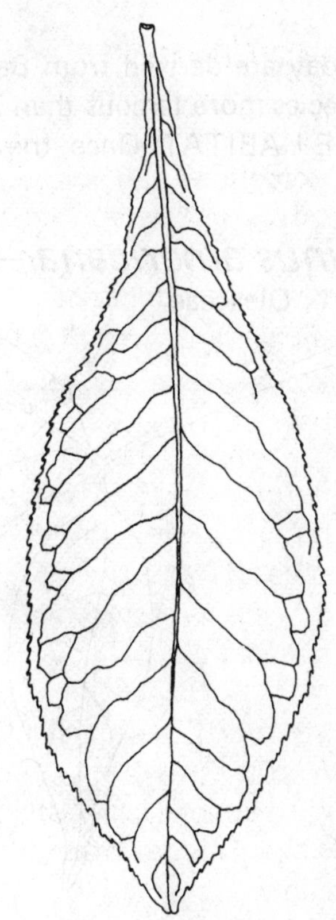

LEAVES: Alternate, simple, 4 to 5" long, obovate-oblong, acute, gradually narrowed into a short petiole, remotely serrate, shiny above, pubescent below.

BUDS: Grayish brown, 1/4 to 1/3" long, usually solitary, round-ovoid, naked, silky pubescent.

STEMS: Moderate, terete, young stems silky; pith rather large, coffee-colored, continuous; leaf-scars half-round, or shield-shaped, scarcely raised; 1 bundle-trace, transverse or V-shaped, compound.

SIZE: 10 to 20′ in height by 6 to 15′ wide in the north; can grow 20 to 30′ in the south.

HARDINESS: Zone 5.

HABIT: Small tree or shrub with upright, spreading branches, often leafless in their lower reaches, giving the plant an open, airy appearance; not unlike *Magnolia virginiana* in habit.

TEXTURE: Medium in all seasons.

LEAF COLOR: Lustrous bright green in summer changing to orange and red in fall. Very handsome foliage.

FLOWERS: Perfect, white petaled, yellow center of stamens, very striking, 3" across, fragrant, solitary, slightly cup-shaped; late July into August and weakly into September.

FRUIT: Woody, 5-valved capsule, 3/5 to 4/5" in diameter.

CULTURE: Somewhat hard to transplant because of sparsely fibrous root system; best to move as a small container or balled and burlapped specimen; requires moist, acid, well-drained soil which has been supplied with ample organic matter; full sun or light shade but best flowering and fall coloration occurs in full sun.

DISEASES AND INSECTS: Wilt caused by a *Fusarium* species is serious.

LANDSCAPE VALUE: A handsome small specimen tree or large shrub valued for the showy white flowers and good fall color. If one is so fortunate to procure this species he/she should provide it a place of prominence in the garden. An aristocrat because of its interesting history.

PROPAGATION: Easily propagated from cuttings taken in late summer or fall. Hormonal treatment results in increased rooting percentages. Seeds should be sown as soon as the fruit has matured. It is important to prevent the seeds from drying out.

ADDITIONAL NOTES: The story has been widely told how John Bartram found this plant in 1770 along the banks of the Alatamaha River in Georgia and collected a few for his garden. Strangely, this plant has never been seen in the wild since 1790, and supposedly all plants in commerce today are derived from Bartram's original collection. I think this story has helped to make the species more famous than is possibly justified.

NATIVE HABITAT: Once, the wilds of Georgia.

Fraxinus americana — White Ash

FAMILY: Oleaceae

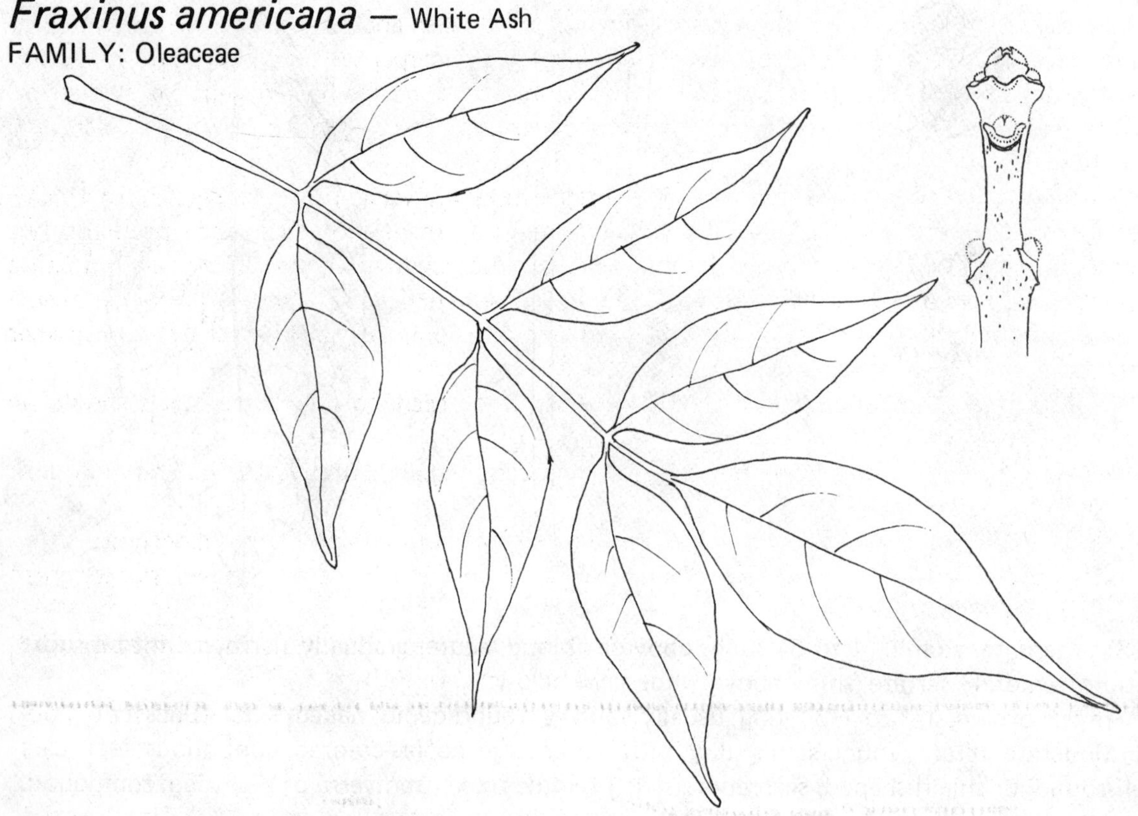

LEAVES: Opposite, pinnately compound, 5 to 9 leaflets, usually 7, stalked, 2 to 6" long, ovate to ovate lanceolate, usually entire, or slightly dentate toward apex, dark green above, glaucous beneath and usually glabrous.

BUD: Terminal present, 2 to 3 pairs of scales, semi-spherical to broadly ovate, scurfy, and more or less slightly downy, rusty to dark brown to sometimes almost black. Terminal about 1/5" long, usually broader than long. Buds inset in the leaf scar.

STEM: Stout, rounded, smooth and shining, grayish or greenish brown often with a slight bloom, brittle, flattened at nodes at right angles to leaf scars. Leaf scars "U" shaped with deep to shallow notch; vascular bundles forming open "C" shape.

SIZE: 50 to 80' in height with a spread of similar proportions, can grow to 120'.

HARDINESS: Zone 3.

HABIT: In youth weakly pyramidal to upright oval, and in old age developing an open and rather round topped crown.

RATE: Medium, 1 to 2' per year over a 10 to 15 year period.

TEXTURE: Medium in leaf; medium-coarse in winter.

BARK: Ashy-gray to gray-brown, furrowed into close diamond-shaped areas separated by narrow interlacing ridges; on very old trees slightly scaly along the ridges.

LEAF COLOR: Dark green above and paler beneath in summer changing to yellow to deep purple and maroon colors in fall. I have seen trees with yellow fall color as well as individuals of dark, intense, maroon color.

FLOWER: Dioecious (possibly polygamo-dioecious), usually imperfect, apetalous, both sexes appearing in panicles before or with the leaves, not ornamentally important.

FRUIT: Samara, 1 to 2" long, 1/4" wide, of no ornamental quality.

CULTURE: Easily transplanted, makes its best growth on deep, moist, well drained soils but also withstands soils which are not excessively dry and rocky; seems to be pH adaptable; full sun; prune in fall; not as adaptable as the Green Ash but much superior to it as an ornamental.

DISEASES AND INSECTS: Ashes are susceptible to many problems and the following list is applicable to the plant types which follow as well as White Ash. Leaf rust, leaf spots (many), cankers (many), dieback has been associated with White Ash and no cause is known, ash borer (can be very destructive), lilac leaf miner, lilac borer, carpenter worm, brown-headed ash sawfly, fall webworm, ash flower gall (flowers develop abnormally and galls are evident on white ash male flowers throughout the winter, caused by a mite), oyster shell scale, and scurfy scale.

LANDSCAPE VALUE: One would wonder if the ashes have any value after reading that impressive list of insects and diseases! Vigorous growing trees do not develop that many problems but homeowners should always be on the lookout and when something seems awry should call a tree specialist or seek help through their county extension office. The White Ash is a handsome native tree for parks and other large areas. I hesitate to recommend it for extensive homeowner use because of size and pest problems.

CULTIVARS: These selected clones are much preferable to seedling grown trees and should be sought out if a White Ash is desired.

'Autumn Applause' – Selected by Wandell Nurseries, Urbana, Illinois for outstanding dark maroon fall color.

'Autumn Purple' – Male, seedless, valued for deep purple autumn color, very handsome.

'Champaign County' – Selected by Wandell Nursery for good habit and smaller, darker green leaves than the species.

'Elk Grove' – Selected by Charles Klehm and Sons Nursery for outstanding habit and beautiful, large, lustrous dark green summer foliage and purple fall foliage.

'Rosehill' – Seedless, dark green summer foliage; bronze red fall color; tolerant of poor, alkaline soils.

PROPAGATION: Seed germinates best with warm stratification at 68 to 86°F for 30 days followed by cold at 41°F for 60 days. Cultivars are budded onto seedling understocks in August in Central Illinois.

RELATED SPECIES:

Fraxinus biltmoreana, Biltmore Ash, is similar to White Ash and by some authorities is considered a variety of White Ash. Differs in the prevailing pubescence of the stems, petioles, and lower surfaces of the leaflets.

NATIVE HABITAT: Nova Scotia to Minnesota, south to Florida and Texas. Introduced 1724.

Fraxinus pennsylvanica — Green Ash. Formerly listed as *F. p. lanceolata* while Red Ash was listed as *F. pennsylvanica.* Both Red and Green are now included in the same species.

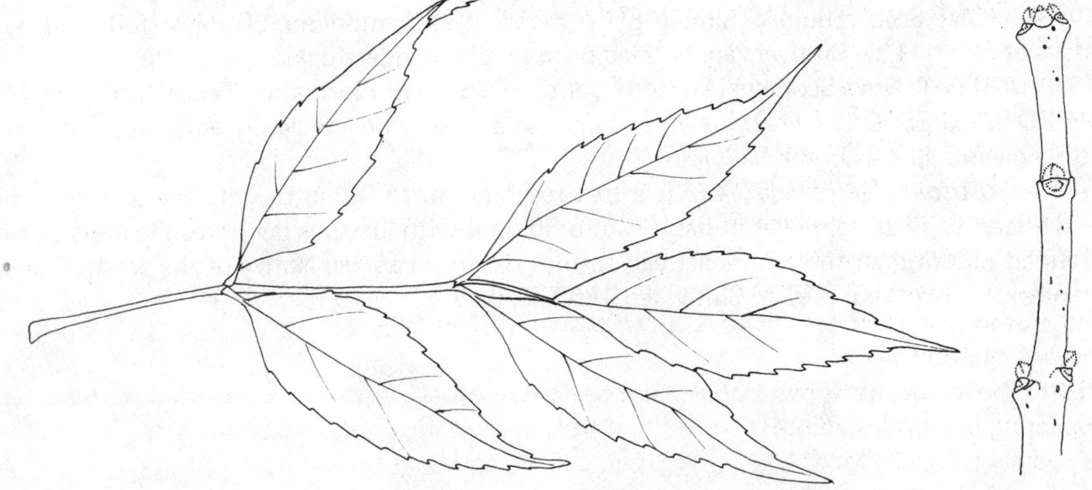

LEAVES: Opposite, pinnately compound, 5 to 9 leaflets, 2 to 5" long, ovate to oblong lanceolate, acuminate, broad-cuneate, crenate serrate or entire, pubescent beneath, prominently so.

BUD: Dark rusty brown, smaller and narrower than those of the White Ash, woolly, set above leaf scar, leaf scars nearly straight across at the top.

STEM: Rounded, rather stout, densely velvety downy or glabrous, leaf scar not notched; vascular bundles forming closed "C" shape.

SIZE: 50 to 60' in height by about 1/2 that in spread, although can grow to over 80'.

HARDINESS: Zone 3.

HABIT: Softly pyramidal when young, developing an upright, spreading habit at maturity with 3 to 5 main branches and many coarse, twiggy branchlets which bend down and then up at the ends. The crown is extremely irregular and the overall habit somewhat difficult to describe. In essence, a mess!

RATE: Fast, 2 to 3' per year in the landscape over a 10 year period. Mr. Earl Cully, a wholesale budded shade tree grower in Jacksonville, Illinois, gets 8 to 12' of growth in a single season.

TEXTURE: Medium in leaf; one of the coarsest trees in winter. I am afraid there are no rivals for sloppy dressing in the winter as Green Ash is head and shoulders above the rest.

BARK: Similar to White Ash.

LEAF COLOR: Variable, but often a shiny medium to dark green in summer changing to yellow in the fall; fall coloration is inconsistent and seed-grown trees provide only disappointment.

FLOWER: See description for White Ash.

FRUIT: Samara, 1 to 2" long, 1/4" or less wide.

CULTURE: Transplants readily and grows about anywhere, hence its tremendous popularity; actually this is strange for it is found native in moist bottomlands or along stream banks; however, once established it tolerates high pH, salt, drought, and sterile soils; requires full sun, prune in fall.

DISEASES AND INSECTS: See White Ash. Borers and scale are significant problems.

LANDSCAPE VALUE: In a way, this tree has been overplanted because of its adaptability. It has been used for streets, lawns, commercial areas, parks, golf courses and about any other area one can think of; best for plains' states where few trees proliferate but somehow has become the favorite of many plant people. One of the real problems is the use of seedling grown trees for they often fruit and in so doing become a significant nuisance.

CULTIVARS:

'Honeyshade' — One of the handsomest forms because of excellent glossy green leaflets, actually does not even look like it belongs to the Green Ash group.

'Marshall's Seedless' — Male form with dark, glossy green foliage; appears to be more vigorous and has less insect problems than the species, yellow fall color.

'Summit' — Female, upright pyramidal, glossy foliage, selection out of Minnesota tends to drop its leaves two weeks earlier in the fall than 'Marshall's Seedless'.

PROPAGATION: Seed requires warm (68°F), moist stratification for 60 days, followed by 120 days at 32 to 41°F. Cultivars are budded onto seedling understocks.

NATIVE HABITAT: Nova Scotia to Manitoba, south to Northern Florida and Texas. Introduced 1824.

RELATED SPECIES: Other *Fraxinus* of landscape importance but of significantly less concern than the previous species in the Midwest.

Fraxinus angustifolia, Narrowleaf Ash, is a tree reaching 60 to 80' in height. The only specimens I have seen were upright-oval in habit (25 to 30' tall) with lustrous dark green leaflets of a more refined nature than the two American species discussed above. Native of the Western Mediterranean and Northern Africa. Cultivated 1800. Zone 5.

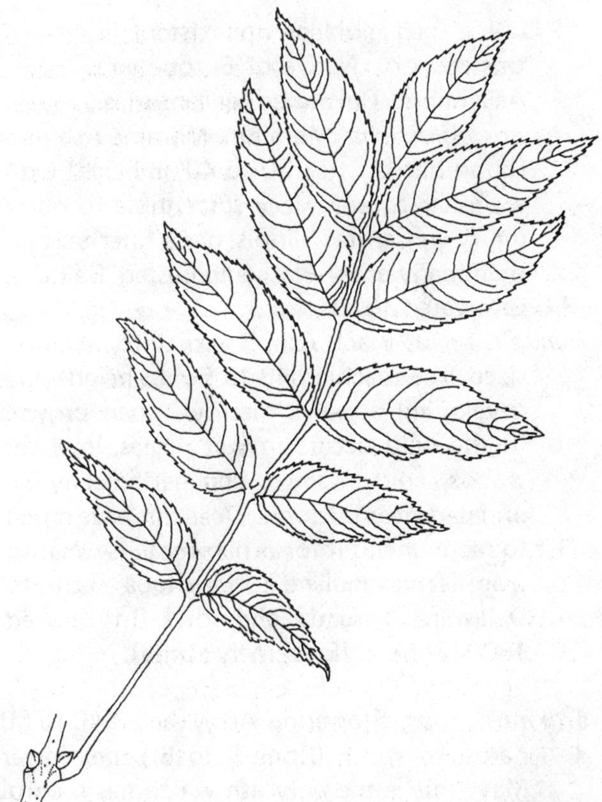

Fraxinus excelsior — Common or European Ash

LEAVES: Opposite, compound pinnate, leaflets 7 to 11, essentially sessile, ovate-oblong to ovate-lanceolate, 2 to 4" long, accuminate, cuneate, serrate, dark green above, lighter green beneath, glabrous except villous along the midrib beneath.

BUDS: Black, pubescent, sessile, with 2 or 3 pairs of opposite scales.

STEM: Usually rounded, somewhat flattened at nodes, glabrous at maturity, grayish or grayish brown.

Fraxinus excelsior, Common or European Ash, grows to 70 to 80′ with a 60 to 90′ spread, reaching on favored sites from 100 to 140′ in height. Forms a round-headed, broad spreading outline, the lower branches up-curving; foliage is dark green in summer and drops off green or develops a casual yellow; prefers a deep, moist, loamy soil and thrives on limestone (calcareous) soils; one of the largest of European deciduous trees and much planted there; has not had overwhelming acceptance in America although many cultivars are available; the following are a few of the more popular.

'Aurea' — Young shoots yellow; older bark yellowish, quite noticeable in winter; fall color deep yellow; slow growing.

'Aurea Pendula' — Branches weeping and forming a flat, umbrella-like head.

'Globosa' — A dense rounded head, 30′ in height with a 20′ spread.

'Gold Cloud' — Yellow stems, leaves turn yellow in the fall.

'Hessei' — One of the most promising cultivars, leaves are simple and prominently toothed, lustrous dark green, very vigorous, upright oval, seedless; has shown good pest resistance compared to the species and other ashes. I have three in our evaluation plots and have found them to be extremely hardy and vigorous; little fall color as the leaves stay green into fall. Leaves remain on the tree very late in the season; trees form a straight sturdy trunk, well filled with branches, and almost flat topped at maturity, 60′, Zone 3. One of the highest rated trees in the Ohio Shade Tree Evaluation Tests.

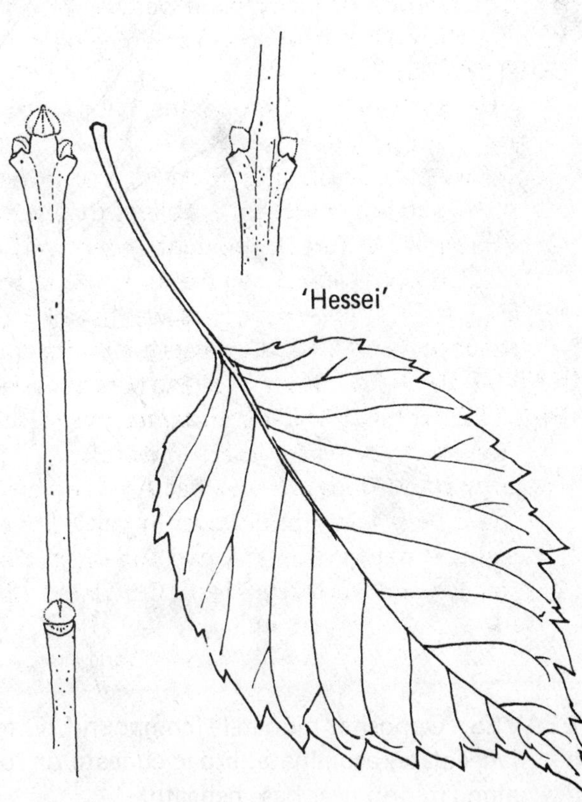

'Pendula' — Branches all weeping, forming a spreading umbrella-like head.

'Rancho' — Small (30′) round headed type. There are numerous other cultivars of Common Ash but their use is negligible or nonexistent in this country. Native of Europe and Asia Minor. Cultivated for centuries.

Fraxinus holotricha 'Moraine', Moraine Ash, is a round headed tree 30 to 40' in height with a similar spread. Very susceptible to borer injury in Central Illinois; has a finer texture than many ashes. Native to Eastern Balkans. Cultivated 1870.

Fraxinus nigra, Black Ash, is a small to medium-sized tree reaching 40 to 50' in height and developing a rather narrow, open crown. In the wild occurs in wet places, low wet woods, cold swamps, and periodically inundated river bottoms. Does not have much to recommend it for ornamental use. Native from Newfoundland to Manitoba, south to Delaware, Virginia and Iowa. Introduced 1800. Zone 2. (Extremely hardy).

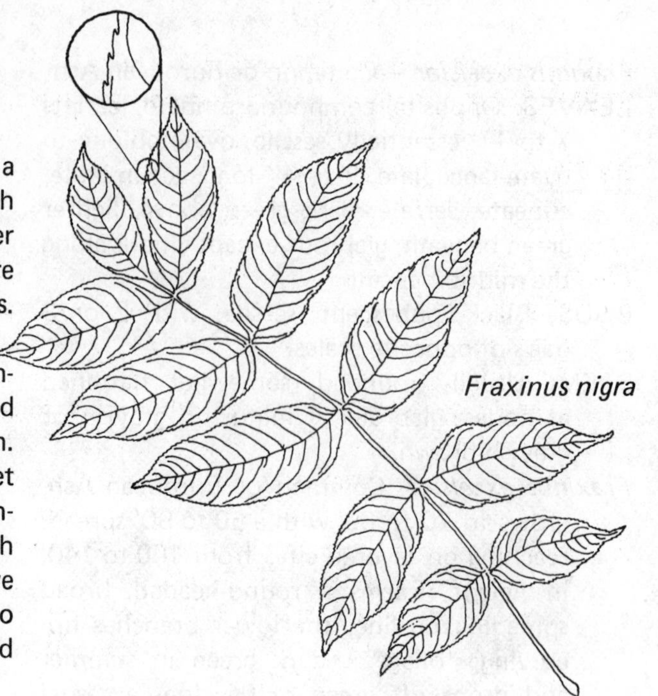

Fraxinus nigra

Fraxinus ornus, Flowering Ash, reaches 40 to 50' in height and develops a rounded, spreading head; hardy to -10°F (Zone 5 to 6); the flowers are showy, fragrant, and borne in 5" panicles in May; this is the only ash which has a corolla and calyx. This species has long been popular in European gardens and has been cultivated there for over 300 years. Native to Southeastern Europe and Western Asia. Introduced 1700.

Fraxinus quadrangulata — Blue Ash

LEAVES: Opposite, pinnately compound, 7 to 11 leaflets, 2 to 5" long, short stalked, ovate to lanceolate, acuminate, broad-cuneate or rounded at base, sharply serrate, dark green, glabrous along midrib near base beneath.

BUD: Dark gray-reddish brown, slightly puberulous or often hairy-tomentose.
STEM: Stout, usually 4-angled and corky-winged, orange-brown, red-hairy, glabrous at maturity. Vascular bundles in a lunate arrangement.
BARK: Rather thin, gray, divided into plate-like scales, often shaggy, inner bark contains substance which turns blue on exposure.

Fraxinus quadrangulata, Blue Ash, grows to 50 to 70′ in height and develops a slender, straight, slightly tapered trunk which supports a narrow, rounded, often irregular crown of spreading branches; leaves are dark green in summer changing to pale yellow in fall; frequents dry, limestone, upland soils; does not seem to be a fast grower and is somewhat difficult to propagate; bark is different from other ashes for on old trunks it is broken into scaly plates; the inner bark contains a mucilaginous substance which turns blue on exposure. Native from Michigan to Arkansas and Tennessee. Introduced 1823. Zone 3.

Fraxinus tomentosa, Pumpkin Ash, is strictly a tree of deep swamps and inundated river bottoms which may grow 80 to 100′ or more. The crown is open and narrow, with small spreading branches; the leaflets are quite large reaching 10″ in length. Native from Western New York to Southern Illinois, Louisiana, and Northwestern Florida. Introduced 1913. Zone 5.

Gaultheria procumbens — Checkerberry

FAMILY: Ericaceae
LEAVES: Alternate, simple, oval to obovate, rarely suborbicular, 3/5 to 1 3/5″ long, obtuse and apiculate, crenate-serrate often with bristly teeth, lustrous dark green above, often variegated, glabrous; petiole—1/6″ long.

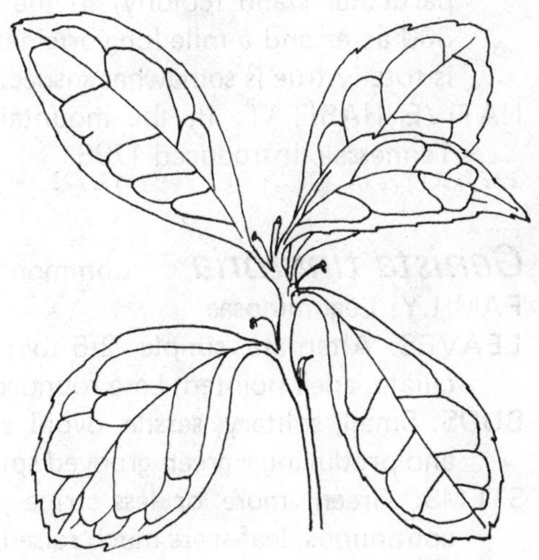

Gaultheria procumbens, Checkerberry, is a low growing (6″), creeping, evergreen ground cover. The leaves turn reddish with the advent of cold weather. When crushed they emit a wintergreen odor and have been a source of this oil in the past. Flowers are perfect, pinkish white, 1/4″ long, nodding, solitary, borne May through September. The fleshy, 2/5″ long scarlet capsule is present in July through April of the following year. The oil is also extracted from the fruits. Culturally, acid, moist, high organic matter soils prove optimum. Using pieces of sod in spring or early fall are the easiest ways of transplanting. Native from Newfoundland to Manitoba, south to Georgia and Michigan. Introduced 1762. Zone 3. Makes a fine ground cover where it can be successfully grown.

Gaylussacia brachycera — Box Huckleberry

FAMILY: Ericaceae
LEAVES: Alternate, simple, 3/4 to 1″ long, elliptic, slightly revolute, glabrous, short-petioled, evergreen, leaves somewhat resembling those of boxwood.
BUDS: Solitary, sessile, ovoid, small, with 2 or some 4 or 5 exposed scales; terminal lacking.
STEM: Slender, roundish; pith small, 3-sided or rounded, continuous; leaf-scars low, crescent-shaped or 3-sided; 1 bundle-trace.

SIZE: 6 to 18" high, spreading indefinitely.
HARDINESS: Zone 5.
HABIT: Dwarf evergreen shrub spreading by underground rootstocks and forming a solid mat.
RATE: Slow.
TEXTURE: Medium-fine in all seasons.
LEAF COLOR: Dark glossy green in all seasons, although when grown in full sun often has a reddish cast.
FLOWERS: Perfect, self-sterile but cross-fertile; white or pinkish, 1/4" long, urn-shaped; late May through early June; borne in short, axillary, few-flowered racemes near the end of the shoot.
FRUIT: Berry-like drupe, bluish, ripening in August.
CULTURE: Another ericaceous plant which requires considerable cultural manipulation if success is to be had; requires an *acid,* loose, well drained soil supplied with organic matter; full sun but preferably partial shade.
DISEASES AND INSECTS: None particularly serious.
LANDSCAPE VALUE: A very lovely, intriguing evergreen ground cover well suited to areas underneath pine trees and rhododendrons where the soil is acid and well drained.
PROPAGATION: Untreated seeds are slow to germinate. Warm followed by cold stratification is recommended. Fluctuating warm temperatures of 68 to 86°F for 30 days followed by 50°F for 27 days and 47 days resulted in 80 percent and 96 percent germination of sound seeds, respectively. Cuttings can also be rooted, preferably softwood.
ADDITIONAL NOTES: Rare American plant, lost to American gardens for a time but was reintroduced through the efforts of the Arnold Arboretum. It has been theorized that one particular stand (colony) in the Amity-Hall area of Central Pennsylvania covering an area of 300 acres and a mile long originated from one plant and is over 12,000-years-old. Whether this is totally true is somewhat suspect but it does make for interesting reading.
NATIVE HABITAT: In the mountains and hills from Pennsylvania to Virginia, Kentucky and Tennessee. Introduced 1796.

Genista tinctoria — Common Woadwaxen or Dyer's Greenwood

FAMILY: Leguminosae
LEAVES: Alternate, simple, 2/5 to 1" long, elliptic-oblong to oblong-lanceolate, nearly glabrous, ciliate, apex pointed; base rounded, margin hairy-fringed.
BUDS: Small, solitary, sessile, ovoid, sometimes developing the first season or collaterally branched and producing a green grooved spine, with some half-dozen scales.
STEMS: Green, more or less stripe-grooved, not spiny; stipules persistent; pith small, rounded, continuous; leaf-scars much raised, minute; 1 indistinct bundle-trace.

SIZE: 2 to 3' high and 2 to 3' wide.
HARDINESS: Zone 2.
HABIT: Low shrub with almost vertical, slender, green, limitedly branched stems; spiky and twiggy in effect.
RATE: Slow, possibly medium.
TEXTURE: Fine to medium-fine in all seasons when well maintained.
STEM COLOR: Green.
LEAF COLOR: Bright green in summer; no fall color.
FLOWERS: Yellow, 1/2 to 3/4" long, produced on erect racemes, 1 to 3" long, occurring on new growth from June to September although peak period is June and limited flowering may occur after that.
CULTURE: Somewhat difficult to transplant and once located should not be moved; prefers hot, sunny location in relatively infertile soils which are dry and loamy or sandy; succeeds in acid or neutral soils and thrives on limestone.
DISEASES AND INSECTS: None serious.

LANDSCAPE VALUE: Good low growing plant for poor, dry soil areas. Will add an element of color to the landscape. The few that I have seen were quite handsome and would make a nice addition to the landscape.

CULTIVARS:

'Plena' — A dwarf, semi-prostrate shrub, with more numerous petals of a more brilliant yellow color.

'Royal Gold' — Stems erect, up to 2' high; flowers golden yellow in terminal and axillary racemes, forming a narrow panicle.

There are numerous geographical varieties which differ in habit, leaf morphology and flower characteristics. Bean noted that *G. tinctoria* in its modern acceptation may be taken to cover a group of allied forms put under one variable species.

PROPAGATION: Seeds should be the preferred method of propagation; however, cuttings collected in late July and August and placed in sand in outdoor frames, rooted the following Spring.

RELATED SPECIES:

Genista pilosa, Silkyleaf Woadwaxen, is a low growing (1 to 1 1/2') procumbent shrub in youth, finally forming a low, tangled mass of slender, twiggy shoots. The leaves and stems are a grayish green and provide a nice contrast. The flowers are bright yellow, produced singly or in pairs from the leaf-axils, forming a crowded 2 to 6" long raceme. Demands sandy, gravelly, dry soils for best growth. Native to much of Europe. Cultivated 1789. Zone 5.

ADDITIONAL NOTES: The woadwaxens (there are numerous species) are not well known in Midwestern gardens. They are popular in Europe where most are found wild. The Morton Arboretum has a small collection which I first saw in the summer of 1975. Most were low growing, spreading shrubs of handsome foliage colors.

NATIVE HABITAT: Europe, Western Asia. Cultivated 1789.

Ginkgo biloba — Ginkgo, often called Maidenhair Tree

FAMILY: Ginkgoaceae

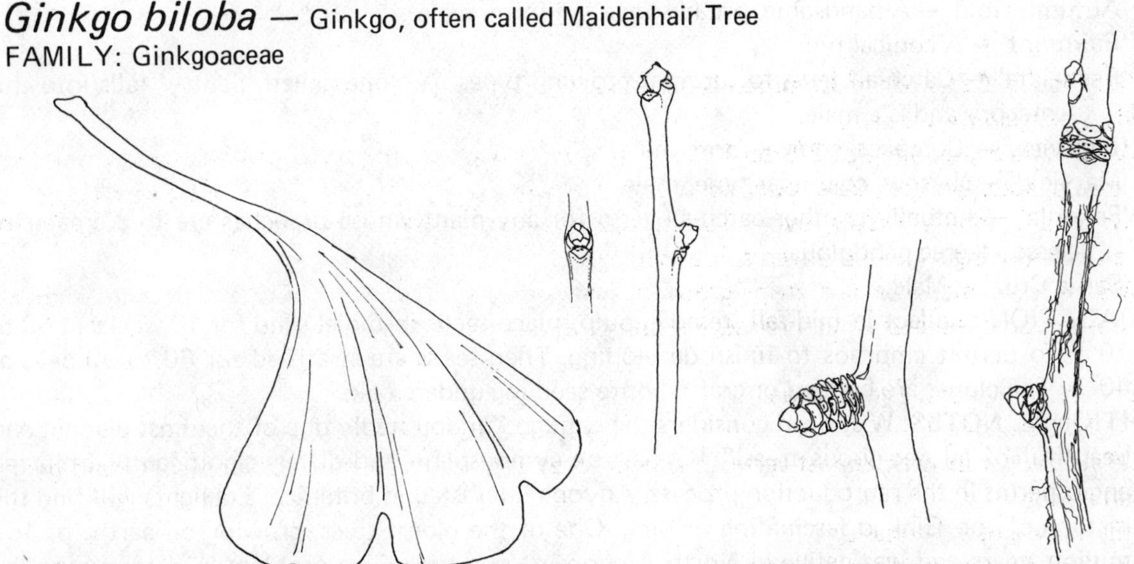

LEAVES: Alternate, simple, in clusters of 3 to 5 on spurs, fan shaped, dichotomously veined, more or less incised or divided at the broad summit, 2 to 3" across.

BUD: Imbricate, mounded, often acute, brownish, borne on spur growth.

STEM: Stout, light brown 1st year, becoming gray with stringy peeling bark; prominent blackish spurs evident.

SIZE: 50 to 80' in height with a tremendously variable spread ranging from 30 to 40' to ultimately wider than high at maturity. The species can grow to 100' or more.

HARDINESS: Zone 4.

HABIT: Usually pyramidal in outline when young; in old age often becoming wide spreading with large, massive, picturesque branches. It is quite difficult to adequately describe the habit of this tree due to the tremendous variation in plants grown from seed. The male tree is supposedly more upright than the pistillate form.

RATE: Slow to medium, probably 10 to 15′ over a 10 to 12 year period although with adequate water and fertilizer this tree will grow very fast.

TEXTURE: Medium in leaf and coarse in winter but not objectionable.

BARK: Usually gray-brown to black combination, ridged and furrowed, actually quite handsome in the overall effect.

LEAF COLOR: Bright green on both surfaces in summer changing to an excellent yellow in fall. Next to *Betula lenta,* Ginkgo is the best tree for yellow fall color in Central Illinois.

FLOWERS: Male are borne in catkins, female usually long pedicelled bearing 1 or 2 ovules, dioecious, not ornamental.

FRUIT: Actually not a true fruit but simply a naked seed; tan to orangish in color, plum-like in shape, 1 to 1 1/2″ long. The fleshy covering on the seed (female gametophyte) is extremely messy and malodorous and, for this reason only male trees should be planted. The sperm which fertilize the egg are motile (swimming) and depend on water for accomplishing their mission. The seed is eaten by the Japanese and is reported to be well flavored.

CULTURE: Transplants easily and established without difficulty; prefers sandy, deep, moderately moist soil but grows in almost any situation; full sun; very pH adaptable; prune in spring; air pollutant tolerant; a durable tree for difficult landscape situations.

DISEASES AND INSECTS: Extremely free of pests although several leaf spots of negligible importance have been reported.

LANDSCAPE VALUE: Excellent city tree, public areas, perhaps too large for street tree use but is used extensively for this purpose. A well developed Ginkgo is an impressive sight; often looks out of place in the small residential landscape because of unique foliage and winter habit.

CULTIVARS:

'Autumn Gold' — A handsome, broad spreading form, male.

'Fairmont' — A conical type.

'Fastigiata' — Catch-all term for upright growing types. A clone called 'Sentry' falls into this category and is a male.

'Lakeview' — Compact, conical form, male.

'Mayfield' — Narrow, columnar type, male.

'Pendula' — Actually another catch-all term for any plant whose branches are to a greater or lesser degree pendulous.

'Santa Cruz' — Male.

PROPAGATION: Collect in mid-fall, remove pulp, place seeds in moist sand for 10 weeks at 60 to 70°F to permit embryos to finish developing. Then seeds are stratified for 60 to 90 days at 40°F. The clones are budded or grafted onto seedling understock.

ADDITIONAL NOTES: W.J. Bean considers the Ginkgo "undoubtedly one of the most distinct and beautiful of all deciduous trees." It is a true gymnosperm and differs significantly from the angiosperms in the reproduction process. Anyone interested in botanical sidelights will find the history of the Ginkgo fascinating reading. One of the oldest trees, growing on earth for 150 million years and was native in North America at one time. The problem in determining the sex of Ginkgo is that they do not "fruit" until they are quite old (20 to 50 years). Always be leary when buying unnamed clones for this reason alone. E.H. Wilson, the great plant explorer, observed numerous trees in China, Japan, and Korea and stated that there is no difference in habit between male and female plants. The literature abounds with conflicts concerning various plant descriptions and, unfortunately, there is no easy way to rectify the incongruities.

NATIVE HABITAT: Eastern China. Introduced 1784.

Gleditsia triacanthos var. *inermis* — Thornless Common Honeylocust

FAMILY: Leguminosae

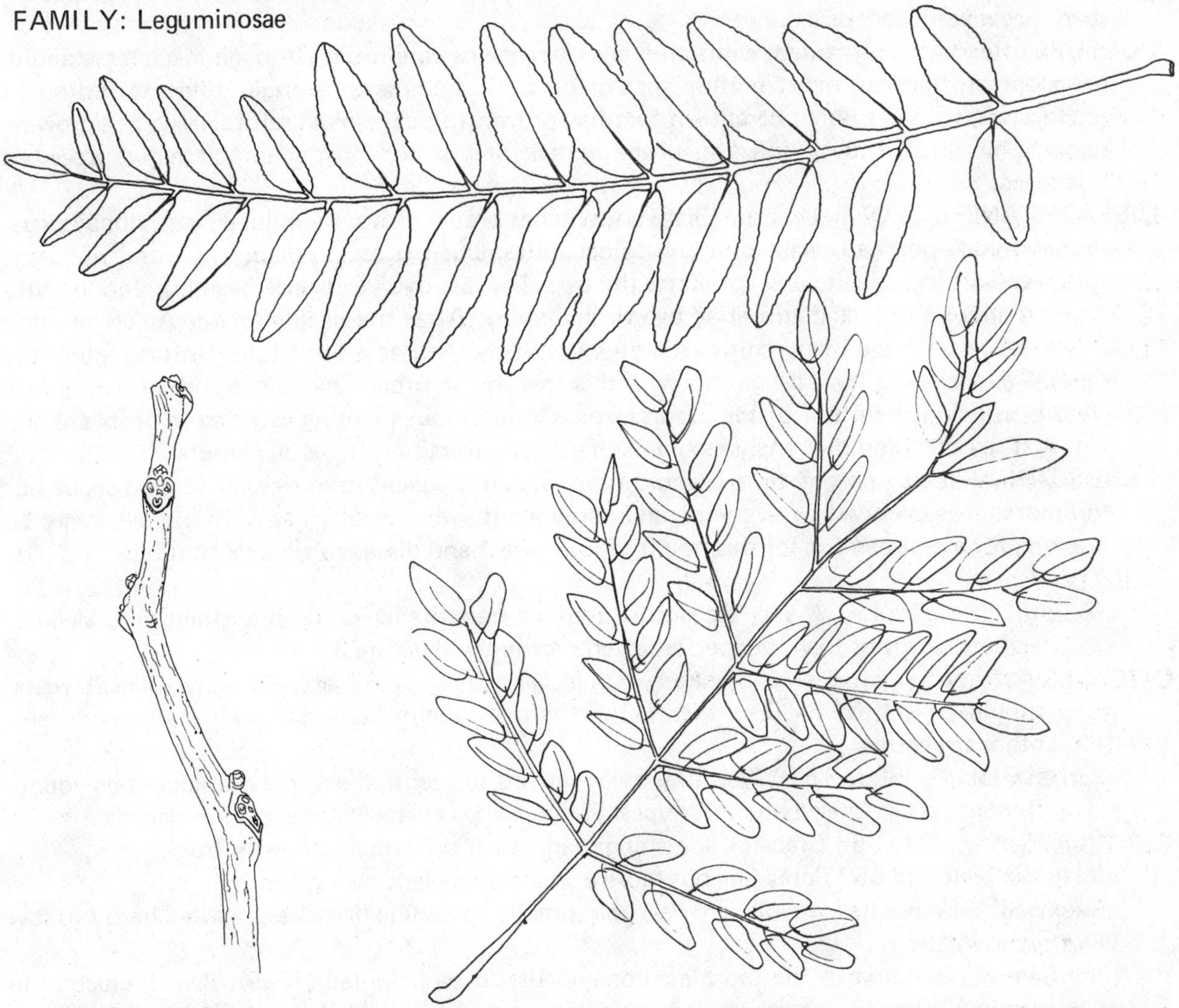

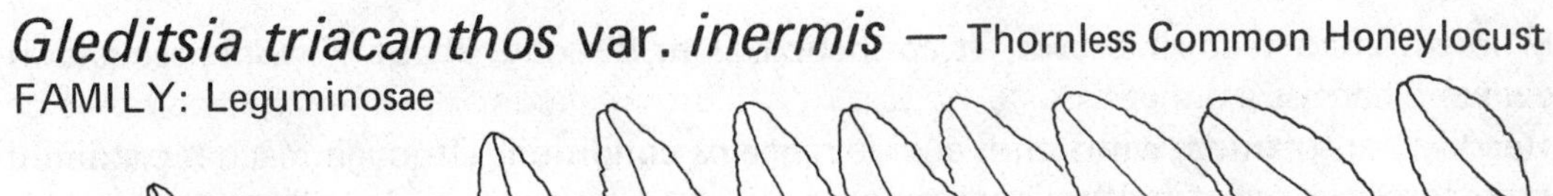

LEAVES: Alternate, pinnately or bipinnately compound, 6 to 8″ long, rachis pubescent all around, grooved; pinnate leaves with 20 to 30 oblong-lanceolate leaflets, 1/3 to 1 1/2″ long, remotely crenate-serrulate, pubescent on midribs beneath; bipinnate leaves with 8 to 14 pinnae, the leaflets 1/3 to 4/5″ long. Base of petiole swollen and enclosing bud.

BUDS: Terminal-absent, laterals small, about 5 more or less distinct at a node, some scaly, others naked.

STEM: Shining, smooth, reddish to greenish brown, often mottled or streaked, zigzag with enlarged nodes.

SIZE: Tremendously variable in the cultivated types but usually in the range of 30 to 70′ in height with a comparable spread; in the wild often grows to over 100 feet.

HARDINESS: Zone 4.

HABIT: Usually a tree with a short trunk and a rather open spreading crown; light-shaded and consequently grass will grow up to the trunk; a very delicate and sophisticated silhouette which, unfortunately, has led to abuse by landscape planners.

RATE: Fast, as a young tree will grow 2′ or more per year over a 10 year period.

TEXTURE: Medium-fine in leaf (almost fine); medium in winter.

BARK: On old trees grayish brown, broken up into long, narrow, longitudinal and superficially scaly ridges which are separated by deep furrows.

LEAF COLOR: Bright green in summer; clear yellow to yellow-green in fall.

FLOWERS: Polygamo-dioecious, perfect and imperfect flowers on same tree, greenish, borne in axillary racemes in June; fragrant and nectar laden; not showy.

FRUIT: Pod, brownish to reddish brown, strap-shaped, 7 to 8" long, about 1" wide; seeds oval, dark brown and hard as a bullet.

CULTURE: Readily transplanted; withstands a wide range of conditions although reaches maximum development on rich, moist bottomlands or on soils of a limestone origin; tolerant of drought conditions; high pH; salt tolerant (in fact has proven to be the most salt-tolerant tree growing along Chicago freeways), full sun; prune in fall; one of our most adaptable native trees but overused.

DISEASES AND INSECTS: Leaf spot, cankers, witches broom, powdery mildew, rust, honeylocust borer, midge pod gall, webworm and spider mites. Our biggest problem in Central Illinois is the webworm which literally defoliates the tree. The last two years have been horrendous with most of the honeylocust appearing brown in August. After the decline of the American Elm, honeylocust and the many cultivars were extensively used as a substitute. Unfortunately the insects and diseases have caught up with this tree in the urban landscapes and let us hope its fate is not similar to that of the predecessor. Monogamous planting can lead to problems and for that reason I would strongly recommend using a diversity of trees and shrubs.

LANDSCAPE VALUE: At one time I would have said an excellent lawn tree for filtered shade but no more. It is overused by everyone and consequently the novelty has worn off. We might be looking for a replacement for this tree if serious insect and disease problems continue.

CULTIVARS:

'Bujotii' ('Pendula') — A very elegant, pendulous tree; branches and branchlets very slender; leaflets narrower than the species, often mottled with white.

'Elegantissima' — Dense, shrubby habit, with elegant foliage; original plant grew 13' in 25 years; should be grafted on *G. t. inermis* understock. Might be suitable under low wires and other structures.

'Green Glory' — (50 to 75') Vigorous grower with strong central leader, pyramidal when young. Retains foliage later than other types. Shows some resistance to webworm damage.

'Imperial' — (30 to 35') Graceful, spreading branches at right angles to main trunk.

'Majestic' — (60 to 65') Spreading but more upright. Excellent dark green foliage.

'Maxwell' — Somewhat irregular grower, horizontally spreading branches; reputed hardy to low temperature.

'Moraine' — The first of the thornless honeylocust to be patented (1949). Broad, graceful in outline; 40 to 50'; fruitless; shows greater resistance to webworm than some of the new introductions; possibly should be considered the standard by which the others are judged.

'Pin Cushion' — Interesting novelty form; foliage is borne in bunches along the stem; I have seen three planted together and the shade produced was not dense enough to protect an ant.

'Ruby Lace' — Purplish bronze foliage, a poor specimen, ungainly.

'Shademaster' — Ascending branches, dark green leaves.

'Skyline' — (45') Pyramidal form with ascending branches, (60 to 90° angle) compact, dark green leaves.

'Sunburst' — (30 to 35') Broad pyramidal head, golden leaves on new growth changing eventually to bright green.

PROPAGATION: Seeds should be scarified in concentrated sulfuric acid for 1 to 2 hours. They will then germinate readily. Cultivars are budded on seedling understock.

ADDITIONAL NOTES: The pods contain a sweetish, gummy substance from which the name honeylocust is derived. The species, *Gleditsia triacanthos*, is laden with multibranched thorns and should not be considered for landscape situations. It should be mentioned that very few of the clones are completely fruitless. The polygamous nature of the flowers usually allows for some perfect flowers and, hence, fruit will occur.

NATIVE HABITAT: Pennsylvania to Nebraska and south to Texas and Mississippi. Introduced 1700.

Gymnocladus dioicus — Kentucky Coffeetree

FAMILY: Leguminosae

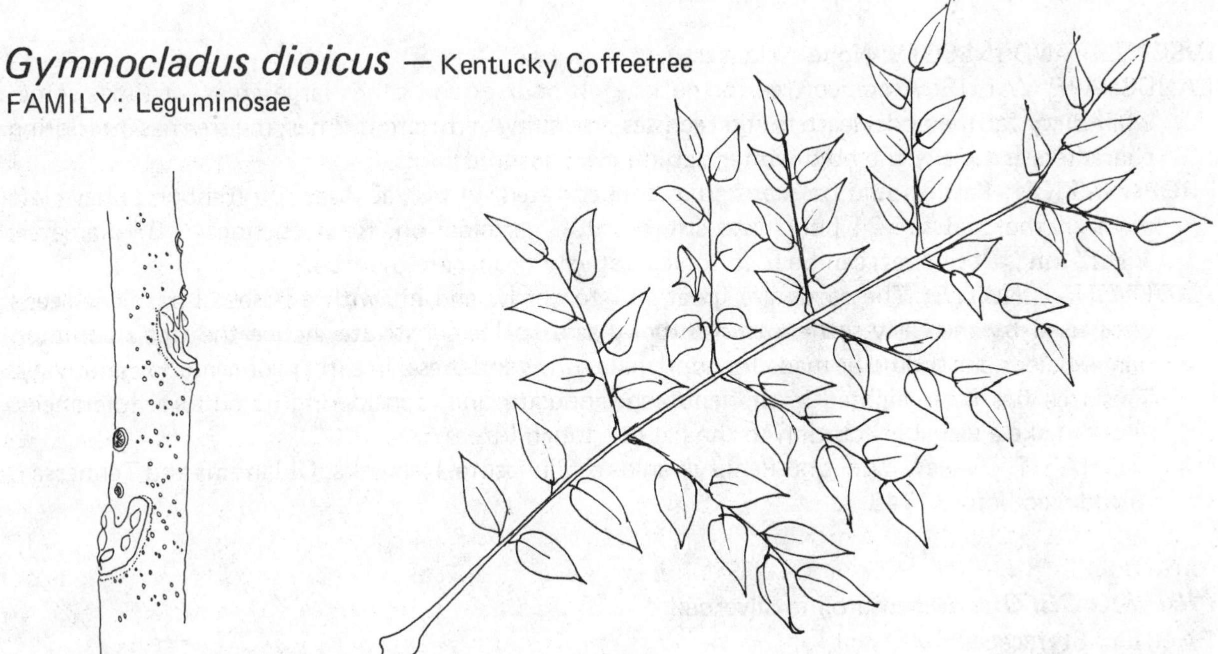

LEAVES: Alternate, bipinnately compound, to 36" long and 24" wide, with 3 to 7 pairs of pinnae, the lowest usually reduced to simple leaflets, the upper with 6 to 14 leaflets; leaflets ovate or elliptic ovate, entire, 2 to 3" long, acute, rounded or cuneate at base, pubescent beneath when young, short petioled, swollen at base.

BUDS: Terminal-absent, laterals—small, bronze, pubescent, partially sunken, scarcely projecting beyond surface of twig, surrounded by an incurved downy rim of bark, axillary bud in depression at top of leaf scar, one or sometimes 2 superposed buds present. Sometimes 2 lateral scales visible.

STEM: Very stout, more or less contorted, brown or slightly greenish, glabrous or often velvety-downy. Pith—wide, salmon-pink to brown.

BARK: Dark brown, characteristically roughened with their tortuous, recurved, scale-like ridges which are distinct even upon comparatively young branches.

SIZE: 60 to 75′ in height by 40 to 50′ in spread although can grow to 90′.

HARDINESS: Zone 4.

HABIT: Usually develops vertically ascending branches which form a narrow, obovate crown; picturesque; bare limbed and somewhat clumsy looking in winter. The finest specimen I know exists on our campus.

RATE: Slow to medium, growing 12 to 14′ over a 10 year period.

TEXTURE: Medium in leaf; coarse, but not offensively so, in winter.

BARK: Rough, with hard, thin, firm and scaly ridges curling outward (recurving) along their edges. Very unique and interesting bark pattern which develops on 1 to 2" diameter branches; grayish brown to dark brown.

LEAF COLOR: One of the latest trees to leaf out in spring, usually emerging about May 5 to May 20 in our area. New leaves are pinkish tinged gradually changing to dark green, almost dark bluish green in summer; fall color is ineffective (some yellow).

FLOWERS: Dioecious or polygamo-dioecious, greenish white; late May to early June; borne in large 8 to 12" long, 3 to 4" wide pyramidal panicles (female); on the male tree the panicle is about 1/3 the length of the female. Interesting on close inspection.

FRUIT: Reddish brown, leathery pod, 5 to 10" long, 1 1/2 to 2" wide, containing a few, large, blackish brown, hard-shelled, rounded seeds imbedded in a sweet, sticky pulp; ripens in October, but hang on tree through winter.

CULTURE: Transplant balled and burlapped into deep, rich, moist soil for best growth; however, adaptable to a wide range of conditions such as chalk (limestone), drought, and city conditions; full sun; prune in winter or early spring; wood may be somewhat brittle.

DISEASES AND INSECTS: None serious.

LANDSCAPE VALUE: A choice tree for parks, golf courses and other large areas, at times somewhat dirty for the pods, leaflets and rachises are falling at different times; the tree has interesting characters especially the bold winter habit and handsome bark.

PROPAGATION: Seed should be scarified in concentrated sulfuric acid for 4 to 6 hours. I have left seeds in the acid for 24 hours and still got 90% germination. Root cuttings, 3/8" diameter, 1 1/2" long, December, can be used to vegetatively propagate the tree.

ADDITIONAL NOTES: The seeds are great fun to throw and hit with a baseball bat. The seeds were used by the early settlers to Kentucky as a coffee substitute, hence the tree's common name. Selections should be made for good male forms and these, in turn, propagated vegetatively. This tree has been slighted in the landscape industry and, considering its cultural tolerances, would make a valuable addition to the list of "tough" trees.

NATIVE HABITAT: New York and Pennsylvania to Minnesota, Nebraska, Oklahoma and Tennessee. Introduced before 1748.

Halesia carolina — Carolina Silverbell

FAMILY: Styracaceae

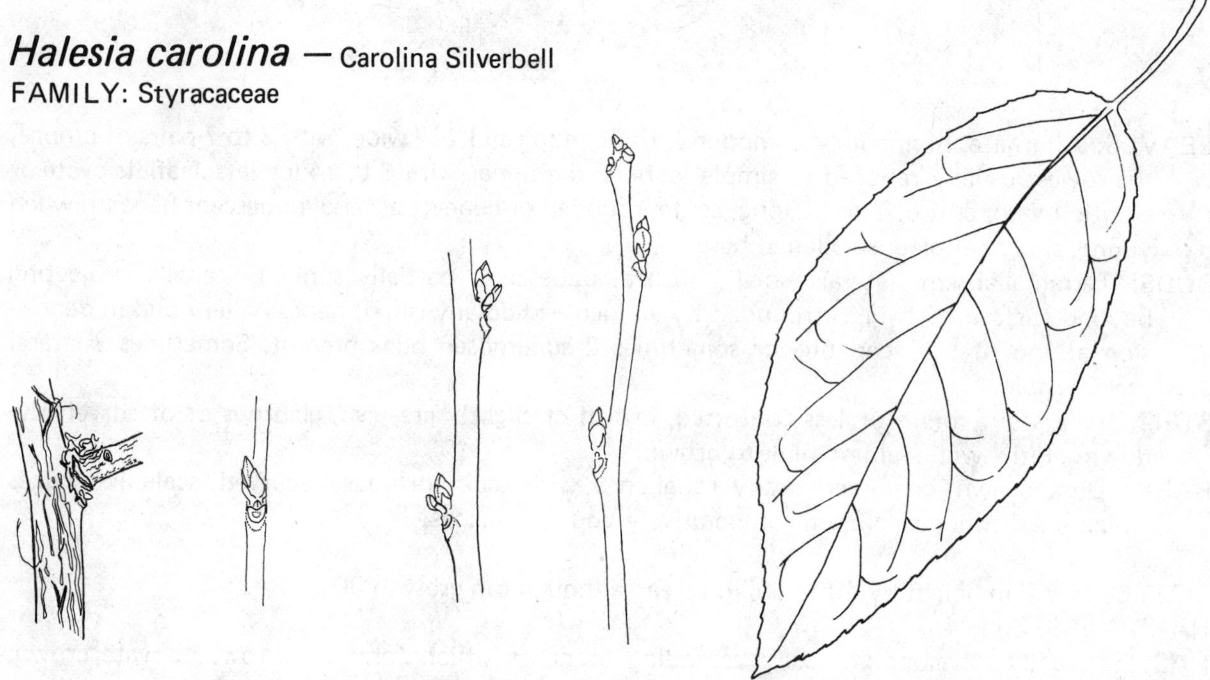

LEAVES: Alternate, simple, ovate or elliptic to ovate-oblong, 2 to 4" long, acute or acuminate, cuneate or rounded at base, serrulate, tomentose at first, soon glabrous above, pubescent beneath; petiole 1/4 to 1/2" long.

BUDS: Terminal-absent, laterals ellipsoid to ovoid, superposed, 1/8" to 1/4" long, with thick, broad-ovate dark red acute puberulous scales rounded on the back, slightly stalked.

STEM: Slender, glabrous or densely pubescent becoming slightly pubescent or remaining glabrous. Pith—white, chambered, 1 bundle trace. Stem becoming stringy on 2nd year wood, 1st year—usually smooth, brown.

SIZE: 30 to 40' in height with a spread of 20 to 35'; supposedly grows up to 80'.

HARDINESS: Zone 4.

HABIT: Low branched tree or shrub with a comparatively narrow head and ascending branches or often with several spreading branches forming a broad, rounded crown.

RATE: Medium, 9 to 12' over a 6 to 8 year period.

TEXTURE: Medium in all seasons.

BARK: Gray to brown to black combination, ridged and furrowed with flat ridges which develop into scaly plates.

LEAF COLOR: Dark yellowish green in summer; changing to yellow or yellow green in fall; usually dropping very early in fall.

FLOWERS: White, rarely pale rose, bell shaped, flowering on year-old wood, 1/2" long; borne in axillary (cymose) 2 to 5-flowered clusters in late April to early May; effective for one week; a subtle beauty not appreciated by most people.

FRUIT: Oblong or obovoid, 4-winged dry drupe, 1 1/2" long, green changing to light brown, effective in September into late fall.

CULTURE: Transplants readily balled and burlapped; prefers rich, well-drained, moist, acid (pH 5 to 6), high organic matter soils; sun or semi-shade; in the wild often occurs as an understory tree on the slopes of mountains, particularly along the streams.

DISEASES AND INSECTS: Exceptionally pest resistant.

LANDSCAPE VALUE: One of my favorite small native trees; often neglected in this country but definitely with a place in shrub and woodland borders; handsome lawn tree; set off best with an evergreen background; rhododendrons grow well beneath silverbells.

PROPAGATION: Seed must be moist stratified at 56° to 86°F for 60 to 120 days, followed by 60 to 90 days at 33 to 41°F. I have collected softwood cuttings from a tree on campus, treated with 1000 ppm IBA/50% alcohol, placed in peat:perlite under mist and received 80 to 90% rooting.

RELATED SPECIES:

Halesia diptera, Two-wing Silverbell, is a shrub, 8 to 15' high, or a small tree growing to 30' in the wild. Similar to *H. carolina* but not as free flowering and therefore not recommended for extensive landscape use. It can be distinguished from *H. carolina* by the 2 (rarely 4) winged drupes. Native from South Carolina and Tennessee to Florida and Texas. Introduced 1758. Zone 6.

Halesia monticola, Mountain Silverbell, is similar to *H. carolina* but differs in having larger flowers, larger fruits and larger habit often reaching 60 to 80' with well developed single or double leaders and a conical habit; some trees develop bushy crowns. Cultivar termed 'Rosea' has pale pink flowers. Native from North Carolina to Tennessee and Georgia in the mountains at altitudes not less than 3,000 feet. Introduced 1897. Zone 5.

ADDITIONAL NOTES: The largest specimens of *H. carolina* and *H. monticola* I have seen are located on the campus of Purdue University, West Lafayette, Indiana. *H. carolina* is about 40 to 50' in height while *H. monticola* is probably 50 to 60'. Both are beautiful specimens and worth seeing. *H. monticola* is not included with *H. carolina* by some authorities and this thinking is probably justified since it is extremely difficult to distinguish between the two species.

NATIVE HABITAT: West Virginia to Florida and Eastern Texas. Introduced 1756.

Hamamelis vernalis — Vernal Witchhazel

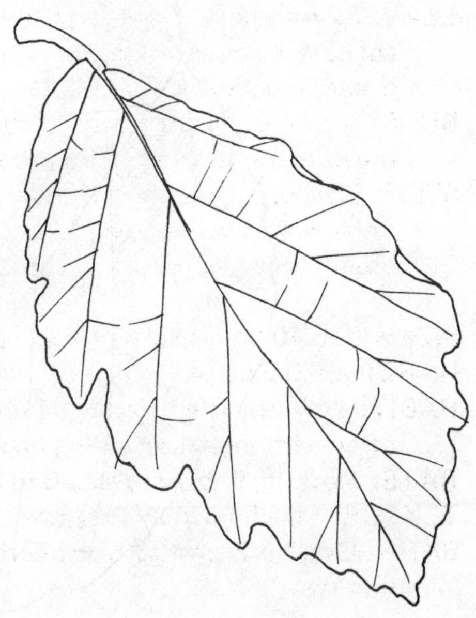

FAMILY: Hamamelidaceae

LEAVES: Alternate, simple, obovate to oblong-ovate, obtusely pointed, narrowed toward the broad cuneate or truncate, rarely subcordate base, 2 to 5" long, coarsely sinuate dentate above the middle, green or glaucescent beneath, glabrous or nearly so, with 4 to 6 pairs of veins; petioles 1/5 to 1/2" long, pubescent. Leaves—thickish.

BUDS: Vegetative—naked, foliose, grayish brown, tomentose. Flower—stalked, rounded, tan, pubescent, usually 3 or 4 per stalk.

STEM: Old—gray, not as smooth as *H. virginiana,* but similar. Young—densely pubescent.

SIZE: 6 to 10' in height by 6 to 10' and greater in spread.

HARDINESS: Zone 5.

HABIT: Multistemmed, dense, rounded shrub, quite neat in appearance compared to *H. virginiana*, but variable in form.

RATE: Slow to medium.

TEXTURE: Medium in leaf and in winter.

STEM COLOR: Older stems, 3-year or greater, assume a grayish brown color; quite attractive.

LEAF COLOR: Medium to dark green in summer, changing to golden yellow in fall, fall color persists for 2 to 3 weeks and has been outstanding in our area.

FLOWERS: Yellow to red, variable, 1/2" across, usually the inner surface of the calyx lobes is red and the petals are yellow, some plants exhibit solid yellow or red; pungently fragrant, late January through February and effective for 2 to 3 weeks, borne in few flowered (3 to 4) cymes. Petals roll up on very cold days and in a protective sense, avoid freeze damage. This "adaptive" mechanism extends the flowering period.

FRUITS: Capsule, dehiscent, 2-valved and splitting and actually expelling the black seeds at maturity; green-yellow to brown and interestingly attractive in a quiet manner.

CULTURE: Supposedly somewhat difficult to transplant; my experience indicated no problem if handled as a container or balled and burlapped specimen, root pruning has been advocated for increasing root development, native on gravelly, often inundated banks of streams, performs best in moist situations, has grown admirably in our poorly-drained, clay soils; does well in full sun or 3/4's shade.

DISEASES AND INSECTS: None serious.

LANDSCAPE VALUE: Durable plant for Central Midwest, used effectively on University of Illinois campus in groupings near large buildings, also in planter boxes, would make a good screen, unpruned hedge. Unusual because of the early flower date. Selections should be made for good floriferous character, dense habit and excellent fall color. I have two selections, one predominantly yellow flowering, the other red which are superior to the type and fortunately both root readily from cuttings.

PROPAGATION: Seed, difficult due to double dormancy but results have been obtained by stratifying seed for 60 days at 68°F plus 90 days at 41°F. Cuttings, collected in early June, wounded, 10 sec. 1000 ppm IBA/50% alcohol dip, placed in sand under mist rooted 70 to 80% in 3 months.

NATIVE HABITAT: Missouri to Louisiana and Oklahoma. Introduced 1908.

Hamamelis virginiana — Common Witchhazel

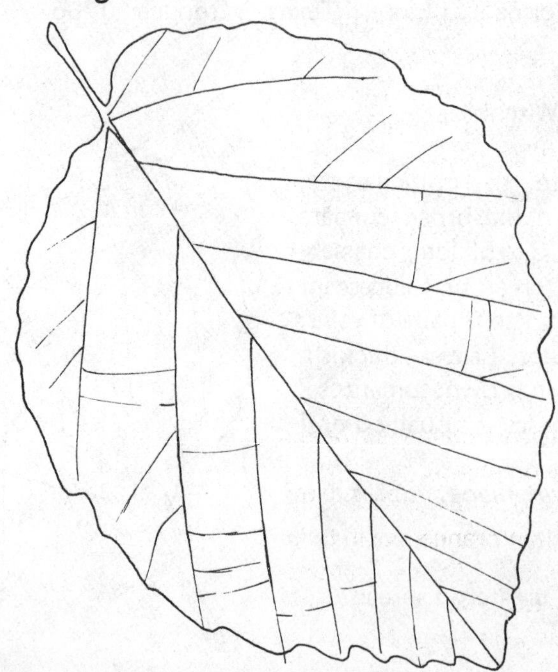

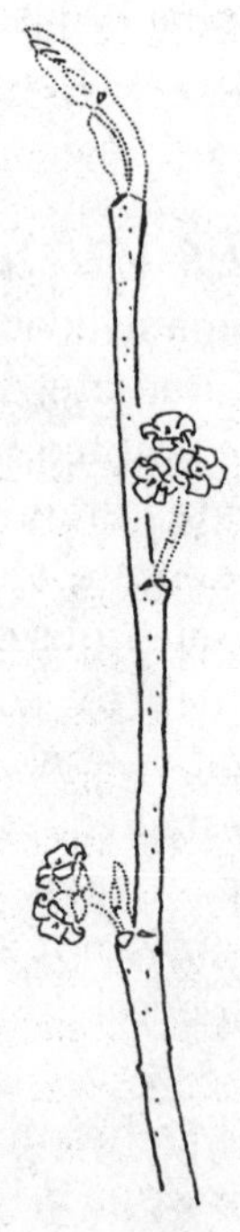

LEAVES: Alternate, simple, obovate or elliptic, obtusely short-acuminate or obtusish, narrowed toward the base and subcordate, rarely broad-cuneate, 3-6" long, coarsely crenate-dentate, nearly glabrous or pubescent on the veins beneath, with 5 to 7 pairs of veins; petioles 1/5 to 3/5" long, pubescent. Leaves—thinnish.

BUDS: Naked, brownish, tomentose. Flower buds—stalked, globose, opening in the fall.

STEM: Slender, older stems—glabrous, smooth, gray. Young stems—brownish, pubescent. Pith—small, green, continuous.

SIZE: 20 to 30' in height by 20 to 25' in spread, possibly 15 to 20' is more appropriate for Midwest.

HARDINESS: Zone 4.

HABIT: Small tree or large shrub with several large, crooked, spreading branches forming an irregular, rounded, open crown.

RATE: Medium.

TEXTURE: Probably would be considered coarse in leaf as well as winter habit, tends toward openness and gangliness.

LEAF COLOR: Medium green in summer yielding to good yellow in the fall.

FLOWERS: Yellow, fragrant, four strap-like petals, 3/4 to 4/5" long, calyx lobes are yellowish brown inside; November, about mid November in Champaign-Urbana. I have observed specimens in full flower in mid October and others as late as early December; flowers are borne in 2 to 4 flowered cymes, effective for about 2 to 3 weeks depending on weather, often in full fall color at the time of flower thus reducing the quality and effectiveness of the flowers.

FRUIT: Capsule, 1/2" long, dehiscing at the distal end; do not discharge the seeds until 12 months after flowering.

CULTURE: Similar to *H. vernalis,* full sun or shade, supposedly somewhat tolerant of city conditions, prefers a moist soil, avoid extremely dry situations.

DISEASES AND INSECTS: None serious, although Wyman noted that when planted near birch trees a peculiar insect makes small galls on the underside of the foliage.

LANDSCAPE VALUE: Native shrub covering much of eastern United States and therefore valuable in a naturalized situation, best reserved for the shrub border, near large buildings in shaded areas. Probably too large for the small residential landscape. Considerable selections could be made for quality and abundance of flower and the absence of foliage during the flowering period.

PROPAGATION: Seed same as described for *H. vernalis.* Cuttings, I have had little success rooting this species; cuttings taken and handled as described for *H. vernalis* yielded 2 to 5% rooting.

RELATED SPECIES:

Hamamelis x *intermedia* is the result of a cross between *H. mollis* and *H. japonica.* Foliage is medium to dark green in summer; reddish in fall (this trait comes from *H. japonica*). Flowers vary from yellow to reddish. The cultivar 'Arnold Promise' has yellow flowers, 1 1/2" diameter; 'Copper Beauty' has reddish flowers; 'Jelena' has an orange tint to the flowers; and 'Ruby Glow' has reddish flowers. These hybrids will grow between 15 and 20' high with a comparable spread.

Hamamelis japonica — Japanese Witchhazel

Leaves: Alternate, simple, suborbicular to broad-ovate or elliptic, rarely obovate, acute or rounded at apex, rounded or subcordate, rarely broad-cuneate at base, 2-4" long, light green and glabrous or slightly pubescent beneath, with usually 6 to 7 pairs of veins; petioles 1/5 to 3/5" long; leaves turn bright yellow orange late in fall. Flowers: Borne in January-February, petals yellow, about 4/5" long, crinkled, strap-like; calyx-lobes—red, reddish brown or greenish inside; slightly fragrant.

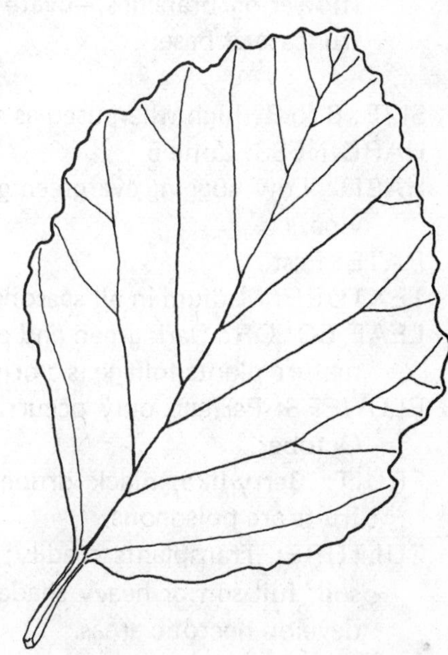

Hamamelis mollis — Chinese Witchhazel

Leaves: Alternate, simple, orbicular-obovate to obovate, short acuminate, obliquely cordate to subcordate at base, 3-6" long, sinuately denticulate, pubescent above, grayish tomentose beneath; petioles stout, 1/5 to 2/5" long, densely pubescent.

Grows to 30' high and forms an upright-oval to rounded outline. The foliage is medium green in summer and changes to bright yellow in fall; flowers are yellow, fragrant, 1 1/2" across; late January through March; in few flowered axillary clusters. Much more floriferous than *H. virginiana* and grows quite well under Central Illinois conditions. Native to Central China. Introduced 1879. Zone 5. 'Brevipetala' has 3/8" long petals of butter yellow color; appears to be a profuse flowerer and is available in the trade.

NATIVE HABITAT: Native from Canada to Georgia, west to Nebraska and Arkansas. Introduced 1736.

Hedera helix — English Ivy

FAMILY: Araliaceae

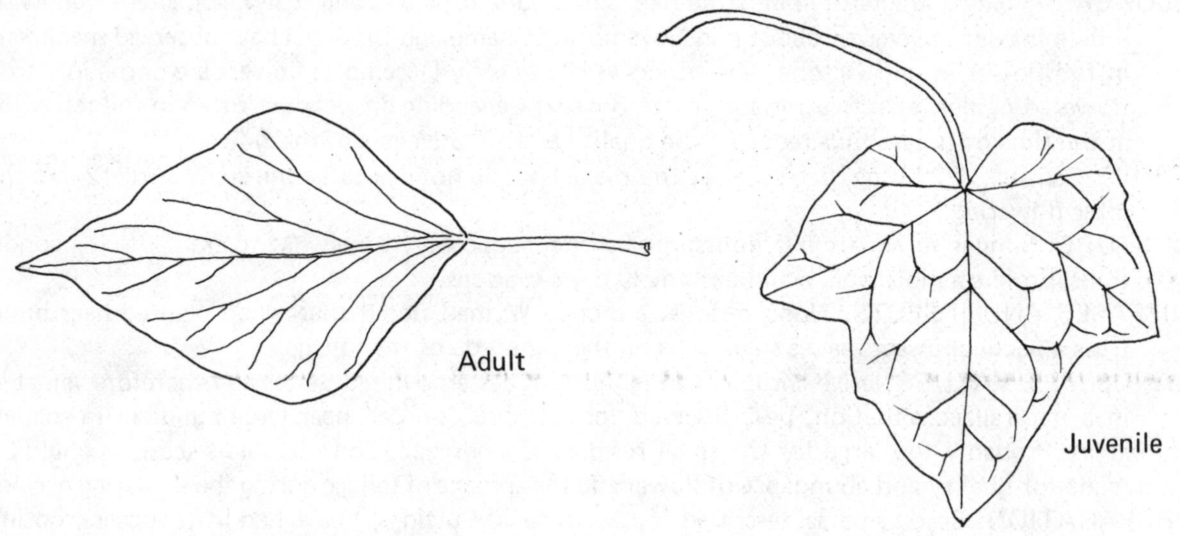

LEAVES: Alternate, simple, of juvenile shoots—3 to 5 lobed, 1 3/5 to 4" long, dark green and usually lustrous above, often with whitish veins, pale or yellowish green beneath; on mature (flowering branches)—ovate to rhombic and often lighter green in color, entire, rounded to truncate at base.

SIZE: 6 to 8" high when used as a ground cover; can climb to 90' as a vine.

HARDINESS: Zone 5.

HABIT: Low hugging evergreen ground cover, rooting at the nodes; or a high climbing, true clinging vine.

RATE: Fast.

TEXTURE: Medium in all seasons.

LEAF COLOR: Dark green and often lustrous above, often with whitish veins on juvenile leaves; on mature plants foliage is a bright, lustrous green without the prominent whitish veins.

FLOWERS: Perfect, only occurring on the "Adult" form, greenish white, borne in globose umbels, October.

FRUIT: Berry-like, black drupe, 1/6" across, April or May following flowering, apparently the fruits are poisonous.

CULTURE: Transplants readily; growth is maximized in rich, fairly moist, organic, well-drained soil; full sun or heavy shade; not a bad idea to protect from winter sun and wind as the leaves develop necrotic areas.

DISEASES AND INSECTS: Bacterial leaf spot and canker, leaf spots, powdery mildews, aphids, caterpillars, mealybugs, scales, and two-spotted mite.

LANDSCAPE VALUE: Ground cover, with many uses, good in heavy shade, can look especially nice when given proper cultural conditions; has a nice effect when grown on trees or buildings; the adult form develops high up in trees or on buildings. The leaf morphology of the adult form is different from the vigorous normal type and the plant becomes quite woody and is often used as a foundation plant.

CULTIVARS:

'Albany' – Possibly an adult form, erect and shrubby in habit.

'Baltica' – A hardy form of the species with smaller leaves.

(var. *baltica*)

'Bulgaria' – Another hardy clone, capable of withstanding the winters in St. Louis. Introduced by Missouri Botanic Garden.

'Hedera Girard' – Foliage lighter green than English Ivy, more of an apple green, with lighter, pronounced veining; texture is heavier and more triangular; hardy, supposedly stands cold weather quite well.

'Rochester' – Another hardy form.

'Rumania' – Similar to 'Bulgaria'.

'Thorndale' – Hardy form with larger leaves than the species.

'Wilson' – Hardy form.

'238th Street' – Supposedly a hardy adult form, not subject to winter burn.

PROPAGATION: Seed, the pericarp must be removed and the seeds stratified. I tried an experiment using whole fruits and those with fruit walls removed. The only germination took place with the seeds which were extracted from the fruit. All seedlings were similar to the juvenile form. Cuttings can be rooted anytime of the year.

NATIVE HABITAT: Europe to Caucasian Mountains. Cultivated since ancient times.

Hibiscus syriacus — Shrub Althea, also called Rose-of-Sharon

FAMILY: Malvaceae

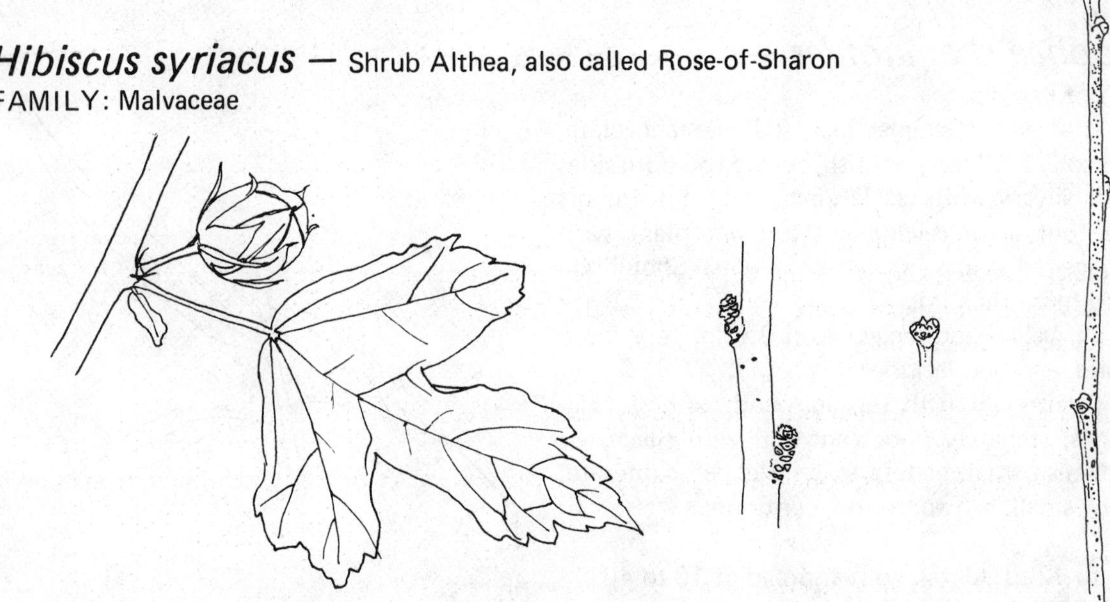

LEAVES: Alternate, simple, palmately veined and 3-lobed, ovate or rhombic-ovate, 2 to 4" long, often coarsely toothed with rounded or acutish teeth, broad-cuneate or rounded at base, glabrous except a few hairs on the veins beneath.

BUDS: Not evident, their position usually occupied by the scars of fallen inflorescences or branch-vestiges.

STEM: Rounded, fluted near the dilated tip, glabrescent, gray; pith—small, white, continuous with green border; leaf-scars crowded at tip, half round or transversely elliptical, raised, shortly decurrent in more or less evident ridges.

FRUIT: A dehiscent, 5-valved, upright, brown capsule which persists through winter and offers a valid identification character.

SIZE: 8 to 12′ in height by 6 to 10′ wide.
HARDINESS: Zone 5.
HABIT: Shrub or small tree, very erect but occasionally spreading, with numerous upright branches.
RATE: Medium.
TEXTURE: Medium in leaf; medium to medium-coarse in winter.
LEAF COLOR: Deep green in summer, holding late or changing to a poor yellow in fall. Very late leafing out in spring.
FLOWERS: Perfect, white to red or purple or violet, or combinations, short stalked, broad campanulate, 2 to 4″ across; July, August through September, solitary on new year's growth.
FRUIT: Dehiscent capsule, 5-valved and persisting through winter.
CULTURE: Move as a small plant (5′ or less), transplants well, grows in about any soil except those which are extremely wet or dry; does best in moist, well-drained soils which have been supplemented with peat moss, leaf mold or compost; pH adaptable; full sun or partial shade; prefers hot weather; prune heavily back in early spring, or prune back to 2 or 3 buds in spring to get large flowers.
DISEASES AND INSECTS: Leaf spots, bacterial leaf spot, blights, canker, rust, aphids, Japanese beetle, mining scale, foliar nematodes and white-fly.
LANDSCAPE VALUE: Valuable for late season flowers, groupings, masses, shrub borders but does not deserve specimen use; has and can be used for screening and hedges; not one of my favorite plants but has certainly been accepted by the gardening public.
CULTIVARS: Too many to discuss. See Wyman's list in *Shrubs and Vines for American Gardens.*
PROPAGATION: Softwood cuttings root readily when treated with IBA and placed under mist.
NATIVE HABITAT: China, India. Introduced before 1600.

Hippophae rhamnoides — Common Seabuckthorn

FAMILY: Elaeagnaceae
LEAVES: Alternate, simple, linear to linear-lanceolate, 4/5 to 2 2/5″ long, acutish, covered on both sides with silvery-white scales. Not common in this area but an excellent salt tolerant plant with orange-red fruits on female plants. Should be used more than it is.
BUDS: Shrivelled and ragged with 2 thin, very loose scales, end bud lacking.
STEM: Commonly with terminal and axillary twig-spines, stellately pubescent and with silvery or brownish small peltate scales; slender, subterete; pith—small, brown, round, continuous.

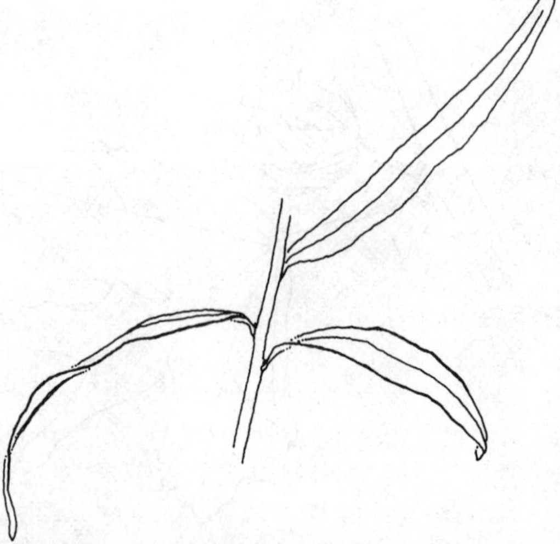

SIZE: 8 to 12 to 30′ tall with a spread of 10 to 40′.
HARDINESS: Zone 3.
HABIT: Large shrub or tree, spreading and irregularly rounded, loose and open. Staminate trees are more erect than the spreading pistillate trees.
RATE: Medium.
TEXTURE: Medium-fine in leaf; medium-coarse in winter.
LEAF COLOR: Silver-green in summer, grayish green in fall.
FLOWERS: Dioecious, yellowish before leaves in March or April, borne in axillary racemes on previous season's branches.

FRUIT: Bright orange, drupe-like, 1/4 to 1/3" long; September, persisting through April of the following year, apparently very acid and birds do not bother it.

CULTURE: A bit difficult to get established; seems to do better in sandy, relatively infertile soil than in rich soil; prefers sand with a moist subsoil; sunny open area; withstands salt spray; actually spreads faster in poor than in fertile soil; supposedly a ratio of 6 females to 1 male is sufficient for pollination, pollen is carried by the wind.

DISEASES AND INSECTS: None serious.

LANDSCAPE VALUE: One of the best plants available for winter fruit color, good for color contrast because of summer foliage and fruit; works well in masses, borders, and along the seashore for stabilizing sand, could be an effective plant for highway use where salt-spray is a problem.

PROPAGATION: I have grown many seedlings but have had a tough time growing them on. Seeds should be stratified for 90 days at 41°F and they will then germinate like beans.

NATIVE HABITAT: Europe to Altai Mountains, Western and Northern China and North and Western Himalayas.

Hovenia dulcis — Japanese Raisintree

FAMILY: Rhamnaceae

LEAVES: Alternate, simple, broad-ovate to elliptic, 4 to 6" long, acuminate, subcordate or rounded and usually unequal or base, coarsely serrate, glabrous or pubescent on veins beneath; petiole 1 1/5 to 2" long; lustrous medium green.

BUDS: Dark brown, hairy, rather small, superposed, sessile, ovoid, with 1 or 2 exposed scales; no terminal.

STEMS: Villous to glabrescent, terete, slender, zig-zag; pith relatively large, pale, continuous, round; leaf-scars round-heart-shaped, somewhat elevated; 3 large bundle traces; no stipule-scars. stipule-scars.

SIZE: Usually listed as reaching 30' under cultivation. The spread would be about 2/3's to equal the height.

HARDINESS: Zone 5, probably safest in the southern areas of Zone 5.

HABIT: Small, handsome tree of upright-oval to rounded outline with clean, ascending main branches and a paucity of lateral branches.

RATE: Medium.

TEXTURE: Medium in all seasons.

LEAF COLOR: Very handsome glossy medium green in summer; yellowish green in fall if, in fact, there is any change. Principally grown for the handsome foliage.

FLOWERS: Perfect, greenish, 1/3" diameter, borne on many-flowered 2" diameter cymes; June and July.

FRUIT: Fleshy drupe, 1/3" diameter, light grayish or brown; the fleshy branches of the inflorescence are reddish; the fleshy branches are sweet and are chewed by the Japanese and Chinese; mature in September-October.

CULTURE: Apparently not too difficult to culture; limited information is available on this species but I have seen the plant performing admirably in a planter on the Southern Illinois Campus at Edwardsville; at the Missouri Botanic Garden, St. Louis; and National Arboretum, Washington, D.C. In all cases the soils, exposures, and maintenance levels were different yet the trees were vigorous and healthy; supposedly thrives in sandy loams.

DISEASES AND INSECTS: Nothing serious.

LANDSCAPE VALUE: Good looking, very clean tree, which would make a small lawn or street tree. Hardiness may be a problem and, as mentioned, the more southerly areas of the midwest would be preferred.

PROPAGATION: Seed is the logical approach. I have attempted and failed due to lack of information concerning proper treatments. Seeds were directly sown after arriving from the Morris Arboretum. Apparently a stratification period of some duration is necessary.

NATIVE HABITAT: China; cultivated in Japan and India. Cultivated 1820.

Hydrangea anomala subsp. *petiolaris* — Climbing Hydrangea

FAMILY: Hydrangeaceae (formerly *H. petiolaris*), (Also included in Saxifragaceae)

LEAVES: Opposite, simple, broad-ovate to ovate-oval, acute or acuminate, cordate or rounded at base, 2 to 4" long, serrate, nearly glabrous, dark green and lustrous above, petioles 4/5 to 1 1/5" long.

BUDS: Imbricate, greenish brown, sometimes tinged red, 2 loosely overlapping scales visible, essentially glabrous.

STEM: Brown, with peeling, exfoliating shaggy bark (handsome), pubescent, developing root-like holdfasts along the internodes.

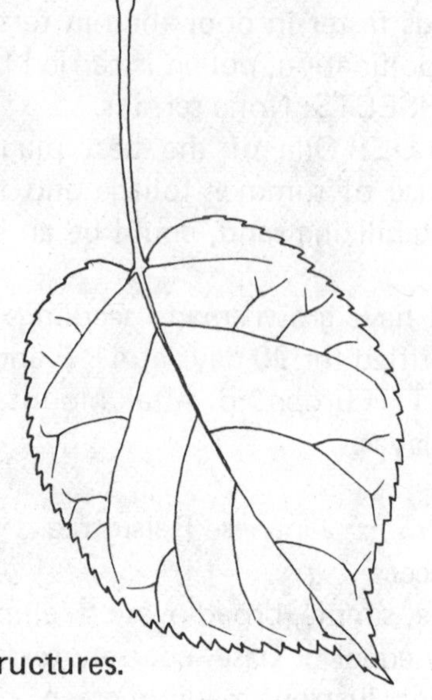

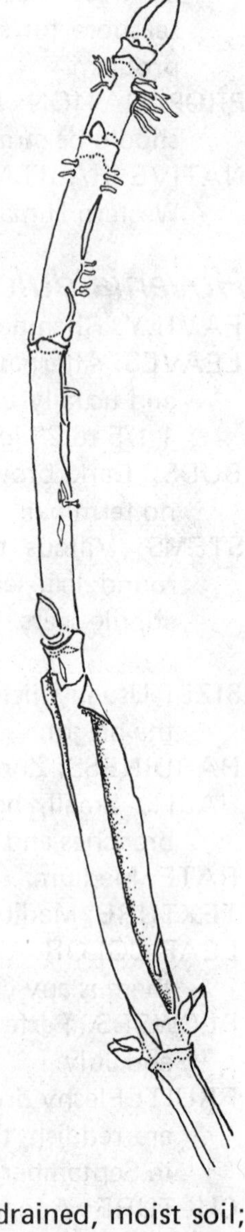

SIZE: Almost unlimited in ability to climb tall trees perhaps 60 to 80' in height. Obviously can be maintained at lower heights but the inherent ability to cover large structures is present. Has been used as a bush in the open, will cover rock piles, walls and other structures.

HARDINESS: Zone 4.

HABIT: True vine clinging and climbing by rootlike holdfasts, interesting in that it develops in more than one plane and gives depth to the structure it is covering. The branches protrude out from the structure to which the vine is attached creating interesting shadows unlike that obtainable with *Parthenocissus* and juvenile *Hedera helix*.

RATE: Slow in the establishment process, but quite vigorous after roots are established.

TEXTURE: Medium-fine in leaf; medium in winter habit.

STEM COLOR: Older stems (3 years or more) develop an exfoliating character much like *Acer griseum* (Paperbark Maple). The bark color is a rich cinnamon-brown and unparalleled by any other hardy vine.

LEAF COLOR: Dark, glossy green in summer foliage, exquisitely handsome, a rare jewel in the crown of vines; the leaves stay green late into fall and abscise green.

FLOWERS: White, late June to early July, effective for 2 weeks or longer, borne in 6 to 10" diameter flat-topped corymbs with the outer flowers sterile and showy (1 to 1 3/4" across) and the inner flowers fertile, dull white, and weakly attractive. Overall flower effect is unrivaled. A specimen in full flower is overwhelming.

FRUIT: Capsule, not important.

CULTURE: Somewhat slow to develop after transplanting, requires rich, well-drained, moist soil; full sun or shade; best used on east or north exposure in adverse climates, should be grown and handled as a container plant to avoid excessive abuse in transplanting.

DISEASES AND INSECTS: None serious compared to those listed for *H. arborescens.*

LANDSCAPE VALUE: The best vine! As Wyman so succinctly stated, "There is no better clinging vine." Excellent for massive effect on brick or stone walls, arbors, trees and any free structure. Becomes quite woody so needs ample support. The extra cultural care required in establishment is rewarded many times over in ornamental assets for the excellent foliage, flowers and winter bark effect make this species a four-season plant.

PROPAGATION: Somewhat difficult to root. I have collected cuttings in July treated with 1000 ppm IBA and received 5% rooting. Supposedly the optimum time to secure cutting wood is late spring or early summer before the stems turn brown.

ADDITIONAL NOTES: Frequently confused with *Schizophragma hydrangeoides,* an allied, but quite distinct climber. The sterile flowers are composed of a single ovate sepal compared to 3 to 5 parted sepals of *H.a. petiolaris* and the leaves are more coarsely toothed.

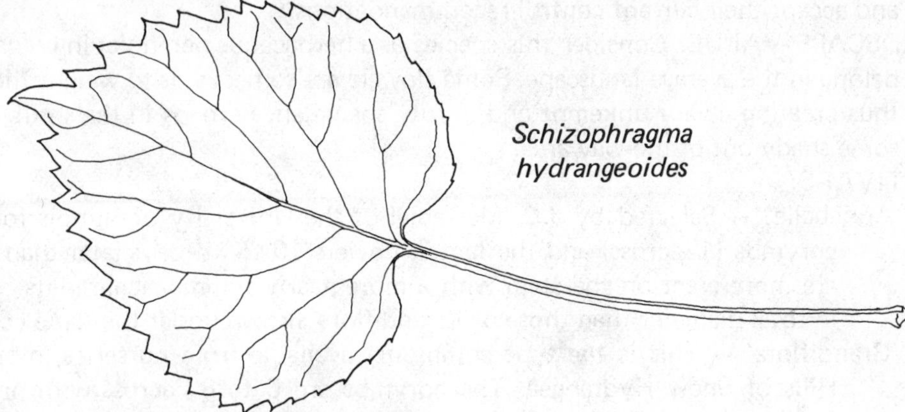

NATIVE HABITAT: Japan, China. Introduced 1865.

Hydrangea arborescens — Smooth Hydrangea

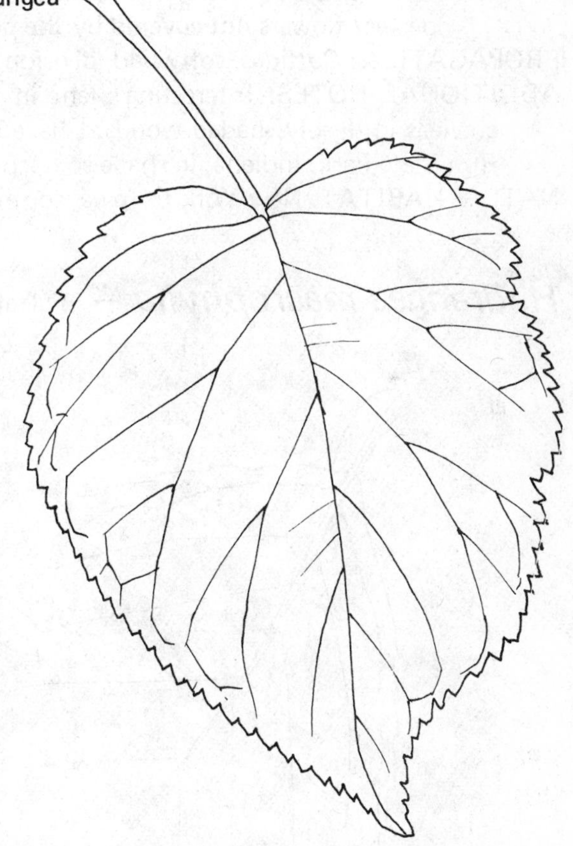

LEAVES: Opposite, simple, ovate to elliptic, acute or acuminate, rounded or cordate at base, 2 to 8" long, serrate, glabrous, or sometimes puberulous beneath. Petioles—4/5 to 2 2/5" long.

BUDS: Imbricate, 4 to 6 scaled, greenish brown, divergent, 1/8" long, glabrous. Much longer than *H. paniculata* buds.

STEM: Slender to medium stout, gray-tan-brown, young branches essentially glabrous, smooth, without gray streaks. Older stems—exfoliating. Pith—relatively large, roundish, continuous, whitish.

SIZE: 3 to 5' in height by 3 to 5' and larger in spread; suckers freely from roots and will cover large areas if not maintained.

HARDINESS: Zone 4.

HABIT: Usually low growing, clumpy shrub with many weak, shreddy barked non-branched canes. Often broader than high at maturity.

RATE: Fast, almost weedy.

TEXTURE: Coarse in leaf, flower and winter habit.

LEAF COLOR: Bright dark green in summer, fall color is green to brown, very nondescript.

FLOWERS: Dull white, late June through September, borne in 4 to 6" diameter, much branched, flattish corymbs with few or no large sterile flowers. Actually the flowers pass from green to white to brown. Probably best to cut off flowers at the early brown stage as they are ornamentally valueless after this time.

FRUITS: Capsule, 8 to 10 ribbed, of no ornamental consequence.

CULTURE: Fibrous rooted, transplants well, very adaptable, however proliferates in rich, well-drained, moist soil; prefers partial shade; often requires supplemental watering in our hot dry summers. Probably should mow it off with a lawnmower in late fall or early spring; flowers on new wood.

DISEASES AND INSECTS: Bacterial wilt, bud blight, leaf spot, powdery mildew, rust, aphids, leaf tier, rose chafer, oystershell scale, two-spotted mite, and nematodes have been reported on this and other species. First have the problem diagnosed by a county agent or university specialist and accept their current control recommendations.

LANDSCAPE VALUE: Consider this species as a herbaceous perennial in colder climates. Does not belong in the average landscape. Some flowers are so heavy as to weight the stem to the ground thus creating a very unkempt and unruly specimen. Perhaps in the shrub border or massing in some shady out-of-the-way area.

CULTIVARS:

'Annabelle' — Selected by J.C. McDaniel of the University of Illinois for its extremely large corymbs (1' across) and the fact it flowers 10 to 14 days later than 'Grandiflora'. Heads are more erect on the stem with a more nearly symmetrical radius, and are usually larger in total diameter than those of 'Grandiflora' grown under the same conditions.

'Grandiflora' — This is the type commonly available from nurseries, often referred to as the Hills of Snow Hydrangea. The corymbs are 6 to 8" across with primarily sterile white flowers. The individual "sterile" showy sepals are larger than 'Annabelle', but the total number of flowers in a head is fewer. The heads are not so radially symmetrical, looking like four parts loosely pushed together, and soon becoming floppy in appearance.

'Sterilis' — Often confused with 'Grandiflora'. Flatter topped head, showing some areas of small perfect flowers not covered by the persisting sepals of the showy flowers.

PROPAGATION: Cuttings, softwood, division of the clumps provide means of increasing plants.

ADDITIONAL NOTES: Interesting plant in its native haunts; often found growing out of rock crevices in deeply shaded woods. I have seen it growing out of the sandstone cliffs in Turkey Run State Park, Indiana, in shade so deep that one could not take an effective photograph.

NATIVE HABITAT: New York to Iowa, south to Florida and Louisiana. Introduced 1736.

Hydrangea macrophylla — Bigleaf Hydrangea

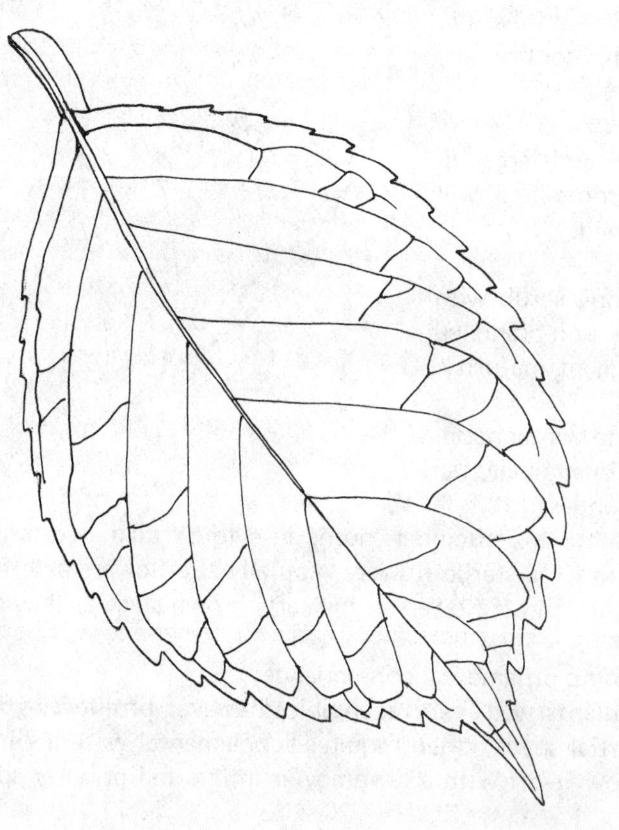

LEAVES: Opposite, simple, thickish, obovate to elliptic or broad-ovate, short-acuminate, broad cuneate at base, 2 3/4 to 6" long, coarsely serrate with triangular obtusish teeth, lustrous medium green above, glabrous or slightly puberulous beneath, petioles stout, 2/5 to 1 1/5" long, leaving large scars, the opposite ones contiguous.

STEMS: Light brown, scarcely branched, often dying back in winter; pith—large, white.

SIZE: 3 to 6' in height but can grow to 10'; spread would be equal to or greater than the height.

HARDINESS: Zone 6. Does not do well in Zone 5 unless extremely well sited. As one goes south and east this becomes a very common plant, however, in the Midwest it is rare to see it in full flower.

HABIT: Rounded, suckering shrub of many erect, usually unbranched, thick stems.

RATE: Fast.

TEXTURE: Medium-coarse in leaf although coarse is a definite possibility; coarse in winter, in fact, irreparably so.

STEM COLOR: Of a light, shiny, gray- or straw-brown color.

LEAF COLOR: Leaves are quite large (4 to 8" long) and are a lustrous medium green in summer. The leaves are quite fleshy (succulent) with a greasy consistency.

FLOWERS: Very difficult to adequately describe the typical species flower because of the numerous selections. The sterile, outer flowers are pink or bluish, entire or toothed, up to 2" or more in diameter; the fertile flowers are usually blue or pink; both are borne in large, broad, flat-topped, much branched, cymose corymbs; July through August.

FRUIT: Capsule, 1/4 to 5/16" long, not showy.

CULTURE: Transplant as a container plant into moist, well-drained soil which has been amended with peat moss, leaf mold and the like. This species requires acid soil and the range of pH 6.0 to 6.5 is suitable for pink flower color while 5.0 to 5.5 suffices for blue color. Will withstand seashore conditions and actually flourish near the shore; full sun or partial shade; pruning is an art with the *Hydrangea* species and one must know the requirements of each type. This species flowers from buds formed on previous season's growth and any pruning should be done right after flowering.

DISEASES AND INSECTS: See under *H. arborescens.*

LANDSCAPE VALUE: Probably a good plant for the shrub border in southern areas. Not adequately winter hardy in the northern states and is often killed back to the ground. The only benefit then is the foliage. This plant and the numerous cultivars are widely planted in the east and south. Makes a good flower display.

CULTIVARS: Unbelievably large number of cultivars many of which are not hardy. W.J. Bean's *Trees and Shrubs Hardy in the British Isles, Vol. II,* and *Hillier's Manual of Trees and Shrubs* offer a wealth of cultivars and the technical information concerning them. Wyman has a list in his book based on observations at the Arnold Arboretum. He considers the following cultivars* among the best for outdoor use.

'Blue Prince'* — Flowers pink or blue. The acidity of the soil dictates the color; see *Additional Note* section.

'Blue Wave' — Ray flowers with four wavy-edged sepals, rich blue on very acid soils, otherwise pink or lilac. A vigorous shrub (6'), and as wide with bold foliage; grows best in light shade, lacecaps type.

'Coerula'* — Perfect flowers a deep blue, ray flowers blue or white.

'Domotoi'* — Double, sterile flowers, pale pink or blue, petals frilled, weak growth, 2 1/2' high; hortensia type.

'Mandshurica'* — Flowers pink or blue, stems dark purple to nearly black. Overwintered in protected areas in the Arnold Arboretum.

'Mariesii'* — A few sterile flowers are scattered among the fertile ones and are similar in shape to the normal ray flowers that edge the inflorescence. Flowers are nearly always pink or mauve-pink (pale blue on very acid soils). Grows 4 to 5' high.

'Nikko Blue'* — Flowers blue, color stable, hortensia type.

'Otaksa' – Flowers pink or blue; red petioles, weak stems. Flowers in large terminal corymbs which weight the stem down. Grows to 3', hortensia.

PROPAGATION: Best to propagate from softwood cuttings of late May or June growth; also semi-hardwood and hardwood cuttings will root. Rooting is hastened with IBA treatment although the rooting percentage will approach 100 without any treatment.

ADDITIONAL NOTES: Quite an interesting species with many lovely garden forms. The cultivars are divided into two groups: the *hortensias* which have essentially sterile flowers that are borne in large globose corymbs. These usually form solid masses of white, pink, and/or blue which are often so heavy they cause the stem to bend. The *lacecaps* have a center of fertile, relatively non-showy flowers and an outer ring of showy, sterile flowers which together afford a pin-wheel effect.

The flower color on some cultivars is strongly affected by the pH of the soil in which they are growing. The ray flowers are often the most affected. The color changes depend on the concentration of *Aluminum* ions in the soil. This depends in turn on the acidity of the soil, being highest on very acid soils and lowest where the soil is alkaline. The color range depends on the cultivar, but the bluest shades are always produced on the most acid soils. A pH range of 5.0 to 5.5 is listed as satisfactory for inducing blue coloration while pH 6.0 to 6.5 and probably slightly higher is best for pink coloration.

NATIVE HABITAT: Japan. Introduced 1790.

Hydrangea paniculata — Panicle Hydrangea

LEAVES: Opposite, sometimes whorled, especially on flowering stems, simple, elliptic or ovate, acuminate, rounded or cuneate at base, 2 to 5" long, serrate, sparingly pubescent or nearly glabrous above, setose pubescent beneath, particularly on the veins.

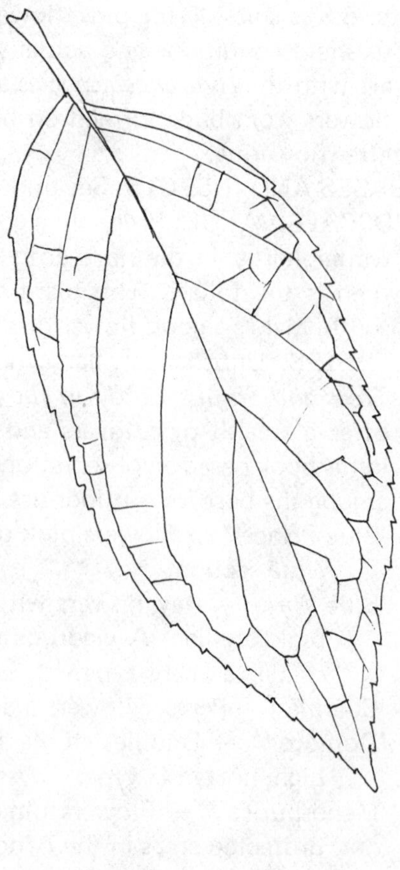

BUDS: Imbricate, rounded, globose, 4 to 6 scaled, glabrous, brownish in color, sometimes with whorled character.

STEM: Stout, reddish brown, bark showing gray vertically streaked areas. Older bark often peeling and more gray in color.

SIZE: 15 to 25' in height by 10 to 20' in spread; quite variable in size, often 10' or less.

HARDINESS: Zone 4.

HABIT: Upright, coarsely spreading small, low-branched tree or large shrub, the branches assuming a semi-arching condition under the weight of the flowers.

RATE: Fast.

TEXTURE: Coarse the year round but peaking when denuded of leaves yet possessed with browned remains of the inflorescence. Actually spent flowers should be removed in September or earlier.

STEM COLOR: Older wood, 1 to 2" or greater, assumes a gray-brown to ridged and furrowed look. Often quite handsome especially when lower branches are removed and the sun shadows are allowed to develop. Especially handsome is the bark on cultivar 'Praecox' when treated in this fashion.

LEAF COLOR: Dark green, possibly a tinge of luster to the summer foliage, fall color is green with a hint of yellow.

FLOWERS: White changing to pink, mid July on, borne in pyramidal panicles approximately 6 to 8" long, the bulk of the flowers are fertile, yellowish white, not showy; a few flowers are sterile and showy as described above, flowers last for long periods while going through the color transformation.

FRUIT: Capsule, ornamentally without appeal.

CULTURE: Similar to *H. arborescens,* prefers good loamy, moist, well-drained soil; sun or partial shade. Remove inflorescences in September as they are then turning brown; flowers on new wood as does *H. arborescens* and can be pruned in winter or early spring, very hardy plant.

DISEASES AND INSECTS: Same as previously described for *H. arborescens.*

LANDSCAPE VALUE: Several astute plantsmen have termed this species a "Monstrosity in the Landscape." Difficult to blend into the modern landscape because of extreme coarseness. Totally disgusting in late fall and winter with inflorescences still evident. Overplanted in the past but little used in modern landscapes. Grows very fast and will provide a large splash of white at a time when few plants are in flower. Possibly should be reserved for the shrub border or the neighbor's yard. I have observed this plant through the seasons and always came to the same conclusion—a "loner" in the landscape.

CULTIVARS:

'Floribunda' — Sterile flowers more numerous but not sufficiently so to conceal the fertile flowers.

'Grandiflora' — Almost all flowers are sterile and large; forming a tight panicle of white then purplish pink and finally brown. The inflorescences can reach sizes of 12 to 18" in length and 6 to 12" wide at the base. This is the most common form and still widely available from nurseries.

'Praecox' — Possesses a smattering of sterile, showy flowers integrated with the fertile, non-showy ones. Majority of the showy flowers are lccated at the base of the inflorescence. Interestingly attractive. Flowers three to six weeks earlier than 'Grandiflora'.

PROPAGATION: Cuttings, softwood, root readily in sand:peat medium. Rooting is hastened with 20 ppm IBA treatment.

NATIVE HABITAT: Japan, Sakhalin, and Eastern and Southern China. Introduced 1861.

Hydrangea quercifolia — Oakleaf Hydrangea

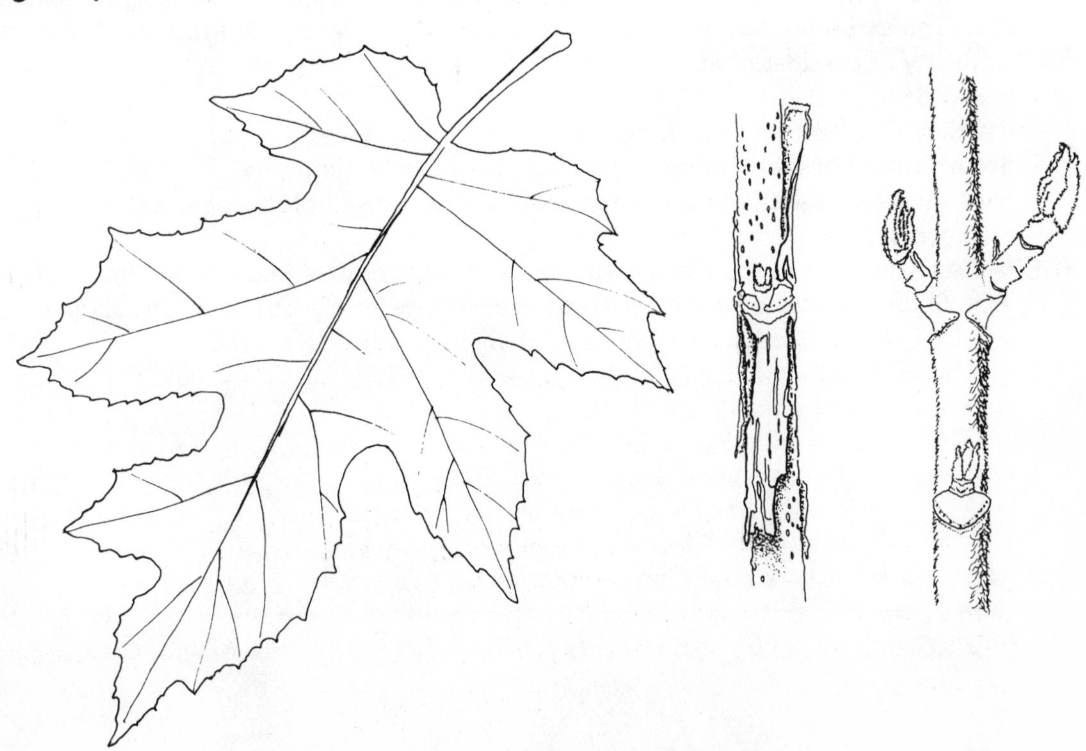

LEAVES: Opposite, simple, ovate to suborbicular in outline, sinuately 3 to 7 lobed, usually truncate at base and decurrent into the petiole, 2 to 8" long, lobes broad, serrate and often slightly lobed, whitish tomentose beneath.

BUDS: Imbricate, 4 to 6 scaled, divergent, brownish tomentose. Terminal—much larger than laterals.

STEM: Stout, pubescent on young growth, brownish, older stems with prominent lenticels, exfoliating cinnamon-brown bark. Pith—light brown, large leaf scars—prominent, inverted, triangular in shape with prominent vascular bundle scars.

SIZE: 4 to 6' in height; spread 3 to 5' and more as it suckers freely from roots.

HARDINESS: Zone 5.

HABIT: Upright, little branched, irregular, stoloniferous shrub forming colonies.

RATE: Slow to medium.

TEXTURE: Pleasantly coarse in leaf; coarse in winter.

STEM COLOR: Young stems intensely brownish tomentose, older stems (3 year and more) exfoliating to expose a rich, reddish brown inner bark. Quite attractive from this aspect but often overlooked.

LEAF COLOR: Deep, dull green, sometimes glossy in summer, changing to shades of red, orangish brown and purple in fall. Quite spectacular in fall color. Seems to be great variability in the fall color among progeny of this species. Selections should be made for this feature alone.

FLOWERS: White, changing to purplish pink and finally brown, outer flowers sterile, 1 to 1 1/2" diameter; fertile flowers numerous, lacking character or good color; late June through July and persisting, borne in 4 to 12" long erect panicles. The cultivars are considerably more showy in flower than the straight species.

FRUIT: Capsule, not showy.

CULTURE: Somewhat tender as a young plant and should be protected in Zone 5; tops usually killed back when winter temperatures go much below zero and flower buds are also killed; requires moist, fertile, well-drained soil; sun or partial (1/2) shade; wise to mulch in the Midwest to maintain a cool, moist root environment; if terminal buds are lost during winter, no flowers will be produced; possibly best to consider this plant for its excellent foliage and if flowering occurs accept it as an added bonus; prune after flowering.

DISEASES AND INSECTS: Observations have led me to believe this species is quite trouble-free; leaf blight has been listed as a problem.

LANDSCAPE VALUE: Somewhat difficult to use in the residential landscape because of coarseness. The shrub border, massing or shady situations offer possibilities. Excellent foliage makes it worthy of consideration.

CULTIVARS:

'Harmony' — Mostly sterile, large paniculate inflorescences, 12" long, white.

'Roanoke' — Loose and more open inflorescence than 'Harmony'.

'Snowflake' — Multiple bracts or sepals emerge on tops of older ones creating a double-flowered appearance.

PROPAGATION: Layers, suckers or cuttings taken soon after midsummer and rooted in bottom heat. Should be treated with IBA (Hormodin #3) or similar strength formulations.

NATIVE HABITAT: Georgia and Florida to Mississippi. Introduced 1803.

Hypericum prolificum — Shrubby St. Johnswort

FAMILY: Guttiferae, Hypericaceae

LEAVES: Opposite, simple, narrow-oblong to oblanceolate, 1 to 3" long, obtuse, dark lustrous green or bluish green above and pellucid-punctate.

STEM: Two-angled, pith—small, green or brown, spongy and finally exavated, older bark exfoliating, light brown.

SIZE: 1 to 4' high by 1 to 4' spread.

HARDINESS: Zone 4.

HABIT: A small, dense little bush with stout, stiff, erect stems, rounded; variable in size.

RATE: Slow.

TEXTURE: Medium-fine in leaf; medium in winter.

BARK: On older stems light brown and exfoliating.

LEAF COLOR: Dark lustrous green in summer, perhaps could be considered bluish green.

FLOWERS: Perfect, 3/4" diameter, bright yellow, late June through July and August, borne in axillary and terminal few-flowered cymes.

FRUIT: A dry, dehiscent, 3-valved capsule; hang on all winter and could be used for dried arrangements.

CULTURE: Best transplanted from a container; does extremely well in dry, rocky soils; full sun or partial shade; pH adaptable; does extremely well in the calcareous soils of Central Illinois. My observations lead me to believe this is an excellent plant for dry, heavy soil areas; prune in early spring.

DISEASES AND INSECTS: Nothing particularly serious afflicts this genus.

LANDSCAPE VALUE: Nice plant for summer color because of excellent yellow (buttercup-colored) flowers; would work well in the shrub border; possibly in groupings or in mass; I do not believe the Hypericums have been adequately explored and developed as landscape plants.

PROPAGATION: Cuttings root readily, softwood collected in June treated with 1000 ppm IBA and placed in sand under mist gave good rooting.

RELATED SPECIES:

Hypericum buckleyi, Blueridge St. Johnswort, is a low growing (1'), spreading, decumbent, yellow flowering shrub. North Carolina to Georgia. Introduced 1889. Zone 5.

Hypericum calycinum, Aaronsbeard St. Johnswort, is a stoloniferous semi-evergreen shrub with procumbent or ascending stems growing 12 to 18" high and spreading 18 to 24". The tops of the plant often winter-kill in severe cold but since it flowers on new wood little damage is done.

The leaves are dark green above and glaucous beneath. The flowers are a screaming bright yellow, 3" across, borne singly or rarely 2 to 3 together on new wood in July through September. Easily transplanted in spring; does well in poor sandy soil; full sun or partial shade; best mowed to the ground to induce new growth each spring. Makes a rather handsome groundcover plant as it grows fast and effectively covers an area in a short time. Roots easily from softwood cuttings (84 percent when taken in early summer and set in sand without hormone treatment in 42 days). Native to Southeastern Europe, Asia Minor. Introduced 1676. Zone 5.

Hypericum densiflorum, Dense Hypericum, grows to 6' in height with 3 to 4' spread. The habit is upright oval, taller than broad and densely twiggy and leafy. The foliage is deep green in summer; flowers are golden yellow, 1/2" across, July through September, borne in many-flowered corymbs. New Jersey to Florida, Missouri and Texas. Introduced 1889. Zone 5.

Hypericum frondosum, Golden St. Johnswort, grows to 3 to 4′ high with a similar spread. Often an upright shrub with rather stout branches; bark is reddish brown and exfoliating; foliage is a very handsome, distinct bluish green; flowers are bright yellow, 1 to 2″ diameter, with the stamens forming a dense brush 3/4″ across, July, solitary. 'Sunburst' is lower growing than the species (2′ by 4′) and makes a lovely facer plant; this cultivar is under test in our woody ornamental evaluation plots and has proven superior for Central Illinois conditions. South Carolina and Tennessee to Georgia and Texas. 1747. Zone 5.

LEAVES: Opposite, simple, entire, ovate-oblong to oblong, 1 to 2 2/5″ long, mucronate, pellucid-dotted.

STEM: With thin exfoliating reddish bark on older branches, branches 2-edged.

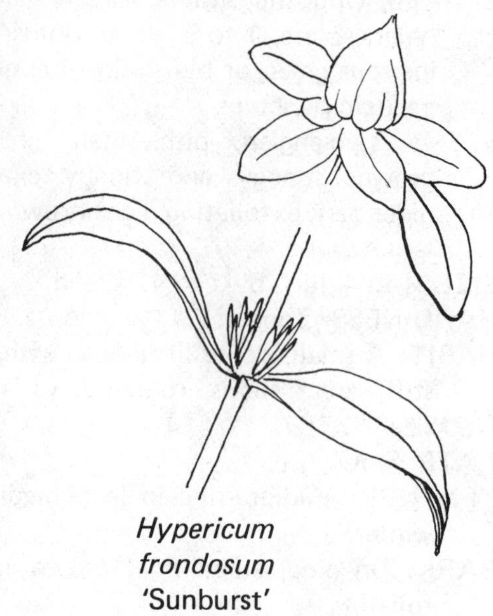

Hypericum frondosum 'Sunburst'

Hypericum kalmianum, Kalm St. Johnswort, grows 2 to 3′ and has bluish green summer foliage. The flowers are bright yellow, 1 to 2″ diameter, July, borne in 3-flowered cymes; a handsome hardy species, confined to cliffs of rivers and lakes from Niagara Falls, north. Quebec and Ontario to Michigan and Illinois. 1760. Zone 4.

Hypericum patulum, Goldencup St. Johnswort, grows to 3′ and is a semi-evergreen to evergreen spreading shrub. Flowers are golden-yellow, 2″ diameter, July, solitary or in cymes. Variety *henryi* is more vigorous than the species, flowers are larger (2 1/2″ across); 'Hidcote' grows to 18″ and as wide with fragrant yellow flowers 2″ in diameter, late June to October (shculd be treated as a herbaceous perennial in the north; 'Sungold' is supposedly more hardy than 'Hidcote'. Japan. 1862. Zone 6 or 7.

NATIVE HABITAT: New Jersey to Iowa and Georgia. Introduced about 1750.

Iberis sempervirens — Candytuft

FAMILY: Cruciferae

LEAVES: Alternate, simple, linear-oblong, 3/5 to 1 1/5″ long, obtuse, entire, dark green.

SIZE: 6 to 12″ high; spreading with time and forming handsome evergreen mats.

HARDINESS: Zone 5.

HABIT: Dwarf evergreen ground cover or shrub of sprawling habit.

RATE: Slow to medium; under good cultural conditions will fill an area reasonably fast.

TEXTURE: Fine in summer; possibly medium in winter as it looks a bit rough.

LEAF COLOR: Dark green and handsome.

FLOWERS: Perfect, white, borne in terminal 1 to 1 1/2″ diameter racemes which engulf the plant and give the appearance of a drift of snow; April-May and lasting for several weeks; spent flowers should be removed.

FRUIT: A silique, orbicular-elliptic, 1/4″ long; not showy.

CULTURE: Easy to transplant; I have moved seedlings and container plants with great success; prefer loose, loamy, average fertility soil. If fertility levels are excessive the plants become loose, leggy and open; full sun or partial shade; pH adaptable; prune heavily after flowering.

DISEASES AND INSECTS: Club root, damping off, downy and powdery mildews, and white rust.

LANDSCAPE VALUE: Excellent plant for early color; contrasts well with tulips and other bulbs; I have used it as drifts interplanted with woody shrubs; even after flowering it can look quite good if it is maintained as described under culture.

CULTIVARS:

'Christmas Snow' ('Snowflake') — Flowers twice, early in season and again in fall.

'Little Gem' — More dwarf than the type, only 6" tall and quite hardy; leaves are smaller, fine in texture.

'Purity' — Similar to 'Little Gem' in habit with larger inflorescences.

PROPAGATION: Seed represents an easy method; sow as soon as mature. Softwood cuttings root easily and I have used this method to reproduce seed-grown plants which were especially floriferous.

NATIVE HABITAT: Southern Europe, Western Asia. Introduced 1731.

Ilex crenata — Japanese Holly

FAMILY: Aquifoliaceae

LEAVES: Alternate, simple, crowded, short-stalked, elliptic or obovate to oblong-lanceolate, 3/5 to 1 1/5" long, acute, cuneate or broad-cuneate, crenate-serrulate or serrulate, lustrous dark green above, glabrous.

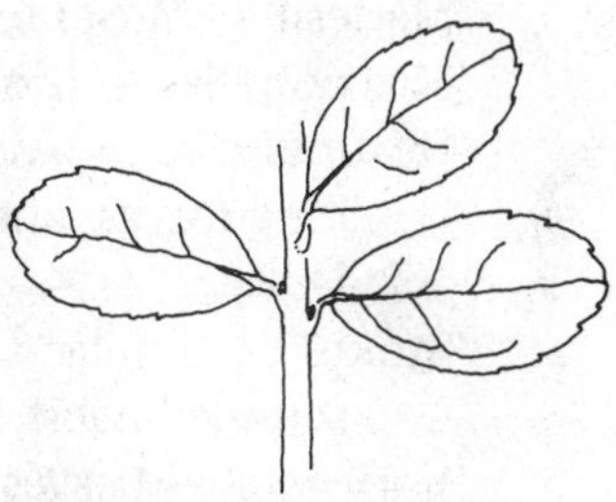

GROWTH HABIT: Except for the species, usually a much branched shrub of dense, rigid, compact habit.

SIZE: Very difficult to ascertain from the literature the actual size of the species, listed as reaching 20' by various authorities; in actuality a shrub of 5 to 10' with a similar or greater spread.

HARDINESS: Zone 5 to 6 depending on cultivar.

HABIT: Usually a dense, multi-branched evergreen shrub of rounded or broad rounded outline.

RATE: Slow.

TEXTURE: Medium-fine in all seasons.

LEAF COLOR: Lustrous dark green in summer and winter.

FLOWERS: Dioecious, unisexual, dull greenish white, staminate in 3 to 7 flowered cymes; pistillate solitary in leaf-axils of current season's growth; May-June. Not at all showy but if one is interested in determining the sex of any particular holly, inspection of the flowers is the only logical way.

FRUIT: Berry-like black drupe, globose, 1/4" diameter, September-October, borne under the foliage and, therefore, somewhat inconspicuous; only female plants have fruits.

CULTURE: Transplants readily balled and burlapped or from a container; prefers light, moist, well-drained, slightly acid soils; sun or shade adaptable; seems to do well in city gardens; prune after new growth hardens off; will withstand severe pruning.

DISEASES AND INSECTS: Nothing as serious as those which occur on American Holly. (see under *I. opaca*)

LANDSCAPE VALUE: Excellent for textural differences in foundation plantings, hedges, and masses. Hedges in Japan have been maintained for so long that they can be walked on. Very handsome and worthwhile landscape plant.

CULTIVARS:

'Black Beauty' — Selected by Girard Nursery, Geneva, Ohio for lustrous dark green foliage, compact habit, and extreme hardiness. Zone 5.

'Border Gem' — Dense, low growing type with lustrous dark green foliage and good hardiness. Zone 5. Has survived winters of -8°F and looked fantastic. 'Hetzii', on the other hand, was severely winter killed at this same temperature.

'Convexa' — (Zone 5) One of the hardiest forms, 40-year-old plant somewhat vase-shaped in habit but extremely dense is 9' tall and 24' wide. Takes pruning for hedging.

'Dwarf Pagoda' — Selected by Dr. Orton from his Holly breeding program at Rutgers University. Female with tiny leaves 5/16" to 7/16" long by 1/4" wide, short internodes, branching irregular; result is an extremely heavy foliage effect and artistic form, 2"/year, hardy to 0°.

'Glass' — (Zone 5) Male clone of *Ilex crenata* 'Microphylla' with compact upright habit and slightly smaller leaves.

'Golden Gem' — Leaves golden, habit low and spreading, the color is best developed in sunny location.

'Green Dragon' — Male clone otherwise similar to 'Dwarf Pagoda'.

'Green Island' — (Zone 5) Loose and open shrub form usually growing twice as broad as tall. 11-year-old plant is 3' by 6'.

'Green Luster' — Similar to above with leaves darker and more lustrous.

'Helleri' — Dwarf, globose, compact form. 26-year-old plant is 4' by 5' with leaves about 1/2" long, Zone 5.

'Hetzii' — (Zone 5) Dwarf clone of *Ilex crenata* 'Convexa'.

'Kingsville Green Cushion' — Dense, low growing form, 10-year-old plant is 8" by 32".

var. *latifolia* — Vigorous growing upright form with large glossy leaves 1 1/2" long and 1/2 to 5/8" wide.

'Mariesii' — Most dwarf of the *I. crenata* forms growing about 1" per year.

'Microphylla' — (Zone 5) Leaves smaller than the species; upright shrub or small tree in habit.

'Rotundifolia' — A somewhat confusing cultivar, but the ones I have seen have large, 1/2 to 1" long leaves, and tend to grow upright rounded to about 8 to 12', called Bigleaf Japanese Holly.

'Stokes' — Similar to 'Helleri' but not as hardy, probably not as globose in habit; low, dense rounded habit.

'Variegata' — Leaves spotted or blotched with yellow.

PROPAGATION: Cuttings root readily, I use 1000 ppm IBA/50% alcohol and achieve 90 percent or greater rooting.

In general, *Ilex* seeds exhibit a deep dormancy that is caused partly by the hard endocarp surrounding the seed coat and partly to conditions in the embryo. According to J. Bon Hartline, an Illinois holly grower, the best way to handle holly seed is as follows. The fruits should be collected in fall, the pulp crushed and washed away. Seeds which float should be discarded, since they are usually not viable. Seeds of *I. crenata, I. vomitoria, I. glabra,* and of some *I. opaca* of southern origin will germinate in a very short time after being properly handled. *Ilex aquifolium, I. cornuta, I. verticillata, I. serrata, I. decidua,* and most *I. opaca* seeds require a longer period—up to 18 months before all seeds germinate. Patience is probably the necessary ingredient in holly seed propagation for it is the length of time rather than the cold treatment which aids germination.

RELATED SPECIES: The following species are excellent plants but not particularly hardy in Zone 5.

Ilex aquifolium, English Holly, is an evergreen tree growing to 30 to 50' (80') in height with a 25 to 35' spread. The foliage is lustrous dark green; the fruits are bright red; native to Southern Europe, Northern Africa and Western Asia. Zone 6 to 7. Sprays are sold at Christmas for decoration.

Ilex cornuta — Chinese Holly

LEAVES: Alternate, short-stalked, oblong-rectangular, 1 1/2 to 4" long, with 3 strong almost equal spines at the broad apex and 1 or 2 spines on each side at the base, or on older plants rounded at the base, lustrous dark green above.

Ilex cornuta, Chinese Holly, is a dense, rounded evergreen shrub reaching 10' in height with a 6 to 10' spread. The foliage is a beautiful lustrous dark green; the fruits bright red and apparently fruits develop without fertilization (parthenocarpy).

'Burfordii' — Leaves entire but with a terminal spine, foliage darker than that of the species and the habit is more globose. A heavy fruiter. I have seen specimens in Georgia which were 10 to 12' high and as wide with an excellent fruit display. The overall effect is that of a dense, rounded, evergreen shrub.

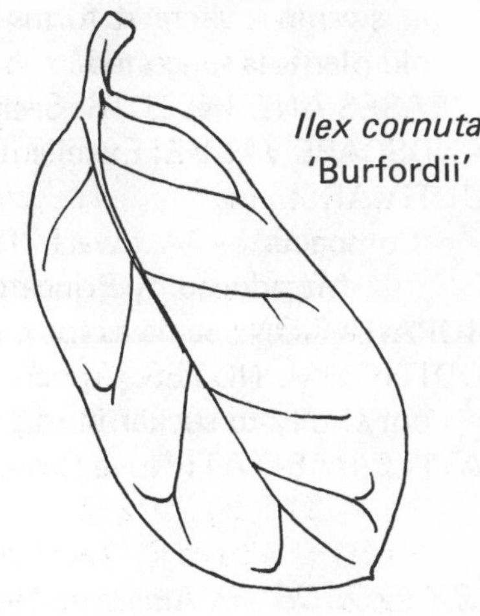

Ilex cornuta 'Burfordii'

'Dwarf Burford' is a dense, slow-growing selection. A 6-year-old plant may be only 18" high and wide. Would be a good choice in restricted growing areas. A fruiting clone. Ultimate height will range between 3 and 8'.

'Carissa' — More compact than 'Rotunda' as it attains a height of 3' and a spread of 4 to 5' in about 8 years.

'Dazzler' — Slow growing compact form with bright red fruits.

'D'Or' — Form with yellow fruits.

'Rotunda' — Good, dense, low growing form.

'Shangri-La' — Fast growing female clone with fruit maturing in June and remaining on the plant until March.

Easily propagated by cuttings; some landscape architects consider it the best broadleaf for the south. Native to Eastern China, Korea. Introduced 1846. Zone 6 to 7. I have a Burford Chinese Holly in my backyard and it survived the winter of 1974-75 without visual injury, however, it is sited in a protected location in an extremely well-drained, acid soil.

ADDITIONAL NOTES: Very handsome plant, not extensively used in Central Illinois but with proper cultivar selection can be successfully grown.

NATIVE HABITAT: Japan and Korea. Introduced 1864.

Ilex glabra — Inkberry

FAMILY: Aquifoliaceae

LEAVES: Alternate, obovate to oblanceolate, 4/5 to 2" long, acute or obtusish, cuneate with few obtuse teeth near apex or entire, dark green and lustrous above, glabrous, leaves are very thin compared to the *I. crenata* forms with which it is often confused.

STEM: Slender, green, pubescent at first, finally glabrous.

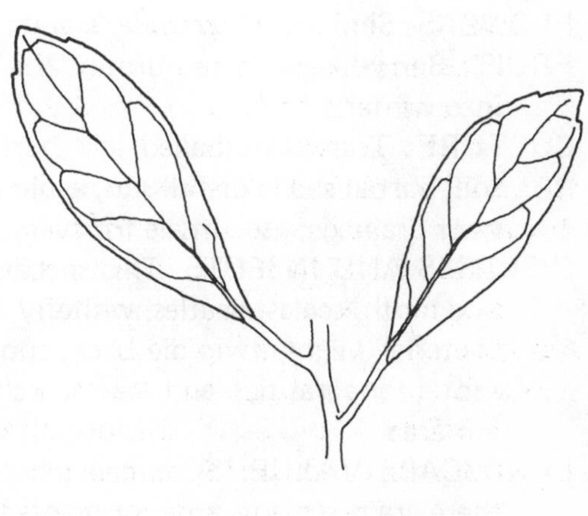

SIZE: 6 to 8' in height by 8 to 10' in spread, however, variable depending on growing conditions.

HARDINESS: Zone 3.

HABIT: Upright, much branched, erect-rounded evergreen shrub, somewhat open with age and often losing the lower leaves.

RATE: Slow.

TEXTURE: Medium in all seasons.

LEAF COLOR: Dark green and often lustrous in summer; sometimes becoming light yellow-green in summer.

FLOWERS: Similar to *I. crenata.*

FRUIT: Berry-like, black drupe, 1/4" diameter, September through until May of the following year. Often hidden by the foliage but usually more showy than *I. crenata* fruits.

CULTURE: Somewhat similar to *I. crenata* except prefers moist, acid soils and in the wild is common in swamps where it forms large clumps. Withstands heavy pruning quite well and renewal of old plants is suggested.

DISEASES AND INSECTS: Seems to be quite free of problems.

LANDSCAPE VALUE: Excellent (especially the cultivar) for foundation, hedges, masses, accent plant.

CULTIVARS:

'Compacta' — A dwarf, female clone with tighter branching and foliage than the species. Introduced by Princeton Nursery; found in a group of seedlings.

PROPAGATION: Same as for *I. crenata.*

ADDITIONAL NOTES: Apparently spreads by underground stems (stolons or rhizomes) and is the only holly to sucker in this manner.

NATIVE HABITAT: Nova Scotia to Florida, west to Mississippi. Introduced 1759.

Ilex opaca — American Holly

FAMILY: Aquifoliaceae

LEAVES: Alternate, elliptic to elliptic-lanceolate, 2 to 4" long, with large remote spiny teeth, rarely nearly entire, dull green above, yellowish green beneath; petiole 1/4 to 1/2" long.

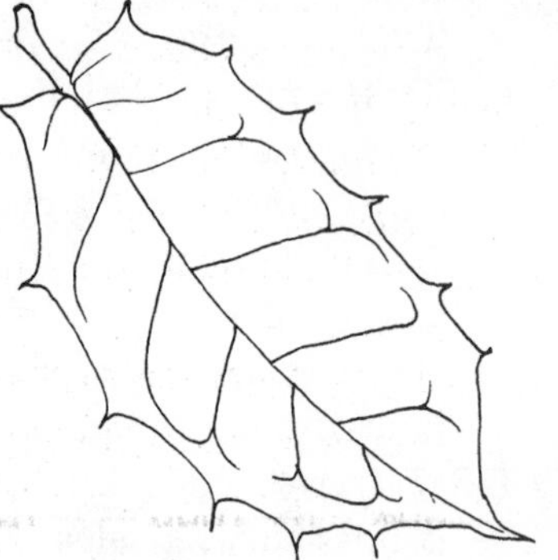

SIZE: 40 to 70' in height with a spread of 18 to 40'; usually much smaller in Central Illinois; 15 to 30' in height would be more reasonable.

HARDINESS: Zone 5, possibly 4 with proper siting.

HABIT: Densely pyramidal in youth with branches to the ground, becoming in age open, irregular, and picturesque, high branching, the branches at a wide angle and contorted.

RATE: Medium in youth, slowing down in older age; Wyman mentioned a tree at Fort Hancock, Sandy Hook, N.J., that was 55' tall and 275-years-old.

TEXTURE: Medium-coarse in all seasons.

LEAF COLOR: Dull, dark yellow green in all seasons; great variation among trees but; in general, not a particularly handsome leaf.

FLOWERS: Similar to *I. crenata;* staminate in 3 to 9-flowered cymes; pistillate solitary.

FRUIT: Berry-like, dull red drupe, 2/5" diameter, borne singly, maturing in October and persisting into winter.

CULTURE: Transplant balled and burlapped in spring into good, moist, loose, acid, well-drained soil; partial shade or full sun, avoid extremely dry, windy, unprotected places; does not tolerate poor drainage; use 1 male for every 2 to 3 females; prune in winter; air pollution tolerant.

DISEASES AND INSECTS: This species is affected by many problems including holly leaf miner, bud moth, scales, beetles, whitefly, berry midge, southern red mite, tar spot, leaf spots, cankers, bacterial blight, twig die back, spot anthracnose, leaf rot, leaf drop, powdery mildews, spine spot (nonparasitic) and leaf scorch (physiological). Leaf miner and scale are troublesome in our area.

LANDSCAPE VALUE: Specimen plant, groupings, requires male and female for fruit set. I feel there are too many superior plants to justify extensive use of this species but the list of cultivars is endless and on the east coast and south this is a favored plant.

CULTIVARS: There are more than 300 cultivars and if one is extremely interested *The International Checklist of Cultivated Ilex,* put out by the U.S. National Arboretum is a must. Desirable characteristics in holly cultivars should include annual bearing, large and bright colored fruits, good foliage, and dense habit.

var. *subintegra* — leaves entire or nearly so.

var. *xanthocarpa* — yellow fruits.

PROPAGATION: Similar to *I. crenata* except some cultivars are grafted.
NATIVE HABITAT: Massachusetts to Florida, west to Missouri and Texas. Introduced 1744.

Ilex pedunculosa — Longstalk Holly

FAMILY: Aquifoliaceae
LEAVES: Alternate, simple, ovate or elliptic, 1 to 3" long, rounded or broad-cuneate at base, acuminate, entire, evergreen, persistent for 3 years.
STEM: Slender, somewhat flattened, brownish green.

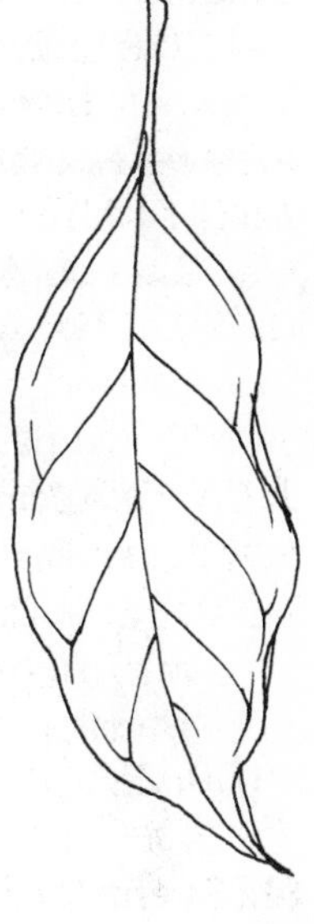

SIZE: 20 to 30' in height but usually smaller under cultivation, perhaps 15'.
HARDINESS: Zone 5, has survived in our rugged field plots under the most adverse conditions: heavy soils, dry, sweeping winds, and intense summer heat.
HABIT: Large shrub or small tree of dense habit and handsome foliage.
TEXTURE: Medium in all seasons.
LEAF COLOR: Very beautiful lustrous dark green in summer; in exposed areas develops a yellow-green cast during winter.
FLOWERS: Similar to *I. crenata.*
FRUIT: Berry-like, bright red drupe, 1/4" diameter, borne singly on 1" or larger pedicels, October and persisting.
CULTURE: Similar to *I. opaca;* from my observations perhaps not as fastidious as to soils.
DISEASES AND INSECTS: None serious, at least I have not seen any serious problems on the few specimens in Champaign-Urbana.
LANDSCAPE VALUE: One of the hardiest evergreen red fruiting hollies; should be used more than it is; apparently not well known.
PROPAGATION: I have had good success with cuttings, in fact, cuttings taken in February rooted 80% with 1000 ppm IBA/50% alcohol.
NATIVE HABITAT: Japan, China. 1892.

Ilex verticillata — Common Winterberry, Black Alder, Coralberry, Michigan Holly

FAMILY: Aquifoliaceae
LEAVES: Alternate, simple, elliptic or obovate to oblanceolate or oblong-lanceolate, 1 2/5 to 3" long, acute or acuminate, cuneate, serrate or doubly serrate, usually pubescent beneath, at least on the veins.
BUD: Smooth, gray-brown, sessile, with 2 to 4 imbricate scales, superposed.
STEM: Dark gray to brown, smooth, pith—green.

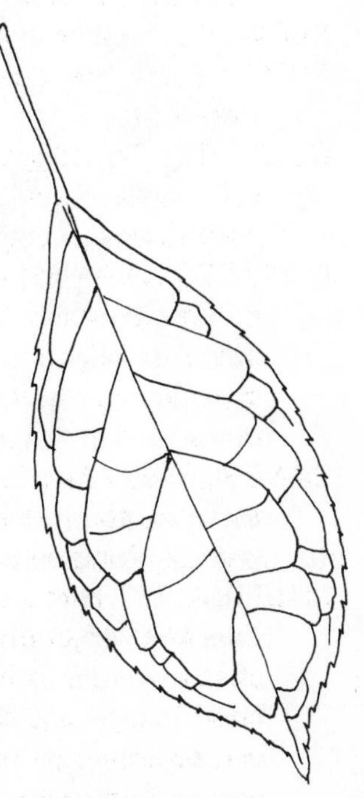

SIZE: 6 to 9' in height with a similar spread, can grow to 20' but this is rare under landscape conditions.
HARDINESS: Zone 3.
HABIT: Oval-rounded, deciduous shrub with dense complement of fine twiggy branches.
RATE: Slow, in youth can be induced into medium growth with adequate fertilizer and water.
TEXTURE: Medium in summer and winter.
LEAF COLOR: Deep rich green in summer; after a heavy freeze the leaves turn blackish, hence, the name Black-alder.
FLOWERS: Similar to *I. crenata,* however, often more than one female flower per node, June.

FRUIT: Berry-like drupe, bright red, 1/4" across and often in pairs, ripening in late August-September and persisting into January depending on bird populations.

CULTURE: Transplant balled and burlapped or as a container plant; adaptable to wet conditions (native to swampy areas) and does well in light and heavy soils; prefers moist, acid (pH 4.5 to 5.5), high organic matter soils; full sun or partial shade.

DISEASES AND INSECTS: Tar spots, leaf spots, and powdery mildew.

LANDSCAPE VALUE: Excellent for mass effect, shrub borders, water side and wet soils; requires male and female for fruit set; I have seen several mass plantings along Illinois highways which were outstanding.

CULTIVARS:

'Cacapon')
'Fairfax') Developed by O.M. Neal, University of West Virginia, supposedly good fruiting clones with excellent winter hardiness.
'Shaver')

'Christmas' or 'X-mas Cheer' – A free-fruiting, red fruited clone.

'Chrysocarpa' – Yellow fruited clone.

'Late Red' – Does not have an official name as of July, 1975; I have seen the parent shrub which is about 8' high and 10' wide with unbelievable quantities of cherry-red fruit, will probably be commercially available in the next year or two; now listed as 'Winter Red'.

'Nana' – Female clone, fruits twice the size of the species, supposedly never grows over 4' tall.

PROPAGATION: Cuttings, softwood, root readily. I have stratified whole fruits for 3 months at 41°F in moist peat and out of approximately 300 fruits ended with 70 seedlings. Alternating warm stratification with cold has been recommended.

RELATED SPECIES:

Ilex decidua – Possumhaw

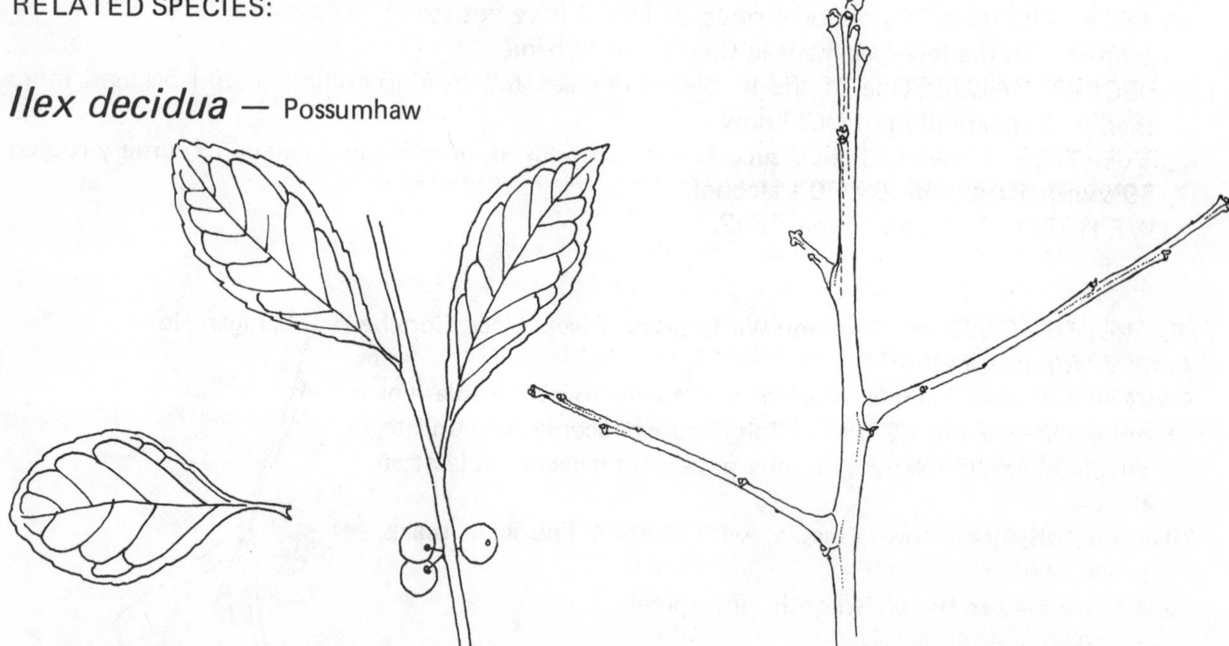

LEAVES: Alternate, simple, obovate to obovate-oblong, 1 2/5 to 3" long, usually obtusish, cuneate, obtusely serrate, dark green and lustrous above and with impressed veins, pale and pubescent on the midrib beneath, thickish, deciduous.

STEM: Grayish, variable, on some plants a very soft gray, on others a grayish brown. The lateral branches are produced in great quantities and result in a very bushy main stem.

Ilex decidua, Possumhaw, will grow to 30' in the wild but 7 to 15' in height with 3/4's that in spread is more reasonable under cultivation. Habit is that of a shrub or small tree, much branched with horizontal and ascending branches. Foliage is dark glossy green in summer; fruits are orange to scarlet, 1/3" diameter and ripen in September, often persisting until the following April; supposedly better adapted to alkaline soils than *I. verticillata;* the stems are usually a very light gray and stand out against an evergreen background. Native from Virginia to Florida, west to Texas. Cultivated 1760. Zone 4-5. Cultivars include:

'Reed' – Heavier fruiter than the species.

'Warren's Red' — Heavier fruiter than the species.

'Byers Golden' — Yellow fruiter.

NATIVE HABITAT: Native in swamps from Nova Scotia to Western Ontario, west to Wisconsin, south to Florida and west to Missouri; the most northerly of the hollies native in America. Introduced 1736.

OTHER HOLLIES OF LANDSCAPE IMPORTANCE

Ilex x *aquipernyi* is the result of crosses between *I. aquifolium* x *I. pernyi.* The habit is densely pyramidal while the foliage is lustrous dark green. 'Aquipern' is a male clone and 'San Jose' a female. 'San Jose' is hardy in Urbana, Illinois but best success is achieved under Zone 6 conditions. The fruits are red and of good size. I have rooted cuttings of 'San Jose' with 100 percent success. Supposedly this hybrid species can grow 20 to 30' high.

Ilex x *fosteri* — Foster's Holly (Botanically listed as *I. attenuata* 'Fosteri')

LEAVES: Evergreen, alternate, simple, elliptic to oblong-ovate, 1 3/5 to 3" long, spiny pointed and with 1 to 4 spreading spiny teeth on each side, glossy green.

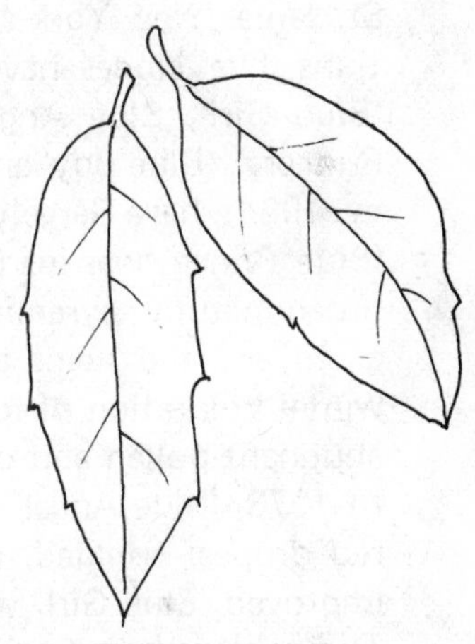

Ilex x *fosteri,* Foster's Holly, represents a group of interspecific hybrids between *Ilex cassine* var. *angustifolia* x *I. opaca.* There are selected clones known as Foster #1 through #5 made by E.E. Foster of Bessemer, Alabama. Foster #2 and #3, the most popular of this group in the south and the ones most often sold as Foster Holly, are used in general landscape work as foundation plants, hedges, and specimen plants. Both #2 and 3 are typically small-leaved, glossy green, with a spiny margin and have a compact, pyramidal growth habit. They are heavily fruited as is *I. cassine.* Foster #4 is a male plant while #1 and 5 are more like inferior forms of *I. opaca* and have been discarded. The Foster hollies are hardy in Zone 6 and based on trials in Urbana and Moline, Illinois do not perform well under Zone 4 or 5 conditions. The wood seems to be hardy but the leaves will turn brown in cold winters. A plant in my yard turned completely brown during the winter of 1975-76 where the coldest recorded temperature was -8° F.

Ilex x 'John Morris' and 'Lydia Morris' represent male and female hybrid hollies selected from seedlings which resulted from crosses between *I. cornuta* x *I. pernyi.* They exhibit a shrub-type habit and possess lustrous dark green, almost black green foliage. The leaves are tightly borne along the stems and are extremely spiny. Very handsome in foliage and the female form produces red fruits. The plants were named after the individuals who donated land for the establishment of the Morris Arboretum, Philadelphia, Pennsylvania. Hardy in Zone 6, shakily so in Zone 5 although Professor J.C. McDaniel has a small plant in his Urbana residence.

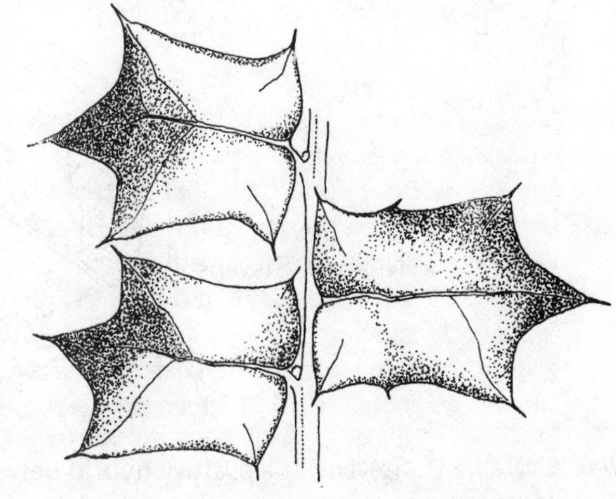

Ilex laevigata, Smooth Winterberry, is closely allied to *I. verticillata* except the fruits are borne singly, are slightly larger, and the leaf petioles are shorter. The plant grows to about 10′, usually with upright branches. The leaves are somewhat glossy, elliptic, oval, or sometimes lanceolate, 1 to 3 1/2″ long, the margins finely serrulate. The fruits are orange-red, 1/3″ diameter, and supposedly can be set without pollination. There is a yellow-fruited cultivar called 'Hervey Robinson'. Native in swamps and low woods from Maine to New Hampshire, south to Northern Georgia. Introduced 1812. Zone 4. The leaves turn yellow in the fall in contrast to the brownish black of *I. verticillata.*

Ilex x *meserveae,* Meserve Holly, represents a group of selected evergreen hollies from interspecific crosses between *I. rugosa,* Prostrate Holly, and *I. aquifolium.* The former species is not particularly attractive as an ornamental but possesses excellent hardiness (Zone 3) while the second, although of the highest landscape quality, is hardy in Zone 7. The initial crosses were made by Mrs. F. Leighton Meserve of St. James, New York and from the seedling populations five clones have been named: 'Blue Boy', 'Blue Girl', Blue Angel', 'Blue Prince' and 'Blue Princess'. 'Blue Boy' and 'Blue Girl', first introduced in 1964, have largely been discarded. In 1972, 'Blue Prince' was introduced. It forms a compact, broad natural pyramid. The leaves are a lustrous green and the stems a purplish blue. There is no winter coloration of foliage. 'Blue Prince' produces abundant pollen and one plant should effectively fertilize all the female hollies in a wide area. In 1973, 'Blue Angel' and 'Blue Princess' were introduced. 'Blue Angel' has large, shiny, deep red drupes; crinkled, dark glossy green foliage; and a full dense habit. 'Blue Princess' is an improved 'Blue Girl' with more abundant fruit and darker, more lustrous bluish green foliage. The habit is broad and shrubby. The best of the lot appear hardy in Zones 4 and 5. Based on observation of plants in Moline and Urbana, Illinois, I would have to rate this group among the hardiest and most ornamental hollies at our landscape disposal. Plants have survived -8°F in Central Illinois without a trace of injury. Cuttings will root readily and with time new and better clones will, no doubt, appear in the trade. Mrs. Meserve was honored for her work and received the American Horticultural Society's Citation for outstanding contributions to Amateur Horticulture.

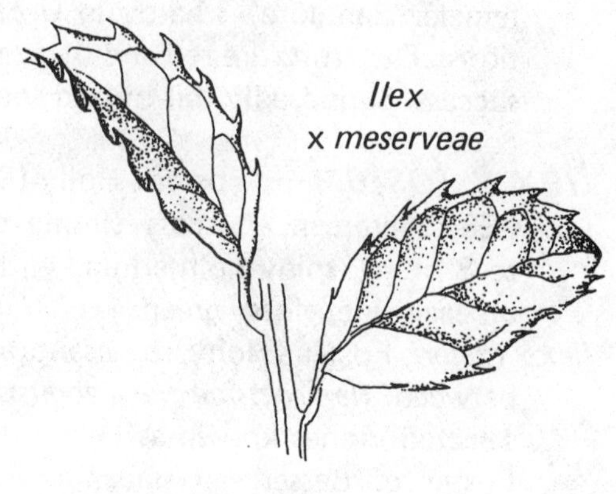

Ilex
x *meserveae*

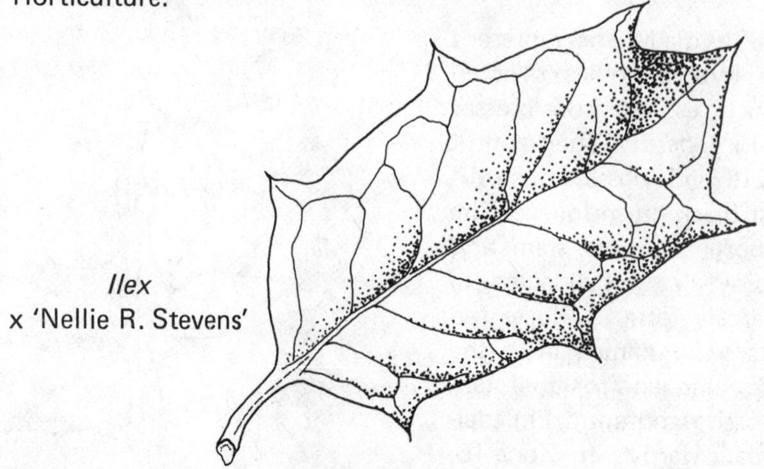

Ilex
x 'Nellie R. Stevens'

Ilex x 'Nellie R. Stevens' is a putitive hybrid between *I. cornuta* x *I. aquifolium.* The habit is that of large evergreen shrub or small pyramidal tree 15 to 25′ high. The leaves are shiny green, slightly bullate, with 2 or 3 teeth on each side. The fruit is red and the female flowers can be effectively pollinated by male *I. cornuta* which flower at a similar time. Heavily fruitful and some fruit may develop parthenocarpically. Hardy in Zone 6. Very vigorous plant and relatively fast growing.

Ilex serrata — Finetooth Holly

LEAVES: Alternate, simple, elliptic or ovate, 4/5 to 2" long, acute or acuminate, serrulate, dull green above, pubescent beneath, deciduous.

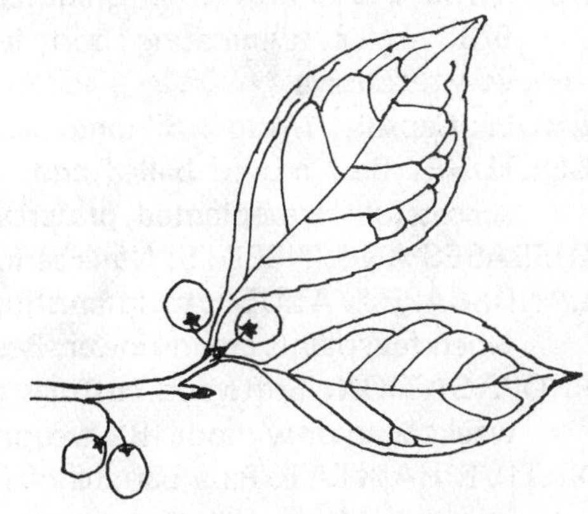

Ilex serrata, Finetooth Holly, is similar to *I. verticillata* except the fruits are smaller (about 1/4" diameter) and not as bright, and the leaves are more finely toothed. The species may grow 12 to 15' high with spreading branches, however, under landscape conditions 4 to 8' is more logical. The red fruits are abundantly borne and extremely showy after the leaves fall. Based on heavy fruited specimens I have seen at the National Arboretum this plant should be given wider landscape consideration. The cultivar 'Leucocarpa' has white fruits while 'Xanthocarpa' sports yellow drupes. A red fruited selection of *I. serrata* x *I. verticillata* is called 'Sparkleberry'. Native to Japan and China. Introduced 1866. Zone 5.

Ilex 'Shin Nien' — The first F_1 American-Chinese holly with the hardiness of *I. opaca* and the superior leaf qualities of *I. cornuta.* The cultivar resulted from a cross between *I.o.* 'Chief Paduke' x *I. cornuta.* The habit is pyramidal; male; hardy in Urbana, Illinois. The leaf surfaces develop a whitish cast in winter and for this reason its ornamental value may be limited. Bred by Professor J.C. McDaniel of the University of Illinois.

Indigofera kirilowii — Kirilow Indigo

LEAVES: Alternate, compound pinnate, 7 to 11 leaflets, sub-orbicular to obovate or elliptic, 2/5 to 1 1/5" long, mucronate, broad cuneate or rounded at base, rounded at apex, bright green above, sparingly appressed-pubescent on both sides.

Indigofera kirilowii, Kirilow Indigo, is a low, dense shrub with erect stems and may grow 3' in height. The foliage is bright green in summer. The flowers are rose-colored, 3/4" long, borne in June and July on dense 4 to 5" long racemes on current season's growth. Extremely adaptable species which does well in calcareous soils; branches may be killed to the ground in severe winters but new shoots quickly develop from the roots. Might be used as a ground cover for difficult areas. The flowers are somewhat masked by the foliage. Native of Northern China, Korea and Southern Japan. Introduced 1899. Zone 4.

Itea virginica — Virginia Sweetspire

FAMILY: Saxifragaceae

LEAVES: Alternate, simple, elliptic or obovate to oblong, acute or short acuminate, usually cuneate at the base, 1 3/5 to 4" long, serrulate, glabrous above, bright green, often sparingly pubescent beneath; petioles 1/5 to 2/5" long.

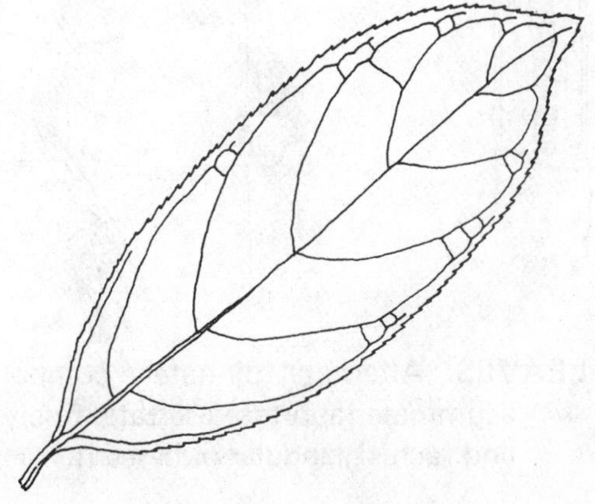

SIZE: 3 to 5' in height, possibly to 10', usually taller than broad at maturity.

HARDINESS: Zone 5.

HABIT: Shrub with erect, clustered branches, branched only near the top.
RATE: Slow to medium.
TEXTURE: Medium.
LEAF COLOR: Bright green in summer changing to scarlet and crimson with the advent of fall. Often persisting quite long in fall.
FLOWERS: Perfect, white, fragrant, borne in upright, dense pubescent racemes, 2 to 6" long, about 5/8" across, terminating short, leafy twigs; June-July; sufficiently abundant to make the bush very attractive.
FRUIT: Capsule, 1/4 to 1/3" long, narrow, pubescent.
CULTURE: Best moved balled and burlapped, however, pieces of the plant can be divided and successfully transplanted; prefers moist, wet, fertile soils and in the wild exists in wet places.
DISEASES AND INSECTS: None serious.
LANDSCAPE VALUE: An interesting native shrub valued for fragrant flowers at a time (July) when few plants are in flower. Best situated in moist or wet areas in the garden; full sun or shade.
PROPAGATION: Softwood cuttings collected in early July rooted 100 percent in sand in four weeks with or without IBA treatment.
NATIVE HABITAT: Pine barrens of New Jersey to Florida, west to Missouri and Louisiana. Introduced 1744.

Juglans — Walnut

FAMILY: Juglandaceae

The walnuts are treated in this text as a group similar to the format under *Carya.* The flowers are imperfect (monoecious); male catkins preformed, appearing as small, scaly, conelike buds, unbranched; female in 2 to 8 flowered spikes. Fruit is a drupe with the outer ovary wall (endocarp and mesocarp) semifleshy; the endocarp is hard and thick walled while the seeds are sweet and quite oily. The flowers are wind pollinated. Walnuts are important timber trees and the Black Walnut, *Juglans nigra,* is a prime timber tree. The following are the more important species.
ADDITIONAL NOTES: Seed of most *Juglans* species have a dormant embryo and the native species also have a hard outer wall. Dormancy can be broken by stratification at temperatures of 34° to 41°F. The cultivars are grafted on seedling understocks.

Juglans cinerea — Butternut

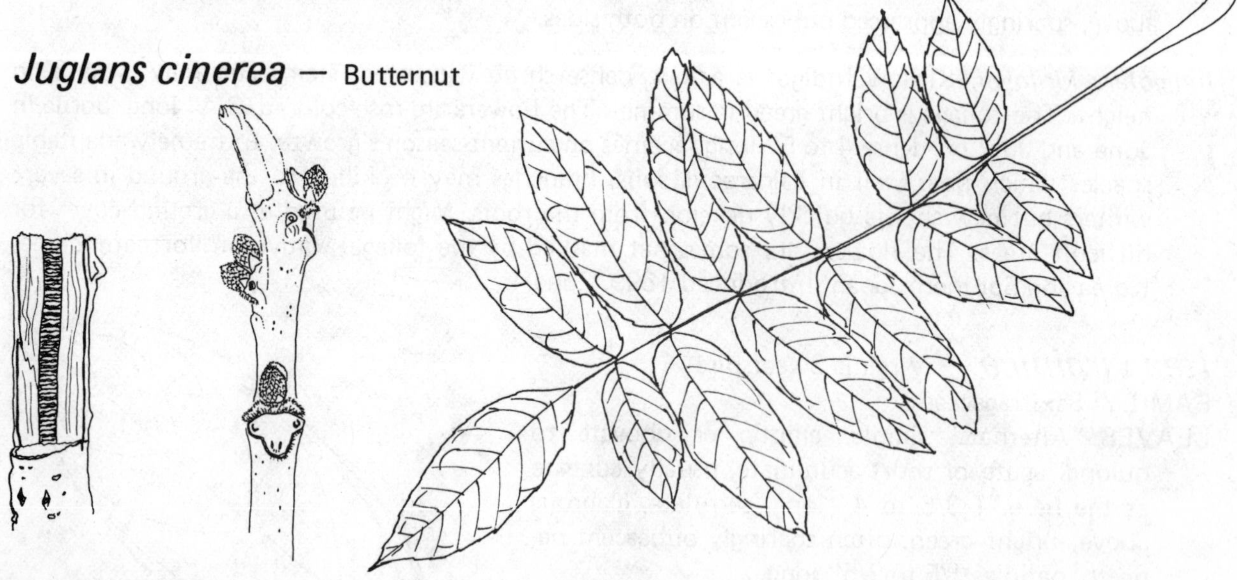

LEAVES: Alternate, pinnately compound, 11 to 19 leaflets, 2 to 5" long, oblong-lanceolate, acuminate, appressed-serrate, finely pubescent above, pubescent and glandular beneath, petiole and rachis glandular-pubescent.

BUDS: Densely pale downy, terminal bud large—2/5 to 4/5" long, flattened oblong to conical, obliquely blunt-pointed; lateral buds smaller, ovate, rounded at apex, 1 to 3 superposed buds generally present above axillary bud.

STEM: Stout, reddish buff to greenish gray, pubescent or smooth, bitter to taste, coloring saliva yellow when chewed. Pith—chocolate brown, chambered. Leaf scar—large, conspicuous, 3-lobed, inversely triangular, upper margin generally convex, seldom slightly notched, surmounted by a raised, downy pad.

BARK: Ridged and furrowed, ridges whitish, furrows grayish black, inner bark becoming yellow on exposure to air, bitter.

Juglans cinerea, Butternut, reaches 40 to 60' in height with a spread of 30 to 50' although it can grow to 100'. The tree is usually round topped with a short, usually forked or crooked trunk and somewhat open, wide-spreading crown of large horizontal branches and stout, stiff branches; relatively slow growing as is true for most walnuts and hickories (excluding *J. nigra*); prefers moist, rich, deep soils of bottomlands although it grows quite well in drier, rocky soils, especially of limestone origin; the seeds are sweet, edible and very oily; the inner bark has mild cathartic properties and was used in older times as an orange or yellow dye. Native from New Brunswick to Georgia, west to the Dakotas and Arkansas. Cultivated 1633. Zone 3. Ranges much further north and occurs at higher elevations than *J. nigra.*

Juglans nigra — Black Walnut

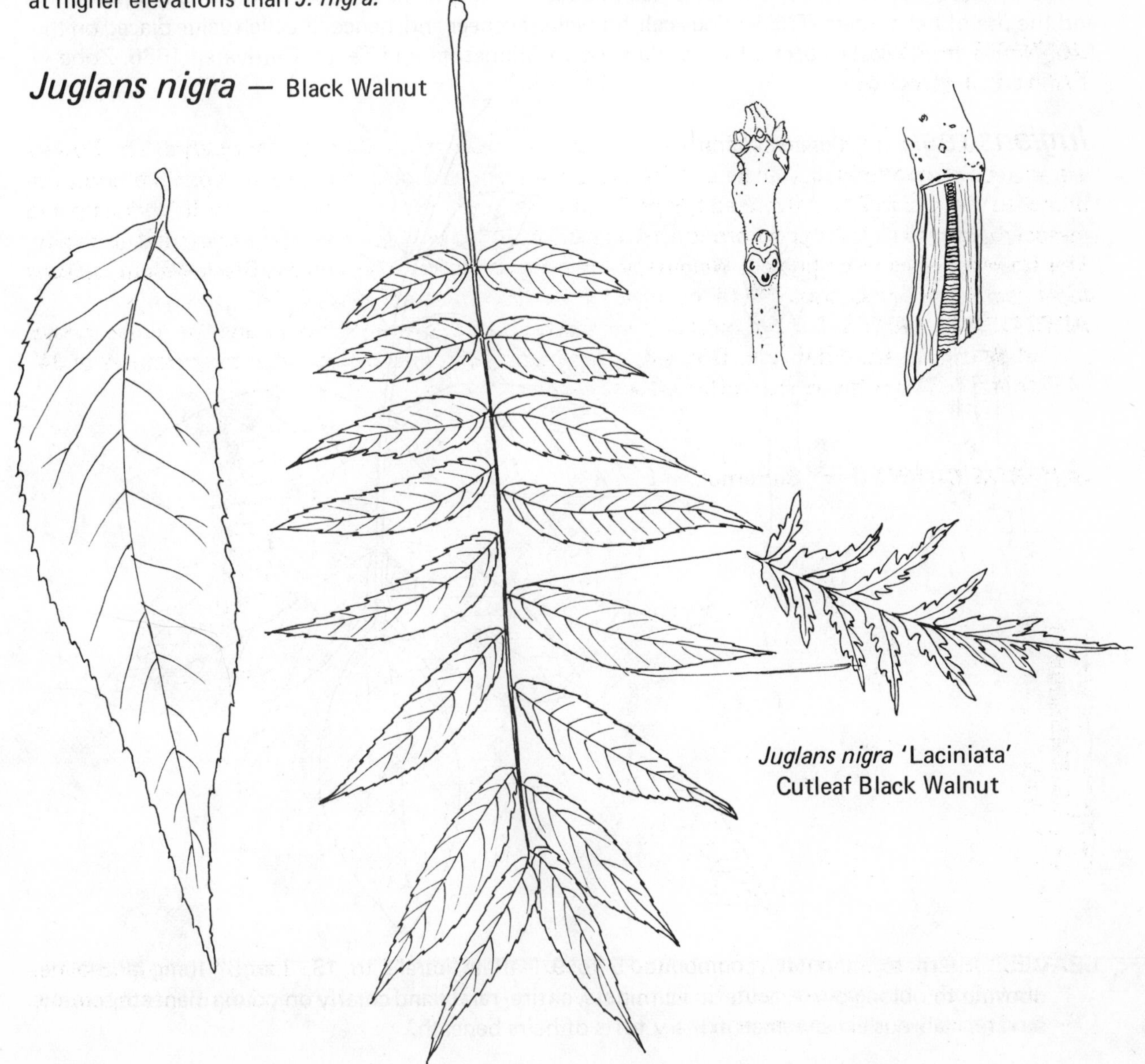

Juglans nigra 'Laciniata'
Cutleaf Black Walnut

LEAVES: Alternate, pinnately compound, 15 to 23 leaflets, 2 to 5" long, ovate-oblong to ovate-lanceolate, acuminate, rounded at base, irregularly serrate, at first minutely pubescent above, finally nearly glabrous and somewhat lustrous, pubescent and glandular beneath, leaves fragrant when crushed.

BUDS: Pale silky-downy; terminal buds ovate, 1/3" long, scarcely longer than broad, lateral buds smaller, often superposed, grayish.

STEM: Stout, densely gray-downy to smooth and reddish buff, bitter to taste and coloring saliva yellow when chewed. Pith—buff, paler than that of Butternut, chambered, open chambers several times wider than intervening diaphragms. Leaf scar—upper margin distinctly notched enclosing axillary bud, no downy pad above leaf scar.

Juglans nigra, Black Walnut, is a large tree to 50 to 75' in height and often a similar spread when open grown. The species may reach a maximum height of 125 to 150'. Usually develops a full, well formed trunk which is devoid of branches a considerable (1/2 to 2/3's) distance from the ground, the crown is oval to rounded and somewhat open; prefers deep, rich, moist soils and here maximum growth occurs; tolerates drier soils but grows much more slowly under these conditions; develops an extensive taproot and is difficult to transplant; the wood is highly prized and has been used for cabinets, gunstocks and many furniture pieces. The wood is so valuable that "Walnut Rustlers" have developed sophisticated techniques to remove trees such as mid-night operations and the use of helicopters. Tremendous call for walnut veneer and, hence, the high value placed on the tree. Native from Massachusetts to Florida west to Minnesota and Texas. Cultivated 1686. Zone 4.

Juglans regia — Persian Walnut

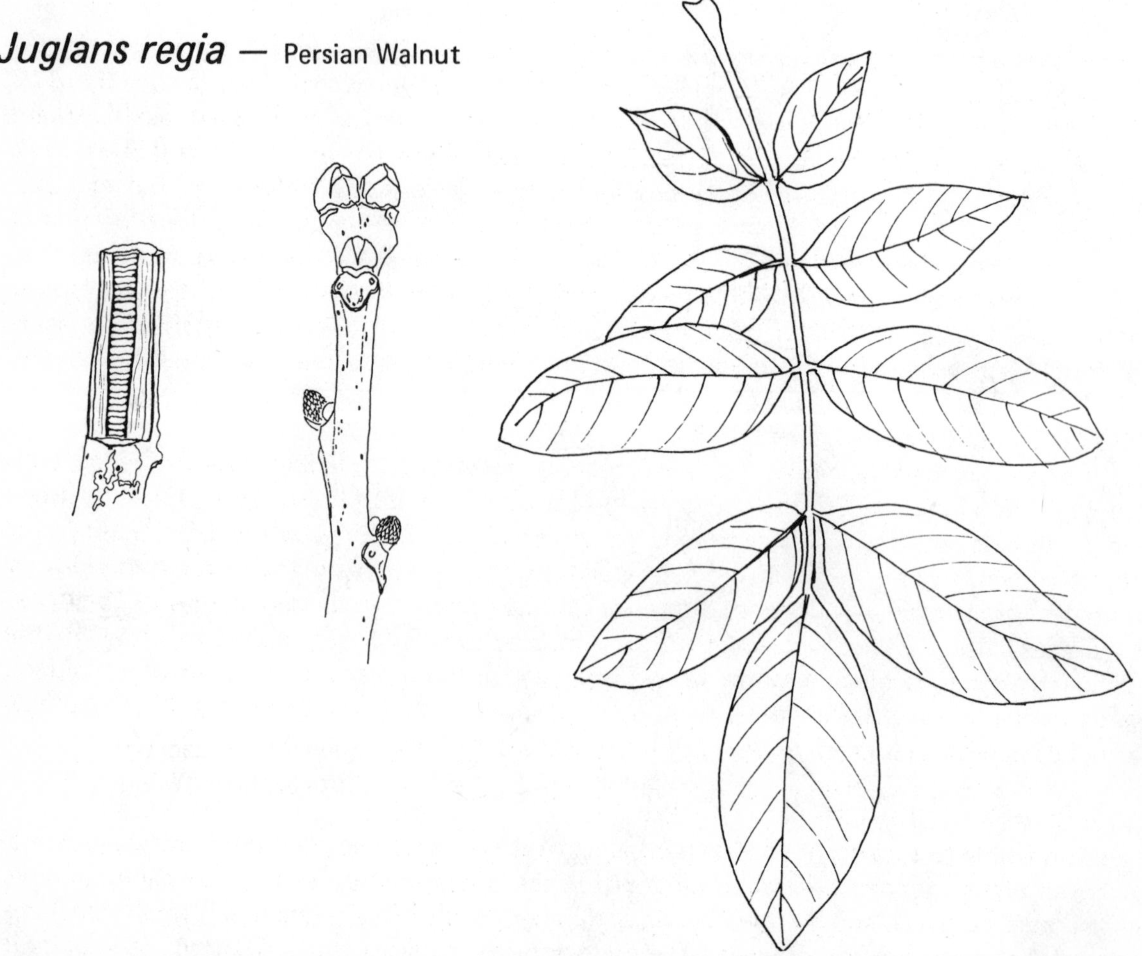

LEAVES: Alternate, pinnately compound, 5 to 9 leaflets, rarely to 13, 2 to 5" long, elliptic to obovate to oblong-ovate, acute or acuminate, entire, rarely and chiefly on young plants obscurely serrate, glabrous except small axillary tufts of hairs beneath.

BUDS: Terminal—2 to 3 fold larger than lateral, 1/5 to 1/3" long, valvate with scales barely overlapping, pubescent, brownish.

STEM: Stout, olive brown when young, grayish on old branches. Pith—uniformly chambered, brownish in color.

Juglans regia — Persian Walnut is a tree which develops a rounded, often spreading and open crown ultimately reaching 40 to 60' in height with a comparable or greater spread. Prefers a deep, dry, light loamy soil; does not do well in wet or poor subsoil areas; like most walnuts should be pruned in summer or fall; nuts are edible, thin shelled and widely available in stores; they do not have the wild, nutty taste of *J. nigra* but are much easier to shell, there are many cultivars of this tree but two which are well adapted to midwestern conditions are 'Carpathian' which was brought to Canada from mountains of Poland and supposedly bears heavy crops even when winter temperatures drop to -40° F, and; 'Hansen' an annual bearer, shells are very thick, easily shelled and the nut meats (seeds) are classed as excellent with the highest percent of kernel reported; the tree is located at Clay Center, Ohio, southeast of Toledo. This particular tree might make a nice ornamental because of quality characters and adaptability to midwestern conditions. Native to Southeastern Europe to Himalayas and China. Long cultivated.

Juniperus — Juniper

Cupressaceae

Junipers would have to rank as the toughest of evergreen landscape plants for they will grow and are used in all parts of the United States and, for that matter, the world. They include 50 to 70 species widely distributed throughout the temperate and subtropical regions of the Northern Hemisphere and south of the equator in Africa. Thirteen species are native to the United States. The majority of types used in landscape plantings are found in the species *J. chinensis, J. communis, J. horizontalis, J. sabina, J. scopulorum* and *J. virginiana,* with a few important cultivars found in *J. conferta, J. procumbens,* and *J. squamata.* For some strange reason the common name of *J. virginiana* is Eastern Redcedar with all other species known as junipers. The wood of the tree species is used for furniture (cedar chests), paneling, novelties, posts, poles, fuel, and pencils. The fleshy cones ("fruits") are used in medicine, varnish and for flavoring an alcoholic beverage known as gin.

MORPHOLOGICAL CHARACTERISTICS

Trees or shrubs; bark of trunk and main branches usually thin, shredding, rarely scaling; buds conspicuous, 1/8" long, scales small, sharply pointed or buds inconspicuous and naked; leaves opposite or ternate, needle-like or scale-like, on young plants always needle-like, on older plants both forms of leaves often found in the same plant, upperside of needle-like leaves with white or blue stomatic bands; male flowers united into an ovoid or oblong catkin, female flowers composed of 3-8 valvate scales, some or all bearing 1-2 ovules; the scales becoming fleshy and united into a berry-like cone; cones variously shaped, brown when young and covered with a thick mealy bloom, afterwards dark blue or blackish blue, ripening the second or third year; seeds elliptic to oblong, obtuse-ended, sometimes somewhat 3-angled in section, glossy brown; cotyledons 2 or 4-6.

GROWTH CHARACTERISTICS

It is impossible to stereotype the junipers as to habit because the species vary from low-growing, ground cover types to larger conical to pyramidal trees (*J. scopulorum* and *J. virginiana*). Among the species and cultivars are narrow, broad, columnar, conical and pyramidal; small and large spreading; globe, slow and fast growing ground cover types. Foliage color varies from dark lustrous green to light green, blue, silver-blue, yellow and shades in between.

CULTURE

Junipers are most successfully moved balled and burlapped or as container plants. In fact, most junipers are now grown in containers, especially the ground cover and shrubby types. They prefer open, sunny locations and light, sandy, low or high pH, moderately moist soils but will grow well in about any situation. They seem to very tolerant of dry, clay soils and some types will grow in sand. They seem to exhibit good air pollution tolerance and will withstand the dirt and grime of cities as well as any conifer. In Illinois they have been used as windbreaks with good success. Some types (*J.c. sargentii, J. conferta* and cultivars) show good salt tolerance. When junipers are located in heavy shade they become open, thin and ratty. Junipers withstand heavy pruning and for this reason make good hedges. A good rule of thumb is "if you cannot grow junipers, then do not bother planting anything else."

DISEASES AND INSECTS

Twig blight *(Phomopsis juniperovora)*, cedar-apple rust, wilt, rocky mountain juniper aphid, bagworm, juniper midge, scale, webworm, redcedar bark beetle, and mites. Junipers have a number of very serious problems including blight (usually manifested in a tip dieback and sometimes whole plants are killed) and bagworm (so bad in Central Illinois that plants are often completely stripped of foliage). *J. horizontalis,* and cultivars (especially 'Plumosa'), *J. procumbens,* and *J. chinensis* 'San Jose' are especially susceptible to blight.

PROPAGATION

Seed and cutting propagation are adequately discussed under *J. chinensis.* Some cultivars are grafted on understocks of *J. virginiana, J. chinensis,* or *J. chinensis* 'Hetzii'. They are pot grafted using a side graft in February or March in the greenhouse.

LANDSCAPE USE

There is no limit to the use of junipers in landscape situations. They make excellent screens, hedges, windbreaks, ground covers, foundations plants, rock garden plants, groupings, and specimens. Because of their ease of culture and ubiquitous landscape value they are often overused almost to the point of monotony. Whole foundation plantings are often composed of nothing but junipers. Another problem is that consideration is seldom given to ultimate landscape size and in a few years plants have overgrown their boundaries. Many of the newer, smaller, better-foliaged types should be used in place of the cumbersome *J.c.* 'Pfitzeriana' and 'Hetzii'. Also it is important to consider the degree of shade in which the junipers will be grown. They can become "ratty" looking in a short time period if sited in too heavy a shade.

ADDITIONAL NOTES

A strong diuretic, oil of juniper, is extracted from juniper berries and these are also used in flavoring gin. The name gin, is abbreviated from *geneva* which in turn is a corruption of *genievre,* the French word for juniper or juneve—its Dutch equivalent. The utilization of juniper berries in the making of gin dates back many centuries. British gin is prepared by distilling a fermenting mixture of maize, rye, and malt. Then the resulting liquid is redistilled after juniper and sometimes coriander have been added.

Juniperus chinensis — Chinese Juniper

LEAVES: Of 2 kinds, adult branches with the ultimate divisions about 1/25" in diameter, clothed with 4 ranks of leaves in opposite pairs which are closely pressed, overlapping and rhombic in outline, 1/16" long, blunt or bluntly pointed, the outer surface convex, green with a paler margin marked with a glandular depression on the back; juvenile leaves awl-shaped, 1/3" long, spreading, in whorls of 3, or in opposite pairs, with a green midrib and 2 glaucous bands above, convex beneath, ending in a spiny point.

CONES: Dioecious, male is yellowish or brownish, numerous, usually borne on adult branchlets, occasionally on branchlets bearing juvenile foliage. Female, ripening the second year, at first whitish blue, bloomy, when ripe brown, sub-globose or top-shaped, 1/3" in diameter, composed of 4 to 8 scales, seeds 2 to 5.

SIZE: Tree to 60-75' in height, averages 15-20' in spread, rarely represented in this country.

HARDINESS: Zone 4.

HABIT: Tree or shrub; most typically an erect, narrow, conical tree; sometimes very slender, sometimes bushy.

RATES: Slow to medium.

TEXTURE: Medium.

LEAF COLOR: Blue-green to grayish green.

FLOWERS: Dioecious; staminate flowers orange-yellow, pistillate yellowish.

FRUIT: Cones globose or oblong irregularly glóbose, 1/4" across, at first whitish blue bloomy, when ripe dark brown; seeds oblong-obtuse or nearly 3-angled, glossy brown.

CULTURE: Transplanted balled and burlapped or from a container, prefers alkaline soils, moist, well drained conditions, full sun or partial shade.

DISEASES AND INSECTS: *Phomopsis* blight (kills young shoots, prevalent in early spring and wet weather).

LANDSCAPE VALUE: Depending on cultivar they can be used as a ground cover, foundation plant, hedge, screen, specimen, and mass planting.

CULTIVARS:

'Ames' — Initially grows as dwarf, wide spreading shrub; however with time develops a central leader. Steel blue foliage initially, turning green when mature.

'Armstrong' — Dwarf form, wide as high, branches horizontally spreading, leaves soft, like those of 'Pfitzeriana', but soft gray green.

'Blaauw' — Foliage is a rich blue green, very dense and compact with an irregular, vase-shaped habit. About 4' high and as wide.

'Blue Point' — Pyramidal form with a tear drop outline, extremely dense branching, blue-gray foliage.

'Blue Vase' — Vase-shaped form, with good summer and winter foliage; supposedly intermediate between upright and spreading type.

'Columnaris Glauca' — Narrowly columnar, 24', loose in branching habit, needles awl-shaped, silvery-gray.

'Fairview' — Narrow-pyramidal, vigorous growing; leaves mostly subulate, on some branches scale-like, bright green. Silver berry-like structures (cones) during late summer and fall.

'Fruitlandii' — Spreading form of vigorous growth, compact, dense with bright green foliage. Actually an improved *J.c.* 'Pfitzeriana Compacta'.

'Hetzii' — Large, rapidly growing, upright spreading form, branches in all directions, 15' by 15' and larger at maturity. Leaves scale-like, glaucous, a few leaves awl-shaped.

'Hetzii Columnaris' — Upright form, similar to 'Keteleeri' with scale and awl-shaped leaves. Needles are bright green.

'Hetzii Glauca' — Semierect form with light blue foliage. Intermediate between the previous two.

'Iowa' — Similar to 'Ames', a little more spreading and not so compact; leaves acicular and scale-like, green with a bluish cast, a free fruiting form.

'Keteleeri' — Broadly pyramidal tree with a stiff trunk and loose, light to medium green foliage, leaves scale-like, very pointed, cones with a recurved stalk, globose, 1/2 to 3/5" across, initially grayish green, finally glossy light green.

'Maney' — Bushy, semi-erect form, as broad as high, leaves acicular, bluish, bloomy.

'Mint Julep' — New from Monrovia. Compact grower with arching branches creating a low fountain-like form, foliage according to Monrovia is a brilliant mint green. Actually looks like a very green Pfitzer.

'Mountbatten' — Dense, pyramidal, narrow form to 12', similar to *J. communis* 'Hibernica'; foliage grayish green, mostly acicular.

'Old Gold' — Similar to Pfitzer only more compact; foliage bronze-gold, persisting during winter.

'Pfitzeriana' — The granddaddy of juniper cultivars. Probably the most widely planted juniper. Wide spreading, variable form, usually listed as growing about 5' high and 10' wide; actually grows 3 times these values. Foliage scale-like and awl-shaped, bright green.

'Pfitzeriana Arctic' — Form with branches that hug the ground, foliage—blue-green. Supposedly growing 18" high and 6' wide. Extremely hardy.

'Pfitzeriana Aurea' — Similar to Pfitzer in growth, branchlets and leaves tinged golden yellow in summer, becoming yellowish green in winter.

'Pfitzeriana Compacta' — Bushy, compact, with greater proportion of awl-shaped leaves.

'Pfitzeriana Glauca' — More dense than Pfitzer with mostly acicular leaves, markedly silver blue in older plants, becoming purplish blue in winter.

'Pfitzeriana Kallay' — Slow growing form with acicular foliage, bright green, mature height 2' and a 6' spread.

'Pyramidalis' — Male, columnar, dense form with ascending branches, leaves acicular, bluish green, very pungent, often sold as *J. excelsa* 'Stricta'.

'Robusta Green' — Upright form with tufted brilliant green foliage. Appears to be similar to 'Keteleeri'.

'San Jose' — Creeping form, 10" high and 6 to 8' wide, spreads irregularly; foliage grayish green, mostly acicular.

var. *sargentii* — Low growing (18" to 2' high), wide spreading (7.5 to 9' wide), branchlets 4-angled, leaves mostly scale-like, small, slightly grooved on back, blue green, bloomy; cones blue, scarcely bloomy; seeds 3; resistant to juniper blight.

var. *sargentii* 'Compacta' — More compact than above with scale-like leaves light green, acicular leaves dark green, with very glaucous green top, margins bounded by a dark green edge.

var. *sargentii* 'Glauca' — Dwarf, much better in growth than 'Compacta'; branchlets thin, feathery; leaves glaucous. 1 1/2' to 6'.

var. *sargentii* 'Viridis' — Similar to var. *sargentii* but leaves light green year round.

'Sea Green' — Compact spreader with fountain-like, arching branches, dark green foliage.

'Sea Spray' — According to Hines Nursery who introduced the shrub it is a better ground cover than 'Blue Rug', 'Bar Harbor' or var. *tamariscifolia.* Grows less than 1' high; center branches stay full and dense; resistant to water molds, root rot and juniper blight; hardy to -20°F. If it meets all the press releases it should prove to be a good juniper.

'Spartan' — A fast, dense grower of tall, pyramidal habit, of rich green color and very handsome appearance.

'Viridis' — Pyramidal, teardrop shape in outline, dense branching, gray green foliage.

'Wintergreen' — Pyramidal, dense, rich green foliage.

PROPAGATION: The seeds should be gathered in the fall as soon as the berry-like cones become ripe. For best germination, seeds should be removed from the fruits and then treated with sulfuric acid for 30 minutes before being stratified, which should be done for about 4 months at 40°F. As a substitute for the acid treatment, 2 to 3 months of warm (70° to 85°F; 21° to 30°C.) stratification or summer planting could be used. Juniper cuttings to be rooted in the greenhouse can be taken at any time during the winter. Taking the cuttings after the stock plants have been exposed to some subfreezing temperatures seems to give better rooting. For propagating in an outdoor cold frame, cuttings are usually taken in late summer or early fall. Lightly wounding the base of the cuttings is sometimes helpful, and the use of indolebutyric acid is also beneficial. A medium-coarse sand or a 1:1 mixture of perlite and sterilized peat moss is a satisfactory rooting medium for juniper cuttings. A greenhouse temperature of about 60°F (15°C) is best for the first 4 to 6 weeks. Maintenance of a humid environment without excessive wetting of the cuttings is desirable, as is a relatively high light intensity. A light, intermittent misting can be used. Bottom heat of about 80°F will aid in rooting.

ADDITIONAL NOTES: The species is almost an unknown entity under cultivation but is adequately represented by the numerous cultivars which vary in size from prostrate, spreading types to upright tree forms. P.J. Van Melle, an American nurseryman, has an interesting hypothesis concerning the numerous cultivars of *J. chinensis.* He says that the original species *J. chinensis* L. was inadequately defined by Linnaeus and that certain true varieties within *J. chinensis* should have been listed as species. He also noted that numerous natural and garden hybrids have occurred between *J. c.* and *J. sabina* all of which are listed under *J. c.* Mr. Van Melle stated that the name *J. chinensis* has come to include "everything but the kitchen stove—a loose aggregate, incapable of definition in terms of a species". He proposed to limit the use of *J. chinensis,* to resuscitate *J. sphaerica* and to raise *J. sheppardii* to specific status. He also proposed a new hybrid species, *J.* x *media,* to contain all the more or less bush-like forms in which *J. sabina* was discernible by the characteristic savin odor of the bruised foliage. He relegated *J. chinensis sargentii* to species level, *J. sargentii.* Van Melle did a considerable amount of study but his work has not been fully accepted by the botanical world. One taxonomist said that "Van Melle is probably right, but a lot more work will have to be done on these junipers before we can accept all he says—it will mean scrapping so much in all the books."

Anyone who has taken a close look and smell of the *J. c.* cultivars will see some truth in Van Melle's hypothesis.

NATIVE HABITAT: China, Mongolia and Japan. Introduced 1767.

Juniperus communis — Common Juniper

LEAVES: Awl-shaped, persisting for 3 years, tapering from the base to a spiny point, sessile, spreading, about 3/5" long, concave above with a broad white band, sometimes divided by a green midrib at the base, bluntly keeled below, needles consistently ternate.

CONES: Usually dioecious, male solitary, cylindrical, 1/3" long. The yellow stamens in 5 to 6 whorls. Female, solitary, green, 1/2" long, ripening the second or third year, green when young, bluish or black when ripe, covered with a waxy bloom; globose or slightly longer than broad, 1/3 to 1/2" diameter with 3 minute points at the top, the 3 scales of which the fruit is composed usually gaping and exposing the seeds. Seeds, 2 to 3, elongated ovoid, 3-cornered, with depressions between.

SIZE: 5-10', (rarely to 15', known to 40') by 8-12' spread.

HARDINESS: Zone 2.

HABIT: A medium-sized tree with ascending and spreading branches or more often a much-branched, sprawling shrub.

RATE: Slow.

TEXTURE: Medium.

BARK: Reddish brown, scaling off in papery sheets.

LEAF COLOR: Gray-green to blue-green in summer; often assuming a yellow or brownish green in winter.

FLOWERS: Dioecious; staminate yellow, pistillate pale yellow.

FRUIT: Cones sessile or short-stalked, globose or broadly ovoid, 1/4" across, bluish black or black, glaucous bloomy, ripening the second or third season; seeds usually 3, elongated ovoid, tricornered with depressions between. (Fruits used as a diuretic, flavoring of Gin.)

CULTURE: Transplants readily; grows on the worst possible land, common on dry, sterile soils, rock outcroppings and waste lands. Withstands wind, tolerant of calcareous soils, will tolerate neutral or slightly acid soils, extremely hardy, full sun.

DISEASES AND INSECTS: Susceptible to Juniper blight and other problems mentioned on the culture sheet.

LANDSCAPE VALUE: A handsome ground cover for sandy soils and waste places, useful for undergrowth and naturalized plantings. Best represented in the landscape by the cultivars.

CULTIVARS:

'Compressa' — Dwarf, fastigiate form, dense, very slow growing, 2 to 3' tall, leaves awl-shaped, thin, with a conspicuous silvery band above, margin narrow, green; dark green beneath.

'Depressa' — Dwarf, broad, prostrate shrub, rarely above 4' high, glaucous band on upper surface with green margin.

'Depressa Aurea' — Yellow foliaged form, otherwise similar to above.

'Gold Beach' — Excellent dwarf form with green foliage, 5 year-old plants are 5" tall and 2' across. In early spring, new growth is yellow, later turning green.

'Hibernica' — Dense, upright in habit, foliage bluish white to near the apex above, margin narrow, green, bluish green beneath. A poor plant.

'Suecica' — Similar to above except the tips of the branchlets droop; leaves bluish green, about as lousy as above.

PROPAGATION: Refer to *J. chinensis.*

ADDITIONAL NOTES: The oil distilled from the fleshy cones ("berries") is used for medicinal and flavoring purposes (gin).

NATIVE HABITAT: *J. communis* has a wider distribution than any other tree or shrub; common in North and Central Europe and also occurs in the mountains of the countries bordering on the Mediterranean. It is also found in Asia Minor, the Caucasus, Iran, Afghanistan, the Western Himalaya, the United States and Canada. In the United States it occurs from New England to Pennsylvania and North Carolina. I have seen old farmland in Massachusetts completely overgrown with this species and the range of forms seemed infinite. One could select cultivars until the cows came home. The whole point is that with junipers we have reached a cultivar glut and the addition of more only compounds and confuses the issue.

Juniperus conferta — Shore Juniper

LEAVES: Crowded, overlapping, awl-shaped, ternate, glaucous green, tapering to a prickly point, deeply grooved above with one band of stomata, convex below and green.

CONES: Produced in abundance, globose, 1/3 to 1/2" diameter, dark blue or bluish black, bloomy at maturity. Seeds, 3, 3-angled, ovate, with longitudinal grooves on back, acuminate.

SIZE: 1 to 1 1/2' in height by 6-9' spread after 15 to 20 years.

HARDINESS: Zone 5-6.

HABIT: Dense, bushy, procumbent evergreen shrub.

RATE: Slow.

TEXTURE: Medium.

LEAF COLOR: Bright bluish green.

FLOWERS: Dioecious, inconspicuous.

FRUIT: Cones subglobose, flat at base, 1/3 to 1/2" across, dark blue or bluish black, bloomy at maturity; seeds, 3, 3-angled, ovate, with longitudinal grooves on back, acuminate.

CULTURE: Tolerant of poor soils, especially adapted to plantings in sandy soils of the seashore and in full sun. Not good for clay soils.

LANDSCAPE VALUE: A low ground cover, especially adapted for planting on sand dunes in the seashore area; actually one of the handsomest of the ground cover type junipers; good in mass, on banks, in planter boxes, around tall shrubs or trees; lovely draped over a wall.

CULTIVARS:

'Blue Pacific' — Low trailing habit and ocean blue-green foliage color.

'Emerald Sea' — Low growing form with blue-green foliage.

PROPAGATION: Refer to *J. chinensis.*

NATIVE HABITAT: Japan and Sakhalin on sandy seashores. Introduced 1915.

Juniperus horizontalis — Creeping Juniper

LEAVES: Conspicuously glaucous, of 2 kinds, mostly scale-like, about 1/6" long, closely appressed, in 4 ranks, ovate to oblong, shortly pointed, each with a glandular depression on the back, the awl-shaped leaves in opposite pairs. Foliage usually turning a plum-purple color in winter. Foliage has a plume-like texture.

CONES: On recurved stalks, bluish or greenish black, 1/4 to 3/4" long. Seeds, 2 to 3.

SIZE: 1 to 2' high by 4 to 8' spread, variable but definitely low growing, spreading type.

HARDINESS: Zone 3.

HABIT: Low growing, procumbent shrub with long, trailing branches forming large mats.

RATE: Slow to medium; may grow to a diameter of 10' over a 10 year period.

TEXTURE: Medium-fine.

LEAF COLOR: Bluish green or steel-blue turning plum purple in winter.

FLOWERS: Dioecious, inconspicuous.

FRUITS: Cones on recurved stalks, about 1/3" across, blue, slightly glaucous; seeds 2-3, seldom produced on cultivated plants.

CULTURE: Adaptable, withstands hot dry situations and slightly alkaline soils, seems to transplant readily, tolerant of heavy soils, native to sandy and rocky soils and exposed situations. Found on sea cliffs, gravelly slopes and in swamps.

DISEASES AND INSECTS: *Phomopsis* blight (Juniper blight) can be extremely serious.

LANDSCAPE VALUE: A low ground-cover valued for its adaptability in sandy and rocky soils as well as tolerating hot, dry, sunny locations. Used for slope plantings and facer evergreens, ground covers, masses, foundations and in containers.

CULTIVARS:

'Alpina' — Dwarf, creeping form, 2' by 5', leaves exclusively awl-shaped, bluish or gray blue, changing to purple in autumn.

'Bar Harbor' — Low growing, spreading form, 1' by 6 to 8', leaves chiefly awl-shaped, loosely appressed, bluish green, turning plum purple in the winter.

'Blue Chip' — Selected by Hill Nursery Co. for low prostrate habit and excellent blue foliage color throughout the year, 8 to 10" high.

'Blue Mat' — Dense, slow growing, prostrate type, with blue-green foliage.

'Douglasii' — Trailing form, 1 to 1 1/2' by 6 to 9', steel blue foliage turning purplish through the winter. Rapid growing form. ('Waukegan')

'Emerald Spreader' — Exceedingly low, ground hugging spreader is heavily set with emerald green branchlets giving it a full, feathery appearance. A Monrovia introduction.

'Emerson' — Low growing form, 1' by 9 to 15', leaves acicular and scale-like, blue foliage color is held throughout the winter, slow growing.

'Glomerata' — Extremely dwarf, 6" high, leaves scale-like, green assuming plum purple color in winter.

'Hughes' — Low growing, 1' by 5', foliage silvery blue, distinct radial branching habit.

'Jade Spreader' — Very low, wide spreading form with dense jade green foliage which creates a heavy mat-like appearance.

'Plumosa' — Wide spreading, dense, compact form, 2' by 10', leaves awl-shaped and scale-like, gray-green, purplish in winter.

'Plumosa Compacta' — Compact form of above, dense branching, flat spreading. Bronze-purple in winter.

'P.C. Youngstown' — Similar to above but stay green all winter.

'Plumosa Fountain' — Flat growing form, 16" by 6', rapid growing.

'Procumbens' — Spreading, prostrate form, 6" by 12 to 15', leaves awl-shaped, soft, glaucous green, becoming bluish green with age.

'Sun Spot' — Similar to 'Waukegan' but spotted yellow throughout the branches.

'Turquoise Spreader' — Wide spreading form, densely covered with soft and feathery branchlets of turquoise green foliage. Vigorous grower.

'Webberi' – Extremely low, mat-like, spreading form of fine texture, bluish green foliage.

'Wiltoni' – Very flat growing form with trailing branches, 4 to 6" by 6 to 8', foliage–intense silver-blue, assumes light purplish tinge in winter, fairly fast growing ('Blue Rug').

PROPAGATION: Refer to *J. chinensis.*

NATIVE HABITAT: North America where it inhabits sea-cliffs, gravelly slopes, even swamps (Nova Scotia to British Columbia, south to Massachusetts, New York, Minnesota, and Montana). Introduced 1836.

Juniperus procumbens — Japgarden Juniper (Listed as a variety of *J. chinensis* by *Hortis III*)

LEAVES: In three's, linear-lanceolate, spiny-pointed about 1/3" long, concave above and glaucous with a green midrib toward the apex, lower surface convex, bluish with 2 white spots near the base below, from which 2 glaucous lines run down the edges of the pulvini. Branchlets with glaucous ridges.

SIZE: 8-12" to 24" high by 10-15' spread.

HARDINESS: Zone 5.

HABIT: A dwarf, procumbent plant with long, wide-spreading, stiff branches.

RATE: Slow, may cover 10' diameter area in 10 years.

TEXTURE: Medium.

LEAF COLOR: Bluish green or gray green.

FLOWERS: Dioecious; staminate yellow, pistillate greenish.

FRUIT: Cones subglobose, 1/3" across; seeds 3, ovoid.

CULTURE: Needs full sun, tolerant of soils, thrives under adverse conditions, needs open situations, supposedly hard to transplant and thrives well on limy soils.

DISEASES AND INSECTS: Tremendously susceptible to *Phomopsis.*

LANDSCAPE VALUE: A handsome ground cover for beds, low borders, terraces, hillsides; can be pruned to retain size. Temper use with knowledge that *Phomopsis* can devastate a planting.

CULTIVARS:

'Nana' – Dwarf, similar to species, forms a compact mat with branches one on top of the other, branchlets vary in length, spreading out as a compact mass of sprays, foliage bluish green, slightly purplish in winter. One of the best!

'Variegata' – The bluish green foliage is streaked with creamy white coloring.

PROPAGATION: Refer to *J. chinensis.*

NATIVE HABITAT: Mountains of Japan. Introduced 1843.

Juniperus sabina — Savin Juniper

LEAVES: Scale-like, 4-ranked, in opposite pairs which are over-lapping, ovate, shortly pointed or blunt at the apex, about 1/20" long, rounded on back, which usually bears a resin gland, leaves on young plants and older branchlets awl-shaped, spreading, straight, 1/6" long, apex sharply pointed, bluish green and with a conspicuous midrib above. Foliage when crushed emits a disagreeable odor and has a bitter taste.

CONES: Dioecious usually. Female cones ripening in the autumn of the first year or the following spring, on recurved stalks, globose to ovoid, about 1/5" diameter, brownish or bluish black, bloomy, composed of 4 to 6 scales, seeds 2 to 3, ovoid, furrowed. Foliage when crushed emits a disagreeable odor and has a bitter taste.

SIZE: 4 to 6' high by 5-10' spread; supposedly can grow to 15'.

HARDINESS: Zone 4.

HABIT: A spreading shrub, upright in habit, stiff, somewhat vase-shaped; distinctly stiff branches borne at a 45° angle to the ground.

RATE: Slow.

TEXTURE: Medium.

LEAF COLOR: Dark green in summer; often a dark dingy green in winter.

FLOWERS: Monoecious or dioecious.

FRUIT: Cones on recurved stalks, ripening in the first season or in the spring of the second season; seeds 1-3, ovoid, furrowed.

CULTURE: Does well on limestone soil, well drained and dry soils, and open, sunny exposures; withstands city conditions.

DISEASES AND INSECTS: Juniper blight, see culture sheet.

LANDSCAPE VALUE: The species does not have a great deal to offer because of poor foliage and ragged nature. The cultivars are quite handsome especially the low growing types. They make excellent groundcovers, mass plants or foundation plants. I noticed that in many reports the var. *tamariscifolia* is listed as moderately to severely injured by juniper blight. I saw several handsome specimens of var. *tamariscifolia* at Purdue University's Horticultural Park, West Lafayette, Indiana, that showed no signs of blight while *J. procumbens, J. procumbens* 'Nana', and *J. horizontalis* and cultivars were heavily infested. Apparently there are different clones in the trade with varying degrees of resistance. An excellent paper evaluating juniper susceptibility to *Phomopsis* appeared in the *Journal of the American Society for Horticultural Science.* 94:609-611 (1969).

CULTIVARS:

'Arcadia' — Growth habit similar to var. *tamariscifolia* but lower, 1' by 4', leaves predominantly scale-like, grass green. Resistant to juniper blight.

'Blue Danube' — Semi-upright yet more horizontal than the species, foliage bluish green, scale-like, awl-shaped inside the plant.

'Broadmoor' — A dwarf, low-spreading, staminate form which looks like a neat form of var. *tamariscifolia* when young, but the plant tends to build up at the center with age. The main branches are strong and horizontally spreading; the branchlets short and reaching upwards; the sprays very short and occurring mainly on the upper side of the branches. The foliage is a soft grayish green and is resistant to juniper blight. This clone as well as 'Arcadia' and 'Skandia' were selected from many thousands of seedlings raised by D. Hill Nursery Co., Dundee, Illinois from seed imported near Petersburgh, Russia in 1933. All have proved resistant to juniper blight.

'Buffalo' — Similar to var. *tamariscifolia* with feathery branches and bright green foliage, 12" high by 8' wide in 10 years.

'Skandia' — Similar to 'Arcadia' with foliage mostly acicular and pale grayish green.

var. *tamariscifolia* — Low spreading, mounded form, branches horizontal, branchlets crowded, leaves awl-shaped, very short, nearly appressed, bluish green; grows 18" tall and 10 to 15' across in 15 to 20 years.

'Variegata' — Dwarf form, 2 to 3' by 3 to 4 1/2', leaves scale-like, sprays streaked white.

'Von Ehron' — Vase-shaped grower, 5' by 5', or according to Wyman 15' by 45', leaves awl-shaped, light green, resistant to juniper blight.

PROPAGATION: Refer to *J. chinensis.*

ADDITIONAL NOTES: A very variable, spreading or procumbent shrub and one in which the numerous named selections are superior to the species type. Some of the cultivars are quite beautiful but do not seem to have the popular appeal of the *J. horizontalis* types.

NATIVE HABITAT: Mountains of Central and Southern Europe. Western Asia, Siberia and Caucasus.

Juniperus scopulorum — Rocky Mountain Juniper, Colorado Redcedar

LEAVES: Scale-like, tightly appressed, rhombic-ovate, apex acute or acuminate, entire, back varying in color, dark or light bluish green, glaucous or light green and obscurely glandular.

CONES: Ripening the second year, globose, 1/4 to 1/3" diameter, dark blue, glaucous bloomy, pulp sweetish; seeds 2, reddish brown, triangular, prominently angled and grooved.

SIZE: 30 to 40′ high by 3 to 15′ wide.
HARDINESS: Zone 5.
HABIT: A narrow, pyramidal tree often with several main stems.
RATE: Slow, most of the cultivars will average 6 to 12″ per year.
TEXTURE: Medium.
BARK: Reddish brown or gray, shredding but persistent.
LEAF COLOR: Varying in color from dark green or bluish green, glaucous or light green.
FLOWERS: Monoecious or dioecious.
FRUIT: Cones nearly globular, to 1/3″ across, dark blue, glaucous bloomy, ripening in the second year, pulp sweetish; seeds 2, triangular, reddish brown, prominently angled, grooved.
CULTURE: Withstands droughty conditions very well. Same requirements as other *Juniperus*.
DISEASES AND INSECTS: *Phomopsis* blight and serves as an alternate host for cedar apple rust.
LANDSCAPE VALUE: Valued for its use as screens, hedges, backgrounds and foundation plants, very nice blue cast to the foliage.
CULTIVARS:

'Blue Heaven' — Neat pyramidal, foliage strikingly blue in all seasons, heavy cone bearer, 20′ in 15 to 20 years.

'Cupressifolia Erecta' — Dense, pyramidal, rich green, with undertones of silvery blue, needle-like foliage.

'Gray Gleam' — Pyramidal, slow growing, male, foliage distinct silvery gray, becoming more brilliant in the winter, grows 15 to 20′ in 30 to 40 years.

'Lakewood Globe' — Compact form with excellent blue-green foliage, 4 to 6′ in 10 years.

'Moffetii' — Pyramidal and dense; foliage heavy, silvery green.

'Montana Green' — Pyramidal, dense, compact, green foliage color.

'Pathfinder' — Narrow, pyramidal tree, regular in outline, leaves in flat sprays, distinctly bluish gray, 20′ high in 15 to 20 years.

'Table Top Blue' — Flat-topped form with silvery blue foliage, grows 5 to 6′ high and 8′ across in 10 years.

'Tolleson's Weeping Juniper' — Silver-blue foliage hangs string-like from arching branches; supposedly cold hardy anywhere in the country.

'Welch' — Narrow, columnar, compact growth habit, to 8′ tall, silvery new growth, changing to bluish green.

PROPAGATION: See under *J. chinensis*.
NATIVE HABITAT: Found wild on dry, rocky ridges, usually above 5,000′, on the eastern foothills of the Rocky Mountains from Alberta to Texas, westward to the coast of British Columbia and Washington, and to Eastern Oregon, Nevada, and Northern Arizona.

Juniperus squamata — Singleseed Juniper

LEAVES: Awl-shaped, over-lapping, in whorls of 3, pressed together or slightly spreading, the upper part free and 1/8 to 1/6″ long, curved, tapering to a sharp point, grayish green with 2 grayish white bands, green beneath, convex, furrowed. Old leaves persisting on the shoots and branchlets as dry brown scales.
CONES: Ellipsoidal, 1/4 to 1/3″ long, reddish brown becoming black when ripe in the second year; scales 3 to 6, pointed; seeds solitary, ovoid, ridged, with 3 to 4 depressions below the middle.

SIZE: Extremely variable and is difficult to ascertain the exact nature of the species. The cultivars are used in landscaping but the species is not cultivated.
HARDINESS: Zone 4.
HABIT: Dwarf, decumbent, ascending or erect shrub; very variable over its wide geographical range; usually low to prostrate shrub, but in some forms capable of being trained as a small tree.
RATE: Slow.
TEXTURE: Medium.

LEAF COLOR: Grayish green with two gray white bands.

FLOWERS: Monoecious; staminate yellow, pistillate green.

FRUIT: Cones elliptic, 1/4 to 1/3" across, reddish brown, changing to purplish black; scales with a triangular mucro; seeds solitary, ovoid, keeled.

CULTURE: Adaptable, tolerates dry soils.

DISEASES AND INSECTS: Susceptible to bagworms.

LANDSCAPE VALUE: Valued for its density and form but difficult to use in the landscape because of foliage color.

CULTIVARS:

var. *expansa* 'Parsoni' — Supposedly a cultivar of *squamata,* however, the foliage looks totally foreign compared to other *squamata* types; 'Parsoni' has a beautiful green foliage and a vase-shaped habit of growth, although I have seen 'Parsoni' in Bernheim Forest Arboretum that was quite prostrate and showed bluish green foliage.

'Meyeri' — Bushy, dense form, 5' by 4', foliage striking blue-white above, needle-like, quite exotic when young but the old dead needles persist and after a time the plant becomes a liability. Often called the Fishtail Juniper; reported to grow as much as 6 to 8' high and 2 to 3' wide in 15 years; known to 20' high.

'Prostrata' — Prostrate, slow growing form, branchlets erect, short, green, leaves—awl-shaped with bluish white bands above, margin broad, green; green and slightly keeled beneath.

'Variegata' — Prostrate, spreading form, 10" by 4 to 5', new growth is cream colored.

PROPAGATION: Refer to *J. chinensis.*

NATIVE HABITAT: Afghanistan, Himalayas, Western China. Introduced 1836.

Juniperus virginiana — Eastern Redcedar

LEAVES: Scale-like leaves arranged in 4 ranks closely pressed and overlapping, about 1/16" long, short or long pointed, free at the apex, often with a small, oval, glandular depression on the back, shorter than the distance from the gland to the leaf-tip. Leaves on older branchlets broader, about 1/12" long becoming brown and withered. Juvenile leaves often present on adult trees, spreading, in pairs 1/5 to 1/4" long, ending in a spiny point, concave and glaucous above, green and convex beneath.

CONES: Dioecious, female cones ripening in one year, sub-globose, ovoid, up to 1/4" long, often glaucous; seeds 1 to 2, ovoid, furrowed, shining brown.

SIZE: 40-50' high by 8-20' spread; extremely variable over its extensive native range.

HARDINESS: Zone 2.

HABIT: Densely pyramidal when young and slightly pendulous in old age.

RATE: Medium.

TEXTURE: Medium.

BARK: A handsome reddish brown, exfoliating in long strips.

LEAF COLOR: Medium green in summer becoming a dirty green in winter.

FLOWERS: Usually dioecious; staminate yellow, pistillate green.

FRUIT: Cones globular or ovoid, about 1/5" across, brownish violet, glaucous bloomy, ripening in the first season; seeds 1-2, ovoid, small, apex blunt-angular, deeply pitted, shining brown.

CULTURE: Easily transplanted balled and burlapped if root pruned. Tolerant of adverse conditions, poor gravelly soils; high pH soils; prefers a sunny, airy location, and a deep moist loam on well drained subsoil. Will tolerate shade only in extreme youth.

DISEASES AND INSECTS: Cedar apple rust and bagworms.

LANDSCAPE VALUE: An excellent specimen and mass if used with care as to color combinations; useful for windbreaks, shelter belts, hedges, and topiary work; the cultivars are the truly ornamental plants of this species; the var. *crebra* is the northern form of the species and tends toward a narrow, conical habit. Most of the selected clones have come from the northern form. The principal value of the species is the wood which is used for cedar chests, closet linings, pencils, carving and small ornamental work.

CULTIVARS:

'Burkii' — Narrow to broad pyramidal, 10 to 25' high, leaves acicular and scale-like, dull blue band above, margin narrow green, green beneath, steel blue with a slight purplish cast in winter.

'Canaertii' — Compact pyramidal form, leaves on young branchlets scale-like, on old ones awl-shaped; dark green; foliage tufted at ends of branches; cones small, grape-like, whitish blue bloomy, usually profusely produced. 20' tall in 15 years.

'Cupressifolia' — Pyramidal, loose; leaves cypress-like, soft yellow-green. Female form. Actually nomenclature is confused on this cultivar. Probably should be called 'Hillspire'.

'Glauca' — Narrow, columnar form to 25', leaves scale-like, appressed, some awl-shaped leaves inside the plant. Silver-blue foliage is best in spring as it turns silver-green in summer.

'Globosa' — Dense, compact form; branchlets crowded, thin, green; brown in winter, 50-year-old plant is about 15' tall.

'Grey Owl' — Similar to Pfitzer in habit with small, appressed, soft silvery gray·foliage. Originated in a batch of 'Glauca' seedlings.

'Hillii' — Dense, columnar, slow-growing form, 6 to 16' high, leaves awl-shaped with a rather broad, bluish white band above, greenish blue beneath, conspicuously purple during winter, 8 to 12' in about 10 years.

'Kosteri' — Bushy form, 3 to 4' by 25 to 30', leaves loosely appressed, grayish blue, assuming a purplish cast, often confused with Pfitzer.

'Manhattan Blue' — Compact, pyramidal form, differing from 'Glauca' by the bluish green foliage. Wyman says it is female, den Ouden & Boom—a male?

'Moon Glow' — Narrow, silver blue foliaged upright type.

'Nova' — Narrow, upright, symmetrical form. Extremely hardy, 10 to 12'.

'Pendula' — Form with spreading branches and pendulous branchlets; leaves mostly acicular, light green, 36 to 45' tall.

'Pyramidalis' — Unfortunately a collective name for pyramidal-growing forms. Hill Nursery Co. has a form named 'Dundee' which falls into the 'Pyramidalis' group. It has soft foliage which turns a purple-green in winter.

'Skyrocket' — Relatively new cultivar of distinct upright habit, very narrow, probably 10 times as high as wide, bluish green needles, mostly acicular.

'Tripartita' — Dwarf, dense form, 4' by 7.5', branches stout, spreading, irregular, branchlets short; leaves acicular, fine, pale green or slightly glaucous. Similar in habit to Pfitzer but does not grow as large.

PROPAGATION: Refer to *J. chinensis.*

ADDITIONAL NOTES: Closely related to *J. scopulorum* but differing in floral characteristics and in its habit of ripening seeds the first year. It can be distinguished from *J. chinensis* by its juvenile leaves being in pairs (rarely 3's) and by the adult leaves which are pointed; and from *J. sabina* by the absence of true savin odor or bitter taste. Apparently this species can hybridize with *J. horizontalis.*

NATIVE HABITAT: East and Central North America, east of the Rocky Mountains. Introduced before 1664.

Kalmia latifolia — Mountain-laurel Kalmia or Mountain-laurel

FAMILY: Ericaceae

LEAVES: Alternate, simple, sometimes irregularly whorled, entire, elliptic to elliptic-lanceolate, 2 to 4" long, acute or short acuminate, cuneate, dark green above, yellowish green beneath, petiole 2/5 to 4/5" long.

SIZE: Variable, 7 to 15' in height with a similar spread, supposedly can grow to 30-36'; often in the midwest landscape reduced to a small 3 to 7' rounded evergreen shrub.

HARDINESS: Zone 4.

HABIT: Large, robust shrub which, if not crowded, is symmetrical and dense in youth; in old age becomes open, straggly, loose, with picturesque, gnarly trunks and limbs.

RATE: Slow, 4 to 8' over a 10 year period.

TEXTURE: Medium in all seasons.

LEAF COLOR: New growth a light yellow green changing to glossy dark green at maturity. Winter foliage color is usually a good dark green.

FLOWERS: Individually the most beautiful flower I know of especially as the buds are opening. Variable from white to pink-rose to deep rose with purple markings within, 4/5 to 1" across, early to mid June, borne in 4 to 6" diameter terminal corymbs, each flower has 10 stamens which on first expanding are held in little cavities in the corolla. The "Knee" (bend) formed by the filament is sensitive, and when the pollen is ripe, if touched, the anther is released. Obviously insect pollination is facilitated in this manner.

FRUIT: Brown dehiscent capsule, 1/4" across, persistent through winter.

CULTURE: Easy to transplant because of fibrous root system; requires acid, cool, moist, well drained soil; full sun or deep shade but flowers best in sunnier locations; remove flowers immediately after fading; mulch to keep soil moist and to reduce cultivation.

DISEASES AND INSECTS: Leaf spot, blight, flower blight, mulberry whitefly, scale, lace bug, azalea stem borer and rhododendron borer.

LANDSCAPE VALUE: Excellent broadleaf evergreen for shady borders; exquisite in mass; magnificent in flower; one of our best and best loved native shrubs; excellent plant for naturalizing; again requires attention to cultural details.

CULTIVARS:

'Alba' — Pure white flowers.

'Fuscata' — Flowers with a broad purple band inside the corolla.

'Myrtifolia')
'Obtusata') Compact growing types less than 6'.

'Polypetala' — Double type with feathery petals.

var. *rubra* — Flowers deep pink.

'Other Cultivars' — Dr. Richard Jaynes, Connecticut Agr. Exp. Station, New Haven, has spent a lifetime studying this species and has many outstanding clones. He has named one 'Pink Surprise', because it is one of the few that roots readily from cuttings.

PROPAGATION: Seed should be directly sown on peat with lights to stimulate growth after germination. The seedlings are extremely small and hard to work with so it is necessary to get some size to them. Cuttings are extremely difficult to root but there are differences in rootability of various clones.

RELATED SPECIES:

Kalmia angustifolia, Lambkill Kalmia, is a low growing (1 to 3') evergreen shrub of rounded spreading habit with 2 forms; one a compact, tufted grower; the other thin and open. Flowers are usually purplish, 2/5" across, in corymbs, June to July; two varieties include var. *rubra* with dark purple flowers and var. *candida* with white flowers; foliage may be poisonous if eaten in large amounts. Native from Newfoundland and Hudson Bay to Michigan and Georgia. Introduced 1736. Zone 2.

ADDITIONAL NOTES: Alfred Rehder called it "One of the most beautiful native American shrubs." Dr. Jaynes recently (1975) published a book on *Kalmia* titled *The Laurel Book* (Hafner Press). It is an excellent treatise on the subject by the authority on the subject.

NATIVE HABITAT: Quebec and New Brunswick to Florida, west to Ohio and Tennessee. Introduced 1734.

Kalopanax pictus — Castor-aralia

FAMILY: Araliaceae

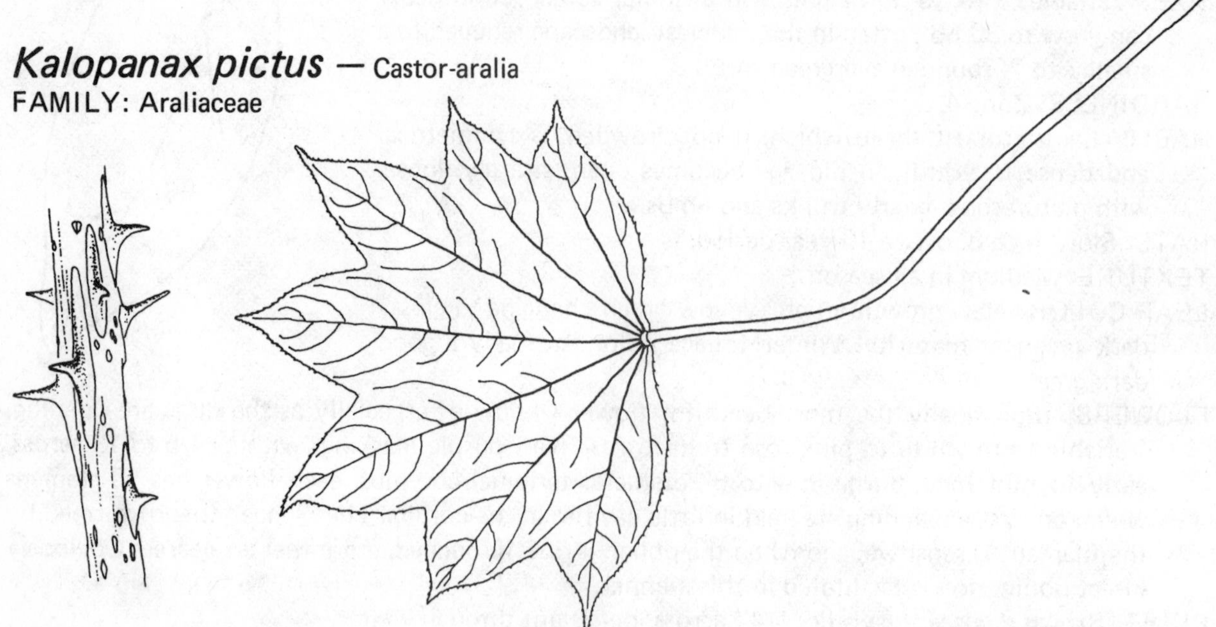

SIZE: 80 to 90' in height in the wild with a spread comparable to height; under cultivation sizes of 40 to 60' would be more in line.

HARDINESS: Zone 4.

HABIT: In youth—upright oval, in old age—assuming a rounded outline with massive, heavy branches and an open appearance.

RATE: Slow until established but thereafter medium. Can grow 12 to 14' in 7 to 10 years upon establishment.

TEXTURE: Medium to medium-coarse in leaf; coarse in winter.

BARK: Armed with stout, broad-based, yellowish prickles.

LEAF COLOR: Dark glossy green above, lighter green beneath, similar in shape to Sweetgum, *Liquidambar styraciflua*; changing to yellow or red in the fall.

FLOWERS: Perfect, white, late July to early August, produced in numerous, small, 1" diameter umbels, forming a large, flattish umbellose-panicle, 12 to 24" across, each individual flower is small, however, they are borne in great quantity; largely hidden by the leaves.

FRUIT: Small drupe, black, late September-October, relished and soon devoured by birds.

CULTURE: Transplant balled and burlapped as a young specimen into deep, rich, moist soil; full sun exposure; prune during spring; supposedly tolerant of alkaline conditions.

DISEASES AND INSECTS: None serious.

LANDSCAPE VALUE: Excellent large shade tree yielding a tropical effect because of the large leaves. Dr. Wyman noted that this species should be used more intensely in the future. There is a handsome small specimen at the Morton Arboretum in Lisle, Illinois.

VARIETY: There is a true variety termed *maximowiczii* with deeply lobed leaves.

PROPAGATION: Dormancy of the seed is related to embryo condition (probably immature) and an impermeable seed coat. Warm plus cold (41°F) stratification for 60 to 90 days may give reasonably prompt germination. Soaking the seeds in sulfuric acid for 30 minutes will substitute for the warm period.

NATIVE HABITAT: Japan, Sakhalin, the Russian Far East, Korea and China. Introduced 1865.

Kerria japonica — Japanese Kerria

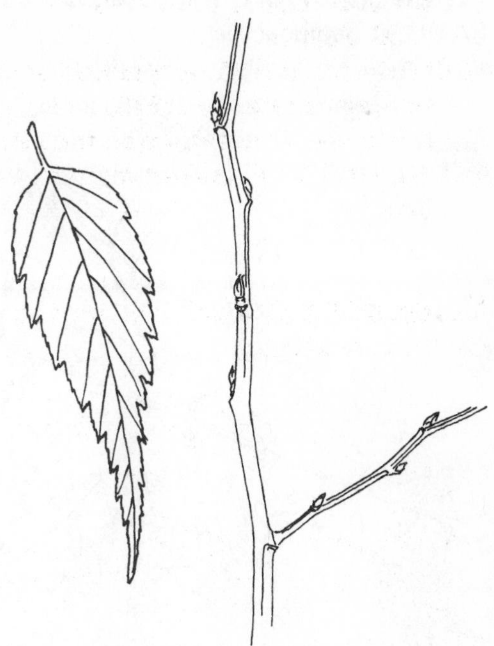

FAMILY: Rosaceae

LEAVES: Alternate, simple, oblong-ovate, acuminate, 4/5 to 2" long, doubly serrate, bright green and glabrous above, paler and slightly pubescent below, petioles 1/5 to 3/5" long.

BUDS: Imbricate, greenish brown, vari-colored, usually 5 exposed scales, glabrous.

STEM: Slender, green throughout winter, zig-zag, glabrous.

SIZE: 3 to 6' in height; spreading, with time, to 6 to 9'.

HARDINESS: Zone 4.

HABIT: Stems distinctly upright arching forming a low, broad, rounded, dense twiggy mass becoming loose with age. Stems are slender, and refined in overall textural quality.

RATE: Somewhat slow in establishment, fast with time.

TEXTURE: Fine in foliage and winter.

STEM COLOR: Distinct yellowish green to bright green in winter, very noticeable and actually not objectionable, adds color to the bleak Midwest landscape in winter especially when used in mass.

LEAF COLOR: Bright green in summer usually exhibiting little change with fall.

FLOWERS: Bright yellow, 1 1/4 to 1 3/4" across, late April to early May (very effective) for 2 to 3 weeks, borne solitary at the terminal of short leafy stems originating from previous year's growth. Sporadically flowers through the season; prune after flowering.

FRUIT: Achene, seldom seen, not showy.

CULTURE: Transplant balled and burlapped or from container, requires loamy, well-drained soil of moderate fertility, does well in full shade; actually best removed from full sun (flowers fade rapidly) and exposed locations; requires considerable pruning for dead branches are constantly evident. Avoid winter damage by planting in a well-drained situation. If fertility levels are too high, the plant becomes weed-like and grows excessively with a resultant reduction in flowers.

DISEASES AND INSECTS: Leaf and twig blight, twig blight, canker, leaf spot, and root rot. The above are possibilities but I have not noticed problems in campus plantings.

LANDSCAPE VALUE: Interesting free-flowering shrub; could be used more extensively; borders, masses, facer plant to hide leggy specimens, possibly on highways or other large public areas where extensive masses of foliage and flowers are welcome and needed; tough plant, seems to withstand considerable abuse.

CULTIVARS:

'Aureo-variegata' — Leaves edged with yellow, 2" long.

'Aureo-vittata' — Branches striped green and yellow.

'Picta' — Leaves edged white, handsome, not obnoxious like many variegated plants; good choice for massing.

'Pleniflora' — Flowers double, nearly ball shaped, 1" in diameter. Flowers are more effective than those of species.

PROPAGATION: Easily rooted using untreated cuttings collected in summer and fall.

NATIVE HABITAT: Central and Western China. Introduced 1834.

Koelreutaria paniculata — Panicled Goldenraintree, Varnish Tree

FAMILY: Sapindaceae

LEAVES: Alternate, pinnate or bipinnately compound to 14" long, 7 to 15 leaflets, ovate to ovate-oblong, 1 1/4 to 3" long, coarsely and irregularly crenate-serrate, at base often incisely lobed, glabrous above, pubescent on the veins beneath or nearly glabrous.

BUD: Terminal-absent, laterals half-ellipsoid, sessile, with 2 exposed scales, brownish.

STEM: Stout, olive-buff, glabrescent leaf scars—raised, rather large, shield-shaped; lenticels—prominent, orange-brown, raised.

SIZE: 30 to 40' in height with an equal or greater spread.

HARDINESS: Zone 5, possibly lower part of 4.

HABIT: Beautiful dense tree of regular rounded outline, sparingly branched, the branches spreading and ascending.

RATE: Medium, 10 to 12' over a 5 to 7 year period.

TEXTURE: Medium in foliage, medium-coarse in winter.

BARK: Light brown, ridged and furrowed on older trunks.

LEAF COLOR: Purplish red when unfolding, bright green at maturity changing to yellow in fall but seldom consistently coloring.

FLOWERS: Perfect, yellow, each about 1/2" wide, borne a 12 to 15" long and wide loose panicle in July, very showy.

FRUIT: Dehiscent, papery, 3-valved capsule, 1 1/2 to 2" long (changing from green to yellow and finally brown); seeds are black, hard, about the size of peas.

CULTURE: Transplants well but best moved balled and burlapped as a small tree; adaptable to a wide range of soils; withstands drouth, heat, wind and alkaline soils; tolerates air pollutants; prefers full sun; prune during winter.

DISEASES AND INSECTS: None particularly serious, although coral-spot fungus, leaf spot, canker, wilt and root rot have been reported.

LANDSCAPE VALUE: Excellent and unrivaled for late yellow flowers; one of the very few yellow flowering trees; excellent as a small lawn tree, for shading a patio; suggested as a street tree although supposedly somewhat weak-wooded. Very lovely to look upon and lay under on a hot July day, choice specimen tree where space is limited.

CULTIVARS:

'Fastigiata' — I have seen this clone at the Arnold Arboretum and found it to be extremely upright; 25' high tree with a 4 to 6' spread. I do not know if it flowers but assume so; raised at Kew Gardens, England.

'September' — Selection by J. C. McDaniel; flowers later than the type, usually in September.

PROPAGATION: Seed has an impermeable seed coat and internal dormancy. Scarification for 60 minutes in concentrated sulfuric acid followed by moist stratification at 41°F for 90 days is recommended. Root cuttings collected in December represent a vegetative means of propagation; very easy to grow from seed. I have raised many seedlings.

NATIVE HABITAT: China, Japan, Korea. Introduced 1763.

Kolkwitzia amabilis — Beautybush

FAMILY: Caprifoliaceae

LEAVES: Opposite, simple, broad-ovate, 1 to 3" long, acuminate, rounded at base, remotely and shallowly toothed or nearly entire, ciliate, dull green above and sparingly hairy, pilose on the veins beneath; Petiole-pilose, about 1/8" long.

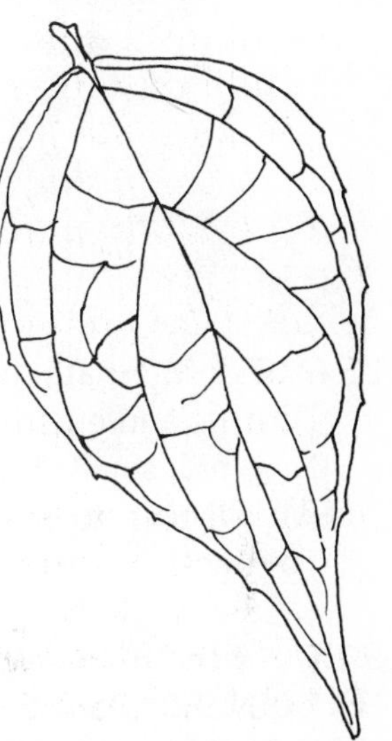

BUDS: Solitary, sessile, ovoid, with 3 or 4 pairs of scales.

STEM: Slender, round, villous at first, later glabrous and developing an exfoliating, brownish bark.

SIZE: 6 to 10' in height and usually slightly smaller in spread.

HARDINESS: Zone 4.

HABIT: Upright arching, deciduous, vase-shaped shrub, somewhat fountain-like in overall effect.

RATE: Fast.

TEXTURE: Medium in leaf; coarse in winter.

BARK: Light grayish brown and often exfoliating on older stems.

LEAF COLOR: Dull green in summer; slightly yellowish to reddish in fall.

FLOWERS: Perfect, pink, yellow in throat, flaring bell-shaped; late May-early June, borne in 2 to 3" diameter corymbs; the principal attribute of this plant is the flower.

FRUIT: Bristly, ovoid, 1/4" long dehiscent capsule, often long persistent.

CULTURE: Easily transplanted balled and burlapped; prefers well drained soil; pH adaptable; full sun for best flowering; older stems should be pruned out every year or to renew plant simply cut it to the ground after flowering; flowers on old wood.

DISEASES AND INSECTS: None serious.

LANDSCAPE VALUE: Probably belongs where it can develop alone, but hardly falls into the category of a specimen plant; probably does best in the shrub border.

CULTIVARS:

'Pink Cloud')
'Rosea') — Clear pink flowers of good size and very floriferous.

PROPAGATION: Seeds can be sown as soon as ripe, or stored in air tight containers in a cool place for up to a year. Plants grown from seeds will often show inferior, washed out, pink flower color. It is best to use softwood cuttings, as they root readily, and select wood from floriferous, good pink-colored plants.

ADDITIONAL NOTES: I have a difficult time acclimating myself to this shrub. In flower it is singularly effective, however, the rest of the year it gives one a headache.

NATIVE HABITAT: Central China. 1901.

Laburnum x *watereri* — Waterer Laburnum, Goldenchain Tree

FAMILY: Leguminosae

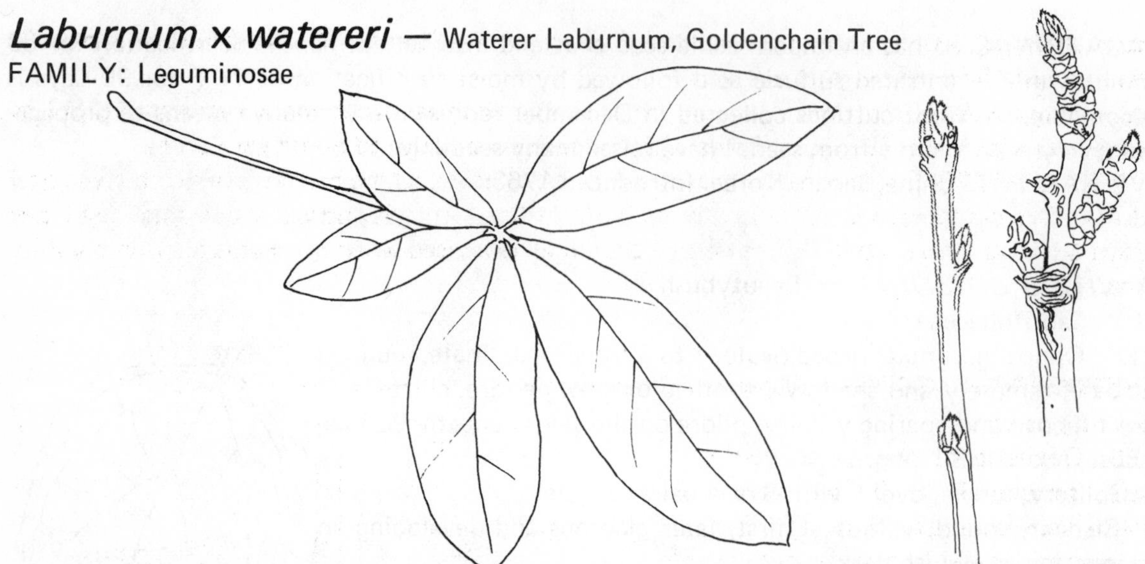

LEAVES: Alternate, trifoliate, elliptic to elliptic-oblong or elliptic-obovate, 1 1/4 to 3" long, usually obtuse and mucronulate, broad cuneate, glabrous at maturity.

BUD: Ovoid, small, 1/16 to 1/8" long, with 2 to 4 exposed silvery-haired scales.

STEM: Slender to stout, olive, without prominent lenticels, green stem color is maintained into old wood.

SIZE: 12 to 15' in height with a spread of 9 to 12'.

HARDINESS: Zone 5.

HABIT: Distinctly upright to round-headed small tree or shrub which usually loses the lower branches and is in need of a facer plant after a period of years.

RATE: Medium, 12 to 18" per year over a 5 to 8 year period.

TEXTURE: Medium-fine in leaf; somewhat coarse in winter condition.

BARK: Olive green in color on young and old branches; eventually developing fissured areas.

LEAF COLOR: Bright green in summer with a bluish tinge; fall color is non-descript.

FLOWERS: Perfect, yellow, 3/4" long, borne on 6 to 10" long, pendulous racemes in late May, extremely beautiful in flower.

FRUIT: Pod, slightly pubescent, October, not ornamentally effective.

CULTURE: Transplant balled and burlapped in spring as a small tree into moist, well drained soil. The plant is adaptable to many situations but prefers light shade in the hot part of the day; will not withstand standing water; also in Urbana-Champaign cold injury can be a problem, actually on the hardiness borderline in our area; withstands high pH conditions; prune after flowering.

DISEASES AND INSECTS: Leaf spot, twig blight, laburnum vein mosaic, aphids and grape mealybug can affect this plant. The twig blight is often a serious problem.

LANDSCAPE VALUE: Good in the shrub border, near buildings, corners of houses; plant in a protected spot such as the east side of the house.

CULTIVARS:

'Autumnale' — Flowers twice, once in spring and again in fall.

'Pendula' — Weeping type, makes an interesting small accent plant.

'Vossii' — Often used as the specific epithet for *L.* x *watereri,* i.e., *L.* x *vossii* when actually 'Vossii' is a superior clone selected for more dense habit and racemes which are up to 2' long.

PROPAGATION: Seed should be scarified in sulfuric acid for 15 to 30 minutes. Cuttings—leaf bud cuttings taken in early summer rooted 80%; cuttings from root sprouts rooted 100%.

RELATED SPECIES:

Laburnum x *watereri* is a hybrid between *L. alpinum* and *L. anagyroides* which has arisen both in gardens and in the wild.

Laburnum alpinum, Scotch Laburnum, is a large shrub or small tree to 30′ and is hardier (Zone 4); less showy in flower than *L.* x *watereri*.

Laburnum anagyroides, Goldenchain Laburnum, is similar to the above in many respects except less hardy and with larger individual flowers. Both species are native to Southern Europe.

ADDITIONAL NOTES: Seeds contain an alkaloid called cytisine, which can be fatal to children and adults. This compound is contained in all parts of the plant. Supposedly, one small seed can prove toxic to a small child. Extreme care should be exercised when using this plant in a public area.

Lagerstroemia indica — Common Crapemyrtle

FAMILY: Lythraceae

LEAVES: Opposite or the upper alternate, simple, 1 to 2 3/4″ long, entire, subsessile, elliptic or obovate to oblong, acute or obtuse, broad-cuneate or rounded at base, glabrous or pilose along the midrib beneath; very small conical and deciduous stipules.

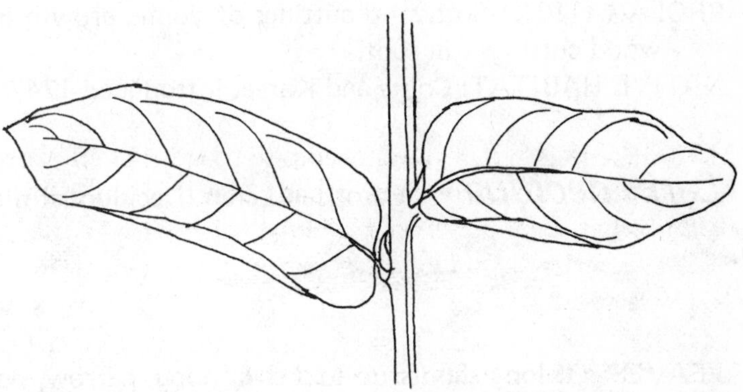

BUDS: Small, solitary, sessile, oblong, somewhat elbowed above base, closely appressed, with 2 acute ciliate scales.

STEMS: Rather slender, angled; pith small, roundish, at length spongy; leaf-scars 4-ranked, separated or approximately in pairs or opposite, nearly round, slightly raised and decurrent from the sides, but concave; 1 bundle-trace, composite, crescent-shaped, sunken; stipule-scars lacking or glandular.

SIZE: Seems variable but based on observations of plants from Washington, D. C.; Raleigh, N. C.; and Athens, GA., a range of 15 to 25′ in height seems reasonable.

HARDINESS: Zone 7, unfortunately we cannot successfully grow this plant in Central Illinois. Trials with several more "hardy" clones met with failure. Even in Southern Illinois success is minimal compared to that obtained in the deep South.

HABIT: Small tree or large shrub of variable habit; often seen in multi-stemmed form with a cloud of foliage reserved for the upper 1/3 of the plant while the basal portion is leafless and only the handsome bark is evident.

RATE: Medium, although probably can be induced into fast growth.

TEXTURE: Medium, possibly medium-fine in all seasons.

BARK COLOR: Smooth, gray, exfoliating and exposing vari-colored underbark which ranges from many handsome shades of brown to gray. The beautiful bark is a real landscape asset. Specimens at the National Arboretum make one drool, especially since the plant cannot be grown in our Central Illinois climate.

LEAF COLOR: New emerging leaves are bronze in color yielding to medium green at maturity. Fall coloration ranges from yellow, orange and red usually with all colors interspersed on the same tree.

FLOWERS: Perfect, each flower 1 to 1 1/2″ wide, color varying from pink to deep red on different plants; produced in 6 to 8″ long and 3 to 5″ wide panicles which terminate the current year's growth; July through September.

FRUIT: A broad-ellipsoidal capsule, about 1/2″ long and persisting for a time.

CULTURE: Transplant as a balled and burlapped or container-grown plant into moist, well-drained soil that has been supplemented with peat moss or leaf mold; prefers full sun; prune by removal of the deadwood or by cutting the plants almost to the ground in spring. This latter approach can be effectively used to keep the larger growing types in bounds. The species prefers hot, sunny climates and, obviously, it is best suited for southern gardens.

DISEASES AND INSECTS: Powdery mildew, black spot, tip blight, leaf spot, root rot, aphid, and Florida wax scale are problems.

LANDSCAPE VALUE: Handsome and very beautiful specimen shrub or tree. Often used in groups and underplanted with a ground cover. The dark green ground cover acts as a foil for the handsome bark. Some of the smaller types are used as hedges.

CULTIVARS: Too numerous to mention. Flower colors range from white, pink, orchid, and dark red. The National Arboretum, Washington, D. C., has an extensive breeding program with *Lagerstroemia*. It is possible that the number of cultivars will swell to even greater proportions. There are new dwarfish types which range in height from 5 to 7 feet and make good foundation plants.

PROPAGATION: Softwood cuttings of young growth in late spring or early summer or semihardwood cuttings will root.

NATIVE HABITAT: China and Korea. Introduced 1747.

Larix decidua — European Larch (Deciduous) (Pinaceae)

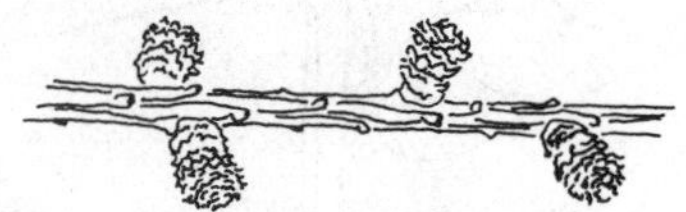

LEAVES: Of long shoots up to 1 1/4" long, narrow, pointed or blunt, those of short shoots 30 to 40 together, 1/2 to 1 1/2" long, narrower and blunter than those of the long shoots, both kinds keeled below, soft, light green, turning yellow in autumn.

BUDS: Terminal of long shoots globose, short-pointed, with many brown pointed scales. Lateral buds shorter, blunter. Buds of short shoots small, rounded.

STEM: Young terminal gray or yellowish, furrowed, without pubescence, those of the second year roughened by cushion-like leaf bases of the previous year. Short shoots dark brown or almost black, marked with as many rings as they are years old, the younger rings downy.

CONES: Ovoid, 1 to 1 1/2" long, 3/4 to 1" wide, scales rounded and entire above, striated, margin sometimes wavy.

SIZE: 70 to 75′ in height by 25 to 30′ in width; can grow 100 to 140′ high.

HARDINESS: Zone 2.

HABIT: Pyramidal, with horizontal branches and drooping branchlets, slender and supple in youth but irregular and lacking in dignity with age; this is a deciduous conifer, i.e., the needles abscise in the fall.

RATE: Medium to fast, 2 1/2′ a year.

TEXTURE: Medium-fine in leaf; medium-coarse in winter.

BARK: On young trees thin, scaly; on old trees, thick, deeply fissured at the base exposing a reddish brown inner bark which contrasts with the grayish brown outer bark.

LEAF COLOR: Bright green in spring becoming a deeper green in summer and finally turning an ochre yellow in the fall.

FLOWERS: Monoecious; in early spring the attractive red, pink, yellow or green female strobili and the smaller yellow male strobili cover the, as yet, leafless branchlets.

FRUIT: Cone (not borne until after 20 years), scales pubescent on the backside, 1 to 1 2/5" long and changing from scarlet to yellow-brown at maturity.

CULTURE: Readily transplanted when dormant. Should have sufficient moisture, well-drained and sunny conditions although larches often grow in wet or even boggy conditions in the wild. Intolerant of shade, dry, shallow, chalky soils and polluted areas. Prune in mid-summer.

DISEASES AND INSECTS: The larch case-bearer is a serious pest. This small insect appears in early May and eventually eats its way into the needles, causing them to turn brown for the remainder of the season. Early and timely spring spraying will control them. Also, cankers, leaf cast, needle rusts, wood decay, larch sawfly, woolly larch, aphid, gypsy moth, tussock moth and Japanese beetle can be problems.

LANDSCAPE VALUE: Very effective for park and large area use as a screen or specimen plant.

CULTIVARS:

'Fastigiata' – Columnar, similar to Lombardy Poplar with short ascending branches.

'Pendula' – Weeping form, extremely pendulous branchlets, excellent plant for weeping habit.

var. *polonica* – The branches and branchlets droop. A true variety found only in small groves in select forests in Poland and Romania.

PROPAGATION: Seeds of most species germinate fairly well without pre-treatment. There seems to be a mild dormancy, however, that varies somewhat among species and lots within species. It can be overcome by cold stratification in a moist medium for 21 to 60 days at 30° to 41°F. Cuttings are difficult to root although low percentages can be achieved with proper timing. The cultivars are grafted.

NATIVE HABITAT: Northern and Central Europe. Introduced in colonial times. The main home of this species lies in the mountains of Central Europe from Southeastern France through the main chain of the Alps eastward to the neighborhood of Vienna. Here it forms beautiful forests, often in association with *Pinus cembra*.

Larix kaempferi (leptolepis) – (Deciduous)

LEAVES: 1 to 1 1/4" long and 1/25" wide. On short spurs 40 or more together, 1 1/2" or longer; upper side of both kinds flat, glaucous, underside keeled and with 2 white bands.

BUDS: Small, oblong or conical, pointed, resinous with bright brown fringed scales.

STEM: Glaucous, covered in varying density with soft brownish hairs or sometimes without hairs, furrowed; short spurs stout, dark brown.

CONES: 3/4 to 1 1/3" long and as broad; scales about 2/5" long and wide, rounded, with the upper edge rolled back giving the extended cones a rosette-like appearance.

SIZE: 70 to 90' in height by 25 to 40' in spread.

HARDINESS: Zone 5.

HABIT: Very open and pyramidal in habit.

RATE: Medium to fast.

TEXTURE: Fine in foliage, coarse in winter.

LEAF COLOR: Green, underside keeled with two white glaucous bands, turning yellowish gold in autumn.

FLOWERS: Inconspicuous, monoecious.

FRUIT: Cones stalked, 1 to 1 1/5" across, scales keeled forming a rosette type of cone.

CULTURE: Readily transplanted when dormant. Should have sufficient moisture, well-drained, sunny situations. Susceptible to drought but tolerant of shallow, acid soils. Intolerant of shade, chalky soils and polluted areas.

DISEASES AND INSECTS: Similar to other larches.

LANDSCAPE VALUE: Best ornamental among the larches but reserved for large areas such as a park, golf course, campus.

CULTIVARS:

'Blue Rabbit' – A narrow, pyramidal form with conspicuously glaucous foliage.

'Dervaes' – Branches horizontal, branchlets drooping; leaves fresh green.

PROPAGATION: As previously described.

Larix kaempferi is difficult to distinguish from *Larix decidua* except shoots of the former are more glaucous, leaves blue-green or glaucous and wider, and broader cones with reflexed scales.

NATIVE HABITAT: Japan. Introduced 1861.

Larix laricina — Eastern or American Larch (Tamarack)

LEAVES: Light bluish green, 4/5 to 1 1/5" long, 1/50" wide, strongly keeled beneath, on short spurs 12 to 30 in a bundle.

BUDS: Rounded, glossy dark red, slightly resinous.

STEM: Thin, at first glabrous, bloomy; later dull or reddish brown.

SIZE: 40 to 80' high by 15 to 30' spread.

HARDINESS: Zone 1.

HABIT: Open and pyramidal with a slender trunk, horizontal branches and drooping branchlets.

RATE: Slow-medium.

TEXTURE: Medium-fine in foliage; coarse in winter.

BARK: Thin and smooth on young stems, later becoming 1/2" to 3/4" thick, gray to reddish brown, scaly.

LEAF COLOR: Bright blue-green foliage turning yellowish in the fall; often showy in fall color.

FLOWERS: Monoecious, sessile, inconspicuous; staminate yellow, pistillate rosy colored.

FRUIT: Cones are small, oval, 2/5" to 3/5" long by 1/3 to 1/2" broad, pendulous, glabrous, green or violet becoming brown when mature.

CULTURE: Moist soils, less tolerant of cultivation than *Larix decidua*. Intolerant of shade and pollution.

DISEASES AND INSECTS: Subject to Larch case-bearer, Larch sawfly, wood rot and several rust fungi.

LANDSCAPE VALUE: Excellent in groves and in moist soil; less tolerant of cultivation than *L. decidua*, best left in its native confines.

CULTIVARS: None important.

PROPAGATION: See previous entry.

NATIVE HABITAT: Northern North America, from the Artic Circle in Alaska and Canada southwards to Northern Pennsylvania, Minnesota and Illinois.

Ledum groenlandicum — Labrador Tea

FAMILY: Ericaceae

LEAVES: Alternate, simple, 3/4 to 2" long, elliptic or ovate to oblong, obtuse, not revolute, glaucous and resinous—lepidote beneath; petiole 1/6 to 1/4" long, evergreen; fragrant when crushed.

BUDS: Solitary, sessile, somewhat compressed, small with about 3 exposed scales; the terminal flower buds large, round or ovoid, with some 10 broad mucronate, glandular-dotted scales.

STEMS: Slender, rounded; young shoots densely covered with rusty tomentum; older branches reddish brown or copper-colored; pith small, somewhat 3-sided, spongy, brownish; leaf-scars mostly low, half-elliptical or bluntly cordate, the lowest transversely linear; 1 bundle-trace.

SIZE: 2 to 4' in height by 2 to 4' in spread.

HARDINESS: Zone 2.

HABIT: Dwarf evergreen shrub with erect branches forming a rounded mass; sometimes procumbent.

RATE: Slow.

TEXTURE: Medium-fine in all seasons.

LEAF COLOR: Deep dark green in all seasons.

FLOWERS: Perfect, white, each flower 1/2 to 3/4" across; borne in 2" diameter corymbs from May through June.

FRUIT: Capsule, about 1/5" long, not showy.

CULTURE: Transplants readily, fibrous rooted; prefers moist, sandy, peaty soils; found in swampy moors of northern latitudes; full sun or partial shade.

DISEASES AND INSECTS: Anthracnose, leaf galls caused by fungi, rusts and leaf spots.

LANDSCAPE VALUE: Another interesting and little known ericaceous plant which is good for moist, swampy areas. The few plants I have seen were extremely attractive.

CULTIVARS:

'Compactum' – Dense, neat shrub to 1' in height with short branches, very woolly stems, short broad leaves, and small flower clusters.

PROPAGATION: Seeds can be grown as described for *Calluna*. Layers and cuttings can also be used.

NATIVE HABITAT: Greenland to Alberta and Washington, south to Pennsylvania and Wisconsin. Introduced 1763.

Leiophyllum buxifolium — Box Sandmyrtle

FAMILY: Ericaceae

LEAVES: Usually alternate, simple, 1/8 to 1/3" long, oblong or obovate-oblong, lustrous dark green above, paler beneath, entire, short-petioled, evergreen.

BUDS: Sessile, solitary, ovoid, appressed, with about 2 exposed scales.

STEMS: Very slender, subterete, pith minute, continuous; leaf-scars more or less broken and then 4-ranked, minute, crescent-shaped or 3-sided, raised; 1 bundle-trace.

SIZE: 1 1/2 to 3' high and spreading 4 to 5'.

HARDINESS: Zone 5.

HABIT: Small evergreen shrub of great variability in the wild; erect, prostrate or decumbent, according to location and altitude; in cultivation usually a dense bush up to 1 1/2' high.

RATE: Slow.

TEXTURE: Fine in all seasons.

LEAF COLOR: Lustrous dark green in summer becoming bronzy with cold weather.

FLOWERS: Perfect, rosy in bud opening to white tipped with pink, each flower about 1/4" diameter; May through June; borne in terminal 3/4 to 1" diameter corymbs.

CULTURE: Transplant balled and burlapped or container-grown plants; prefer moist, sandy, acid soil supplied with peat and leaf mold; full sun or partial shade; will not tolerate drought, not an easy plant to establish but like *Ledum* and *Epigaea* is well worth the effort.

DISEASES AND INSECTS: None serious.

LANDSCAPE VALUE: Dainty and unusual plant for the rock garden; blends well with other broadleaf evergreens.

PROPAGATION: Seed as described for *Calluna*; root cuttings, layering and stem cuttings also work. One authority noted the best method is by cuttings made of shoots 1 to 1 1/2" long in July or August, placed in peat:sand and provided bottom heat.

ADDITIONAL NOTES: The only species within the genus; resembles *Ledum* but can be distinguished by the small, quite glabrous, short-stalked to almost sessile leaves. The species is usually divided into three varieties.

NATIVE HABITAT: New Jersey southward, westward into the mountains of the Carolinas, Tennessee, and Eastern Kentucky. Introduced 1736.

Lespedeza bicolor — Shrub Bushclover

Lespedeza bicolor, Shrub Bushclover, is an upright, somewhat open, loosely branched shrub which grows 6 to 9' high and slightly less in spread. The foliage is dark green above and grayish green beneath in summer. The flowers are rosy-purple, 2/5" long, produced in 2 to 5" long racemes on current season's growth, and are borne from the leaf-axils from the uppermost 2' of the stem. Does best in light, sandy, well-drained soil. Often dies back in severe winters but like *Indigofera* develops new shoots from the roots and will produce flowers on the new growth. The flowers are not overwhelming and the shrub only has value for late summer flower. Native of Manchuria, Northern China, and Japan. Introduced 1856. Zone 4.

Leucothoe fontanesiana (catesbaei) — Drooping Leucothoe or Fetterbush

FAMILY: Ericaceae

LEAVES: Alternate, simple, ovate-lanceolate to lanceolate, 2 to 5" long, long-acuminate, rounded or broad-cuneate at base, appressed ciliate-serrulate on margins, lustrous dark green above, lighter beneath, glabrous, evergreen.

STEM: Long, slender, with little or no lateral branch development; greenish to reddish in color.

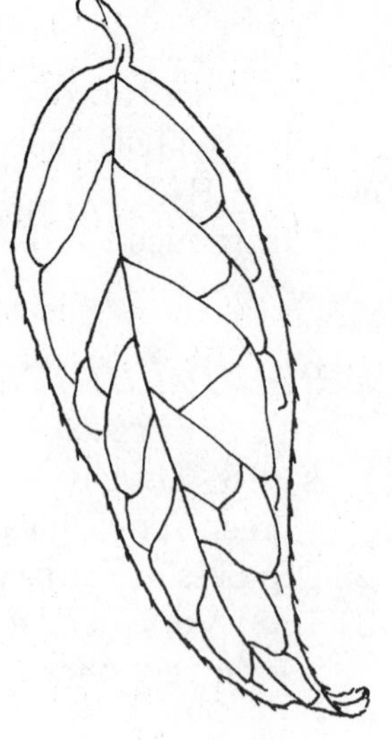

SIZE: 3 to 6′ by 3 to 6′.

HARDINESS: Zone 4.

HABIT: Very graceful evergreen shrub with long, spreading, arching branches clothed with long pointed leaves and weighted down by the flowers; almost fountain-like in habit.

RATE: Slow to medium, 3 to 5′ in 4 to 5 years.

TEXTURE: Medium in all seasons.

LEAF COLOR: New growth of bright green or bronzy color eventually changing to lustrous dark green at maturity; develops a bronze to purplish coloration in winter.

FLOWER: Perfect, white, fragrant, 1/4" long; mid-May, borne in 2 to 3" long axillary racemes under the foliage.

FRUIT: Capsule.

CULTURE: Transplants readily, best moved as a container plant in spring; prefers acid, moist, well drained, organic soil; will not withstand drought or sweeping, drying winds; prefers partial to full shade but will grow in full sun if not too dry; rejuvenate by pruning to ground after flowering.

DISEASES AND INSECTS: Leaf spots can be troublesome as at least 8 species of fungi infect *Leucothoe*. Basically a trouble-free plant.

LANDSCAPE VALUE: Good facer plant, hides leggy plants, nice cover for a shady bank, massing, grouping or shrub borders; contrasts nicely with dull rhododendron foliage, good as undergrowth plant.

CULTIVARS:

'Girard's Rainbow' — Chance seedling, new shoots are reddish changing to pink, then to yellow, green and copper variations.

'Nana' — Dwarf form, 30-year-old plants are less than 2′ tall but are 6′ across.

'Trivar' — Another clone with multicolored foliage.

PROPAGATION: Direct sow the seed as described for *Calluna*. Cuttings collected in June root readily when treated with 1000 ppm IBA/50% alcohol in peat:perlite under mist.

RELATED SPECIES:

Leucothoe axillaris, Coast Leucothoe, is receiving wide favor in the nursery trade as a potential replacement or substitute for *L. fontanesiana*. Apparently it is not as susceptible to leaf spot and has a similar habit and evergreen nature. Grows 2 to 4′ high (6′) and 1 1/2 times that in width, with spreading branches zig-zagged towards the end. The leaves are leathery, dark glossy green. Flowers develop in axillary racemes, 1 to 2 1/2" long, white, in April and May. This species is not particularly common in cultivation and in many respects resembles *L. fontanesiana*. It differs in comparatively shorter and broader, abruptly pointed leaves. Native from Virginia to Florida and Mississippi in lowland areas. Introduced 1765. Supposedly hardy in Zone 6, but based on observation of plants at Millcreek Valley Park, Youngstown, Ohio and in Lake County, Ohio, nursery area, I would place it in Zone 5.

NATIVE HABITAT: Virginia to Georgia and Tennessee. Introduced 1793.

Libocedrus decurrens (Calocedrus decurrens) — California Incensecedar

LEAVES: In 4's closely pressed, equal in size, oblong-obovate, apex finely pointed and free, narrowing to base, dark green; on ultimate branches about 1/4" long; on main shoots about 1/2" long, lateral pair boat-shaped, almost wholly ensheathing the facial pairs; glandular, emitting an aromatic odor when crushed.

STEM: Branchlets flattened, terminating in dense, fan-like sprays in which the ultimate branches point forward at an acute angle.

SIZE: 30 to 50' high by 8 to 10' wide; can grow to 125 to 150' high in the wild. (Cupressaceae)

HARDINESS: Zone 5.

HABIT: Stiff or narrowly columnar in youth, very regular in outline, with a distinct formal character even in old age.

RATE: Slow-medium, in proper soil and atmosphere may grow 50 to 70' after 3C to 50 years.

TEXTURE: Medium.

BARK: Thin, smooth, and grayish green or scaly and tinged with red on young stems; on old trunks—thick (3 to 8"), yellowish brown to cinnamon-red, fibrous, deeply and irregularly furrowed.

LEAF COLOR: Shiny dark green, borne in vertical sprays.

FLOWERS: Monoecious, rarely dioecious, inconspicuous.

FRUIT: Cones pendent, cylindric, 4/5" long by 2/5" broad, reddish brown or yellowish brown when ripe in early autumn, remaining on the tree until spring; lowest pair of cone-scales half as long as the others; seeds 1/3 to 1/2" long.

CULTURE: Prefers moist, well-drained, fertile soil; full sun or light shade, not tolerant of smoggy or wind swept conditions.

DISEASES AND INSECTS: A heart rot caused by *Polyporus amarus* is this tree's most destructive single enemy. Other conspicuous, but seldom damaging, diseases are a brooming *Gymnosporangium* rust and a leafy mistletoe.

LANDSCAPE VALUE: Handsome specimen for large areas and formal plantings; not used enough; the plant that your neighbor will wonder about.

PROPAGATION: Propagated by seed, which requires a stratification period of about 8 weeks at 32° to 40°F. for good germination. I have had poor success trying to grow this species.

ADDITIONAL NOTES: Habit is broadly conical in the wild with spreading branches; in cultivated trees the branches are usually short and the outline is columnar. Most trees in cultivation appear to be the cultivar 'Columnaris' which is narrow, columnar.

NATIVE HABITAT: Western United States from Oregon to Nevada and Lower California. Introduced 1853.

Ligustrum amurense — Amur Privet

FAMILY: Oleaceae

LEAVES: Opposite, simple, entire, elliptic to oblong, 1 to 2" long, obtuse to acute, rounded or broad cuneate at base, ciliolate, glabrous except on midrib beneath.

BUDS: Sessile, ovoid, small, with 2 or 3 pairs of exposed scales, brownish; typical for most privets.

STEM: New growth purplish, pubescent, older stems gray with some pubescence.

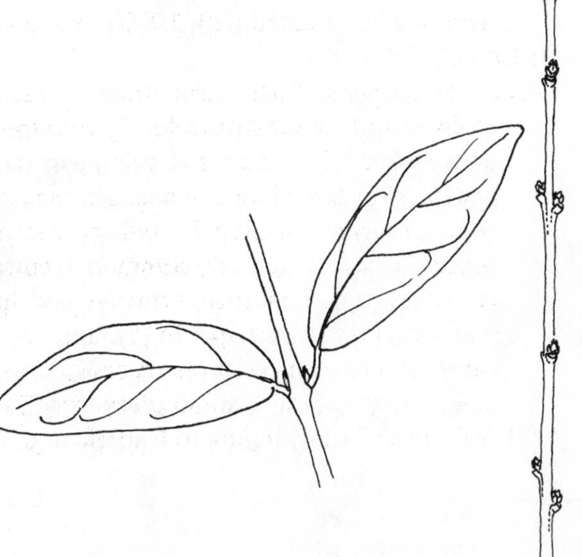

SIZE: 12 to 15' high and 2/3's that in width or with a spread equal to the height.

HARDINESS: Zone 3.

HABIT: Dense, upright, multi-stemmed shrub with a weak pyramidal outline.

RATE: Fast. All privets are fast growing shrubs.
TEXTURE: Medium-fine in leaf and in winter condition.
LEAF COLOR: Medium to dark green in summer; no fall coloration of any consequence.
FLOWERS: Perfect, creamy white, unpleasantly fragrant; early to mid June, 2 to 3 weeks, borne in axillary 1 to 2" long panicles; flower effect is often lost because of use in hedges and flowers are cut off.
FRUIT: Berry-like drupe, black, 1/4 to 1/3" long, September-October, not particularly showy.
CULTURE: Transplant readily bare root, adaptable to any soil except those which are extremely wet; pH adaptable, full sun up to 1/2 shade, tolerant of smoke and grime of cities; do well in dry soils; prune after flowering.
DISEASES AND INSECTS: Anthracnose, twig blight (affects *L. vulgare* more so than this species), leaf spots, galls, powdery mildew, root rots, privet aphid, leaf miners, scales, privet thrips, mealybugs, Japanese weevil, mites, whitefly and nematodes. In spite of this impressive array of problems, privets, in general, do very well and rarely require spraying. The key is selecting the most reliable and hardy species.
LANDSCAPE VALUE: Hedging purposes, withstands pruning about as well as any plant; tends to be overused; there are many better hedging plants.
PROPAGATION: As a graduate student at the University of Massachusetts I was always attempting to propagate plants which were growing on campus. In winter I collected a quantity of *L. amurense* fruits and directly sowed one lot while removing the pericarp and cleaning the seed before sowing the second lot. The first batch did not germinate while batch two came up like beans. Apparently there is a chemical or physical barrier to germination which resides in the fruit wall. The usual recommendation for seed is 3 months at 41°F. in a moist medium. Softwood cuttings root readily, in fact, I do not know why people would bother to propagate this group of plants any other way.
RELATED SPECIES:
Ligustrum x *ibolium*, Ibolium Privet, is a cross between *L. ovalifolium* and *L. obtusifolium*. It is more handsome than *L. amurense* for the foliage is a dark glossy green. Zone 4. Originated in Connecticut.

Ligustrum obtusifolium — Border Privet

LEAVES: Opposite, simple, entire, elliptic to oblong or oblong-obovate, 4/5 to 2" long, acute or obtuse, cuneate or broad-cuneate, glabrous above, pubescent beneath or only on midrib.
STEM: Green when young, possibly with a slight purplish tinge, pubescent. Older stems gray, somewhat pubescent.

Ligustrum obtusifolium, Border Privet, grows 10 to 12' tall with a spread of 12 to 15'. Usually a multi-stemmed shrub of broad horizontal outline, broadest at the top, much branched and twiggy with wide spreading branches. The foliage is medium to dark green in summer, sometimes turning russet to purplish in fall. Flowers are white, unpleasantly fragrant, early to mid June and later, borne in 3/4 to 1 1/2" nodding panicles usually numerous on short axillary branches. Fruit is black to blue-black, slightly bloomy, 1/4" long, berry-like drupe which ripens in September and persists. Probably the best growth habit of the *Ligustrum* species and makes a good screen, background or hedge plant. The variety *regelianum* is low (4 to 5') with horizontal spreading branches and leaves regularly spaced in a flat plane to give this plant a unique appearance. Extensively used for highway plantings, works well in mass especially on banks and other large areas. Japan. Introduced 1860. Zone 3.

Ligustrum x *vicaryi*, Golden Vicary Privet or Golden Privet, goes under many names in the trade. Result of a cross between *L. ovalifolium* 'Aureum' and *L. vulgare*. The habit is somewhat vase-shaped and the leaves are golden yellow the entire growing season especially if the plant is used in a sunny location. I do not find this shrub palatable but nurserymen claim they cannot grow enough of it. To each his own! If one must have golden foliage this plant is probably as good as any. Can grow 10 to 12' high so should be afforded adequate garden space. If grown in the shade the foliage turns a sickly yellow-green and the only medicine which cures this malady is full sun. Reports from the Minnesota Landscape Arboretum indicate that Vicary is not hardy with them, however, they have a form called the 'Hillside Strain' which looks similar but does not winter kill. I would guess this strain has significant *L. vulgare* blood based on leaf characteristics. Vicaryi is rated Zone 5 and Hillside Zone 4. Golden Vicary originated in the garden of Vicary Gibbs, Middlesex, England, before 1920.

Ligustrum vulgare — European Privet

LEAVES: Opposite, simple, entire, oblong-obovate to lanceolate, 1 to 2 2/5" long. Obtuse to acute, glabrous, dark green.

STEM: Young branches green and minutely pubescent.

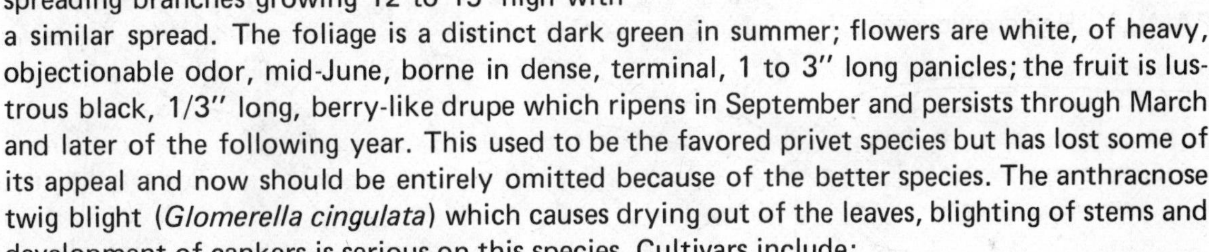

Ligustrum vulgare, European or Common Privet, is a stout, much branched shrub with irregularly spreading branches growing 12 to 15' high with a similar spread. The foliage is a distinct dark green in summer; flowers are white, of heavy, objectionable odor, mid-June, borne in dense, terminal, 1 to 3" long panicles; the fruit is lustrous black, 1/3" long, berry-like drupe which ripens in September and persists through March and later of the following year. This used to be the favored privet species but has lost some of its appeal and now should be entirely omitted because of the better species. The anthracnose twig blight (*Glomerella cingulata*) which causes drying out of the leaves, blighting of stems and development of cankers is serious on this species. Cultivars include:

'Densiflorum' — Upright form with dense habit; maintaining this, if unclipped, for at least 20 years.

var. *italicum* — Holds the leaves longer than any variety.

'Lodense' — Low, dense, compact form; 22-year-old plant was only 4 1/2' tall. Extremely susceptible to a blight for which there is no cure.

'Pyramidale' — Excellent hedge plant, somewhat pyramidal in habit. Native to Europe, Northern Africa, naturalized in eastern North America. Zone 4.

NATIVE HABITAT: Northern China. Introduced 1860.

Lindera benzoin — Spicebush

FAMILY: Lauraceae

LEAVES: Alternate, simple, oblong-obovate, 3 to 5" long, acute or short acuminate, cuneate at base, entire, light green above, pale beneath.

BUDS: Small, superposed, upper collaterally arranged producing green ovoid stalked flower buds, vegetative buds with 3 scales, end bud lacking.

STEM: Rounded, slender, green or olive-brown with pale lenticels; pith—large, round, white, continuous. All parts of the plant are aromatic when broken.

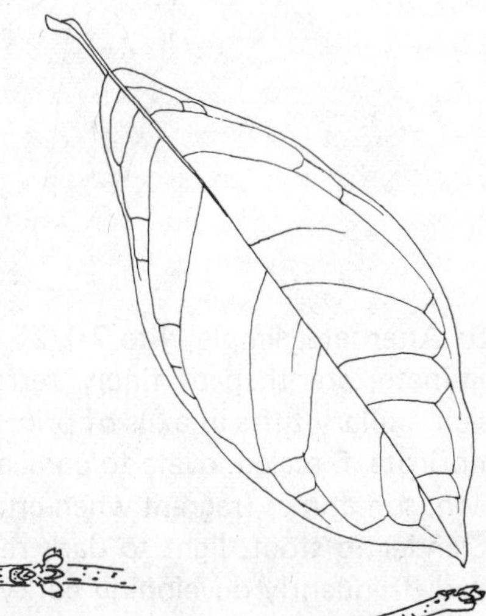

SIZE: 6 to 12' high with a similar spread.

HARDINESS: Zone 4.

HABIT: Usually a rounded shrub in outline, somewhat loose and open.

RATE: Slow.

TEXTURE: Medium in all seasons.

LEAF COLOR: Light green in summer changing to yellow in fall.

FLOWERS: Dioecious or polygamous, greenish yellow, early to mid-April before the leaves, in axillary clusters.

FRUIT: Drupe, 2/5" across, scarlet, September, seldom seen since it is showy only after the leaves fall and is borne only on pistillate plants, nevertheless, very ornamental.

CULTURE: Difficult to transplant because of coarsely fibrous root system and somewhat slow to reestablish; does best in moist, well-drained soils; full sun or 1/2 shade; does adequately in dry soils.

DISEASES AND INSECTS: None serious.

LANDSCAPE VALUE: Good shrub for the shrub border or naturalizing; I have seen it growing in deep woods; nice for the early yellow flowers and yellow fall color.

PROPAGATION: Seed should be stratified for 30 days at 77°F, followed by 90 days in peat at 34° to 41°F or 105 days in sand at 41°F. Cuttings of half-ripe (greenwood) shoots will root.

ADDITIONAL NOTES: The fruits are lovely and remind one of the fruits of *Cornus mas*. They are a brilliant scarlet and singularly eye-catching in the autumn landscape.

NATIVE HABITAT: Maine to Ontario and Kansas, south to Florida and Texas. Introduced 1863.

Liquidambar styraciflua — American Sweetgum

FAMILY: Hamamelidaceae

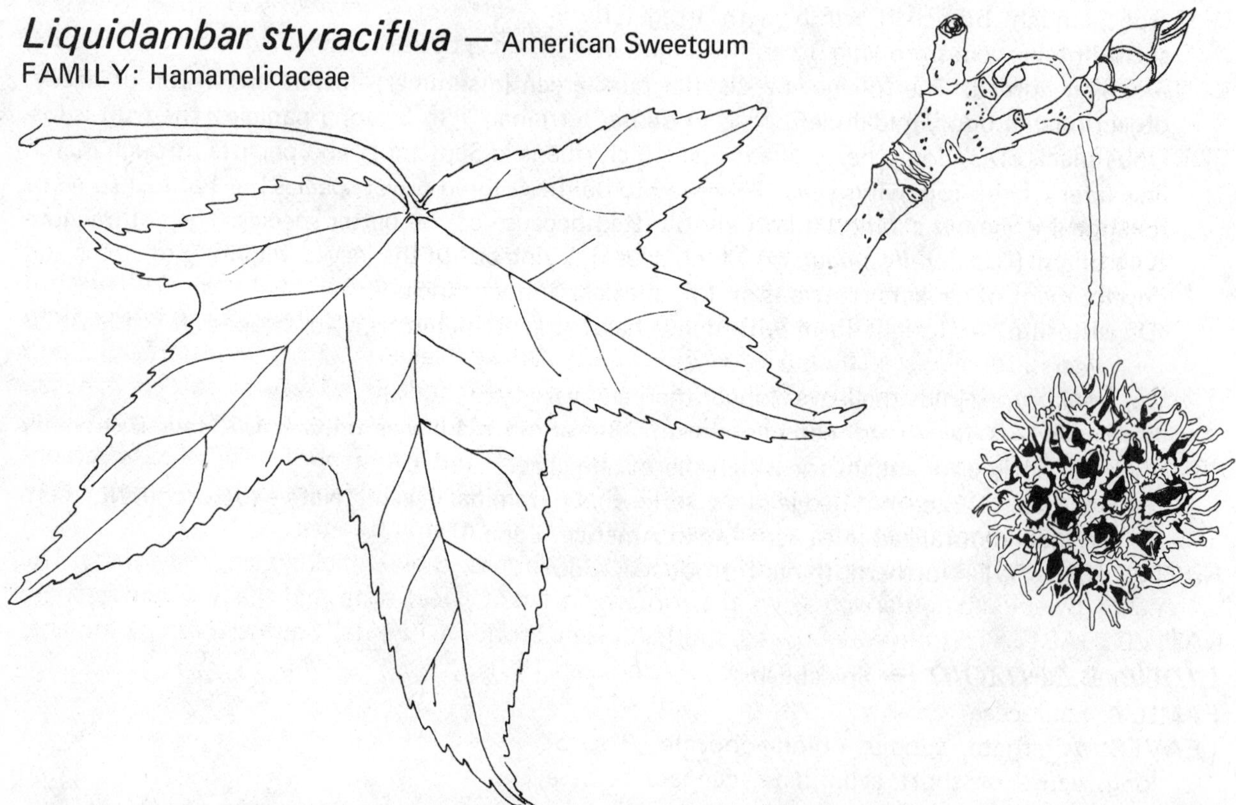

LEAVES: Alternate, simple, 4 to 7 1/2" wide and about as long, 5 to 7 lobed with oblong-triangular acuminate, star-shaped, finely serrate lobes, dark green and lustrous above, paler beneath except axillary tufts in axils of principal veins.

BUD: Imbricate, 6 scaled, ovate to conical, 1/4 to 1/2" long terminal; laterals smaller, reddish green-brown, sometimes fragrant when crushed; lateral buds divergent.

STEM: Slender to stout, light to dark reddish or yellowish brown, aromatic, rounded or somewhat angled, frequently developing corky wings during the second year. Pith—star-shaped and solid, white or brownish.

SIZE: 60 to 75′ in height with a spread of 2/3's to equal the height. Can reach 80 to 120′ in the wild.

HARDINESS: Zone 5.

HABIT: Decidedly pyramidal when young, of very neat outline; often with an oblong to rounded crown at maturity.

RATE: Medium to fast, 2 to 3′ per year in moist soil; 1 to 2′ per year in dry soil; 20.3′ high and 14.5′ wide after 10 years in Oregon test.

TEXTURE: Medium to medium-fine in leaf; medium-coarse in winter.

BARK: Grayish brown, deeply furrowed into narrow, somewhat rounded, ridges.

LEAF COLOR: Very beautiful, deep, glossy green above in summer, changing to rich yellow-purple-red tones in the fall. There is great variability in fall colors. I have seen sweetgums which were totally disappointing and others which should be propagated vegetatively for their fall color alone. Holds leaves very late in fall.

FLOWERS: Monoecious, staminate are green and borne in racemes; pistillate, borne terminally in globose heads, not showy.

FRUIT: Syncarp of dehiscent capsules, 1 to 1 1/2″ diameter, persisting into winter, the seeds are brownish and winged. The fruit can be quite messy.

CULTURE: Transplant balled and burlapped in spring into deep, moist, slightly acid soil; full sun; the root system is fleshy and consequently is not greatly fibrous and takes a while to re-establish. In the wild the tree occurs as a bottomland species on rich, moist, alluvial soils but is found on a great variety of sites; prune during the winter; not a good plant for city plantings and small areas where roots are limited in their development.

DISEASES AND INSECTS: Bleeding necrosis, leaf spots, sweetgum webworm, caterpillars, cottony-cushion scale, sweetgum scale, walnut scale; iron chlorosis can be a problem on high pH soils.

LANDSCAPE VALUE: Excellent lawn, park, or street tree but needs large area for root development. Used extensively on west coast. Avoid polluted areas.

CULTIVARS:

'Burgundy' – Leaves turn claret (wine-color) in fall.

'Festival' – Slender, columnar type.

'Levis' – Branches show no corky bark character; leaves color brilliantly in autumn.

'Moraine' – More uniform and faster growing than the species; upright-oval habit with a medium branch texture and brilliant red fall color. I have seen this cultivar at the Ohio Agricultural Research and Development Shade Tree Evaluation Plots, Wooster, Ohio, and was impressed by the excellent dark, glossy green foliage, as well as the good habit.

'Variegata' – Leaves marked with yellow; an unusual and somewhat interesting variegated type.

PROPAGATION: Seeds exhibit only a shallow dormancy, but germination rate is considerably increased by cold, moist stratification at 41°F for 15 to 90 days in moist sand. Cuttings: Leafy softwood cuttings taken with a heel can be rooted under mist in summer.

ADDITIONAL NOTES: Wood is used for plywood, furniture, cabinet making, and other uses. The name Sweetgum is derived from the sap which has a sweet taste and gummy consistency.

NATIVE HABITAT: Connecticut, and south to New York to Florida, Southern Ohio, Indiana, Illinois, Missouri to Texas and Mexico. Introduced 1681.

Liriodendron tulipifera — Tuliptree, also called Tulip Magnolia, Tulip Poplar, Yellow Poplar, and Whitewood.

FAMILY: Magnoliaceae

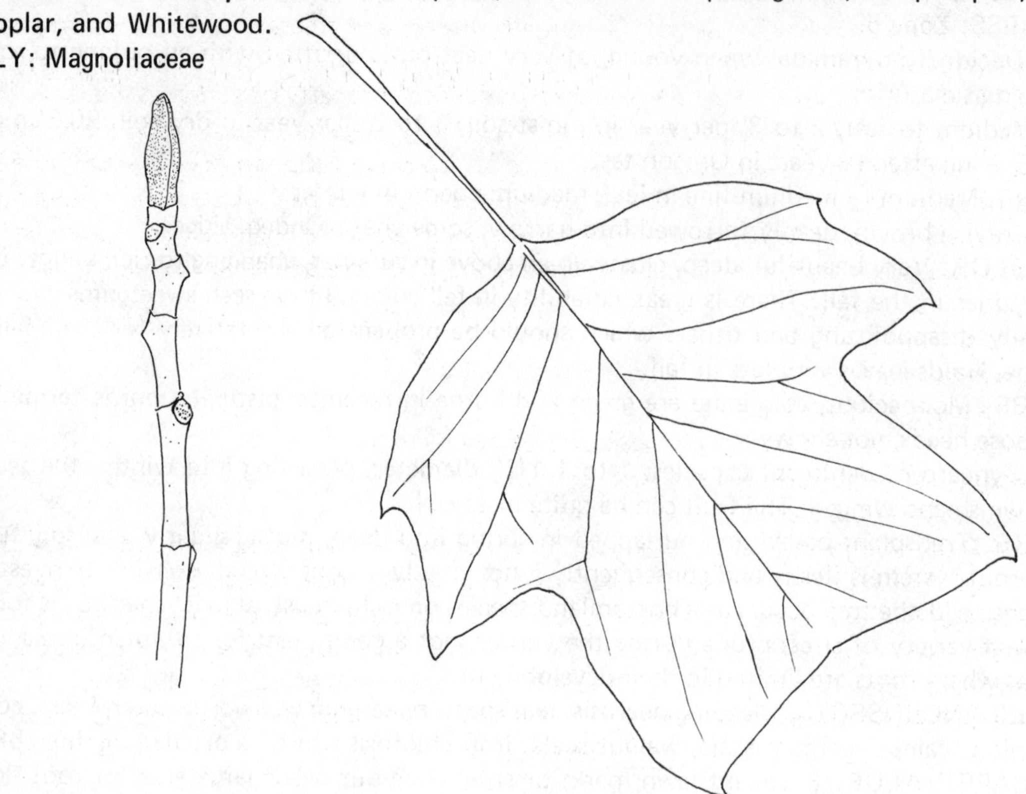

LEAVES: Alternate, simple, lobed, 3 to 6" across, broad truncate apex, with a short acuminate lobe in each side and usually 1 or 2, rarely 3 or 4, acute or short-acuminate lobes on each side near the rounded or truncate base, bright green above, paler beneath.

BUDS: Valvate, terminal—1/2" long, greenish to reddish brown, covered with a bloom, white dotted, entire bud resembling a duck's bill.

STEM: Slender to stout, lustrous greenish to red-brown, sometimes bloomy, aromatic when broken but with intensely bitter taste; distinct stipular scars surrounding stem; pith—chambered.

SIZE: 70 to 90' in height with a spread of 35 to 50'; can grow to 150' and greater.

RATE: Fast, 15 to 20' over a 6 to 8 year period.

TEXTURE: Medium in leaf and winter.

BARK: Brownish; furrowed into close, interlacing, rounded ridges which are separated by grayish crevices.

LEAF COLOR: Bright green in summer, changing to golden-yellow or yellow in fall.

FLOWERS: Perfect, with 6 greenish yellow petals in 2 rows; 3 sepals, interior of the corolla an orangish color; mid-May to early June; solitary; often takes 10 to 20 years to flower from seed; flowers are often borne high in the tree and are missed by the uninitiated.

FRUIT: Cone-like aggregate of samaras, 2 to 3" long, eventually turning brown in October and persisting through winter.

CULTURE: Transplant balled and burlapped in spring into deep, moist, well-drained loam; the root system is fleshy and often poorly branched; full sun; pH adaptable although prefers a slightly acid soil; prune in winter; has been used for street tree plantings in narrow tree lawns and usually develops leaf scorch or simply dies after a time.

DISEASES AND INSECTS: Cankers, leaf spots, powdery mildews, root and stem rot, *Verticillium* wilt, leaf yellowing (physiological disorder), aphid, scale, and tuliptree spot gall. Aphids are a real problem in Central Illinois. The insect secretes liberal quantities of "honeydew" and the leaves of the plants are often coated with this substance which is then overrun with the sooty mold fungus, which causes a blackening and unsightliness of the leaves. The leaf yellowing problem can be a headache with newly planted as well as established trees which do not receive adequate water. The leaves abscise prematurely and create a mess that requires constant attention.

LANDSCAPE VALUE: Not a tree for the small residential property or streets; should be restricted to large areas and this type of situation only; a very large and magnificent plant when fully grown and developed; somewhat weak-wooded, although variation occurs among individuals, and often breaks up in ice and severe storms. This tree has been abused and misused by landscape people for so long that they think they are doing the right thing by planting it along streets. My only thought is, "Does a weak-wooded, 150′ tree constantly dropping leaves belong in your backyard?"

CULTIVARS:

'Aureo-marginatum' — Leaves margined with yellow.

'Compactum' — Dwarf form.

'Crispum' — Leaves broader than long, with wavy margins.

'Fastigiatum' — Narrow, upright to 35′, novelty.

'Tortuosum' — Contorted stems.

PROPAGATION: Seeds should be stratified in bags of peat moss or sand for 60 to 90 days at 41°F. Cuttings, July collected, made with basal cut 1/2″ below node, rooted 52%.

ADDITIONAL NOTES: Wood is used for furniture and other products; one of our tallest native Eastern American deciduous species and can grow to 190′. The showy flowers depend on honeybees for cross-pollination and the honey is supposedly of excellent quality.

NATIVE HABITAT: Massachusetts to Wisconsin, south to Florida and Mississippi. Cultivated 1663.

Liriope spicata — Lilyturf, often called Creeping Lilyturf or Liriope.

FAMILY: Liliaceae

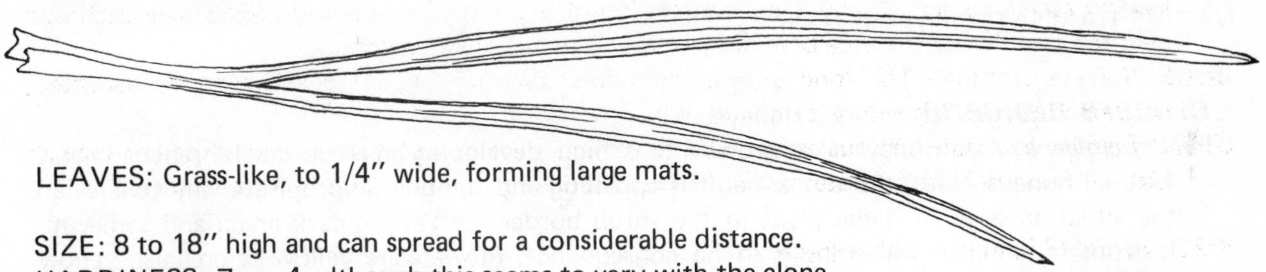

LEAVES: Grass-like, to 1/4″ wide, forming large mats.

SIZE: 8 to 18″ high and can spread for a considerable distance.

HARDINESS: Zone 4, although this seems to vary with the clone.

HABIT: Grass-like in overall appearance.

RATE: Slow.

TEXTURE: Depending on cultivar fine to medium fine as some have wider blades than others as well as different foliage colors.

LEAF COLOR: Medium to deep green in summer often becoming yellowish or brownish green in cold weather.

FLOWERS: Lilac to almost white, each flower 1/6 to 1/4″ wide; July through August; borne on upright 4 to 8″ spikes; very attractive in flower but seldom given plaudits for this feature.

FRUIT: Berry, blue-black, 1/4″ diameter, October and persisting. I have seen heavily fruited plants in January on the University of Georgia campus.

CULTURE: Of the easiest culture; transplant as a small pot plant or from pieces of sod into about any soil; prefer well-drained soils and will endure heat, drought and salt spray. Perform extremely well in heavy shade or full sun; should be planted about 12″ apart and will completely cover an area in a single season; not a bad idea to mow off old foliage in the spring and divide every few years.

DISEASES AND INSECTS: None serious.

LANDSCAPE VALUE: Quality ground cover which can be used in poor soils, in all degrees of shade, on slopes and banks, as edging plants, and under trees and shrubs. This plant is used extensively in the south and east and is comparable to the *Pachysandra* and *Vinca* which we utilize so freely in the north. Liriope offers a distinctly different textural effect compared to most ground covers. There is a small planting on the University of Illinois campus which is a beautiful grass-green in summer but with the advent of cold weather takes on a sickly yellow-brown-green combination. I was amazed at the trememdous quantity of *Liriope* used in the south. The University of Georgia campus is extremely beautiful with its massive Water Oaks, *Quercus nigra*, and other large trees which are underplanted with extensive beds of *Liriope* and *Hedera helix*. The fruiting seems to be much more profuse on southern plants. I noted that the variegated leaf type was not as heavy a fruiter as the green-leaved types.

PROPAGATION: Usually by division of the parent plant. This seems to be an efficient way of increasing plant numbers.

RELATED SPECIES: There is a considerable confusion concerning *Liriope* and a related genus *Ophiopogon*. An attempt is made here to alleviate the confusion.

Liriope muscari, Big Blue Lilyturf, grows to 2′ high and has wider leaves than those of *L. spicata* which are only about 1/4″ in diameter. *L. muscari* is considerably coarser than *L. spicata* and has bluish green foliage. The flowers are lilac-purple on spikes about as high as the leaves and develop in September. There is a cultivar 'Variegata' which has yellow-striped leaves. This clone was much in evidence throughout the south. Native to Japan and China. Zone 6.

Ophiopogon species are similar to *Liriope* but differ only in minor characteristics except they are slightly less hardy (Zone 7) and the flowers are borne well down in the foliage, whereas those of *Liriope* are above the leaves. *O. jaburan* grows to 3′ with leaves 1/4 to 1/2″ wide and flowers ranging from white to lilac. The cultivars 'Aureus' and 'Variegatus' have leaves striped with yellow. *O. japonicus* grows 6 to 15″ with leaves 1/8″ wide and flowers violet or bluish tinted. Very dense and handsome evergreen groundcover which is admirably displayed in the National Arboretum, Washington, D.C. Both are native to Japan and the latter is also found in Korea.

NATIVE HABITAT: China and Japan.

Lonicera alpigena — Alps Honeysuckle

Lonicera alpigena, Alps Honeysuckle, grows 4 to 8′ high, developing an erect, much branched habit. Like all honeysuckles, the winter habit is appalling and the only appropriate way to alleviate the situation is to hide the plant in the shrub border. Leaves are dark green and somewhat lustrous in summer; fall color is of no consequence. Flowers are yellow or greenish yellow, tinged dull red or brown-red; effective in May; borne in axillary peduncled pairs; each flower about 1/2″ long. The fruits are red, up to 1/2″ long, cherry-like, often united for a portion of their length. This is a rather distinct species because of the long flower stalks, large leaves and large fruits. The cultivar 'Nana' is a low, slow-growing form; a 63-year-old plant being only 3′ high. Native to the mountains of Central and Southern Europe. Introduced 1600. Zone 5.

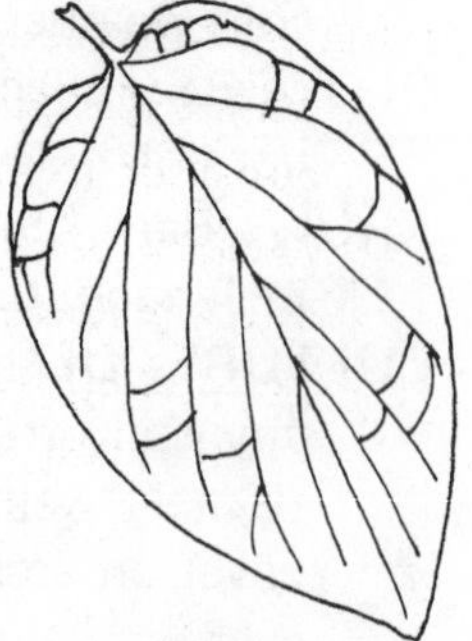

Lonicera x *bella*, Belle Honeysuckle, is the result of crosses between *L. morrowi* and *L. tatarica*. The hybrids were first raised in the Münden Botanic Garden from seeds received from the St. Petersburg (Russia) Botanic Garden before 1889. The plants will grow 8 to 10′ high and 8 to 12′ wide. The shrub develops a dense, rounded habit with spreading, somewhat arching branches. The foliage is bluish green in summer. Flowers vary in degrees of pink and usually fade to yellow. They are evident in early to mid-May in Central Illinois. The fruit is a red, 1/4″ diameter berry which becomes effective in late June and July often persisting into fall but does not rival *L. tatarica* for abundance or showiness. Several selections have been made from the seedling populations and the best include "Atrorosea'—buds pink, flowers white with tips of petals tinged pink; 'Candida'—pure white flowers; and 'Rosea'—flowers deep pink. Zone 4.

Lonicera fragrantissima — Winter Honeysuckle

FAMILY: Caprifoliaceae

LEAVES: Opposite, simple, very short petioled, elliptic to broad-ovate, 1 1/5 to 2 4/5" long, acute, setose-ciliate, glabrous above, setose on the midrib.

BUDS: Imbricate, sessile, with numerous 4-ranked scales; slightly pubescent.

STEM: Slender, glabrous, light, often lustrous brown, pith—white, solid or slightly excavated.

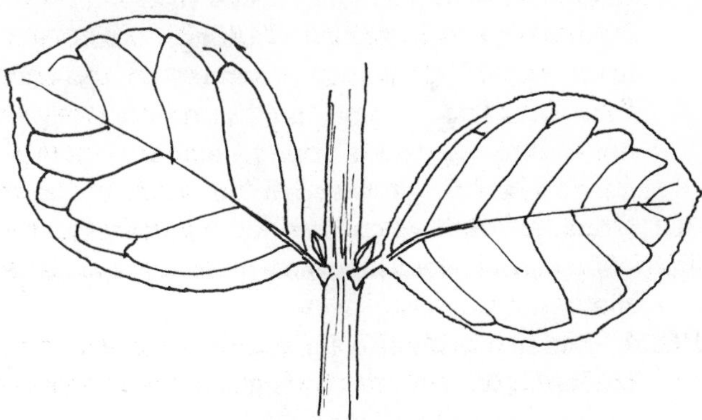

SIZE: 6 to 10' high (15') by 6 to 10' in spread.

HARDINESS: Zone 5 (4).

HABIT: Wide-spreading, irregular growing deciduous shrub with tangled mass of slender recurving branches. Holds foliage very late in fall (November).

RATE: Fast.

TEXTURE: Medium in leaf; medium-coarse in winter; this is true for most of the larger honeysuckles.

LEAF COLOR: Dark bluish or grayish green in summer; foliage holds late and falls green or brown.

FLOWERS: Creamy white, lemon-scented and extremely fragrant, relatively small; late March-early April for a 3 to 4 week period; borne in axillary peduncled pairs before the leaves. Not very showy but certainly among the most fragrant of woody flowering shrubs.

FRUIT: Berry, 1/4" diameter, red, late May-early June.

CULTURE: The following discussion applies to the honeysuckle descriptions which follow. Transplants readily, adapted to many soils and pH levels; prefers good loamy, moist, well-drained soil; abhors extremely wet situations; full sun; pruning should be accomplished after flowering and, in fact, when honeysuckles become overgrown the best treatment is to cut them back to the ground as they readily develop new shoots.

DISEASES AND INSECTS: Leaf blight, leaf spots, powdery mildews, woolly honeysuckle sawfly, four-lined plant bug, planthopper, greenhouse whitefly, flea beetle, looper caterpillar, long-tailed mealybug, fall webworm, and a few scale species.

LANDSCAPE VALUE: Makes a good hedge plant, nice for fragrance, could be integrated into the shrub border; worthwhile to force branches inside in late winter.

PROPAGATION: Most species show some embryo dormancy and stratification in moist media for 30 to 60 days at 41°F. is recommended. Some species have hard seed coats and warm followed by cold stratification is recommended. Cuttings of most species (softwood collected in June) root with ease under mist.

NATIVE HABITAT: Eastern China. Introduced 1845.

Lonicera x *heckrottii,* often called the Everblooming or Goldflame Honeysuckle, is a vine of unknown origin although the parentage was purported to be *L. americana* x *L. sempervirens*. I would consider it the most handsome of the climbing honeysuckles. The flower buds are carmine and as they open the yellow, inside the corolla, is exposed. The outside gradually changes to a pink color and the total flower effect is strikingly handsome. The flowers are borne in elongated peduncled spikes, with several remote whorls; June and continuing throughout the summer. Fruit is red and apparently sparsely produced. Zone 4.

Lonicera japonica — Japanese Honeysuckle

LEAVES: Opposite, simple, ovate to oblong-ovate, 1 1/5 to 3" long, acute to short-acuminate, rounded to subcordate at base, pubescent on both sides when young, later glabrate above; petiole—1/5" long.

BUD: Small, solitary, covered with 2 pubescent scales, superposed, sessile.

STEM: Reddish brown to light brown, covered with soft pubescence, twining; pith—excavated.

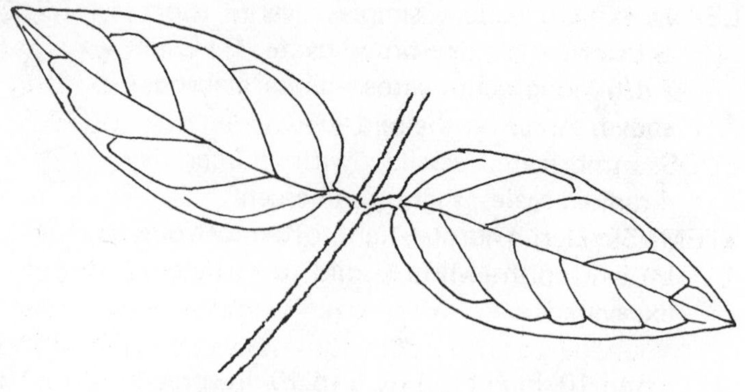

Lonicera japonica, Japanese Honeysuckle, is a weedy twining vine growing from 15 to 30'. The foliage is semi-evergreen in Central Illinois and of dark green color. Flowers are white, tinged pink or purple, turning yellow, fragrant; June through September, borne in peduncled pairs. Usually a solid mass of white and yellow during June; fruit is a black, 1/4" diameter berry ripening in August through October; a good, quick ground cover, bank cover, or support cover but has escaped from cultivation and has become a noxious weed in the south. 'Halliana' has pure white flowers which change to yellow, very fragrant; vigorous grower. Japan, China, Korea. 1806. Zone 4.

'Aureo-reticulata' is an interesting cultivar with yellow netted markings throughout the leaf; the overall effect is that of reverse chlorosis; best grown in full sun; an interesting novelty plant.

Lonicera korolkowii, Blueleaf Honeysuckle, is a loose, open, irregular shrub with slender, spreading and arching branches growing 6 to 10' high and as wide although one authority listed mature size between 12 and 15' high with an equal spread. The downy shoots and pale, sea green, pubescent leaves give the shrub a striking gray-blue hue and hence the name Blueleaf Honeysuckle. The flowers are rose-colored (pinkish), each flower about 2/3" long (corolla), borne in peduncled pairs from the leaf axils of short lateral branchlets in late May. The fruit is a bright red berry which matures in July and August. Culturally this species is more difficult to establish than other honeysuckles and should be transplanted balled and burlapped. This is one reason why Blueleaf Honeysuckle is seldom seen in the trade. The cultivars include 'Aurora' with moderate purplish pink flowers and a profuse flowering nature, and 'Floribunda' which supposedly is more floriferous than the species. There is a variety *zabelii* which has deeper rose-pink flowers and glabrous leaves broader than the species. This variety is often confused with the cultivar 'Zabelii' which is purported to belong to *L. tatarica*. Native to Soviet Central Asia, bordering parts of Afghanistan and Pakistan. Introduced 1880. Zone 4.

Lonicera maackii — Amur Honeysuckle

LEAVES: Opposite, simple, ovate-elliptic to ovate-lanceolate, 2 to 3" long, acuminate, broad-cuneate, rarely rounded at base, usually pubescent only on the veins on both sides; petiole—1/8 to 1/5" long, glandular—pubescent.

BUDS: Gray, pubescent, oblong or acute.

STEM: Grayish brown, short pubescent on current year's growth, finally glabrous; pith—brown, excavated in internodes, solid at nodes.

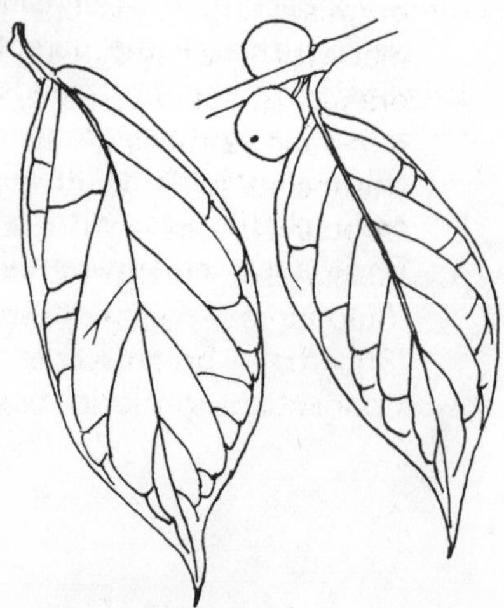

Lonicera maackii, Amur Honeysuckle, is a large, upright, spreading, leggy, deciduous shrub reaching 12 to 15' in height with a similar spread. The foliage is a medium to dark green in summer and the fall color is ineffective. The flowers are white changing to yellow, 4/5" long, late May creeping into early June, borne in axillary peduncled pairs. The fruit is a red, 1/4" diameter berry which ripens in October and is eaten by the birds. Variety *podocarpa* flowers in early June, Zone 4 hardiness, and is a better flowerer. The birds deposit the seeds in old shrub borders, hedges, wasteland and before one knows Amur Honeysuckle has taken over. Manchuria and Korea. Introduced 1855-1860. Zone 2.

Lonicera morrowii — Morrow Honeysuckle

LEAVES: Opposite, simple, elliptic to ovate-oblong or obovate-oblong, 1 to 2" long, acute or obtusish and mucronulate, rounded at base, sparingly pubescent above at least when young, soft-pubescent beneath; petiole 1/12 to 1/8" long.

BUDS: Small, somewhat puberulent, small and blunt.

STEM: Grayish to light brown, pubescent when young, older stems a distinct gray.

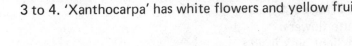

Lonicera morrowii, Morrow Honeysuckle, grows 6 to 8' high and 6 to 10' wide forming a broad, rounded, dense, tangled mound with branches and foliage to the ground. Foliage is a grayish to bluish green in summer. Flowers are creamy-white changing to yellow, 3/5" long, mid to late May, in peduncled pairs. Fruit is a blood-red, 1/4" diameter berry ripening in July and August. Better than many honeysuckles as the foliage hugs the ground. Japan. 1975. Zone 3 to 4. 'Xanthocarpa' has white flowers and yellow fruits.

Lonicera sempervirens — Trumpet Honeysuckle

LEAVES: Opposite, simple, very short-petioled or subsessile, elliptic or ovate to oblong, 1 1/5 to 3" long, obtuse or acutish, usually cuneate, dark green above, glaucous beneath and sometimes pubescent, 1 or 2 pairs below the inflorescence connate into an oblong disk, rounded or mucronate at ends. More or less evergreen; new growth —reddish.

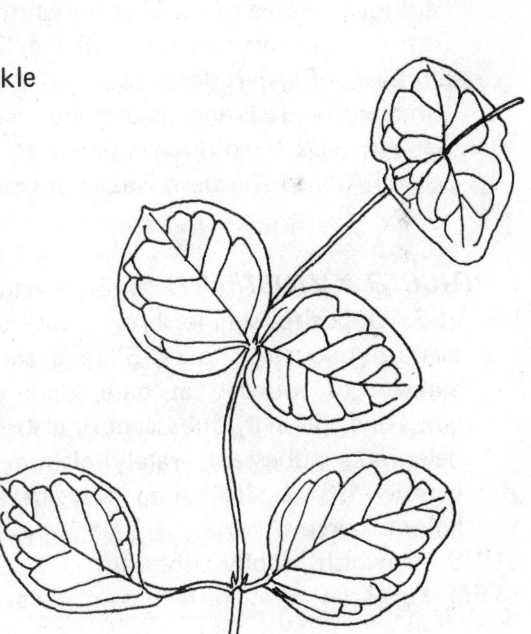

STEM: Twining, straw colored, glabrous; pith—excavated.

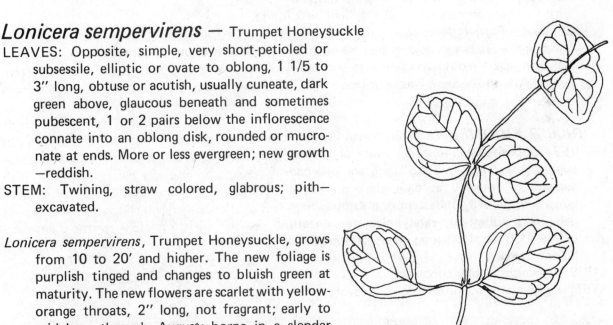

Lonicera sempervirens, Trumpet Honeysuckle, grows from 10 to 20' and higher. The new foliage is purplish tinged and changes to bluish green at maturity. The new flowers are scarlet with yellow-orange throats, 2" long, not fragrant; early to mid-June through August; borne in a slender peduncled spike. Fruit is a bright red, 1/4" berry which ripens in September and is effective through November. The cultivars include:

'Magnifica' – bright red flowers.

'Sulphurea' – yellow flowers.

'Superba' – bright scarlet flowers.

Connecticut to Florida, west to Nebraska and Texas. 1686. Zone 3.

Lonicera tatarica — Tatarian Honeysuckle

LEAVES: Opposite, simple, ovate to ovate-lanceolate, 1 to 2 2/5" long, acute to acuminate, rarely obtusish, rounded or subcordate at base; petiole 1/12 to 1/4" long.

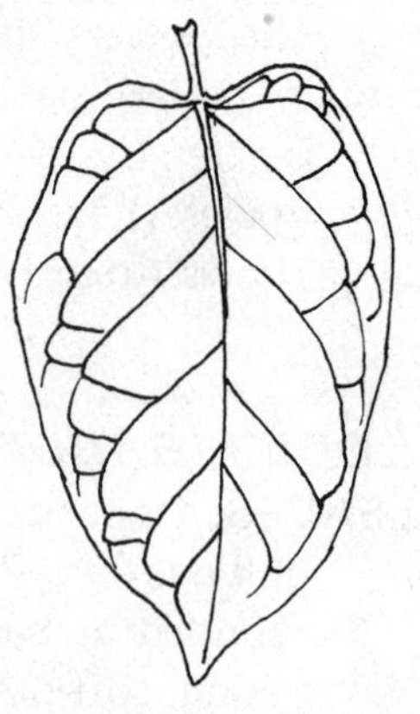

BUDS: Flattened, closely appressed, elongated, with valvate lower scales, glabrous.

STEM: Green at first, finally brownish, glabrous; pith—brown, excavated.

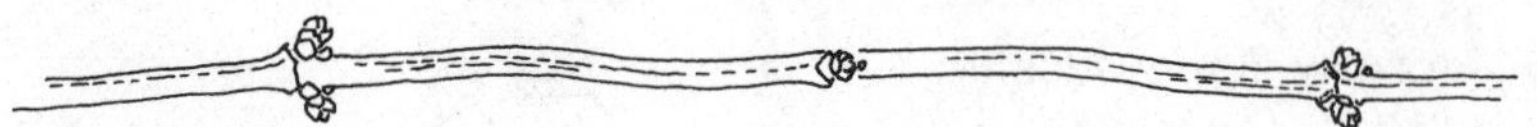

Lonicera tatarica, Tatarian Honeysuckle, grows 10 to 12' in height with a 10' spread. The general habit is upright, strongly multi-stemmed with the upper branches arching and the overall effect one of a dense, twiggy mass. Foliage is bluish green in summer; flowers are pink to white (profusely borne), 3/5 to 4/5" long, May 5 to 15, soon after the leaves develop, borne in peduncled pairs in the axils of the leaves. Fruit is a red, 1/4" diameter berry which colors in late June into July and August. Often considered the "best" of the honeysuckles because of the many cultivars which include:

'Alba' — Flowers pure white.
'Arnold Red' — Darkest red flowers of any honeysuckle.
'Grandiflora' — Large white flowers. Sometimes called 'Bride'.
'LeRoyana' — Dwarf variety, 3' tall, poor flowerer, valued solely for dwarf character.
'Lutea' — Pink flowers, yellow fruit.
'Morden Orange' — Pale pink flowers and good orange fruits.
'Nana' — Flowers pink, dwarf habit, 3' high at 9 years.
'Parvifolia' — One of the best for white flowers.
'Rosea' — Flowers rosy pink outside, light pink inside.
'Sibirica' — Flowers deep rose.
'Virginalis' — Buds and flowers are rose-pink. Largest flowers of any *L. tatarica* form.
'Zabelii' — Dark red flowers similar to 'Arnold Red'.

Central Asia to Southern Russia. Introduced 1752. Zone 3.

Lonicera xylosteum — European Fly Honeysuckle

LEAVES: Opposite, simple, broad-ovate or elliptic-ovate to obovate, 1 to 2 2/5" long, acute, broad-cuneate to rounded at base, dark or grayish green and sparingly pubescent or glabrous above, paler and pubescent, rarely glabrate beneath, petiole—1/8 to 1/3" long. Margins sometimes hairy fringed.

BUDS: Brownish, woolly pubescent.

STEM: Pubescent, gray, pith—brown, excavated.

Lonicera xylosteum, European Fly Honeysuckle, develops into a rounded mound with spreading arching branches; grows to 8 to 10' with a spread of 10 to 12'. Foliage is grayish green (has somewhat of a blue effect). The flowers are white or yellowish white, 2/5" long, often tinged reddish; mid-May; borne in peduncled pairs. Fruit is a dark red berry ripening in July and August. 'Claveyi' is a 3 to 6' dwarf form recommended for hedges; 'Hedge King' is another selection by Clavey Nurseries and is a distinct narrow, upright grower which would be suitable for hedges. 'Emerald Mound' or 'Nana' is one of the very finest low growing, mounded honeysuckles. The foliage is a rich, bluish green and about the handsomest of any honeysuckle. I have seen this cultivar used in mass at the Minnesota Landscape Arboretum and must admit was handsomely impressed. Roots easily from cuttings and should become more popular with exposure. Ultimate landscape size should run 3′ with a 4 1/2 to 6′ spread. Do not move in leaf. Europe to Altai. Long cultivated. Zone 4.

Maackia amurensis — Amur Maackia

FAMILY: Leguminosae

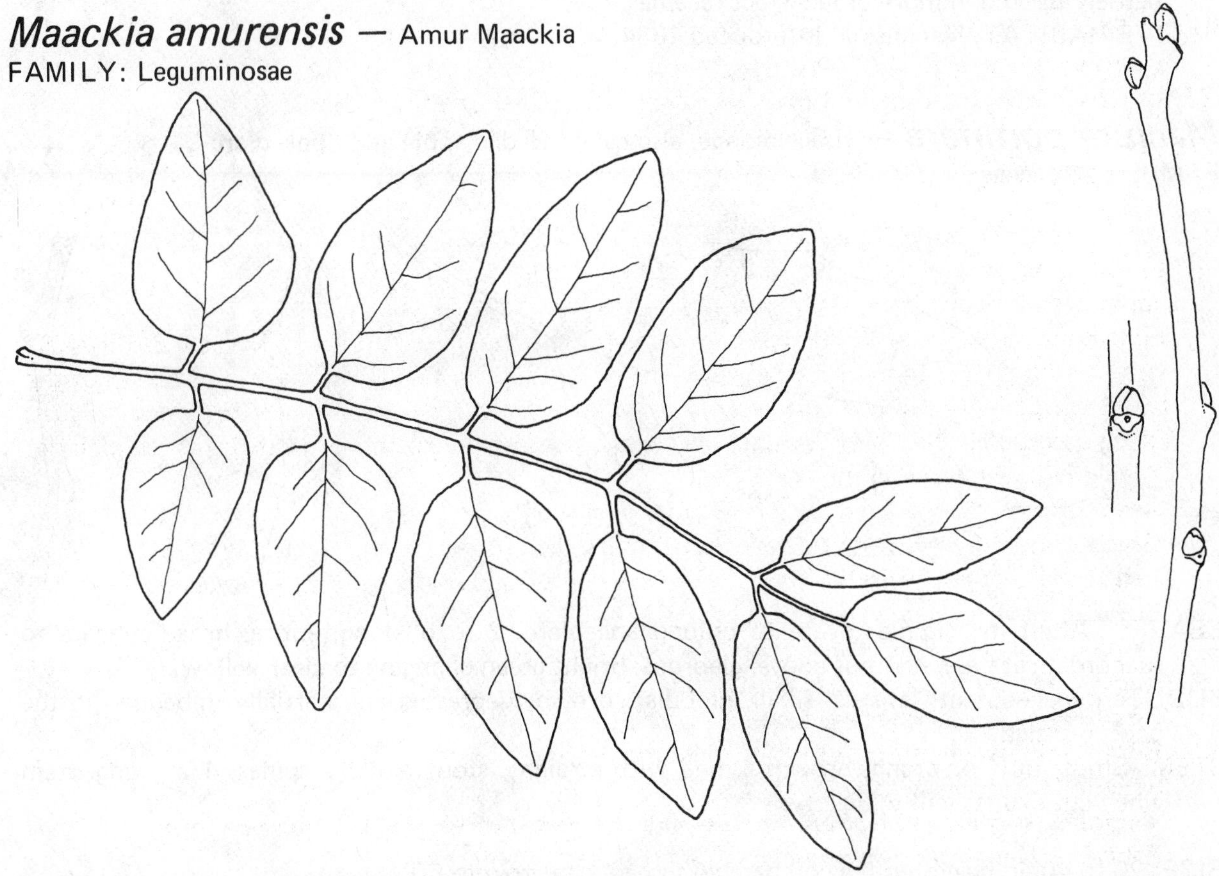

LEAVES: Alternate, compound, odd-pinnate, leaflets opposite or nearly so, short stalked, 7 to 11, elliptic to oblong-ovate, 2 to 3 1/2″ long, short acuminate, rounded at base, glabrous, grayish green when unfolding finally turning a dark green.

BUDS: Two exposed pale-margined scales; dark brown, somewhat ovoid, plumpish, similar in shape to the buds of *Koelreutaria*.

STEM: Dark grayish brown to black, usually glabrous; somewhat dingy in color and texture in winter.

SIZE: Probably 20 to 30′ under cultivation but can grow to 45′ in the wild.

HARDINESS: Zone 5.

HABIT: Small, round headed tree; quite dapper in outline when properly grown.

RATE: Slow, 12′ over a 20 year period according to an English source.

TEXTURE: Medium in all seasons.

BARK: Peeling with maturity, rich, shining brown; developing a curly consistency.

LEAF COLOR: Initially somewhat grayish green finally dark green; fall color is nonexistent.

FLOWERS: Perfect, dull white, closely set on stiff erect racemes, 4 to 6″ long, sometimes branched at the base; July and August.

FRUIT: Pod, 2 to 3″ long, 1/3″ wide, flat.

CULTURE: Performs best in good, loose, well-drained, acid or alkaline soil; preferably sunny exposures.

DISEASES AND INSECTS: Nothing particularly serious.

LANDSCAPE VALUE: Of interest for the late summer flowers. The few young specimens I have seen had very clean foliage and appeared quite vigorous.

PROPAGATION: Seed may be soaked in hot water (190°F) overnight, then sown.

ADDITIONAL NOTES: A little-known genus which is closely related to *Cladrastis* and may have by some authorities been put in that genus. It differs from *Cladrastis* in that the leaf-buds are solitary and not hidden by the base of the petiole; the leaflets are opposite and the flowers are densely packed in more or less erect racemes.

NATIVE HABITAT: Manchuria. Introduced 1864.

Maclura pomifera — Osage-orange, also called Hedge-apple and "bois d'arc".

FAMILY: Moraceae

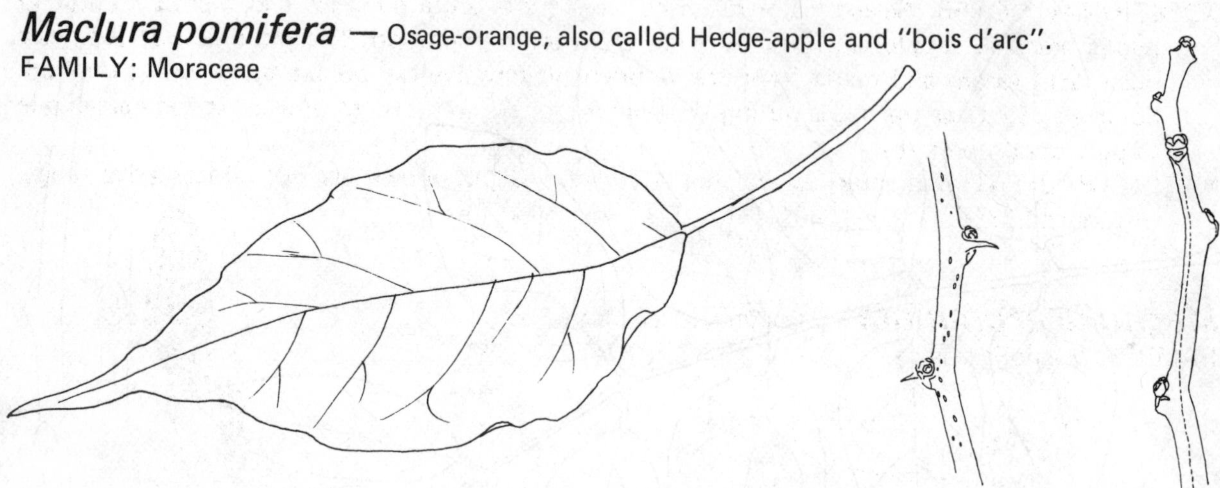

LEAVES: Alternate, simple, ovate to oblong-lanceolate, 2 to 5" long, entire, broad-cuneate to subcordate at base, lustrous above, glabrous, bright green changing to clear yellow.

BUD: Terminal—absent, laterals—small, globular, brown, depressed and partially imbedded in the bark, 5-scaled.

STEM: Stout, buff or orange-brown, armed with straight, stout axillary spines, 1/2" long, stem when cut exudes milky juices.

SIZE: 20 to 40' in height with a comparable spread, can grow to 60'.

HARDINESS: Zone 4.

HABIT: Usually develops a short trunk and low, rounded, irregular crown composed of stiff, spiny, interlacing branches; some of the branches show a pendulous tendency.

RATE: Fast, 9 to 12' over a 3 to 5 year period.

TEXTURE: Medium in leaf; coarse in fruit and winter.

BARK: On old trunks, the bark develops ashy-brown or dark orange-brown with irregular longitudinal fissures and scaly ridges; the wood itself is of a characteristic orange color.

LEAF COLOR: Bright, shiny medium green in summer; fall color varies from yellow-green to a good yellow.

FLOWERS: Dioecious, inconspicuous; female borne in June in dense globose heads on short penduncles; male in subglobose or sometimes in elongated racemes; ornamentally worthless.

FRUIT: A large, globose syncarp of drupes covered with a mamillate rind; yellow-green in color; becoming effective in September and lethal in October if one is sitting under the tree; usually fall after ripening. A real mess.

CULTURE: One of our very tough and durable native trees; transplants readily; the poorer the site the better; withstands wetness, dryness, wind, extreme heat, acid and high pH conditions once established; full sun; selections could be made for inner city areas and other impossible sites where few plants will grow.

DISEASES AND INSECTS: None serious, although a few leaf spots have been reported.

LANDSCAPE VALUE: Has been used for hedgerows in the plains states; not worth recommending for the residential landscape; has potential for rugged, polluted areas; wood is valuable for making bows and is amazingly rot resistant; I have seen patios made out of osage-orange logs which were quite handsome; the wood contains about 1% 2,3,4,5-tetrahydroxystilbene, which is toxic to a number of fungi and thus probably explains the decay resistance.

CULTIVARS:

var. *inermis* – A thornless type; also many people (nurserymen) are interested in selecting superior clones and, no doubt, the future will yield several cultivars.

PROPAGATION: Seeds exhibit a slight dormancy which can be overcome by stratification for 30 days at 41°F or by soaking in water for 48 hours. Softwood cuttings taken in July rooted 32% without treatment and 100% in 42 days after treatment with IAA.

ADDITIONAL NOTES: Select male trees; the large fruits are a nuisance and a problem around public areas as people will invariably use them for ammunition. The wood is used for fence posts, bow-wood, and rustic furniture. A bright yellow dye can be extracted from the wood. Squirrels often eat the seeds during the winter months and it is not unusual to see a small pile of pulp under the trees.

NATIVE HABITAT: Arkansas to Oklahoma and Texas but grown far out of its native range. Introduced 1818.

Magnolia acuminata — Cucumbertree Magnolia

FAMILY: Magnoliaceae

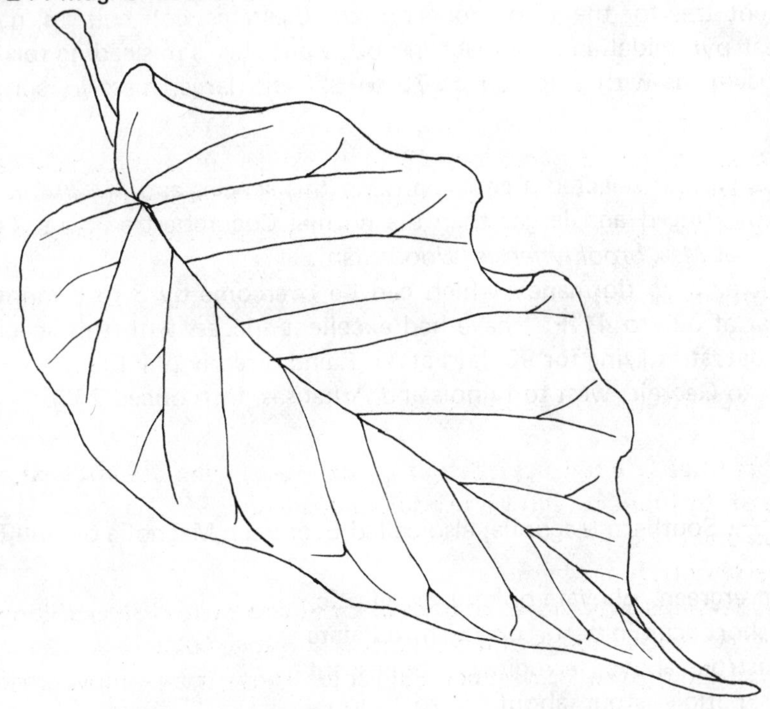

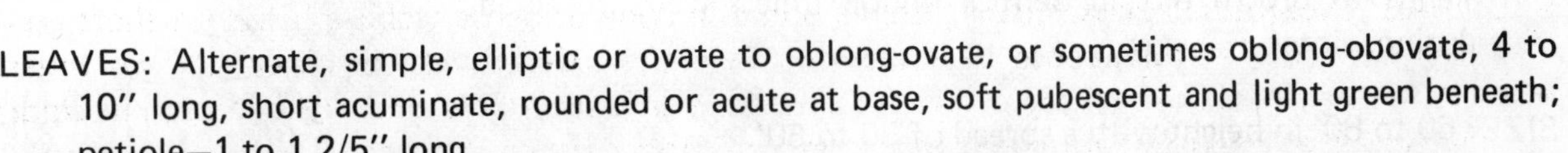

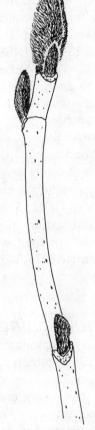

LEAVES: Alternate, simple, elliptic or ovate to oblong-ovate, or sometimes oblong-obovate, 4 to 10" long, short acuminate, rounded or acute at base, soft pubescent and light green beneath; petiole–1 to 1 2/5" long.

BUDS: Greenish to whitish, pubescent, covered (as is true for all magnolias) with a single keeled scale which on abscising leaves a distinct scar which appears as a fine line encircling the stem.

STEM: Moderate, brownish or reddish brown; the leaf scars U-shaped; emits a spicy odor when bruised.

SIZE: 50 to 80' in height with a comparable spread at maturity; in youth a distinctly pyramidal tree and the spread is always considerably less than the height.

HARDINESS: Zone 4.

HABIT: Pyramidal when young (20 to 30 years of age), in old age developing a rounded to broad-rounded outline with massive wide spreading branches. An open grown Cucumbertree Magnolia is a beautiful specimen.

RATE: Medium to fast, 10 to 15′ over a 4 to 6 year period.

TEXTURE: Medium-coarse in leaf; coarse in winter.

LEAF COLOR: Dark green in summer, abscising green or brown in fall; some trees develop a soft ashy-brown fall color which is actually quite attractive.

FLOWERS: Perfect, often self-sterile, however, some trees are self-fertile, greenish yellow, 2 1/2 to 3″ long, late May to early June; borne solitarily; not particularly showy for the flowers are borne high in the tree and often are masked by the foliage; seedling grown trees may not flower until 20′ or more in height.

FRUIT: Aggregate of follicles, pinkish red; October, briefly persisting, 2 to 3″ long, looks like a small cucumber, hence the name Cucumbertree.

CULTURE: Transplant balled and burlapped in early spring into loamy, deep, moist, well drained, slightly acid soil; does not tolerate extreme drouth or wetness; full sun or partial shade; does not withstand polluted conditions; do not plant too deep; prune after flowering; another of the fleshy rooted type trees which have a minimum of lateral roots and practically no root hairs; trees which fall into this category are often difficult to transplant and care should be taken in the planting process.

DISEASES AND INSECTS: Basically free from problems; scale can occur now and then.

LANDSCAPE VALUE: Excellent tree for the large property; parks, estates, golf courses, naturalized areas. The trees appear pyramidal and compact in youth but this is misleading for I have seen several 60 to 70′ specimens with a spread of 70 to 85′ and large, massive, spreading branches.

CULTIVARS:

'Woodsman' — J. C. McDaniel has selected a cross between this species and *M. liliflora*. The flowers are light purple tinged and larger than the normal Cucumbertree type. Technically, the cross is listed as *M.* x *brooklynensis* 'Woodsman'.

PROPAGATION: Seeds exhibit embryo dormancy which can be overcome by 3 to 6 months of stratification in moist peat at 32° to 41°F. I have had excellent success with this species by removing the fleshy seed coat; stratifying for 90 days at 41°F and directly planting.

NATIVE HABITAT: New York to Georgia, west to Illinois and Arkansas. Introduced 1736.

Magnolia grandiflora — Southern Magnolia, also called Evergreen Magnolia or Bull Bay.

FAMILY: Magnoliaceae

LEAVES: Alternate, simple, evergreen, obovate-oblong or elliptic, 5 to 10″ long, obtusely short-acuminate or obtusish, cuneate at base, dark green and lustrous above, ferrugineous-pubescent beneath, firmly coriaceous, petioles stout, about 4/5 to 1″ long. Tends to brown out in Central Illinois unless well protected during winter.

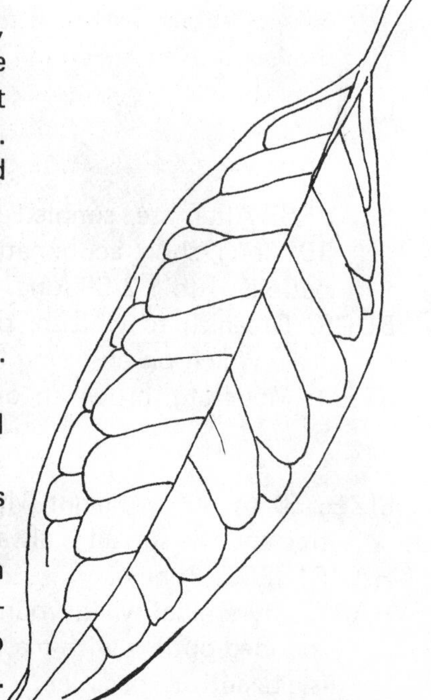

SIZE: 60 to 80′ in height with a spread of 30 to 50′.

HARDINESS: Zone 6.

HABIT: Densely pyramidal, low branching, stately evergreen tree.

RATE: Slow to medium.

TEXTURE: Even though the leaves are extremely large, the overall textural effect is medium-coarse.

LEAF COLOR: Lustrous dark green above, often ferrugineous pubescent beneath.

FLOWERS: Perfect, creamy white, beautifully fragrant (better than the best perfume), 8 to 12″ in diameter, solitary, June, sporadically thereafter, usually with 6 petals. May take as long as 15 to 20 years for trees to flower which have been grown from seed.

FRUIT: Aggregate of follicles, 3 to 5" long, splitting open to expose the red seeds; usually ripen in early fall.

CULTURE: Transplant balled and burlapped or from a container in early spring; soil should be rich, porous, acidulous and well drained; full sun or partial shade; some authorities indicate it does best in partial shade, supposedly will tolerate as little as 3 hours of sunlight per day; must be protected from winter winds and sun in northern areas; does not do well in Central Illinois and often the foliage is badly browned in winter.

DISEASES AND INSECTS: Practically problem free.

LANDSCAPE VALUE: Specimen, widely used and planted in the southern states; needs room to develop; a very worthwhile and handsome tree.

CULTIVARS:

'Goliath' – Superior flowering form with large flowers up to 12" across. The leaves are broad, rounded and blunt at the end and glossy green.

'Lanceolata' – Narrow pyramidal form, leaves narrower than species, rusty tomentose beneath. (Same as var. *exoniensis*)

'St. Mary' – Flowers at a younger age than most *M. grandiflora* forms. Leaves are conspicuously brown on the under surface.

'Samuel Sommer' – Form of rapid growth, strong ascending habit and large (10 to 14" diameter) creamy white petals.

There are numerous other cultivars which are of minimal importance to northern gardners.

PROPAGATION: Seed exhibits embryo dormancy and should be stratified for 3 to 6 months at 32 to 41°F. Cuttings—softwood root without great difficulty.

NATIVE HABITAT: North Carolina to Florida and Texas. Cultivated 1734.

Magnolia kobus — Kobus Magnolia

LEAVES: Alternate, simple, broad-obovate to obovate, 2 to 4" long, abruptly pointed, tapering to the cuneate base, light green beneath and pubescent on the veins, finally glabrous or nearly so; petioles—2/5 to 3/5" long.

Magnolia kobus, Kobus Magnolia, in youth develops a pyramidal crown and eventually becomes round-headed. The tree grows 30 to 40' high and often develops a multiple-stem character. The young branches are fragrant when crushed. The foliage is medium to dark green in summer and does not develop good fall color. The flowers are white, slightly fragrant, 4" across or less; 6 to 9 petals, with a faint purple line at the base outside, petals soon falling; April. Does not flower well when young and may take as long as 20 to 30 years to reach full flowering potential although there is variation in this respect among progeny. Easily propagated from cuttings. I have seen several old specimens (35') in flower at Cave Hill Cemetery, Louisville, Kentucky; they were like a white cloud. This and *Magnolia stellata* are among the earliest magnolias to flower. Variety *borealis* represents a more vigorous, robust, larger (growing 70 to 80' high), pyramidal tree than the species. The leaves are 6 to 7" long and the flowers average up to 5" across. A seedling of variety *borealis* grown by Sargent of the Arnold Arboretum was still sparse flowering when almost 30-years-old, but 15 years later was making a fine display and bore more flowers in succeeding years. Native to Japan. Introduced 1865. The species is hardy in Zone 5, the variety in Zone 4. Supposedly excellent for all types of soil, including limestone.

Magnolia liliflora — Lily Magnolia

The scientific name is now *M. quinquepeta*. Needless to say it will take considerable time before this epithet is accepted and used.

LEAVES: Alternate, simple, entire, obovate or elliptic-ovate or short acuminate, tapering at base, 4 to 7" long, dark green and sparingly pubescent above, light green beneath and finely pubescent on the nerves.

BUDS: End bud enlarged, hairy.

STEM: Glabrous except near the tip.

Magnolia liliflora, is a rounded, shrubby growing plant reaching 8 to 12' in height with a similar spread. The flowers are purple outside and usually white inside, 6 petals; late April to early May, just as leaves are developing; borne singly.

Cultivars:

'Gracilis' — More narrow, fastigiate habit, with narrower flower petals.

'Nigra' — Larger flowers (5" across), dark purple outside and light purple inside, makes a less straggly bush than the species.

'O'Neill' — Clone was selected by Professor J. C. McDaniel for good vigorous habit and very dark purple flowers.

Considered to be a native of China. Zone 5.

Magnolia macrophylla — Bigleaf Magnolia

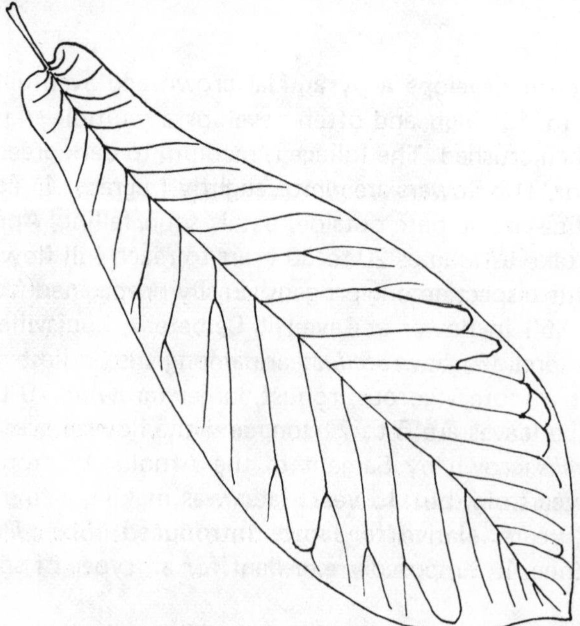

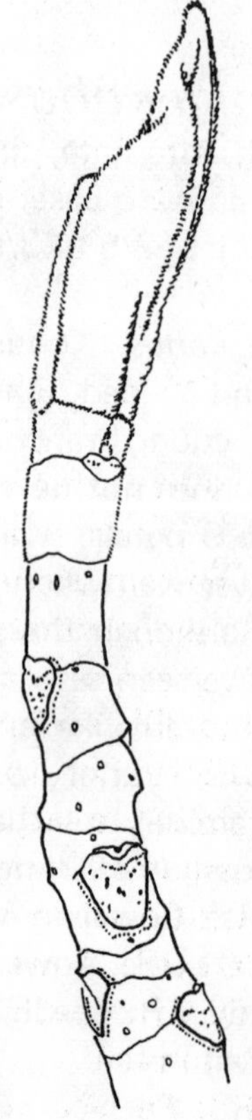

LEAVES: Alternate, simple, entire, oblong-obovate, 12 to 32" long, obtuse, subcordate—auriculate at base, glaucescent and finely pubescent beneath.

BUDS: Large, tomentose, 1/2 to 1" long.

STEM: Stout, pubescent at first, finally glabrous, coarse-textured.

Magnolia macrophylla, Bigleaf Magnolia, is a round-headed, cumbersome giant reaching 30 to 40′ in height. The flowers are creamy-white, 8 to 10″ and sometimes 14″ across, 6 petals, fragrant; June; solitary. The leaves are extremely large (12 to 30″ long) and the tree gives an overall coarse appearance which makes it difficult to use in the landscape. An interesting native tree which occurs limitedly from Kentucky to Florida west to Arkansas and Louisiana. 1800. Zone 5.

Magnolia x soulangiana — Saucer Magnolia

FAMILY: Magnoliaceae

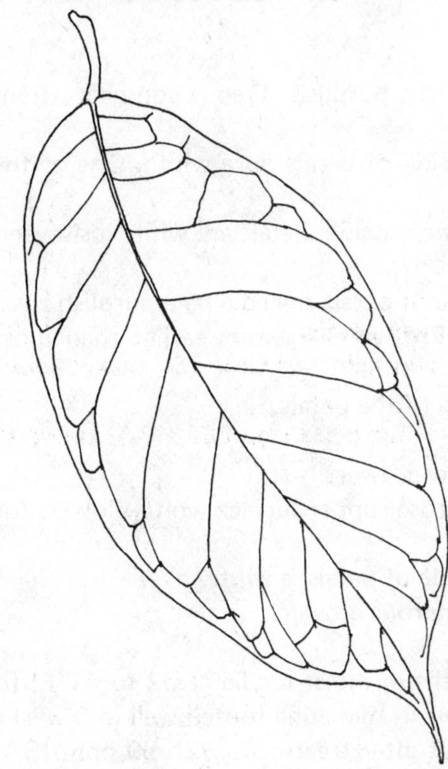

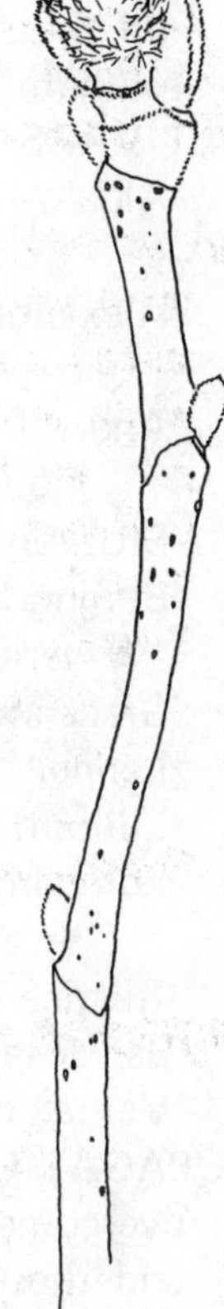

LEAVES: Alternate, simple, 3 to 6″ long, obovate to broad-oblong; apex narrow and more or less abruptly short-pointed; base taper-pointed.

BUDS: Pubescent, silky to the touch, 1/2 to 3/4″ long.

STEM: Brown, glabrous, with grayish lenticels, fragrant when crushed, with prominent stipular scars.

SIZE: 20 to 30′ in height with a variable spread, often about the same as height.

HARDINESS: Zone 5.

HABIT: Usually a large spreading shrub or small, low-branched tree with wide-spreading branches.

RATE: Medium, 10 to 15′ over a 10 year period.

TEXTURE: Coarse in leaf; perhaps medium to medium-coarse in winter.

BARK COLOR: A handsome gray on older trunks, usually smooth, often with Sapsucker damage.

LEAF COLOR: Medium to deep flat green in summer; sometimes (but not usually) an attractive brown in fall.

FLOWERS: Perfect, white to pink to purplish (variable when seed grown), usually the outside of the petals are flushed pinkish purple while the inside is whitish, 5 to 10″ diameter, campanulate, before the leaves in mid to late April; borne solitary.

FRUIT: Aggregate of follicles, August-September.

CULTURE: The following discussion applies to the other magnolias in this section with one notable exception. Magnolias have a fleshy root system with minimal lateral roots and root hairs and should be transplanted balled and burlapped or from a container; soil should be moist, deep, acid (pH 5.0 to 6.5), and supplemented with leaf mold or peat moss; prefer full sun but will withstand light shade; do not plant too deep; prune after flowering.

DISEASES AND INSECTS: Black mildews, leaf blight, leaf spots (at least 15 different ones), dieback, *Nectria* canker, leaf scab, wood decay, algal spot, magnolia scale, Tuliptree scale, and other scales. Although the list is quite impressive I have not witnessed many problems on magnolias in Central Illinois.

LANDSCAPE VALUE: Small specimen tree, often over-used but with ample justification; flowers when 2 to 4' tall; could be used in groupings, near large buildings or in large tree lawns; roots need ample room to develop; one serious problem is that late spring frosts and freezes often nip the emerging flower buds; in fact, 1 out of every 3 or 4 years would be a conservative estimate for almost total flower loss in Central Illinois.

CULTIVARS:

'Alba' — Flowers white, outside of petals colored very light purplish. Tree is compact. (Syn: 'Superba' or 'Alba Superba')

'Alexandrina' — Flowers flushed rose purple outside, inside of petals pure white. One of the larger and earlier flowering varieties.

'Andre LeRoy' — Flowers are dark pink to purplish on the outside. Petals are white inside and flowers decidedly cup-shaped.

'Brozzoni' — Flowers 10" across when fully open. Outside of petals tinged a pale purplish rose.

'Burgundy' — Flowers are deep purple color of Burgundy wine. Flowers earlier than most varieties.

'Grace McDade' — Flowers are white with pink at the base of the petals.

'Lennei' — Dark purplish-magenta flowers.

'Lilliputian' — Smaller flowers and habit than species. Slow grower.

'Lombardy Rose' — Lower surface of the petals is dark rose, upper surface white, flowers for several weeks.

'Rustica Rubra' — Rose-red flowers, 5 1/2" diameter; inside of petals is white.

'San Jose' — Large flowers, rosy-purple, fragrant, and a vigorous grower.

'Verbanica' — Late flowerer, slow grower.

PROPAGATION: Seed should be stratified for 3 to 6 months in moist media at 32 to 41°F. to overcome embryo dormancy. Softwood cuttings collected in mid-June rooted well in 3 weeks and those collected in late June rooted 100% in 35 days after treatment with 50 ppm IBA.

RELATED SPECIES: *M.* x *soulangiana*, Saucer Magnolia, is a hybrid species and the two parents are *M. denudata*, Yulan Magnolia, and *M. liliflora*, Lily Magnolia.

Magnolia denudata — Yulan Magnolia

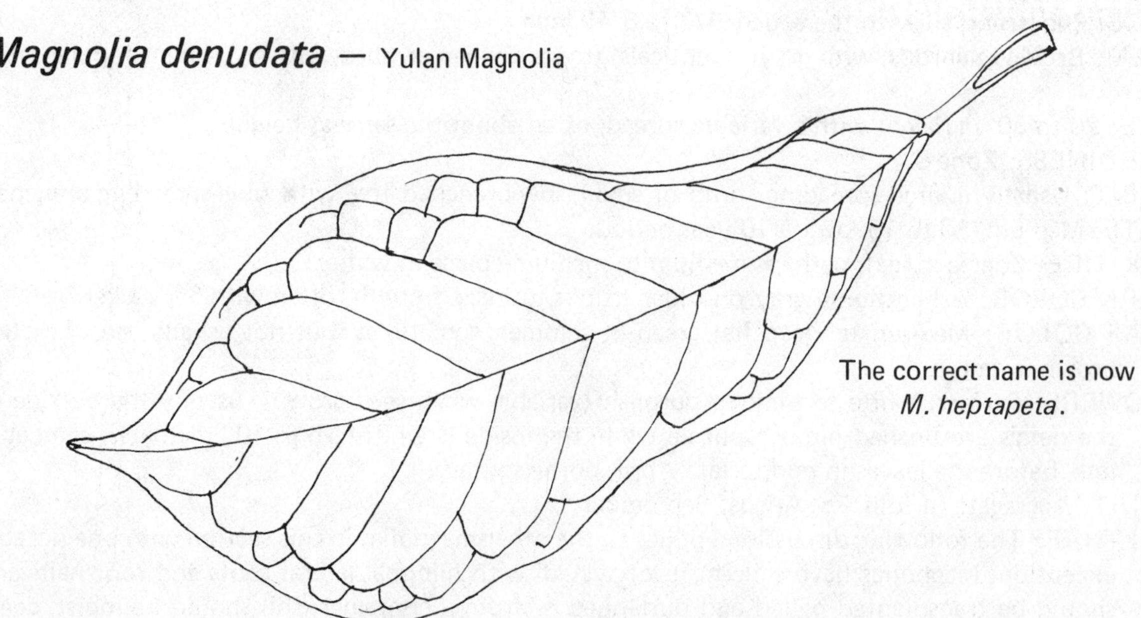

The correct name is now *M. heptapeta*.

LEAVES: Alternate, simple, entire, obovate to obovate-oblong, 4 to 6" long, short acuminate, tapering at base, sparingly pubescent above, light green beneath and minutely pubescent chiefly on the nerves and slightly reticulate.

Magnolia denudata, is a small tree growing 30 to 40' high with a similar spread. The flowers (9 petals) are white, fragrant, 5 to 6" across and open before *M. soulangiana* (early April) and are borne singly. The cultivar 'Purpurascens' has rose-red flowers outside, pink inside. Unfortunately this species responds to early warm spells and the flowers are often injured by late freezes. Very beautiful when unadulterated by the weather. Central China. 1789. Zone 5.

Magnolia x *loebneri*, Loebner Magnolia, is considered a cross between *M. stellata* x *M. kobus*. The tree can grow to 50' but 20 to 30' with a slightly greater spread is more logical. The flowers are white, 12 petals, fragrant; mid to late April; borne singly.

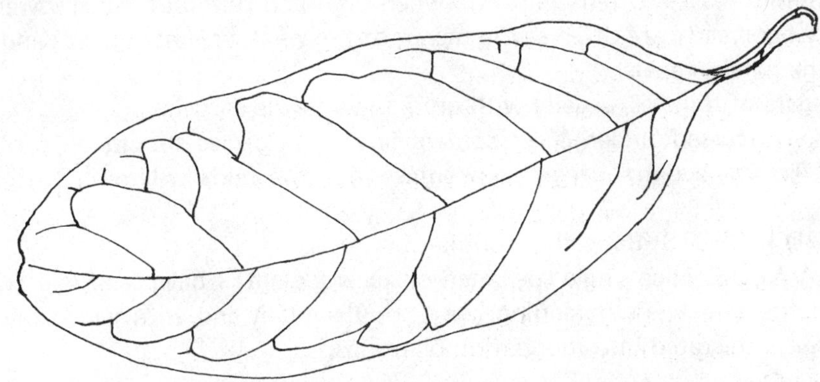

'Ballerina' — J. C. McDaniel introduced this clone. Superior flowering form as is 'Spring Song' which hold their good pure white petal color much longer than the species. 'Ballerina' rooted 88 percent in 8 weeks when treated with 10,000 ppm IBA/50 percent alcohol, quick dip and placed in sand under mist.

'Leonard Messel' — 12 petals, purplish pink on outside, white within.

'Merrill' — Flowers early, often after 5 years from seed, and *M. kobus* often takes 20 years. The petals number 15 and are slightly larger than those of *M. stellata*. Very vigorous tree growing about twice as fast as Star Magnolia.

Magnolia stellata — Star Magnolia

FAMILY: Magnoliaceae

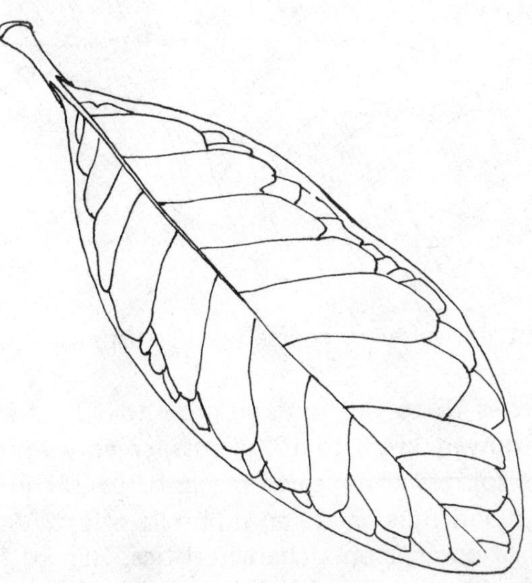

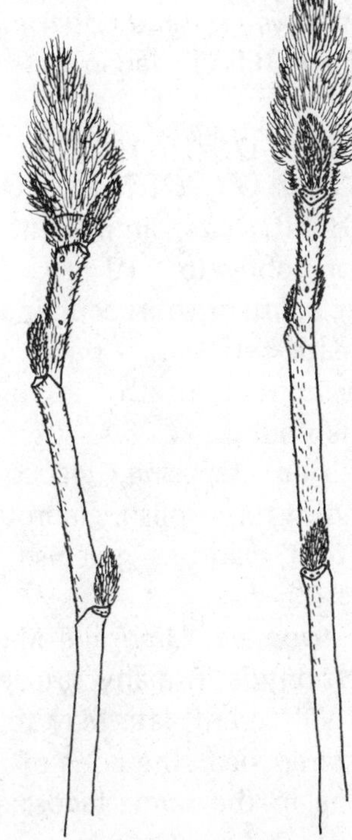

LEAVES: Alternate, simple, entire, obovate or narrow elliptic to oblong-obovate, 2 to 4" long, obtusely pointed or obtusish, gradually tapering at base, glabrous and dark green above, light green and reticulate beneath and glabrous or appressed-pubescent on the nerves.
BUDS: Densely pubescent, 1/3" to 1/2" long.
STEM: Slender, brown, glabrous, densely set.

SIZE: 15 to 20' in height with a spread of 10 to 15'.
HARDINESS: Zone 4.
HABIT: Dense shrub or small tree usually of thick constitution from the close-set leaves and stems.
RATE: Slow, 3 to 6' over a 5 to 6 year period.
TEXTURE: Medium in all seasons; possibly medium-fine.
LEAF COLOR: Dark green in summer; often yellow to bronze in fall.
FLOWERS: White, double, fragrant, 3" in diameter, 12 to 15 petals, early to mid April, solitary, flowers before leaves; often flowering when less than one foot tall. Flowers are delicate and since they open early are often at the mercy of the weather. Late freezes and wind can severely damage the petals (tepals).
FRUIT: Aggregate of follicles, usually with only a few fertile carpels.
CULTURE: As discussed under *M.* x *soulangiana* this species should be protected as much as possible. Try to avoid southern exposures since the buds will tend to open fastest in this location.
DISEASES AND INSECTS: Basically, trouble-free.
LANDSCAPE VALUE: Nice single specimen or accent plant; I have seen it used against red brick walls and the effect is outstanding; very popular plant and with justifiable reason; could be, and often is, integrated into foundation plantings.
CULTIVARS:

'Centennial' — Originated at Arnold Arboretum, larger petals (1 3/5 to 2" long), more open flower habit (5 1/2" across), and petals are without pink.

'Pink Star' — Flower buds and open flowers are pink, eventually fading to white.

'Rosea' — Flower buds pink, fading white at maturity.

'Rubra' — Flowers are purplish rose.

'Waterlily' — Buds pink, eventually white and slightly larger than those of the species. Upright, bushy grower.

PROPAGATION: Softwood cuttings collected in June and early July, treated with 1000 ppm IBA, rooted well in sand under mist.
NATIVE HABITAT: Japan. Introduced 1862. Zone 5.

Magnolia tripetala — Umbrella Magnolia

LEAVES: Alternate, simple, entire, oblong-obovate, 10 to 22" long, acute or short acuminate, cuneate at base, pale and pubescent beneath, at least while young.
BUDS: Long, tapering, glaucous, greenish to purplish, glabrous. 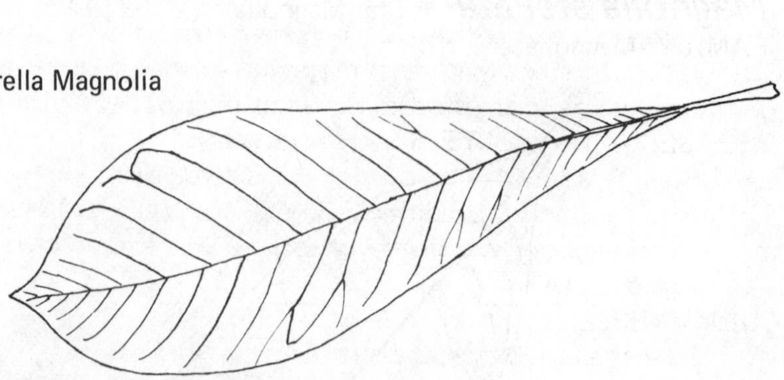
STEM: Stout, glabrous, greenish, leaf scar—large, oval; very coarse textured stems.

Magnolia tripetala, Umbrella Magnolia, reaches 15 to 30' but can grow to 40'. It is similar to *M. macrophylla* in many respects but the flowers are 6 to 10" across, creamy-white, and unpleasantly fragrant, late May to early June, solitary. The leaves reach 10 to 24" in length and are clustered near the ends of the branches and thus create an umbrella effect. Very difficult to utilize in the home landscape because of cumbersome characteristics. Ranges from Southern

Pennsylvania to Northern Georgia and Alabama, and west to Central Kentucky and Southwestern Arkansas. Introduced 1752. Zone 4. A hybrid between this and *M. virginiana* is called *M.* x *thompsoniana*. Professor J. C. McDaniel has selected a clone and named it 'Urbana'. The leaves are a lustrous green, the flowers creamy white, about 3 to 5" across, fragrant, and open over a long period from late May through June.

Magnolia virginiana — Sweetbay Magnolia, also called Laurel or Swamp Magnolia

FAMILY: Magnoliaceae

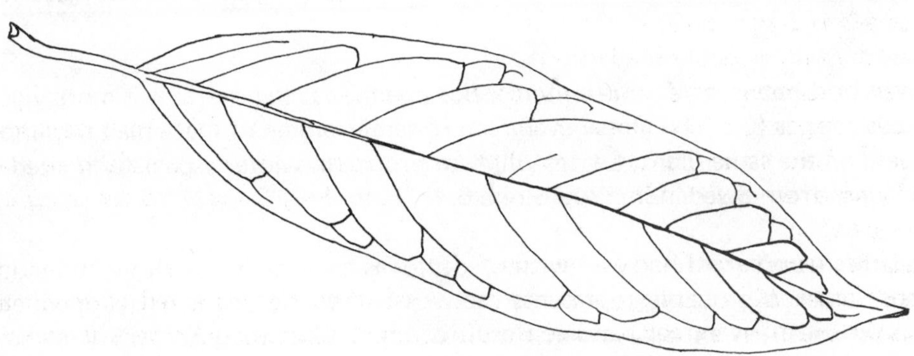

LEAVES: Alternate, simple, entire, semi-evergreen, elliptic to oblong-lanceolate, 3 to 5" long, acute or obtuse, broad cuneate at base, rarely rounded, dark lustrous green above and glaucous beneath.

BUDS: Sparsely pubescent, somewhat silky.

STEM: Green, slender, glaucous, with prominent diaphragms.

SIZE: In the North 10 to 20' by 10 to 20'. In the southern part of its range can grow to 60' or more.

HARDINESS: Zone 5.

HABIT: Small, multi-stemmed, deciduous shrub of loose, open, upright spreading habit in the north; semi-evergreen in the south.

RATE: Medium to fast.

TEXTURE: Medium in all seasons.

LEAF COLOR: Dark green and often lustrous above, distinctly glaucous beneath in summer.

FLOWERS: Creamy white, lemon-scented, 2 to 3" diameter, 9 to 12 petals, June, solitary; usually not produced in great abundance, often continuously on leafy shoots from June to September; apparently slow to flower in youth.

FRUIT: Aggregate of follicles, 2" long, dark red.

CULTURE: Different than most magnolias in that it does well in wet and even swampy soils. Also tolerates shade; detests drouth; seems to grow best in warm climates.

DISEASES AND INSECTS: See previous entry.

LANDSCAPE VALUE: I have always considered this a lovely, graceful, small patio or specimen tree for Zone 5 and 6 conditions. The foliage is handsome especially as the wind buffets the leaves around exposing the silvery underside. Winter damage is a distinct possibility in the northern range of Zone 5.

CULTIVARS:

var. *australis* — More pubescent branches and petioles.

PROPAGATION: Easy to root from softwood cuttings. Treat with 1000 ppm IBA, place in sand under mist.

NATIVE HABITAT: Massachusetts to Florida and Texas, near the coast. Introduced 1688.

Mahoberberis

X *Mahoberberis* is the result of intergeneric crosses between *Mahonia* and *Berberis*. The foliage varies from evergreen to semievergreen and from simple to compound on the same plant.

Flowers and fruits are sparse or nonexistent. Having seen the following hybrids I would have to rate them poor quality ornamentals. They do have some interest for the plant collector and are chiefly found in arboreta although, to my surprise, I discovered several plants in Cave Hill Cemetery, Louisville, Kentucky.

M. x *aquicandidula* resulted from a cross between *M. aquifolium* and *B. candidula*. The leaves are a leathery, dark glossy green, 1 to 1 1/2" long, with 3 to 5 sharp spines on each margin of the leaf. The foliage turns brilliant scarlet, claret and other red-purple combinations in the winter. The habit is somewhat open and stiff and not attractive. Will probably grow 3 to 6' at maturity. Zone 6, possibly 5.

M. x *aquisargentiae* is a hybrid between *M. aquifolium* x *B. sargentiana*. In general it is more vigorous than the previous species (6'). The glossy evergreen to semievergreen foliage may be simple or compound pinnate on the same plant. Leaves will turn bronze in winter especially if sited in full sun. First introduced from Sweden in 1948. Zone 6.

M. x *neubertii* is the first *Mahoberberis* I had ever witnessed. It was growing in the shrub collection at the Arnold Arboretum and probably represents the worst of the lot. It is leggy, open, and the leaves are of a dull, semi-evergreen nature. Result of crosses between *Berberis vulgaris* x *Mahonia aquifolium.* Grows 4 to 6' high. Zone 5.

Mahonia aquifolium — Oregongrapeholly or Oregon Grapeholly or Oregon Hollygrape depending on who or what is writing the common name.

FAMILY: Berberidaceae

LEAVES: Alternate, odd pinnate, 5 to 9 leaflets, ovate to oblong-ovate, 1 2/5 to 3" long, rounded or truncate at base, sinuately spiny-dentate, lustrous dark green above, rarely dull, extremely stiff and leathery, usually turning purplish in winter.

BUDS: Rather small except for the terminal which is ovoid with half-a-dozen exposed scales.

STEM: Roundish, stout; pith—large, pale, continuous; leaf scars—narrow, low, half encircling the stem.

SIZE: 3 to 6', will grow to 9' in height; spread of 3 to 5'.

HARDINESS: Zone 4 to 5.

HABIT: Limited branching evergreen shrub with upright, heavy stems, often stoloniferous in habit. Actually there seem to be two forms, one low and broad, dense and rounded; the other taller with upright branches, irregular and open, with lustrous foliage.

RATE: Slow, 2 to 3' over a 3 to 4 year period.

TEXTURE: Medium in summer; medium-coarse in winter.

LEAF COLOR: Reddish bronze when unfolding, changing to light, glossy yellow-green and finally lustrous dark green in summer; changing to purplish bronze in fall.

FLOWERS: Perfect, bright yellow, borne in fascicled, erect, terminal racemes, late April. Very handsome in flower. Has slightly fragrant flowers but not to the degree of *Mahonia bealei*.

FRUIT: True berry, blue-black, bloomy, 1/3" diameter, August-September; look like grapes and, therefore, the common name grape holly; fruit may persist into December.

CULTURE: Transplant balled and burlapped into moist, well-drained, acid soil; avoid hot dry soils and sweeping winds; sun but preferably shade; tends to brown up very badly in Central Illinois unless sited in a protected location.

DISEASES AND INSECTS: Leaf rusts, leaf spots, leaf scorch (physiological problem caused by sweeping winds and winter sun), barberry aphid, scale, and whitefly.

LANDSCAPE VALUE: Foundation plant, shrub border, specimen, shady area. Not the best of the broadleaves but certainly not the worst; has a place in the landscape but should be used with discretion.

CULTIVARS:

'Atropurpureum' — Leaves dark reddish purple in winter.

'Compactum' — Dwarf form with very glossy green leaves and a bronze winter color; grows about 24" to 36" in height, hardy to -10°F.

'Golden Abundance' — Heavy yellow flowers are borne against bright green foliage; plants are vigorous, erect and dense, and covered with blue berries (Zone 5).

'Mayhan Strain' — A dwarf form with glossy foliage and fewer leaflets per leaf and the leaflets arranged more closely on the rachis. The Mayhan Nursery who introduced this cultivar claims it is the result of 25 years of selection and the form can be maintained by seed propagation. Plants should grow between 20 and 30".

'Moseri' — Leaves in the first year pale green and more or less tinted with pink or red.

'Orange Flame' — Blazing bronze-orange new foliage, contrasts with wine-red or deep green older leaves, erect grower, stout stems, needs full sun.

PROPAGATION: Seed should be stratified for 90 days at 41°F and should not be allowed to dry out after it is collected. Softwood and hardwood cuttings root well, and division of the parent plant is an alternate method for increasing numbers.

RELATED SPECIES:

Mahonia bealei, Leatherleaf Mahonia, is a clumsy, upright, coarse evergreen shrub growing to 10 to 12'. The foliage is dull, dark, blue-green and very coriaceous; texture is coarse; flowers are lemon yellow and extremely fragrant, mid to late April, 3 to 6" long inflorescence; fruit is bluish black berry maturing in August. Native to China. Introduced 1845. Zone 6.

Mahonia nervosa, Cascades Mahonia, is a low, suckering, evergreen shrub rarely reaching more than 12 to 18"; flowers are yellow and borne in 8" racemes; fruit purplish blue, 1/4" diameter. Western North America.

Mahonia repens, Creeping Mahonia, is a low (10"), stoloniferous ground cover plant of stiff habit. Flowers are deep yellow, April, borne in small racemes, 1 to 3" long; fruit is black, grape-like, covered with a blue bloom, 1/4" diameter, August-September. British Columbia to Northern Mexico and California. Introduced 1822. Zone 5.

NATIVE HABITAT: British Columbia to Oregon. Introduced 1823.

Malus — Flowering Crabapple (Rosaceae)

I doubt if any treatment of flowering crabapples will ever be complete for as I write this someone is ready to introduce a new clone into the trade. The actual number of crabapple types is open to debate but across the country one could probably find 400 to 600 types. Crabapples tend to be cross fertile and freely hybridize. If one checked the parentage of many clones he or she would find that it was an open pollinated seedling, meaning that any number of trees within proximity of the fruiting tree could be the parent(s). We have a nice collection of crabapples on the University of Illinois campus and I have collected fruits from many types and enjoyed watching the potpourri of seedlings which resulted. The diversity of foliage colors (light green, dark green, various tints of purple); leaf morphology (serrate, lobed, incised); and vigor (some seedlings grow 3 to 4 times faster than others) can be attributed to the heterogenous genetic pool contributed by the many different parents. I was told a particular mass planting on campus was *M. hupehensis*, Tea Crabapple, a triploid which comes true-to-type from seed. The plants did not have the typical vase-shaped habit of the species and I found out why when the first group of seedlings developed. The leaves were different colors, shapes and sizes indicating anything but a species which breeds true from seed.

I have attempted to assemble a fairly representative list of crabapples which are often grown and available from nurseries. The salient characteristics of flower, fruit, size and diseases are included. Many crabapples are almost worthless because of extreme susceptibility to apple scab, rust, fire blight, leaf spot and powdery mildew. Unfortunately, the most susceptible types seem to be the most popular (i.e. Almey, Hopa, Eleyi, Bechtels, Red Silver). Considering the tremendous number of crabapples available only a handful or so meet the stringent requirements of excellent flower, fruit, habit and disease resistance. Many types are slightly susceptible to certain disease(s) and are perfectly acceptable provided their limitations are understood. I have used Dr. Lester Nichols, Pennsylvania State University, disease ratings based on his many years of collecting data regarding disease susceptibility. In certain instances no data were available and no evaluation is given. I have cross-checked many references in regard to the flower and fruit characters and strongly recommend the following references for further reading: TREES FOR AMERICAN GARDENS by Donald Wyman; TREES AND SHRUBS HARDY IN THE BRITISH ISLES, VOL II by W. J. Bean; CRAB-APPLES OF DOCUMENTED AUTHENTIC ORIGIN, National Arboretum Contribution No. 2 by Roland Jefferson; and FLOWERING CRABAPPLES by Arie den Boer.

The following twelve crabapples are my favorites (note the selection is not necessarily based on disease resistance as was strongly suggested in the above discussion).

M. x *astrosanguinea* — Carmine Crabapple
M. floribunda — Japanese Crabapple
M. 'Golden Hornet'
M. halliana var. parkmanii
M. hupehensis — Tea Crabapple
M. 'Makamik'
M. purpurea 'Lemoine'
M. sargentii — Sargent Crabapple
M. 'Selkirk'
M. 'Snowdrift'
M. 'White Angel'
M. 'White Cascade'

There are few other trees or shrubs which approach the beauty of a crabapple tree in full flower. Ornamental crabapples are an outstanding group of small flowering trees for Midwestern landscape planting. They are valued for foliage, flowers, fruit, and variations in habit or size. By using different species and cultivars, the flowering period can be extended from late April to late May and early June with colors ranging from white through purplish red.

The small fruits, borne in the fall, are also effective, with colors of red, yellow, and green. Other features of this group are the small size (rounded, horizontal, pendulous, fastigiate, and vase-shaped). Crabapples are suited for home grounds, schools, parks, commercial and public buildings, and highway plantings.

CHARACTERISTICS

Deciduous trees and shrubs, rarely half evergreen; most are between 15 and 25′ in height at maturity.

Shape: Range from low mound-like plants to narrow upright or pendulous types.

Branches: Alternate, upright, horizontal, or drooping, rarely with spinescent branches.

Buds: Ovoid, with several imbricate scales.

Flowers: White to pink or carmine to red to rose. Single flowers have 5 petals. Flowers occur in umbel or corymb-like racemes. Petals are small, suborbicular or obovate. Stamens 15 to 20, usually with yellow anthers. Ovary is inferior, 3 to 5 celled, styles present vary from 2 to 5, connate at base, perfect.

Fruit: A pome with persistent or deciduous calyx; colors range from red to yellow to green. If fruit is 2″ in diameter or less, it is a crabapple. If the fruit is larger than 2″, then it is classified as an apple.

HABITAT

There exist approximately 20 to 30 species of crabapples in the temperate regions of North America, Europe, and Asia. Currently, at least 100 to 200 types of crabapples are grown in North American nurseries, with at least 300 to 400 additional types in arboretums and botanical gardens (roughly 400 to 600 types).

GENERAL CULTURE

Crabapples are quite adaptable to varying soil conditions, but have been observed to do best in a heavy loam. The soil, regardless of type, should be well drained, moist, and acid (pH 5.0 to 6.5). Most crabapples are hardy in the Midwest and should be planted in full sun for best development of flowers and fruits. The Asiatic forms are much more resistant to insects and diseases than are the forms native to North America.

Generally crabapples require little pruning, but if any is done, it should be completed before early June. Most crabapples initiate flower buds for the next season in mid-June to early July and pruning at this time or later would result in decreased flower production the following year. Pruning may be done, however, to remove sucker growth, open up the center of the plant to light and air, to cut off out-of-place branches, and shape the tree.

PROPAGATION

Practically all flowering crabs are self-sterile and are propagated by budding, grafting, or from softwood cuttings. Two crabapples are, however, commonly propagated from seed and come entirely true to type; *hupenhensis* and *toringoides*. The Sargent Crabapple is also frequently propagated from seed, but a considerable variation in size occurs. The seeds must be after-ripened for 2 to 3 months at 60-65°F to overcome radical dormancy and then maintained at 40-45°F for 2 to 3 months to overcome epicotyl dormancy.

Crabapples are often grafted, using a whip graft, or are budded in mid to late August. Understocks include the common apple; *M. robusta* and *M. sieboldii* seedlings have proven acceptable as has *M. baccata* where hardiness is a factor. In addition to grafting and budding, a few crabapples such as Arnold, Carmine, Sargent, or Japanese Flowering are propagated from softwood cuttings taken from mid-June through July.

DISEASES AND INSECTS

Fireblight. The diseased plants have the appearance of being scorched by fire. The first visible signs of infection are often a drying up of the tips of young shoots and bud-clusters. The disease is caused by bacteria which are spread by aphids, leaf hoppers, and even bees. Carelessness in handling diseased leaves and branches, and failure to adequately disinfect pruning equipment contributes to the spread of the disease. Control of this disease is difficult. Cultural control practices such as pruning out diseased branches and avoiding excessive nitrogen fertilization should be employed.

Cedar Apple Rust (Asiatic varieties are resistant). The disease appears on apple leaves in May as yellow leaf spots which subsequently enlarge, resulting in heavy leaf drop. The disease has as an alternate host, Redcedars *(Juniperus virginiana).* Galls appear on Redcedars in early April and spores produced by these galls later infect apple trees.

Cultural control is possible by keeping a minimum distance of 500′ between apple and Redcedar plants. The disease can be prevented from spreading to apples by spraying the Redcedar galls when they form in early April with either 2 ppm Acti-Dione, or Cycloheximide (1 actispray tablet in 2 gallons of water). Crabapples can be sprayed with ferbam (Fermate 2 lb/100 gallons water) when the galls appear on Junipers (about mid-April to mid-May). Make 4 to 5 applications at 7 to 10 day intervals.

Apple Scab. The native North American species and hybrids and the native apple (*Malus pumila*) are quite susceptible to this disease. Fruits show darkened, leathery spots with many small cracks. The leaves also have darkened spots which may look black or velvety. For control of scab use liquid lime sulfur in late March before flowers show any color, and repeat the application in a week or ten day intervals until petals have dropped and the fruits have set. Liquid lime sulfur will leave an unsightly white residue on surfaces and should be used when wind is negligible. As a substitute for liquid lime sulfur, Captan or Cyprex can be used. Apply both when leaves start to open and continue weekly applications through June.

Canker. Two species of fungi cause cankers on the trunks of crabapples. They often gain entrance through wounds made by lawn mowers and other maintenance equipment.

Scale. Three types, San Jose, Oyster Shell, or Putman. Adequate control can be obtained by either using a dormant oil (1/15) as a spray before bud break or with malathion (2 or 3 applications at 1 1/2-4 lbs/100 gallons water) at mid-May when the scales are in the crawling stage.

Borers (may be a serious problem). For cultural control, keep the plants growing well with adequate fertilization and watering practices.

Aphids. A serious problem generally only on native species. Adequate control can be obtained by spraying the trees with malathion at the rate of 2 1/2-4 lbs/100 gallons water.

Other insects include alder lace bug, leafhoppers, several foliage feeding caterpillars, and European red mite, all of which can be controlled.

Malus 'Adams'
FLOWERS: Single, 1 1/2" diameter, carmine bud and flowers, fading to dull pink, annual.
FRUIT: Red, 5/8" diameter.
HABIT: Rounded and dense, 24'.
DISEASES: Very resistant, proving to be a superior crabapple.

Malus 'Aldenham'
FLOWERS: Single and semidouble, expanding buds maroon-red, open purplish red fading to deep purplish pink, 1 4/5" across.
FRUIT: Dark maroon-red to maroon-purple, shaded side green to bronze, 4/5" diameter.

Malus 'Almey'
FLOWERS: Single, expanding buds deep maroon or purple-red, open purple-red with claw and base of petals and center vein pale lavender to nearly white, 1 4/5" diameter.
FRUIT: Maroon, approximately 1" across.
DISEASES: Very susceptible to diseases, especially scab.

Malus x *arnoldiana (floribunda* x *baccata)*
FLOWERS: Single, buds rose-red, flower phlox pink outside fading to white inside, 2" diameter, fragrant, annual or alternate.
FRUIT: Yellow and red, 5/8" diameter.
HABIT: Mounded, dense branching. 20'.
DISEASES: Susceptible to scab and fireblight.

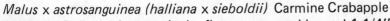

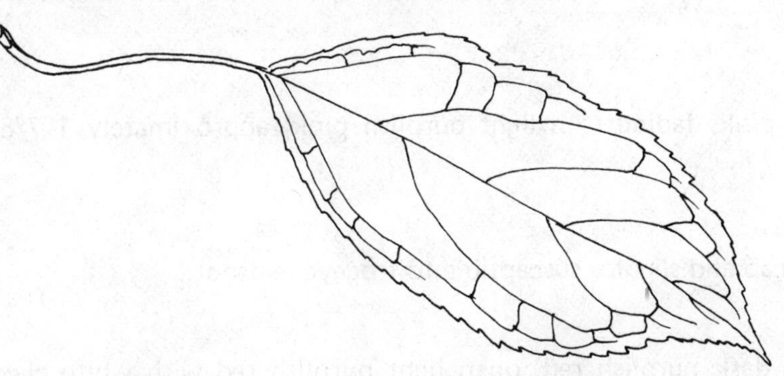
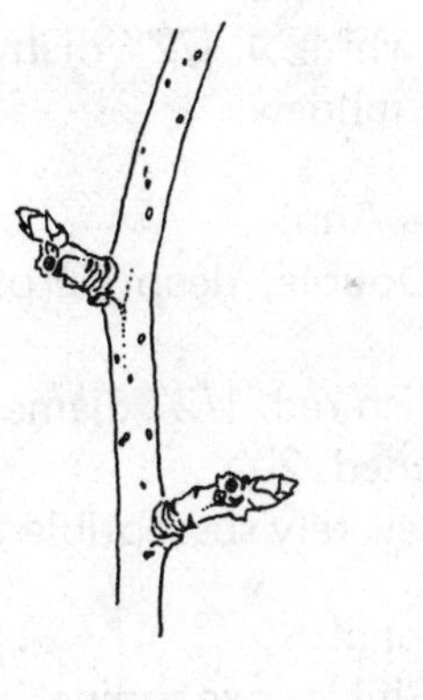
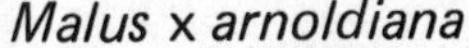
Malus x *arnoldiana*

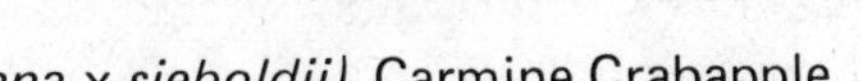
Malus x *astrosanguinea (halliana* x *sieboldii)* Carmine Crabapple
FLOWERS: Bud crimson, single, flower rose madder and 1 1/4" diameter, annual.
FRUIT: Dark red, 3/8" diameter, not ornamental.
HABIT: Mounded, almost shrub-like, dense branching, 15 to 20', very lovely small crabapple.
DISEASES: Very resistant to scab; variable to fireblight.

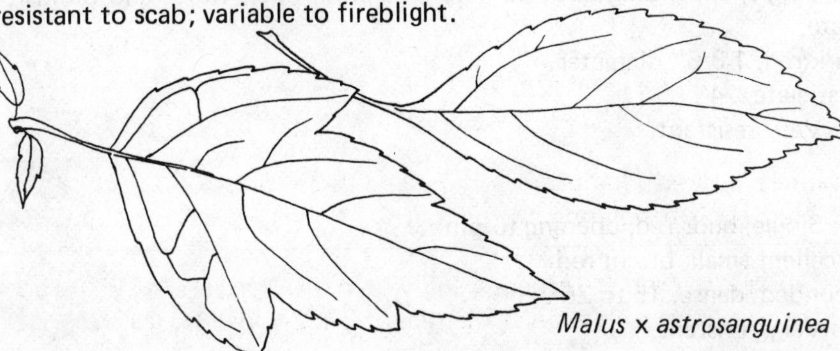
Malus x *astrosanguinea*

Malus baccata Siberian Crabapple
FLOWERS: Single, white, 1 1/2" diameter, very fragrant, annual.
FRUIT: Bright red or yellow, 3/8" thick.
HABIT: Tree, 20 to 50' high, forming a rounded, wide-spreading head of branches.
DISEASES: Susceptible to scab; variable to fireblight.

M. b. 'Columnaris'
FLOWERS: Single, open pure white, 1 3/5" across, buds creamy-white.
FRUIT: Yellow with a red cheek, approximately 1/2" diameter.
HABIT: Distinctly upright columnar tree probably 4 to 5 times as tall as wide. Does not seem to flower and fruit well, at least this was true for few trees I have observed.
DISEASES: Supposedly very susceptible to fireblight.

M.b. var. *gracilis*
White flowers, 1 3/8" diameter, more dense than the species with tips of the branches slightly pendulous.

M.b. 'Jackii'
FLOWERS: Single, expanding buds white with touch of pink, open pure white, approximately 1 3/5" diameter.
FRUIT: Purplish or maroon-red, tan on shaded side, 1/2" diameter.
HABIT: An upright type with leaves of a remarkably deep green for a crabapple; probably grow to 20 to 40'.
DISEASES: Slightly susceptible to fireblight and powdery mildew.

M.b. var. *mandshurica*
Flowers white, 1 1/2" diameter, the first crabapple to flower. Slightly susceptible to scab and powdery mildew.

Malus 'Barbara Ann'
FLOWERS: Double, deep purplish pink, fading to a light purplish pink, approximately 1 7/8" diameter.
FRUIT: Purplish red, 1/2" diameter.
HABIT: Rounded, 20'.
DISEASES: Severely susceptible to scab and slightly susceptible to frogeye leafspot.

Malus 'Baskatong'
FLOWERS: Single, expanding buds dark purplish red, open light purplish red with white claw, 1 4/5" diameter.
FRUIT: Dark purplish red with many russet marks, 1" diameter.
HABIT: Tree 30'.
DISEASES: Very resistant.

Malus 'Beauty'
FLOWERS: Single, expanding buds pink to rose-pink, open white and pinkish white, 2" diameter, alternate.
FRUIT: Dark red, 1 3/5" diameter.
HABIT: Fastigiate, 24'.
DISEASES: Very resistant.

Malus 'Beverly'
FLOWERS: Single, buds red, opening to pink.
FRUIT: Excellent small, bright red.
HABIT: Rounded, dense, 15 to 25'.
DISEASES: Very resistant.

Malus 'Blanche Ames'
FLOWERS: Semidouble, 1 1/2" diameter, pink and white, annual.
FRUIT: Yellow, 1/4" diameter.
HABIT: Rounded and dense (24').
DISEASES: Resistant to scab.

Malus 'Bob White'
FLOWERS: Buds cherry colored, flowers fade to white, 1" diameter, fragrant, alternate or annual.
FRUIT: Yellow, 5/8" diameter.
HABIT: Rounded, dense branching, 20'.
DISEASES: Resistant to scab.

Malus 'Coralburst'
FLOWERS: Double, coral-pink buds open to double rose-pink flowers.
HABIT: Dainty, dwarf type forming a rounded bushy head, grows to 8'.
DISEASES: Resistant to scab, mildew and fireblight.

Malus coronaria Wild Sweet Crabapple
FLOWERS: Single, white tinged with rose, fragrant like violets, 1 1/2 to 2" diameter, pink in bud.
FRUIT: Yellowish green, 1 to 1 1/2" diameter, orange-shaped, very harsh and acid.
HABIT: A tree 20 to 30' with a short trunk and a wide spreading head of branches.
DISEASES: Extremely susceptible to diseases.

M.c. 'Charlottae'
FLOWERS: Double (12-18 petals), expanding buds flesh pink, open pale pink, 2" diameter, annual.
FRUIT: Dark green, 1 1/5" diameter.
DISEASES: Susceptible to diseases.

M.c. 'Neuwlandiana'
FLOWERS: Double, expanding buds rose-red, open pink, 2 1/5" diameter, annual.
FRUIT: Yellowish green, 1 3/5" diameter.

Malus 'Dolgo'
FLOWERS: White, 1 3/4" diameter, fragrant, flowering well in alternate years.
FRUIT: Bright red, 1 1/4" diameter.
HABIT: Open, but vigorous, 40'.
DISEASES: Very resistant.

Malus 'Donald Wyman'
FLOWERS: Single, expanding buds pink, opening to white.
FRUIT: Glossy bright red, approximately 3/8" diameter.
DISEASES: Slightly susceptible to powdery mildew.

Malus 'Dorothea'
FLOWERS: Semidouble, 10 to 16 petals, expanding buds carmine, open-rose pink not fading to white, approximately 1 4/5" diameter.
FRUIT: Yellow, approximately 1/2" diameter.
HABIT: Rounded, dense branching, 25'
DISEASES: Severely susceptible to scab and fireblight, slightly susceptible to powdery mildew.

Malus 'Eleyi' (often listed as *M. purpurea* cv. Eleyi)
Similar to 'Almey'. Very susceptible to disease.

Malus 'Evelyn'
FLOWERS: Single, expanding buds deep rose-red, open rose-red to deep rose-red, 1 2/5" diameter.
FRUIT: Greenish yellow and red, 1 2/5" diameter.
HABIT: Erect, 20'.
DISEASES: Very resistant.

Malus 'Flame'
FLOWERS: Single, white, 1 1/2" diameter, expanding buds pink, open white, annual.
FRUIT: Bright red, 4/5" across.
HABIT: Rounded, dense, 25'.
DISEASES: Extremely susceptible to diseases.

Malus floribunda Japanese Flowering Crabapple
FLOWERS: Buds deep pink to red, flowers gradually fading white, 1-1 1/2" diameter, fragrant, annual.
FRUIT: Yellow and red, 3/8" diameter.
HABIT: Broad-rounded and densely branched, 15-25', one of the best crabapples, one that all others are compared to.
DISEASES: Slightly susceptible to scab and powdery mildew; moderately susceptible to fireblight.

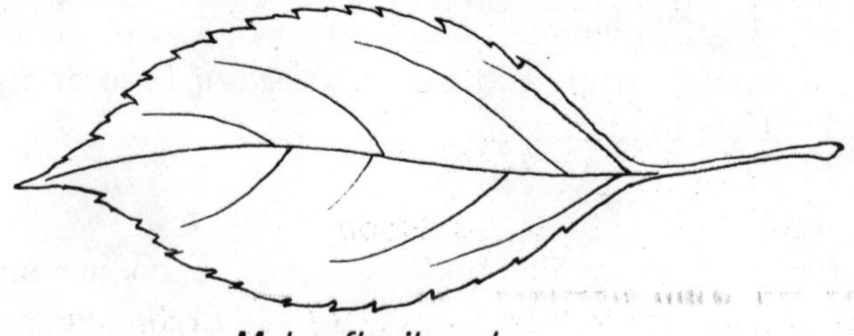

Malus floribunda

Malus 'Gibbs Golden Gage'
FLOWERS: Single, buds pink, open white.
FRUIT: Yellow, 1" diameter.
DISEASES: Resistant.

Malus 'Golden Hornet'
FLOWERS: Single, white, 1 1/5" diameter.
FRUIT: Yellow, 1" diameter, very freely borne and remaining long on the tree.
DISEASES: Resistant to scab.

Malus 'Gorgeous'
FLOWERS: Single, 1 1/4" diameter, pink buds followed by white flowers, annual.
FRUIT: Glossy red, 1" diameter, abundantly produced.
HABIT: Dense, rounded, 25-30'.
DISEASES: Resistant to scab.

Malus 'Gwendolyn'
FLOWERS: Single, pink flowers.
FRUIT: Red.
DISEASES: Resistant.

Malus halliana var. *parkmanii*
FLOWERS: Double (15 petals), neyron rose, 1 1/4" diameter, annual.
FRUIT: Dull red, 1/4" diameter.
HABIT: Upright, almost vase-shaped, dense branching, 15'.
DISEASES: Resistant to scab.

Malus 'Henry F. Dupont'
FLOWERS: Single and semidouble (5-10 petals), expanding buds purplish red to deep rose-red, open light purplish pink, fading to pale magenta, 1 1/2" diameter, annual.
FRUIT: Brownish red, 1/2" diameter.
HABIT: Low rounded, 20'.
DISEASES: Severely susceptible to scab and fireblight, slightly susceptible to powdery mildew.

Malus 'Hopa'
FLOWERS: Single, expanding buds dark red to purplish red, open rose-pink with almost white star in the center, approximately 1 1/2 to 2" diameter.
FRUIT: Bright red or crimson, usually yellowish on shaded side, approximately 3/4 to 1" diameter.
HABIT: 20 to 25' forming a dense rounded crown.
DISEASES: This, along with the old standards 'Almey' and 'Eleyi' should be on the discard list because of extreme disease susceptibility especially to apple scab. In 1973 and 1974 the trees were defoliated by early August.

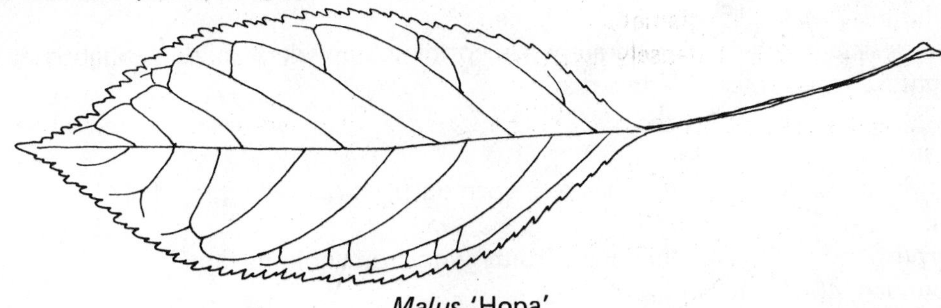

Malus 'Hopa'

Malus hupehensis (triploid, comes true to type from seed) Tea Crabapple
FLOWERS: Deep pink buds, gradually fading white, 1 1/2" diameter, fragrant, alternate.
FRUIT: Greenish yellow to red, 3/8" diameter.
HABIT: Vase-shaped, decidedly picturesque, 20-25'.
DISEASES: Severely susceptible to fireblight; have not noticed any problems with trees on University of Illinois campus.

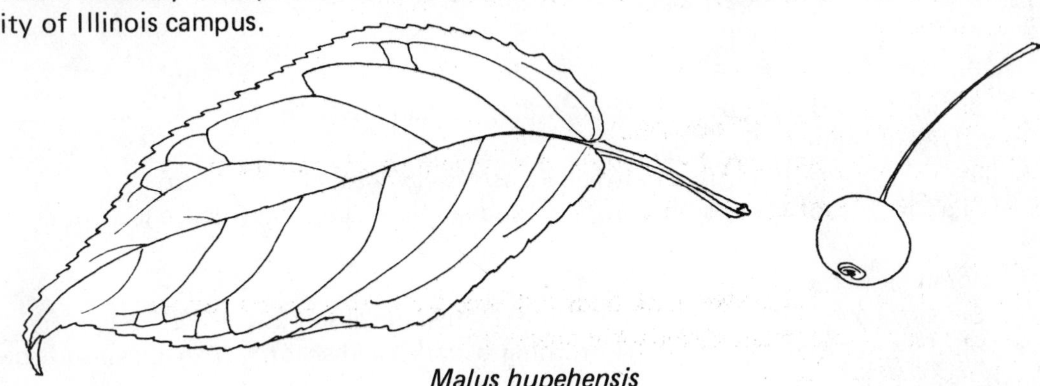

Malus hupehensis

Malus 'Indian Magic'
FLOWERS: Single, deep pink.
FRUIT: Small glossy red, changing to orange, persisting.
DISEASES: Moderately susceptible to scab.

Malus ioensis 'Plena'
FLOWERS: Double (33 petals), buds and flowers pink, 2" diameter, fragrant.
FRUIT: Green, 1 1/8" diameter, few produced.
HABIT: Rounded, open, 30'.
DISEASES: Extremely susceptible to diseases.

Malus 'Katherine'
FLOWERS: Double (15-24 petals), expanding buds deep pink, open pink fading to white, 2" diameter, annual.
FRUIT: Yellow with a red cheek, 2/5" diameter.
HABIT: Loose and open, 20'.
DISEASES: Resistant to scab and fireblight.

Malus 'Lady Northcliffe'
FLOWERS: Single, expanding buds rose-red, open pale pink fading to white, 1" diameter.
FRUIT: Yellow and red, 3/5" diameter.
DISEASES: Resistant to scab.

Malus 'Liset'
FLOWERS: Single, expanding buds dark crimson, approximately 1 1/2" diameter.
FRUIT: Dark crimson to maroon-red, glossy, approximately 1/2" diameter.
HABIT: Columnar, dense, 15'.
DISEASES: Resistant to scab, moderately susceptible to powdery mildew. Slightly susceptible to fireblight, resistant to cedar apple rust.

Malus 'Makamik'
FLOWERS: Single, expanding buds dark red, open purplish red fading to a lighter tint, 2" diameter, annual.
FRUIT: Purplish red, 3/4" diameter, good fruiter with fruits holding late.
HABIT: Rounded, 40', bronze foliage.
DISEASES: Resistant to scab, moderately susceptible to mildew, slightly susceptible to fireblight.

Malus 'Marshall Oyama'
FLOWERS: Single pink buds followed by white flowers, 1 5/8" diameter, annual.
FRUIT: Yellow and red, 1" diameter.
HABIT: Narrowly upright.
DISEASES: Resistant to scab and fireblight.

Malus 'Mary Potter'
FLOWERS: Single, expanding buds pink, open white, 1" diameter.
FRUIT: Red, 1/2" diameter.
HABIT: Similar to *M. sargentii* (a cross between *M. astrosanguinea* x *M. sargentii*).
DISEASES: Slightly susceptible to scab, powdery mildew, fireblight, and frogeye leaf spot.

Malus 'Oekonomierat Echtermeyer'
FLOWERS: Single, expanding buds deep purplish red, open purplish pink, 1 3/5" diameter.
FRUIT: Purplish red before ripening, later turning a dark reddish brown to greenish brown, 1" diameter.
HABIT: Semi-weeping, 15'.
DISEASES: Extremely susceptible to diseases.

Malus 'Ormiston Roy'
FLOWERS: Single, expanding buds rose-red turning pale rose-pink, open white, 1 3/5" diameter, annual.
FRUIT: Orange-yellow with reddish blush.
DISEASES: Resistant.

Malus 'Pink Spires'
FLOWERS: Pink.
FRUIT: Purplish red.
HABIT: Upright grower with copper-colored fall foliage.
DISEASES: Moderately susceptible to scab, slightly to fireblight and leaf spot.

Malus 'Prince Georges'
FLOWERS: Double (50-61 petals), expanding buds deep rose-pink, open light rose-pink, 2" diameter, annual.
FRUIT: Not known to produce fruit.
HABIT: Upright, dense, 15 to 20'.
DISEASES: Resistant.

Malus 'Profusion'
FLOWERS: Single, expanding buds deep red, open purplish red fading to purplish pink, 1 3/5" across.
FRUIT: Oxblood red, 1/2" diameter.
DISEASES: Moderately susceptible to powdery mildew.

Malus pumila 'Niedzwetzkyana'
Young leaves, flowers, fruit including the flesh, and bark and wood of branches red. This form is a parent of many crabapples. Resistant to fireblight and variable resistance to scab.

Malus purpurea 'Lemoine'
FLOWERS: Single and semidouble, expanding buds dark red, open purple-red to crimson fading to lighter shades, 1 1/2" diameter, annual.
FRUIT: Purplish red, 5/8" diameter.
HABIT: Dense, 25', leaves purplish when unfolding and becoming deep green later.
DISEASES: Highly resistant to scab and fireblight.

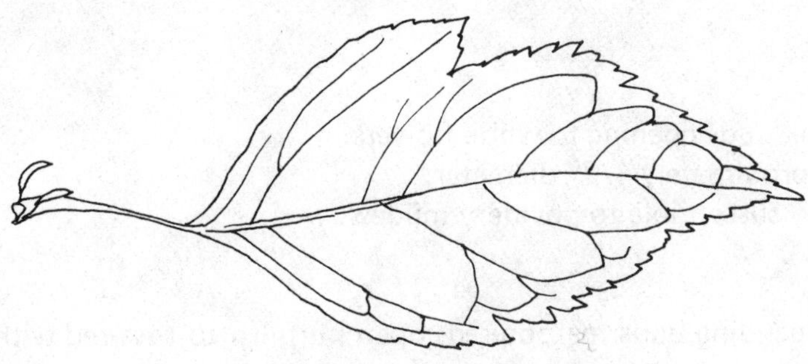

Malus purpurea 'Lemoine'

Malus 'Radiant'
FLOWERS: Single, expanding buds deep red, open deep pink, annual.
FRUIT: Bright red, approximately 1/2" diameter.
HABIT: Compact upright grower, 25 to 30'. Young leaves purplish changing to green.
DISEASES: Very susceptible to scab.

Malus 'Red Jade'
FLOWERS: Single, expanding buds deep pink, open white, 1 3/5" diameter, alternate.
FRUIT: Glossy red, 1/2" in diameter, birds like the fruits.
HABIT: Weeping, 15' ±, of a graceful pendulous nature.
DISEASES: Moderately susceptible to scab and powdery mildew.

Malus 'Red Jewel'
FLOWERS: White, single.
FRUIT: Bright cherry red, less than 1/2" diameter, persisting with color until mid-December.
DISEASES: Moderately susceptible to scab.

Malus 'Red Silver'
FLOWERS: China rose color, 1 1/2" diameter, single, alternate.
FRUIT: Purplish red, 3/4" diameter.
HABIT: Dense, 30'.
DISEASES: Extremely susceptible to scab.

Malus 'Red Splendor'
FLOWERS: Single, expanding buds rose-red, open pink to rose-pink, 1 4/5" diameter.
FRUIT: Red, 3/5" diameter.
DISEASES: Slightly susceptible to scab; moderately to fireblight.

Malus x *robusta*
FLOWERS: Single and semidouble, expanding buds white with trace of pink, open pure white, 1 3/5" diameter, alternate.
FRUIT: Yellow and red to dark crimson, 1" diameter.
HABIT: Oval-shaped, dense branching, 40'.
DISEASES: Resistance to scab; variable to fireblight.

M. r. 'Erecta'
Upright habit when young, with maturity opens up as side branches are often weighted down with fruits.

M. r. 'Persicifolia'
Excellent red ornamental fruits, 3/4" diameter. Hang on late in season, slightly susceptible to scab.

Malus 'Rocki'
FLOWERS: Single, pink buds opening to white flowers.
FRUIT: Bright red, approximately 1/2" diameter.
DISEASES: Moderately susceptible to powdery mildew.

Malus 'Rosseau'
FLOWERS: Single, expanding buds maroon-red, open purplish to rose-red with white claw, 1 3/5" diameter.
FRUIT: Carmine to light jasper red, 1" diameter, annual.
HABIT: Rounded, dense, 40'.
DISEASES: Resistant to scab and fireblight.

Malus 'Royal Ruby'
FLOWERS: Double, red-pink, 1 to 2" across, annual.
FRUIT: Red, 1/2" across, limitedly produced.
HABIT: Vigorous tree to 10 to 15' with dark green foliage.
DISEASES: Severely susceptible to scab.

Malus 'Royalty'
FLOWERS: Single, crimson, almost purple, annual.
FRUITS: Dark red, 5/8" diameter.
HABIT: 15', one of the best purple-foliaged forms; leaves are glossy purple in Spring, a purple, tinted green in mid-Summer, and brilliant purple in Fall.
DISEASES: Severely susceptible to scab, slightly susceptible to fireblight.

Malus sargentii Sargent Crabapple
FLOWERS: Single, red in bud opening white, 1/2" diameter, fragrant, annual.
FRUIT: Dark red, 1/4" diameter, birds like them.
HABIT: Mounded, dense branching, wide spreading, 6-8' high, twice that in spread.
DISEASES: Slightly susceptible to scab, fireblight and leaf spot.

M. s. 'Rosea'
Similar to species except flower buds darker red.

Malus x *scheideckeri*
FLOWERS: Double (10 petals), pale pink, 1 1/2" diameter, annual.
FRUIT: Yellow to orange, 5/8" diameter.
HABIT: Upright, dense, 20'.
DISEASES: Extremely susceptible to diseases.

Malus 'Selkirk'
FLOWERS: Rose-red, 1 1/2" diameter, single, annual.
FRUIT: Glossy purplish red, 4/5" diameter.
HABIT: Open, somewhat vase-shaped, 25', extremely flower bud hardy, has flowered profusely in 1973, '74 and '75. Looks like a superior crab for the Midwest.
DISEASES: Moderately susceptible to scab and powdery mildew.

Malus sieboldii var. *arborescens*
FLOWERS: Pink buds, fading white, fragrant, 3/4" diameter.
FRUIT: Yellow to red, 1/2" diameter, bearing annually.
HABIT: Mounded, dense branching, 30'.

Malus sieboldii 'Fuji'
FLOWERS: Double, expanding buds purplish red, open greenish white with occasional traces of purplish red, approximately 1 1/2" diameter.
FRUIT: Orange, approximately 1/2" diameter.
HABIT: Oval, 25'.
DISEASES: Slightly susceptible to powdery mildew.

Malus sieboldii var. *zumi*
FLOWERS: Single, pink in bud becoming white after opening, 1 to 1 1/4" diameter, alternate.
FRUIT: Red, 1/2" diameter.
HABIT: Small tree of pyramidal habit.
DISEASES: Moderately susceptible to scab.

Malus sieboldii var. *zumi* 'Calocarpa'
FLOWERS: Single, expanding buds deep red, open white to pinkish white, 1 2/5" diameter, fragrant, annual, at least based on flower production in 1973, '74 and '75 on our campus trees.
FRUIT: Bright red, 1/2" diameter.
HABIT: Pyramidal, dense branching, 25'.
DISEASES: Slightly susceptible to scab, powdery mildew and severely susceptible to fireblight.

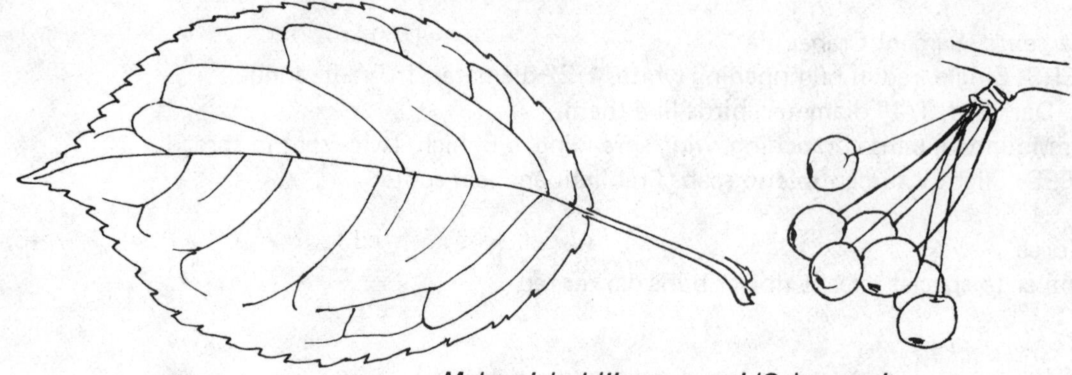

Malus sieboldii var. *zumi* 'Calocarpa'

Malus 'Sissipuk'
FLOWERS: Single, expanding buds deep carmine, open rose-pink fading to pale pink, 1 1/8" diameter, annual.
FRUIT: Dark maroon-purple to oxblood red, 1" diameter.
HABIT: Rounded, 40'.
DISEASES: Resistant to scab and fireblight.

Malus 'Snowdrift'
FLOWERS: Single, expanding buds red, open white, 1" diameter, annual.
FRUIT: Orange-red, 2/5" diameter.
HABIT: Rounded, dense, good vigorous grower, 15 to 20'.
DISEASES: Slightly susceptible to scab and fireblight.

Malus spectabilis Chinese Crabapple
FLOWERS: Often double, deep rosy-red in bud, paling to blush-tint when fully open, 2" diameter.
FRUIT: Yellow, 3/4 to 1" diameter, poor fruiter.
HABIT: A tree to 30' forming a rounded head of branches as wide as high.

Malus spectabilis 'Riversii'
FLOWERS: Pink, double (9-12 petals), 2" diameter, alternate bearer.
FRUIT: Green, 1 1/4" diameter, not effective.
HABIT: Open, 25'.
DISEASES: Highly resistant to fireblight; variable to scab.

Malus 'Spring Snow'
FLOWERS: White.
FRUIT: Few to none.
HABIT: Rounded, 20'.
DISEASES: Severely susceptible to scab. Slightly susceptible to cedar apple rust and fireblight.

Malus 'Tanner'
FLOWERS: Single, white, 1 1/2" diameter.
FRUIT: Red, 5/8" diameter, alternate.
HABIT: Low, 20'.

Malus 'Tina'
FLOWERS: Single, white with yellow centers, pink to red buds.
FRUIT: Red, small.
HABIT: Supposedly a dwarf Sargent type with low spreading form, 12 to 18" plant was 3 to 3 1/2' wide.

Malus toringoides var. *macrocarpa*
FLOWERS: White, 3/4" diameter, fragrant, alternate, expanding buds pink or pinkish white.
FRUIT: Pear shaped, 1" diameter, yellow on shaded side, red on sunny side.
HABIT: Upright, pyramidal branching, dense.
DISEASES: Resistant to scab and rust.

Malus 'Van Eseltine'
FLOWERS: Double (13-19 petals), expanding buds deep rose-red to rose-pink, often pink fading to pale pink, 2" diameter, alternate bearer.
FRUIT: Yellow, with brown or light carmine cheek, 3/4" diameter.
HABIT: Narrowly upright, 20', vase-shaped crown.
DISEASES: Severely susceptible to scab and fireblight.

Malus 'Vanguard'
FLOWERS: Single, rose-pink, 2" diameter, annual.
FRUIT: Red, 3/4" diameter.
HABIT: Dense, somewhat vase-shaped, 18'.

Malus 'White Angel' (also termed 'Inglis')
FLOWERS: Single, 1" diameter, pure white, heavy flowerer, expanding buds pink.
FRUIT: Glossy red, 3/4 to 1" diameter, heavy fruiter, almost overbears.
HABIT: Tends toward a rounded tree; has not been around long enough to adequately evaluate.

Malus 'White Candle'
FLOWERS: Semi-double, white, one reference said pale pink, 1 1/2" diameter, borne in great quantity.
FRUIT: Red, 5/8" diameter, limitedly produced.
HABIT: 12 to 15' by 2 to 3' wide, good upright type.
DISEASES: Slightly susceptible to scab and fireblight.

Malus 'White Cascade'
FLOWERS: Single, white, buds crimson red and flowers uniformly from top to bottom, gives the appearance of a cascading waterfall.
FRUIT: Yellow, small.
HABIT: 10 to 15', gracefully pendulous.
DISEASES: Resistant, based on current data; has not been extensively tested.

Malus 'Winter Gold'
FLOWERS: Single, expanding buds deep carmine, open white, 1 1/5" diameter, alternate.
FRUIT: Yellow, occasionally with orange to pink blush, 1/2" diameter.
HABIT: Tree, 30'.
DISEASES: Slightly susceptible to powdery mildew and fireblight.

Malus yunnanensis
FLOWERS: White, 3/5" diameter.
FRUIT: Red, 2/5 to 3/5" diameter.
HABIT: Tree, 30'.
DISEASES: Resistant to scab.

Menispermum canadense — Common Moonseed

FAMILY: Menispermaceae

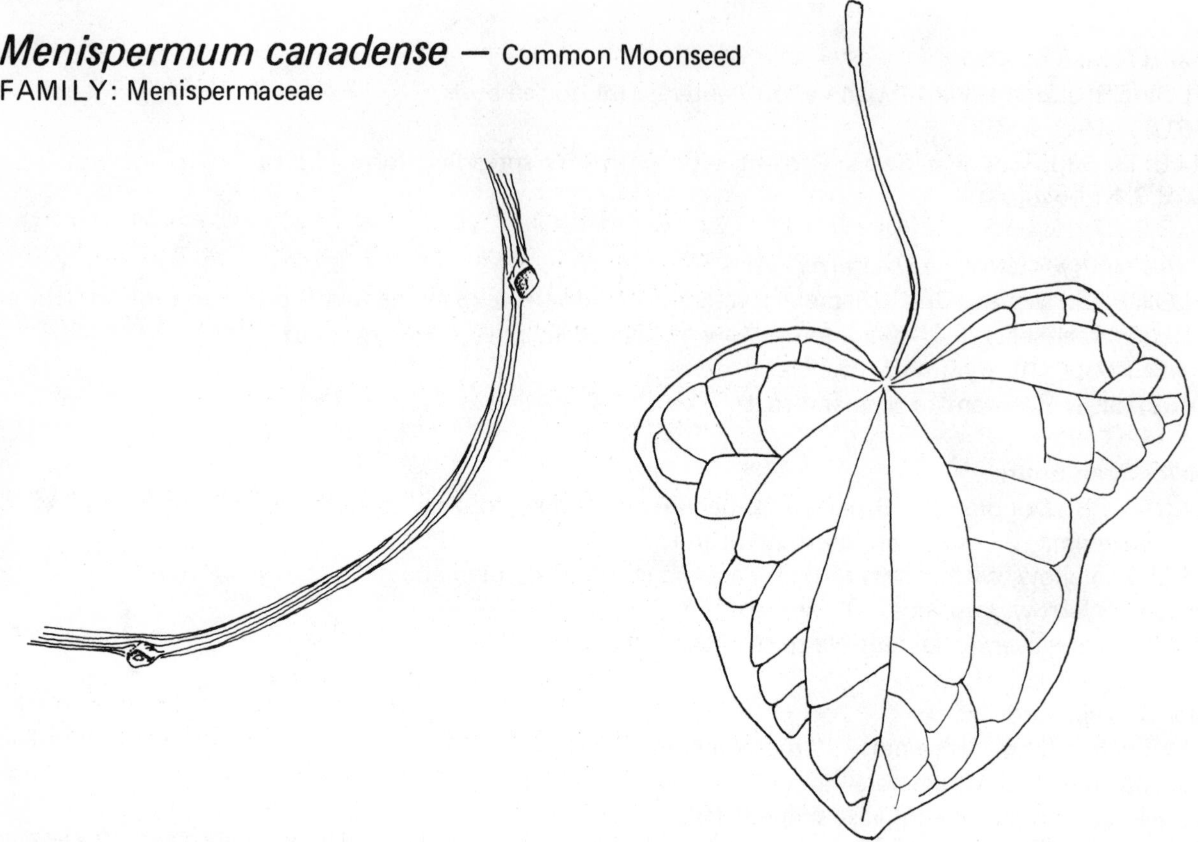

LEAVES: Alternate, simple, slender-petioled, orbicular-ovate, 4 to 10" long, acute or obtuse, rounded or truncate at base, entire or shallowly angulate-lobed, slightly pubescent beneath or nearly glabrous at maturity; petioles 2 to 6" long.

BUDS: Small, hairy, superposed, with the uppermost developing the inflorescence and the lower covered by the leaf scar, about 3 scaled.

STEM: Round, fluted, pith—white, solid, sieve tubes prominent, visible to the naked eye, green becoming buff to shiny brown, glabrescent, leaf scars raised, crater-like.

Menispermum canadense, Common Moonseed, is a deciduous, twining vine growing 10 to 15' and more. The stems are very slender and require support. The foliage is dark green in summer and the leaves are quite large (4 to 10") which makes for effective screening; very adaptable, grows back quickly (6 to 10' in a single season); easily propagated by division; Quebec and Manitoba to Georgia and Arkansas. 1646. Zone 4. Almost a weed.

Metasequoia glyptostroboides — Dawn Redwood (Deciduous) (Taxodiaceae)

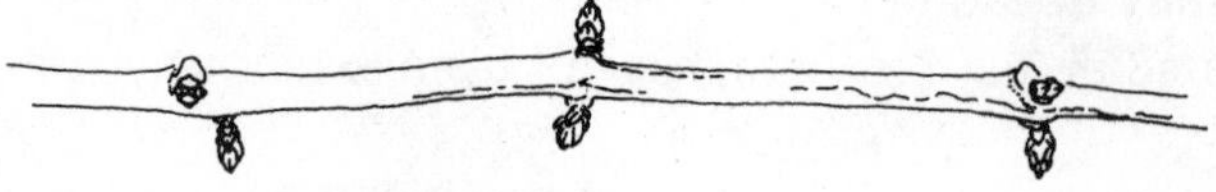

LEAVES: Deciduous, opposite in arrangement, linear, flattened, straight or slightly curved, pectinately arranged, 1/2" long and 1/16" broad on mature trees; upper surface is bright green with a narrowly grooved midvein, lower surface bearing obscure lines of stomata, lighter green or slightly glaucous, the midrib slightly raised.

BUDS: Non-resinous (opposite), usually in pairs at the base of deciduous branchlets but sometimes solitary between the branchlets; ovoid or ellipsoid, 1/10 to 1/5" long, 1/20 to 1/8" wide; scales light reddish or yellowish brown with a linear keel.

STEM: Branchlets of 2 kinds, persistent and deciduous. The persistent—bright, reddish brown when young, shallowly ridged, carrying the deciduous branchlets, numerous vegetative buds and a few leaves. The green deciduous branchlets are up to about 3" long, usually arranged distichously, more or less horizontal, ribbed with the long decurrent bases of up to 50 to 60 or more leaves.

SIZE: 70 to 100′ in height by 25′ spread, known to 120′ high.

HARDINESS: Zone 5.

HABIT: Pyramidal, conical, with a single straight trunk in youth; supposedly developing a broad-rounded crown with age. The Missouri Botanic Garden has a beautiful complement of trees which were grown from seed distributed to them by the Arnold Arboretum. The trees are 35 to 50′ high and probably 25 to 30 years of age. Their habits are like feathery cones with a tapering trunk broadening to a buttressed base.

RATE: Fast (50′ in 15 to 20 years); 30-year-old tree on William and Mary College campus is over 120′ high.

TEXTURE: Fine.

BARK: Reddish brown when young, becoming darker, grayish, fissured and exfoliating in long narrow strips.

LEAF COLOR: Bright green above changing to brown in fall.

FLOWERS: Monoecious; male flowers in racemes or panicles.

FRUIT: Cones pendulous, on long stalks, globose or cylindrical, 3/5 to 4/5" across, dark brown and mature the first year.

CULTURE: Easy to transplant; performs best in moist, deep, well-drained, slightly acid soils; is not well adapted to chalky soils; full sun; often grows late into summer and early fall and is damaged by an early freeze; should be well sited such as on a hill rather than a low area; seldom requires pruning due to neat, uniform conical habit.

DISEASES AND INSECTS: Recently the National Arboretum has lost some trees through canker infestations; prior to this there were no known serious problems; usually if a tree is around long enough and has been planted in sufficient numbers some insect or disease catches up with it.

LANDSCAPE VALUE: I have changed my opinion of this tree since I first learned it in my plant materials courses at Ohio State in 1963. At that time the tree was . . . well . . . just another tree but through closer association I find it a very lovely ornamental well suited to parks, golf courses and other large areas. Would make a very effective screen, grouping or for use in lining long drives or streets. Where it can be grown without problem of freeze damage it should be given adequate consideration.

CULTIVARS:

'National' — Habit conspicuously narrow-pyramidal.

PROPAGATION: Seeds, if viable, germinate without difficulty; softwood and hardwood cuttings root readily. Leafy cuttings root easily under mist if taken in summer and treated with indolebutyric acid at 20,000 ppm by the concentrated-dip method.

ADDITIONAL NOTES: This species was only known in fossil remains but was rediscovered growing in the remote village of Mo-tao-chi in the Chinese province of Szechuan. The Arnold Arboretum sent an expedition to the area and collected seeds which were shared with other arboreta and botanical gardens around the world. This species has been growing and reproducing itself for 50 million years.

NATIVE HABITAT: Native of Eastern Szechuan and Western Hupeh, China. Introduced 1947-1948.

Mitchella repens — Patridgeberry, also called Twinberry and Squawberry

FAMILY: Rubiaceae

LEAVES: Opposite, simple, 1/5 to 4/5" long, petioled, orbicular-ovate, obtuse, subcordate or rounded; lustrous above, often variegated with whitish lines; evergreen.

SIZE: 2"±

HARDINESS: Zone 3.

HABIT: Low growing, ground-hugging evergreen cover.

RATE: Slow.

TEXTURE: Fine.

LEAF COLOR: Dark green and lustrous above, often with variegated or whitish lines.

FLOWERS: White or pinkish, possibly tinged with purple, 2/5" long, fragrant; borne over an extended period in late spring and early summer in short peduncled pairs (hence the name Twinberry).

FRUIT: Berry-like drupe, red, 1/4" diameter, fall into winter; in the wild it is not uncommon to see flowers and fruits appearing at the same time.

CULTURE: Best moved in sods being careful to maintain as much soil as possible; requires acid, moist, well-drained soil which has been abundantly supplied with acid leafmold or peat; requires shade; is sensitive to the encroachment of man.

DISEASES AND INSECTS: Several leaf diseases have been reported but none are serious.

LANDSCAPE VALUE: A worthwhile groundcover for the lover of plants. Requires special attention and without it should not even be considered. The plants are collected from the wild and sold at Christmas time. There is one firm in Vermont which sells the Patridge-berry bowl, which consists of Rattlesnake plantain, moss and the above.

NATIVE HABITAT: Nova Scotia to Ontario and Minnesota; south to Florida, Arkansas and Texas. Introduced 1761.

Morus alba — White or Common Mulberry

FAMILY: Moraceae

LEAVES: Alternate, simple, undivided or lobed, dimorphic, serrate or dentate, ovate to broad-ovate, 2 to 7" long, acute or short acuminate, rounded or cordate at base, dark green and usually smooth above, pubescent on veins beneath or nearly glabrous.

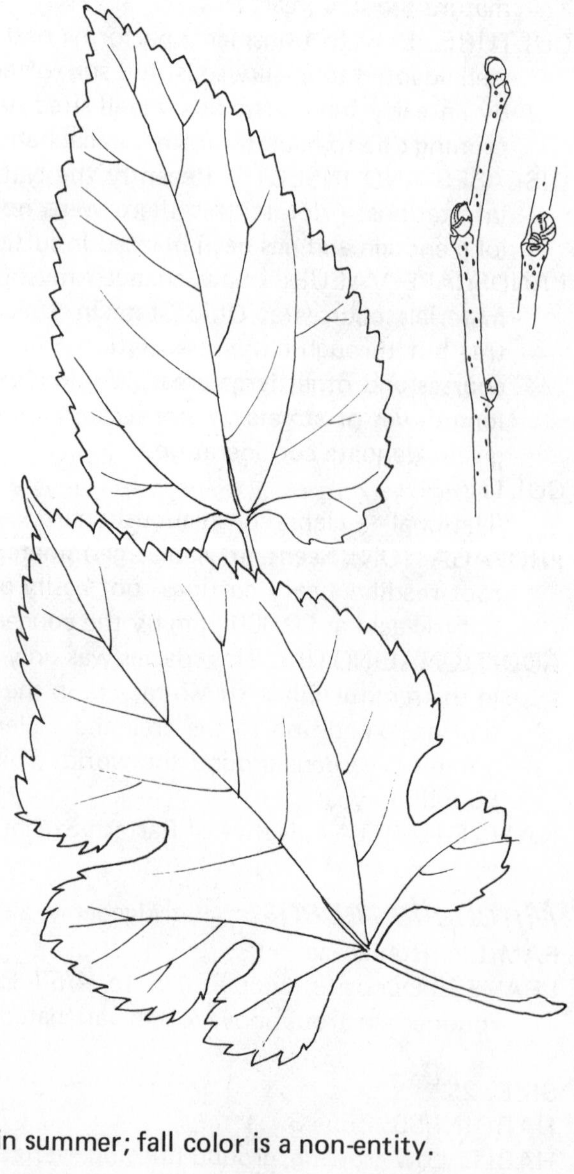

BUDS: Imbricate, terminal—absent, laterals—small, 1/8" long, ovoid, 3 to 6 scales, appressed, sharp or blunt pointed, light brown to reddish brown, often set oblique to leaf scar. Margins of bud scales somewhat finely hairy.

STEM: Slender, yellowish green to brownish gray, smooth, more or less shining. Slightly sweetish if chewed, bark exuding a white juice if cut on warm days.

SIZE: 30 to 50' in height with a comparable spread.

HARDINESS: Zone 4.

HABIT: Usually an extremely dense, round topped tree with a profusion of tight-knit slender branches. Often develops a witches' broom which gives the tree a messy, unkempt appearance. Definitely one of the original garbage can trees; probably without equal in this respect.

RATE: Fast; 10 to 12' over a 4 to 6 year period.

TEXTURE: Coarse throughout the year.

BARK: On young branches (1 to 4") an ashy-orange or light orangish brown, on larger trunks a brown color.

LEAF COLOR: Variable, often a lustrous dark green in summer; fall color is a non-entity.

FLOWERS: Polygamo-dioecious (monoecious or dioecious according to Rehder), greenish, both sexes in stalked axillary pendulous catkins; not showy.

FRUIT: Multiple fruit of small fleshy drupes; white, pinkish or purplish violet, sweet, but insipid, 1/2 to 1" long, late June to July; somewhat similar in size and shape to blackberry; birds love them and create fantastic messes because of cathartic properties.

CULTURE: Transplants readily, adaptable, withstands drouth, urban and seaside conditions; full sun to light shade; prune in winter; similar to *Maclura* in cultural adaptability.

DISEASES AND INSECTS: Bacterial blight on leaves and shoots, leaf spots, cankers, powdery mildews, scales, two-spotted mites and other pests. In the southern states this species is infested with many more problems.

LANDSCAPE VALUE: None; according to a landscape architect whose name will remain anonymous this tree has excellent color, texture, and form. Possibly she and I are thinking of different trees. About the only beneficiaries are the birds and the silkworms. The tree was originally imported from China for the silkworm industry and unfortunately escaped and is now naturalized in Asia, Europe and America.

CULTIVARS:

'Chaparral' — Non-fruiting weeping type.

'Kingan' — A type with leathery, lustrous foliage; fruitless; fast growing; drought resistant and apparently somewhat salt resistant as it is often used for seashore plantings.

'Pendula' — A form with slender pendulous branches and gnarled twisted growth habit; often in evidence in older landscapes; interesting but grotesque (also called Teas Weeping Mulberry), a fruiting clone.

'Pyramidalis' — Upright clone.

'Stribling' — Another fruitless, fast growing clone.

var. *tatarica* — Called the Russian Mulberry, hardiest of all the mulberries.

'Urbana' — Weeping, fruitless clone named by J. C. McDaniel.

PROPAGATION: Seed, stratify for 60 days at 41°F to improve germination. Cuttings collected in late October rooted 30% without treatment and 87% in 13 weeks with IBA.

RELATED SPECIES:

Morus rubra, Red Mulberry, reaches 40 to 70' in height with a 40 to 50' spread and is taller, more open, and irregular than *M. alba*. Fruits are red turning dark purple, juicy, edible and relished by birds. Native from Massachusetts to Florida, west to Michigan, Nebraska, Kansas and Texas. Introduced 1629. A better tree than *M. alba* and more fastidious as to soil requirement; prefering rich, moist situation.

NATIVE HABITAT: China. Introduced into Jamestown, Virginia with the early settlers.

Myrica pensylvanica — Northern Bayberry

FAMILY: Myricaceae

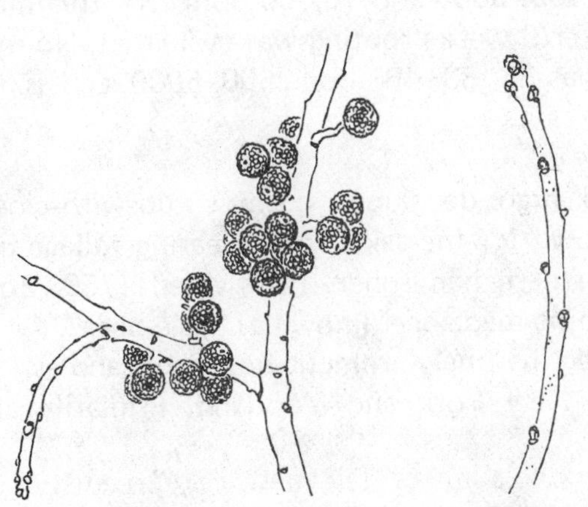

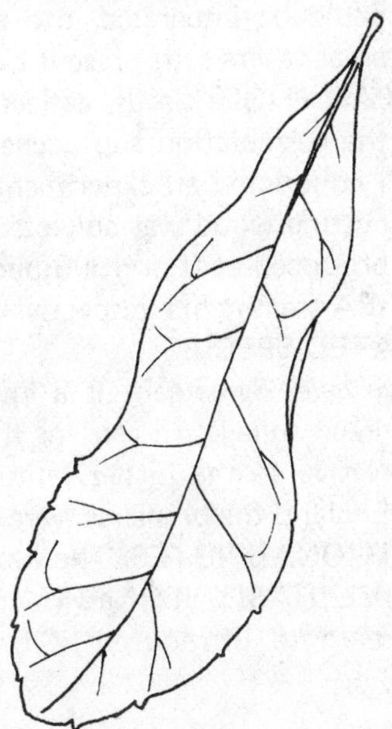

LEAVES: Alternate, simple, obovate to oblong-obovate or oblong, 1 3/5 to 4" long, 3/5 to 1 3/5" wide, obtuse or acutish, shallowly toothed toward apex or entire, lustrous dark green and pubescent above, pubescent beneath, resin-dotted, leaves aromatic when bruised.

BUD: Small, solitary, sessile, subglobose or ovoid, with 2 to 4 exposed scales, end-bud absent.

STEM: Rounded or angular, stoutish, resin-dotted when young; pith small, somewhat angled, continuous, green.

FRUIT: A small gray, waxy coated drupe which persists throughout the winter. An excellent identification feature.

SIZE: 9' is a good average for height, however, quite variable ranging from 5 to 12' in height and could equal that in spread. Tends to colonize and therefore forms large clumps.

HARDINESS: Zone 2.

HABIT: Deciduous to semi-evergreen, upright, rounded, and fairly dense shrub. Actually difficult to describe the habit of this plant; must be seen to be fully appreciated. Usually deciduous in midwestern states.

RATE: Medium from old wood, probably fast from shoots which develop from roots.

TEXTURE: Medium in foliage, possibly could be considered medium-fine; medium in winter habit. A very handsome specimen in winter because of interesting branch pattern and the gray, waxy fruits.

LEAF COLOR: Deep lustrous green dotted with resin glands beneath, leaves have a leathery texture, very aromatic when crushed as are all parts of the plant; fall color is nonexistent.

FLOWERS: Monoecious or dioecious, tends toward the dioecious character so male and female plants are required for good fruit development; not showy, the flowers borne in catkins with male consisting of varying number of stamens; the female of a one-celled ovary with two stalkless stigmas. Sepals and petals are absent. Flowering in late March to early April before the leaves.

FRUIT: Drupe, 1/6" across, grayish white, endocarp covered with resinous, waxy coating, effective from September through April and later of the following year, borne in great quantities and usually covering the stems of female plants.

CULTURE: Transplant balled and burlapped or as a container plant; thrives in poor, sterile, sandy soil; has performed well in our heavy clay soils in the Central Illinois region; appears to be extremely adaptable; full sun to 1/2 shade, withstands salt spray. Chlorosis is a problem on high pH soils but can be corrected with soil treatments or iron sprays.

DISEASES AND INSECTS: None serious.

LANDSCAPE VALUE: Excellent plant for massing, border, combines well with broadleaf evergreens, could be integrated into the foundation plantings, possibly for highway plantings and other areas where salts present a cultural problem; could be used in many poor soil sites.

PROPAGATION: Seeds, collect in October, remove the wax, stratify in moist peat for 90 days and the germination approaches 100%. I have had excellent success with this procedure. Cuttings, I conducted an experiment using 0, 1000, 2500, 5000 and 10,000 ppm IBA treatments. The cutting wood was collected June 14, and after 8 weeks rooting was evaluated. No roots were produced at 0 or 1000 ppm IBA. Rooting was 36, 53, 46% for 2500, 5000, and 10,000 ppm IBA treatments, respectively.

RELATED SPECIES:

Myrica gale, Sweetgale, is a low growing, 2 to 4' high, deciduous, bushy shrub with glossy, dark green foliage. In gardens the Sweetgale is grown for the sake of its pleasing foliage fragrance. Native to the higher latitudes of all the northern hemisphere. Cultivated 1750. Zone 1. In England the branches were used to flavor a home-made beer known as "gale-beer".

ADDITIONAL NOTES: The wax is used for making the finely aromatic bayberry candles.

NATIVE HABITAT: Newfoundland to Western New York and Maryland. Primarily along the seashore. Introduced 1725.

Neviusia alabamensis — Snow-wreath

FAMILY: Rosaceae

LEAVES: Alternate, simple, 1 1/2 to 2 4/5" long, ovate to ovate-oblong, acute or acuminate, doubly serrate, those of shoots slightly lobed, nearly glabrous, medium green.

BUDS: Glabrate, rather small, solitary, sessile, ovoid, ascending, with about 6 somewhat keeled or striate scales.

STEMS: Golden-brown, puberulent, slender, long, somewhat zig-zag, decurrently ridged from the nodes; pith relatively large, rounded, white, continuous; round-cordate, slightly raised and decurrent; 3 bundle-traces, more or less doubled; stipules persistent as small scabs from the decurrent ridges above leaf-scar.

SIZE: 3 to 6' high with an equal spread.

HARDINESS: Zone 5 (4), growing at Morton Arboretum, Chicago, Illinois.

HABIT: Upright deciduous shrub of somewhat straggly, open appearance with arching branches.

RATE: Slow to medium.

TEXTURE: Medium-fine in leaf; medium in winter.

FLOWERS: Perfect, apetalous, white, borne in 3 to 8 flowered cymes in early to mid-May. The stamens are the showy part of the flower and give a very feathery appearance to the plant.

FRUIT: Achene, of no ornamental consequence.

CULTURE: Apparently of easy culture; there is little available information on this species since it is so rare.

DISEASES AND INSECTS: None serious.

LANDSCAPE VALUE: A novelty item for the plantsman who wants something different. The flowers are quite showy and interesting.

PROPAGATION: Probably would root easily from softwood cuttings; division of the plant works quite well; I have received dormant divisions from the Morton Arboretum and had good success by potting them and growing them on in the greenhouse.

NATIVE HABITAT: One species in Alabama. Introduced about 1860.

Nyssa sylvatica — Black Tupelo, also known as Black Gum, Sour Gum, and Pepperidge.

FAMILY: Nyssaceae

LEAVES: Alternate, simple, obovate or elliptic, 2-5" long, entirely or remotely toothed, acute or obtusish, cuneate or sometimes rounded at base, lustrous dark green above, glaucescent beneath, pubescent on veins or glabrous at maturity. Leaves acid to the taste.

BUDS: Imbricate, 1/8 to 1/4" long, ovoid, vari-colored, yellow-brown to red-brown, smooth or slightly downy at tip. Usually brownish on tip of scales.

STEM: Slender, glabrous or nearly so, grayish to light reddish brown, producing numerous short slow growing spurs. Pith—chambered. Bundle traces 3, distinct, forming cavern-like entrance to stem.

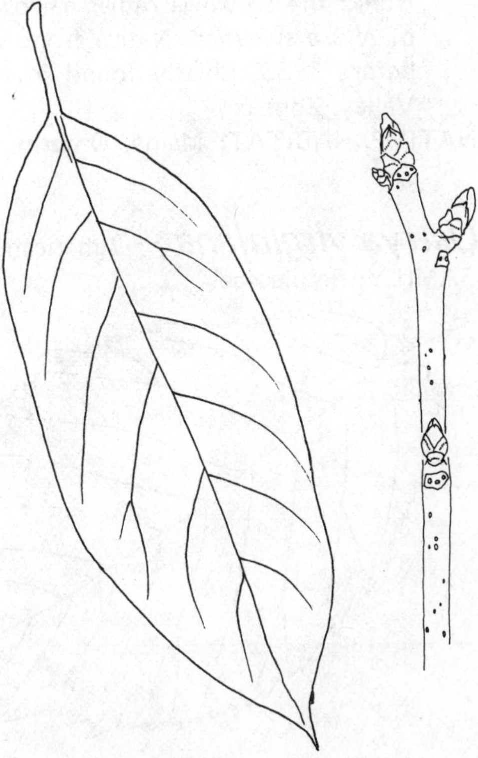

SIZE: 30 to 50' in height with a spread of 20 to 30'; can grow to 100' or more but this size is rare.

HARDINESS: Zone 4.

HABIT: One of our most beautiful native trees; somewhat pyramidal when young with densely set branches, some of which are pendulous; in old age the numerous spreading and often horizontal branches form an irregularly rounded or flat-topped crown. I have seen 60′ specimens in Spring Grove Cemetery which were distinctly upright-oval in outline. Apparently there is great variation in mature habit. The young trees take on the appearance of *Q. palustris*.

RATE: Slow to medium, 12 to 15′ over a 10 to 15 year period.

TEXTURE: Medium-fine in leaf; medium-coarse in winter.

BARK: Dark gray, at times almost black, broken into thick irregular ridges which are checked across into short segments, giving it a block-like or alligator hide appearance.

LEAF COLOR: Dark glossy green in summer changing to fluorescent yellow to orange to scarlet to purple colors in the fall. One of our best, most consistent, and most beautiful trees in fall.

FLOWERS: Polygamo-dioecious, appearing with the leaves, small, greenish white, borne in (female) axillary penduncled clusters; the male in many-flowered peduncled clusters. Not ornamentally effective.

FRUIT: Oblong drupe, 1/2″ long, bluish black, ripening late September through early October and eaten by many species of birds and mammals.

CULTURE: Difficult to transplant because of taproot; move balled and burlapped in early spring; prefers moist, well drained, acid (pH 5.5 to 6.5), deep soils; however, in the wild it is found on dry mountain ridges, burned over forest land, or abandoned fields, and in cold mountain swamps; does not tolerate high pH soils; full sun or semi-shade and sheltered locations from winds are preferred; prune in fall.

DISEASES AND INSECTS: Cankers, leaf spots, rust, tupelo leaf miner and scale. None are particularly serious in Central Illinois.

LANDSCAPE VALUE: Excellent specimen tree, acceptable street tree in residential areas, not for heavily polluted areas, outstanding summer and fall foliage and habit, lovely in a naturalized area.

PROPAGATION: Seeds exhibit moderate embryo dormancy and moist stratification for 60 to 90 days at 41°F is beneficial.

RELATED SPECIES:

Nyssa aquatica, Water Tupelo, is one of the most characteristic of southern swamp trees and is found on sites which are periodically under water. The distinguishing differences from *Nyssa sylvatica* include larger leaves to about 7″ long and larger fruit (about 1″ long) and of reddish purple color. The trunk bulges conspicuously at the base but tapers rapidly to a long, clear trunk; the crown is rather narrow and open. The wood is commerically important as is that of *Nyssa sylvatica*. Native from Virginia to Southern Illinois, Florida and Texas. Introduced before 1735. Chiefly found in the Atlantic and Gulf Coastal Plains and Mississippi River Valley. Zone 6.

NATIVE HABITAT: Maine, Ontario, Michigan to Florida and Texas. Introduced before 1750.

Ostrya virginiana — American Hophornbeam, also known as Ironwood.

FAMILY: Betulaceae

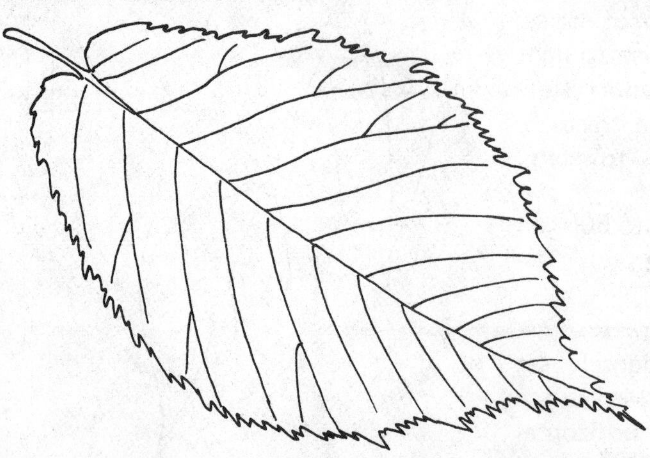

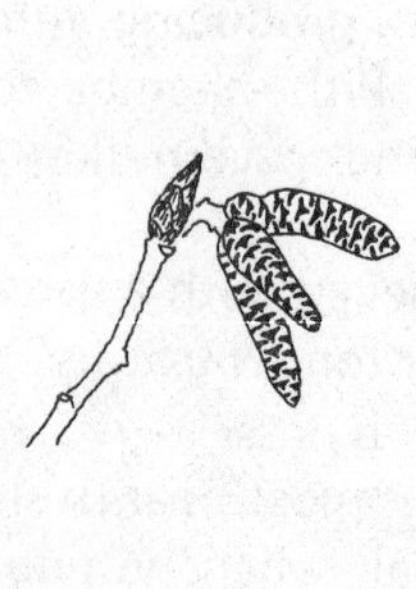

LEAVES: Alternate, simple, 2 1/2 to 5" long, sharply and doubly serrate, veins forking at ends.

BUDS: Imbricate, small, 1/8 to 1/4" long, narrowly ovate, pointed, glabrous or finely downy, slightly gummy especially within, strongly divergent; terminal bud absent. Scales, longitudinally striate.

STEM: Slender, dark reddish brown, often zigzag, for the most part smooth and shining.

FRUIT: Nutlet, enclosed in hop-like sac. Staminate catkins, abundantly present, usually in 3's, good winter identification characters.

SIZE: A small tree averaging 25 to 40' in height and 2/3's to equal that in spread. The tree can reach 60' but this is seldom attained.

HARDINESS: Zone 4.

HABIT: Very graceful small tree with many horizontal or drooping branches usually forming a rounded outline; somewhat pyramidal in youth.

RATE: Slow, probably 10 to 15' over a 15 year period.

TEXTURE: Medium-fine in leaf, medium in winter.

BARK: Grayish brown, often broken with narrow, longitudinal strips which are free at each end.

LEAF COLOR: Medium green in summer changing to yellow or reddish in the fall; foliage is little troubled by insects and diseases.

FLOWERS: Monoecious, male catkins usually grouped in 3's and visible throughout winter; female visible in spring, a catkin.

FRUIT: A nut(let), enclosed in an inflated involucre and resembling the fruit of Hops, hence, the name Hophornbeam.

CULTURE: Transplant balled and burlapped or from a container in early spring into a cool, moist, well drained, slightly acid soil, although is often found in the wild growing in rather dry gravelly or rocky soil, full sun or partial shade, prune in winter or early spring, somewhat slow to re-establish after transplanting.

DISEASES AND INSECTS: None serious.

LANDSCAPE VALUE: Handsome medium sized tree for lawns, parks, golf courses, naturalized areas, and possibly streets. The species has performed well in city plantings and very narrow tree lawns.

PROPAGATION: Seeds have an internal type of dormancy which is difficult to overcome. Warm followed by cold seems to be the best treatment.

NATIVE HABITAT: Cape Breton, Ontario to Minnesota, south to Florida and Texas. Introduced 1690.

Oxydendrum arboreum — Sourwood, also called Sorrel Tree or Lily of the Valley Tree.

FAMILY: Ericaceae

LEAVES: Alternate, simple, slender-petioled, elliptic-oblong to oblong-lanceolate, 3 to 8" long, acuminate, broad-cuneate, serrulate, glabrous above, sparingly pubescent on veins beneath; petiole—1/3 to 3/5" long.

BUDS: Small, conical—globose, solitary, sessile, with about 6 scales; terminal lacking.

STEM: Glabrous or sparingly pubescent, olive or bright red, slender.

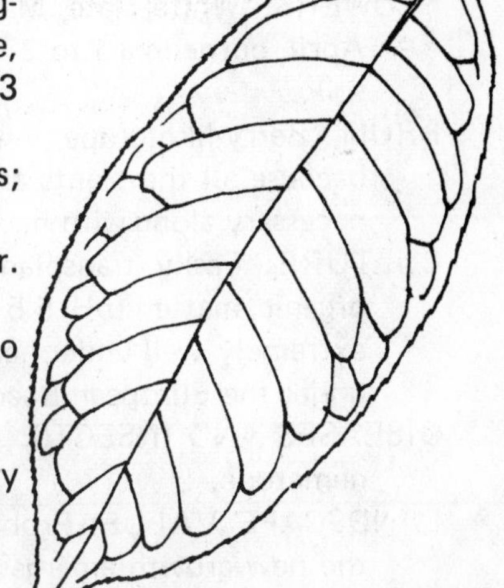

SIZE: 25 to 30' in height and approximately 20' in spread; can grow to 50 to 75'.

HARDINESS: Zone 5, possibly 4.

HABIT: Pyramidal tree, with rounded top and drooping branches; very lovely outline.

RATE: Slow, 14 to 15' over a 12 to 15 year period.

TEXTURE: Medium in all seasons.

BARK: Gray, thick, deeply furrowed, and has rather scaly ridges.
LEAF COLOR: Lustrous dark green in summer; brilliant scarlet in fall.
FLOWERS: White, urn-shaped, 1/4" long, fragrant, late June to early July in 4 to 10" long and wide drooping racemose-panicles, excellent flowering tree.
FRUIT: Dehiscent capsule.
CULTURE: Transplant as a young tree balled and burlapped into acid, peaty, moist, well-drained soil; full sun or partial shade although flowering and fall color are maximized in sun, the pH should run 5.5 to 6.5 if possible.
DISEASES AND INSECTS: Leaf spots and twig blight, neither of which are serious.
LANDSCAPE VALUE: Truly an all season ornamental; excellent specimen plant; it has so many attributes that it should only be considered for specimen use. Many gardeners feel, among native trees, this is second only to Flowering Dogwood.
PROPAGATION: Seed, see under *Calluna*. Softwood cuttings, short side shoots taken with a heel rooted 80% when taken in late July, treated with 90 ppm IBA, and placed in sand:peat. They did not root well in sand; untreated cuttings did not root at all.
NATIVE HABITAT: Pennsylvania to Florida west to Indiana and Louisiana. 1747.

Pachysandra terminalis — Japanese Pachysandra or Spurge

FAMILY: Buxaceae
LEAVES: Alternate, simple, obovate to ovate, 2 to 4" long, glabrous, dentate, 3-nerved at base, dark green and lustrous above, petiole—2/5 to 1 1/5" long.
STEM: Borne upright, greenish.

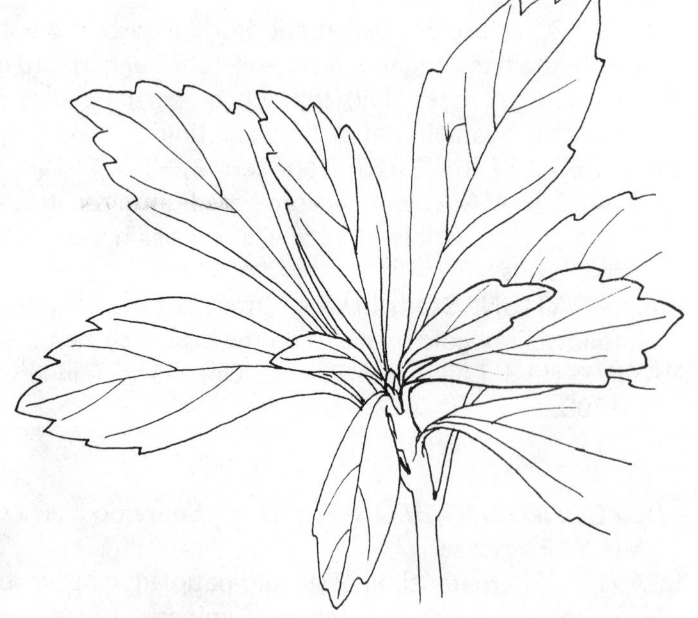

SIZE: 6 to 12" high.
HARDINESS: Zone 4.
HABIT: Evergreen ground cover spreading by stolons (rhizomes).
RATE: Slow.
TEXTURE: Medium, possibly medium-fine in all seasons.
LEAF COLOR: New growth is a lovely light green which gradually changes to lustrous dark green.
FLOWERS: White, late March to early April; borne in a 1 to 2" long upright spike.
FRUIT: Berry-like drupe, whitish, 2/5" long. Some plantings rarely produce fruits. This is probably because all the plants are of one clone. The plant is probably self-sterile and several clones are necessary along with bees to insure fruit set.
CULTURE: Easily transplanted; prefers moist, well drained, acid soil abundantly supplied with organic matter (pH 5.5 to 6.5 is ideal); prefers shade and actually yellows in full sun; does extremely well under heavily shaded and shallow rooted trees. I have seen established plantings under the European Beech which is one of the densest shaded trees.
DISEASES AND INSECTS: Leaf blight, *Pachysandra* leaf tier, scale, mites and northern root-knot nematode.
LANDSCAPE VALUE: Probably the best ground cover for deep shade; singularly beautiful when the new growth emerges; one of my favorites; siting is important and in exposed locations of sun and wind extensive foliar discoloration and damage occur.

CULTIVARS:

'Green Carpet' – A superior cultivar because the foliage is not trailing in habit but grows close to the ground, forming a low, neat ground cover. Foliage color is a deeper green than the species.

'Variegata' ('Silver Edge') – Leaves prominently mottled with white, is not as vigorous as the species and does not develop in shade as the species.

PROPAGATION: Cuttings root readily with 1000 ppm IBA, stuck in peat: perlite under mist.

RELATED SPECIES:

Pachysandra procumbens, Alleghany Pachysandra, is similar to the above species except with semi-evergreen foliage, larger flowers, and lighter green foliage. West Virginia to Florida. Introduced 1800. Zone 4.

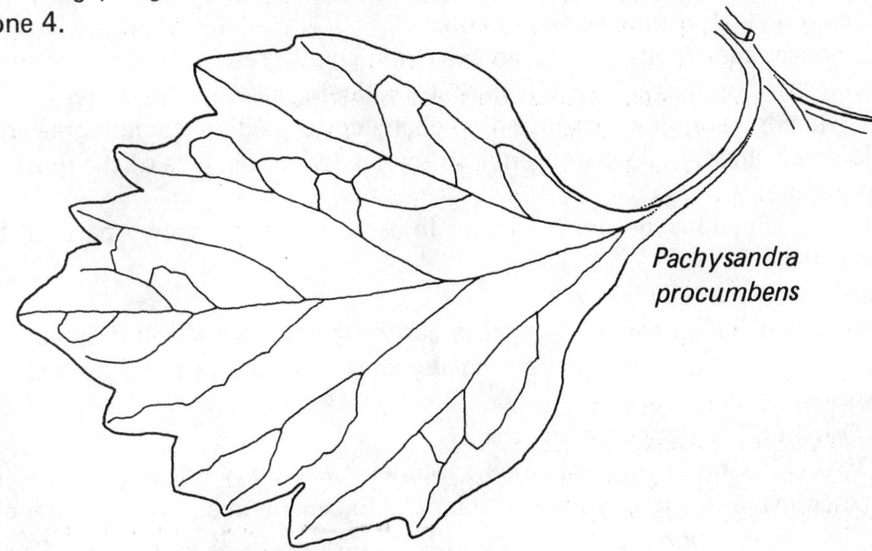

NATIVE HABITAT: Japan. Introduced 1882.

Parrotia persica – Persian Parrotia

FAMILY: Hamamelidaceae

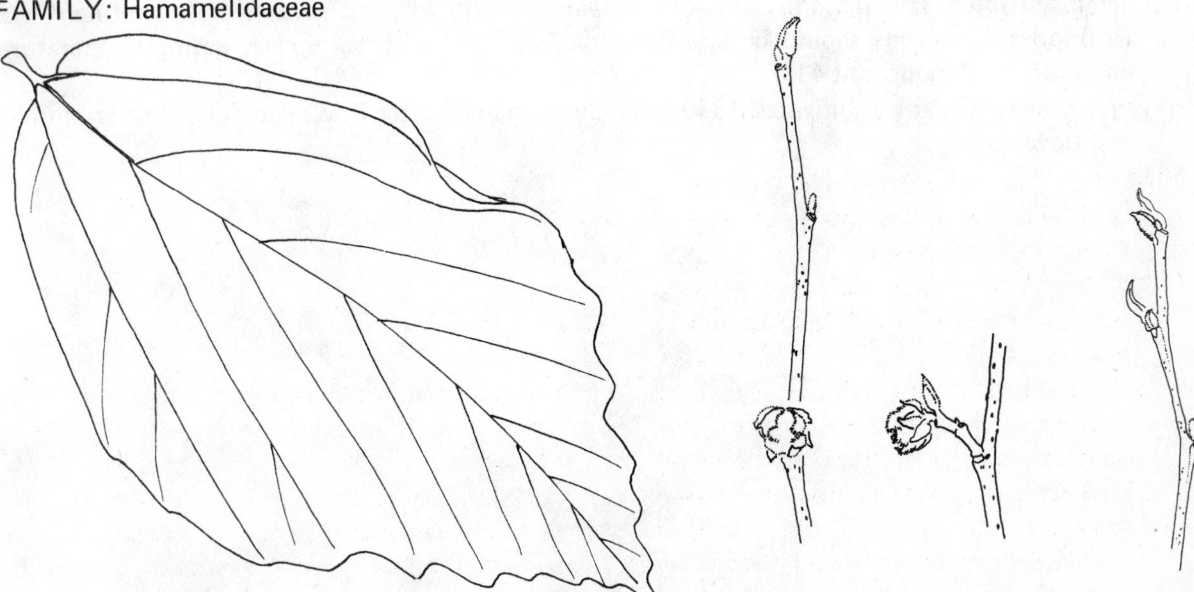

LEAVES: Alternate, short petioled, sinuate-dentate, with large lanceolate caducous stipules, oval to obovate-oblong, obtuse, rounded to sub-cordate at base, 2 to 4" long, coarsely crenate-dentate above the middle, stellate pubescent on both sides, medium to dark green, similar in shape to witchhazel and fothergilla leaves; petioles 1/12 to 1/4" long.

BUDS: Vegetative—stalked, with 2 outer scales, tomentulous, brownish; flower buds—globose, about 1/3" diameter, quite pubescent, brownish black.

STEM: Slender, brownish, pubescent when young, finally becoming grayish brown and glabrous with maturity.

SIZE: 20 to 40′ in height with a spread of 15 to 30′.

HARDINESS: Zone 5.

HABIT: Small single stemmed tree or large multistemmed shrub with an oval-rounded head of upright, ascending branches.

RATE: Medium, 10′ over a 6 to 8 year period.

TEXTURE: Medium in leaf; medium-fine in winter.

BARK: Older branches and trunks develop an exfoliating gray, green, white, brown color reminiscent of *Pinus bungeana*, Lacebark Pine. The bark is a welcome asset in the winter landscape.

LEAF COLOR: Reddish purple when unfolding changing to medium to dark green during summer and developing brilliant yellow to orange to scarlet fall color. One of the most beautiful trees for foliage effect.

FLOWERS: Perfect, apetalous, before the leaves in early April, the showy parts of the flower are the crimson stamens.

FRUIT: A capsule, ornamentally ineffective.

CULTURE: Transplant balled and burlapped in early spring; prefers well drained, loamy, slightly acid (pH 6.0 to 6.5) soils; will tolerate chalky soils; full sun, but will do well in light shade; prune in spring.

DISEASES AND INSECTS: Very pest-free tree.

LANDSCAPE VALUE: One of the best small specimen trees that I know of. The foliage, bark and pest resistance make it a tree worth considering. Excellent small lawn or street tree, could be integrated into foundation plantings around large residences; is definitely a topic of conversation; a fine accent plant. The largest specimen I know of is located at the Biltmore Estate, Ashville, N.C. It is worth the trip just to see this one plant.

PROPAGATION: Cuttings—I have had 100% success with July cuttings treated with 1000 ppm IBA/50% alcohol and placed under mist. Other investigators reported cuttings taken in late January rooted 33% in sand:peat without treatment and 56% in 16 weeks after treatment with Hormodin #3. Seeds should be stratified for five months at warm, fluctuating temperatures and then for 3 months at 41°F.

NATIVE HABITAT: Iran, cultivated 1840, one species named after F. W. Parrot, German naturalist and traveler.

Parthenocissus quinquefolia — Virginia Creeper also called Woodbine.

FAMILY: Vitaceae

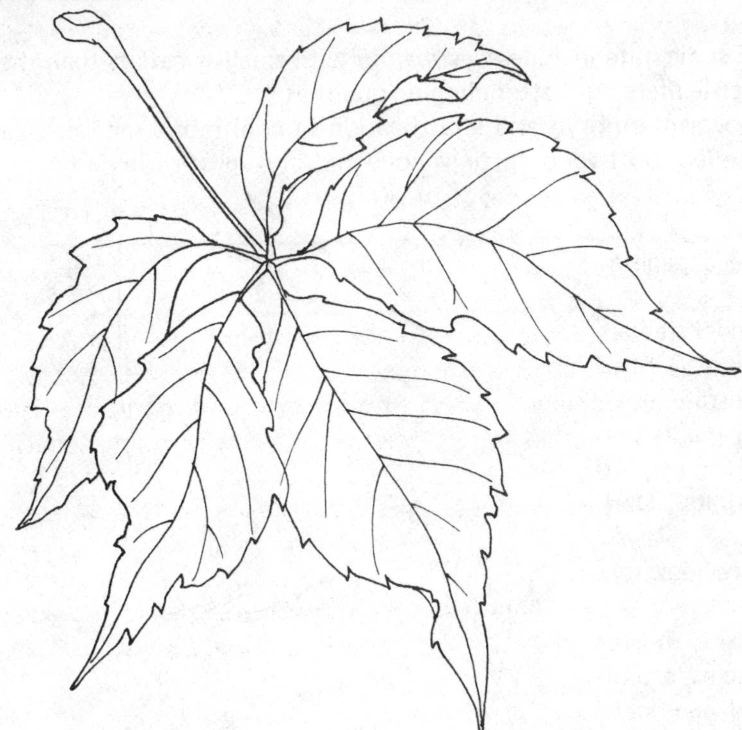

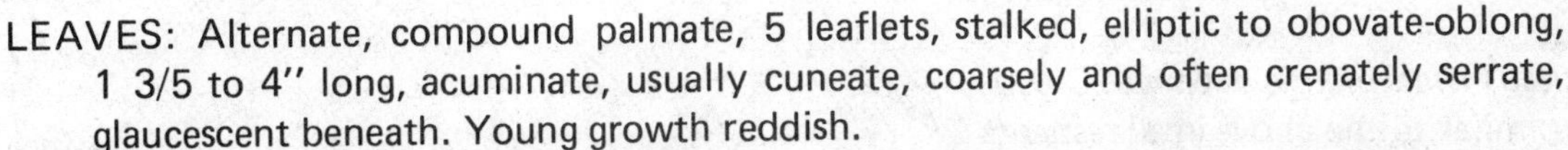

LEAVES: Alternate, compound palmate, 5 leaflets, stalked, elliptic to obovate-oblong, 1 3/5 to 4" long, acuminate, usually cuneate, coarsely and often crenately serrate, glaucescent beneath. Young growth reddish.

BUDS: Often collateral, brownish, sessile, round-conical, with 2 to 3 exposed scales, end-bud absent.

STEM: Round, pith—white, tendrils with 5 to 12 branches ending in adhesive tips, longer than those of *P. tricuspidata,* color is a light brown, prominently lenticelled, usually pubescent; leaf scars distinctly concave.

SIZE: 30 to 50' and more.

HARDINESS: Zone 3.

HABIT: Deciduous vine with tendrils which have 5 to 8 branches each ending in adhesive like tips; has the ability to literally cement itself to the wall and therefore needs no support.

RATE: Fast, 6 to 10' and beyond in a single season.

TEXTURE: Medium in leaf, somewhat coarse in winter.

LEAF COLOR: Rich deep green in summer; usually a purple red to crimson red in fall; first of all woody plants to color effectively; often noticeable in the tops of tall trees.

FLOWERS: Greenish white, July, in cymes which usually form terminal panicles; totally ineffective as they are borne under the foliage.

FRUIT: Berry, 1/4" diameter, bluish black, bloomy, September-October, and only effective after the leaves have fallen.

CULTURE: Supposedly coarsely fibrous and slow to reestablish but I have never had any problem rooting or growing it; best grown in containers and moved from them to the final growing area; tolerates just about any kind of soil; full sun or full shade; exposed, windy conditions; polluted situations, city conditions; actually difficult to kill.

DISEASES AND INSECTS: Canker, downy mildew, leaf spots, powdery mildew, wilt, beetles, eight-spotted forester, leaf hoppers, scales and several other insects. The University of Illinois buildings are covered with this and Japanese Creeper and I have not seen problems on any of the plantings.

LANDSCAPE VALUE: Excellent, tough, low maintenance cover for walls, trellises, rock piles; can be an asset if used properly. The ivy covered walls of most Universities are not ivy covered but "creeper" covered.

CULTIVARS: Two varieties of some note include *engelmannii* with smaller leaflets than the species and *saint-paulii* with smaller leaflets but better clinging qualities.

PROPAGATION: Seed has a dormant embryo and stratification in cool moist sand or peat for 60 days at 41° F is recommended. Softwood cuttings collected in August rooted 90% in 20 days without treatment.

RELATED SPECIES:

Parthenocissus tricuspidata — Japanese Creeper.

LEAVES: Alternate, simple, slender stalked, broad-ovate, 4 to 8" wide, 3-lobed with acuminate coarsely serrate lobes, or, chiefly on the young plants and basal shoots, smaller and partly 3-foliate with stalked leaflets. Dark glossy green above.

BUDS: Brownish—similar to previous species.

STEM: Squarish, tendrils 5 to 12, shorter than those of previous species, prominent, vertically arranged lenticels, usually glabrous.

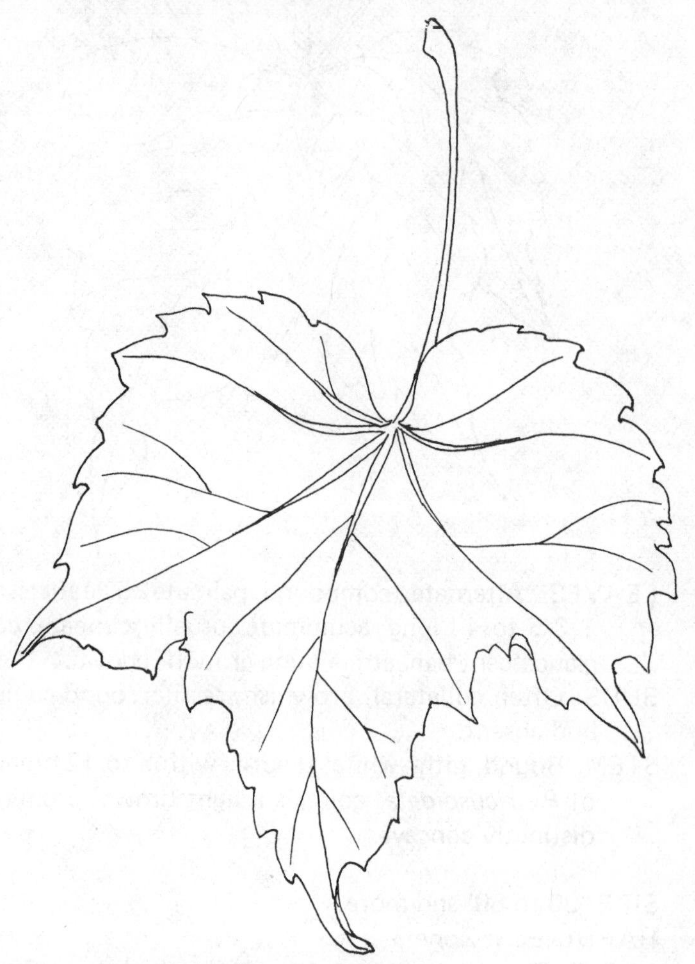

Parthenocissus tricuspidata, Japanese Creeper, is similar to the above in all respects except the foliage is usually more lustrous, the leaf is simple and 3-lobed and it is possibly not as hardy. It is excellent and can be used in the same situations as Virginia Creeper. Japan. Central China. 1862. Zone 4.

NATIVE HABITAT: New England to Florida and Mexico, west to Ohio, Illinois and Missouri. Introduced 1622.

Paulownia tomentosa — Royal Paulownia, also called Empress Tree or Princess Tree.

FAMILY: Schrophulariaceae, sometimes placed in Bignoniaceae.

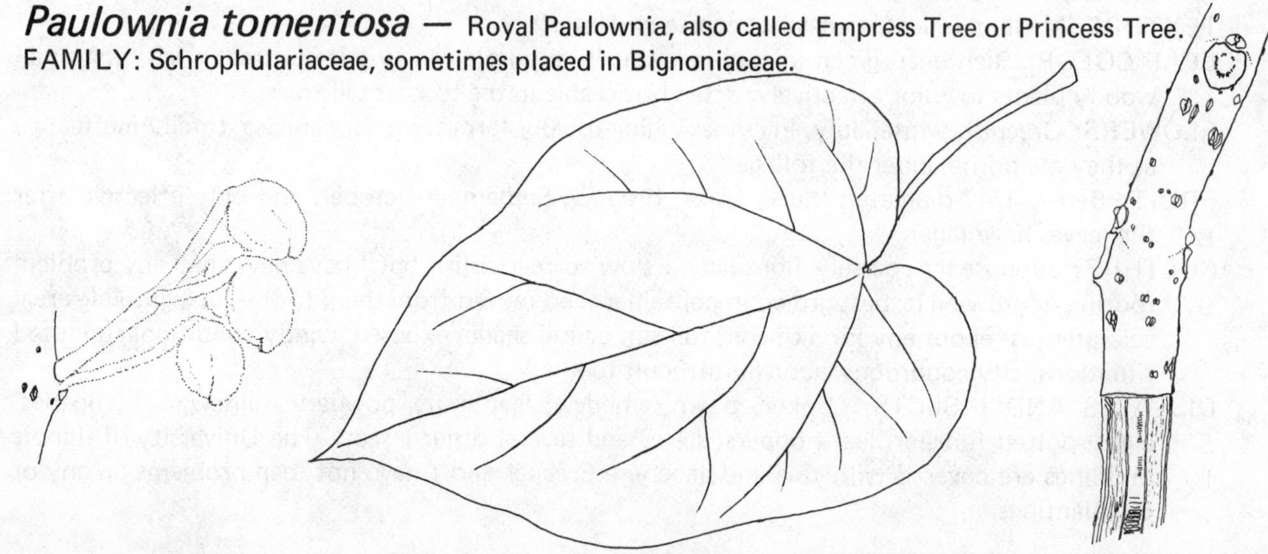

LEAVES: Opposite, simple, broad-ovate to ovate, 5 to 10" long, acuminate, cordate, entire or sometimes shallowly 3-lobed, pubescent above, tomentose beneath. Velvety pubescence on lower side of leaf.

BUDS: Similar to *C. speciosa*.

STEM: Pubescent when young, heavily lenticelled, with lip-like shape. Olive-brown color.

PITH: Chambered, *Catalpa* pith is continuous.

FLOWER: Panicle, formed in late summer. Individual flower buds appear as light brown, pubescent spheres through winter.

SIZE: 30 to 40′ in height with an equal spread.

HARDINESS: Zone 5.

HABIT: Rounded, open crown; resembles *C. bignonioides* in habit.

RATE: Fast, 14 to 17′ in 4 to 5 years and can grow as much as 8 to 10′ in a single year; the wood tends to be somewhat brittle.

TEXTURE: Coarse in all seasons.

LEAF COLOR: Medium to dark green in summer, fall color of no consequence as the leaves usually fall off green.

FLOWERS: Pale violet with darker spots and yellow stripes inside, 2" long, vanilla scented, borne in April before the leaves in 8 to 12" long pyramidal panicles. Flower buds are formed during the summer prior to flowering and are a brown color and very evident during the winter. Unfortunately the flower buds are often killed during the winter and this has been the case in Urbana, Illinois.

FRUIT: Ovoid, beaked capsule, 1 to 2" long, not ornamentally overwhelming.

CULTURE: Transplant balled and burlapped in early spring into moist, deep, well drained soil; will tolerate a wide range of soils but does best in the type mentioned; full sun or partial shade; and sheltered from wind; withstands air pollutants and does well along coastal areas; prune in winter.

DISEASES AND INSECTS: Seldom troubled although leaf spots, mildew and twig canker have been reported.

LANDSCAPE VALUE: Falls in the same category as *Catalpa* except probably less desirable because of messiness and in northern climates the uncertainty of flowers. Possibly for parks and other large areas; very dense shaded and therefore difficult to grow grass under.

PROPAGATION: The seeds exhibit no dormancy but light is necessary for germination. Fresh seed had a germination capacity of 90 percent in 19 days with alternating temperatures of 68° and 86°F. Eight hours of light were supplied during the 86°F cycle.

NATIVE HABITAT: China. Introduced 1834. Escaped from cultivation from Southern New York to Georgia.

Paxistima canbyi — Canby Paxistima (formerly spelled Pachistima), also called Rat-stripper.

FAMILY: Celastraceae

LEAVES: Opposite, simple, linear-oblong or narrow-oblong, 1/4 to 1" long, short-petioled, revolute and usually serrulate above the middle, lustrous dark green, evergreen.

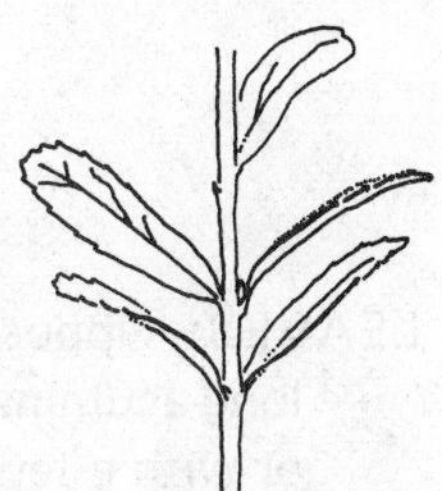

BUD: Solitary, sessile, ovoid, appressed, very small, with about 2 pairs of exposed scales; the terminal somewhat larger with more visible scales.

STEM: Very slender, somewhat 4-sided, the bark becoming corky-thickened and transversely checked; pith minute, rounded, brownish, and spongy; leaf-scars minute, crescent-shaped, somewhat raised; 1 indistinct bundle-trace.

SIZE: 1 to 2′ in height by 3 to 5′ in spread at maturity.

HARDINESS: Zone 5, possibly 4, performing quite well in Champaign-Urbana which is in the northen range of Zone 5.

HABIT: Low growing evergreen shrub with decumbent branches which often root when in contact with the soil; relatively neat and compact.
RATE: Slow, can grow 12" high by 2 to 3' wide in 3 to 4 years.
TEXTURE: Fine in all seasons.
LEAF COLOR: Lustrous dark green in summer becoming bronzish in cold weather.
FLOWERS: Perfect, reddish, 1/5" across; early May, borne in few-flowered cymes, not particularly showy.
FRUIT: Leathery capsule, 1/6" long, of no ornamental consequence.
CULTURE: Easily transplanted, but best moved as a container-grown plant; prefers moist, acid well drained soil which has been well supplied with organic matter; in the wild it is found on rocky soils; full sun or partial shade although is denser and more compact in full sun; rarely requires fertilizer or pruning.
DISEASES AND INSECTS: Leaf spot of minor consequence and scale have been reported.
LANDSCAPE VALUE: Good evergreen groundcover which once established requires little or no attention; excellent when used in combination with broadleaf evergreens; makes a good facer plant or low hedge; does not appear too often in Midwestern gardens but is used extensively on the east coast.
PROPAGATION: Plants can be divided; cuttings can be rooted easily; I have taken cuttings in late July, treated them with 1000 ppm IBA, placed them under mist and had good success. Another investigator collected softwood cuttings in summer, treated them with Hormodin #2 and had 100% rooting in 6 weeks.
NATIVE HABITAT: Mountains of Virginia and West Virginia. Cultivated 1880.

Phellodendron amurense — Amur Corktree

FAMILY: Rutaceae

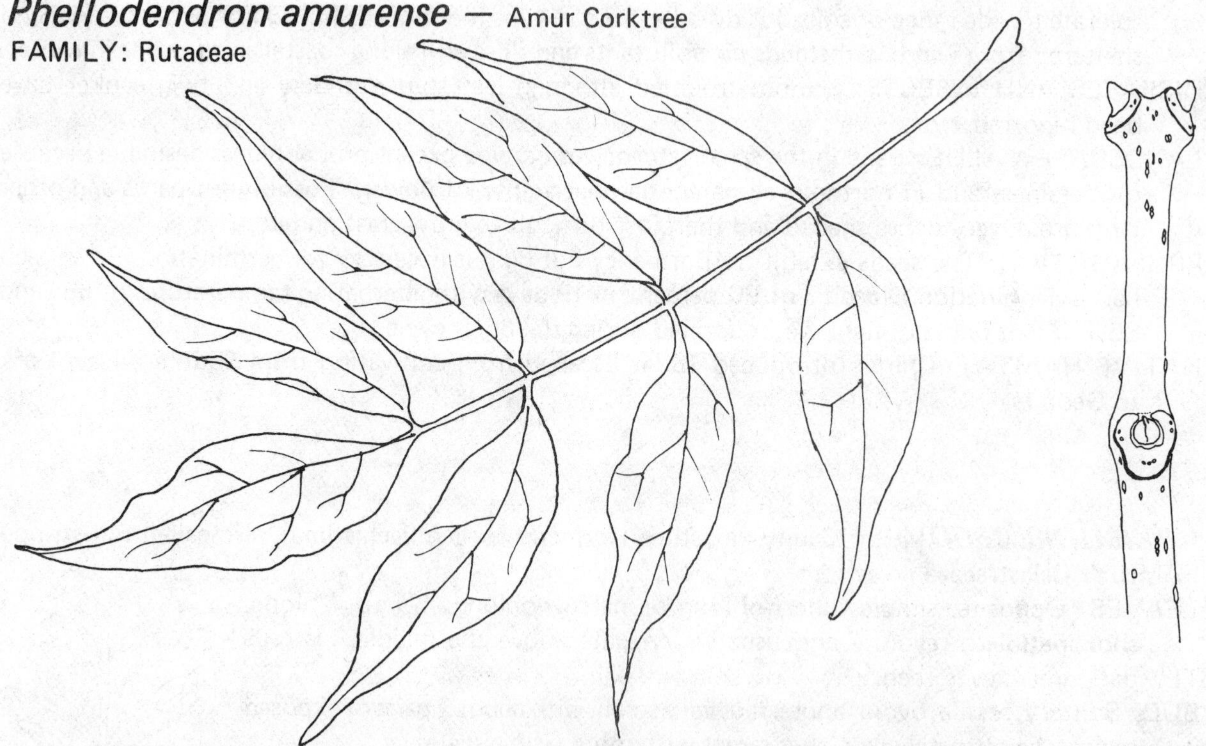

LEAVES: Opposite, pinnately compound, 5 to 13 leaflets, ovate to lance-ovate, 2 to 4" long, long-acuminate, rounded or narrowed at base, dark green and lustrous above, glabrous beneath or with a few hairs along the base of the midrib.
BUD: Solitary, half-ellipsoid, compressed from the sides, silky with red or bronzed hairs so as to mask the overlapping of the two scales, enclosed by base of petiole.
STEM: Stout, orange-yellow or yellowish gray, changing to brown, lenticels prominent, leaf scars horseshoe-shaped, raised, rather large with bud setting in the "U" formed by the leaf scar. Inner bark of young stems usually a bright yellowish green.

SIZE: 30 to 45′ in height with an equal or greater spread.
HARDINESS: Zone 3.
HABIT: Broad spreading tree with a short trunk and an open, rounded crown of a few large, often horizontally arranged branches.
RATE: Medium, 10 to 12′ over a 5 to 8 year period.
TEXTURE: Medium in leaf; would probably be considered coarse in winter habit.
BARK: On old trunks, ridged and furrowed into a cork-like pattern, gray-black in color, very beautiful and unusual bark pattern but does not develop until old age.
LEAF COLOR: Deep, often shiny green in summer, changing to yellow or bronzy yellow in fall and briefly persisting.
FLOWERS: Dioecious, yellowish green, borne in 2 to 3 1/2″ long panicles in late May to early June.
FRUIT: Subglobose, black, 1/2 to 3/5″ diameter drupe, with strong odor when bruised; ripening in October and persisting into winter; borne only on female trees.
CULTURE: Transplants readily, has a fibrous, shallow, wide spreading root system; does well on many types of soils; withstands acid or alkaline conditions, drouth and polluted air; full sun; prune in winter.
DISEASES AND INSECTS: Unusually free of pests.
LANDSCAPE VALUE: Light headed shade tree of unique interest for bark, excellent in parks and other large areas, possibly for residential landscapes with lots of 10,000 square feet or more; not for streets although has been used for that purpose.
PROPAGATION: Seeds germinate like beans without any treatment. I have directly sowed seed and also stratified seed and then planted. The differences in germination percentage were negligible although the percent was slightly higher with stratification.
RELATED SPECIES:
Phellodendron lavallei, Lavalle Corktree, is similar to *P. amurense* but not as suitable for cultivation and supposedly grows somewhat taller.
Phellodendron sachalinense, Sakhalin Corktree, tends to be more regularly vase-shaped than the irregularly branching habit of *P. amurense*. The hardiest (Zone 3) of the corktrees. Native to Korea, Northern Japan, Western China. Introduced 1877.
ADDITIONAL NOTES: The Arnold and Morton Arboreta have beautiful specimens of this species. The effect is strongly oriental and the trees must be seen in the mature state to be fully appreciated.
NATIVE HABITAT: Northern China, Manchuria. Introduced 1856.

Philadelphus coronarius — Sweet Mockorange

FAMILY: Saxifragaceae
LEAVES: Opposite, simple, ovate to ovate-oblong, 1 3/5 - 3″ long, acuminate, broad cuneate or rounded at the base, remotely denticulate or dentate, glabrous except bearded in the axils of veins beneath and somethimes hairy on the veins.
BUDS: Solitary, sessile, with 2 nearly valvate, mostly hairy scales, the terminal lacking.
STEM: Young branches glabrous or slightly pilose; bark reddish to chestnut-brown, exfoliating on old stems; pith—moderate, rounded, pale or white, continuous.

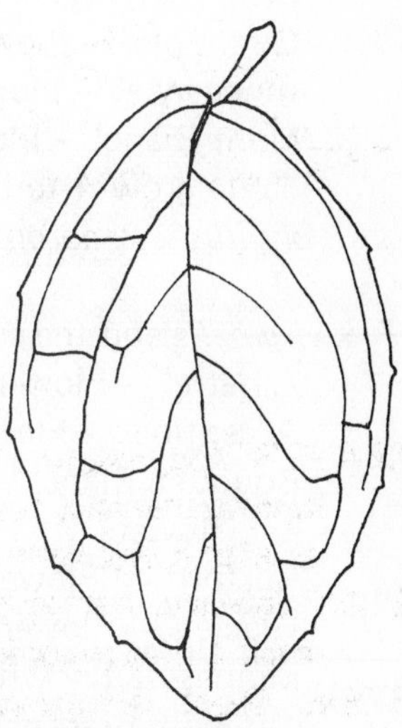

SIZE: 10 to 12′ by 10 to 12′.
HARDINESS: Zone 4.
HABIT: Large rounded shrub with stiff straight ascending branches, arching with age, often leggy, straggly.
RATE: Fast.
TEXTURE: Somewhat coarse in all seasons.

BARK: Exfoliating, orangish brown.

LEAF COLOR: Medium, non-descript green in summer; no change in fall.

FLOWER: Perfect, white, 1 to 1 2/3" across, very fragrant; late May to early June; borne in 5 to 7-flowered racemes.

FRUIT: Four valved dehiscent capsule, persisting.

CULTURE: Transplant readily; not particular as to soil; full sun or light shade; prefer moist, well drained soil supplied with organic matter and here make their best growth; should be pruned after flowering either by removing old wood or cutting to the ground; the root system on mockorange is more extensive and woody than the tops. I dug several large specimens out of our yard and simply could not believe the mass of roots.

DISEASES AND INSECTS: Canker, leaf spots, powdery mildews, rust, aphids, leaf miner and nematodes. None of these are serious.

LANDSCAPE VALUE: Old favorite for sweetly-scented flowers; does not have much to recommend it for the modern landscape. Some of the floriferous cultivars are much better than the species.

CULTIVARS:

'Aureus' — Yellow foliage, a real lemon in any garden.

'Nanus' — Dwarf type about 4'.

PROPAGATION: Cuttings can be taken and rooted with good success about any time of the year.

NATIVE HABITAT: Southern Europe, Italy to Caucasia. Cultivated 1560.

Other *Philadelphus* types of some worth include:

Philadelphus x *cymosus* and the cultivars:

'Banniere' — Flowers semidouble, 1 1/2 - 2 1/2" diameter, fragrant.

'Conquete' — Flowers single, 2" diameter, very fragrant, one of the best.

'Norma' — Flowers single, 1 3/4" diameter.

'Perle Blanche' — Flowers single, 1 1/2" diameter, one of the most fragrant.

The plants in this group grow 6 to 8' high; tend to be rather open and lanky; hardy in Zones 4 to 5; result of crosses between *P.* x *lemoinei* x *P. grandiflorus.*

P. x *lemoinei* and the cultivars:

'Avalanche' — Flowers single, 1" diameter, 4' high with arching branches and one of the most fragrant.

'Belle Etoile' — Flowers single, 2 1/4" diameter, 6' high.

'Boule d'Argent' — Flowers double, 2" diameter, 5' high.

'Erectus' — Flowers single, 1" diameter, 4' high, good compact, upright habit.

'Fleur de Neige' — Flowers single, 1 1/4" diameter and very fragrant.

'Girandole' — Flowers double, 1 3/4" diameter, 4' high.

'Innocence' — Flowers single, 1 3/4" diameter, 8' high, one of the most fragrant forms.

'Mont Blanc' — Flowers single, 1 1/4" diameter, 4' high, one of the hardier forms.

Plants grow 4 to 8', are very fragrant and hardy in Zone 5. Result of crosses between *P. microphyllus* x *P. coronarius.*

P. x *virginalis* and the cultivars:

'Albatre' — Flowers double, 1 1/4" diameter, 5' high.

'Argentine' — Flowers double, 2" diameter, 4' high.

'Bouquet Blanc' — Flowers single, 1" diameter, 6' high, moundlike habit and covered with flowers.

'Burford' — Flowers single to semidouble, 2 1/4 - 2 1/2" diameter.

'Glacier' — Flowers double, 1 1/4" diameter, 5' high.

'Minnesota Snowflake' — Fragrant, white, double, 2" diameter flowers, 8' in height and clothed with branches. Supposedly withstanding temperatures as low as -30°F.

'Virginal' — Flowers double, 2" diameter, 9' high, very fragrant.

Plants grow 5 to 9', are hardy in Zone 5. Result of crosses between *P.* x *lemoinei* x *P. nivalis plena*.

All *Philadelphus* types require about the same care—none. They are vigorous, easy to grow plants but are strictly of single season quality. In flower they are attractive to some but the rest of the year (about 50 weeks) are real eyesores. My garden space and labor are too valuable to waste on shrubs which only return a small interest. Consider these factors before extensively planting shrubs of this type.

Photinia villosa — Oriental Photinia

FAMILY: Rosaceae

LEAVES: Alternate, simple, 1 1/5 to 3 1/5" long, short-stalked, obovate to oblong-obovate, acuminate, cuneate, finely and sharply serrate, glabrous above, villous beneath with 5 to 7 pairs of veins, firm at maturity; petioles 1/25 to 1/5" long.

BUDS: Sessile, solitary, ovoid, acute, with about 4 somewhat keeled and mucronate scales; terminal lacking.

STEM: Moderate or rather slender, rounded with large lenticels; pith rather small, continuous; leaf-scars 2-ranked, linear, crescent-shaped or somewhat 3-lobed, somewhat raised; 3 bundle-traces.

SIZE: 10 to 15' high; usually less in spread.

HARDINESS: Zone 4.

HABIT: A large shrub, but can be trained as a tree, often with an irregular, obovoid crown; usually taller than broad.

RATE: Medium.

TEXTURE: Medium throughout the year.

LEAF COLOR: Dark green above, villous beneath in summer changing to reddish bronze in fall.

FLOWERS: White, 1/2" across, May into June; borne in 1 to 2" diameter corymbs, terminating short side branches.

FRUIT: Pome, bright red, 1/3" long; effective in October and persist for a time if not consumed by the birds; inflorescence is conspicuously warty.

CULTURE: Best to move balled and burlapped; prefers well-drained soil; full sun or light shade; pruning is rarely required.

DISEASES AND INSECTS: Leaf spots, powdery mildews, fireblight. Fireblight can be a very serious problem and for this reason the plant is often not grown.

LANDSCAPE VALUE: Makes a good specimen or shrub border plant. The fruits and fall color are attractive. Extensive use limited by fireblight susceptibility.

PROPAGATION: Softwood, semi-hardwood, or hardwood cuttings will root without great difficulty.

NATIVE HABITAT: Japan, Korea, China. Introduced about 1865.

Physocarpus opulifolius — Common Ninebark, also Eastern Ninebark

FAMILY: Rosaceae

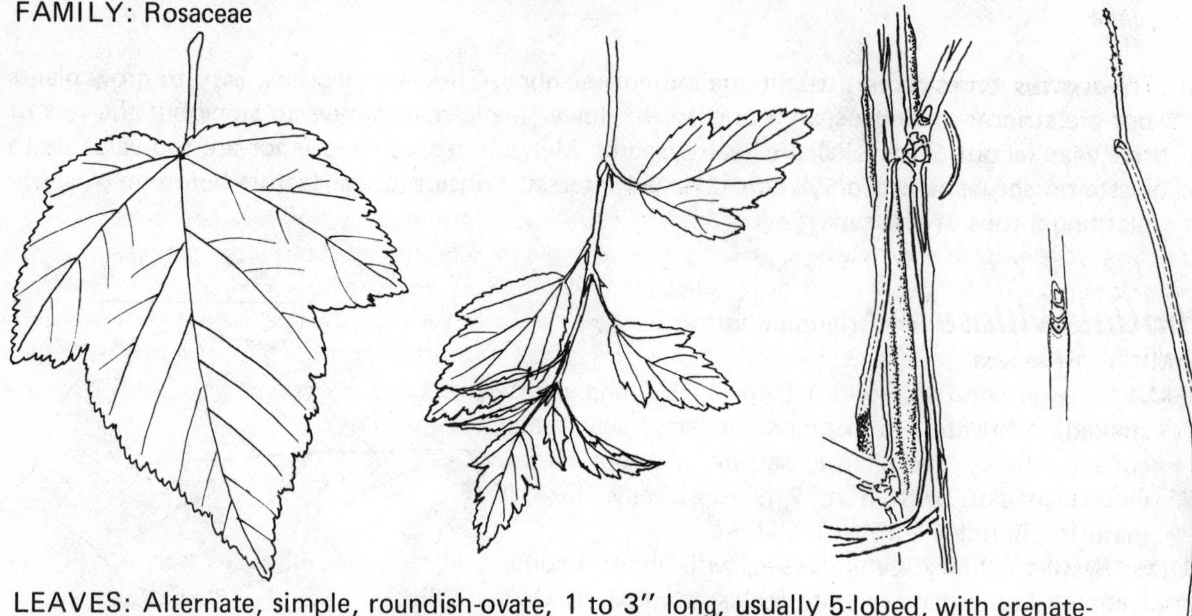

LEAVES: Alternate, simple, roundish-ovate, 1 to 3" long, usually 5-lobed, with crenate-dentate obtuse or acutish lobes, glabrous or nearly so beneath.

BUDS: Imbricate, appressed, basically glabrous, usually 5-scaled, brown.

STEM: Young—shiny red-brown, glabrous. Old—brown, exfoliating in papery strips. Pith—brownish, stems distinctly angled from base of leaf scars.

SIZE: 5 to 9' in height; spread of 6 to 10'.

HARDINESS: Zone 2.

HABIT: Upright, spreading shrub with stiffly recurved branches, rounded and dense in foliage but quite ragged in winter.

RATE: Medium to fast.

TEXTURE: Somewhat coarse in leaf, definitely coarse in winter.

LEAF COLOR: Flat green (medium) in summer; fall color yellowish to bronze; has not been effective in Central Illinois.

FLOWERS: White or pinkish, each flower about 2/5" diameter, May, borne in many flowered, 1 to 2" diameter corymbs, effective but not overwhelming.

CULTURE: Easily transplanted, adapted to difficult situations, full sun or partial shade, very tough individual resembling spirea in character.

DISEASES AND INSECTS: None serious.

LANDSCAPE VALUE: Quite coarse and therefore difficult to use in the small home landscape. Massing, border, possibly a screen; limited in usefulness because of limited ornamental assets. Bark on older stems (1/2" diameter or larger) exfoliates into papery strips exposing a rich brown inner bark. Unfortunately this character is masked by the foliage and dense tangle of stems.

CULTIVARS:

var. *intermedius* — A handsome low growing (4'), fine textured form with darker green foliage than the species. Preferable for modern gardens because of refined and humble character.

'Luteus' — Leaves initially yellow gradually changing to yellowish green.

var. *nanus* — Another dwarf form (2') with smaller, less deeply lobed leaves.

PROPAGATION: Cuttings, easily propagated from softwood cuttings taken in summer. Such cuttings rooted better in sand:peat than in sand, and better at 60°F than 70°F. November cuttings rooted 80% in 53 days without treatment.

ADDITIONAL NOTES: The Minnesota Landscape Arboretum has a large collection of ninebarks and after looking over the entire group still came away with the opinion that about anything is better than a *Physocarpus*.

NATIVE HABITAT: Quebec to Virginia, Tennessee and Michigan. Introduced 1687.

Picea – Spruce

Pinaceae

The spruces represent an interesting group of usually tall, symmetrical, conical trees. Numerous cultivars occur within selected species (*P. abies, P. glauca, P. pungens*) but are limitedly available in the trade. The genus includes nearly 40 species which are largely restricted to the cooler regions of the Northern Hemisphere. No less than 18 of these are confined to China but some of the newer Chinese species are difficult to separate. *Picea* is the ancient latin name of the spruces, derived from pix=pitch. The wood is strong for its weight and is of primary importance in the manufacture of pulp and paper. The resinous bark exudations of *P. abies* furnish the so-called Burgundy pitch which is the basic compound for a number of varnishes and medicinal compounds; while the new leafy shoots are used in brewing spruce beer. Sounding boards for musical instruments are made from the wood of *P. abies*. Healing salves from gums and aromatic distillations of *P. glauca* and *P. mariana* are made, as well as ropes from the roots of *P. abies* and *P. glauca*.

MORPHOLOGICAL CHARACTERISTICS

Monoecious trees, pyramidal or conical; bark usually thin, scaly on old trees, sometimes furrowed at base; branches whorled; branchlets with prominent leaf-cushions (pulveni), separated by incised grooves and produced at the apex into a peg-like stalk bearing the leaf and left when the leaves fall; winter–buds ovoid or conical; scales imbricated, with or without resin; leaves spirally, often pectinately arranged, on underside of branchlets usually 4 angled, stomatiferous on all 4 sides or compressed and stomatiferous only on the upper or ventral side which appears by twisting of leaves to be the lower one; usually with 2 marginal resin-ducts; male flowers axillary; female flowers terminal; cones mostly hanging, ovoid to oblong-cylindrical, not shattering at maturity; scales suborbicular to rhombic-oblong, subtended by small bracts; seeds 2 to each scale, compressed; wing large, thin, obovate or oblong.

GROWTH CHARACTERISTICS

Most spruces are large trees of pyramidal to conical outline of a very formal nature. This tends to limit their usefulness as they dominate a small landscape because of their size and strong vertical lines. Retention of foliage and branches results in dense, attractive trees even after many years. *Picea glauca* 'Conica' is one of the few dwarf types available in the trade. *Picea abies* alone contains over 135 cultivars, only a few of which possess merit for landscape use.

CULTURE

Spruces should be transplanted balled and burlapped and, because of the shallow, spreading root system, large specimens can be transplanted successfully. Spruces prefer a moderately moist, well drained soil although perform well in the clay soils of the midwest. They do not grow well under hot, dry, polluted conditions. *P. omorika, P. orientalis* and *P. pungens* are more tolerant of dry conditions than other species. Usually little pruning is necessary but plants can be touched up in spring when the new growth is approximately one-half developed to create a denser plant. Selected species can be used for hedges as they tolerate heavy pruning.

DISEASES AND INSECTS

Canker (*Cytospora*), needle casts, rusts, wood decay, spruce gall aphid, cooley spruce gall aphid, other aphids, spruce budworm, spruce bud scale, spruce needle miner, pine needle scale, spruce epizeuxis, sawflies, white pine weevil, spruce spider mite and bagworm. The three most prevalent pests in the midwest appear to be mites, aphids and bagworms.

PROPAGATION

Seeds of most *Picea* species germinate promptly without pretreatment, but cold stratification has been used for a few species. Cuttings have been used in isolated cases but percentages were usually low and this does not represent a practical method of propagation. Grafting is used on the cultivars of *P. abies* and especially the blue-foliaged forms of *P. pungens*. A side graft is used on seedlings of the species.

LANDSCAPE VALUE

Spruces are used extensively in large scale landscape plantings such as parks, golf courses, highways, and public buildings. The dense compact character of even older specimens provides attractive dependable evergreens which change little in effect over a long period of time. The symmetrical form results in plants with strong outlines and formal habit.

Textural variations are not great; however, some differences in branching habit can be used for different effect, i.e. the stiff branching of *P. pungens* contrasts with the pendulous branching of *P. abies*. Color contrasts are more distinctive and include light, dark, and yellow greens, and many shades of blue. Because of the conspicuous character of many of the so-called Blue Spruces, care and discretion should be used in locating these plants in the landscape. One of the stigmas of our landscapes has been the placement of these plants in prominent places, especially in the front of the property, which detracts from all other plantings as well as the house.

Selected forms are effective as hedges, screens, windbreaks, specimens, and plantings near large buildings.

SPRUCE SPECIES SELECTED
(The best spruces for the midwest)

Picea abies
Picea glauca
Picea omorika
Picea orientalis
Picea pungens

Picea abies — Norway Spruce

LEAVES: Persistent for several years, those on the upper side of the stem more or less overlapping and pointing forwards, those on the lower side spreading right and left and exposing the stem; rhombic in cross-section, 1/2 to 1" long, stiff, straight or curved, ending in a blunt, horny point; light or dark green with 2 or 3 stomatic lines on each side, often shining green.

BUDS: Reddish or light brown, not resinous, scales often with spreading tips, about 1/4" long, rosette shape.

STEM: Reddish brown or orangish brown, glabrous or with minute scattered hairs.

CONES: Pendulous, cylindrical, 4 to 6" long, brown when mature. Cone scales without undulations, persisting through winter.

SIZE: 40 to 60' in height by 25 to 30' spread; can grow to 100' and more.
HARDINESS: Zone 2.
HABIT: Pyramidal with pendulous branchlets; stiff when young, graceful at maturity.
RATE: Medium to fast especially in youth; may grow 75' high after 50 years.
TEXTURE: Medium.
BARK: Usually thin on young trees; on old trees thick with small, thin gray flaking surface scales.

LEAF COLOR: Bright green in youth changing to lustrous dark green with 2 to 3 stomatic lines on each side.

FLOWERS: Monoecious, male flowers are axillary and infrequent whereas female flowers are terminal, spread on the crowns of the trees and reddish pink in color.

FRUIT: Cones are cylindrical, 4 to 6″ long, pendulous, light brown, purple or green before maturity.

DISEASES AND INSECTS: Susceptible to red spider, spruce gall aphid, budworm and borers.

LANDSCAPE VALUE: Much overplanted, with old age (30 years) loses its form and its usefulness. Commonly used as a windbreak, shelters or as a temporary specimen.

CULTURE: The following applies to all spruces covered in this book unless other specifics are listed under a particular plant. Transplant balled and burlapped in large sizes (3 to 4′ and greater); move readily because of shallow spreading root system; perform best in moderately moist, sandy, well drained soils but can be planted in most average soils provided adequate moisture is available especially in the early years of establishment; prefer a cold climate; prune in early spring either by removing a selected branch or, if a hedge is desired, by pruning the young growth.

CULTIVARS:

'Maxwellii' — Dwarf, globular, flattened; branches short, stiff, branchlets spreading.

'Nidiformis' — Dwarf, dense, broad, nest-like shrub, 3 to 6′ high.

'Pendula' — Branches and branchlets extremely pendulous.

'Procumbens' — Dwarf, broad shrub, 3 to 4′ high, branches horizontal and heaping up; branchlets crowded, thin, stiff.

'Pumila' — Dwarf, globular, flattened, compact, very broad, 3 to 4′ high, lower branches spreading, upper ones nearly erect; branchlets dense, regularly set, directed slightly forward, stiff, flexible, light to reddish brown.

PROPAGATION: Seed does not require a stratification period and can be directly sowed. Optimum period for rooting cuttings appears to be from November to February. Cuttings rooted better when taken in December. Cuttings root best when taken from the lower portion of old trees and should be made from the full length of the current year's growth. Cuttings generally rooted better if made with the basal cut at or slightly above the base of the current year's growth. Rooting was better in 1 sand:1peat, than in sand. Hormonal treatments did not prove significantly beneficial for enhancing rooting.

NATIVE HABITAT: Northern and Central Europe, growing in extended forests, in plains and in the mountains. Introduced in colonial times.

Picea glauca — White Spruce

LEAVES: Persistent for several years, crowded on the upper side of the stem, pale green or glaucous, about 1/2″ long, incurved, ending in an acute or roundish horny point; quadrangular in cross-section. Fetid when bruised.

BUDS: Up to 1/4″ long with rounded chestnut-brown scales, apex blunt, not resinous.

STEM: Slender, glabrous, often glaucous, becoming dark yellowish brown or pale brown in their second year; usually emitting a fetid mouse-like odor when bruised.

CONES: Cylindric, blunt, 1 to 2 1/2″ long and 1/2 to 3/4″ in diameter, pale brown when ripe.

SIZE: 40 to 60′ in height by 10 to 20′ in spread; size descriptions for this species vary significantly with author. Supposedly can grow to 90-120′.

HARDINESS: Zone 2.

HABIT: A broad, dense pyramid in youth, becoming a tall, fairly narrow dense spire, compact and regular, with ascending branches.

RATE: Medium.

TEXTURE: Medium.

BARK: Thin, flaky or scaly, ashy brown; freshly exposed layers somewhat silvery.

LEAF COLOR: Glaucous green with 2 to 3 stomatic lines above and 3 to 4 beneath.

FLOWERS: Inconspicuous, moneocious; staminate, pale red becoming yellow, pistillate purple.

FRUIT: Annual, stalked, pendulous, cylindrical cones 1 to 2 1/2", green when young and light brown when mature.

DISEASES AND INSECTS: Susceptible to trunk and root rot, spruce budworm, European sawfly and red spiders.

CULTURE: Transplants readily; makes its best growth on moist loam or alluvial soils; and although found on many different sites, it is typical of stream banks, lake shores and adjacent slopes. One of the most tolerant spruces as it withstands wind, heat, cold, drought and crowding. Best in full sun, but quite tolerant of some shade.

LANDSCAPE VALUE: Useful as a specimen, mass, hedge, windbreak. Widely used in the plains states because of its adaptability. Probably should be relegated to secondary garden status in the eastern states because of superior evergreen alternatives.

CULTIVARS:

var. *albertiana* – Slow growing, compact, narrow pyramidal tree. Apparently there is considerable hybridization between *P. glauca* and *P. engelmannii* and this gives rise to numerous forms which have been classed as varieties by some authorities.

'Conica' – Often called the Dwarf Alberta Spruce and Dwarf White Spruce. This natural dwarf (could be listed as var. *conica*) was found by J. G. Jack and Alfred Rehder at Lake Laggan, Alberta, Canada as they awaited the train to bring them back to the Arnold Arboretum. The plants become broadly conical with time. The foliage is light green, densely set, and the needles radiate around the stem. Growth is very slow (about 2 to 4" per year). Interesting specimen or novelty plant.

'Densata' – This again could and often is listed correctly as var. *densata*. This is a slow growing conical type reaching 20 to 40' after 40 to 80 years. The few trees on our campus are much denser and more ornamental than the species.

PROPAGATION: Seed requires no pretreatment. Cuttings collected in late July rooted 84 to 90% and better than cuttings taken earlier or later. Treatment with IAA did not affect rooting. *P. g.* 'Conica' cuttings collected in December rooted better in sand:peat than sand, and the percentage was increased by 70 ppm IBA/24 hour soak. There are other reports which indicate this plant can be successfully rooted from cuttings.

RELATED SPECIES:

Picea engelmannii, Engelmann Spruce, is a large, narrow, almost spire-like, densely pyramidal tree with ascending branches. In the eastern states this species may grow 40 to 50' high in 40 to 60 years but in its native range can grow 100 to 120' tall. The needles are 4-sided, blue-green, about 1"± long and emit a rank odor when crushed. The bark is thin and broken into large purplish brown to russet-red, thin, loosely attached scales. Maximum growth is made on deep, rich, loamy soils of high moisture content. Wyman considers this species one of the better spruces for ornamental planting. Several cultivars include: 'Argentea' which has silvery gray needles and 'Glauca' with needles bluish to steel blue. Native to the Rocky and Cascade Mountains and Northeastern California. Zone 5.

Picea mariana, Black Spruce, is a small to medium-sized tree which grows 30 to 40' tall and develops a limited spread. The habit is distinctly conical, spire-like. The needles are 4-sided, dull bluish green, more or less glaucous, 1/4 to 1/2" long. The cones are small, 3/4 to 1 1/2" long, ovoid, purplish and turn brown at maturity. The bark is broken into thin, flaky, grayish brown to reddish brown scales, 1/4 to 1/2" thick, freshly exposed inner scales somewhat olive-green. This is a cold climate tree and in the southern part of its range is commonly restricted to cool sphagnum bogs; in the far north it is found on dry slopes but makes its best growth on moist, well drained alluvial bottoms. The cultivar 'Doumetii' is a slow growing densely pyramidal form which can be propagated by cuttings. Wyman makes reference to a 20-year-old tree in the Arnold Arboretum that was 8' tall, and 9' in branch spread. Native to Northeastern United States and transcontinental through Canada. Zone 2.

NATIVE HABITAT: Northern United States and transcontinental through Canada.

Picea omorika — Serbian Spruce

LEAVES: Overlapping and directed forwards on upper side of branchlets, 2/5 to 4/5" long, 1/25 to 1/12" wide, apex short pointed on young plants, rounder on old plants, compressed, flat, keeled on both sides, dark green, without stomata above; glaucous white with 4 to 6 distinct stomatic bands on either side of the midrib beneath.

SIZE: 50 to 60' by 20 to 25' spread after 50 to 60 years, can grow to 100'.
HARDINESS: Zone 4.
HABIT: A tree with a remarkably slender trunk and short ascending or drooping branches forming a very narrow, pyramidal head.
RATE: Slow.
TEXTURE: Medium.
BARK: Thin, scaling off in platelets, coffee-brown in color.
LEAF COLOR: The upper surface is a glossy dark green in contrast to the lower with its two prominent white stomatic lines.
FLOWERS: Inconspicuous, monoecious, purple.
FRUIT: Cones are oblong-ovoid, 1 3/5 to 2 3/5" long, blue-black when young, shining cinnamon brown when ripe.
CULTURE: Prefers a deep rich soil that is both moist and well-drained. Furthermore, grows on limestone and acid peats, and will benefit from winter protection from strong winds. Likes a dry atmosphere and semi-shade, supposedly tolerates city air.
DISEASES AND INSECTS: Subject to aphids, budworm and borers.
LANDSCAPE VALUE: Noted for its excellent foliage and narrow, pyramidal growth; considered excellent for the northeastern states. Would make an excellent evergreen street tree.
CULTIVARS:

'Nana' — A small, densely conical bush of compact habit.

'Pendula' — A very beautiful, slender tree with drooping, slightly twisted branches.

PROPAGATION: Seed requires no pretreatment. Cuttings taken in winter from 4-year-old trees rooted moderately well. Rooting was improved by treatment with 200 ppm IBA/24 hour soak.
ADDITIONAL NOTES: Perhaps the most handsome of the spruces. The habit is more graceful and refined than most. Should be used in preference to other spruces when it can be located.
NATIVE HABITAT: Southeastern Europe (Yugoslavia).

Picea orientalis — Oriental Spruce

LEAVES: Very short, 1/4 to 1/2" long, 4-sided, lustrous dark green, blunt or rounded at the apex, with 1 to 4 lines of stomata on each surface.

SIZE: 50 to 60' in height after about 60 years, can grow to 120'.
HARDINESS: Zone 4.
HABIT: A dense, compact pyramid with horizontal branches that are often pendulous.
RATE: Slow.
TEXTURE: Medium.
BARK: Brown, exfoliating in thin scales.
LEAF COLOR: Lustrous dark green with 1 to 4 stomatic lines on each side, needles very short and tightly set.
FLOWERS: Inconspicuous, monoecious; carmine-red.
FRUIT: Cones short stalked, nodding, ovoid-cylindrical, 2 to 4" long by approximately 1" wide, purple when young turning brown when mature.
CULTURE: Will tolerate poor, gravelly soils. Plant where winters are not excessively cold or dry; has done well in Midwest as a young tree; protect from harsh winter winds.
LANDSCAPE VALUE: Because of its graceful and attractive habit it has value as a specimen spruce for small areas; much superior to Norway and White; may suffer browning of foliage in severe

winters; there are many fine specimens in Spring Grove Cemetery, Cincinnati and Cave Hill Cemetery, Louisville, Kentucky. Once one sees this tree he or she wonders why Norway and White are ever planted.

CULTIVARS:

'Aurea' — Young shoots golden yellow in spring, changing to green, often with a general golden sheen all over the leaves.

'Gowdy' — Supposedly a very narrow columnar form with small rich green leaves.

'Gracilis' — A slow growing densely branched form developing into a small, conical tree; 15 to 20' tall.

'Pendula' (now called 'Weeping Dwarf') — A compact, slow-growing form with pendulous branchlets.

PROPAGATION: Seed requires no pretreatment.

NATIVE HABITAT: Asia Minor, Caucasus.

Picea pungens — Colorado Spruce

LEAVES: Spreading more or less all around the stem, but more crowded above than below, stout, rigid, incurved and very prickly, 3/4 to 1 1/4" long, varying in color on different trees, dull green, bluish or silvery-white, 4-sided with about 6 stomatic lines in each side. Needles with acid taste when chewed.

BUDS: Broadly conical to nearly spherical, apex blunt, yellowish brown, not resinous; scales loosely appressed, apex often reflexed, the lowest ones keeled, long pointed.

STEM: Stout, without pubescence, glaucous at first becoming orange-brown with age.

CONES: Cylindrical but slightly narrowed at each end, 2 to 4" long, pale shining brown when mature, prominent undulating lines in each cone scale.

SIZE: 90 to 135' in height by 20 to 30' spread. (In Illinois, 30 to 60' in height with a 10 to 20' spread.)

HARDINESS: Zone 2.

HABIT: A broad, dense, regular pyramid with horizontal stiff branches to the ground; becoming open, poor and dingy in age.

RATE: Slow-medium, 30 to 50' after 35 to 50 years. Very stiff and coarse in outline.

TEXTURE: Medium to coarse.

LEAF COLOR: Usually gray-green to blue-green; young growth soft, silvery blue-gray.

FLOWERS: Monoecious; staminate orange, pistillate greenish or purple and inconspicuous.

FRUIT: Cones oblong, cylindrical, short-stalked, 2 to 4" long, green when young turning light or yellow-brown when ripe.

CULTURE: It prefers a rich and moist soil in full sunlight although is more drought tolerant than other *Picea*.

DISEASES AND INSECTS: Subject to spruce gall aphid (causes tips of branches to die), spruce budworm and spider mites.

LANDSCAPE VALUE: Overused; popular as a specimen but hard to combine well with other plants; acceptable in dry climates; can be used in mass plantings. One of the standard practices in past years has been the use of this plant or a blue-foliaged type in the front yard where it immediately detracts from the rest of the landscape.

CULTIVARS:

'Argentea' — Foliage silvery white; a collective name for cultivars with silvery colored leaves.

'Bakerii' — Deeper blue than foliage of 'Argentea' and possibly better than 'Moerheimii'. After 32 years a specimen in the Arnold Arboretum was only 12' tall and 6' across.

'Coerulea' — Foliage bluish white.

var. *glauca* — Foliage bluish green. The variety from which the best cultivars are selected.

'Hoopsii' — Dense, pyramidal form with spreading branches, foliage extremely glaucous. Perhaps the most glaucous form and the best grower, my number one choice.

'Hunnewelliana' – Dense pyramidal form of light blue foliage. Thirty-two-year-old tree is 15' tall and 8' across.

'Mission Blue' – Intense blue foliage color, compact, symmetrical grower.

'Moerheimii' – Compact, dense growing form with very blue foliage, sometimes with longitudinal young shoots. Retains blue color in winter. An irregular grower.

'Pendens' – ('Koster'). This form develops a horizontal trunk with pendulous branches and must be staked to develop tree form.

'Thompsonii' – ('Thompson'). Symmetrical pyramidal tree of a whitish-silver-blue foliage color, more intense than the above varieties although somewhat similar to 'Hoopsii', but leaves at least twice as thick, one of the best.

PROPAGATION: Seed requires no pretreatment. Cuttings can be rooted and are best taken in winter although cuttings taken in April rooted 80% in eight weeks after treatment with 100 ppm IBA/24 hour soak. Most of the cultivars are grafted onto seedling understocks. This is usually done in January and February in the greenhouse and the grafted plants are placed under lath or lined out in the spring.

NATIVE HABITAT: Southwestern United States; Rocky Mountains from Colorado to Utah to New Mexico and Wyoming. Introduced about 1862.

Pieris japonica — Japanese Pieris, also mistakenly called Andromeda

FAMILY: Ericaceae

LEAVES: Alternate, simple, obovate-oblong to oblanceolate, 1 1/5 to 3" long, crenate-serrate, lustrous dark green above, lighter green beneath, glabrous. New growth is a bronze-purple color.

FLOWERS: Buds form in summer prior to year of flowering and offer a valid identification characteristic.

SIZE: 9 to 12' in height by 6 to 8' in spread.

HARDINESS: Zone 5.

HABIT: Upright evergreen shrub of neat habit with stiff, spreading branches and dense rosette like foliage.

RATE: Slow, 4 to 6' in 5 to 8 years.

TEXTURE: Medium in all seasons.

LEAF COLOR: New growth a rich bronze; changing to lustrous dark green at maturity.

FLOWER: Perfect, weakly fragrant, white, urn-shaped, 1/5" long, mid to late March, borne in 3 to 6" long slightly pendulous panicles, effective for 2 to 3 weeks.

FRUIT: Dehiscent capsule.

CULTURE: Transplant balled and burlapped or as a container plant into moist, acid, well-drained soil which has been supplemented with peat moss or organic matter; full sun or partial shade; supposedly not as fastidious as to acid soil requirement as other ericaceous plants; prune after flowering; shelter from wind.

DISEASES AND INSECTS: Leaf spots, dieback (*Phytophthora*), lace bug (very prevalent in eastern states where it has made the culture of *Pieris* very difficult; sucks juices from leaves and causes yellowing to browning of foliage), Florida wax scale, two-spotted mite, nematodes.

LANDSCAPE VALUE: Excellent large specimen broadleaf evergreen, works well in the shrub border, in mass, or blended with other broadleaf evergreens.

CULTIVARS:

'Compacta' – Compact form with leaves about 1/2 those of the species.

'Crispa' – Leaves with wavy margins.

'Dorothy Wycoff' — Compact form, dark-red flower buds, red to dark pink flowers.
'Pink Bud' — Buds and newly opened flowers pink.
'Pygmaea' — Leaves small, 1/2 to 1" long and very narrow; feathery in effect.
'Variegata' — Leaves with white margins.
'White Caps' — Exceptionally long inflorescences.

PROPAGATION: Seed, as discussed for other Ericaceae. Cuttings root readily, see under *Leucothoe*. Seed was collected in November, 1975, and directly sowed on peat and placed under mist. Within 21 days excellent germination had occurred.

RELATED SPECIES:

Pieris floribunda, Mountain Pieris, is a handsome evergreen shrub of neat, bushy habit, low and rounded, with rather stiff branches and dense, dark green, 1 to 3" long leaves; will grow 2 to 6' high with a similar or greater spread. Flowers are white, fragrant, borne in 2 to 4" long, dense, upright panicles; April for 2 to 4 weeks; very handsome small rounded shrub which has not been used enough in American gardens; not afflicted by the lacebug like the Japanese Pieris; also is tolerant of higher pH soils than most Ericaceae. Seed can be sown as soon as ripe however cuttings have proved somewhat difficult to root. Native to Virginia and Georgia. Introduced 1800. Zone 4.

An F_1 hybrid between the Japanese and Mountain Pieris has resulted in a clone called 'Brouwer's Beauty' which is dense and compact in habit; the leaves are dark green and shiny; the new foliage a distinct yellow-green. Panicles are horizontal but slightly arched. Flower buds are deep purplish red. Roots easier than *Pieris floribunda*; cuttings should be taken in the fall and placed in plastic tents and a peat:perlite medium. Previously, this clone was thought to be resistant to the lace bug but recent controlled tests have shown that the hybrid is susceptible when exposed to large numbers of lace bugs.

ADDITIONAL NOTES: The flower buds are formed the summer prior to flowering and are exposed all winter. They are quite attractive and do add ornamental appeal to the landscape.

NATIVE HABITAT: Japan. Cultivated 1870.

Pinus — Pine

Pinaceae

Of all the needle-type evergreens pines seem to show the greatest diversity of habit, distribution and ornamental characteristics. There are about 90 species distributed throughout the Northern Hemisphere from the Arctic Circle to Guatemala, the West Indies, North Africa and the Malayan Archipelago. Most are large trees however several species are dwarfish or shrubby and over their native range may vary from dense, compact, slow growing types (3') to large trees (75', *Pinus mugo*). The pines are of primary importance in the production of timber, pulp, and paper manufacture. Turpentine, pine-wood oils, wood tars, and rosin are obtained from the wood of several species. The leaf oils of several species are used in the manufacture of medicines and the seeds of several others are suitable for food ("pine nuts"). Generally, pines are considered more tolerant of adverse soil and climatic conditions than species *Picea* and *Abies*.

MORPHOLOGICAL CHARACTERISTICS

Evergreen, monoecious trees of various heights, tall, rarely shrubby; crowns of young to middle-aged trees pyramidal, older flat-topped or arched-umbelliformly branched; trunk of isolated trees usually large at base, rapidly tapering, that of forest-grown trees straight, lower branches shredding; bark usually thick, rough, furrowed or scaly; branches whorled; branchlets appearing as long shoots and as spurs; long shoots on seedling plants up to the third year with needle-like leaves, afterwards with dry-membranous (soon deciduous) scale-like leaves, in the axils of which arise the spurs; one year long shoots regularly grow from winter-buds producing a single internode, consisting of a leafless base, which often bears the male flowers, a longer upper part bearing foliage and ending in a terminal bud, surrounded by a whorl of smaller buds, one or more of which may be replaced by female flowers, or the long shoot consisting of 2 internodes, each with a leafless base, a leaf-bearing portion, and a whorl of buds; some species produce occasionally shoots that bear juvenile leaves until advanced in age; such often appear from adventive buds; terminal buds varying in different species regarding the shape and character of their scales, resinous or not; leaves of three kinds: Leaves borne on seedling-plants, solitary, spirally arranged, linear lanceolate, entire or margin fringed, soon deciduous, except the basal portion; adult leaves, needle-like, borne in clusters of 2, 3 or 5, margin often minutely toothed, the section semi-circular in the 2-leaved species, triangular in the 3- to 5-leaved ones, persistent 2 or more years; sheaths of the leaf-bundles persistent, deciduous or partly so; cones variable in outline, symmetrical or oblique, remaining on the tree unopened for many years; scales thin, or thick and woody, the exposed part of each scale (apophysis) thickened, showing a terminal or dorsal protuberance or scar, called the umbo, which is often pointed with a prickly point, boss or stout hook; seeds 2 to each scale, nut-like or ovoid, appressed, the kernel surrounded by a shell, winged or not; cotyledons 4-15.

GROWTH CHARACTERISTICS

It is difficult to stereotype the growth habits of pines but the majority are pyramidal, more or less symmetrical trees in youth becoming more round-topped, open and picturesque with age. There is considerable interest in the dwarf types and many selections have been made among species. One of the most beautiful of all upright types is *Pinus strobus* 'Fastigiata' which carries its plume-like foliage on strongly ascending branches and maintains a full complement of branches into old age.

CULTURE

Pines, with the exception of small seedlings or liners, should be moved balled and burlapped. If large plants have been properly root pruned transplanting is accomplished with little difficulty. Most pines will develop a tap root and therefore are difficult to transplant from the wild.

Pines are more tolerant of adverse soil, exposure, and city conditions than *Abies* and *Picea*. The two needle types are considered more tolerant than the three which are greater than the five. *Pinus sylvestris* and *P. nigra* are adapted to many soil types while *P. mugo, P. pungens, P. banksiana* and *P. thunbergii* are more satisfactory in sandy soils. *Pinus nigra, P. pungens, P. thunbergii* and *P. virginiana* exhibit salt spray tolerance. Several species such as *P. jeffreyi, P. thunbergii* and *P. wallichiana* are on the hardiness borderline in the upper midwest.

Pines withstand pruning and can be maintained as hedges and screens. Removing one-half of the new candle-growth (usually in June) will result in the formation of lateral buds below the cut. Christmas tree growers use machete's or power equipment for pruning.

DISEASES AND INSECTS

Late damping-off and root rot, dieback, tip blight, stem blister rust, Comandra blister rust, cankers, *Cenangium* twig blight, leaf cast, needle blight, needle rust, shrub pine needle rust, littleleaf, white-pine aphid, European pine shoot moth, Nantucket pine moth, sawflies, pine webworm, pine false webworm, pine needle scale, pine needle miner, pine spittlebugs, pine tortoise scale, red pine scale, pales weevil, pine root collar weevil, white pine shoot borer, white pine tube moth, white pine weevil, Zimmerman pine moth, bark beetles.

Physiological problems include:

White pine blight—browning of current season's needles especially in Northeastern United States; primary cause is unknown.

Stunt—on *Pinus resinosa*; possibly from poor soil drainage.

Air pollutants—including sulfur dioxide and ozone, produce tip burn or speckling of leaves.
Salt—significant damage to trees located along highways which are heavily salted. Damage is usually evident only on side of tree facing the highway.

PROPAGATION

All species are grown from seed and the stratification requirements vary significantly (see specific requirements which are listed under each species). Recently there has been considerable interest in producing seed-grown dwarf types. Cones are collected from witches' broom type growths and the resultant progeny are usually dwarfish in habit.

Grafting is used on many of the cultivars. A side graft is usually used on seedlings of the species. Cuttings have also been rooted but the percentage was usually low.

LANDSCAPE USE

The tree species and cultivars of pine are used extensively in large scale landscape plantings such as parks, golf courses, estates, cemeteries, industrial grounds, shopping centers, and public buildings. More advantage is usually found in using a few or individual specimen plants, rather than mass planting, because of the interesting outlines and branching habits. Variations in color from blue to dark green and in texture from fine to coarse makes possible the creation of many landscape effects.

Large dense specimens or groups should be used carefully, if at all, on small properties because of the massive and overpowering effects, unwanted shade in winter, and interference with air movement.

Selected forms can be used near the house or other small buildings, as hedges, screens, windbreaks, or specimens.

The continuing trend to large scale landscaping will increase the demand for high quality, landscape size pines in the future.

Pine List
According to Needle Number

FIVE NEEDLE TYPES

PRIMARY

Pinus aristata	Bristlecone Pine
Pinus cembra	Swiss Stone Pine
Pinus flexilis	Limber Pine
Pinus koraiensis	Korean Pine
Pinus parviflora	Japanese White Pine
Pinus peuce	Balkan Pine
Pinus strobus	Eastern White Pine
Pinus wallichiana	Himalayan Pine

SECONDARY

Pinus balfouriana	Foxtail Pine

THREE NEEDLE TYPES

PRIMARY

Pinus bungeana	Lacebark Pine

SECONDARY

Pinus ponderosa	Ponderosa Pine
Pinus rigida	Pitch Pine
Pinus taeda	Loblolly Pine

TWO NEEDLE TYPES

PRIMARY

Pinus densiflora	Japanese Red Pine
Pinus mugo	Swiss Mountain Pine
Pinus nigra or *P. nigra nigra*	Austrian Pine
Pinus resinosa	Red Pine
Pinus sylvestris	Scotch Pine

SECONDARY

Pinus banksiana	Jack Pine
Pinus echinata	Shortleaf Pine
Pinus pungens	Table Mountain Pine
Pinus thunbergii	Japanese Black Pine
Pinus virginiana	Scrub Pine

Pinus aristata — Bristlecone Pine, also called Hickory Pine.

LEAVES: Borne 5 together, bluish green, persistent for 14 to 17 years, commonly dotted with white resinous exudations, 4/5 to 1 3/5″ long; leaf sheaths curling back into small rosettes, remaining 2 to 4 years at the base of the leaf.

SIZE: 8 to 20′ with an irregular spread; can grow to 40′ but this would take many years.
HARDINESS: Zone 5.
HABIT: Dwarf, shrubby and picturesque in youth and in old age.
RATE: Slow, in fact extremely so, 16-year-old plant being only 4′ high.
TEXTURE: Medium.
LEAF COLOR: Dark green with white resinous exudations giving the leaf a bluish white cast.
FLOWERS: Monoecious and inconspicuous.
FRUIT: Cones sessile, cylindrical-ovoid, 2 to 4″ long by 1 3/5″ broad, apex blunt, a bristle-like prickle at the edge of each pine scale.
CULTURE: Will succeed in poor, dry, rocky soils whether alkaline or acid, dislikes shade and will not tolerate smoke-polluted air.
DISEASES AND INSECTS: Refer to general culture sheet.
LANDSCAPE VALUE: Suitable for rock garden or used as an accent plant. Could possibly be used as a foundation plant because of its picturesque growth habit, makes a nice bonsai or patio plant.
PROPAGATION: Seeds have no dormancy and will germinate immediately upon collection. I have raised many seedlings and the only requirement is that damping-off be controlled.
ADDITIONAL NOTES: Depending on what source you believe this species is one of the oldest living plants on earth. Estimates range from 2000 to 7000 years, however, several trees in the

4000 to 5000 year-old category have been adequately documented. One authority reported a 4900-year-old tree in Eastern Nevada. Trees may attain only an inch diameter in a century.

Often referred to as foxtail pine because of the length of needle retention and the bushy effect of the foliage. *Pinus balfouriana*, Foxtail Pine, is a related type but does not develop the resinous exudations.

NATIVE HABITAT: Southwestern United States from the mountains along the Nevada-California border east through the highlands of Nevada, Utah, Colorado, Northern Arizona and Northern New Mexico.

Pinus banksiana — Jack Pine

LEAVES: In pairs, persisting 2 or 3 years (olive green), stiff, curved or slightly twisted, 3/4 to 2" long, margin with minute or rudimentary teeth, apex short-petioled, stomata on each surface.

BUDS: Dark brown, 1/8 to 1/4" long, cylindrical, resinous with closely pressed scales.

STEM: Smooth, glabrous, pale yellowish green, reddish or brown the second year.

SIZE: 35 to 50' in height, known to 70'; irregularly spreading but usually less than height.

HARDINESS: Zone 2.

HABIT: Pyramidal in youth; open, spreading, often shrubby and flat-topped at maturity.

RATE: Slow-medium.

TEXTURE: Medium; possibly coarse in winter as needles often form a sickly yellow-green.

BARK: Thin, reddish brown to gray on young stems, becoming dark brown and flaky; on old trunks furrowed into irregular thick plates.

LEAF COLOR: Young leaves light green to dull dark green; yellow-green in winter.

FLOWERS: Monoecious; staminate clustered, yellowish.

FRUIT: On some trees, nearly all mature cones remain closed; on others most of them open. closed cones subjected to temperatures of 140°F will open.

CULTURE: Easily transplanted if root pruned. Not good in limestone soils, but will survive in almost pure sand and extremely cold climates. Desires full sun, dry, sandy and acid soils. Grows in soils too poor for most plants.

LANDSCAPE VALUE: Not especially ornamental but adaptable as windbreaks, shelterbelts and mass plantings in sand. Also valued for its extreme hardiness and suitability to the colder regions. I have seen considerable plantings in poor soil regions of southern Indiana.

CULTIVARS:

'Uncle Fogy' — Weeping form, can be grafted to an upright standard and grown as a weeping tree or used as a ground cover. In 10 years, one plant had spread 15' and was 2' high.

PROPAGATION: Seeds have no dormancy, or only a slight one, and will germinate immediately upon collection after a light stratification.

ADDITIONAL NOTES: Species serves as a valuable pioneer tree on poor sandy soils, but, except on the very poorest, is eventually replaced by Red or White Pine. Parboiling the male flowers to remove excess resin supposedly makes them suitable for eating.

NATIVE HABITAT: Most northerly of North American species—grows near the Arctic Circle, south to Northern New York and Minnesota.

Pinus bungeana — Lacebark Pine

LEAVES: 3, remaining 3 to 4 years, stiff, apex sharp-pointed, 2-4" long, 1/12" wide, margins finely toothed, inside slightly rounded, made by the raised midrib, with stomatic lines on both sides, bright medium green. Needles are very stiff and rigid as well as sharp to the touch.

SIZE: 30 to 50' with a 20 to 35' spread, can grow to 75'.

HARDINESS: Zone 4.

HABIT: Rounded to pyramidal, often with many trunks in youth; becoming open, picturesque, flat-topped and broad-spreading with age.
RATE: Slow.
TEXTURE: Medium.
BARK: Exfoliating in patches like a planetree, young stems greenish with irregular whitish or brownish areas interspersed; one of the most handsome pines for bark character.
LEAF COLOR: Bright green.
FLOWERS: Monoecious, clustered.
FRUITS: Cones 1 to 2, terminal or lateral, subsessile, ovoid, 2 to 3" long, approximately 2" across, light yellowish brown; scale-end broader than high, cross-keeled, with a reflexed, triangular spine.
CULTURE: Transplant balled and burlapped if root pruned. Prefers well-drained soils and sunny conditions; supposedly tolerates limestone.
DISEASES AND INSECTS: See culture sheet.
LANDSCAPE VALUE: A good specimen tree valued for its striking, showy white bark; excellent on corners of large buildings; and places where bark can be viewed.
ADDITIONAL NOTES: The National Arboretum, Washington, D. C., has many handsome specimens. Has a place in almost every garden; one of the most beautiful of introduced pines; first observed by Dr. Bunge near Peking in 1831, cultivated in a temple garden.
NATIVE HABITAT: China. Introduced 1846.

Pinus cembra — Swiss Stone Pine (Arolla Pine)

LEAVES: 5, remaining 4 to 5 years, densely set, rather stiff, straight, 2 to 3" (5") long, scarcely 1/25" wide, apex blunt-pointed, margins finely toothed, dark green outside, innersides with bluish white stomatic lines; leaf sheaths falling the first year.
STEMS: Covered with dense, orange-colored pubescence the first year; becoming grayish black the second year.

SIZE: 30 to 40' in height, occasionally 70' with a spread of 15 to 25'.
HARDINESS: Zone 2.
HABIT: A narrow, densely columnar pyramid in youth; and becoming open and flat-topped with spreading, drooping branches when mature; extremely upright in youth.
RATE: Slow, rarely reaches 25' after 25 or 30 years.
TEXTURE: Medium.
LEAF COLOR: Lustrous dark green outside, innersides with bluish white stomatic lines.
FLOWERS: Monoecious, clustered and inconspicuous.
FRUIT: The cones are terminal, short-stalked, erect-ovoid, apex blunt, 2 to 3" long by 1 2/5 to 2 1/5" broad. Greenish violet at first turning purplish brown when mature. Cones never open but fall in the spring of the third year.
CULTURE: Requires a well-drained, loamy soil in full sun. Transplants better than most other pines. Soil must be well-drained and slightly acid; should be located in an open area with free air movement.
DISEASES AND INSECTS: See culture sheet.
LANDSCAPE VALUE: A picturesque and hardy tree; useful as a specimen or mass; very handsome pine but somewhat slow growing.
CULTIVARS:

'Columnaris' — More narrow and columnar in habit than the species.

PROPAGATION: Seed should be stratified in moist medium for 90 to 270 days at 33 to 41°F.
NATIVE HABITAT: Mountains of Central Europe and Southern Asia. Introduced 1875.

Pinus densiflora — Japanese Red Pine

LEAVES: 2, remaining 3 years, slender, twisted, soft, 3 to 5" long, 1/25" wide, apex acute, margins finely toothed, with inconspicuous stomatic lines on each side. The needles appear as if tufted and are borne somewhat upright along the stems.

STEMS: Initially greenish, more or less downy, eventually orange-yellow, somewhat glaucous, glabrous.

SIZE: 40 to 60' in height with a similar spread at maturity, can grow to 100'.

HARDINESS: Zone 4.

HABIT: The trunks are frequently crooked or leaning, branches horizontally spreading and the crown is rather broad and flat; very irregular even in youth as it is an open, floppy grower.

RATE: Slow.

TEXTURE: Medium.

BARK: Orangish to orangish red when young, peeling off in thin scales; in old age grayish at the base, fissured into oblong plates.

LEAF COLOR: Bright, bluish green turning yellowish green to pale green in the winter.

FLOWERS: Monoecious, inconspicuous.

FRUIT: Cones sub-terminal, short-stalked, solitary or in clusters, conical-ovoid to oblong, somewhat oblique at the base, 1 2/5 to 2" long by approximately 1" broad, dull tawny yellow opening the second year and remaining 2 to 3 years on the tree.

CULTURE: Prefers a well-drained, slightly acid soil and sunny conditions.

DISEASES AND INSECTS: See culture sheet.

LANDSCAPE VALUE: Used as a specimen because of its interesting form and decorative, orange-red bark; also favorite subject for bonsai.

CULTIVARS:

'Globosa' — Rounded, spreading shrub, the trunk is semi-prostrate. Slow growing (15' in 50 years.)

'Oculus-draconis' — Each leaf marked with two yellow lines and when viewed from above shows alternate yellow and green rings.

'Prostrata' — Main stems bend and branches follow the contour of the ground.

'Umbraculifera' — Dwarf, umbrella-like head, to 9 feet or more tall; branches densely borne, upright spreading, very beautiful especially when the bark color is developed.

PROPAGATION: Seed requires no stratification.

NATIVE HABITAT: Japan. Introduced 1854.

Pinus flexilis — Limber Pine

LEAVES: In fives, persisting 5 to 6 years, densely crowded on the ends of the branchlets, pointing forwards, rigid, curved or slightly twisted, 2 to 3" long, margins entire, apex sharp-pointed, 3 to 4 lines of stomata on each surface, dark green to a slight glaucous dark green.

BUDS: Ovoid, slender, sharply pointed, 3/8" long.

STEM: Tough, flexible, glabrous or minutely tomentulous, actually can be tied in knots.

SIZE: 30 to 50' in height by 15 to 35' in spread.

HARDINESS: Zone 2.

HABIT: Dense, broad pyramidal in youth; becoming a low, broad, flat-topped tree at maturity.

RATE: Slow.

TEXTURE: Medium.

BARK: In youth smooth, silvery white to light gray or greenish gray; on old trunks dark brown to nearly black, separated by deep fissures into rectangular to nearly square, superficially scaled plates or blocks.

LEAF COLOR: Dark bluish green; very attractive.

FLOWERS: Monoecious; staminate clustered, rose color becoming purple, then tan brown.

FRUIT: Cones subterminal, short-stalked, cylindric ovoid, 3 to 6" long, erect when young and spreading when mature, light brown.

CULTURE: Transplants well balled and burlapped if root pruned. Does best in moist, well-drained soil and prefers sun or partial shade. Adapted for planting on rocky slopes.

DISEASES AND INSECTS: See culture sheet.

LANDSCAPE VALUE: A handsome specimen or mass; Wyman noted than an 80-year-old tree in the Arnold Arboretum was only 30' tall.

CULTIVARS:

'Columnaris' — Fastigiate, upright form, good for narrow areas.

'Glauca' — Foliage bluish green, much more so than the species.

'Glenmore' — Leaves longer and more silvery in color.

'Nana' — Dwarf, bushy form, extremely slow growing.

PROPAGATION: Seed should be stratified for 21 to 90 days at 35 to 41°F.

RELATED SPECIES: Categorized as one of the stone pines. A related species is *P. albicaulis*, Whitebark Pine, which differs in its smaller ovoid cones, 2 1/2" long, and the fact they remain closed at maturity.

NATIVE HABITAT: Rocky Mountains of Western North America, Alberta to Northern Mexico, east to Texas.

Pinus mugo — Swiss Mountain Pine

LEAVES: In pairs persisting five or more years, rigid, curved, medium to dark green, 1 to 2" (1 1/2 to 3") long, margins finely toothed, apex short, blunt, horny point; stomatic lines on both surfaces; basal sheath up to about 3/5" long.

BUDS: Oblong ovoid, 1/4 to 1/2" long with reddish brown scales encrusted with resin, scales closely appressed.

STEM: Young stems short, without down, green at first with prominent ridges becoming brown to blackish brown.

SIZE: 15 to 20' in height by 25 to 30' spread; but can grow 30 to 80' tall and as wide.

HARDINESS: Zone 2.

HABIT: Very variable, prostrate or pyramidal; usually low, broad-spreading and bushy, at least the types available from nurseries.

RATE: Slow.

TEXTURE: Medium.

BARK: Brownish gray, scaly, split in irregular plates but not scaling off on old trunks; a good identification feature on 1/2" to 2 to 3" diameter stems are the regular bumpy protuberances which result when the leaves abscise.

LEAF COLOR: Medium-green, often yellowish green in winter especially on the tips of the needles.

FLOWERS: Monoecious and inconspicuous.

FRUIT: Cones, subterminal, sessile or short stalked, erect, horizontal, or slightly pendulous, solitary or 2-3(-4) together, ovoid or conical-ovoid, 4/5 to 1 2/5" long by 3/5 to 1 3/5" broad, apex surrounded by a darker ring; at maturity grayish black.

CULTURE: Moves well balled and burlapped if root pruned. Prefers a deep, moist loam in sun or partial shade. Can be pruned annually to thicken plant and keep dwarf.

DISEASES AND INSECTS: Subject to rusts, wood rots, borers, sawflies and especially scale (often very serious).

LANDSCAPE VALUE: The species is seldom used; valued chiefly for its dwarf cultivars which are useful in landscape plantings, especially for foundations, low masses, groupings.

CULTIVARS:

'Compacta' — Very dense and globose, 40-year-old plant was 4 by 5'.

'Gnom' — Twenty-five-year-old plant is 15" high and 36" wide.

var. *mugo* — Low growing form of the species usually less than 8′ tall and about twice that in width. Variable due to seed source.

var. *pumilio* — Usually prostrate grower.

'Slavinii' — Forty-year-old plant is 3 by 5′.

PROPAGATION: Seeds have no dormancy and will germinate immediately upon collection.

ADDITIONAL NOTES: Perhaps one of the most confusing pines for the homeowner because of tremendous variability in size. The cute, diminutive, prostrate plant that comes from the garden center and is placed in the foundation planting often becomes 10 to 15′ tall although it was advertised as a 2 to 4′ low growing evergreen. One of the real problems with this and other plants is that they do not read the advertisements.

This species includes a number of varieties or geographical forms which are difficult to classify, as the variations in habit are not always correlated with the character of the cones and appear to be due in many cases to soil, climate, and other growing conditions, or perhaps to hybridization with other species. Nomenclature is sometimes confused on this species as it is listed as *Pinus montana mugo* and other odd things.

NATIVE HABITAT: Mountains of Europe from Spain to the Balkans. Introduced 1779.

Pinus nigra var. *nigra* — Austrian Pine

LEAVES: In pairs persisting about 4 years, very dense on the branchlets, stiff, straight or curved, 4 to 6″ long, 1/16 to 1/12″ wide, margins minutely toothed, apex a thickened horny point, sharp to the touch, 12 to 14 lines of stomata on each surface, dark green.

BUDS: Ovoid to oblong or cylindrical, 1/2 to 1″ long, abruptly contracted to a sharp point; scales light brown, resinous.

STEM: Young stems without down (pubescence), yellowish brown, ridged, the branchlets as they lose their leaves becoming roughened by the persistent leaf bases.

SIZE: 50 to 60′ in height by 20 to 40′ in spread but can grow to 100′ or more.

HARDINESS: Zone 4.

HABIT: Densely pyramidal when young becoming a large, broad, flat-topped tree with a rough, short trunk and low, stout, spreading branches.

RATE: Medium, 35 to 50′ after 20 to 30 years.

TEXTURE: Medium-coarse.

BARK: Dark brown furrows, usually with gray or gray-brown mottled ridges; quite attractive.

LEAF COLOR: Dark, shining green.

FLOWERS: Staminate clustered, yellow; pistillate yellow-green.

FRUIT: Solitary or in clusters, sub-sessile, ovoid-conical, 2 to 3″ long, 1 to 1 1/4″ wide before opening; tawny-yellow initially, becoming brown; scales about 1″ long, transversely keeled near the apex which often ends in a more or less persistent prickle.

CULTURE: A very hardy tree that withstands city conditions better than other pines. Very tolerant of soils, if moist. Will stand some dryness and exposure. Resists heat and drought, less fastidious in its soil requirements than most pines, will succeed in fairly heavy clay; tolerates seaside conditions.

DISEASES AND INSECTS: In recent years this pine has exhibited severe dieback in Illinois and other midwestern states. Some of the dieback has been attributed to *Diplodia* tip blight, however, whole trees have died in a single season so probably multiple factors are involved.

LANDSCAPE VALUE: An adaptable species with very stiff needles making a good specimen, screen, or windbreak. Can also be used for mass planting.

CULTIVARS:

'Hornibrookiana' — (originated as a witches broom), needles 2 1/2″ long, very compact, dwarf and rounded, 30-year-old plant is 2′ tall and 6′ across.

'Pryamidalis' — A narrow pyramidal plant with closely ascending branches.

PROPAGATION: Seeds have no dormancy and will germinate immediately upon collection.

ADDITIONAL NOTES: A somewhat confusing pine often listed as *P. nigra* or *P. nigra austriaca*. It is another species somewhat like *P. mugo* and has many geographical varieties and subspecies. Den Ouden and Boom noted that it is a fine tree for garden planting and a forest tree with good economic properties. On the other side of the ledger, Dallimore and Jackson stated that under cultivation it is usually a rough, heavily branched tree, too sombre for ornamental planting and of little value as a timber tree as its wood is coarse and knotty. One wonders if these authorities are discussing the same plant.

NATIVE HABITAT: It is a native of Europe, from Austria to Central Italy, Greece and Yugoslavia. Introduced 1759.

Pinus parviflora — Japanese White Pine

LEAVES: 5, persisting 3 to 4 years, crowded, rather stiff, usually twisted, forming brush-like tufts at the ends of the branches, 4/5 to 1 3/5" long, 1/25" wide, apex usually blunt, margins finely toothed, without stomata outside, inner sides with 3 to 4 stomatic lines; leaf sheaths falling.

STEM: Greenish brown, finally light gray, short, minutely downy, older stems glabrous.

SIZE: 25 to 50' in height with a similar or greater spread at maturity.

HARDINESS: Zone 5.

HABIT: Dense, conical pyramid when young developing wide-spreading branches, flat-topped head and picturesque character with age.

RATE: Slow.

TEXTURE: Medium.

BARK: On young trees smooth, gray, eventually becoming darker gray and platy, scaly on old trunks.

LEAF COLOR: Bluish green, sometimes grass green with 3 to 4 stomatic bands on inner sides of needles.

FLOWERS: Monoecious and inconspicuous.

FRUIT: Cones nearly terminal, almost sessile, horizontally spreading, straight, ovoid to nearly cylindrical, 1 3/5 to 3" long, spreading widely when ripe, remaining 6 to 7 years on the tree; scales few, broad wedge-shaped, thick, leathery-woody, brownish red; scale-end undulate, slightly incurved; umbo inconspicuous.

CULTURE: Full sun, average moisture; good drainage essential. Tolerant of most soils, even clay loam.

DISEASES AND INSECTS: See culture sheet.

LANDSCAPE VALUE: A choice, extremely graceful small conifer whose low stature and fine-textured foliage make it a perfect tree for small places, good for the sea coast as it is somewhat salt tolerant.

CULTIVARS:

'Brevifolia' — Low, open pyramid or a rounded bush. Slow growing.

'Bergmann' — Spreading, rounded shrub with many leaders of equal size.

PROPAGATION: Seed should be stratified for 90 days at 33 to 41°F in moist medium.

NATIVE HABITAT: Japan. Introduced 1861.

Pinus peuce — Balkan or Macedonian Pine

LEAVES: 5, remaining 3 years, densely bundled, 3 to 4" long, 1/36" wide, apex pointed, straight, rather stiff, margin finely toothed, both inner sides with 3 to 5 lines.

STEM: Thickish, greenish, in the 2nd year grayish green or brownish gray, glabrous.

SIZE: 30 to 60' in height with a relatively narrow spread; can grow to 100' and specimens of this size grow in Bulgaria.

HARDINESS: Zone 4.

HABIT: Narrow pyramid, sometimes columnar in form.
RATE: Slow.
TEXTURE: Medium.
BARK: Gray-brown, thin, on old trees develops a scaly character.
LEAF COLOR: Green to gray-green.
FLOWERS: Monoecious and inconspicuous.
FRUIT: Cones terminal, short-stalked, solitary or 3 to 4 together, spreading or deflexed, nearly cylindrical, 3 to 6" long by approximately 1" broad, light brown and resinous.
CULTURE: Full sun, moist soils with good drainage and move balled and burlapped if root pruned.
LANDSCAPE VALUE: Best used in large, open areas such as a park.
PROPAGATION: Seed may require no stratification or up to 60 days.
ADDITIONAL NOTES: Somewhat resembles *P. cembra* in outline; closely allied to *P. wallichiana*, but differs in its narrow habit, smaller branches, and shorter, stiffer needles which are less spreading; the green, glabrous shoots distinguish it from *P. cembra*.
NATIVE HABITAT: Balkans, confined to limited areas in Albania, Bulgaria, Greece and Yugoslavia. Introduced 1863.

Pinus ponderosa — Ponderosa Pine, Western Yellow Pine

LEAVES: In three's, sometimes two's, remaining 3 years, densely crowded on the branchlets, rigid, curved, 5 to 10" long, 1/20 to 1/12" wide, margins minutely toothed, apex a sharp, horny point; stomatic lines on each surface, dark or yellowish green.
BUDS: Oblong, cylindrical, 4/5" long, acute, resinous; scales closely appressed, reddish brown.
STEM: Young stems stout, glabrous, orange-brown or greenish at first eventually becoming nearly black; with the odor of vanilla when bruised.

SIZE: 150 to 230' in height in the wild, averages 60 to 100' under cultivation, spread 25 to 30'.
HARDINESS: Zone 5.
HABIT: Narrow, columnar when young; with time develops an irregularly cylindrical and narrow crown, with numerous short stout branches, the lower ones often drooping; very old trees have short conical or flat-topped crowns and are devoid of branches for one-half or more of their height.
RATE: Medium, 75' after 40 to 50 years.
TEXTURE: Medium to coarse.
BARK: Brown-black and furrowed on vigorous or young trees, yellowish brown to cinnamon-red and broken up into large, flat, superficially scaly plates separated by deep irregular fissures on slow-growing and old trunks.
LEAF COLOR: Dark or yellowish green.
FLOWERS: Monoecious, staminate clustered, yellow; pistillate red, in pairs.
FRUIT: Cones terminal, solitary or 3 to 5 together, nearly sessile, spreading or slightly recurved, symmetrical, ovoid or oblong-ovoid, 3 to 6" long, 1 2/5 to 2" broad, light reddish brown, shining, after falling often leaving a few of the basal scales attached to the branchlet, umbo broad triangular, terminated by a stout usually recurved prickle.
CULTURE: Transplant balled and burlapped if root pruned; prefers a deep, moist, well-drained loam; sunny, open exposure; intolerant of shade, hurt by late frosts; resistant to drought; tolerates alkaline soils.
LANDSCAPE VALUE: Valuable forest tree but not recommended for areas outside of which it is native. Useful for mass planting and shelter belts.
PROPAGATION: Seeds have no dormancy and will germinate immediately upon collection.
RELATED SPECIES:
Pinus contorta, Lodgepole Pine, is widespread throughout Western North America and from my limited observations more ornamentally attractive than *P. ponderosa*. It differs from *P. ponderosa* in that the needles are in fascicles of 2, 1 1/2" long, yellowish green to dark green and

twisted; the cones are about 1 1/2" long, mostly remaining unopened and attached for many years. There are two distinct varieties: one termed *P. c. contorta*, Shore Pine (Zone 7), is a small tree 25 to 30' high characterized by a short contorted trunk and a dense, irregular crown of twisted branches, many of which extend nearly to the ground; the other *P. c. latifolia*, Lodgepole Pine (Zone 5), grows 70 to 80' high and develops a long, clear, cylindrical trunk and short, narrow, open crown. The Shore Pine tends to establish in wet, boggy areas and is seldom found far from tidewater while the Lodgepole Pine performs best in moist, well drained, sandy or gravelly soils, although it grows on a variety of soils. Native habitat is Western North America.

Pinus jeffreyi, Jeffrey Pine, differs from the previous two species in the blue-green twisted needles and the 9" long cones which open and fall at maturity. Similar to *P. ponderosa* in habit and other respects. Can endure great extremes of climate and is somewhat more frost hardy. The Morton Arboretum has several 40' specimens which are rather attractive. Potentially can grow 90 to 100' under favorable conditions. Native from Southern Oregon to Lower California. Zone 5.

ADDITIONAL NOTES: The most important pine in Western North America; furnishes more timber than any other American pine and is second only to Douglas-fir in total annual production; thrives under widely different conditions and in many kinds of soils from low elevations to a considerable altitude, on light and moist soils; on dry, arid land; on dried-up river-beds and lakes where there is a deep and rich soil; and on almost bare rocks. The most abundant growth takes place on light, deep, moist, well drained soils.

NATIVE HABITAT: Western North America.

Pinus resinosa — Red Pine

LEAVES: In two's persisting 4 years, densely arranged on the branches, slender, snap when bent, 5 to 6" long, margins finely and regularly toothed, apex sharp-pointed, stomata in ill defined lines on each surface, medium to dark green.

BUDS: Ovoid or narrow conical, about 1/2" long, resinous, with some of the scales free at the tips.

STEM: Glabrous, stout, pale brown or yellowish green.

SIZE: 50 to 80' in height with a variable spread; can grow to 125' and more. I have never seen a Red Pine larger than 50' in the Midwest.

HARDINESS: Zone 2, can withstand seasonal variations of 40 to 60°F below zero to 90 to 105°F above.

HABIT: When growing in the open the trunk is short and develops a heavily branched crown in youth; in old age the crown is somewhat symmmetrically oval with the characteristic tufted foliage which separates it from the ragged, unkempt Jack Pines and the plumelike tops of the White Pine.

RATE: Medium, 50' after 25 to 30 years.

TEXTURE: Medium.

BARK: On young trees scaly, orange-red; eventually breaking up into large, flat, reddish brown, superficially scaly plates, irregularly diamond-shaped in outline.

LEAF COLOR: Lustrous, dark green.

FLOWERS: Monoecious, clustered; staminate red, pistillate reddish.

FRUITS: Cones subterminal, solitary or two together, sessile, horizontally spreading, symmetrical, ovoid-conical, narrowing rapidly to the apex, approximately 2" long by 1 to 2" broad and light brown.

CULTURE: Transplant balled and burlapped if root pruned. Does well on exposed, dry, acid, sandy or gravelly soils, full sun, susceptible to sweeping winds. Extremely cold tolerant (-40 to -60°F).

LANDSCAPE VALUE: A picturesque and desirable tree which survives under adversity; good on exposed and sterile soils, for groves and windbreaks, best in northern areas.

PROPAGATION: Seeds have no dormancy and will germinate immediately upon collection.

ADDITIONAL NOTES: Sometimes termed Norway Pine; it is said that early settlers mistook it for Norway Spruce, and also that it grew in abundance near the town of Norway, Maine. Very tolerant of sandy soils and ranks behind *P. banksiana* in its ability to invade cutover land.
NATIVE HABITAT: Newfoundland and Manitoba, south to the mountains of Pennsylvania, west to Michigan.

Pinus rigida — Pitch Pine

LEAVES: In three's lasting 2 years, spreading, rigid, slightly curved and twisted, 3 1/2 to 4 1/2" long, margins finely toothed, ending in a horny point.
BUDS: Cylindrical or conical, sharp-pointed, 1/4 to 3/4" long, scales pressed together but often free at the tips, usually resinous.
STEM: Stout with many buds, green at first, becoming dull orange-brown in the second year, prominently ridged.

SIZE: Variable, 40 to 60' in height by 30 to 50' in spread although can grow to 100'. Often dwarfed by its environment for on exposed sites it is very grotesque while in better situations a tall trunk and small open crown develop.
HARDINESS: Zone 4.
HABIT: Open, irregular pyramid in youth, becoming gnarled and more irregular with age.
RATE: Medium in youth becoming slower.
TEXTURE: Medium.
BARK: Initially dark and very scaly; eventually 1 to 2" thick at the base of old trees and smoother with brownish yellow, flat plates separated by narrow irregular fissures.
LEAF COLOR: Yellowish, orange-green at first, becoming a dark green.
FLOWERS: Monoecious, staminate yellow, pistillate light green tinted rose.
FRUIT: Cones lateral, in whorls of 3 to 5, seldom solitary, 2 2/5" long, stalked or nearly sessile, deflexed when young, spreading at right angles when mature, rather symmetrical, ovoid-conical, light brown and remaining 2 or more years on the tree.
CULTURE: Prefers a light, sandy, acid, moist, well-drained soil; however, is found along the coast on peat soils of Atlantic White-cedar swamps (*Chamaecyparis thyoides*); open, sunny exposure; susceptible to sweeping winds; appears to be somewhat salt tolerant; able to survive on the driest, sandiest, most unproductive sites.
LANDSCAPE VALUE: Not highly ornamental but excellent for poor soils, wildernesses and solitary places.
PROPAGATION: Seed requires no stratification.
ADDITIONAL NOTES: A tree of great diversity in form, habit, and development. One of the few conifers that produces sprouts from cut stumps or when injured by fire. Produces anywhere from 1 to 3 whorls of branches in a single season which is unusual for a pine. Also produces cones very early as 12-year-old trees often bear quantities of seeds. I have seen it all over Cape Cod in the sandiest of soils.
NATIVE HABITAT: Eastern North America in sandy uplands.

Pinus strobus — Eastern White Pine

LEAVES: In five's remaining 2 to 3 years, slender, bluish green, 3 to 5" long, margins finely toothed, white stomatic lines on the two inner surfaces.
BUDS: Ovoid, with a sharp point, 1/4" long, resinous, some scales free at the tips.
STEM: Slender with tufts of short hairs below the insertion of the leaf bundles, usually without down elsewhere, greenish to light greenish brown.

SIZE: 50' to 80' in height by 20 to 40' in spread; can grow to 150' and more.
HARDINESS: Zone 3.

HABIT: In youth a symmetrical pyramid of soft, pleasant appearance; in middle-age and on old trees the crown is composed of several horizontal and ascending branches, gracefully plumelike in outline and very distinctive when compared to other conifers.

RATE: Fast, probably the fastest growing pine; becoming 50 to 75′ tall in 25 to 40 years.

TEXTURE: Medium-fine.

BARK: Thin, smoother, grayish green when young, becoming darker with age; dark grayish brown on old trunks and deeply furrowed longitudinally into broad scaly, 1 to 2″ thick ridges.

LEAF COLOR: Light bluish green, however, greatly variable.

FLOWERS: Monoecious; staminate clustered, yellow; pistillate pink.

FRUIT: Cones subterminal, pendent, 6 to 8″ long by 1 3/5″ broad, stalked, cylindrical, often curved, apex pointed, resinous and light brown. Mature in autumn of second year.

CULTURE: Easily transplanted because of wide-spreading and moderately deep root system with only a vestige of a taproot; makes its best growth on fertile, moist, well-drained soils however is found on such extremes as dry, rocky ridges and wet sphagnum bogs; light demanding but can tolerate some shade; humid atmosphere; quite susceptible to sweeping winds and branches are often lost in strong storms; is extremely intolerant of air pollutants (ozone, sulfur dioxide) and salts.

DISEASES AND INSECTS: Two very serious pests include the White Pine blister rust, a bark disease, which eventually kills the tree; and the White Pine weevil which kills the terminal shoots thus seriously deforming the tree to the extent they become bushy and have been called "Cabbage Pines".

LANDSCAPE VALUE: A very handsome and ornamental specimen or mass; valuable for parks, estates and small properties. Also makes a beautiful sheared hedge. One of our most beautiful native pines.

CULTIVARS:

'Compacta' — A dense rounded type, slow growing, appears to be a catch-all term for dwarfish clones.

'Contorta' — An open, irregular, pyramidal form with slightly twisted branchlets. Forty-year-old plant is 18′ high.

'Fastigiata' — Narrowly upright and columnar when young developing a wider character with age as the branches ascend at a 45° angle from the trunk. Ultimately about three times as tall as wide. I have seen several large (70′) specimens of this clone and they were beautifully formed and not at all harsh like many of the fastigiate plants.

var. *glauca* — Leaves are a light bluish green and of beautiful color. A specimen in the Arnold Arboretum is 60′ high and 60′ wide.

'Minima' — Dense, low spreading type, wider than high; 1″ per year.

'Nana' — Bushy, irregular pyramid becoming open with age; 75-year-old plant is 16′ high.

'Pendula' — Very interesting weeping type with long branches which sweep the ground; must be trained in youth to develop a leader.

'Prostrata' — Another rounded, dwarf type; 20-year-old plant is 8′ by 7′.

'Pumila' — Roundish plant with central shoot elongating.

PROPAGATION: Seed should be stratified for 60 days. Pines, in general, are difficult or impossible to root from cuttings; however, considerable work has been undertaken with White Pine. Cuttings can be rooted but the percentages were low averaging from 0 to 34% depending on the tree sampled. Several investigators have rooted fascicles with some success.

ADDITIONAL NOTES: Often produces cones at an early age, sometimes when not more than 10′ high; very aggressive and quickly seeds in abandoned fields so much so it received the name "Old Field Pine". Largest of northeastern conifers and a very valuable timber species. Great variation in needle color, resistance to salts and air pollutants. In the Central Illinois area trees are beautiful and keep their good bluish green color through the winter while others turn yellowish green. Selections could be made for superior traits and adaptability to various climatic and environmental conditions.

NATIVE HABITAT: Southern Canada, Great Lake states, the Northeast, and the Appalachian Mountains.

Pinus sylvestris — Scotch Pine

LEAVES: In pairs persisting about 3 years, variable in length, twisted, stiff, 1 to 4" long, short-pointed, margins minutely toothed, glaucous with many well-defined lines of stomata on the outer side, blue-green in color.

BUDS: Oblong-ovate, 1/4 to 1/2" long, pointed with lanceolate, fringed scales, the upper ones free at the tips, brown, resinous.

STEM: Green when young, dull grayish yellow or brown in the second year, marked with prominent bases of the scale leaves.

SIZE: 30 to 60' in height with a spread of 30 to 40'; can grow to 80 to 90' high.

HARDINESS: Zone 2.

HABIT: In youth an irregular pyramid with short, spreading branches, the lower soon dying, becoming in age very picturesque, open, wide-spreading and flat- or round-topped, almost umbrella-shaped.

RATE: Medium when young; slow with age.

TEXTURE: Medium.

BARK: On the upper portion of the stems orangish or orangish brown, thin, smooth, peeling off in papery flakes, thick towards the base, grayish or reddish brown, fissured into irregular longitudinal scaly plates.

LEAF COLOR: Bluish green frequently changing to yellowish green in the winter.

FLOWERS: Monoecious, inconspicuous.

FRUIT: Cones mostly solitary to 2-3 together, long- or short-stalked, 1 3/5 to 3" long, symmetrical or oblique, gray or dull brown, falling at maturity; umbo small, obtuse.

CULTURE: Transplants easily balled and burlapped if root pruned. Will grow on a variety of soils as long as they are well-drained. Poor, dry sites will support this tree. It must be allowed full sunlight; preferably acid soils.

LANDSCAPE VALUE: Valued for its more than usual picturesque character; useful as a distorted specimen or in masses and on waste lands. Not suitable for underplanting or shelter belts. It cannot be considered a good shade tree, but for displaying unique form and color among the pines it is outstanding.

CULTIVARS:

'Argentea' — Leaves are a pronounced silvery color. Cones also silvery tinged.

'Fastigiata' — Columnar, narrow in habit, about the narrowest of any of the pines; often called Sentinel Pine, tends to break-up in heavy ice and snow.

'Watereri' — A slow growing, densely pyramidal to flat-topped form with steel-blue needles, almost as high as wide when young; the orange bark character develops very nicely as well.

PROPAGATION: Seeds have no dormancy and will germinate without stratification.

ADDITIONAL NOTES: One of the most popular pines for Christmas tree use; has largely superseded Balsam Fir and other pines as the number one tree. The great problem with Scotch Pine is the tremendous variability in needle length and color, hardiness, habit, and adaptability due to geographic races or strains. Five major groups of variants are recognized by Dallimore and Jackson and one starts to realize why some Scotch Pines have bluish needles, others yellowish green, etc. after reading their interesting discussion.

NATIVE HABITAT: One of the most widely distributed pines, ranging from Norway and Scotland to Spain, Western Asia and Northeastern Siberia; naturalized in some places in the New England states.

Pinus thunbergii — Japanese Black Pine (Listed as *P. thunbergiana* by *Hortus III*).

LEAVES: Two, densely crowded, twisted, more or less spreading, 2 1/2 to 7" long, 1/12" wide, apex stiff, fine pointed, rigid, margins finely toothed, with stomatic lines on each surface; leaf sheaths 1/2" long, ending in two long, thread-like segments, persistent; very lustrous dark green.

BUDS: One of the few conifers in which the buds provide a good identification feature. The terminal buds characteristically ovoid-cylindrical, apex sharp-pointed, 1/2 to 3/4" long, not resinous; scales appressed, tips free, gray or silvery white (very prominent), fimbriated.

STEM: Light brown, glabrous, ridged with the scale leaves persisting during the first year; in the second and third year blackish gray.

SIZE: 20 to 80' in height with a greatly variable spread.

HARDINESS: Zone 5.

HABIT: Broadly pyramidal, dense, irregular shape at maturity with spreading often pendulous branches; even in youth does not show a regular growth pattern.

RATE: Medium.

TEXTURE: Medium.

BARK: On old trees blackish gray, soon becoming fissured into elongated irregular plates.

LEAF COLOR: Dark green, very handsome.

FLOWERS: Monoecious, inconspicuous.

FRUIT: Cones subterminal, solitary or clustered, short-stalked, spreading, symmetrical, ovoid to conical, 1 3/5 to 2 2/5" long, 1 1/5 to 1 3/5" wide; scale end flattened, shiny light brown; umbo depressed, small, obtuse or with a minute prickle.

CULTURE: Transplants easily balled and burlapped if root pruned; makes its best growth on moist, fertile, well drained soils; will grow on sandy soils and has been used for reclaiming sand dunes and other protective work near the shore; supposedly quite salt tolerant and has been used where foliar salts present a cultural problem; best in full sun.

LANDSCAPE VALUE: Because of its tolerance of salt spray it is invaluable for seashore plantings and useful in stabilizing sand dunes; also a good accent or bonsai plant.

CULTIVARS:

'Oculis-draconis' — The needles are striped with two yellow bands.

PROPAGATION: Seeds have no dormancy and will germinate immediately upon planting.

NATIVE HABITAT: Japan. Introduced 1855.

Pinus virginiana — Virginia (Scrub) Pine, Jersey Pine, Spruce Pine, Poverty Pine

LEAVES: In two's remaining 3 to 4 years, twisted, spreading, stout, 1 1/4 to 2 1/4" long, margins with minute, irregular teeth, apex sharp-pointed, grayish green.

BUDS: Ovoid with a short point, 1/3 to 1/2" long, resinous with closely pressed scales.

STEM: Young—slender, purplish with a pale bloom.

SIZE: 15 to 40' in height by 10 to 30' spread.

HARDINESS: Zone 4.

HABIT: A broad, open pyramid, becoming flat-topped, the branches springing irregularly from the stem; finally low, straggling, scrubby; with long, outstretched limbs.

RATE: Slow.

TEXTURE: Medium.

BARK: Thin and smooth, eventually scaly-plated, reddish brown, 1/4 to 1/2" thick.

LEAF COLOR: Yellow-green to dark green.

FLOWERS: Monoecious; staminate orange-brown, pistillate pale green.

FRUIT: Cones 2 to 4 together or solitary, short stalked or sessile, spreading or deflexed, oblong-conical, symmetrical, 1 3/5 to 3" long by 1 to 1 2/5" broad, apex blunt, dark brown; maturing in the second autumn but often persistent after that. Cones sharp due to prickly-like appendage.

CULTURE: Does well in poor, dry soils where other pines will not grow. Best on clay loam or sandy loam, dislikes shallow, chalky soils; open, sunny exposure.

LANDSCAPE VALUE: Not very ornamental but valuable as a cover for dry and barren soils.

PROPAGATION: Seeds have no dormancy or a slight one and may require 30 days of stratification.

ADDITIONAL NOTES: Chief merit lies in its ability to reproduce and grow on heavy, clay land where few other plants will grow, both on virgin soil and impoverished farm land.
NATIVE HABITAT: Long Island, New York, southwestward to Central Alabama, in the Appalachian, Ohio Valley, Piedmont, and part of the Coastal Plain regions.

Pinus wallichiana — Himalayan Pine (Bhutan Pine); also called *P. griffithii*.

LEAVES: Five, persisting 3 to 4 years, on young shoots more or less erect, the older ones spreading or drooping, slender, flaccid, creating a feathery effect, 5 to 8" long, apex sharp pointed, grayish green, margin minutely toothed, with glaucous-white stomatic lines inside, outside green; leaf sheaths about 4/5" long, soon falling.

SIZE: 50 to 80' high under landscape conditions but may grow to 150'; spread is variable but the few large specimens I have seen were 1/2 to 2/3's the height.
HARDINESS: Zone 5.
HABIT: Loosely and broadly pyramidal when young; graceful, of elegant habit and often feathered with branches to the ground in old age. Tends to be more wide-spreading than many pines as it approaches maturity.
RATE: Slow-medium.
TEXTURE: Medium.
LEAF COLOR: Gray-green.
FLOWERS: Monoecious, inconspicuous.
FRUIT: Cones subterminal, solitary, stalked, 1 to 2" long, erect when young; pendulous the second year, cylindrical, 6 to 10" long by approximately 2" broad, light brown when ripe and very resinous.
CULTURE: Listed as somewhat difficult to transplant and should be moved as a young (2 to 3' high) plant to a permanent location; soil requirements are similar to those for White Pine and a sandy, well drained, acid loam is best; full sun; not recommended for shallow, chalky soils; severe winter winds can result in needle browning; withstands atmospheric pollutants better than most conifers; in extremely exposed locations the top becomes thin and weak when the tree is 25 to 40' high and, therefore, a sheltered position is desirable.
LANDSCAPE VALUE: Excellent and beautiful pine for large areas, very graceful in effect; a lovely specimen tree; apparently there are differences in hardiness among nursery-grown trees (related to origin of seed) for some trees will do well in the Midwest and others succumb after a difficult winter. The Morton Arboretum has a lovely, well formed specimen from which seed or scion wood should be collected for the Central States.
CULTIVARS: There is a yellow-banded clone which is listed as 'Oculis-draconis' by some authorities, however, Den Ouden and Boom categorize the clone as 'Zebrina' which they describe as having leaves barred, marked an inch below the apex with a cream-colored band, otherwise green and gold. I have seen this cultivar at the National Arboretum in their Gottelli Conifer Collection. Perhaps as striking and interesting a cultivar as one could hope to see among the pines. There are three 'Oculis-draconis' clones, one is *P. densiflora*, another is *P. thunbergii*, and the above. All are interesting but difficult to blend into the average landscape. For the hobby gardener they offer a worthwhile challenge.
PROPAGATION: Seeds have no dormancy or a slight one and may require 15 days of stratification.
NATIVE HABITAT: Temperate Himalaya. At 6,000 to 12,500' elevation, extending westward to Afghanistan and eastward to Nepal. Introduced 1827.

Platanus x *hybrida (acerifolia)* — London Planetree — result of a cross between *P. orientalis* x *P. occidentalis.*

FAMILY: Platanaceae

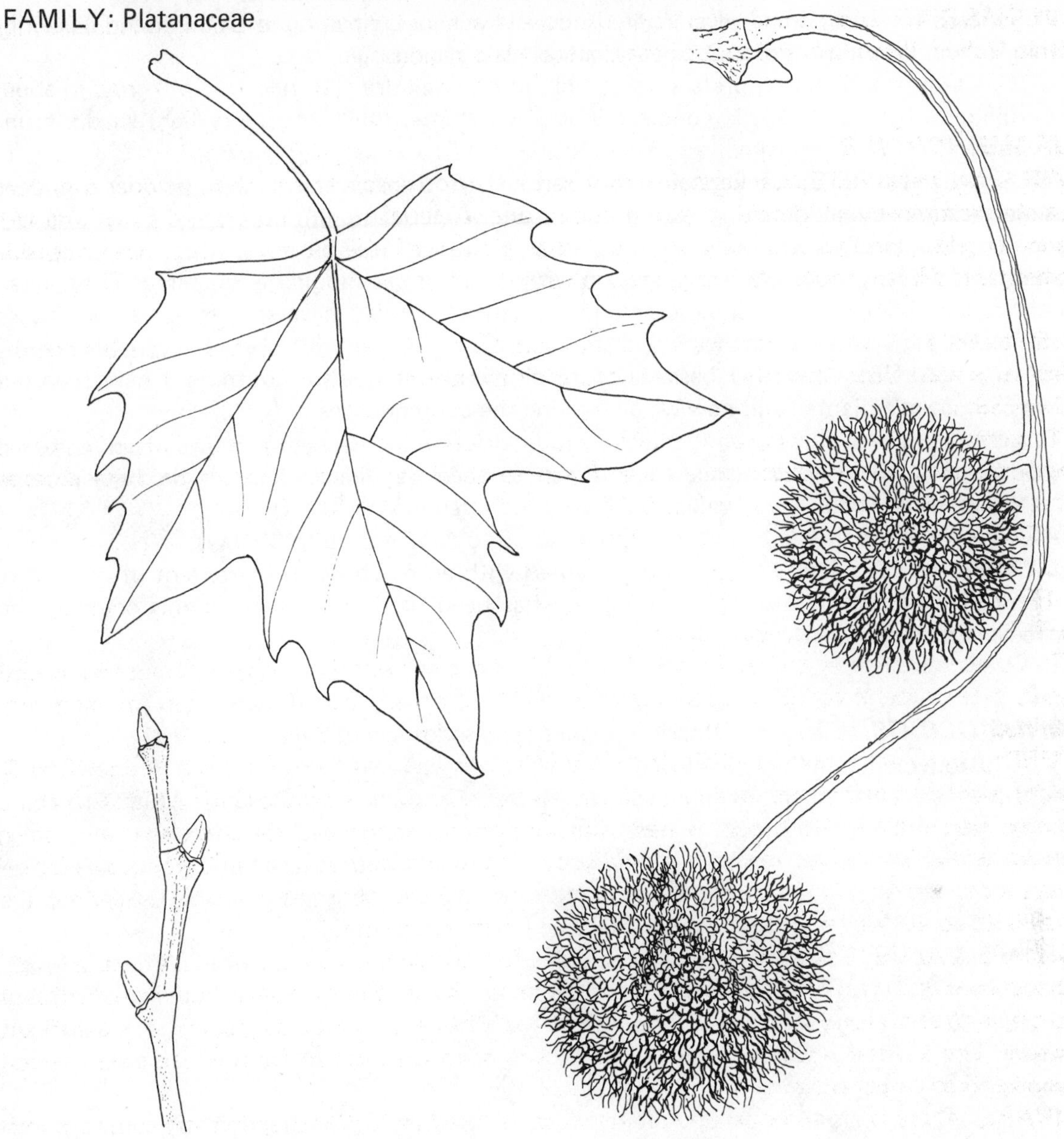

LEAVES: Alternate, simple, truncate to cordate, 5 to 10" wide, 3 to 5 lobed, with triangular-ovate or broad triangular, not or sparingly toothed lobes, with acute or rounded sinuses extending 1/3 the length of the blade, glabrous or nearly so at maturity.

BUDS: Similar to *P. occidentalis.*

STEM: Similar to *P. occidentalis.*

BARK: Olive-green to creamy, exfoliating. Actually the best asset of the tree.

SIZE: 70 to 100' in height with a spread of 65 to 80' although can grow to 120' or more.

HARDINESS: Zone 4.

HABIT: Pyramidal in youth developing with age a large, open, wide spreading outline with massive branches; does not spread as much as *P. occidentalis* but nonetheless is still not acceptable for street tree use.

RATE: Medium, 35' over a 20 year period.

TEXTURE: A bum in all seasons, coarse throughout the year.

LEAF COLOR: Flat medium green in summer; repugnant brown in fall.

FLOWER: Monoecious, unisexual flowers, not showy.

FRUIT: Syncarp (multiple fruit) of elongated obovoid achenes, ripening in October and persisting late into winter, usually borne 2 together although 3's and singles occur.

CULTURE: Easily transplanted; prefers deep, rich, moist, well drained soils, but will grow in about anything; withstands high pH conditions and pollutants; full sun or very light shade; prune in winter.

DISEASES AND INSECTS: Cankerstain (very serious), *Botryosphaeria* canker, powdery mildew, cankers caused by illuminating gas and dog urine, American plum borer, and Sycamore lace bug. The London Planetree was once touted as a "Super" tree by many people and was soon overplanted. Many diseases have caught up with it and its use should be tempered. The cankerstain fungus is especially troublesome and in Central Illinois I have seen trees badly infested with lacebug.

LANDSCAPE VALUE: Limited, I hesitate to recommend this tree for anything. I have seen our own campus overplanted and now we are paying the consequences.

CULTIVARS:

'Bloodgood' — Greater resistance to anthracnose than the species. One of the highest rated trees in the Shade Tree Evaluation Tests conducted at Wooster, Ohio.

PROPAGATION: Seeds should be moist stratified at 35 to 41°F for 45 to 60 days.

ADDITIONAL NOTES: This species is not troubled with anthracnose to the extent of our native American Planetree. Withstands pruning and has been used as a hedge in this country and especially Europe.

Platanus occidentalis — American Planetree, also known as Sycamore, Buttonwood, and Buttonball-tree

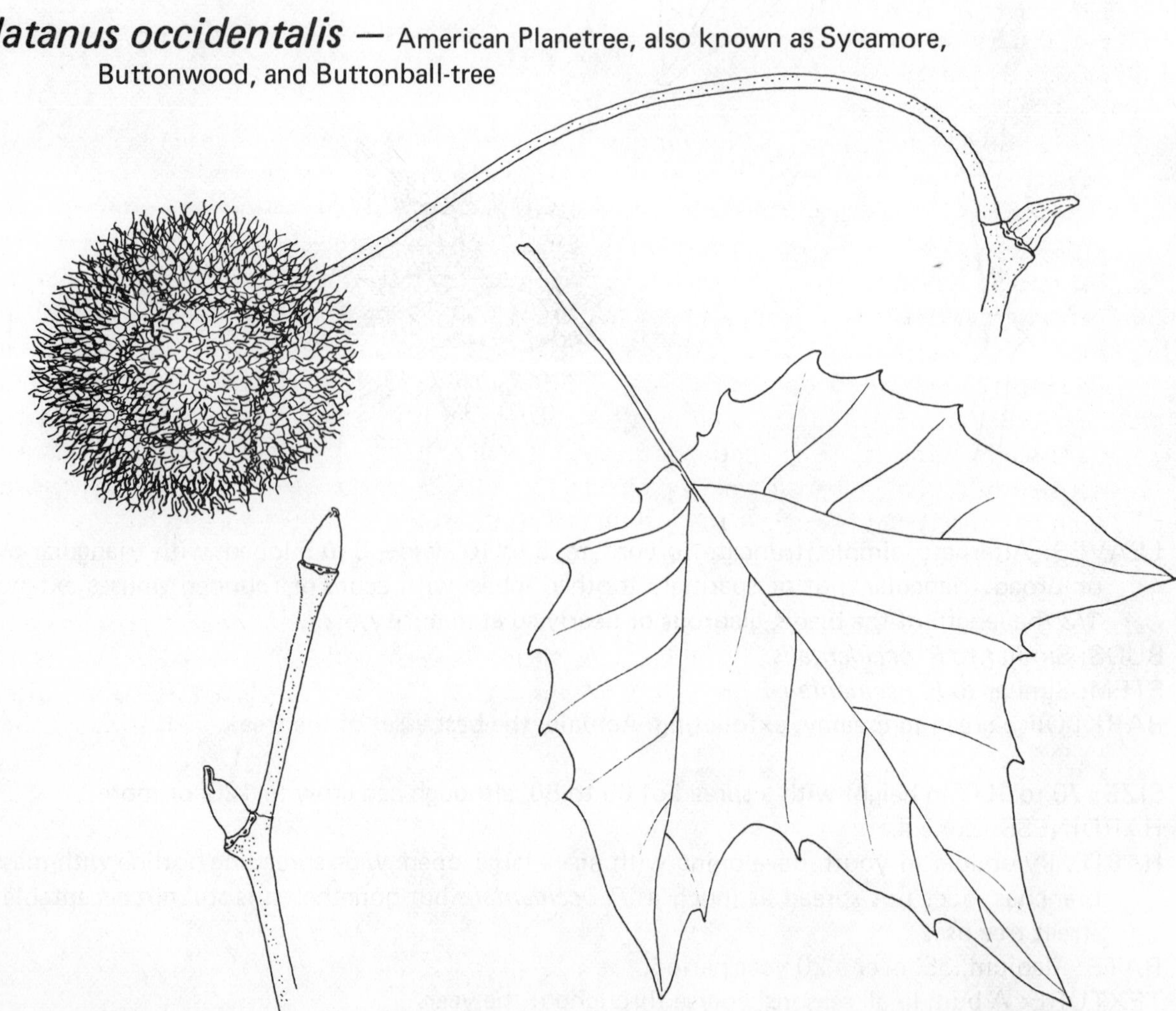

LEAVES: Alternate, simple, truncate or cordate, rarely cuneate, 4 to 9" wide, often broader than long, 3- or sometimes 5-lobed with shallow sinuses and broad-triangular lobes, broader than long, coarsely toothed or rarely entire, floccose-tomentulose when young, at maturity pubescent only along veins beneath.

BUDS: Terminal-absent, laterals—large, 1/4 to 3/8" long, conical, blunt pointed, smooth, shiny, dark reddish brown, with single visible scale formed within petiole base. Second scale green, gummy, innermost scale covered with long rusty hairs; divergent.

STEM: Rather stout, round, smooth or pubescent, shiny yellow-orange-brown, generally zigzag.

BARK: Red brown and scaly near base, exfoliating on upper trunk exposing lighter colored (white to creamy white) inner layers.

FRUIT: Multiple, globose fruit of achenes, borne singly.

SIZE: 75 to 100' in height with a similar or greater spread; can grow to 150' and next to *Liriodendron tulipifera* is one of our tallest eastern native deciduous trees.

HARDINESS: Zone 4.

HABIT: Usually a tree with a large, massive trunk and a wide spreading open crown of massive, crooked branches. A behemoth in the world of trees. A striking and impressive specimen especially in winter when the white mottled bark stands out against the cold gray sky. The best description of habit would be irregular.

RATE: Fast.

TEXTURE: Coarse, but humanely so.

BARK: Mostly smooth, very light grayish brown, flaking off in large, irregular, thin pieces and exposing the grayish to cream-colored inner bark which gradually becomes whitish and produces the impressive mottled appearance.

LEAF COLOR: Flat medium green in summer; fall color is tan to brown and unrewarding.

FLOWERS: Similar to *P.* x *hybrida.*

FRUIT: Also similar except the fruits are borne singly.

CULTURE: Similar to, but not as tolerant as *P.* x *hybrida;* found native in bottomlands and along the banks of rivers and streams; attains its greatest size in deep, moist, rich soils.

DISEASES AND INSECTS: Anthracnose, leafspots, aphids, sycamore plant bug, Sycamore tussock moth, scales, bagworms, borers, ad infinitum. Anthracnose is a serious problem as it affects developing leaves and stems; there is a dieback followed by a witches broom type development beneath the dead area. Two wet seasons (1973 and 1974) in Champaign-Urbana have been ideal for the spread of this disease and I do not think you could find a good looking American Planetree in the two cities.

LANDSCAPE VALUE: If native to an area do not remove the tree(s), however, do not plant it. I have seen it used for street tree planting in Urbana, Illinois! The tree is simply too large and is constantly dropping leaves, twigs and fruits. If people only considered all the factors regarding each tree they plant perhaps much maintenance and trouble could be avoided, but . . . !

PROPAGATION: Supposedly no pregermination treatment is necessary.

RELATED SPECIES:

Platanus orientalis, Oriental Planetree, is one of the parents of *P.* x *hybrida* and mentioned here because of its resistance to Anthracnose which was apparently transmitted to the London Planetree. Similar to other species except the leaves are more deeply incised; the fruits are borne 3 to 6, rarely 2's and the bark is a gray color. Not particularly hardy, Zone 7.

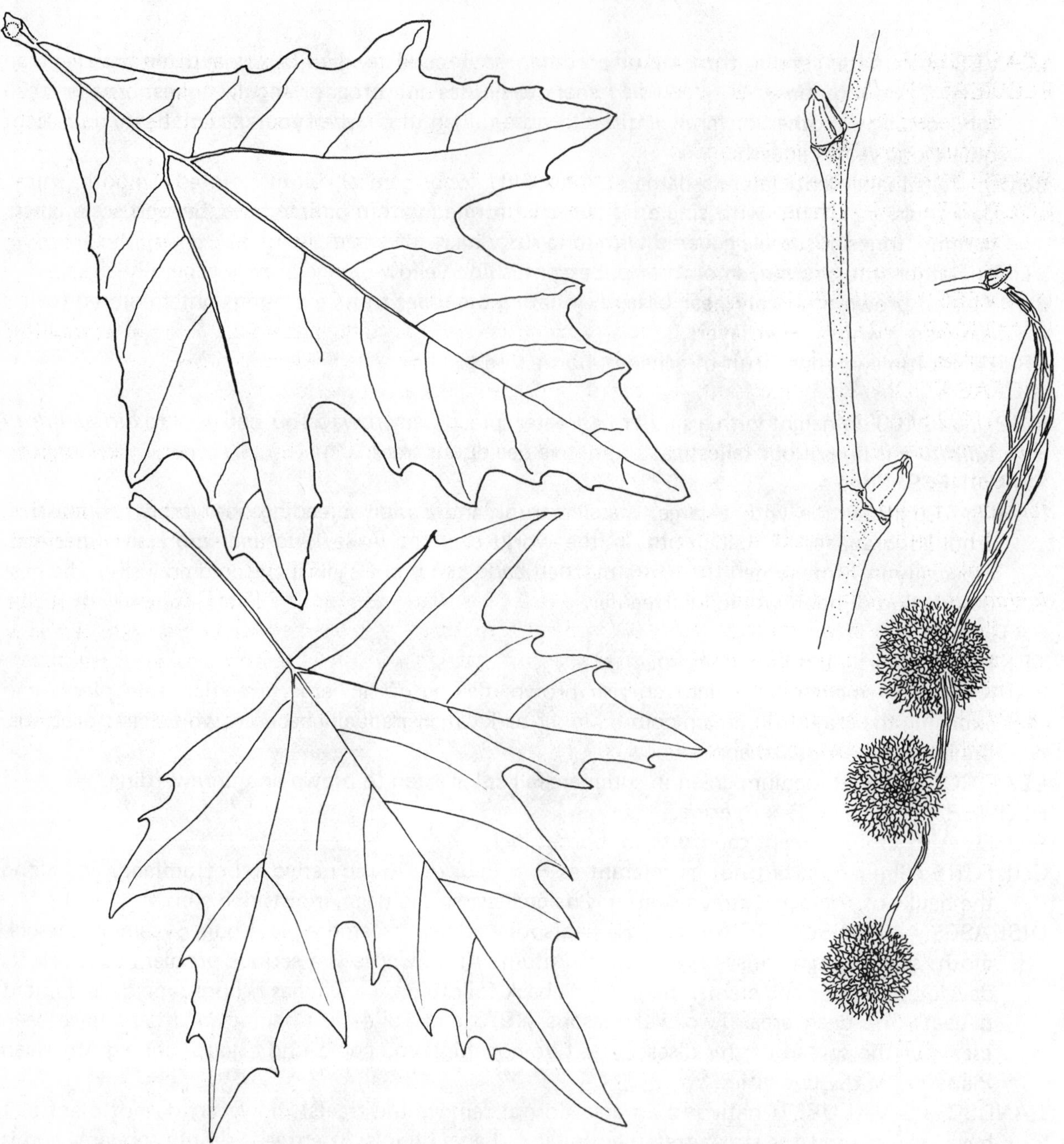

ADDITIONAL NOTES: The wood is heavy, hard, tough and coarse grained, and is used for furniture, boxes, crates and butcher's blocks.

NATIVE HABITAT: Ranges from Maine to Ontario and Minnesota, south to Florida and Texas. Introduced 1640.

Polygonum aubertii — Silvervine Fleeceflower, Silver Lace Vine

FAMILY: Polygonaceae

LEAVES: Alternate, simple, 1 1/2 to 3 1/2" long, ovate to oblong-ovate, hastate at base, usually undulate at margin; petioles 1 1/5 to 2" long.

SIZE: 25 to 35'.

HARDINESS: Zone 4.

HABIT: Twining deciduous vine of rampant growth.

RATE: Fast, as much as 10 to 15' in one growing season is not unreasonable.

TEXTURE: Medium in foliage; rather coarse in winter.

LEAF COLOR: Bright green when mature; reddish, bronze-red when emerging and developing.

FLOWERS: Perfect, white or greenish white, sometimes slightly pinkish, fragrant, about 1/5" diameter; borne in numerous, slender panicles along the upper part of the branches; July, August, and through September.

FRUIT: Three angled achene; now showy, not setting freely.

CULTURE: Easily transplanted; rapidly spreads by underground stems (rhizomes); the smallest segment of which will produce a new plant; full sun or shade; seems to do well in dry soils; almost a weed because of its ebullient, vigorous habit.

DISEASES AND INSECTS: Japanese Beetle can be a problem.

LANDSCAPE VALUE: A vigorous rapidly growing vine with good foliage. Valued for its adaptability; makes a good, quick cover. This might be used where few other vines will grow.

PROPAGATION: Easily increased by stem cuttings or by dividing pieces of sod.

RELATED SPECIES:

The nomenclature is confused within this group of plants and some of the names almost appear "homemade".

Polygonum reynoutria offers the biggest dilemma, for it is widely advertised in nursery catalogs but is limitedly discussed in botanical literature. Wyman and Bailey noted that *P. reynoutria* had pink flowers developing from deep red buds and grows only 4 to 6" high.

Polygonum cuspidatum compactum, Low Japanese Fleeceflower, grows to 2' and has greenish white flowers and small reddish fruits. Wyman also reported a few roots which were planted in a vacant spot in the perennial border developed into an eight foot square in a short period of time. Often offered in the trade as *P. reynoutria.*

LEAVES: Alternate, simple, short-oval to orbicular-ovate, 3 to 6" long, abruptly pointed, with an abrupt or truncate base, petiole about 1" long.

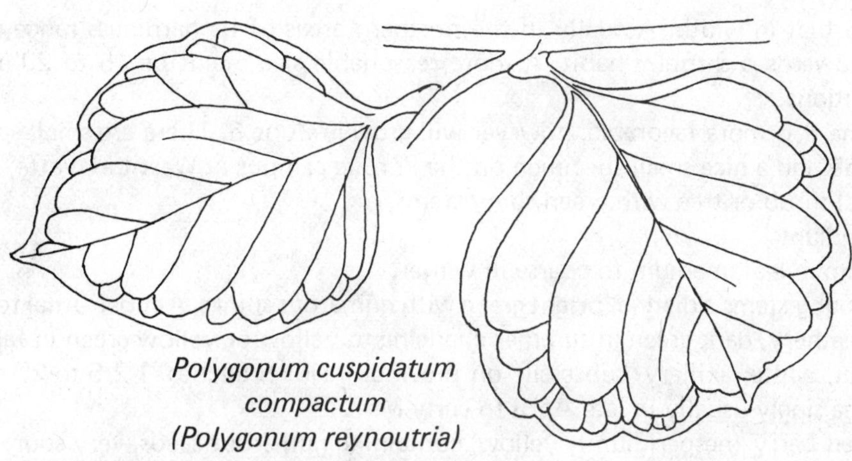

Polygonum cuspidatum compactum (Polygonum reynoutria)

ADDITIONAL NOTES: There are several *Polygonum* plantings on the University of Illinois campus which grow 1 to 2' high and have pinkish flowers. They die back after a hard freeze and look unsightly in the winter only to arise with reddish leaves in April. I noticed considerable variation in size, as some plants grow about a foot while others become almost vine-like and grow to 3'.

NATIVE HABITAT: Western China. Introduced 1899.

Poncirus trifoliata — Hardy-orange

FAMILY: Rutaceae

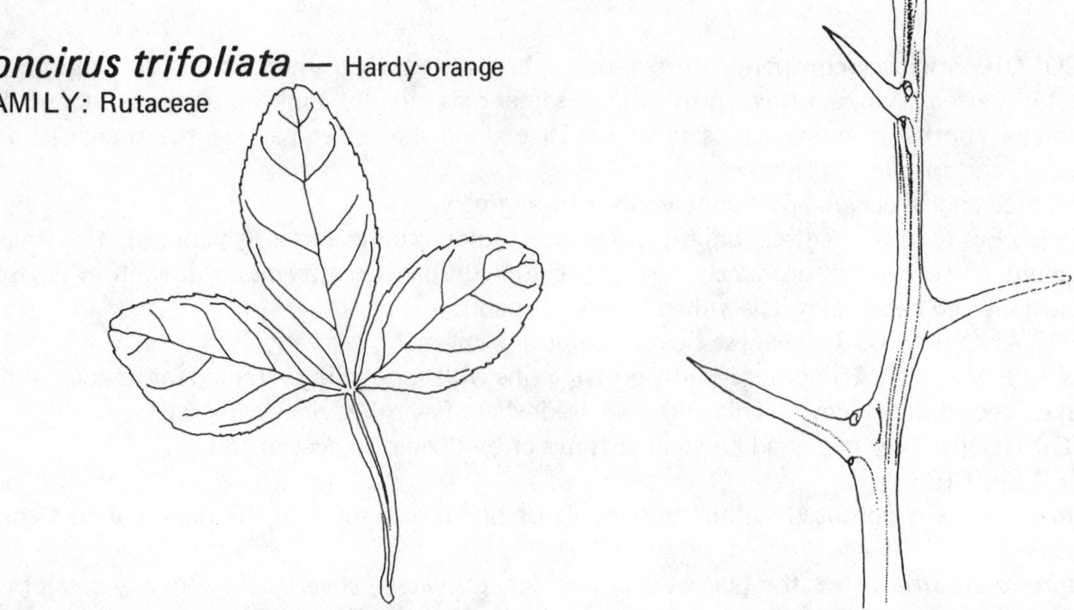

LEAVES: Alternate, tri-foliolate, terminal leaflet obovate to elliptic, 1 to 2 1/2" long, obtuse or emarginate, cuneate, crenulate, sub-coriaceous, the lateral ones similar, but smaller and usually elliptic-ovate, very oblique at base; petiole 1/3 to 1" long; dark green.

BUDS: Glabrous, rather small, solitary, sessile, subglobose, with about 3 exposed scales; terminal lacking.

STEMS: Glabrous, glossy green, triangular, dilated into the thorns at nodes, rather stout; pith large, white, homogenous; leaf scars very small, elliptical, scarcely raised; bundle-trace 1, crescent-shaped; no stipule-scars, 1 to 4 stout spines, occasionally to 3" long. Green stem color and very prominent broad-based spines are good winter identification characters.

SIZE: 30' tall, 2/3 that in width. Actually in the northern areas of its hardiness range this species tends more towards a shrubby habit. A more reasonable size might be 15 to 20' under Midwestern conditions.

HARDINESS: Zone 6 is more favorable, however will grow in Zone 5. There are small specimens in Urbana, Illinois and a nice small specimen on the Purdue campus at West Lafayette, Indiana.

HABIT: Small, oval shrub or tree with green spiny stems.

RATE: Slow to medium.

TEXTURE: Medium in leaf; medium to coarse in winter.

STEM COLOR: Young stems a distinct bright green with numerous spines. Almost lethal to the touch.

LEAF COLOR: Leathery, dark green in summer changing to yellow or yellow-green in fall.

FLOWERS: Perfect, white, axillary, subsessile on previous year's branches, 1 2/5 to 2" across, very fragrant, borne singly usually in late April to early May.

FRUIT: A modified berry (hesperidium), yellow, containing numerous seeds, very sour, ripening in September or October.

CULTURE: Easy to transplant, prefers well drained, acid and probably sandy soils; once established in the right situation it proves to be a vigorous grower.

DISEASES AND INSECTS: None serious.

LANDSCAPE VALUE: More of a novelty plant than anything else in the north. Used in the south for hedging because of its dense growth and thorny character. Even a dumb football player would not attempt to penetrate this hedge!

PROPAGATION: Seeds germinate like beans when stratified for 90 days at 41°F in a moist medium. One of my former students collected fruits from a tree in the Missouri Botanic Garden, St. Louis, and after stratification subsequent germination averaged 95 percent plus. Softwood cuttings taken in summer rooted after treatment with 50 ppm IBA/17 to 24 hr. soak. Cuttings taken in late October failed to root without treatment, but rooted 76 percent after treatment with 50 ppm NAA/24 hour soak.

NATIVE HABITAT: Northern China, Korea. Introduced about 1850.

Populus alba — White Poplar, Silver-leaved Poplar

FAMILY: Salicaceae

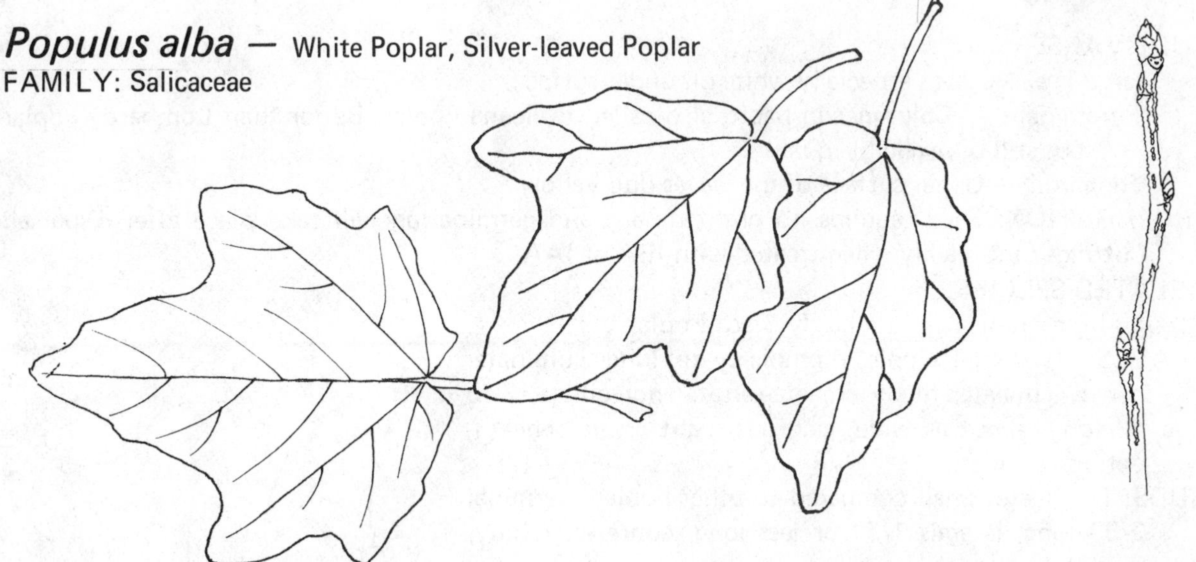

LEAVES: Alternate, simple, on long shoots, palmately 3 to 5 lobed with triangular coarsely toothed lobes, acute, subcordate or rounded at base, 2 to 5" long, dark green above, white-tomentose beneath; on short branches, smaller, ovate to elliptic-oblong, sinuate-dentate, usually gray tomentose beneath, petioles tomentose.

BUDS: Imbricate, small, ovate to conical, light chestnut brown, appressed, shining or more or less covered especially toward base with cottony wool; laterals 1/5 to 1/4" long, terminals larger.

STEM: Slender or sometimes stout, greenish gray, densely covered with thick whitish-cottony wool which can be readily rubbed off. Pith—5 pointed, star-shaped.

BARK: On young trunks characteristically light greenish gray or whitish, often with dark blotches; base of older trunk deeply furrowed into firm dark ridges.

SIZE: 40 to 70' in height with a similar spread; can grow to 90' or greater.

HARDINESS: Zone 3.

HABIT: Usually a wide spreading tree with an irregular, broad, round-topped crown; spreading abundantly by root suckers. Tends to be weak-wooded and susceptible to breakage in storms.

TEXTURE: Medium-coarse in leaf; coarse in winter.

BARK: Greenish gray to whitish, marked with darker blotches, the bases of old trunks becoming fissured, with blackish ridges.

LEAF COLOR: Dark green above and silvery white beneath, the lower surface coated with a thick, matted tomentum; the leaves fall very early in the fall and usually show no coloration although yellowish and reddish have been listed by various authorities.

FLOWERS: Not important, see under *P. deltoides.*

FRUITS: Not important, see under *P. deltoides.*

CULTURE: Easy to grow, does well under any conditions but prefers moist, deep loam; pH adaptable; full sun; prune in summer or fall as it "bleeds" if pruned in winter and spring; air pollution tolerant.

DISEASES AND INSECTS: Poplars, in general, are affected by a whole host of diseases. They are poor ornamental trees and are continually dropping leaves, twigs and other debris. The following pests are the more common and include *Cytospora* canker, poplar canker, fusarium canker, hypoxylon canker, septoria canker, branch gall, leaf blister, leaf spots, leaf rusts, powdery mildew, dieback, aphids, bronze birch borers, poplar borer, red-humped caterpillar, poplar tent maker, scales and imported willow leaf beetle. If anyone plants poplars they deserve the disasters which automatically ensue.

LANDSCAPE VALUE: I hesitate to recommend this tree for anything since it becomes a nuisance and liability after a time. Wood is brittle, roots will clog drain tiles, sewers and water channels; avoid this pest.

CULTIVARS:

var. *nivea* — Leaves especially white on under surface.

'Pyramidalis' — Columnar in habit, also called Bolleana Poplar. Better than Lombardy Poplar but still of negligible quality.

'Richardii' — Upper surface of the leaves dull yellow.

PROPAGATION: Seed requires no pretreatment and germination will take place after dispersal. Cuttings root readily when treated with IBA or IAA.

RELATED SPECIES:

Populus nigra 'Italica' — Lombardy Black Poplar

LEAVES: Alternate, simple, rhombic-ovate, long-acuminate, narrow-cuneate, finely crenate-serrate, non-ciliate, 2 to 4" long, about as wide, glabrous, light green beneath, petioles slender.

BUDS: Imbricate, small compared to other poplars; terminal 2/5" long, laterals 1/3" or less long, appressed, shiny, reddish brown, glabrous.

STEM: Slender, round, lustrous brown.

GROWTH HABIT: Easily recognizable because of decidedly upright habit, often used for screen on old farm properties.

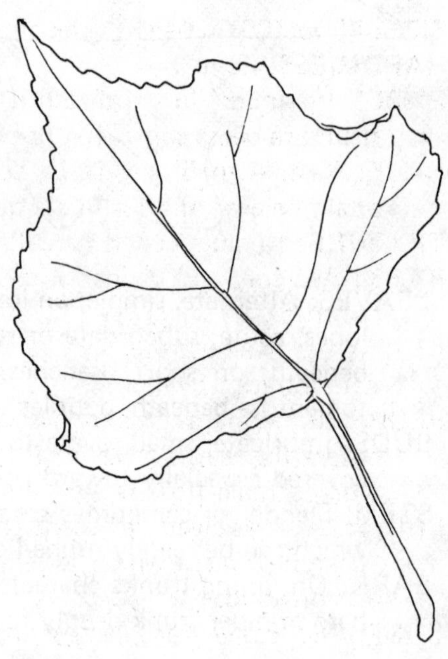

Populus nigra 'Italica', Lombardy Black Poplar, is an upright, fast growing, weedy cultivar that was introduced into this country in colonial times; can grow to 70 to 90' with a spread of 10 to 15' in 20 to 30 years but seldom attains this size because of a canker disease which develops in the upper branches and trunk for which there is no cure. Substitutes might include *Populus alba* 'Pyramidalis', *Alnus glutinosa* 'Fastigiata', although none will grow as fast as Lombardy; a male clone.

NATIVE HABITAT: Central to Southern Europe to Western Siberia and Central Asia. Long cultivated. Naturalized in North America. Introduced 1784.

Populus deltoides — Eastern Cottonwood, also called Eastern Poplar.

FAMILY: Salicaceae

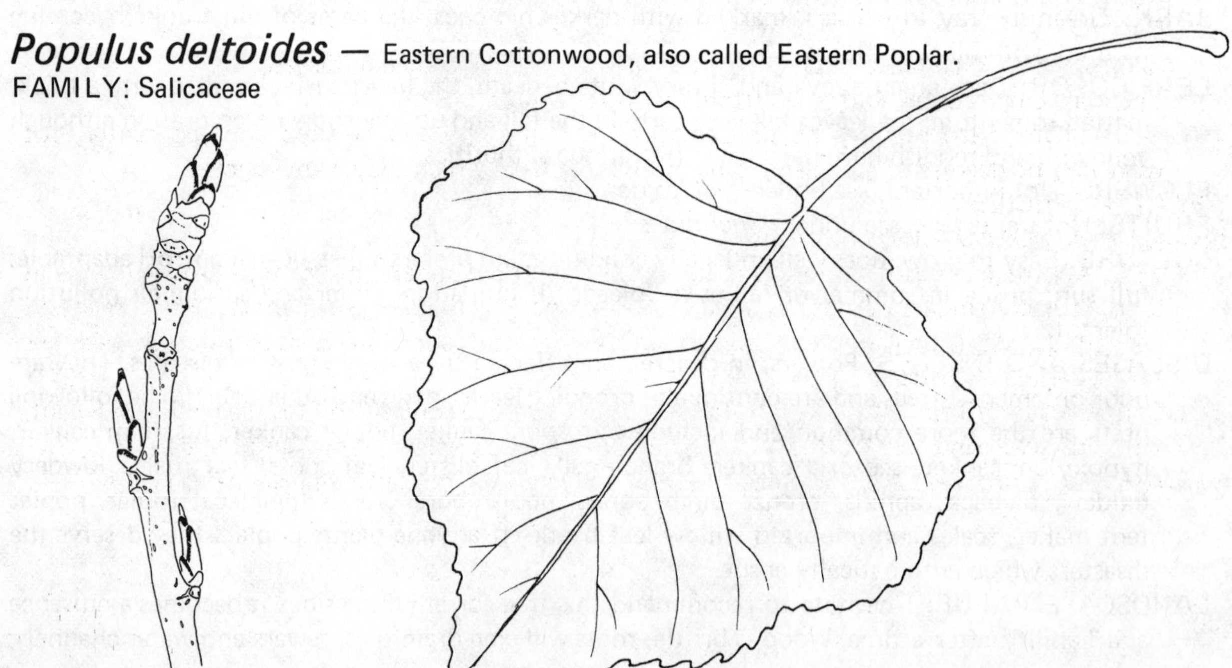

LEAVES: Alternate, simple, deltoid-ovate or broad-ovate, acuminate, subcordate to truncate and with 2 or 3 glands at base, 3 to 5" long, coarsely crenate-dentate with curved teeth, entire at base and apex, densely ciliate, bright green below, glabrous.

BUDS: Imbricate, terminal—1/2 to 3/4" long, 6 to 7 visible scales, conical acute, shiny chestnut brown, resinous.

STEM: Stout, yellowish to greenish yellow, round or marked especially on vigorous trees with more or less prominent wings running down from the two sides and bases of the leaf-scars. Also quite ragged in appearance.

SIZE: 75 to 100' in height spreading 50 to 75'.

HARDINESS: Zone 2.

HABIT: Pyramidal in youth but developing a broad vase-shaped habit in old age with the branching structure being somewhat open, irregular and ragged.

RATE: Fast, 4 to 5' a year in rich moist soil is not uncommon, in fact, in two years trees may attain heights of 30' and diameters of nearly 5".

TEXTURE: Medium-coarse in leaf, coarse in winter.

BARK: Ash-gray and divided into thick, flattened or rounded ridges separated by deep fissures on old trunks.

LEAF COLOR: Lustrous light to medium green in summer, abscising early in fall and usually only with a trace of yellow.

FLOWERS: Applies to most *Populus;* Dioecious, anemophilous, in pendulous catkins appearing before the leaves, individual flowers (both sexes) solitary, inserted on a disk and subtended by a bract; male flowers with either 6 to 12, or 12 to many stamens; female with a single pistil.

FRUIT: 3 or 4-valved dehiscent capsule, 1/4 to 1/3" long, the seeds are tufted and represent the "cottony" mass which is seen under and around the trees at dispersal time; hence the name Cottonwood.

CULTURE: Easily transplanted and grown, prefers moist situations along waterways but tolerates dry soils; very common on moist alluvial soils through the plains and prairie states; tolerates saline conditions and pollutants; very pH adaptable; a short-lived species and trees over 70 years old deteriorate rapidly.

LANDSCAPE VALUE: Little, except in the difficult plains states; a messy tree often dropping leaves, flowers, fruits, twigs and branches; will break up in storms as the wood is light, soft and weak; impressive in river bottoms and should remain there.

CULTIVARS:

'Siouxland' — Male form, good dark green leaves, some resistance to disease.

The male clones often sold as "Cottonless Cottonwoods".

PROPAGATION: Seed requires no pretreatment. Cuttings can also be used and apparently root with varying degrees of ease depending on the tree from which they were selected.

RELATED SPECIES:

Populus grandidentata — Bigtooth Aspen

LEAVES: Alternate, simple, on long shoots, 3 to 4" long, acuminate, truncate to broad-cuneate at base, coarsely sinuate dentate with callous mucronate teeth, dark green above, gray tomentose beneath at first, soon glabrescent and glaucescent, those of short branches elliptic, with sharper teeth, petiole glabrescent.

BUDS: Imbricate, 1/8 to 1/4" long, 6 to 7 visible scales, ovate to conical, pointed, generally divergent, dull, dusty-looking, due to fine, close, pale pubescence especially at margin of scales.

STEM: Stout, round, reddish brown or somewhat yellowish brown, older stems greenish gray.

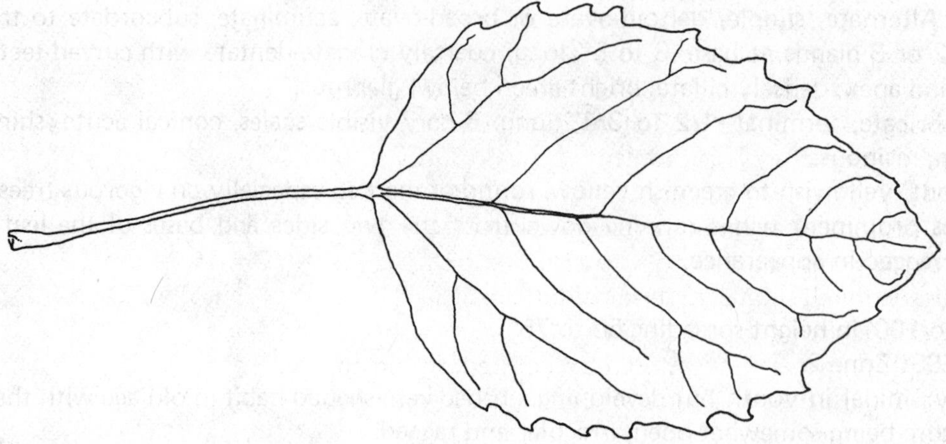

Populus grandidentata, Bigtooth Aspen, is normally a medium-sized tree reaching 50 to 70′, with a spread of 20 to 40′. Often pyramidal in youth with a central leader, developing an oval, open, irregular crown at maturity; very fast growing (65′/20 years); reaches best development on moist fertile soils but will grow on dry, sandy or gravelly soils; ornamental assets are few but it is valuable for pulp wood and other wood uses. Native from Nova Scotia to Ontario and Minnesota south to North Carolina, Tennessee, Illinois and Iowa. Introduced 1772. Zone 3.

Populus tremula 'Erecta' – Upright European Aspen

LEAVES: Alternate, simple, thin, suborbicular to ovate, rounded or acute at apex, truncate or subcordate at base, sinuately crenate-dentate, 1 to 3″ long, tomentose when emerging, quickly glabrous, glaucescent beneath; gray-green; petioles flattened, glabrous, often as long as the blade.

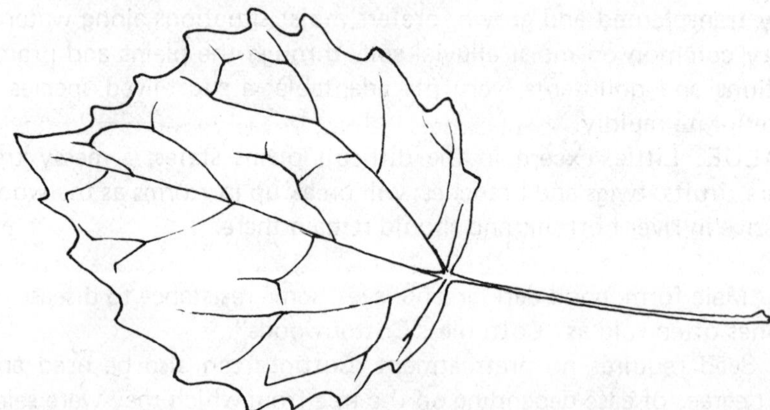

Populus tremula 'Erecta', Upright European Aspen, is an excellent, narrowly fastigiate tree which was found in the forests of Sweden. It may prove to be a substitute for the canker-infested Lombardy Poplar. Based on evaluations of plants in our trial gardens the leaves contract a severe leaf spot and in 1975 were defoliated by early August. Specimens at the Minnesota Landscape Arboretum appeared in outstanding condition. Perhaps the tree is best adapted to colder climates. The species is native to Europe, Northern Africa, Western Asia and Siberia. Zone 2.

Populus tremuloides — Quaking Aspen

LEAVES: Alternate, simple, thin, ovate to orbicular, short-acuminate, truncate to broad-cuneate at base, finely glandular-serrate, 1 1/2 to 3" long, lustrous dark green above, glabrous and glaucescent beneath, leaves of suckers ovate, large, glabrous.

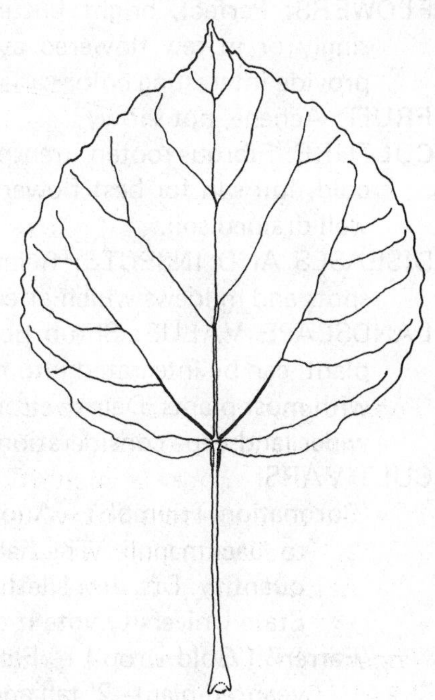

BUDS: Terminal-imbricate, conical, sharp-pointed, sometimes very slightly resinous, 6 to 7 scaled, reddish brown; laterals-incurved, similar to terminal but smaller.

STEM: Slender, lustrous, reddish brown.

BARK: Smooth, greenish white to cream-colored; in old age furrowed, dark brown or gray, roughened by numerous wartlike excrescences.

Populus tremuloides, Quaking Aspen, is the most widely distributed tree of North America. It is fast growing, relatively short-lived and attains heights of 40 to 50' with a spread of 20 to 30'. Pyramidal and narrow when young, usually with a long trunk and narrow, rounded crown at maturity. Indifferent as to soil conditions and over its range can be found in moist, loamy sands to shallow rocky soils and clay. The leaves flutter in the slightest breeze, hence the name Quaking Aspen. The fall color is a good yellow. Ornamentally not important because of disease and insect problems but, nonetheless, an interesting tree. The wood is important for pulpwood and other uses. Native from Labrador to Alaska, south to Pennsylvania, Missouri, Northern Mexico and Lower California. Introduced 1812. Zone 1.

NATIVE HABITAT: Quebec to North Dakota, Kansas, Texas, Florida. Introduced 1750.

Potentilla fruticosa — Bush Cinquefoil

FAMILY: Rosaceae

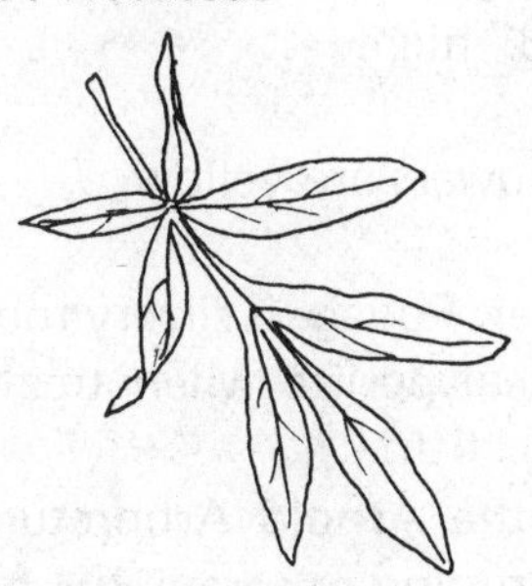

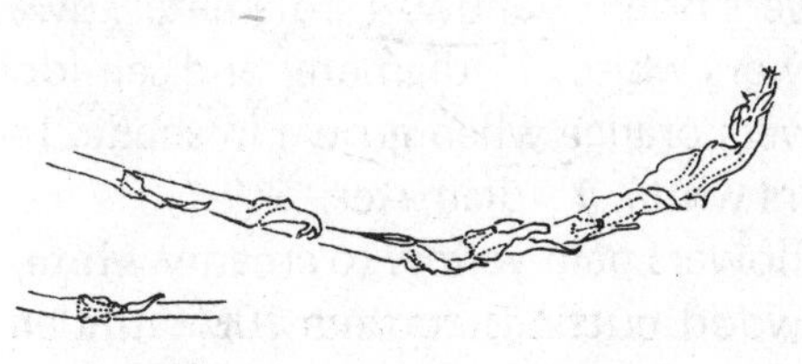

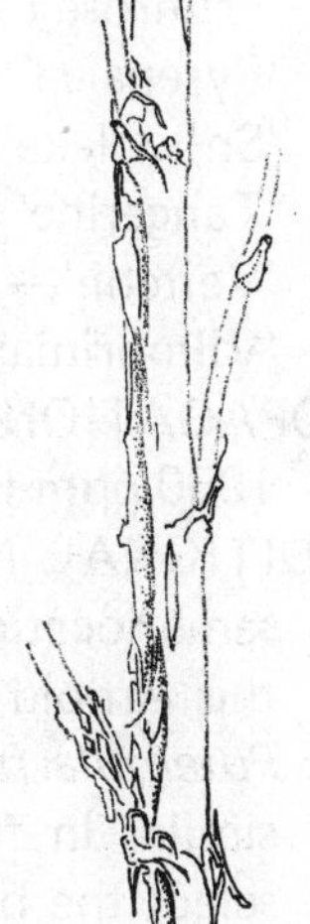

LEAVES: Alternate, compd. pinnate, 3 to 7 leaflets, usually 5, sessile, elliptic to linear-oblong, acute, 2/5 to 1" long, with revolute margin, more or less silky.

STEMS: Shiny brown, slender, wispy.

SIZE: 1 to 4' in height and 2 to 4' or larger in spread. Dainty in size considerations.

HARDINESS: Zone 2.

HABIT: Very bushy shrub with upright slender stems forming a low, rounded to broad-rounded outline.

RATE: Slow.

TEXTURE: Fine in leaf; medium-fine in winter. Refined, graceful appearance in foliage.

STEM COLOR: Interesting in winter if framed by a new snow; brown in color.

LEAF COLOR: Silky gray-green when unfolding changing to bright green in mature leaf; fall color is green to yellow-brown, not ornamental.

FLOWERS: Perfect, bright buttercup yellow, about 1" across, June through until frost, borne singly or in few flowered cymes, excellent color addition to any garden; numerous cultivars provide interesting color variation.

FRUIT: Achene, not showy.

CULTURE: Fibrous rooted, transplants well, of easy culture, withstands poor, dry soils and extreme cold, full sun for best flower although they seem to do well in partial shade; best in a fertile, well-drained soil.

DISEASES AND INSECTS: Relatively free from insect and disease pests. There are several leaf spots and mildews which affect the plant but they are rarely serious.

LANDSCAPE VALUE: Shrub border, massing, edging plant, low hedge, perennial border, facer plant, can be integrated into the foundation planting and will add a degree of color unattainable with most plants. Dainty clean foliage, good flower color and length of flowering period justify wider landscape consideration.

CULTIVARS:

'Coronation Triumph' — Another large clone, 3 to 4', with a softer green foliage cast compared to 'Jackmannii'. The habit is dense, full, and mounded, and the flowers are borne in great quantity. Drs. Jim Klett, South Dakota State University and Dale Hermann, North Dakota State University vote it one of the best for their area.

'Farreri' ('Gold Drop') — Flowers deep yellow, 3/4" diameter, leaves very small. Twenty-five year-old-plant—2' tall and 3' across.

'Friedrichsenii' — Flowers creamy white to pale yellow, 1" diameter. Fifty-eight year old plant is 4 1/2' high and 6' across.

'Grandiflora' — Flowers bright yellow, 1 3/8" diameter, with large leaves. Ultimate height about 6'.

'Jackmannii' — A larger form, 3 to 4' high, good medium green foliage color, and a profusion of bright yellow flowers; has performed well in the midwest.

'Katherine Dykes' — Lemon-yellow flowers; arching, rounded; may contract leaf spot.

'Maanely's' (Moonlight) — Flowers pale yellow, 1" diameter.

var. *mandshurica* — Flowers white, 1" diameter, leaves with dense white pubescence on both surfaces. Dwarf form about 1 1/2' tall.

'Primrose Beauty' — Pale yellow flowers, outstanding foliage; low growing.

'Pyrenaica' — Flowers bright yellow, 1" diameter, dwarf—6 to 18" high.

'Snowflake' — Flowers white, 1" diameter and semidouble.

'Tangerine' — Flowers orange when grown in shade. In full sun flowers are yellow.

'Veitchii' — Flowers white, 1" diameter.

'Vilmoriniana' — Flowers pale yellow to creamy white, 1" diameter. Foliage is silvery tomentose.

PROPAGATION: Softwood cuttings rooted 100% under mist in peat:perlite when treated with 1000 ppm IBA.

ADDITIONAL NOTES: Wyman noted that one cultivar grown in the Arnold Arboretum in the same location for 60 years was 3' tall and had never required pruning or spraying. I have seen the Arnold Arboretum's and the Minnesota Landscape Arboretum's extensive collections of *Potentilla fruticosa* and wondered how anyone could separate them without labels. Many look similar in flower color, habit, and foliage characteristics. The logical approach would be to select the best 5 or 10 and use this as a guide. From what I understand continued breeding and selection is occurring so, no doubt, more clones will inundate an already confused group of plants. Their extreme hardiness and summer flowering sequence make them valuable landscape plants.

NATIVE HABITAT: Northern hemisphere.

Prinsepia sinensis — Cherry Prinsepia

FAMILY: Rosaceae

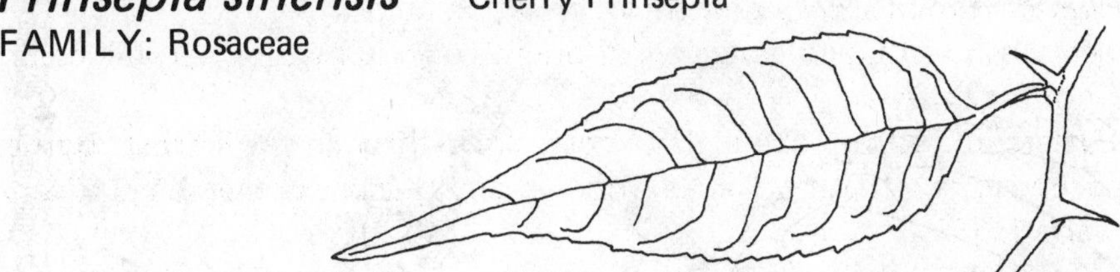

LEAVES: Alternate, simple, ovate-lanceolate to lanceolate, 2 to 3" long, long acuminate, entire or sparingly serrulate, finely ciliate, otherwise glabrous, bright green; slender petioled.

BUDS: Small, indistinctly scaly, concealed in brown hairs; buds may develop into spines.

STEM: Long and slender, round, spiny (1/4 to 2/5" long), light gray-brown; pith chambered.

SIZE: 6 to 10' in height and as wide.

HARDINESS: Zone 4.

HABIT: Haystack to rounded, dense, spiny shrub well adapted for hedges and screens.

RATE: Medium.

TEXTURE: Medium in leaf; perhaps medium-coarse in winter.

LEAF COLOR: Bright green in summer; fall color of little consequence.

FLOWERS: Perfect, small, light yellow, borne in fascicles of 1 to 4 on previous year's wood in March-April, each flower about 3/5" diameter, worthwhile but not overwhelming.

FRUITS: Red, cherry-like, 3/5" long, subglobose or ovoid drupe which ripens in July and August and is effectively digested by birds.

CULTURE: Easily transplanted, of undemanding culture, requiring only fertile, well-drained soil and open, sunny location; probably best to renewal prune when plants become overgrown; withstands pruning quite favorably.

DISEASES AND INSECTS: One of its principal merits is resistance to pests.

LANDSCAPE VALUE: Not a very common shrub but one certainly worth considering for hedges, screens or barriers. Quite serviceable shrub and requires minimal maintenance. The only places I have seen the shrub were in the Arnold and Minnesota Landscape Arboreta.

PROPAGATION: Seeds can be sown as soon as ripe in August or stored over winter and then sown. No cold stratification period is apparently required. Softwood cuttings can also be rooted without difficulty.

RELATED SPECIES:

Prinsepia uniflora, Hedge Prinsepia, is a rather thorny, moderately dense aggregate of light gray branches growing 4 to 5' high with a similar spread. The Minnesota Landscape Arboretum has both species growing side by side and the growth habit and foliage characteristic differences become immediately evident. The leaves are very dark green, 1 to 2 1/2" long and not as densely borne as those of *P. sinensis.* The flowers are similar while the fruits are globose, about 1/2" across, dark purplish red, bloomy, maturing in late summer. This species would also make a good hedge or barrier and on the basis of foliage color is superior to *P. sinensis.* Native to Northwestern China. Introduced 1911. Zone 4. Rare in cultivation.

ADDITIONAL NOTES: One of the first shrubs to leaf out in spring, making it about the first of all woody plants to develop green foliage.

NATIVE HABITAT: Manchuria. Cultivated 1896.

Prunus avium — Mazzard or Sweet Cherry

FAMILY: Rosaceae

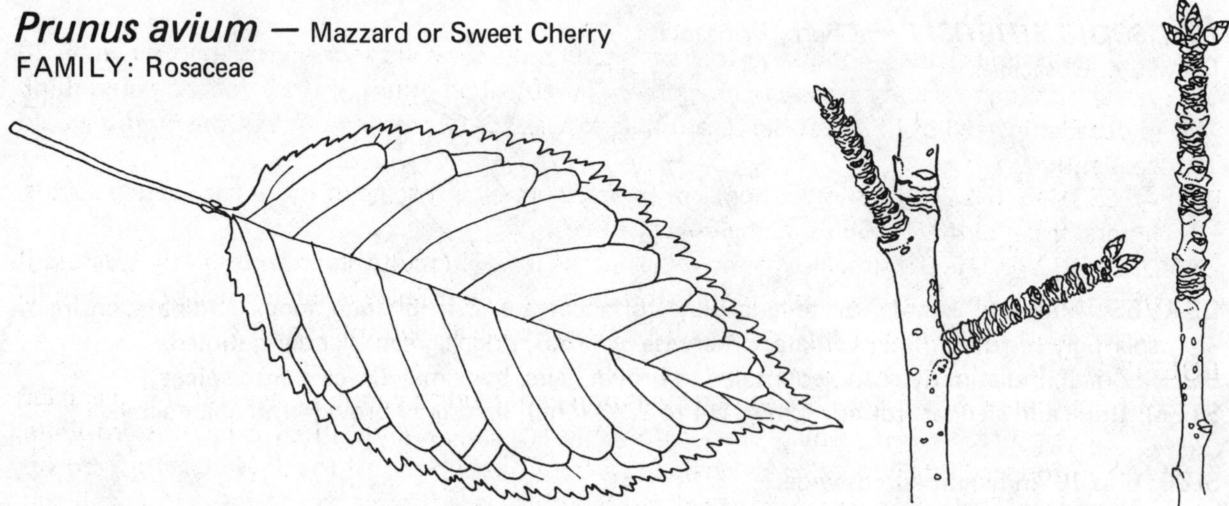

LEAVES: Alternate, simple, oblong-ovate, 2 to 6" long, acuminate, unequally serrate, dull and often slightly rugose above, more or less pubescent beneath, of soft texture, petioles—1 3/5" long with prominent glands.

Prunus avium, Mazzard or Sweet Cherry, is a large tree of conical shape growing to 70′ or more but usually under cultivation reaches 30 to 40′ with a similar spread. The foliage is a deep green in summer and turns yellow to bronze in fall. Flowers are white, 1 to 1 1/2" diameter, fragrant; mid to late April, in several flowered umbels. The fruit is a reddish black drupe about 1" in diameter. This is the species from which most of our popular sweet cherry clones are derived. The cultivar 'Plena' has double white 1 1/2" diameter flowers with as many as 30 petals and is superior to the species for flower effect. There are other clones of limited importance. Europe, Western Asia. Cultivated since ancient times. Zone 3. One of the hardiest cherries and might be used where the Oriental types are not hardy.

Prunus cerasifera — Cherry Plum or Myrobalan Plum

FAMILY: Rosaceae

LEAVES: Alternate, simple, toothed, 1 1/2 - 2 1/2" long, ovate, elliptic or obovate, apex pointed, broadly wedge-shaped or rounded, without glands on the petiole.

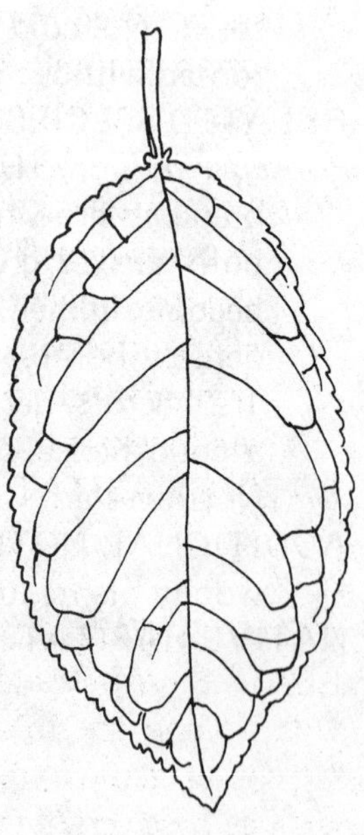

SIZE: 15 to 30′ by 15 to 25′.

HARDINESS: Zone 3.

HABIT: Small, shrubby tree, twiggy and rounded, with ascending, spreading branches.

RATE: Fast.

TEXTURE: Medium in all seasons.

LEAF COLOR: Deep green in summer, often bronze-red in fall.

FLOWERS: Perfect, white, 4/5 to 1" across, sickeningly fragrant; sometime in April before the leaves, often around early to mid April; usually borne solitary.

FRUIT: Reddish, slightly bloomy drupe, approximately 1" across, July or August.

CULTURE: This discussion applies to the *Prunus* species. Transplant bare root or balled and burlapped in spring; any average soil is acceptable but should be well drained; pH adaptable; full sun; prune after flowering although potential fruits will be cut off; keep trees vigorous as there are numerous serious insects and diseases associated with *Prunus;*

they are not particularly pollution tolerant and in most cases are short-lived (approximately 20 years) although certain species are much more durable than others; if the gardener would think in decades instead of lifetimes the pleasurable experience of growing some of the *Prunus* would be just that.

DISEASES AND INSECTS: Almost hopeless to list them all but some of the worst include aphids, borers, scale, tent caterpillars, and a host of others.

LANDSCAPE VALUE: This species has no value but the following cultivars are extensively (overused) used for specimens, groupings, and in foundation plantings. There is something about a purple-leaved beast that excites people to spend money on basically worthless plants.

CULTIVARS:

'Atropurpurea' – Upright, dense branching form with reddish purple foliage and 3/4" diameter, light pink flowers, which open before the leaves (usually). Often called Pissard Plum, introduced into France from Persia (now Iran) through the efforts of Mr. Pissard, gardener to the Shah. For best foliage color the purple-leaved forms should be sited in full sun.

'Hollywood' – Foliage first appears green as it unfolds, then turns a deep purple.

'Nigra' – Foliage very dark purple and color is retained through the summer. Flowers are single, pink and 5/8" in diameter.

'Pendula' – Form with pendulous branches.

'Thundercloud' – Excellent form which retains its deep purple foliage color.

'Vesuvius' – Large deep purple leaves highlight this form.

PROPAGATION: *Prunus* seeds have an embryo dormancy and require a period of after ripening in the presence of oxygen and moisture to overcome it. Softwood cuttings of *P. cerasifera* rooted 20% without treatment and 100% in 4 weeks after treatment with 30 ppm NAA which is the most effective hormone for this species.

RELATED SPECIES:

Prunus x *blireiana,* Blireiana Plum, is a hybrid between *P. cerasifera* 'Atropurpurea' and *P. mume.* It is a rounded, dense branching tree with reddish purple foliage and double, light pink, 1" diameter flowers in late April; fruits are purplish red and lost in the foliage so as not to be effective; 24' high; Zone 5.

Prunus x *cistena* – Purpleleaf Sand Cherry

A cross between *P. pumila* x *P. cerasifera* 'Atropurpurea'. Small shrub (8') often planted for reddish purple foliage and edible blackish purple fruit.

Prunus x *cistena,* Purpleleaf Sand Cherry, is a cross between *P. pumila* and *P. cerasifera* 'Atropurpurea' and grows 7 to 10' tall usually with a slightly smaller spread. The foliage is intensely reddish purple and stays effective throughout summer. The flowers are single, pinkish, fragrant, borne after the leaves have developed in early May; fruits are blackish purple. Zone 2.

NATIVE HABITAT: Western Asia, Caucasia.

Prunus glandulosa — Dwarf Flowering Almond

LEAVES: Alternate, simple, ovate-oblong or oblong to oblong-lanceolate, 1 to 3 1/2" long, acute, rarely acuminate, broad-cuneate at base, crenate-serrulate, glabrous beneath or slightly hairy on midrib, petioles–1/4" long.

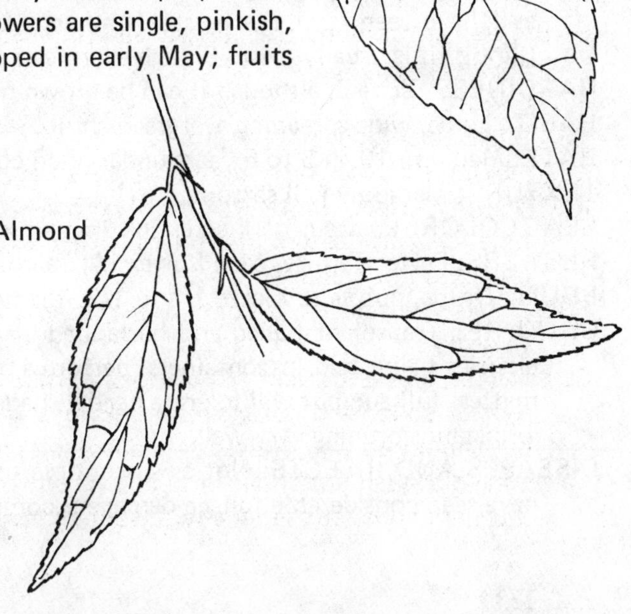

Prunus glandulosa, Dwarf Flowering Almond, is the bargain basement shrub of many discount stores. It grows 4 to 5′ tall and 3 to 4′ wide and is a spreading, weakly multi-stemmed, straggly shrub. The summer foliage is light green; flowers are pink or white, single or double; late April to early May, one or two together; fruits are red, 1/2″ across and rarely produced; chief value is in the flowers; basically a very poor plant, single season quality, appearing distraught and alone in summer, fall and winter. Central and Northern China, Japan. Introduced 1835. Zone 4.

Prunus 'Hally Jolivette' is the result of a cross of *P. subhirtella* x *P. yedoensis* crossed back on *P. subhirtella* by Dr. Karl Sax of the Arnold Arboretum. It is a rounded, dense branching, shrubby tree growing to 15′ and of relatively fine texture. The flowers are pink in bud, opening white, double, 1 1/4″ diameter and effective over a 10 to 20 day period in late April to early May as the flowers do not all open at once. One of the very nicest *Prunus* developed by a great cytologist at the premier Arboretum in the United States. Zone 5. 1940.

Prunus maackii, Amur Chokecherry, is an interesting rounded, dense branching tree growing to 45′ with 2 to 3″ long racemes of white flowers in early to mid-May. The bark is a handsome brownish yellow and peels off in thin strips like that of the Paper Birch. Korea, Manchuria. Introduced 1878. Zone 2. May suffer from borers in hot, dry climates.

Prunus maritima, Beach Plum, is a rounded dense bush growing 6′ and more. The flowers are white, single or double, 1/2″ across; May; 2 to 3 together; fruits a dull purple, 1/2 to 1″ diameter, sometimes crimson, ripening in August and relished for jams and jellies. This species abounds on Cape Cod, Massachusetts and is one of the Cape Coders' cherished plants. A good salt tolerant species which grows along the coast from Maine to Virginia. Introduced 1818. Zone 3. Variety *flava* is a yellow fruited form apparently found wild on the Cape.

Prunus laurocerasus — Common Laurelcherry

FAMILY: Rosaceae

LEAVES: Alternate, simple, 2 to 6″ long, usually oblong or obovate-oblong, acuminate, cuneate to rounded at base, obscurely serrate to nearly entire, glabrous; petioles 1/5 to 2/5″ long, evergreen, round nectar-discs on back.

BUDS: Solitary or collaterally multiple, sessile, subglobose or mostly ovoid, with usually 6 exposed scales.

STEMS: Slender or moderate, subterete or somewhat angled from the nodes, occasionally spine tipped; pith roundish or angled, pale or brown, continuous; leaf scars raised on a cushion flanked by the stipule vestiges or scars, half-round or half-elliptical, small; 3 bundle-traces, usually minute.

SIZE: Often listed as growing 10 to 18′ high and under ideal conditions might become 25 to 30′ but as I have seen it in the North (Amherst, Mass.; Youngstown and Columbus, Ohio; Urbana, Illinois) it is usually a 4 to 6′ high evergreen shrub of spreading habit.

HARDINESS: Zone 6, although it can be grown north of this area with some success.

HABIT: Large, wide spreading evergreen shrub.

RATE: Medium, 10′ in 5 to 6 years under good conditions.

TEXTURE: Medium in all seasons.

LEAF COLOR: Lustrous dark green in summer; loses some of its sheen in cold climates.

FLOWERS: Perfect, white, each flower 1/4″ across; late May; borne in 2 to 5″ long racemes.

FRUIT: Drupe, purple to black, 1/3 to 1/2″ diameter; late summer.

CULTURE: Transplant balled and burlapped or from a container. Lately I have seen most laurelcherries being sold in containers; performs best in well drained soil supplemented with organic matter; full sun but will tolerate partial shade as well as salt spray; avoid excessive fertilization; withstands pruning very well.

DISEASES AND INSECTS: Not as susceptible to the problems which beset the tree *Prunus* but I have seen considerable foliage damage accomplished by insects.

LANDSCAPE VALUE: Relatively handsome hedge plant; popular in the south; is not too successfully used north of Philadelphia.

CULTIVARS:

'Otto Luyken' — Broad spreading dwarf form; old plants may be 3' high and 6 to 8' wide; keeps its small dwarf habit into old age.

'Schipkaensis' — Shrubby form with Zone 5 hardiness; leaves not as big as the species.

'Zabeliana' — Good clone with leaves narrower than the species; Zone 5 hardiness; growing 3 to 5' high by 5 to 8' wide in 4 to 5 years.

PROPAGATION: Cuttings taken in late summer rooted 90 percent in sand:peat in 7 weeks without treatment.

NATIVE HABITAT: Southeastern Europe and Asia Minor. Introduced 1576.

Prunus padus — European Birdcherry

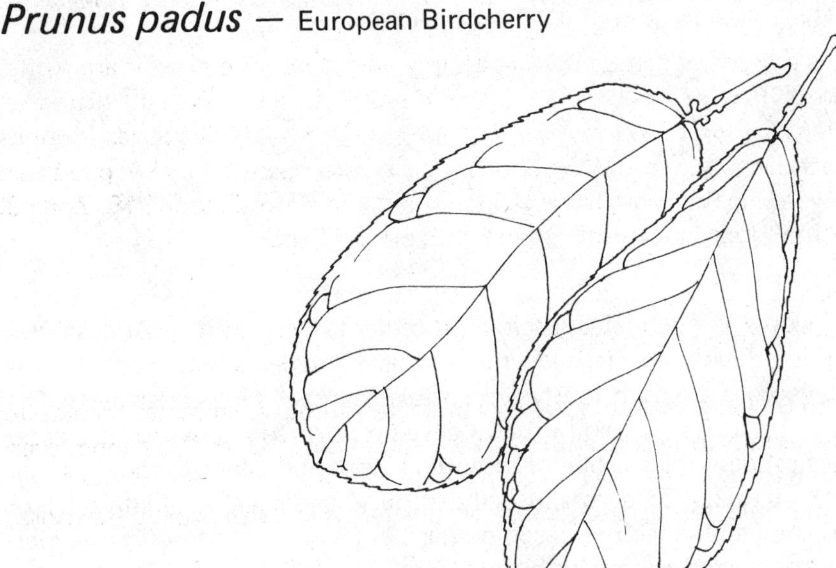

LEAVES: Alternate, simple, toothed, 2 1/2 to 5" long, obovate to elliptic, apex abruptly taper pointed, base wedge-shaped, rounded or slightly cordate, teeth fine, very sharp, grayish and hairless beneath or with axillary tufts, petiole-glandular.

Prunus padus, European Birdcherry, is a medium sized (30 to 40'), rounded, low branched tree with ascending branches. The foliage is a dark, dull green in summer. The flowers are white, fragrant, 2/5 to 3/5" across; mid April to early May; borne in drooping loose racemes 3 to 6" long. The fruit is black, 1/4 to 1/3" across, July to August. This is the first tree to leaf out on the campus and the new, lustrous light green leaves are a welcome sight after a difficult Midwestern winter. Several cultivars include:

'Commutata' — Individual flowers 1/2" in diameter and flowers 3 weeks before other forms.

'Plena' — Flowers large and double, remaining effective longer than any other form.

'Spaethii' — Racemes somewhat pendulous.

'Watereri' — Racemes 8" long, quite effective in flower.

Europe, Northern Asia, to Korea and Japan. Zone 3. It is one of the best looking *Prunus* species on our campus.

Prunus pensylvanica, Pin or Wild Red Cherry, is a small, slender, often shrubby tree with branches spreading at a broad angle forming a round-topped, oblong head. Size varies from 25 to 40' in height by 18 to 25′ in spread. This is a very rapid grower and can quickly develop in abandoned areas. The leaves are a lustrous deep green in summer changing to yellow and red in fall. The flowers are white, 1/2″ across; May-June; borne in 2 to 5-flowered umbels or short racemes. Fruit is a light red, 1/4″ diameter, globose, sour drupe which ripens in July through August. Very adaptable species as it forms a pioneer association on cut-over or burned-over forest lands; intolerant of shade and soon yields to other species. A useful "nurse" type tree much in the mold of Gray Birch in this respect. Native from Labrador west to British Columbia, south to North Carolina and Colorado. Introduced 1773. Zone 2.

Prunus persica — Common Peach

LEAVES: Alternate, simple, elliptic-lanceolate or oblong lanceolate, broadest about or slightly above the middle, 3 to 6″ long, long-acuminate, broad cuneate, serrate or serrulate, glabrous, dark green, often lustrous; petioles glandular, 2/5 to 3/5″ long.

STEM: Offers a valid identification characteristic for the upper portion is often reddish while the lower part is greenish; the stem has a somewhat grainy appearance.

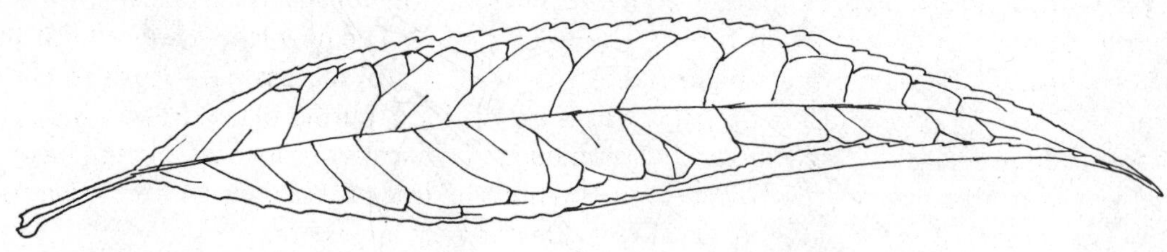

Prunus persica, Peach, as most people know, yields luscious, succulent, tasty fruit in August. Yet the production of peaches is a highly specialized and technical art demanding considerable time, investment and luck. Peaches are notoriously susceptible to insect and disease pests. The Common Peach grows from 15 to 25′ tall and usually develops a spread equal to or greater than its height. The habit is best described as one of ascending limbs and a low, broad, globular crown. The flowers are pink, 1 to 1 2/5″ across, usually solitary, and develop in late April or early May before the leaves. Actually, a mature peach orchard in flower is a magnificent experience. Flowers are often injured in cold winters or by late frosts. The fruit is a large, 3″ diameter, almost globular, yellow and/or reddish, pubescent drupe which matures in August. Peaches present many problems culturally and the homeowner should not be discouraged if they fail. The best approach is to avoid peaches altogether. There are many single, semi-double or double flowered forms of the common peach which are beautiful in flower but almost impossible to keep in good condition. The colors range from white through pink to variegated to deep red. Since first arriving on the Illinois campus I have watched a double pink peach flower spectacularly in 1973 and 1974, but the consistent munching by the borers resulted in the death of the tree in 1975. The temptation to buy these forms based on flower alone is overwhelmingly appealing and, consequently, one's enthusiasm must be tempered with the knowledge that the peach is prone to insects and diseases. The peach is native to China and has been cultivated since ancient times. Zone 5. There are numerous cultivars of both the fruiting and double-flowered forms and it is wise to check with the local nurseryman for the best types for your area.

Prunus sargentii — Sargent Cherry

LEAVES: Alternate, simple, purplish or bronzy when unfolding, elliptic-obovate to oblong-obovate, 3 to 5″ long, long acuminate, rounded or sometimes subcordate at base, sharply serrate with acuminate teeth, glabrous and glaucescent beneath; petiole 4/5 to 1 1/5″ long.

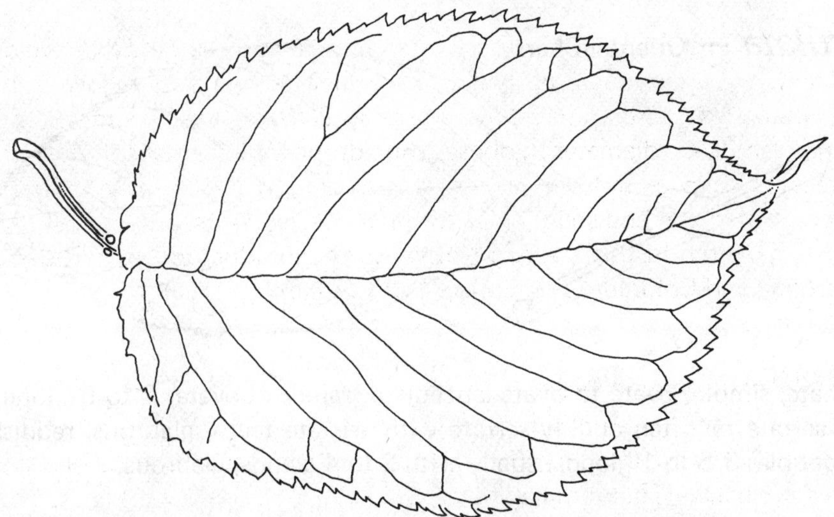

Prunus sargentii, Sargent Cherry, is one of the most useful cherries available. It grows 40 to 50′ in height with a spread approximately equal to height. The foliage is an excellent shiny dark green in summer and changes to bronze or red in the fall. The new leaves are reddish tinged as they emerge. The flowers are single, pink, 1 1/5 to 1 3/5″ across; late April to early May; borne in 2 to 4 flowered sessile umbel. Fruit is a 2/5″ long, purple black drupe which ripens in June and July. Both the species and 'Columnaris' (a narrow, columnar clone) have proved excellent in evaluations at the Shade Tree Evaluation Plots at Wooster, Ohio. Native to Japan. Introduced 1890. Zone 4. Possibly one of, if not, the best large cherry.

Prunus serotina — Black Cherry

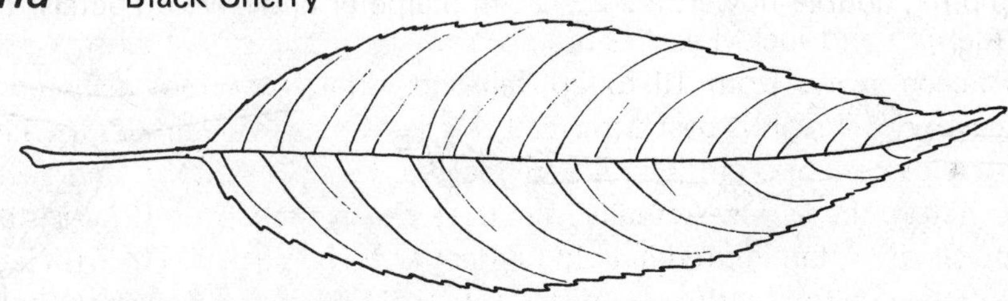

LEAVES: Alternate, simple, oblong-ovate to lance-oblong, 2 to 5″ long, acuminate, cuneate, serrulate with small incurved callous teeth, lustrous, medium to dark green above, light green beneath and often villous along the midrib; petioles—1/4 to 1″ long, glandular.

Prunus serotina, Black Cherry, is a common sight over much of the eastern United States. It is an oval headed tree with pendulous branches, commonly growing 50 to 60′ tall but occasionally reaching 100′. The leaves are a lustrous dark green in summer. Flowers are white, 2/5″ across; May; borne in pendulous, 4 to 6″ long racemes. Fruits are red changing to black, 2/5″ across, ripening in August and September and have a pleasant bitter-sweet and winy flavor and are often used for making wine and jelly. Valuable timber tree especially since it is used in the manufacture of furniture. Very adaptable tree making its best growth on deep, moist, fertile soils but is also found growing on rather dry, gravelly, or sandy soils in the uplands. Ontario to North Dakota, Texas and Florida. Introduced 1629. Zone 3.

Prunus serrula is a small, vigorous tree growing to 30′. The main ornamental asset is the glistening surface of the polished red-brown, mahogany-like bark. Flowers are small, 1 to 3, May, with the foliage. Fruit is a 1/2″ long red drupe. Very difficult to find commercially but worth seeking. Handsome in winter when the bark is maximally exposed. Central China. Introduced 1907. Zone 5.

Prunus serrulata — Oriental Cherry

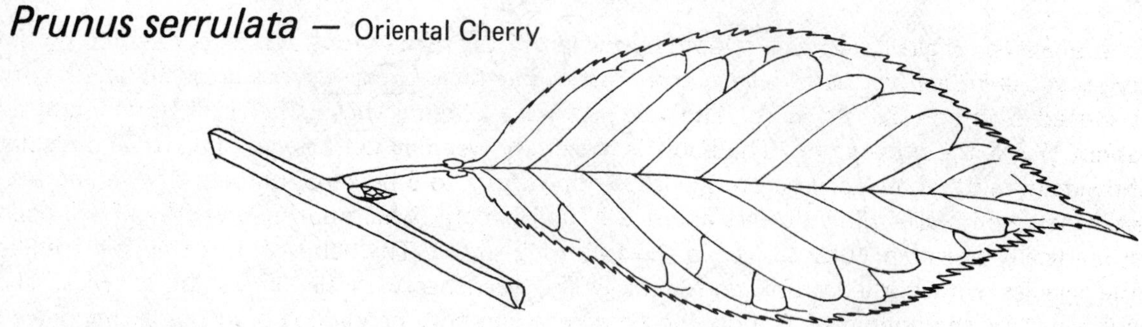

LEAVES: Alternate, simple, ovate to ovate-lanceolate, rarely obovate, 2 to 5" long, abruptly long acuminate, serrate or often doubly serrate with aristate teeth, glabrous, reddish brown when unfolding; petioles 3/5 to 1" long, usually with 2 to 4 glands, glabrous.

Prunus serrulata, Oriental Cherry, is a large tree growing 50 to 75' however it is not a factor in the modern landscape for the numerous cultivars are much preferable. Most cultivars grow 20 to 25' with a vase-shaped or upright habit. The new foliage is often reddish tinged and eventually changes to lustrous dark green at maturity. The flowers are greatly variable but range from single to doubles, white to pinks, and from 1/2 to 2 1/2" diameter. They usually flower in late April to early May and are borne profusely along the stems, usually before or with the leaves. They are usually grafted on *P. avium,* Mazzard Cherry, at heights of 4 to 6'. The three hardiest cultivars and possibly the best for the Midwest include:

'Fugenzo' — 2 1/2" diameter, rosy pink flowers fading to a light pink, double with about 30 petals.

'Kwanzan' — Probably the most popular and hardiest of all the double flowered types. The deep pink, double flowers are 2 1/2" in diameter and have 30 petals. The tree grows 12 to 18' high.

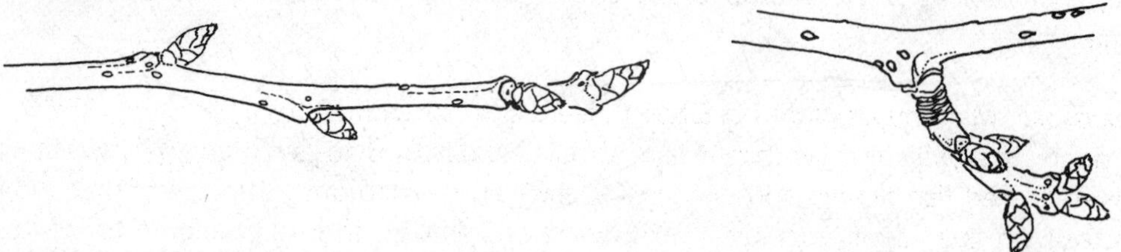

'Shirofugen' — Double pink flowers up to 2 1/2" in diameter which quickly fade white as the flowers mature.

There are over 120 cultivars and many are very difficult to distinguish. Donald Wyman has an excellent discussion on the Oriental Cherry in *Trees for American Gardens.* Japan, China, Korea. Zone 5 to 6, depending on the clone.

Prunus subhirtella — Higan Cherry

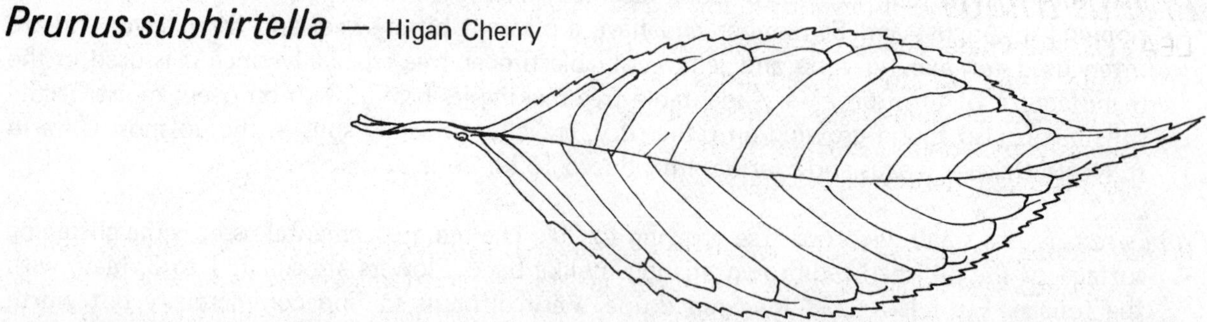

LEAVES: Alternate, simple, ovate to oblong-ovate, 1 to 4" long, acuminate, sharply and often doubly serrate, pubescent on veins beneath, with about 10 pairs of veins; petioles pubescent, 1/4" long, glandular.

Prunus subhirtella, Higan Cherry, is seldom cultivated in the species form but is represented by the types var. *pendula,* var. *autumnalis,* and 'Yae-shidare-higan'. These types grow 20 to 40' with a spread of 15 to 30' or more. The var. *pendula,* Weeping Higan Cherry, is usually grafted about 6' on the understock. The habit is gracefully weeping with single pink, 1/2" diameter flowers in mid to late April before the leaves, borne in 2 to 5 flowered umbels. The var. *autumnalis* has semidouble pink flowers about 3/4" in diameter which during a warm fall will open sporadically and then fully flower in the following spring. The habit on this tree is more like the species with forked trunk and erect twiggy branches with slender whiplike twigs. The cultivar 'Yae-shidare-higan' is a double flowered type with pendulous branches and appeared quite floriferous with longer lasting flowers than the var. *pendula.* The species is a very variable one giving rise to many different forms and flower colors. Japan. Introduced 1894. Zone 5.

Prunus tomentosa — Manchu Cherry, Nanking Cherry

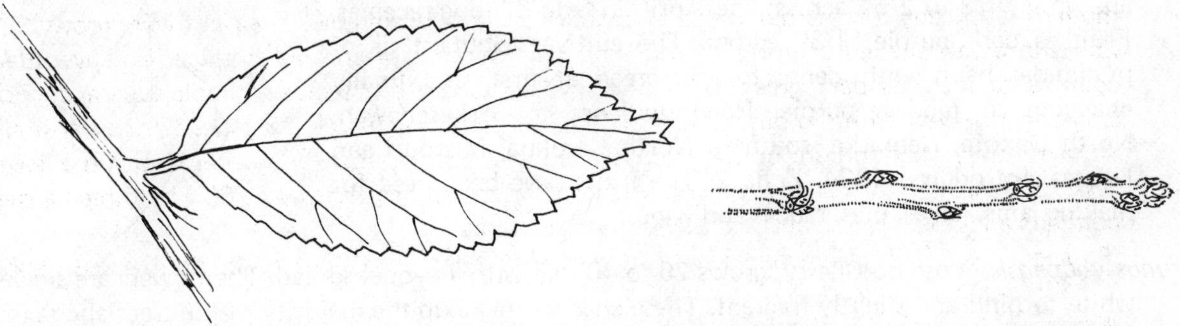

LEAVES: Alternate, simple, obovate to elliptic, 2 to 3" long, abruptly acuminate, unequally serrate, rugose, dull dark green and pubescent above, densely villous beneath; petioles 1/12 to 1/6" long, glandular.

Prunus tomentosa, Manchu or Nanking Cherry, is a broad spreading, densely twiggy shrub, becoming more open, irregular and picturesque with age. It grows 6 to 10' high and spreads to 15'. The bark is shiny reddish brown and exfoliating. Leaves are medium green in summer and extremely tomentose on the lower surface. The flowers are pinkish in bud changing to white, fragrant, 3/5 to 4/5" across; early to mid-April; appears to be one of the earliest flowering *Prunus* species in the Midwest. The fruits are scarlet, 2/5" across, edible, ripening in June through July. Could be used in mass plantings or the shrub border for the early flowers and fruits are valuable. North and Western China, Japan, Himalayas. Cultivated 1870. Zone 2. 'Leucocarpa' has white fruits.

Prunus triloba — Flowering Plum, Flowering Almond

LEAVES: Alternate, simple, broad-elliptic to obovate, 1 to 2 1/2" long, broad cuneate at base, acuminate or sometimes 3-lobed at apex, coarsely and doubly serrate; slightly pubescent beneath; petiole—1/5" long.

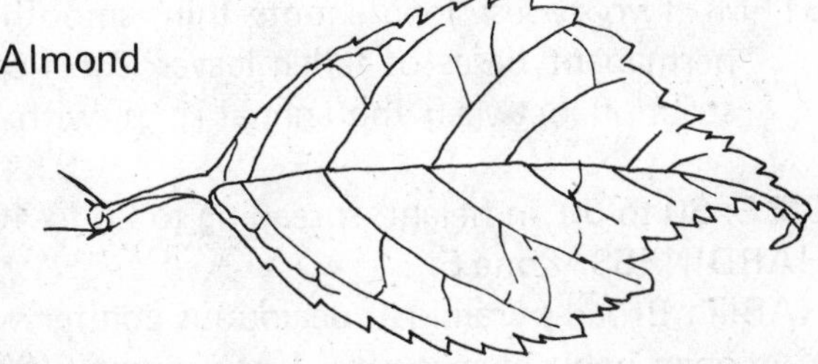

Prunus triloba, Flowering Plum, is a large (12 to 15'), cumbersome, clumsy shrub with tree-like qualities. The foliage is a medium green in summer and turns yellow to bronze in fall. The flowers are double, pinkish, about 1 to 1 1/2" across, borne in late April. They are often nipped by a late freeze and severely injured. I have never seen any fruit on the plants on our campus. This species has always been somewhat confusing. Dr. Rehder listed the double flowering type as *P. t. multiplex* and noted this was or is the original *P. triloba. P. t. simplex*

is the single flowered type and bears fruits. Perhaps Dr. Rehder's treatment is a simplification. China. Introduced 1885. Zone 5.

Prunus virginiana — Common Chokecherry

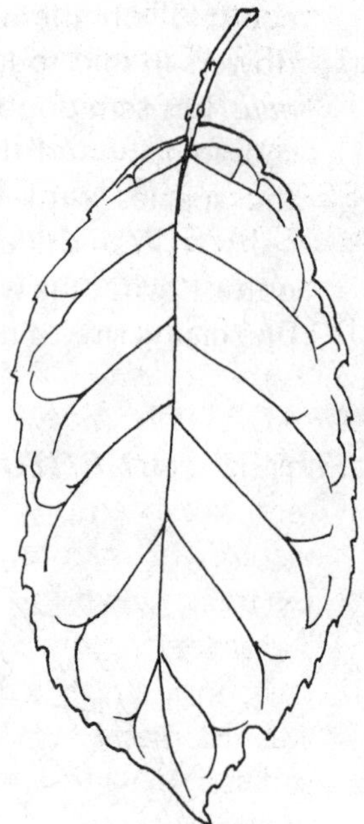

LEAVES: Alternate, simple, broad-elliptic to obovate, 1 3/5 to 5" long, abruptly acuminate, broad-cuneate to rounded at base, closely serrulate, dark green above, glaucescent or grayish green beneath, glabrous except axillary tufts of hair; petioles—2/5 to 4/5" long, glandular.

Prunus virginiana, Common Chokecherry, can grow 20 to 30' tall with a spread of 18 to 25'. It is a small tree or shrub with crooked branches and slender twigs forming an oval-rounded crown. Flowers are white, 1/3 to 2/5" across; late April; in 3 to 6" long racemes. Fruit is dark purple, 1/3" across. The cultivar 'Shubert' is of pyramidal habit with dense foliage, green at first, and finally changing to reddish purple. Newfoundland, to Sasketchewan, North Dakota, Nebraska, south to North Carolina, Missouri and Kansas. Introduced 1724. Zone 2. The fruits have been used for making jams, jellies, pies, sauces and wine.

Prunus yedoensis, Yoshino Cherry, grows 20 to 40' tall with an equal spread. The flowers are single, white to pink and slightly fragrant. These cherries make up the majority of the trees about the Tidal Basin in Washington D.C.

'Perpendens' — Irregular pendulous branches.

'Akebono' — Soft pink, double flowers. Supposedly this tree can be grown from seed, cuttings, or grafted on *P. avium.*

P. avium seems to be a common understock for many of the Oriental Cherries. Cultivated in Japan, supposed to be a hybrid between *P. serrulata* x *P. subhirtella.* Introduced 1902. Zone 5.

Pseudolarix kaempferi — Golden-larch (Pinaceae), formerly *P. amabilis*

LEAVES: Scattered and spreading; leaves are often curved, 1 1/4 to 2 2/5" long, 1/12 to 1/6" wide, apex long pointed, soft, light green and rounded above, keeled beneath, margins thin with 2 conspicuous gray bands of stomata.

BUDS: Of long shoots ovoid, pointed, surrounded by long pointed brown scales with free tips, which fall away soon after the leaves develop in spring; of short shoots similar in shape with persistent scales; axillary buds rounded with short-pointed deciduous scales.

STEM: Two types: long shoots thin, smooth, bloomy, brown in the second year, roughened by permanent bases of fallen leaves; short spurs longer than those of *Larix,* with a distinct constriction between the annual rings, with 15 to 30 umbelliformly spreading leaves at the end.

SIZE: 30 to 50' in height, spreading to 20 to 40'; can grow to 120'.

HARDINESS: Zone 5.

HABIT: Broad-pyramidal, deciduous conifer with wide-spreading horizontal branches and a rather open habit at maturity. I have a small (6') specimen in my garden which is already quite open. Wyman noted that trees up to 30 to 40' high may be almost as wide as tall.

RATE: Slow, in fact the oldest tree in the United States is 100 years but only 45' tall.

TEXTURE: Medium.

LEAF COLOR: Soft, light green above, bluish green beneath in summer turning a clear golden yellow in autumn.

FLOWERS: Monoecious, borne on separate branches of the same tree, opening in May or June.

FRUIT: Cones solitary, ovoid, erect, 2 to 3" long by 1 1/2 to 2" wide, ripening in autumn of the first year; glaucous, bloomy, green to purplish during summer; ripening brown to reddish brown, very beautiful but borne in the upper reaches of the tree so as to be reduced in ornamental effectiveness.

CULTURE: Transplants readily balled and burlapped; requires a light, moist, acid, deep, well-drained soil; does not effectively tolerate high pH soils; prefers full sun although I have seen it in partially shaded situations; protect from wind; somewhat resistant to air pollutants.

DISEASES AND INSECTS: None serious.

LANDSCAPE VALUE: Truly a beautiful specimen in large areas, grows slowly enough that it can be integrated into the small landscape.

CULTIVARS:

'Annesleyana' — Dwarf, bushy; short horizontal, pendent branches; leaves densely set.

PROPAGATION: Seeds are the usual method of reproduction, however, it is difficult to obtain fertile seeds. A specimen at the Missouri Botanic Garden has coned rather heavily but no viable seed has been produced. Den Ouden and Boom and Dallimore and Jackson noted that seeds were difficult to obtain from China in a fresh state, but fertile seeds are frequently produced on trees grown in Italy. On a recent trip (1976) to the Holden Arboretum, Dick Munson, the Propagator, showed me numerous seedlings he had grown from seed collected off a grove of trees in Mentor, Ohio. He was kind enough to show me the parent trees and needless to say I was impressed. We discussed the problems of seed propagation and theorized that the trees are self-sterile and the fact that several seedling grown trees were in close proximity contributed to cross pollination and viable seed production. Perhaps this is the reason the tree in the Missouri Botanic garden does not develop viable seed. Seeds will germinate without pretreatment, but 60 days at 41°F will result in more uniform germination.

NATIVE HABITAT: Eastern China at altitudes of 3000 to 4000'. Introduced 1854.

Pseudotsuga menziesii — Douglasfir (Pinaceae)

formerly listed as *P. douglasii* and *P. taxifolia*

LEAVES: Pectinate with a V-shaped arrangement between the 2 lateral sets, straight, 1 to 1 1/2" long, thin, shining dark green above, with 2 white bands of stomata beneath, smelling of camphor when bruised.

BUDS: Ovoid-conical, imbricate, apex pointed, to 2/5" long, shining chestnut brown, mostly resinous at base.

STEM: Yellowish green initially becoming gray to brown, minutely pubescent or almost glabrous.

CONES: Three to 4" long, 1 1/2 to 2" wide, light brown, bracts are prominent and extend beyond the scales, persistent into winter.

SIZE: Under Midwestern landscape conditions will grow 40 to 80' in height with a 12 to 20' spread; can grow to 200' and greater.

HARDINESS: Zone 4 to 6, depending on the seed source.

HABIT: An open, spiry pyramid with straight stiff branches; the lower drooping, upper ascending, dense in youth becoming loose with age.

RATE: Medium, will grow 12 to 15' over a 10 year period; this rate based on observations taken with trees growing on University of Illinois campus. One authority noted the tree might grow 40 to 100' high after 50 to 75 years and 1 to 2' a year when young; he leaves himself a pretty safe estimating range!

TEXTURE: Medium.

BARK: On young stems smooth except for resin blisters; on old trunks often divided into thick reddish brown ridges separated by deep irregular fissures; becoming 6 to 24" thick.

LEAF COLOR: Depends largely on the seed source. The Rocky Mountain, Colorado type is bluish green and hardy in Zone 4, this is the type which should be grown in the Midwest; the other type is restricted to the Pacific slope where there is ample atmospheric moisture. This type has dark green foliage and is less hardy (Zone 6). This type is the largest growing and can grow to 300′ and more.

FLOWERS: Monoecious, on two year-old wood; staminate axillary, pendulous; pistillate terminal, with exserted, three-pointed bracts, handsome rose-red when young.

FRUIT: Cones pendulous, oval-ovoid, 4″ long by 1 1/2 to 2″ broad three-pronged bracts, light brown; borne on 25 year-old trees.

CULTURE: Transplants well balled and burlapped. Prefers neutral or slightly acid, well-drained, moist soils. Fails on dry, poor soils. Sunny, open, roomy conditions; injured by high winds, does best where there is an abundance of atmospheric moisture.

DISEASES AND INSECTS: Cankers (a number of species), leaf casts (similar to leaf spots), leaf and twig blight, needle blight, witches broom, aphids, Douglasfir bark beetle, scales, spruce bud-worm, pine butterfly, Zimmerman pine moth, tussock moth, gypsy moth, and strawberry root weevil.

LANDSCAPE VALUE: One of the noblest forest trees, very ornamental under cultivation; an excellent specimen or group or mass; not suited for underplanting or windbreaks; its use should be tempered in the dry windy areas of the Midwest. Makes a nice short needle Christmas tree.

CULTIVARS:

'Compacta' – Compact, conical form with short, dry green needles.

'Fastigiata' – Conical, branches crowded, branchlets erect, leaves densely radial, short; good looking clone.

var. *glauca* – More compact with slightly more ascending branches than the species. Leaves bluish green. Hardy to Zone 4.

'Pendula' – Branches and branchlets held close to the stem.

PROPAGATION: Several recent papers on rooting Douglasfir discuss various factors related to successful rooting and would make interesting reading for propagators. See *J. Amer. Soc. Hort. Sci.* 99:551-555 and *Forest Science* Volume 21.

ADDITIONAL NOTES: There is considerable confusion related to the various types of Douglasfir and every individual seems to have a different story to tell. The following information is based on the current thinking of the foresters and coincides pretty well with what most knowledge-able plantsmen relate. *P. menziesii* includes two geographic varieties: (1) the Coast Douglasfir (var. *menziesii*) is fast growing, long-lived, and sometimes becomes over 300′ tall and attains a diameter of 8 to 10′. The foliage is typically of a yellow green color, although some trees show bluish green, and the cones are often 4″ long and have straight, more or less appressed bracts; (2) the Rocky Mountain Douglasfir (var. *glauca*) is slower growing, shorter lived, and seldom exceeds 130′ in height. The foliage is bluish green but others with yellowish green needles are found standing together. The cones are smaller, barely 3″ in length, with much-exserted and strongly reflexed bracts. Unfortunately in certain areas the two varieties overlap and here intermediate forms are found. Variety *glauca* is widely grown and used for Christmas trees and ornamental plantings in the Northeastern United States.

The most important lumber producing tree in the United States. The wood has exceptional strength and is widely used for heavy structural timber; also used for plywood and pulp. One of the best short-needled Christmas trees because the needles do not easily fall off as is the case with *Abies* (fir) and *Picea* (spruce).

NATIVE HABITAT: Rocky Mountains and Pacific coast (British Columbia to Mexico).

Ptelea trifoliata — Hoptree, also called Wafer-ash or Stinking-ash

FAMILY: Rutaceae

LEAVES: Alternate, tri-foliate, leaflets ovate to elliptic-oblong, 2 1/2 to 5″ long, narrowed at ends, sometimes acuminate, the lateral ones oblique at base, smaller, entire, or obscurely crenulate, lustrous dark green above and glabrous below.

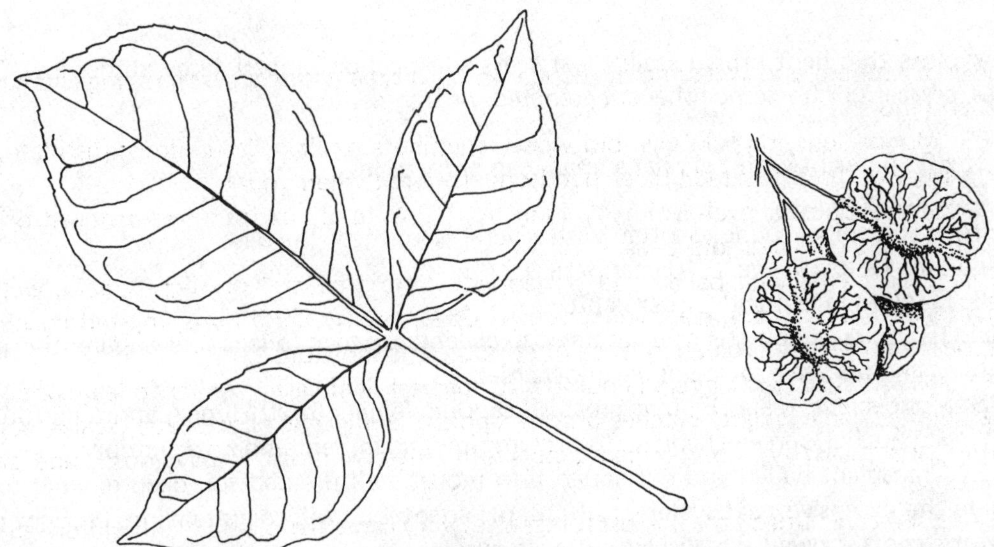

BUDS: Moderate, closely superposed in pairs, very low-conical, sessile, hidden beneath petiole bases, breaking through the leaf scars, not distinctly scaly, silvery-silky; terminal lacking (Hidden beneath petiole bases).

STEMS: Glabrous, buff, moderate, warty and dotted, terete; pith rather large, roundish, continuous, white; leaf scars somewhat raised, rather long, horseshoe shaped when torn by buds; 3 bundle-traces; no stipule scars.

SIZE: 15 to 20′ high.
HARDINESS: Zone 4.
HABIT: Large tree or small shrub of a bushy, rounded nature.
RATE: Slow to medium.
TEXTURE: Medium in leaf; coarse in winter.
BARK: Dark gray, smooth, except for warty protuberances.
LEAF COLOR: Lustrous dark green in summer; yellow-green in fall.
FLOWERS: Small, polygamous, greenish white, borne in terminal corymbs on short lateral branches; June; not particularly showy.
FRUIT: A compressed, broadly winged, suborbicular, 2-sided, indehiscent samara; brownish at maturity, rather conspicuous; effective August through September. The common name is derived from the shape and appearance of the parts.
CULTURE: Very adaptable species which performs maximally in dry, sandy or rocky situations and is often found in river valleys.
DISEASES AND INSECTS: Various leaf spots and a rust disease; none of which are serious.
LANDSCAPE VALUE: None, however an interesting native plant covering much of the Eastern United States.
PROPAGATION: The seed germinates slowly, probably because of embryo dormancy. Germination can be hastened by stratification in sand or peat for 3 to 4 months at 41°F.
ADDITIONAL NOTES: The fruits have been used as a substitute for hops, hence the reason for the first common name. The bark has been utilized in medicinal preparations. The fruits and bark contain a bitter substance.
NATIVE HABITAT: Ontario and New York to Florida, west to Minnesota. Introduced 1724.

Pterocarya fraxinifolia — Caucasian Wingnut

FAMILY: Juglandaceae
LEAVES: Alternate, pinnately compound, 8 to 18″ long; rachis terete, glabrous; leaflets 11 to 20, ovate-oblong to oblong-lanceolate, acuminate, sharply serrate, 3 to 5″ long, thin, glabrous except stellate hairs in the axils and along the midrib beneath; shiny, handsome dark green.
BUDS: Red-brown, rather large, superposed, the upper distinctly stalked or elongating the first year; naked with folded leaves.
STEMS: Red-brown, moderate or rather stout, rounded; pith moderate, angular, chambered with

rather close thin light brown scales; leaf scars elliptical or 3-lobed, large, rather low, 3 bundle-traces, crescent or horseshoe shaped, crenated, or fragmented.

SIZE: 30 to 50′ in height with a similar spread, can grow to 90′.
HARDINESS: Zone 5.
HABIT: Broad spreading, rounded, often with several stems near the base.
RATE: Medium, 12 to 15′ over a 10 year period.
TEXTURE: Medium in leaf and winter habit.
LEAF COLOR: Dark glossy green in summer, excellent summer foliage and apparently quite free of insects and diseases; fall color is yellow green.
FLOWERS: Monoecious; male—5″ long greenish catkins; female to 20″ long, catkin-like, June.
FRUIT: Winged nut(let), green changing to brown; ripening in September to October.
CULTURE: Transplant balled and burlapped into moist, well drained soil deep enough to accommodate the extensive root system; full sun; pH adaptable; will tolerate wind, drought and hard soil if the roots are well established; prune in summer.
DISEASES AND INSECTS: None serious.
LANDSCAPE VALUE: Very handsome specimen plant which could be successfully used for large areas such as parks, schools, and golf courses. The largest specimen I have seen was very broad spreading and made an excellent shade tree; much superior to ashes, honeylocusts and weak wooded maples but little known; handsome foliage and interesting fruits.
PROPAGATION: Seeds should be stratified for 90 days at 41°F. Cuttings taken in summer and made from young shoots with a heel will sometimes take root.
NATIVE HABITAT: Caucasia to Northern Iran. Introduced 1782.

Pterostyrax hispidus — Fragrant Epaulettetree

FAMILY: Styracaceae
LEAVES: Alternate, simple, oblong to obovate-oblong, 3 to 7 1/2″ long, acute or short-acuminate, rounded or cuneate at base, minutely denticulate, glabrous above, sparingly pubescent beneath at least on veins, petiole 2/5 to 4/5″ long; bright green.
BUDS: Moderate, sessile, usually solitary; terminal elongated, hairy, and naked; the lateral ovoid, glabrate with 2 exposed scales.
STEMS: Quickly shredding gray bark, rounded, rather slender; pith moderate, rounded, continuous, white; leaf scars 2-ranked, finally broadly crescent-shaped, somewhat raised; indistinct bundle-trace; stipule-scars lacking.

SIZE: 20 to 30′ tall with a similar or greater spread although can grow to 45′.
HARDINESS: Zone 5.
HABIT: A round-headed small tree which develops an open head, and slender spreading branches.
RATE: Medium, 12 to 14′ in about 8 years.
TEXTURE: Medium-coarse in leaf; medium in winter.
LEAF COLOR: Bright green above, silvery-green beneath in summer; yellow-green in fall. Foliage is quite handsome and free of pest problems.
FLOWERS: White, perfect, fragrant, borne in large, 5 to 10″ long, pendulous panicles which terminate short lateral branches; June after the leaves have matured; trees start to flower when 8 to 10′ high.
FRUIT: A 2/5″ long, cylindric, 10 ribbed, densely bristly, dry drupe.
CULTURE: Transplant balled and burlapped in spring into moist, well drained, preferably acid soil; full sun; and in northern areas protect from strong winds and extremes of temperature; prune in winter.
DISEASES AND INSECTS: None serious.
LANDSCAPE VALUE: Supposedly quite difficult to locate in commerce, but it does have possibilities for the small residential landscape. The flowers are extremely handsome and develop when a limited number of plants are offering color.

PROPAGATION: Softwood cuttings rooted 30% in 48 days after treatment with IBA, 1:250, in talc.
NATIVE HABITAT: Japan. Introduced 1875.

Pyracantha coccinea — Scarlet Firethorn

FAMILY: Rosaceae
LEAVES: Alternate, simple, narrow-elliptic to lanceolate or oblanceolate, rarely ovate-oblong, acute, rarely obtusish, cuneate, 4/5 to 1 3/5" long, closely crenulate-serrulate, slightly pubescent beneath at first.
STEMS: Woolly at first, becoming glossy brown with spines 2/5 to 3/5" long.

SIZE: 6 to 18' in height with an equal spread. This shrub can get out of hand and considerable pruning is necessary to keep it in bounds.
HARDINESS: Zone 6.
HABIT: Semi-evergreen to evergreen shrub with stiff, thorny branches and an open habit if left unpruned.
RATE: Medium to fast.
TEXTURE: Medium in leaf; coarse in winter.
LEAF COLOR: Lustrous dark green in summer becoming brownish in winter in unprotected areas; if sited well will maintain considerable green foliage.
FLOWERS: Perfect, whitish, 1/3" across, early June, borne in 1-2" diameter, 2 to 3" long compound corymbs; quite showy in flower as the inflorescences literally shroud the plants.
FRUIT: Berry-like pome, 1/4" diameter, orange-red, ripening in September and persisting into winter.
CULTURE: Move as a container plant in spring into well-drained soil; does quite well where soil is dry in summer; full sun for best fruiting although will do well in partial shade; pH 5.5 to 7.5; pruning can be accomplished anytime; very difficult to transplant and once established should be left in that area; makes a good plant for container production.
DISEASES AND INSECTS: Fireblight can be serious, scab affects the fruits turning them a dark sooty color, twig blight, leaf blight, root rot, aphid, lace bug, and scales.
LANDSCAPE VALUE: Often used as an informal hedge or barrier plant, good for espaliers on walls, trellises and the like; fruit is the outstanding attribute; hardiness is a problem and selected cultivars must be used. Ohio State University campus has a large complement of *Pyracantha* and it is spectacular in the fall.
CULTIVARS:

'Aurea' — Form with yellow fruits.

'Chadwicki' — (Zone 5) Hardy form and a prolific fruiter, fruits are orange-red.

'Kasan' — (Zone 5) Orange-red fruits.

'Lalandi' ('Lalandei') — (Zone 5) Probably the most widely grown and one of the hardiest, with orange-red fruits.

'Lalandi Monrovia' — Orange-red fruits and slightly less hardy than 'Lalandi'.

'Runyani' — Another orange-fruited form.

'Thornless' — Red fruiting, thornless form supposedly as hardy as 'Lalandi'.

'Wyattii' — Orange-red fruits prolifically produced, hardy to Zone 5, tolerant of poor soil.

PROPAGATION: Seed should be stratified for 90 days at 41°F. Softwood cuttings root readily under mist; treatment with IBA is recommended to hasten rooting.
ADDITIONAL NOTES: The cultivar 'Mohave' developed at the U.S. National Arboretum is hardy to -10°F. It grows upright, is densely branched with glossy foliage and 2" creamy white flowers; fruit is orange-red and usually starts to color in August. The cultivar is resistant to scab

and fireblight. I had a specimen under trial in our field plots but it was lost in the winter of 1974-1975.

NATIVE HABITAT: Italy to Western Asia. Introduced 1629.

Pyrus calleryana 'Bradford' — Bradford Callery Pear

FAMILY: Rosaceae

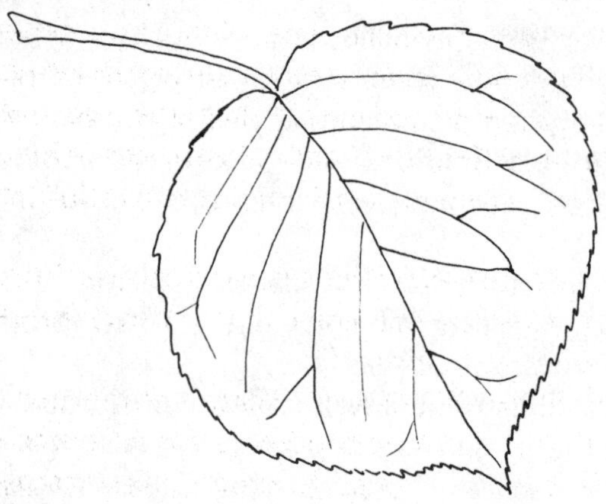

LEAVES: Alternate, simple, broad-ovate to ovate, 1 1/2 to 3" long, rarely elliptic-ovate, short acuminate, rounded or broad - cuneate at base, crenate, usually quite glabrous, stipules — strap-like.

BUDS: Large, terminal and laterals of approximately same size, ovoid, elongated, 1/2" long, intensely woolly, grayish brown.

STEM: Stout, brownish, sometimes exhibiting ridges running from base of leaf scar, generally white woolly pubescent, especially below terminal; gradually changing to smooth, glossy brown at maturity.

This discussion is concerned with the cultivar Bradford and not the species.

SIZE: 30 to 50' in height with a 20 to 35' spread.

HARDINESS: Zone 4.

HABIT: Moderately conical (pyramidal) in youth and old age.

RATE: Medium, 12 to 15' over an 8 to 10 year period.

TEXTURE: Medium-fine in leaf; medium in winter.

BARK: Brown, nondescript.

LEAF COLOR: Outstanding glossy dark green in summer changing to glossy scarlet and purple shades in fall; very spectacular in fall color.

FLOWERS: White, 1/3" across, malodorous, late April to early May, borne in 3" diameter corymbs before or with the leaves; the tree looks like a white cloud in full flower.

FRUIT: Small pome, 1/2" or less across, russet, dotted, hidden by the foliage; not ornamentally effective.

CULTURE: Easy to transplant balled and burlapped if moved in late winter or early spring; several Illinois nurserymen will not move them in leaf; very adaptable to many different soils; tolerates dryness, pollution, and should be sited in full sun; prune in winter or early spring.

DISEASES AND INSECTS: Resistant to fireblight which is so troublesome to the Common Pear, *Pyrus communis.* Basically free of pests.

LANDSCAPE VALUE: One of our finest street trees, lawn trees, and all around general purpose plants; works well in malls and planters; very fine tree and has received wide acceptance in east coast landscaping. I have noticed very few in Central Illinois but hope to see more in the future.

PROPAGATION: Seeds of the species require cold (32 or 36°F) for 60 to 90 days. Isolated reports indicated 'Bradford' could be rooted from cuttings. In late spring and summer of 1976, Ms. Sue Burd, one of my graduate students, initiated a rooting study with crabapples, silverbells, serviceberries, birch and Bradford Pear. The treatments consisted of IBA, NAA and a combination applied at 0, 2500, 10,000, 20,000, or 30,000 ppm. Cuttings were collected every two weeks or monthly depending on the plant in question. Bradford Pear rooted, 0, 70, 80, 30 and 50 percent under the IBA concentrations, respectively. Rooting was nil under NAA or combination treatments. When the study is completed the results will be published in *The Plant Propagator.*

OTHER CULTIVARS:

'Aristocrat' – Selection made by Carlisle Nursery, Independence, Kentucky; differs from 'Bradford' in more horizontal branch formation, glossier and darker green leaves with a wavier edge, fall foliage is more consistently red or red-purple, tree at 6 years old is 12' tall and 10' wide with a 3" trunk diameter; like 'Bradford' and 'Chanticleer' it is thornless.

'Chanticleer' – Supposedly similar to 'Bradford', cone-shaped habit, reaching 30' in height with a 15' spread.

'Fauriei'– Often listed as a variety and by some authorities considered a species. The Korean Pear has the same shiny leaves, tiny fruit, excellent fall color, but is slower growing and wider than 'Bradford', forming a sturdy medium sized tree.

'Select' – An evenly branched, cone-shaped clone of relatively dense constitution. Young trees flower as well or better than Bradford; thornless; handsome for its formal nature; Dr. Ed Hasselkus considers it superior in habit compared to other Callery forms. Much denser than 'Aristocrat' which seems to be open and loose in outline.

RELATED SPECIES:

Pyrus communis – Common Pear

LEAVES: Alternate, simple, orbicular-ovate to elliptic, acute or short acuminate, subcordate to broad-cuneate, 3/4 to 3" long, crenate-serrulate, glabrous or villous when young.

BUDS: Imbricate, conical, sharp pointed, smooth or slightly hairy, terminal about 1/3" long, laterals —small, generally divergent and not flattened or at times on vigorous shoots both flattened and appressed.

STEM: Stout, glabrous or slightly downy, yellowish green or sometimes with tinge of brown; stubby branched, slow-growing fruit spurs abundant.

BARK: Grayish brown, smooth on young branches, with age longitudinally fissured into flat-topped ridges which are further broken by transverse fissures into oblong scales.

FRUIT: A large fleshy pome.

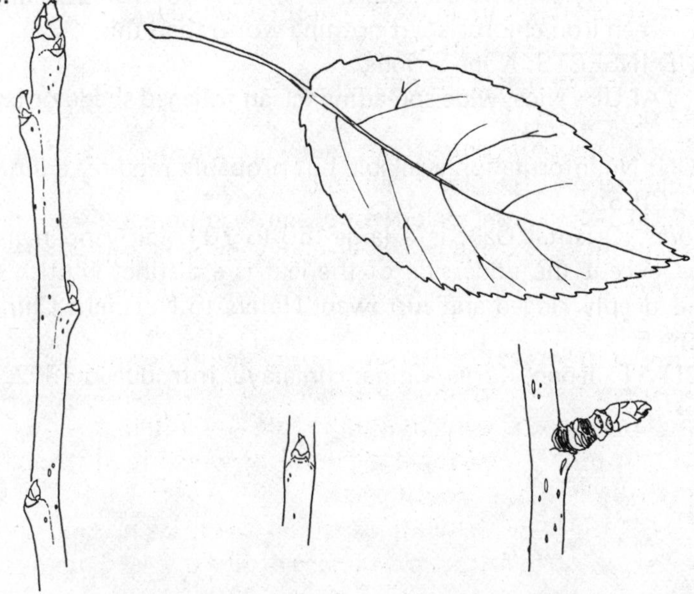

Pyrus communis, Common Pear, is only mentioned here because it is sometimes trained as an espaliered plant. Tremendous fireblight susceptibility and not recommended for ornamental purposes although the white flowers are quite showy and malodorous.

Pyrus salicifolia, Willowleaf Pear, reaches 25′ and possesses graceful, silvery-gray, willow-like leaves. Unfortunately it is very susceptible to fireblight.

Pyrus ussuriensis, Ussurian Pear, is the hardiest of all pears. The habit is dense, rounded, 40 to 50′; the leaves are a handsome, glossy dark green in summer changing to red and reddish purple in the fall. Flowers may be faintly pink in bud, finally white; 1 1/3″ across, April-May. The fruit is 1 to 1 1/2″ diameter, greenish yellow, subglobose pome. It, along with *P. calleryana,* is the least susceptible to fireblight. For colder climates it would prove a valuable ornamental. Northeastern Asia. Introduced 1855. Zone 4.

NATIVE HABITAT: *Pyrus calleryana* is native to China. Introduced 1908.

Quercus acutissima — Sawtooth Oak

FAMILY: Fagaceae

LEAVES: Alternate, simple, 3 1/2 to 7 1/2″ long, obovate-oblong to oblong, acute, broad-cuneate or rounded at base, serrate with bristle-like teeth terminating the 12 to 16 parallel veins, lustrous dark green, glabrous above, glabrous beneath except axillary tufts of hairs, pubescent when unfolding, petioles 3/4 to 1″ long; leaf looks like a *Castanea* leaf in many respects and is often confused with same.

BUDS: Imbricate, pubescent, almost woolly, grayish brown, 1/4″ long; somewhat similar to *Q. velutina* in appearance but not as angled.

SIZE: 35 to 45′ in height. I have seen trees taller than wide and others wider than tall. Probably great variation in seed grown material although the trend is toward a broad, rounded outline.

HARDINESS: Zone 5 to 6.

HABIT: Dense, broad pyramid in youth; varying in old age from oval-rounded to broad-rounded.

RATE: Slow over a period of years; initially medium.

TEXTURE: Pleasantly medium in foliage; medium to medium-coarse in winter.

BARK: Deeply ridged and furrowed.

LEAF COLOR: Dark lustrous green in summer; often a good clear yellow in fall.

FRUIT: Acorn, sessile, involucre with long, spreading and recurving scales, inclosing about 2/3 of the nut.

CULTURE: Apparently of fairly easy culture. There is not a great deal of literature available on this tree. I have seen iron chlorosis but nothing worse than this.

DISEASES AND INSECTS: None serious.

LANDSCAPE VALUE: Nice, wide spreading; clean foliaged shade or lawn tree. Could be used more than it is.

PROPAGATION: No information available but probably requires a limited cold treatment.

RELATED SPECIES:

Quercus variabilis, Oriental Oak, is a large (60 to 70′), fairly open tree with foliage similar to *Q. acutissima* except the underside of the leaf is a distinct whitish tomentose. The bark is very corky and deeply ridged and furrowed. Native to Northern China, Korea, Japan. Introduced 1861. Zone 5.

NATIVE HABITAT: Japan, Korea, China, Himalaya. Introduced 1862.

Quercus alba — White Oak

FAMILY: Fagaceae

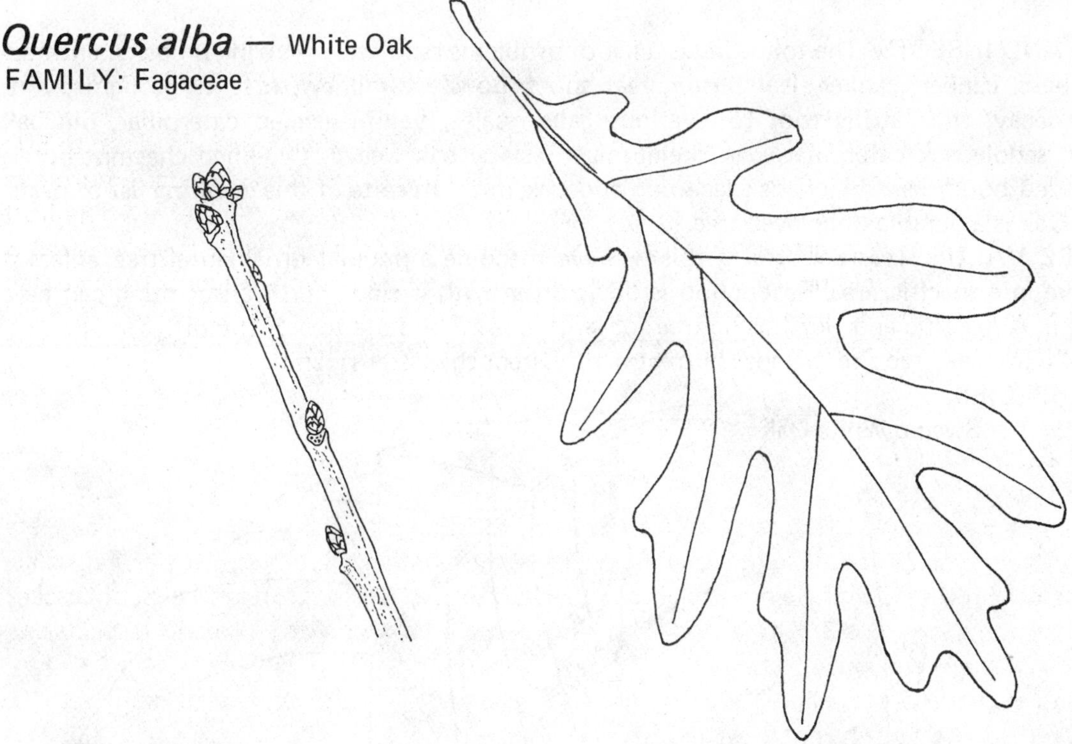

LEAVES: Alternate, simple, 4 to 8 1/2" long, obovate to oblong-obovate, narrowed at base, with 5 to 9 oblong and obtuse, entire lobes, dark green.

BUDS: Imbricate, broadly ovate, blunt, reddish brown to brown in color, 1/8" long, sometimes slightly hairy, usually glabrous.

STEM: Stout, brown to purple, angled, sometimes covered with bloom.

SIZE: 50 to 80' in height by 50 to 80' in spread; can grow well over 100' in the wild.

HARDINESS: Zone 4.

HABIT: Pyramidal when young, upright-rounded to broad-rounded with wide spreading branches at maturity. Very imposing specimen when full grown.

RATE: Slow to medium, 12 to 15' over a 10 to 12 year period, very slow after first 20 to 30 years.

TEXTURE: Medium in leaf; medium to coarse in winter but with a strong, bold appearance.

BARK: On old trunks light ashy-gray, variable in appearance, often broken into small, vertically arranged blocks, scaly on the surface; later irregularly plated, or deeply fissured, with narrow rounded ridges.

LEAF COLOR: Grayish and pinkish when unfolding changing to dark green in summer, almost tends toward a blue-green; fall color varies from brown to a rich red to wine color and lasts for a long period of time.

FLOWERS: The following discussion concerns the flowers of the genus *Quercus* and is applicable to most species covered in this text. Monoecious, appearing on the old or new growth; staminate catkins pendent, clustered; individual flowers comprising a 4 to 7 lobed calyx which encloses 6 stamens, rarely 6 to 12; pistillate flowers solitary or in few to many-flowered spikes from the axils of the new leaves; individual flowers consisting of a 6 lobed calyx surrounding a 3 (rarely 4 to 5) celled ovary, the whole partly enclosed in an involucre.

FRUIT: Nut, solitary or paired, sessile or short stalked, 1/2 to 3/4" long, ovoid-oblong, enclosed for 1/4 of its length in a light chestnut-brown, bowl-like cup (involucre).

CULTURE: Transplant balled and burlapped as a small tree; found on many types of soil although performs maximally in deep, moist, well-drained soils; prefer acid soils pH 5.5 to 6.5; full sun; prune in winter or early spring. There is a delicate balance in forest situations and when man encroaches and builds roads and houses in white oak timber the trees often gradually decline and die. This is, in part, due to compaction, ruination of mycorrhizal associations and removal of the recycled organic matter from under the trees.

DISEASES AND INSECTS: The following is a list of problems reported occurring on oaks: anthracnose, basal canker, canker, leaf blister, leaf spots, powdery mildew, rust, twig blights, wilt, wood decay, shoe string root rot, various galls, scales, yellow-necked caterpillar, pin oak sawfly, saddleback caterpillar, oak skeletonizer, asiatic oak weevil, two-lined chestnut borer, flatheaded borer, leaf miner, oak lace bug and oak mite. In spite of this inspiring list of pests, White Oak is a durable, long-lived tree.

LANDSCAPE VALUE: It is doubtful if this will ever become a popular ornamental tree unless it is native in a specific area. Production is difficult, growth is slow, and transplanting can be a problem. A majestic and worthwhile tree for large areas. The state tree of Illinois.

PROPAGATION: Seed requires no special treatment. Direct sow after ripening.

RELATED SPECIES:

Quercus bicolor – Swamp White Oak

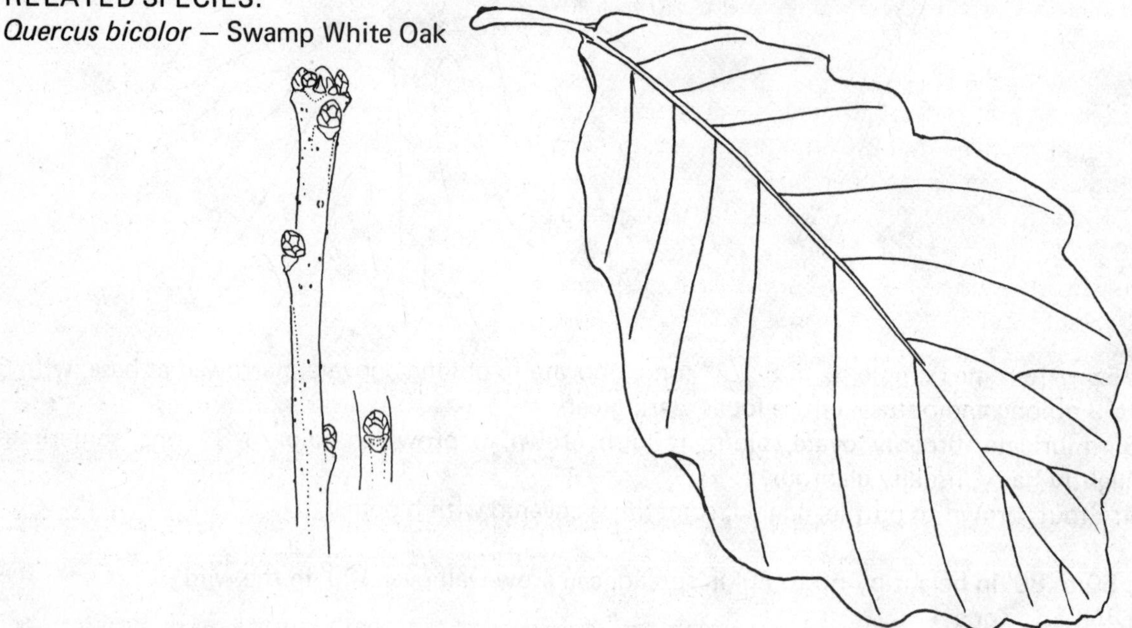

LEAVES: Alternate, simple, 4 to 6″ long, oblong-obovate to obovate, coarsely sinuate-dentate with 6 to 10 pairs of entire usually obtuse teeth, or sometimes lobed halfway to the midrib, dark green above, whitish tomentose or grayish green and velvety beneath. Leaf with a very velvety feel, also leathery overall texture.

BUDS: Imbricate, broadly ovate, light chestnut brown, 1/8″ long, coated with pale down above the middle.

STEM: Stout to slender, yellowish green to reddish brown.

BARK: Flaky, grayish brown, divided by deep longitudinal fissures into rather long flat ridges.

Quercus bicolor, Swamp White Oak, grows 50 to 60′ in height with an equal or greater spread; forms a broad, open, round-topped crown and a short, limby trunk; the acorn is about 1″ long, usually paired, borne on slender peduncles 1 to 4″ long; found in the wild in low lying and more or less swampy situations, often occurring in moist bottom lands and along the banks of streams; requires acid soil; I have observed very severe chlorosis on this species in Central Illinois. Native Quebec to Georgia, west to Michigan and Arkansas. Introduced 1800.

ADDITIONAL NOTES: The most important species of the White Oak group. The wood is used for furniture, flooring, interior finishing, boat building, wine and whiskey casks. The acorn is edible and is eaten by many kinds of birds and mammals. Best to boil in water to remove tannins.

NATIVE HABITAT: Maine to Florida, west to Minnesota and Texas. Introduced 1724.

Quercus imbricaria — Shingle Oak, also known as Laurel Oak

LEAVES: Alternate, simple, 2 1/2 to 6" long, oblong or lanceolate, acute at apex with bristle-like tip, revolute margin, dark green and glabrous above, pale green or brownish and pubescent beneath.

BUDS: Imbricate, ovoid, sharp pointed, 1/8" long, brownish, often slightly hairy.

STEM: Slender, green-brown, lustrous, glabrous.

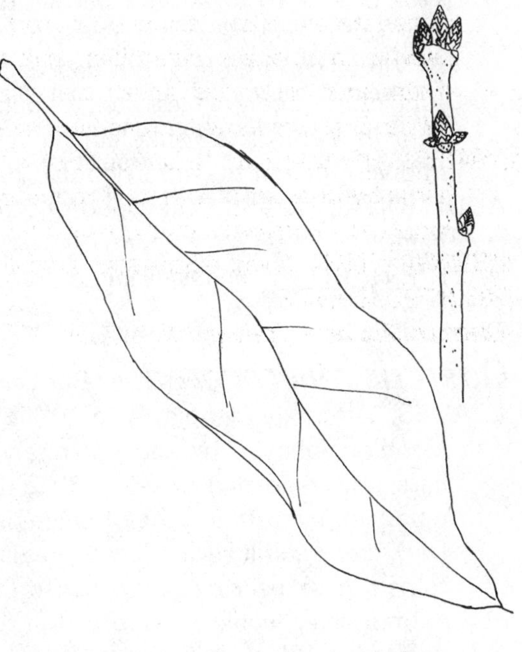

SIZE: 50 to 60' in height, developing a comparable or slightly greater spread, can grow to 80 to 100' in height.

HARDINESS: Zone 4.

HABIT: Pyramidal to upright-oval in youth assuming a broad-rounded outline in old age, often with drooping lower lateral branches.

RATE: Slow to medium, 1 to 1 1/2' per year over a 10 to 20 year period.

TEXTURE: Medium in leaf, medium-coarse in winter.

BARK: Gray-brown, close, eventually with broad low ridges separated by shallow furrows.

LEAF COLOR: Bright red when first unfolding changing to a lustrous dark green in summer and assuming brown to russet-red colors in fall.

FRUIT: Nut, sub-globose, about 5/8" long, the nut enclosed 1/2 to 1/3 in a thin bowl-shaped cup with appressed red-brown scales.

CULTURE: Transplants with less difficulty than many oaks, prefers moist, rich, deep, well drained, acid soil although is tolerant of drier soils; somewhat tolerant of city conditions; full sun.

DISEASES AND INSECTS: See under White Oak.

LANDSCAPE VALUE: Does quite well in the Midwest and has been used for lawn, street, park, golf course and other large areas. Accepts pruning very well and can be used for hedges. The leaves persist into winter and aid in screening or breaking the wind.

PROPAGATION: Seed, stratify in moist sand or peat for 30 to 60 days at 41° F.

RELATED SPECIES:

Quercus phellos — Willow Oak

LEAVES: Alternate, simple, 2 to 4" long, 3/8 to 3/4" wide, narrowly elliptical or lance-shaped, entire on margins, tipped with a bristle.

BUD: Imbricate, 1/8" long, ovoid, sharp-pointed, chestnut brown.

STEM: Slender, smooth, somewhat lustrous, reddish brown to dark brown.

BARK: Older, becoming nearly black and roughened by deep irregular furrows and thick, more or less scaly ridges.

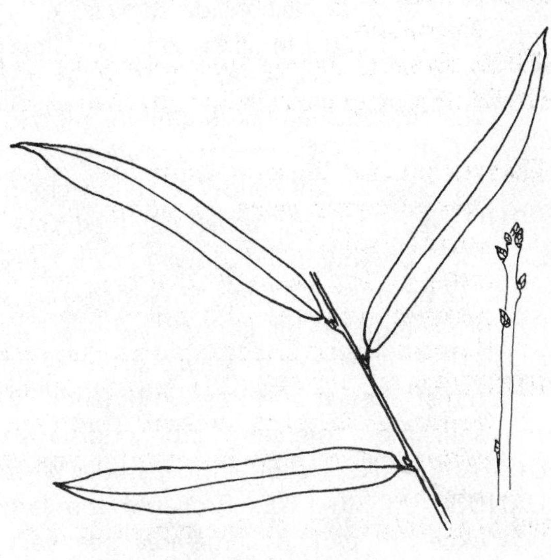

Quercus phellos, Willow Oak, native from New York to Florida, west to Missouri and Texas, occurs in extreme Southern Illinois. Introduced 1723. Can grow to 40 to 60' in height with a spread of 30 to 40' although may reach 90 to 100' in ideal locations; a pyramidal tree in youth developing a dense oblong to oval crown at maturity; leaves are a light to bright green in summer changing to yellow and russet red in fall; a relatively fast growing oak often averaging 2′ per year over a 10 to 20 year period; occurs as a bottom land tree on poorly drained, loamy or clay soils; transplants more readily than most oaks for the tap root is not as extensive as Bur or White Oak; prefers acid soil and full sun; nuts are solitary or paired, 1/2″ or less long, subglobose, more or less stellate pubescent, light yellowish- or greenish-brown, enclosed at the base in a thin saucer-like cup; a very handsome oak best reserved for southern areas of the Midwest, one of the most popular shade and street trees in the south.

ADDITIONAL NOTES: The wood of Shingle Oak was used to make shingles, hence, the common name.

NATIVE HABITAT: Pennsylvania to Georgia, west to Nebraska and Arkansas. Introduced 1724.

Quercus macrocarpa — Bur Oak, also called Mossycup Oak

LEAVES: Alternate, simple, 4 to 10″ long, obovate to oblong-obovate, cuneate or rarely rounded at base, lower portion of leaf with 2 to 3 pairs of lobes, upper 5 to 7 pairs of ovate-obtuse lobes. Dark green and lustrous above, grayish or whitish tomentulose beneath. Leaf shaped like a fiddle.

BUD: Imbricate, conical to broadly ovate, sharp pointed or blunt, 1/8 to 1/4″ long, pale pubescence covering entire bud, often with stipular structures arising out of clustered buds.

STEM: Stout, yellowish brown, smooth or downy, stems on some trees developing corky ridges after first year.

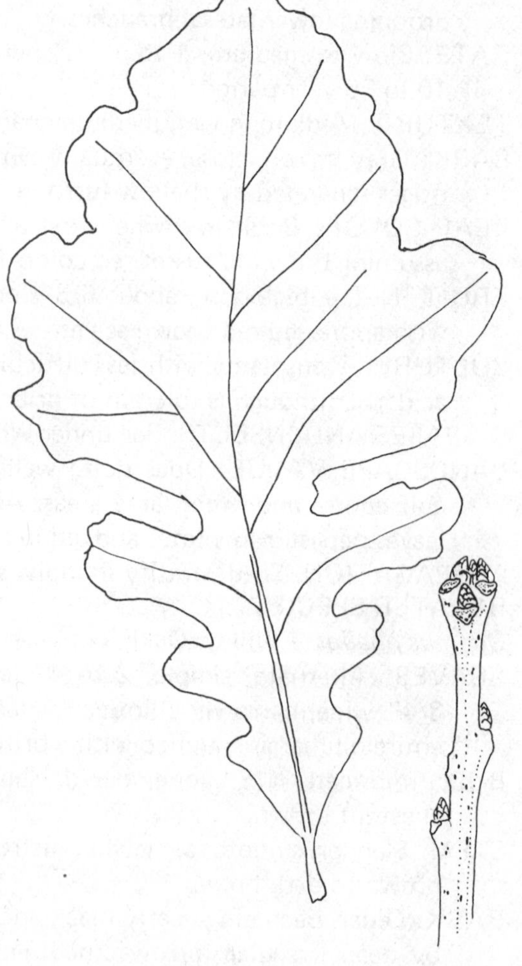

SIZE: 70 to 80′ in height with an equal or slightly greater spread, can grow to over 100′.

HARDINESS: Zone 2.

HABIT: Weakly pyramidal to oval in youth gradually developing a massive trunk and a broad crown of stout branches.

RATE: Slow, over a 20 year period 15 to 20′ of growth could be considered average.

TEXTURE: Coarse in all seasons, but majestically so.

BARK: Rough, developing deep ridged and furrowed character, usually dark gray in color.

LEAF COLOR: Often lustrous dark green in summer, fall color is dull yellow to yellow-green.

FRUIT: Nut, solitary, usually stalked, 3/4 to 1 1/2″ long, broadly ovoid, downy at the apex, enclosed 1/2 or more in a deep cup which is conspicuously fringed on the margin.

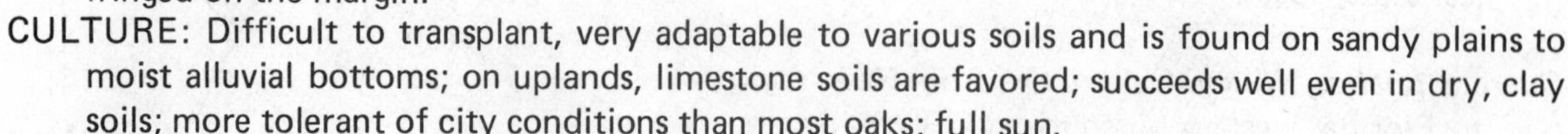

CULTURE: Difficult to transplant, very adaptable to various soils and is found on sandy plains to moist alluvial bottoms; on uplands, limestone soils are favored; succeeds well even in dry, clay soils; more tolerant of city conditions than most oaks; full sun.

DISEASES AND INSECTS: See under White Oak.

LANDSCAPE VALUE: Probably too large for the average home landscape, however makes an excellent park or large area tree; very impressive and inspiring tree; there is one specimen in Urbana, Illinois over 90′ tall and estimated at 300 years of age.

PROPAGATION: No pretreatment is required although 30 to 60 days at 41°F in moist sand or peat is suggested.

NATIVE HABITAT: Nova Scotia to Pennsylvania, west to Manitoba and Texas. Introduced 1811.

Quercus muehlenbergii — Chinkapin Oak, also called Yellow Chestnut Oak

LEAVES: Alternate, simple, 4 to 6 1/2" long, oblong to oblong-lanceolate, acute or acuminate, usually rounded at base, coarsely toothed, with about 8 to 13 pairs of acute and mucronate often incurved teeth, lustrous dark yellow-green above, whitish tomentulose beneath.

BUDS: Light brown or pale margined, ovoid or conical-ovoid, end bud narrow, sharp, usually over 3/16" long.

STEM: Glabrous, brown, rounded, slender.

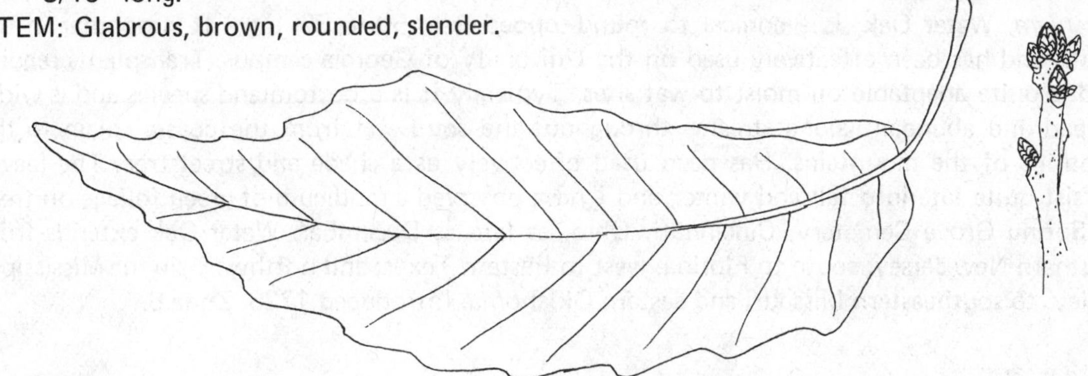

SIZE: 40 to 50' under landscape conditions but can, and often does, grow 70 to 80' tall in the wild. Spread is usually greater than height at maturity.

HARDINESS: Zone 5.

HABIT: Weakly rounded in youth but of dapper outline; with maturity developing an open, rounded crown.

RATE: Medium in youth, slowing down with age.

TEXTURE: Medium in leaf; medium-coarse in winter.

BARK: Ashy-gray, more or less rough and flaky.

LEAF COLOR: Dark, lustrous yellowish green in summer; fall color varies from yellow to orangish brown to brown.

FRUIT: Acorn, subsessile, globose-ovoid to ovoid, 3/5 to 4/5" long, inclosed about 1/2 by the thin cup; scales small, appressed.

CULTURE: Like many oaks, somewhat difficult to transplant; in the wild is found on dry limestone outcrops and soils with an alkaline reaction; prefers rich bottomlands and there attains its greatest size.

DISEASES AND INSECTS: None particularly serious.

LANDSCAPE VALUE: Actually quite an attractive tree especially in old age. If native in an area it is worthwhile saving. I doubt if it will ever become a popular landscape tree.

PROPAGATION: No seed pretreatment is necessary.

NATIVE HABITAT: Vermont to Virginia, west to Nebraska, Mexico and Texas. Introduced 1822.

Quercus nigra — Water Oak, also called Possum Oak

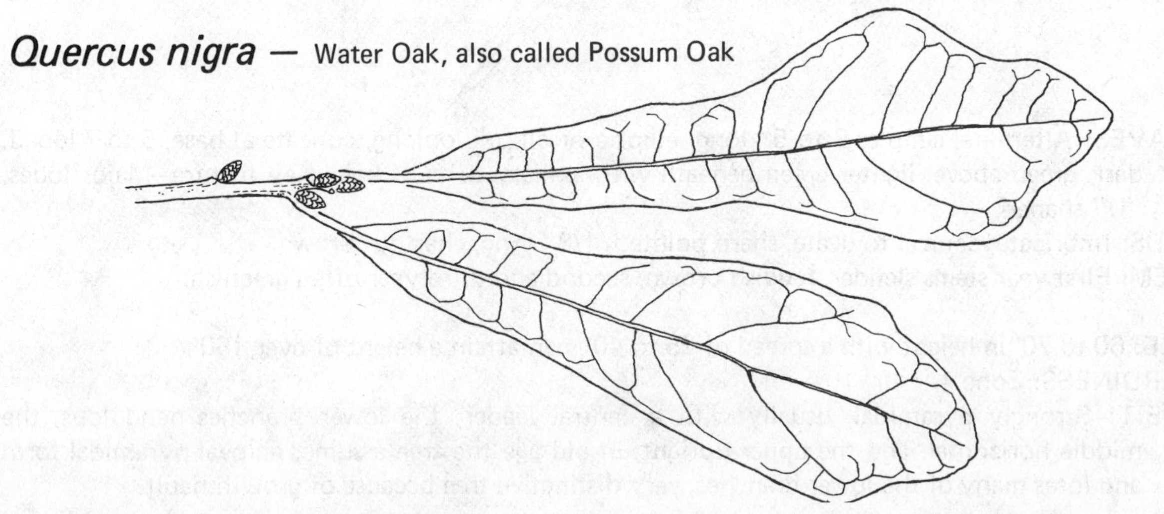

LEAVES: Alternate, simple, exceedingly variable as to size and shape, obovate, 3-lobed at apex or sometimes entire, rarely pinnately lobed above the middle, 3 to 7" long, dull bluish green above, paler beneath, soon glabrous except for axillary tufts of brown hairs.
BUDS: Ovoid, pointed, prominently angled, smooth, reddish brown, 1/8 to 1/4" long.
STEM: Slender, smooth, dull red to brown.

Quercus nigra, Water Oak, is a conical to round-topped tree, 50 to 80' high. It is popular in the south and has been effectively used on the University of Georgia campus. Transplants readily and is quite adaptable on moist to wet sites. Typically it is a bottomland species and is widespread and abundant along streams throughout the southeast from the coastal plain to the foothills of the mountains. Has been used effectively as a shade and street tree. The leaves persist quite late into fall and winter and I have observed a modicum of green foliage on trees in Spring Grove Cemetery, Cincinnati, Ohio, as late as December. Water Oak extends from southern New Jersey, south to Florida, west to Eastern Texas; and northward, in the Mississippi valley, to southeastern Missouri and eastern Oklahoma. Introduced 1723. Zone 6.

Quercus palustris — Pin Oak, also called Swamp Oak

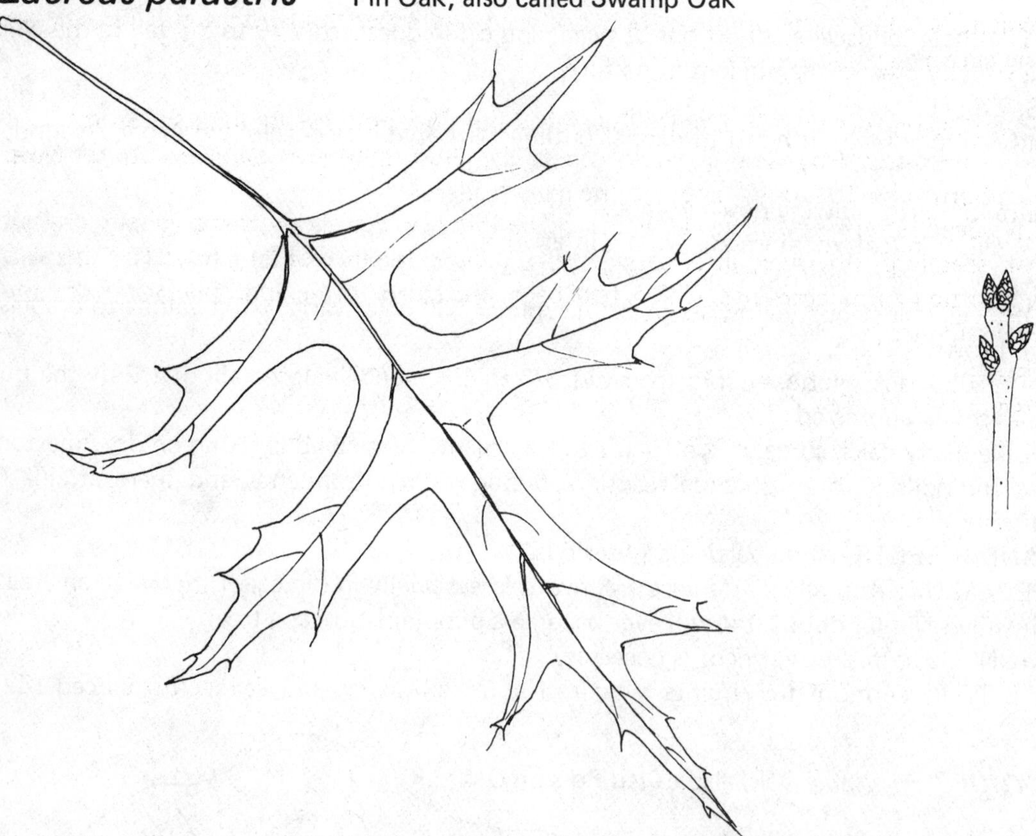

LEAVES: Alternate, simple, 3 to 5" long, elliptic or elliptic oblong, cuneate at base, 5 to 7 lobed, dark green above, lighter green beneath with axillary tufts of hair. Key feature—Major lobes, "U" shaped.
BUDS: Imbricate, conical to ovate, sharp pointed, 1/8" long, chestnut brown.
STEM: First year stems slender, reddish brown, second and third year often greenish.

SIZE: 60 to 70' in height with a spread of 25 to 40', can attain a height of over 100'.
HARDINESS: Zone 4.
HABIT: Strongly pyramidal, usually with a central leader; the lower branches pendulous, the middle horizontal, and the upper upright; in old age the tree assumes an oval-pyramidal form and loses many of the lower branches; very distinctive tree because of growth habit.

RATE: One of the faster growing oaks, 12 to 15′ over a 5 to 7 year period.

TEXTURE: Medium in leaf; medium-coarse in winter.

BARK: Grayish brown, thinnish, smooth and with age develops narrow, relatively shallow ridges and furrows.

LEAF COLOR: Dark glossy green in summer changing to russet, bronze or red in fall; fall coloration is variable and usually only fair in Central Illinois.

FRUIT: Nut, solitary or clustered, 1/2″ long, nearly hemispherical, light brown, often striate, enclosed only at the base in a thin, saucer-like cup.

CULTURE: Readily transplanted because of shallow, fibrous root system; will tolerate wet soils and is found in the wild on wet clay flats where water may stand for several weeks; actually prefers moist, rich, acid, well-drained soil; very intolerant of high pH soils and iron chlorosis can be a significant and disastrous problem with this species; somewhat tolerant of city conditions; tolerant of sulfur dioxide; full sun.

DISEASES AND INSECTS: Galls are often a problem; iron chlorosis can be serious but can be corrected; the use of capsules (ferric ammonium citrate) placed in the tree has proven very effective and has worked over a three year period.

LANDSCAPE VALUE: Probably the most widely used native oak for landscaping; possesses interesting habit and has been used for lawn, park, golf courses, commercial landscapes and streets. Personally I feel there are many superior oaks and other tree species but this oak has outstanding customer appeal.

CULTIVARS:

'Crown Rite' (Crown Right) — Similar to 'Sovereign' but does not develop bark splitting.

'Sovereign' — Introduced by Cole Nursery, Circleville, Ohio; the lower branches do not weep but are borne at a 90° to 45° angle to the main leader.

PROPAGATION: Seed, stratify at 32 to 41°F for 30 to 45 days; 'Sovereign' was originally grafted on Pin Oak seedlings, however, after several years a graft incompatability resulted. This was solved by grafting onto seedlings which had been produced from nuts collected from the original Sovereign tree.

RELATED SPECIES:

Quercus coccinea — Scarlet Oak

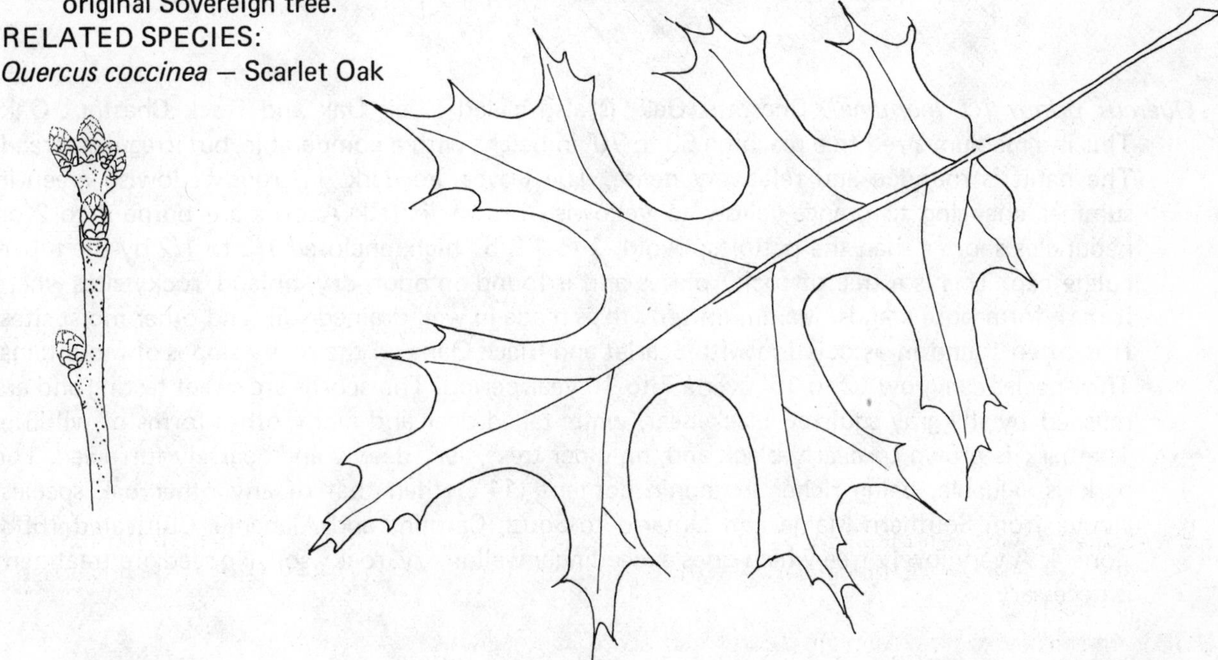

LEAVES: Alternate, simple, 3 to 6″ long, oblong or elliptic, truncate or rarely broadly cuneate at base, with 7, rarely 9, bristle tipped lobes, bright green and glabrous beneath. Major lobes, "C" shaped.

BUDS: Imbricate, broadly ovate, blunt apex, 1/8 to 1/4″ long, dark reddish brown, pale woolly pubescence above middle.

STEM: Light brown to red-brown, glabrous.

Quercus coccinea, Scarlet Oak, grows to 70 to 75′ in height by 40 to 50′ in width under landscape conditions but can reach 100′ in the wild. Habit is somewhat similar to Pin Oak but becomes more rounded and open at maturity; will grow 1 1/2 to 2′ per year over a 10 to 20 year period; foliage is an excellent glossy dark green in summer changing to scarlet in the fall; fruit is solitary or paired, 1/2 to 1″ long, oval to hemispherical, reddish brown, rarely striate, often with concentric rings near the apex, 1/3 to 1/2 enclosed in a deep bowl-like cup; less tolerant of adverse conditions than Pin Oak and Red Oak and rarely available in the nursery trade; generally found on dry, sandy soils; usually does not develop chlorosis problems to the degree of Pin Oak; native range extends from Maine to Florida, west to Minnesota and Missouri, Zone 4. Introduced 1691.

NATIVE HABITAT: Massachusetts to Delaware, west to Wisconsin and Arkansas. Introduced before 1770.

Quercus prinus — Chestnut Oak, Basket Oak

LEAVES: Alternate, simple, obovate to obovate-oblong, 4 to 6″ long, acute or acuminate, cuneate or rounded at base, coarsely and regularly toothed, with 10 to 14 pairs of obtusish, often mucronate teeth, lustrous dark yellow green, grayish tomentulose beneath; petioles 3/5 to 1 2/5″ long.

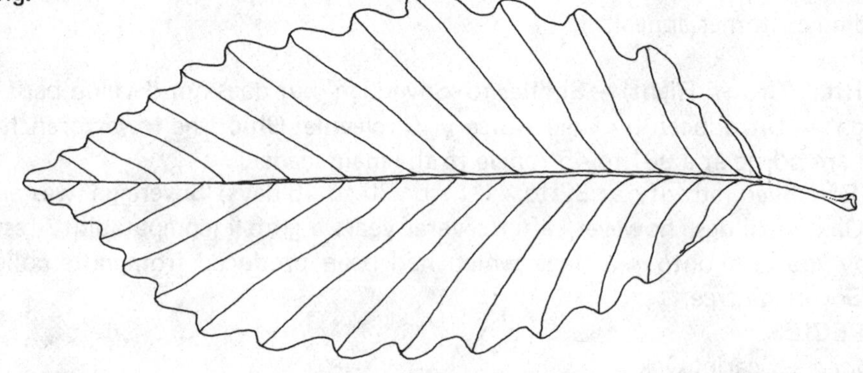

Quercus prinus (Q. montana), Chestnut Oak, is also called Rock Oak and Rock Chestnut Oak. This is a medium-sized tree reaching 60 to 70′ in height with a comparable, but irregular spread. The habit is rounded and relatively dense. The leaves are dark, lustrous yellowish green in summer changing to orange-yellow to yellowish brown in fall. Acorns are borne 1 to 2 on peduncles shorter than the petioles; ovoid, 1 to 1 2/5″ high, enclosed 1/3 to 1/2 by the tuberculate cap. This is a tree of rocky places and is found on poor, dry, upland, rocky sites where it may form pure stands. Maximum growth is made in well-drained soils and other moist sites. It is often found in association with Scarlet and Black Oaks on the rocky slopes of mountains. This species can grow 12 to 15′ over a 7 to 10 year period. The acorns are sweet tasting and are relished by the gray squirrel, black bear, white-tailed deer and many other forms of wildlife. The bark is brown to nearly black and, on older trees, very deeply and coarsely furrowed. The bark is valuable, being richer in tannin content (11%) than that of any other oak species. Native from Southern Maine and Ontario to South Carolina and Alabama. Cultivated 1688. Zone 4. A very lovely tree which does exceedingly well in dry, rocky soil. No seed pre-treatment is necessary.

Quercus robur — English Oak, Truffle Oak

LEAVES: Alternate, simple, 2 to 5" long, obovate to obovate-oblong, auriculate base, 3 to 7 pairs of rounded lobes, glabrous, dark green above, pale bluish green beneath. Key feature, ear-lobe-like leaf base (auriculate).

BUDS: Imbricate, rounded, plump, angled, 1/4", chestnut brown, scales fringed with hairs.

STEM: Glabrous, reddish brown, often purplish.

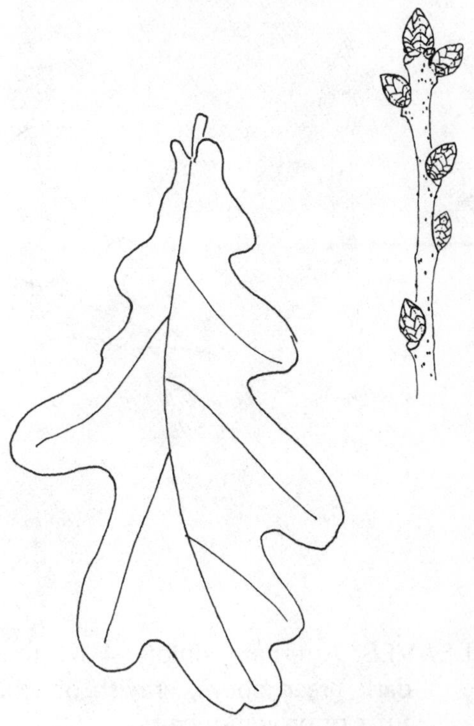

SIZE: The species can reach 75 to 100' or more in height with a comparable spread.

HARDINESS: Zone 4.

HABIT: Large, massive, broadly rounded, open-headed tree with a short trunk; too large for the average landscape.

RATE: Medium in leaf; probably would be considered coarse in winter.

BARK: Deeply furrowed.

LEAF COLOR: Dark green in summer; fall color in Central Illinois is nil, for the leaves either abscise green or persist and change to a nondescript brown.

FRUIT: Nut, 1 to 2" long, enclosed 1/3 by the cup, borne on 1 to 3" long peduncle.

CULTURE: Transplant balled and burlapped, prefers good, well-drained soil, seems to be pH tolerant; full sun.

DISEASES AND INSECTS: Mildew is often a serious problem on the species and the cultivar 'Fastigiata'.

LANDSCAPE VALUE: The species is widely used in Europe; good tree for parks and other large areas; too many better native oaks to justify extreme excitement over this introduced species.

CULTIVARS:

'Asplenifolia' — Leaves deeply cut, fern-like, fine texture; very rare in this country even in arboreta.

'Atropurpurea' — Leaves supposedly a dark purple, however, Wyman noted that the tree in the Arnold Arboretum had faintly purplish green leaves, with the color differing only slightly from the species.

'Concordia' — Leaves are bright yellow when they first appear in the spring. Should be sited in partial shade as the leaves will sun-scorch. There is a 25 to 30' high specimen in Spring Grove Cemetery which is rather striking when the leaves first emerge.

'Fastigiata' — Distinctly upright and columnar in habit, however, some variation does occur because the cultivar is often grown from seed. It comes 80 to 90 percent true. A mature tree may be 50 to 60' in height but only 20' wide.

PROPAGATION: Seed, no pretreatment necessary.

NATIVE HABITAT: Europe, Northern Africa and Western Asia. Long cultivated.

Quercus rubra — Red Oak

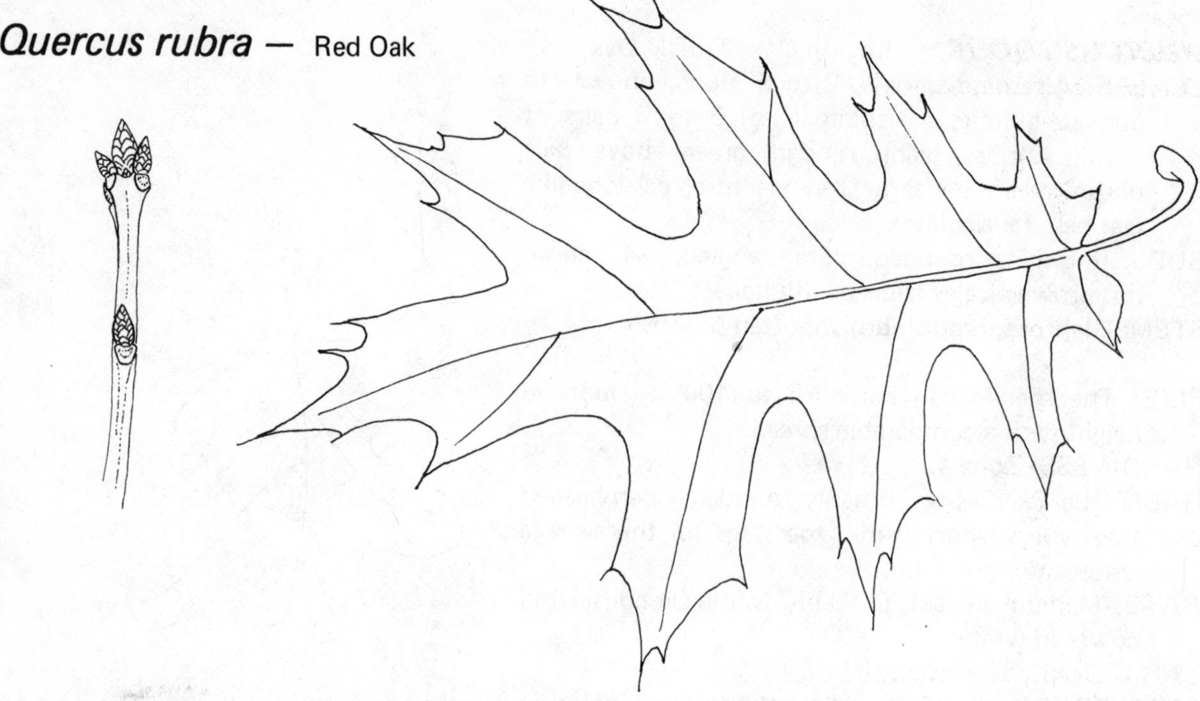

LEAVES: Alternate, simple, 4 1/2 to 8 1/2" long, oblong, cuneate at base, 7 to 11 lobed, lustrous dark green above, grayish or whitish or sometimes pale yellow-green beneath with axillary tufts of brownish hairs.

BUDS: Imbricate, oval to ovate, 1/6 to 1/3" long, chestnut brown, sharp pointed, smooth or with rusty hairs at extreme apex. Scales—margin slightly hairy.

STEM: Stout, reddish to greenish brown, glabrous.

BARK: With distinct flat gray areas intermingled with ridged and furrowed areas.

SIZE: 60 to 75' in height with a spread of 40 to 50', although can grow to over 100' in the wild.

HARDINESS: Zone 4.

HABIT: Rounded in youth and in old age often round-topped and symmetrical.

RATE: Another oak of fast growth, many individuals relegate the oaks to slow status, however, there are significant exceptions; Red Oak can grow 2' per year over a 10 year period.

TEXTURE: Medium in leaf and winter.

BARK: On old trunks brown to nearly black and broken up into wide, flat-topped gray ridges, separated by shallow fissures; on very old trees often deeply ridged and furrowed.

LEAF COLOR: Lustrous dark green in summer changing to russet-red to bright red in fall.

FRUIT: Nut, solitary or paired, 3/4 to 1" long, variable in shape, but usually subglobose, enclosed at the base in a flat, thick, saucer-like cup.

CULTURE: Transplants readily because of negligible taproot; prefers sandy loam soils which are well-drained and on the acid side; withstands the polluted air of cities; full sun; seems to do quite well in Central Illinois although not as widely planted as Pin Oak.

DISEASES AND INSECTS: Basically free of problems, although the problems listed under White Oak are limitedly applicable to this species.

LANDSCAPE VALUE: Valuable fast growing oak for lawns, parks, golf courses and commercial areas.

PROPAGATION: Seed, stratify at 32° to 38°F for 30 to 45 days.

RELATED SPECIES:
Quercus velutina – Black Oak

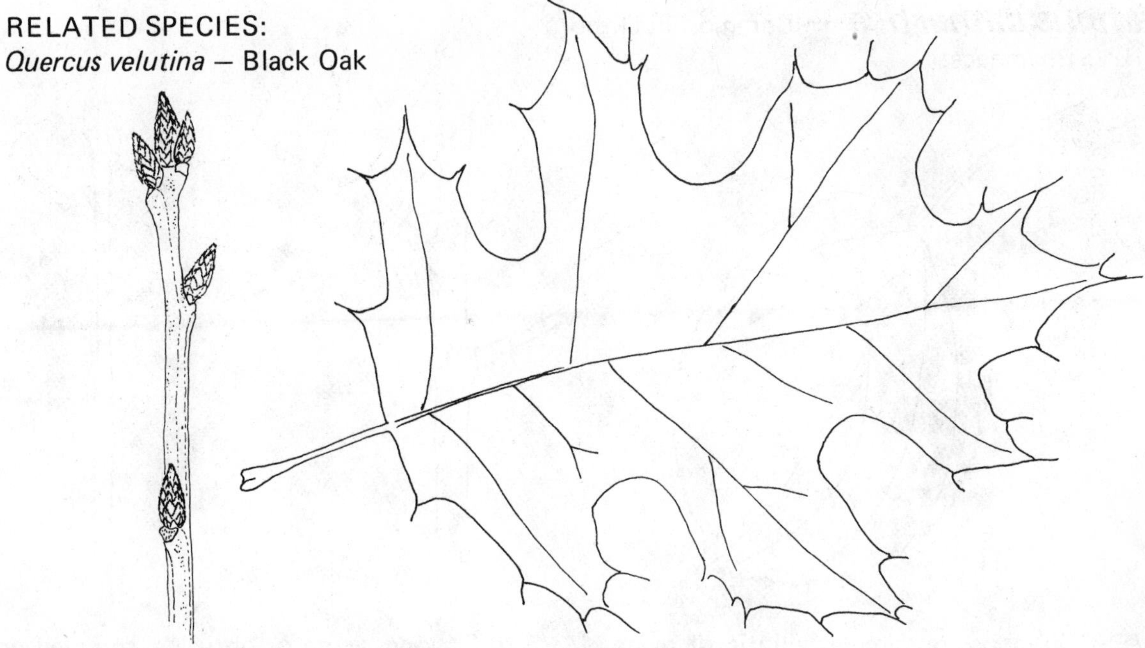

LEAVES: Alternate, simple, 4 to 10" long, ovate, oblong, cuneate to truncate, 7 to 9 lobes, lustrous dark green above, glabrous except in axils of veins.

BUDS: Imbricate, ovate to conical, 1/6 to 1/2" long, narrowed to a sharp point, generally 5-sided, strongly angled, covered with pale yellowish gray to dirty-white pubescence.

STEM: Stout, reddish brown or reddish, mottled with gray, tasting bitter if chewed and coloring saliva yellowish.

Quercus velutina, Black Oak, reaches 50 to 60' in height and the spread is variable for the crown is often quite irregular and can be narrow or wide-spreading, elongated or rounded; extensive tap root and for this reason is somewhat difficult to transplant; makes best growth on moist, rich, well-drained, acid soils but is often found on poor, dry, sandy, or heavy clay hillsides; not an important tree in commerce; fruit is solitary or paired, 1/2 to 3/4" long, ovoid to hemispherical, often striate, light red-brown, 1/4 to 1/3 enclosed in a deep bowl-like cup; bark is nearly black on old trunks, deeply furrowed vertically, and with many horizontal breaks; inner bark bright orange or yellow. Native from Maine to Florida, west to Minnesota and Texas. Introduced 1800.

ADDITIONAL NOTES: Oaks hybridize freely and there are abundant hybrids evident in landscapes and the wild. Red and Black Oak are associated in the wild and frequently hybrids occur.

NATIVE HABITAT: Nova Scotia to Pennsylvania, west to Minnesota and Iowa. Introduced 1800.

Rhamnus cathartica — Common Buckthorn

FAMILY: Rhamnaceae

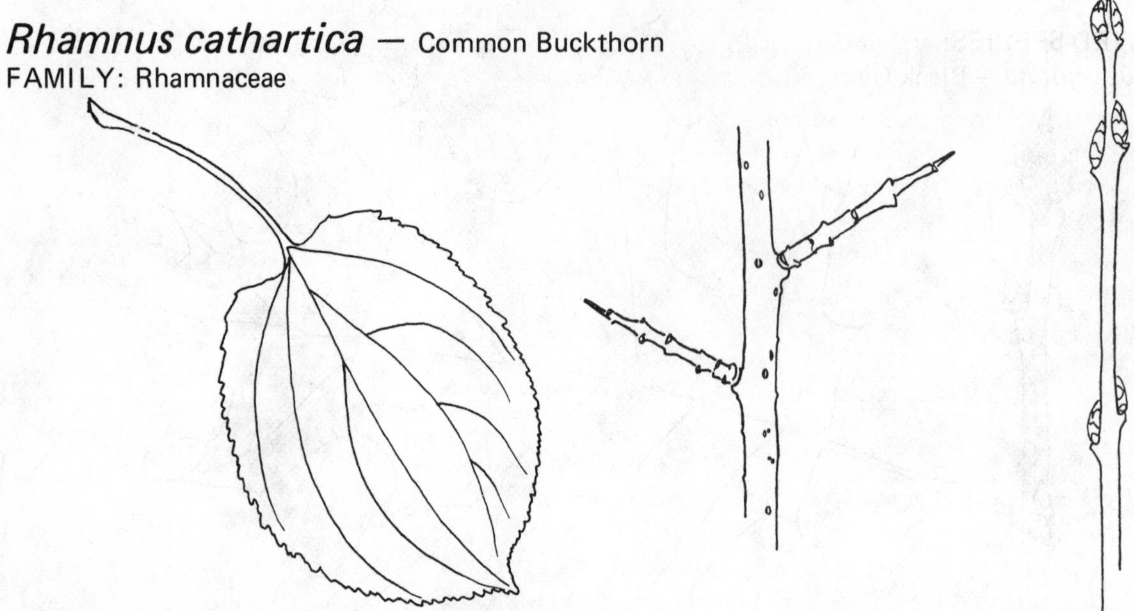

LEAVES: Subopposite, simple, elliptic or ovate, 1 3/5 to 3" long, acute or obtusish, rounded or subcordate at base, sometimes broad-cuneate, crenate-serrulate, dark glossy green above, light green and usually glabrous beneath, with 3 to 5 pairs of veins; petiole 1/4 to 1" long.

BUDS: Imbricate, appressed, elongated, brownish black, and glabrous.

STEM: Slender, somewhat grayish, glabrous, terminal bud a modified spine usually as long as or longer than the buds.

SIZE: 18 to 25' in height with a comparable spread.

HARDINESS: Zone 2.

HABIT: Large shrub or low branched tree with a rounded, bushy crown of crooked, stoutish stems.

RATE: Medium to fast.

TEXTURE: Medium in leaf; coarse in winter.

LEAF COLOR: Dark glossy green in summer, very clean foliage throughout the growing season, excellent if foliage is the only ornamental asset desired; fall color is a disappointing green to yellowish green.

FLOWERS: Unimportant, polygamous or dioecious, small, yellowish green, May, borne in 2 to 5 flowered umbels.

FRUIT: Berry-like drupe, 1/4" diameter, black, not particularly effective, birds like them.

CULTURE: Easily transplanted, adapted to difficult conditions, withstands urban environments; a very tough, durable tree for areas where few other trees will survive. The fruits are eaten by the birds and the seeds deposited in hedge-rows, shrub borders and other out-of-the-way places. Can actually become a weed.

DISEASES AND INSECTS: Leaf spots, rust, powdery mildew, aphids, scales. None are serious except the rust (*Puccinia coronata*) which can cause considerable damage to oats. Eradication of buckthorn is recommended control measure.

LANDSCAPE VALUE: Possibly as a background, screen or hedge under difficult growing conditions.

PROPAGATION: Seed, 60 to 90 days in moist peat at 41°F. Cuttings, would probably root easily from softwood material but I cannot find absolute references and am simply inferring this.

RELATED SPECIES:

Rhamnus davurica – Dahurian Buckthorn. 25 to 30', spreading shrub or small tree, with stout often spinescent stems; foliage lustrous dark green; fruit is black much like *R. cathartica*, extremely hardy and durable, well-adapted to difficult situations, limitedly available in commerce.

NATIVE HABITAT: Europe and Western and Northern Asia, naturalized in Eastern United States.

Rhamnus frangula — Glossy Buckthorn, also called Alder Buckthorn

LEAVES: Alternate, simple, oval or obovate to obovate-oblong, 1 1/5 to 3" long, acute, rounded or broad-cuneate at base, entire, dark lustrous green above, lighter green and often slightly pubescent beneath, with 8 or 9 pairs of veins; petiole 1/4 to 1/2" long.

BUDS: Terminal—naked, pubescent, brownish, foliose, much larger than laterals; laterals—brownish, depressed imbricate, small.

STEM: Slender, pubescent on young stems, eventually becoming glabrous. Prominently lenticelled on young and old stems.

SIZE: 10 to 12' possibly to 18' in height and probably 8 to 12' or greater in spread.

HARDINESS: Zone 2.

HABIT: Upright, spreading, large shrub or small, low-branched tree with long arching branches yielding an upright-oval outline; quite gangly and open.

RATE: Medium to fast.

TEXTURE: Medium in leaf; medium-coarse in winter.

LEAF COLOR: Dark glossy green in summer changing to greenish yellow or yellow in fall. In Central Illinois the fall color is a poor greenish yellow.

FLOWERS: Unimportant, polygamous or dioecious, creamy green, bees love them.

FRUIT: Berry-like drupe, 1/4" across, in maturation passes from red to purple-black, effective from late July through September.

CULTURE: Transplants well, adaptable, sun or partial shade, prefers well-drained soil. I noticed where students have made paths through the hedges (*Rhamnus frangula* 'Columnaris') a significant decrease in height is evident on either side of the path compared to nontrafficked areas. Widely used and promoted.

DISEASES AND INSECTS: Until 1975 no serious problems had been reported. However, many of the hedge plants on the University of Illinois campus exhibit a dieback disorder typical of canker or wilt infestation. Don Schoeneweiss reported in the *Plant Disease Reporter* in Volume 58:937 that low temperature stresses predisposed Tallhedge to the fungus *Tubercularia ulmea*. He was consistently able to isolate the fungus from stem cankers that were girdling the shoots.

LANDSCAPE VALUE: Species is worthless for landscape considerations; falls into the weed character for the birds deposit the seeds everywhere and plants are found in unexpected places.

CULTIVARS:

'Aspenifolia' — Cut-leaf variety of very fine texture, slow growing, but interesting; not common.

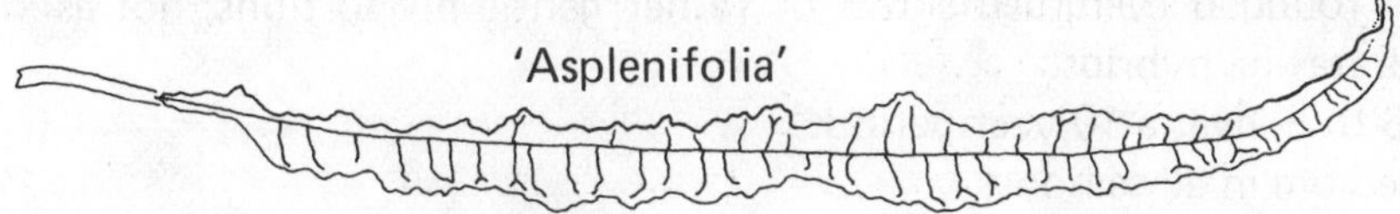

'Columnaris' — Narrow, upright deciduous shrub prized for hedges, has been overused in the Midwest. The insects and diseases may be catching up, much as is the case with Common Honeylocust.

PROPAGATION: Seed, 60 days in moist peat at 41°F.

NATIVE HABITAT: Europe, Western Asia, North Africa; naturalized in Eastern and Midwestern United States.

Rhododendrons

The genus *Rhododendron* comprises over 900 species and infinite numbers of cultivars due to the ability of the species to freely hybridize. The improvements in rhododendrons (foliage, flower color and quality, hardiness and growth habit) have come about through hybridization. There is a need for cold hardy forms with good flower color. Many of the hardy types available are endowed with the lavender-purple-magenta colors offensive to many people. Rhododendrons are indigenous to many parts of the world but the strongest concentrations of hardy, colorful, useful types exist in China, Japan and the eastern United States. Greatest cultural success in the States is achieved in the Pacific Northwest and the eastern United States where soils and atmospheric conditions are close to optimum. The following list is not complete and was not intended to be. The types listed represent some of the hardier and more common forms which could possibly be grown in this area. A good rhododendron display is without equal and a recent poll of gardeners (asking them their favorite shrub) indicated rhododendrons were *numero uno*. For additional information see Bower's or Leach's books on rhododendrons as they are excellent references.

Differences in Rhododendrons and Azaleas

Actually, all azaleas are now included in the genus *Rhododendron*. There are not clear cut lines for distinguishing *all* azaleas from *all* rhododendrons but

1. True rhododendrons are usually evergreen but there are exceptions such as *R. mucronulatum* and *R. dauricum*.
2. True rhododendrons have 10 or more stamens and leaves are often scaly or with small dots on their undersurface.
3. Azaleas are mostly deciduous.
4. Azalea flowers have mostly 5 stamens, leaves are never dotted with scales and are frequently pubescent.
5. Azalea flowers are largely funnel-form while rhododendron flowers tend to be bell-shaped.

Rhododendron carolinianum — Carolina Rhododendron

FAMILY: Ericaceae

LEAVES: Evergreen, alternate, simple, elliptic to narrow-elliptic, 2 to 3" long, acutish or abruptly short-acuminate, broad cuneate, glabrous above, ferrugineous scaly, often very densely so beneath, sometimes glaucescent; petiole 1/5 to 2/5" long. Leaves aromatic when bruised.

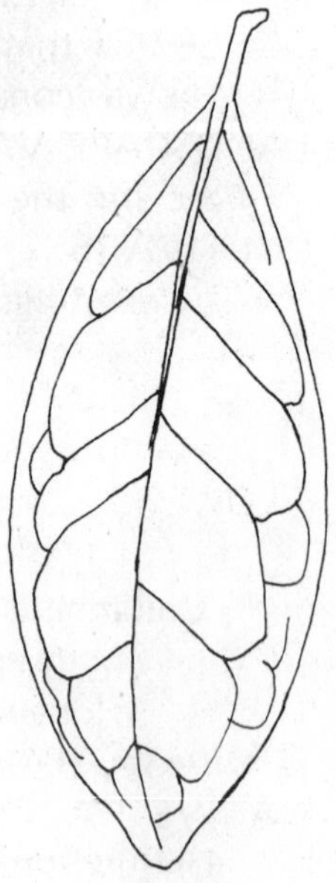

SIZE: 3 to 6' in height with a similar or greater spread.

HARDINESS: Zone 4 to 5.

HABIT: Small, rounded evergreen shrub of rather gentle proportions; not as coarse as Catawba hybrids.

RATE: Slow, 3 to 5' over a 10 year period.

TEXTURE: Medium in all seasons.

LEAF COLOR: Dark green in summer; usually assuming a purplish tinge in cold climates.

FLOWERS: Perfect, varies from pure white to pale rose, rose and lilac-rose in color; borne in terminal, umbel-like 3" diameter racemes (trusses) in mid-May.

FRUIT: Dehiscent capsule.

CULTURE: See under Broadleaf Evergreen. Rhododendrons are extremely sensitive to salinity, high pH (chlorosis), and winter injury.

DISEASES AND INSECTS: Botrytis blotch, bud and twig blight, gray blight, *Botryosphaeria* canker, crown rot, dieback, dampening-off, azalea petal blight, azalea gall, leaf spots, leaf scorch, powdery mildew, rust, shoot blight, shoestring root rot, wilt, rhododendron aphid, azalea stem borer, azalea leaf tier, black vine and strawberry weevils, giant hornet, Japanese beetle, asiatic garden beetle, lace bugs, red-banded leafhopper, azalea leaf miner, rhododendron tip midge, mites, mealybugs, pitted ambrosia beetle, rhododendron borer, scales, thrips, rhododendron whitefly, nematodes, stem girdling caused by woodpeckers. Rhododendrons are troubled by many pests and their culture is often fraught with difficulty. Good cultural practices will reduce the incidence of disease and insect damage.

LANDSCAPE VALUE: Like all rhododendrons a nice plant for the shrub border, groupings, massing, foundations. Should be sited in a slightly shaded area and out of strong winter sun and wind.

CULTIVARS:

var. *album* – White flowers.

var. *lutem* – Mimosa yellow flowers; like most rhododendrons this species exhibits great variation when grown from seed.

PROPAGATION: See under *Calluna*. I have raised many seedlings with a minimum of effort. Cuttings are somewhat difficult to root but when taken in August and treated with a hormone and fungicide will give a reasonable percentage.

NATIVE HABITAT: Blue Ridge Mountains of Carolinas and Tennessee.

Rhododendron catawbiense — Catawba Rhododendron

FAMILY: Ericaceae

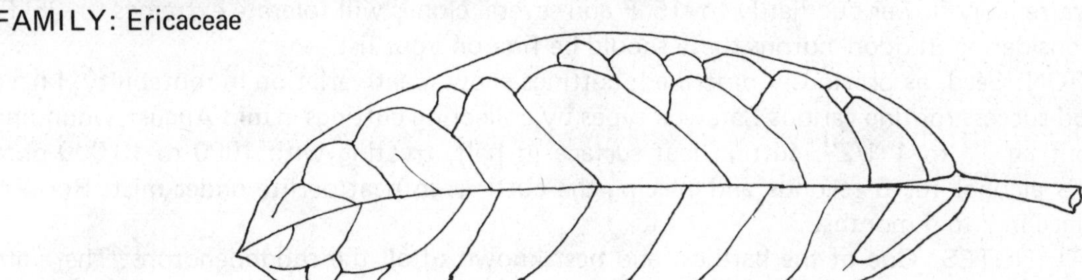

LEAVES: Alternate, simple, elliptic to oblong, 2 to 5" long, obtuse and mucronulate, rounded at base, dark green above, light green below, glabrous, of leathery texture.

FLOWER BUDS: Large–1/2" long, scaly, pointed, yellowish green.

STEM: On new growth, yellowish green changing to brown with age.

SIZE: 6 to 10' in height rarely 15 to 20'; spread 5 to 8' or more.

HARDINESS: Zone 4.

HABIT: Heavy evergreen shrub with large, dense foliage to the ground; often leggy in unfavorable locations; usually taller than wide although does assume a rounded appearance on occasion.

RATE: Slow.

TEXTURE: Medium-coarse in all seasons.

LEAF COLOR: Dark green, very handsome; often in winter under exposed conditions will develop a yellow-green color.

FLOWERS: Lilac-purple, sometimes purplish rose, with green or yellow-brown markings on the inside of the corolla, 2 to 2 1/2" diameter; mid to late May, borne in 5 to 6" diameter umbel-like racemes (trusses).

FRUIT: Rusty, hairy capsule.

CULTURE: See under Broadleaf Evergreen.

DISEASES AND INSECTS: See under *R. carolinianum*.

LANDSCAPE VALUE: Very handsome and esthetic broadleaf evergreen; the flowers are beautiful but the foliage is equally valuable. Beautiful when used in mass; hardy to -30°F.

CULTIVARS:

var. *album* – One of the best whites for cold climates, buds pink, open to pure white; foliage is usually a good dark glossy green.

'America' – Brilliant clear red, very floriferous, forming a broad bush.

'Boursault' — Buds purple, turning rosy-lilac, compact grower.

'Compactum' — Form which stays less than 3' tall.

'Cunningham' (often called 'Cunningham's White') — Low growing, white flowering form.

'English Roseum' — Light rose, vigorous upright grower, large foliage.

'Grandiflora' — Purplish rose.

'Lee's Dark Purple' — Buds deep purple, opening to medium purple, broad, compact bush, of vigorous constitution.

'Mrs. C. S. Sargent' — Rich carmen rose flowers, spotted yellow; a worthy selection for cold areas.

'Nova Zembla' — Red flowers, perhaps not as intense as 'America'; quite cold tolerant and heat resistant, probably one of the best for the midwest.

'Parson's Gloriosum' — Compact, conical trusses of lavender flowers, compact yet tall growth habit; dense, dark green foliage.

'Purpureum Elegans' — Flowers bishop's violet with orange-brown markings, 3" diameter.

'Purpureum Grandiflorum' — Imperial-purple, red-orange markings, 2 1/4" diameter.

'Roseum Elegans' — The old stand-by, lavender pink flowers and reliability in flowering; suffering temperature extremes without injury.

The above cultivars represent the most hardy, fool-proof clones of Catawba Rhododendron. They are reliably flower bud hardy to -15°F and several clones will tolerate extremes to -25°F. When considering Rhododendrons these should be first on your list.

PROPAGATION: Seed, as previously described; cuttings show great variation in rootability. I have had good success rooting various Catawba types by collecting cuttings in mid-August, wounding for about an 1" to 1 1/2", cutting leaf surface in half, treating with 1000 to 10,000 ppm IBA/50% alcohol for 5 seconds and placing the cuttings in peat:perlite under mist. Rooting takes place in 2 to 4 months.

ADDITIONAL NOTES: One of the hardiest and best known of all the rhododendrons. There are many cultivars but not too many are good for hot and cold conditions like we have in Central Illinois.

NATIVE HABITAT: Alleghenies, West Virginia, Southwest to Georgia and Alabama.

Rhododendron mucronulatum — Korean Rhododendron

FAMILY: Ericaceae

LEAVES: Alternate, simple, deciduous, elliptic to elliptic-lanceolate, 1 1/5 to 2 2/5" long, acute or obtusish, very aromatic when crushed.

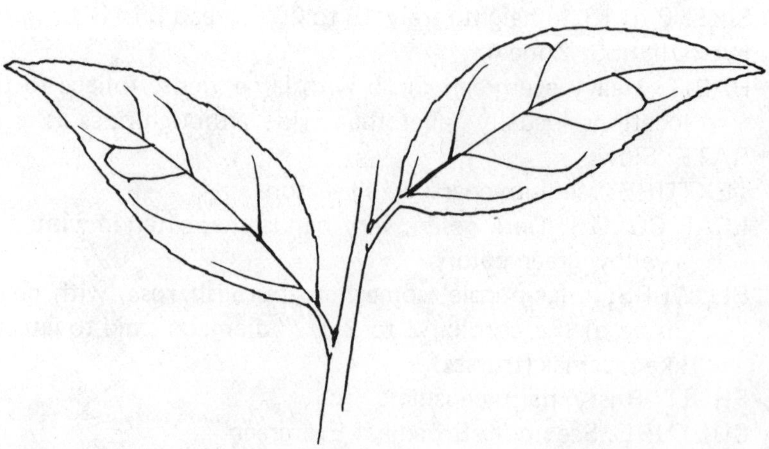

SIZE: 4 to 8' in height with a similar spread.

HARDINESS: Zone 4.

HABIT: Deciduous shrub of upright-oval to rounded outline with clean branching and foliage characteristics.

RATE: Slow.

TEXTURE: Medium-fine in foliage; medium in winter.

LEAF COLOR: Soft green in summer changing to shades of yellow and bronzy crimson in fall.

FLOWERS: Bright rosy purple, 1 1/2" long and 1 1/2" wide; mid to late March, 3 to 6 together at the ends of the branches. Flowers well before the leaves and often as the buds are opening a freeze will kill or injure them. Siting is very important and a protected location where the south and southwestern sun will not hit them in February and March is recommended.

CULTURE: See under Broadleaf Evergreens.

DISEASES AND INSECTS: See under *R. carolinianum*.

LANDSCAPE VALUE: First of all the hardy rhododendrons and azaleas to flower in Northeastern United States. Very lovely in a shrub border. I have 5 scattered around the Northeast corner of my house and they make nice foundation plants because of compactness and good foliage as well as lovely early flower.

CULTIVARS:

'Cornell Pink' – Soft pink flowers, unadulterated by the magenta present in the flowers of the species. I have seen this cultivar in flower but was not impressed by the color, even though the description is listed as soft pink the color appeared a deeper pink.

PROPAGATION: Seed, very easy; softwood cuttings collected in July rooted 50%. I have grown many seedlings of this species and also rooted many cuttings. One of the seedlings flowered in spring of 1975 and was a beautiful soft pink (apple-blossom like). Currently I am growing the plant on, trying to secure cutting wood.

NATIVE HABITAT: Northern China, Manchuria, Korea, and Northern Japan. Introduced 1882.

Rhododendron schlippenbachii — Royal Azalea

FAMILY: Ericaceae

LEAVES: Alternate, simple, usually 5 at ends of the branches, appear as if whorled, short-petioled, obovate or broad-obovate, 2 to 4'' long, truncate or rounded to emarginate at apex, mucronate, cuneate, slightly undulate, sparingly pubescent when young, later glabrous except on veins beneath, dark green above, pale beneath.

SIZE: 6 to 8' high and as wide at maturity.

HARDINESS: Zone 4.

HABIT: Upright-rounded deciduous shrub.

RATE: Slow.

TEXTURE: Medium in all seasons.

LEAF COLOR: Dark green in summer; yellow, orange, crimson in fall.

FLOWERS: Pale to rose pink, no trace of magenta, fragrant, early to mid-May; 3 to 6 together in a 2 1/4 to 3'' diameter inflorescence. One of the most delicate and beautiful of the azaleas for northern gardens.

CULTURE: Seems to do better on high pH soils than other Ericaceae; pH 6.5 to 7 would be acceptable; may have a higher calcium requirement than other types.

LANDSCAPE VALUE: One of the finest azaleas, flowers open just as the leaves are expanding; no adequate way to do justice to the beauty of this plant by the written word.

PROPAGATION: Seed as previously described. Cuttings taken in late May and treated with a hormone (IBA) will give a fair percentage.

ADDITIONAL NOTES: This species comes fairly true from seed as it fails to hybridize freely with other species.

NATIVE HABITAT: Korea, Manchuria. Introduced 1893.

Other Rhododendrons

Rhododendron arborescens, Sweet Azalea, is a deciduous, erect stemmed, loosely branched shrub growing from 8 to 20' in height with an equal spread; foliage is bright green in summer and dark glossy red in fall; flowers are white, 1 1/2 to 2'' diameter, after the leaves in early June, fragrant odor like heliotrope; best native white azalea that is hardy in the north; prefers light, consistently moist, acid soil. Native from Southern Pennsylvania to Georgia and Alabama; grows chiefly on the banks of mountain streams. Introduced before 1814. Zone 4.

Rhododendron 'Boule de Neige' is listed as a Caucasian hybrid and is one of the finest white flowering types. The evergreen foliage is a dark, lustrous green and the habit is compact and of a rounded outline. Zone 5, possibly 4.

Rhododendron calendulaceum, Flame Azalea, is a deciduous, loosely branched shrub of upright habit, usually as wide as high (4 to 6' tall by a comparable spread). The summer foliage is medium green and the fall color yellow-green; flowers vary from yellow to orange to scarlet, 2", early June, in loose trusses; colors range from lemon to dark yellows, tawny, apricot, salmon, deep flesh color, pinkish, brilliant shades of orange and scarlet. Most showy and one of the most notable American azaleas (a parent of the Ghent hybrid race); retains flowers for nearly two weeks, excellent in naturalistic setting or mass planting. Native to mountains of Pennsylvania south to Georgia. Zone 5.

Rhododendron 'Exbury Hybrids' are also called the Knap Hill or deRothschild Hybrids. They are deciduous, upright growing types with medium green summer foliage and yellow, orange, red fall colors; flowers range from pink, creams, yellows, near whites to orange, rose and red, borne in 2 to 3" diameter, 18 to 30 flowered trusses in mid to late May. Some of the better clones include Exbury types:

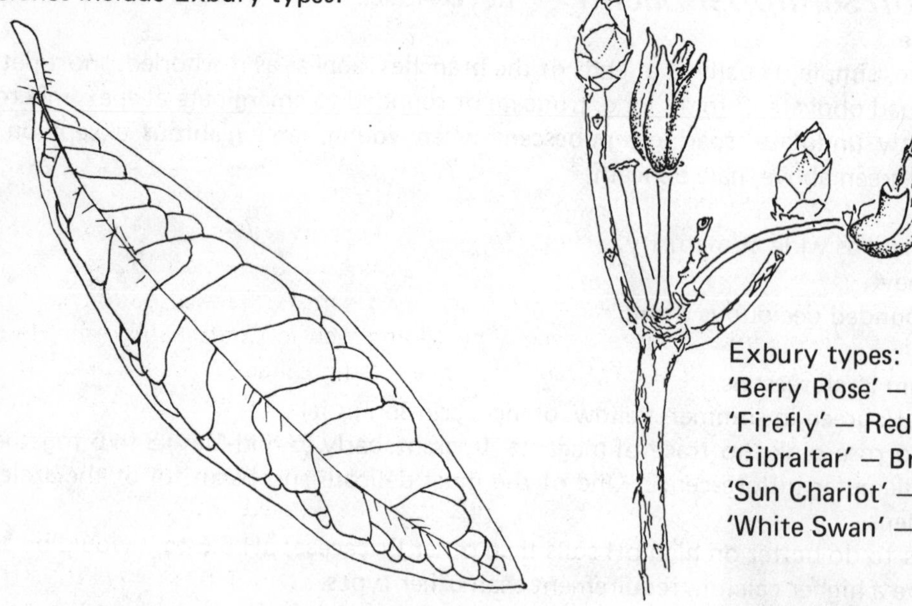

Exbury types:
'Berry Rose' – Rose pink.
'Firefly' – Red.
'Gibraltar' – Brilliant orange.
'Sun Chariot' – Yellow.
'White Swan' – White.

Knaphill types:
'Bullfinch' – Deep red.
'Flamingo' – Pink.
'Golden Oriole' – Yellow.
'White Throat' – Double white.

These hybrids are a result of crosses involving several species including *R. calendulaceum, R. arborescens, R. occidentale, R. molle.* Zone 5.

Rhododendron 'Gable Hybrids' are a mixed lot but offer a quality range of colors and they are considered the hardiest evergreen azaleas for Zone 5 conditions. They were developed by the late Joseph Gable, a rhododendron hybridizer at Stewartstown, Pennsylvania. Other hybrid groups which fall into this same milieu include those developed by Girard (Geneva, Ohio), Pride (Butler, Pennsylvania), Shammarello (S. Euclid, Ohio). I have several of Girard's hybrids in my yard and they are performing quite nicely. These plants grow 2 to 4' high and as wide in 4 to 6 years. The foliage is a shiny dark green, about 1" long, although there is considerable variation among clones. The flowers arrive in late April to early May and are about 2" across.

The plants are usually solid masses of color at this time. A few named cultivars include 'David Gable', rosy-pink; 'Forest Fire', blood red; 'Girard's Red', brilliant red (looks exceptionally good); 'Girard's Rose', rose; 'Louis Gable', salmon pink; 'Purple Splendor', rich purple; 'Rosebud', bright pink; 'Rose Greeley', white; 'Stewartstonian', bright clear red, with lustrous *dark* green foliage.

Rhododendron x *gandavense*, Ghent Azaleas, are deciduous 6 to 10' shrubby growers with flower colors ranging from pure white, pure yellow, to combinations of pink, orange and scarlet; flowers are single or double, the doubles with numerous overlapping petals, 1 1/2 to 2" across. The hybrids were developed by crossing several species and some of the select clones are hardy to -20°F. Cultivars:

'Bouquet De Flore' — Bright pink.
'Coccinea Speciosa' — Orange.
'Daviesii' — White.
'Gloria Mundi' — Orange-yellow-red combination.
'Narcissiflora' — Double yellow.
'Pallas' — Orange-red.

Developed in Ghent, Belgium.

Rhododendron kaempferi was formerly listed as *R. obtusum kaempferi* but is now considered a species. The kaempferi hybrids can grow to 10' and 5 to 6' after 5 to 10 years. The leaves are dark green, semi-evergreen to deciduous and turn reddish tones in fall and winter. The flowers range in color from salmon-red, orange-red, pink, to rosy-scarlet and white; each flower 1 3/4 to 2 1/2" long and wide, funnel-shaped, 1 to 4 per truss. This is a very variable species and apparently has interbred with *R. obtusum* producing large hybrid swarms which dot the mountainsides of Japan. Usually found in sunny positions on hillsides, by the sea, on active volcanos and also in thickets, pinewoods and deciduous forests. Several cultivars of merit include: 'Barbara', deep pink; 'Fedora', deep pink (doing well in Central Illinois); 'Herbert', lavender orchid (also performing well); 'Holland', deep red; 'Mikado', bright red; 'Othello', orange-red; 'Thais', crimson; 'Wilhelmina Vuyk' ('Palestrina'), white; and 'Zampa', violet-red. These hybrids resulted from crosses between *R. kaempferi* x Malvatica (unknown, but thought to be a hybrid of 'Hinodegiri' x *R. mucronatum*). The species is found wild on the main islands of Japan from sea-level to the lower hills below 2600 feet. Introduced 1892.

Rhododendron keiskei, Keisk Rhododendron, grows to 4 to 5' high and is of scraggly habit; evergreen in foliage; lemon-yellow flowers, early to mid-May, 3 to 5 flowers per cluster; it is one of the few evergreen rhododendrons with pale yellow flowers. Japan. Zone 5.

Rhododendron x *kosterianum* — Mollis Hybrid Azaleas

LEAVES: Alternate, simple, entire, 1 1/2 to 4" long, obovate to oblong-ovate; apex bluntish, with a gland-like tip; base wedge-shaped; margin-hairy on upper surface or becoming hairless, bristly-hairy on veins beneath.

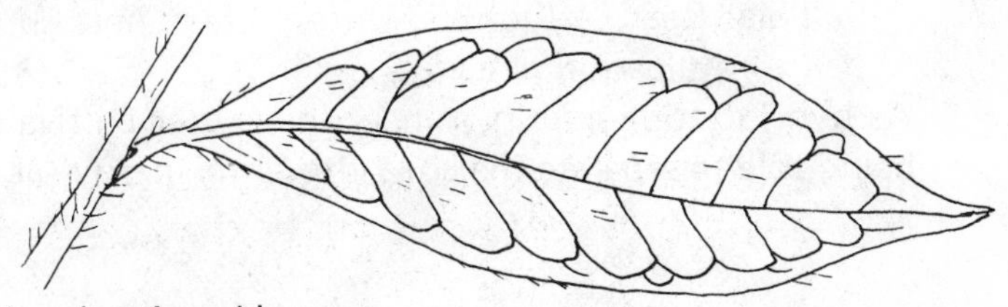

BUDS: Large—1/4 to 1/2", imbricate, tip of scales tinged brown.

Rhododendron x *kosterianum*, Mollis Hybrid Azaleas, are somewhat similar to the Exbury group in flower characteristics but usually smaller and not as hardy; foliage is deciduous; resulted from crosses between *R. molle* x *R. japonicum*. Cultivars worth considering include:

'Christopher Wren' — Yellow.
'Consul Ceresole' — Rose-pink.
'Koster's Brilliant' — Orange-red.
'Snowdrift' — White.

My experience has been that they are easy to grow from seed.

Rhododendron x *laetivirens*, Wilson Rhododendron, is a small (2 to 4′ by 2 to 6′), low growing, glossy leaved, evergreen shrub with pink to purplish flowers; makes a good, neat, small evergreen plant in rock garden or for foundation planting. Zone 4. Result of a cross between *R. carolinianum* x *R. ferrugineum.*

Rhododendron maximum, Rosebay Rhododendron, grows to 4 to 15′ in the north but can grow to 30′; habit is loose and open; leaves are large (4 to 8″ long) and evergreen (dark green); flowers are rose colored to purplish pink, spotted with olive-green to orange, 1 to 2″ across, June, requires moist, acid soil and shade protection. Cultivars:

var. *album* — White flowers.

var. *purpureum* — Deep pink to purple flowers.

Native to Nova Scotia and Ontario to Georgia, Alabama and Ohio. Introduced 1736. Zone 3.

Rhododendron nudiflorum, Pinxterbloom Azalea, is a low, much branched, almost stoloniferous, deciduous shrub which averages 4 to 6′ in height but ranges from dwarfish (2′) to relatively large (10′) shrubs over the native habitat. The foliage is bright green in summer turning dull yellow in fall. The flowers vary in color from impure white or pale pink to deep violet and open in late April or early May. The flowers are fragrant, each about 1 1/2″ across, borne 6 to 12 together before the leaves. This species is adapted to dry, sandy, rocky soils. A useful plant for naturalizing, and along with *R. calendulaceum* and *R. viscosum* was used in the development of the Ghent hybrids. Native from Massachusetts to North Carolina and Ohio. Introduced 1730. Zone 3.

Rhododendron obtusum, Hiryu Azalea, is a spreading, dense evergreen shrub with glossy green leaves up to 1 1/4″ long. The flowers are reddish violet, but bright red, scarlet and crimson forms occur. Each flower may be 3/4 to 1″ across, funnel-shaped, 1 to 3 per truss. Found wild in highly acid soil on three mountains in Kyushu, Japan. Introduced about 1844. Zone 6. There are a number of cultivars which have been derived from *R. obtusum, R. kaempferi, R. kuisianum,* and *R. satense*. This group has the name Kurume Azaleas and while often considered dwarf they will develop into dense, well-preserved 4 to 6′ high plants. Many of the clones have been used for greenhouse forcing and are simply not hardy in the northern areas. The range of colors travels from white to pink, lavender, scarlet, salmon and all shades in between. Some of the hardier clones that I am familiar with include:

'Amoenum' — Flowers rich magenta, double (hose in hose), small and dense, twiggy, old variety, hardier than most, Zone 5.

'Eureka' — Flowers pink, hose-in-hose, medium, spreading.

'Hershey's Red' — Bright red, double.

'Hino-Crimson' — Flowers crimson-red, low to medium.

'Hinodegiri' — Flowers vivid red, 1 1/2″ across, low and compact.

'Polar Bear' — Flowers white, hose-in-hose, upright, performing well in our woody plant evaluation plots.

As hybridization continues new and better cultivars will appear in the trade. The real crux is being able to separate the good flowering, hardy (at least to -10°) types from the rest of the lot.

Rhododendron P.J.M.
LEAVES: Small, 1 to 2 1/2" long, usually elliptic; dark green above, changing to purple in winter, essentially hairless, rusty-scaly beneath, thick, leathery.
BUDS: Rounded and much smaller than those of *R. catawbiense.*

Rhododendron 'P.J.M. Hybrids' resulted from crosses between *R. carolinianum* and *R. dauricum sempervirens*. The P.J.M. Hybrids are a group of plants and, therefore, there may be differences in flower colors. The plant grows from 3 to 6' in height and is of rounded outline, the foliage is evergreen, dark green in summer and turning plum purple in fall; the flowers are vivid, bright lavender pink and occur in mid to late April; the flowers occur heavily every year as the plant sets little or no seed. Zone 4 hardiness. Dr. Donald Wyman said the 'P.J.M. Hybrids' were the most promising rhododendrons that have originated in New England during the past 25 years. Originated in the Weston, Nurseries, Hopkinton, Massachusetts. 1943. Many people do not like the "dirty, squalid lavender-pink flowers" but when the choice of rhododendrons is limited this is a bright element in the landscape.

Rhododendron poukhanense, Korean Azalea, grows to 3 to 6' and spreads that much or more; develops into a broad mat on exposed locations; foliage is dark green in summer; orange to red-purple in fall; flowers are rose to lilac-purple, 2" across, slightly fragrant, mid-May, 2 to 3 flowers together. The variety *yedoense* has double flowers of a similar color; native to Korea. Zone 4 to 5. Has performed well in our evaluation plots.

Rhododendron 'Purple Gem' is a rounded, dwarf, evergreen type with small leaves and light purple flowers in mid-April. Hardy to -15°F; a cross between *fastigiatum* x *carolinianum.*

Rhododendron 'Ramapo' is another compact form with glaucous foliage, bright-violet pink flowers in early April and -25°F hardiness.

Rhododendron roseum, Roseshell Azalea, is a deciduous 2 to 8', rarely to 15' tall, much branched shrub with numerous spreading branches; spread is comparable to height; foliage is bright green in summer; green to bronze in fall; flowers are bright pink with clove-like scent, May, borne 5 to 9 per cluster before or with the leaves; superior to *R. nudiflorum* and *R. canescens*; extremely hardy, with marked tolerance to high pH. Native to New Hampshire and Southern Quebec to Virginia, west to Illinois and Missouri. Introduced 1812. Zone 3.

Rhododendron smirnowii, Smirnow Rhododendron, is an evergreen shrub growing 6 to 8' high and as broad in 15 years. The foliage is dark green above with thick woolly tomentum beneath. The flowers are rose or rosy-pink and the corolla is frilled; each flower is 1 1/2" long and 2" across; May; in 5 to 6" wide trusses. Very distinct and handsome rhododendron in flower. Has been used for breeding work because of good hardiness (Zone 4), flower and foliage. Will become increasingly evident in American gardens as its merits are extolled. Native to Caucasus, 5,000 to 8,000 feet. Introduced 1886.

Rhododendron vaseyi, Pinkshell Azalea, grows 5 to 10' in height; the habit is irregular upright; foliage is deciduous, medium green in summer changing to light red in fall; flowers are clear rose, before leaves, 1 1/2" diameter, early to mid-May, 5 to 8 flowers per inflorescence; one of the hardy American types; var. *album* has white flowers; native to the Blue Ridge Mountains of North Carolina. Zone 4.

Rhododendron viscosum, Swamp Azalea, grows 1 to 8′ by 3 to 8′ and is of loose, open habit with numerous spreading, very hispid branches; flowers are white, rarely pink, clove-like scent, late June, 4 to 9 flowers per inflorescence. Maine to South Carolina in swamps. Cultivated 1731. Zone 3.

Rhododendron 'Windbeam' is another very hardy (-25°F) evergreen type of low, semi-dwarf habit, with white flowers becoming suffused with pink. It is a cross between *carolinianum* and *racemosum*.

Rhododendron yakusimanum is a dense, mounded, evergreen rhododendron growing about 3′ tall and 3′ wide. The foliage is dark green with a woolly indumentum beneath; the flowers are bright rose in bud opening to white in full flower (sort of an apple blossom effect), about 10 campanulate flowers in a truss; hardy from -5 to -15°F, used extensively in hybridizing and superior clones are available; one reference indicated a 20-year-old plant may be only 3′ by 5′. Native to Yakusima Island, Japan.

Rhodotypos scandens — Black Jetbead

FAMILY: Rosaceae

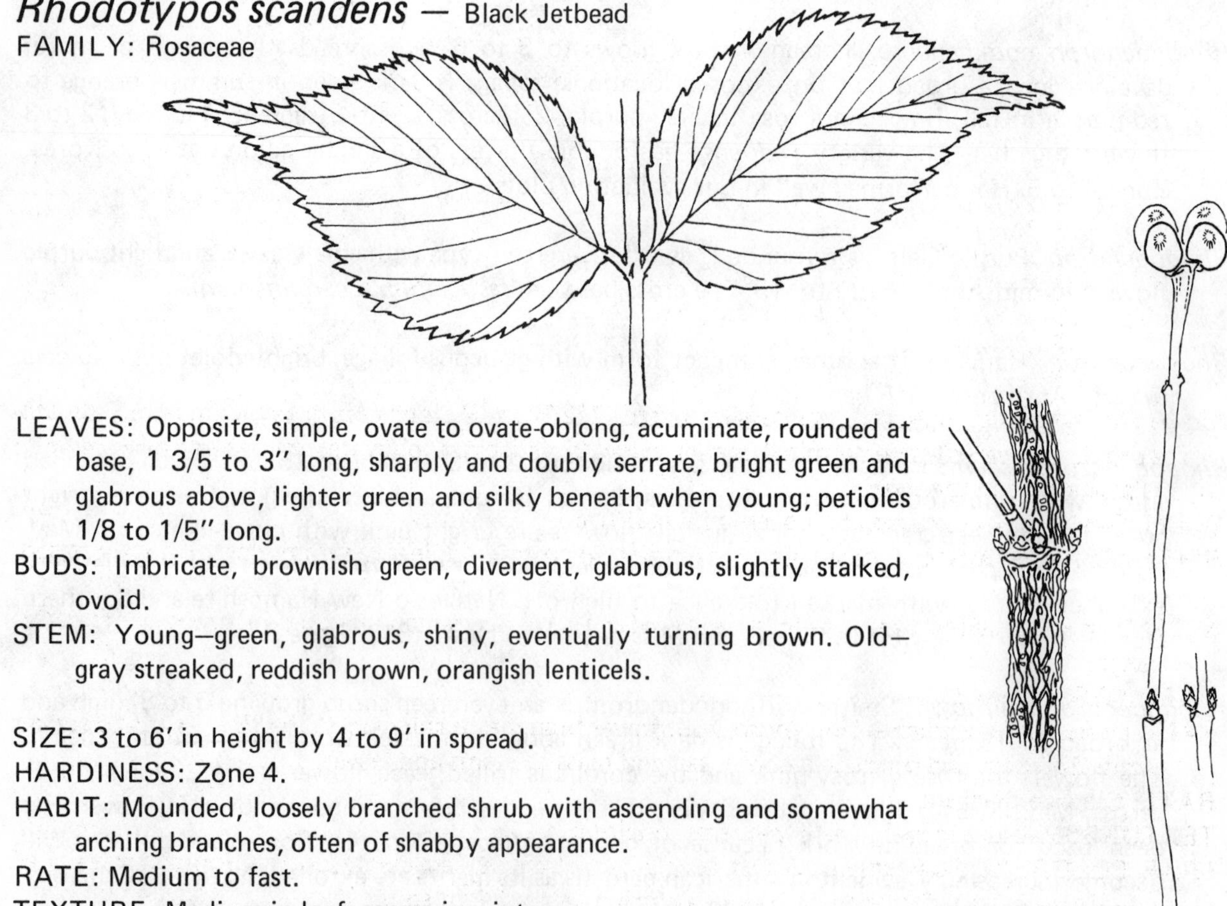

LEAVES: Opposite, simple, ovate to ovate-oblong, acuminate, rounded at base, 1 3/5 to 3″ long, sharply and doubly serrate, bright green and glabrous above, lighter green and silky beneath when young; petioles 1/8 to 1/5″ long.

BUDS: Imbricate, brownish green, divergent, glabrous, slightly stalked, ovoid.

STEM: Young—green, glabrous, shiny, eventually turning brown. Old—gray streaked, reddish brown, orangish lenticels.

SIZE: 3 to 6′ in height by 4 to 9′ in spread.

HARDINESS: Zone 4.

HABIT: Mounded, loosely branched shrub with ascending and somewhat arching branches, often of shabby appearance.

RATE: Medium to fast.

TEXTURE: Medium in leaf; coarse in winter.

LEAF COLOR: Various authors report dark green the typical summer foliage color, however, I feel the color tends toward a bright green. Fall color is green with a slight tinge of yellow.

FLOWERS: White, 1 to 2″ diameter, 4 petaled (unusual for Rosaceae), mid-May to early June, borne singly.

FRUIT: Drupe, 1/3″ long, hard, 3 to 4 in a group, shining black, October and persistent into the following spring and summer. Neither flowers or fruits are showy but do offer a degree of interest in the garden.

CULTURE: Readily transplanted, very tolerant of differing soil conditions, tolerates full sun or shade, crowding and polluted conditions.

DISEASES AND INSECTS: Trouble free.

LANDSCAPE VALUE: Tough, durable plant for rugged conditions; good in shady areas, shrub border. There are too many superior ornamental shrubs to justify extensive use of this species.

PROPAGATION: Cuttings, softwood taken in late spring root readily. Actually easy to root any time the plant is in leaf.

NATIVE HABITAT: Japan and Central China. Introduced 1866.

Rhus aromatica — Fragrant Sumac

FAMILY: Anacardiaceae

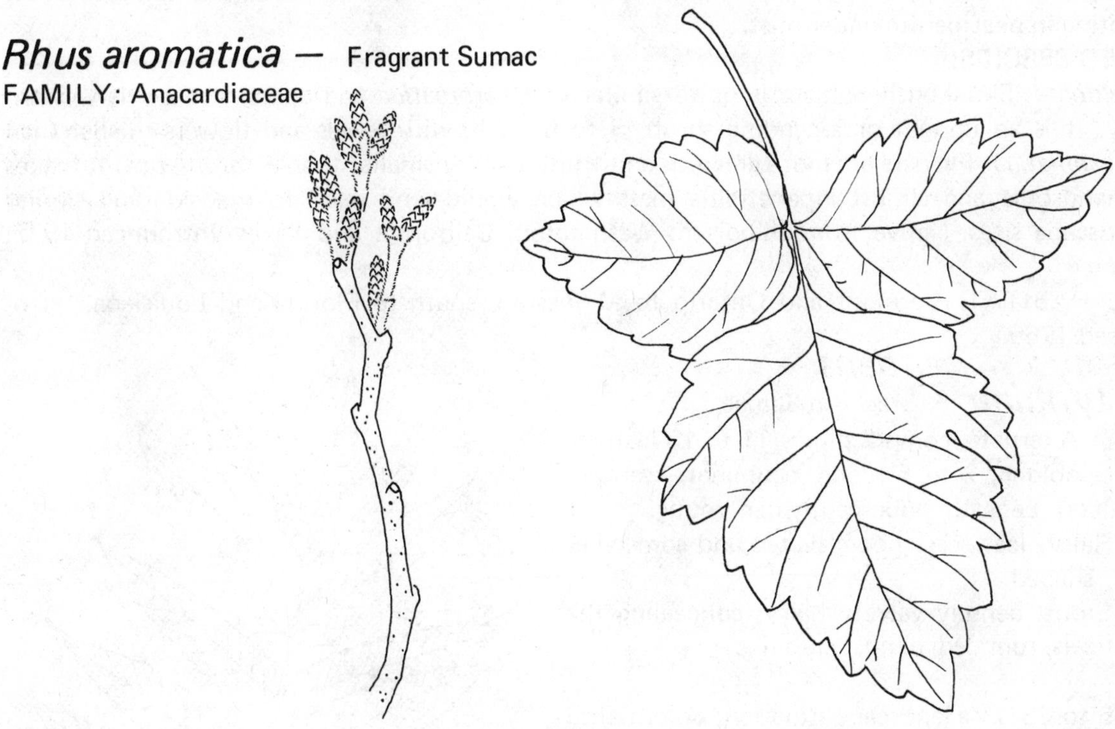

LEAVES: Alternate, trifoliate, subsessile, ovate, 1 2/5 to 3" long, acute or acuminate, crenate-serrate, pubescent, the terminal leaflet cuneate and often obovate, the lateral ones oblique and rounded at the base.

BUDS: Small, yellow, pubescent, covered by leaf scar.

STEM: Slender, pubescent, aromatically fragrant when bruised, leaf scars circular, distinctly raised.

SIZE: 2 to 6', possibly larger, with a spread of 6 to 10', extremely variable in size over its native range.

HARDINESS: Zone 3.

HABIT: Low, irregular spreading shrub with lower branches turning up at the tips. Tends to sucker from the roots and produce a dense, tangled mass of stems and leaves.

RATE: Slow to medium.

TEXTURE: Medium in leaf, medium-coarse in winter habit.

LEAF COLOR: Medium green, almost blue-green effect, often glossy on the upper surface. Fall color orange to red to reddish purple, coloring best on light soils.

FLOWERS: Polygamous or dioecious, yellowish, mid to late March, borne in approximately 1" catkins (male) or short panicles at ends of branches (female). Male catkin persistent and exposed through late summer, fall and winter.

FRUIT: Red (female plants only), August-September and briefly persisting, hairy drupe, 1/4" diameter.

CULTURE: Fibrous root system, easily transplanted, adaptable, withstands 1/2 to 3/4 shade or full sun.

DISEASES AND INSECTS: None serious although various wilts, leaf spots, rusts, aphids, mites, and scales have been noted.

LANDSCAPE VALUE: Excellent fast cover for banks, cuts and fills, massing, facing, could be used as ground cover especially the following cultivars. This plant has the ability to develop roots as the stems touch the soil and is therefore useful for stabilizing banks or slightly sloping areas.

CULTIVARS:

'Green Globe' — Grows to 6', forms a rounded, dense shrub.

'Gro-low' — Low, wide-spreading habit, excellent glossy foliage, 2 to 4' high.

PROPAGATION: Seed, (H_2SO_4), 60 minutes or softwood cuttings, July, 1000 ppm IBA gave 100% rooting in peat:perlite under mist.

RELATED SPECIES:

Rhus trilobata, Skunkbush Sumac, is quite similar to *R. aromatica* and appears to be its western ally. It is an upright or ascending shrub, 3 to 6' high, with leaves and flowers smaller than *R. aromatica*. Flowers are more greenish and fruits slightly smaller than *R. aromatica*. It makes a handsome and almost inpenetrable mass which would lend itself to roadside and similar landscape sites. Native from Illinois to Washington, California and Texas. Introduced 1877. Zone 4.

NATIVE HABITAT: Vermont and Ontario to Minnesota, south to Florida and Louisiana. Introduced 1759.

Rhus typhina — Staghorn Sumac

LEAVES: Alternate, compd. pinn., 11 to 13 leaflets, lance-oblong, 2 to 5" long, acuminate, serrate, glaucous beneath, pubescent when young.

BUDS: Hairy, leaf scars not elevated and somewhat "C" shaped.

STEM: Stout, densely velvety hairy; concealing the lenticels, rounded; almost club-like.

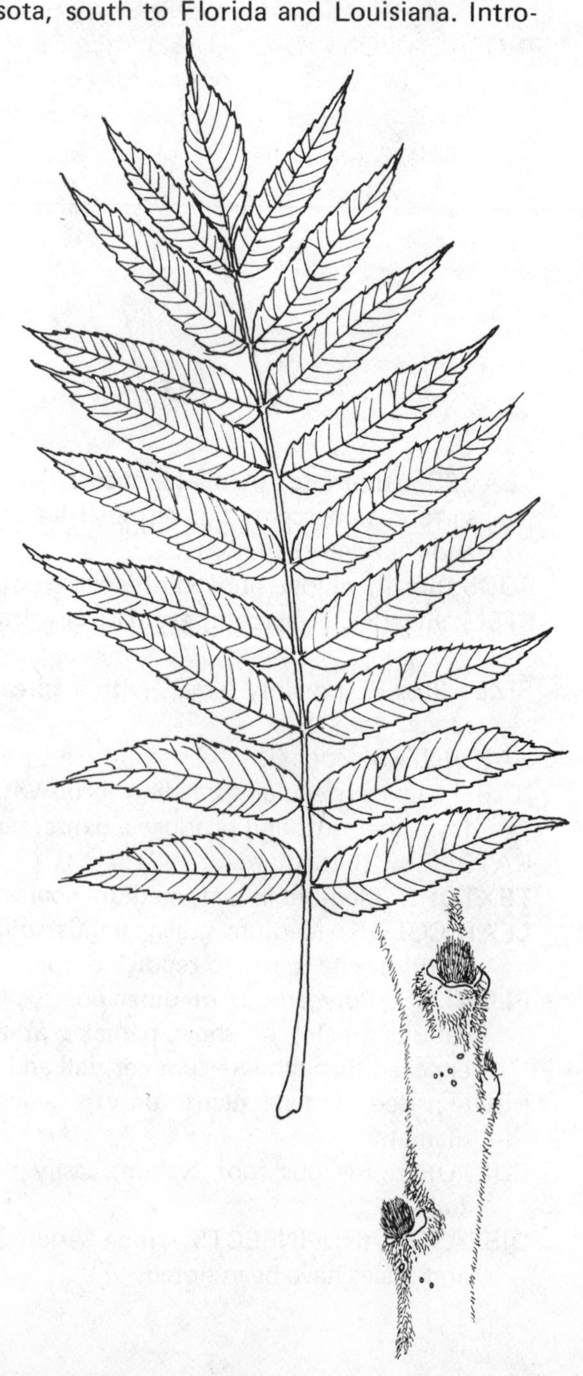

SIZE: 15 to 25' in a landscape situation; potential to 30-40' in the wild. Spread is usually equal to or greater than height.

HARDINESS: Zone 3.

HABIT: A large, loose, open, spreading shrub or a gaunt, scraggly tree with a flattish crown and rather picturesque branches resembling the horns on a male deer, hence the name Staghorn.

RATE: Fast when development occurs from root suckers. Slow to medium on old wood.

STEM: Dense, velvety pubescent persisting into 2 and 3-year-old branches.

TEXTURE: Species—medium in summer, coarse in winter. Cultivars ('Laciniata' and 'Dissecta') fine in foliage, coarse in winter.

LEAF COLOR: Dull to bright green in summer, orange and scarlet in fall.

FLOWERS: Dioecious, greenish, late June to early July, borne in dense hairy panicles, 4 to 8" long.

FRUIT: Crimson, late August through April, densely hairy drupe.

CULTURE: Easily transplanted, adapted to many soil types however prefers a well-drained soil, not a plant for poorly drained areas. Tolerates very dry, sterile soil; often seen along railroad tracks; suckers profusely and tends to form wide spreading colonies.

DISEASES AND INSECTS: Same as described under *Rhus aromatica* except *Verticillium* is often prevalent in Staghorn Sumac.

LANDSCAPE VALUE: Massing, naturalizing, waste areas, perhaps banks, cuts and fills. Actually hard to kill this plant due to its ability to sucker freely from roots. Should not be used as a specimen, foundation or container plant. Tends to be overused, especially the cutleaf forms. An interesting plant but its use should be tempered.

CULTIVARS:

'Dissecta' – Similar to 'Laciniata' but leaflets more deeply divided.

'Laciniata' – Leaflets deeply divided creating a fine-textured ferny appearance.

PROPAGATION: Seed (H_2SO_4) for 50 to 80 minutes. Cuttings, root pieces collected in December placed in moist sand:peat yielded plants in 2 months.

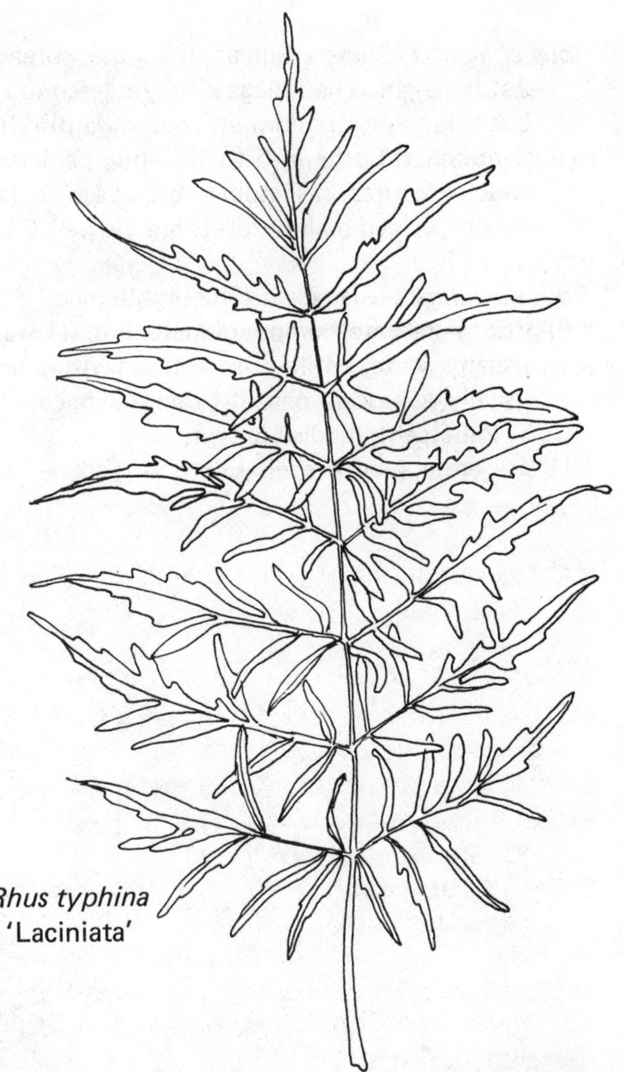

Rhus typhina 'Laciniata'

RELATED SPECIES:

Rhus chinensis – Chinese Sumac

LEAVES: Alternate, compd. pinnate, 7 to 13 leaflets, subsessile, ovate to ovate oblong, 2 to 5" long, acute or short acuminate, coarsely crenate-serrate, brownish pubescent beneath, rachis and often the petiole conspicuously winged, pubescent.

BUDS: Pubescent; almost woolly, gray-brown in color, leaf scars not elevated, "C" shaped.

STEM: Yellowish brown, glabrous to minutely pubescent, lenticels prominent.

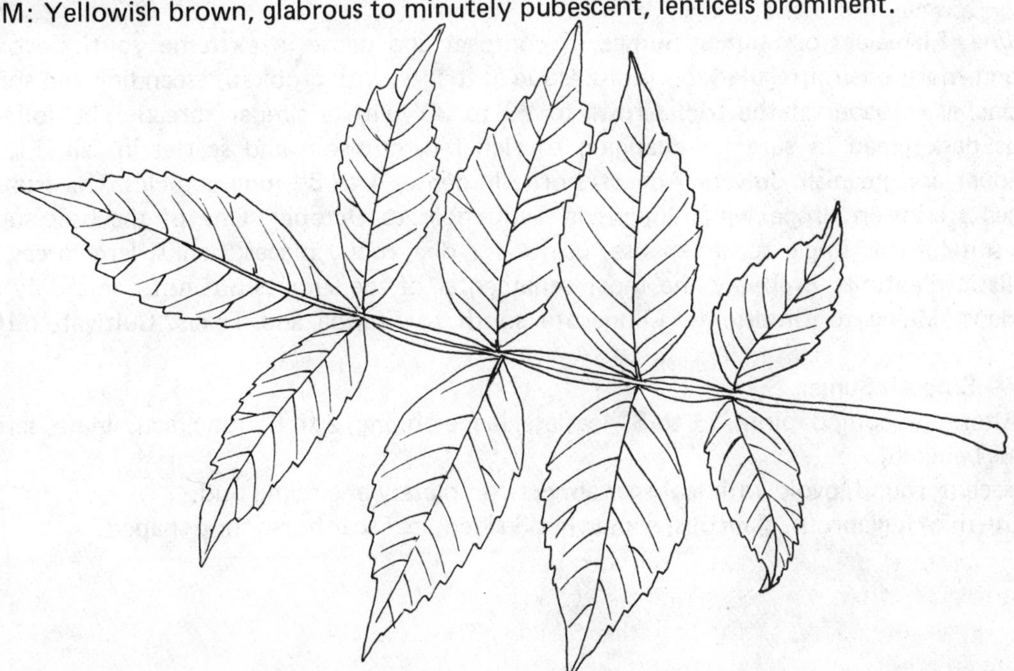

Rhus chinensis, Chinese Sumac, is a loose, spreading, suckering shrub or flat headed tree growing to 24′ in height. The foliage is bright green in summer and can change to orangish red tones in fall but this color is seldom realized in Central Illinois. The flowers are yellowish white, August into September, borne in 6 to 10″ long panicles. The fruit is a densely pubescent orange-red drupe which matures in October. Best used in large areas, naturalistic settings, possibly the shrub border; valued mainly for its late flower. China, Japan. Cultivated 1784. Zone 5.

Rhus copallina — Flameleaf (Shining) Sumac

LEAVES: Alternate, compd. pinnate, 9 to 21 leaflets, oblong-ovate to lance-ovate, 1 3/5 to 4″ long, usually acute, entire or sometimes with a few teeth near the apex, glabrous and lustrous above, usually pubescent beneath, rachis winged, pubescent.

BUDS: Pubescent, reddish brown.

STEM: Terete, reddish, puberulous, leaf scars—"U" shaped.

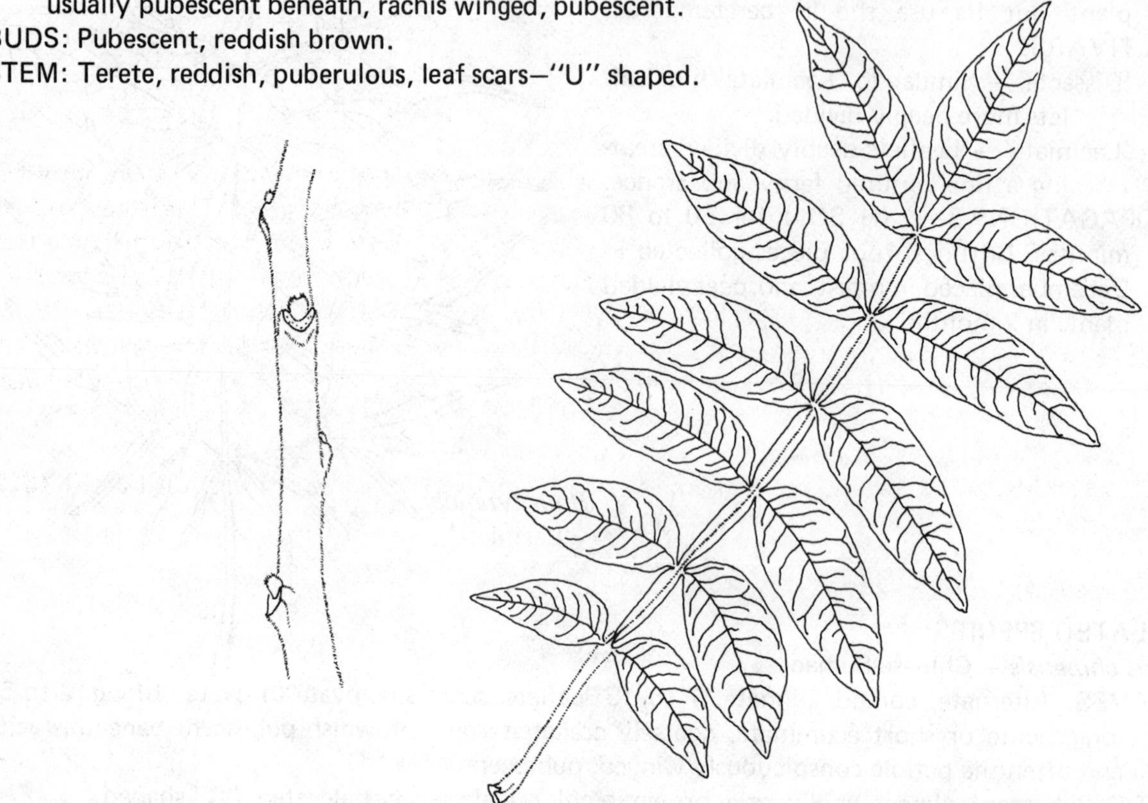

Rhus copallina, Flameleaf or Shining Sumac, is compact and dense in extreme youth becoming more and more open, irregular and picturesque as it ages, with crooked, ascending and spreading branches; broader at the top. Grows to 20 to 30′ with a similar spread. The foliage is lustrous dark green in summer changing to rich red, crimson, and scarlet in fall. Flowers (dioecious) are greenish, July to August, borne in dense, 4 to 8″ long panicles. The fruit is a pubescent, crimson drupe which ripens in September to October. One of the best sumacs and is suitable for single specimen use; useful for dry, rocky places, banks, large areas, and naturalistic plantings. Probably the most ornamental of the sumacs but not commonly seen in gardens. Maine to Ontario to Minnesota south to Florida and Texas. Cultivated 1688.

Rhus glabra — Smooth Sumac

LEAVES: Alternate, compd. pinn., 11 to 31 leaflets, lance-oblong, 2 to 5″ long, acuminate, serrate, glaucous beneath.

BUDS: Pubescent, round, ovoid with leaf scar almost completely encircling bud.

STEM: Stout (thick), glabrous, glaucous, somewhat 3-sided, leaf-scar horse-shoe shaped.

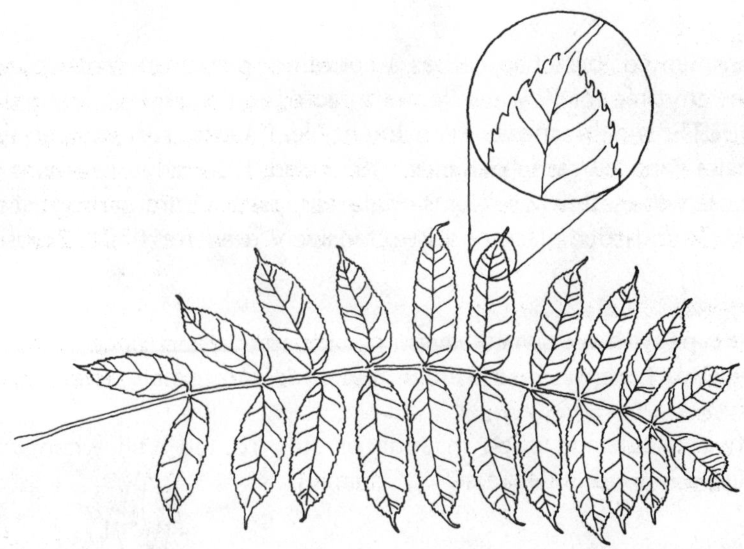

Rhus glabra, Smooth Sumac, grows 9 to 15′ high with a comparable spread. Usually grows in colonies as it suckers and develops in all directions from the mother plant. This is very evident in plantings which occur along railroad tracks and other waste areas. The foliage is medium green in summer changing to excellent orange-red-purple combinations in fall. Flowers are dioecious, greenish, July, borne in 6 to 10″ long panicles. Fruit is a scarlet, hairy drupe which persists late into winter. Good plant for mass plantings, highways, dry, poor soil areas. The cultivar 'Laciniata' has leaflets which are deeply cut and lobed. The essential difference between this species and *R. typhina* is the lack of pubescence on the young stems. Maine to British Columbia, south to Florida and Arizona. Cultivated 1620. Zone 2.

NATIVE HABITAT: Quebec to Ontario, south to Georgia, Indiana and Iowa. Cultivated 1629.

Ribes alpinum — Alpine Currant

FAMILY: Saxifragaceae

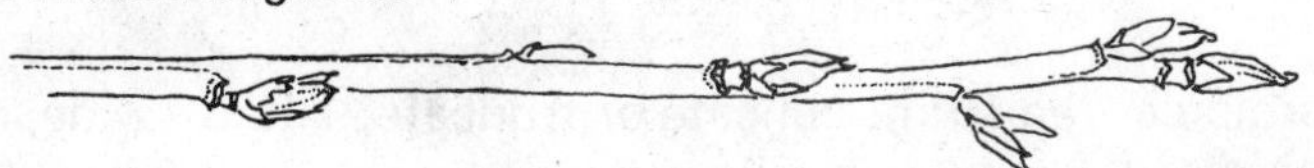

LEAVES: Alternate, simple, roundish or ovate, truncate or subcordate, 1 1/5 to 2″ across, 3- rarely 5-lobed, with obtuse or acute dentate lobes, bright green.

BUDS: Stalked, large, imbricate, distinctly gray-tan in winter.

STEM: Light to chestnut brown, often lustrous, with conspicuous ridges running down from edges of leaf scars, unarmed.

SIZE: 3 to 6′ high (15′) by twice that in spread.

HARDINESS: Zone 2.

HABIT: Densely twiggy, rounded shrub; erect in youth with stiffly upright stems and spreading branches.

RATE: Medium.

TEXTURE: Medium-fine in leaf; medium in winter.

STEM COLOR: Straw colored on young stems; old becoming deep brown and shredding.

LEAF COLOR: Deep bright green in summer; poor yellow in fall; one of the first shrubs to leaf out in spring.

FLOWERS: Polygamo-dioecious, greenish yellow, early April; borne in racemes; staminate with 20 to 30 flowers in 1 to 2″ long inflorescence; female smaller.

FRUIT: Juicy berry, scarlet, 1/4 to 1/3″ diameter; June-July; attractive but seldom seen in cultivation as male clones seem to dominate.

CULTURE: Easily transplanted, best handled as a container plant; tolerant of any good soil; full sun or shade; prune anytime for flowers are not a factor.

DISEASES AND INSECTS: Anthracnose, cane blight, leaf spots, rust, currant aphid, imported currant worm, scales, and currant bud mite. 1973 and 1974 were very wet seasons and leaf spot and anthracnose were serious problems. Male supposedly immune to rust diseases.

LANDSCAPE VALUE: Good hedge plant and is extensively used for that purpose, mass, good in semi-shady areas.

CULTIVARS:

'Aureum' – Dwarf type with yellowish leaves.

'Green Mound' – Dwarf, dense, 2 to 3' high and wide form; male; shows good resistance to leaf diseases.

PROPAGATION: Softwood cuttings taken in June or July rooted well when treated with IBA, 1000 ppm, and placed in sand under mist.

RELATED SPECIES:

Ribes odoratum – Clove Currant

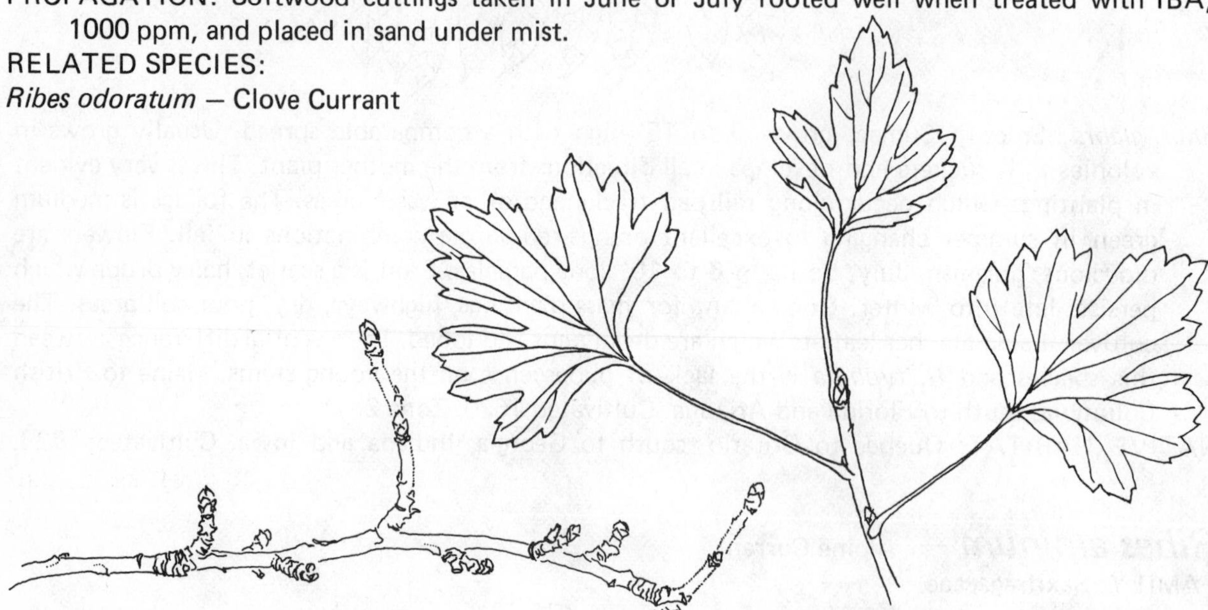

LEAVES: Alternate, simple, ovate or orbicular-reniform, cuneate or truncate, 1 to 3" wide, deeply 3-5 lobed, with coarsely dentate lobes, glabrate or puberulous beneath.

STEM: Pubescent, grayish brown.

Ribes odoratum, Clove Currant, grows 6 to 8' and is an irregular shrub of ascending, arching stems, usually surrounded by a mass of young suckering growth, loose and open with age. It is not the neatest shrub and selection for dwarf attributes would be worthwhile. Foliage is bright green in summer; briefly yellowish just before dropping in fall (could have reddish tones). Flowers (dioecious) are yellow, fragrant, odor of cloves; early to mid-April; borne in 5- to 10-flowered, usually nodding racemes. Fruit is a black berry, 1/3" across, June or July. Good shrub for the border or where early spring odor is desired. It is an alternate host for White Pine Blister Rust (*Cronartium ribicola*). South Dakota to Western Texas, east to Minnesota and Arkansas. Zone 4.

NATIVE HABITAT: Europe. Cultivated 1588.

Robinia pseudoacacia — Black Locust, also Common Locust, Yellow or White Locust

FAMILY: Leguminosae

LEAVES: Alternate, pinnately compound, 6 to 14" long, 7 to 19 leaflets, elliptic or ovate, 1 to 2" long, entire, rounded or truncate and mucronate at apex, dark bluish green, glabrous beneath or slightly pubescent when young.

BUD: Terminal—absent, laterals—minute, rusty-downy, 3 to 4 superposed, generally close together.

STEM: Slender, brittle, often zigzag, light reddish to greenish brown, smooth or nearly so, more or less angled with decurrent ridges from base and outer angles of leaf scars, generally spiny with paired stipular prickles at nodes, about 1/2" long.

SIZE: Would average 30 to 50' in height with a spread of 20 to 35' although can grow 70 to 80' high.

HARDINESS: Zone 3.

HABIT: Often an upright tree with a straight trunk and a narrow oblong crown and becoming ragged and scraggly with age; will develop thickets as it freely seeds, and develops shoots from roots; some forms are spreading in habit with several trunks.

RATE: Fast, will average 2' or greater per year over a 10 year period.

BARK: Reddish brown to almost black, deeply furrowed into rounded, interlacing, fibrous, superficialy scaly ridges.

LEAF COLOR: Dull, dark blue-green above; very strongly contrasting with the light and dark green of other trees; leaves fall early or show a slight yellow-green in fall.

FLOWERS: Perfect, 1" across, extremely fragrant, borne in dense racemes 4 to 8" long in late May to early June, flowers at a young age, effective for 7 to 10 days.

FRUIT: Pod, flat, brown-black, 2 to 4" wide, maturing in October and persisting for a time.

CULTURE: Transplants very easily, extremely adaptable to varied soils and climates; will grow in about any soil except those that are permanently wet; reaches maximum development on moist, rich, loamy soils or those of limestone origin; tolerant of dry conditions and saline environments; will grow on sandy, sterile soils; has the ability to fix atmospheric nitrogen and in this way partially creates its own nitrogen supply. This is true for many legumes as well as alders, bayberry, sweetfern and others. Prune in late summer or fall for locusts "bleed" in spring.

DISEASES AND INSECTS: Canker, dampening-off, leaf spots, powdery mildews, wood decay, witches' broom, locust borer, carpenterworm, locust leaf miner, locust twig borer, and scales. The most destructive pest is the locust borer which can riddle whole trees or whole plantations. The wood is extremely hard and durable yet this borer can destroy it like balsa wood. Tree vigor is the important factor, for fast-growing trees exhibit the greatest resistance.

LANDSCAPE VALUE: An "alley cat" type tree which can survive under the toughest of conditions. Good for stripped-mined areas; highway cuts and fills; sandy, poor soils; shelter plantations and afforestation purposes; not recommended for the home landscape, but definitely has a place in difficult areas. The flowers are exceedingly fragrant from which bees produce a delicious honey.

CULTIVARS:

'Aurea' — New leaves emerge yellow and the color persists for a time but eventually yields to the normal blue-green.

'Bessoniana' — Somewhat similar to 'Umbraculifera' but less dense.

'Decaisneana' — Flowers are light rose in color.

var. *dependens* — Possesses pendulous branches.

'Erecta' — A columnar form; if one looks at enough seedling populations he/she could select erect types with little difficulty.

'Purple Robe' — A form which looks similar to R. 'Idaho'. The flowers are a rose-pink, slightly fragrant, and occur in late May to early June. Interesting for flower color.

'Semperflorens' — Flowering throughout the summer.

'Umbraculifera' — Forms a dense umbrella-like canopy 20' high and 20' wide but bears few or no flowers; susceptible to borers and ice.

PROPAGATION: Seed dormancy is caused by an impermeable seed coat and seeds should be scarified in sulfuric acid, soaked in hot water or mechanically scarified. Root cuttings 1/4 to 1" diameter, and 3 to 8" long gave 25% plants; the younger the tree and roots the better.

RELATED SPECIES AND CULTIVARS:

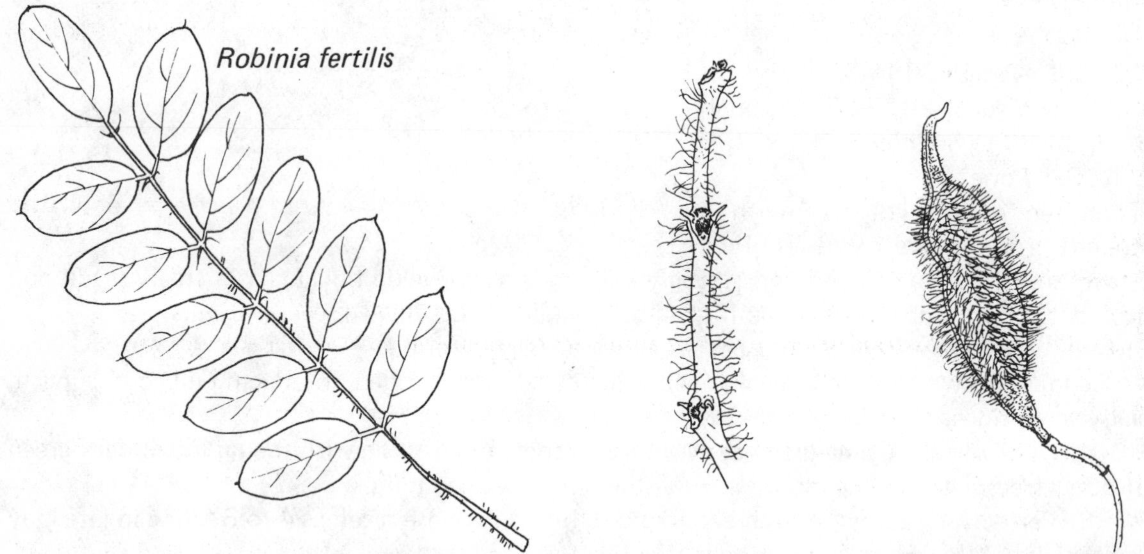

Robinia fertilis, no common name, and *R. hispida*, Bristly or Roseacacia Locust, are closely related species. *Robinia fertilis* sets fruits and seeds while *R. hispida* does not or only sparingly so. Most of my observations lead me to believe we are looking at *R. fertilis* and not the Bristly Locust. Both are small, spreading, suckering shrubs in the 6 to 10' category with prominent hispid petioles and branches; the foliage is a blue-green and the flowers rose colored or pale purple, scentless; borne in 2 to 4" long pendulous, hispid racemes; usually quite showy; their cultural requirements are similar to *R. pseudocacia*; both are good plants for stabilizing sandy banks and sterile, dry, impoverished soils. *R. hispida* is native from Virginia and Kentucky to Georgia and Alabama. Introduced 1758. Zone 5, while *R. fertilis* ranges from North Carolina to Georgia. Cultivated 1900. Zone 5.

Robinia 'Idaho', Idaho Locust, will grow 25 to 40' with a spread of 15 to 30', tends to be more open than *R. pseudocacia* in habit; flowers are dark purplish red, 1" long, borne in 6 to 8" pendent racemes in late May to early June; the parentage is unknown but presumably *R. pseudocacia* is one of the parents; very popular in semiarid parts of the west that suffer extremes of heat and cold (Zone 3 and 4); supposedly meets the stringent requirements for street tree use; medium in growth rate.

NATIVE HABITAT: Pennsylvania to Georgia, west to Iowa, Missouri and Oklahoma. Introduced 1635.

Rosa — Rose

The infinite number of roses available to the gardener makes it impossible to discuss the subject adequately in this book. There are many books on the subject of roses and they should be consulted for more complete information. The floribundas, grandifloras, hybrid teas, and climbers represent groups of roses which must be cuddled and coddled. The flower color range is infinite, and there are wide variations in foliage and habit characteristics among the above types. Several characteristics which are common include lack of winter hardiness and distinct disease susceptibility. Other roses which are termed old fashioned or species types offer a touch of class for every garden. They have, in a sense, been shoved aside for the newer, more floriferous, more fragrant, double, ever-blooming types. The following discussion applies to only the species types. An excellent article concerning rose breeding and particularly the use of the good species roses for increasing hardiness and disease resistance appeared in *HortScience* 10(6):564-567. 1975.

Rosa multiflora — Japanese Rose, also referred to as Multiflora Rose

FAMILY: Rosaceae

LEAVES: Alternate, odd-pinnate, usually 9 leaflets, 3/5 to 1 1/5" long, obovate to oblong, acute or obtuse, serrate, pubescent.

CANES: Usually with paired and occasionally scattered prickles; prickles short, recurved, more or less enlarged and flattened at base.

SIZE: 3 to 4 to 10′ in height and may spread 10 to 15′.

HARDINESS: Zone 5.

HABIT: A fountain with long, slender, recurving branches; eventually forming an impenetrable tangle of brush suitable only for burning.

RATE: Fast; too fast for most farmers who have this species in their fields.

TEXTURE: Medium in leaf; somewhat repulsive in winter (medium-coarse).

LEAF COLOR: Very lustrous bright green in summer; fall color, at best, is a sickly yellow.

FLOWERS: White, about 1" across, fragrant; June; borne in many-flowered corymbs.

FRUIT: Red, 1/4" globular to egg-shaped hip which is effective in August and into winter.

CULTURE: Same as described under *R. rugosa* although this species may be more invasive. Seems to tolerate dry, heavy soils very well.

DISEASES AND INSECTS: None serious.

LANDSCAPE VALUE: None in the residential landscape; has received a lot of attention for conservation purposes; makes a good place for all the "critters" to hide, yet can be a real nuisance, for the birds deposit the seeds in fence rows and open areas, and soon one has a jungle. Use this species with the knowledge that none of your gardening friends in the immediate vicinity will ever speak to you again.

CULTIVARS: Variety *cathayensis* has pale pink, 2/5 to 4/5" diameter flowers which are borne in few- to many-flowered rather flat corymbs. Variety *inermis* is a thornless type. I have not seen this but it would be a worthwhile addition. The prickles can be "deadly". 'Platyphylla' — Double form, flowers a deep pink. According to Wyman, it is not a very vigorous grower.

PROPAGATION: Cuttings as described under *R. rugosa*. Seed should be stratified for 120 days.

NATIVE HABITAT: Japan, Korea. Escaped from cultivation in the United States. Introduced 1868.

Rosa rugosa — Rugosa Rose, also called Saltspray Rose

FAMILY: Rosaceae

LEAVES: Alternate, odd-pinnate; leaflets 5 to 9, 4/5 to 2" long, elliptic to elliptic obovate, acute or obtusish, serrate, lustrous, rugose dark green and glabrous above, glaucescent, reticulate, and pubescent beneath, thick and firm; petioles tomentose and bristly.

CANES: Stout, densely bristly, prickly, downy.

SIZE: 4 to 6′ high by 4 to 6′ wide.

HARDINESS: Zone 2.

HABIT: A sturdy shrub with stout, upright stems, filling the ground and forming a dense mat.

RATE: Fast.

TEXTURE: Medium in leaf; medium-coarse when undressed.

LEAF COLOR: Lustrous, deep, rugose green in summer then briefly yellowish in fall.

FLOWERS: Perfect, rose-purple to white, 2 1/2 to 3 1/2" across, fragrant; June through August, often found sporadically in September and October; solitary or few in clusters.

FRUIT: Hip (for lack of better terminology), actually an urn-shaped structure which encloses achenes, about 1" across, brick-red; maturing in August through fall. The flowers and fruit are handsomely displayed against the dark green foliage.

CULTURE: Easy to grow, prefers well-drained soil which has been supplemented with organic matter; sunny and open; pH adaptable, however, a slightly acid soil is best; salt tolerant; possibly one of the most trouble-free roses. I have seen the species growing in pure sand not 100 feet from the Atlantic Ocean on Cape Cod, Mass. The plant really stands out against the white sands, the dull green beach grass, and silvery wormwood (*Artemesia*).

DISEASES AND INSECTS: Roses have about as many problems as *Prunus* and a complete listing is impossible. The most common include: black-spot (a leaf disease), powdery mildew, various cankers, rusts, virus diseases, aphids, beetles, borers, leafhopper, scales, rose-slug, thrips, mites, ad infinitum.

LANDSCAPE VALUE: Rugosa Rose is a valuable plant for difficult sites: banks, cuts, fills, sandy soils, and saline environments. Very beautiful in foliage, flower and fruit. Has escaped from cultivation in the Northeastern United States and is often apparent along the sandy shores of the ocean. It is also called Saltspray Rose because of its tolerance. Withstands pruning and is often used in hedges. Has been used in hybridization work because of its extreme vigor and ease of culture which would be worthwhile traits to impart to offspring.

CULTIVARS:

'Alba' – Single, white flowered type.

'Albo-plena' – Double, white flowered type.

'Plena' – Double, fuchsia-purple flowers.

'Rosea' – Single, rose flowers.

PROPAGATION: The seeds (actually achenes) of most species exhibit dormancy which is principally due to seedcoat conditions rather than embryo dormancy. Cold stratification at 40°F for 90 to 120 days is recommended for *R. rugosa*. Cuttings can be effective with the species roses. Hardwood cuttings should be taken from November through early March, stored in sand or peat at 35° to 40°F and planted outside in spring, with only about 1" of the upper end of the cutting protruding. Softwood cuttings should be taken in July, August, and September with all but the top leaf removed. Rose cuttings respond to IBA and Hormodin #1 or a quick-dip of 1000 ppm IBA.

ADDITIONAL NOTES: The species roses, of which *R. rugosa* is a member, are not as prone to the disease and insects as the hybrid types. They are more vigorous and less exacting as to culture. The fruits of *R. rugosa* are supposed to make the finest jelly.

NATIVE HABITAT: Northern China, Korea, Japan. Introduced 1845.

Other Species Roses

Rosa carolina — Carolina Rose

LEAVES: Alternate, pinnately compound, leaflets usually 5, rarely 7, 2/5 to 1 1/5 long, elliptic to lance-elliptic, rarely oblanceolate, acute or obtuse, sharply serrate with ascending teeth, glabrous beneath, pubescent on veins or nearly glabrous; stipules narrow; in autumn the leaves turn a dull red of varying shades.

CANES: Often covered with scattered and paired prickles and bristles when young, sometimes rather sparsely so later; prickles slender, usually not flattened except on vigorous branches, mostly straight.

HABIT: 3 to 6′, freely suckering shrub composed of erect branches forming dense thickets.

FLOWERS: Pink, single, 2 to 2 1/2″ across, solitary or 2 or 3 together; June into July. Variety *alba* has white flowers.

FRUIT: Red, 1/3″ diameter, urn- or pear-shaped, supposedly persisting into winter and maintaining good color.

NATIVE HABITAT: Maine to Wisconsin, Kansas, Texas and Florida. Introduced 1826. Zone 4. Common in low wet grounds and borders of swamps and streams.

Rosa x *harisonii* — Harrison's Yellow Rose

HABIT: Upright shrub growing 4 to 6′ high.

FLOWERS: Yellow, double, about 2″ diameter, borne over a two week period in early June; very dependable flowering shrub; has a somewhat unpleasant odor.

FRUIT: Nearly black, small, not ornamentally effective.

ADDITIONAL NOTES: The specific epithet is often spelled *harrisoni*. Zone 5.

Rosa hugonis — Father Hugo Rose

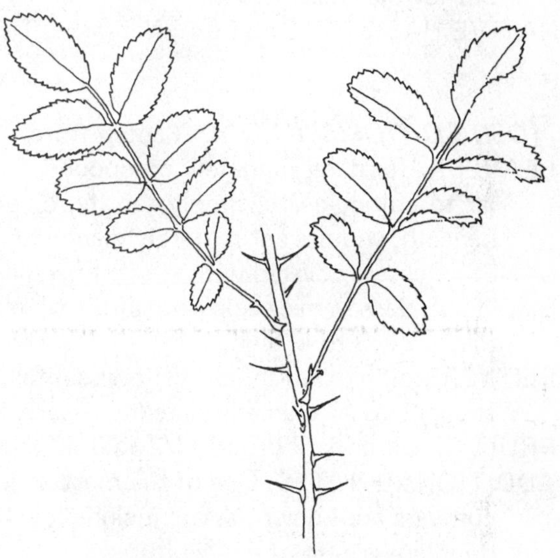

LEAVES: Alternate, pinnately compound, 5 to 13 leaflets, 3/10 to 4/5″ long, oval to obovate or elliptic, obtuse, sometimes acutish, finely serrate, glabrous, or slightly villose on the veins when unfolding.

CANES: Often reddish, with scattered prickles, usually also bristly at least at base of non-flowering young growth; prickles stout, straight, flattened, often red.

HABIT: Medium sized (6 to 8′) shrub with upright, arching canes and a twiggy rounded habit; often broader than high.

FLOWERS: Single, canary yellow, 2 to 2 1/2″ diameter, solitary; May-June.

FRUIT: Scarlet turning blackish red, nearly globular, about 1/2″ across, ripening in August.

ADDITIONAL NOTES: One of the more common species roses; often found in older gardens. Good, free flowering, bright yellow shrub. Looks a little ragged when not in flower.

NATIVE HABITAT: Central China. Introduced 1899. Zone 5.

Rosa omeiensis — Omei Rose

LEAVES: Alternate, pinnately compound, usually 5 to 9 leaflets, 2/5 to 1 2/5″ long, oblong or elliptic-oblong, acutish, cuneate, serrate, glabrous, puberulous on midrib beneath; petioles puberulous and prickly.

HABIT: Large spreading shrub with rich green, finely divided leaflets which give the plant a fern-like appearance. Can grow 10 to 15′ high and as wide.

FLOWERS: White, single, 1 to 1 1/2″ across, June, not overwhelmingly effective.

FRUIT: Pear-shaped, 1/3 to 3/5″ long, glossy orange-red; borne on yellow stalks; maturing in July-August, falling soon after maturation.

ADDITIONAL NOTES: Fruits are especially beautiful as are the large broad based, translucent ruby-red prickles which provide winter interest and make for interesting flower-arranging effects. Variety *chyrsocarpa* has yellow fruits. Variety *pteracantha* has much enlarged prickles often forming wide wings along the stem, reddish.

NATIVE HABITAT: Western China. Introduced 1901. Zone 4.

Rosa setigera — Prairie Rose, also called Michigan Rose or Climbing Rose

LEAVES: Alternate, pinnately compound, leaflets 3, rarely 5, 1 1/5 to 3 1/2" long, ovate to oblong-ovate, short-acuminate, serrate, pubescent on veins beneath. Lustrous dark green in summer; fall colors often a combination of bronze-purple, red, pink, orange and yellow.

CANES: With scattered or paired prickles; prickles strong, usually recurved, enlarged and flattened at base; stems, petioles and peduncles often glandular-pubescent. Stems green or reddish, often dark purple with a bloom.

HABIT: A wide spreading shrub with arching and spreading canes which may extend 15' in a single season. May grow to 15' but usually shorter; when climbing over flat ground grows 3 to 4' in height.

FLOWERS: Deep pink fading to white, nearly scentless, single, about 2" across; borne in few-flowered corymbs in late June through early July.

FRUIT: Red, globular, 1/3" diameter, maturing in fall.

ADDITIONAL NOTES: One of the latest flowering species roses; quite hardy (Zone 4) and has been used in breeding work; might be a good plant for difficult areas along highways; definitely not for the small garden.

NATIVE HABITAT: Ontario to Nebraska, Texas and Florida. Introduced 1810.

Rosa spinosissima — Scotch Rose

LEAVES: Alternate, pinnately compound, 5 to 11 leaflets, usually 7 to 9, 2/5 to 4/5" long, orbicular to oblong-ovate, simply serrate, or doubly glandular-serrate, glabrous, sometimes glandular beneath; stipules entire, rarely glandular-dentate.

CANES: Densely covered with straight needle-like bristles and prickles.

HABIT: A dense, free-suckering shrub of mound-like, symmetrical habit, often forming thickets; may grow 3 to 4' high.

FLOWERS: Pink, white, or yellow; solitary, single, but numerous on short branches along the stems, 1 to 2" diameter; late May—early June.

FRUIT: Black or dark brown, 1/2 to 3/4" diameter; effective in September.

ADDITIONAL NOTES: One of the most widely distributed rose species; very variable and numerous cultivars are known; assets include low habit, profuse flowering, variation in flower color, size, doubleness; also of easy culture.

NATIVE HABITAT: Europe, Western Asia, naturalized in Northeastern United States. Cultivated before 1600. Zone 4.

Rosa virginiana — Virginia Rose

LEAVES: Alternate, pinnately compound, 7 to 9 leaflets, 4/5 to 2 2/5" long, usually acute at ends, serrate with ascending teeth; upper stipules dilated.

CANES: Reddish, with mainly paired prickles, sometimes variously prickly; prickles thick based, flattened, straight or often hooked.

HABIT: A low to medium-sized shrub which often forms a dense mass of erect stems. Will grow to 6' in height.

FLOWERS: Pink, single, solitary or 2 to 3 together, 2 to 2 1/2" across; June.

FRUIT: Red, about 1/2" diameter, ripening late and persistent through winter.

ADDITIONAL NOTES: One of the more handsome native roses. The summer foliage is excellent glossy dark green and changes to first purple then to orange-red, crimson and yellow in autumn. The fruits are a bright glistening red and persist into winter. The canes are reddish with many paired prickles and are attractive in winter. Can be used as an effective barrier or low hedge, and when it has overstepped boundaries it can be cut to the ground and will develop quickly to excellent form; excellent in sandy soils, particularly by the sea.

NATIVE HABITAT: Newfoundland to Virginia, Alabama and Missouri. Introduced before 1807. Zone 3.

Rosa wichuriana — Memorial Rose

LEAVES: Alternate, pinnately compound, 7 to 9 leaflets, 2/5 to 1" long, suborbicular to broad-ovate or obovate, usually obtuse, coarsely serrate, lustrous above and beneath, glabrous, stipules dentate; lustrous dark green.

CANES: With scattered prickles; prickles sparse, strong, and recurved.

HABIT: A procumbent shrub, of semi-evergreen nature, with long green canes trailing over the ground and rooting; will climb if supported. Probably stays in the 8 to 16' category from a height aspect.

FLOWERS: Pure white, fragrant, single, about 2" across, borne in few- to many-flowered pyramidal corymbs in June and July.

FRUIT: Red, about 1/2" long, egg-shaped; maturing in September-October.

ADDITIONAL NOTES: This species makes an excellent ground cover. I have seen it used on highway slopes where it does an excellent job of holding the soil as well as adding a touch of beauty. Has been used in breeding work and is a parent of many of the modern climbers. Good plant because of its ease of culture and freedom from insects and diseases.

NATIVE HABITAT: Japan, Korea, Taiwan, Eastern China. Introduced into North America by the Arnold Arboretum. Zone 5.

Salix alba — White Willow

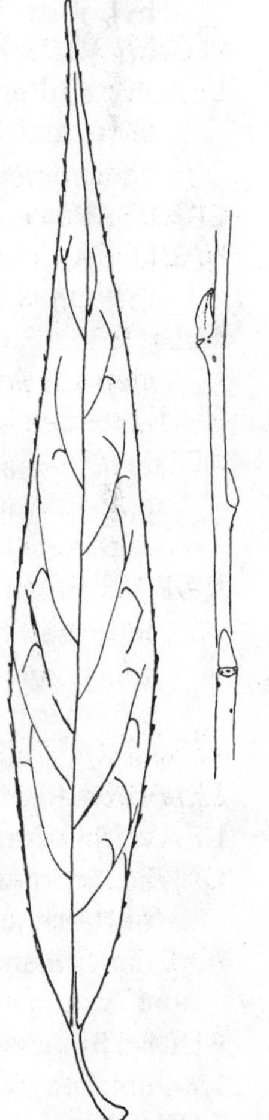

FAMILY: Salicaceae

LEAVES: Alternate, simple, lanceolate, 1 1/2 to 4" long, acuminate, cuneate, serrulate, glaucous and silky beneath; petiole 1/4 to 1/2" long, with small glands; stipules—lanceolate.

BUDS: Terminal—absent, laterals about 1/5" long, oblong, rounded at apex, smooth, more or less silky-downy, flattened and appressed against stem. A single bud scale visible, rounded on back, flattened toward the twig.

STEM: Rather slender, light yellow-green, smooth and shining or dull with more or less dense covering of fine silky hairs, bitter to taste.

SIZE: 75 to 100' in height with a spread of 50 to 100'.

HARDINESS: Zone 2.

HABIT: Large, low branching tree with long branches and flexible stems forming a broad, open, round topped crown.

RATE: Extremely fast, 3 to 4'/year over a 20 year period.

TEXTURE: Fine in leaf, medium in winter.

BARK: Yellowish brown to brown, somewhat corky, ridged and furrowed; I saw a beautiful specimen at Smith College Botanic Garden, Northampton, Mass., with a distinctly corky-textured bark.

LEAF COLOR: Bright green above, glaucous green beneath (silvery) in summer; fall color is negligible. Willows are one of the first plants to leaf out in spring and the last to drop their leaves in the fall.

FLOWERS: Dioecious, entomophilous and also anemophilous; male and female borne in upright catkins; the males are quite showy and represent the "Pussy" willow character which is familiar to everyone.

FRUIT: Two-valved capsule containing a number of cottony or silky hairy seeds.

CULTURE: Easily transplanted because of fibrous, spreading, suckering root system; prefer moist soils and are frequently found along streams, ponds, rivers and other moist areas; full sun, pH adaptable but apparently do not like shallow, chalky soils; prune in summer or fall.

DISEASES AND INSECTS: Willows like poplars are afflicted by numerous problems such as bacterial twig blight, crown gall, leaf blight, black canker, cytospora canker, many other cankers, gray scab, leaf spots, powdery mildew, rust, tar spot, aphids, imported willow leaf beetle, pine cone gall, basket willow gall, willow lace bug, willow flea weevil, mottled willow borer, poplar borer, willow shoot sawfly, willow scurfy scale and other selected insects.

LANDSCAPE VALUE: One of the best upright willows for landscape use; good for moist, wet places where little else will grow; wood is actually tougher than *Populus* but still very susceptible to ice and wind storms; tends to be a dirty street tree as do all willows because leaves, twigs, branches and the like are constantly dropping throughout the season.

CULTIVARS:

'Chermesina' — Stems bright red.

'Sericea' — Form with whitish leaves, often listed as var. *sericea*.

'Tristis' — Called the Golden Weeping Willow and certainly one of the hardiest and most beautiful of the weeping types; sometimes listed as *S. vitellina pendula* in the trade and also as *S. alba* 'Niobe'.

'Vitellina' — Has bright yellow stems.

PROPAGATION: Seeds have no dormancy and germinate within 12 to 24 hours after falling on moist or wet sand. There is no dormancy known in any species. All willows are easily propagated by soft or hardwood cuttings at anytime of the year. Just collect the cuttings and stick them. The stems have pre-formed root initials.

RELATED SPECIES: The willows are not extensively treated in this text (or for that matter any text) for they are hopelessly confused botanically. There are about 250 species generally confined to the northern hemisphere and about 75 species grow in North America. They hybridize freely and it is often difficult to distinguish hybrids from species. The following are used in landscaping to one degree or another but are not enthusiastically recommended by this author.

Salix babylonica — Babylon Weeping Willow

LEAVES: Alternate, simple, lanceolate to linear-lanceolate, 3 to 6" long, acuminate, cuneate, serrulate, dark green above, grayish green beneath, with distinct venation, glabrous; petiole 1/5" long, stipules rarely developed, ovate-lanceolate.

Salix babylonica, Babylon Weeping Willow, grows 30 to 40' with a comparable spread; a very graceful, refined tree with a short, stout trunk and a broad, rounded crown of weeping branches which sweep the ground; where hardy (Zone 6) should be given preference; foliage is dark green; 'Annularis' is a cultivar with spirally curled leaves. China. Introduced 1730.

Salix x *blanda*, Wisconsin Weeping Willow, is a hybrid between *S. babylonica* and *S. fragilis* with increased hardiness (Zone 4). Not as desirable as *S. babylonica* and *S.* x *elegantissima* because the branches are 1/2 as long. The term 'Niobe' has been attached to this hybrid species but whether it is a synonym is not actually known.

Salix caprea — Goat Willow

LEAVES: Alternate, simple, broad-elliptic to oblong, 2 to 4" long, acute, rarely rounded at base, irregularly and slightly toothed or nearly entire, pubescent at first, finally glabrate, rugulose and dark green above, gray-pubescent beneath and reticulate; petiole 1/3 to 2/3" long; stipules oblique—reniform, serrate.

BUDS: Stout at maturity, medium sized to large, 1/6 to 2/5" long, colored and clothed as the twigs, purplish brown.

STEM: Stout, yellowish brown to dark brown, pubescent to glabrescent.

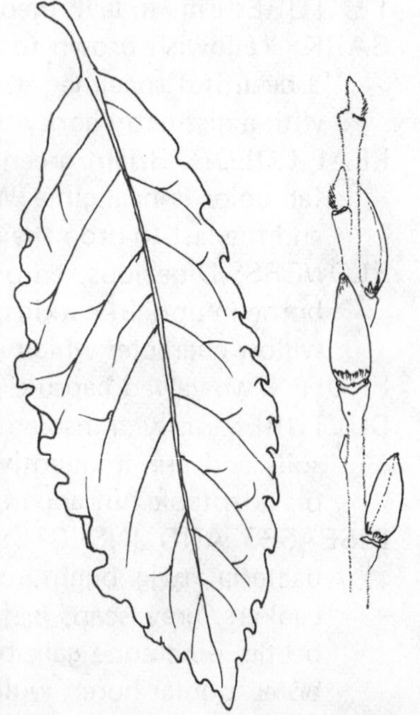

Salix caprea, Goat Willow, is a small tree growing to 15 to 25' with a 12 to 15' spread; the only asset is the large (1" long) male catkins which appear in March and early April and are affectionately referred to as Pussy Willows because of the softness of the catkins. This species is often confused with *S. discolor*, the true

Pussy Willow, which is native to wet areas over much of the eastern United States, however, *S. discolor* has smaller catkins and seems to be more susceptible to canker than *S. caprea. S. caprea* is hardy to Zone 4 and native from Europe to Northeastern Asia and Iran.

Salix x *elegantissima*, Thurlow Weeping Willow, is another hybrid probably of *S. babylonica* x *S. fragilis*. This is the best substitute for the Babylon Weeping Willow in the North (Zone 4).

Salix gracilistyla, Rosegold Pussy Willow, is allied with *S. discolor* and *S. caprea* by virtue of being grown for its showy, 1 1/4" long, male, pinkish or reddish tinged catkins. It is lower growing (6 to 10') than the other species and for this reason may be better suited to the small landscape. The leaves are grayish or bluish gray and offer a foliage contrast not available from the other species. Japan, Korea. Cultivated 1900. Zone 5.

Salix matsudana 'Tortuosa', Corkscrew Hankow Willow, is a tree to 30' in height with upright spreading, contorted and twisted branches. A rather sickening sight in any landscape but unfortunately widely sold and bought. An oddity with little to recommend it. China, Korea. Introduced 1923. Zone 4.

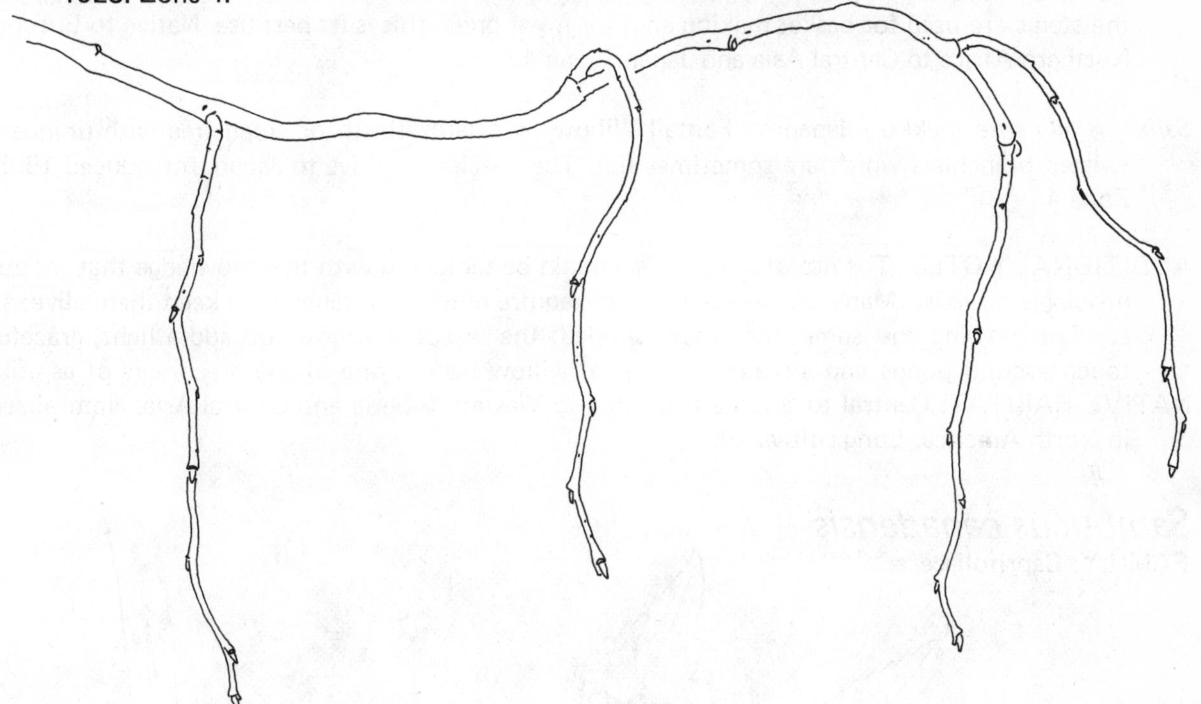

Salix pentandra — Laurel Willow

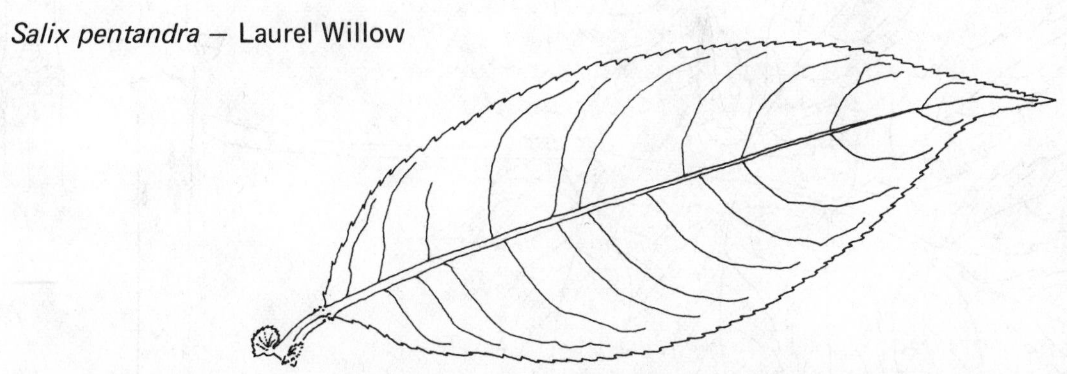

LEAVES: Alternate, simple, elliptic to ovate to elliptic-lanceolate, 1 3/5 to 5" long, short-acuminate, rounded or subcordate at base, glandular-denticulate, lustrous dark green above, lighter beneath, midrib yellow; petiole 1/4 to 2/5" long, glandular; stipules oblong-ovate, often small.

Salix pentandra, Laurel Willow, has the most handsome foliage of all the willows. The leaves are a lustrous, polished, shimmering dark green in summer; grows to 60′ but usually much less with an oval compact form. The few I have seen in Central Illinois were so infested with leaf disease that by August there were no leaves on the tree. Where leaf diseases do not present a problem it could be an interesting specimen. Native to Europe. Zone 4.

Salix purpurea — Purpleosier Willow

LEAVES: Alternate or opposite, simple, oblanceolate, rarely oblong-obovate, often opposite, 2 to 4″ long, acute or acuminate, cuneate, serrulate toward the apex, dull green above, pale or glaucous beneath, glabrous or slightly pubescent at first, turning black in drying; petiole 1/6 to 1/3″ long; stipules small or wanting.

BUDS: Frequently opposite, remarkable for being opposite or subopposite, glabrous.

STEM: Slender tough branches, purplish at first, light gray or olive gray, glabrous.

Salix purpurea, Purpleosier Willow, is a rounded, dense, finely branched shrub 8 to 10′ tall; the cultivar 'Nana' is a smaller growing type; the specimens on our campus are horrendous looking and without ornamental appeal; possibly for wet areas but avoid it unless absolutely necessary; the stems are used for basket making and, for my money, this is its best use. Native to Europe, Northern Africa to Central Asia and Japan. Zone 4.

Salix sachalinense 'Sekko', Japanese Fantail Willow, is a large shrub or small tree with uniquely twisted branchlets which are sometimes flat. The species is native to Japan. Introduced 1905. Zone 4.

ADDITIONAL NOTES: The use of any willow should be tempered with the knowledge that serious problems do exist. Many are short-lived and require much maintenance to keep them alive; all are fast growing and somewhat weak wooded; the weeping willows do add a light, graceful touch around ponds and streams; extract of willow bark is one of the precursors of aspirin.

NATIVE HABITAT: Central to Southern Europe to Western Siberia and Central Asia. Naturalized in North America. Long cultivated.

Sambucus canadensis — American Elder

FAMILY: Caprifoliaceae

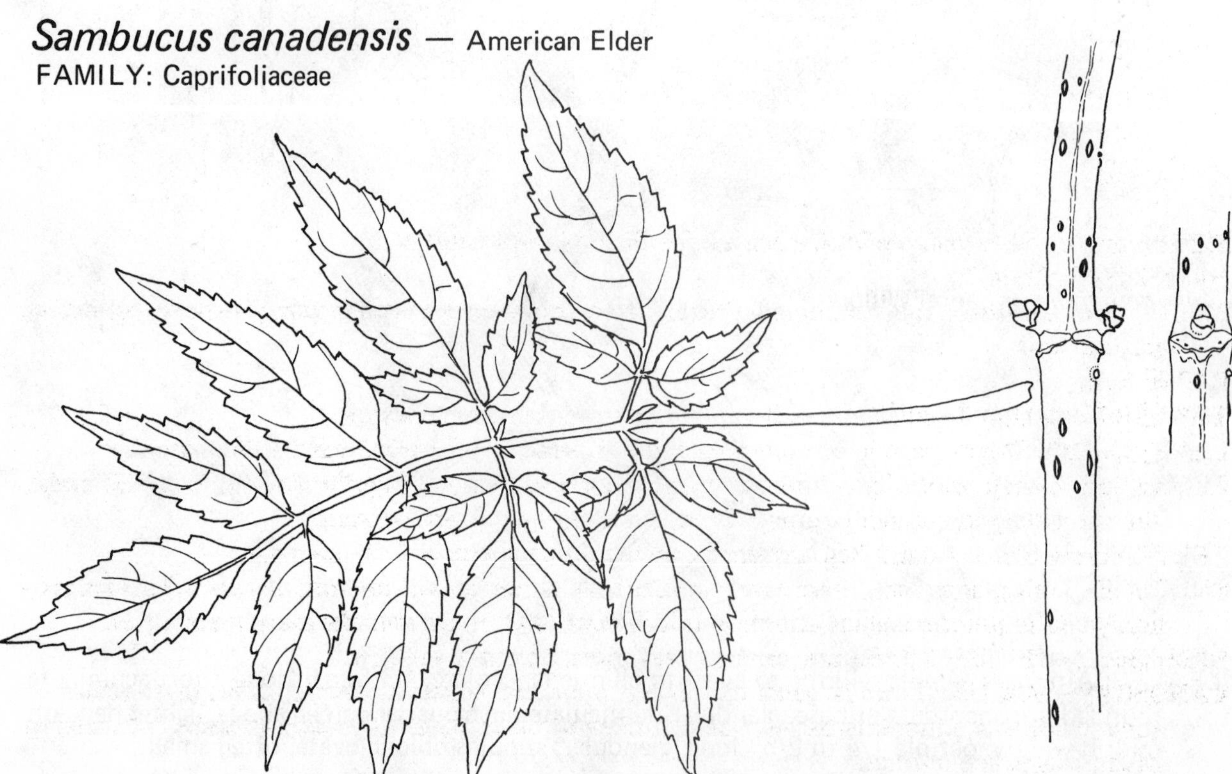

LEAVES: Opposite, compd. pinn., usually 7 leaflets, short stalked, elliptic to lanceolate, 2 to 6" long, acuminate, sharply serrate, bright green, slightly puberulous on the veins beneath or nearly glabrous.

BUDS: Solitary or multiple, terminal mostly lacking, brown, few-scaled, small, 1/8" long.

STEM: Stout, pale yellowish gray, heavily lenticellate, glabrous, pith—white. Leaf scars broadly crescent-shaped or 3- or 4-sided, large, more or less transversely connected.

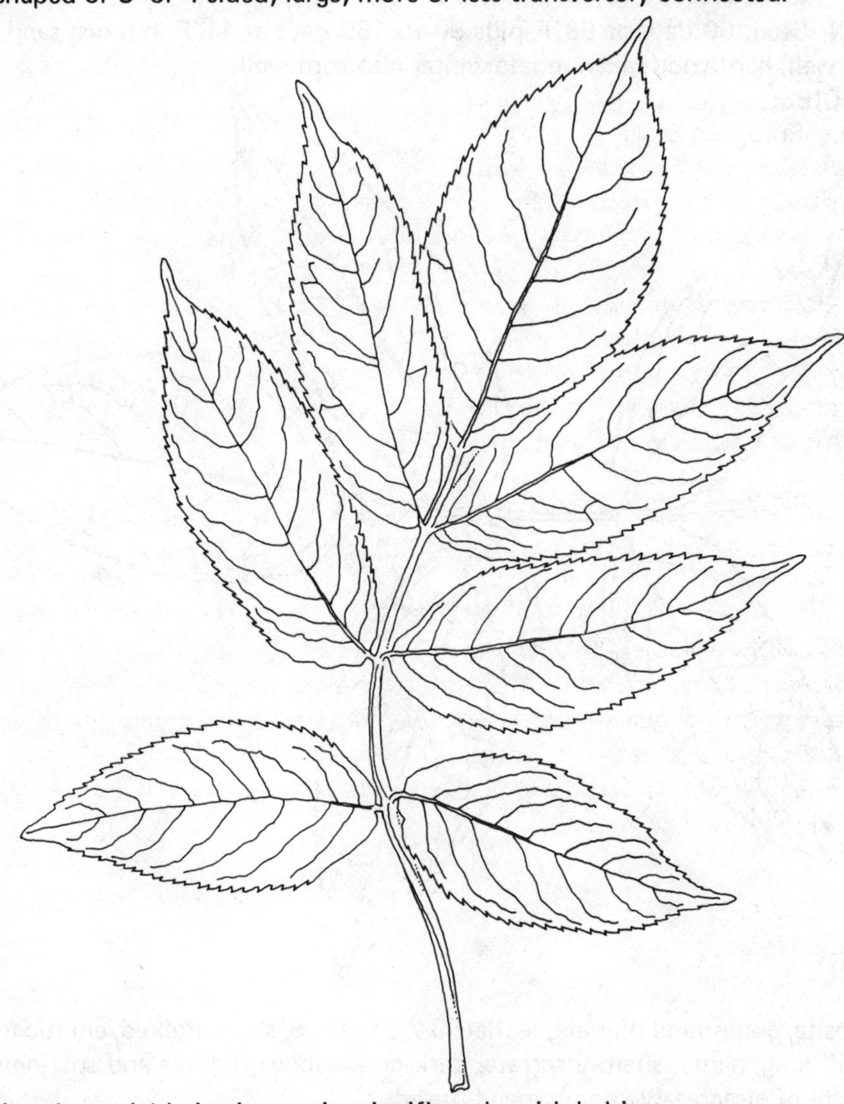

SIZE: 5 to 12', quite variable in size, varies significantly with habitat.

HARDINESS: Zone 3.

HABIT: Stoloniferous, multistemmed shrub, often broad and rounded with branches spreading and arching.

RATE: Fast.

TEXTURE: Medium in foliage (usually quite dense); very coarse in winter.

LEAF COLOR: Bright green in summer; fall color is generally an insignificant yellow-green.

FLOWERS: Perfect, white, late June-early July, borne in 5-rayed, slightly convex, 6 to 10" wide, flat topped cymes. Usually quite profuse and covering the entire plant.

FRUIT: Purple-black, August-September, berry-like drupe about 1/4" in diameter.

CULTURE: Transplants well, does best in moist soils although will tolerate dry soils. Suckers profusely and requires constant attention if it is to be kept in presentable, decent condition.

DISEASES AND INSECTS: Borers, cankers, leaf spots, powdery mildew.

LANDSCAPE VALUE: Fruit is good for jellies, wine and attracting birds, difficult to utilize in home landscape situations because of its unkempt habit. Potential near wet areas, naturalizing effect, roadside plantings.

CULTIVARS:

'Acutiloba' – Leaflets very deeply divided.

'Adams' – Numerous fruits, large clusters.

'Aurea' – Cherry red fruit, foliage yellow, grows vigorously and looks good throughout the growing season.

'Maxima' – Flower clusters 13" in diameter.

PROPAGATION: Seed, 60 days at 68°F plus 90 to 150 days at 41°F in moist sand. Cuttings, softwood root well; hardwood taken in late winter also root well.

RELATED SPECIES:

Sambucus nigra – European Elder

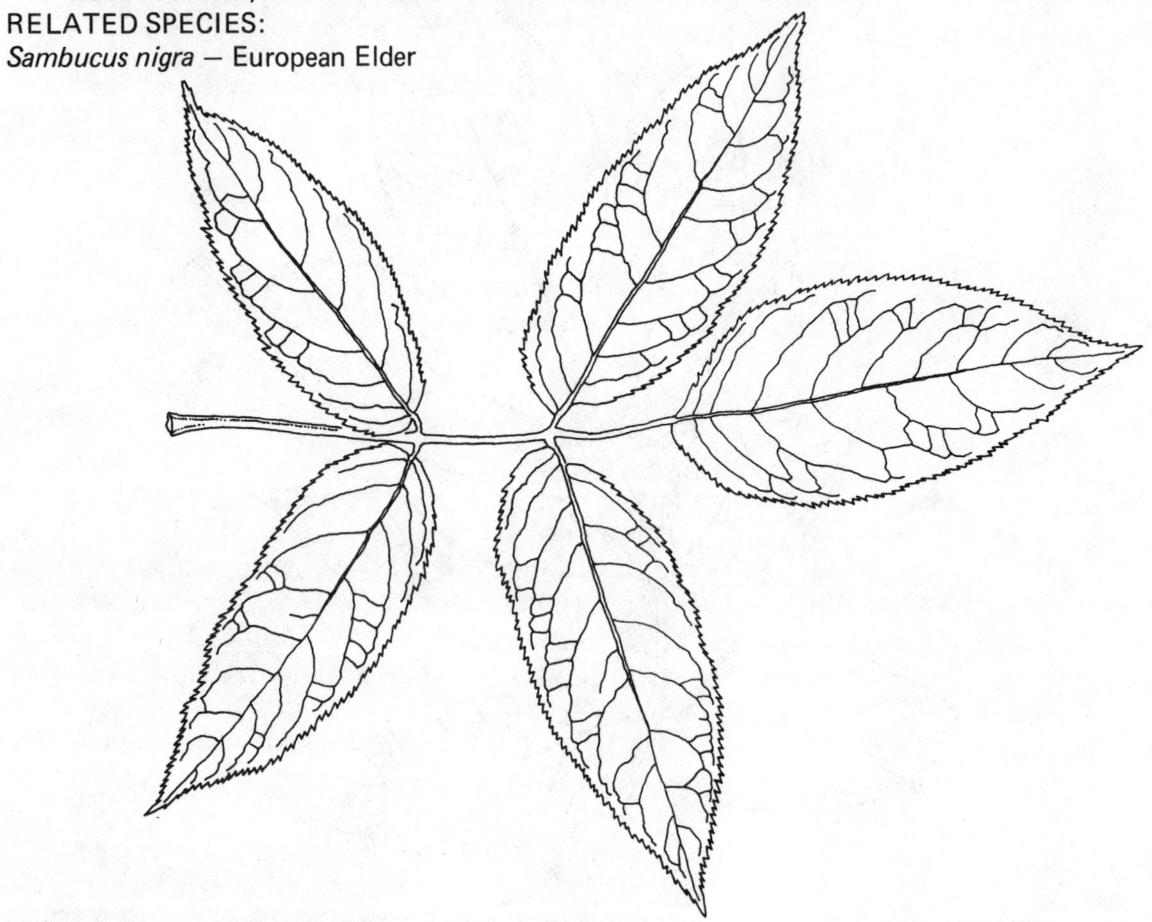

LEAVES: Opposite, compound pinnate, leaflets 3-7, usually 5, short-stalked, elliptic to elliptic-ovate, 1 3/5 to 5" long, acute, sharply serrate, dark green above, lighter and sparingly hairy on the vein beneath, of disagreeable odor when bruised.

Sambucus nigra, European Elder, grows 20 to 30' high. The foliage is dark green in summer and of a disagreeable odor when bruised. Flowers are yellowish white and borne in 5 to 8" diameter, 5-rayed, flat-topped cymes. The fruit is lustrous black. There are numerous cultivars associated with this species. Europe, Northern Africa, Western Asia. Zone 5.

Sambucus pubens, Scarlet Elder, grows 12 to 24' high with a similar spread. The flowers are yellowish white, May, borne in 5" long pyramidal panicle. The fruit is red or scarlet, drupe, 1/5 to 1/4" diameter, ripening in late June into July, quite effective. The cultivar 'Dissecta' has deeply divided leaflets. The buds are solitary, 4-scaled, brown and the stems are light brown with a brown pith. Found in rocky woods from Newfoundland to Alaska, south to Georgia and Colorado. Introduced 1812. Zone 4.

Sambucus racemosa, European Red Elder, grows to 12' and has flowers and fruits similar to *S. pubens*. Native to Europe, Western Asia. Cultivated 1596.

NATIVE HABITAT: Nova Scotia and Manitoba to Florida and Texas. Introduced 1761. Found in damp, rich soil.

Sassafras albidum — Common Sassafras

FAMILY: Lauraceae

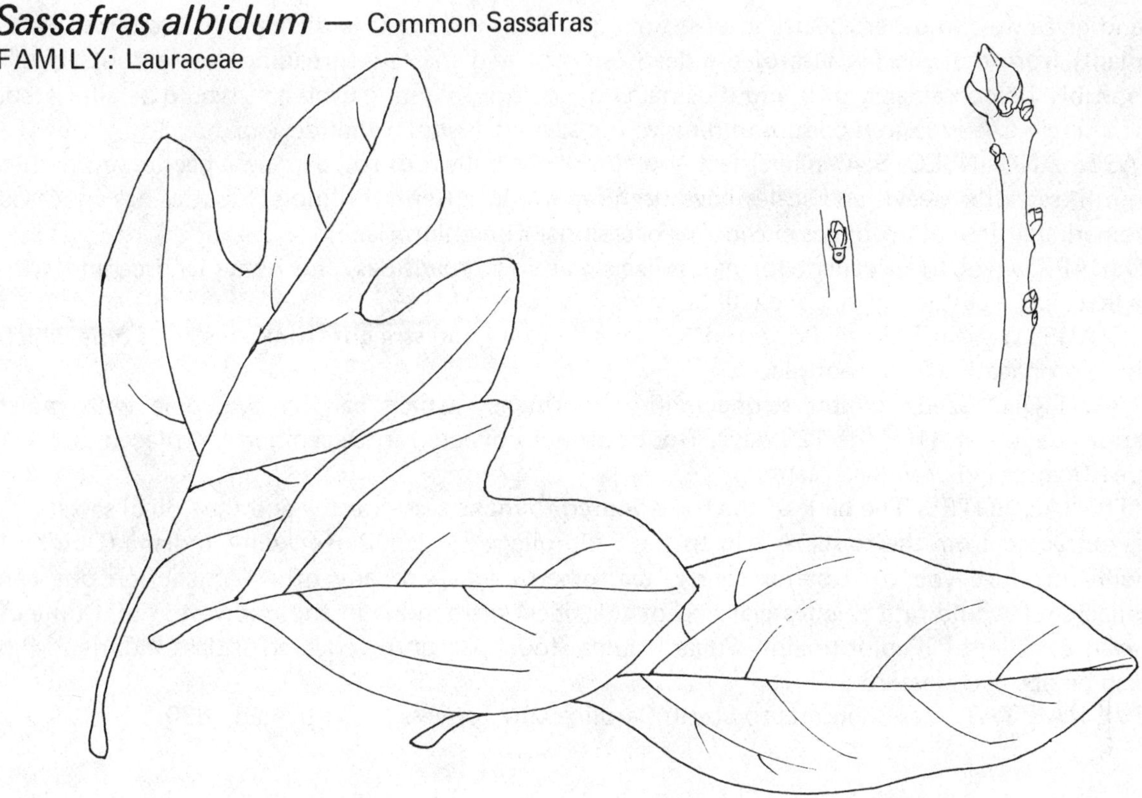

LEAVES: Alternate, simple, ovate to elliptic, 3 to 5" long, entire or 1 to 3 lobed, acutish or obtuse, cuneate at base, bright green above, glabrous and glaucous beneath; leaves are entire, mitten-shaped or three lobed.

BUDS: Solitary, ovoid, sessile, about 4 scales, green-tinged with red toward tip; lateral buds small, divergent; terminal buds large, 2/5" long.

STEM: Bright yellowish green, often reddish where exposed to light, glabrous and glaucous. Spicy-aromatic to both smell and taste. Sympodial branching.

SIZE: 30 to 60' in height with a spread of 25 to 40'.

HARDINESS: Zone 4.

HABIT: Pyramidal, irregular tree or shrub in youth; with many short, stout, contorted branches which spread abruptly to form a flat topped, irregular, round-oblong head at maturity; often sprouting from roots and forming extensive thickets.

RATE: Medium, 10 to 12' over a 5 to 8 year period.

TEXTURE: Medium in all seasons, very intriguing winter silhouette results from the sympodial branching habit.

BARK: Dark reddish brown, deeply ridged and furrowed, forming corky ridges that are easily cut across with a knife.

LEAF COLOR: Bright to medium green in summer changing to tones of yellow to deep orange to scarlet and purple in fall. One of our most outstanding native trees for fall color. A sassafras thicket in October is unrivaled.

FLOWERS: Usually dioecious, yellow, fragrant, developing before the leaves in April, borne in terminal racemes, 1 to 2" long.

FRUIT: Drupe, 1/2" long, dark blue, ripening in September but quickly falling or devoured by birds; the fruit stalk (pedicel) is scarlet and very attractive at close range; many people think the pedicel is the fruit.

CULTURE: Move balled and burlapped in early spring into moist, loamy, acid, well drained soil; full sun or light shade; in the wild often found in acid, rocky soil; has a strong tendency to invade abandoned fields and form dense thickets; as a pioneer tree it is somewhat intolerant and gives way to other species after a time; prune in winter; it is difficult to establish (transplant) from the wild because of the deep tap root and the few spreading, lateral roots; could possibly be container grown and thus many of the transplanting problems would be alleviated. If a single tree is desired be sure to remove the suckers (shoots) that develop.

DISEASES AND INSECTS: Cankers, leaf spots, mildew, wilt, root rot, Japanese beetle, promethea moth, sassafras weevil and scales have been reported. In Central Illinois Sassafras has appeared remarkably free of problems except for occasional iron chlorosis.

LANDSCAPE VALUE: Excellent for naturalized plantings, roadsides, and home landscaping; with a little extra cultural effort one will be rewarded manyfold.

CULTIVARS: William Flemer, Princeton Nurseries, has a good straight trunked, strong type which he is propagating from root pieces.

PROPAGATION: Seeds exhibit strong embryo dormancy which can be overcome with moist stratification at 41°F for 120 days. Root cuttings collected in December and placed in 2:1:1 peat:loam:sand produced plants.

ADDITIONAL NOTES: The bark of the roots is used to make sassafras tea and the "oil of sassafras" is extracted from the roots. A trip to the Fall Foliage Festival in Rockville, Indiana (October) will introduce you to sassafras candy, tea, bread and about any other concoction one can imagine. I would rate this festival one of the finest attractions in the midwest at that time of year. Excellent fall color (mainly Sugar Maples), food, pageantry, covered bridges and friendship can be observed (eaten).

NATIVE HABITAT: Massachusetts to South Carolina and Tennessee. Cultivated 1630.

Sciadopitys verticillata — Umbrella-pine or Japanese Umbrella-pine (Pinaceae)

LEAVES: Of 2 kinds, some small and scale-like scattered on the shoot, but crowded at its end and bearing in their axils a whorl of 20 to 30 linear flat leaves, furrowed on each side, more deeply beneath; dark glossy green, thick, almost prehistoric in appearance. The way the needles radiate around the stem creates an "umbrella" effect.

STEM: At first green, later brown, glabrous.

BARK: Thin, nearly smooth, gray to grayish brown, exfoliating in long strips.

SIZE: 20 to 30' by 15 to 20'; can grow to 60 to 90' high.

HARDINESS: Zone 5.

HABIT: A compact, spirelike, broadly pyramidal tree in youth, with a straight stem and horizontal branches spreading in whorls, stiff and twiggy, the young branchlets with the leaves crowded at the ends; with age the branches become more pendulous and spreading and the whole habit loose.

RATE: Slow, extremely slow, perhaps 6" a year.

TEXTURE: Medium-coarse, one of the most interesting conifers for textural effect.

LEAF COLOR: Dark green and glossy above.

FLOWERS: Monoecious; female solitary, terminal and subtended by a small bract, male flowers in dense clusters.

FRUIT: Cones oblong-ovate, compressed, narrowly winged. Cones are green at first, ripening to brown the second year.

CULTURE: Transplant balled and burlapped, prefers a rich, moist, acid soil and sunny, open locations, late afternoon shade is advantageous in hot areas; protection from wind is desirable.

DISEASES AND INSECTS: None serious.

LANDSCAPE VALUE: F. B. Robinson called it "a queer tree of odd texture; can be used as an accent or specimen." L. H. Bailey termed it "one of the most handsome and distinctive of conifers." For foliage effect as well as texture this conifer ranks among the best. Could be integrated into a foundation planting, rock garden or border.

PROPAGATION: Either warm stratification for 100 days in moist sand at 63 to 70°F or cold for 90 days in moist, acid peat at 32 to 50°F have been recommended for inducing prompt germination. A combination of the two may be more effective. Cuttings taken in January rooted 92% in sand:peat in 20 weeks after treatment with 100 ppm NAA for 24 hours. Cuttings from 7-year-old trees collected in January and treated with 20 ppm IBA rooted 70% in 8 months. In 32 weeks there was 43% rooting of untreated cuttings taken in August.

NATIVE HABITAT: Restricted in a wild state to the Valley of the Kiso-gawa in Central Hondo, and to Koya-san and its immediate neighborhood in east central Hondo; the best trees being found in steep, rocky, sheltered situations.

Shepherdia canadensis — Russet Buffaloberry

FAMILY: Elaeagnaceae

LEAVES: Opposite, simple, 4/5 to 2" long, elliptic to ovate, obtuse; dark green and sparingly scurfy above; silvery stellate pubescent below; often much of the pubescence is brown; petioles—short, stellate—pubescent.

BUDS: Rather small, solitary or multiple, stalked, oblong, with 2 or 4 valvate scales.

STEMS: Red-brown, scurfy, scaly, not spiny; nearly terete, rather slender; leaf-scars half-round, minute, slightly raised; 1 bundle-trace; pith—small, round, continuous.

SIZE: 6 to 8' high and as wide, varies from 3 to 9' high.

HARDINESS: Zone 2.

HABIT: Small, loosely-branched shrub of rounded outline.

RATE: Slow to medium.

TEXTURE: Medium in all seasons.

LEAF COLOR: Silver-green to gray-green in summer; upper surface green, lower silvery mixed with brown scales. Like most members of the Elaeagnaceae does not color well in the fall.

FLOWERS: Dioecious, small, yellowish, 1/6" across; in short axillary spikes or the pistillate often solitary; April to early May; not showy.

FRUIT: Drupe-like, yellowish red, insipid, ovoid, 1/6 to 1/4" long; effective in June and July.

CULTURE: Easily grown and tolerates the poorest of soils; does well in dry or alkaline situations; prefers sunny open position.

DISEASES AND INSECTS: Several leaf spots, powdery mildew, and a rust have been reported but none are serious.

LANDSCAPE VALUE: Actually of no value where the soil is good and better shrubs can be grown. Has possibilities along highways and other rough areas where poor soils, lousy maintenance, and salt are the rule.

CULTIVARS: 'Xanthocarpa' — Yellow-fruited type.

PROPAGATION: Seed has an embryo dormancy and should be stratified for 60 to 90 days at 41°F. The seed coats are hard and an acid scarification for 20 to 30 minutes proves beneficial.

RELATED SPECIES:

Shepherdia argentea, Silver Buffaloberry, is a thorny shrub, sometimes nearly tree-like, growing 6 to 10' high, although it may reach 18'. The foliage is silvery on both surfaces and much more gray in appearance than *S. canadensis*. The flowers and fruits are similar to the above species with only minor exceptions. The fruits of both species have been used for jellies. Native to Minnesota and Manitoba to Sasketchewan, Kansas and Nevada. Introduced 1818. Zone 2.

ADDITIONAL NOTES: I have seen both species, but only in arboreta, and was not intrigued by either. They are extremely cold- and drought-tolerant as well as alkaline soil adaptable and should be used in areas where these conditions prevail.

NATIVE HABITAT: Newfoundland to Alaska, south to Maine, Ohio, Northern Mexico and Oregon. Introduced 1759.

Sophora japonica — Japanese Pagodatree, often called Scholar-tree

FAMILY: Leguminosae

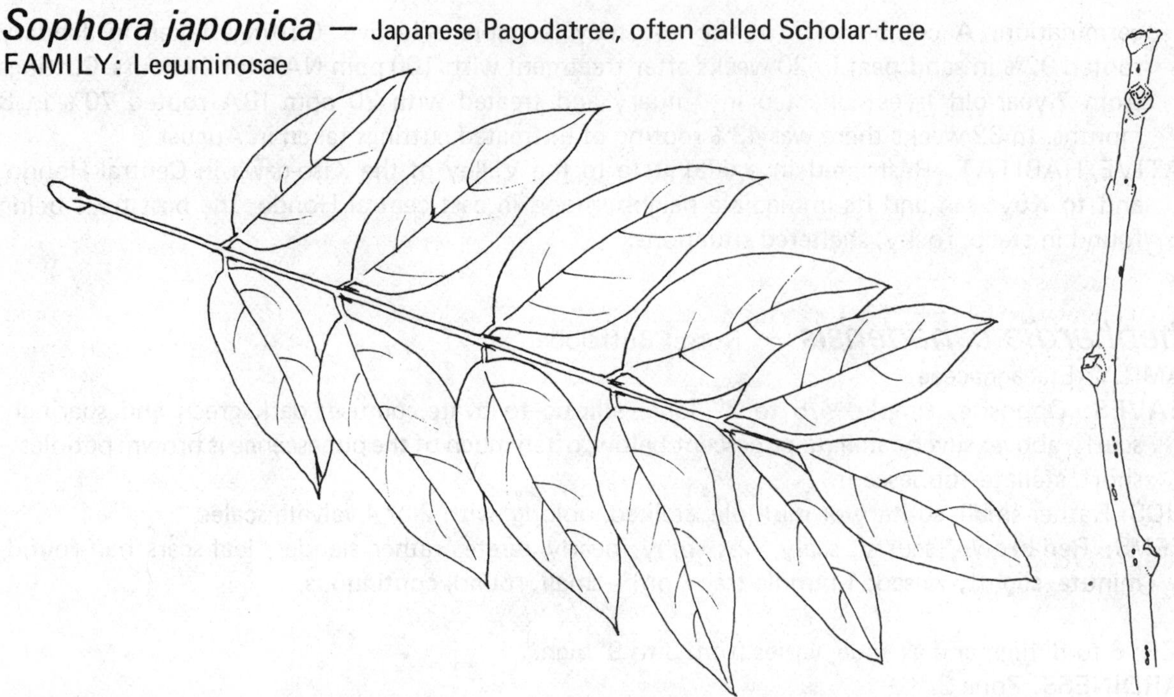

LEAVES: Alternate, pinnately compd., 6 to 10" long, 7 to 17 leaflets, entire, ovate to lance-ovate, 1 to 2" long, acute, broad-cuneate to rounded at base, medium to dark green and lustrous above, glaucous beneath and closely appressed-pubescence.

BUDS: Blackish, woolly, sessile, indistinctly scaly, concealed by the leaf scar, end bud lacking; base of petiole swollen and enclosing bud.

STEM: Slender, glabrous, green on 1 through 4 and 5-year-old wood.

SIZE: 50 to 75' in height with a comparable spread although great variation occurs.

HARDINESS: Zone 4.

HABIT: Dense when young, usually upright, spreading with a broadly rounded crown at maturity; casts a light shade.

RATE: Medium to fast, 10 to 12' in a 5 to 6 year period.

TEXTURE: Medium-fine in leaf; medium in winter.

BARK: On old trunks somewhat Black Locust-like except pale grayish brown in color.

LEAF COLOR: Medium to dark lustrous green in summer; green color holds late and little fall color develops.

FLOWERS: Perfect, creamy-white, mildly fragrant; borne in 6 to 12" long and wide terminal panicles in late July through mid-August; very showy in flower, unfortunately trees grown from seed do not flower until about 10 to 15 years of age. This could be solved by grafting or budding mature flowering wood onto seedling understocks.

FRUIT: Pod, bright green changing to yellow and finally yellow brown, 2 to 3" long, 1 to 6 seeded; October, and may remain all winter; after the pods abscise the inflorescences remain.

CULTURE: Transplant balled and burlapped as a young specimen; prefers loamy, well-drained soil; actually somewhat tender when young to cold, but once over 1 1/2" caliper diameter seems to be fine; once established withstands heat and drouth well; also tolerant of polluted conditions; prune in fall; tends to be a "floppy" grower and is somewhat difficult to train into a central leader with a nice head.

DISEASES AND INSECTS: Canker, damping-off of seedlings, twig blight, powdery mildew and leaf hoppers. The potato leaf hopper can kill young stems and this in turn results in a witches' broom.

LANDSCAPE VALUE: Good tree for city conditions, lawns, poor soil areas, parks, golf courses; excellent flower and good foliage are principal assets.

CULTIVARS:

'Fastigiata' — Upright growth habit.

'Pendula' — Weeping form, seldom flowers, quite interesting when used as an accent or formal specimen.

'Regent' — Selection by Princeton Nurseries with faster growth rate, straighter growth habit, large oval crown, deep glossy leaves, and flowers younger (6 to 8 years old).

PROPAGATION: Seeds require a weak scarification in acid to break down the impermeable seed coat, easy to grow from seed.

ADDITIONAL NOTES: Last of the large ornamental trees to flower in the north; used around Buddhist temples; yellow dye can be extracted from the flowers by baking them until brown and then boiling them in water. A very distinctive and aesthetically handsome tree in flower; should be used more extensively.

NATIVE HABITAT: China, Korea. Introduced 1747.

Sorbaria sorbifolia — Ural Falsespirea

FAMILY: Rosaceae

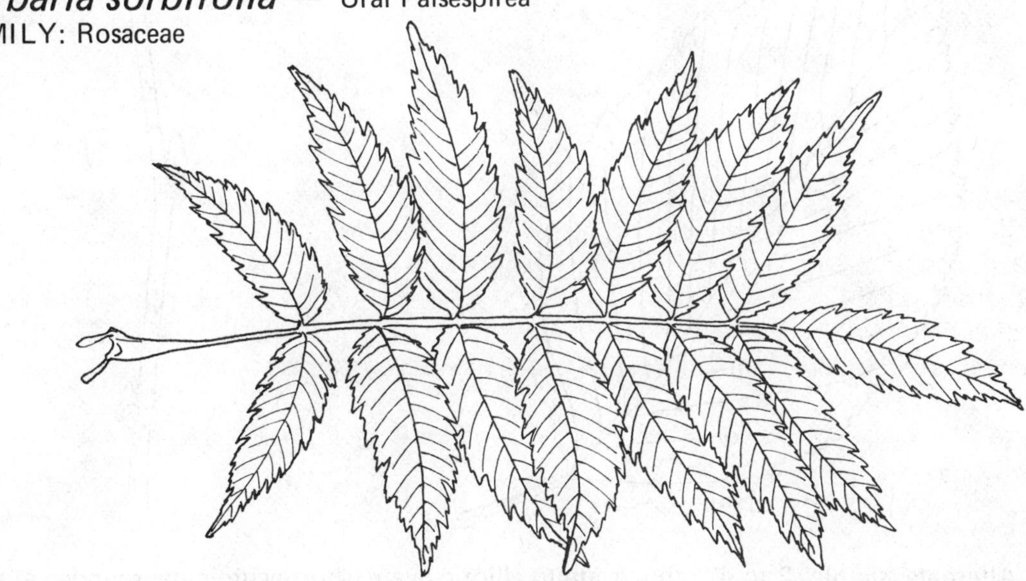

LEAVES: Alternate, pinnately compound, 13 to 23 leaflets, lanceolate to ovate-lanceolate, long acuminate, 2 to 4" long, doubly serrate, usually glabrous or nearly so beneath, resembles mountainash foliage.

STEM: Young—usually green or pink, often somewhat downy, gray-brown when old and glabrous; pith—large, brown, continuous.

SIZE: 5 to 10' in height with a similar spread.

HARDINESS: Zone 2.

HABIT: Erect, almost herbaceous shrub, with foliage similar to European Mountainash; spreads rapidly by suckers.

RATE: Fast.

TEXTURE: Many people say the texture is coarse but I feel if the shrub is properly pruned and maintained the texture is at worst medium in summer; tends toward coarseness in winter.

LEAF COLOR: Has a reddish tint when unfolding gradually changing to bright deep green in summer; fall color is not effective.

FLOWERS: Perfect, white, 1/3" across; late June into July; borne in large, terminal, fleecy, 4 to 10" panicles; very effective and, in fact, outstanding in flower.

FRUIT: Dehiscent capsule.

CULTURE: Transplants readily, very fibrous rooted, suckers and spreads profusely; prefers moist, well drained, organic soil; tends to become dwarfed in dry soils; full sun or light shade; pH adaptable; prune in early spring before growth starts as the flowers are produced on current season's growth, cut off old flowers; relatively easy plant to grow however it is not widely known.

DISEASES AND INSECTS: None serious.

LANDSCAPE VALUE: Excellent plant for the shrub border, for massing, grouping, might make a good bank cover as it freely suckers and spreads; is one of the first shrubs to leaf out in spring; they need considerable room to spread and are not reserved for small planting areas.

PROPAGATION: Fantastically easy to root from softwood, greenwood or hardwood cuttings, preferably in sand under mist.

NATIVE HABITAT: Northern Asia from Ural to Japan. Cultivated 1759.

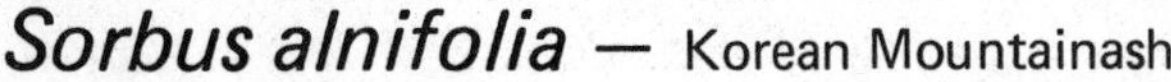

Sorbus alnifolia — Korean Mountainash

FAMILY: Rosaceae

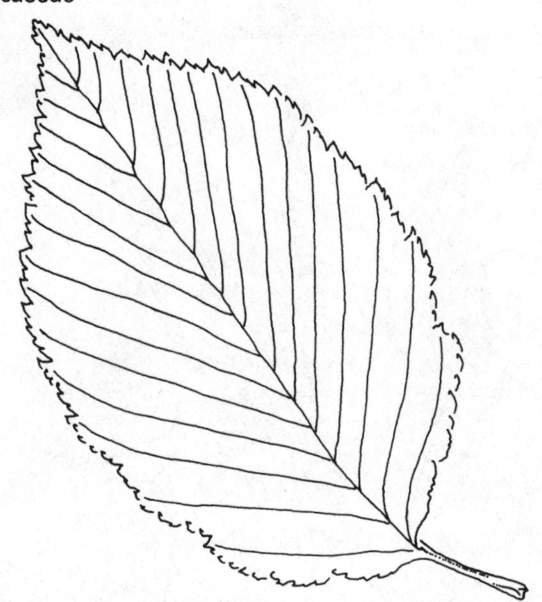

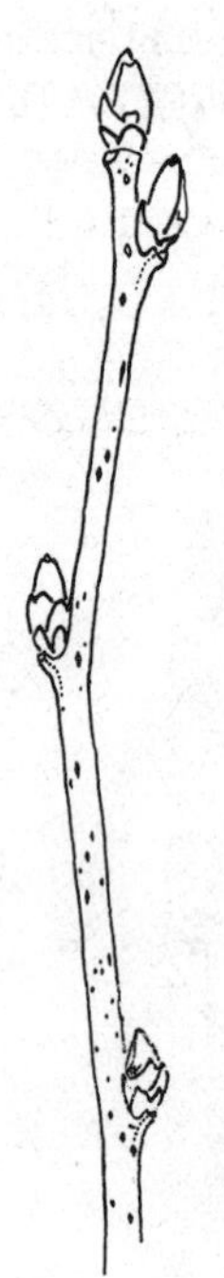

LEAVES: Alternate, simple, 2 to 4" long, ovate to elliptic-ovate, short-acuminate, rounded at base, unequally serrate, glabrous above, glabrous or slightly pubescent beneath, on vigorous shoots sometimes pubescent, with 6 to 10 pairs of veins. Leaf shape resembles *Fagus* to a degree; lustrous bright green.

BUDS: Oblong, terminal bud scarcely larger than the lateral, solitary, sessile, with several dark margined scales, the inner of which are more or less pubescent with long hairs often matted in gum.

STEM: Moderate, large lenticels, continuous; pith roundish, brownish, continuous; leaf scars raised, crescent-shaped or linear; bundle traces 3; stipular scars lacking.

SIZE: 40 to 50' in height by 20 to 30' in spread although can grow to 60'.

HARDINESS: Zone 5 (4).

HABIT: Pyramidal when young developing a weakly pyramidal-oval outline at maturity.

RATE: Medium to fast, 10 to 12' over a 5 to 7 year period.

TEXTURE: Medium in all seasons.

BARK: Gray on old trunks, almost beech-like. The first time I witnessed Korean Mountainash was at the Arnold Arboretum and was instantly taken by the beautiful foliage, flowers, bark and habit. One of my favorite all around trees; unfortunately, not very well known.

LEAF COLOR: Lustrous bright green in summer changing to orange and scarlet in fall; the leaves are simple and do not look anything like what we normally consider a mountainash leaf; look like beech leaves.

FLOWERS: Perfect, white, 3/4" in diameter, borne in 6 to 10 flowered, flat topped corymbs in mid May. I cannot say enough about the flower—overwhelming, perhaps, but then . . .

FRUIT: Pome, orange to scarlet, 3/8" diameter, ripening in September.

CULTURE: Transplant balled and burlapped into any well drained soil; very pH adaptable; does not withstand polluted conditions; prune in winter or early spring; Donald Wyman noted that it was one of the most successful of the flowering trees introduced by the Arnold Arboretum from Japan and requires little cultural attention.

DISEASES AND INSECTS: Discussed under *Sorbus aucuparia*. The least susceptible to borer injury.

LANDSCAPE VALUE: Specimen tree for lawns; not for streets or downtown city areas. The best of the mountainash. Difficult to believe it is even related to the genus *Sorbus*.

PROPAGATION: Seeds require 60 days or more of cold stratification at 33°F in moist medium.

RELATED SPECIES: Other species which you may find of interesting ornamental value include *S. folgneri,* Folgner Mountainash; *S. intermedia,* Swedish Mountainash; and *S. thuringiaca,* all of which are simple-leaved species.

NATIVE HABITAT: Central China to Korea and Japan. Introduced 1892.

Sorbus aucuparia — European Mountainash

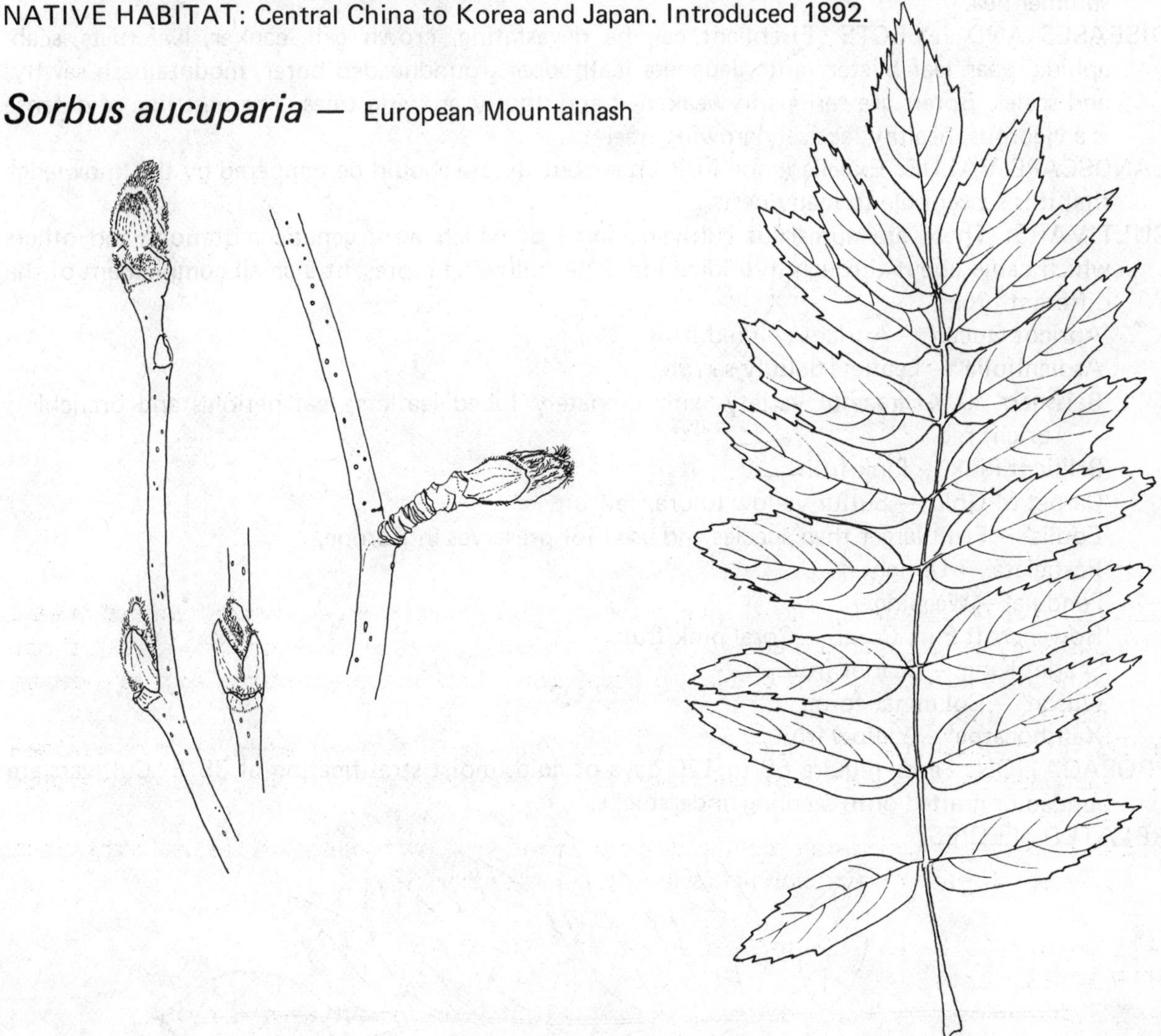

LEAVES: Alternate, pinnately compound, 9 to 15 leaflets, oblong to oblong-lanceolate, acute or obtusish, 3/4 to 2" long, serrate, usually entire in lower third, dull green above, glaucescent beneath and pubescent, at least when young.

BUDS: Terminal—large, woolly, 1/2" long; lateral often reduced with several scales, the inner of which are more or less pubescent, reddish brown.

STEM: Young branches pubescent, becoming glabrous, grayish brown and shiny when older.

SIZE: 20 to 40′ in height with a spread of 2/3's to equal the height.

HARDINESS: Zone 3.

HABIT: Erect and oval in youth forming an ovate or spherical, gracefully open head at maturity.

RATE: Medium, 25 to 30′ over a 20 year period.

TEXTURE: Medium-fine in leaf, medium or medium-coarse in winter.

BARK: Light grayish brown in color, usually smooth, but often somewhat slightly roughened on old trunks.

LEAF COLOR: Flat, dull green in summer; fall color ranges from green to yellow to reddish.

FLOWERS: White, 2/5″ across, malodorous, borne in 3 to 5″ diameter flat-topped corymbs in mid to late May. Effective, but not outstanding.

FRUIT: Small, berry-like pome, 1/4″ diameter, orange-red; late August into September, very handsome.

CULTURE: Transplant balled and burlapped into well drained loam; prefers acid soils and is often short-lived on chalky soils; has problems in Central Illinois not the least of which is extreme summer heat.

DISEASES AND INSECTS: Fireblight can be devastating, crown gall, canker, leaf rusts, scab, aphids, pear leaf blister mite, Japanese leafhopper, roundheaded borer, mountainash sawfly, and scales. Borers are serious in weakened and poorly growing trees. The best line of defense is a vigorous, healthy, actively growing tree.

LANDSCAPE VALUE: Excellent for fruit effect but its use should be tempered by the knowledge that it is susceptible to many pests.

CULTIVARS: There are numerous cultivars, some of which were genetic mutations and others which came about through hybridization. The following represent a small complement of the different types.

'Apricot Queen' – Apricot colored fruit.

'Asplenifolia' – Leaflets doubly serrate.

'Beissneri' – A graceful variety with pinnately lobed leaflets; leaf petioles and branchlets bright red.

'Brilliant Pink' – Pink fruit.

'Carpet of Gold' – Sulfur yellow to orange fruit.

'Edulis' – Fruit larger than species and used for preserves in Europe.

'Fastigiata' – Upright.

'Pendula' – Weeping.

'Rowencroft Pink Coral' – Coral pink fruit.

'Scarlet King' – Scarlet fruit.

'Wilson' – Columnar form.

'Xanthocarpa' – Yellow fruits.

PROPAGATION: Seeds require 60 to 120 days of cold, moist stratification at 38°F. Cultivars are budded or grafted onto seedling understocks.

RELATED SPECIES:

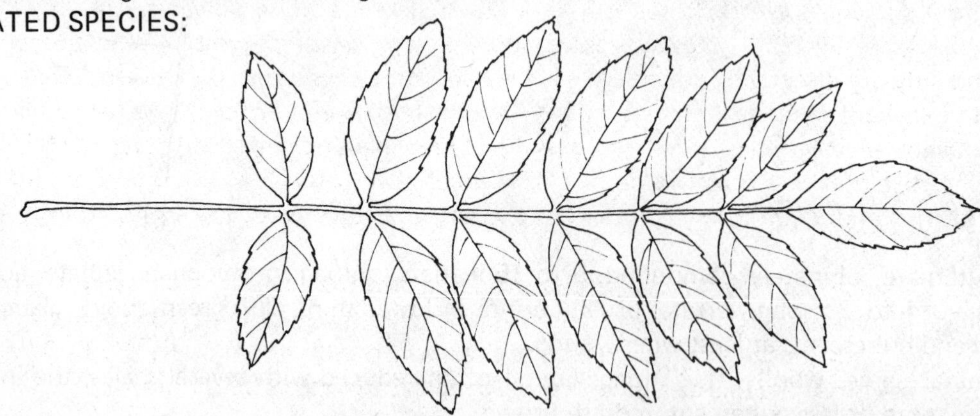

Sorbus americana, American Mountainash, is a northern species which grows from 10 to 30′ and is usually a small tree or shrub with a short trunk of spreading slender branches that form a narrow, open, round topped crown. Hardy to Zone 2 (-35 to -50°F), it frequents borders of cold swamps and bogs, or grows in a stunted form on relatively dry soils; grows slowly and is short-lived; flowers are white; fruit a brilliant orange-red; ranges from Newfoundland to Manitoba, south to Michigan, and North Carolina along the Appalachian Mountains.

Sorbus aria, Whitebeam Mountainash, is a tree which develops a broad-pyramidal or ovoid head. This species grows 35 to 45′ tall and has simple, leathery, lustrous dark green leaves (upper surface) while the lower surface is white-tomentose in summer. Fall color varies from pale green to golden brown to reddish. Flowers are white, about 3/5″ across, borne in 2 to 3″ terminal corymbs in May. Fruit is a 1/2″ diameter, orange-red or scarlet, berry-like pome which ripens in September through October. The leaves are quite different from what we associate with a "normal" mountainash leaf. The Royal Botanic Garden, Hamilton, Ontario, has an interesting collection of *Sorbus*. Native to Europe, long cultivated, Zone 5. There are several cultivars of note: 'Aurea' — a type with yellow foliage; var. *majestica* — fruits are as much as 5/8″ in diameter and the leaves reach 7″ in length.

Sorbus cashmiriana, Kashmir Mountainash, develops a conical crown and grows 20 to 40′ high with an equal spread. The flowers are pinkish white, 3/4″ diameter, and borne in mid to late May. The foliage is dark green and compound pinnate. In fall the leaves may change to a good red. The white fruits are about 3/8″ diameter and are often tinged pink; the fruit stalks are pink to red in color. This species has been used in hybridizing with *S. aucuparia* by European nurserymen. Some of the cultivars include 'Carpet of Gold', yellow fruits; 'Kirsten Pink', dark pink fruits; and 'Maidenblush', pale pink fruits. Native to Himalayas; introduced 1949 into the Arnold Arboretum. Zone 4. Wyman considers this species well worthy of a trial wherever mountainashes are grown.

Other species of some interest, but limited landscape acceptability, include *S. decora*, Showy Mountainash; and *S. discolor*, Snowberry Mountainash. I have seen both these species and was quite impressed by their fruit displays.

NATIVE HABITAT: Europe to Western Asia and Siberia, and naturalized in North America.

Spiraea albiflora — Japanese White Spirea

LEAVES: Alternate, simple, short-petioled, lanceolate, acuminate, cuneate, 2 1/2″ long, coarsely or sometimes doubly serrate, with callous-tipped teeth, medium to dark green above; glabrous and bluish green beneath.

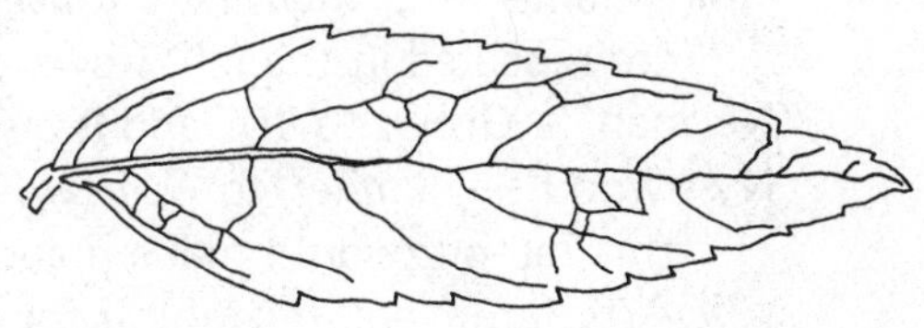

Spiraea albiflora, Japanese White Spirea, could be equated with a white flowered Anthony Waterer. The habit is low (1 1/2′), rounded, dense and the large, white corymbs which appear in late June and July are effectively foiled against the handsome medium to dark green foliage. Would make an excellent facer plant, mass, or filler in the shrub border. Flowers on new wood so can be effectively rejuvenated in early spring. Cultivated in Japan. Introduced before 1868. Zone 4. Sometimes listed as *S. japonica alba* or 'Alba' which is actually a synonym. Roots very readily from cuttings and is infinitely superior to the large, cumbersome, unkempt, straggly spireas.

Spiraea bullata, Crispleaf Spirea, makes a rather intriguing, low (12 to 15″), groundcover type plant. The foliage is thickish and bullate, medium to dark green above, grayish green beneath. Flowers are deep rosy-pink, borne in small, dense corymbs which form a terminal 1 3/5 to 3″ diameter corymb; June-July. Valuable as a dwarf shrub. Japan. Cultivated 1880. Zone 4.

Spiraea x *bumalda* — Bumalda Spirea

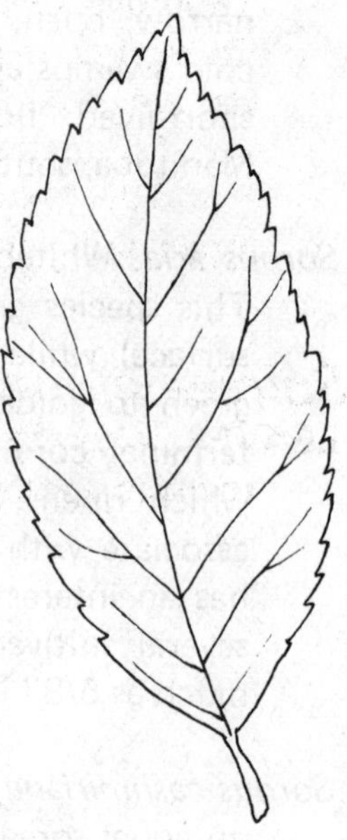

FAMILY: Rosaceae

LEAVES: Alternate, simple, toothed, 1-3" long, ovate lanceolate, apex pointed; base narrowed; teeth mostly doubled, sharp; dark green above; pinkish-red-purple when young.

STEM: Brown, slightly angled in cross section, somewhat lined or ridged, glabrous.

SIZE: 2 to 3' high and 3 to 5' wide.

HARDINESS: Zone 4 (5).

HABIT: A broad, flat topped, low shrub, densely twiggy with erect branches.

RATE: Fast.

TEXTURE: Medium-fine in all seasons.

LEAF COLOR: Pinkish to reddish when unfolding changing to dark bluish green at maturity.

FLOWERS: White to deep pink, mid June into August, borne in 4 to 6" flat-topped corymbs; flowers on new growth.

FRUIT: Dry, brown follicle.

CULTURE: Easy to transplant; tolerant of many soils except those which are extremely wet; prefer full sun in open areas; pruning must be based on type of wood upon which flowers are produced. *S.* x *bumalda* should be pruned in early spring before growth starts.

DISEASES AND INSECTS: Subject to many of the problems that afflict other members of the Rosaceae. Fireblight, bacterial hairy root, leaf spot, powdery mildews, root rot, spirea aphid, oblique-banded leaf roller, scales, caterpillars and root-knot nematode.

LANDSCAPE VALUE: Good filler or facer plant, can be used as a low massing plant, possibly as a bank cover for it suckers from the roots. Like most spireas has been overused.

CULTIVARS:

'Anthony Waterer' — Grows about 2' high and twice as wide; new growth deep reddish purple; flowers deep pink; widely evident in older landscapes.

'Crispa' — Form with twisted leaves, 2' high, rose-pink flower in June-July.

'Froebeli' — 3 to 3 1/2' high with deep pink flowers.

'Gold Flame' — 2' high, new foliage is mottled with red, copper, and orange and these colors are repeated in the fall; flowers are compact.

'Norman' — Grows to 10" and is quite compact.

'Nyeswood' — Similar to *S. j. alpina* but larger growing. Very tight knit and dense and, for this reason, would make a good facer or mass plant. I first saw this plant at the Holden Arboretum and mistook it for *S. j. alpina.* Flowers are pink; foliage a deep blue-green.

Spiraea japonica — Japanese Spirea

LEAVES: Alternate, simple, ovate to ovate-oblong, acute, cuneate, 4/5 to 3" long, doubly incised-serrate, pale or glaucescent beneath and usually pubescent on the veins; petioles about 1/8" long.

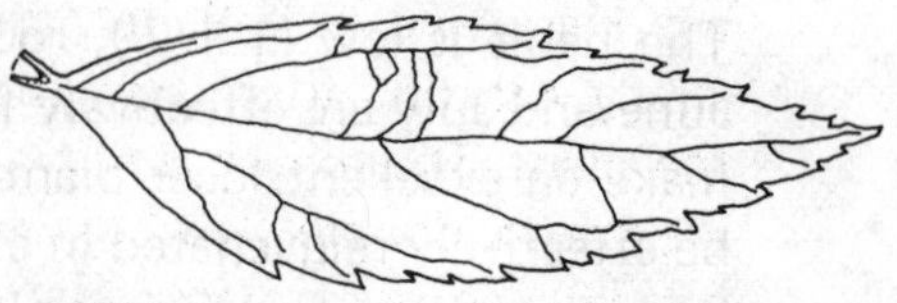

Spiraea japonica, Japanese Spirea, grows 4 to 5' high and is composed of upright stiff branches. Not as preferable as *S.* x *bumalda* types because of larger size and coarser texture. The flowers vary from pale to deep pink to white, in flat-topped corymbs, June through July. Several clones include:

'Atrosanguinea' — With deep rose-red, 4 to 5" diameter flowers. This clone is supposed to have the deepest red flowers of any spirea, however, I found it difficult to separate (by flower color) this from Anthony Waterer although they were growing within 15' of each other at the Minnesota Landscape Arboretum.

'Ovalifolia' or var. *ovalifolia* – White flowers borne in 3 to 5" diameter corymbs.

'Ruberrima' – Flowers deeper pink than the species.

var. *alpina* – A very dainty, low growing (less than one foot), fine-textured, pink flowered type which flowers in June or July. Makes a nice edging plant or limited mass or grouping.

Japan. Cultivated 1870. Zone 4.

var. *alpina*

Spiraea nipponica 'Snowmound' – Snowmound Nippon Spirea

LEAVES: Alternate, simple, obovate to oval, broadly cuneate, 3/5 to 1 1/5" long, crenate at the rounded apex, rarely entire.

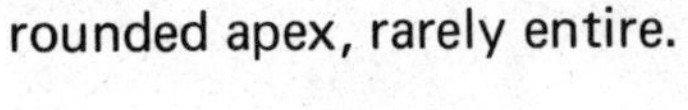

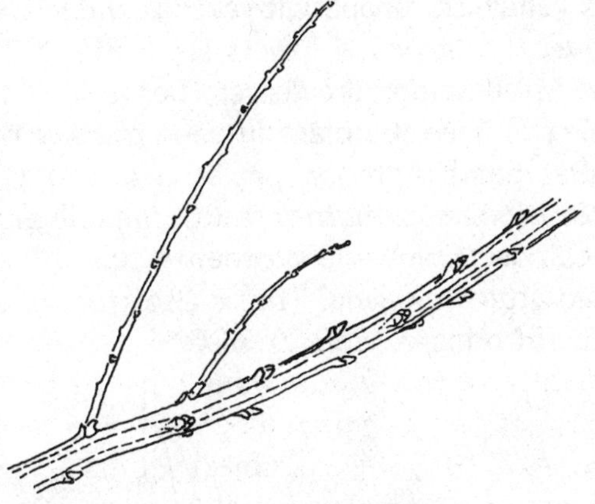

Spiraea nipponica 'Snowmound', Snowmound Nippon Spirea, has performed admirably in our woody plant test plots and appears to be a superior replacement for *S.* x *vanhouttei*. The plant grows 3 to 5' high and as wide, with small blue green leaves and white flowers appearing in late May into June. It maintains a neater, denser outline than Vanhoutte. There have been reports of isolated branches dieing out but I have not observed this on campus plants. The species is native to Japan. Cultivated 1908. Zone 4.

Spiraea prunifolia – Bridalwreath Spirea

LEAVES: Alternate, simple, elliptic to elliptic-oblong, acute at ends, 4/5 to 2" long, denticulate, glabrous or finely pubescent beneath, dark green and lustrous above.

STEMS: Zig-zag, slender, angled, shiny brown, glabrous.

Spiraea prunifolia, Bridalwreath Spirea, is an old favorite (I do not know why) growing 4 to 9' tall and 6 to 8' wide. It is an open, coarse, straggly shrub, often leggy, upright and limitedly spreading with foliage on the upper 50% of the plant. The foliage is shiny dark green in summer and of no consequence in fall. The flowers are white, double, 1/3" diameter; mid to late April; borne in 3 to 6 flowered sessile umbels. I really see no use for this plant in modern gardens, it belongs to the "Over the hill gang". Korea, China, Formosa. Cultivated 1864. Zone 4.

Spiraea thunbergii — Thunberg Spirea

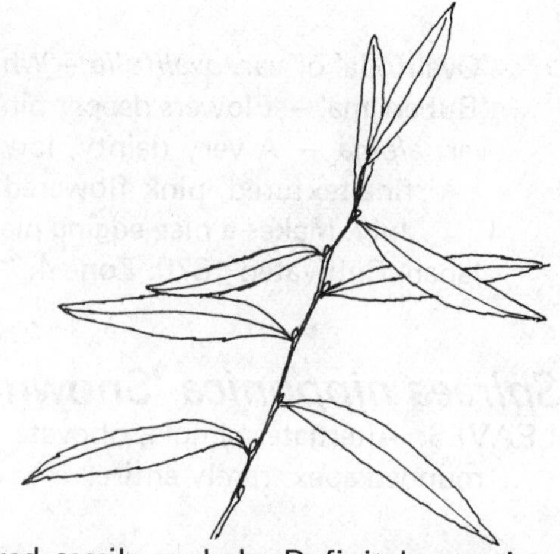

LEAVES: Alternate, simple, linear-lanceolate, acuminate, 4/5 to 1 3/5" long, sharply serrate, glabrous.

STEM: Extremely slender and fine, slightly angled, zig-zag, light brown, glabrous.

Spiraea thunbergii, Thunberg Spirea, grows 3 to 5' tall and 3 to 5' wide. It is a bushy, slender-branched, tiny leaved shrub, rather loosely spreading and arching and very twiggy. Foliage is yellowish green in summer and turns yellowish, tinged with orange and bronze in fall (not very effective). Flowers are white, 1/3" across, early April before the leaves; borne in 3 to 5 flowered sessile umbels. Definitely requires pruning to keep the plant in good condition as it becomes straggly and open. Relatively fine-textured plant. Another species, *S. arguta*, Garland Spirea, is similar to the above and in fact is a cross between *S. multiflora* x *S. thunbergii*. I cannot see a great deal of difference in the two. The cultivar 'Compacta' grows to 4' tall. All flower on old wood and pruning should be accomplished after flowering. This is also true for *S. prunifolia* and *S.* x *vanhouttei*. Native to Japan, China. Introduced 1830. Zone 4.

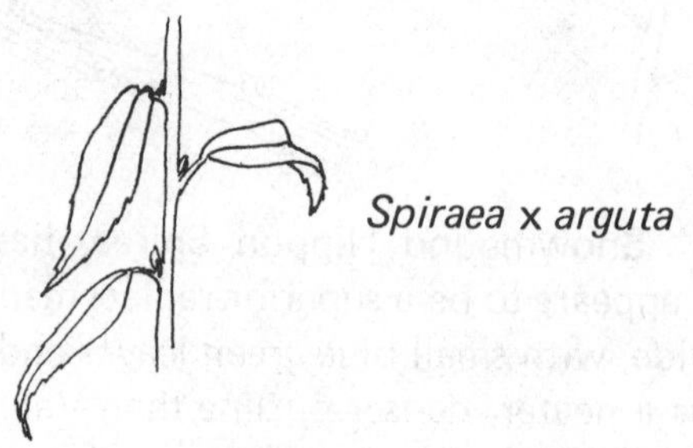

Spiraea x *arguta*

Spiraea x *vanhouttei* — Vanhoutte Spirea

LEAVES: Alternate, simple, toothed, often obscurely 3-lobed, 3/4 to 1 1/2" long, rhombic-ovate or somewhat obovate; apex pointed; base tapering, teeth irregular, coarse, often incised, minutely tipped, present above the middle; pale bluish green, glabrous.

STEM: Slender, brown, rounded, glabrous.

Spiraea x *vanhouttei,* Vanhoutte Spirea, grows 8 to 10' high and spreads 10 to 12'. The habit is fountain-like or vase-shaped, round-topped with arching branches recurving to the ground, making a tall broad mound. Foliage is a dull bluish green in summer and fall color is nonexistent. Flowers are white, 1/3" across; late April-early May; borne in many flowered umbels. Very showy in flower. I was spraying weed killer on our lawn and had a bit left over and decided to apply the rest to the Vanhoutte Spireas which were left by the previous owner. To my surprise the herbicide did not effect the plant in the slightest. I think this says something for its toughness. This is undeniably the most popular of all the spireas and is a hybrid between *S. cantoniensis* x *S. trilobata*. The arching, fountain-like habit coupled with the profusion of white flowers has contributed to its popularity with the masses.

PROPAGATION: All spireas root readily from softwood cuttings taken in June or July. An IBA treatment usually improves rooting but is not necessary in most cases.

Staphylea trifolia — American Bladdernut

FAMILY: Staphyleaceae

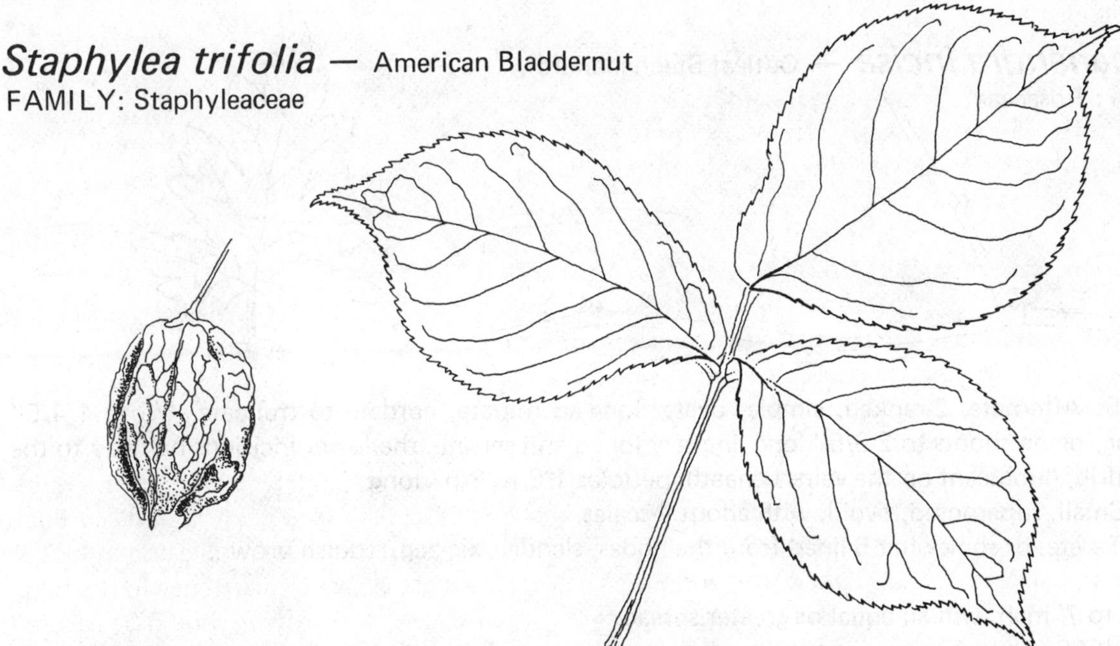

LEAVES: Opposite, compound pinnate, 3 leaflets, elliptic to ovate, 1 2/5 to 3" long, acuminate, sharply and unequally serrate, pubescent beneath, sometimes glabrate at maturity.

BUDS: Four-scaled, solitary, ovoid, glabrous; terminal—usually lacking.

STEM: Moderate, rounded, glabrous; pith—large, continuous, white.

SIZE: 10 to 15' in height, usually taller than wide at maturity.

HARDINESS: Zone 3.

HABIT: Upright, heavily branched, suckering shrub with smooth striped bark forming a solid aggregate of brush; sometimes wide spreading.

RATE: Medium to fast.

TEXTURE: Medium in leaf; medium-coarse in winter.

BARK: Light, greenish gray with linear white fissures, branchlets at first pale green with white lenticels, downy; later brownish purple; finally ashen gray.

LEAF COLOR: Bright green when emerging eventually turning pale green in summer; developing pale dull yellow in fall.

FLOWERS: Perfect, greenish white, bell-shaped, borne in nodding panicles or umbel-like racemes, abundant; April-May.

FRUIT: A 3-lobed, 1 to 1 1/2" long, inflated capsule, pale green changing to light brown; effective in September.

CULTURE: Prefers damp, moist, well-drained soils; performs better under cultivation than in native haunts; in the wild is often loose and open, but under cultivation takes on a more dense, vigorous nature.

DISEASES AND INSECTS: None serious.

LANDSCAPE VALUE: Not a great deal; could be used in naturalizing; best reserved for parks and other low maintenance areas.

PROPAGATION: Seed apparently possesses a double dormancy. Do not allow the seed to dry out before stratification; 3 months warm followed by 3 months at 40°F is recommended. Softwood and hardwood cuttings root easily.

RELATED SPECIES:

Staphylea colchica, Colchis Bladdernut, is somewhat similar to the above but the leaflets are usually in 5's and the orange-blossom fragrant flowers are borne later, usually in late May or June. It, too, is a suckering, upright shrub growing to 12'. Native to Caucasus. Introduced 1850. Zone 6.

ADDITIONAL NOTES: The most interesting aspect of bladdernuts is the inflated, balloon-like fruit.

NATIVE HABITAT: Quebec to Ontario and Minnesota, south to Georgia and Missouri. Cultivated 1640.

Stephanandra incisa — Cutleaf Stephanandra

FAMILY: Rosaceae

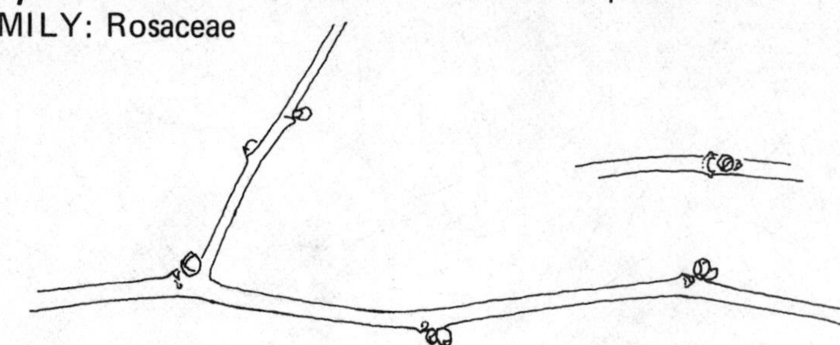

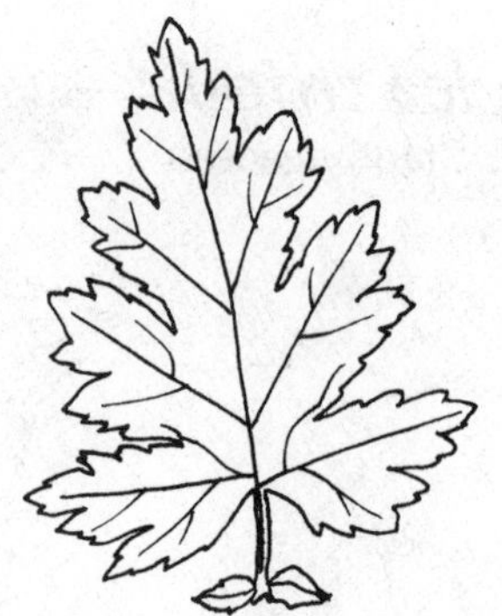

LEAVES: Alternate, 2-ranked, simple, ovate, long-acuminate, cordate to truncate, 4/5 to 1 4/5" long, or on shoots to 2 3/5" long, incisely lobed and serrate, the lower incisions halfway to the midrib, pubescent on the veins beneath; petioles 1/8 to 2/5" long.

BUDS: Small, superposed, ovoid, with about 4-scales.

STEM: Terete, or somewhat 5-lined from the nodes, slender, zig-zag, reddish brown.

SIZE: 4 to 7' high with an equal or greater spread.

HARDINESS: Zone 4.

HABIT: Graceful shrub with dense, fine textured foliage and wide spreading, arching slender branches.

RATE: Fast.

TEXTURE: Fine in leaf; medium in winter.

STEM COLOR: Cinnamon-brown.

LEAF COLOR: Tinged red when unfolding, later bright green; red-purple or red-orange in fall.

FLOWERS: Greenish white, small; early June; borne in loose terminal panicles, 4/5 to 2 2/5" long; not particularly showy, in fact, I did not know the two small plants in my yard were flowering, although I walk past them every day, until I was doing some hand weeding and inadvertently gazed upon the flowers.

FRUIT: Follicle.

CULTURE: Easy to transplant, best moved as a container plant; prefers moist, well-drained soil that has been supplemented with peat moss or leaf mold, although tolerant of most soils; full sun or light shade; in exposed, windswept areas the very delicate young branches may be killed, at least near the tips, in winter; simply prune back to live tissue before new growth starts; tends to root wherever the stems touch the soil.

DISEASES AND INSECTS: None serious.

LANDSCAPE VALUE: The species could be used for hedges, massing, screens, or in the shrub border while the low growing cultivar 'Crispa' makes an excellent facer, bank cover, or ground cover plant.

CULTIVARS:

'Crispa' — Handsome form which grows 1 1/2 to 3' tall.

PROPAGATION: Roots readily from cuttings taken at any time of the year. I have used softwood (June and July collected) cuttings and had 100% success.

NATIVE HABITAT: Japan, Korea. Cultivated 1872.

Stewartia ovata — Mountain Stewartia

FAMILY: Theaceae

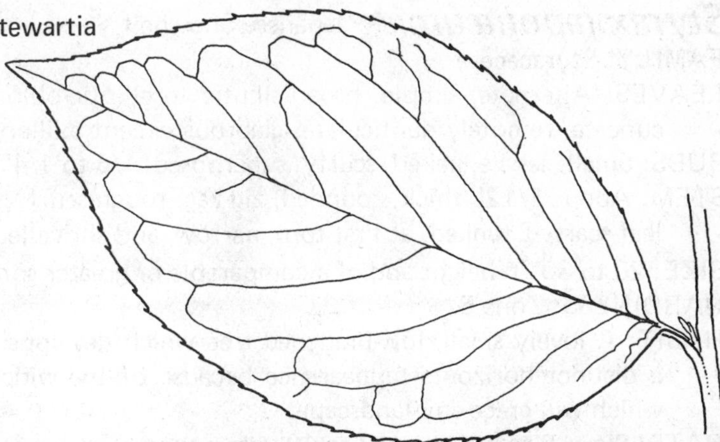

LEAVES: Alternate, simple, ovate or elliptic to ovate-oblong, 2 to 5″ long, acuminate, usually rounded at the base, remotely serrulate, sparingly pubescent and grayish green beneath; petiole 1/8 to 3/5″ long.

BUDS: Moderate, solitary or superposed, sessile, compressed fusiform, with 2 or 3 exposed scales.

STEM: Moderate, subterete; pith—rounded, somewhat spongy.

SIZE: 10 to 15′ high.

HARDINESS: Zone 5.

HABIT: Large shrub or small tree with spreading branches and a bushy habit.

RATE: Slow.

TEXTURE: Medium in leaf and winter.

BARK: Dark brown bark flakes off to expose green inner bark; very lovely bark pattern.

LEAF COLOR: Dark green in summer; beautiful orange to scarlet in fall.

FLOWERS: Perfect, white with purple stamens, 4″ diameter; July.

FRUIT: Woody, sharply 4-angled, 3/5 to 4/5″ long capsule.

CULTURE: Difficult to transplant and should be moved as a small (4 to 5′ or less) container or balled and burlapped plant in early spring. The soil should be moist, acid (pH 4.5 to 5.5), abundantly supplemented with leaf mold or peat moss. They do best where there is sun most of the day, but shade during the hottest periods. They seldom require pruning.

DISEASES AND INSECTS: Basically free of problems.

LANDSCAPE VALUE: One of the very finest specimen plants; a lovely sight in all seasons. It should not be wasted and hidden in some obscure corner of the landscape. The flowers, fall color and bark are among the best.

CULTIVARS:

var. *grandiflora* — Has larger flowers than the species, up to 4″ diameter.

PROPAGATION: Seeds should be given a warm treatment for 150 to 180 days at fluctuating temperatures of 68 to 86°F and then a 90 day cold treatment at 41°F. Softwood cuttings should be taken in June or July. They require hormonal treatment (IBA 2500 ppm has worked well for us) and preferably mist. Rooting varies among the species but should average 80 to 90 percent.

RELATED SPECIES:

Stewartia koreana, Korean Stewartia, grows to 35 to 45′ and is dense and pyramidal in habit. Foliage is dark green in summer and turns orange-red in fall. Flowers are white, 3″ in diameter, with yellow, conspicuous stamens; July; bark is similar to the above species. This is supposedly the hardiest of the Stewartias and, like the others, is difficult to find in the trade. Korea. 1917. Zone 5.

Stewartia pseudo-camellia, Japanese Stewartia, grows to 60′ with smaller white flowers than the other species. The bark is more colorful than that of other species, being red and peeling off in large flakes. Japan. 1874. Zone 5.

NATIVE HABITAT: North Carolina and Tennessee to Florida. Cultivated 1800.

Styrax japonicum — Japanese Snowbell

FAMILY: Styracaceae

LEAVES: Alternate, simple, broad-elliptic to elliptic-oblong, 4/5 to 3" long, acute to acuminate, cuneate, remotely denticulate, glabrous except axillary tufts beneath; medium to dark green.

BUDS: Small, sessile, naked, scurfy, superposed; 1/6 to 1/4" long.

STEM: About 1/12" thick, rounded, zig-zag, rough-scurfy; pith small, rounded, continuous, green; leaf scars—2 ranked, at first torn, narrow, and shrivelled, finally broadly crescent-shaped.

SIZE: 20 to 30' in height and of a comparable or greater spread.

HARDINESS: Zone 5.

HABIT: A lovely small, low-branched tree which develops a rounded to broad-rounded crown and a distinct horizontal appearance because of the wide-spreading branches. A very dainty tree which will grace any landscape.

RATE: Slow, 9 to 10' over a 7 to 10 year period.

TEXTURE: Medium-fine in leaf; medium in winter.

BARK: Quite handsome gray-brown of smooth consistency but showing irregular, orangish brown, and interlacing fissures.

LEAF COLOR: Medium to dark green in summer, unusually pest free; changing to yellow or reddish in the fall. Foliage is borne on the upper part of the branches and does not significantly detract from the flowers which are somewhat pendulous.

FLOWERS: Perfect, 3/4" diameter, pendulous, bell-shaped, white flowers; borne 3 to 6 in clusters on short lateral branches in June. The dainty flowers are especially noticeable when viewed from below and for this reason the tree makes a nice patio specimen.

FRUIT: Dry drupe, ovoid, about 1/2" long, grayish in color and somewhat attractive; effective in August.

CULTURE: Transplant balled and burlapped in early Spring into a moist, acid, well drained soil which has been abundantly supplemented with peat moss or organic matter; full sun or partial shade; prune in winter.

DISEASES AND INSECTS: Amazingly trouble-free.

LANDSCAPE VALUE: A handsome small tree for any situation: Excellent near the patio, in the lawn, or in the shrub border. It is another of the unknown trees which is worthy of extensive landscape use.

PROPAGATION: Softwood cuttings, treated with IBA will root readily under mist. *S. obassium* rooted well when collected in mid-July. Seeds apparently exhibit a double dormancy and warm stratification for 5 months followed by cold for 3 months is recommended.

RELATED SPECIES:

Styrax obassium — Fragrant Snowbell, is a small tree or shrub which develops dense, ascending branches and can grow to 30'. The flowers are white, fragrant, borne in 4 to 8" long racemes in June. The leaves are dark green and quite large (3 to 8" long) and detract slightly from the quality and intensity of the flowers. The leaves apparently do not develop a good fall color. The fruit is a 4/5" long, ovoid dry drupe. Native to Japan. Introduced 1879. Zone 6. This species is not as hardy as *S. japonicum*.

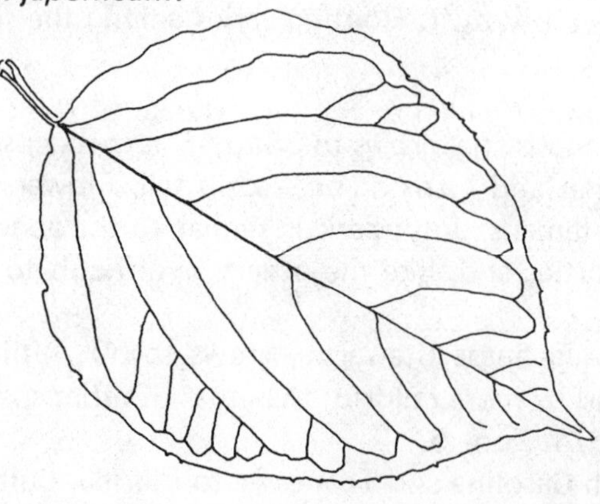

ADDITIONAL NOTES: I have seen both species and perhaps am biased but believe *S. japonicum* more aesthetic and culturally adapted to northern conditions.

NATIVE HABITAT: China, Japan. Introduced 1862.

Symphoricarpos albus — Common Snowberry

FAMILY: Caprifoliaceae

LEAVES: Opposite, simple, oval to elliptic-oblong, 4/5 to 2" long, obtuse; on shoots often sinuately lobed, pubescent beneath.

STEM: Slender, rounded, pubescent; pith—brownish, excavated.

SIZE: 3 to 6' by 3 to 6'.

HARDINESS: Zone 3.

HABIT: Bushy, deciduous shrub with numerous ascending shoots, densely fine and twiggy.

RATE: Fast.

TEXTURE: Medium in leaf; however, in winter extremely sorrowful.

LEAF COLOR: Bluish green in summer; no effective fall color.

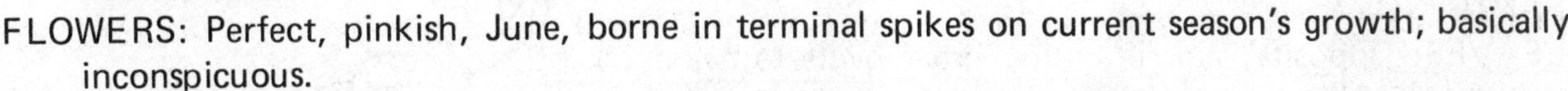

FLOWERS: Perfect, pinkish, June, borne in terminal spikes on current season's growth; basically inconspicuous.

FRUIT: Berry-like drupe, white, 5/8" diameter, September through November; most ornamental asset of this shrub.

CULTURE: Transplants easily, very tolerant of any soil; native on limestone and clay; full sun to medium shade; suckers profusely and tends to spread extensively, prune in early spring so current season's growth can produce flowers.

DISEASES AND INSECTS: Anthracnose (two genera affect the host, one causes a discoloration of the fruit, the other a spotting of the leaves), berry rot (fruits turn yellowish or brown and are affected by a soft, watery rot), leaf spots, powdery mildews, rusts, stem gall, aphids, snowberry clearwing, scale and glacial whitefly.

LANDSCAPE VALUE: Not a very valuable plant but fruit can be interesting, useful in heavily shaded situations and for holding banks, cuts, fills, etc.

CULTIVARS:

var. *laevigatus* — Taller (6'), leaves larger and broader, fruit larger.

PROPAGATION: Immersion in H_2SO_4 for 40 to 60 minutes followed by warm and then cold stratification will assist in breaking seed dormancy. Cuttings are extremely easy to root, softwood taken in June, July, August, rooted readily.

RELATED SPECIES:

Symphoricarpos x *chenaultii*, Chenault Coralberry, is a cross between *S. microphyllus* x *S. orbiculatus*. The plant is a low spreading arching shrub growing about 3' high. Flowers are pink; fruit is pink or white and tinged pink; the cultivar 'Hancock' is a beautiful low growing type with small leaves and good ground cover possibilities, a 12-year-old plant is 2' tall and 12' wide; Chenault Coralberry fruits differ from those of Indiancurrant Coralberry in that the side away from the sun is white. Zone 4.

Symphoricarpos x *doorenbosii* is a hybrid between *S. albus laevigatus* and *S. chenaultii*. The cultivar 'Mother of Pearl' is one of the best clones, with whitish fruits tinged a pale pink. 'Magic Berry' and 'White Hedge' are two other clones.

Symphoricarpos orbiculatus — Indiancurrant Coralberry or Buckbrush

LEAVES: Opposite, simple, elliptic or ovate, 3/5 to 1 2/5" long, obtuse or acutish, rounded at base, glaucescent and pubescent beneath.

STEM: Pubescent when young, pith—continuous.

Symphoricarpos orbiculatus, Indiancurrant Coralberry or Buckbrush, grows 2 to 5' by 4 to 8' and develops into a spreading arching shrub. The foliage is a dull green (possibly blue-green) in summer and hangs on late in fall. The flowers are yellowish white flushed rose, borne in June or July, in dense and short axillary clusters and terminal spikes. The fruit is a purplish red, 1/6 to 1/4" diameter berry-like drupe, maturing in October and persisting late into winter; 'Leucocarpus' has white or whitish fruit. New Jersey to Georgia, Kansas and Texas, west to South Dakota. 1727. Zone 2.

ADDITIONAL NOTES: The *Symphoricarpos* have limited ornamental value but fruit and shade tolerance are definite assets. Should be used sparingly, however, the cultivar 'Hancock' deserves further use.

NATIVE HABITAT: Nova Scotia to Alberta, south to Minnesota and Virginia. Introduced 1879.

Syringa amurensis japonica — Japanese Tree Lilac, correct scientific name is now *S. reticulata.*

FAMILY: Oleaceae

LEAVES: Opposite, simple, entire, broad-ovate to ovate, 2 to 5 1/2" long, rounded or subcordate, dark green above, grayish green and reticulate beneath and glabrous or slightly pubescent.

BUDS: Sessile, subglobose, with 4 pairs of scales, end bud frequently absent, brownish.

STEM: Stout, shiny brown, heavily lenticelled resembling cherry bark, glabrous.

SIZE: 20 to 30' in height; 15 to 25' in spread.

HARDINESS: Zone 4.

HABIT: Large shrub or small tree with stiff, spreading branches developing a somewhat oval to rounded crown.

RATE: Medium, 9 to 12' over a 6 to 8 year period.

TEXTURE: Medium in all seasons.

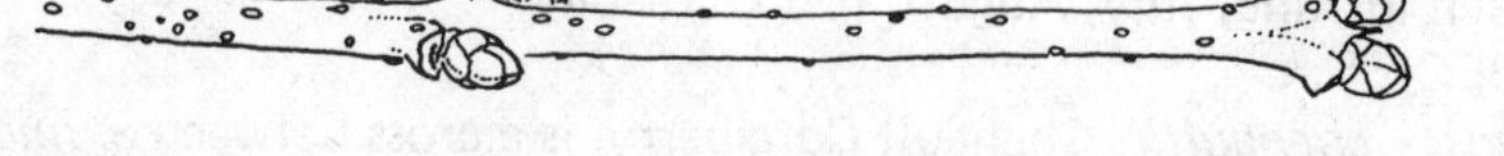

BARK: Cherry-like, reddish brown to brownish on young and old stems, marked with prominent horizontal lenticels.

LEAF COLOR: Dark green in summer; like most lilacs no good fall color.

FLOWERS: Perfect, white, fragrant, early to mid-June, effective for 2 weeks, borne in large terminal 6 to 12" long and 6 to 10" wide panicles; extremely showy in flower.

FRUIT: Warty, dehiscent, 4/5" long capsule.

CULTURE: This discussion applies to the lilac species which follow. Transplant balled and burlapped, actually lilacs are easy to move; soil should be loose, well-drained and slightly acid although lilacs seem to be pH adaptable; full sun for best flowering; pruning should be done after flowering or if a plant is overgrown (applies to multi-stemmed clones) cut it to the ground for complete rejuvenation; should be good air movement, seem to prefer cool summers.

DISEASES AND INSECTS: Bacterial blight, *Phytophthora* blight, leaf blights, leaf spots, powdery mildew (bad on Common Lilac, Persian Lilac), wilt, other minor pathological problems, ring spot virus, witches' broom, frost injury (in late spring young leaves may be injured by near freezing temperatures), graft blight (occurs on lilacs grafted on privet), leaf roll necrosis (caused by various air pollutants), lilac borer, leopard moth borer, caterpillars, giant hornet, lilac leaf miner, scales and several other insects of negligible importance. It should be evident that lilacs require a certain degree of maintenance. I have seen the borer and scale insects decimate large shrubs and whole plantings.

LANDSCAPE VALUE: Possibly the most trouble-free lilac; excellent specimen tree, street tree, good in groups or near large buildings. One of my favorite lilacs; I think there is a need for selection of superior flowering and foliage types within this species.

PROPAGATION: Seed dormancy is variable but cold stratification for 30 to 90 days at 34° to 41°F is recommended. I have attempted to grow this lilac from seed, however, all attempts met with failure. The seed, in all cases, was purchased from an unknown source and perhaps this was the problem. Cuttings which I collected in June rooted 90 percent when treated 10,000 ppm IBA/50 percent alcohol and placed in sand under mist. Root formation was extremely profuse and the cuttings that did not root showed good callus formation.

RELATED SPECIES:

Syringa pekinensis — Pekin Lilac

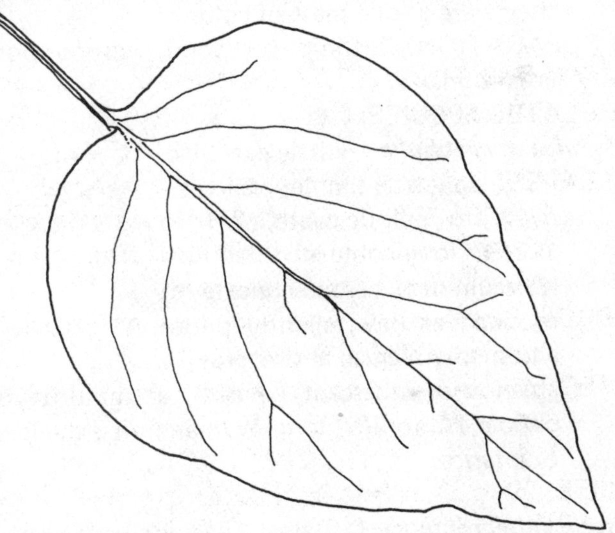

LEAVES: Opposite, simple, ovate to ovate-lanceolate, 2 to 4" long and 4/5 to 1 2/5" broad, acuminate, cuneate, dark green above, grayish green beneath and scarcely veined, quite glabrous; petiole 3/5 to 1" long.

Syringa pekinensis, Pekin Lilac, is somewhat similar to the above but smaller (15 to 20') with a more informal (multistemmed) habit and finer texture throughout. The leaves and stems are smaller and finer. The flowers are yellowish white (creamy) and appear before *S. a. japonica* in 3 to 6" long panicles. I have seen plantings in various arboreta where the two plant types were flowering at about the same time. The habit tends to be bushy, spreading and rounded. The bark is often quite handsome and adds significantly to the plant's landscape assets. There is a clone named 'Pendula' with drooping branches. Northern China. Introduced 1881. Zone 4.

ADDITIONAL NOTES: Both plant types deserve further use. The Pekin Lilac is interesting but from what I can gather little known and little grown.

NATIVE HABITAT: Japan. Introduced 1876.

Syringa meyeri — Meyer Lilac, in the trade often referred to as *S. palibiniana* or possibly *S. velutina*.

FAMILY: Oleaceae

LEAVES: Opposite, simple, elliptic-ovate to sometimes elliptic-obovate, 4/5 to 1 3/5" long, acute or obtusish, glabrous above, scarcely paler beneath and pubescent on the veins near base, with 2 to 3 pairs of veins from base nearly to apex, dark green, somewhat lustrous, with a reddish purple rim around margin of young leaves; petiole 1/5 to 2/5" long.

SIZE: 4 to 8′ high and 1 1/2 times that in spread.
HARDINESS: Zone 5.
HABIT: Small, dense, neat, broad-rounded, mounded shrub.
RATE: Slow.
TEXTURE: Medium-fine in leaf; medium in winter.
LEAF COLOR: New leaves rimmed with a purplish margin, finally turning dark green; fall color is nonexistent.
FLOWERS: Violet-purple (I see pink in them but most of the botanical descriptions do not), early to mid May, effective for 10 to 14 days, fragrant but not the soft fragrance associated with Common Lilac; literally cover the entire plant and are spectacular. One of the best for flower effect.
FRUIT: Capsule.
CULTURE: Does well in the Midwest, does not contract mildew like other species, requires little or no maintenance.
LANDSCAPE VALUE: Very handsome lilac, will start to flower when about one foot high; extremely floriferous; best used in shrub border with an evergreen background, flowers before leaves are fully developed; the flower buds emerge very early and can be injured by a late freeze. In spring of 1974 the plants on campus did not have one flower (late frost), in 1975 they were a solid mass of color.
PROPAGATION: Cuttings, softwood, will root but the percentage has not been high under our test conditions.
RELATED SPECIES:

Syringa microphylla – Littleleaf Lilac
LEAVES: Opposite, simple, orbicular-ovate to elliptic-ovate, 2/5 to 1 3/5″ long, obtuse or abruptly acuminate, broad-cuneate to rounded at base, slightly pilose and medium green above, grayish green and pubescent beneath, at maturity only on the veins, ciliolate, or nearly glabrous, petiole 1/5 to 2/5″ long. Wyman noted the leaves are about the same size and shape as those of *L. tatarica.*

Syringa microphylla, Littleleaf Lilac, is a very handsome, broad spreading, dense shrub usually about 1 1/2 to 2 times as broad as tall; 6′ by 9-12′; the medium green leaves are about one-quarter the size of those of *S. vulgaris*; flowers are rosy-lilac, fragrant, borne in small 1 1/2 to 2 1/2″ long panicles in late May into early June and often flowering sporadically again in September. Makes a nice plant for the shrub border, in groupings, possibly a free-standing hedge; 'Superba' has single, deep pink flowers, grows twice as broad as tall; native to Northern China. Introduced 1910; Zone 4.

Syringa velutina – Manchurian Lilac
LEAVES: Opposite, simple, larger than those of *S. meyeri* or *S. microphylla*, 2 to 5″ long, elliptic to ovate-oblong, acuminate, broad-cuneate or rounded at base, slightly pubescent to glabrous above, densely pubescent beneath or pilose only on midrib or veins; petiole 1/5 to 2/5″ long.

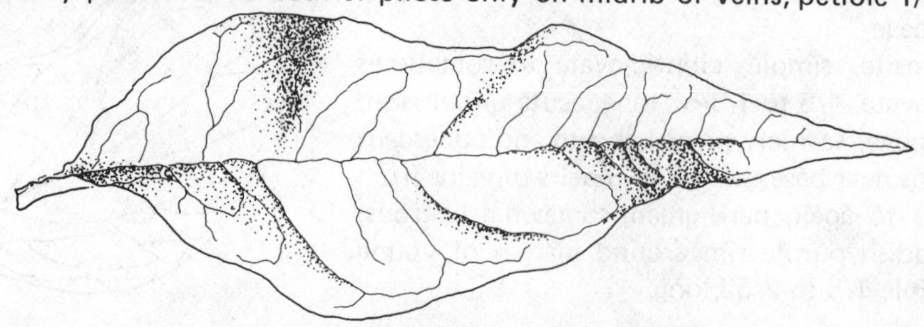

Syringa velutina, Manchurian Lilac, is confused (and justifiably so) with the above species. *S. velutina* is a more upright, vigorous shrub (9′) than *S. meyeri*. Otherwise the characteristics appear similar. 'Miss Kim' is a clone listed as growing 3′ high and 3′ wide with 3″ panicles of purple buds which open to fragrant icy blue flowers. I have seen this clone growing in the Holden Arboretum and, at that time, it was 6′ high and 4 to 5′ wide. Northern China, Korea. Cultivated 1902. Zone 3. The so called *S. palibiniana* is used in the nursery trade and does not really exist. One is buying either *S. meyeri* or *S. velutina* or, perhaps, *S. microphylla*.

NATIVE HABITAT: Northern China. Introduced 1908.

Syringa villosa — Late Lilac

FAMILY: Oleaceae

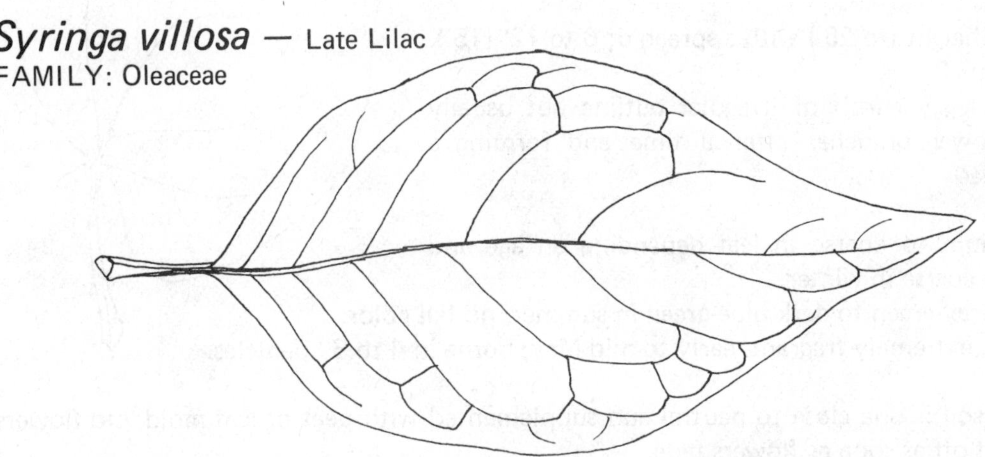

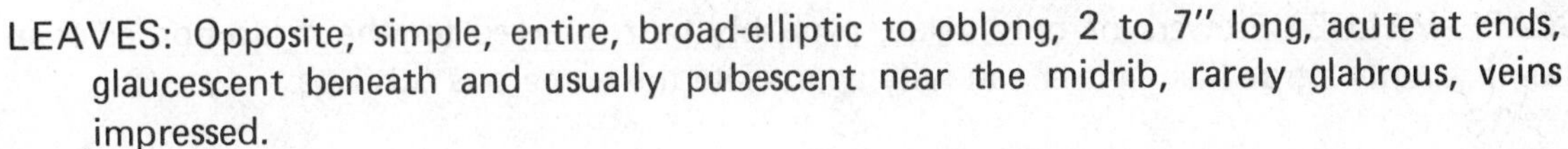

LEAVES: Opposite, simple, entire, broad-elliptic to oblong, 2 to 7″ long, acute at ends, glaucescent beneath and usually pubescent near the midrib, rarely glabrous, veins impressed.

SIZE: 6 to 10′ high and 4 to 10′ wide.
HARDINESS: Zone 2.
HABIT: Bushy shrub of dense habit with erect or ascending, stout, stiff branches.
RATE: Slow to medium.
TEXTURE: Medium in leaf and winter.
LEAF COLOR: Medium green in summer.
FLOWERS: Rosy lilac to white, not as fragrant as *S. vulgaris*, with a curious odor similar to privet; late May possibly into early June; borne in dense pyramidal 3 to 7″ long panicles.
FRUIT: Capsule.
CULTURE: See under *S. a. japonica*.
DISEASES AND INSECTS: See under *S. a. japonica*.
LANDSCAPE VALUE: Nice lilac for the shrub border.
CULTIVARS: The Preston Lilacs are the result of crosses between *S. villosa* and *S. reflexa*. They are extremely hardy (Zone 2) and possess many of the morphological features of *S. villosa*.

'Audrey' — Phlox purple, with 7″ by 6″ panicles.

'Donald Wyman' — Deepest pink to almost reddish flowers with buds and flowers the same color.

'Handel' — Amaranth rose buds fading to white when open with tight 5″ by 3″ panicles.

'Isabella' — Pink flowers and the largest pyramidal panicles.

PROPAGATION: Softwood cuttings, the softer the better.
ADDITIONAL NOTES: Despite the lack of overwhelming fragrance this group of lilacs deserves landscape consideration because of lateness and quantity of flowers. The habit is also quite neat, dense, and compact.
NATIVE HABITAT: China. Cultivated 1802.

Syringa vulgaris — Common Lilac

FAMILY: Oleaceae

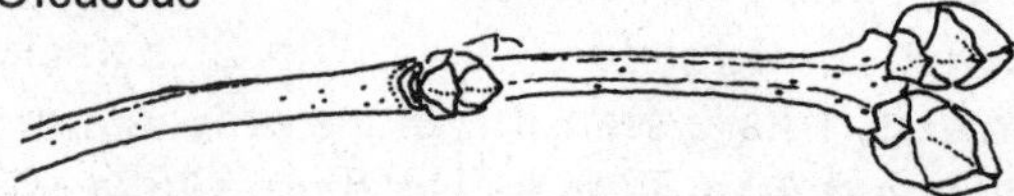

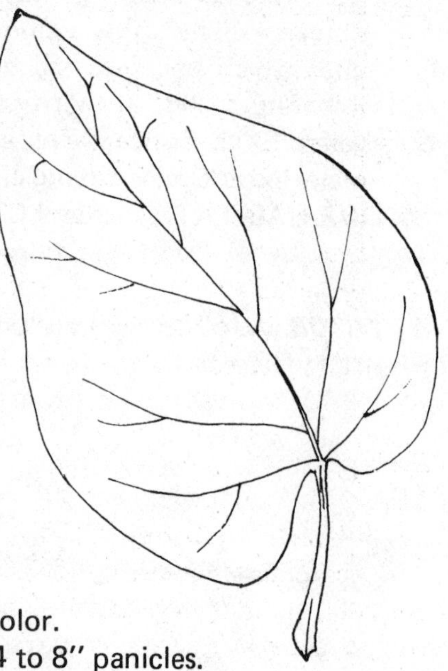

LEAVES: Opposite, simple, entire, ovate or broad-ovate, 2 to 5" long, acuminate, truncate or subcordate, broad-cuneate, glabrous; petiole—3/5 to 1 1/5" long. Dark green, often bluish green.

SIZE: 8 to 15' in height (to 20') with a spread of 6 to 12' (15').
HARDINESS: Zone 3.
HABIT: Upright leggy shrub of irregular outline but usually devoid of lower branches after a time and forming a cloud-like head.
RATE: Medium.
TEXTURE: Medium to coarse in leaf depending on age and size of plant; coarse in winter.
LEAF COLOR: Gray-green to dark blue-green in summer; no fall color.
FLOWERS: Lilac, extremely fragrant, early to mid May; borne in 4 to 8" panicles.
FRUIT: Capsule.
CULTURE: Best soil is one close to neutral and supplemented with peat or leaf mold; old flowers should be cut off as soon as flowers fade.
LANDSCAPE VALUE: Flowers of only value, probably best reserved for the shrub border or in groupings; only a true lilac fancier can fully appreciate the numerous cultivars.
CULTIVARS:

var. *alba* — White flowering type.

There are over 400, possibly 800 to 900 different clones and it is hopeless to attempt to list them. Donald Wyman has a valuable list in his *Shrubs and Vines for American Gardens* based on observations of the lilac collections at the Arnold Arboretum.

PROPAGATION: Softwood cuttings under mist; semi-hard wood or mature cuttings also work; or can dig up suckers and replant.
RELATED SPECIES:

Syringa x *chinensis* — Chinese Lilac

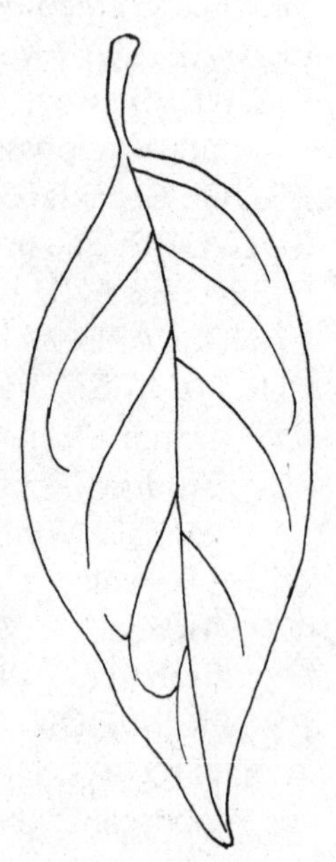

LEAVES: Opposite, simple, entire, ovate-lanceolate, 1 3/5 to 3" long, acuminate, cuneate; petiole—3/5" long.
BUDS: Smaller and more refined than those of *S. vulgaris*.

Syringa x *chinensis*, Chinese Lilac, also listed as *S. rothomagensis*, is a hybrid between *S. vulgaris* and *S. persica.* The shrub is graceful, broad spreading, round-topped, with arching branches, more delicate and more profuse in flower than *S. vulgaris*. Grows to 8 to 15' tall and as wide. Flowers are purple-lilac, fragrant, mid-May, borne in large and loose 4 to 6" long panicles; one of the more handsome hybrid lilacs and often spoken of as the first hybrid lilac, originated as a chance seedling at Rouen, France, 1777. Midway in leaf size and habit between Persian and Common Lilac. Can become ratty looking like *S. vulgaris* and proper pruning techniques are a must. The cultivar 'Alba' has white flowers, and 'Saugeana' has lilac-red flowers.

Syringa laciniata — Cutleaf Lilac

LEAVES: Opposite, simple, all or partly 3 to 9 lobed, very interesting and different leaf texture for a lilac.

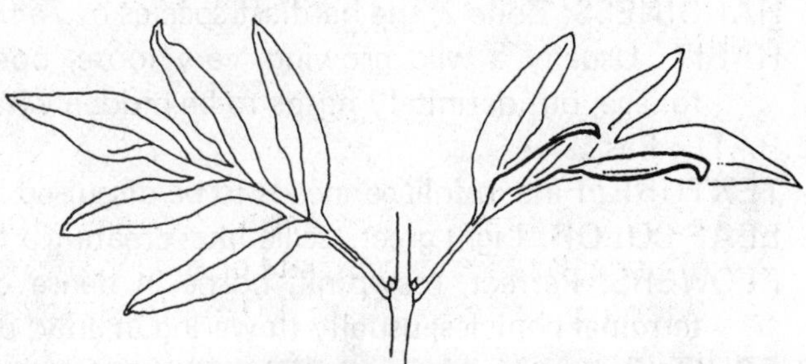

Syringa laciniata, Cutleaf Lilac, is a somewhat confused entity and at one time was listed as a variety of *S. persica*. The habit is low, dense, rounded-mounded to about 6′ in height. The small, pale lilac flowers are often borne all along the stems in May. The lacy, fine-textured foliage is an unusual asset and quite striking when one considers the usual foliage complement of most *Syringa*. Hardy to at least Zone 4 as I have seen a thriving specimen in the Wisconsin Landscape Arboretum. Considered native to Turkestan and China.

Syringa persica — Persian Lilac

LEAVES: Opposite, simple, lanceolate, 1 1/5 to 2 2/5″ long, acuminate, cuneate, dark green above, often infested with mildew to a degree that the leaves assume a whitish cast.

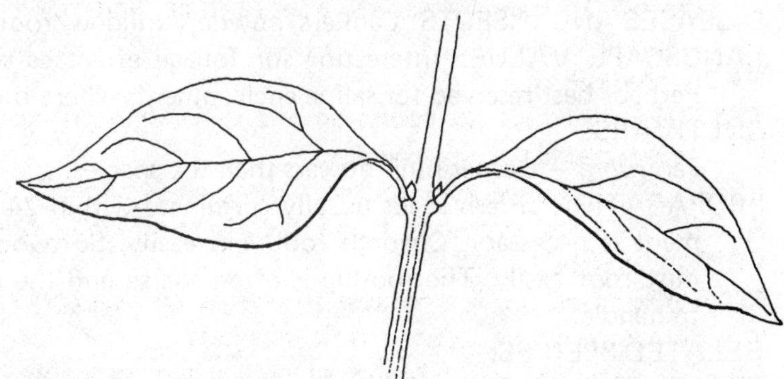

Syringa persica, Persian Lilac, is a graceful shrub with upright, arching branches reaching 4 to 8′ in height and spreading 5 to 10′. The foliage is bluish green; flowers are pale lilac, fragrant, mid-May, borne profusely in broad, 2 to 3″ long panicles. A nice small lilac with a mass of flower when properly grown, good plant for the shrub border. Iran to Northwestern China. Introduced 1614. Zone 5. According to Wyman this may not be a true species and, in fact, may be a hybrid between *S. laciniata* x *S. afghanica* since it is almost completely sterile and probably has not been found wild in any country.

ADDITIONAL NOTES: Two of the nicest lilac collections I have seen are located at the Arnold Arboretum and Royal Botanic Garden, Hamilton, Ontario, Canada.

NATIVE HABITAT: Southern Europe. Cultivated 1563.

Tamarix pentandra — Five-stamen Tamarix

FAMILY: Tamaricaceae

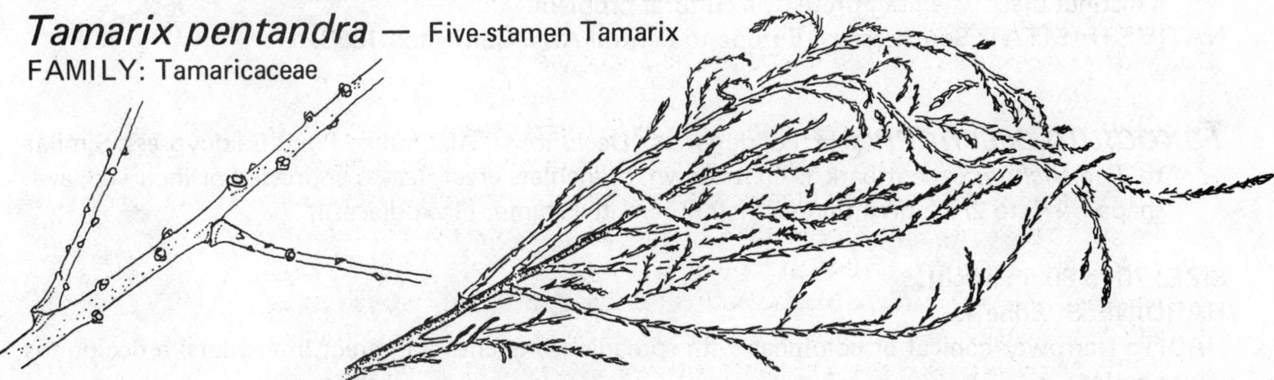

LEAVES: Alternate, simple, lanceolate to ovate, acute, glaucous, small, usually scale-like, bright green; similar to juniper foliage.

BUDS: Small, sessile, rounded, compressed against twig, solitary or quickly becoming concentrically multiple, with about 3 exposed scales.

STEM: Slender, elongated, rounded; pith small, rounded, continuous.

SIZE: 10 to 15′ high; usually less in spread.

HARDINESS: Zone 2; the hardiest species of *Tamarix*.

HABIT: Usually a wild growing, very loose, open shrub; can be attractive with its fine-textured foliage, but definitely needs to be hidden when defoliated.

RATE: Fast.

TEXTURE: Fine in foliage; needs to be disguised in winter (coarse).

LEAF COLOR: Light green, scale-like; creating a feathery appearance.

FLOWERS: Perfect, rosy-pink, borne in dense or slender 1 to 3" long racemes which form large terminal panicles; usually flowering in July; quite attractive.

FRUIT: Capsule, inconsequential.

CULTURE: Root systems are usually very sparse and, for this reason, care should be exercised in planting; container-grown plants are the best bet; prefer well-drained soil; full sun; not really particular as to soil and can grow in sand; ideal for seashore plantings as they are fantastically salt tolerant; prune back this species in early spring since it flowers on new growth.

DISEASES AND INSECTS: Cankers, powdery mildew, root rot, wood rot, and scales.

LANDSCAPE VALUE: Interesting for foliage effect as well as flowers but its uses are limited. Perhaps best reserved for saline environments where it does amazingly well.

CULTIVARS:

var. *rubra* — Deeper pink flowers than the species.

PROPAGATION: Fresh seeds usually germinate within 24 hours after imbibing water. No pretreatment is necessary. Cuttings root very easily. Softwood cuttings, placed in peat:perlite under mist root easily. The rooting is often sparse and the roots are coarse and somewhat difficult to handle.

RELATED SPECIES:

Tamarix odessana, Odessa Tamarix, grows to 6', is of neater habit than the above species and best suited for small gardens. The flowers are pink, borne on new growth in panicles in July. Should be pruned before new growth starts in the spring. Native to the Caspian region. Introduced about 1885. Zone 4.

Tamarix parviflora, Small-flowered Tamarix, grows 12 to 15' high, flowers on previous year's growth and should be pruned immediately after flowering. The flowers are light pink and usually develop in late May through early June. Supposedly very similar to *T. odessana* except it is larger in size and flowers earlier. Native to Southeastern Europe. Cultivated 1853. Zone 4.

ADDITIONAL NOTES: This genus does not seem to like high fertility soils, and I have noticed decline in container-grown specimens under high nutritional status. The plants also become more open and leggy than normal when grown under high fertility. This is a genus which has a distinct place when salt presents a cultural problem.

NATIVE HABITAT: Southeastern Europe to Central Asia. Cultivated 1883.

Taxodium ascendens — Pondcypress (Deciduous). Also called Pond Baldcypress. Similar to *T. distichum* except bark is light brown; branchlets erect, leaves appressed or incurved, awl-shaped, 1/5 to 2/5", bright green, rich brown in autumn. (Taxodiaceae)

SIZE: 70 to 80' in height.

HARDINESS: Zone 4.

HABIT: Narrowly conical or columnar with spreading branches and erect branchlets; a deciduous conifer.

RATE: Slow to medium (18' in 20 years).

TEXTURE: Fine in foliage; medium in winter.

LEAF COLOR: Bright green changing to rich brown in autumn.

FLOWERS: Monoecious; male flowers ovoid, forming terminal and drooping panicles; female flowers scattered near the ends of branches of the previous year, sub-globose.

FRUIT: Cones short-stalked, globose or ovoid, 2/5 to 1 1/5" across, purplish and resinous when young, ripening the first year.

CULTURE: Easy to transplant, adaptable, prefers swampy, moist soils, full sun and open areas, performs well on upland soils, extremely wind firm.

DISEASES AND INSECTS: None serious.

LANDSCAPE VALUE: Specimen for parks, large areas, wet and dry places.

CULTIVARS:

'Nutans' – Branches short, horizontal, some ascending parallel with the trunk; branchlets crowded, closely set.

'Prairie Sentinel' – An Earl Cully introduction. Very tall in relation to width, 60' tall and 10' wide with very soft, fine-textured foliage. Does well on upland soil and on very moist sites.

PROPAGATION: *Taxodium* seeds exhibit an apparent internal dormancy which can be overcome by 90 days of cold stratification, preceded by a 5 minute soak in ethyl alcohol. Pondcypress seeds respond well to 60 to 90 days of stratification at 38°F in peat moss, preceded by 24 to 48 hour soak in 0.01% nitric acid.

ADDITIONAL NOTES: This species is now listed as a variety by several authors under the name *nutans*. I have treated it as a species, however, this may not be the case although everyone does not agree on the classification.

NATIVE HABITAT: Southeastern United States (Virginia to Florida and Alabama). Cultivated 1789.

Taxodium distichum – Common Baldcypress (Deciduous)

LEAVES: Spirally arranged on the branchlets, 2-ranked on the deciduous shoots, linear-lanceolate, apiculate, 1/3 to 3/4" long, delicate green in spring, yellowish green in summer, rich brown in autumn.

BUDS: Alternate, near tip of stem rounded, with overlapping, sharp-pointed scales; smaller lateral buds also present, and from them leafy, budless branches arise which fall in autumn.

STEMS: Of two kinds: lateral branchlets green, deciduous; young branchlets green, becoming brown the first winter.

SIZE: 50 to 70' high by 20 to 30' wide, can grow to 100' and more.

HARDINESS: Zone 4, Baldcypress has been planted far north of its natural range. There are specimens in Minnesota, southern Canada and a few 75-year-old trees in Syracuse, New York. Some of these trees have withstood temperatures of -20 to -30°F.

HABIT: A lofty, deciduous conifer of slender, pyramidal habit, almost columnar in youth, with a stout, straight trunk buttressed at the base and short, horizontal branches, ascending at the ends, the lateral branchlets pendulous; sometimes becoming irregular, flat-topped and picturesque in old age.

RATE: Medium, 50 to 70' high in 30 to 50 years.

TEXTURE: Medium-fine in leaf; medium in winter.

LEAF COLOR: Bright yellow-green in spring; it darkens in summer to a soft sage green. In autumn it becomes a russet or soft brown.

FLOWERS: Monoecious, staminate in drooping panicles; pistillate cones are subglobose, comprising several spirally arranged peltate scales, each bearing 2 erect, basal ovules.

FRUIT: Cones globular or obovoid, short-stalked, approximately 1" across, purple and resinous when young. It matures the first year.

CULTURE: Transplants readily balled and burlapped; makes its best growth on deep, fine, sandy loams with plenty of moisture in the surface layers and moderately good drainage. In the wild it is seldom found on such places and occurs primarily in permanent swamps where it forms pure stands; very adaptable tree to wet, dry and well drained soil conditions; soils should be acid for chlorosis will occur on high pH soils; several trees on our campus were almost golden yellow and when treated with a trunk injection of ferric ammonium citrate they greened up within a month. Exceptionally wind firm and even winds of hurricane force rarely overturn them.

DISEASES AND INSECTS: Twig blight, wood decay, cypress moth, spider mites, and a gall forming mite.

LANDSCAPE VALUE: A stately tree, conventional and fastidious under cultivation; a decided accent of texture and of form. In parks or large estates it makes a distinctive specimen; good for wet areas; possibly a worthwhile highway plant or street tree.

CULTIVARS:

'Monarch of Illinois' — Truly a handsome specimen. Wide spreading, the parent tree has a limb spread of 65' and a height of 85'. This type of growth habit is unusual for this species.

'Pendens' — Pyramidal form; branches nearly horizontal, nodding at the tips, branchlets drooping.

'Shawnee Brave' — Form with narrow pyramidal habit. Parent tree is 75' tall and 18' across. Has street tree and single specimen possibilities.

PROPAGATION: As previously discussed under *T. ascendens*. I have rooted cuttings with 30 to 40% success using very soft growth; 1000 ppm IBA, under mist, in peat:perlite.

NATIVE HABITAT: Southeastern and South Central United States (Delaware to Florida, west to Southern Illinois, Missouri, Arkansas and Louisiana). Introduced 1640.

Taxus — Yew

Taxaceae

The genus *Taxus* is considered to include the highest quality needle type evergreens in landscape use. The quality characteristics include slow to moderate growth rate, resistance to insects and diseases, excellent year-round color, wide variations in form, compact growth habit, winter hardiness, and ease of propagation. *T. canadensis* and *T. brevifolia* are native to this country; however, the important ornamental cultivars are found in the species *T. cuspidata* and *T.* x *media* with a few excellent types in the species *T. baccata*. Many of the *T. baccata* types are tender and may be damaged or discolored during winter in the midwest. In addition to the factors mentioned above, the colorful red seed is an effective ornamental feature on some cultivars. Literature has it that Robin Hood made his bows from the yew tree.

Unfortunately the nomenclature of *Taxus* is as confused as is any genus. This has come about because of the lack of clear distinguishing features between cultivars, and the indiscriminate naming of cultivars by numerous plantsmen. This problem is particularly serious in the *T. cuspidata* and *T.* x *media* types; whereas the naming of *T. baccata* types, which have been under cultivation for hundreds of years, is less confused. A collection of *Taxus* was begun at the Ohio Agricultural Research and Development Center in Wooster in 1942. This collection, containing over 100 cultivars, is the largest in the world and is intended to serve as a base for selecting outstanding forms which, after positive identification, are being disseminated throughout the world.

MORPHOLOGICAL CHARACTERISTICS

Evergreen trees and shrubs with reddish to brown bark and spreading and ascending branches. Branchlets are green. Leaves are glossy or dull dark green above, lighter green below, flat and needle-like, abruptly pointed or tapering and acute. *T. baccata* types usually have sickle shaped leaves. Leaves are arranged radially or in a flat plane. Winter buds are small and scaly. With rare exceptions, plants are dioecious with the *male flowers globose* and the *female flowers appearing as small stalked conical buds.* The seeds are brown and nut-like covered by an attractive fleshy red aril, ripening the first year; cotyledons 2. If one is interested in securing "fruiting" plants the morphological differences italicized above are worth remembering.

GROWTH CHARACTERISTICS

There is a wide variation in habit, size, growth rate, and textural effects. Practically all cultivars are compact and retain a dense character with age, without extensive pruning. In addition to overall form, line and textural effects vary because of differences in branching habit and degree of compactness. Foliage color is essentially dark green with some variations to lighter greens and a few cultivars with yellow foliage. *Taxus* retain high quality characteristics indefinitely, and under good conditions, will continue to increase in value with age.

CULTURE

Taxus are most effectively moved balled and burlapped and can be planted in spring or fall with good success. Some growers are producing container yews and this represents an alternate choice to balled and burlapped specimens. Yews require a fertile soil, sufficient moisture, and *excellent* drainage. Anything less than *excellent* drainage results in growth reductions or death of yews. Yews do equally well in sun or shade but should be kept out of sweeping winds. Often, in winter, the needles will brown or yellow because of desiccation. All, except some of the *T. baccata* cultivars, are reliably hardy in the midwest. Very few yews are used in Minnesota and areas with similar low temperatures.

Many of the cultivars are naturally compact and symmetrical and relatively little corrective pruning is necessary. *Taxus* can be pruned severely and it is possible to maintain plants at determined sizes and shapes by frequent pruning or shearing. This is particularly advantageous in the culture of formal *Taxus* hedges or screens where early spring pruning followed by removal of "feather growth" in the summer will maintain the desired form. Although it is common practice to shear *Taxus* into tight, formally shaped plants, more interesting and attractive plants will result from pruning rather than shearing to retain the natural habit and appearance of the cultivar. The tight pruning results in the formation of green meatballs, cubes, rectangles and other odd shapes.

DISEASES AND INSECTS

Needle blight, twig blight, root rot, other fungus diseases, twig browning, black vine weevil, strawberry root weevil, taxus mealybug, grape mealybug, scales, ants, termites, and nematodes.

PROPAGATION

Although *T. cuspidata capitata* is usually propagated from seed, all other cultivars are propagated by cuttings taken in late summer through winter and rooted in cold frames and greenhouses. Specific recommendations are listed under *T. canadensis*.

LANDSCAPE VALUE

Probably the only negative comment one can apply to yews is that they are overused. Their ubiquitous landscape uses make them a favorite choice of landscape designers. They appear, almost to the point of monotony, in hedges, foundations, groupings, broad masses and as facer plants.

The moderate growth rate, uniform habit, high quality appearance, and maintenance free aspect result in *Taxus* being classed as the best shrubby needle-type evergreen for landscape use. However, it should be emphasized that *T. baccata, T. cuspidata* and *T. media* can grow 40 to 50′ in height.

Taxus baccata — English Yew (Common Yew)

LEAVES: Spirally arranged, spreading all around in erect shoots but appearing more or less 2-ranked on horizontal shoots, linear, 1/2 to 1 1/4" long, convex and shining on the upper surface, with recurved margins and a prominent midrib, paler and yellowish green beneath with ill-defined lines of stomata, gradually tapering at the apex to a horny point.

STEM: Branchlets surrounded at the base by brownish scales.

SIZE: 36 to 60' high by 15 to 25' spread; usually smaller; tremendous number of clones all varying in size and shape.

HARDINESS: Zone 6 (5).

HABIT: Tree or shrub-like, wide-spreading and densely branched; broad-rounded, rounded or shrubby.

RATE: Slow.

TEXTURE: Medium.

BARK: Reddish brown, furrowed, thin, scaly, flaky.

LEAF COLOR: Dark green and lustrous above.

FLOWERS: Usually dioecious, male strobili stalked, globose, arising from the axils of the leaves on the undersides of the branchlets of the previous year, each consisting of 6 to 14 stamens with short filaments; female strobili solitary, green, from the leaf axils.

FRUIT: Seeds solitary, bi- seldom tri- or quadrangular, slightly compressed, 1/4" long, 1/5" broad, olive brown; aril roundish, red.

CULTURE: Well-drained, sun or shade, does well on chalky soils as well as acid soils. Prefers a moist, sandy loam. See culture sheet.

DISEASES AND INSECTS: *Taxus* mealybug, black vine weevil, *Taxus* scale, yew-gall midge.

LANDSCAPE VALUE: Useful in gardens and parks, in shade, for undergrowth, hedges, screens and foundation plantings. Used extensively for topiary work in England. Not outstandingly hardy in Zone 5 and inferior to *T.* x *media* and *T. cuspidata* types for that reason.

CULTIVARS: Den Ouden and Boom list over 100 cultivars of this species. Apparently cultivated in England for over 1000 years and numerous selections have been made. The following might be considered among the best.

'Adpressa' — Female form with a rounded, bush-like habit, needles about 3/5" long.

'Aurea' — Bushy, compact form, branchlets yellow when young, leaves with yellow margins with color most pronounced on the lower leaf surface; 30-year-old specimen is 8 by 15'.

'Dovastoniana' — Tree form, 9 to 15' high with horizontal branches and pendulous branchlets, needles almost blackish green. Male form.

'Elegantissima' — Compact form although with wide spreading branches, leaves striped a pale yellow and sometimes whitish, female, bears seeds prolifically.

'Erecta' — Raised from seed of the Irish Yew, wider than high; one old specimen in Kew Garden is 24' high by 90' in circumference.

'Fastigiata' — Most popular and picturesque of all forms, fastigiate with all branches rigidly upright in habit, leaves blackish green above, streaked with dull green and a narrow, slightly shining midrib beneath.

'Lutea' — Broad-spreading form, 9 to 15' wide with yellow seeds.

'Nana' — Dwarf form not exceeding 3', leaves much smaller and darker than the species.

'Pygmaea' — Dwarf form to 15" high, very dense and compact, leaves shining light green.

'Repandens' — Dwarf, wide-spreading form with the tips of the branchlets pendulous, leaves flat, shining dark green above, dull green below, Zone 5, very good looking plant.

'Washingtonii' — Open, loose form, 4.5 to 6' high and wide, branchlets yellowish green, leaves tinted a rich gold.

PROPAGATION: Most clonal selections of yews are propagated by cuttings, which root easily. Seedling propagation is little used, owing to the variation appearing in the progeny, the complicated seed dormancy conditions, and the slow growth of the seedlings. Side or side-veneer grafting is practiced for those few cultivars which are especially difficult to start by cuttings.

ADDITIONAL NOTES: Yews are mong the most toxic of plants. They appear to be poisonous all seasons of the year. The toxic principal is taxine. Foliage, bark, or seeds, whether dry or green, are toxic to people and to all classes of livestock. The fleshy red arils are not poisonous as the toxic principal is contained in the hard part of the seed. This is not digested and is passed so no harm is done. I had a veterinarian in one of my off-campus courses and while discussing yews he mentioned he had seen cows who had died from eating yew foliage and the amount removed from their stomach was very small in relation to their total body weight.

NATIVE HABITAT: Europe, Northern Africa, Western Asia.

Taxus canadensis — Canadian Yew

LEAVES: Densely set, in 2 ranks, 2/5 to 4/5" long, 1/16 to 1/12" wide, apex abruptly short pointed, with a slightly raised midrib above and below, flat dark green, assuming a reddish tint in winter.

SIZE: 3 to 6' by 6 to 8' broad.

HARDINESS: Zone 2.

HABIT: Often prostrate, loose, straggling; leaders prostrate and rooting in the ground; very straggly shrub compared to other yew types.

RATE: Slow.

TEXTURE: Medium.

LEAF COLOR: Flat, dark green assuming a reddish tint in winter.

FLOWERS: Monoecious, inconspicuous.

FRUIT: Seeds broader than high, aril light red.

CULTURE: Moist, sandy loam; sun or shade; transplanted balled and burlapped. Will not tolerate heat and drought.

DISEASES AND INSECTS: None serious.

LANDSCAPE VALUE: Suitable as a ground cover but only for underplanting in cool, shaded situations. The hardiest of the yews.

CULTIVARS:

'Stricta' — Branches stiffly upright yet the plant is wider than high at maturity.

PROPAGATION: Yew seeds are slow to germinate; natural germination not taking place until the second year. Seeds have a strong but variable dormancy that can be broken by warm plus cold stratification. One recommendation is to hold the seeds for 90 to 210 days at 60°F followed by 60 to 120 days at 36 to 41°F. Another recommendation specifies prechilling the seed for 270 days at 37° to 41°F. Most yews root readily from cuttings and the recommended practice is to procure cutting wood from October through January. The cuttings are treated with a hormone dip or powder (IBA, 5000 to 10,000 ppm quick dip or Hormodin #3) and placed in sand or sand:peat. Misting is used although I have placed flats of yew cuttings under the bench, watering them only when other plants need water and had excellent success. Rooting time is rather long and 2 to 3 months would probably represent an average time span from sticking to rooting.

NATIVE HABITAT: Newfoundland to Virginia, Iowa and Manitoba. Introduced 1800.

Taxus cuspidata — Japanese Yew

LEAVES: Short-stalked, mostly not distinctly 2-ranked, upright and irregularly V-shaped, straight or slightly curved, slightly leathery, apex rather abruptly sharp-pointed, 1/2 to 1" long, 1/12 to 1/8" wide, dull to dark lustrous green above, paler beneath with 2 yellowish green bands.

BUDS: Ovoid-oblong, chestnut brown, composed of overlapping, concave, ovate scales more or less keeled on the back.

SEEDS: Ovoid, about 1/5" long, aril—red.

SIZE: 10 to 40′ with an equal or greater spread; usually smaller depending on cultivar—see cultivar list for specifics.
HARDINESS: Zone 4.
HABIT: Crown erect or flattened, broad or narrow, of irregular habit and spreading or upright-spreading branches; can be grown as a tree or multistemmed shrub.
RATE: Slow.
TEXTURE: Medium.
BARK: On old tree-like specimens is a handsome reddish brown.
LEAF COLOR: Dark lustrous green above, yellowish green beneath.
FLOWERS: Dioecious, solitary, inconspicuous.
FRUIT: Seeds ovoid, about 1/5″ long by 1/6″ broad, compressed, aril red, seldom yellow.
CULTURE: Transplants well balled and burlapped. Prefers a moist, sandy loam although adaptable, must be well-drained, shade or sun, superior to other conifers in shade. Sun and wind may cause needles to turn yellowish brown. Furthermore, it endures the dust and smoke of city atmospheres surprisingly well and withstands any amount of pruning.
DISEASES AND INSECTS: None serious, see culture sheet.
LANDSCAPE VALUE: Excellent for many purposes: foundation plantings, hedges, screens, bonsai, masses, groupings, bank covers.
CULTIVARS:

'Aurescens' — Low, compact, slow-growing form, 1 by 3′, leaves of the current year's growth deep yellow, after first season changing gradually to green, male.

'Capitata' — Usually a pyramidal form, can be maintained in a tightly pruned form, however will grow to 40 to 50′.

'Densa' — Low shrub form, two times as broad as tall with extremely dark green leaves, 40-year-old specimen is 4 by 8′. Fruiting clone. One of the best dwarf forms.

'Expansa' — According to Wyman a name applied to many *Taxus cuspidata* seedlings with a vase-shaped habit. This form has an open center, loose foliage and branches at a 45 to 60° angle from the base. About 1 1/2 to 2 times as broad as high; male and female clones available.

'Intermedia' — Dwarf, round, compact, slow-growing form, leaves densely set, resembles 'Nana' with the same heavy plump dark green leaves; starts growth earlier in the season and grows faster.

'Jeffrey's Pyramidal' — Heavy fruiting, pyramidal form.

'Nana' — Slow-growing form with spreading branches, twice as wide as high. Forty-year-old plant—10 by 20′. Excellent fruiting form.

'Pyramidalis' — Pyramidal form with dark green leaves. Introduced by Hill's.

'Thayeri' — Slow-growing, wide-spreading form with branches at a 30° angle with ground and forming a flat-topped head. Centers are full. About twice as wide as high.

PROPAGATION: Cuttings of most clones will root readily. *Taxus cuspidata capitata* is often grown from seed as it comes fairly true-to-type. Cuttings from *capitata* should be collected from vertical terminal growth as laterally-spreading cuttings will develop into spreading types.
ADDITIONAL NOTES: The new growth on *Taxus* is a lovely soft yellow-green which develops in May and is effective for about one month. The emphasis on well-drained soil cannot be stressed enough. *Taxus* do not tolerate "wet feet" for any period of time. Even if they do not die the growth is often reduced. About the best advice is to plant high if the soil is hopelessly wet and use raised beds. Pruning can be accomplished about any time but early in the growing season is often recommended. Hard, close pruning is not recommended as this results in the formation of a shell of foliage and a very formal appearance. The best way is to hand prune removing the longest growth every other year and thus creating an "unpruned" effect.
NATIVE HABITAT: Japan, Korea, Manchuria. Introduced 1853.

Taxus x *media* — Anglojap Yew (*T. cuspidata* x *T. baccata*)

Similar to *T. cuspidata* is many respects, however, differing in olive color of the branchlets which do not change to brown the second year, the blunt bud scales and the distinct two-ranked leaves.

SIZE: Variable.

HARDINESS: Zone 4.

HABIT: Broad-pyramidal, medium-sized tree to large shrub, of spreading habit often with a central leader. Actually, it is very difficult to ascertain the exact habit and size of the Anglojap types since they are hybrids and the growth characters they exhibit are variable. I have seen the excellent *Taxus* collection at Wooster, Ohio, and it is here that growth differences are very evident. The plants have not been pruned and have developed naturally. It is extremely difficult to identify *Taxus* by needle characteristics and when they have been pruned into little squares, balls and hedges in the landscape, there is no hope. Often nurserymen sell *Taxus* "spreaders" which could be about anything.

RATE: Slow.

TEXTURE: Medium.

LEAF COLOR: Similar to *T. cuspidata*; dark green, often lustrous above, lighter green beneath.

FLOWERS: Dioecious, inconspicuous.

FRUIT: Fleshy, red aril.

CULTURE: Transplants well balled and burlapped. Prefers a moist, sandy, acid loam, must be well-drained, shade or sun.

DISEASES AND INSECTS: See culture sheet.

LANDSCAPE VALUE: Depending on the cultivar, may be used for hedges, screens, foundations, and mass plantings.

CULTIVARS:

'Amherst' — Male clone, slow-growing, dense, compact form; 12-year-old specimen is 6 by 9'.

'Berryhilli' — A female clone, dense growing spreading type, 20-year-old plant is 5 by 9'.

'Brownii' — Male clone with a densely rounded habit, foliage dark green, 9 by 12' after 15 to 20 years.

'Densiformis' — Dense, shrub-like form, twice as wide as high, needles bright green, first year branchlets greenish brown in winter.

'Halloriana' — Broad, compact form, branches erect, sprays erect, leaves densely set, dark green.

'Hatfieldii' — Dense, broad pyramidal form, leaves dark green; 20-year-old plant is 12 by 10'. A very excellent clone; predominantly male.

'Hicksii' — Male and female clones, columnar in habit, needles lustrous dark green above, lighter green beneath. Similar to the Irish Yew but more hardy; 20' high after 15 to 20 years.

'Kelseyi' — Erect, dense, compact form taller than broad, free fruiting female form. Very dark green needles; 20-year-old plant is 12 by 9'.

'Sentinalis' — Very narrow form, female; 10-year-old plant is 8 by 2'.

'Stoveken' — Male, excellent columnar form; 20-year-old specimen is 12 by 6'.

'Vermeulen' — Female, slow-growing, rounded type; 20-year-old plant is 8 by 9'.

'Wardii' — Wide-spreading, dense form, foliage dark green; 20-year-old plant is 6 by 19'.

PROPAGATION: Propagated vegetatively (cuttings) if their individual character is to be retained.

ADDITIONAL NOTES: A hybrid species first raised by T. D. Hatfield of the Hunnewell Pinetum, Wellesley, Massachusetts about 1900. Since that time numerous selections have been made and often it is difficult to tell if one is looking at a *T. cuspidata, T. baccata* or *T.* x *media* type. Unfortunately nurserymen have confounded the issue by indiscriminately naming clones which they thought were better and introducing them. When one sees a whole nursery block of a certain yew next to another block, specific differences are noticeable such as foliage color, needle density, and habit; but once they have been massacred in the landscape by the hedge shears (worst landscape tool ever invented), there is no effective way to distinguish between and among different clones.

A recent publication titled "A Study of the Genus *Taxus*" is available from the OARDC, Wooster, Ohio, as Research Bulletin 1086. The publication contains a wealth of information on the *Taxus* collection at Wooster, early history of yews, the development of the Hatfield yews, morphology, sex and fruiting characteristics, propagation, culture and an extensive treatment of *Taxus* species, clones, and cultivars. Written by Drs. R. A. Keen and L. C. Chadwick and should prove invaluable for anyone interested in this most important group of landscape evergreens.

Thuja – Arborvitae

Cupressaceae

The genus *Thuja* constitutes a major group of small to medium size evergreens used extensively in landscape plantings. Many cultivars of different form, size, and with varied foliage color are available. Five species in cultivation are native in North America and Eastern Asia. *T. orientalis* is the least hardy of the species and is used extensively on the West Coast and in the South. Some cultivars of *T. occidentalis* are of good quality; however, many types have a tendency to discolor in the winter, with center foliage browning in the fall. *T. plicata* and *T. standishi* have the best foliage characteristics of the species. *T. koraiensis* is not common in cultivation, but has proven hardy in Central Illinois. *T. occidentalis* and *T. plicata* are important timber trees, the wood being used extensively for shingles, shakes, siding and poles. Arborvitae are not considered to be of the highest quality because of winter discoloration, loss of foliage and a thin and "ratty" appearance with age. Because of this, many types tend to decrease rather than increase in value, especially in congested planting sites. The cultivars 'Nigra' and 'Techny' are very valuable for they maintain good dark green foliage color in all seasons.

MORPHOLOGICAL CHARACTERISTICS

Evergreen small trees and shrubs with thin scaly bark and spreading or erect branches. Juvenile leaves are needle-like and the mature foliage scale-like and imbricate in four rows with glands sometimes on the back. The lateral leaves nearly cover the facial ones with branchlets flattened in one plane. Flowers are monoecious with male types yellow and female types rounded and forming a bluish rounded cone. Cones solitary, ovoid or oblong; scales 8-12, with a thickened apical ridge or process, the 2 or 3 middle pairs fertile; seeds 2-3 beneath each scale, thick, wing broad or thick, or seeds wingless; cotyledons 2.

GROWTH CHARACTERISTICS

Arborvitaes are usually dense, pyramidal trees but vary from narrow- to broad-pyramidal. Numerous cultivars have been selected from *T. occidentalis* and *T. orientalis* and a selected few are available in the trade. Cultivars range from dwarf, rounded shapes, to globe, to narrow-upright types with foliage colors of yellow, bluish and various shades of green.

CULTURE

Arborvitaes should be planted in fertile, moist, well drained soils, although in the wild the species may be found on wet and dry soils, however, maximum growth is not realized on these sites. They are easily transplanted balled and burlapped about any time of year. Arborvitaes perform best in full sun, although light shade is acceptable. In heavy shade plants become loose, open and lose their dense constitution. The characteristic winter browning of *T. occidentalis* and cultivars results in an unsightly plant. *T. orientalis* also suffers from low temperature stresses and probably should be avoided in Zone 5 gardens. Pruning can be accomplished prior to growth in the spring. Usually extensive pruning is not necessary and if heavy pruning is practiced the result is similar to that achieved with tightly pruned yews.

DISEASES AND INSECTS

Leaf blight, juniper blight, tip blight, arborvitae aphid, cedar tree canker, arborvitae leaf miner, mealybug, scales, and other pests.

(Physiological Diseases)

Leaf browning and shedding—inner leaves may be dropped in the fall.

Winter browning—caused by rapid temperature changes.

In general, arborvitaes exhibit few serious insect and disease problems.

PROPAGATION

Seeds do not usually require a stratification period although selected seed lots have exhibited dormancy. Stratification in a moist medium at 34 to 41°F for 30 to 60 days will stimulate prompt germination. Cuttings are taken in late summer through early winter. See specific recommendations under the species descriptions. Cultivars are also rooted from cuttings.

LANDSCAPE USE

Arborvitaes have received wide acceptance in landscaping and are commonly used in foundations and as screens, windbreaks, accent plants, or hedges. They make excellent tall hedges and screens and, to a degree, have become stereotyped in these roles. The yellow-foliaged forms should be used with discretion for they detract from surrounding plantings. Arborvitaes will always be popular landscape plants but some of the new cultivars should be used in preference to the seedling-grown material.

Thuja occidentalis — Eastern Arborvitae, American Arborvitae, White Cedar

LEAVES: Scale-like, abruptly pointed, those on the main axis conspicuously glandular; on the branchlets sometimes inconspicuously so, dark green above, pale green below, emitting a tansy-like odor when bruised.

BRANCHLETS: Alternate, compressed, flat; sprays horizontal, laterally compressed.

CONES: Oblong, 1/3 to 1/2″ long, yellowish and erect when young, brown and pendent when mature at the end of the first summer, scales 8 to 10, usually 4 fertile with a minute mucro at apex.

SIZE: 40 to 60′ high, usually less, by 10′ to 15′ spread.

HARDINESS: Zone 2.

HABIT: A dense, often broad-pyramidal tree with short ascending branches to the ground which end in flat, spreading, horizontal sprays. Usually there is one trunk but multiple trunks do occur. This is a good feature for separating this species from *T. orientalis* which develops many leaders and takes on a more dense bushy appearance with the sprays borne in strong vertical planes.

RATE: Slow to medium.

TEXTURE: Medium-fine.

BARK: Reddish to grayish brown, 1/4″ to 1/3″ thick, fibrous, forming a more or less close network of connecting ridges and shallow furrows, grayish on the surface.

LEAF COLOR: Flat green in summer changing to a yellow-brownish-green in winter.

FLOWERS: Monoecious, terminal, solitary.

FRUIT: Cones oblong, 2/5″ long, light brown; scales 8 to 10, usually 4 fertile, with a minute mucro at apex; seeds 1/8″ long, compressed; wing round the seed, narrow, emarginate.

CULTURE: Readily transplanted balled and burlapped if root pruned. Must be grown in areas with considerable atmospheric moisture as well as soil moisture. Requires a deep, well drained soil; thrives in marshy loam; full sun; tolerant of pruning; susceptible to strong wind, snow or ice damage, very tolerant of limestone soils.

DISEASES AND INSECTS: Subject to bagworm, heart rot and red spider mites; see culture sheet.

LANDSCAPE VALUE: Useful as a specimen or accent, good for hedges, shelterbelts and commonly used as a foundation plant. At times is over-used in landscape plantings. The cultivars 'Nigra' and 'Techny' are excellent for the Midwest. The species becomes yellow or brownish green in winter and is a rather ugly sight.

CULTIVARS:

'Aurea' – Broad shrub with golden yellow leaves.

'Boothii' – Dwarf, globular, dense, foliage bright green, broader than tall, flat-topped at maturity.

'Douglasii Aurea' – Pyramidal, slender, 30 to 45' tall, branchlets spreading; sprays yellow, grading to yellowish green at base. Leaves golden yellow, bronzed in winter.

'Ellwangeriana' – Juvenile form, conical, sometimes broad-pyramidal, 6 to 9' tall, leaves on developed branches and branchlets–scale-like, other leaves linear, spreading, acicular.

'Ericoides' – Juvenile form, dwarf, compact, rounded, 3' tall and wide, leaves linear, spreading in pairs, flat, apex sharp pointed, yellowish green in summer, brownish in winter.

'Globosa' – Dwarf, globular, 4.5 to 6' high and wide; leaves green, slightly grayish green in winter.

'Holmstrup' – Compact, slow growing, pyramidal form with bright green, tight, bunchy foliage, 5' by 2'.

'Little Gem' – Dwarf, globose, dense form, broader than tall, 4.5 to 6' in diameter, leaves dark green, slightly brown in winter.

'Lutea' – Pyramidal, narrow, 30 to 36' high, sprays and leaves golden yellow, light yellowish green on underside of branchlets.

'Nigra' – Pyramidal form with good dark green foliage persisting through the winter.

'Pyramidalis' – Narrow pyramidal, formal in outline with bright green soft textured foliage.

'Robusta' – Synonym for pyramidal, vigorous growing forms.

'Rosenthali' – Pyramidal, compact, slow-growing, 9 to 15' high, leaves shining dark green. Good hedge form.

'Spiralis' – Narrow pyramidal, slender, 30 to 45' high, branches short; branchlets spirally arranged, sprays somewhat fernleaf-shaped; leaves dark green.

'Techny' ('Mission') – Pyramidal form, excellent dark green foliage year-round, good hedge plant, slow growing.

'Umbraculifera' – Dwarf, globose, depressed, compact form, 3 to 4.5' high, leaves thin, green, glaucous, bloomy, probably most glaucous form.

'Wareana' – Pyramidal, low, dense, leaves bright green, without a brown tinge; 35-year-old plant is 8' tall.

'Woodwardii' – Globular form, wider than high, foliage dark green, turning brown in winter, 72-year-old plant–8' by 18'. A popular form.

PROPAGATION: Cuttings made from current year's wood, taken with a heel, rooted well when taken each month in November through March. Cuttings taken in and after January rooted a little more quickly.

NATIVE HABITAT: Eastern North America (Nova Scotia to Manitoba, south to North Carolina, Tennessee and Illinois). Introduced about 1536.

Thuja orientalis — Oriental Arborvitae, now listed as *Biota orientalis*

LEAVES: Smaller than those of other species, distinctly grooved on the back, those on main axis about 1/12" long, triangular, ending in a blunt point, not pressed close to the shoot, those on the finer spray about 2/3's as long, closely pressed, green on both surfaces, bearing minute stomata, giving off a slightly resinous odor when bruised. Branchlets arranged in a vertical plane.

CONES: Ovoid, fleshy, glaucous green before ripening, 2/5 to 4/5" long, 6 to 8 scales, each with horn-like process or hook.

SIZE: 18 to 25′ high by 10 to 12′ in width, however can grow 30 to 40′ high but this is seldom realized under cultivation.

HARDINESS: Zone 5 or 6.

HABIT: A large shrub or small tree of dense, compact, conical or columnar habit when young with the branchlets held vertically, becoming in age loose and open and not so markedly vertical; composed of many slender branches which tend to bend and break in ice and snow.

RATE: Slow to medium.

TEXTURE: Medium-fine.

LEAF COLOR: Bright yellow-green to grass-green in youth changing to a darker green when older.

FLOWERS: Monoecious, terminal, solitary.

FRUIT: Cones globose-ovate, 2/5 to 4/5″ long, fleshy, bluish before ripening; scales usually 6, ovate, each with a horn-like projection, the uppermost sterile; seeds 2 to each scale, ovoid, about 1/8″ across; wingless.

CULTURE: Transplant balled and burlapped, tolerant of moist soils except those that are extremely wet or dry. Needs less moisture than *T. occidentalis*, best if the winter atmosphere is dry, protect from sweeping winds; pH adaptable.

DISEASES AND INSECTS: Bagworm and red spider mites.

LANDSCAPE VALUE: Useful for hedges and specimens but not of value in the north central states although commonly sold; used extensively in the south.

CULTIVARS:

'Aurea Nana' — Dwarf, dense, globular to ovoid form to 5′ tall, foliage light yellow-green, slightly brownish in winter; probably can reach 15′.

'Baker' — Bright green foliage, densely set needles and broad conical shape; does well in hot dry places; grows 5 to 8′ high in 8 to 10 years.

'Compacta' — Pyramidal, dense, formal, slow-growing form, foliage glaucous green, tips plum colored in winter.

'Sieboldii' — Bright green foliage on a dense mounded plant that rarely exceeds 3′ in height.

'Westmont' — Compact, globe-shaped, slow growing type with rich dark green foliage tipped with yellow from spring to fall.

PROPAGATION: Seed germination is relatively easy but stratification of seeds for 60 days at about 40°F may be helpful. Cuttings of this species are more difficult to root than those of *T. occidentalis*. Small, softwood cuttings several inches long, taken in late spring, can be rooted in outdoor mist beds if treated with a root-promoting chemical.

ADDITIONAL NOTES: Always looks ragged in Central Illinois, especially during the winter; should not be used; if an arborvitae is desired, *T. occidentalis* cultivars should be the first choice. The scientific name is listed by some authorities as *Biota orientalis*.

NATIVE HABITAT: Korea, Manchuria and Northern China. Introduced before 1737.

Thuja plicata — Giant (Western) Arborvitae

LEAVES: On leading shoots parallel to the axis, ovate, long-pointed, each with an inconspicuous resin gland on the back, up to 1/4″ long, the points free; those on the ultimate divisions smaller, about 1/8″ or less long, ovate, short and bluntly pointed, closely overlapping and often without glands, glossy dark green above, usually faintly streaked with white beneath but on some branchlets remaining green; emitting a tansy-like odor when bruised.

STEM: Branches horizontal, often pendent at the ends; branchlets in the same plane, much divided, the small lateral shoots falling after 2 or 3 years; often fern-like or stringy in appearance.

SIZE: 50 to 70′ high and 15 to 25′ wide; can grow in areas of the northwest to 180 to 200′ high.

HARDINESS: Zone 5.

HABIT: A narrow, pyramidal tree with a buttressed base and often with several leaders; usually maintaining the lower branches.

RATE: Slow.

TEXTURE: Medium.

BARK: Cinnamon-red on young stems; gray on old trunks, 1/2 to 1" thick, fibrous, and forming a closely interlacing network.

LEAF COLOR: A good dark green in summer and winter.

FLOWERS: Monoecious, small, inconspicuous; staminate yellowish, pistillate pinkish.

FRUIT: Cones erect, cylindric-ovoid, 1/2" long, green in summer, brown in winter; scales 8 to 10, elliptic-oblong with usually the middle pair fertile; seeds winged; the wing notched apically.

CULTURE: Transplants readily balled and burlapped; prefers moist, well drained, fertile soils and in the wild is found on moist flats, slopes, the banks of rivers and swamps, and is even found in bogs; occasionally found on dry soils but growth is usually stunted; moist atmosphere; full sun or partial shade; pH adaptable.

DISEASES AND INSECTS: Bagworm and heart rot.

LANDSCAPE VALUE: Useful as a specimen or for hedges in formal and semi-formal plantings, groupings, screens.

CULTIVARS:

'Atrovirens' – Possibly the best of the large, pyramidal arborvitae types, excellent shining dark green foliage, an excellent hedge form.

'Fastigiata' – Supposedly a good columnar clone with a straight slender outline.

PROPAGATION: Dormant seed lots have been encountered occasionally on which stratification in a moist medium at 34° to 41°F for 30 to 60 days stimulated prompt germination (variation among seed lots). Seed treatments with potassium nitrate or gibberellic acid have been tested on a limited scale as an alternative for cold stratification. Cuttings rooted well when taken in January.

ADDITIONAL NOTES: Extremely handsome conifer; probably better than *T. occidentalis* from an ornamental standpoint. Principal timber tree used for shingle manufacture in the United States and Canada. Is used for poles, posts, piling, boxwood, house-building, garden buildings, summerhouses and greenhouses because of its durability. The Indians used the split trunks for totem poles and hollowed-out trunks for canoes. They used the inner bark for fiber which was woven into mats, baskets and hats. The roots are so tough that they were used for fish hooks.

NATIVE HABITAT: Alaska to Northern California and Montana. Introduced 1853.

Thymus serpyllum — Mother-of-Thyme

It is difficult to justify this in a woody plant manual but for sheer beauty in a rocky, dry area of the garden Thyme is unrivaled.

FAMILY: Labiatae

LEAVES: Opposite, simple, 1/5 to 1/2" long, short petioled, ovate or elliptic to oblong, obtuse, broad-cuneate, glabrous beneath or pubescent and ciliate; floral leaves similar.

SIZE: 1" to 3" high.

HARDINESS: Zone 4.

HABIT: Prostrate, weak subshrub or nearly herbaceous perennial; spreading, trailing, with rooting stems which ascend at the ends.

RATE: Slow.

TEXTURE: Fine in leaf; hardly noticeable in winter.

LEAF COLOR: Medium green although the numerous cultivars offer grayish, bluish, yellowish green, whitish margined, and yellowish colored foliage.

FLOWERS: On the species is rosy-purple, 1/4" long; June through September; borne in dense terminal heads. The flowers are beautiful and one can walk by Thyme without ever noticing it underfoot but the bright flowers make it come alive. The bees appreciate the flowers and from same manufacture a delicious honey.

CULTURE: Easily moved as clumps or from containers in spring; prefers dry, calcareous, well drained soil in a sunny location; if over-fertilized or the soil is too rich the stems become tall and weak and the plant loses its dainty character; plant 6 to 12" apart and they will fill in adequately in one growing season; makes an excellent cover for gentle slopes, a filler among rocks, dry walks, ledges or a crevice plant for walls, terraces, sidewalk cracks and the like.

DISEASES AND INSECTS: Apparently there are very few problems associated with the species although root rot and the ground mealybug have been noted.

LANDSCAPE VALUE: My first thorough introduction to this plant came as a graduate student when I took care of the Amherst, Massachusetts, Garden Club's 18th Century Garden. It was always a delight to watch the barren, sterile small stems yield the soft green and gray foliage in May after a long Massachusetts winter. The soft carpet was possibly the nicest bed I have ever slept upon and also the most fragrant. As discussed under culture this species and the many cultivars are well adapted for rocky, dry slopes, as an edging plant, ground cover or among stepping stones; will endure a modicum of mowing and occasional tramping.

CULTIVARS: I have had great difficulty locating specific names for many of the different flowering and foliage clones which exist. The following names represent my "best" attempts.

'Albus' — Possesses white flowers.

'Coccineus' — Has bright red flowers.

'Lanuginosus' — A type with gray-pubescent leaves and the appropriate name, Woolly Mother-of-Thyme.

'Roseus' — A pink flowering clone.

Other clones include one with lavender flowers; one with white leaf margins; one with yellow coloring in the leaves; lemon-scented thyme has yellow-green foliage.

PROPAGATION: Very easy to root from cuttings or simply divide the plant.

RELATED SPECIES: Other species include *T. lanicaulis,* Woolly-stem Thyme, and *Thymus vulgaris,* Common Thyme, which has been used for seasoning since earliest times. Both species are ornamentally inferior to *T. serpyllum* but are worth the effort for the collector and true plantsman.

NATIVE HABITAT: Europe, Western Asia, Northern Africa. Cultivated for centuries.

Tilia americana — American Linden (Basswood)

FAMILY: Tiliaceae

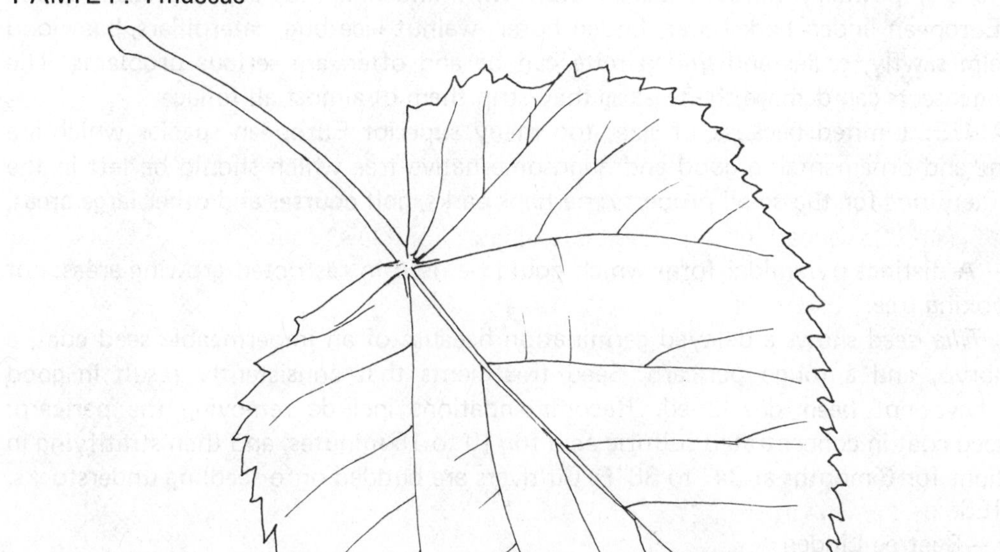

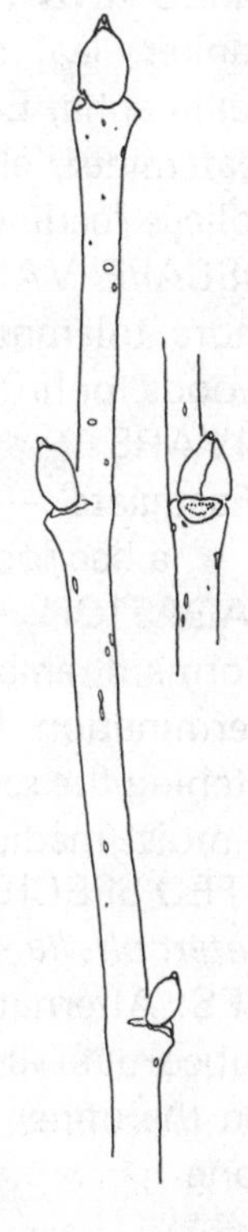

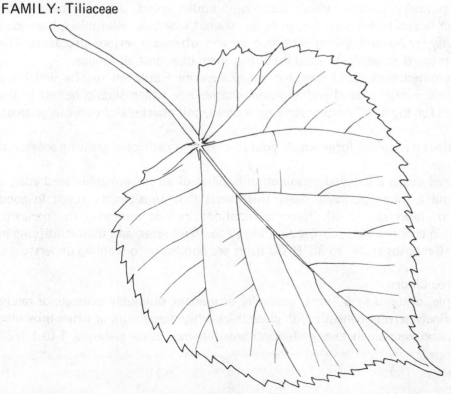

LEAVES: Alternate, simple, broad-ovate, 4 to 8" long, abruptly acuminate, cordate to truncate at base, coarsely serrate with long-pointed teeth, light green beneath, with tufts of hair on the axils of the lateral veins, wanting at base; petiole 1 to 2" long.

BUDS: Terminal—absent, laterals—1/8 to 2/5" long, somewhat flattened, often lopsided, divergent, brown, reddish brown or greenish, smooth or slightly downy at apex. Bud shaped like a teardrop.

STEM: Slender, smooth, shining brown or greenish red, covered with a bloom, generally zigzag.

SIZE: 60 to 80' in height with a spread of 1/2 to 2/3's the height, but can grow to 100' or more.

HARDINESS: Zone 2.

HABIT: Tall, stately tree with numerous, slender, low hung spreading branches; pyramidal in youth; at maturity the lower drooping down then up, forming a deep, ovate, oblong, or somewhat rounded crown.

RATE: Medium, 20 to 30' over a 20 year period although some authorities indicate the tree may grow 2 to 3' over a 10 to 20 year period. Soil conditions largely govern the growth rate.

TEXTURE: Coarse in all seasons.

BARK: Gray to brown, broken into many long, narrow, flat topped, scaly ridges.

LEAF COLOR: Dark green above, paler green beneath, sometimes changing to pale yellow in the fall; usually the leaves fall off green or yellow-green in Central Illinois. Leaves tend to develop a brownish cast in mid-September and actually become unsightly. This seems even more pronounced if the summer was extremely dry.

FLOWERS: Perfect, pale yellow, 3/5" long, fragrant, borne in 5 to 10 flowered, 2 to 3" wide pendulous cymes in mid to late June. Bees supposedly make the finest honey from these flowers.

FRUIT: Not clearly defined, but termed a nutlike structure, 1/3 to 1/2" long, grayish tomentose. Of no ornamental value.

CULTURE: Transplants readily; prefers deep, moist, fertile soils and here reaches maximum size but will grow on drier, heavier soils and is often found in the wild on the slopes of hills, even in rocky places; seems to be pH adaptable; full sun or partial shade; not particularly air pollutant tolerant.

DISEASES AND INSECTS: Anthracnose occasionally occurs on the European lindens, leaf blight, canker, leaf spots, powdery mildew, *Verticillium* wilt, linden aphid, Japanese beetle, elm calligrapha, European linden bark borer, linden borer, walnut lace bug, caterpillars, basswood leaf miner, elm sawfly, scales and linden mite can be and often are serious problems. The foliage feeding insects can damage the trees as they strip them of almost all foliage.

LANDSCAPE VALUE: Limited because of size; too many superior European species which are more tolerant and ornamental; a good and handsome native tree which should be left in the woods; definitely not for the small property; perhaps parks, golf courses and other large areas.

CULTIVARS:

'Fastigiata' — A distinct pyramidal form which could be used in restricted growing areas; not a bad looking tree.

PROPAGATION: *Tilia* seed shows a delayed germination because of an impermeable seed coat, a dormant embryo, and a tough pericarp. Seed treatments that consistently result in good germination have not been developed. Recommendations include removing the pericarp; etching the seed coat in concentrated sulfuric acid for 10 to 15 minutes, and then stratifying in a moist medium for 3 months at 34° to 38°F. Cultivars are budded onto seedling understocks.

RELATED SPECIES:

Tilia heterophylla — Beetree Linden

LEAVES: Alternate, simple, ovate, 3 to 5" long, gradually acuminate, obliquely truncate or rarely subcordate at base, finely serrate beneath with close thick white tomentum or often brownish on the upper leaves, and with small tufts of reddish brown hairs; petiole glabrous, 1 to 1 1/2" long.

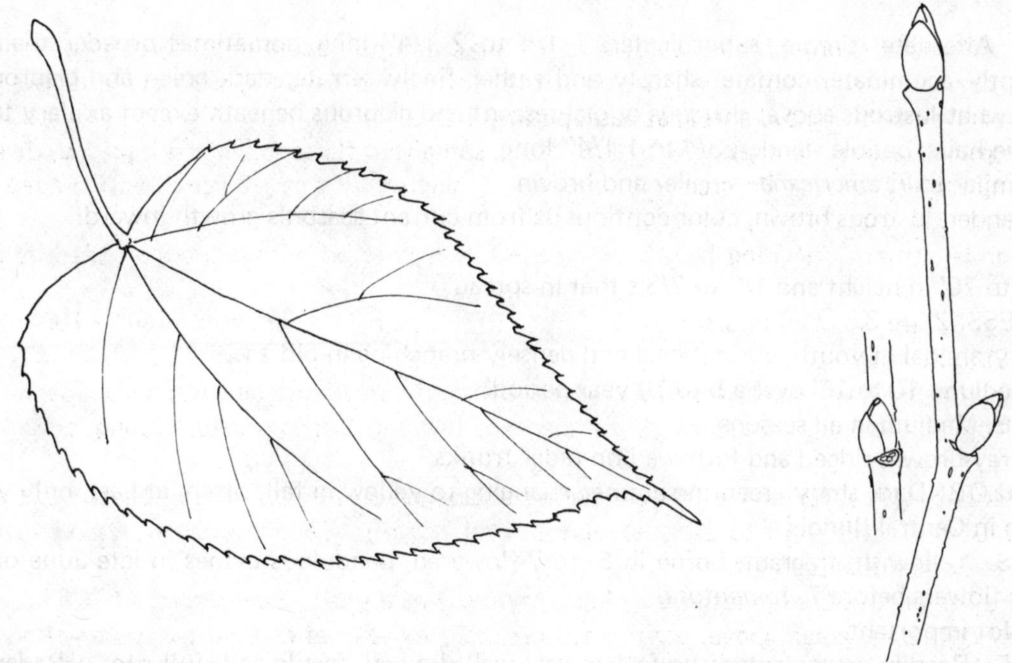

BUDS: Terminal-absent—laterals 1/4 to 1/2" long, prominently pointed, reddish maroon.
STEM: Glabrous, relatively stout, reddish maroon.

Tilia heterophylla, Beetree Linden, also called White Basswood, is similar to the preceding but is typically a southern species. Morphologically, very similar except for undersurface of leaf, which is densely whitish; flowers smaller (1/4" long) and 10 to 25 per inflorescence. I have reason to suspect that many of the trees in Champaign-Urbana are, in fact, *T. heterophylla* and possibly were bought from southern nurseries. Native from West Virginia to Northern Florida, Alabama and Indiana. Cultivated 1755. Zone 5.

ADDITIONAL NOTES: The wood of this tree is used for many purposes including furniture, boxes, cooperage, wooden ware, veneer and food containers. The tough inner bark is sometimes used for making rope.

NATIVE HABITAT: Northern half of Eastern United States. Introduced 1752.

Tilia cordata — Littleleaf Linden

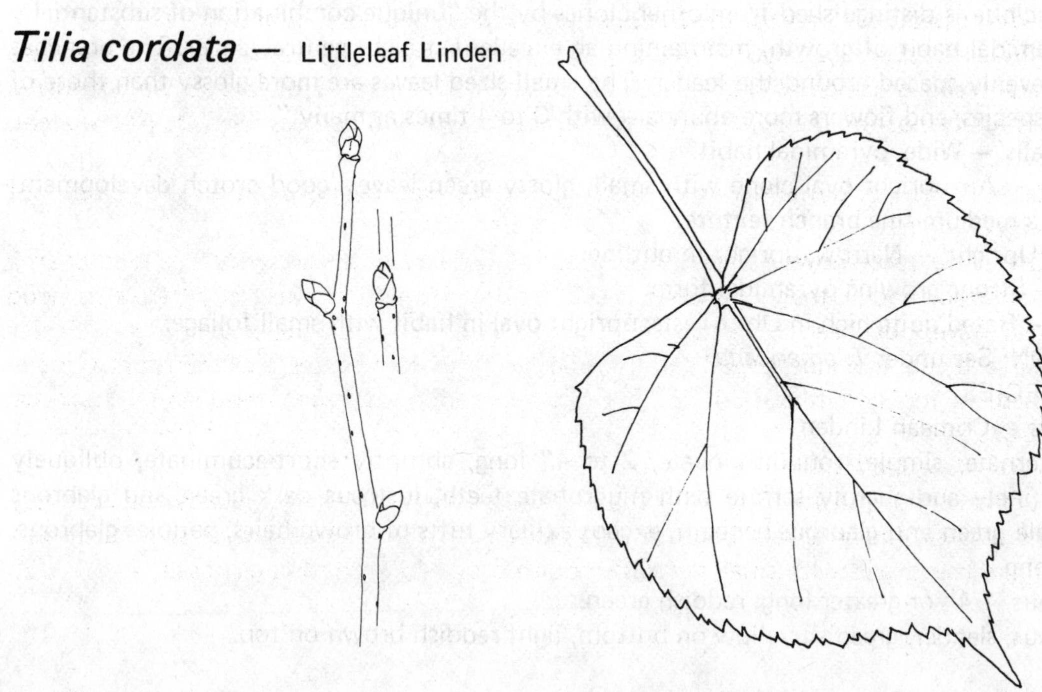

LEAVES: Alternate, simple, suborbicular, 1 1/4 to 2 1/4" long, sometimes broader than long, abruptly acuminate, cordate, sharply and rather finely serrate, dark green and glabrous and somewhat lustrous above, glaucous or glabrescent and glabrous beneath except axillary tufts of brown hairs; petiole slender, 3/4 to 1 1/4" long.

BUDS: Similar to *T. americana*—smaller and brown.

STEM: Slender, lustrous brown, color continuous from current season's growth inward.

SIZE: 60 to 70' in height and 1/2 to 2/3's that in spread.

HARDINESS: Zone 3.

HABIT: Pyramidal in youth; upright-oval and densely branching in old age.

RATE: Medium, 10 to 15' over a 5 to 10 year period.

TEXTURE: Medium in all seasons.

BARK: Gray-brown, ridged and furrowed on older trunks.

LEAF COLOR: Dark shiny green in summer changing to yellow in fall; often, at best, only yellow-green in Central Illinois.

FLOWERS: Yellowish, fragrant, borne in 5- to 7-flowered, pendulous cymes in late June or early July; flowers before *T. tomentosa.*

FRUIT: Not important.

CULTURE: Readily transplanted; prefers moist, well drained, fertile soil; full sun; pH adaptable; supposedly quite pollution tolerant; one of the best street and city trees.

DISEASES AND INSECTS: See under *T. americana*. Aphids often a problem.

LANDSCAPE VALUE: Excellent shade tree for lawn, large areas, streets, planters, malls and about any place a real quality tree is desired; can be pruned (and quite effectively) into hedges; the Europeans tend to use the tree much more as a hedge than do the Americans.

CULTIVARS:

'Chancellor' — Fastigiate in youth becoming pyramidal with age; fast growing; has good crotch development.

'Greenspire' — Maintains a single leader with a nice branching habit, widely used as a street tree, result of a cross between cultivar 'Euclid' and a selection from the Boston Parks; does well under difficult conditions.

'Handsworth' — Young stems are a light yellow-green; supposedly quite striking especially on young trees.

'June Bride' — According to the introducers, Manbeck Nurseries, Inc., New Knoxville, Ohio, this clone is distinguished from other clones by the "unique combination of substantially pyramidal habit of growth, maintaining an excellent straight central leader. The branches are evenly spaced around the leader. The small-sized leaves are more glossy than those of the species, and flowers more abundant with 3 to 4 times as many."

'Pyramidalis' — Wide, pyramidal habit.

'Rancho' — An upright oval clone with small, glossy green leaves; good crotch development; and a medium-fine branch texture.

'Swedish Upright' — Narrow, upright in outline.

'Turesi' — Strong growing pyramidal form.

'XP110' — Rated quite high in Ohio Tests; upright oval in habit with small foliage.

PROPAGATION: See under *T. americana.*

RELATED SPECIES:

Tilia x *euchlora* — Crimean Linden

LEAVES: Alternate, simple, roundish ovate, 2 to 4" long, abruptly short-acuminate, obliquely cordate, finely and sharply serrate with mucronate teeth, lustrous dark green and glabrous above, pale green and glabrous beneath, except axillary tufts of brown hairs; petioles glabrous, 1 to 2" long.

BUDS: Glabrous, 1/4" or greater long, reddish green.

STEM: Glabrous, slender, greenish yellow on bottom, light reddish brown on top.

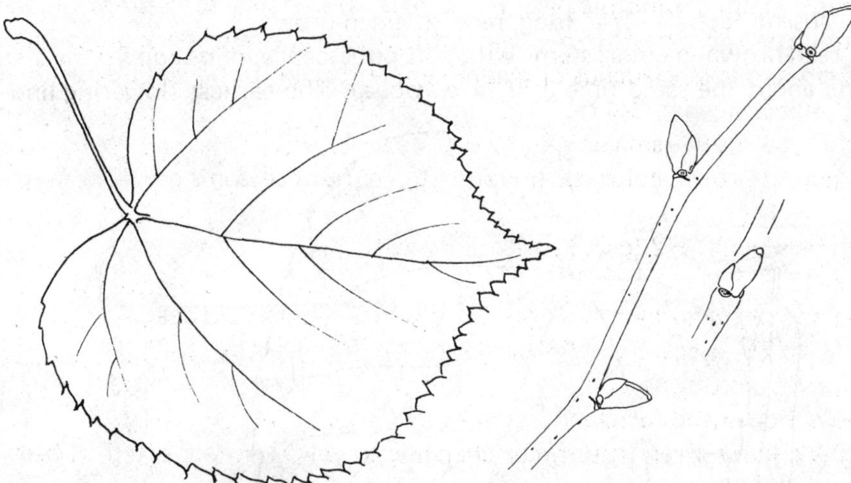

Tilia x *euchlora*, Crimean Linden, is the result of a cross between *T. cordata* x *T. dasystyla*. This tree grows to 40 to 60′ high and half that in spread. The leaves are a lustrous dark green. Other features are similar to *T. cordata*. The cultivar 'Redmond' is a form with a dense, pyramidal habit and larger, less glossy leaves. It was introduced by the Plumfield Nurseries of Fremont, Nebraska, in 1927; supposedly the result of a cross between *T.* x *euchlora* and *T. americana*. The few trees I have seen look more like *T. americana* than *T.* x *euchlora*. Zone 5.

Tilia x *europaea* – European Linden, also listed as *T. vulgaris*.

LEAVES: Alternate, simple, broad-ovate, 2 to 4″ long, short-acuminate, obliquely cordate or nearly truncate, sharply serrate, dark green and glabrous above, bright green beneath and glabrous except axillary tufts of hair, petioles 1 to 2″ long.

Stems and buds usually intensely red–maroon, buds and stems smaller, more refined than those of *T. heterophylla*. Flowers earlier than *T. cordata* and *T.* x *euchlora*, usually around early June.

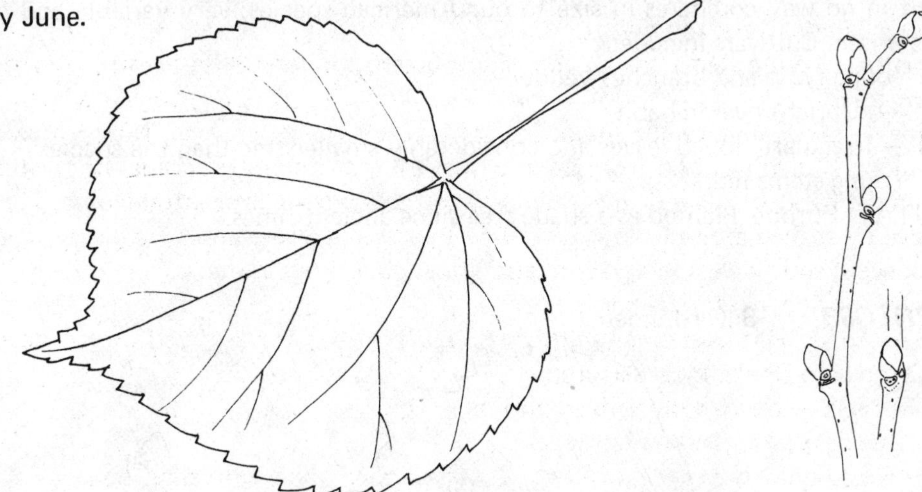

Tilia x *europaea*, European Linden, is another hybrid with *T. cordata* and *T. platyphyllos* the parents; pyramidal in youth and develops a more rounded habit in old age than the previous species. Tends to sucker from the base and also forms burls on the trunk. Probably not preferable to *T. cordata* and her cultivars. Zone 3. A cultivar 'Pallida' is a vigorous, pyramidal grower with good crotch development.

Tilia platyphyllos – Bigleaf Linden

LEAVES: Alternate, simple, roundish ovate, 2 to 5″ long, abruptly acuminate, obliquely cordate, sharply and regularly serrate, dull and short pubescent or glabrous above, light green and pubescent beneath, especially on the veins, rarely nearly glabrous; petiole pubescent, 3/5 to 2″ long.

BUDS: Terminal—absent, laterals—1/4" long, reddish green-brown.

STEM: Reddish green-brown in color; stems with soft pubescence, pilose on young stems.

FLOWERS: Borne about the same time as *T.* x *europaea*. The earliest flowering lindens in Central Illinois.

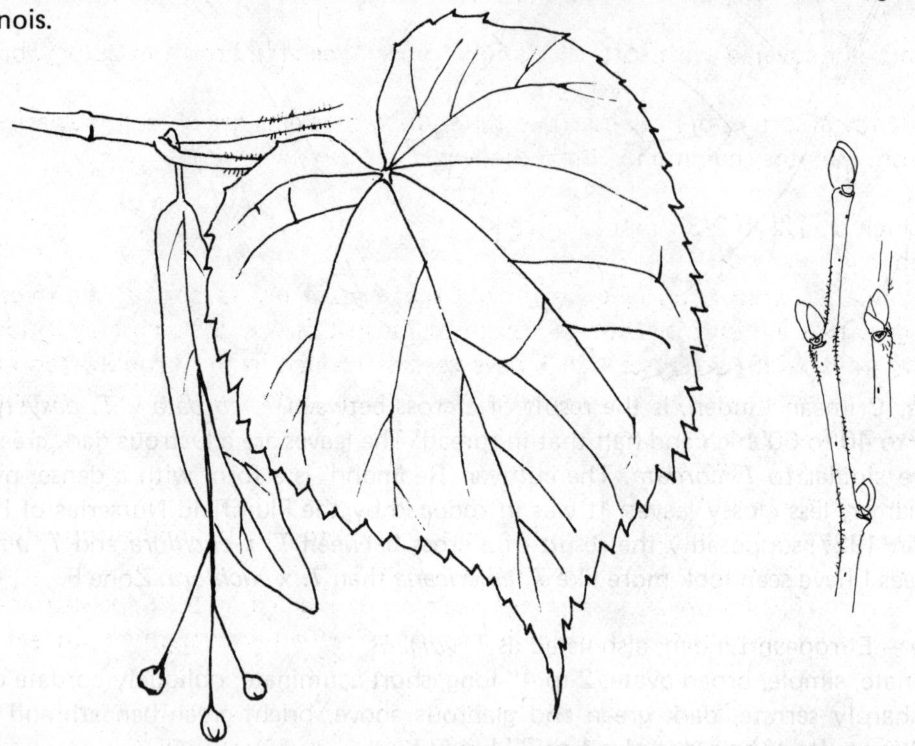

Tilia platyphyllos, Bigleaf Linden, grows to 60 to 80' and larger; not extensively planted in this country although the few large specimens I have seen were extremely beautiful in foliage (dark green) and outline (similar to *T. cordata*). It has the largest leaves of the European species but in no way compares in size to our American species; very variable and numerous types have arisen. Cultivars include:

'Aurea' – Young twigs and branches yellow.

'Fastigiata' – Upright-oval in habit.

'Laciniata' – Irregularly lobed leaves and considerably smaller tree than the species.

'Rubra' – Young stems red.

NATIVE HABITAT: Europe. Planted as a shade tree since ancient times.

Tilia tomentosa — Silver Linden

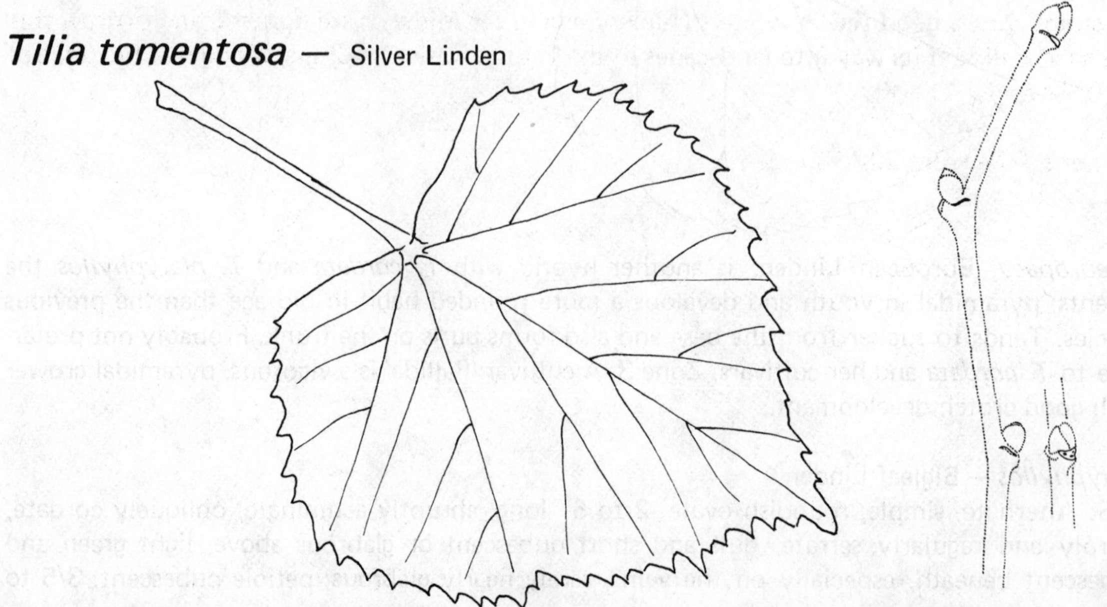

LEAVES: Alternate, simple, suborbicular, 2 to 4" long, abruptly acuminate, cordate to nearly truncate at base, sharply and sometimes doubly serrate or even slightly lobulate, dark green and slightly pubescent above at first, white tomentose beneath; petiole 1 to 1 1/2" long, tomentose.

BUDS: Often partially covered with soft, short pubescence; green-red-brown in color; about 1/4" long.

STEM: Covered with a soft, short pubescence; the pubescent stems separate this species and *T. petiolaris* from the other commonly grown lindens.

SIZE: 50 to 70' high by 1/2 to 2/3's that in spread.

HARDINESS: Zone 4.

HABIT: Pyramidal when young, upright-oval in old age; one of my favorite shade trees; can be effectively grown as a multiple-stemmed specimen for in this way the light gray, smooth bark is maximally enjoyed. The largest tree I have seen is located in the Arnold Arboretum and grows next to an equally large and beautiful *T. cordata*. Both are about 60' in height with upright oval habits.

RATE: Medium, similar to *T. cordata*.

TEXTURE: Medium throughout the seasons.

BARK: Light gray and smooth, almost beech-like on trunks up to 8 to 10" and eventually developing gray-brown color and ridged and furrowed character.

LEAF COLOR: Lustrous, shimmering, glistening, gleaming dark green on the upper surface; silvery tomentose beneath; when the wind is blowing a nice soft effect is created as both leaf surfaces are exposed.

FLOWERS: Yellowish white, fragrant, supposedly narcotic to bees; late June to early July; borne in 7 to 10-flowered pendulous cymes, the last *Tilia* to flower in Central Illinois.

FRUIT: See under *T. americana*.

CULTURE: See under *T. cordata*.

DISEASES AND INSECTS: See under *T. cordata*.

LANDSCAPE VALUE: Good street tree as it tolerates heat and drouth better than other lindens. I highly recommend this for residential plantings as it is a very beautiful ornamental shade tree.

CULTIVARS:

'Fastigiata' – An upright clone.

PROPAGATION: See under *T. americana*.

RELATED SPECIES:

Tilia mongolica, Mongolian Linden, is a small (30'), graceful, pyramidal tree. The leaves are small, 1 1/2 to 3" long and deeply cut (almost lobed), which makes the leaf unlike any linden leaf; the stems turn a good red in winter. Nurserymen in the Midwest are now starting to grow this tree so it will find its way into landscapes in the future. Native to China, Mongolia. Introduced 1880. Zone 4.

Tilia petiolaris – Pendent Silver Linden

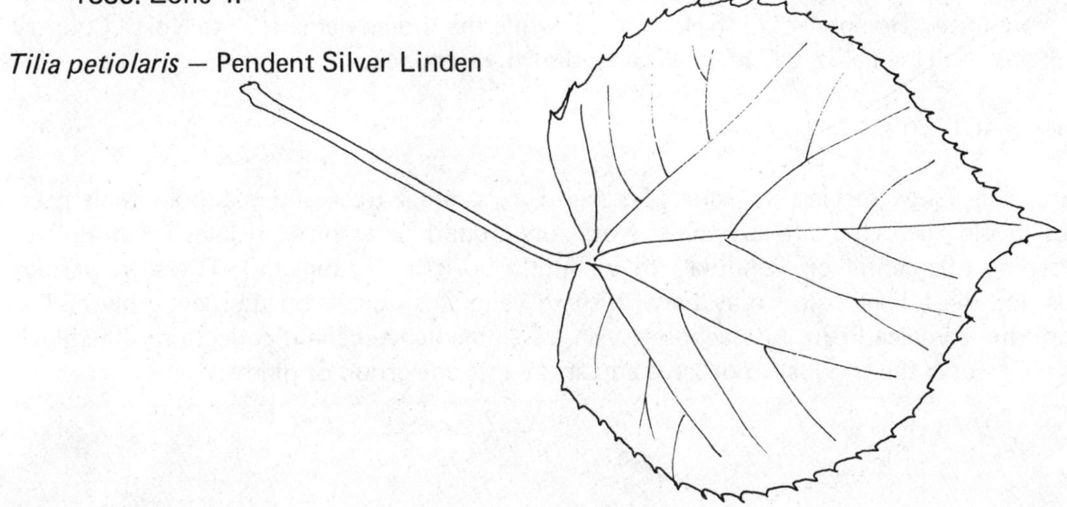

Tilia petiolaris, Pendent Silver Linden, is closely allied to *T. tomentosa*, but differs chiefly in the pendulous, graceful branches; makes a beautiful specimen tree and the 60′ specimen on the University of Illinois campus is the largest I know of in the Midwest. Unfortunately this specimen is surrounded by a black-topped bicycle parking area and in 1976 I noticed considerable top die back which would indicate the stresses have caught up with the tree. Supposedly the bees find the flowers narcotic or poisonous and can be found in large numbers on the ground under such trees. I have not noticed strange bee-havior around our campus tree. It is interesting to note that although this tree is listed as a species it is usually grafted. I would be interested in knowing what percentage of seed-grown trees exhibit the weeping tendency. Dr. Donald Wyman considers it the most beautiful of the lindens. Native to Southeastern Europe. Introduced 1840. Zone 5.

NATIVE HABITAT: Europe, planted as a shade tree since ancient times.

Tsuga – Hemlock

Pinaceae

If I were forced to select one conifer for my garden it would certainly be *Tsuga canadensis*. The species has multitudinous uses and the infinite variation in seed-grown material has resulted in the selection of many excellent cultivars. The number of *Tsuga* species used in landscaping is small but they are considered among the most graceful and beautiful of large evergreen conifers. Fourteen species have been reported, four occurring in the United States and the others in the Himalayas, China, Taiwan, and Japan. *Tsuga heterophylla* is the most important timber-producing species. Hemlock bark contains between 7 and 12 percent tannin, and in the United States that of *T. canadensis* was one of the principal commercial sources for many years.

MORPHOLOGICAL CHARACTERISTICS

Evergreen trees of graceful pyramidal habit with slender horizontal to drooping branches. The bark is cinnamon-red color and furrowed. Buds are rounded and not resinous. Needles, borne on petioles, spirally arranged, more or less 2 ranked, flattened and grooved above, with 2 white stomatic bands below. Needle margin is toothed or entire and the apex is rounded, notched, or blunt pointed. Male flowers are catkins and axillary on previous year's shoots. The greenish female flowers are terminal on previous year's lateral shoots with imbricated scales. Cones are pendulous and often produced in abundance.

According to Jenkins in *Arnoldia* 6: no. 11-12 (1946) the name *Tsuga* is derived from a Japanese word, composed of the elements 'tree' and 'mother', meaning Tree-mother. Concerning the common name Hemlock, Sudworth states that the New York Indians use the descriptive name Oh-neh-tah, pronounced Hoe-o-na-dia, or Hoe-na-dia, while the Indian name for the North Country (now Canada) was also Hoe-nadia, which means a land of the Hemlock.

GROWTH CHARACTERISTICS

Generally, the *Tsuga* species are stately, graceful, pyramidal trees and maintain their good characteristics in old age. The cultivars range from low ground cover types ('Coles Prostrate') to gracefully weeping ('Sargentii' or 'Pendula') to distinctly upright ('Fastigiata'). There are various globose types and the foliage colors may be whitish to yellow especially on the new growth. The Arnold Arboretum, Jamaica Plain, Massachusetts, has assembled an excellent collection of hemlock variants. It is well worth the trip just to observe and study this one group of plants.

CULTURE

Hemlocks should be moved balled and burlapped in either spring or fall. They can be planted on many soil types; however, good drainage, cool, acid soils, and adequate moisture are necessary. They will not thrive under hot, extremely dry conditions. Sweeping winds may be detrimental. They will withstand full shade; however, partial shade is preferable and best growth is attained in full sunlight. They will not withstand air pollution and are susceptible to salt damage. Pruning can be accomplished in spring or summer. Hemlocks withstand heavy pruning and for this reason are often used for hedges.

DISEASES AND INSECTS

Leaf blight, cankers, blister rust, needle rust, sapwood rot, hemlock borer, hemlock looper, spruce leaf miner, hemlock fiorinia scale, grape scale, hemlock scale, spider mites and other pests. Physiological diseases:

Sunscorch, drought injury—Hemlocks are more sensitive to drought than most other narrow leaf evergreens especially when sited in southern exposures and rocky slopes.

PROPAGATION

Seed dormancy is variable in hemlock, with some seed lots requiring pregermination treatment and others germinating satisfactorily without treatment. Cold stratification of mature seeds shortens incubation time and may substantially increase germinative energy, and is therefore recommended. General recommendation for *T. canadensis, T. caroliniana, T. heterophylla,* and *T. mertensiana* is 60 to 120 days at 41°F in moist sand. Some success has resulted from the use of cuttings but timing is critical and the rooting percentages are low. Most of the cultivars are grafted onto species understocks.

LANDSCAPE USE

Tsuga canadensis is used extensively for specimen, hedge, screen and grouping purposes. Often it is used in foundation plantings but care must be exercised to keep it in bounds over the years. This is quite simple for it can be maintained at a height of 3 to 5 feet by judicial pruning. *Tsuga caroliniana* is less common in landscapes but, by some authorities, is considered a better plant because of greater pollution tolerance. The habit of Carolina Hemlock is probably a bit more stiff than Eastern Hemlock. *Tsuga canadensis* makes one of the best evergreen hedges especially if pruned correctly. If individual shoots are removed every year (rather than shearing the entire plant) a more aesthetically pleasing effect is achieved.

Several cultivars make excellent landscape plants and are often found in the trade.

Tsuga canadensis 'Bennett' — A spreading compact type, broader than high.

'Coplen' — A compact pyramid with a single leader, slow growing.

'Pendula' or 'Sargentii' — Shrub semi-globose, broader than high, dome-shaped in full age; branches and branchlets pendulous.

Bean separated the two cultivars 'Pendula' and 'Sargentii', but according to Jenkins the nurseryman's stock has all been derived from the 4 original plants found near the summit of Fishkill Mountain (near Beacon City, on the Hudson River) by General Joseph Howland about 1870. The finder grew one in his own garden at Matteawan, N.Y., gave the second to Henry Winthrop Sargent (after whom the plant was named), of Fishkill; the third to H. H. Hunnewell, of Wellesley, Mass., and the fourth to Prof. C. S. Sargent of the Arnold Arboretum. The second and third are dead but the first and fourth have made fine specimens. Most of the plants in cultivation have been grown from grafts; however, there are also seedlings, so some variation can be expected.

Tsuga canadensis — Canadian (Eastern) Hemlock

LEAVES: Almost regularly 2-ranked, linear, obtuse or acutish, 1/4 to 2/3" long, obscurely grooved, green above, with 2 whitish bands beneath, toothed.
BUDS: Minute, ovoid, with hairy scales, light brown.
STEM: Young stems slender, grayish brown, very hairy.
CONES: Small, ovoid, 1/2 to 1" long on slender stalks; light to medium brown.

SIZE: 40 to 70' in height by 25 to 35' in spread; known to 100' and more.
HARDINESS: Zone 3.
HABIT: Softly and gracefully pyramidal in youth with tapering trunk becoming pendulously pyramidal with age.
RATE: Medium, 25 to 50' in 15 to 30 years.
TEXTURE: Fine.
BARK: Flaky and scaly on young trees, brown; soon with wide, flat ridges; on old trees heavily and deeply furrowed; freshly cut surfaces showing purplish streaks.
LEAF COLOR: New spring growth—light yellow-green changing to a dark, glossy green, underside of needles with two glaucous bands.
FLOWERS: Monoecious; staminate light yellow, pistillate pale green.
FRUIT: Cones slender, stalked, ovoid, apex nearly blunt, 1/2 to 1" long by approximately 1/2" broad, brown at maturity.
CULTURE: Transplants well balled and burlapped if root pruned. Amenable to pruning. It is an excellent subject for moist, well-drained, acid soils, rocky bluffs or sandy soils. Unlike most conifers tolerates shade well. Can grow in full sun as long as it has good drainage and organic matter in the soil and there is no strong, drying wind to contend with. Heavy soil from which water is unable to drain is not suitable. Does not tolerate wind or drought. Plant in sheltered locations, avoiding windswept sites and polluted conditions.
DISEASES AND INSECTS: Leaf blight, cankers, blister rust, needle rust, sapwood rot, hemlock borer, hemlock looper, spruce leaf miner, hemlock fiorinia scale, grape scale, hemlock scale, spider mites, bagworm, fir flat headed borer, spruce budworm, gypsy moth, and hemlock sawfly.

Two physiological problems include sunscorch which occurs when temperatures reach 95°F and above. The ends of the branches may be killed back for several inches. Another problem is drought injury for hemlocks are more sensitive to prolonged periods of dryness than most other narrow-leaved evergreens. Plants may die during extended dry periods. For all the problems mentioned, hemlocks under landscape conditions prove to be reliable, handsome ornamentals if given proper cultural care.

LANDSCAPE VALUE: Makes an extremely graceful evergreen hedge of value in almost any situation except city conditions. Excellent for screening, accent plant and foundation planting. The most commonly planted of the hemlocks, popular over a wide area; one of our best evergreens.
CULTIVARS:

var. *sargentii* or *pendula* – Graceful, round and moundlike in habit of growth with slightly pendulous branches. Two or three times broader than tall, probably the best and most well known of hemlock cultivars. (Also listed as 'Sargentii' and 'Pendula'.)

See introduction sheet for additional cultivars.

PROPAGATION: Seed dormancy is variable so to insure good germination it is advisable to stratify the seeds for 2 to 4 months at about 40°F. Layering has also been used successfully. Cuttings have been successfully rooted but timing is important. Hormonal treatment is necessary. Percentages ranged from 60 to 90% depending on sampling time and hormonal strength.
NATIVE HABITAT: Nova Scotia to Minnesota, south along the mountains to Alabama and Georgia.

Tsuga caroliniana — Carolina Hemlock

LEAVES: Radiating around the stem, linear, 3/5 to 4/5" long, about 1/12" wide, apex blunt or slightly notched, entire, glossy green above, with 2 distinct white bands beneath, margins narrow, green.

BUDS: Ovoid to roundish, apex blunt, pubescent.
STEM: Light reddish brown when young, finely pubescent or nearly glabrous.

SIZE: 45 to 60′ in height by 20 to 25′ spread.
HARDINESS: Zone 4.
HABIT: Airy, spiry-topped tree with a tapering trunk and short, stout, often pendulous branches forming a handsome, evenly pyramidal head. More compact and of darker green color than *T. canadensis*.
RATE: Slow to medium, not as fast as *T. canadensis*.
TEXTURE: Medium.
BARK: Reddish brown, deeply fissured, scaly.
LEAF COLOR: Glossy green above, lighter green below.
FLOWERS: Monoecious, inconspicuous.
FRUIT: Cones short-stalked, oblong-cylindrical, 4/5 to 1 2/5″ long.
CULTURE: Transplants well balled and burlapped if root pruned. Needs moist, well-drained soils; partially shaded, sheltered exposure and will not tolerate droughty conditions.
LANDSCAPE VALUE: Performs better than *T. canadensis* under city conditions, and probably as good a landscape plant but not as well known.
CULTIVARS:

'Arnold Pyramid' – Pyramidal, dense, with a rounded top.
'Compacta' – Dwarf, low growing and very dense.

PROPAGATION: Same as for *T. canadensis*.
ADDITIONAL NOTES: Easily separable from *T. canadensis* by the way the foliage radiates around the stem forming a bottle-brush-like effect.
NATIVE HABITAT: Southeastern United States (Southwestern Virginia to Northern Georgia in the Blue Ridge Mountains).

Ulmus americana — American Elm, also known as White, Gray, Water or Swamp Elm.

FAMILY: Ulmaceae
LEAVES: Alternate, simple, ovate-oblong, 3 to 6″ long, acuminate, unequal at base, doubly serrate, glabrous and rough above, pubescent or nearly glabrous beneath; petioles 1/5 to 1/3″ long.
BUDS: Terminal—absent; laterals—small, often placed at one side of leaf scar, ovate-conical, pointed, 1/6″ long, slightly flattened and more or less appressed against the stem, light reddish brown, smooth and shining or slightly pale-downy; flower buds stouter, obovate, appearing as if stalked. Scales generally with darker and more or less hairy-edge margins.

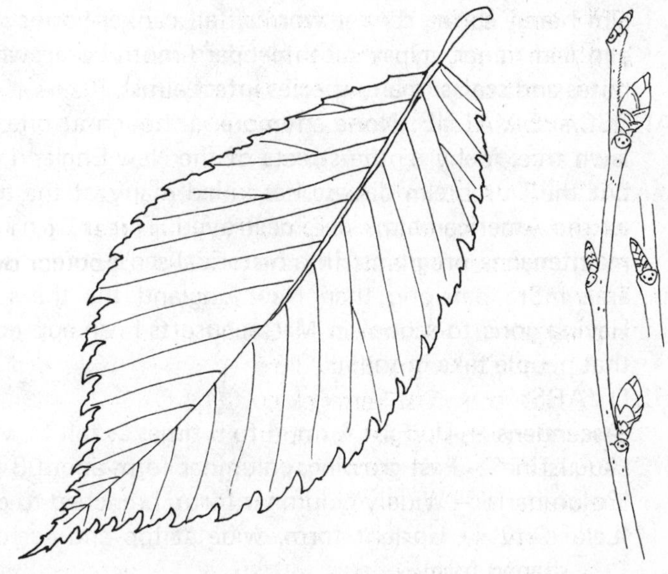

STEM: Slender, round, red-brown; pubescent at first, becoming glabrous, (sometimes maintaining pubescence).

SIZE: 60 to 80′ with a spread of 1/2 to 2/3's the height.
HARDINESS: Zone 2.

HABIT: 3 distinct habits are recognized and include the vase-shaped form in which the trunk divides into several erect limbs strongly arched above and terminating in numerous slender, often pendulous branchlets, the whole tree a picture of great beauty and symmetry; a form with more widely spreading, less arching branches, often called the "oak-form"; and a narrow form with branchlets clothing the entire trunk. The largest known American Elm in the United States is located at Trigonia, Tennessee and is 160′ high with a branch spread of 147′.

RATE: Medium to fast, 10 to 12′ in 5 years. This rate of growth is common for many elms.

BARK: Dark gray-brown with broad, deep, intersecting ridges, or often scaly; outer bark in cross section shows layers of a whitish-buff color alternating with thicker dark layers.

LEAF COLOR: Lustrous dark green in summer; yellow in fall; great variation in intensity of coloration.

FLOWERS: Polygamo-monoecious, greenish red, in fascicles of 3 or 4, March, interesting but not too showy.

FRUIT: Samara, 1/2″ long, maturing in late May through June, not ornamental.

CULTURE: Easily transplanted because of shallow, fibrous, wide spreading, gross feeding root system; prefer rich moist soils but grows well under a variety of conditions. In the wild the tree is a common inhabitant of wet flats where standing water may accumulate in the spring and fall; prune in fall.

DISEASES AND INSECTS: The elms are, unfortunately, subject to many pests and I have often wondered why they have been treated as royalty when they are so fallible. Many of the pests are devastating and control measures are simply not effective or available. The following list should provide an idea of the potential problems which may beset "your" elm. Wetwood (*Erwinia mimipressuralis*) is a bacterial disease which appears as a wilt, branch dieback, and internal and external fluxing of elms. A pipe is often placed in the tree to relieve the tremendous gas pressure that builds up; no control known. Cankers (at least 8 species cause cankers and dieback of stems and branches), Dutch elm disease (devastating and uncontrollable), bleeding canker, leaf curl, leaf spots (there are so many fungi that cause leaf spots that only an expert can distinguish one from another), powdery mildews, *Cephalosporium* wilt, *Verticillium* wilt, wood decay, phloem necrosis (apparently caused by a mycoplasm), mosaic, scorch, woolly apple aphid, elm leaf curl aphid, Japanese beetle, smaller European elm bark beetle, elm borer, spring canker worms, fall cankerworms, elm cockscomb gall, dogwood twig borer, elm leaf miner, gypsy moth, leopard moth borer, white marked tussock moth, elm calligrapha, mites and scales (many species infest elms).

LANDSCAPE VALUE: None anymore, although at one time extensively used as a street and large lawn tree. Many of the streets of the New England towns and cities were arched with this tree but the Dutch elm disease has killed many of the trees. People somehow have the notion that all the American elms were destroyed. This is by no means true and many cities have extensive maintenance programs. In a historical sense, there is no tree more American and no geographic area more patriotic than New England the the splendid American Elm is worth the visit. Having gone to school in Massachusetts I can appreciate the legacy of these elms and the pride that people take in them.

CULTIVARS:

'Ascendens' — Upright form, 4 to 5 times as tall as wide, branches high up on trunk.

'Augustine' — Fast growing, columnar form about 3 times as high as broad.

'Columnaris' — Widely columnar form, branched to ground, 3 times as high as broad.

'Lake City' — Upright form, wide at top and narrow at base, however, not the typical vase-shaped form.

'Littleford' — Columnar, 3 times as high as wide.

'Moline' — Good, rugged, moderately vase-shaped form, has survived the Dutch elm disease on our campus.

var. *pendula* — Pendulous branches, but vase-shaped habit.

'Princeton' — Large leathery foliage, vigorous, and supposedly resistant to elm leaf beetle (foliage feeder).

WASHINGTON - Selected for crown resistance to D. Elm disease, good glossy foliage, 70 to 80' ft. high

PROPAGATION: Seeds of some lots show dormancy and should be stratified at 41°F for 60 to 90 days in moist medium although some seeds do not require any treatment. In the long run it is probably safer to stratify. Cuttings also root quite readily; those taken in early June rooted 94% with IBA treatment.

RELATED SPECIES:

Ulmus rubra — Slippery Elm

LEAVES: Alternate, simple, obovate to oblong, 4 to 8" long, long acuminate, very unequal at base, doubly serrate, very rough above, densely pubescent beneath (scabrous), petioles 1/6 to 1/5" long.

BUDS: Terminal-absent, laterals about 1/4" long, dark brown—nearly black at tips of scales, especially at tips with long rusty hairs; flower buds more or less spherical.

STEM: Rather stout, light grayish brown, pubescent, roughened by numerous raised lenticels, strongly and characteristically mucilaginous if chewed.

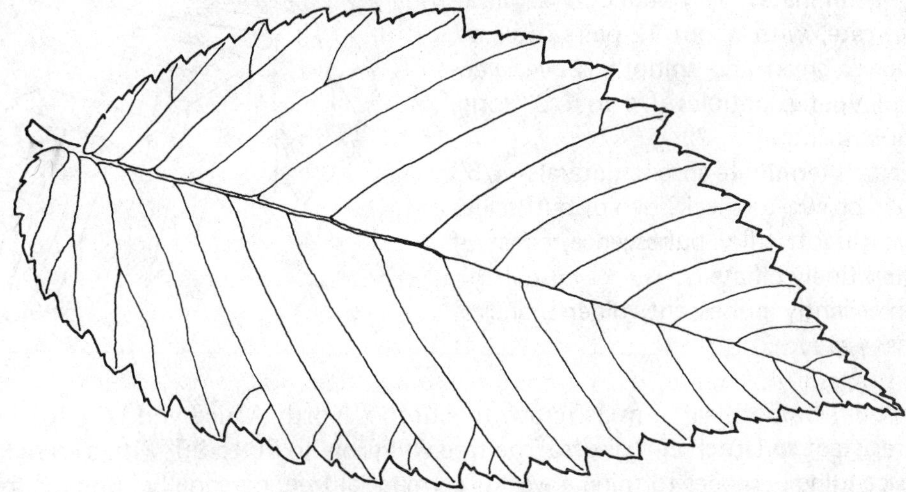

Ulmus rubra, Slippery Elm, is a close cousin of American Elm and often goes under the names Red, Gras, or Moose Elm. The tree grows to 40 to 60' with a somewhat vase-shaped habit but the branchlets are more ascending (upright) than those of American Elm. The ornamental value is limited and this species actually becomes a weed as it tends to infest unkempt shrub borders, hedges, fence rows and other idle ground; prefers moist, rich, bottomland soils but also grows on dry, limestone soils. The name "Slippery" developed because of the mucilaginous inner bark which was chewed by the pioneers to quench the thirst. Native from Quebec to Florida, west to the Dakotas and Texas covering much the same range as *Ulmus americana*. Cultivated 1830. Zone 3.

Two other native elm species worth mentioning include *Ulmus thomasii*, Rock or Cork Elm, and *U. serotina*, September or Red Elm. The former has an oblong crown and the trunk usually remains unbranched; it is found on dry gravelly uplands and rocky slopes but attains its best development in rich bottomland soils; the wood is heavy, hard and tough; the finest of all woods; hence the name Rock Elm. The wood was used in the construction of automobile bodies and refrigerators. It is now used for furniture, agricultural implements, hockey sticks, ax handles and other items which require a wood which will withstand strains and shocks. Native from Quebec to Tennessee, west to Nebraska. Introduced 1875. Zone 2. The latter elm, *U. serotina*, is a southern species ranging from Kentucky to Alabama, north to Georgia and Southern Illinois. Cultivated 1903. Zone 5.

ADDITIONAL NOTES: The extensive use of one tree such as the American Elm is an example of foolhardy landscaping. The tree is tremendously ornamental and was overplanted. The diseases caught up with the tree and the results were disastrous. Urbana and Champaign were called the "cities of the elms" but Dutch elm disease changed all that and it is now a treasure hunt to find a good specimen. Unfortunately, people do not seem to learn by their mistakes and now Honeylocust has been and is being used in wholesale fashion for cities, residences and about everywhere. I strongly urge a diversified tree planting program encompassing many different species and cultivars. One of our newer buildings was landscaped with 300 Honeylocust. Don't people know there are superior trees?

NATIVE HABITAT: Newfoundland to Florida, west to the foot of the Rockies. Introduced 1752.

The following elms are introduced species and are not treated extensively in this text. However, they are used in landscaping and should be known and recognized as entities which must be dealt with.

Ulmus carpinifolia — Smoothleaf Elm

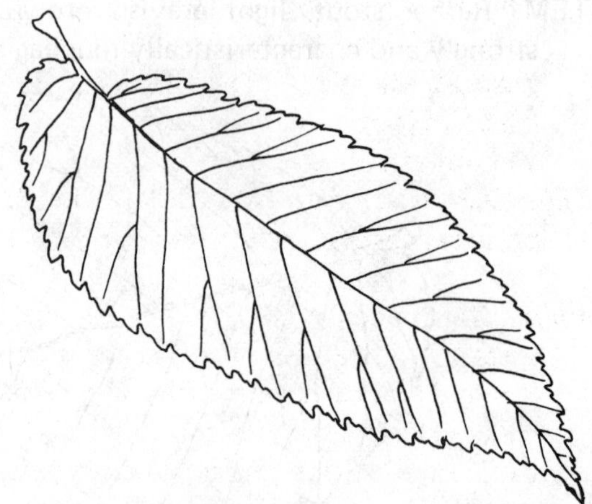

LEAVES: Alternate, simple, elliptic to ovate or obovate, acuminate, very oblique at base, doubly serrate, with about 12 pairs of veins, lustrous dark green and smooth above, glabrous when young, petioles 1/4 to 1/2" long, usually pubescent.

BUDS: Imbricate, terminal—absent, laterals—1/8" long, deep brown to black, ovoid, bud scales covered with soft silky pubescence, edges of scales often finely ciliate.

STEM: Brown, slightly pubescent, older branches turning ashy-gray.

Ulmus carpinifolia, Smoothleaf Elm, is native to Europe, North Africa and Western Europe. Supposedly resistant to Dutch elm disease; the tree will grow to 70 to 90' with a straight trunk and slender ascending branches forming a weakly pyramidal tree; personally I find the tree attractive but again it is an elm and subject to all the pests; the foliage is a lustrous dark green in summer. The following cultivars are reasonably important in the trade and include:

'Bea Schwarz' — Resistant to Dutch elm disease.

'Christine Buisman' — Resistant to Dutch elm disease.

'Koopmanni' — Small tree with dense branches and upright oval head.

'Pendula' — Form with gracefully pendulous branches.

'Sarniensis' — Narrowly upright in habit.

'Umbraculifera' — Usually grafted high on species, forms a single-trunked tree with a densely globose head.

'Urban Elm' — Result of crosses among *Ulmus hollandica* var. *vegeta* x *Ulmus carpinifolia* x *Ulmus pumila,* resistant to Dutch elm disease. Developed at ARS Shade Tree Laboratory, Delaware, Ohio. Grows fast on various soil types, has dark green foliage, and is tolerant of drought, pollution, soil compaction and restricted root space. Should make a good tree for heavily urbanized areas.

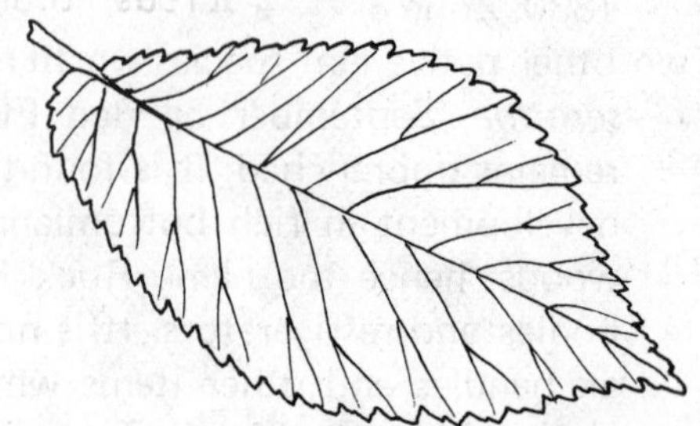

'Umbraculifera'

Ulmus glabra — Scotch Elm

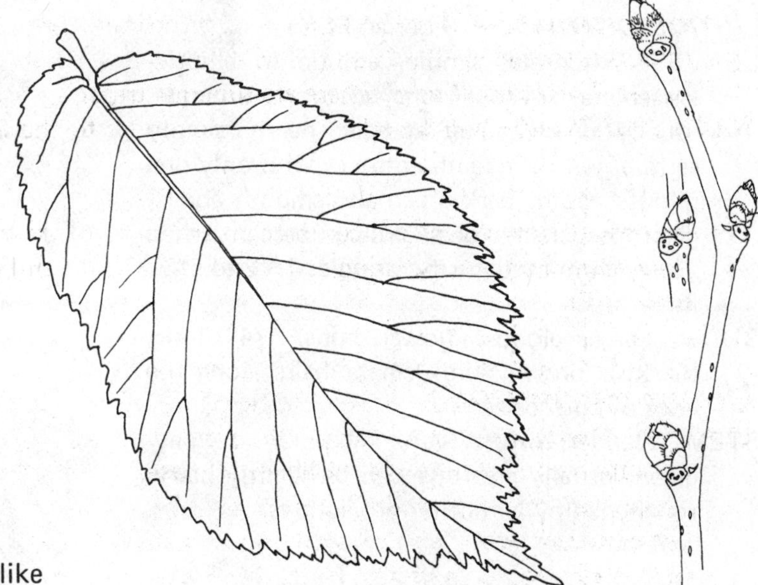

LEAVES: Alternate, simple, very short petioled, oblong-obovate to elliptic or obovate, 3 to 6" long, abruptly acuminate, very unequal at base, sharply and doubly serrate, scabrous above, pubescent beneath; rarely nearly glabrous; petioles—1/8 to 1/4" long.

BUDS: Imbricate, terminal—absent, laterals—1/4" long, vegetative buds dark chestnut brown to brown-black with hispid bud scales. Flower buds, globose and not as pubescent.

STEM: Dark gray-brown with bristly-like pubescence, distinctly hairy.

Ulmus glabra, Scotch Elm, is a large, massive, rather open tree growing from 80 to 100′ with a spread of 50 to 70′. The foliage is dark green in summer and green to yellow to brown in fall. I would not recommend the species but the cultivars 'Camperdownii' and 'Pendula' are worthwhile. The former is a round headed, pendulous branched type that is usually grafted about 6 to 7′ high on the understock while the latter, although often confused with 'Camperdownii' is a flat-topped tree with horizontal branches and branchlets pendulous. Native to Northern and Central Europe, Western Asia. Zone 4.

Ulmus x *hollandica*, Dutch Elm, is a whole group of trees which resulted from crossing *U. carpinifolia* x *U. glabra* and the progeny supposedly intermediate between the two parents.

Ulmus parvifolia — Chinese Elm

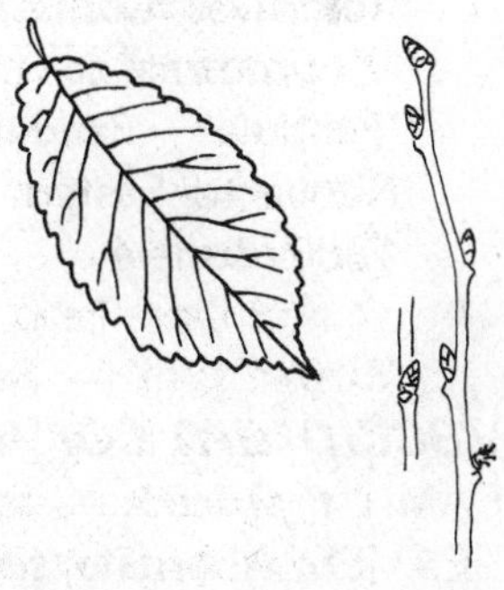

LEAVES: Alternate, simple, elliptic to ovate or obovate, 3/4 to 2" long, acute or obtusish, unequally rounded at base, simply or nearly serrate, lustrous and smooth above, pubescent beneath when young, subcoriaceous at maturity; petioles 1/4 to 1/2" long.

STEM: Gray brown, glabrous, often pubescent, slender, very fine in texture.

BUDS: Small, 1/10 to 1/8" long, brown. Smallest buds of any elm, slightly pubescent. Easy to recognize because of late flower and fruit dates—September-October.

BARK: Mottled (rather than ridged and furrowed like other elms), exfoliating in irregular spots, exposing lighter bark beneath.

Ulmus parvifolia, Chinese Elm, is a broad, round-topped tree often with pendulous branchlets growing 40 to 50′ in height with a similar or slightly greater spread; the foliage is a shiny dark green in summer and turns yellow to reddish in fall; resistant to Dutch elm disease; the bark is often a beautiful mottled combination of green, gray, orange and brown areas; I would rate it excellent in this respect; this is the true Chinese Elm and should not be confused with the inferior *U. pumila*, Siberian Elm; this species flowers in August through September. Native to Northern and Central China, Korea, and Japan. Introduced 1794. Zone 5. Softwood cuttings root well.

Ulmus pumila — Siberian Elm

LEAVES: Alternate, simple, elliptic to elliptic-lanceolate, 3/4 to 3" long, acute or acuminate, usually nearly equal at base, nearly simply serrate, with the teeth entire or with only one minute tooth, dark green and smooth above, glabrous beneath or slightly pubescent when young, firm at maturity; petioles 1/12 to 1/6" long.

BUDS: Large, globose flower buds, 1/4" long, blackish brown, with ciliate hairs along the edge of bud scales.

STEM: Slender, brittle, very light gray or gray-green, usually glabrous, can be slightly hairy, roughened by lenticellar projections.

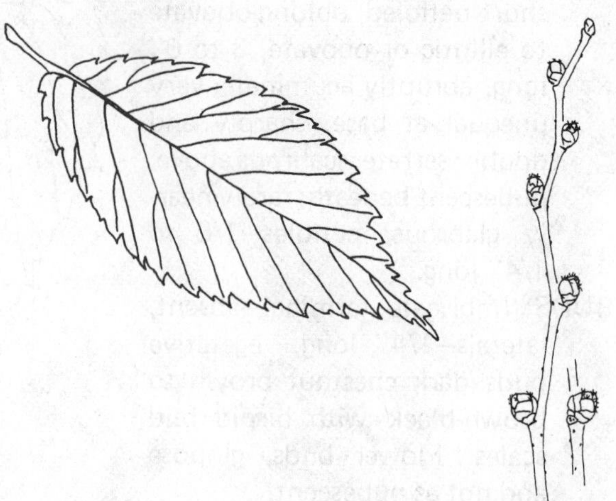

Ulmus pumila, Siberian Elm, is a 50 to 70' high tree with a spread equal to 3/4's the height. The habit is rather open, with several large ascending branches with flexible, breakable, pendulous branchlets. The growth is fast and the wood brittle; the tree grows under any kind of conditions; the foliage is dark green and loved by insects; a poor ornamental tree that does not deserve to be planted—anywhere! Resistant to Dutch elm disease and phloem necrosis; one of, if not, the world's worst tree; I have seen whole streets and cemeteries, planted with this species; the initial growth is fast but the ensuing branch breakage, messiness, and lack of ornamental assets appalling. Several cultivars have been introduced which would seem to have preference over the species. They include:

'Coolshade' — Resistant to breakage in ice storms compared to species (*pumila* x *rubra*).

'Dropmore' — Fast growing form with small neat foliage, hardy in Dropmore, Manitoba, Canada.

'Hamburg Hybrid' — Stronger wooded than species, fast growing, 4 to 6' per year (*americana* x *pumila*).

'Improved Coolshade' — Fast growing, uniform habit, hardy, drought resistant and resistant to breakage from wind and ice (*pumila* x *rubra*).

'Pendula' — Pendulous branches.

Native to Eastern Siberia, Northern China and, unfortunately, was not left there. Cultivated 1860. Zone 4.

Vaccinium corymbosum — Highbush Blueberry

FAMILY: Ericaceae

LEAVES: Alternate, simple, ovate to elliptic-lanceolate, 1 to 3" long, acutish, entire.

STEM: Slender, yellow-green to reddish in winter, warty; pith—solid, green. Overall effect is quite handsome in winter especially with snow as a background for the red-stemmed branches.

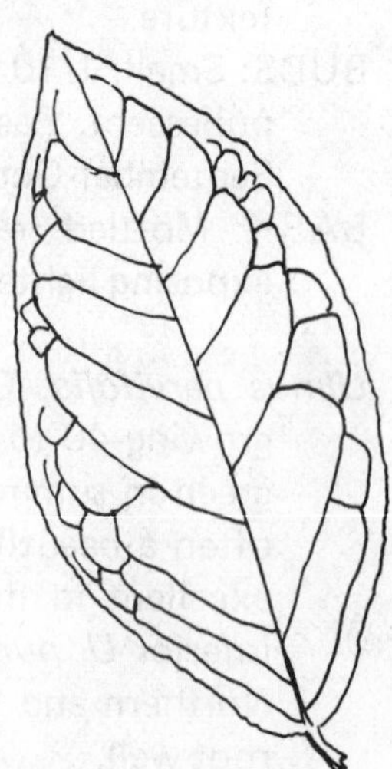

SIZE: 6 to 12' in height with a spread of 8 to 12'.

HARDINESS: Zone 3.

HABIT: Upright, multi-stemmed shrub with spreading branches forming a rounded, dense, compact outline, especially under cultivation.

RATE: Slow.

TEXTURE: Medium in all seasons.

LEAF COLOR: Dark green, almost dark blue green, in summer; changing to yellow, bronze, orange or red combinations in fall; very excellent fall coloring shrub.

FLOWERS: White, possibly tinged pink or pinkish, urn-shaped, 1/3" long, May, just before leaves completely unfold; borne in axillary racemes in great quantities.

FRUIT: Berry, blue-black, bloomy, 2/5" across or larger depending on the cultivar, edible but require a good complement of sugar; late July through August.

CULTURE: Transplant balled and burlapped or from a container into moist, acid, organic, well-drained soils (pH 4.5 to 5.5); native to somewhat swampy soils but does extremely well under acid, sandy conditions; chlorosis is a significant problem and pH of the soil should be the first concern of anyone desiring to culture blueberries. Actually they are very easy to grow if given the above conditions. Mulching is a good idea to reduce injury around roots and preserve moisture; prune after fruiting; full sun or partial shade.

DISEASES AND INSECTS: Actually the cultivated blueberries are subject to many insects and diseases. If the shrub is being grown for ornamental rather than commercial purposes no extensive control program is necessary and there are usually sufficient fruits for a few pies, jams, and the birds.

LANDSCAPE VALUE: Could blend well into the shrub border or small garden plot. Two or three bushes will provide many quarts of berries. It is wise to check with the local extension service or your state university to determine the best cultivars for your area.

PROPAGATION: Seed, some species germinate immediately, others germinate over a long period of time. Cuttings, especially softwood, collected in June root readily under mist in peat:perlite when treated with 1000 ppm IBA, I have had good success this way.

RELATED SPECIES:

Vaccinium angustifolium, Lowbush Blueberry, is a low, straggly, open growing shrub reaching 6" to 2' in height and spreading to 2'. The foliage is lustrous blue green in summer changing to bronze, scarlet and crimson in fall. The flowers are white, 1/4" long, April-May, racemes. The fruit a bluish black, bloomy, very sweet berry, 1/4 to 1/2" across. Does extremely well in dry, acid, poor soils and is the main fruit crop in the state of Maine (6 to 9 million dollar enterprise). Newfoundland to Sasketchewan south to the Mountains of New Hampshire and New York. Introduced 1772. Zone 2.

NATIVE HABITAT: Maine to Minnesota, south to Florida and Louisiana. Introduced 1765. Zone 3.

Vaccinium macrocarpon — American Cranberry

FAMILY: Ericaceae

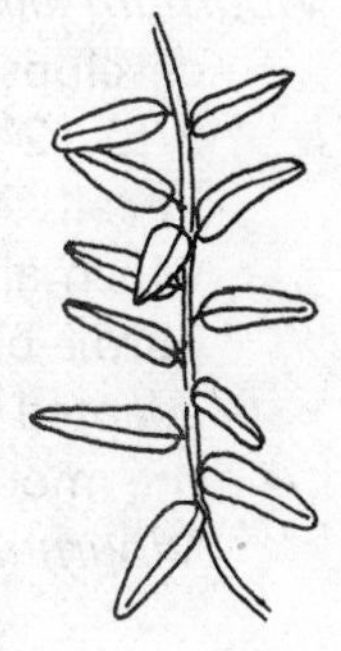

LEAVES: Alternate, simple, 1/4 to 3/4" long, elliptic-oblong, flat or slightly revolute, slightly whitened beneath, evergreen, short-petioled; lustrous dark green in summer assuming purplish tones in fall.

BUDS: Small or minute, solitary, sessile, with 2 apparently valvate scales or the larger with some half-dozen scales; terminal deciduous.

STEMS: Slender, very obscurely 3- or 5-sided or distinctly angled; pith small, nearly round, continuous; leaf-scars small or minute, half-rounded or crescent-shaped, somewhat elevated; 1 bundle-trace.

SIZE: 2 to 6" in height, spread is indefinite.

HARDINESS: Zone 2.

HABIT: Low, dense, small-leaved evergreen ground cover.

RATE: Slow to medium; I have grown plants in containers with excellent success.

TEXTURE: Beautifully fine in all seasons.

LEAF COLOR: Glossy medium to dark green in summer; new growth is often bronzy; during cold weather the foliage takes on a reddish bronze cast.

FLOWERS: Perfect, pinkish, corolla deeply 4-cleft with revolute linear-oblong lobes; borne solitary, axillary, nodding, jointed with pedicel; May-June; not showy but interesting from a morphological viewpoint.

FRUIT: Berry; red, 2/5 to 4/5" across; ripening in September or October.

CULTURE: Transplant as a container grown plant into a moist, high organic matter soil; in the wild is found growing in moist sphagnum bogs; full sun, possibly light shade; most important to keep the roots cool and moist.

DISEASES AND INSECTS: Several associated with commercial production but nothing of consequence for the homeowner to worry about.

LANDSCAPE VALUE: A novelty evergreen ground cover which is quite handsome. I have had good success with container-grown plants which were transplanted into a 1/2 soil:1/2 sphagnum peat mixture.

PROPAGATION: Cuttings are extremely easy to root. Softwood cuttings treated with 1000 ppm IBA, placed in peat:perlite under mist rooted 80+ percent in 6 weeks.

RELATED SPECIES:

Vaccinium vitis-idaea, Cowberry, may grow to 10". The evergreen foliage is lustrous dark green above and paler and black dotted beneath; turns metallic mahogany in winter. The flowers are white or pinkish, campanulate, 4-lobed, 1/4" long; May through June; borne in short subterminal nodding racemes. The fruit is a dark red, 2/5" diameter berry with an acid, bitter taste; ripens in August. Culturally it performs best on moist, peaty soil and in full sun. The variety *minus,* Mountain Cranberry, is lower growing (4" rarely 8") and hardier (Zone 2) than the species. The variety ranges from Labrador to Massachusetts to Alaska and British Columbia (Cultivated 1825) while the species is native to Europe and Northern Asia. Cultivated 1789. Zone 5. I have seen the variety *minus* in Maine and have come to cherish and appreciate it for the refined, dainty habit and the excellent evergreen foliage.

ADDITIONAL NOTES: The American Cranberry is the source of the cranberries which we relish during the holidays and for that matter the rest of the year. Massachusetts is the leading state in cranberry production and a trip to old Cape Cod at harvesting time (or for that matter any time) is well worth the effort. Very interesting crop as far as cultural and nutritional practices are concerned and anyone interested should consult a text on modern fruit production.

NATIVE HABITAT: Newfoundland to Sasketchewan, south to North Carolina, Michigan and Minnesota. Introduced 1760.

Viburnum alnifolium — Hobblebush

Viburnum alnifolium, Hobblebush, is a straggling shrub with pendulous outer branches; often develops a procumbent habit and roots develop where the branches touch the ground; reaches 9 to 12′ in height. The summer foliage is medium green and develops a reddish or deep claret in fall. The flowers are borne in flat-topped, 3 to 5" diameter cymes—the outer flowers of which are sterile, white, about 1" diameter and produced in mid-May. The fruit is a red, finally purple-black drupe about 1/3" long which matures in September. This species is maximally adapted to shady, moist areas. Native to New Brunswick and Michigan to North Carolina in the mountains. Introduced 1820. Zone 3. Apparently there has been a name change for *Viburnum lantanoides* is appearing in the literature.

Viburnum x *burkwoodii* — Burkwood Viburnum

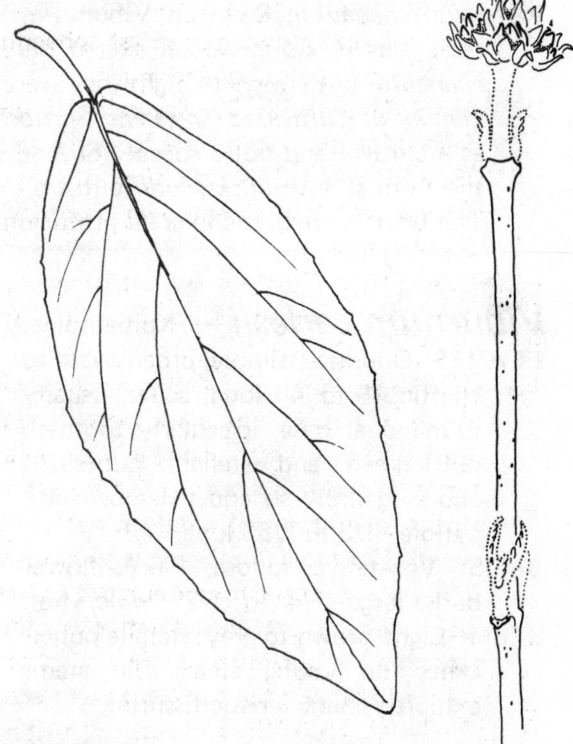

FAMILY: Caprifoliaceae

LEAVES: Opposite, simple, oblong, 1 1/2 to 2 1/2" long, lustrous dark green above, a bit rough to the touch, much lighter beneath and tomentose; veins—rusty brown in color; margins—toothed.

BUDS: Vegetative—foliose and tomentose.

STEM: Light tan in color, tomentose.

FLOWER: Clustered (cymose), 1/2" across, grayish pubescent.

SIZE: 8 to 10' with spread about 2/3's height.

HARDINESS: Zone 5.

HABIT: Upright, multistemmed, often tangled mass of stems yielding a somewhat straggly appearance.

RATE: Slow to medium.

TEXTURE: Medium in foliage, yields a medium-coarse appearance in winter, primarily because of its irregular growth habit.

LEAF COLOR: Lustrous dark green above; light gray-brown tomentose beneath. Holds green color late, tends toward a semi-evergreen character; fall color is a sporadic wine-red.

FLOWERS: Pink in bud to white in flower, spicy, aromatic fragrance, mid to late April, effective for 7 to 10 days, hemispherical cyme approximately 2 to 3" across.

FRUIT: Red changing to black, July-August, drupe, usually sparsely produced and of insignificant ornamental importance.

CULTURE: Most viburnums require a slightly moist, well-drained soil, are pH adaptable but prefer a slightly acid situation, probably should be moved balled and burlapped or as a container specimen, small plants can be handled bare root, avoid sulfur sprays as many viburnums are defoliated by them. A very serviceable group of plants of easy culture provided the soil is well-drained.

DISEASES AND INSECTS: Bacterial leaf spot, crown gall, shoot blight, leaf spots, powdery mildew, rusts, downy leaf spot, spot anthracnose, spray burn (caused by sulfur sprays), viburnum aphid, asiatic garden beetle, citrus flatid planthopper, tarnished plant bug, thrips, potato flea beetle, dogwood twig borer, and seven scale species. Although the list is impressive the viburnums are relatively free of major problems.

LANDSCAPE VALUE: Excellent choice for the shrub border, works well with broadleaf evergreens, fragrance permeates the entire garden.

CULTIVARS: 'Mohawk' resulted from a backcross of *V.* x *burkwoodii (V. carlesii* Hemsl. x *V. utile* Hemsl.) x *V. carlesii* made in 1953. The cultivar was selected for the dark red (Currant Red) flower buds which open to white petals with red-blotched (Currant Red) reverse; abundant inflorescences; strong, spicy clove fragrance; compact growth habit; and foliage resistant to bacterial leaf spot and powdery mildew. The brilliant red flower buds appear several weeks before the flowers begin to open, and extend the effective ornamental period of the plant to several weeks rather than a few days as with other *V. carlesii* types. The strong, spicy clove fragrance is very pleasant and noteworthy attribute of 'Mohawk'. The glossy, dark green leaves, which turn a brilliant orange-red in autumn are highly resistant to bacterial leaf spot and powdery mildew. The original plant is a compact shrub 7' in height with spreading branches to 7 1/2'. 'Mohawk' has been hardy as far north as Ithaca, New York. In colder regions the plant may survive, but the naked flower buds may be frost damaged.

PROPAGATION: I have rooted cuttings from June-July collected wood with 100% efficiency, cuttings were dipped in 1000 ppm IBA/50% alcohol situation.

RELATED SPECIES:

Viburnum chenaultii, Chenault Viburnum, is an extremely confused entity and in many respects resembles *V.* x *burkwoodii* except the leaves are smaller. I have seen specimens labeled as *V. chenaultii* but always thought they were *V.* x *burkwoodii.* Rehder does not list this species in his *Manual of Cultivated Trees and Shrubs* and *Hillier's Manual of Trees and Shrubs* lists the plant as a cultivar and not a species. Several specimens I have seen were actually larger in size than the normal *V.* x *burkwoodii* but a bit more compact in the density of branching and leaves. The flowers are borne in great profusion and literally cover the shrub in late April or early May.

Viburnum carlesii — Koreanspice Viburnum

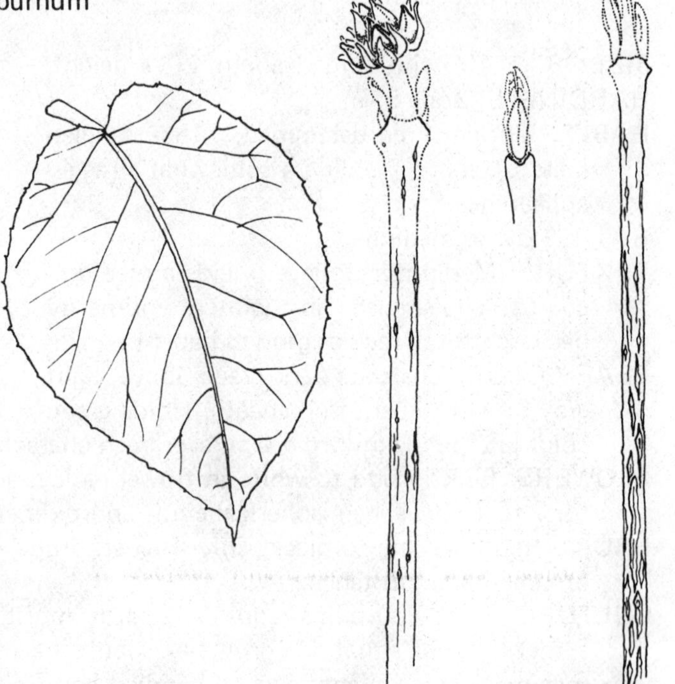

LEAVES: Opposite, simple, broad-ovate to elliptic, 1 to 4″ long, acute, usually rounded at base, irregularly toothed, dull green and stellate pubescent above, densely so and paler beneath, petiole—1/5 to 2/5″ long.

BUDS: Vegetative foliose, hairy; flower buds large—1/4 to 1/2″ wide, flat.

STEM: Light brown to gray, stellate pubescence on young stem. Old stems exhibit a characteristic fissuring.

SIZE: 4 to 5′ possibly to 8′ in height, by 4 to 8′ in width.

HARDINESS: Zone 4.

HABIT: Rounded, dense shrub with stiff, upright spreading branches.

RATE: Slow.

TEXTURE: Medium in summer and winter, clean in appearance.

LEAF COLOR: Dull dark green, very pubescent on the upper epidermis; reddish to wine-red in fall color, not consistent in coloration.

FLOWERS: Perfect, pink to red in bud, opening white, each individual flower 2/5 to 3/5″ across, pleasantly fragrant; late April to early May; in dense hemispherical cymes, 2 to 3″ across, often termed semi-snowball type flowers. Flowers are at their best when leaves are 1/2 to 2/3 mature size.

FRUIT: Drupe, 2/5″ diameter, red changing to black(not effective), August to September.

CULTIVARS: 'Cayuga' is the result of a backcross made in 1953 of *V. carlesii* Hemsl. x *V.* x *carlcephalum* Burk. ex Pike (*V. carlesii* x *V. macrocephalum* Fort.). 'Cayuga' is distinct in producing abundant inflorescenses with pink buds (Rose Opal) that open to white flowers in late April; compact growth habit; and medium textured foliage, with tolerance to bacterial leaf spot and powdery mildew. The leaves, which are less susceptible to bacterial leaf spot and powdery mildew than those of *V. carlesii*, are a darker green, smaller and not as coarse as those of *V.* x *carlcephalum*. In the autumn the foliage turns a dull orange-red. Although the inflorescences of 'Cayuga' are smaller than those of *V.* x *carlcephalum*, their greater numbers present a mass effect and a more ornamental plant. The flowers open from one side of the inflorescence in such a way that nearly all inflorescences have pink buds accenting the white, waxy flowers. 'Cayuga' is a compact, spreading, deciduous shrub to 5′ high. Plants have been hardy as far north as Ithaca, New York.

'Compacta' — More dense and compact than the species, about 2/3's the height.

PROPAGATION: Cuttings, softwood, with IBA treatment.

RELATED SPECIES:

V. bitchiuense — Bitchiu Viburnum

This species is similar to *V. carlesii* but with smaller leaves, more slender stems and looser habit; flowers are smaller; Japan. Cultivated 1909. Zone 5. Possibly more reliable than *V. carlesii.*

Viburnum x *carlcephalum,* Carlcephalum or Fragrant Viburnum, grows 6 to 10′ with an equal spread. Habit is somewhat open and loose. Foliage is dark green in summer changing to reddish purple in fall. The flowers are white, fragrant, late April to early May, borne in 5″ diameter hemispherical cymes. Fruit is a drupe which changes from red to black, however, it is seldom effective. Excellent plant for the shrub border for the spicy scented flowers perfume the entire garden. Result of a cross between *V. carlesii* x *V. macrocephalum*. Originated in England in 1932 at the Burkwood and Skipworth Nursery.

Viburnum x *juddii* — Judd Viburnum. Result of a cross between *V. carlesii* and *V. bitchiuense* with the best features of both parents. I feel it is superior to *V. carlesii* and may eventually replace it in northern areas.

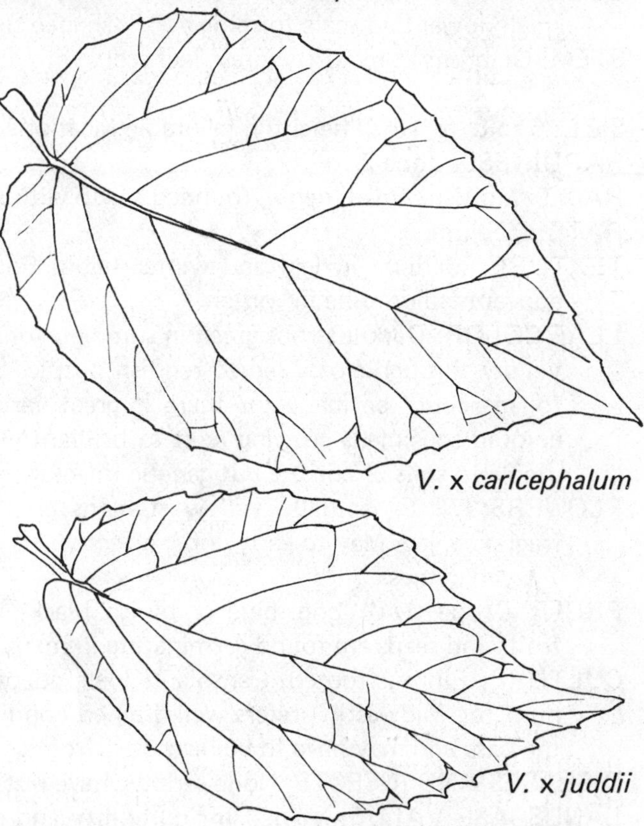
V. x *carlcephalum*

V. x *juddii*

Viburnum macrocephalum, Chinese Snowball Viburnum, is a dense, rounded shrub growing 6 to 10′ high. The flowers are white, each individual floret 1 1/5″ across, late May to early June, borne in 3 to 8″ diameter hemispherical cymes. Extremely showy in flower but requires a protected location and well-drained soil. I have seen it flowering in Columbus, Ohio, in protected areas. The foliage is semi-evergreen in the south. Does not fruit as the flowers are sterile. The var. *keteleeri* is the wild form and has sterile marginal flowers and fertile inner flowers. China. Introduced 1844. Zone 6.

NATIVE HABITAT: Korea. Introduced 1812.

Viburnum dentatum — Arrowwood Viburnum

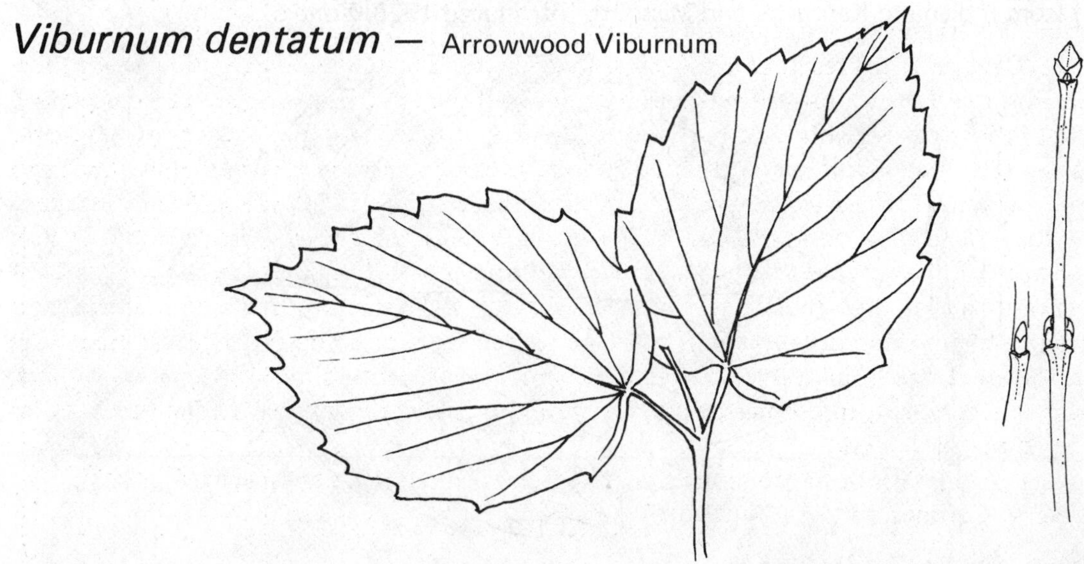

LEAVES: Opposite, simple, suborbicular to ovate, 1 to 3" long, short acuminate, rounded or subcordate, coarsely dentate, glabrous and lustrous above, glabrous beneath or bearded in the axils of the veins, with 6 to 10 pairs of veins, petiole 2/5 to 1" long.

BUDS: Imbricate (one of the few viburnums with imbricate buds), usually appressed, brownish, small, lower bud scale forming a "V"-shaped notch, glabrous.

STEM: Glabrous at maturity, gray, leaf scars with ciliate hairs around the margins.

SIZE: 6 to 8' to 15' in height in favorable locations, spread 6 to 15'.

HARDINESS: Zone 2.

HABIT: Multistemmed, dense, rounded shrub with spreading, finally arching branches.

RATE: Medium.

TEXTURE: Medium in leaf and winter habit. Some specimens are so delicately branched as to appear medium-fine in winter.

LEAF COLOR: Dark lustrous green in summer, sometimes without the sheen, fall color ranges from yellow through glossy-red to reddish purple. Selections for superior clones both in habit and foliage could be made for there is great variability within this species. I have seen poor fall colored specimens growing next to brilliant glossy red forms. The differences were not attributable to soils or climate but genetic differences.

FLOWERS: White, actually yellow stamens create a creamy color rather than pure white, no fragrance, late May to early June, effective 10 to 14 days, borne in 2 to 4" diameter flat-topped 7-rayed cymes.

FRUIT: Drupe, 1/4" long, blue or bluish black, late September through October; birds like the fruits and seeds are found germinating in many out-of-the-way places.

CULTURE: Fibrous rooted, transplants well, adapted to varied soils (possibly most durable viburnum for Midwest), prefers well-drained conditions, sun or partial shade. Suckers freely from the base and may have to be restricted from getting out of bounds.

DISEASES AND INSECTS: None serious, have not noticed any problems on the Midwest plantings.

LANDSCAPE VALUE: Valued for durability and utility, the ornamental characters are secondary to other viburnums, good in hedges, groupings, masses, filler in shrub border. University of Illinois has effectively employed this shrub for screening parking lots.

PROPAGATION: Seed, 180 to 510 days at fluctuating temperatures of 68 to 86°F, followed by 15 to 60 days at 41 to 80°F. Cuttings, softwoods are easy to root.

RELATED SPECIES:

Viburnum molle, Kentucky Viburnum, is a loose, open, multi-stemmed shrub reaching 10 to 12' in height. The bark exfoliates in thin flakes exposing a brownish inner bark. The leaves are dark green in summer. The flowers are whitish, borne in long-stalked, 2 to 3" diameter cymes in June. The fruit is a bluish black, 2/5" long drupe which is effective in August through September. Native from Indiana to Kentucky and Missouri. Introduced 1923. Zone 5.

ADDITIONAL NOTES: Indians used the strong shoots which developed from the roots for the shafts of their arrows, hence, the name Arrowwood.

NATIVE HABITAT: Eastern United States, New Brunswick to Minnesota, south to Georgia.

Viburnum dilatatum — Linden Viburnum

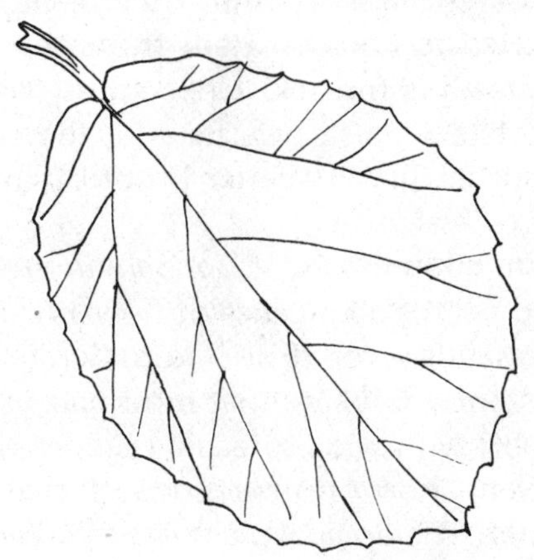

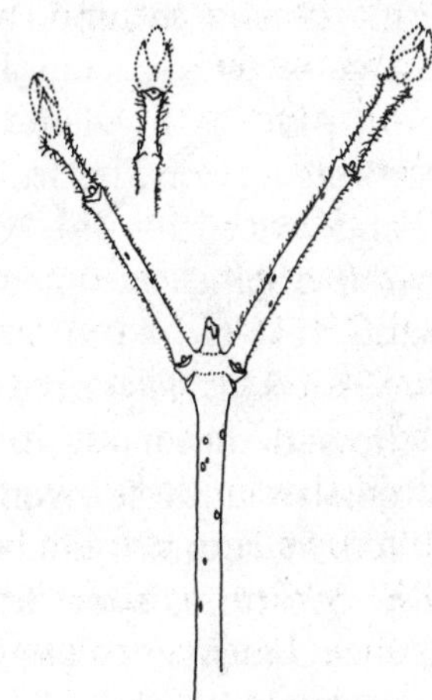

LEAVES: Opposite, simple, suborbicular to broad-ovate or obovate, 2 to 5" long, abruptly short acuminate, rounded or subcordate at base, coarsely toothed, hairy on both sides, with 5 to 8 pairs of veins, petiole 1/5 to 3/5" long.

BUDS: Imbricate, slightly pubescent, 4 to 6 bud scales, blunt, brownish, often with a tinge of red in the scales.

STEM: Young branches hispid when young, lenticels—orange (prominent).

SIZE: 8 to 10' in height, 2/3's to equal that in spread.

HARDINESS: Zone 5 (4).

HABIT: Often upright, somewhat leggy and open; also dense and compact in other forms.

RATE: Slow-medium.

TEXTURE: Medium in leaf, medium to coarse in winter.

LEAF COLOR: Dark green, often lustrous changing to an inconsistent russet-red in fall.

FLOWERS: White, late May to early June, effective 7 to 10 days, borne in pubescent (pilose), flat-topped, 3 to 5" diameter cymes.

FRUIT: Drupe, 1/3" long, bright red, cherry red or scarlet (excellent color), September to October and often persisting into December when fruit takes on appearance of withered red raisins. I have seen fruiting cymes heavy enough to bend the branches. Plant several clones for best fruiting.

CULTURE: Easily transplanted, adaptable, full sun for best fruiting.

DISEASES AND INSECTS: None serious.

LANDSCAPE VALUE: Specimen, shrub border, all purpose shrub ornamentally valuable in three seasons. Outstanding for fruits, however, little used in Midwestern gardens compared to the normal garden variety (forsythia, deutzia) shrubs.

CULTIVARS:

'Catskill' is a dwarf growing *V. dilatatum* seedling selection made in 1958 from plants raised from seed obtained from Japan. 'Catskill' was selected for the compact growth habit; smaller and rounder leaves; and good autumn coloration. The compact, wide spreading growth habit has been constant. The smaller, dull, dark green leaves, which are more nearly rounded than on most *V. d.* plants, assume good yellow, orange, and red fall coloration. The creamy-white inflorescences are produced in May on new growth. The dark red (Brick Red to Currant Red) fruit clusters, which are dispersed over the plant, ripen in mid-August and provide a display until mid-winter. The original plant, now 13 years old, is 5′ high and 8′ wide.

'Iroquois' resulted from a cross of two *V. d.* selections made in 1953. The cultivar was selected for large, thick textured, dark green leaves; abundant inflorescences of creamy-white flowers; large, glossy, dark scarlet fruits; and dense, globose growth habit. The heavy textured foliage is ornamental in all seasons, glossy green in summer, and orange-red to maroon in autumn. In mid-May the inflorescences transform the plant into a mound of creamy-white. The glossy, red (Orient Red to Cardinal Red) fruits are larger than those on most *V. d.* plants. The flat, wide spreading fruit clusters contrast well with the dark green leaves. The fruit, which ripens in late August, persists after the leaves have fallen, and often the dried fruits are in abundance in mid-winter if not eaten by birds earlier. The original specimen is 9′ high and 12 1/2′ wide.

'Oneida' resulted from a cross of *V. dilatatum* Thunb. x *V. lobophyllum* Graebn. made in 1953. This deciduous shrub was selected for the abundance of flowers in May and sporadic flowers throughout the summer; the glossy, dark red (Fire Red to Cardinal Red) fruit that persists until late winter; and the thin textured foliage that turns pale yellow and orange-red in autumn; and upright growth habit with wide spreading branches. Because of the two or three sporadic flowering periods, abundant fruit is produced that ripens in August and persists on the plant until mid-winter. The original plant has grown to a height of 10′ and a width of 9 1/2′.

'Xanthocarpum'. Form with showy yellow fruits.

PROPAGATION: Cuttings, softwood, June with 1000 ppm IBA solution, peat:perlite under mist yielded 90% rooting.

RELATED SPECIES:

Viburnum acerifolium — Mapleleaf Viburnum

LEAVES: Opposite, simple, suborbicular to ovate, 3-lobed, sometimes slightly so, 2 to 4″ long, rounded to cordate at base, the lobes acute to acuminate, coarsely dentate, slightly pubescent above, more densely so and with black dots beneath; petiole 2/5 to 1″ long.

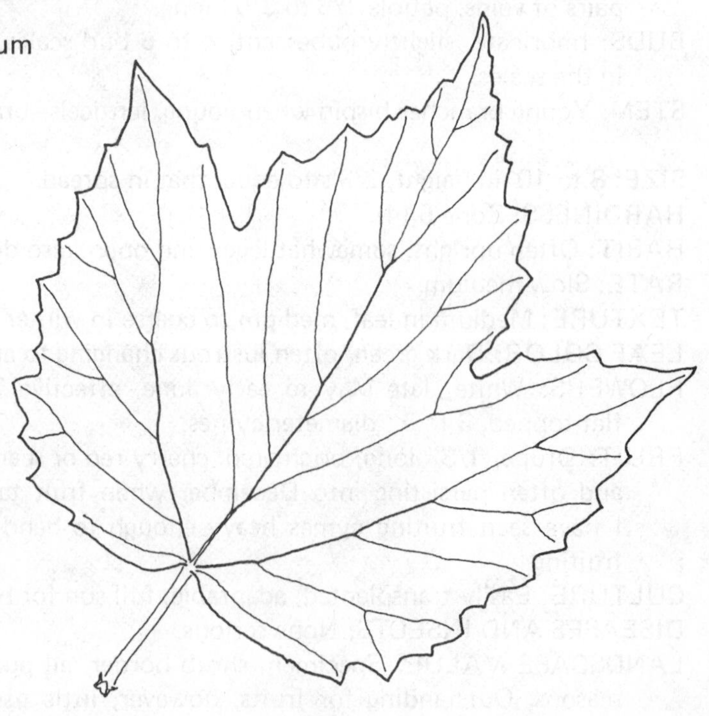

Viburnum acerifolium, Mapleleaf Viburnum, is a low, sparse shrub growing 4 to 6′ tall and 3 to 4′ wide. The foliage is bright green in summer changing to reddish purple in fall. The flowers are yellowish white, early June, borne in 1 to 3″ diameter cymes. The fruit is a black, 1/3″ long drupe which ripens in September. An extremely shade tolerant species reserved for naturalizing. New Brunswick to Minnesota, south to North Carolina. Introduced 1736. Zone 3.

Viburnum cassinoides — Witherod Viburnum

LEAVES: Opposite, simple, elliptic or ovate to oblong, 1 1/5 to 4″ long, acute or bluntly acuminate, obscurely dentate or denticulate, nearly glabrous.

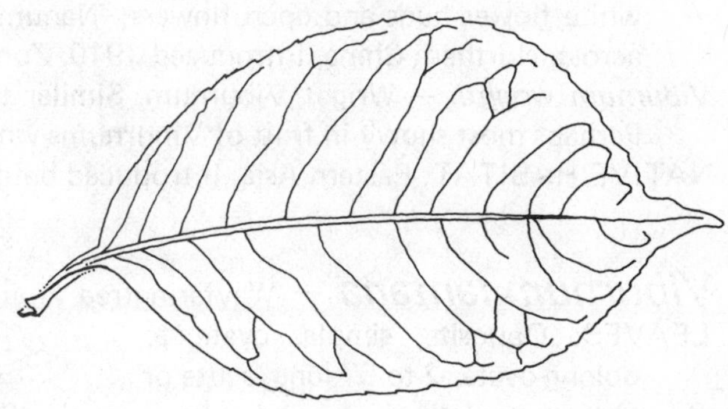

Viburnum cassinoides, Witherod Viburnum, grows 5 to 6′ tall with a similar spread but can reach 10′ in height. It is a handsome dense shrub, compact and rounded with spreading finally slightly arching branches. The foliage is bright green in summer changing to orange-red, dull crimson, and purple in fall. The flowers are creamy white, late June to early July, borne in 2 to 5″ diameter flat topped cymes. The fruit is the most beautiful attribute as it changes from green to pink, then from red to blue before becoming black in September. Often all colors are present in the same infructescence (fruiting cluster). A very lovely but little used shrub which has a place in naturalizing, massing, and the shrub border. I have seen it used effectively in a mass planting at the Holden Arboretum, Mentor, Ohio. A similar species is *V. nudum*, Smooth Witherod, which is less hardy and native to southeastern United States. *V. cassinoides* is native from Newfoundland to Manitoba and Minnesota, south to North Carolina. Introduced 1761. Zone 2.

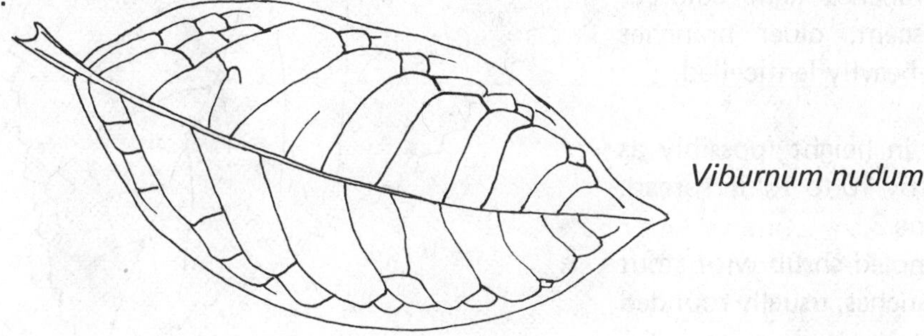

Viburnum nudum

Viburnum farreri — Fragrant Viburnum

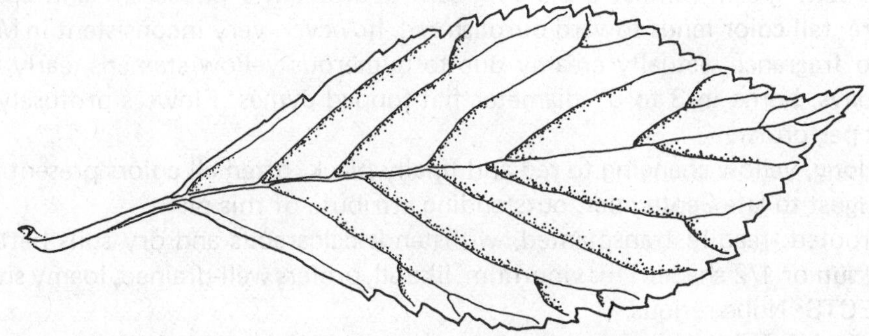

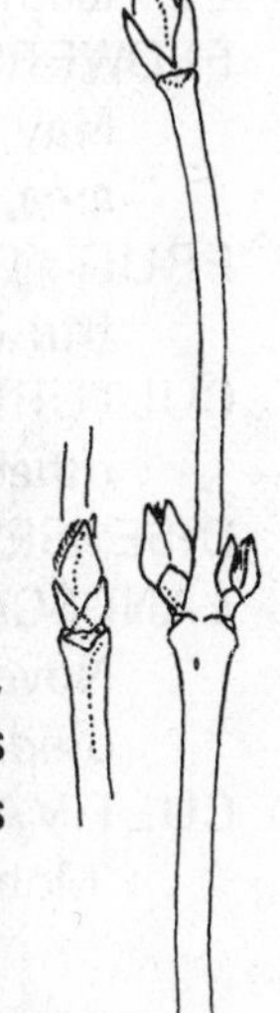

LEAVES: Opposite, simple, elliptic, 1 3/5 to 3″ long, acute, broad-cuneate or cuneate, serrate with triangular teeth, sparingly pubescent above and pubescent on veins beneath, finally glabrous or nearly so, with 5 to 6 pairs of veins and the veinlets impressed above and below, dark green; petiole 2/5 to 3/5″ long, purplish.

Viburnum farreri (fragrans), Fragrant Viburnum, grows 8 to 12′ tall with a similar spread. The foliage is dark green in summer changing to reddish purple in fall. The flowers are pinkish red in bud opening to white tinged with pink, early to mid-April before the leaves, borne in 1 to 2″ long panicle; one of the earliest Viburnums to flower.

Fruit colors red, finally black and is effective in July to August. The cultivar 'Album' has white flower buds and open flowers; 'Nanum' is a dwarf type growing 2 to 3' tall and 4 to 6' across. Northern China. Introduced 1910. Zone 5.

Viburnum wrightii – Wright Viburnum. Similar to *V. dilatatum* but with larger leaves and fruits. Perhaps most showy in fruit of Viburnums which can be grown in the North.

NATIVE HABITAT: Eastern Asia. Introduced before 1845.

Viburnum lantana — Wayfaringtree Viburnum

LEAVES: Opposite, simple, ovate to oblong-ovate, 2 to 5" long, acute or obtuse, cordate to rounded at base, rather closely denticulate, sparingly stellate-pubescent and wrinkled above, stellate-tomentose beneath, petiole–2/5 to 1 1/5" long, very uniform serrations and a strong reticulate venation pattern.

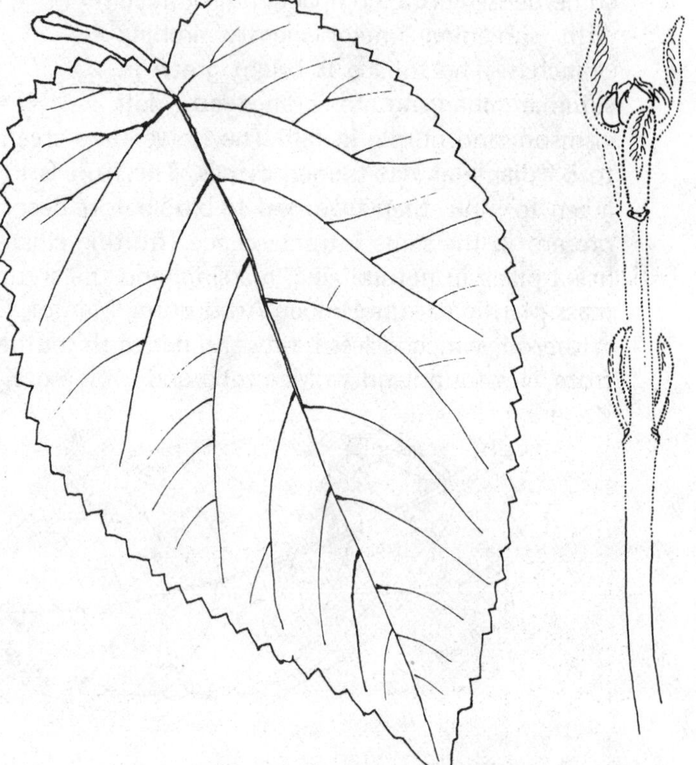

BUDS: Naked, foliose, whitish tomentose. Flower buds similar to *V. carlesii*.

STEM: Young branches light colored, scurfy pubescent, older branches gray, usually heavily lenticelled.

SIZE: 10 to 14' in height (possibly as large as 20') by 10 to 15' in spread.

HARDINESS: Zone 3.

HABIT: Multistemmed shrub with stout spreading branches, usually rounded in outline.

RATE: Medium.

TEXTURE: Medium in leaf, often quite ragged in winter habit, appearing coarse.

LEAF COLOR: Dull dark green (almost a bluish green), leaves quite pubescent and somewhat leathery in texture; fall color tends toward purplish red, however, very inconsistent in Midwest.

FLOWERS: White, no fragrance, actually creamy due to numerous yellow stamens, early to mid-May, 10 to 14 days, borne in 3 to 5" diameter flat-topped cymes. Flowers profusely in our area, a consistent performer.

FRUIT: Drupe, 1/3" long, yellow changing to red and finally black, often all colors present in same fruiting cyme, August to late September, outstanding attribute of this plant.

CULTURE: Fibrous rooted, readily transplanted, withstands calcareous and dry soils better than other viburnums, sun or 1/2 shade. This viburnum, like all, prefers well-drained, loamy situation.

DISEASES AND INSECTS: None serious.

LANDSCAPE VALUE: Used for hedges, screens, massing, shrub border; foliage persists until November in Central Illinois. Winter coarseness should be considered before this species is used extensively.

CULTIVARS:

'Mohican' – A seedling selected in 1956 from a population grown from *V. l.* seed received from Poland. The plant, as a deciduous shrub, was selected for compact growth habit; thick, dark green leaves; fruit that turns orange-red and maintains an effective display for 4 or more weeks; and resistance to bacterial leaf spot. The creamy-white flowers and expanding pale green leaves appear together for a week in early May. The orange-red fruit (Jasper Red to Blood Red) begins to ripen in early July and remains effective for 4 or more weeks, whereas fruit on other *V. l.* plants pass rapidly from orange to black. The original specimen in 15 years has grown to 8 1/2′ high and 9′ wide.

'Rugosum' – Leathery-leaf form with larger and darker green leaves which are more handsome than those of the species.

PROPAGATION: Cuttings, softwood, root easily.

NATIVE HABITAT: Europe, Western Asia, occasionally escaped from cultivation in Eastern United States.

Viburnum lentago — Nannyberry Viburnum, Sheepberry

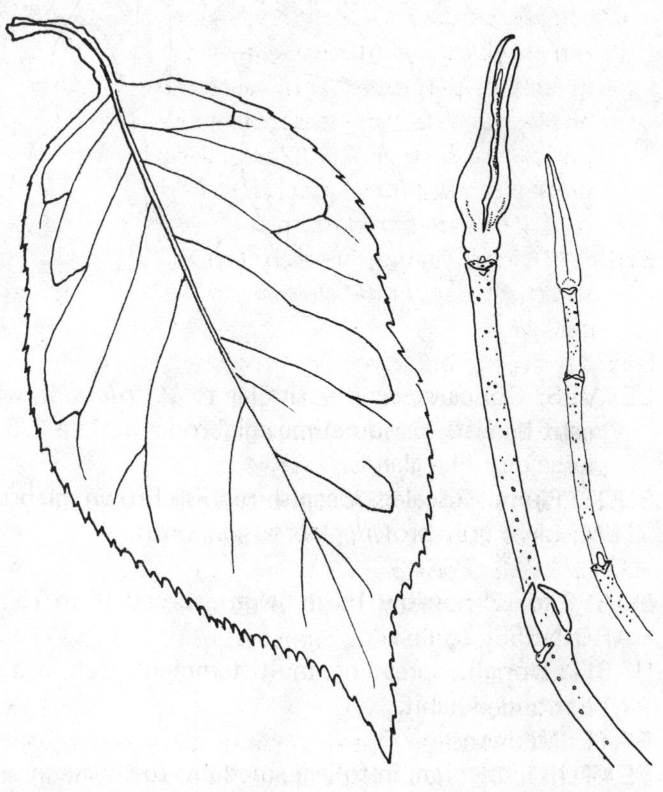

LEAVES: Opposite, simple, ovate to elliptic-obovate, 2 to 4″ long, acuminate, broad cuneate to rounded at base, finely toothed, glabrous or scurfy on the veins beneath, petiole—2/5 to 1″ long, mostly winged with wavy margin.

BUDS: Vegetative—valvate in nature, long pointed, slightly curved, lead-gray in color; Flower buds—fat at base and tapering to a long point, both about 1″ long.

STEM: Slightly pubescent to essentially glabrous, brownish in color.

SIZE: 15 to 18′ possibly to 30′ in height, spread quite variable, often 6 to 10′ and more.

HARDINESS: Zone 2.

HABIT: Shrub or small tree with slender finally arching branches, somewhat open at maturity; often suckering.

RATE: Medium.

TEXTURE: Medium in leaf, medium-coarse in winter.

LEAF COLOR: Soft yellow green when unfolding, gradually changing to glossy medium green. Fall color develops purplish red but is not guaranteed in the Midwest. Often poor green and falls off as such.

FLOWERS: White, no fragrance, appearing creamy due to yellow stamens, early to mid May, 7 to 10 days, borne in 3 to 8″ diameter, flat cymes. Flower is good but color is typical of many viburnums.

FRUIT: Drupe, 1/2″ long, bluish black, bloomy, September to October and often December in our area; common name is derived from smell of the fruits.

CULTURE: Fibrous rooted, transplants readily, often suckers profusely forming a thicket, adaptable to a wide range of conditions, sun or shade, native species of great durability.

DISEASES AND INSECTS: Often covered with mildew especially when grown in shaded areas. Spray with Karathane. Usually no serious problems are encountered.

LANDSCAPE VALUE: Ideal shrub for naturalizing, works well in shrub borders, as a background or screen plant and limitedly for specimen use. Good winter food for the birds.

PROPAGATION: Seed, 150 to 270 days at 68 to 86°F fluctuating temperatures followed by 60 to 120 days at 41°F. Cuttings, softwood; from personal experience this species roots easily from softwood cuttings.

NATIVE HABITAT: Hudson Bay to Manitoba, south to Georgia and Mississippi.

Viburnum opulus — European Cranberrybush Viburnum

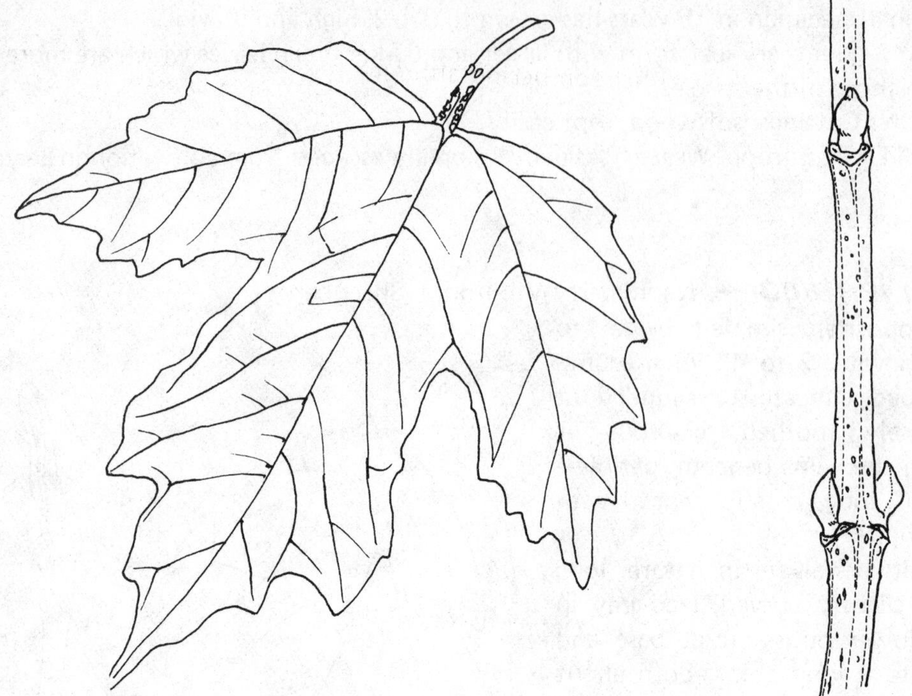

LEAVES: Opposite, simple, similar to *V. trilobum*, with rather shorter, more-toothed lobes, pubescent beneath or sometimes glabrous; petiole 2/5 to 4/5" long, with narrow groove and a few large disk-like glands.

BUDS: Plump, 2 scaled, greenish-reddish brown, glabrous, shiny; scales connate.

STEM: Light gray-brown, glabrous, smooth.

SIZE: 8 to 12' possibly 15' in height, spread 10 to 15'.

HARDINESS: Zone 3.

HABIT: Upright, spreading, multistemmed shrub, often with arching branches to the ground creating a rounded habit.

RATE: Medium.

TEXTURE: Medium in foliage; medium to coarse in winter, can look "ratty" in winter.

LEAF COLOR: Good glossy dark green in summer, changing to yellow-red and reddish purple in fall. Not a consistent fall coloring shrub in Midwest. Often leaves show no change, simply falling off green.

FLOWERS: White, outer ring of flowers sterile and showy, inner flowers fertile and inconspicuous creating a pin-wheel effect, mid May, borne in 2 to 3" diameter, flat-topped cymes. Flowers are handsome and interesting because of unique combination of sterile and fertile flowers in same inflorescence.

FRUIT: Berry-like drupe, bright red, ripening in September-October and persisting into winter, each fruit is about 1/4" diameter and globose in shape. The fruits often shrivel through the winter months and take on the appearance of dried red raisins.

DISEASES AND INSECTS: Often infested with aphids (plant lice) but this is more common on the cultivar 'Roseum'. Can be controlled with malathion or similar compounds.

LANDSCAPE VALUE: Shrub border, screen, large areas, massing, excellent for its showy flower and fruit display. The following cultivars are excellent landscape plants.

CULTIVARS:

'Compactum' — Excellent plant where space is limited, 1/2 the size of the species in height and extremely dense in habit. Excellent in flower and fruit. Excellent in masses, fruit makes a brilliant show. Probably should be considered over the species in the smaller, more restricted planting areas of the modern landscape.

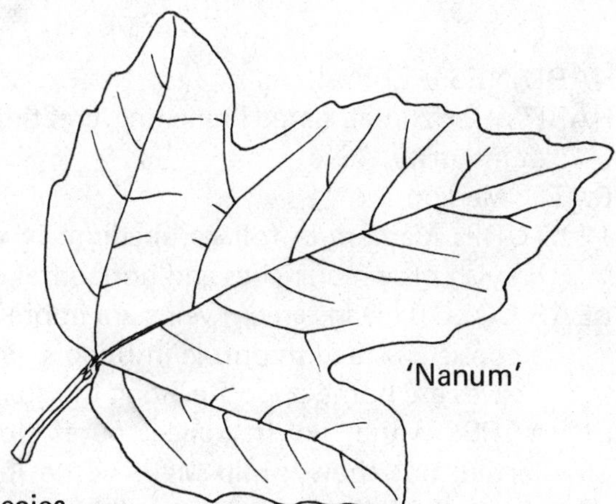

'Nanum' – Dwarf form, much branched and dense, 18 to 24" in height and 1 1/2 times that in spread; I have seen specimens between 4 and 5' high; supposedly never flowers or fruits but, again, I have seen several isolated flowering and fruiting specimens. Makes a good filler or facer plant; can be used for low hedges; will not withstand wet, poorly drained conditions, and in wet weather contracts significant leaf spot.

'Notcutt' – Supposedly more vigorous than the species.

'Roseum' – The European Snowball or Guilder-rose, a form with sterile flowers which is extremely showy in flower. The 2 1/2–3" diameter inflorescences literally cover the shrub in mid-May. An old favorite more apt to be located around older residences. Aphids infest this form quite heavily and often distort the young leaves and stems.

'Xanthocarpum' – Form with yellowish gold fruits, quite attractive.

PROPAGATION: Seed, 60 to 90 days at fluctuating temperatures of 68 to 86°F followed by 30 to 60 days at 41°F. Cuttings are easy to root. I have had 100% success with softwood and greenwood cuttings.

NATIVE HABITAT: Europe, Northern Africa and Northern Asia.

Viburnum plicatum tomentosum — Doublefile Viburnum

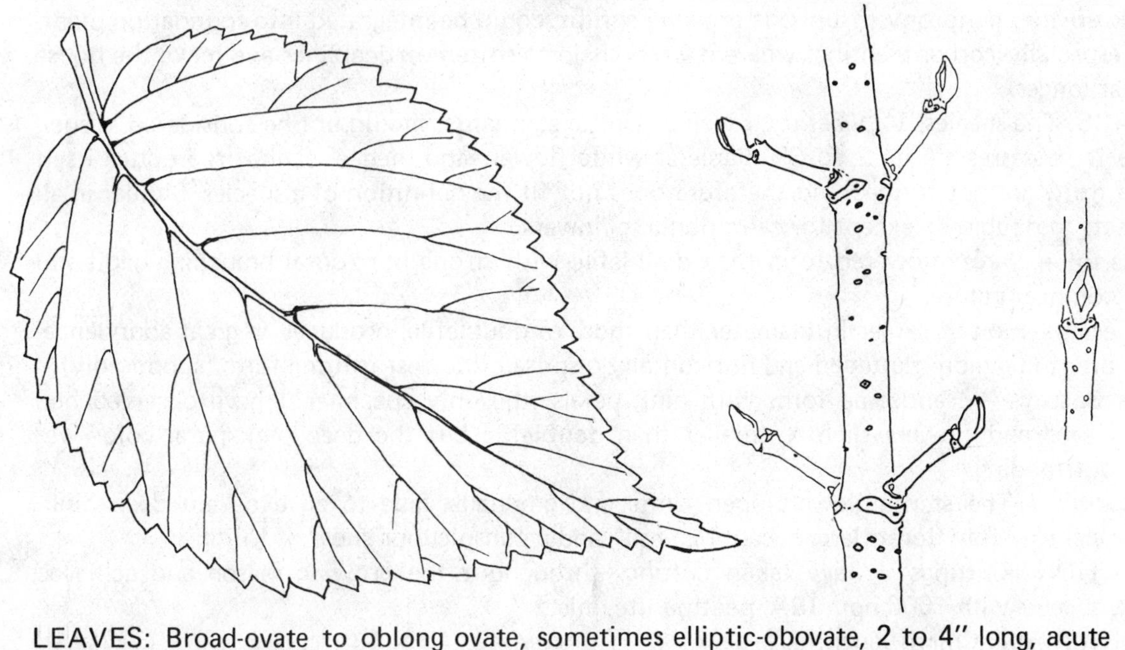

LEAVES: Broad-ovate to oblong ovate, sometimes elliptic-obovate, 2 to 4" long, acute or abruptly acuminate, rounded to broad-cuneate, dentate-serrate, dark green and nearly glabrous above, stellate-pubescent beneath, with 8 to 12 pairs of nearly straight veins, petiole–2/5 to 4/5" long.

BUDS: Vegetative buds–naked, foliose, pubescent; Flower buds–valvate, angular, tan-brown, hairy, appressed to stem or divergent.

STEM: Young branches with stellate tomentose, older branches dark gray or brownish, orangish lenticels, many small branches (2 at node) forming a fishbone effect.

SIZE: 8 to 10' in height, usually slightly wider than tall at maturity (9 to 12'), one old plant at Bicton outside Bristol, England, was 10' tall and 20' wide, but this is unusual.

HARDINESS: Zone 4.

HABIT: Horizontal, tiered branching, creating a stratified effect, appearing rounded to broad-rounded at maturity.

RATE: Medium.

TEXTURE: Medium in foliage, medium in winter. Extremely handsome in winter because of clean grayish brown branches and horizontal habit.

LEAF COLOR: Dark green, veins are impressed creating a ridge-furrowed effect; fall color has been a consistent reddish purple in Illinois. Possibly, best viburnum for fall color in Central Midwest. Leaves are borne opposite along the stems and tend to hang down creating a "dog-eared" effect.

FLOWERS: White, no fragrance, outer flowers sterile, 4-lobed, pure snow white; inner flowers fertile, not showy; mid May; borne in 2 to 4" diameter flat-topped cymes which are borne above the foliage creating a milky way effect along the horizontal branches. A choice specimen of Doublefile Viburnum is without equal.

FRUIT: Drupe, 1/3" long, bright red changing to black, July and August, usually devoured by birds before completely ripened. One of the earliest viburnums to display excellent fruit color.

CULTURE: Fibrous rooted, transplants well, demands moist, well-drained soil, from my own observations this plant will not tolerate heavy, clayey, poorly-drained soils. I have grown well-branched 3 to 4' specimens in two growing seasons from cuttings without special care.

DISEASES AND INSECTS: None serious, although I have observed stem dieback in wet areas. I am not sure if the problem is of a pathological or physiological nature.

LANDSCAPE VALUE: Possibly the most elegant of flowering shrubs. One of the best specimens I have had the privilege of viewing is located on the Amherst College campus, Amherst, Massachusetts. A choice specimen when placed near red brick buildings where the snow-white flowers are accentuated; massing, screen, shrub border. Blends well into a border as the horizontal lines break up the monotony of upright growing shrubs, could be integrated into foundation plantings especially corner plantings where it would help to soften vertical lines and make the house appear longer.

CULTIVARS: The species, *V. plicatum*, by all botanical standards, should not be considered as such since it possesses sterile 2 to 3" diameter white flowers and, hence, cannot reproduce itself since fruits are not formed and therefore does not fit the definition of a species. Similar in all respects to doublefile except for carnation-like flowers.

'Lanarth' — Larger flowered form than doublefile with strong horizontal branching habit and compact nature.

'Mariesii' — Flowers larger in diameter than those of doublefile, produced in great abundance; branching more flattened and horizontally disposed; the best fruiting form (supposedly).

'Pink Beauty' — Handsome form with pink petals, the only specimen I have observed had leaves and flowers slightly smaller than doublefile but the deep pink petal color was outstanding.

'Roseum' — The sterile flowers open white and gradually fade to an excellent deep pink.

'Rowallane' — Ray florets larger than 'Mariesii', and a conspicuous show of fruits.

PROPAGATION: Cuttings, I have taken cuttings throughout the growing season and achieved 100% success with 1000 ppm IBA, peat:perlite, mist.

NATIVE HABITAT: China, Japan.

Viburnum prunifolium — Blackhaw Viburnum

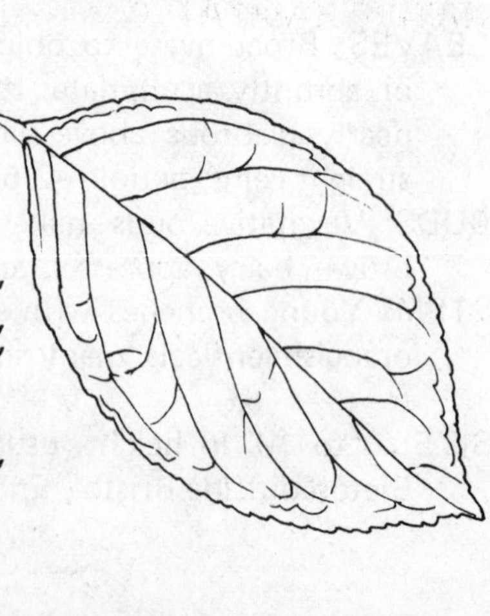

LEAVES: Opposite, simple, broad-elliptic to ovate, 1 to 3" long, acute or obtuse, rounded at base or broad-cuneate, serrulate, glabrous or nearly so, petiole not narrowly winged, 1/3 to 2/3" long.

BUDS: Vegetative and flower buds short pointed, valvate, lead colored, about 1/2" long.

STEM: Glabrous, usually short and stiff in nature.

SIZE: 12 to 15′ in height by 8 to 12′ in width.

HARDINESS: Zone 3.

HABIT: Round headed tree or multistemmed shrub, stiffly branched, similar to *Crataegus* in growth habit. Robinson described this species as "a puritan with a rigidity of character similar to some of the hawthorns."

RATE: Slow to medium.

TEXTURE: Medium in leaf; handsomely coarse in winter.

LEAF COLOR: Dark green, handsome, clean foliage in summer changing to purplish in the fall. Various authorities have described the fall color as shining red, dull deep red or bronze.

FLOWERS: White, actually creamy due to numerous yellow stamens, mid May, borne in 2 to 4″ diameter flat-topped cymes.

FRUIT: Drupe, up to 1/2″ long, bluish black, bloomy, September through fall, fruit is palatable and has been used for preserves since colonial days.

CULTURE: Transplants well, adaptable to many soil types, sun or shade conditions.

DISEASES AND INSECTS: None serious.

LANDSCAPE VALUE: Interesting as a small specimen tree, massing, shrub border, groupings. Habit is somewhat similar to hawthorns.

CULTIVARS:

'Mrs. George Large' — Not widely known but very handsome for its more compact habit, distinct leathery green summer foliage and maroon fall color. I first observed this form at Purdue University's Horticultural Park and was impressed by the overall attractiveness.

RELATED SPECIES:

Viburnum rufidulum — Southern or Rusty Blackhaw. Handsome lustrous green foliage, more pubescent plant parts, and slightly less hardy (Zone 6) than the species. Worthwhile specimen where it can be grown.

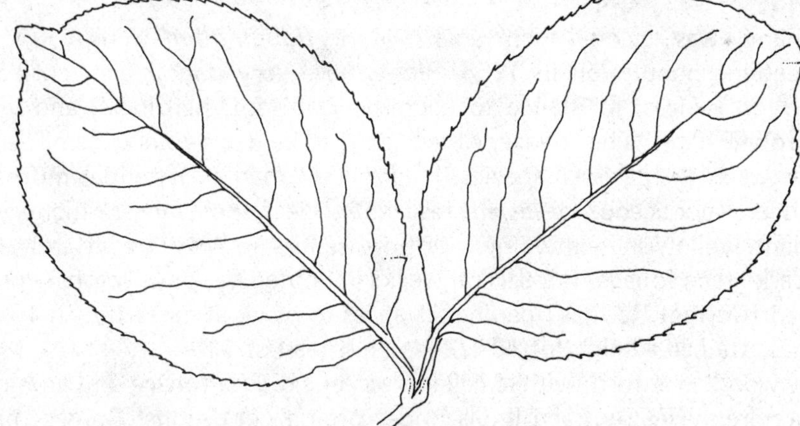

NATIVE HABITAT: Connecticut to Florida, west to Michigan and Texas.

Viburnum x *rhytidophylloides* — Lantanaphyllum Viburnum

A hybrid of *V. lantana* x *V. rhytidophyllum.*
Similar to *V. rhytidophyllum* except leaves broader and less rugose.

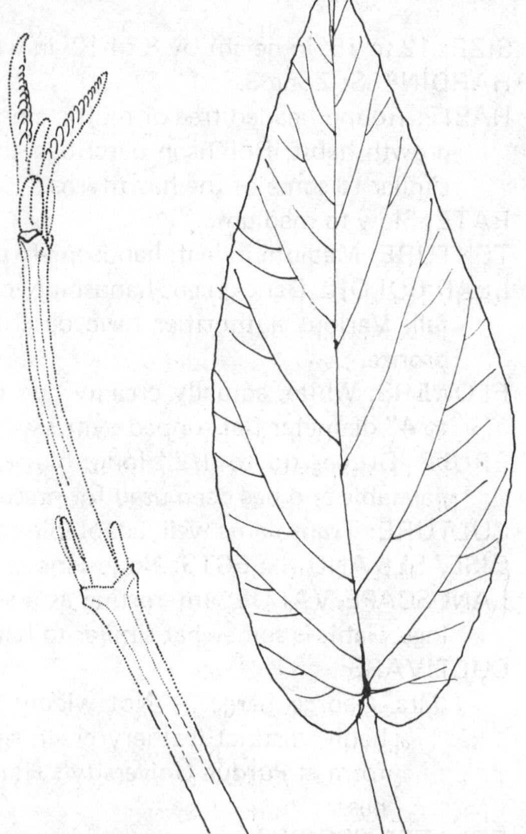

SIZE: 8 to 10′ possibly 18′ in height, spread would probably equal height at maturity.

HARDINESS: Zone 5.

HABIT: Upright, spreading shrub with slightly arching branches. Eventually somewhat rounded in outline.

RATE: Medium.

TEXTURE: Medium to coarse in summer and winter because of large evergreen leaves.

LEAF COLOR: Dark leathery green above, light brown and extremely tomentose beneath. The foliage has a bold coarseness which is quite attractive.

FLOWERS: White (creamy), often sparingly produced, May, borne in 3″ diameter flat-topped cymes. Flowers are not showy on this plant.

FRUIT: Drupe, reddish changing to black, late August through September, usually of limited ornamental consequence.

CULTURE: Transplants well, adaptable, sun or partial shade, best sited in a protected location in Central Midwest, hardier than *V. rhytidophyllum.*

LANDSCAPE VALUE: Possibly should replace *V. lantana* because of excellent foliage although flower and fruit are not as good. Could be utilized for screen, foundation plant, blended with other broadleaf evergreens.

CULTIVARS:

'Alleghany' was selected from an F_2 *V. rhytidophyllum* Hemsl. x *V. lantana* L. 'Mohican' seedling population in 1958. Plants have very dark green, coriaceous leaves; abundant inflorescences; resistance to bacterial leaf spot; hardiness; and vigorous, dense, globose growth habit. The foliage, which tends to be deciduous to semi-persistent, is intermediate between the parental species. It is smaller than *V. r.*, and is more leathery than *V. l.* The rugose, coriaceous leaves are resistant to leaf spot and are highly ornamental. The abundant, yellowish white flower inflorescences in May are effectively displayed above the dark green foliage. For several weeks in September and October the fruit becomes brilliant red (Currant Red) as ripening advances to black at maturity. In 13 years the original plant has attained a height of 10 1/2′ and a spread of 11′.

'Willowwood' — A form with excellent lustrous rugose foliage and arching habit. Has performed admirably in Central Illinois under prairie conditions. Comes through the winter with foliage in good condition. I have seen this cultivar flowering in October on the Purdue University campus at West Lafayette, Indiana. Result of a cross made by Henry Tubbs of Willowwood Farm, Gladstone, New Jersey.

PROPAGATION: Cuttings, softwood dipped in 1000 ppm IBA solution rooted 100%.

ADDITIONAL NOTES: I had never seen abundant fruit on this species until the summer of 1975 when I visited the nursery at Spring Grove Cemetery. There were many viburnums in close proximity and the fruit set was simply unbelievable on *V. rhytidophylloides* and *V. lantana*. This seems to emphasize the importance of using closely related species or different clones of viburnum to insure cross pollination and abundant fruiting.

Viburnum rhytidophyllum — Leatherleaf Viburnum

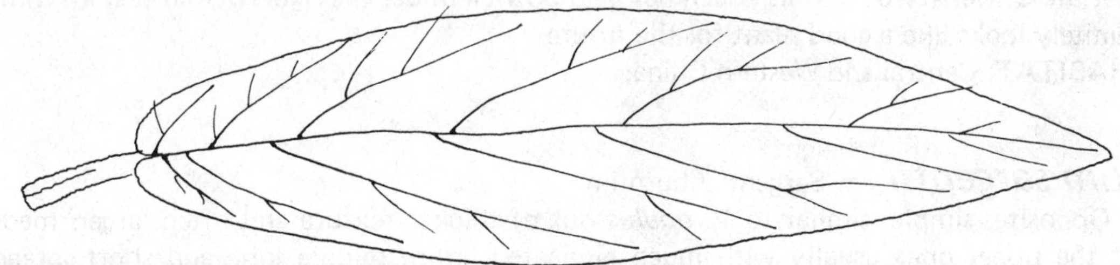

LEAVES: Opposite, simple, ovate-oblong to ovate-lanceolate, 3 to 7" long, acute or obtuse, rounded or subcordate at base, entire or obscurely denticulate, lustrous dark green, glabrous and strongly wrinkled above, prominently reticulate beneath and gray or yellowish tomentose, petiole—2/5 to 1 1/5" long.

BUDS: Vegetative—large, rusty colored, tomentose, foliose. Flower buds borne in flat cymes, 1 1/2-2" across, evident throughout winter.

STEM: Gray to brown in color with stellate pubescence on young stems, older stems glabrous.

SIZE: 10 to 15' in height with a similar spread.

HARDINESS: Zone 5, although in severe winters will be killed to the ground. Usually develops new shoots the following spring as the roots are not injured.

HABIT: Upright, strongly multistemmed shrub, often somewhat open with age, usually upright-rounded to rounded in outline.

RATE: Medium.

TEXTURE: Possibly coarse in foliage, usually coarse in winter.

LEAF COLOR: Dark, lustrous, leathery green above, gray to brownish tomentose beneath, semi-evergreen in the north and with proper siting (in a micro-climate) will maintain most of its foliage. I rate this plant very high because of its excellent foliage.

FLOWERS: Yellowish white, mid May, borne in 4 to 8" diameter, 7 to 11 rayed, flat-topped cymes. The color is not outstanding but the quantity and size of the flowers are ornamental assets. The naked flower buds are formed in August-September of the year prior to flowering and are interesting because of large cymes on which they are borne. Flowers are slightly fragrant.

FRUIT: Drupe, 1/3" long, red changing to black, September, October through December. Prior to 1973 I had never observed good fruiting on this species. In 1973 I found three specimens on the north side of a house in Urbana, Illinois, literally weighted down with beautiful bright red fruits. Often viburnums are somewhat self-sterile and do not fruit heavily unless different clones are present. Perhaps what I stumbled upon were three clones of Leatherleaf. Needless to say, cuttings were collected, rooted, and are now developing in my garden.

CULTURE: Transplants well, well-drained soil aids hardiness, shelter from wind and winter sun, seems to tolerate heavy shade (3/4's).

DISEASES AND INSECTS: None serious.

LANDSCAPE VALUE: Excellent specimen where it can be grown without coddling, blends well with other broadleaf evergreens, possibly massing or as a background plant.

CULTIVARS: Wyman mentions a variety *roseum* which has pink flower buds but opens yellowish white.

PROPAGATION: Cuttings, I have taken cuttings throughout the growing season and achieved 100% success.

RELATED SPECIES:

Viburnum x *pragense* is the result of a cross between *V. rhytidophyllum* and *V. utile*. It is an attractive semi-evergreen shrub with lustrous, dark green, elliptic, 2 to 4" long leaves. The flowers are creamy white, buds pink, and produced in terminal cymes in May. This

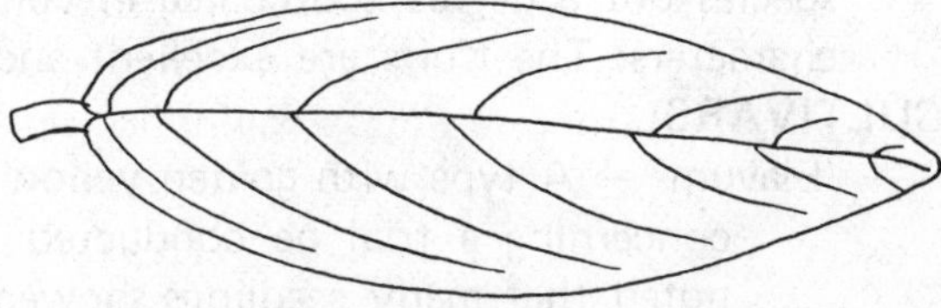

hybrid was raised in Prague and is extremely hardy. There is one plant in our woody plant test plots at the University of Illinois which has held up well under the rigors of Midwestern winters. It definitely looks like a good plant for the future.

NATIVE HABITAT: Central and Western China.

Viburnum sargentii — Sargent Viburnum

LEAVES: Opposite, simple, similar to *V. opulus* but of thicker texture and often larger, medium green, the upper ones usually with much elongated entire middle lobe and short spreading lateral lobes, sometimes oblong-lanceolate and without lobes; petiole 4/5 to 1 4/5" long with large disk-like glands, pinkish or reddish in color.

BUDS: Oblong, or flask-shaped, mostly appressed, scurfy; scales closely valvate or connate as a closed sac; green to red in color.

STEMS: Straw-colored to brownish; often of polished appearance; thickish for a viburnum stem, about 1/3" diameter.

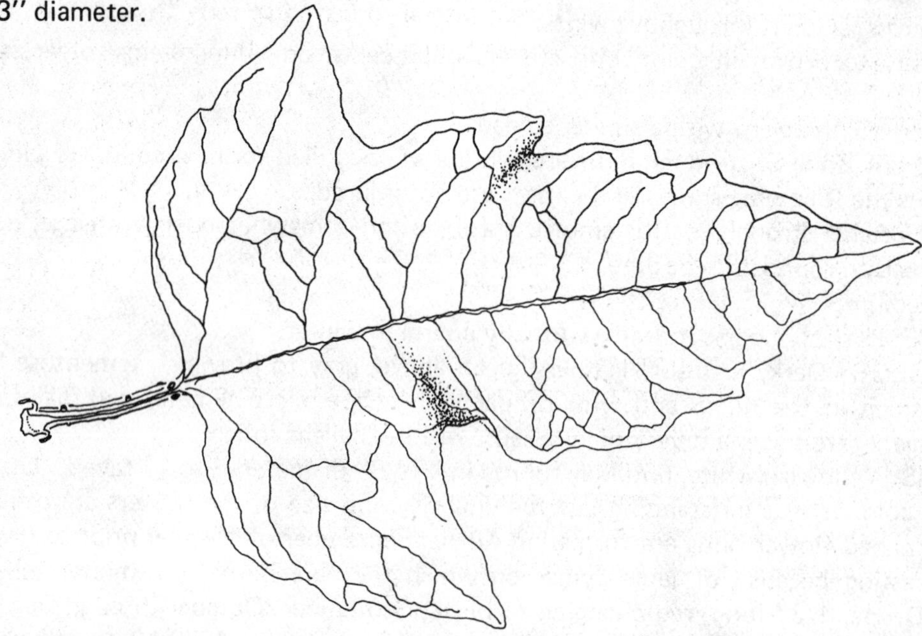

SIZE: 12 to 15' high and 12' to 15' in width.

HARDINESS: Zone 4.

HABIT: Multistemmed upright-rounded to rounded shrub of relatively coarse texture. Somewhat similar to *V. opulus* but not as handsome.

RATE: Medium, I noticed a specimen at Purdue's Horticultural Park which exhibited extreme vigor.

TEXTURE: Would have to be rated coarse in all seasons.

LEAF COLOR: Medium green in summer; often assuming yellowish to reddish tones in fall.

FLOWERS: White, borne in flat-topped cymes on a 4/5 to 2" long stalk; sterile outer flowers about 1" or slightly greater in diameter; the anthers are purple and differ from the yellow anthers of *V. opulus*. Flowers in late May.

FRUITS: Scarlet, 2/5" long, berry-like drupe; effective in August through October.

CULTURE: Similar to other viburnums.

DISEASES AND INSECTS: None particularly serious.

LANDSCAPE VALUE: More vigorous than *V. opulus* and more resistant to aphids. Interesting species but a degree too coarse in comparison to other viburnums with similar ornamental characters. The fruits are excellent and of a bright, translucent red, lasting well into winter.

CULTIVARS:

'Flavum' — A type with golden yellow translucent fruit. Wyman has an interesting anecdote concerning a trial he conducted growing seedlings from the yellow-fruited form. He noted that many seedlings showed yellowish leaf petioles and others reddish. The seedlings with yellowish petioles fall colored yellowish green; those with reddish petioles fall colored red. Obviously the fruit will also follow the same trends exhibited in petiole color.

PROPAGATION: Easily propagated by cuttings. Seed probably possesses a double dormancy similar to *V. opulus* and a warm stratification of 60 to 90 days followed by cold for 30 to 60 days should suffice.

NATIVE HABITAT: Northeastern Asia. Introduced 1892.

Viburnum setigerum — Tea Viburnum ✱

LEAVES: Opposite, simple, 2 to 5" long, acuminate, rounded at base, remotely denticulate, flat, soft blue-green above, glabrous except silky hairs on the veins beneath, with 6 to 9 pairs of veins, petiole 2/5 to 4/5" long, glabrous.

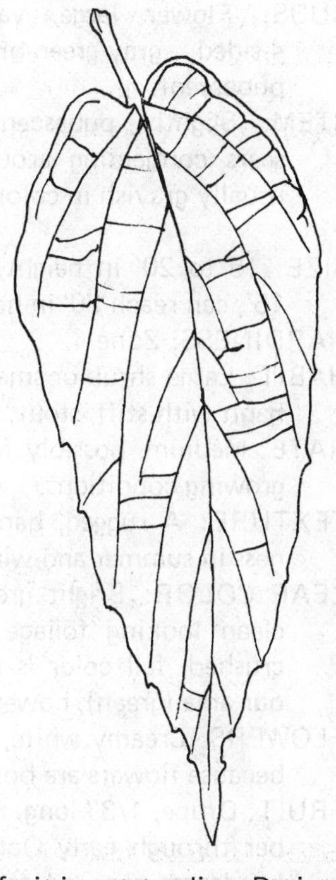

BUDS: Imbricate, terminal—green with red; lateral—green with red tip, large and glabrous. Very prominent, imbricate-scaly bud. Usually with 3 to 5 visible scales.

STEM: Glabrous, smooth, gray and usually stout.

SIZE: 8 to 12' tall, 2/3's that in width.

HARDINESS: Zone 5.

HABIT: Upright, multistemmed, often leggy at the base, but if used properly the leggy character is minimized.

RATE: Slow, possibly medium.

TEXTURE: Medium-coarse in foliage; coarse in winter.

LEAF COLOR: Flat, soft blue-green, interesting foliage in summer; fall color is inconsistent but can develop reddish purple.

FLOWERS: White, mid to late May, borne in 1 to 2" diameter, 5-rayed, flat-topped cymes; limitedly ornamental.

FRUIT: Drupe, 1/3" long, bright red, October into late fall, very effective, possibly the most handsome fruiter among the viburnums.

CULTURE: Similar to other viburnums.

DISEASES AND INSECTS: None serious.

LANDSCAPE VALUE: Shrub border situations because of leggy habit, fruit is outstanding. Derives its name from the fact that the leaves were used for making tea.

CULTIVARS:

'Aurantiacum' — Orange fruited form.

PROPAGATION: I have rooted this species from leafy cuttings collected in September.

NATIVE HABITAT: Central and Western China. Introduced 1901.

Viburnum sieboldii — Siebold Viburnum

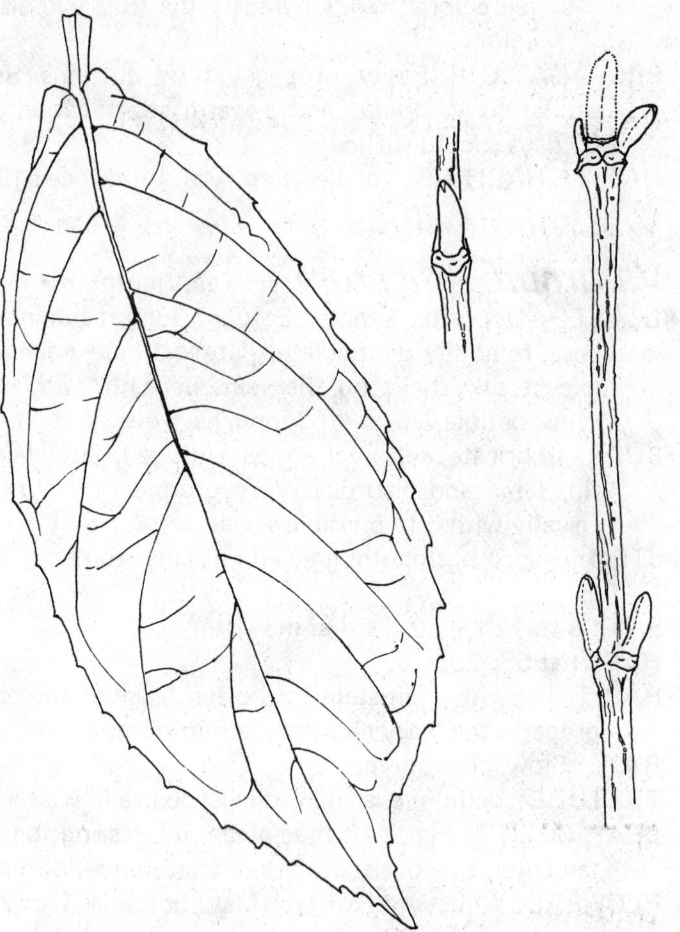

LEAVES: Opposite, simple, elliptic or obovate to oblong, 2 to 5" long, acute to rounded, broad-cuneate, coarsely crenate-serrate, bright green above, stellate pubescent chiefly on the veins beneath, with 7 to 10 pairs of prominent veins, petiole 1/3 to 3/5" long; leaves when crushed, emitting a fetid odor.

BUDS: Flower large, valvate, angled, 4-sided, gray-green-brown, slightly pubescent.

STEM: Slightly pubescent, stout, leaf scars connecting around the stem, usually grayish in color.

SIZE: 15 to 20' in height, spread 10 to 15', can reach 30' in height.

HARDINESS: Zone 4.

HABIT: Large shrub or small tree of open habit with stiff, stout, rigid branches.

RATE: Medium, possibly fast under ideal growing conditions.

TEXTURE: A rugged, handsome coarseness in summer and winter.

LEAF COLOR: Bright green, extremely clean looking foliage, very fetid if crushed, fall color is nonexistent in our area (green), however, various authors indicated red-purple a possibility.

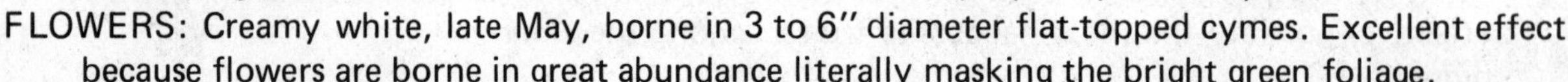

FLOWERS: Creamy white, late May, borne in 3 to 6" diameter flat-topped cymes. Excellent effect because flowers are borne in great abundance literally masking the bright green foliage.

FRUIT: Drupe, 1/3" long, rose-red to red changing to black, effective for two weeks in mid September through early October, birds seem to devour the fruits, however, the inflorescences are handsome rose-red and remain effective for two to four weeks after the fruits are gone. The fruit must be seen to be fully appreciated and the result is usually love at first sight.

CULTURE: Transplants well, adaptable, prefers moist, well-drained soils, tolerates partially shady situations, definitely needs sufficient moisture as leaf scorch will develop under dry soil conditions.

DISEASES AND INSECTS: None serious.

LANDSCAPE VALUE: Specimen, against large buildings, blank walls, groupings; open habit, excellent foliage, flowers and fruits make it worthy of consideration for many landscape situations.

CULTIVARS: 'Seneca' resulted from a self-pollination of *V. s.* The plant was selected for the abundant, large, pendulant inflorescences of firm red fruit on red pedicels which persist on the plant up to 3 months before turning black and falling. The massive, creamy-white panicles are produced in May to early June as the young foliage unfolds. The panicles are supported on stout, spreading branches that are picturesque at all seasons. The pendulant, multiple-colored clusters of orange-red (Indian Yellow to Jasper Red) ripening to Blood Red fruit are spectacularly displayed above the coriaceous, green foliage. Birds normally eat the fruit of *V. s.* before it has matured, leaving only the red pedicels which provide an ornamental display. However, the fruit of 'Seneca' is very firm and is not devoured by birds even when the fruit becomes fully ripe. Although 'Seneca' is tree-like and has attained a height of 14 feet and a width of

13 1/2′, the plant can be trained with several branches from the base and kept as a large spreading shrub. This cultivar will undoubtedly equal in size plants of the species and be as much as 30′ with gnarled trunk.

PROPAGATION: Cuttings, softwood—root easily.

NATIVE HABITAT: Japan. Cultivated 1880.

Viburnum trilobum — American Cranberrybush Viburnum

LEAVES: Opposite, simple, broad-ovate, 2 to 5″ long, rounded or truncate at base, lobes acuminate, coarsely dentate, sometimes the middle lobe elongated and entire, pilose on the veins beneath or nearly glabrous, petiole 2/5 to 1/5″ long with shallow groove and small dome-shaped, usually stalked glands.

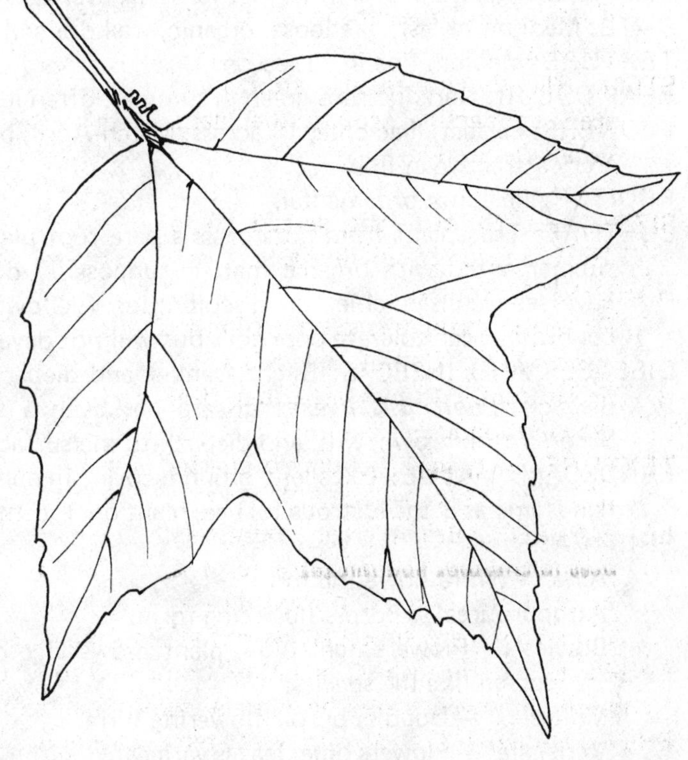

BUDS: Similar to *V. opulus*, sometimes sticky, green-reddish and smooth, with 2 connate outer scales.

STEM: Gray-brown, glabrous, with a waxy appearance.

SIZE: 8 to 12′ in height, spread 8 to 12′.

HARDINESS: Zone 2.

HABIT: Similar to *Viburnum opulus*, round topped and fairly dense.

RATE: Medium.

TEXTURE: Medium in foliage; medium to coarse in winter.

LEAF COLOR: Lustrous medium to dark green changing to yellow through red-purple in fall.

FLOWERS: White, similar to *V. opulus,* mid to late May, 3 to 4 1/4″ diameter, flat-topped cymes. Extremely handsome, possibly better than *V. opulus* but not as available through nurseries.

FRUITS: Drupe, 1/3″ long, bright red, early September through fall into February, holds better than *V. opulus*, edible, use for preserves.

CULTURE: Native species, transplants well, prefers good, well-drained soil, sun or partial shade, should be more adaptable than *V. opulus* due to wide native range, however, limitedly planted.

DISEASES AND INSECTS: None serious.

CULTIVARS:

'Compactum' — Excellent compact, dwarf form with good flowering and fruiting habit. I prefer this to the species because of its neat habit. Grows about 1/2 the size of species.

'Andrews', 'Hahs', and 'Wentworth' have been selected for larger fruits.

PROPAGATION: Cuttings, softwood, root easily.

NATIVE HABITAT: New Brunswick to British Columbia, south to New York, Michigan, South Dakota and Oregon.

Vinca minor — Common Periwinkle

FAMILY: Apocynaceae

LEAVES: Opposite, simple, evergreen, entire, 1/2 to 1 1/2" long, elliptic, oblong or elliptic-ovate, acutish or obtuse, lustrous dark green above, lighter green beneath, petiole short—1/2 to 1/5" long, exuding a milky juice when broken.

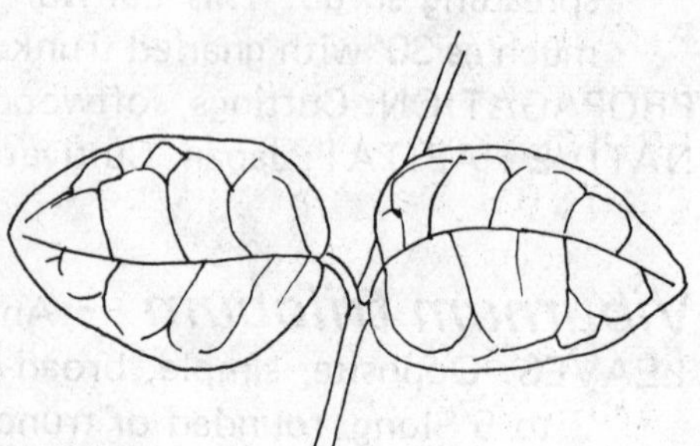

SIZE: 3 to 6" ground hugging plant.

HARDINESS: Zone 4.

HABIT: Low growing, prostrate, mat forming, evergreen ground cover.

RATE: Medium to fast; in a loose, organic, well drained soil will fill in very fast.

TEXTURE: Medium-fine in all seasons.

LEAF COLOR: Dark lustrous green in summer, often losing some of the sheen in winter.

FLOWERS: Perfect, lilac-blue, 1" across, March-April, borne solitary, on 3/5 to 1 1/5" long pedicels. Very attractive in flower.

FRUIT: Follicle, not ornamental.

CULTURE: Transplant from pots or as a bare root plant into moist, well drained soil abundantly supplemented with organic matter; supposedly does equally well in full sun or shade but I have seen considerable leaf discoloration (yellowing and browning) in winter under full sun conditions; can tolerate poor soils but will not develop and fill in as fast.

DISEASES AND INSECTS: Blight, canker and dieback, leaf spots, and root rot. The canker and dieback (*Phomopsis livella*) disease has been a significant problem in Illinois. The shoots become dark brown, wilt, and dieback to the surface of the soil.

LANDSCAPE VALUE: Excellent ground cover, in spite of problems; the dainty blue flowers are handsome as is the lustrous foliage; plant on 1' centers.

CULTIVARS:

'Alba' — White flowering form.

'Atropurpurea' — Purple flowering form.

'Bowles' — Flowers light blue, plant grows vigorously but is a clumpy grower and does not spread like the species.

'Multiplex' — Double, purple flowering form.

'Variegata' — Flowers blue, leaves variegated with rich yellow.

PROPAGATION: Extremely easy to root from cuttings.

NATIVE HABITAT: Europe and Western Asia, cultivated since ancient times; escaped from cultivation.

Vitex negundo — Chastetree

FAMILY: Verbenaceae

LEAVES: Opposite, digitate, leaflets usually 5, sometimes 3, 1 1/5 to 2 1/2" long, stalked, elliptic-ovate to lanceolate, entire or serrate, grayish, tomentulose beneath; petiole 3/5 to 2" long.

BUDS: Superposed, sessile or the upper commonly developing the first season, subglobose, the 1 or 2 pairs of leaf-rudiments or scales concealed in pubescence.

STEMS: Compressed at nodes, quadrangular with obtuse or flattened angles, rather slender; pith relatively large, more or less angled, white, continuous and homogeneous; leaf-scars U-shaped, rather small, low; the surface usually torn and the solitary bundle-trace indistinct.

SIZE: Difficult to predict since the plants are often frozen to the ground; the height in one growing season might be 3 to 5' but if no damage is done, over the years the plant may grow to 15'.

HARDINESS: Zone 6, often listed as 5 but shakily so.

HABIT: Not a bad looking plant in leaf; develops a loosely branched, airy, open outline.

RATE: Fast.

TEXTURE: Medium-fine in leaf; medium-coarse in winter.

LEAF COLOR: Grayish green cast in summer; nothing to speak of in the way of fall color.

FLOWERS: Small, lilac or lavender, in loose clusters forming slender spikes collected into terminal panicles 5 to 8" long; effective in August.

FRUIT: A small drupe; of no consequence.

CULTURE: Transplant as a container plant into loose, well-drained soil; full sun; prefer hot weather; well-drained situation definitely aids in reducing winter injury; if pruning is necessary, cut the plant to within 6 to 12" of the ground in spring.

DISEASES AND INSECTS: Several leaf spots and a root rot have been reported but are not serious.

LANDSCAPE VALUE: Possibly a plant for the shrub border; should almost be treated as a herbaceous perennial in the north; interesting foliage texture and late season flowers.

CULTIVARS:

'Heterophylla' – Leaves finely cut.

PROPAGATION: Softwood cuttings of this species taken in July rooted 4 percent without treatment and 64 percent in 22 days after treatment with IBA. Softwood cuttings rooted 100 percent in sand:peat in 32 days after treatment with 100 ppm IAA/24 hours.

RELATED SPECIES:

Vitex agnus-castus, Chastetree, is not as hardy as the above species. The flowers are more prominent, lilac or pale violet, fragrant, and occur from June-July through September. This species grows 8 to 10' high. The cultivars include 'Alba' with white flowers and 'Rosea' with pink flowers. A variety *latifolia* is supposedly more vigorous and hardier than the species. I remember learning the variety in my plant material courses at Ohio State, for it was always necessary to hunt through the old Horticultural garden to see if we could find a few live branches. Native to Southern Europe and Western Asia. Introduced 1570. Zone 6 or 7.

NATIVE HABITAT: China, India. Introduced about 1697.

Weigela florida — Old Fashioned Weigela

FAMILY: Caprifoliaceae

LEAVES: Opposite, simple, short-petioled to sub-sessile, elliptic to ovate-oblong, or obovate, 2 to 4" long, acuminate, rounded to cuneate at base, serrate, glabrous above except on midrib, pubescent or tomentose on veins beneath.

STEM: With 2 rows of hairs running from node to node, gray-brown, scurfy with large circular lenticels, pith—moderate, pale brown, continuous.

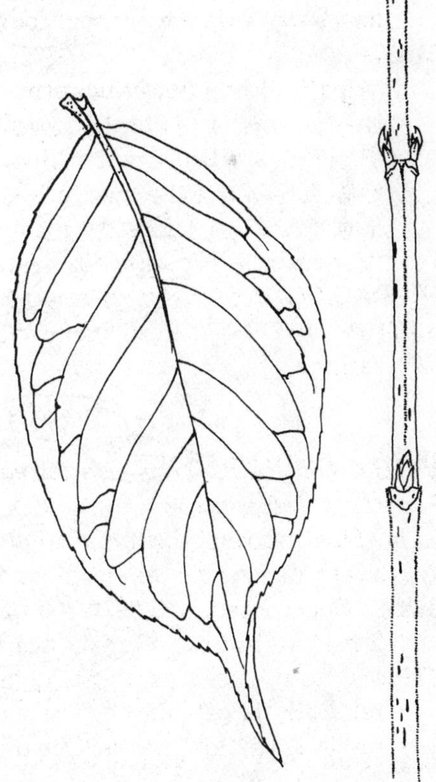

Weigela florida, Old Fashioned Weigela, (Caprifoliaceae) is a spreading, dense, deciduous, rounded shrub with coarse branches which eventually arch to the ground (6 to 9' high by 9 to 12' wide). Foliage is medium, nondescript green in summer. Flowers are perfect, rosy-pink, borne in late May to early June, singly or several in axillary cymes on short branches of last year's branches, also sporadically flowering on current season's growth. Fruit is a capsule. Adaptable, but prefers a well-drained soil and sunny location, find a lot of dieback and considerable pruning after flowering is necessary to keep it in shape; quite resistant to pests; best uses are in the shrub border, groupings or massing. Some of the better cultivars include:

'Bristol Snowflake' – White, with some pink.

'Candida' – Pure white.

'Conquerant' — Rose.
'Dame Blanche' — Almost pure white.
'Floreal' — Purplish pink.
'Foliis Purpuriis' — Pink flowers with purplish green foliage, dwarf, for a 20-year-old plant is densely rounded and 4' tall.
'Gracieux' — White and magenta.
'Richesse' — Pale Pink.
'Seduction' — Magenta-rose.
'Styriaca' — Purplish pink.
'Vanicek' — One of the best for red flower color as well as hardiness, sometimes referred to as 'Newport Red'.
'Variegata' — Flowers deep rose, leaves edged pale yellow, compact grower, about 4 to 6' high.
'Variegata Nana' — Most dwarf of the weigelas—3' tall—same foliage as above.
var. *venusta* — Leaves smaller, flowers rosy pink, very hardy, Zone 4.
Easily rooted from cuttings. Northern China, Korea. 1845. Zone 5.

Wisteria floribunda — Japanese Wisteria

FAMILY: Leguminosae

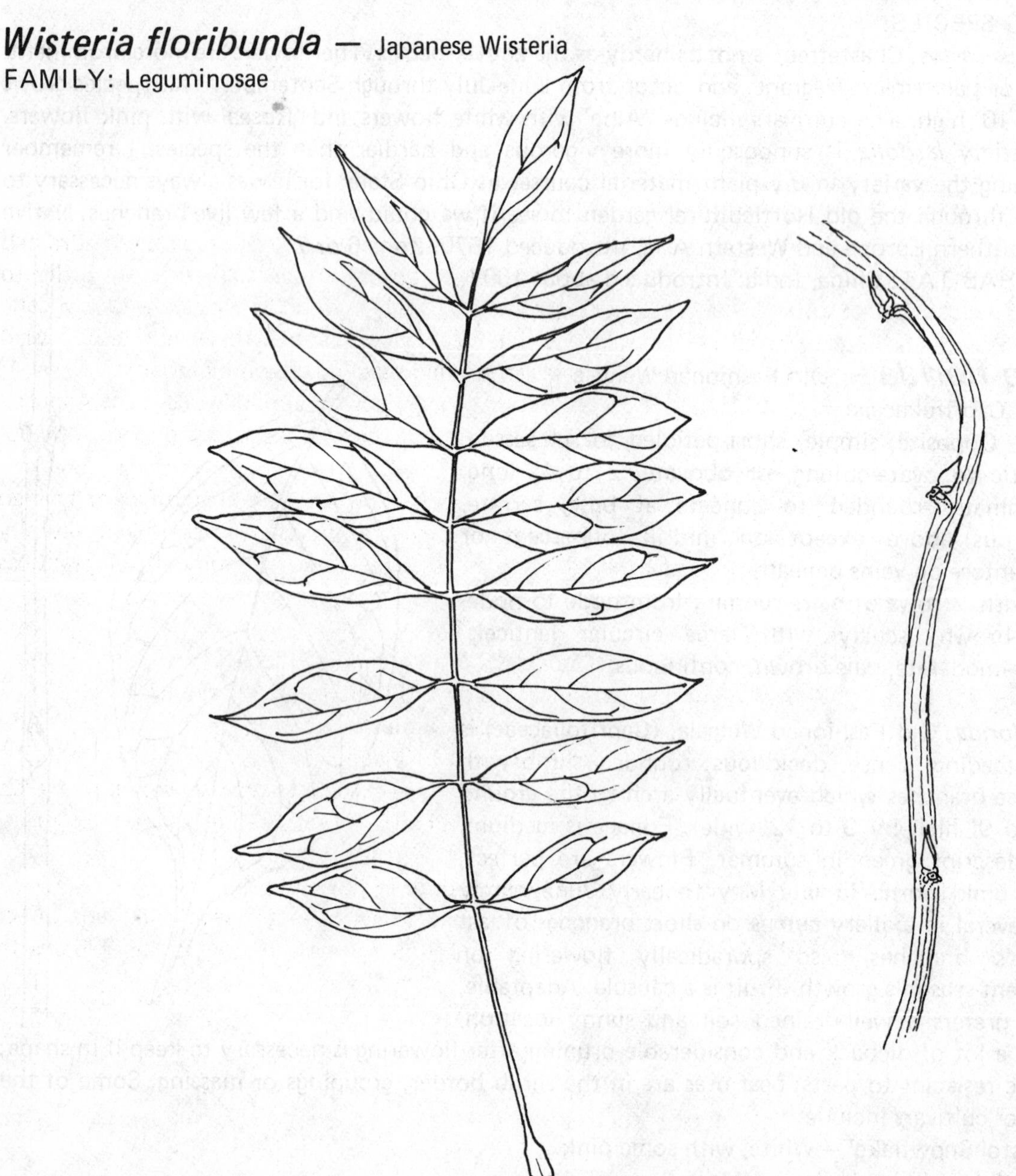

LEAVES: Alternate, pinnately compound, 13 to 19 leaflets, ovate-elliptic to ovate-oblong, 1 3/5 to 3" long, acuminate, rounded at base, rarely broad cuneate, appressed pubescent when young, soon nearly glabrous.

BUDS: Narrowly oblong and acute at the tip with 3 outer scales, one scale usually surrounding the entire bud, reddish brown, pubescent, appressed.

STEM: Twines right to left, somewhat angled, light tan or brown changing to gray-brown, 2 spine-like projections at the base of the leaf scar.

SIZE: 30' or more.

HARDINESS: Zone 4.

HABIT: Stout vine, climbing by twining stems which turn right to left, developing twisted woody trunk several inches in diameter and requires considerable support.

RATE: Fast, as is true with most vines; will grow to 10' in a single season once established.

TEXTURE: Medium in leaf; somewhat coarse in winter.

BARK: On old trunks, a grayish color.

LEAF COLOR: Bright green, usually late to leaf out, mid to late May; no fall color of any consequence.

FLOWERS: Perfect, violet or violet blue, on old wood, each flower 3/5 to 4/5" long, slightly fragrant, mid to late-May; borne in slender 8 to 20" racemes, the flowers opening from the base to the apex; very lovely as the flowers open before or just as leaves emerge; not too many vines rival it for flower effect.

FRUIT: Pod, brown, 4 to 6", October persisting into winter, glabrous.

CULTURE: Supposedly hard to transplant and slow to establish, however, I have grown many in containers and have had no difficulty establishing them; plant in deep, moist, well-drained loam; pH adaptable although it is often reported they do better at a higher pH; in order to insure successful culture it is wise to use nitrogen sparingly for this promotes excess vegetative growth, use superphosphate, root prune, cut back vigorous growth leaving only 3 or 4 buds, plant in full sun and use named cultivars rather than seedling grown material.

DISEASES AND INSECTS: Crown gall, leaf spots, stem canker, powdery mildew, root rot, tobacco mosaic virus, sweet potato leaf beetle, Japanese mealybug, citrus flata planthopper, fall webworm, black vine weevil and scale.

LANDSCAPE VALUE: Excellent flowering vine, nice over patios, on large structures, or trained into a tree form; needs ample support and metal pipe is recommended for it will actually crush wood supports with time; not the easiest plant to keep flowering and cultural practices must be fairly precise.

CULTIVARS:

'Alba' – Racemes 11" long, moderate fragrance, dense, white, 13 leaflets.

'Issai' – Racemes 12" long, moderate fragrance, violet to bluish violet, 17 leaflets.

'Kyushaki' – Racemes 26" long, fragrance fair, reddish violet to violet.

'Longissima Alba' – Racemes 15" long, good fragrance, 13 leaflets, white.

'Macrobotrys' – Racemes 18-36" long (60"), fragrance excellent, reddish violet to violet.

'Murasaki Noda' – Racemes 10" long, fragrance fair, 15 leaflets, reddish violet to violet.

'Rosea' – Pink form.

'Violacea Plena' – Only wisteria with double flowers, poor in flower, violet.

PROPAGATION: Seeds germinate readily without treatment. I have collected seed in fall and direct sowed them with good results. July cuttings rooted 80% without treatment and 100% with 25 ppm IBA.

RELATED SPECIES:
Wisteria sinensis — Chinese Wisteria

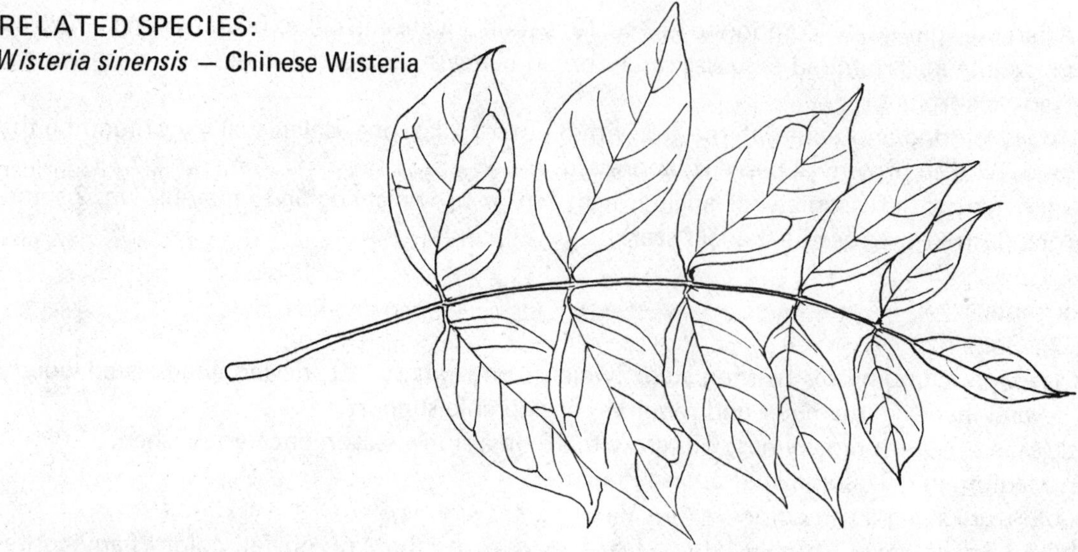

LEAVES: Alternate, pinnately compound, 7 to 13 leaflets, ovate-oblong to ovate-lanceolate, 2 to 3" long, abruptly acuminate, usually broad-cuneate at base, ciliate, densely appressed-pubescent at first, glabrate at maturity.

Wisteria sinensis, Chinese Wisteria, is similar to the above except the flower is a blue-violet, about 1" long, not as fragrant, late May, borne in dense, 6 to 12" long racemes, all flowers of one raceme opening at about the same time; fruit is a pod, 4 to 6" long, densely velutinous; var. *alba* has white flowers and 'Jako' is a selected form of *alba* with extremely fragrant flowers; China. 1916. Zone 5.

NATIVE HABITAT: Japan. Introduced 1830.

Xanthorhiza simplicissima — Yellowroot

FAMILY: Ranunculaceae

LEAVES: Alternate, clustered, long-stalked, pinnate or bipinnate, leaflets usually 5, 1 1/2 to 2 3/4" long, ovate to ovate-oblong, incisely toothed, sometimes serrate; of bright green color.

BUDS: Lateral buds solitary, sessile, ovoid-oblong, compressed and flattened against stem, with about 3 scales; terminal buds much larger, fusiform, terete, with about 5 scales, red-brown.

STEMS: Outer bark yellowish brown; inner bark yellow; branchlets pale greenish gray; pith large, round, continuous; leaf-scars low, slightly curved, more than half encircling twig; about 11 bundle-traces.

ROOTS: Long, slender, deep yellow; hence, the name Yellowroot.

SIZE: 2 to 3' in height and spreading freely as it suckers from the roots.

HARDINESS: Zone 4.

HABIT: A flat-topped groundcover with erect stems and celery-like leaves, filling the ground as a mat.

RATE: Medium.

TEXTURE: Medium in all seasons.

STEM AND ROOT COLOR: The inner bark and roots are yellow.

LEAF COLOR: Bright green in summer; very handsome foliage, fall color may develop golden yellow and orange.

FLOWERS: Brownish purple, 1/6" across; star-shaped, usually occurring before the leaves in late April or early May; borne in 2 to 4" long racemes.

FRUIT: Follicle, not effective.

CULTURE: Transplant in spring or fall; best to divide old plants and space these 18 to 24" apart; prefers moist, well-drained soils and here makes its best growth; will do well in heavy soils;

does well under average conditions but is less invasive in dry soils; full sun or partial shade; thrives along streams and moist banks.

DISEASES AND INSECTS: None serious.

LANDSCAPE VALUE: A very desirable ground cover for moist areas; little known and grown; makes a very solid mat; the more I see it the more I believe it has been slighted by American gardeners.

PROPAGATION: Most effective method is by division of the parent plant; root cuttings will also work.

ADDITIONAL NOTES: From the juice (sap) the Indians developed a yellow dye.

NATIVE HABITAT: New York to Kentucky and Florida. Introduced 1776.

Zelkova serrata — Japanese Zelkova

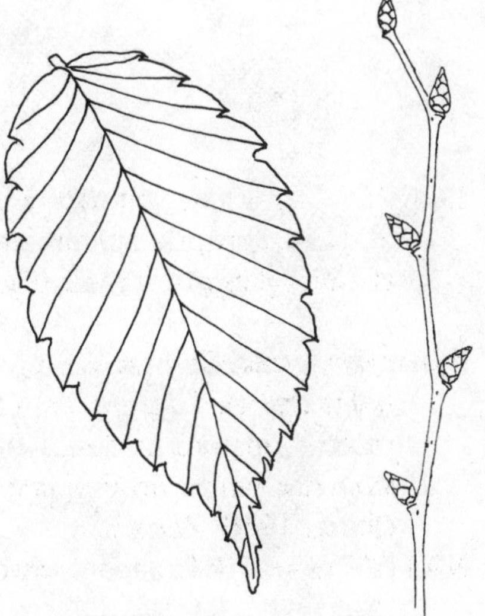

FAMILY: Ulmaceae

LEAVES: Alternate, simple, ovate to oblong-ovate, 1 1/4 to 2" long, or on shoots to 5" long, acuminate or apiculate, rounded or subcordate at base, sharply serrate with acuminate teeth, with 8 to 14 pairs of veins, somewhat rough above, glabrous or nearly so beneath; petioles 1/12 to 1/5" long.

BUDS: Ovoid, acutish, with many imbricate dark brown, broad scales; diverge at 45° angle from stem.

STEM: Pubescent when young, glabrous at maturity, brown.

BARK: Beautiful. Resembles that of Chinese Elm.

SIZE: 50 to 80' in height with an equal spread.

HARDINESS: Zone 5.

HABIT: In youth, a low branched vase-shaped tree; in old age maintaining a similar form with many ascending branches.

RATE: Medium, possibly fast in youth, 10 to 12' over a 4 to 6 year period.

TEXTURE: Medium-fine in leaf; medium in winter.

BARK: In youth cherry-like, reddish brown, heavily lenticelled; in old age often exfoliating with a character not unlike that of Chinese Elm, *U. parvifolia*.

LEAF COLOR: Dark green in summer; yellow-orange-brown in fall, possibly deep red.

FLOWERS: Polygamous, male clustered in axils of lower leaves, female in axils of upper leaves; not showy; flowers in April-May with the leaves.

FRUIT: A small drupe, about 1/6" across, ripening in fall.

CULTURE: Transplants readily balled and burlapped; prefers moist, deep soil; once established supposedly very wind and drouth tolerant. Young trees are susceptible to frost; pH adaptable; prune in fall.

DISEASES AND INSECTS: Susceptible to some of the problems which beset the elms, however, resistant to Dutch elm disease. The trees I have observed were much cleaner than the elms.

LANDSCAPE VALUE: Very handsome tree because of good foliage, interesting growth habit and handsome bark; well suited to lawns, residential streets, parks, large areas; considered as a replacement for the American Elm but this has not, and will never, come about.

CULTIVARS:

'Village Green' — Selected by Princeton Nurseries, the tree grows more rapidly than ordinary seedlings and develops a smooth, straight trunk; the dark green foliage turns a rusty red in fall; much hardier than trees of Japanese origin and is highly resistant to Dutch elm disease and to leaf eating and bark beetles.

PROPAGATION: Seeds germinate without pretreatment but percentage is better when stratified at 41°F for 60 days (this was my own personal experience). I have rooted cuttings taken from seedlings with 100% success when treated with 1000 ppm IBA.

RELATED SPECIES: *Zelkova carpinifolia*, Elm Zelkova, and *Zelkova sinica*, Chinese Zelkova, are beautiful trees with Zone 6 hardiness. Recommended for southern areas.

NATIVE HABITAT: Japan, Korea. Introduced 1862 into America.

BIBLIOGRAPHY

Agricultural Research Service. U.S.D.A. 1970. *Crabapples of Documented Authentic Origin.* Washington, D.C. 107 p.

Agricultural Research Service. U.S.D.A. 1973. *International Checklist of Cultivated Ilex.* Supt. of Doc., U.S. Gov. Printing Office. Washington, D.C. 84 p.

Apgar, Austin C. 1892. *Trees of the Northern United States.* American Book Co., N.Y. 224 p.

Apgar, Austin C. 1910. *Ornamental Shrubs of the United States.* American Book Co., N.Y. 352 p.

Bailey Hortorium. 1976. *Hortus III.* Macmillan Co. New York. 1290 p.

Bailey, Liberty Hyde. 1948. *The Cultivated Conifers in North America.* Macmillan Co. N.Y. 404 p.

Bailey, Liberty Hyde. 1933. *How Plants Get Their Names.* Macmillan Co. N.Y. 209 p.

Bailey, Liberty Hyde. 1949. *Manual of Cultivated Plants.* Macmillan Co. N.Y. 1116 p.

Bailey, Liberty Hyde. 1914. *The Standard Cyclopedia of Horticulture.* Vols. I, II, III. Macmillan Co. N.Y. 3639 p.

Bean, W.J. 1973. *Trees and Shrubs Hardy in the British Isles,* 8th Ed. Vols. I, II, III. John Murray Ltd. London. Each 800 p.

Benson, Lyman. 1959. *Plant Classification.* D.C. Heath and Co., Lexington, MA. 688 p.

Blackburn, Benjamin. 1952. *Trees and Shrubs in Eastern North America.* Oxford University Press. N.Y. 358 p.

Blakeslee, Albert Francis, and Chester Deacon Jones. 1972. *Northeastern Trees in Winter.* Dover Publications, Inc. N.Y. 264 p.

Bloom, Adrian. *Conifers for Your Garden.* American Garden Guild. 145 p.

Bowers, Clement Gray. 1960. *Rhododendrons and Azaleas.* Macmillan Co. N.Y. 525 p.

Britton, Nathaniel Lord, and Addison Brown. 1912. *Illustrated Flora of the Northern United States, Canada and the British Possessions,* Vols. I, II, III. Charles Scribner's Sons. N.Y.

Brooklyn Botanic Gardens' Plants and Gardens Handbooks covering a multitude of subjects. Book list available from Brooklyn Botanic Garden, 1000 Washington Avenue, Brooklyn, N.Y. 11225.

Brown, H. P. 1938. *Trees of Northeastern United States.* Christopher Publishing House. Boston, Mass. 488 p.

Butcher, D. 1964. *Knowing Your Trees.* American Forestry Assoc. Washington, D.C. 349 p.

Carter, Cedric J. 1970. *Illinois Trees: Selection, Planting and Care.* Ill. Nat. Hist. Survey. Urbana, Ill. 123 p.

Carter, Cedric J. 1964. *Illinois Trees: Their Diseases.* Ill. Nat. Hist. Survey. Urbana, Ill. 96 p.

Core, Earl L., and Nelle P. Ammons. 1958. *Woody Plants in Winter.* Boxwood Press, California. 218 p.

Crockett, James Underwood. 1971. *Evergreens.* Time-Life Series. Time-Life Books. N.Y. 160 p.

Crockett, James Underwood. 1972. *Flowering Shrubs.* Time-Life Series. 160 p.

Crockett, James Underwood. 1972. *Lawns and Ground Covers.* Time-Life Series. 160 p.

Crockett, James Underwood. 1972. *Trees.* Time-Life Series. 160 p.

Curtis, Carlton C., and S. C. Bausor. 1943. *The Complete Guide to North American Trees.* Collier Books. New York, N.Y. 342 p.

Curtis, Ralph W., John F. Cornman, and Robert G. Mower. 1962. *Vegetative Keys to Common Ornamental Woody Plants.* New York State College of Agriculture. Cornell University, Ithaca, N.Y. 83 p.

Dallimore, W., and Bruce A. Jackson. 1967. *A Handbook of Coniferae and Ginkgoaceae.* St. Martin's Press. N.Y. 700 p.

Dame, Lorin L., and Henry Brooks. 1972. *Trees of New England.* Dover Publications, Inc. N.Y. 196 p.

Deam, Charles C. 1921. *Shrubs of Indiana.* State of Indiana Publication No. 44. Ind. 350 p.

denBoer, Arie F. 1959. *Ornamental Crabapples.* American Association of Nurserymen. 226 p.

English, L. L. 1970. *Illinois Trees and Shrubs: Their Insect Enemies.* Ill. Nat. Hist. Survey. Urbana, Ill. 91 p.

Fernald, Merritt Lyndon. 1950. *Gray's Manual of Botany.* 8th ed. American Book Co. 1632 p.

Frederick, William H. Jr. 1975. *100 Great Garden Plants.* Alfred A. Knopf. N.Y. 207 p.

Foley, Daniel J. 1972. *Ground Covers for Easier Gardening.* Dover Publ. Inc., N.Y. 224 p.

Forest Service, U.S.D.A. 1974. *Seeds of Woody Plants in the United States,* Agriculture Handbook No. 450. Supt. of Doc. U.S. Gov. Printing Office. Washington, D.C. 883 p.

Gilmour, J. S. L. 1969. *International Code of Nomenclature of Cultivated Plants.* International Assoc. for Plant Taxonomy. Utrecht, Netherlands. 32 p.

Grimm, William Carey. 1962. *The Book of Trees.* Stackpole Co. Harrisburg, Pa. 493 p.

Grimm, William Carey. 1968. *Recognizing Flowering Wild Plants.* Stackpole Co. Harrisburg, Pa. 319 p.

Grimm, William Carey. 1970. *Home Guide to Trees, Shrubs and Wildflowers.* Stackpole Books. Harrisburg, Pa. 320 p.

Hansell, Dorothy E., ed. 1970. *Handbook on Hollies.* The American Horticultural Magazine. Mt. Vernon, Va. 333 p.

Harlow, William M. 1942. *Trees of the Eastern United States and Canada.* Whittlesey House. N.Y. 512 p.

Harlow, William M. 1946. *Fruit Key and Twig Key.* Dover Publications, Inc. N.Y. 56 p.

Harlow, William M., and Ellwood S. Harrar. 1969. *Textbook of Dendrology,* 5th Ed. McGraw-Hill Book Co. 512 p.

Harrar, Ellwood S., and J. George Harrar. 1962. *Guide to Southern Trees,* 2nd Ed. Dover Publications, Inc. N.Y. 709 p.

Hepting, George H. 1971. *Diseases of Forest and Shade Trees of the United States.* Agricultural Handbook No. 386. U.S.D.A. Forest Service. Supt. of Doc. U.S. Gov. Printing Office. Wash. D.C. 658 p.

Hillier and Sons. *Hilliers' Manual of Trees and Shrubs.* Yelf Brothers Limited. England. 576 p.

Hosie, R. C. 1973. *Native Trees of Canada.* Information Canada. Ottawa. 380 p.

Hume, Harold H. 1953. *Hollies.* Macmillan Co. N.Y. 237 p.

Hyams, Edwards. 1965. *Ornamental Shrubs for Temperate Zone Gardens.* A.S. Barnes and Co. N.Y. 315 p.

Jaynes, Richard A. 1975. *The Laurel Book.* Hafner Press. N.Y. 180 p.

Johnson, H. 1973. *The International Book of Trees.* Simon and Schuster, Inc. N.Y. 286 p.

Jones, George Neville. 1971. *Flora of Illinois.* University of Notre Dame, Notre Dame, Indiana. 401 p.

Keeler, Harriet L. 1916. *Our Northern Shrubs.* Charles Scribner's Sons. N.Y. 519 p.

Kelsey, Harlan P., and William A. Dayton. 1942. *Standardized Plant Names,* 2nd Ed. J. Horace McFarland Co. Harrisburg, Pa. 675 p.

Knobel, Edward. 1972. *Identify Trees and Shrubs by Their Leaves.* Dover Publications, Inc. N.Y. 47 p.

Kumlier, Loraine L. 1946. *The Friendly Evergreens.* Rinehart. N.Y. 237 p.

Lanjouw, J. 1966. *International Code of Botanical Nomenclature.* International Assoc. for Plant Taxonomy. Utrecht. Netherlands. 402 p.

Lawrence, George H. M. 1951. *Taxonomy of Vascular Plants.* Macmillan Co. N.Y. 823 p.

Leach, David G. 1961. *Rhododendrons of the World.* Charles Scribner's Sons. N.Y. 544 p.

Lemmon, Robert S. 1952. *The Best Loved Trees of America.* The American Garden Guild. Garden City, N.Y. 254 p.

Lentz, A. N. *Common Forest Trees of New Jersey.* Ext. Bull. 396. Coop. Ext. Service Rutgers Univ. New Brunswick, N.J.

Li, Hui-lin. 1963. *The Origin and Cultivation of Shade and Ornamental Trees.* Univ. of Penn. Press. Philadelphia, Pa. 282 p.

Li, Hui-lin. 1972. *Trees of Pennsylvania, The Atlantic States and the Lake States.* Univ. of Pennsylvania Press. Philadelphia, Pa. 276 p.

Logan, Harry Britton. 1974. *A Traveler's Guide to North American Gardens.* Charles Scribner's Sons. New York. 253 p.

Makins, F. K. 1948. *The Identification of Trees and Shrubs.* E.P. Dutton and Co., Inc. N.Y. 350 p.

Mohlenbrock, Robert H. *Forest Trees of Illinois.* State of Ill. Dept. of Conservation. Div. of Forestry. 178 p.

Nelson Jr., Wm. R. 1975. *Landscaping Your Home.* Circ. 111. U. of I. Coop. Ext. Service. Champaign, Ill. 246 p.

Ouden, P. Den, and B. K. Boom. 1965. *Manual of Cultivated Conifers.* M. Nijhoff. The Hague. Netherlands. 526 p.

Otis, Charles Herbert. 1954. *Michigan Trees.* Univ. of Michigan Press. Ann Arbor. 333 p.

Petrides, George A. 1972. *A Field Guide to Trees and Shrubs,* 2nd Ed. Houghton Mifflin Co. Boston, Mass. 428 p.

Pirone, Pascal P. 1970. *Diseases and Pests of Ornamental Plants,* 4th Ed. Ronald Press Co. N.Y. 546 p.

Powell, Thomas and Betty. 1975. *The Avant Gardener.* Houghton Mifflin Co. Boston, Mass. 263 p.

Preston, Richard J. 1947. *Rocky Mountain Trees.* Iowa State College Press. Ames, Iowa. 285 p.

Preston, Richard J. 1961. *North American Trees.* The M.I.T. Press. Mass. 395 p.

Rehder, Alfred. 1940. *Manual of Cultivated Trees and Shrubs,* 2nd Ed. Macmillan Co. N.Y. 996 p.

Reisch, Kenneth W., Philip C. Kozel, and Gayle A. Weinstein. 1975. *Woody Ornamentals for the Midwest.* Kendall/Hunt Publ. Co., Dubuque, Iowa. 293 p.

Robinette, Gary. 1967. *The Design Characteristics of Plant Materials.* American Printing and Publishing, Inc. Madison, Wisc. 244 p.

Robinson, Florence B. 1941. *Tabular Keys for the Identification of Woody Plants.* Garrard Press. Champaign, Ill. 156 p.

Robinson, Florence B. 1960. *Useful Trees and Shrubs.* Garrard Publishing Co. Champaign, Ill.

Sargent, Charles Sprague. 1965. *Manual of the Trees of North America,* Vols. I and II. Dover Publications, Inc. N.Y. 934 p.

Schuler, Stanley. 1973. *The Gardener's Basic Book of Trees and Shrubs.* Simon and Schuster. N.Y. 319 p.

Settergren Carl, and R. E. McDermott. 1969. *Trees of Missouri.* Agr. Exp. St. Univ. of Missouri. Columbia, Mo. 123 p.

Shosteck, Robert. 1974. *Flowers and Plants.* New York Times Book Co. 329 p.

Smith, Alice Upham. 1969. *Trees in a Winter Landscape.* Holt, Rinehart and Winston of Canada, Ltd. 207 p.

Stephens, H. A. 1967. *Trees, Shrubs and Woody Vines in Kansas.* Univ. Press of Kansas. Lawrence, Kansas. 250 p.

Sudworth, George B. 1967. *Forest Trees of the Pacific Slope.* Dover Publications, Inc. N.Y. 455 p.

Symonds, George W. D. 1958. *The Tree Identification Book.* William Morrow and Co. Inc. N.Y. 272 p.

Symonds, George W. D. 1963. *The Shrub Identification Book.* M. Barrows and Co. N.Y. 379 p.

Taylor, Norman. 1961. *Taylor's Encyclopedia of Gardening.* Houghton Mifflin Co. Boston, Mass. 1329 p.

Tehon, Leo R. 1942. *Field Book of Native Illinois Shrubs.* Nat. Hist. Survey Div. Urbana, Ill. 300 p.

Trelease, William. 1931. *Winter Botany*, 3rd Ed. Dover Publications, Inc. N.Y. 396 p.

Viereck, Leslie A., and Elbert L. Little. 1972. *Alaska Trees and Shrubs.* Agriculture Handbook No. 410. U.S.D.A. Forest Service. Supt. of Doc. U.S. Gov. Printing Office. Wash. D.C. 265 p.

Viertel, Arthur T. 1970. *Trees, Shrubs, and Vines.* Syracuse University Press. Syracuse, N.Y.

Welch, H. J. 1966. *Dwarf Conifers.* Charles T. Branford Co. Mass. 334 p.

Whitehead, Stanley B. 1956. *The Book of Flowering Trees and Shrubs.* Frederick Warne and Co. Ltd. N.Y. 246 p.

Wilson, E. H. 1925. *America's Greatest Garden: The Arnold Arboretum.* The Stratford Co. Boston. 123 p.

Wilson, E. H. 1926. *Aristocrats of the Garden.* The Stratford Co. Boston. 312 p.

Wilson, E. H. 1928. *More Aristocrats of the Garden.* The Stratford Co. Boston. 288 p.

Wilson, E. H. 1930. *Aristocrats of the Trees.* The Stratford Co. Boston. 279 p.

Wyman, Donald 1954. *The Arnold Arboretum Garden Book.* D. Van Nostrand Co., Inc. 354 p.

Wyman, Donald. 1956. *Ground Cover Plants.* Macmillan Co. N.Y. 175 p.

Wyman, Donald. 1965. *Trees for American Gardens.* Macmillan Co. N.Y. 502 p.

Wyman, Donald. 1969. *Shrubs and Vines for American Gardens.* Macmillan Co. N.Y. 613 p.

Wyman, Donald. 1971. *Wyman's Gardening Encyclopedia.* Macmillan Co. N.Y. 1221 p.

Wyman, Donald. 1975. *Dwarf Shrubs.* Macmillan Co. N.Y. 137 p.

GLOSSARY OF TAXONOMIC TERMS COMMONLY EMPLOYED IN THE IDENTIFICATION OF WOODY PLANTS

a-: prefix indicating not or without.
abortive: defective, barren, not developed.
abruptly pinnate: without a terminal leaflet.
abscission: the separating of a leaf from a self healing, clean-cut scar.
acaulescent: stemless or apparently so. Ex: *Taraxacum, Dodecatheon, Primula.*
accessory buds: those found beside or above the true bud at a node.
accessory fruit: one whose conspicuous tissues have not been derived from those comprising the pistil of the fl. Ex: in strawberry *(Fragaria)* the fleshy part of the fr. is of receptacular and not of pistillate origin. An accessory fr. may or may not also be an aggregate fr. (it is so in the strawberry and not so in the banana).
accessory parts of a flower: the petals and sepals.
achene: a dry indehiscent one-seeded fruit. Ex: fr. of members of the Compositae.
acicular: needle-shaped. Ex: lvs. of *Pinus,* spines of some cacti.
acorn: the fruit of oaks, a thick walled nut with a woody cup-like base.
actinomorphic: of regular symmetry, applied to perianth whorls, as opposed to zygomorphic.
aculeate: prickly.
acuminate: having an apex whose sides are gradually concave and tapering to a point.
acute: having an apex whose sides are straight and taper to a point.
adherent: a condition existing when two dissimilar organs touch each other (sometimes seemingly fused) but not grown together.
adnate: fused with unlike parts, as in the fusion of a filament to a petal.
adventitious: arising from an unusual or irregular position.
aerial rootlets: those produced above ground, especially as in climbing organs of a vine.
aestivation: the arrangement of floral parts (especially sepals and petals) in the bud.
aggregate flower: a flower heaped or crowded into a dense cluster.
aggregate fruit: one formed by the coherence or the connation of pistils that were distinct in the flower (as in *Rubus*) when the pistils of separate flowers (as in mulberry) make up the fr. it is designated as a multiple fruit.
akene: a small dry indehiscent fruit with one seed free inside the thin pericarp.
alternate: an arrangement of leaves or other parts not opposite or whorled; parts situated one at a node, as leaves on a stem: like parts succeeding each other singly with a common structure.
ament: see catkin.
amplexicaul: encircling the stem.
anastomosing: netted, applied to the veins of a lf.; the marginal reticulations closed.
androecium: stamens of a fl. as a unit.
anemophilous: describes flowers that are pollinated by wind.
angiospermous: having seeds borne within a pericarp.
angular: of pith; not rounded in cross section.
annual: maturing and living one season only.
annular: shaped like a ring.
anterior: on the front side, away from the axis, toward the subtending bract.
anther: pollen-bearing part of a stamen, borne at the top of a filament, or sessile.
anthesis (an-thee-sis): that period of fl. development when pollen is shed from the anther; also used to designate the act of flowering or the time of fl. expansion.
apetalous: without petals. Ex: fls. of grasses.
apex: the tip or terminal end.
apical: describes the apex or tip.
apiculate: ending abruptly in a short pointed tip.
apocarpous: having separate carpels; frequently applied to a gynoecium of several pistils.

apophysis: that part of the cone scale that is exposed when the cone is closed.
appressed: pressed close to the stem, not spreading.
arboreal, arboreous: treelike or pertaining to trees.
arching: curving gracefully.
arcuate venation: pinnate, with the secondary veins curving and running parallel to the margin.
areole: small pit or raised spot, often bearing a tuft of hairs, glochids, or spines.
aril: a fleshy appendage of the seed.
aristate: bearing a stiff bristle-like awn or arista, or tapered to a very slender stiff tip. Ex: awns of many grasses, apices of many calyx-teeth.
armed: provided with a sharp defense such as thorns, spines, prickles or barbs.
aromatic: fragrantly scented, at least if broken or crushed.
articulate: having nodes or joints where separation may naturally occur.
ascending: curving indirectly or obliquely upward. Ex: branches of *Taxus canadensis.*
assurgent: rising at an angle, not straight upwards.
attenuate: showing a long gradual slender taper; usually applied to apices, but equally appropriate for bases of leaves, petals, etc.
auriculate: bearing ear-like appendages, as the projections of some leaf and petal bases.
awl-shaped: tapering to a slender stiff point.
awn: a bristle-like appendage.
axil: belonging to the axis. See placentation.
axillary: in the axil.
axis: the main stem or central support of a plant.
baccate: pulpy, fleshy.
barbed: bristles, awns, etc. provided with terminal or lateral spine-like hooks that are bent sharply backward. Ex: pappus on fruits of beggar's ticks.
bark: a dead outer protective tissue of woody plants, derived from the cortex. Varies greatly in appearance and texture; often including all tissue from the vascular cambium outward.
basal: pertaining to the extremity of an organ by which it is attached to its support; said of lvs. when at base of plant only. See rosette.
basifixed: attached basally as ovules or anthers.
beak: a long prominent point. Ex: on lettuce *(Lactuca)* or dandelion *(Taraxacum)* frs.
beaked: ending in a point, especially on fruits.
bearded: having long hairs.
berry: a fleshy indehiscent pulpy multi-seeded fr. resulting from a single pistil. Ex: tomato.
bi-: prefix indicating twice or doubly.
biennial: of two season's duration, normally flowering, fruiting and dying the second growing season from time of seed germination.
bifid: two-cleft, as in apices of some petals and leaves. Ex: petals of some *Lychnis* or leaves of *Bauhinia.*
bifurcate: forked, as some Y-shaped hairs.
bilabiate: two-lipped, often applied to a corolla or calyx: each lip may or may not be lobed or toothed. Ex: corolla of snapdragon *(Antirrhinum)* and most members of the mint family *(Labiatae).*
bipinnate: twice pinnate.
bisexual: stamens and pistil present in the one fl.
biternate: twice ternate; a structure basically ternate, but whose primary divisions are again each ternate. Ex: lvs. of some columbines *(Aquilegia)* and meadow-rues *(Thalictrum).*
bladder-like: inflated, empty with thin walls.
blade: the expanded part of lf. or petal; lamina.
bloom: a waxy coating found on stems, leaves, flowers and fruits, usually of a grayish cast and easily removed.
bole: stem of a tree.
boss: a raised usually pointed projection.

bract: a much-reduced lf., often scale-like and usually associated with a fl. or infl.
branch: one of the coarser divisions of a trunk or main branch.
branchlet: smaller, a division of the branch.
bristle: a stiff hair.
broad-elliptic: wider than elliptic.
broad-ovate: wider than ovate.
bronzing: turning a metallic bronze or coppery color, especially of foliage after a winter.
bud: a structure of embryonic tissues, which will become a leaf, a flower, or both, or a new shoot. Especially the stage in which a growing point spends the winter or a dry season. May be naked or enclosed in scales.
bud scale: a modified leaf or stipule (there may be one, a few, or many) protective of the embryonic tissue of the bud.
bud scale scar: the mark left by the sloughing off of the bud scale.
bulb: a modified underground stem comprised of shortened central axis surrounded by fleshy scale-like lvs.
bulbil: small bulbs arising around parent bulb.
bulblet: small bulbs arising in leaf axils.
bullate: with the surface appearing as if blistered between the veins. Ex: Savoy cabbage.
bundle scar: seen in the leaf scar, the broken ends of the woody vascular strands that connected the leaf and the stem.
bur: any rough or prickly seed envelope.
burl: a knot or woody growth of very irregular grain.
bush: a low several stemmed shrub with no single trunk.
caducous: falling off early or prematurely.
calcarate: having a spur.
calcicole: a plant growing best on limey soils.
callus: a hard protuberance, or the new tissues formed in response to a wound.
calyx: the outer set of perianth segments or floral envelope of a flower, usually green in color and smaller than the inner set.
campanulate: bell-shaped.
cane: a long woody pliable stem rising from the ground.
canescent: having a gray hoary pubescence.
capillary: hair-like; very slender.
capitate: headlike, in a dense rounded cluster.
capsule: a dry dehiscent fruit produced from a compound pistil. Ex: fruit of a tobacco, *Catalpa, Dianthus*.
carinate: keeled; with longitudinal ridge or line.
carpel: one of the foliar units of gynoecium. See pistil.
carpophore: elongated axis bearing a gynoecium and projecting between the carpels.
caryopsis: the fruit of members of the grass family; not basically distinct from an achene.
castaneous: dark brown.
catkin: a spike-like infl. comprised of scaly bracts subtending unisexual fls., often somewhat flexuous and pendulous but not necessarily so. Ex: infl. of willows *(Salix)* and poplars *(Populus)*.
caudate: bearing a tail-like appendage. Ex: spadices of some aroids.
caulescent: having an evident leaf-bearing stem above ground.
cauliflorous: flowering from the trunk or main branches directly or on short specialized spurs.
cauline: of or belonging to the stem.
ceriferous: waxy.
cernuous: drooping or nodding.
cespitose: growing in tufts or dense clumps.
chalaza: basal part of ovule, where it is attached to the funiculus.
chaff: dry, thin, membranous bract, particularly those subtending the fls. of the *Compositae*.
chaffy: covered with small thin dry scales or bracts.

chambered: of pith, divided into empty horizontal chambers by cross partitions.
channeled: grooved lengthwise.
chartaceous: of papery or tissue-like texture.
ciliate: marginally fringed with hairs, often minutely so and then termed "ciliolate."
cinereous: ash colored.
circinate: rolled coil-wise from top downward. Ex: unopened fern fronds.
circumscissile: opening or dehiscing by a line around the fr. or anther, the top (valve) coming off as a lid. Ex: fr. of *Portulaca* or *Plantago.*
cladophyll: a flattened, foliaceous stem having the form and function of a leaf, but arising in the axis of minute bract-like often caducous true leaf. Ex: the so-called leaves of *Ruscus* and *Asparagus*.
clasping: a stalkless leaf, with the base partly surrounding the stem.
clavate: club-shaped, as a baseball bat.
claw: the constricted petiole-like base of petals and sepals of some flowers. Ex: petals of flowers of mustard family, of *Cleome.*
cleft: divided to or about the middle into divisions.
cleistogamous: describes a small, closed self-fertilized flower, usually near the ground.
climbing plant: one which raises its foliage by supporting itself on surrounding objects, by twining stem or tendrils, grasping rootlets, or scrambling.
clone: a group of plants derived vegetatively from one parent plant, identical to each other and to the parent.
close bark: not broken up or scaly.
clustered: of leaves, crowded so as not to be clearly opposite or alternate, also said of whorled condition.
coalescent: two or more parts united.
coarse (texture): consisting of large or rough parts.
coherent: two or more similar parts or organs touching one another in very close proximity by the tissues not fused. Ex: the two ovaries of asclepiadaceous flowers. (By some the term treated as if synonymous with connate.)
collateral buds: accessory buds to either side of the true lateral bud at a node.
columella: the carpophores in umbellifer fruits.
column: the structure formed by union of filaments in a tube (as in mallows) or of the filaments and style of orchids.
commisure: the edge or face of two adjoining structures.
comose: tufted with hairs. Ex: milkweed seeds.
compact: arranged in a small amount of space, dense habit.
complete flower: one which has corolla, calyx, stamens and one or more pistils.
composite: compound.
compound leaf: a leaf of two or more leaflets, in some cases (Citrus) the lateral leaflets may have been lost and only the terminal lft. remain. *Ternately compound* when the lfts. are in 3's; *palmately compound* when three or more lfts. arise from a common point to be palmate (if only three are present they may be sessile); *pinnately compound* when arranged along a common rachis or if only three are present at least the terminal lft. is petioled; *odd-pinnate* if a terminal lft. is present and the total number of lfts., for the lf. is an odd-number; *even-pinnate* if no terminal lft. is present and the total is an even number.
compound pistil: a pistil comprised of two or more carpels. The number of cells or locules within the ovary may or may not indicate the number of carpels. An ovary having more than one complete cell or locule is always compound, but many one-celled ovaries are compound also. A pistil having a one-celled ovary, but more than one placenta or more than one style or more than one stigma, or any combination of these duplicities, may be presumed to be compound insofar as taxonomic considerations are concerned.
compressed: flattened from the sides.
concave: curved like the inner surface of a sphere.

conduplicate: folded together lengthwise.
cone: a coniferous fruit, having a number of woody, leathery, or fleshy scales, each bearing one or more seeds, and attached to a central axis.
conelet: a young, immature first season cone, in the pines.
conical: cone shaped, as the young form of many spruces.
coniferous: cone bearing.
confluent: blending together, not easily distinguishable as separate.
connate: like parts fused together into one, fused into a tube. Ex: filaments of a mallow androecium, or anthers of a Composite flower.
connective: the tissues between the two anthers of a stamen, often much elaborated when the anther cells are separated. Ex: *Salvia.*
connivent: a synonym of coherent.
constricted: squeezed or compressed as if by shrinking or tightening.
continuous pith: solid and without interruption.
convex: curved like the outer surface of a sphere.
convulate: rolled up lengthwise; in flower buds when overlapping of one edge of a perianth segment by the next while the other margin is overlapped by its preceding member.
coppice: growth arising from sprouts at the stump, bushy.
cordate: heart-shaped, with a sinus and rounded lobes; properly a term applied only to bases of leaves and bracts, but frequently employed to designate a structure of ovate outline and heart-shaped base.
coriaceous: of leathery texture. Ex: *Buxus* lf.
corky ridges: elongated warts or strips of soft springy wood.
corm: a solid bulb-like underground stem not differentiated into scales, often depressed-globose in form, bearing scale-like buds on surface, usually tunicated. Ex: *Gladiolus, Crocus.*
cormel: small corm arising from base of parent corm.
corolla: the usually petaloid, inner whorl or floral envelopes; when the parts are separate and distinct they are petals and the corolla is said to be *polypetalous;* when connate in whole or in part the distal parts are teeth, lobes, divisions, or segments and the corolla is said to be gamopetalous.
corona: a crown; an appendage or extrusion that stands between the corolla and stamens; an outgrowth of perianth tissue in the "cup" of *Narcissus,* or of the androecium in the milkweeds.
corymb: a more or less flat-topped indeterminate infl. whose outer fls. open first. Ex: *Viburnum,* some verbenas.
costate: having longitudinal ribs or veins.
cotyledon: the primary leaves of the embryo, present in the seed.
creeping: running along at or near the ground level and rooting occasionally.
cremocarp: a dry dehiscent 2 seeded fruit of the *Umbelliferae,* each half a mericarp.
crenate: rounded teeth on mgn. Ex: lvs. of some *Coleus.*
crenate-serrate: having a mixture of blunt and sharp teeth.
crenulate: having very small rounded teeth.
crested: with an elevated and irregular or toothed ridge; found on some seeds or some floral parts.
crisp-hairy: with kinky hair or tomentum.
crown: the upper mass or head of a tree, also a central point near the ground level of a perennial herb from which new shoots arise each year.
cruciform: cross shaped.
cucullate: hooded.
culm: stem of grasses and sedges.
cultigen: a plant arising through domestication and cultivation.
cultivar: a cultivated variety.
cultivated: maintained by man.
cuneate: wedge-shaped with essentially straight sides, the structure attached at the narrow end.
cuspidate: with an apex somewhat abruptly and concavely constricted into an elongated sharp-pointed tip.

cuticle: an outer film of dead epidermal cells, often waxy.
cyathium: the infl. characteristic of *Euphorbia,* the fls. condensed and congested within a bracteate envelope, emerging at anthesis.
cymbiform: boat-shaped.
cyme: a more or less flat-topped determinate infl. whose outer fls. open last. Ex: elderberry *(Sambucus).*
cymose: of or arranged on cymes.
cymule: a diminutive cyme. Ex: *Armeria.*
deciduous: falling off, as lvs. of a tree.
decompound: more than one compound.
decumbent: reclining on ground with tip ascending.
decurrent: extending down the stem.
decussate: with alternating pairs at right angles to each other, as pairs of opposite lvs. on a stem.
deflexed: synonym of reflexed.
defoliation: casting off or falling off of leaves.
dehiscent: splitting open, the sides or segments of the splitting organ usually termed valves; *loculicidally* dehiscent when the split opens into a cavity or locule, *septicidally* dehiscent when at point of union of septum or partition to the side wall, *circumscissilely* when the top valve comes off as a lid. *Poricidally* when by means of pores whose valves are often flap-like. The term is commonly applied to anthers or seed pods.
deliquescent: the primary axis or stem much branched. Ex: branching of an elm tree.
deltoid: triangular.
dense: crowded together, thick, compact.
dentate: having marginal teeth whose apices are perpendicular to the margin and do not point forward.
denticulate: slightly or minutely dentate.
denuded: naked through loss of covering.
depressed: flattened, as if compressed somewhat.
determinate: said of an inflorescence when the terminal flower opens first and the prolongation of the axis is thereby arrested.
di-: prefix indicating two.
diandrous: having an androecium of two stamens.
diaphragmed pith: having horizontally elongated cells with thickened walls spaced throughout the pith like the rungs of a ladder.
dichlamydeous: having both a corolla and a calyx.
dichotomous: forked in pairs.
diclinous: with unisexual flowers.
dicot: angiospermous plant having two cotyledons.
didynamous: in two pairs of different length.
diffuse: loosely or widely spreading, an open form.
digitate: palmate.
dimorphic: having two forms.
dioecious: having unisexual fls., each sex confined to a separate plant, said of species.
disarticulate: to fall away leaving a clear cut scar.
discoid: having only disk fls. as an infl. of a member of the Compositae family.
disk: (1) a glandular elevation about the base of a superior ovary; (2) the flattened receptacle of the infl.; (3) a flattened extremity as a stigma or as on the tendrils of some climbing vines.
disk flower: the tubular fl. in the center of the usual Composite infl. Ex: daisy, aster.
disposed: arranged.
dissected: divided in narrow, slender segments.
distal: toward the apex, away from the base.
distichous: two-ranked, with lvs., lfts. or fls. on opposite sides of a stem in the same plant.
distinct: separate, not united with parts of like kind. Compare with "free".

diurnal: blossoms opening only during the day.
divaricate: spreading very wide apart.
divergent: spreading broadly.
divided: separated to the base into divisions.
dormant: in a restive or non vegetative state, especially a winter condition.
dorsal: the black or outer surface.
dorsiventral: referring to a front-to-back plane.
dotted: describes the underside of a leaf having a pattern of spots or hair glands visible.
double flower: one with more than the usual number of petals, colored sepals or bracts.
double serrate: serrations bearing minute teeth on margins.
doubly compound: bi-pinnate.
diadelphous: in two sets, applied to stamens. In many legumes the androecium is comprised of 10 stamens: 9 in one set, 1 in the other.
doubly crenate, dentate, or serrate: having small teeth of the given kind within the larger ones.
downy: pubescent with fine soft hairs.
drooping: hanging from the base, suggesting wilting.
drupaceous: drupe-like.
drupe: a fleshy indehiscent fr. whose seed is enclosed in a stony endocarp. Ex: date, cherry.
drupelet: a small drupe. Ex: raspberry.
duct: generally, a water conducting tube, also a canal through the wood carrying resin, latex or oil.
dwarf: an atypically small plant.
dwarf shoots: spur shoots.
ebracteate: without bracts.
echinate: with stout bluntish prickles.
eglandular: without glands.
ellipsoid: three dimensional shape of ellipse, football shaped.
elliptic-oblong: a shape between the two forms.
elliptical: having the outline of an ellipse, broadest at middle and narrower at each end.
elongate: lengthened.
emarginate: with a shallow notch at the apex.
emergences: appendages other than hairs.
endemic: confined to a small geographic area.
endocarp: the inner layer of the pericarp.
ensiform: sword-shaped.
entire: having a margin without teeth or crenations.
entomophilous: describes flowers that are pollinated by insects.
ephemeral: persisting for one day only, of short duration. Ex: fls. of *Neomarica, Tradescantia.*
epidermis: the outer superficial layer of cells.
epigynous: borne on the ovary; said of the fl. when the ovary is inferior, or of stamens when apparently borne on the gynoecium.
epitrophic: more nourished and developed on the upper side.
equitant: overlapping in two ranks. Ex: lvs. of *Iris.*
erect: upright habit of growth.
erose: having a margin appearing eroded or gnawed; of a jaggedness not sufficiently regular to be toothed. Ex: leaf apices of the fish-tail palm *(Caryota).*
espalier: any plant trained lattice fashion in one plane.
established: growing and reproducing without cultivation.
estipulate: without stipules.
evanescent: describes veins grown very faint near the margin.
even-pinnate: results in a lack of the terminal leaflet, since each one is paired.
evergreen: having green foliage throughout the year.
excavated: describes pith which is hollow between the nodes.
excurrent: extending beyond the margin or tip. Ex: awns of some grasses.

exfoliate: to peel off in shreds or thin layers, as bark from a tree.
exotic: foreign, not naturalized.
exserted: projecting beyond, as stamens beyond a corolla.
exstipulate: without stipules.
extrorse: facing outward from the center; in the case of anthers, dehiscing outward; a character most accurately determined by a cross-section of the anther.
falcate: sickle-shaped.
falls: outer whorl of perianth segments of an iridaceous fl., often broader than the inner and, in some *Iris,* drooping or flexuous.
farinaceous: with a powdery or mealy coating.
fasciated: abnormally much flattened, and seemingly several units fused together.
fascicle: a close cluster. Ex: lvs. of white pine.
fastigiate: branches erect and close together.
felty: having compressed matted fibers.
fenestrate: perforated with opening or with translucent areas. Ex: lvs. of *Monstera deliciosa.*
ferrugineous: rust colored.
fertile: capable of producing fruit and seed.
fibrous: having long narrow shreds or flakes.
filament: that portion of a stamen comprising the stalk.
filamentous: thread-like.
filiform: long and very slender; thread-like.
fimbriate: fringed.
fine texture: consisting of small rather delicate parts.
firm bark: close, not broken into loose or shaggy parts.
fissured bark: torn lengthwise, with vertical furrows.
fistulose: hollow and cylindrical.
fistulous: describes a hollow stem with excavated pith.
flabellate: fan-like.
flaccid: limp.
flaking: shreddy, with shorter fragments.
flat: a low horizontal habit of growth.
fleshy: applied to a fruit somewhat pulpy or juicy at maturity, as opposed to a dry hard or papery fruit.
flexous: waxy.
floccose: having surface with tufts of soft woolly hair, often rubbing off easily.
floret: technically a minute flower; applied to the flowers of grasses and Composites.
flower: an axis bearing one or more pistils or one or more stamens or both: when only the former, it is a *perfect flower* (I.E. bisexual or hermaphroditic). The androecium represents a series or whorls, derived from a spiral condition adjoining the pistil. When this perfect flower is surrounded by a perianth represented by two floral envelopes (the inner envelope comprising the corolla, the outer the calyx), it is a *complete flower.*
flower scar: marks remaining after the abscission of the flower parts.
fluted: having rounded lengthwise ridges.
foliaceous: leaf-like in color and form.
foliage: leaves.
-foliate: -leaved.
-foliolate: -leafleted.
follicle: a dry dehiscent fruit opening only along one suture and the product of a single carpel (simple ovary). Ex: peony, columbine, milkweed.
form: a subdivision of a species which occurs occasionally in the wild, seldom breeds true, and does not develop a natural population or distribution.
foveola: a pit.
fragmented: not continuous, especially of vascular bundle scars.

free: separate in that it is not joined to other organs; as petals free from calyx or calyx free from capsule. Contrast with "distinct".
free-central: see placentation.
fringed: ciliate with glands or scales rather than hairs.
frond: a leaf, once applied only to leaves of ferns but now to leaves of palms also.
fruit: technically a ripened ovary with its adnate parts, the seed-containing unit characteristic of all Angiosperms. The term is also employed loosely for all similar structures as the "fruit" of a Cycad which in reality is a naked seed or the "fruit" of the Blue Cohosh (an Angiosperm) which also is a naked seed: all are functionally fruiting structures.
fruticose: shrubby, in sense of stems being woody.
fugacious: falling or withering very early.
fulvous: tawny, a dull grayish yellow color.
funiculus: the stalk by which an ovule is attached to the ovary wall.
funnelform: the tube gradually widening. Ex: corolla of morning-glory.
furcate: forked.
furrowed: having longitudinal channels or grooves.
fuscous: grayish brown.
fusiform: spindle-shaped; tapering to each end from a smaller mid-section.
galea: a helmet. Ex: *Aconitum.*
gamopetalous: the petals united, at least at base, to form a corolla of one piece; the corolla coming off from the fl. as a single unit.
geniculate: bent like a knee.
genus: a group of species possessing fundamental traits in common but differing in other lesser characteristics.
gibbous: swollen on one side, usually basally. Ex: snapdragon corolla.
glabrate: becoming glabrous with maturity, but as seen under a lens is noted to be not quite so prior to maturity.
glabrous: not hairy. Note: a glabrous surface need not be smooth, for it may be bullate or rugose.
gland: a general term applied to oil-secreting organs, or sometimes an obtuse projection or a ring at base of a structure.
glandular: bearing glands.
glandular-pubescent: glands and hairs intermixed.
glandular-punctate: see punctate.
glaucescent: slightly glaucous.
glaucous: covered with a waxy bloom or whitish material that rubs off readily. Ex: the bloom on many sorts of grape.
globose: having a round or spherical shape.
globular: circular.
glochid: a minute barbed spine or bristle. Ex: the components of the tawny hair-like tufts on many species of *Opuntia.*
glomerate: in dense or compact clusters, usually applied to flowers.
glossy: shining, reflecting more light than if lustrous.
glume: a stiff chaff-like bract, usually applied to the two empty bracts at base of grass spikelets.
glutinous: sticky.
granular: minutely roughened.
grooved: marked with long narrow furrows or channels.
ground cover: a plant that grows near the ground densely, and spreads.
gum: a fluid sticky resin.
gymnospermous: plant bearing naked seeds without an ovary.
gynoecium: collectively the female element of a fl.; a collective term employed for the several pistils of a single fl. when referred to as a unit; when only one pistil is present the two terms are synonymous.
gynophore: a stalk bearing a pistil above point of stamen attachment. Ex: *Cleome.*

habit: the general aspect or mode of growth of a plant.
habitat: the type surrounding in which a plant grows.
hair: superficial outgrowth, trichome.
hairy: pubescent with longer hairs.
hardened: conditioned by various factors to withstand environmental stresses; contrast with succulent growth which is very vulnerable.
hardy: capable of enduring winter stresses.
hastate: having the shape of an arrow-head and the basal lobes pointed outwards at or nearly at right angles to the mid-rib.
head: a short dense infl. of variable form, as in *Compositae* (daisy) family, *Eryngium,* or many clovers.
helicoid: spiraling like a snail shell.
herb: a plant dying to the ground at the end of the season; one whose aerial stems are soft and succulent without appreciable parenchymatous xylem tissue; a plant not woody in texture.
herbaceous: having no persistent woody stem above ground.
herbage: vegetative parts of an herb.
hermaphrodite: bisexual.
hesperidium: a fleshy berry-like fr. with hard rind and definite longitudinal partitions. Ex: orange.
heterogamous: bearing two kinds of flowers.
heterogeneous: not uniform in kind of flowers.
hidden bud: bud covered by the petiole base and therefore inconspicuous.
hilum: the scar on a seed marking its point of attachment.
hip: fruit of the rose.
hippocrepiform: horseshoe-shaped.
hirsute: with rough coarse hairs, usually rather long.
hirtellous: minutely hirsute.
hispid: with stiff or bristly hairs.
hispidulous: minutely hispid.
hoary: with a close white or whitish pubescence.
hirsute: pubescent with coarse or stiff hairs.
hollow: describes pith with a central cavity.
homogamous: bearing only one kind of flower.
homogeneous: all of one kind and texture, continuous pith.
hooked: bent like a hook, having a hook.
horizontal: with broad faces parallel to the ground.
humifuse: spreading over the ground.
husk: outer covering of the seed or fruit.
hyaline: translucent when viewed in transmitted light.
hybrid: plant resulting from a cross between two or more other plants which are more or less alike.
hydrophyte: an aquatic plant.
hypanthium: the cup-like "receptacle" derived from the fusion of perianth parts and on which are seemingly borne the stamens, corolla, and calyx. Ex: fuchsia, plum.
hypocrateriform: see salverform.
hypogynous: borne on the torus or receptacle, beneath or at base of ovary; said of stamens, petals or calyx when the ovary is superior or above their point of attachment.
hypotrophic: more nourished and developed on the under side.
imbricated: overlapping, as shingles on a roof.
imperfect flower: one which lacks either stamens or pistils.
impressed: bent inward, furrowed as if by pressure.
incised: cut by sharp and irregular incisions more or less deeply, but intermediate between toothed and lobed.
included: not protruding as stamens not projecting beyond a corolla; opposed to exserted.
incomplete flower: one which lacks any one or more of these parts: calyx, corolla, stamens, and pistils.

incumbent: having cotyledons which within the seed lie face to face with the back of one lying against the hypocotyl; anthers are incumbent when turned inwards.
incurved: bent into an inward curve.
indehiscent: not opening regularly, as a capsule or anther.
indeterminate: said of those kinds of infl. whose terminal fls. open last, hence the growth or elongation of the main axis is not arrested by the opening of first flowers.
indigen: plant native and original to a region.
indumentum: with a generally heavy covering of hair: a general term without precise connotation.
indurate: hardened.
indusium: the epithelial excrescence that, when present, covers or contains the sporangia of a fern when the latter are in sori.
inferior: beneath, below; said of an ovary when situated below the apparent point of attachment of stamens and perianth; a fl. having such an ovary is said to be epigynous.
inflated: bladder like, loose and membraneous about the seed.
inflorescence: the method of flower-bearing; the disposition of flowers on the axis (or axes).
infundibular: funnel-shaped.
inner bark: cortical tissues inside the protective outer layers but outside the wood.
internode: the part of an axis between two nodes.
interrupted: not continuous, smaller parts or lack of parts between normal ones.
introduced: brought intentionally from another region for purposes of cultivation.
introrse: turned or faced inward, toward the central axis; said of stamens whose anthers dehisce on the side facing inward.
involucel: a secondary involucre.
involucral: of the involucre.
involucrate: having an involucre.
involucre: one or more whorls or series of small lvs. or bracts that are close underneath a fl. or infl.; the individual bracts termed phyllaries by some. Ex: subtending the heads of most members of the *Compositae.*
involute: a longitudinal curving or rolling upwards as opposed to revolute.
irregular flower: a flower that can be cut longitudinally into two equal halves at only one place; one having some parts different from other parts in the same series; a flower that is not symmetrical when in face view; a zygomorphic flower.
isodiametric: as broad as tall.
jointed: having nodes or points of real or apparent articulation.
jugum: a pair, as of leaflets.
junctures: winter nodes.
juvenile: an early phase of plant growth, usually characterized by non-flowering, vigorous increase in size, and often thorniness.
keel: of a papilionaceous corolla, the two front petals united along lower margin into a boat-shaped structure enveloping the pistil and stamens.
key: a small indehiscent fruit with a wing.
knees: pointed or domelike outgrowths from baldcypress roots, rising above the water.
labellum: a modified petal; the enlarged spreading or pouch-like lip of the orchid flower.
labiate: lipped, as in the corolla of most mints; as a proper noun, a member of the *Labiatae* family.
lacerate: irregularly torn or cleft.
laciniate: slashed into narrow pointed incisions.
lactiferous: milky.
lacuna: a cavity, hole or gap.
lageniform: gourd-shaped.
lamellae: thin flat plates or laterally flattened ridges.
lamellate: made up of thin plates.
lamina: a blade.
lanate: woolly; with long intertwined curly hairs.

lanceolate: much longer than wide, broadest below the middle and tapering to the apex.
lanuginose: cottony or woolly; downy, the hairs somewhat shorter than in lanate.
lanulose: very short woolly.
lateral: borne at or on the side, as flowers, buds or branches.
lateral bud: a bud borne in the axil of a previous season's leaf.
latex: milky sap.
lax: loose; the opposite of congested.
leader: the primary or terminal shoot, trunk of a tree.
leaf: the whole organ of photosynthesis, characterized by an axillary bud most of the year.
leaflet: a foliar element of a compound leaf.
leaf ratio: the fraction obtained by dividing length by width.
leaf scar: the mark remaining after the leaf falls off a twig.
legume: a dry fruit dehiscing along both sutures and the product of a single carpel (simple ovary). Ex: pea, most beans.
lemma: the outer or lowermost bract of the two immediately inclosing a grass flower.
lenticel: a small corky spot on young bark made of loosely packed cells, providing gaseous exchange between the inner tissues and the atmosphere.
lenticular: lens-shaped, the sides usually convex.
lepidote: covered with minute scurfy scales.
liana: a tropical woody vine.
lignified: woody, hardened.
ligulate: strap-shaped; a leaf blade with the sides essentially parallel and abruptly terminated.
ligule: (1) a strap-shaped organ; (2) (in grasses) a minute projection from the top of the leaf sheath; (3) the strap-shaped corolla in the ray flowers of Composites.
limb: the expanded, and usually terminal, part of a petal (as in *Dianthus*), or of a gamopetalous corolla as distinguished from the often constricted tube.
linear: long and very narrow, as in blades of grass.
lineate: lined; bearing thin parallel lines.
lined: lightly ridged or ribbed.
lingulate: tongue-shaped.
lip: one of the parts of an unequally divided corolla or calyx; these parts are usually two, the upper lip and the lower lip, although one lip is sometimes wanting; the seemingly lower lip of orchid fls. (the labellum) has this position because of a twisting of the pedicel or receptacle.
lobe: a projecting part or segment of an organ as in a lobed ovary or stigma; usually a division of a lf., calyx, or petals cut to about the middle (i.e. midway between margin and midrib).
locule: a cell or compartment of an ovary, anther or fruit.
loculicidal: see dehiscent.
lodicule: minute, gland-like structure at base of grass ovary.
loment: a legume constricted between the seeds (as in peanut) or which separates into one-seeded articulations (as in *Desmodium* or *Lespedeza*).
loose: not compact, irregularly formed.
lorate: strap-shaped.
lunate: crescent-shaped, as a quarter moon.
lustrous: having a slight metallic gloss, less reflective than glossy.
lyrate: having a pinnately compound leaf with the terminal lft. much larger than the lateral lfts. and the latter becoming progressively smaller basally.
macrospore: the larger of two spores (as in *Selaginella*) which on germination produces the female gametophyte; synonymous with megaspore.
marcescent: withering, but the remains persisting.
margin: the edge of a leaf.
marginal: pertaining to the margin.
matted: growing densely, forming a low close ground cover or compact tufts.
mature: a later phase of growth characterized by flowering, fruiting, and a reduced rate of size increase.

mealy: having a mottled, granular appearance.
membranaceous: of parchment-like texture.
meristem: nascent tissue, capable of developing into specialized tissues.
-merous: referring to the number of parts; as fls. 3-merous, in which the parts of each kind (as petals, sepals, stamens, etc.) are 3 each or in multiples of 3.
metamorphosed: changed from one state to a different one.
microspore: the smaller of two kinds of spores (as in *Selaginella*) which on germination produces the male gametophyte; sometimes applied to a pollen grain.
microsporangium: the microspore-containing case; an anther sac.
midrib: the primary-rib or mid-vein of a leaf or lft.
milky sap: whitish in color, often thicker than water.
monadelphous: said of stamens when united by their filaments. Ex: hollyhock.
moniliform: constricted laterally and appearing bead-like.
monocarpic: fruiting once and then dying. Ex: some palms and most bamboos.
monocot: angiospermous plant having only one cotyledon.
monoecious: a species with unisexual fls., having both sexes on the same plant. Ex: corn.
monogymous: having a gynoecium of one pistil.
monopodial: continuing growth from a terminal bud each year.
mossy: describes a matted growth habit, with small overlapping foliage.
mound: plant having a massive form, full to the ground.
mucilaginous: slimy.
mucro: a short, sharp, abrupt tip.
mucronate: abruptly terminated by a mucro.
mucronulate: minutely mucronate.
multiple buds: a terminal or lateral bud crowded by many accessory buds.
multiple fruit: one formed from several fls. into a single structure having a common axis, as in pineapple or mulberry.
mummy: a dried shrivelled fruit.
muricate: rough, due to presence of many minute spiculate excrescences on the epidermis.
muriform: with markings, pits, or reticulations arranged like bricks of a wall; as on some seed coats and achenes.
mutation: a sudden change in genetic material resulting in an altered individual. Generally disadvantageous to survival.
naked bud: one without scales.
naked flower: one having no floral envelopes (perianth).
nascent: in the act of being formed.
native: inherent and original to an area.
naturalized: thoroughly established, but originally from a foreign area.
navicular: coat-shaped, as glumes of most grasses.
nectary: a nectar-secreting gland; may be a protuberance, a scale, or a pit.
needle: the slender leaf of many conifers.
nerve: a slender rib or vein, especially unbranched.
netted venation: the veins reticulated and resembling a fish net; the interstices close.
neutral flower: a sterile fl. consisting of perianth without any essential organs.
nocturnal: opening at night and closing during the day.
nodding: drooping, bending over.
node: a joint on a stem, represented by point of origin of a leaf or bud; sometimes represented by a swollen or constricted ring, or by a distinct leaf scar.
nodulose: having small, swollen knobs; knot-like.
notched: with v-shaped indentations.
nut: a dry, indehiscent, 1-celled, 1-seeded fruit having a hard and bony mesocarp; the outermost endocarp may be fibrous or slightly fleshy.
nutlet: diminutive nut; applied to one of the four nucules of the fruit of the mint family.
ob-: prefix indicating the inverse.
obcordate: the apex being cordate.
oblanceolate: inversely lanceolate.
oblate: flattened at the poles.

oblique: lop-sided, as one side of a leaf base larger, wider or more rounded than the other.
oblong: longer than broad; rectangular; the sides nearly parallel.
oblong-lanceolate: a shape in between the two forms.
oblong-obovate: a shape in between the two forms.
obovate: inversely ovate, broadest above the middle.
obovoid: three dimensional shape of obovate, pear shaped.
obsolete: rudimentary.
obtuse: rounded, approaching the semi-circular.
ochrea: a nodal sheath formed by fusion of the two stipules. Ex: *Rumex, Polygonum.*
odd-pinnate: see compound.
odoriferous: aromatic but questionably pleasant.
oligo-: a prefix meaning few, as oligospermous—few-ovuled.
opposite: two at a node, as leaves.
operculate: provided with a cap or lid (the operculum).
orbiculate: circular or disk-shaped. Ex: leaf of common nasturtium.
orthotropous: said of an ovule or seed when straight and erect, the hilum at the base and micropyle at the apex.
osier: a long lithe stem.
oval: twice as long as broad, widest at the middle, both ends rounded.
ovary: the ovule-bearing part of a pistil; one borne above the point of attachment of perianth and stamens is a *superior ovary:* when below attachment of these floral envelopes it is an *inferior* or *hypogenous ovary:* when intermediate or surrounded by an hypanthium it is a *half-inferior* or *perigynous ovary.*
ovate: egg-shaped in outline, broadest below the middle, like an oval.
ovate-oblong: a combination of the two forms.
ovoid: said of a solid that is three-dimensionally egg-shaped.
ovulate: bearing ovules.
ovule: the egg-containing unit of an ovary, which after fertilization becomes the seed.
paired: occurring in twos.
palate: the projecting part of the lower lip of a bilabiate corolla that closes the throat of the corolla or nearly does so. Ex: toad-flax, snapdragon.
palea (Palet): the inner of the two bracts immediately subtending a grass flower; the lower one is the lemma.
palmate: digitate, radiating, fan-like from a common point, as leaflets of a palmately compound lf. or veins or palmately-veined lf.
palamatifid: cut palmately about half-way down.
pandurate: fiddle-shaped.
panicle: an indeterminate infl. whose primary axis bears branches of pedicelled fls. (at least basally so); a branching raceme.
paniculate: bearing panicles.
papilionaceous: having a pea-like corolla that is comprised of standard, wings and keel.
papillate: bearing minute, pimple-like protuberances (Papillae).
pappillose: with small nipple-like projections.
pappus: the modified calyx of Composites, borne on the ovary (usually persisting on the achene) and represented by hairs, bristles, awns, scales, or others.
parallel: especially of veins, running side by side from base to tip.
parallel venation: the veins extending in more or less parallel fashion from base to apex.
parenchyma: unspecialized living cells, present in the pith.
parietal: borne on the side walls of an ovary (or capsule), or on invaginations of the wall that form incomplete partitions or septae within the ovary.
parted: cleft or cut not quite to the base.
pectinate: comb-like or pinnatifid with very close narrow divisions or parts; also used to describe spine conditions in cacti when small lateral spines radiate as comb-teeth from areole.
pedate: a palmately divided or compound lf. whose two lateral lobes are again cleft or divided.
pedicel: the stalk of a flower or fruit when in a cluster or when solitary.
peduncle: the stalk of a fl. cluster or a single fl. when that fl. is solitary, or the remaining member of a reduced infl. (as in *Euphorbia* where a constriction designates the "break" between peduncle and pedicel).

pellucid: clear or translucent, said of minute glandular dots that can nearly be seen thru when viewed in transmitted light.
peltate: having the petiole attached inside the margin, such a lf. is typically shield-shaped.
pendulous: more or less hanging or declined.
penniveined: pinnately arranged.
percurrent: the main trunk continuing through to the top.
perennial: of three or more seasons duration.
perfect flower: having both functional stamens and pistils.
perfoliate: the leaf-blade surrounding the stem. Ex: *Uvularia perfoliatus.*
perianth: the two floral envelopes of a fl.; a collective term embracing both corolla and calyx as a unit; often used when it is not possible to distinguish one series from the other (as in most monocots) and the parts then called tepals.
pericarp: a term used by some to designate a fruit; technically, the ovary wall.
periderm: a protective layer of corky cells.
perigynous: borne around the ovary but not fused to it, as when calyx, corolla and stamens are borne on the edge of a cup-shaped hypanthium. Ex: coral-bells, fuchsia, evening-primrose.
persistent: adhering to position instead of falling, whether dead or live.
personate: concealed; a corolla whose tube is closed by a palate, as in snapdragon.
perulate: scale-bearing, as a scaly bud.
petal: one unit of the inner floral envelope or corolla of a polypetalous fl., usually colored and more or less showy.
petaloid: a structure not a petal (for example a sepal) that is of the color and shape of a petal; resembling a petal.
petiole; leaf-stalk.
petiolule: leaflet-stalk.
phylloclad: a branch, more or less flattened, functioning as a leaf. Ex: Christmas cactus.
phyllodium: a flattened, expanded petiole without blade and functioning as a lf. Ex: some spp. *Acacia.*
phyllotaxy: arrangement of lvs. or of floral parts on their axis.
picturesque: striking in an unusual way.
pilose: shaggy with soft hairs.
pinked: notched.
pinna: the lft. of a compound lf.; of ferns, the primary division attached to the main rachis; feather-like.
pinnate: compounded with the lfts. or segments along each side of a common axis or rachis; feather-like.
pinnatifid: pinnately cleft or parted.
pinnatisect: pinnately cut to midrib or almost to it.
pinnule: the lft. of a pinna; a secondary lft. of a pinnately decompound lf.
pistil: the unit of the gynoecium comprised of ovary, style and stigma: it may consist of 1 or more carpels; the former with a single placenta is a *simple pistil,* the latter with 2 or more carpels is a *compound pistil.* See carpel or ovary.
pistillate: having no functional stamens (staminodia may be present) in the flower.
pith: the central part of a twig, usually lighter or darker than the wood.
pitted: marked with small depressions.
placenta: that place in the ovary where ovules are attached. A location, not a structure.
placentation: the arrangement of ovules within the ovary. Several types are recognized, among them are: *parietal placentation* (see parietal), *axile placentation,* the ovules borne in the center of the ovary on the axis formed by the union and fusion of the septae (partitions) and usually in vertical rows; in 2-celled ovaries they are borne in the center and on the cross partition or on a proliferation of it often filling the loculi; *free central placentation,* the ovules borne on a central column with no septae present; *basal placentation,* the ovules few or reduced to one and borne at the base of the ovary, the solitary ovule often filling the cavity; *lamellate placentation,* the ovules completely sunken in spongy ovarian and receptacular tissues with only the discoid stigmas exserted.
plicate: folded, as in a folding fan, or approaching this condition.
plugged pith: having cross partitions at the nodes.

plumose: feather-like, plumy.
pod: a dry dehiscent fruit; a general term.
pollen: microspores contained within an anther; sometimes agglutinated into a mass.
pollinium: an agglutinated, coherent mass of pollen. Ex: milkweeds, orchids.
polycarpic: flowering and fruiting many times. See monocarpic.
polygamo-dioecious: having male and female fls. on separate plants, but these plants having perfect flowers as well.
polygamous: bearing unisexual and bisexual flowers on the same plant.
polypetalous: with a corolla of separate petals. See corolla.
polysepalous: having a calyx of separated sepals.
pome: a type of fleshy fruit represented by the apple, pear and related genera, resulting from a compound ovary.
poricidal: see dehiscence.
porrect: said of cactus spines when the laterals are at right angles to the central one of an areole.
posterior: at or toward the back; opposite the front; nearest the axis; away from the subtending bract.
preformed: already having definite structure, such as leaves within a bud.
prehensile: clasping or coiling in response to touch.
prickle: an excrescence of bark that is small, weak, and spine-like.
prominent: projecting outward, conspicuous.
primocane: the first year's shoot or cane of a biennial woody stem. Ex: *Rubus.*
procumbent: lying flat on the ground but the stem not rooting at nodes or tip.
prostrate: lying flat on the ground; a general term.
protandrous: with anthers maturing before the stigma.
protogynous: having stigma receptive to pollen before pollen is released from anthers of same fl.
proximal: toward the base, away from the apex.
pruinose: having a coarse, granular, dust-like, waxy bloom.
pseudo-terminal bud: seemingly the terminal bud of a twig, but actually the upper-most lateral bud with its subtending lf. scar on one side and the scar of the terminal bud often visible on opposite side.
puberulent: minutely pubescent as viewed with a lens.
pubescent: covered with short soft hairs; a general term.
pulvinate: cushion-shaped.
pulvinus: a minute gland or a swollen base of the petiole or petiolule responding to vibrations. Ex: sensitive-plant *(Mimosa).*
punctate: with translucent or covered dots, depressions, or pits.
pungent: terminated by a sharp stiff point; sharp and acid to taste or smell.
pustular: blistery, usually minutely so.
pyramidal: broadest at base, tapering apically; pyramid-shaped.
pyrene: the pit or "seed" of a drupelet.
pyriform: pear-shaped.
pyxidium: pyxis: a capsule dehiscing circumscissilely.
quadrangular: four angled, of pith or a twig.
raceme: a simple indeterminate inflorescence with pedicelled flowers.
racemose: having flowers in racemes.
rachilla: a diminutive or secondary axis; a branch of a rachis; the minute axis bearing the individual florets in grass and sedge spikelets; the secondary axes of decompound fern fronds.
rachis: axis bearing leaflets or the primary axis of an infl.; the axis bearing pinnae of a fern frond.
radial: arranged around and spreading from a common center.
radiate: (1) said of a Composite infl. when bearing ray fls.; (2) star-shaped or spreading from a common center.
radical: of or pertaining to the root.
radicle: the embryonic root of a seed.
ramified: branched.
ramiform: branching.
ranked: foliage is arranged in longitudinal planes around the stem.
raphides: needle-like crystals in plant tissues.
ray: (1) the ligulate or lorate corolla of some composite flower; (2) the fl. of a Composite having a ligulate or strap-shaped corolla; (3) the axes of an umbel or umbel-like inflorescence.

receptacle: a torus; the distal end of a flower-bearing axis, usually more or less enlarged, flattened, or cup-like on which some or all of the flower parts are borne. Ex: *Compositae, Onagraceae.*
reclining: having an axis that is falling back or bent down from the vertical.
recurved: bent or curved backward, usually roundly or obtusely so. See reflexed.
reduced: smaller or simpler than normal.
reduplicate: said of buds whose components have their edges rolled outward in aestivation.
reflexed: bent abruptly backward or downward.
regular flowers: (1) a flower that can be cut longitudinally into two equal halves along an indefinite number of radii; (2) one having the parts of any one series all alike and uniformly disposed about the axis, as petals all alike, sepals all alike, etc.; a symmetrical or actinomorphic fl.
remote: widely spaced.
reniform: kidney-shaped.
repandate: having a weakly sinuate margin, one slightly uneven.
repent: creeping along the ground and rooting at the nodes.
replum: the partition separating the two loculi or cells or cruciferous fruits.
resin duct: a lengthwise or transverse canal carrying resins.
resinous: secreting a viscid exudate.
reticulate: like a net, the interstices closed.
retrorse: turned back or downwards, usually applied to armament or vesture.
retuse: notched slightly at a usually obtuse apex.
revolute: rolled toward the back, as a margin tightly or laxly rolled along the lower side.
rhizome: an underground stem distinguishable from a root by presence of nodes, buds or scale-like lvs.
rhombic: with four nearly equal sides, but unequal angles, diamond shaped.
rhombic-ovate: somewhere between egg and diamond shaped.
rhomboidal: of the shape of a rhomboid.
rib: conspicuous vein of a lf.; a prominent ridge.
root: the descending axis of the plant, without nodes and internodes, usually underground.
rootlet: a subdivision of a root, also an aerial root.
rosette: a crown of lvs. radiating from a st. and at or close to the surface of the ground.
rostellum: a small beak: a projection from the distal edge of the stigma in many monandrial orchids.
rostrate: beaked.
rosulate: in rosettes, or rosette-like in form.
rotate: wheel-shaped, a corolla whose limb flares out at right angles to the fl. axis and with no conspicuous tube produced; a flat circular or disc-like limb.
rotund: orbicular and inclining to be oblong.
rudiment: the beginning of an undeveloped member.
rufous: reddish brown.
rugose: wrinkled, usually covered with wrinkles.
ruminate: mottled in appearance, in a surface or tissue due to dark and light zones or irregular outline.
runcinate: pinnatifidly incised, the incision sharp and pointing backward. Ex: some *Taraxacum* leaves.
runner: a slender trailing shoot that usually roots at the tip and some nodes.
saccate: bag-shaped, pouchy.
sagittate: shaped like an arrow-head with the basal lobes pointing directly downward (backward) or inward.
salverform: said of a corolla with a slender tube and an abruptly expanded flat limb extending at right angles to the tube. Ex: *Phlox, Galium,* most primulas.
samara: a dry indehiscent fruit bearing a wing (the wing may be limb-like or envelop the seed and be wafer-like). Ex: maple, ash, *Ptelea.*
sarmentose: producing long flexuous runners.
scabrous: rough or gritty to the touch; rough-pubescent.
scalariform: said of pits or pith partitions when arranged like ladder rungs.
scale: a small and usually dry bract or vestigial leaf or a structure resembling such.
scandent: climbing, usually without tendrils.
scape: a leafless peduncle arising from the basal rosette of a few or no basal leaves; sometimes a few scale-like lvs. or bracts may be borne on it; a scape may be one or many-flowered.
scapose: bearing its fls. on a scape.
scar: the mark left from a former attachment.

scarious: thin, dry, membranous and usually translucent margins or parts that are not green in color.
scattered: not in any patterned arrangement, especially of vascular bundle scars.
schizocarp: a dry dehiscent fr. that splits into two halves. Ex: maple.
scorpioid-cyme: a determinate infl. (often seemingly indeterminate) that is coiled with the fls. 2-ranked and borne alternately at the right and the left. Ex: forget-me-not, heliotrope.
scrambler: plant that climbs without twining or grasping in some way.
scurfy: describes a surface covered with bran-like particles.
scutate: like a small shield.
secund: one-sided, in that the fls. are seemingly borne in a one-sided infl.
seed: a fertilized ripened ovule that contains an embryo.
segment: a portion of a leaf or perianth that is divided but not compound.
semi-cordate: partly heartshaped.
semi-evergreen: green for only a part of the winter, or only part of the foliage fully evergreen.
sepal: one of the units comprising the calyx; a usually green foliaceous element subtending the corolla.
septate: divided by partitions.
septicidal: see dehiscence.
septum: a partition.
sericeous: see silky.
serotinous: produced late in the season, late to open; having cones that remain closed long after the seeds are ripe.
serrate: saw-toothed, the teeth pointing forward.
serrulate: minutely serrate.
sessile: without a stalk.
seta: a bristle.
setaceous: bristle-like.
setose: covered with bristles.
shaggy: covered with or resembling long rough woolly hair.
sheath: any elongated, more or less tubular structure enveloping an organ or part.
shrub: a woody plant that is never tree-like in habit and produces branches or shoots from or near the base.
silicle: the short fr. of some crucifers, which is usually not more than 1 1/2 times as long as wide.
silique: the elongated fr. of some crucifers, usually 3 times as long as wide or longer.
silky: covered with soft appressed fine straight hairs; sericeous.
simple: said of a lf. when not compound, of an infl. when unbranched.
sinuate: with a strongly wavy margin.
sinus: the space between two lobes, segments, or divisions; as of lvs. or perianth parts.
smooth: not roughened, not warty.
solitary: occurring alone, not paired or clustered.
sori: see sorus.
sorus: cluster of sporangia (of ferns), appearing usually as a dot on the dorsal surface of a frond.
spadix: a fleshy usually club-shaped axis on which are borne fls. and which is generally enveloped by a spathe; the infl. of most *Araceae;* sometimes employed for the branched infl. of palms.
spathe: the bract or modified leaf surrounding or subtending a flowering infl. (usually a spadix); it may be herbaceous, colored, and "flower-like" as in the calla-lily or the anthurium, or hard, dry and woody in many palms. By some the term is restricted to members of the *Araceae.*
spathe valves: one or more herbaceous or scarious bracts that subtend an inflorescence or a flower.
spatulate: spoon-shaped.
species: a natural group of plants composed of similar individuals which can produce similar offspring; usually including several minor variations.
spicate: with spikes.
spicula: a cymule or small cyme.
spike: (1) a usually unbranched, elongated, simple, indeterminate infl. whose fls. are sessile; the fls. may be congested or remote; (2) a seemingly simple infl. whose "fls." may actually be composite heads (Liatris).
spikelet: (1) a secondary spike; (2) one part of a compound infl. which of itself is spicate; (3) the floral unit, or ultimate cluster, of a grass infl. comprised of fls. and their subtending bracts.
spine: an excrescence of st., strong and sharp-pointed. Ex: spines of hawthorns.

spinescent: more or less spiny.
spinose: beset with spines.
spirally arranged: the actual pattern of alternate leaves.
spongy: porous, as parenchyma cells of the pith.
sporangium: a spore-containing case, as in ferns.
spore: a minute reproductive body comprised of a single gametophytic cell.
sporocarp: a body containing sporangia or spores.
sporophyll: a spore-bearing leaf.
spray: a branchlet with foliage.
spreading: growing outward or horizontally.
spur: a tubular or sac-like projection from a fl. and usually from a sepal or petal.
squamate: with small scab-like projection from a fl. and usually from a sepal or petal.
squamose: covered with small scales, more coarsely so than when lepidote.
squarrose: with branches spreading and recurved at the ends.
stalk: a supporting structure of a leaf, flower or fruit.
stalked bud: a bud whose outer scales are attached above the base of the bud axis.
stamen: the unit of the androecium and typically comprised of anther and filament, sometimes reduced to only an anther; the pollen-bearing organ of a seed plant.
staminate: describes an imperfect flower with only functional stamens, male.
staminate flower: see flower.
staminode (staminodium): a sterile stamen reduced to a non-functional filament-like stalk, a gland, or sometimes expanded and petal-like; borne in the same or adjacent whorl as the functional stamens.
standard: (1) of a papilionaceous fl., the upper usually expanded, more or less erect petal; (2) the erect petals of an iris fl. as opposed to the broader and often drooping falls.
stellate: star-like; stellate hairs having radiating branches or are separate hairs aggregated in star-like clusters; hairs once or twice forked often are treated as stellate.
stellate-pubescent: with hairs in small starlike tufts.
stem: the primary axis of a plant having foliage and flowers opposed to the root axis.
sterigma: the raised base from which some small evergreen leaves finally fall (spruces).
sterile: barren, not able to produce seed.
stigma: the usually distal end of the pistil that receives the pollen, of varied shapes and surfaces.
stipe: (1) a naked stalk; (2) the petiole of a fern frond.
stipel: a stipule of a lft.
stipellate: having stipels at the base of the leaflets.
stipular, stipulate: having stipules at the base of the leaves.
stipule: a basal appendage of a petiole, usually one at each side, often ear-like and sometimes caducous.
stipule scar: a pair of marks left after the stipules fall off, to either side of the leaf scar.
stolon: a horizontal stem that roots at its tip and there gives rise to a new plant.
stoloniferous: bearing slender stems just on or under the ground which roots at the tips.
stoma: a minute pore in the epidermis, especially in the lower surface on the leaf.
stomatiferous: bearing stomata.
stone: the hard usually one-seeded endocarp of a drupe.
stratified: arranged in horizontal layers.
striate: with fine longitudinal lines, channels or ridges.
strict: rigidly erect.
strigose: with sharp, stiff, straight and appressed hairs.
strobilus: a cone.
style: the more or less elongated part of a pistil between the stigma and the ovary.
stylopodium: a disk-like enlargement at the base of a style.
subcontinuous pith: with occasional but not regular gaps.
submerged bud: a bud hidden by the petiole or embedded in the callus of the leaf scar.
subopposite: pairs of leaves close but not exactly at the same level on the stem.
subpetiolar: under the base of the petiole.
subtend: to stand immediately beneath.
subulate: awl-shaped.

succulent: thickened, juicy, fleshy tissues that are more or less soft in texture.
sucker: a shoot arising from the roots or from beneath the surface of the ground; also the adhering discs of a vine.
suffrutescent: a plant whose stems are woody basally but herbaceous above, dying back to the woody portion at the close of each growing season. Ex: *Alyssum saxatile,* rock rose, *Pachysandra.*
sulcate: deeply grooved lengthwise.
superficial: on the surface, not connected to inner tissues.
superior ovary: see ovary.
superposed bud: accessory bud above the true lateral bud.
supine: lying flat, face upwards.
suture: a line of dehiscence or groove marking a face of union.
syconium: the fruit of a fig.
symmetrical: actinomorphic or regular (flower) to the extent that the parts of the several series (calyx, corolla, stamens) are each of the same number.
symmetrical flower: one having the same number of parts in each envelope (calyx and corolla).
sympetalous: the petals united at least at the base; synonym for gamopetalous.
sympodial: continuing growth by the development of an axillary bud and not the terminal bud, season after season.
sympodial inflorescence: a determinate infl. that simulates an indeterminate infl., as if a scorpioid cyme were straight rather than circinate.
syncarp: a fleshy aggregate fruit.
syncarpous: having a gynoecium with all the carpels united.
syngenesious: stamens connate by their anthers in a cylinder about the style. Ex: *Compositae* family.
tailed: said of anthers having caudal appendages.
tapering: gradually decreasing towards an end.
taxonomy: the area of botany dealing with the classifying and naming of plants.
tendril: a modified stem or leaf, usually filiform, branched or simple, that twines about an object providing support.
tepal: a segment of perianth not differentiated into calyx or corolla. Ex: tulip, magnolia.
terete: cylindrical, or at least circular in cross section.
terminal: at the tip or distal end.
ternate: in threes.
testa: the outer coat of a seed.
tetradynamous: with an androecium of 6 stamens, four longer than the other two, as in Cruciferae.
texture: the effect of the surface structure.
thallus: a foliaceous organ, not differentiated into the stem and foliage and not bearing true roots.
thicket: a dense growth of shrubs, a copse.
thorn: a modified twig which has tiny leaf scars and buds; can be single or branched.
throat: the opening into the lower end of a gamopetalous corolla, the point where the limb joins the tube.
thyrse: compact panicle-like infl. whose distal end is indeterminate and the lateral branches determinate. Ex: lilac *(Syringa vulgaris).*
tomentose: densely woolly, the hairs soft and matted.
tomentulose: diminutive of tomentose; delicately tomentose.
tomentum: the dense matted hairs.
toothed: the margin broken up into small rather regular segments.
torsion: twisting.
torose: cylindrical with constrictions at intervals, slightly moniliform.
torulose: twisted or knobby; irregularly swollen at close intervals.
torus: see receptacle.
trailing: prostrate and not rooting.
translucent: transmitting light but diffuse enough to distort images.
transverse ridge: one which runs across the stem from one leaf scar to its pair on opposite twigs.
tree: a woody plant with one main stem at least 12 to 15 feet tall, and having a distinct head in most cases.
triangular-ovate: a flattened angular egg shape.
trichoma: a bristle.

trifid: three-cleft.
trifoliate: three-leaved. Ex: *Trillium.*
trifoliolate: with a leaf of three lfts.
tripinnate: with compounded pinnules.
triternate: a biternate lf. again divided in 3's. Ex: many spp. *Thalictrum.*
triquetrous: three-angled.
truncate: as if cut off at right angles to the primary axis; a term applicable to bases or apices.
tuber: a short, thickened organ, usually—but not necessarily—an underground stem.
tubercle: a miniature tuber, tuber-like body or projection.
tubular: having petals, sepals, or both united into a tube.
tuft: a clump of hairs growing close together.
tumid: swollen.
tunic: a coat about an organ, often fibrous or papery. Ex: about the crocus corm or tulip bulb.
tunicated: with concentric layers, often of fleshy scales. Ex: onion bulb.
turion: a young shoot or sucker. Ex: asparagus stalk.
turbinate: inversely conical, top-shaped.
turgid: swollen to firmness.
twig: the shoot of a woody plant representing the growth of the current season.
twiggy: having many divergent twigs.
twig scar: mark left by the sloughing of a length of dead twig tissue.
twining: the stem winding about a support.
umbel: an indeterminate infl., usually but not necessarily flat-topped with the pedicels and peduncles (termed rays) arising from a common point, resembling the stays of an umbrella.
umbellate: having umbels.
umbellet: a secondary umbel.
umbo: a conical projection arising from the surface.
unarmed: without a sharp defense such as spines or bristles.
uncinate: hooked at the tip.
undulate: wavy, as a leaf margin.
unguiculate: narrowed into a petiole-like base; clawed.
unijugate: a compound lf. reduced to a single pair of leaflets.
unilateral: one-sided.
unilocular: one-celled or with a single cavity.
unisexual flowers: of one sex only. See flower.
urceolate: urn-shaped; constricted at the throat.
utricle: a small dry thin-walled, usually dehiscent, 1-seeded fruit; an achene whose pericarp is loose and readily removed. Ex: *Amaranthus.*
vaginate: sheathed.
valvate: (1) dehiscing by valves; (2) meeting by the edges without overlapping, as lvs. or petals in the bud.
valve: a separable part of a dehiscent fruit or stamen; the unit into which a capsule splits or divides in dehiscing.
variegated: striped, margined or mottled with a color other than green, where green is normal.
variety: subdivision of a species having a distinct though often inconspicuous difference, and breeding true to that difference. More generally also refers to clones.
vascular bundle: a discrete group of conducting vessels.
vascular bundle scar: a minute spot within the leaf scar where the vessels were positioned.
vasiform: an elongated funnel-shaped object.
vein: a vascular rib of the leaf.
velutinous: clothed with a velvety indumentum comprised of erect straight dense moderately firm hairs.
venation: arrangement of veins.
ventral: relating to the anterior or inner face or part of an organ, the opposite of dorsal.
ventricose: a one-sided swelling or inflation, more pronounced than gibbous.
venulose: with very fine veins.
vernal: related to spring.
vernation: the arrangement of leaves within a bud.

verrucose: having a wart-like surface.
versatile: moving freely because of attachment near the middle, as an anther attached crosswise medianly to the filament.
vertical: having broad faces perpendicular to the earth.
verticil: a whorl.
verticillate inflorescence: one with the flowers in whorls about the axis, the whorls remote from one another (as in many salvias) or congested into head-like structures (catnip). Such whorls are false-whorls since they are actually sessile cymes arranged opposite one another in the axils of opposite bracts or leaves.
verticillate: arranged in whorls.
vesicle: a small bladdery sac or cavity filled with air or fluid.
vestige: the remains of an exhausted or dead member.
vesture: any substance on or arising from the surface rendering it other than glabrous.
vexillum: the petal of a papilionaceous corolla known also as the standard; the upper broad petal.
villous: having long, soft, shaggy hairs that are not matted.
vine: a slender-stemmed climbing or trailing plant.
virgate: wand-like; long straight and slender.
viscid: sticky or with appreciable viscosity.
vittatae: the oil tubes of *Umbelliferae,* especially of their fruits.
voluble: twining.
warty: marked with rounded tubercles, rougher than granules.
watery sap: thin and clear.
wavy: alternating concave and convex curves.
weeping: dropping conspicuously, pendent.
whorl: arrangement of three or more structures arising from a single node.
whorled: in a whorl, as leaves.
wilt: to become limp and lose turgor through a deficit of water.
wing: (1) the lateral petal of a papilionaceous flower; (2) a dry, thin, membranous appendage.
wither: to dry up and shrivel.
wood: a dead, hard xylem tissue.
woolly: having long, soft, more or less matted hairs; like wool.
x: indicates a hybrid.
zig-zag: bent back and forth at the nodes.
zone: an area restricted by a range of annual average minimum temperatures, used in describing hardiness.
zygomorphic: irregular, not symmetrical.

SCIENTIFIC NAME INDEX

COMMON NAME INDEX